D0181243

Greece

Korina Miller
Kate Armstrong, Michael Stamatios Clark, Chris Deliso,
Des Hannigan, Victoria Kyriakopoulos

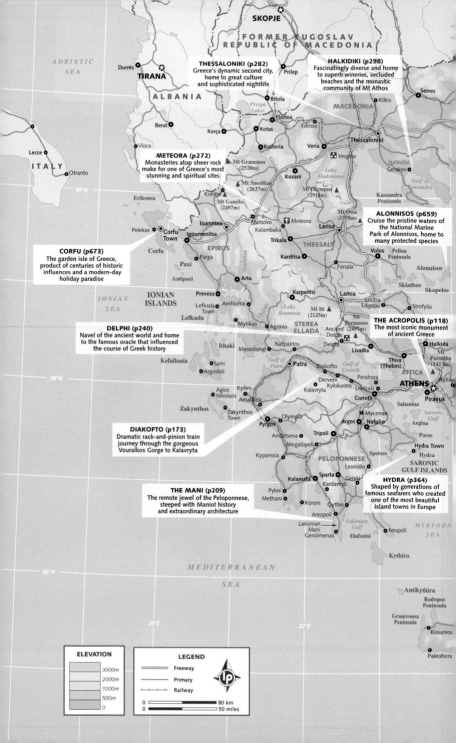

SKOPJE

FORMER YUGOSLAV
REPUBLIC OF MACEDONIA

ADRIATIC
SEA

Durrës

TIRANA

ALBANIA

THESSALONIKI (p282)
Greece's dynamic second city,
home to great culture
and sophisticated nightlife

HALKIDIKI (p298)
Fascinatingly diverse and home
to superb wineries, secluded
beaches and the monastic
community of Mt Athos

Serres

Prilep

Kilkis

Bitola

Prespa
Lakes

Florina

Edessa

MACEDONIA

Berat

Korça

Kotas

Veria

Thessaloniki

Vlora

Kastoria

Vergina

Halkidiki
Gerakini

Gulf of
Kassandra

METEORA (p272)
Monasteries atop sheer rock
make for one of Greece's most
stunning and spiritual sites

Mt Grammos
(2520m)

Kozani

Mt Olympus
(2918m)

Kassandra
Peninsula

ITALY

Lecce

Otranto

40°N

Erikousa

Mt Smolikas
(2637m)

Konitsa

Mt Gamila
(2497m)

Ioannina

Metsovo

Meteora

Mt Ossa
(1978m)

Lake
Aliakmonas

Larisa

Kalambaka

THESSALY

Volos

Pelion
Peninsula

ALONNISOS (p659)
Cruise the pristine waters of
the National Marine
Park of Alonnisos, home to
many protected species

Pelekas

Corfu
Town

Igoumenitsa

EPIROS

Trikala

Karditsa

Farsala

Alonnisos

CORFU (p673)
The garden isle of Greece,
product of centuries of historic
influences and a modern-day
holiday paradise

Corfu

Paxi

Parga

Skiathos

Skopelos

Antipaxi

Arta

Preveza

Karpenisi

Lamia

Loutra
Edipsou

Strofylia

IONIAN
SEA

IONIAN
ISLANDS

Lefkada
Town

Lefkada

Amfilohia

Mytikas

Agrinio

Lake
Kremasta

Mt Iti
(2125m)

Mt
Parnassos
(2457m)

Ancient
Delphi

Delphi

THE ACROPOLIS (p118)
The most iconic monument
of ancient Greece

Halkida

Mt
Parnitha
(1413m)

DELPHI (p240)
Navel of the ancient world and home
to the famous oracle that influenced
the course of Greek history

Ithaki

Messolongi

Nafpaktos

STEREA
ELLADA

Livadia

Thiva
(Thebes)

ATTICA

Kafina

38°N

Kefallonia

Sami

Argostoli

Gulf of
Patra

Patra

Diakofto

Derveni

Xylokastro

Perahora

Loutraki

Gulf of
Corinth

Corinth

ATHENS

Piraeus

Saronic
Gulf

Agios
Nikolaos

Kyllini

Amaliada

Kalavryta

Mycenae

Salamina

Aegina

Zakynthos

Zakynthos
Town

Olympia

Pyrgos

Argos

Nafplio

Poros

DIAKOFTO (p173)
Dramatic rack-and-pinion train
journey through the gorgeous
Vouraïkos Gorge to Kalavryta

Andritsena

Tripoli

Megalopoli

PELOPONNESE

Spetses

Hydra Town

Hydra

SARONIC
GULF ISLANDS

Kyparissia

Leonidio

HYDRA (p364)
Shaped by generations of
famous seafarers who created
one of the most beautiful
island towns in Europe

THE MANI (p209)
The remote jewel of the Peloponnese,
steeped with Maniot history
and extraordinary architecture

Kalamata

Sparta

Geraki

Pylos

Methoni

Kardamyli

Koroni

Gythio

Areopoli

Lakonian
Mani

Gerolimenas

Lakonian
Gulf

Elafonisi

Neapoli

MYRTOÖN
SEA

Kythira

MEDITERRANEAN

36°N

SEA

Antikythira

Rodopos
Peninsula

Gramvousa
Peninsula

Kissamos

20°E

22°E

Paleohora

ELEVATION

3000m
2000m
1000m
500m
0

LEGEND

Freeway
Primary
Railway

0   80 km
0   50 miles

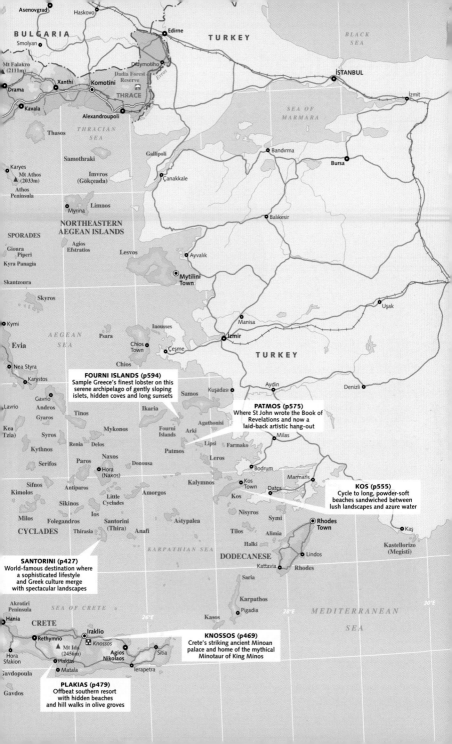

FOURNI ISLANDS (p594)
Sample Greece's finest lobster on this serene archipelago of gently sloping islets, hidden coves and long sunsets

PATMOS (p575)
Where St John wrote the Book of Revelations and now a laid-back artistic hang-out

KOS (p555)
Cycle to long, powder-soft beaches sandwiched between lush landscapes and azure water

SANTORINI (p427)
World-famous destination where a sophisticated lifestyle and Greek culture merge with spectacular landscapes

KNOSSOS (p469)
Crete's striking ancient Minoan palace and home of the mythical Minotaur of King Minos

PLAKIAS (p479)
Offbeat southern resort with hidden beaches and hill walks in olive groves

On the Road

KORINA MILLER Coordinating Author

It's very quiet. All I can hear is the hissing and popping of the crater as I stand deep within it. It's early morning and we're alone. Around me is the moonscape of the volcano of Nisyros (p551), the caldera rising up to the lush landscape that spills down to the shore. Beautiful, other-worldly and – it can't be denied – rather pongy.

KATE ARMSTRONG Who says we authors don't go to the ends of the earth for our readers? Here I am at Cape Tenaro (p213), Greece's southernmost point. Cape Tenaro lighthouse sits in a historical treasure trove in the magnificent Mani. The walk there – via a rocky path – with views of Roman ruins, inlets and the ocean, makes you feel like you're on the edge of the world.

MICHAEL STAMATIOS CLARK

When I reached the Serpentine Organic Garden oasis (p267) in Tsangarada on the Pelion Peninsula, via a rocky forest path, I found a hidden hillside of greenery and colour, even a family of ducks annoyed by my presence. We worked it out, though, and I was able to grab a bit of shade on a hot summer's day.

CHRIS DELISO They seldom come more iconic than Georgios the elder. With a long beard and an unbreakable olive-wood cane, this black-clad elder descended on me in Rethymno's bus station, bearing 700 years of Cretan history and an ever so slight whiff of Crete's famous firewater, *raki*. Fifteen minutes later the history lesson was over and the other waiting tourists, like all of Crete's would-be past invaders, had left the scene.

VICTORIA KYRIAKOPOULOS Where did you say that bar was? Getting the low-down on new bars, restaurants and the latest hotspots in Athens (p147) is serious business involving serious research and leg work. Walking around exploring Athens is always full of surprises and rewards, with new places to discover all the time.

DES HANNIGAN Always find time for an acropolis; but not just your common or garden Athenian pile of old rocks. This is the Mycenaean acropolis of Koukounaries (p402) near Naousa, on Paros. Unbeatable viewpoint, enough old stones to stir the imagination and rarely anyone else there. Don't all rush.

For full author biographies see p777

Greece Highlights

We've roamed the length and breadth of Greece in search of its ultimate offerings. Some are age-old sights that continue to beckon – towering ancient ruins, powder-soft beaches, charismatic cities and traditional white-washed villages. Others we've stumbled upon, such as remote, nearly forgotten islands, silent boat trips through wildlife reserves, or mazes of medieval alleyways. You're sure to find your own hidden gems, but to whet your appetite, here are our authors' top finds. Share yours at lonelyplanet.com/greece.

KRZYSZTOF DYDYNSI

1 ATHENS

Greece's bustling capital, Athens (p101), has a way of surprising even the most jaded visitor. The historic centre under the magnificent Acropolis is part open-air museum, part open-air lounge, teeming with alfresco cafes, bars and restaurants and an almost festive atmosphere, especially at night. Summer or winter, where else could you experience such an anarchic yet exhilarating mix of culture and history, urban jungle and urban chic, restless energy and hedonistic lifestyle?

Victoria Kyriakopoulos

METEORA

You're not likely to forget the first moment the magnificent Meteora (p272) come into view – soaring pillars of rock that jut heavenward, and a handful of monasteries at the top (some dating from the 14th century). The rope ladders that once enabled the monks to reach the top have long been replaced by steps carved into the rock. Today, these spectacular stone towers beckon rock climbers from around the world.

Michael Stamatios Clark

ANDREW BAIN

2

SANTORINI

Santorini (p427) is frontline Greek tourism – sensational, glamorous and indulgent. I love its glitter and the crowds of fellow tourists feasting on curiosity and expectation. Most of all, I love its local people who manage to preserve a Greek way of life that is still rooted in quiet corners of the island.

Des Hannigan

CRAIG PERSHOUSE

3

TREVOR CREIGHTON

4

HORA SFAKION

Honorary capital of Crete's stony southern badlands, the whimsical port village of Hora Sfakion (p492) is full of rugged individuals and other local characters. It's a relaxing place to circle the wagons for a couple of days, plan coastal boat trips and enjoy some good swimming and seafood, while listening to traditional music and local legends invoking Sfakia's strong-willed independent streak.

Chris Deliso

SAMOS

Lush Samos (p595) is intensely appealing, with its sweet red wine, hidden sandy coves, cool mountain villages and remarkable ancient sites. It's also one of the sharpest dressed of the northeastern Aegean Islands, where chic young partiers enjoy drinks in bars overlooking the hypnotically illuminated sea until late into the night.

Chris Deliso

CHRIS DELIS

6

GEORGE TSAFOS

5

OLYMPIA

Rub shoulders with the ghost of Milo of Kroton, the famous wrestler, or take a swipe at the boxer, Diagoras of Rhodes. At Olympia (p226), past and present merge magically. As you emerge from the tunnel into the Olympic stadium, it's hard to ignore thousands of cheering spectators. Ghosts they may be, but this surreal experience is guaranteed to make your arm hairs stand on end. Get there early to avoid throngs of mere mortals.

Kate Armstrong

JOHN ELK

7

ANGELOKASTRO

The ruined fortress of Angelokastro (p683), on Corfu's west coast, rises above everything, especially the crowds. It's one of those reassuring places where land and water meet sensationally; a great knuckle of rock soaring above the glittering Ionian Sea, a green pelt of olive trees and cypresses at its back. I return there often, not as a writer to record its mere statistics, but because I like it. Its name derives from the 11th-century Byzantine rulers of Corfu. Its fortifications repulsed Ottoman attack three times. You climb steeply to the lonely ruins – ancient Kerkyra beneath your feet – and just know that this lofty place must also have been a refuge and lookout long before the Byzantines.

Des Hannigan

ANCIENT DELPHI

Arrive early to catch the magic of the sun's rays pouring over the Sanctuary of Athena (p243) at Delphi, the centre of the ancient Greek world. Only three columns remain of the magnificent Sanctuary of Athena, but that's enough to let your imagination soar. Nearby, the Sacred Way meanders past the Temple of Apollo (p242) where the Delphic oracle uttered prophecies that sent armies to battle and lovers to swoon.

Michael Stamatios Clark

8

NOBORU KOMINE

KALYMNOS

Kalymnos (p565) has the best of both worlds. In the spirited main town, tourists blend into the bustle of teeming streets and an animated harbour, while local sponge harvesters sort through their daily catch, and teenagers zip past on mopeds. Meanwhile, just up the road you can hop on a fishing boat to tiny Telendos Islet (p570), where time stands still and tourists put their feet up to watch the sun sink into the horizon.

Korina Miller

WAYNE WALTON

ISTOCK // STEPHEN FRENCH

9

10

PARGA

The jewel in the crown of the Epirot Riviera, Parga (p350) is an alluring, laid-back resort flanked by sandy beaches and olive groves, and crowned by a Venetian castle. Despite the summer crowds, the white-plastered backstreets – with their sleepy cats, chattering elders and scampering children – help the village retain its authenticity. With atmospheric dining and sleeping options, and quick access to ancient sites and some Ionian islands, Parga is a great base for further adventures and offers a taste of the Italian-flavoured Epiros of old.

Chris Deliso

CHRIS CHRIS

12 AEGINA

Of all Greek islands, Aegina (p356), in the Saronic Gulf, seems the least insular. About half an hour by ferry from dockside Piraeus, its back streets – with their no-nonsense domestic bustle – are cheerfully unglamorous and un-touristy. This island seethes also with Greek history and traditions. Its highpoints are the 5th-century-BC Temple of Aphaia (p359) and the Temple of Apollo (p358). But, it is medieval Paleohora (p359) that absorbs me most of all; a tumbling rocky hillside covered with vivid wildflowers in spring and peppered with over thirty chapels, several now restored. You head back to Aegina's happy chaos with a smile.

Des Hannigan

©MOM/P.DENDRINOS

11 NATIONAL MARINE PARK OF ALONNISOS

The crystal-blue waters of this marine park (p661) are considered the most pristine in Greece. Many of the smallest islets are off-limits to any human visitors in order to protect the delicate habitat of the endan-gered Mediterranean monk seal and Eleanora's falcon, among others. On our boat, the gregarious captain impresses the visitors with his know-ledge and respect for the marine life. It helps that he's stocked up with lunch and plenty of wine.

Michael Stamatios Clark

GEORGE TSAFI

13 THE MANI

Although it can no longer be described as 'remote' or 'rarely visited', the Mani (p209) holds a magic unlike any-where else in Greece. For centuries, the feuding families were literally, a law unto themselves, and this has contrib-uted to its unique and very special historical, cultural and physical landscapes. With everything from rugged rocky highlands reminiscent of Scotland, to hidden lush green oases, or from small fishing tavernas to severe rock-solid tower houses, this pocket of the Peloponnese is well worth exploring at leisure. Maniots are proud people, and this is reflected in their cuisine and hospitality.

Kate Armstrong

PREVELI BEACH

Preveli Beach (p480) comprises one of Greece's most instantly recognisable stretches of sand. Bisected by a freshwater river and flanked by cliffs concealing sea caves, Preveli is all about soaking up the sun in special company, under the sacred gaze of a magnificent monastery situated high above.

Chris Deliso

15

CHRIS CHRISTO

PELION PENINSULA

The Pelion Peninsula (p261) is criss-crossed by old cobblestone trails that connect mountain villages to the small bays that dot the eastern coast, like this one at Damouhari (p266). The trails are well marked and along the way, you're just as likely to encounter a small herd of goats as you are a car or motorbike. It's also likely that the trail will end near a good Greek taverna or *ouzerie* (place serving ouzo and appetisers).

Michael Stamatios Clark

16

MICHAEL STAMATIOS CLARK

14

WAYNE WALTON

RHODES OLD TOWN

Getting lost in the Old Town (p518) is a must. Only then will you find yourself removed from the throngs of tourists and meandering down twisting, turning, cobbled alleyways with archways above and squares opening up ahead of you. The beauty of the Old Town lies in these hidden corners, where your imagination will take off with flights of medieval fancy.

Korina Miller

HANIA

The pretty former Venetian port town of Hania (p483) features a shimmering, pastel-hued waterfront backed by an evocative old town full of winding stone lanes and atmospheric guest houses and restaurants.

Chris Deliso

CHRIS DELI

18

EGMONT STRIGL/ALAMY

SAMOTHRAKI

Exotic Samothraki (p632) has a strong spiritual vibe, as the ancient Thracians realised when building their Sanctuary of the Great Gods – one of Greece's top archaeological sites – here around 1000 BC. This jungle island remains for the true initiates, with its mountainous interior, cool river, rock pools and waterfalls to explore. Camp on the beach, strum a guitar, and peace out on this little-known northeastern Aegean classic.

Chris Deliso

GEORGE TSAFC

19

SHOW AT THE ODEON OF HERODES ATTICUS

Few theatres in the world evoke the palpable sense of history and awe you feel when sitting on the worn marble seats of this ancient amphitheatre (p122), with the floodlit Acropolis as a backdrop, watching anything from the staging of ancient drama and contemporary Greek performers to the world's leading ballets.

Victoria Kyriakopoulos

Contents

Regional Map Contents

Northern Greece p279

Central Greece p237

Ionian Islands p672

Evia & the Sporades p644

Northeastern Aegean Islands p586

Athens & Attica pp108–16

Peloponnese pp168–9

Saronic Gulf Islands p356

Cyclades p373

Dodecanese p513

Crete pp458–9

Destination Greece

What is it that calls so many of us to Greece? Perhaps it's the endless miles of aquamarine coastline with some of Europe's cleanest beaches. Or the ancient sights that you've read about all your life and want to see with your own eyes. Maybe it's the slow-paced island life where days melt from one to the next, or the adrenalin-rushing possibilities of the mountainous terrain. It's easy to understand how so many myths of gods and giants originated in this vast and varied landscape, with wide open skies and a sea speckled with islands. Greece is also the birthplace of drama and democracy, of western science and medicine. It's been said that, in many ways, we are all the sons and daughters of Ancient Greece. Perhaps we're simply being called home.

Once you arrive, it's not too difficult to find the Greece you were hoping for, whether it's the pulsing nightclubs of Mykonos or the solemnity of Meteora; the grandeur of Delphi or the earthiness of Metsovo; the rugged Cretan hillsides and the lush wildflowers of spring. You'll quickly become acquainted with the melancholy throb of *rembetika* (blues songs), the tang of homemade tzatziki, and the ability of the ancient sights to unleash an imagination you might not have realised you had.

Nevertheless, while ancient sights might take the limelight in many tourist itineraries, the Greeks certainly aren't stuck in the past. Sure, it's easy to find remote, traditional villages with brilliant white buildings and roaming donkeys and goats, but the shepherd will likely be talking on their mobile phone and making a date for the local, trendy cafe. Athens has a firm grip on style and sophistication to rival any European capital. The Greek modern art scene is fresh and vibrant, and the political scene is passionate. It's a nation that welcomes and even insists upon change – from the unstoppable urban renewal taking place in Athens to the internet cafes found on the smallest islands and modern, impressive museums popping up around the nation. There are few cultures that embrace the past so fondly while simultaneously welcoming the future with open arms.

Like everywhere, it's not always smooth sailing in Greece. When problems do arise, they're debated and handled with a strong will, as is evident in the heated conversations outside the local *kafeneio* (coffee house). The past three decades of increased wealth and improved living standards have gone hand in hand with rising unemployment, growing public debt and a credit crunch that's left many Greeks disillusioned and angry. The government's proposals of reforms in pensions and labour, plans for privatisation, and alleged corruption, incited many Greeks to take to the street in massive strikes and protests.

Since the early '70s, battles between youth and the police have been a mainstay of Greek society. Increases in youth unemployment and downward mobility have added fuel to the youth movement and protests in December 2008 resulted in the death of a 15-year-old, shot by the Athenian police in the student neighbourhood of Exarhia. News of the shooting quickly spread (largely via texting, Facebook and Twitter) and hundreds of youth took to the streets in a social uprising that lasted for days and threatened to topple the government.

The colossal fires of 2007 also sparked distrust in the government for the way in which they were (or weren't) dealt with. Today you'll find student groups, environmental charities and locals teamed up with expats working to reforest the country. Greeks are, in general, becoming increasingly aware of environmental degradation, with calls for bans on sprawling development

FAST FACTS

Population: 11.26 million

Percentage of women: 50%

Life expectancy: 80 years

Inhabitants per square kilometre: 87

Tourists: 18.8 million annually

GDP: US$345 billion

Per capita income: US$32,005

Inflation: 1.57%

Unemployment: 9.3%

External debt: US$92.19 billion

and more opportunities to recycle. Climate change, diminished water supplies and the rising of sea levels are very real concerns for Greeks. But the debate is often tangled in the mixed interests of locals versus developers or backdoor deals with local government.

On the global front, Greece has become a truly multicultural nation in recent years and the pros and cons of this are another hot topic of conversation. Once an emigrant country, with thousands of Greeks moving to North America and Australia, and later a popular refuge for expats, Greece now sees a huge influx of illegal migrants from Afghanistan, Iraq and Africa who cross the border from Turkey. As islands such as Samos struggle to house boatloads of migrants, there is mounting criticism from the international community on the poor conditions and treatment of refugees and immigrants in Greece. With the lowest acceptance rate in Europe for asylum requests (only 379 out of 20,000 were accepted in 2008), many illegal immigrants and refugees simply disappear into Greece's informal economy or attempt to cross into other European countries. Others linger in shanty towns and deportation centres.

All of this would have once been discussed in a haze of smoke at the local *kafeneio* but in July 2009, Greece brought in antismoking laws similar to those across Europe, meaning all public places should be smoke free. Greeks are some of the heaviest smokers in Europe and it will be interesting to see how well this law is enforced, particularly in the small villages, remote islands and party hubs. It seems likely that the majority will continue to rule.

Despite these passionate debates and controversy, Greece is essentially a laid-back place. Lounge at the cafe over an endless coffee, stroll along the seafront, park yourself on the beach and take your time over meals and you'll fit right in. Greeks know how to enjoy life and are renowned as some of the most hospitable people on the globe. Their generosity and warmth is as genuine as the soft sand between your toes and the warmth of the Aegean sun.

Getting Started

WHEN TO GO

Spring and autumn are the best times to visit Greece; specifically May, June, September and October. Most of the country's tourist infrastructure goes into hibernation during winter, particularly on the islands (and in some places you'll be hard-pressed to find a hotel or restaurant open). Some of the smaller islands close completely as islanders head off to alternative homes on the mainland for a few months. Many hotels, seasonal cafes and restaurants close their doors from the end of October until mid-April; bus and ferry services are either drastically reduced or cancelled.

The cobwebs are dusted off in time for Orthodox Easter (usually in April; see p23), when the first tourists start to arrive. Conditions are perfect between Easter and mid-June, when the weather is pleasantly warm in most places; beaches and ancient sites are relatively uncrowded; public transport operates at close to full schedules; and there's a bigger variety of accommodation options to choose from.

Mid-June to the end of August is high season, when everything is in full swing and the majority of festivals take place. It's also very hot – in July and August the mercury can soar to 40°C (over 100°F) in the shade just about anywhere in the country; most beaches are crowded; many ancient sites are swarming with tour groups; and in some places, accommodation is booked solid. The high season starts to wind down in September and conditions are ideal once more until the end of October.

See Climate (p714) for more information.

By November the endless blue skies of summer have disappeared. November to February are the wettest months and it can get surprisingly cold. Snow is common on the mainland and in the mountains of Evia and Crete; it even occasionally snows in Athens. But there are also plenty of sunny days and some visitors prefer the tranquillity that reigns at this time of year.

COSTS & MONEY

Prices have rocketed since the adoption of the euro in 2002 and, although they appear to be levelling off, Greece is no longer the cheap country it once was. While tiny hole-in-the-wall restaurants continue to deliver hearty meals for low prices, eating out anywhere more upmarket has become a pricey venture.

DON'T LEAVE HOME WITHOUT...

Bags feel twice as heavy in the heat. Clothes also dry super fast under the Greek sun, so don't take more than you really need.

- A few novels or a deck of cards to while away the hours spent riding ferries.
- A shady hat, sunglasses and sunblock – indispensable in Greece's hot climate.
- An inflatable neck pillow and eye shades – for those long bus and train journeys.
- Lonely Planet's *Greek phrasebook* – talk like the locals.
- CDs – life-saving if you rent a car in a remote area.
- A bathing suit in your daypack – for those unexpected coves and beaches.
- Sturdy, nonslip shoes – many sights, historic towns and villages have slippery, rocky paths.
- A penchant for octopus – it's on nearly every island menu.
- Insect repellent – to ward off mosquitoes and sand fleas.

Accommodation has also skyrocketed, making many of the budget options not really worth the price and many of the midrange options appearing much more worthwhile.

A rock-bottom daily budget for a solo traveller is about €50. This would mean buses, staying in youth hostels or camping, and only occasionally eating in restaurants or taking ferries. Allow €100 per day if you want your own room and plan to eat out, travel about and see the sights. If you want comfortable rooms and restaurants all the way, you will need closer to €150 per day. These budgets are for individuals travelling in high season (mid-June to late August). Couples sharing a room can get by on less.

HOW MUCH?

Local telephone call per minute €0.30

Minimum taxi fare €4

Single Greek coffee €2

City bus ticket €1

Greek salad €6

Your money will go much further if you travel during the quieter months of May to mid-June and September to October. Particularly on the islands, accommodation is a lot cheaper outside high season. You will also be able to negotiate better deals if you stay a few days. Families can achieve considerable savings by looking for self-catering apartments and shopping for food and drink at supermarkets and local produce markets. Travelling by boat can also save money as children under five board for free and you can save a night's accommodation.

Prices quoted throughout this book are for the high season of mid-June to late August.

TRAVELLING RESPONSIBLY

As with many popular European destinations, Greece's environment is pushed to the limit each year by the massive influx of tourists. While the bigger picture can seem rather overwhelming to an individual tourist (p90), there are a number of things you can do that can help lessen the impact without compromising your holiday.

The first thing to consider is how you will travel to Greece. While short vacations don't always offer the luxury of avoiding the carbon footprints involved in flying (see p762), reaching Greece from the rest of Europe by train and/or boat is a viable option for those with a little more time. See p728 for options. The experience of long-distance train travel can also be a highlight of your trip.

Next consider when you're going to travel. Visiting Greece on the shoulder seasons – early spring or autumn – means the weather is more bearable and puts less pressure on precious resources such as food and water. This is particularly true on the islands.

Once you're there, how you get around can make a difference to the environment. Not everyone (in fact, very few of us!) have the gumption and stamina to tackle the hilly, hot terrain on bicycle, but you can opt for local buses and trains rather than planes or rented cars, or for fast, fuel-economic ferries rather than slow gas-guzzlers. We've got all of the information you need to tackle the local transport; see p731 and p738 for more details.

Water scarcity is a serious problem throughout much of Greece; a number of islands are without their own source. It's impractical to avoid buying bottled water entirely. On some of the remote and smaller islands, tap water is not safe to drink (unless you boil or purify it); always ask locally. When buying bottled water, choose Greek brands (which are everywhere) rather than European brands that have travelled further and therefore come with a larger carbon footprint. You can also cut down on water use by not requesting hotels to wash your towels daily and by taking quick showers.

'Organic' and 'green' are increasingly popular buzzwords in Greece. The rise in agrotourism means more options for staying in local, environmentally friendly places. You'll also find increasing options for recycling and for buying organic food, and for guided activities such as

TOP 10

GREEN CHOICES

Green doesn't have to mean composting toilets and a holiday without showers. Here are excellent ways to enjoy your vacation and do your bit for the earth at the same time.

1 Milia (p498) – mountaintop ecolodges

2 National Marine Park of Alonnisos (p661) – preserve of the Mediterranean monk seal

3 Serpentine Organic Garden (p267) – volunteering on these lush sustainable grounds

4 Tilos (p547) – for rare birds

5 Octopus Sea Trips (p404) – ecofriendly family activities

6 Hydra (p364) – car- and scooter-free

7 Thrassa Eco-Tourism Guesthouse (p331) – organic food and outdoor activities

8 Masticulture Ecotourism Activities (p611) – traditional cultivation of mastic trees, olive trees and grapevines

9 feel ingreece (p667) – catch a glimpse of wild ponies

10 2407 Mountain Activities (p215) – hop on a bike to explore in and around the Taÿgetos Mountains

SET IN GREECE

Get inspired with some Greek scenery in these critically acclaimed films.

1 *Mediterraneo* (1991) – an award-winning comedy about Italian soldiers stranded on tiny Kastellorizo during WWII

2 *For Your Eyes Only* (1981) – Roger Moore travels around Greece secret-agent style

3 *Captain Corelli's Mandolin* (2001) – not as good as the book, but great scenes of Kefallonia

4 *The Guns of Navarone* (1961) – iconic war film, starring Anthony Quinn and Gregory Peck, on Rhodes

5 *Mamma Mia* (2008) – taking the world by storm, this ABBA-based musical is filmed on Skopelos, the Pelion Peninsula and Skiathos

6 *Zorba the Greek* (1964) – Anthony Quinn's steamy performance as an uptight English writer who finds love on Crete; the famous beach dance scene was at Stavros, near Hania

7 *Never on a Sunday* (1960) – Greece's big star Melina Mercouri received an Oscar nomination for her role as a prostitute in Piraeus

8 *Lara Croft Tomb Raider* (2001–02) – Lara Croft went diving off Santorini

9 *Shirley Valentine* (1989) – this classic foreign romance fantasy takes place in Mykonos

10 *My Life in Ruins* (2009) – Nia Vardalos led her tour bus around Athens and the Peloponnese

ADRENALIN KICKS

Greece isn't all about lazing on the beaches.

1 Hiking through mountain villages in the Lousios Gorge (p197)

2 Rock climbing seaside cliffs (p569)

3 Diving in clear waters (p654)

4 Kitesurfing with the world's best (p536)

5 Scaling steep rock pinnacles (p275)

6 Walking scenic cobblestoned mule pathways (p262)

7 Hiking into the depths of a volcanic crater (p554)

8 Walking in wildflower meadows (p659)

9 Hiking the pristine Pindos Mountains through the stone-and-slate villages of the magical Zagorohoria region (p342)

10 Swimming at the semitropical pink-sand beach of Elafonisi (p498)

hiking and cycling. As much of Greek cuisine is based on local produce, restaurant proprietors are catching on to the movement and advertising their dishes as locally sourced and, in many cases, organically grown. Shops are also selling local, organic herbs, honey, soap and other wares as souvenirs, making it possible to support the local economy and the environment in one go. You'll find many of these greener options listed in our GreenDex (p803).

TRAVEL LITERATURE

Travel writers can be a great source of inspiration for those planning to follow in their footsteps.

92 Acharnon Street (John Lucas; 2007) A view into contemporary Greece from the perspective of a visiting English professor at the University of Athens. It reflects the changes that took place during the '80s and covers politics to poetry.

Eurydice Street: A Place In Athens (Sofka Zinovieff; 2004) An engaging tale of an expat in Athens. The book takes in customs, etiquette, culture and modern history. Recommended by Greeks for its accuracy of modern Greek culture.

Falling for Icarus: A Journey Among the Cretans (Rory MacLean; 2004) The author journeys to Crete to live out his dream of constructing and flying his own plane and entwines his tale with history, myths and portrayals of village life.

It's All Greek to Me! (John Mole; 2004) The humorous and much-acclaimed account of an English family converting a stone ruin into a home on Evia, including their outlandish attempts to 'fit in'.

My Family and Other Animals (Gerald Durrell; 1977) The classic, witty story of a childhood spent on Corfu, told by a now-famous naturalist and conservationist. Not surprisingly, flora and fauna find their way into the pages.

The Colossus of Marousi (Henry Miller; 1975) Few writers have matched the enthusiasm expressed in this classic tale. Miller's fervour never flags as he leaps from one adventure to the next.

INTERNET RESOURCES

There is a huge number of websites providing information about Greece.

EOT (Greek National Tourist Organisation; www.gnto.gr) For concise tourist information.

Greece Online (www.greece-on-line.gr) An interactive map that lets you pinpoint things like beaches, museums, ski resorts or airports.

Greek Travel Pages (www.gtp.gr) One-stop site with access to ferry schedules, accommodation listings and destination details.

Lonely Planet (www.lonelyplanet.com) Get the latest updates and ask questions before you go or dispense advice when you get back.

Ministry of Culture (www.culture.gr) Details of events, sights, galleries, monuments and museums.

Travel Guide to Greece (www.greektravel.com) Matt Barrett's comprehensive site to travelling in Greece.

Events Calendar

Attending a Greek festival or event can easily be a highlight of your trip. Atmospheric and jubilant, they're often seen as an excuse for a good party. Below are some of the main events; there are also countless religious festivals that towns and entire islands celebrate with great gusto. Ask locally, and see also the destination chapters.

JANUARY

FEAST OF   1 Jan
AGIOS VASILIOS (ST BASIL)
A church ceremony followed by the exchanging of gifts, singing, dancing and feasting; the *vasilopita* (golden glazed cake for New Year's Eve) is cut and the person who gets the slice containing a coin will supposedly have a lucky year.

EPIPHANY   6 Jan
(BLESSING OF THE WATERS)
The day of Christ's baptism by St John is celebrated throughout Greece. Seas, lakes and rivers are blessed; with the largest ceremony held at Piraeus (p158).

GYNAIKOKRATIA   8 Jan
The villages of the prefectures of Rodopi, Kilkis and Seres in northern Greece hold a day of role reversal. Women spend the day in *kafeneia* (coffee houses) while the men stay at home to do the housework.

PATRAS CARNIVAL   mid-Jan–early Mar
This Peloponnesian festival in Patra (p171) features a host of minor events leading up to a wild weekend of costume parades, colourful floats and celebrations in late February or early March. For more details check www.carnivalpatras.gr.

FEBRUARY

CARNIVAL SEASON   3 weeks before Lent
Prior to the fasting of Lent, carnival season has many regional variations, but fancy dress, feasting, traditional dancing and general merrymaking prevail. The Patra carnival (above) is the largest, while the most bizarre is on Skyros (p667).

CLEAN MONDAY   Mon before Ash Wed
(SHROVE MONDAY)
On the first day of Lent (a day which is referred to as Kathara Deftera), people take to the hills throughout Greece to enjoy picnics together and fly kites.

MARCH

INDEPENDENCE DAY   25 Mar
The anniversary of the hoisting of the Greek flag by independence supporters at Moni Agias Lavras is celebrated with parades and dancing. This act of revolt marked the start of the War of Independence.

APRIL

ORTHODOX EASTER   40 days after
the start of Lent
The Lenten fast ends on Easter Sunday with the cracking of red-dyed Easter eggs, feasting and dancing. This is the most important festival in the Greek Orthodox religion. The Monastery of St John the Theologian on Patmos (p575), in the Dodecanese, is a great place to witness it.

FEAST OF AGIOS   23 Apr or 1st Tue
GEORGIOS (ST GEORGE)   following Easter
The feast day of St George, the country's patron saint and the patron saint of shepherds, is celebrated at several places, but with particular exuberance in Arahova (p247), near Delphi, in central Greece. Expect dancing, feasting and much merriment.

MAY

MAY DAY   1 May
This occasion is marked by a mass exodus from towns to the country. During picnics, wildflowers are gathered and made into wreaths to decorate houses.

ANASTENARIA   21 May
This fire-walking ritual takes place in the village of Langadas, near Thessaloniki. Villagers clutching icons dance barefoot on burning charcoal.

JUNE

NAVY WEEK
early Jun

Celebrating their long relationship with the sea, fishing villages and ports throughout the country host historical re-enactments and parties.

NAFPLION FESTIVAL
mid-Jun

Featuring Greek and international performers, this classical music festival in the Peloponnese uses the Palamidi fortress (p187) as one of its concert venues. Check out www.nafplionfestival .gr for details.

FEAST OF
ST JOHN THE BAPTIST
24 Jun

This widely celebrated holiday sees Greeks make bonfires of the wreaths made on May Day.

ROCKWAVE FESTIVAL
end of Jun

With major international artists (such as Moby, The Killers and Mötley Crüe) and massive crowds, this festival (p138) is held on a huge parkland at the edge of Athens. See www.rockwavefestival .gr for more.

HELLENIC FESTIVAL
Jun-Aug

The most prominent Greek summer festival features local and international music, dance and drama staged at the Odeon of Herodes Atticus (p122) in Athens and the world famous Theatre of Epidavros (p193), near Nafplio in the Peloponnese.

JULY

WINE & CULTURE
FESTIVAL
early Jul-end Aug

Held at Evia's coastal town of Karystos, this festival (p649) includes theatre, traditional dancing, music and visual-art exhibits. It ends with a sampling of every local wine imaginable.

FOLEGANDROS FESTIVAL
late Jul

This week-long festival (p442) features music and feasting at a range of locations around the island's beautiful old *hora* (main town).

SPEED WORLD CUP
Jul or Aug

Kitesurfers from around the world hit Karpathos (p536) for its excellent surfing conditions and big prize money. Event dates change annually; check www.speedworldcup.com for more details.

AUGUST

AUGUST MOON FESTIVAL
full moon

The full moon is celebrated with musical performances at historical venues such as the Acropolis (p118) in Athens and other sites around the country. Check local papers for details.

FEAST OF THE ASSUMPTION
15 Aug

Assumption Day is celebrated with family reunions; the whole population is seemingly on the move on either side of the big day. Thousands make a pilgrimage to Tinos to its miracle-working icon of Panagia Evangelistria (p379).

CRACKIN' HOLIDAY

Forget Christmas or birthdays. In Greece, the biggest day of the year is Easter when communities joyously celebrate Jesus' Resurrection. The festival begins on the evening of Good Friday with the *perifora epitafiou*, when a shrouded bier (representing Christ's funeral bier) is carried through the streets in a moving candle-lit procession. One of the most impressive of these processions climbs Lykavittos Hill (p131) in Athens to the Chapel of Agios Georgios. If you visit churches early in the morning on Good Friday, you'll often see the bier being decorated with countless flowers.

Resurrection Mass starts at 11pm on Saturday night. At midnight, packed churches are plunged into darkness to symbolise Christ's passing through the underworld. The ceremony of the lighting of candles that follows is the most significant moment in the Orthodox year, for it symbolises the Resurrection. Its poignancy and beauty is spellbinding. The ceremony ends with candle-lit processions through the streets and fireworks representing the sound of the boulder rolling away from in front of Jesus' tomb.

The Lenten fast ends on Easter Sunday with the cracking of red-dyed Easter eggs, symbolising the blood of Christ and new life – taken together this represents the new life given through Christ's resurrection on the cross. An outdoor feast of roast lamb takes place in the afternoon, followed by Greek dancing. The day's greeting is '*Hristos anesti*' (Christ is risen), to which the reply is '*Alithos anesti*' (truly He is risen).

WHAT'S IN A NAME?

Religious festivals flood the Greek calendar. In fact, according to tradition, every day of the year is dedicated to a saint or a martyr. Christian Greeks are more likely to celebrate the day for the saint they are named after than their birthday. On a person's name day, greet them with *hronia polla* (good wishes and prosperity) and, if you go to visit or meet them out, take them a small gift. Islands and towns also celebrate the day of their patron saint with church services in historic chapels, feasting and often some dancing.

SEPTEMBER

GENNISIS TIS PANAGIAS 8 Sep

The birthday of the Virgin Mary is celebrated throughout Greece with religious services and feasting.

EXALTATION OF THE CROSS 14 Sep

Celebrated throughout Greece with processions and hymns.

OCTOBER–NOVEMBER

FEAST OF AGIOS DIMITRIOS 26 Oct

This feast day, commemorating St Dimitrios, is celebrated in Thessaloniki (p291) with wine drinking and revelry.

OHI (NO) DAY 28 Oct

Metaxas' refusal to allow Mussolini's troops passage through Greece in WWII is commemorated with remembrance services, parades, feasting and dance.

THESSALONIKI INTERNATIONAL FILM FESTIVAL mid-Nov

Around 150 films are crammed into 10 days of screenings around the city. For details, check out www.filmfestival.gr.

DECEMBER

CHRISTMAS DAY 25 Dec

Christmas is celebrated with religious services and feasting plus added 'Western' features, such as Christmas trees, decorations and presents.

Itineraries
CLASSIC ROUTES

A CYCLADES CIRCLE
Two Weeks / Athens to Athens

The Cyclades are by far the most popular and best known of the Greek islands. Start with a couple of days sightseeing in **Athens** (p102), before catching a ferry from **Rafina** (p164). The first port of call is classy **Andros** (p374), with its fine beaches and art galleries. Move along to **Tinos** (p378), a pilgrimage island for many Orthodox Christians. Next in line is chic **Mykonos** (p386), famous for its bars and beaches, and stepping-off point for the sacred island of **Delos** (p395). **Naxos** (p406), the greenest and most fertile of the Cyclades, is a great place for walkers. The sheer cliffs of the volcanic caldera at **Santorini** (Thira; p427), created by one of the largest eruptions ever recorded, are a sight not to be missed. Start your return leg with a couple of days partying on youthful **Ios** (p423), then recover on nearby **Paros** (p397) with its plethora of fine beaches and more mellow nightlife. Swing west on a weekly ferry to demure **Sifnos** (p447) with its olive grove, oleanders, almonds and junipers. Finally, visit discrete **Kythnos** (p453) and mingle with the Athenian yacht crowd.

Heading southeast from Athens, this circular route covers several hundred kilometres, taking you to the jewels of the Cyclades and back to Athens.

THE GRAND TOUR   One Month / Athens to Ancient Delphi

A month is long enough to experience the huge variety of attractions (both ancient and modern) that Greece has to offer.

From bustling **Athens** (p102), head to the pretty Venetian city of **Nafplio** (p186) in the Peloponnese. Nafplio, first capital of independent Greece, is the perfect base for day trips to **Ancient Mycenae** (p184) and the celebrated **Theatre of Epidavros** (p193). Head south from here to the attractive fishing town of **Gythio** (p208) to catch a ferry across to **Kissamos** (p500) on Crete, possibly stopping at the delightfully unspoiled island of **Kythira** (p231) on the way. It's certainly worth calling in at either the charming **Hania** (p483) or **Rethymno** (p473) on the journey along Crete's northern coast to the capital **Iraklio** (p460) and the ruins of **Knossos** (p469). From Iraklio, jump across to not-to-be-missed **Santorini** (Thira; p427) and start island hopping north. Consider unwinding for a few days at some of the smaller islands such as **Anafi** (p438) and **Koufonisia** (p417), both perfect for beach lovers, before hitting the bars and clubs of hedonistic **Mykonos** (p386). Mykonos also has weekly flights to cosmopolitan **Thessaloniki** (p282) in northern Greece. Thessaloniki is a pleasant surprise to many travellers; a sophisticated city with some fine Roman and Byzantine architecture and a lively nightlife. Walkers will certainly want to call at **Mt Olympus** (p311) on the way to the amazing rock monasteries of **Meteora** (p272), home of hermit monks. The last stop is at unforgettable **Ancient Delphi** (p241), former home of the mysterious Delphic oracle and steeped in Ancient Greek history; just the place to ask what to do next.

A month-long epic trip, taking you through the Peloponnese, Crete, the Cyclades and back to the mainland through northern and central Greece.

MAINLY MAINLAND

Two Weeks / Igoumenitsa to Athens

If entering Greece from Italy with your own transport, Igoumenitsa is a good place to start exploring the natural and historic wonders of the mainland.

Do not linger in **Igoumenitsa** (p352), the busy entry port in Greece's far northwest; head across the mountains to **Ioannina** (p337) with its arresting lakeside location, Ottoman monuments and social life. Head northwards to the **Zagorohoria** (p342), unlike anything else you will see in Greece. Cross the Pindos Mountains via the less-travelled northern route to **Kastoria** (p319), a pretty lakeside town. Now make a beeline for the **Prespa Lakes** (p317), where tranquillity reigns over landscapes of water and mountains. Visit the artists' town of **Florina** (p315) and cruise through western Macedonia with an overnight stop in **Edessa** (p314) – famous for its tumbling waterfalls. Spend some time in bustling **Thessaloniki** (p282) before heading to the home of the ancient gods at **Mt Olympus** (p311), a mere 90-minute drive south. Passing through the **Vale of Tembi** (p258) you enter the sprawling plains of Thessaly where monks built monasteries atop pinnacles of rock at stunning **Meteora** (p272). Heading south, the route takes you across agricultural plains and mountains to the sea once more near **Lamia** (p254), not far from where ancient hero Leonidas stood his ground against invading Persians at **Thermopylae** (p254). A fast highway now leads on to Athens, a detour from which leads you to **Thiva** (Thebes; p238). From here choose the less-travelled mountain route via Erythres to approach **Athens** (p102).

This circuitous 1000km-long route takes in the more spectacular scenery of the north plus the centre's most visited attraction, Meteora, and finally leads you to Athens along less-travelled routes.

ROADS LESS TRAVELLED

EASTERN ISLAND RUN   Three Weeks / Rhodes to Alexandroupoli

This route takes travellers island hopping north from Rhodes through the islands of the Dodecanese and the Northeastern Aegean, finishing in Alexandroupoli.

Spend a few days on **Rhodes** (p512), exploring the atmospheric old city and visiting the spectacular **Acropolis of Lindos** (p526) before setting sail for **Tilos** (p547). This laid-back island has escaped the ravages of development and is a great place for walkers. The next stop is **Nisyros** (p551), with its breathtaking volcano and lush flora. Call briefly at **Kos** (p555) to lounge on long, sandy beaches and then hop on a ferry to **Patmos** (p575), an island that St John the Divine found sufficiently inspiring to pen his *Book of Revelations*. Patmos has good connections to ultra-laid-back **Ikaria** (p587), where you can laze at some of the Aegean's best beaches before continuing to **Chios** (p604) and its fabulous mastic villages of the south. The next stop is **Lesvos** (Mytilini; p616), birthplace of the poet Sappho, and producer of Greece's finest ouzo and arguably some of the country's finest olive oil. **Limnos** (p627) is little more than a transit point on the journey north to **Samothraki** (p632) and the Sanctuary of the Great Gods. The final leg is to the Thracian port of **Alexandroupoli** (p327), where travellers will find good transport connections to Thessaloniki and Athens.

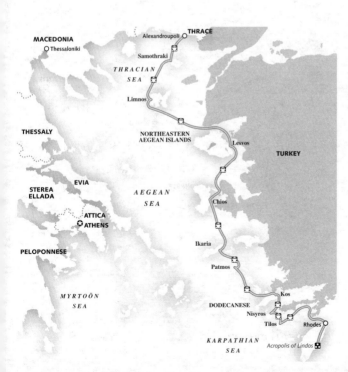

Starting in the far south of Greece, this leisurely 800km-long trip hops through the Dodecanese to the north-eastern Aegean islands with lots of beaches and stunning scenery en route.

EXPLORING THE PELOPONNESE
Two Weeks / Athens to Athens

This route mixes island life with the ancient sights and villages of the Peloponnese peninsula. It's only a short hop from Athens but it feels worlds away.

Jump on a ferry from **Athens** (p101) to Methana from where you can visit the ancient theatre of **Epidavros** (p192) and take in some star-lit classical performances. Next head to graceful **Nafplio** (p186) with its mansions, museums and lively port. From here, it's easy to do day trips to the impressive acropolis at **Tiryns** (p192) and the citadel of **Mycenae** (p184). Head west from Nafplio to the medieval village of **Dimitsana** (p197), perched high on a hill and a magnet for hikers. A detour north will take you to the sanctuary of **Ancient Olympia** (p227) where you can stand in the stadium that first hosted the Games. South of Dimitsana is the World Heritage–listed **Mystras** (p202), the massive ruins of an ancient fortress town that was the last stronghold of the Byzantine Empire. If you enjoy stretching your legs, head south to the rugged and remote **Mani** (p209). Explore the Taÿgetos Mountains and tiny, isolated coves. Walk out to one of mainland Europe's most southerly points at **Cape Tenaro** (p213), mentioned in Homer's 'Iliad'. Follow the coast east to spectacular **Monemvasia** (p205), Greece's answer to France's Mont St-Michel, and spend at least a day exploring the medieval cobbled alleyways and staying in atmospheric lodgings within the walls. A short journey south brings you to Neapoli where you can hop on a ferry to the unspoilt island of **Kythira** (p231) with its fine beaches and tiny villages. From here, another ferry will return you to Athens.

This 900km-long route through the Peloponnese peninsula takes in some of Greece's most beautiful medieval towns and historic sights, and dramatic scenery that's ideal for hikers.

TAILORED TRIPS

ON THE GO

If you really fancy a vacation that combines a number of activities beyond beaching it and dining then listen up. Start with some relaxing fly fishing on the Aoös River near **Konitsa** (p346) in Epiros. After a lunch of freshly caught trout, try walking the **Vikos Gorge** (p344) and maybe follow that with a mountain hike to **Drakolimni** (Dragon Lake; p343). Now take your gear south and check out some fast windsurfing at **Vasiliki** (p691) on the island of Lefkada. When surfed out and you've caught your breath, trek on southwards across the Gulf of Corinth to the deep southwest of the Peloponnese at **Karitena** (p196) where you can white-water raft or hot dog a fast-flowing river and or simply hike. Now hop on a slow ferry to **Crete** (p457) from the southern Peloponnese and really do some walking. Hike the Trans-European E4 walking trail (p486) and take in the spectacular **Samaria Gorge** (p491) while you are at it. Allow a good week for this very challenging slog. Now cruise to **Rhodes** (p512) and take in some super scuba-diving and when done with exploring the depths, zip across the water to kitesurf at **Mikri Vigla** (p411) on Naxos. Exhausted?

NORTHERN ANTIQUITIES

Make Thessaloniki your base and seek out some of the lesser-known but no less spectacular sites of the sprawling regions of Epiros, Macedonia and Thrace. This itinerary is best accomplished with your own transport.

Revel for a day or two in the vibrant nightlife of **Thessaloniki** (p282) and visit its numerous museums, then head west to the ancient Macedonian capital of **Pella** (p310), where you can admire the ruins of Alexander the Great's home base. See the stunning tomb of Alexander's father Phillip of Macedon at nearby **Vergina** (p313), the north's singularly most impressive archaeological site. Cross the looming Pindos Mountains to **Ioannina** (p337) from where you can easily visit the splendid amphitheatre and oracle of **Dodoni** (p341), the eerie underground site of ancient Hades at the **Nekromanteio of Afyra** (p352), close to the Epirot coast, and the Roman-era settlement of **Nikopolis** (p350). Cross back to Macedonia and take another breather in Thessaloniki before heading east. The first stop will be **Philippi** (p306), a Roman site where Christianity was first accepted in Europe and close to the busy port of **Kavala** (p306) with its archaeological museum. Do not miss out on the spectacular **Sanctuary of the Great Gods** (p634) on the island of Samothraki where the Winged Victory of Samothrace was found (now on display in the Louvre in Paris).

History

PREHISTORY

The discovery of a Neanderthal skull in a cave on the Halkidiki peninsula of Macedonia confirmed the presence of humans in Greece 700,000 years ago; and bones and tools from as far back as Palaeolithic times (around 6500 BC) have been found in the Pindos Mountains.

Pastoral communities emerged during Neolithic times (7000–3000 BC), primarily in the fertile region that is now Thessaly. These well-organised people grew barley and wheat; bred sheep and goats; and used clay to produce pots, vases and stylised representations of idols as figures of worship.

By 3000 BC settlements had developed into streets, squares and mud-brick houses. The villages were organised around a large palace-like structure that belonged to the tribal leader. The most complete Neolithic settlements in Greece are Dimini (inhabited from 4000 to 1200 BC) and Sesklo, near Volos.

Around 3000 BC Indo-European migrants introduced the processing of bronze into Greece and from there began three remarkable civilisations: Cycladic, Minoan and Mycenaean.

Greece Before History, by Priscilla Murray and Curtis Neil Runnels, is a good introduction to Greece's earliest days.

ARTISTIC & CULTURAL LEGACIES
Ancient Civilisations
CYCLADIC CIVILISATION

The Cycladic civilisation – centred on the islands of the Cyclades – comprised a cluster of small island communities that relied primarily on Neolithic farming methods and fishing. However, their society developed a sophisticated artistic temperament.

The most striking legacy of this civilisation is the carving of the statuettes from Parian marble – the famous Cycladic figurines. The statuettes depicted images of the Great Mother (a form of early worship, see p35 for more details). Other remains include bronze and obsidian tools and weapons, gold jewellery, and stone and clay vases and pots. Cycladic sculptors are also renowned for their impressive, life-sized *kouroi* (marble statues), carved during the Archaic period.

Scholars divide the Cycladic civilisation into three periods: Early (3000–2000 BC), Middle (2000–1500 BC) and Late (1500–1100 BC).

MINOAN CIVILISATION

The Minoans – named after King Minos, the mythical ruler of Crete – were the first advanced civilisation to emerge in Europe, drawing their inspiration from two great Middle Eastern civilisations: the Mesopotamian and the Egyptian.

TIMELINE

7000–3000 BC	3000–1100 BC	1700–1550 BC
For 4000 years the early inhabitants of the Greek peninsula live a simple agrarian life, growing crops and herding animals. Communities with housing and planned streets begin to appear by around 3000 BC.	The discovery of blending copper and tin into a strong alloy gives rise to the Bronze Age. Trade gains traction; increased prosperity sees the birth of the Cycladic and Minoan – and later, the Mycenaean – civilisations.	Santorini erupts with a cataclysmic explosion, one of the largest volcanic events in recorded history, causing a Mediterranean-wide tsunami that scholars suggest contributed to the destruction of Minoan civilisation.

The Minoan civilisation reached its peak during the Middle period; around 2000 BC the large palace complexes of Knossos, Phaistos, Malia and Zakros were built, marking a sharp break from Neolithic village life. Evidence uncovered in these grand palaces on Crete indicates a sophisticated society, splendid architecture and wonderful detailed frescoes. It had highly developed agriculture, an extensive irrigation system and advanced hydraulic sewerage systems (that included the use of ventilation shafts).

The advent of bronze enabled the Minoans to build great boats, which helped them establish a powerful *thalassocracy* (prosperous maritime trade). As accomplished sailors, they exported their wares to Asia Minor (the west of present-day Turkey), Europe and North Africa, as well as to continental Greece. They used tremendous skill to produce fine pottery and metalwork of great beauty.

Scholars are still debating about the sequence of events that led to the ultimate demise of the Minoans. Scientific evidence suggests the civilisation was weakened by a massive tsunami and ash fallout attributed to the eruption of a cataclysmic volcano on Thira (Santorini) around 1500 BC. Some argue a second, powerful quake a century later decimated the society. And others blame the invading Mycenaeans.

> Most archaeologists split the Minoan civilisation into three phases: Early (3000–2100 BC), Middle (2100–1500 BC) and Late (1500–1100 BC).

MYCENAEAN CIVILISATION

The decline of the Minoan civilisation coincided with the rise of the first great civilisation on the Greek mainland, the Mycenaean (1600–1100 BC), which reached its peak between 1500 and 1200 BC. The civilisation is named after the ancient city of Mycenae, though it's also called the Achaean civilisation, after the Indo-European branch of migrants who had settled in mainland Greece and absorbed many aspects of Minoan culture.

Mycenaean society was characterised by independent city-states such as Corinth, Pylos, Tiryns and, most powerful of them all, Mycenae. Powerful monarchs ruled from imposing palaces heavily fortified within massive walls on easily defensible hill tops. The Mycenaeans adorned their palaces with frescoes and documented commercial transactions on tablets in Linear B (a form of Greek language 500 years older than the Ionic Greek used by Homer). But their most impressive legacy is the production of magnificent gold masks, refined jewellery and metal ornaments, the best of which are in the National Archaeological Museum in Athens (p127).

The collapse of the Mycenaean civilisation came around 1200 BC, and is often attributed to Dorian incursion (see Geometric Age, p34); however, scholars are still considering whether natural disasters are responsible.

> *The Man Who Deciphered Linear B*, by Andrew Robinson, tells of the fascinating story of Michael Ventris, the young genius who cracked the code in 1952, solving one of archaeology's greatest linguistic mysteries.

1500–1200 BC	1200–800 BC	800–700 BC
The rigid and authoritarian Mycenaean culture from the Peloponnesian mainland usurps much of the Cretan and Cycladic cultures. Goldsmithing is a predominant feature of Mycenaean life.	The Dorian tribes herald a 400-year period of obscurity in terms of international trade; but they excel in the use of iron weaponry and ironwork in architecture, and develop striking geometric designs on pottery.	Homer composes the 'Iliad' and the 'Odyssey' around this time. The two epic poems are Greece's earliest pieces of literary art, and are still praised for their poetic genius.

Geometric Age

The Dorians were an ancient Hellenic people who had settled in the Peloponnese by the 8th century BC. Their origins remain uncertain: they are generally thought to have come from Epiros or northern Macedonia, but some historians argue that they only arrived from that direction because they had been driven out of Doris, in central Greece, by the Mycenaeans.

In the 11th or 12th century BC these warriorlike people fanned out to occupy much of the mainland, seizing control of the Mycenaean kingdoms and enslaving the inhabitants. The Dorians heralded a traumatic break with the past, and the following 400-year period is often referred to as Greece's 'dark age'. But their influence was not all negative. They brought iron with them and developed a new style of pottery, decorated with striking geometric designs; although art historians are still divided on whether these were merely refinements of the sophisticated oriental forms and designs perfected by Ionians in Attica. The Dorians also helped introduce the polytheistic religion (see opposite), which combined pagan beliefs with Eastern mythology.

Greek is Europe's oldest written language, second only to Chinese in the world. It is traceable back to the Linear B script of the Minoans and Mycenaeans. For more on Linear B script, try www.ancientscripts.com/linearb.html.

Archaic Age

During the Archaic period, about 1000–800 BC, Greek culture developed rapidly; many of the advancements in literature, sculpture, theatre, architecture and intellectual endeavour began; this revival overlapped with the Classical age (the two eras are often classified as the Hellenic period). Advances included the Greek alphabetic script (of Phoenician origin, though the Greeks introduced the practice of indicating vowels within the script); the verses of Homer (which created a sense of a shared Mycenaean past); the founding of the Olympic Games (p38); and central sanctuaries such as Delphi (a neutral meeting ground for lively negotiations and ceremonial reconciliations). These common bonds gave Greeks a sense of national identity and emerging platforms to express intellect and opinion, and to determine regional political strategy.

By about 800 BC Greece had begun to settle into a new social and political structure. The Dorians had developed into a class of landholding aristocrats and Greece had been divided into a series of independent city-states. The most powerful of these were Argos, Athens, Corinth, Elis, Sparta and Thiva (Thebes).

The city-states strived for autonomy; most abolished monarchic rule in favour of an aristocratic form of government, usually headed by an *arhon* (chief magistrate) who ruled by a rudimentary consensus. The population often disliked aristocrats for their inherited privileges and some city-states fell to the rule of tyrants (who seized their position rather than inheriting it) – after Kypselos, the first tyrant of Corinth, started the practice in Corinth around 650 BC. (While today the word 'may have darker over-

800–650 BC	700–500 BC	594 BC
Independent city-states begin to emerge in the Archaic Age as the Dorians develop. Aristocrats rule these ministates while tyrants occasionally take power by force. The Greek alphabet emerges from Phoenician script.	Having originated around 1000 BC in the Peloponnese, the Spartans come to play a decisive role in Greek history. Politically and militarily, the Spartans dominate for around 200 years.	Solon, a ruling aristocrat in Athens, introduces rules of fair play to his citizenry. His radical rule-changing – in effect creating human and political rights – is credited as being the first step to real democracy.

tones, in ancient times tyrants were often seen as being on the side of ordinary citizens.) Kypselos was responsible for removing the ruling aristocracy from power and establishing a set of laws that redistributed wealth and allowed the city's citizens to regain control over their lands.

PAGANISM TO MONOTHEISM

Early Worship

The origins of ancient Greek worship are found in antiquity (c 3000 BC); later the worship focuses mainly on 12 major and minor deities – essentially a pastiche of various pagan gods, goddesses, belief systems and fertility cults of indigenous tribes and settlers. Surviving representations include terracotta (or stone) statuettes of the Great Mother (the earth goddess) found in early Greek tombs and sanctuaries, depictions on fresco fragments or gold pieces, and lists of the names of gods found on clay tablets.

It was the Dorians who dispensed with fertility goddesses and adopted the Mycenaean gods Poseidon, Zeus and Apollo. New deities such as Aphrodite (originally from Asia) were introduced later; paving the way for the Greek religious pantheon as personified in Greek mythology (see p53) and general Hellenic texts.

Christianity

St Paul had visited Greece several times in the 1st century AD and made many converts. The definitive boost to the spread of Christianity in this part of the world came with the conversion of the Roman emperors and the rise of Constantinople and the Byzantine Empire, which blended Hellenic culture with Christianity.

In 394 Christianity emerged as the state's official religion under Emperor Theodosius I. He outlawed the worship of all Greek (and Roman) gods, now branded as pagan; this proclamation forced the closure of 'heathen' temples, such as those at Delphi, Olympia and the Parthenon – many were converted to Christian churches – while all public pagan activities were banned or suspended, including the Olympic Games. Athens remained an important cultural centre until 529, when Emperor Justinian forbade the teaching of classical philosophy in favour of Christian theology, then seen as the supreme form of all intellectual endeavour.

Greek Orthodox Church

Although Constantinople fell in 1453 under Turkish Ottoman rule, Islamic doctrine tolerated the Byzantine Orthodox faith, which the Turks designated a secular administrative body. Paradoxically, while the exarchs (Orthodox bishops) retained spiritual authority over the Greek people, this enabled the Church to become the custodian of Greek identity by maintaining the links with tradition, culture and language. (However, there were tremendous political and economic advantages to embracing Islam and mass conversions were still common.)

These days, the Church still does not have the same Church–State separation as many other Western countries. The Church is vocal about its strong opposition to non-Orthodox denominations and continues to influence political public policy (eg after years of controversy, cremation was only recently legalised in Greece). For more on religion, see p60.

490 BC	480 BC	479 BC
Athens invokes the ire of the distant Persians by supporting insurgencies within Persian territorial domains. Seeking revenge, the Persian king Darius sends an army to teach Greece a lesson but is defeated at Marathon.	Darius' son and heir Xerxes seeks revenge for the defeat at Marathon. The enormous forces sent to crush Greece defeat Leonidas at Thermopylae and then sack Athens, but are routed at sea off Salamis (Salamina).	The Greeks pay back their defeat at the hands of Xerxes by smashing the Persian army of Mardonius at the decisive Battle of Plataea under the Spartan leader Pausanias. The Persian Wars are finally over.

Democracy

The seafaring city-state of Athens, meanwhile, was still in the hands of aristocrats when Solon was appointed *arhon* in 594 BC with a mandate to defuse the mounting tensions between the haves and the have-nots. He cancelled all debts and freed those who had become enslaved because of them. Declaring all free Athenians equal by law, Solon abolished inherited privileges and restructured political power, establishing four classes based on wealth. Although only the first two classes were eligible for office, all four could elect magistrates and vote on legislation, forming the basis of a mainly representative civic governance model. Solon's reforms have become regarded as a harbinger of the ideological democratic system found in most current Western legal traditions.

Scientists have recently discovered a bronze and wood astronomical instrument, known as the Antikythera Mechanism, which helped the ancients plot the four-year Olympiad cycle.

Classical Age

During Greece's archetypal golden age, from the 6th to 4th centuries BC, many of the city-states enjoyed increased economic reform, political prosperity and greater cultural creativity. The historians Herodotus and Thucydides documented political narratives and wrote of significant events of the time. Literature and drama also bloomed during this period, led by notable figures such as Aeschylus, Euripides and Sophocles who contributed dramatic tragedies, and Aristophanes who inspired political satire with his comedies; their contributions still influence current Western culture. Athens in particular reached its zenith, especially once the territorial wrangling between Athens, Sparta, and the Persians (see The Persian Wars, p38) had been resolved.

After defeating the Persians, the disciplined Spartans retreated to the Peloponnese, while Athens basked in its role as liberator. In 477 BC it founded the Delian League, the naval alliance that was based on Delos and was formed to liberate the city-states still occupied by Persia, and to defend against further Persian attack. The alliance included many of the Aegean islands and some of the Ionian city-states in Asia Minor. Swearing allegiance to Athens and making an annual contribution to the treasury of ships (later just money) were mandatory and Athens punished recalcitrant members of the alliance; the league, in effect, transformed into an Athenian empire.

Homer's classic work, the 'Iliad', relates in poetic epithet a mythical episode of the Trojan War. Its sequel, the 'Odyssey', recounts the epic adventures of Odysseus and his companions in their journey home from the Trojan War.

Indeed, when Pericles became leader of Athens in 461 BC, he moved the treasury from Delos to the Acropolis. He used the treasury's funds to construct new buildings and grander temples on the Acropolis, to replace those destroyed by the Persians, and to link Athens to the port of Piraeus with long, parallel fortification walls designed to withstand any future onslaught.

Athens' elegant temples and monuments built during this time, such as the Parthenon (p120) and the Erechtheion (p121), and were the pinnacle of architectural brilliance as well as enduring symbols of power. Elsewhere, many fine temples were also being constructed, including the Temple of Zeus

477 BC	461–32 BC	431–21 BC
Seeking security while building a de facto empire, the Athenians establish a political and military alliance called the Delian League. Many city-states and islands join the new club.	New Athenian leader Pericles shifts power from Delos to Athens and uses the treasury wealth of the Delian League to fund massive works, including the construction of the magnificent Parthenon, an enduring legacy.	The military might of Sparta runs afoul of the commercial and artistic clout of Athens over an alliance with Corcyra. The spat becomes a full-blown war of attrition, with Athens barricaded and the Peloponnese embargoed.

THE SPARTANS

During the battle of Thermopylae in 480 BC, one of the most celebrated battles in history, a few hundred soldiers held an entire Persian army at bay and died to a man doing so. What kind of soldiers could display such selfless bravery? Spartan ones, of course.

Admired and feared, the Spartans were held in mythic awe by their fellow Greeks for their ferocious and self-sacrificing martial supremacy, marching into battle in a disciplined, lock-stepped phalanx, living (and very often dying) by the motto 'return with your shield or on it'.

They were the product of harsh ideology. Every Spartiate (usually the male full citizen) was by definition a soldier (hoplite), who began his training almost from birth. Poor recruits were weeded out early – a citizens' committee decided which newborn babies did not pass muster (they would then be left on a mountain top to die).

The surviving children endured 13 years of training to foster supreme physical fitness from the age of seven, and suffered institutionalised beating 'competitions' to toughen them up.

All hoplites were bound to military service until the age of 60, lived in barracks until the age of 30 (even if married) and were obliged to eat at the *phiditia* (mess hall). Shame and often death awaited retreaters, cowards and those who didn't live up to their tough code of battle.

But the Spartiates were the lucky ones. Helots, Sparta's slaves, had no rights at all and those suspected of any kind of misdemeanour were hunted and killed by Sparta's secret police.

A measure of the contempt in which the Spartiates held their helots (and also a sign of their galloping paranoia) came after the Peloponnesian Wars (in which Sparta was the ultimate victor). Dwindling numbers of Spartiates meant that the lower orders had to fight as well. Asked by their helot masters to pick 2000 of their bravest, these fighting helots, who thought they were to be made full citizens, were then executed en masse.

Although admired by some Greek thinkers, most notably Plato (albeit from the safety of an easygoing democracy), an authoritarian system that could motivate a body of men to sit calmly under a hail of arrows also necessarily stifled individual initiative and the introduction of new ideas.

This rigidity and lack of innovation contributed, along with the exhausting Peloponnesian Wars, to the decline of Sparta, which did not quite know what to do with its dominance. The battle of Leuctra in 371 BC was the first major defeat of the Spartans in open battle and marked the beginning of the collapse of their power.

(p228) at Olympia and the Temple of Poseidon (p162) at Sounion. It was also during this Classical period that sculptors developed a more naturalistic, aesthetic style for marble pieces and bronze casts; and it was Pericles who commissioned the Athenian sculptor Pheidias to create the enduring marble friezes of the Parthenon.

With the Aegean Sea safely under its wing, Athens began to look westwards for further expansion, bringing it into conflict with the Sparta-dominated Peloponnesian League. A series of skirmishes and provocations subsequently led to the Peloponnesian Wars (p39).

The web portal www .ancientgreece.com is great for all things ancient and Greek.

413–404 BC	399 BC	371–62 BC
A second war between Sparta and Athens breaks out over the distant colony of Sicily, ending an eight-year truce. The Spartans break the Athenian siege and Sparta assumes total dominance.	Socrates stands at trial accused of corrupting the young with his pedagogical speeches. A jury condemns Socrates to death. Rather than appealing for voluntary exile, Socrates defiantly accepts a cup of hemlock.	Thiva (Thebes), a small city-state, is in ascendancy and gains control after it wins a land defeat against Sparta at Leuctra. But nine years of Theban dominance ends at the hands of a Spartan-Athenian alliance.

ORIGINAL OLYMPICS

The Olympic tradition emerged around the 11th century BC as a paean to the Greek gods in the form of contests, attended initially by notable men – and women – who assembled before the sanctuary priests and swore to uphold solemn oaths. By the 8th century attendance had grown from a wide confederacy of city-states, and the festival morphed into a male-only major event lasting five days at the site of Olympia (p227). A ceremonial truce was enforced for the duration of the games. Crowds of spectators lined the tracks, where competitors vied for an honourable (and at times dishonourable) victory in athletics, chariot races, wrestling and boxing. Three millennia later, while the scale and scope of the games may have expanded considerably, the basic format is essentially unchanged.

Hellenistic Age

In the century following the Peloponnesian Wars, the battle-weary city-states came under the rule of the Macedonian king Philip II, but it would be his young son and successor, Alexander the Great (p41), who would extend the Hellenistic idea across a vast empire.

Alexander's campaigns of expansion were aimed at uniting the Greeks and spreading Greek language and culture throughout the wider empire. However, the city-states felt disempowered by the loss of autonomy under the monarch. The Greeks now perceived themselves as part of a larger empire, and it is this concept that characterises the Hellenistic society. Contemporary arts, drama, sculpture and philosophy reflected growing awareness of a new definition of Greek identity.

The Histories, written by Herodotus in the 5th century BC, chronicles the conflicts between the ancient Greek city-states and Persia. The work is considered to be the first narrative of historical events ever written.

Hellenism continued to prosper even under Roman rule (p41). As the Roman province of Achaea, Greece experienced an unprecedented period of peace for almost 300 years, known as the Pax Romana. The Romans had always venerated Greek art, literature and philosophy, and aristocratic Romans sent their offspring to the many schools in Athens. Indeed, the Romans adopted most aspects of Hellenistic culture, spreading its unifying traditions throughout their empire.

The Romans were also the first to refer to the Hellenes as Greeks, derived from the word *graikos* – the name of a prehistoric tribe.

WAR & CONQUEST
The Persian Wars

Athens' rapid growth as a major city-state also meant heavy reliance on food imports from the Black Sea; and Persia's imperial expansion westward threatened strategic coastal trade routes across Asia Minor. Athens' support for a rebellion in the Persian colonies of Asia Minor sparked the Persian drive to destroy the city. Persian emperor Darius spent five years suppress-

359 BC	336 BC	334–323 BC
In the north, the Macedonians are on the rise as King Philip II seizes the initiative in the power vacuum. He seeks alliances with Sparta and Athens on a promise to wage war again on Persia.	Philip's son Alexander assumes leadership of Macedonia following the untimely murder of his father. Within a few years the new king takes up the challenge against Persia laid down by the slain Philip.	Alexander the Great sets out to conquer the known world. Thebes (Thiva) is the first victim, followed by the Persians, the Egyptians and finally the peoples of today's central Asia. He dies in 323 BC.

ing the revolt and remained determined to succeed. A 25,000-strong Persian army reached Attica in 490 BC, but was defeated when an Athenian force of 10,000 outmanoeuvred it at the Battle of Marathon.

When Darius died in 485 BC, his son Xerxes resumed the quest to conquer Greece. In 480 BC Xerxes gathered men from every nation of his empire and launched a massive, coordinated invasion by land and sea. Some 30 city-states met in Corinth to devise a defence (others, including Delphi, sided with the Persians). This joint alliance, the Hellenic League, agreed on a combined army and navy under Spartan command, with the strategy provided by the Athenian leader Themistocles. The Spartan king Leonidas led the army to the pass at Thermopylae, near present-day Lamia, the main passage into central Greece from the north. This bottleneck was easy to defend and, although the Greeks were greatly outnumbered, they held the pass – until a traitor showed the Persians another way over the mountains, from where they turned to attack the Greeks. The Greeks retreated, but Leonidas, along with 300 of his elite Spartan troops, fought to the death in a heroic last stand.

The Trial of Socrates by IF Stone frames in a contemporary investigative light Plato's version of events surrounding the philosopher Socrates' life and death.

The Spartans and their Peloponnesian allies fell back on their second line of defence, an earthen wall across the Isthmus of Corinth, while the Persians advanced upon Athens. Themistocles ordered his people to flee the city, the women and children to seek refuge at Salamis (today's Salamis) and the men to sea with the Athenian naval fleet, while the Persians razed Athens to the ground. The Persian naval campaign, however, was not successful. By skilful manoeuvring, the Greek warships trapped the larger Persian ships in the narrow waters off Salamis, where the smaller, more agile Greek vessels carried the advantage. Xerxes returned to Persia in disgust, leaving his general Mardonius to subdue Greece. The result was quite the reverse; a year later the Greeks, under the command of the Spartan general Pausanias, obliterated the Persian army at the Battle of Plataea.

The Peloponnesian Wars

The Peloponnesian League was essentially a military coalition governed by Sparta, who maintained political dominance over the Peloponnesian region. Athens' growing imperialism threatened Spartan hegemony; the ensuing power struggle was to last almost 30 years.

In *The Peloponnesian War,* Thucydides sets out a historical narrative of the quarrels and warfare between Athens and Sparta.

FIRST PELOPONNESIAN WAR

One of the major triggers of the first Peloponnesian War (431–421 BC) was the Corcyra incident, in which Athens supported Corcyra (present-day Corfu) in a row with Corinth, its mother city. Corinth called on Sparta to help and the Spartans, whose power depended to a large extent on Corinth's wealth and allegiance, duly rallied to the cause.

86 BC–AD 224	324	394
Roman expansion inevitably includes Greek territory. First defeating Macedonia at Pydna in 168 BC, the Romans ultimately overtake the mainland and establish the Pax Romana. It lasts 300 years.	The AD 250 invasion of Greece by the Goths signals the decline of Pax Romana and in 324 the capital of the empire is moved to Constantinople. Christianity gains traction.	Christianity is declared the official religion. All pagan worship of Greek and Roman gods is outlawed. Christian theology supplants classical philosophy.

Athens knew it couldn't defeat the Spartans on land, so it abandoned Attica and withdrew behind its mighty walls, opting to rely on its navy to put pressure on Sparta by blockading the Peloponnese. Athens suffered badly during the siege; plague broke out in the overcrowded city, killing a third of the population – including Pericles – but the defences held firm. The blockade of the Peloponnese eventually began to hurt and the two cities negotiated an uneasy truce.

SECOND PELOPONNESIAN WAR

The truce lasted until 413 BC, when the Spartans went to the aid of the Sicilian city of Syracuse, which the Athenians had been besieging for three years. The Spartans ended the siege, and destroyed the Athenian fleet and army in the process.

Despite this, Athens fought on for a further nine years before it finally surrendered to Sparta in 404 BC. Corinth urged the total destruction of Athens, but the Spartans felt honour-bound to spare the city that had saved Greece from the Persians. Instead, they crippled it by confiscating its fleet, abolishing the Delian League and tearing down the walls between the city and Piraeus.

The Rise of Macedon

The Greeks were by now engineering their own decline. Sparta began a doomed campaign to reclaim the cities of Asia Minor from Persian rule, bringing the Persians back into Greek affairs where they found willing allies in Athens and an increasingly powerful Thebes (Thiva). The rivalry between Sparta and Thebes culminated in the decisive Battle of Leuctra in 371 BC, where Thebes, led by Epaminondas, inflicted Sparta's first defeat in a pitched land battle. Spartan influence collapsed and Thebes filled the vacuum. In a surprise about-turn, Athens now allied itself with Sparta, and their combined forces met the Theban army at Mantinea in the Peloponnese in 362 BC. Thebes won the battle, but Epaminondas was killed; and without him, Theban power soon crumbled.

However, the political influence of the major city-states had by now been significantly eroded. Their strength waning, they were unable to combat the new power in the north, Macedon – geographically the modern *nomós* (prefecture) of Macedonia – which was gathering strength under its monarch, Philip II.

In 338 BC, Philip II marched into Greece and defeated a combined army of Athenians and Thebans at the Battle of Chaironeia. In a move that signalled the beginning of the end of the autonomous city-state structure, Philip called together all the city-states (except Sparta who resisted alliance) at Corinth and persuaded them to swear allegiance to Macedonia by promising to campaign against Persia. But before the monarch could

Philip II engaged the philosopher Aristotle to tutor the teenage Alexander, who was greatly inspired by Homer's 'Iliad'. Alexander retained a strong interest in the arts and culture throughout his life.

529	1204	1209
Athens' cultural influence is dealt a fatal blow when Emperor Justinian outlaws the teaching of classical philosophy in favour of Christian theology, by now regarded as the ultimate form of intellectual endeavour.	Marauding Frankish Crusaders sack Constantinople. Trading religious fervour for self-interest, the Crusaders strike a blow that sets Constantinople on the road to a slow demise.	Geoffrey de Villehardouin parcels out the Peloponnese into fiefs; he paves the way for his nephew, another Geoffrey, who appoints himself Prince of Morea (the name given to medieval Peloponnese).

realise those ambitions, a Macedonian noble assassinated Philip in 336 BC. His son, 20-year-old Alexander, became king.

Alexander the Great

Philip II's death had been the signal for rebellions throughout the budding empire, but Alexander wasted no time in crushing them, making an example of Thebes by razing it to the ground. After restoring order, he turned his attention to the Persian Empire and marched his army of 40,000 men into Asia Minor in 334 BC.

After a few bloody battles with the Persians, most notably at Issus (333 BC), Alexander succeeded in conquering Syria, Palestine and Egypt – where he was proclaimed pharaoh and founded the city of Alexandria. He then pursued the Persian king, Darius III, defeating his army in 331 BC. Alexander continued his reign east into what is now Uzbekistan, Balkh in Afghanistan and northern India. His ambition was now to conquer the world, which he believed ended at the sea beyond India, but his soldiers grew weary and in 324 BC forced him to return to Mesopotamia, where he settled in Babylon. The following year, at the age of 33, he fell ill suddenly and died. His generals swooped like vultures on the empire and, when the dust settled, Alexander's empire had been carved up into independent kingdoms.

Macedonia lost control of the Greek city-states to the south, which banded together into the Aetolian League, centred on Delphi, and the Achaean League, based in the Peloponnese. Athens and Sparta joined neither.

> 'Although officially under the auspices of Rome, some major Greek cities were given the freedom to self-govern'

FOREIGN RULE
Roman Era

While Alexander the Great was forging his vast empire in the east, the Romans had been expanding theirs to the west, and now they were keen to start making inroads into Greece. After several inconclusive clashes, they defeated Macedon in 168 BC at the Battle of Pydna.

The Achaean League was defeated in 146 BC and the Roman consul Mummius made an example of the rebellious Corinthians by destroying their city. In 86 BC Athens joined an ill-fated rebellion against the Romans in Asia Minor staged by the king of the Black Sea region, Mithridates VI. In retribution, the Roman statesman Sulla invaded Athens and took off with its most valuable sculptures. Greece now became the Graeco-Roman province of Achaea. Although officially under the auspices of Rome, some major Greek cities were given the freedom to self-govern to some extent. As the Romans revered Greek culture, Athens retained its status as a centre of learning. During a succession of Roman emperors, namely Augustus, Nero and Hadrian, Greece experienced a period of relative peace, the Pax Romana (see p38), which was to last until the middle of the 3rd century AD.

1453	1460	1684–87
Greece becomes a dominion of the Ottoman Turks after they seize control of Constantinople (modern-day İstanbul), sounding the death knell for the Byzantine Empire.	By 1460 the Morea falls to the Turks and centuries of power struggles between the Turks and Venetians follows.	The Venetians expel the Turks from the Peloponnese in a campaign that sees Venetian troops advance as far as Athens.

The Byzantine Empire & the Crusades

The Pax Romana began to crumble in AD 250 when the Goths invaded Greece, the first of a succession of invaders spurred on by the 'great migrations' of the Visigoths and then the Ostrogoths from the middle Balkans.

In an effort to resolve the conflict in the region, in AD 324 the Roman Emperor Constantine I, a Christian convert, transferred the capital of the empire from Rome to Byzantium, a city on the western shore of the Bosphorus, which was renamed Constantinople (present-day İstanbul). While Rome went into terminal decline, the eastern capital began to grow in wealth and strength as a Christian state (see the boxed text, p35). In the ensuing centuries, Byzantine Greece faced continued pressure from the Persians and Arabs, but it managed to retain its stronghold over the region.

But it is ironic that the demise of the Byzantine Empire was accelerated by fellow Christians from the west – the Frankish Crusaders. The stated mission of the Crusades was to liberate the Holy Land from the Muslims, but in reality they were driven as much by greed as by religious zeal. The first three Crusades passed by without affecting the area, but the leaders of the Fourth Crusade (in the early part of the 13th century) decided that Constantinople presented richer pickings than Jerusalem and struck a deal with Venice, who had helped prop up the Crusades.

Constantinople was sacked in 1204 and much of the Byzantine Empire was partitioned into fiefdoms ruled by self-styled 'Latin' (mostly Frankish or western-Germanic) princes. The Venetians, meanwhile, had also secured a foothold in Greece. Over the next few centuries they acquired all the key Greek ports, including Methoni, Koroni and Monemvasia in the Peloponnese (then known as the Morea), and the island of Crete, and became the wealthiest and most powerful traders in the Mediterranean.

Despite this sorry state of affairs, Byzantium was not yet dead. In 1259 the Byzantine emperor Michael VIII Palaeologos recaptured the Peloponnese and made the city of Mystras his headquarters. Many eminent Byzantine artists, architects, intellectuals and philosophers converged on the city for a final burst of Byzantine creativity. Michael VIII managed to reclaim Constantinople in 1261, but by this time Byzantium was a shadow of its former self.

Greece is home to the oldest mosque in Europe. The mosque at Didymotiho (p332) was built by Ottoman Sultan Bayazit I in the late 14th century.

Ottoman Rule

Constantinople was soon facing a much greater threat from the east. The Seljuk Turks, a tribe from central Asia, had first appeared on the eastern fringes of the empire in the middle of the 11th century. The Ottomans (the followers of Osman, who ruled from 1289 to 1326) supplanted the Seljuks as the dominant Turkish tribe. The Muslim Ottomans began to expand rapidly the areas under their control and by the mid-15th century were harassing the Byzantine Empire on all sides.

1770s & 1780s	1814	1821
Catherine the Great of Russia dislodges the Turks from the Black Sea coast and assigns several towns with Ancient Greek names. She offers Greeks financial incentives and free land to settle the region, and many accept.	The underground Hellenic Independence organisation known as the Filiki Eteria (Friendly Society) is established in the town of Odessa on the Black Sea coast. Its influence spreads throughout Greece.	On 25 March, Bishop Germanos of Patra (a member of the Filiki Eteria) signals the beginning of the War of Independence on the mainland. Greece celebrates this date as its national day of Independence.

On 29 May 1453, Constantinople fell under Turkish Ottoman rule (referred to by Greeks as *turkokratia*). Once more Greece became a battleground, this time fought over by the Turks and Venetians. Eventually, with the exception of the Ionian Islands (where the Venetians retained control), Greece became part of the Ottoman Empire.

Ottoman power reached its zenith under Sultan Süleyman the Magnificent, who ruled between 1520 and 1566. His successor, Selim the Sot, added Cyprus to their dominions in 1570, but his death in 1574 marked an end to serious territorial expansion. Although they captured Crete in 1669 after a 25-year campaign, the ineffectual sultans that followed in the late 16th and 17th centuries saw the empire go into steady decline.

Venice expelled the Turks from the Peloponnese in a three-year campaign (1684–87) that saw Venetian troops advance as far as Athens. During this campaign, Venetian artillery struck gunpowder stored inside the ruins of the Acropolis and badly damaged the Parthenon.

The Ottomans restored rule in 1715, but never regained their former authority. By the end of the 18th century pockets of Turkish officials and aristocrats had emerged throughout Greece as self-governing cliques that made cursory gestures of obligation to the sultan in Constantinople. Also, some Greeks had gained influence under the sultan's lax leadership or enjoyed privileged administrative status; they were influential church clerics, wealthy merchants, landowners or governors, ruling over the provincial Greek peasants. But, there also existed an ever-increasing group of Greeks, including many intellectual expatriates, who aspired to emancipation.

Russia campaigned to liberate its fellow Christians in the south, and sent Russian agents to foment rebellion, first in the Peloponnese in 1770 and then in Epiros in 1786. Both insurrections were crushed ruthlessly – the latter by Ali Pasha (1741–1822), the Ottoman governor of Ioannina (who would proceed to set up his own power base in defiance of the sultan).

INDEPENDENCE

In 1814 businessmen Athanasios Tsakalof, Emmanuel Xanthos and Nikolaos Skoufas founded the first Greek independence party, the Filiki Eteria (Friendly Society). The underground organisation's message spread quickly. Supporters believed that armed force was the only effective means of liberation, and made generous financial contributions to the Greek fighters.

Ali Pasha's private rebellion against the sultan in 1820 gave the Greeks the impetus they needed. On 25 March 1821, the Greeks launched the War of Independence. Uprisings broke out almost simultaneously across most of Greece and the occupied islands. The fighting was savage and atrocities were committed on both sides; in the Peloponnese 12,000 Turkish inhabitants

The poet Lord Byron was one of a large group of philhellenic volunteers who played an active role in fanning the independence cause. Byron's war effort was cut short when he died in 1824.

1822–29	1827	1827–31
Independence is declared at Epidavros on 13 January 1822, but fighting continues for another seven years. The Ottomans capitulate and accept the terms of the Treaty of Adrianople.	British, French and Russian forces sink the combined Turkish-Egyptian naval fleet in the Battle of Navarino (at Pylos, in the Peloponnese); a decisive action in the War of Independence.	Ioannis Kapodistrias is appointed prime minister of a fledgling government with its capital in the Peloponnesian town of Nafplio. Discontent ensues and Kapodistrias is assassinated.

A FEMALE FORCE

Greek women have played a strong role in Greek resistance movements throughout history and Laskarina Bouboulina (1771–1825), a celebrated seafarer, is one such woman. She became a member of Filiki Eteria (Friendly Society), a major organisation striving for independence against Ottoman rule. Originally from Hydra, she settled in Spetses from where she commissioned the construction of and commanded – as a lady admiral – several warships that were used in significant naval blockades (the most famous vessel being the *Agamemmnon*). She helped maintain the crews of her ships and a small army of soldiers, and supplied the revolutionaries with food, weapons and ammunition, using her ships for transportation. Her role in maritime operations significantly helped the independence movement. However, political factionism within the government led to her postwar arrest and subsequent exile to Spetses, where she died.

Distinguished as a national heroine, streets across Greece bear her name and her image appeared commemoratively on the (now-disused) one-drachma coin. Moreover, her great-granddaughter, Lela Karagiannis, also fought with the resistance in WWII. There are statues dedicated to both women in Spetses Town; and Bouboulina's home is now a private museum (see p370).

were killed after the capture of the city of Tripolitsa (present-day Tripoli), while the Turks retaliated with massacres in Asia Minor, most notoriously on the island of Chios.

The campaign escalated, and within a year the Greeks had captured the fortresses of Monemvasia, Navarino (modern Pylos) and Nafplio in the Peloponnese, and Messolongi, Athens and Thebes. The Greeks proclaimed independence on 13 January 1822 at Epidavros.

Eugène Delacroix' oil canvas, The Massacre at Chios (1824), was inspired by the events in Asia Minor during Greece's War of Independence in 1821. The painting hangs in the Louvre Museum in Paris.

Regional differences over national governance twice escalated into civil war (in 1824 and 1825). The Ottomans took advantage and by 1827 the Turks (with Egyptian reinforcements) had recaptured most of the Peloponnese, as well as Messolongi and Athens. The Western powers intervened and a combined Russian, French and British naval fleet sunk the Turkish-Egyptian fleet in the Battle of Navarino in October 1827. Sultan Mahmud II defied the odds and proclaimed a holy war, prompting Russia to send troops into the Balkans to engage the Ottoman army. Fighting continued until 1829 when, with Russian troops at the gates of Constantinople, the sultan accepted Greek independence with the Treaty of Adrianople (independence was formally recognised in 1830).

THE MODERN GREEK NATION

The Greeks, meanwhile, had been busy organising the independent state they had proclaimed several years earlier. In April 1827 they elected Ioannis Kapodistrias, a Corfiot and former diplomat of Russian Tsar Alexander I, as the first president of the republic; and chose Nafplio, in the Peloponnese, as the capital.

1833	1862–63	1863–64
The powers of the Entente (Britain, France and Russia) decree that Greece should be a monarchy and dispatch Prince Otto of Bavaria to Greece to be the first appointed monarch in modern Greece.	The monarchy takes a nosedive and King Otto is deposed in a bloodless coup. The British return the Ionian Islands (a British protectorate since 1815) to Greece, in an effort to quell Greece's expansionist urges.	The British engineer the ascension to the Greek throne of Danish Prince William, later crowned King George I. His 50-year reign begins with a new constitution in 1864.

However, there was much dissension within Greek ranks. Kapodistrias was assassinated in 1831 after he had ordered the imprisonment of a Maniot chieftain, part of a response to undermine rising discontent and rebellion among the many parties (including leaders of the independence movement) whose authority had been weakened by the new state.

Amid the ensuing anarchy, Britain, France and Russia declared Greece a monarchy. They set on the throne a non-Greek, 17-year-old Bavarian Prince Otto, who arrived in Nafplio in January 1833. The new kingdom (established by the London Convention of 1832) consisted of the Peloponnese, Sterea Ellada, the Cyclades and the Sporades.

After moving the capital to Athens in 1834, King Otto proved to be an abrasive ruler who had alienated the independence veterans by giving the most prestigious official posts to his Bavarian court. However, by the end of the 1850s most of the stalwarts of the War of Independence had been replaced by a new breed of university graduates (Athens University was founded in 1817).

The Great Idea

Greece's foreign policy (dubbed the 'Great Idea') was to assert sovereignty over its dispersed Greek populations. Set against the background of the Crimean conflict, British and French interests were nervous at the prospect of a Greece alliance with Russia against the Ottomans, especially as in 1862 Otto had been ousted in a bloodless coup.

British influence in the Ionian Islands had begun in 1815 (following a spell of political ping-pong between the Venetians, Russians and French). The British did improve the islands' infrastructure and many locals adopted British customs (such as afternoon tea and cricket). But, Greek independence put pressure on Britain to give sovereignty to the Greek nation, and in 1864 the British left. Meanwhile, Britain simultaneously eased onto the Greek throne the young Danish Prince William, crowned King George I in 1863. His 50-year reign eventually brought some stability to the country, beginning with a new constitution in 1864 that established the power of democratically elected representatives.

In 1881 Greece acquired Thessaly and part of Epiros as a result of a Russo-Turkish war. But Greece failed miserably when, in 1897, it tried to attack Turkey in the north in an effort to reach *enosis* (union) with Crete (who had persistently agitated for liberation from the Ottomans). The bid drained much of the country's resources and timely diplomatic intervention by the great powers prevented the Turkish army from taking Athens.

Crete was placed under international administration, but the government of the island was gradually handed over to Greeks, and in 1905 the president of the Cretan assembly, Eleftherios Venizelos, announced Crete's union with Greece (although this was not recognised by international law until 1913).

'King Otto alienated the independence veterans by giving the most prestigious official posts to his Bavarian court'

1883	1896	1912–13
Greece completes construction of the Corinth Canal that cuts through the Isthmus of Corinth. The engineering feat opens a link between the Aegean and Ionian Seas.	The staging of the first modern Olympic Games in Athens marks Greece's coming of age. Winners receive a silver medal and olive crown, and second and third places receive a bronze medal and a laurel branch, respectively.	The Balkan Wars erupt when Greece and Serbia initially side with Bulgaria against Turkey over the territory of Macedonia. Then Greece and Serbia fight for the same territory against Bulgaria. Greece's territory expands.

Venizelos went on to become prime minister of Greece in 1910 and was the country's leading politician until his republican sympathies brought about his downfall in 1935.

Balkan Wars

Although the Ottoman Empire was in its death throes at the beginning of the 20th century, it had still retained Macedonia. This was a prize coveted by the newly formed Balkan countries of Serbia and Bulgaria, as well as by Greece, and led to the outbreak of the Balkan Wars (1912 and 1913). The outcome was the Treaty of Bucharest (August 1913), which greatly expanded Greek territory (and with it its fertile agricultural resources). Its borders now took in the southern part of Macedonia (which included Thessaloniki, the vital cultural centre strategically positioned on the Balkan trade routes), part of Thrace, another chunk of Epiros, and the northeastern Aegean Islands, as well as recognising the union with Crete.

WWI & Smyrna

In March 1913 a lunatic assassinated King George, and his son Constantine became the monarch. King Constantine, who was married to the sister of the German emperor, insisted that Greece remain neutral when WWI broke out in August 1914. As the war dragged on, the Allies (Britain, France and Russia) put increasing pressure on Greece to join forces with them against Germany and Turkey, promising concessions in Asia Minor in return. Prime Minister Venizelos favoured the Allied cause, placing him at loggerheads with the king. The king left Greece in June 1917, replaced by his second-born son, Alexander, who was more amenable to the Allies.

Greek troops served with distinction on the Allied side, but when the war ended in 1918 the promised land in Asia Minor was not forthcoming. Venizelos then led a diplomatic campaign to further the case and, with Allied acquiescence, landed troops in Smyrna (present-day İzmir in Turkey) in May 1919, under the guise of protecting the half a million Greeks living in the city. (However, the occupation of Smyrna stirred internal resentments and helped spark a series of sanguinary reprisals against its local Muslim population.) With a seemingly viable hold in Asia Minor, Venizelos ordered his troops to march ahead, and by September 1921 they'd advanced as far as Ankara. But by this stage foreign support for Venizelos had ebbed and Turkish forces, commanded by Mustafa Kemal (later to become Atatürk), halted the offensive. The Greek army retreated but Smyrna fell in 1922, and tens of thousands of its Greek inhabitants were killed.

The outcome of these hostilities was the Treaty of Lausanne in July 1923, whereby Turkey recovered eastern Thrace and the islands of Imvros and Tenedos, while Italy kept the Dodecanese (which it had temporarily acquired in 1912 and would hold until 1947).

Prince Philip, the Duke of Edinburgh, was part of the Greek royal family – born in Corfu as Prince Philip of Greece and Denmark in 1921. Former king of Greece Constantine is Prince William's godfather and Prince Charles' third cousin.

1914	1919–23	1924–34
The outbreak of WWI sees Greece initially neutral but eventually siding with the Western Allies against Germany and Turkey on the promise of land in Asia Minor.	Greece embarks on the 'Great Idea' campaign to unite the former Hellenic regions, including those in Asia Minor. It fails and leads to a population exchange between Greece and Turkey in 1923, often referred to as the Asia Minor catastrophe.	Greece is proclaimed a republic and King George II leaves the country. The Great Depression counters the nation's return to stability. Monarchists and parliamentarians under Venizelos tussle for control of the country.

The treaty also called for a population exchange between Greece and Turkey to prevent any future disputes. Almost 1.5 million Greeks left Turkey and almost 400,000 Turks left Greece. The exchange put a tremendous strain on the Greek economy and caused great bitterness and hardship for the individuals concerned. Many Greeks abandoned a privileged life in Asia Minor for one of extreme poverty in emerging urban shanty towns in Athens and Thessaloniki.

The Republic of 1924–35

The arrival of the Greek refugees from Turkey coincided with, and compounded, a period of political instability unprecedented even by Greek standards. In October 1920 King Alexander died from a monkey bite and his father Constantine was restored to the throne. But the ensuing political crisis deepened and Constantine abdicated (again) after the fall of Smyrna. He was replaced by his first son, George II, who was no match for the group of army officers who seized power after the war. A republic was proclaimed in March 1924 amid a series of coups and counter-coups.

A measure of stability was attained with Venizelos' return to power in 1928. He pursued a policy of economic and educational reform, but progress was inhibited by the Great Depression. His antiroyalist Liberal Party began to face a growing challenge from the monarchist Popular Party, culminating in defeat at the polls in March 1933. The new government was preparing for the restoration of the monarchy when Venizelos and his supporters staged an unsuccessful coup in March 1935. Venizelos was exiled to Paris, where he died a year later. In November 1935, King George II reassumed the throne (by a likely gerrymander of a plebiscite) and he installed the right-wing General Ioannis Metaxas as prime minister. Nine months later, Metaxas assumed dictatorial powers with the king's consent, under what many believed to be the pretext of preventing a communist-inspired republican coup.

WWII

Metaxas' grandiose vision was to create a utopian Third Greek Civilisation, based on its glorious ancient and Byzantine past, but what he actually created was more like a Greek version of the Third Reich. He exiled or imprisoned opponents, banned trade unions and the recently established Kommounistiko Komma Elladas (KKE, the Greek Communist Party), imposed press censorship, and created a secret police force and fascist-style youth movement. But Metaxas is best known for his reply of *ohi* (no) to Mussolini's ultimatum to allow Italians passage through Greece at the beginning of WWII, thus maintaining Greece's policy of strict neutrality. The Italians invaded Greece, but the Greeks drove them back into Albania.

On 25 November 1942 a coalition of Greek resistance groups, aided by the British, blew up the Gorgopotamos railway bridge near Lamia in Sterea Ellada, sabotaging for weeks German supply routes through the country.

1935	1940	1941–44
The monarchy is restored and King George II is reappointed to the throne. Right-wing General Ioannis Metaxas adopts the role of prime minister while introducing dictatorial measures of governance.	On 28 October Metaxas famously rebuffs the Italian request to traverse Greece at the beginning of WWII. The Italians engage Greek forces and are driven back into Albania.	Germany invades and occupies Greece. Monarchists, republicans and communists form resistance groups that, despite infighting, drive out the Germans after three years.

A prerequisite of Hitler's plan to invade the Soviet Union was a secure southern flank in the Balkans. The British, realising this, asked Metaxas if they could land troops in Greece. He gave the same reply as he had given the Italians, but then died suddenly in January 1941. The king replaced him with the more timid Alexandros Koryzis, who agreed to British forces landing in Greece. Koryzis committed suicide when German troops invaded Greece on 6 April 1941. The Nazis vastly outnumbered the defending Greek, British, Australian and New Zealand troops, and the whole country was under Nazi occupation within a few weeks. The civilian population suffered appallingly during the occupation, many dying of starvation. The Nazis rounded up more than half the Jewish population and transported them to death camps.

Numerous resistance movements sprang up. The dominant three were Ellinikos Laïkos Apeleftherotikos Stratos (ELAS), Ethnikon Apeleftherotikon Metopon (EAM) and the Ethnikos Dimokratikos Ellinikos Syndesmos (EDES). Although ELAS was founded by communists, not all of its members were left wing, whereas EAM consisted of Stalinist KKE members who had lived in Moscow in the 1930s and harboured ambitions of establishing a postwar communist Greece. EDES consisted of right-wing and monarchist resistance fighters. These groups fought one another with as much venom as they fought the Germans with, often with devastating results for the civilian Greek population.

The Germans began to retreat from Greece in October 1944, but the communist and monarchist resistance groups continued to fight one another.

Civil War

By late 1944 the royalists, republicans and communists were polarised by interparty division and locked in a serious battle for control. The British-backed provisional government was in an untenable position: the left was threatening revolt, and the British were pushing to prevent the communists from further legitimising their hold over the administration – influence the communists gained during the German occupation – in an effort to augment British hopes to reinstate the Greek monarchy.

On 3 December 1944 the police fired on a communist demonstration in Plateia Syntagmatos (Syntagma Sq) in Athens, killing several people. The ensuing six weeks of fighting between the left and the right, known as the Dekemvriana (events of December), marked the first round of the Greek Civil War. British troops intervened and prevented an ELAS-EAM coalition victory.

In February 1945 formal negotiations for reconciliation between the government and the communists fell flat, and the friction continued. Many civilians on all political sides were subjected to bitter reprisals at the hands of leftist groups, the army or rogue right-wing vigilantes, who threatened

1944–49	1967–74	1973
The end of WWII sees Greece descend into civil war, pitching monarchists against communists. The monarchists recover in 1946, but the civil war takes its toll and many Greeks emigrate in search of a better life.	Right- and left-wing factions continue to bicker, provoking in April 1967 a right-wing military coup d'état by army generals who establish a junta. They impose martial law and abolish many civil rights.	On 17 November tanks ram the gates of the Athens Polytechnio (Technical University) and troops storm the school buildings in a bid to quash a student uprising against the junta. More than 20 students die.

political enemies with widespread intimidation and violence. The royalists won the March 1946 election (which the communists had unsuccessfully boycotted), and a plebiscite (widely reported as rigged) in September put George II back on the throne.

In October the left-wing Democratic Army of Greece (DSE) was formed to resume the fight against the monarchy and its British supporters. Under the leadership of Markos Vafiadis, the DSE swiftly occupied a large swath of land along Greece's northern border with Albania and Yugoslavia.

In 1947 the USA intervened and the civil war developed into a setting for the new Cold War theatre. Communism was declared illegal and the government introduced its notorious Certificate of Political Reliability (which remained valid until 1962), which declared that the document bearer was not a left-wing sympathiser; without this certificate Greeks could not vote and found it almost impossible to get work. US aid did little to improve the situation on the ground. The DSE continued to be supplied from the north (by Yugoslavia, Bulgaria and indirectly by the Soviets through the Balkan states), and by the end of 1947 large chunks of the mainland were under its control, as well as parts of the islands of Crete, Chios and Lesvos.

In 1949 the tide began to turn when the forces of the central government drove the DSE out of the Peloponnese; but the fighting dragged on in the mountains of Epiros until October 1949, when Yugoslavia fell out with the Soviet Union and cut the DSE's supply lines.

The civil war left Greece politically frayed and economically shattered. More Greeks had been killed in three years of bitter civil war than in WWII, and a quarter of a million people were homeless.

The sense of despair became the trigger for a mass exodus. Almost a million Greeks headed off in search of a better life elsewhere, primarily to countries such as Australia, Canada and the USA.

> Women exercised their right to vote in general elections (granted by parliament in 1952) in 1956. Lina Tsaldari was the first woman to hold a cabinet post, as minister of social welfare.

Reconstruction & the Cyprus Issue

After a series of unworkable coalitions, the electoral system was changed to majority voting in 1952 – which excluded the communists from future governments. The November 1952 election was a victory for the right-wing Ellinikos Synagermos (Greek Rally) party, led by General Alexander Papagos (a former civil-war field marshal). General Papagos remained in power until his death in 1955, when he was replaced by Konstandinos Karamanlis.

Greece joined NATO in 1952, and in 1953 the USA was granted the right to operate sovereign bases. Intent on maintaining support for the anticommunist government, the USA gave generous economic and military aid.

Cyprus resumed centre stage in Greece's foreign affairs. Since the 1930s Greek Cypriots (four-fifths of the island's population) had demanded union

1974	1981	1981–90
A botched plan to unite Cyprus with Greece prompts the invasion of Cyprus by Turkish troops and results in the fall of the military junta. This acts as a catalyst for the restoration of parliamentary democracy in Greece.	Greece joins the EU, effectively removing protective trade barriers and opening up the Greek economy to the wider world for the first time. The economy grows smartly.	Greece acquires its first elected socialist government (PASOK) under the leadership of Andreas Papandreou. The honeymoon lasts nine years. The conservatives ultimately reassume power.

with Greece, while Turkey had maintained its claim to the island ever since it became a British protectorate in 1878 (it became a British crown colony in 1925). Greek public opinion was overwhelmingly in favour of union, a notion strongly opposed by Britain and the USA on strategic grounds.

In 1956 the right-wing Greek Cypriot National Organisation of Cypriot Freedom Fighters (EOKA) took up arms against the British. In 1959, after extensive negotiations, Britain, Greece and Turkey finally agreed on a compromise solution whereby Cyprus would become an independent republic the following August, with Greek Cypriot Archbishop Makarios as president and a Turk, Faisal Kükük, as vice president. The changes did little to appease either side. EOKA resolved to keep fighting, while Turkish Cypriots clamoured for partition of the island.

The 1963 political assassination of Grigoris Lambrakis is described in Vassilis Vassilikos' novel *Z*, which later became an award-winning film.

Back in Greece, Georgios Papandreou, a former Venizelos supporter, founded the broadly based Centre Union (EK) in 1958, but elections in 1961 returned the National Radical Union (ERE), Karamanlis' new name for Greek Rally, to power for the third time in succession. Papandreou accused the ERE of ballot rigging, and the political turmoil that followed culminated in the murder, in May 1963, of Grigoris Lambrakis, the deputy of the communist Union of the Democratic Left (EDA). All this proved too much for Karamanlis, who resigned and went to live in Paris.

The EK finally came to power in February 1964 and Papandreou wasted no time in implementing a series of radical changes. He freed political prisoners and allowed exiles to come back to Greece, reduced income tax and the defence budget, and increased spending on social services and education.

Colonels, Monarchs & Democracy

The political right in Greece was rattled by Papandreou's tolerance of the left, and a group of army colonels, led by Georgios Papadopoulos and Stylianos Patakos, staged a coup on 21 April 1967. They established a military junta with Papadopoulos as prime minister. King Constantine tried an unsuccessful counter-coup in December, after which he fled to Rome, then London.

The colonels declared martial law, banned political parties and trade unions, imposed censorship and imprisoned, tortured and exiled thousands of dissidents. In June 1972 Papadopoulos declared Greece a republic and appointed himself president.

On 17 November 1973 tanks stormed a building at the Athens Polytechnio (Technical University) to quell a student occupation calling for an uprising against the US-backed junta. While the number of casualties is still in dispute (more than 20 students were reportedly killed and hundreds injured), the act spelt the death knell for the junta.

Shortly after, the head of the military security police, Dimitrios Ioannidis, deposed Papadopoulos. In July 1974 Ioannidis tried to impose unity with

1999	2004	2007
Turkey and Greece experience powerful earthquakes within weeks of each other that result in hundreds of deaths. The two nations respond to each disaster by pledging mutual aid and support, initiating a warming of diplomatic relations.	Greece successfully hosts the 28th Summer Olympic Games amid much muffled rumour that infrastructure would not be complete in time. Greece also wins the European football championship.	Vast forest fires devastate much of the western Peloponnese as well as parts of Evia and Epiros, causing Greece's worst ecological disaster in decades. Thousands lose their homes and 66 people perish.

Cyprus by attempting to topple the Makarios government in Cyprus; Makarios got wind of an assassination attempt and escaped. The junta replaced him with the extremist Nikos Sampson (a former EOKA leader) as president. Consequently, mainland Turkey sent in troops until they occupied northern Cyprus, partitioning the country and displacing almost 200,000 Greek Cypriots who fled their homes for the safety of the south (reportedly more than 1500 Cypriots remain missing).

The junta dictatorship collapsed. Karamanlis was summoned from Paris to take office and his New Democracy (ND) party won a large majority at the November elections in 1974 against the newly formed the Panhellenic Socialist Union (PASOK), led by Andreas Papandreou (son of Georgios). A plebiscite voted 69% against the restoration of the monarchy and the ban on communist parties was lifted. (The exiled former royal family still lives in London, where it continues to use its royal titles. A dispute between the former king, Constantine, and the government over the family's assets was settled in 2002 and the royal family members now often return to Greece as private citizens.)

For an insight into the 1967 colonels' coup read Andreas Papandreou's account in Democracy at Gunpoint.

The 1980s &1990s

When Greece became the 10th member of the EU in 1981, it was the smallest and poorest member. In October 1981, Andreas Papandreou's PASOK party was elected as Greece's first socialist government. PASOK ruled for almost two decades (except for 1990–93). PASOK promised ambitious social reform, to close the US air bases and to withdraw from NATO. US military presence was reduced, but unemployment was high and reforms in education and welfare were limited. Women's issues fared better: the dowry system was abolished, abortion legalised, and civil marriage and divorce were implemented.

Economic scandal, a series of general strikes, and fundamental policy wrangling over the country's education system damaged PASOK, and in 1990 Konstantinos Mitsotakis led the ND back to office. Intent on redressing the country's economic problems – high inflation and high government spending – the government imposed austerity measures, including a wage freeze for civil servants and steep increases in public-utility costs and basic services.

By late 1992 corruption allegations were being levelled against the government. By mid-1993 Mitsotakis supporters had abandoned the ND for the new Political Spring party; the ND lost its parliamentary majority and an early election in October returned Andreas Papandreou's PASOK party.

Papandreou stepped down in early 1996 due to ill health and he died on 26 June. His departure produced a dramatic change of direction for PASOK, with the party abandoning Papandreou's left-leaning politics and electing experienced economist and lawyer Costas Simitis as the new prime minister (who won a comfortable majority at the October 1996 polls).

2007	2008	2009
General elections are held in September and the conservative government of Konstandinos Karamanlis returns to power for a second consecutive term.	Police shoot and kill a 15-year-old boy in Athens following an alleged exchange between police and youths. This sparks a series of urban riots nationwide.	PASOK secures the vote in the European Parliamentary elections in early June. George Papakonstadinou heads the Greek contingency, represented by 22 members of the European Parliament (MEPs).

The 21st Century

The Simitis government focused almost exclusively on the push for further integration with Europe. This meant, in general terms, more tax reform and austerity measures, and by 2004 PASOK's popularity was in decline, and Georgios Papandreou replaced Simitis. Greece changed course when the ND party won the March 2004 general election, with Konstandinos Karamanlis as prime minister.

The new millenium has seen living standards increase and billions of euros poured into large-scale infrastructure projects across Greece, including the redevelopment of Athens – spurred on largely by its hosting of the 2004 Olympic Games. However, rising unemployment, ballooning public debt, slowing inflation and the squeezing of consumer credit have taken their toll. Public opinion soured further in 2007 when Karamanlis' government was widely criticised for its handling of the emergency response to severe summer fires, which were responsible for widespread destruction throughout Greece. Nevertheless, snap elections held in September 2007 returned the conservatives, albeit with a diminished majority.

'The new millenium has seen living standards increase and billions of euros poured into large-scale infrastructure projects across Greece'

Over recent years, a series of massive general strikes and blockades have highlighted mounting electoral discontent. Hundreds of thousands of people have protested against proposed radical labour and pension reforms and privatisation plans that analysts claim will help curb public debt. The backlash against the government reached boiling point in December 2008, when urban rioting broke out across the country, led by youths outraged by the police shooting of a 15-year-old boy in Athens following an alleged exchange between police and a group of teenagers. Youths hurled stones and firebombs at riot police who responded with tear gas. Concern is growing over political tangles in an ongoing investigation regarding alleged corruption among state executives (on both sides of the political fence) in connection with the Siemens Hellas group. This follows another controversy that involved land-swap deals between a monastery and the government, which some commentators believe to have gone heavily in the monastery's favour, at the expense of taxpayers. A general election held in October 2009, midway through Karamanlis' term, saw PASOK take back the reins in a landslide win against the conservatives.

Greece continues to face the challenge of resolving its sometimes abrasive relationship with its Balkan neighbour, Former Yugoslav Republic of Macedonia (FYROM), over the contentious issue of it adopting the nomenclature of Macedonia (a topic negotiated between the two nations via UN-mediated dialogue). Relations with Turkey these days are more neighbourly. Greece supports Turkey's steps towards EU-ascension, and is urging joint action between the two nations to manage illegal immigration across Greece's borders. But Greece has expressed rumblings of concern since Turkey declared its intention to explore for oil and gas in the eastern Aegean, sparking a diplomatic headache.

2009	2009	2009
On 20 June, the much-acclaimed new Acropolis Museum holds its official inauguration. A public-relations campaign still rages for the repatriation of the Parthenon Marbles from the British Museum.	Greece raises concerns over Turkey's intention to explore for oil and gas off the coasts of Kastellorizo and Cyprus. Diplomatic tension mounts when locals spot Turkish jets flying low over several eastern Aegean Islands.	Konstandinos Karamanlis calls for an early general election. Socialist PASOK, under Georgios Papandreou, wins the October election with a landslide result against the conservatives.

A Who's Who of the Ancient Greek Pantheon

Richard Waters

Ancient Greece revolved around a careful worship of 12 central gods and goddesses. A visitor to Greece 2500 years later should not neglect a nod to them; picture Poseidon and his pet Kraken lurking in the navy deeps of the Aegean, sniff the pine-scented forests and listen for Pan's footfalls between the cicada song. So representative was the Olympian pantheon in its human aspect – the wanton lustfulness of Zeus, the boozy revelry of Dionysos – that the Greek gods were to survive even the invasion of the Romans who were happy to plunder and rename them for their own worship. Below is the pecking order of the deities (with equivalent Roman names).

ZEUS (JUPITER)

Heavyweight champ of Mt Olympus, lord of the skies and master of disguise in pursuit of mortal maidens. Wardrobe includes shower of gold, bull, eagle and swan.

POSEIDON (NEPTUNE)

God of the seas, master of the mists and younger brother of Zeus. He dwelt in a glittering underwater palace.

HERA (JUNO)

Protector of women and family, the queen of heaven is also the embattled wife of Zeus. She was the prototype of the jealous, domineering wife.

HADES (PLUTO)

God of death, he ruled the underworld, bringing in newly dead with the help of his skeletal ferryman, Charon. Serious offenders were sent for torture in Tartarus, while heroes enjoyed eternal R&R in the Elysian Fields.

ATHENA (MINERVA)

Goddess of wisdom, war, science and Guardian of Athens. The antithesis of Ares (see p54), Athena was deliberate and where possible, diplomatic in the art of war. Heracles, Jason (of Jason and the Argonauts fame) and Perseus all benefited from her patronage.

APHRODITE (VENUS)

Goddess of love and beauty. The curvy lady of the shell was said to have been born whole on the waves. When she wasn't cuckolding her unfortunate husband, Hephaestus, she and her cherubic son Eros (Cupid) were enflaming hearts and causing trouble (cue the Trojan War).

APOLLO (PHOEBUS)

God of music, the arts and fortune-telling, Apollo was also the god of light and an expert shot with a bow and arrow. It was his steady hand which guided Paris' arrow towards Achilles' only weak spot – his heel – thus killing him.

'Ancient Greece revolved around a careful worship of 12 central gods and goddesses'

ARTEMIS (DIANA)

The goddess of the hunt and twin sister of Apollo was, ironically, patron saint of wild animals. By turns spiteful and magnanimous, she was closely associated with the sinister Hecate, patroness of witches.

ARES (MARS)

God of war. Zeus' least favourite of his progeny. Not surprisingly, Ares was worshipped by the bellicose Spartans and may today have felt at home among soccer hooligans.

HERMES (MERCURY)

Messenger of the gods, patron saint of travellers, the handsome one with a winged hat and sandals. He was always on hand to smooth over the affairs of Zeus, his father.

HEPHAESTUS (VULCAN)

God of craftsmanship, metallurgy and fire, this deformed and oft derided son of Zeus made the world's first woman of clay, Pandora, as a punishment for man. Inside that box of hers were the evils of mankind.

HESTIA (VESTA)

Goddess of the hearth, she protected state fires in city halls from where citizens of Greece could light their brands. She remained unmarried, inviolate.

THE MYTHS, THE MYTHS!

Some of the greatest stories are to be found in the Greek myths. Confound fellow travellers with your classical erudition using our whistle-stop tour!

'Some of the greatest stories are to be found in the Greek myths'

HERACLES (HERCULES)

The most celebrated, endearing hero of ancient Greece. The bearded one was set 12 labours of penitence for mistakenly killing his family (Hera blinded him with madness). These included slaying the Nemean Lion and the Lernian Hydra (see opposite); capturing the Ceryneian Hind and the Erymanthian Boar; cleaning the Augean Stables in one day; slaying the Stymphalian Birds; capturing the Cretan Bull; stealing the man-eating Mares of Diomedes; obtaining the Girdle of Hippolyta and the oxen of Geryon; stealing the Apples of the Hesperides; and capturing Cerberus (see opposite).

THESEUS

The Athenian hero volunteered himself as a one of seven men and maidens in the annual sacrifice to the Minotaur, the crazed half-bull–half-man offspring of King Minos of Crete (see also opposite). Once inside its forbidding labyrinth (from which none had returned) Theseus, aided by Princess Ariadne (who had a crush on him courtesy of Aphrodite's dart) loosened a spool of thread to find his way out once he'd killed the monster.

ICARUS

Along with Deadalus (his father and a brilliant inventor), Icarus flew off the cliffs of Crete pursued by King Minos and his troops. Using wings made of feathers and wax, his father instructed him to fly away from the midday sun. Boys will be boys, Icarus thinks he's Jonathan Livingston Seagull…glue melts, feathers separate, bird-boy drowns. And the moral is: listen to your father.

TOP FIVE MYTHICAL CREATURES

- **Medusa**: She of the bad hair day, punished by the gods for her inflated vanity. Even dead, her blood is lethal.
- **Cyclops**: One-eyed giant. Odysseus and his crew were trapped in the cave of one such cyclops, Polyphemus.
- **Cerberus**: The three-headed dog of hell, he guards the entrance to the underworld – under his watch no-one gets in or out.
- **Minotaur**: This half-man–half-bull mutant leads a life of existential angst in the abysmal labyrinth, tempered only by the occasional morsel of human flesh.
- **Hydra**: Cut one of its nine heads off and another two will grow in its place. Heracles solved the problem by cauterizing each stump with his burning brand.

PERSEUS

Perseus' impossible task was to kill the gorgon, Medusa (see above). With a head of snakes she could turn a man to stone with a single glance. Armed with an invisibility cap and a pair of flying sandals from Hermes, Perseus used his reflective shield to avoid Medusa's stare. Having cut off her head and secreted it in a bag, it was shortly unsheathed to save Andromeda, a princess bound to a rock in her final moments before being sacrificed to a sea monster. Medusa turns it to stone, Perseus gets the girl.

OEDIPUS

You can run but you can't hide…having been abandoned at birth, Oedipus learned from the Delphic oracle that he would one day slay his father and marry his mother. On the journey back to his birthplace, Thiva (Thebes), he killed a rude stranger and then discovered the city was plagued by a murderous Sphinx (a winged lion with a woman's head). The creature gave unsuspecting travellers and citizens a riddle; if they couldn't answer it they were dashed on the rocks. Oedipus succeeded in solving the riddle, felled the Sphinx and so gained the queen of Thiva's hand in marriage. On discovering the stranger he'd killed was his father and that his new wife was in fact his mother, Oedipus ripped out his eyes and exiled himself.

The Culture

THE GREEK PSYCHE

Greeks have long lived in the shadow of their ancient ancestors' illustrious cultural and artistic legacy. If history is a country's burden, then the baggage of centuries of foreign occupation, colonisation, war, political turmoil, isolation, poverty and mass emigration also weighs heavily on the Greek psyche. The exotic 1960s image of Greece as a nation of carefree pleasure-seeking Zorbas may have reflected their resilience and spirit, but not the complexity of the Greek character.

The World of the Ancient Greeks (2002), by archaeologists John Camp and Elizabeth Fisher, is a broad and in-depth look at how the Greeks have left their imprint on politics, philosophy, theatre, art, medicine and architecture.

The Greeks are undeniably passionate, fiercely independent and proud of their heritage. While their ancestry can give them a smug sense of cultural superiority, they are well aware of their present-day underdog status in the new Europe and are more firmly focused on building a future.

Since they came hurtling into the EU in 1981 as the smallest and poorest nation on the block, Greeks have been struggling to catch up with the radical, fast-tracked social changes, modernisation and economic reforms that are still sweeping the country.

The resounding success of the Athens 2004 Olympic Games was a major turning-point in changing the perception of Greece as a European backwater, while Greece's euphoric European Cup football triumph that same year also boosted morale and national pride.

Freedom and self-determination has only been a recent phenomenon but these days the resilience of Greek culture and traditions are being tested by globalisation, market forces and radical social change. The current generation of Greeks is dealing with a massive generational and technological divide; multilingual children playing games on their mobile phones while their illiterate grandfathers still get around on a mule. In the major shift from a largely poor, agrarian existence to increasingly sophisticated urban dwellers, Greeks are also delicately balancing cultural and religious mores. The younger generation of Greeks is multilingual, educated, far less insular and increasingly more widely travelled. They are also living in a wealthier and far more multicultural society.

As Greeks continue to reinvent themselves, the Greek psyche presents some intriguing paradoxes.

Greeks have an undeniable zest for life, but aren't into making plans, with spontaneity a refreshing aspect of social life. They like to flaunt their newfound wealth with top brand-name clothing and flashy cars, and they are prone to displays of excess, especially in spending on entertainment. In many ways the chain-smoking, mobile-phone-addicted, consumerist Greeks are making up for lost time.

Greeks are among the world's biggest mobile phone users, with more than 11.9 million mobile phones connected, which is more than the estimated population of 11.2 million people.

Greeks have long enjoyed a reputation as loyal friends and generous hosts. They pride themselves on their *filotimo* (dignity and sense of honour), and their *filoxenia* (hospitality, welcome, shelter), which you will find in even the poorest household.

Yet this hospitality and generosity seems to extinguish in the public sphere, where surly civil servants show a distinct lack of interest in customer service. The notion of the greater good often plays second fiddle to personal interests and there is little sense of collective responsibility in relation to issues such as the environment. The pride Greeks have in their homes rarely extends to public spaces.

Greeks have a residual mistrust of authority and little respect for the state; personal freedom and democratic rights are almost sacrosanct and there is an aversion to the Big Brother approach of over-regulated Western nations (in 2009, Greece banned Google Earth's street-view function after an outcry over invasion of privacy). This inherent insubordinate streak means rules and regulations are routinely ignored. Many visitors are indeed surprised to learn there are road rules at all. Despite hefty fines, wearing a seatbelt is treated as an optional inconvenience; creative and inconsiderate parking is the norm; dangerous overtaking is rife; and you'll often see people riding motorbikes, carrying their helmets as they chat on their mobile phones. New smoking bans introduced in 2009 were set to test the nation – heralded by some commentators as 'the second civil war'.

Patronage features prominently at all levels of society; nepotism is an accepted state of affairs, a by-product of having to rely on personal networks to survive. It's still almost impossible to make any headway with Greece's bloated bureaucracy (or in many cases get a job) without *meson* (the help of a friend or family member working within the system). Greeks are masters at getting around the system, demonstrating almost admirable impudence or *poniria* (low cunning), though corruption is the more serious manifestation of this attitude. The infamous *fakelaki* (little envelope of cash) remains a common way to cut red tape, from jumping the queue for surgery to dealing with the tax office or building permits. Transparency International ranks Greece among the most corrupt countries in Europe.

Greece is both Mediterranean and Balkan and has long straddled East and West, so it's not surprising that Greeks have a very different character to the rest of Europe. Most Greeks are forthright and argumentative. They thrive on news, gossip and political debate and, while they will mercilessly malign their governments and society, they are defensive about external criticism and can be fervently nationalistic. Greeks have a work-to-live attitude and pride themselves on their capacity to enjoy life. They are social animals and enjoy a rich communal life, eating out regularly and filling the country's myriad cafes and bars. They travel and socialise in packs, with family or their *parea* (company of friends). Solitude is neither valued nor sought.

Unlike many Western cultures where people avoid eye contact with strangers, Greeks are unashamed about staring and blatantly observing (and commenting on) the comings and goings of people around them. Few subjects are off limits, from your private life and why you don't have children, to how much money you earn or how much you paid for your house or shoes. And they are just as likely to tell you their woes and ailments rather than engage in polite small-talk.

Greeks are notoriously late and are masters of the last minute, as the 2004 Olympics proved. Turning up to an appointment on time is often referred to as 'being English'. It's almost as if they resent the sense of

> Greeks are the EU's biggest smokers: 37.6% of people over 15 are heavy smokers, and women smoke as much as men. In 2009 smoking bans were optimistically extended to restaurants, bars and nightclubs.

> Greeks have their own distinctive body language – 'yes' is a swing of the head and 'no' is a curt raising of the head (or eyebrows), often accompanied by a 'ts' click-of-the-tongue sound.

WISHING WELL

Greetings are one of the endearing features of daily life in Greece. Whether it stems from superstition or an excess of good will, Greeks seem to have a wish for every occasion. They won't just wish you *kali orexi (bon apetit)*, but also *kali honepsi* (good digestion) and *kali xekourasi* (good rest) or *kali diaskedasi* (good entertainment). On the first day of the week it's *kali evdomada* (good week), each month *kalo mina* (a good month), while the start of summer brings *kalo kalokeri* (good summer) and the end of the holidays *kalo himona* (good winter). When you purchase something it's *kaloriziko* (good luck) and a new business is greeted with *kales doulies* (good work) or challenges with *kali dynami* (good strength) and every possible *kalo* permutation.

obligation; some speculate that this stems from centuries of answering to foreign masters.

Greeks remain very ethnocentric, while anti-Americanism is another interesting undercurrent of the Greek psyche. Apart from general resistance to American hegemony, it originates from what many regard as undue US interference in Greek affairs during the civil war (p48); suspected CIA involvement in the colonels' coup in 1967; US indifference over Cyprus; and its interventions in the Middle East and the Balkans. Protest can take an irrational anti-American focus, but can be as benignly passive aggressive as refusing to serve Coca-Cola.

Stereotypes about Greek men being mummies' boys are not totally unfounded, while AIDS and the sexual liberation of Greek women have virtually killed off the infamous Greek lover and the *kamaki* (literally a fishing trident; the term refers to the once widespread practice of 'fishing' for foreign women) that made the Greek islands a magnet for foreign women in the 1970s and '80s à la *Shirley Valentine*.

THE GOOD LIFE

Greece remains one of Europe's friendliest, safest and most relaxed countries. In the evenings, especially in summer, you will see people of all ages out on their *volta* (evening walk), walking along seafront promenades or through town centres, dressed up and refreshed from their afternoon siesta (albeit a dying institution). Restaurants, cafes, theatres, cinemas, bars and live-music venues seem to thrive and the lively street life in Athens and most major towns is something that strikes most visitors. Another is that children are out late at night, socialising with their parents or playing nearby.

Summer holidays are the highlight of the year and the country virtually shuts down mid-August when most people take off for the islands, beaches or their ancestral villages. One of the peculiarly Greek social talking points is how many swims you've had each summer.

While some things haven't changed, the standard of living for the average Greek has changed beyond all recognition, especially in the past two decades. Greeks are visibly wealthier, as the new generation of Athenian yuppies in designer clothes, clutching the latest mobile phones and driving new cars will attest. Well-to-do farmers drive the latest 4WD pick-up truck and the shepherds have mobile phones. More Greeks are now travelling and studying abroad. Greek children, meanwhile, are now the fattest in the EU and many teenagers are addicted to internet games.

High levels of home ownership, generational wealth and family support structures – plus a decade of economic boom times – go a fair way to explaining a lifestyle that is pretty much out of sync with average incomes. Greek wages remain among the lowest in the EU, yet the cost of living has risen dramatically, particularly since the introduction of the euro in 2002.

But after 10 years of economic boom times, Greece was conceding a slide into recession by 2009 (ironically having been propped up by a black-market economy estimated by various studies at up to 30% of the country's GDP). Greek households have also been living beyond their means, with the use of credit cards, loans and *dosis* (instalment schemes) skyrocketing.

Overeducated middle-class youth, dubbed the €700 generation (the average postgraduation monthly wage), remain highly dependent on family and largely disenchanted by career prospects, having lost the sense of possibility engendered by the 2004 Olympics. Youth disenchantment, along

Greece has compulsory 12-month military service for all males aged 19 to 50. Women are accepted into the Greek army, though they are not obliged to join and rarely do so.

with a general political malaise, partly fuelled the social unrest and rioting following the police shooting of a teenager in December 2008.

Huge disparities in the overall standard of living and a stark rural–city divide persist. There has also been a perceptible increase in the number of junkies, homeless people and beggars on the streets of Athens and other major towns.

PEOPLE & SOCIETY

Greece's population was estimated at 11.2 million in 2009, with a third of the population living in the Greater Athens area. Greece has become a largely urban society, with more than two-thirds of the population living in cities and less than 15% living on the islands.

However, regional development, decentralisation and the improved lot of many regional communities has stemmed the tide of people moving to Athens (other than new immigrant arrivals). Young people are less likely to leave major regional growth centres such as Larisa, Iraklio or Ioannina, while people are also escaping overpopulated Athens for the regions. Greece has an ageing population and a declining birth rate, with large families a thing of the past.

Greece's main population growth has been the flood of migrants who have arrived since 1991 – about 1.5 million migrants are estimated to be living in Greece legally, illegally or with indeterminate status. Immigrants are estimated to make up one-fifth of the workforce. Greece's inadequate migration system and painfully slow asylum processes have failed to cope with the massive influx of new arrivals, drawing international criticism.

Greece's remote islands have seen an increase in new arrivals (such as economic migrants, as well as asylum seekers). It's reported that these significant increases are causing major social problems, especially on smaller islands unable to cope with the number of arrivals, which can exceed their resident population.

> 'Extended family plays an important role in daily life, with grandparents often looking after grandchildren while parents work or socialise'

Family Life

Greek society remains dominated by the family. It's uncommon for Greek children to move out of home before they are married, unless they are going to university or find work in another city. While this is slowly changing among professionals and people marrying later, low wages are also keeping young people at home.

Parents strive to provide homes for their children when they get married, with many families building apartments for each child above their own (thus the number of unfinished buildings you see).

Extended family plays an important role in daily life, with grandparents often looking after grandchildren while parents work or socialise. The trade-off is that children look after their elderly parents, rather than consign them to nursing homes. This has become increasingly difficult in villages, where foreign women are brought in to look after elderly parents.

Greeks attach great importance to education, with the previous generation determined to provide their children the opportunities they lacked. Greece has the highest number of students in the EU studying at universities abroad, though many end up overeducated and underemployed.

Greeks retain strong regional identities and affiliations, despite the majority having left their ancestral villages for the cities or abroad. Even the country's remotest villages are bustling during holidays, elections and other excuses for homecomings. One of the first questions Greeks will ask a stranger is what part of Greece they come from.

The Greek church is vehemently opposed to gay marriage and a widely publicised 2008 attempt to challenge a loophole in civil law (that a 1982 law does not specify that a civil union must involve a man and a woman) was later annulled by a Greek court.

Multiculturalism

Greece has been a largely homogenous society and not so long ago the concept of multiculturalism was tantamount to regional differences. The disparate *xenoi* (foreigners) living in Greece were mostly the odd Hellenophile and foreign women married to locals, especially on the islands.

But with the influx of economic migrants, Greece is becoming an inadvertently more multicultural society. Bulgarian women look after the elderly in remote villages, Polish kitchen-hands work on the islands, Albanians dominate the manual labour force, Chinese businesses have sprung up all over Greece, African hawkers flog fake designer bags and CDs on the streets and Pakistanis gather for weekend cricket matches in Athens car parks.

Migration and multiculturalism are posing major challenges for both society and the State, both of which were ill-prepared for dealing with this inward wave of people (see the boxed text, p62). Economic migrants exist on the social fringe, but as they seek Greek citizenship and try to integrate into mainstream society, community tolerance, prejudice, xenophobia and notions of Greek identity and nationality are being tested.

Albanians make up roughly two-thirds of the migrant population and have become an economic necessity in the agriculture and construction sectors, and in the menial labour and domestic work that Greeks no longer want to do. Many have settled with their families all over Greece but remain largely stigmatised.

The new arrivals also include more than 150,000 people of Greek descent who repatriated from the former Soviet Union and Balkan states after the fall of communism.

Mixed marriages are becoming common, especially in rural areas where Eastern European brides fill the void left by Greek women moving to the cities. While there is still a long way to go before migrants are accepted into the community, there is recognition that they keep the economy going. Greece's illegal immigration problems have also sparked anti-immigrant rallies by far-right fringe groups.

Until recently Greece's only recognised ethnic minority were the 300,000 Muslims in western Thrace (mostly ethnic Turks exempt from the 1923 population exchange), who continue to have a difficult time, despite being Greek-born.

Very small numbers of Vlach and Sarakatsani shepherds live a semi-nomadic existence in Epiros, while you will come across Roma (Gypsies) everywhere in Greece, especially in Macedonia, Thrace and Thessaly.

Religion & Identity

The New Testament was first written in Greek, around AD 350. It was not translated into English until around 1526.

The Orthodox faith is the official and prevailing religion of Greece and a key element of Greek identity, ethnicity and culture. There is a prevailing view that to be Greek is to be Orthodox. While the younger generation aren't generally devout nor attend church regularly, most observe the rituals and consider their faith part of their identity. Between 94% and 97% of the Greek population belong at least nominally to the Greek Orthodox Church, though the migrant population is changing the dynamic.

During consecutive foreign occupations, the church was the principal upholder of Greek culture, language and traditions and helped the Greeks

THE BIG SPLIT

Greece was one of the first places in Europe where Christianity emerged, with St Paul reputedly first preaching the gospel in AD 49 in the Macedonian town of Philippi. He later preached in Athens, Thessaloniki and Corinth. After Constantine the Great officially recognised Christianity in AD 313 (converted by a vision of the Cross), he transferred the capital of the Roman Empire to Byzantium (today's İstanbul) in AD 330.

By the 8th century AD differences of opinion and increasing rivalry emerged between the pope in Rome and the patriarch of the Hellenised eastern Roman Empire. One dispute was over the wording of the Creed, which stated that the Holy Spirit proceeds 'from the Father', but Rome added 'and the Son'. Other points of difference included Rome decreeing priests had to be celibate, while Orthodox priests could marry before becoming ordained; and the Orthodox Church forbade wine and oil during Lent.

Their differences became irreconcilable, and in the great schism of AD 1054 the pope and the patriarch went their separate ways as the Roman Catholic Church and the Orthodox Church (Orthodoxy means 'right belief').

The Greek Orthodox Church is closely related to the Russian Orthodox Church; together they form the third-largest branch of Christianity.

maintain a sense of unity. Under Ottoman rule, religion was the most important criterion in defining a Greek. The Church still exerts significant social, political and economic influence in Greece, which doesn't have the same Church–State separation as other Western countries (priests are paid by the state). Until recently, Greece was one of the few European countries where religious affiliation appeared on national identity cards. Non-Orthodox Greeks can still have a hard time joining the civil service or military; civil marriages have only been recognised since the early 1980s; and cremation was only recently legalised after much controversy.

The Greek year is centred on the saints' days and festivals of the church calendar. Namedays (celebrating your namesake saint) are celebrated more than birthdays, and baptisms are an important rite. Most people are named after a saint, as are boats, suburbs and train stations.

You will notice taxi drivers, motorcyclists and people on public transport making the sign of the cross when they pass a church, and many Greeks will go to a church when they have a problem, to light a candle to the relevant saint. There are hundreds of tiny churches dotted around the countryside, predominantly built by individual families dedicated to particular saints. The tiny iconostases or chapels you see on roadsides are either shrines to people who died in road accidents or similar dedications to saints. If you wish to look around a church or monastery, you should always dress appropriately. Arms should be covered, women should wear skirts that reach below the knees and men should wear long trousers.

While religious freedom is part of the constitution, the only other officially recognised religions in Greece are Judaism and Islam, despite the existence of everything from Greek Jehovah's Witnesses to Scientologists. While there is tolerance of non-Orthodox faiths, they still face legal and administrative impediments.

The recent wave of migrants has significantly increased the Muslim population of Athens, where many makeshift mosques operate. Construction of an official mosque, though approved at the official level (both government and Church leaderships publicly support it), remains mired in controversy and delays.

There are more than 50,000 Catholics, mostly of Genoese or Frankish origin and living in the Cyclades, especially on Syros, where they make up

'The Church still exerts significant social, political and economic influence in Greece'

THE GREEK DIASPORA

Greece was until recently a nation of emigrants, with more than five million people of Greek descent living in 140 countries. The biggest migration waves were in the 15 years before the Balkan Wars, after the 1922 Asia Minor purge and the postwar period in the 1950s and '60s.

The largest Greek communities abroad include an estimated three million in the US and Canada. Melbourne, Australia, claims to have the third-largest population of Greek-speakers in the world (300,000), after Athens and Thessaloniki.

Nostalgia and ties with the home country remain strong, with a significant number of Greeks living abroad or of Greek descent returning for annual holidays or retiring in Greece. They own property and are involved in the country's political and cultural life, while a steady stream of young second- and third-generation Greeks are also repatriating.

The Greek state promotes Greek language, culture and religion abroad and funds a world body representing the Greek diaspora. There were also controversial moves to give Greeks living abroad the right to vote in elections.

40% of the population. Polish and Filipino migrants make up the majority of Athens' Catholics.

Greek Jews number about 5000, with small Jewish communities in Ioannina, Larisa, Halkida and Rhodes (dating back to the Roman era) and Thessaloniki, Kavala and Didymotiho (mostly descendants of 15th-century exiles from Spain and Portugal). In 1941 the Nazis transported 46,000 (90%) of Thessaloniki's Jews to Auschwitz; most never returned.

In recent years there has been a resurgence of interest in the polytheistic religion of the Ancient Greek gods. Fringe revival groups claimed a victory in 2006, after a Greek court recognised the Ellinais group as a 'cultural association with a religious goal'. All forms of pagan worship were outlawed by the Roman state in the 4th century AD, and were later renounced by the Greek Orthodox Church.

Women in Society

Greek women have a curious place in Greek society and the male–female dynamic throws up some interesting paradoxes. Despite the machismo, it is very much a matriarchal society. Men love to give the impression that they rule the roost but, in reality, it's often the women who run the show both at home and in family businesses.

'Men love to give the impression that they rule the roost but it's often the women who run the show'

Despite sexual liberation, education and greater participation in the workforce, 'mother' and 'sex object' are still the dominant role models and stereotypes, which Greek women play on with gusto. Chauvinism and sexism seem to be an entrenched and largely accepted part of the social dynamic, though there are low-key women's groups fighting for equal opportunity.

Old attitudes towards the 'proper role' for women have changed dramatically since the 1980s, when dowry laws were abolished, legal equality of the sexes established and divorce made easier.

While there have been many benefits for mothers in the public sector (such as leaving work earlier to pick up school children and earlier retirement for women with school-age children), Greek women generally do it tough in the male-dominated workplace. Women are significantly under-represented in the workforce compared with their EU or international counterparts, often earning less than men and struggling to even find the corporate ladder.

There are capable women in prominent positions in business and government, though more often than not they also happen to be the wives or daughters of prominent or wealthy men. Women – who did not even vote in national elections until 1952 – hold only 16% of seats in parliament.

In conservative provincial towns and villages, women still maintain traditional roles, though women's agricultural cooperatives play a leading role in regional economies and in the preservation of culinary and cultural heritage. On the domestic front, Greek women (at least the older generation) are famously house-proud and take great pride in their culinary skills. It's still relatively rare for men to be involved in housework or cooking, and boys are waited on hand and foot. Girls are involved in domestic chores from an early age, though the new generation of bleached-blonde Athenian women are more likely to be found in the gym or beauty salon than in the kitchen.

Politics & the Media Circus

Greeks love their newspapers and gorge on news and politics. You will often see men standing outside *periptera* (street kiosks) reading the day's juicy front-page headlines from the gallery of daily papers on display. Greece has a disproportionate number of newspapers and TV stations given its population – 30 national dailies (including 10 sports dailies) and seven national TV networks. Newspapers, like most Greeks, are mostly openly partisan, with papers representing the gamut of political views from conservative to communist. The line between news and opinion is often blurred, with more reams dedicated to commentators and diatribe than straight news coverage.

In 2009, Lesbians from the island of Lesvos lost a bid in the Greek courts to stop the world's lesbians monopolising the term, which stems from the island's famous poet (and lesbian icon), Sappho.

Newspaper readership has, however, dramatically declined since the advent of private TV and radio in 1989. Papers and magazines have fought back with gimmicks, competitions, magazine inserts and free DVDs and gifts, but the poor industry outlook claimed its first victim in 2009, when daily *Eleftheros Typos* closed down after 26 years.

With the exception of the more straight-shooting public broadcasters, TV news is highly sensationalist and parochial, dominated by domestic news and society scandals. Dramatic music, repetitive footage and multiple screens with talking heads (usually shouting at the same time) are a key feature.

Given the partisan nature of newspapers and the sensationalist TV news coverage, the country's media owners play an extremely influential role in shaping public opinion. Media ownership is spread among a handful of major players, while the contentious entangled relationship between media owners, journalists, big business and the government, coined *diaplekomena* (intertwined), regularly raises its head.

ARTS
Theatre

Drama in Greece dates back to the contests staged at the Ancient Theatre of Dionysos in Athens during the 6th century BC for the annual Dionysia festival. During one of these competitions, Thespis left the ensemble and did a solo performance which is regarded as the first true dramatic performance – thus the term 'thespian'.

Aeschylus (c 525–456 BC) is the so-called 'father of tragedy'; his best-known work is the Oresteia trilogy. Sophocles (c 496–406 BC), regarded as the greatest tragedian, is thought to have written more than 100 plays, of which only seven survive. These include *Antigone*, *Electra* and his most famous play, *Oedipus Rex*. Sophocles, whose complex plots dealt mainly with tales from mythology, won first prize 18 times at the Dionysia festival.

Euripides (c 485–406 BC), whose most famous works are *Medea*, *Andromache*, *Orestes* and *Bacchae*, was more popular than either Aeschylus or Sophocles because his plots were considered more exciting. He wrote 80 plays, of which 19 are extant (although *Rhesus* is disputed).

DON'T WORRY

You see men stroking, fiddling and masterfully playing with them everywhere – the de-stressing worry beads that are not just an enduring tradition but a fashion statement. There are many theories about the origins of the *komboloï* – one is that Greeks first improvised with Islamic rosary beads to mock their enemy's religious habits; another is that they derived from Orthodox monks' rosaries. *Komboloïa* (plural) were traditionally made from amber, but coral, handmade beads, semiprecious stones and synthetic resin are also widely used. Most of the ones you see in souvenir shops are plastic but you can get *komboloïa* worth more than €10,000 and rare old ones are collector's items.

Aristophanes (c 427–387 BC) wrote comedies – often ribald – that dealt with topical issues: *The Wasps* ridicules Athenians who resorted to litigation over trivialities; *The Birds* pokes fun at Athenian gullibility; and *Ploutos* deals with the unfair distribution of wealth.

You can see plays by the Ancient Greek playwrights at the Athens and Epidavros festivals (p137), and at various historic venues and festivals around the country. Drama continues to feature prominently in domestic arts. Athens supports a lively winter theatre scene, with more than 200 theatres presenting anything from Sophocles to Beckett, as well as popular slapstick comedies and political satires (presented in Greek).

The most distinguished modern Greek playwrights are the father of postwar drama Iakovos Kambanellis, Yiorgos Skourtis and Pavlos Matessis, whose plays have been translated and performed outside Greece.

Literature
FROM HOMER TO ZORBA

The first, and greatest, ancient Greek writer was Homer, author of the 'Iliad' and 'Odyssey', telling the story of the Trojan War and the subsequent wanderings of Odysseus. Nothing is known of Homer's life; where or when he lived, or whether, as it's alleged, he was blind. The historian Herodotus thought Homer lived in the 9th century BC, and no scholar since has proved or disproved this.

Collected Poems by George Seferis and *Selected Poems* by Odysseus Elytis are excellent English translations of these Greek poets.

Herodotus (5th century BC) was the author of the first historical work about Western civilisation. His highly subjective account of the Persian Wars, however, led some to regard him as the 'father of lies' as well as the 'father of history'. The historian Thucydides (5th century BC) was more objective in his approach, but took a high moral stance. He wrote an account of the Peloponnesian Wars and also the famous *Melian Dialogue,* which chronicles talks between the Athenians and Melians prior to the Athenian siege of Melos.

Pindar (c 518–438 BC) is regarded as the pre-eminent lyric poet of Ancient Greece. He was commissioned to recite his odes at the Olympic Games. The greatest writers of love poetry were Sappho (6th century BC) and Alcaeus (5th century BC), both of whom lived on Lesvos. Sappho's poetic descriptions of her affections for women gave rise to the term 'lesbian'.

Dionysios Solomos (1798–1857) and Andreas Kalvos (1796–1869), who were both born on Zakynthos, are regarded as the first modern Greek poets. Solomos' *Hymn to Freedom* became the Greek national anthem. Other notable literary figures include Alexandros Papadiamantis (1851–1911) from Skyros, and poet Kostis Palamas (1859–1943).

The best-known 20th-century poets are George Seferis (1900–71), who won the 1963 Nobel Prize in Literature, and Odysseus Elytis (1911–96), who won the same prize in 1979.

The most celebrated novelist of the early 20th century is Nikos Kazantzakis (1883–1957), whose unorthodox religious views created a stir. His novels, all of which have been translated into English, are full of drama and larger-than-life characters, such as the magnificent title character in *Alexis Zorbas* (Zorba the Greek) and the tortured Captain Michalis in *Freedom and Death*, two of his finest works.

Another of the great prose writers was Stratis Myrivilis (1892–1969), whose works includes *Life in the Tomb*, *Vasilis Arvanitis* and *The Mermaid Madonna*.

Delve into contemporary Athens' underbelly with Petros Markaris' fine detective novels *The Late Night News* (2005) and *Zone Defence* (2007), featuring the Rebus-like Inspector Haritos.

CONTEMPORARY WRITERS

Greek has a thriving publishing industry, including many small independent publishers. About 7500 new titles are published annually, including 1700 local works of literature. Unfortunately very little contemporary fiction is translated into English.

Leading contemporary Greek writers who have been translated include Thanassis Valtinos, Rhea Galanaki, Ziranna Ziteli and Ersi Sotiropoulou, who wrote the acclaimed 1999 novel *Zigzagging Through the Bitter Orange Trees*. Playwright Kostas Mourselas' bestselling novel *Red-Dyed Hair* was made into a popular TV series, while Ioanna Karystiani's award-winning *Swell*, was due to be published in English in 2010.

Uncle Petros and Goldbach's Conjecture by Apostolos Doxiadis, an unlikely blend of family drama and mathematical theory, tells the story of a mathematical genius' attempt to solve a problem that has defied the world's greatest minds.

Apostolos Doxiadis wrote the international bestseller, *Uncle Petros and Goldbach's Conjecture* (2000), while award-winning children's writer and criminologist Eugene Trivizas has published more than 100 books, including the international hit, *The Three Little Wolves and the Big Bad Pig*.

Also making small inroads into foreign markets are Vangelis Hatziyiannidis, who wrote the award-winning *Four Walls* and *Stolen Time* and Alexis Stamatis, author of *Bar Flaubert* and *The Seventh Elephant*.

Kedros' modern literature translation series includes Dido Sotiriou's *Farewell Anatolia* and Maro Douka's *Fool's God*. A younger voice in translation is author and newspaper columnist Amanda Mihalakopoulou, with her book of interwoven short stories, *I'd Like*.

Panos Karnezis bypassed the translation issue by writing in English. *The Birthday Party* follows his well-received novel *The Maze* and short stories, *Little Infamies*. Best-selling author, Soti Triandafyllou, also wrote her latest novel, *Poor Margo*, in English.

The Greek Book Centre reviews the latest Greek books and has author profiles in the Ithaca Online (www.ekabi.gr) journal.

Fine Arts
PAINTING

Art historians have been largely left to rely on decorated terracotta pots as evidence of the development of Greek painting, given the lack of any comprehensive archaeological record.

The few exceptions include the famous frescoes unearthed on Santorini, now housed in the National Archaeological Museum (p127) in Athens. Painted in fresco technique using yellow, blue, red and black pigments, with some details added after the plaster had dried, they are stylistically similar to the paintings of Minoan Crete.

Greek painting came into its own during the Byzantine period. Byzantine churches were usually decorated with frescoes on a dark blue background with a bust of Christ in the dome, the four Gospel writers in the pendentives supporting the dome and the Virgin and Child in the apse. They also

EL GRECO

One of the geniuses of the Renaissance, El Greco ('The Greek' in Spanish), was in fact a Cretan named Dominikos Theotokopoulos. His grounding in the tradition of late-Byzantine fresco painting was during a time of great artistic activity in Crete, following the arrival of painters fleeing Ottoman-held Constantinople.

In his early 20s, El Greco went to Venice but came into his own after he moved to Spain in 1577, where his highly emotional style struck a chord with the Spanish. He lived in Toledo until his death in 1614. His fight for art and freedom was the subject of a €7 million biopic *El Greco* (2007).

A handful of El Greco's works are in Greece. In Athens you can see *Concert of Angels, The Burial of Christ* and *St Peter* at the National Art Gallery (p130), as well as two signed works in the Benaki Museum (p128). El Greco's *View of Mt Sinai, The Monastery of St Catherine* and *Baptism of Christ* hang in Iraklio's Historical Museum of Crete (p464).

featured scenes from the life of Christ (Annunciation, Nativity, Baptism, Entry into Jerusalem, Crucifixion and Transfiguration) and figures of the saints. In later centuries the scenes in churches and icons involved more detailed narratives, including cycles of the life of the Virgin and the miracles of Christ. The 'Cretan school' of icon painting, influenced by the Italian Renaissance and artists fleeing to Crete after the fall of Constantinople, combined technical brilliance and dramatic richness.

With little artistic output under Ottoman rule, modern Greek art per se started after independence, when painting became more secular in nature. Artists specialised in portraits, nautical themes and representations of the War of Independence, including major 19th-century painters such as Dionysios Tsokos, Theodoros Vryzakis, Nikiforos Lytras and Nicholas Gyzis, who was a leading artist of the Munich school (where many Greek artists of the day went). Lytras' *The Naughty Grandchild* set a record for a Greek artist when it was sold for more than €1 million at a London auction in 2006.

From the first decades of the 20th century, artists such as Konstantinos Parthenis, Fotis Kontoglou, Konstantinos Kaleas and, later, the expressionist George Bouzianis were able to use their heritage and incorporate various developments in modern art.

Significant artists of the '30s generation were cubist Nikos Hatzikyriakos-Ghikas, surrealist Nikos Engonopoulos, Yiannis Tsarouhis and Panayiotis Tetsis.

Other leading 20th-century artists include Yannis Moralis, Dimitris Mytaras, Yannis Tsoklis and abstract artists Yannis Gaitis and and Alekos Fassianos.

For a comprehensive run-down of arts and cultural events and exhibitions around Greece, check out www.elculture.gr.

Many internationally known Greek artists live abroad, including Paris-based Pavlos, known for his distinctive use of paper, and kinetic artist Takis. New York–based artists include neon installation artist Stephen Antonakos and sculptor/painter Chryssa.

Athens has a burgeoning contemporary arts scene (p129), with regular shows by local and international artists at a host of galleries centred mostly in Psyrri, Kolonaki and Metaxourghio. A much-anticipated new Museum of Contemporary Art (p130) is being built at the former Fix brewery in Athens. The National Art Gallery (p130) in Athens and the Rhodes Art Gallery have the most extensive collections of 20th-century art. You can also see work by leading contemporary artists in the Athens metro.

SCULPTURE

The extraordinary sculptures of Ancient Greece hold pride of place in the collections of the great museums of the world, revered for their beauty and form.

Prehistoric Greek sculpture has been discovered only recently, most notably the remarkable figurines produced in the Cyclades from the high-quality marble of Paros and Naxos in the middle of the 3rd millennium BC. Their primitive and powerful forms have inspired many artists since.

Displaying an obvious debt to Egyptian sculpture, the marble sculptures of the Archaic period are true precursors of the famed Greek sculpture of the classical period. The artists of this period moved away from the examples of their Asian predecessors and began to represent figures that were true to nature, rather than flat and stylised. For the first time in history a sculpted shape was made to reproduce the complex mechanism of the human body. Seeking to master the depiction of both the naked body and of drapery, sculptors of the period focused on *kouroi* (figures of naked youths), with their set symmetrical stance and enigmatic smiles. Many great *kouros* sculptures and draped female *kore* can be admired at the National Archaeological Museum (p127) and the Acropolis Museum (p122) in Athens.

The sculptures of the classical period show an obsession with the human figure and with drapery. Unfortunately, little original work from this period survives. Most freestanding classical sculptures described by ancient writers were made of bronze and survive only as marble copies made by the Romans.

The quest to attain total naturalism continued in the Hellenistic period; works of this period were animated, almost theatrical, in contrast to their serene Archaic and classical predecessors. These were revered by later artists such as Michelangelo, who was at the forefront of the rediscovery and appreciation of Greek works in the Renaissance. The end of the Hellenistic age signalled the decline of Greek sculpture's pre-eminent position. The torch was handed to the Romans, who proved worthy successors. Sculpture in Greece never again attained any degree of true innovation.

Two of the foremost modern Greek sculptors from Tinos, where marble sculpture endures, were Dimitrios Filippotis and Yannoulis Halepas. Yiannis Kounellis is a pioneer of the Arte Provera movement, while Giorgos Zongolopoulos is best known for his trademark umbrella sculptures.

Modern Greek and international sculpture can be seen at the National Sculpture Gallery (p130) in Athens.

Greek Art and Archaeology by John Griffiths Pedley is a super introduction to the development of Greek art and civilisation.

POTTERY

The painted terracotta pots of ancient Greece, excavated after being buried throughout Greece over millennia, have enabled us to appreciate in small measure the tradition of ancient pictorial art.

Practised from the Stone Age on, pottery is one of the most ancient arts. At first vases were built with coils and wads of clay, but the art of throwing on the wheel was introduced in about 2000 BC and was then practised with great skill by Minoan and Mycenaean artists.

Minoan pottery is often characterised by a high centre of gravity and beaklike spouts, with flowing designs of spiral or marine and plant motifs. Painted decoration was applied as a white clay slip (a thin paste of clay and water) or one that fired to a greyish black or dull red. The Archaeological Museum in Iraklio (p463) has a wealth of Minoan pots.

Mycenaean pottery-shapes include a long-stemmed goblet and a globular vase with handles resembling a pair of stirrups. Decorative motifs are similar to those on Minoan pottery but are less fluid.

The 10th century BC saw the introduction of the Protogeometric style, with its substantial pots decorated with blackish-brown horizontal lines around the circumference, hatched triangles and compass-drawn concentric circles. This was followed by the new vase shape and more crowded decoration of the Geometric period, painted in a lustrous brown glaze on the light surface of the clay, with the same dark glaze used as a wash to cover the undecorated areas. Occasionally a touch of white was added. By the early 8th century BC figures were introduced, marking the introduction of the most fundamental element in the later tradition of classical art – the representation of gods, men and animals.

By the 7th century BC Corinth was producing pottery with added white and purple-red slip. These pots often featured friezes of lions, goats and swans, and a background full of rosettes. In 6th-century-BC Athens, artists used red clay with a high iron content. A thick colloidal slip made from this clay produced a glossy black surface that contrasted with the red and was enlivened with added white and purple-red. Attic pots, famed for their high quality, were exported throughout the Greek empire during this time and today grace the collections of international museums.

Reproductions of all these styles are available at souvenir shops throughout the country. Some contemporary ceramicists are making pots using ancient firing and painting techniques, while Minoan-style pottery is still made in Crete. The island of Sifnos continues its distinctive pottery tradition. You can also find traditional potters in the northern Athenian suburb of Marousi, once one of the big pottery centres of Greece.

Music

Greece's strong and enduring musical tradition dates back at least to the 2000 BC Cycladic figurines found holding musical instruments resembling harps and flutes. Ancient Greek musical instruments included the lyre, lute, *piktis* (pipes), *kroupeza* (a percussion instrument), *kithara* (a stringed guitarlike instrument), *avlos* (a wind instrument), *barbitos* (similar to a cello) and the *magadio* (similar to a harp).

The ubiquitous six- or eight-stringed bouzouki, the long-necked lute-like instrument most associated with contemporary Greek music, is a relative newcomer to the scene. The *baglamas* is a baby version of the bouzouki used in *rembetika* (blues songs) while the *tzouras* is halfway between the two.

The plucked strings of the bulbous *outi* (oud), the strident sound of the Cretan *lyra* (lyre), the staccato rap of the *toumberleki* (lap drum), the *mandolino* (mandolin) and the *gaïda* (bagpipe) bear witness to a rich range of musical instruments that share many characteristics with instruments all over the Middle East, as do the flat multistringed *santouri* and *kanonaki*.

The Greek *tetrahordo* (four pairs of strings) bouzouki was introduced into popular Irish music in the 1960s, and spawned its progeny, the Irish bouzouki.

TRADITIONAL MUSIC

Every region in Greece has its own musical tradition. Regional folk music is divided into *nisiotika* (the lighter, more upbeat music of the islands), and the more grounded *dimotika* of the mainland – where the *klarino* (clarinet) is prominent and lyrics refer to hard times, war and rural life. The music of Crete, represented in the world-music scene as a genre in its own right, remains the most dynamic traditional form, with a local following and regular performances and new recordings by folk artists. Folk music can be heard in *panigyria* (open-air festivals) around Greece during summer.

Byzantine music is mostly heard in Greek churches these days, though Byzantine hymns are performed by choirs in concerts in Greece and abroad and the music has influenced folk music.

Greece's music has always reflected the country's history and politics. Traditional folk music was shunned by the Greek bourgeoisie during the period after independence, when they looked to Europe – and classical music and opera – rather than their eastern or 'peasant' roots.

In the 1920s the underground music known as *rembetika* (see the boxed text, p70) became popular, entering the mainstream after WWII.

In the '50s and '60s a popular musical offshoot of *rembetika* – known as *laïka* (urban folk music) took over and the clubs in Athens became bigger, glitzier and more commercialised. The late Stelios Kazantzidis was the big voice of this era, along with Grigoris Bithikotsis.

During this period another style of music emerged, led by two outstanding composers – the classically trained Mikis Theodorakis and Manos Hatzidakis. Known as *entehni mousiki* or 'artistic' music, they drew on *rembetika* and instruments such as the bouzouki but had more symphonic arrangements. They brought poetry to the masses by creating popular hits from the works of Seferis, Elytis, Ritsos and Kavadias.

Composer Yiannis Markopoulos continued this new wave by introducing rural folk-music and traditional instruments such as the *lyra*, *santouri*, violin and *kanonaki* into the mainstream and bringing folk performers such as Crete's legendary Nikos Xylouris to the fore.

During the junta years Theodorakis' and Markopoulos' music became a form of political expression (Theodorakis' music was banned and the composer jailed). Theodorakis is one of Greece's most prolific composers, though somewhat to his dismay he is best known for the classic 'Zorba' tune.

Road to Rembetika: Music of a Greek Sub-Culture: Songs of Love, Sorrow and Hashish by Gail Holst-Warhaft is a fine account of the genre, as is Ed Emery's translation of Elias Petropoulos' *Songs of the Underworld: The Rembetika Tradition*.

MUSICAL HERITAGE

Georgios Xylouris grew up with music – his late father was the legendary Cretan singer and *lyra* (lyre) player Nikos Xylouris – and it remains his passion.

'Greece has a very rich musical tradition and music remains the most important form of cultural expression,' he says. 'We sing and play music at all events, happy and sad, from love songs to the dirges improvised by women.'

The different musical traditions found across Greece reflect the way people live, the environment and history of the area. Traditional folk music is the music of the rural and regional areas, while *laïka* (urban folk music) and *entehni mousiki* (artistic music) is the urban music of the cities.

While there are parts of Greece where traditional music is dead and nothing new is being produced, Xylouris says there are also places like Crete, where traditional music is alive and thriving.

'In Crete, music is in the blood and one of the reasons the music has stayed alive is that there are always new lyrics because of the popularity of *mantinadhes* (rhyming couplets). Having new lyrics helps create new music.'

In the last 15 years there has been a revival in traditional musical and in young musicians learning to play traditional instruments such as the *lyra* or *kanonaki* (flat, multistringed instrument). Much contemporary Greek music now draws heavily on traditional music and instruments and there is a healthy local music scene.

'In winter in Athens there are many live-music venues with constantly changing line-ups where you can hear today's contemporary musicians play every night of the week. In summer, there are festivals and concerts all over Greece, in every town.'

Georgios Xylouris runs a specialist Greek music store (p152) in Athens and presents a radio show covering the gamut of Greek music.

REMBETIKA

Rembetika is often referred to as the Greek 'blues', because of its urban folk-music roots and themes of heartache, hardship, drugs, crime, and the grittier elements of urban life. The etymology of the term *rembetika* is highly disputed, as is its transliteration. The rhythms and melodies are a hybrid of influences, with Byzantine and Ancient Greek roots.

Two styles make up what is broadly known as *rembetika*. The first emerged in the mid- to late 19th century in the thriving port cities of Smyrna and Constantinople, which had large Greek populations, as well as in Thessaloniki, Volos, Syros and Athens. Known as Smyrneika or Cafe Aman music, it had a rich vocal style with haunting *amanedes* (vocal improvisations), occasional Turkish lyrics and a more oriental sound. The predominant instruments were the violin, *outi* (oud), guitar, mandolin, *kanonaki* and *santouri* (flat, multistringed musical instruments).

In Piraeus, *rembetika* was the music of the underclass and the bouzouki and *baglamas* (baby version of the bouzouki) became the dominant instruments. When the bulk of refugees from Asia Minor ended up in Piraeus after the 1922 population exchange (many also went to America where *rembetika* was recorded in the 1920s), it became the music of the ghettos. The lyrics reflected the bleaker themes of their lives; the slums, hash dens and prisons, infused with defiance, nostalgia and lament. Markos Vamvakaris, acknowledged as the greatest *rembetis* (musician who plays *rembetika*), became popular with the first bouzouki group in the early 1930s, which recorded at the Columbia factory in Athens. He revolutionised the sound of popular Greek music.

The protagonists of *rembetika* songs were often the *manges,* the smartly dressed (often hashish-smoking and knife-carrying), street-wise outcasts who spent their evenings singing and dancing in the *tekedhes* (the hash dens that inspired many of the lyrics).

Although hashish was illegal, the law was rarely enforced until Metaxas did his clean-up job in 1936, attempting to wipe out the subculture through censorship, police harassment, raids on *tekedhes* and arresting people carrying a bouzouki (and apparently cutting off half their slick moustaches and lopping their pointy shoes). Many artists soon stopped performing and recording, though the music continued clandestinely.

After WWII a new wave of *rembetika* performers and composers emerged, including Vasilis Tsitsanis, Apostolos Kaldaras, Yiannis Papaioannou, Georgos Mitsakis and Apostolos Hatzihristou; one of the greatest female *rembetika* singers, Sotiria Bellou, also appeared at this time. Their music later morphed into lighter *laïka* (urban folk music), with the lyrics reflecting more social and sentimental themes. It was played in bigger clubs with electrified orchestras, losing much of the essence of the original music.

Rembetika's anti-authoritarian themes made the genre popular among political exiles and left-wing activists during the junta years.

Interest in genuine *rembetika* was revived in the late 1970s to early '80s – particularly among students and intellectuals, and it continues to be popular today.

CONTEMPORARY & POP MUSIC

All of the different Greek musical styles are still heard today, with most leading performers drawing on *rembetika, laïka* and regional music at some stage in their careers. Comparatively few Greek performers have made it big on the international scene – 1970s icons Nana Mouskouri and kaftan-wearing Demis Roussos remain the best known.

Greek music veteran George Dalaras has covered the gamut of Greek music and collaborated with Latin and Balkan artists, as well as Sting, while Dionysis Savopoulos is known as the Dylan of Greece. Distinguished women of Greek music include Haris Alexiou, Glykeria, Dimitra Galani and Eleftheria Arvanitaki.

Contemporary Greek music also includes elements of folk rock, heavy metal, rap and electronic dance music, as well as a host of music that fits no established category, reflecting a strong underground music scene. The pop-rock band Raining Pleasure is breaking into Europe with English lyrics.

Stand-out new-generation artists include Cypriot-born 'modern trouba-dour' Alkinoos Ioannides, with his brand of rocky folk-inspired songs and ballads, as well as singer-songwriters Thanasis Papakonstantinou, Dimitris Zervoudakis and Miltiadis Pashalidis.

Acclaimed vocal artist Savina Yannatou, along with ethnic jazz fusion artists Kristi Stasinopoulou and Mode Plagal, are making a mark on the world-music scene, while other notable musicians include the band Haïnides and guitarist Ahilleas Persidis.

Greece's answer to Madonna is Anna Vissi, while the youth vote was firmly with pop idol Mihalis Hatziyiannis and Greek-Swedish singer Elena Paparizou, who claimed Greece's first-ever Eurovision Song Contest win in 2005 (a feat heart-throb Sakis Rouvas failed to repeat in his two attempts). The big *laïka* performers include Yiannis Ploutarhos and Antonis Remos, while siren Despina Vandi has broken into the US dance charts.

During summer you can see Greece's leading acts in outdoor con-certs around the country. In winter they perform in clubs in Athens and Thessaloniki. The popular nightclubs known as *bouzoukia* are glitzy, ex-pensive, cabaret-style venues where the bouzouki reigns supreme. Musical taste can sometimes takes a back seat in second-rate clubs referred to as *skyladhika* or dog houses – apparently because the crooning singers resemble a whining dog.

> The comprehensive www .rebetiko.gr has an extensive discography and database of more than 2500 songs, while Matt Barrett gives a history and personal guide to the main players in modern Greek music at www .greektravel.com/music/ index.html.

CLASSICAL MUSIC

For a nation without a strong classical Western tradition, Greece has spawned a surprisingly formidable list of soloists and conductors, many of whom lived abroad.

Sopranos Elena Kelessidi and Irini Tsirakidou are following in the foot-steps of original opera diva Maria Callas. Greece's best-known conductor was composer Dimitris Mitropoulos, who led the New York Philharmonic in the 1950s, while Loukas Karytinos is Greece's leading conductor. Greece's most distinguished composers include Stavros Xarhakos and the late Yannis Xenakis. Mezzo-soprano Agnes Baltsa and acclaimed pianist Dimitris Sgouros are internationally known, while Greece's answer to Andrea Bocelli is tenor Mario Frangoulis.

Composer Vangelis Papathanasiou is best known for film scores, in-cluding Oscar-winner *Chariots of Fire, Blade Runner* and more recently *Alexander*. Stamatis Spanoudakis wrote the excellent soundtrack to *Brides*, while Evanthia Remboutsika and Eleni Karaindrou have also written award-winning film scores.

> The *syrtaki* dance, immortalised by Anthony Quinn in the final scene of *Zorba the Greek*, was in fact a dance he impro-vised, as he had injured his leg the day before the shoot and could not perform the traditional steps and leaps originally planned.

Dance

Dancing has been part of social life in Greece since the dawn of Hellenism. Some folk dances derive from the ritual dances performed in ancient Greek temples. The *syrtos* is depicted on ancient Greek vases and there are refer-ences to dances in Homer's works. Many Greek folk dances are performed in a circular formation; in ancient times, dancers formed a circle in order to seal themselves off from evil influences or would dance around an altar, tree, figure or object. Dancing was part of military education; in times of occupation it became an act of defiance and a way to keep fit.

Dance styles often reflect the climate of the region or disposition of the participants, and dance is a way of expressing sorrow and joy.

In Epiros, the stately *tsamikos* is slow and dignified, reflecting the often cold and insular nature of mountain life. The Pontian Greeks, on the

---

RECOMMENDED LISTENING

40 Hronia Tsitsanis Original recordings of the classics of Vasilis Tsitsanis by some of the leading Greek singers.

Anthologio A musical journey with Greece's most formidable female singer Haris Alexiou, covering her most memorable hits from 1975 to 2003.

Auti I Nyhta Menei A double-CD of some of the most memorable songs from the voice of an era, Stelios Kazantzidis.

Dinata (2008) Songstress Eleftheria Arvanitaki's best compilation from 1986 to 2007.

Hatzidakis at the Roman Agora Double-CD compilation spanning Manos Hatzidakis' works from 1947 to 1985, or his timeless classical recording.

Itane Mia Fora A two-CD collection covering a broad range of music from Crete's favourite son, Nikos Xylouris.

Me Ton Grigori An anthology of Grigoris Bithikotsis, one of the greatest Greek voices, with songs covering the gamut of Greek music.

Mode Plagal III (2001) The third self-titled album by this contemporary jazz-folk fusion band features some distinguished vocalists, including Savina Yiannatou, Eleni Tsaligopoulou, Theodora Tsatsou and Yota Vei.

Neroponti (2009) The latest album from Alkinoos Ioannidis.

Stin Agora Tou Kosmou (1993) The album that launched Alkinoos Ioannidis' career.

Ta Rembetika An excellent two-CD compilation of original recordings of *rembetika* from Greece's national broadcaster, featuring all the foremost exponents of the genre.

The Very Best of Mikis Theodorakis A special-edition three-CD set covering the acclaimed composer's music from 1960 to 2000.

The Very Best of Stavros Xarhakos A good compilation of the composer's work sung by great Greek voices such as Xylouris and Bithikotsis.

To Hamogelo tis Tzokontas Manos Hatzidakis' timeless classical recording.

---

contrary, have vigorous and warlike dances such as the *kotsari*, reflecting years of altercations with their Turkish neighbours. On Crete you have the graceful and slow *syrtos*, the fast and triumphant *maleviziotiko* and the dynamic *pentozali*, which has a slow and fast version, in which the leader impresses with high kicks and leaps.

The islands, with their bright and cheery atmosphere, give rise to light, springy dances such as the *ballos* and the *syrtos*, while the graceful and most widely known Kalamatianos, originally from Kalamata, reflects years of proud Peloponnese tradition. The so-called 'Zorba dance', or *syrtaki*, is a stylised dance for two or three men or women with linked arms on each other's shoulders, though the modern variation is danced in a long circle with an ever-quickening beat.

Women and men until recently danced separately (or often used handkerchiefs to avoid skin contact) and had their own dances, while courtship dances such as the *sousta* were danced together.

The often spectacular solo male *zeïmbekiko*, with its whirling, meditative improvisations, has its roots in *rembetika*, often danced while drunk or high on hashish. Women have their own sensuous *tsifteteli*, a svelte, sinewy show of femininity evolved from the Middle Eastern belly dance.

The best place to see traditional dancing is at festivals around Greece and at the Dora Stratou Dance Theatre in Athens (p148).

Contemporary dance in Greece is gaining prominence, with leading local dance troupes taking their place among the international line-up at the prestigious Kalamata International Dance Festival and the Athens International Dance Festival (p138). Acclaimed choreographer Dimitris Papaioannou was the creative director of the Athens 2004 Olympics' opening and closing ceremonies.

The memorable opening-credits track from the 1994 film *Pulp Fiction* was based on surf guitar legend Dirk Dale's 1960s version of '*Misirlou*' – originally recorded by a Greek *rembetika* band around 1930.

Cinema

Cinema in Greece took off after the end of the civil war and peaked in the 1950s and early '60s when domestic audiences flocked to a flurry of comedies, melodramas and musicals being produced by the big Greek studios. The 1950s also saw the arrival of significant directors such as Michael Cacoyiannis (1950s classics *Zorba the Greek* and *Stella*) and Nikos Koundouros, while more social themes were tackled in the 1960s.

After those heydays, Greece's film industry was in the doldrums, largely due to the demise of the studios after the advent of TV, inadequate funding and state film policy. Film production decreased dramatically – from its peak in 1967–68 when 118 films were made in one year to the 15 to 20 films made annually since the late '80s.

The problem was compounded by filmmakers taking on writer, director and producer roles, as well as the type of films being produced. The 'new Greek cinema' of the '70s and '80s was largely slow-moving, cerebral epics loaded with symbolism and generally too avant-garde to have mass appeal.

The leader of this school is award-winning film director Theodoros Angelopoulos, winner of the Golden Palm award at the 1998 Cannes Film Festival for *Eternity and a Day*. Angelopoulos, known for his long takes and slow pans, is considered one of the few remaining 'auteur' filmmakers. His films have won international acclaim, including the epic *Alexander the Great* (1980), *Travelling Players* (1975), *Landscape in the Mist* (1988) and *Ulysses' Gaze* (1995), starring Harvey Keitel.

Another internationally known Greek director is Paris-based Costa-Gavras, who made his name with the 1969 Oscar-winning *Z*, a political thriller based on the murder of communist deputy Grigoris Lambrakis in Thessaloniki by right-wing thugs. His recent films include *Amen* (2003), *The Axe* (2005) and *Eden is West* (2009).

The 1990s saw a shift in cinematic style, with a new generation of directors achieving moderate commercial successes with lighter social satires and themes, and a more contemporary style and pace. These included Sotiris Goritsas' *Balkanizater* (1997), Olga Malea's *Cow's Orgasm* (1996) and *The Mating Game* (1999), Nikos Perakis' *Female Company* (1999) and the hit comedy *Safe Sex* (2000), directed by Thanasis Reppas and Mihalis Papathanasiou.

But Greece hasn't had a major international hit since *Zorba*, and beyond the festival circuit few have made an impact outside Greece. Two major mainstream films that gained international cinematic releases outside Greece – the first in many years – were Tasos Boulmetis' *A Touch of Spice* (*Politiki Kouzina*; 2003) and Pantelis Voulgaris' 2004 hit *Brides* (*Nyfes*), which was executively produced by Martin Scorsese. Perakis' chauvinistic but fun 2005 comedy *Sirens in the Aegean* was a big local hit, as was the high-budget *El Greco* (2007), and Malea's 2007 comedy *First Time Godfather*.

The latest wave of filmmakers is attracting international attention with films that present a grittier, up-close and candid look at contemporary Greek life, a shift from the idealised and romanticised views from the past. Directors to watch include Konstantinos Giannaris, whose provocative documentary-style films such as *From the Edge of the City* and his most recent release *Hostage* seem to split audiences and critics alike. Dennis Iliadis directed his first American film, *Last House on the Left* (2009), a remake of the classic horror film, on the back of his 2004 movie *Hardcore*, about young prostitutes in Athens. Writer-director Yorgos Lanthimos won the new talent (Un Certain Regard) section at Cannes in 2009 for

Costas Ferris' acclaimed movie *Rembetiko* (1983), is based on the life of Marika Ninou, a refugee from Smyrna who became a leading *rembetika* singer in Piraeus.

Pantelis Voulgaris' acclaimed 2004 film *Brides* follows the fortunes of one of the 700 Greek mail-order brides who set off for America in the 1920s on the SS *Alexander*, bound for unknown husbands and lives.

his drama *Dog Tooth (Kynodonta)*, the first major prize at the festival for Greece in a decade.

Greece's most prestigious film event is the annual Thessaloniki International Film Festival (p291) in November, which has been going for 50 years.

Television

Greek TV offers a jumble of programs from histrionic comedy series, talk shows and soap operas to Greek versions of reality TV, game shows and star-producing talent shows, including *Fame Story* and *Greece Has Got Talent*. Prime-time TV is dominated by news and locally produced shows, with significant investment in original Greek TV series, though in recent years many programs have been adaptations of foreign show (such as *The Nanny*).

Popular comedies are generally hammed up and loud, though there have also been some excellent dramas in recent years tackling social themes such as immigration, single mothers and life in rural Greece. The most popular show in 2009 was actor-comedian Lakis Lazopoulos' satirical news show *Al Tsantiri News*.

TV reflects Greek stereotypes and local preoccupations, as well as attitudes to gender roles and sexual mores, one example being younger women often portrayed in relationships with much older men, while comedies such as *Seven Deadly Mothers-in-Law* play on well-known stereotypes. Outlandish weather girl Petroula's nightly forecasts are a mind-boggling recent addition to Greece's TV offerings (and a YouTube hit).

SPORT

Football (soccer) remains the most popular spectator sport in Greece, followed by basketball and volleyball. For a brief time after Greece's astounding football victory in the 2004 European Cup, Greece was the reigning European champion in both football and basketball (2005 winners). This followed the resounding success of the Athens 2004 homecoming Olympic Games, but little of international note has since happened in the Greek sporting arena.

Football's first division is dominated by the big glamour-clubs of the league: Olympiakos of Piraeus and Panathinaikos of Athens, with their rivalry occasionally interrupted by AEK Athens and PAOK from Thessaloniki. Olympiakos has dominated the domestic game and in 2009 clinched the Greek Championship for the fifth consecutive year and claimed its 14th double after a spectacular 15–14 win in a penalty shootout with AEK.

Greek soccer teams have attracted some top international players in recent years, but hooliganism and violence at soccer matches has affected attendance at games. Greece normally fields two teams in the European Champions League, but remains in the shadow of Europe's soccer heavyweights.

Greece is, however, one of the powerhouses of European basketball, and the sport is enjoying a new golden age. It first gained popularity after the Greek team won the European Championship in 1987, for a while overtaking football as business tycoons bought the big clubs and paid big money for broadcast rights. Panathinaikos, Olympiakos and AEK also dominate Greek basketball. Panathinaikos won its fifth Euroleague title in 2009, while Olympiakos, AEK, Aris and PAOK have also won European titles.

'Football (soccer) remains the most popular spectator sport in Greece'

The future bodes well for Greek basketball following recent European wins by Greek under-20 teams.

Greece's interest in other sports was boosted during the Athens Olympics, where Greek athletes won a record 16 Olympic medals. The Greek medal tally at Beijing was a quarter of that, and the Games were marred by a doping scandal that saw most of the weightlifting team and several other athletes suspended (forcing Greece to introduce tougher antidoping legislation).

Since 2004, some of Athens' world-class Olympic sports stadiums have attracted international sporting events and track meetings, but most are still awaiting their new fate and many are being turned into entertainment complexes.

The second Athens Open in tennis was held in 2009, while the XVII Mediterranean Games are to be held in 2013 in Volos and Larisa.

Food & Drink

Greek cuisine has been experiencing a welcome renaissance, with renewed interest in traditional cooking, and an emphasis on Greece's diverse regional cuisine and produce – the sort of food few people seem to cook at home any more. This is great for travellers, who have long suspected that the food served in the average tourist taverna bore little resemblance to that served at the kitchen table – and certainly didn't do the cuisine justice.

One of delights of travelling around Greece has always been exploring regional variations and specialities and discovering there's so much more to Greek cuisine than *mousakas* (p79) and charcoal-grilled meat and seafood (which admittedly Greeks do exceptionally well).

Steeped in ritual, Greece's culinary tradition incorporates mountain village food, island cuisine, exotic flavours introduced by Greeks from Asia Minor, and influences from various invaders and historical trading partners. Rustic Greek cooking reflects the bounty of the land, its diverse topography and the resourcefulness that comes from subsistence living during hard times. Greeks are good at making a delicious meal out of fresh, simple ingredients, while virgin olive oil is key to making many vegetable dishes and legumes taste so good.

Greeks are sticklers for fresh produce, often travelling great distances to dine on the day's catch in remote fishing villages or eat in village tavernas, where the meat is local and the vegetables came from the owner's garden. They still prefer shopping for seasonal produce at weekly farmers street markets than supermarkets.

The new generation of Greek chefs is experimenting with contemporary Greek cuisine based on traditional recipes and regional gourmet delights. Overall, Greece's dining scene has become increasingly diverse, with more international style and ethnic cuisine in Athens, the bigger islands and larger towns.

Whether it's dining alfresco at a rickety table by the sea, enjoying fine wine and modern Greek cuisine in style in Athens or eating boiled goat in a mountain village, dining out in Greece is never just about what you eat, but the whole sensory experience.

The Glorious Foods of Greece by Diane Kochilas is a must for any serious cook; an insightful regional exploration, laced with history, personal anecdotes and glorious recipes.

THE GREEK KITCHEN

The essence of traditional Greek cuisine lies in its fresh, seasonal local produce and generally simple, unfussy cooking that brings out the rich flavours of the Mediterranean.

The majority of Greek dishes are simply seasoned with salt, pepper, lemon juice and delightfully pungent Greek oregano. Parsley, garlic and dill are also widely used, while the use of spices such as cinnamon, cloves and cumin varies across the regions.

Olive oil is indeed the elixir of Greece, with extra-virgin oil produced commercially and in family-run groves all over the country. The best and majority of olive oil is produced in the southern Peloponnese and the islands of Crete, Lesvos and Corfu.

Vegetables, pulses and legumes – key elements of the healthy Mediterranean diet – feature prominently in Greek cooking, made tastier with plentiful use of olive oil and herbs. Beans and pulses are the foundation of the winter diet.

Meat was once reserved for special occasions but has become more prominent in the modern diet, often added to vegetable stews, such as green beans. Lamb and pork dominate, though kid goat is also common. Beef

Greeks consume more oil per capita than any other people: 30L annually. Greece is the third-largest producer of olives and olive oil (more than 80% of which is extra-virgin, compared to 45% in Italy), but exports much of its finest oil to Italy, where it is mixed and sold as Italian.

SAY CHEESE

Greeks are the world's biggest per capita consumers of cheese, eating around 25kg per capita annually – more than the French and Italians. Widely used in cooking in both savoury and sweet dishes, cheese is also an accompaniment to most meals. Greece produces many different types of cheeses, with infinite variations in taste due to the different microclimates. Several Greek cheeses have gained appellation of origin status. Most are made from the milk of the nation's 16 million goats and sheep.

Feta, the national cheese, has been produced for about 6000 years from sheep's and/or goat's milk. Only feta made in Greece can be called feta, an EU ruling that will eventually apply worldwide.

Graviera, a nutty, mild Gruyère-like sheep's-milk cheese, is made around Greece, but is a speciality of Crete, where it is often aged in caves or stone huts *(mitata)*, Naxos and Tinos.

Other excellent cheeses include *kaseri*, similar to provolone, the ricotta-like whey cheese *myzithra*, and the creamy *manouri* from the north. *Myzithra* is also dried and hardened and grated in pastas. *Anthotyro*, a low-fat soft unsalted whey cheese similar to *myzithra*, and the hardened sour *xynomyzithra* are made on Crete.

Other distinctive regional cheeses include *galotiri* and *katiki*, strong white spreadable cheeses from Epiros and Thessaly; *ladotyri*, a hard golden cheese from Mytilini preserved in olive oil; the semisoft smoked *metsovone* from Epiros; and *mastelo* from Chios.

The popular skillet-fried cheese, *saganaki*, is made from firm, sharp cheeses, such as *kefalotyri* or *kefalograviera*, while *formaella*, from Arahova, is also ideal grilled.

(mostly imported) and chicken are widely used, often in tomato-based stews *(kokkinisto)*, with special dishes reserved for the *kokoras* (cockerel or rooster). At home, lamb and chicken are commonly prepared with lemon and oregano and baked with potatoes. Pork is the meat commonly used in *gyros* (meat slivers cooked on a vertical rotisserie; usually eaten with pitta bread) or souvlaki. Rabbit is delicious cooked in a *stifadho* (sweet stew cooked with tomato and onions). Almost every part of the animal is used – from the delicacy *ameletita* (literally 'unmentionables'), which are fried sheep's testicles to *kokoretsi* (spicy, spit-roasted offal wrapped in intestines) and the hangover-busting *patsas* (tripe soup).

Fish has long been an essential ingredient, and fish from the Mediterranean and Aegean Seas are tasty enough to be cooked with minimum fuss – best grilled whole and drizzled with *ladholemono* (a lemon and oil dressing). Smaller fish such as *barbouni* (red mullet) and *maridha* (whitebait) are lightly fried.

The ubiquitous Greek salad (*horiatiki*, translated as 'village salad') is *the* summer salad, made of fresh tomatoes, cucumber, onions, feta and olives (sometimes garnished with purslane, peppers or capers). Other summer favourites include dishes such as *yemista* (tomatoes and seasonal vegetables stuffed with rice and herbs). Lettuce and cabbage salads are served outside the summer. *Horta* (wild or cultivated greens) make a great warm or cold salad, drizzled with olive oil and lemon.

A variety of cheeses is used in sweet and savoury dishes and appears on every table (above). Greece's exceptional tangy, thick-strained yoghurt, usually made from sheep's milk, is rich and flavourful and ideal for breakfast with thick aromatic thyme honey, walnuts and fruit. A Greek staple with a myriad regional variations of pastry and fillings is the *pita* (pie), the most common being the *tyropita* (cheese pie) and *spanakopita* (spinach pie). Typical Greek pasta dishes include *pastitsio* (a thick spaghetti and meat bake) and the hearty *youvetsi*, slow-cooked lamb or beef in a tomato sauce with *kritharaki* (orzo or rice-shaped pasta).

There are more than 300 edible *horta* (wild or cultivated greens) in Greece, though identifying the full range of edible greens is a dying art. Rare and difficult-to-find mountain greens fetch high prices.

Bread is a mandatory feature of every meal and traditionally used to scoop up food in lieu of a knife. The most common is the white crusty *horiatiko* (village) loaf.

DINING OUT

Eating out with family and friends is an integral part of social life, and Greeks eat out regularly regardless of socioeconomic status. Meals are rowdy affairs and most people still prefer the informal, relaxed taverna style of dining, normally sharing a range of dishes. This is why meat and fish are often sold by the kilo, not per portion. (Greeks are fussy about fresh food, especially seafood).

Most restaurants charge for bread and small dips or nibbles served on arrival. Frozen ingredients, especially seafood, are usually indicated on the menu with an asterisk. Service charges are included but it is customary to leave a small tip.

The key to picking a restaurant is to find where locals are eating, rather than 'tourist' tavernas (touts and big illuminated photos and signs are a dead giveaway). Hotel recommendations can be tricky as some have deals with particular restaurants or may suggest one run by a relative.

Try to adapt to local eating times – a restaurant that was empty at 7pm might be heaving at 11pm (for more details see Habits & Customs, p82).

While there are plenty of stylish upscale eateries in inspiring settings, some of the most memorable meals will be in the most unexpected places, with minimum fuss and ambience. Solo diners remain a curiosity but are looked after. Most tavernas are open all day, but many upmarket restaurants open for dinner only.

Mezedhes & Starters

Greeks love to share a range of mezedhes (appetisers), often making a full meal of them (or adding a main or two). Common mezedhes include dips, such as *taramasalata* (fish roe), tzatziki (yoghurt, cucumber and garlic) and *melitzanosalata* (aubergine), *keftedhes* (meatballs), *loukaniko* (sausage) and *saganaki* (skillet-fried cheese).

Vegetarian mezedhes include rice-filled dolmadhes (see p83), deep-fried zucchini or aubergine slices and *yigantes* (lima beans in tomato and herb

---

Acclaimed London chef Theodore Kyriakou sails in search of recipes for *A Culinary Voyage Around the Greek Islands*, a delectable sequel to *The Real Greek at Home* and *Real Greek Food*.

WHERE TO EAT & DRINK

Bar-restaurant A more recent urban concept, they become incredibly loud after 11pm.

Estiatorio A restaurant, where you pay more for essentially the same dishes as in a taverna or *mayireio* (below), but with a nicer setting and formal service. These days it also refers to an upmarket restaurant serving international cuisine.

Kafeneio One of the oldest institutions, a *kafeneio* (coffee house) serves Greek coffee, spirits and little else (though in rural villages it may serve food), and remains largely the domain of men.

Mayireio Specialises in traditional home-style one-pot stews, casseroles and baked dishes (known as *mayirefta*).

Mezedhopoleio Offers lots of small plates of mezedhes (appetisers).

Ouzerie Traditionally serves tiny plates of mezedhes with each round of ouzo. The Cretan equivalent is a *rakadhiko* (serving raki) while in the north you will find *tsipouradhika* (premises serving *tsipouro*, a variation on the local firewater; see also The Tsipouradhika, p261).

Psarotaverna Tavern or restaurant that specialises in fish and seafood.

Psistaria A taverna specialising in char-grilled or spit-roasted meat.

Taverna The most common, casual, family-run (and child-friendly) place, where the waiter arrives with bread and cutlery in a basket; usually has barrel wine, paper tablecloths and fairly standard menus.

Zaharoplasteio A cross between a patisserie and a cafe (though some only cater for takeaway and gifts).

FISHY BUSINESS

One of the most memorable culinary treats in Greece is a simply grilled fish freshly plucked out of the water by local fishermen, ideally eaten by the seaside. These days, fish has become a bit of a luxury, largely as a result of overfishing, and there's certainly not enough caught locally to cater for millions of tourists each summer. The fish on your plate could just as well be from Senegal or from a fish farm, but some places charge the same regardless. Many tavernas on the islands will tell you they have no fish on the menu because their local fishermen didn't catch any.

Most places will state if the fish and seafood is frozen, though sometimes only on the Greek menu (indicated by the abbreviated 'kat' or an asterisk). Smaller fish are often a safer bet – the odder the sizes, the more chance that they are local and fresh.

Fish is usually sold by weight and it is customary to go into the kitchen and choose your fish (go for firm flesh and glistening eyes). Check the weight (raw) so you know what to expect on the bill as the price for fresh fish starts at around €50 per kilo.

See the food glossary (p85) for common fish names.

---

sauce). The Cyclades specialise in a range of fritters, such as *kolokythokeftedhes* (with zucchini), *revythokeftedhes* (with chick pea) or *domatokeftedhes* (with tomato).

Typical seafood *mezedhes* are pickled or grilled *ohtapodi* (octopus), marinated *gavros* (anchovies), *lakerda* (cured fish), mussel or prawn *saganaki* (usually fried with tomato sauce and cheese), crispy fried calamari and fried *maridha*.

Soup is not usually eaten as a starter, but can be an economical and hearty meal in itself. You'll occasionally come across home-style soups, such as the national dish, *fasolada* (bean soup), *fakes* (lentils) or chicken soup with rice and *avgolemono* (egg and lemon). In island tavernas you are more likely to find a *psarosoupa* (fish soup) with vegetables or *kakavia* (a bouillabaisse-style speciality laden with various fish and seafood; made to order).

Mains

Tavernas normally have a selection of one-pot stews, casseroles and *mayirefta* (ready-cooked oven-baked meals) and food cooked to order *(tis oras)*, such as grilled meats. *Mayirefta* are usually prepared early and left to cool, which enhances the flavour (they are often better served lukewarm, though many places microwave them).

The most common *mayirefta* are *mousakas* (layers of eggplant or zucchini, minced meat and potatoes topped with cheese sauce and baked), *boureki* (a cheese, zucchini and potato bake), *pastitsio* and *yemista*. Other tasty dishes include rabbit or beef *stifadho* and *soutzoukakia* (spicy meatballs in tomato sauce).

Tasty charcoal-grilled meats – most commonly *païdakia* (lamb cutlets) and *brizoles* (pork chops) – are usually ordered by the kilo. Restaurants tend to serve souvlaki – cubes of grilled meat on a skewer, rather than *gyros*.

Seafood mains include octopus in wine with macaroni, grilled *soupies* (cuttlefish), squid stuffed with cheese and herbs or rice, and fried salted cod served with *skordalia* (a lethal garlic and potato dip).

Sweet Treats

Greeks traditionally serve fruit rather than sweets after a meal but there's no shortage of delectable Greek sweets and cakes, as the proliferation of *zaharoplasteia* (sweet shops) will attest. Sweets are offered to guests with coffee or taken as gifts when visiting someone's home.

Vefa's Kitchen is a weighty 750-page bible of Greek cooking from TV cooking matron Vefa Alexiadou, with 650 recipes, including some from leading Greek chefs around the globe.

Traditional sweets include baklava, *loukoumadhes* (ball-shaped dough-nuts served with honey and cinnamon), *kataïfi* (chopped nuts inside shredded angel-hair pastry), *rizogalo* (rice pudding) and *galaktoboureko* (custard-filled pastry). Dodoni and Kayak are excellent local ice cream brands and it is worth looking out for places selling *politiko pagoto* (Constantinople-style ice cream). Traditional syrupy fruit preserves, *ghlika kutalyu* (spoon sweets), are served on tiny plates as a welcome offering, but are also delicious as a topping on yoghurt or ice cream.

REGIONAL SPECIALITIES

While you'll find the staple dishes throughout Greece, seek out the diverse regional variations and specialities. Some areas have dishes unheard of in other parts of Greece, such as *kavourma*, the smoked water buffalo made around Serres, or pies made with nettles in northern Greece. Local cuisine is invariably influenced by the produce of the region, from the oil-rich foods of the Peloponnese to the red peppers in Florina, the giant beans of Prespa in the north, to the foraged wild greens and herbs of the barren Cyclades.

For the largest collection of Greek recipes online try www.greek-recipe.com or www.gourmed.com, or check out Diane Kochilas' Greek Food TV segments on YouTube.

The cuisine of northern Greece is influenced by the eastern flavours introduced by Asia Minor refugees, and uses less olive oil and more peppers and spices than the rest of the country. Thessaloniki and its mezes culture has had the gastronomic upper hand over Athens, while northern coastal towns of Volos are known for seafood mezedhes such as fried mussels or mussel pilaf. Ioannina's specialities include crayfish, frogs legs and *kokoretsi*, while Epiros is one of Greece's biggest cheese-producing regions.

The Peloponnese is known for simpler herb-rich one-pot dishes. As the biggest producers of olive oil, it is not surprising that the Peloponnese and Crete have the biggest variety of *ladhera* (vegetable dishes baked or stewed with plenty of olive oil).

The cuisine of the Ionian Islands (which were never under Turkish rule) has an Italian influence, seen in dishes such as *sofrito*, a braised meat with garlic-and-wine sauce.

Cretan specialities include spiky wild artichokes, *soupies* with wild fennel or *horta*, *hohlii* (snails) and *dakos* (rusks moistened and topped with tomato, olive oil and cheese). *Volvoi* (bitter bulbs) are pickled on Crete and elsewhere.

For a cinematic feast, Tassos Boulmetis' 2003 film *Politiki Kouzina* (A Touch of Spice) is a bittersweet story about Greek refugees from Turkey, told through a boy's passion for food.

Santorini and the Cyclades are renowned for their *fava* (split pea purée served with lemon juice and finely cut red onions), sun-dried tomato fritters and wild capers. On Sifnos, *revithadha* (a local chick-pea stew) is slow-cooked overnight in a specially shaped clay pot.

You'll find excellent cured meats across Greece, from the vinegar cured *apaki* (Crete), olive-oil stored *pasto* (the Mani) and specialities, such as *louza* (Tinos and Mykonos) and *siglino* (Crete and Peloponnese).

Look out for regional sweet specialities, such as *amygdhalota* (almond sweets) from Andros, and Thessaloniki's favourite *bougatsa* (creamy semolina/custard pudding wrapped in a pastry envelope, baked and sprinkled with icing sugar).

Quick Eats

Souvlaki is still the favourite fast food, both the *gyros* and skewered versions wrapped in pitta bread, with tomato, onion and lashings of tzatziki. *Tyropites* (cheese pies) and *spanakopites* (spinach pies) can be found in every bakery and food store. Another favourite snack is the *koulouri* (round, sesame-covered fresh pretzel-like bread) sold by street vendors. There are plenty of *fastfoudadika* (burger and fast-food chains) in major cities.

MADE IN GREECE

Feta cheese was the first Greek product to gain the same protected status as Parma ham and champagne, but several other local products are also being recognised as officially Greek, including ouzo, *tsipouro* (distilled spirit similar to ouzo) and Greece's other popular spirit, *tsikoudia* (see p84).

One of the more obscure Greek products is mastic, the aromatic resin from the mastic trees that grow almost exclusively on the island of Chios. Most people associate it with chewing gum, liqueur, or the sticky white fondant sweet served in a glass of water, but it is also used to flavour pastries and other foods, and its medicinal benefits are promoted through mastic-based natural skin products and pharmaceuticals.

Greece is also one of the biggest producers of organic red saffron – *Krokos kozanis* is grown in villages around the northern town of Kozani – one of the few areas in the world suitable for cultivation of high-quality saffron.

Another local delicacy is *avgotaraho* (botargo), a distinctive fish roe (usually grey mullet) from Messolongi on the west coast, which is preserved in beeswax.

VEGETARIANS & VEGANS

A legacy of lean times and the Orthodox faith's fasting traditions mean vegetables feature prominently in the Greek kitchen, making it easier and tastier to go vegetarian in Greece.

Ladhera are the mainstay of religious fasts. Look for popular vegetarian dishes, such *fasolakia yiahni* (green bean stew), *bamies* (stuffed okra) and *briam* (oven-baked vegetable casserole). Artichokes and aubergines are also widely used, while vine-leaf or cabbage dolmadhes and *anthoi* (stuffed zucchini flowers) are a staple. Beans and pulses are widely used, and you will often find dishes such as *yigantes* on the menu. Of the wild greens, *vlita* (amaranth) are the sweetest, but other common varieties include wild radish, dandelion, stinging nettle and sorrel.

FEASTS & CELEBRATIONS

Religious rituals and cultural celebrations inevitably involve a feast, or have their special treats. Every morsel is laced with symbolism, from Christmas biscuits to the spit-roast lamb for Easter. Even the 40-day Lenten fast has its culinary attractions, with special dishes that have no meat or dairy products (or oil if you go strictly by the book).

Red-dyed boiled eggs are an integral part of Easter festivities, both for cracking and decorating the *tsoureki* (a brioche-style bread flavoured with mastic) and *mahlepi* (mahaleb cherry kernels). The Resurrection Mass on Saturday night is followed by a supper that includes *mayiritsa* (offal soup), while on Easter Sunday you will see lambs cooking on spits all over the countryside.

Christmas is a more low-key celebration, with pork the traditional dish for Christmas Day. A golden-glazed cake called *vasilopita* (with a coin inside) is cut at midnight on New Year's Eve, giving good fortune to whoever gets the lucky piece.

Lenten sweets include halva, both the Macedonian-style version made from tahini (sold in blocks in delis) and the semolina dessert often served in tavernas after a meal.

In agricultural areas many harvest festivals are dedicated to local produce, from the Aubergine Festival (see p199) in Leonidio in the Peloponnese (which has a distinctive long purple local variety) to Aegina's Fistiki Fest (p358), celebrating the island's excellent pistachio industry.

The healthy Mediterranean diet has become a victim of changing lifestyles and the rise of fast-food/junk-food culture, with Greeks recording the highest obesity rates in the EU.

DOS & DON'TS

■ Do ask what the local speciality is in each region.

■ Do look in the pots in the kitchen to select your meal.

■ Do select your own fish and get it weighed.

■ Don't insist on paying if you are invited out – it insults your host.

■ Don't refuse a coffee or drink – it's a gesture of hospitality and goodwill.

HABITS & CUSTOMS

Hospitality is a key element of Greek culture, from the customary glass of water served on arrival to the complimentary fruit at the end of the meal. Meals are commonly laid out in the middle of the table and shared, making it a more social dining experience (it also means meals can be stretched to accommodate extra and unexpected guests, as is often the case). Greeks generally order way too much food and notoriously over-cater at home, preferring to give it away or even throw it out than not have enough.

Culinaria Greece, edited by Marianthi Milona, is a fine weighty tome exploring Greek cuisine, with recipes, history, and useful guide to Greek products and wine, and plenty of photos.

Breakfast is commonly a cigarette and a cup of coffee, and maybe a *koulouri* or *tyropita* eaten on the run, though you'll find Western-style breakfasts in tourist areas.

While changes in working hours are affecting traditional meal patterns, lunch is still usually the big meal of the day and does not start until after 2pm. Cafes do a roaring postsiesta afternoon trade. Most Greeks wouldn't think of eating dinner before sunset, which coincides with shop closing hours, so restaurants often don't fill up until after 10pm.

Dining is a drawn-out ritual, so go easy on the mezedhes, because there will usually be much more to come. The pace of service can be slow by Western standards, but the staff is not in a rush to get you out of there either. The table is not generally cleared until you ask for the bill, which was traditionally (and in many places still is) brought out with complimentary fruit or sweets and in some cases a shot of liquor.

It's impolite to start drinking before everyone's glass is full and they've done the customary toast, *'Ya mas'*. Greeks generally don't drink coffee after a meal and many old-style tavernas don't offer it.

EATING WITH KIDS

Greeks love children and tavernas are very family-friendly, where it seems no one is too fussed if children play between the tables. You might find a children's menu in some tourist areas but kids mostly eat what their parents eat. For more information on travelling with children, see p713.

COOKING COURSES

For comprehensive articles about Greek products and cuisine, including a glossy maga-zine with recipes that you can download, check out www.kerasma.gr.

Several well-known cooking writers and chefs run cooking courses, mostly during spring and autumn.

Aglaia Kremezi and her friends open their kitchens and gardens on the island of Kea for six-day hands-on **cooking workshops** (www.keartisanal.com).

Award-winning Greek-American food writer Diane Kochilas runs week-long courses at her **Glorious Greek Kitchen Cooking School** (www.dianekochilas.com) course on her ancestral island Ikaria in July and August, as well as cooking classes and culinary tours around Athens.

Crete's **Culinary Sanctuaries** (www.cookingincrete.com), run by Greek American chef and food writer Nikki Rose, combines cooking classes, farm tours, hiking and cultural excursions.

DRINKS
Wine

Krasi (wine) predates the written record in Greece, with the wine god Dionysos tramping the vintage before the Bronze Age. By the time of Greek Independence in 1821, however, there was barely a wine industry, with most wine made for personal consumption. It wasn't until the 1960s that Greeks began producing wine commercially – and the infamous retsina (resinated wine) became Greece's best known wine export.

But in the past 20 years, Greek wine has been revolutionised by a new generation of progressive, internationally trained winemakers. Apart from foreign wine varieties being produced, age-old indigenous Greek varietals are being revived and are producing fine wines that are increasingly being recognised internationally for their unique flavours. White wines include *moschofilero, assyrtiko, athiri, roditis, robola* and *savatiano*. Greek reds include *xynomavro, agiorgitiko* and *kotsifali*. A rose *agiorgitiko* is the perfect summer wine. Before ordering red in summer, check that it is not chilled.

During the 1960s urbanisation in Athens and parallel tourism boom, bottled retsina took over from the casks that tavernas used to ferment it in – and was imported around the world.

Greek wines are produced in relatively small quantities, making many essentially boutique wines (and priced accordingly). House wine can vary dramatically in quality (white wine is often the safer bet), and is ordered by the kilo/carafe. Few tavernas serve wine by the glass.

Dessert wines include excellent muscats from Samos, Limnos and Rhodes, Santorini's Vinsanto, Mavrodafne wine (often used in cooking) and Monemvasia's Malmsey sweet wine.

Meanwhile, retsina nowadays retains a folkloric significance with foreigners. It does go well with strongly flavoured food (especially seafood) and you can still find some fine homemade retsina. Wineries are also producing a more lightly resinated and new-age retsina.

TRAVEL YOUR TASTE BUDS

You will discover a range of culinary treats on your travels around Greece. Look out for the following.

ahinosalata – sea urchin eggs with lemon juice, for a super-sea taste

anthoi – zucchini flowers stuffed with rice and herbs

bekri mezes – spicy meat pieces cooked in tomato and red wine

bougatsa – Thessaloniki's famous baked creamy semolina/custard pudding wrapped in pastry, and sprinkled with icing sugar

dolmadhes – vine or cabbage leaves stuffed with rice and herbs

domatokeftedhes – tasty tomato fritters from the Cyclades

fava – yellow split-pea purée from Santorini

gavros marinatos – delicious marinated anchovies

hohlii bourbouristoi – Crete's famous snail dish, fried with vinegar and rosemary

horta – wild or cultivated greens; nutritious and delicious

keftedhes – small meatballs made with minced lamb or pork

melitzanosalata – a tangy roast aubergine purée

saganaki – a sharp, hard cheese skillet-fried until crispy on the outside and soft in the centre

spetsofai – a spicy sausage and pepper stew, originally from Volos and Pelion

taramasalata – a thick pink or white purée of fish roe, potato, oil and lemon juice

tyrokafteri – a spicy feta cheese–based dip

THE ART OF OUZO

Ouzo is Greece's most famous but misunderstood tipple. While it can be drunk as an aperitif, for most Greeks ouzo has come to embody a way of socialising – best enjoyed during a lazy, extended summer afternoon of seafood mezedhes (appetisers) by the beach. Ouzo is sipped slowly and ritually to cleanse the palate between tastes (it also cuts through the oiliness of some foods). It is served in small bottles or *karafakia* (carafes) with water and a bowl of ice cubes, and is commonly drunk on the rocks, diluted with water (it turns a cloudy white). In some regions they prefer it straight (and claim the ice crystalises the sugar and alcohol, making you drunk quicker). Whatever the case, mixing it with cola is a foreign abomination.

Made from distilled grapes in a similar way to grappa or *raki* (Cretan fire water), ouzo is also distilled with residuals from fruit, grains and potatoes and flavoured with spices, primarily aniseed, giving it that liquorice flavour. The best ouzo is produced in Lesvos (Mytilini), particularly Plomari, named after the region where it is widely made. There are more than 360 brands of ouzo.

These days more ouzo is drunk in Germany than Greece, where Johnnie Walker dominates and the trendy young things are downing mojitos.

Spirits

Greece's main firewater is *tsipouro*, a highly potent spirit produced from fermented distilled grape skins. Crete produces a similar but smoother variation called *raki* or *tsikoudia*. Greek brandies tend to be sweet and flowery in the nose, the dominant brand being Metaxa. Also look out for sweet liqueurs such as Mastiha from Chios (served chilled), citrus-flavoured Kitro from Naxos, Kumquat from Corfu and sweet, cinnamon-flavoured Tentura from Patra.

The Illustrated Greek Wine Book by Nico Manessis is the definitive guide, tracing the history of Greek wine and profiling leading Greek wine-makers and wine regions. Also check out www .greekwine.gr.

Beer

Greeks are not big beer drinkers, consuming about half the EU per capita average. The most common beer is locally brewed Amstel and Heineken. Major Greek brands include Mythos and Alfa, while smaller brewer, Craft, has draught beer on tap at bars around the country.

Boutique breweries produce some fine brews. Look out for Vergina, a lager produced by the Macedonian Thrace brewery, the organic Piraiki beer made in Piraeus, Hillas from Rodopi and Crete's Rethymniaki blonde and dark lagers. Corfu produces a unique nonalcoholic ginger beer called Tsitsibira.

Hot Beverages

A legacy of Ottoman rule, Greek coffee has a rich aroma and distinctive taste. It is brewed in a *briki* (narrow-top copper pot) – traditionally on a hot sand apparatus called a *hovoli* – and served in a small cup. It should be sipped slowly until you reach the mudlike grounds at the bottom (don't drink them) and is best drunk *metrios* (medium, with one sugar).

The ubiquitous frappé is the iced instant coffee concoction that you see everyone drinking. Espresso coffee also comes in a refreshing chilled form (*freddo*) or *freddo cappuccino*.

While *tsai* (tea) is usually a sorry story (hot water and a cheap-brand teabag), the chamomile and *tsai tou vounou* (mountain teas) that grow wild all over Greece are excellent. Crete's endemic Diktamo (dittany) is known for its medicinal qualities, while the island's other reputedly medicinal tipple (found in many parts of Greece) is *rakomelo* – warm raki with honey and cloves.

EAT YOUR WORDS

Get behind the cuisine scene by getting to know the language. For pronunciation guidelines see p767.

Food Glossary

STAPLES

αλάτι	a·*la*·ti	salt
αυγά	a·*vgha*	eggs
βούτυρο	*vu*·ti·ro	butter
γάλα	*gha*·la	milk
ελαιόλαδο	e·le·*o*·la·dho	olive oil
ελιές	e·*lyes*	olives
ζάχαρη	*za*·ha·ri	sugar
μέλι	*me*·li	honey
ξύδι	*ksi*·dhi	vinegar
πιπέρι	pi·*pe*·ri	pepper
τυρί	ti·*ri*	cheese
ψωμί	pso·*mi*	bread

MEAT, FISH & SEAFOOD

αρνί	ar·*ni*	lamb
αστακός	a·sta·*kos*	lobster
βοδινό	vo·dhi·*no*	beef
γαρίδες	gha·*ri*·dhes	prawns
ζαμπόν	zam·*bon*	ham
καλαμάρι	ka·la·*ma*·ri	squid
κατσικάκι	ka·tsi·*ka*·ki	kid (goat)
κέφαλος	*ke*·fa·los	grey mullet
κολιός	ko·li·*os*	mackerel
κοτόπουλο	ko·*to*·pu·lo	chicken
κουνέλι	ku·*ne*·li	rabbit
λαγός	la·*ghos*	hare
μαρίδα	ma·*ri*·dha	whitebait
μοσχάρι	mos·*ha*·ri	veal
μπαρμπούνια	bar·*bu*·nya	red mullet
μύδια	*mi*·di·a	mussels
ξιφίας	ksi·*fi*·as	swordfish
ροφός	ro·*fos*	blackfish
σαρδέλες	sar·*dhe*·les	sardines
σουπιά	su·*pia*	cuttlefish
σφυρίδα	sfi·ri·da	grouper
φαγρί/λιθρίνι/μελανούρι	fa·*ghri*/li·*thri*·ni/me·la·*nu*·ri	bream
χταπόδι	okh·ta·*po*·dhi	octopus
χοιρινό	hyi·ri·*no*	pork

FRUIT & VEGETABLES

αγγινάρα	ang·gi·*na*·ra	artichoke
αρακάς	a·ra·*kas*	peas
βλήτα	*vli*·ta	greens, seasonal/amaranth
καρότο	ka·*ro*·to	carrot
κεράσι	ke·*ra*·si	cherry
κρεμμύδια	kre·*mi*·dhi·a	onion
λάχανο	*la*·ha·no	cabbage
λεμόνι	le·*mo*·ni	lemon

μελιτζάνα	me·li·*dza*·na	aubergine
μήλο	*mi*·lo	apple
ντομάτα	do·*ma*·ta	tomato
πατάτες	pa·*ta*·tes	potatoes
πιπεριές	pi·per·*yes*	peppers
πορτοκάλι	por·to·*ka*·li	orange
ροδάκινο	ro·*dha*·ki·no	peach
σκόρδο	*skor*·dho	garlic
σπανάκι	spa·*na*·ki	spinach
σπαράγγι	spa·*rang*·gi	asparagus
σταφύλια	sta·*fi*·li·a	grapes
φράουλα	*fra*·u·la	strawberry
(άγρια) χόρτα	(*a*·ghri·a) *hor*·ta	greens, seasonal (wild)

DRINKS

καφές	ka·*fes*	coffee
κρασί (κόκκινο/άσπρο)	kra·*si* (*ko*·ki·no/*a*·spro)	wine (red/white)
μπύρα	*bi*·ra	beer
νερό	*ne*·ro	water
τσάι	*tsa*·i	tea

Environment

THE LAND

Think Greece and you'll likely picture rugged mountains, indigo water and innumerable islands. These are certainly the dominating features of the Greek landscape which was shaped by submerging seas, volcanic explosions and mineral-rich terrain. Mountains rise over 2000m and occasionally tumble down into plains, particularly in Thessaly and Thrace, while the Aegean and Ionian Seas flow between and link together the country's farthest flung islands.

No matter where you go in Greece, it's impossible to be much more than 100km from the sea. The country is made up of a mainland peninsula and around 1400 islands, of which 169 are inhabited. The mainland is 131,944 sq km, with an indented coastline stretching for 15,020km. Meanwhile, the islands fill 400,000 sq km of territorial waters and are divided into six groups: the Cyclades, the Dodecanese, the islands of the Northeastern Aegean, the Sporades, the Ionian and the Saronic Gulf Islands. The two largest islands, Crete and Evia, are independent of the island groups.

During the Triassic, Jurassic and Cretaceous and even later geological periods, Greece was a shallow oxygen-rich sea. The continuous submerging of land created large tracts of limestone through the whole submarine land mass. Later, as the land emerged from the sea to form the backbone of the current topography, a distinctly eroded landscape with crystalline rocks and other valuable minerals began to appear, marking the spine that links the north and south of the mainland today. Limestone caves are a major feature of this karst landscape, shaped by the dissolution of a soluble layer of bedrock.

Volcanic activity once regularly rocked Greece with force – one of the world's largest volcanic explosions was on Santorini around 1650 BC. Today earthquakes continue to shake the country on a smaller scale but with almost predictable frequency. In 1999, a 5.9-magnitude earthquake near Athens killed nearly 150 people and left thousands homeless. In 2008, three separate quakes of 6.5-magnitude shook the Peloponnese but caused little damage. To check out Greece's explosive past, visit the craters of Santorini (p427), Nisyros (p551) and Polyvotis (p554).

Greece is short on rivers, with none that are navigable. The largest are the Aheloös, Aliakmonas, Aoös and Arahthos, all of which have their source in the Pindos Mountains of Epiros. The long plains of the river valleys, and those between the mountains and the coast, form Greece's only lowlands. The mountainous terrain, dry climate and poor soil leave farmers at a loss and less than a quarter of the land is cultivated. Greece is, however, rich in minerals, with reserves of oil, manganese, bauxite and lignite.

WILDLIFE

Animals

Greece's relationship with its fauna has not been a happy one. Hunting of wild animals is a popular activity with Greeks as a means of providing food. This is particularly true in mountainous regions where the partisanship of hunters is legendary. Despite signs forbidding hunting, Greek hunters often shoot freely at any potential game. This can include rare and endangered species, however the main game is often wild boars which have been around since antiquity. Considered destructive and cunning animals, the number of wild boars has increased in recent decades, likely due to a lower number of predators. Many argue that hunting is an important means of culling them.

The Greek Orthodox Church is the second-largest landowner in Greece.

Greece is the most seismically active country in Europe, with more than half of the continent's volcanic activity.

There are also an increasing number of wild boar breeding farms and you will find boar on many menus.

In areas widely inhabited by humans, you are unlikely to spot any wild animals other than the odd fox, weasel, hare or rabbit scurrying out of your way. The more remote mountains of northern Greece support a wide range of wildlife including decreasing populations of brown bear and gold jackal which survive in Epiros and Macedonia. The grey wolf also lives here while wild dogs and shepherds' dogs with bad attitudes often roam the higher pastures on grazing mountains and should be given a wide berth if encountered.

Wolves have never been popular creatures in Greece. In many Greek myths, the bad guy was turned into a wolf as punishment; in others, wolves were frequently the villains.

Greece has an active snake population and in spring and summer you will inevitably spot these wriggling reptiles on roads and pathways all over the country. Fortunately the majority are harmless, though the viper and the coral snake can cause fatalities (see p765). Lizards are in abundance and there is hardly a dry-stone wall without one of these curious creatures clambering around.

Birdwatchers have a field day in Greece as the country is on many north–south migratory paths. Lesvos (Mytilini; p616) in particular draws a regular following of birders from all of Europe who come to spot some of more than 279 recorded species that stop off at the island annually. Storks are more visible visitors, arriving in early spring from Africa and returning to the same nests year after year. These are built on electricity poles, chimney tops and church towers, and can weigh up to 50kg; keep an eye out for them in northern Greece, especially in Thrace (p322).

Bird lovers should head to www.ornithologiki.gr for articles, links and heaps of info on the habitats and environmental protection of their feathered friends.

Lake Mikri Prespa (p317) in Macedonia has the richest colony of fish-eating birds in Europe, including species such as egrets, herons, cormorants and ibises, as well as the rare Dalmatian pelican – Turkey and Greece are now the only countries in Europe where this large bird is found. The wetlands at the mouth of the Evros River (p330), close to the border with Turkey, are home to two easily identifiable wading birds – the avocet, which has a long curving beak, and the black-winged stilt, which has extremely long pink legs.

Upstream on the Evros River in Thrace, the dense forests and rocky outcrops of the 72-sq-km Dadia Forest Reserve (p331) play host to the largest range of birds of prey in Europe. Thirty-six of the 38 European species can be seen here, and it is a breeding ground for 23 of them. Permanent residents include the giant black vulture, whose wingspan reaches 3m, the griffon vulture and the golden eagle. Europe's last 15 pairs of royal eagle nest on the river delta.

The Society for the Protection of Prespa works with the Dalmatian pelican and the pygmy cormorant. If you're planning a visit, www.spp.gr has details on what you can see when.

About 350 pairs (60% of the worlds' population) of the rare Eleonora's falcon nest on the island of Piperi (p664) in the Sporades and on Tilos (p547), which is also home to the very rare Bonelli's eagle and the shy, cormorant-like Mediterranean shag.

For information regarding the oldest and largest wildlife rehabilitation centre in Greece and southern Europe, see the Hellenic Wildlife Hospital (p360).

ENDANGERED SPECIES

One could argue that all the native animals of Greece are endangered, given the encroaching and invasive nature of human development over a generally small land mass. The brown bear, Europe's largest land mammal, still manages to survive in very small numbers in the Pindos Mountains, the Peristeri Range that rises above the Prespa Lakes, and in the mountains that lie along the Bulgarian border. If you want to see a bear in Greece nowadays you're better off heading for the Arcturos Bear Sanctuary in the village of Nymfeo in Macedonia as it's extremely rare to see one in the wild.

The grey wolf, which is protected under the European Bern Convention, is officially classified as stable however, at last count, there were only an estimated 200–300 surviving in the wild and it's believed that up to 100 are killed annually by farmers' indiscriminate (and illegal) use of poison baits in retaliation for the occasional marauding and mauling of their flocks. The Greek Government and insurance companies pay compensation for livestock lost to wolves but it doesn't appear to slow the killings. The surviving wolves live in small numbers in the forests of the Pindos Mountains in Epiros, as well as in the Dadia Forest Reserve area. Head to the wolf sanctuary near Aetos in Macedonia for a better chance to see one.

The golden jackal is a strong candidate for Greece's most misunderstood mammal. Although its diet is 50% vegetarian (and the other 50% is made up of carrion, reptiles and small mammals), it has traditionally shouldered much of the blame for attacks on stock and has been hunted by farmers as a preventative measure. Near the brink of extinction, it was declared a protected species in 1990 and now survives only in the Fokida district of central Greece and on the island of Samos.

Between 1974 and 1980 an estimated 4000 jackals were hunted and killed on the Peloponnesian peninsula alone.

Endangered Marine Species

Claiming top position for Europe's most endangered marine mammal, the monk seal *(Monachus monachus)* ekes out an extremely precarious existence in Greece. Approximately 200 to 250 monk seals, about 90% of Europe's minuscule population, are found in both the Ionian and Aegean Seas. Small colonies also live on the island of Alonnisos (p659) and there have been reported sightings on Tilos (p547). Pervasive habitat encroachment is the main culprit for their diminished numbers.

The waters around Zakynthos (p702, see also At Loggerheads, p707) are home to the last large sea turtle colony in Europe, that of the endangered loggerhead turtle *(Caretta caretta)*. The loggerhead also nests in smaller numbers on the Peloponnese and on Crete. Greece's turtles have many hazards to dodge – fishing nets, boat propellers, rubbish, sun-loungers and beach umbrellas. It doesn't help that the turtles' nesting time coincides with the European summer holiday season.

Overfishing has severely impacted Greece's dolphin populations. Once spotted during almost any ferry trip, a number of the species are now considered vulnerable, while the number of common dolphins *(Delphinus delphis)* has dropped from 150 to 15 in the past decade. The main threats to dolphins are a diminished food supply and entanglement in fishing nets. In the early 1990s, the striped dolphin also fell victim to an infection called morbillivirus which killed several thousand in the Mediterranean Sea, including many in Greek waters.

The Sea Turtle Protection Society of Greece, Archelon, runs monitoring programs and is always looking for volunteers. For details, visit www .archelon.gr.

Plants

Greece is endowed with a variety of flora unrivalled elsewhere in Europe. The wildflowers are spectacular, with more than 6000 species, some of which occur nowhere else, and more than 100 varieties of orchid. They continue to thrive because most of the land is inadequate for intensive agriculture and has therefore escaped the ravages of chemical fertilisers.

The regions with the most wildflowers are the Lefka Ori mountains of Crete (p457) and the Mani area (p209) of the Peloponnese. Trees begin to blossom as early as the end of February in warmer areas and the wildflowers start to appear in March. During spring the hillsides are carpeted with flowers, which seem to sprout even from the rocks. By summer the flowers have disappeared from everywhere but the northern mountainous regions. Autumn brings a new period of blossoming.

For details and pictures of the thousands of mountain flowers you may to stumble across in Greece, check out www .greekmountainflora.info.

WHERE TO PARK

- Mt Olympus National Park (p311) – Home to Greece's tallest mountain, rich flora and considered the home of the gods

- Mt Parnitha National Park (p165) – Very popular wooded parkland north of Athens; home to the red deer

- National Marine Park of Alonnisos (p661) – Covers six islands and 22 islets in the Sporades and is home to monk seals, dolphins and rare birdlife

- Parnassos National Park (p246) – Towering limestone and scenic views down to Delphi

- Prespa Lakes (p317) – One of Europe's oldest lakes, steeped in wildlife and tranquillity

- Samaria Gorge (p491) – Spectacular gorge on Crete and a refuge for the *kri-kri* (Cretan goat)

- Cape Sounion (p162) – A cape with panoramic views and home to the Temple of Poseidon

- Vikos-Aoös National Park (p343) – Excellent hiking with caves, canyons and dense forest

- Bay of Laganas (see At Loggerheads, p707) – An Ionian refuge for loggerhead turtles

- Iti National Park (p255) – Tranquil stretches of forest, meadows and pools and home to eagles, deer and boar

---

The forests that once covered ancient Greece have been decimated by thousands of years of clearing for grazing, boat building and housing. More recently, they've suffered from severe forest fires (see Environmental Issues, below). Northern Greece is the only region that has retained significant areas of native forest and here you will find mountainsides covered with dense thickets of hop hornbeam *(Ostrya carpinifolia)*, noted for its lavish display of white clustered flowers. Another common species is the Cyprus plane *(Platanus orientalis insularis)*, which thrives wherever there is ample water. It seems as if every village on the mainland has a plane tree shading its central square.

Herbs in Cooking is an illustrative book by Maria and Nikos Psilakis that can be used as both an identification guide and a cookbook for Greek dishes seasoned with local herbs.

Herbs grow wild throughout much of Greece and you'll see locals out picking fresh herbs for their kitchen. Locally grown herbs are also increasingly sold as souvenirs and are generally organic.

NATIONAL PARKS

National Parks were first established in Greece in 1938 with the creation of Mt Olympus National Park, followed quickly by the establishment of Parnassos National Park. There are now 10 parks and two marine parks which aim to protect the unique flora and fauna of Greece. Facilities for visitors are often basic; abundant walking trails are not always maintained and the clutch of basic refuges are very simple. Chances are, you'll hardly notice as you'll be so gob-smacked by the surroundings.

Most of the parks are surrounded by buffer zones protecting an inner wilderness area. Some activities, such as grazing, woodcutting, camping and fish farms, are permitted in the buffer areas, but no activities other than walking are allowed in the protected area. For a rundown of Greece's parks, see the boxed text, above.

ENVIRONMENTAL ISSUES

Greece is belatedly becoming environmentally conscious. Global awareness, a greater sensitivity on the part of younger generations, and sheer financial inducements from funding bodies are shifting Greece's devil-may-care attitude of yesteryear to a growing awareness that the environmental rape and pillage of a land cannot go on forever.

General environmental awareness remains at a low level, especially where litter is concerned. The problem is particularly bad in rural areas, where roadsides are strewn with soft-drink cans and plastic packaging hurled from passing cars. Environmental education has begun in schools and recycling is more commonly seen in city centres, but it will be a long time before community attitudes change.

Long-standing problems such as deforestation and soil erosion date back thousands of years. Live cultivation and goats have been the main culprits, while firewood gathering, shipbuilding, housing and industry have all taken their toll.

Forest fires are a major problem, with many thousands of hectares destroyed annually, often in some of the most picturesque areas of Greece. The increasing scale of recent fires is blamed on rising Mediterranean temperatures and high winds. Massive fires on Mt Parnitha and in the Peloponnese in the summer of 2007 destroyed large tracts of that area's vegetation, as well as entire villages, and changed the face of the landscape for hundreds of years to come.

The result is that the forests of ancient Greece have all but disappeared. Epiros and Macedonia in northern Greece are now the only places where extensive tracts remain. This loss of forest cover has been accompanied by serious soil erosion. Many locals argue that the government continues to be ill-prepared to deal with the annual fires and that its attempts to address the problem are slow, with long overdue reforestation programs that it is felt are not enough.

Illegal development of mainly coastal areas and building in forested or protected areas has gained momentum in Greece since the 1970s. Despite attempts at introducing laws to stop the land-grab and protests by locals and environmental groups, corruption and the lack of an infrastructure to enforce the laws means little is done to abate the problem. The issue is complicated by population growth and increased urban sprawl, as upwardly mobile residents from inner Athens head to the outskirts. The developments often put a severe strain on the environment, including water supplies and endangered wildlife. A few spectacularly outrageous, purely-for-profit developments have been torn down in recent years, however in more cases, the illegal buildings have been legalised. Often this is deemed necessary due to social need, whereby demolition would leave residents with no alternative affordable housing.

Global warming is playing havoc with the Greek thermometer and it's believed that by the end of the century, the average temperature in Athens will rise by 8°C, while some 560 sq km of coastal land will be flooded. Areas at greatest risk include the Evros Delta, Corfu, Crete and Rhodes. It's predicted that a simultaneous decline in rainfall will mean a severe shortage of water throughout the country.

MARINE ISSUES

In its vast amounts of sea territory, Greece's marine life leads a precarious life. In many respects, tourism has been the cause of much of the demise of the Greek seas, as well as the motivation for cleaning them up. Legislation aimed at preventing water pollution has been noticeably effective at keeping the quality of Greece's seawater at a respectable level of salinity. Water clarity in the Saronic Gulf – once notoriously polluted – is now almost on a par with the further reaches of the Aegean archipelago. The country's bathing water quality is now rated as number two in Europe by the European Commission. Nevertheless, foreign ships continue to be threats as many illegally discharge their waste into the sea.

www.cleanupgreece.org.gr promotes programs and events aimed at building awareness of the protection of Greece's environment.

The current advance of global warming means that 0.4% of Greece's land mass is predicted to be submerged by water before the end of the century.

Loggerhead turtle hatchlings use the journey from the nest to the sea to build up their strength. Helping the baby turtles to the sea can actually lower their chances of survival.

A more endemic problem lies in overfishing – a problem that is admittedly Mediterranean-wide. While Greeks love their fresh-fish restaurants and will pay a premium to eat at them, finding the fresh fish is getting increasingly difficult, with fish-farming becoming more common. Greece now produces more than 60,000 tons per annum of farmed fish, and around 60% of the EU's sea bass and sea bream.

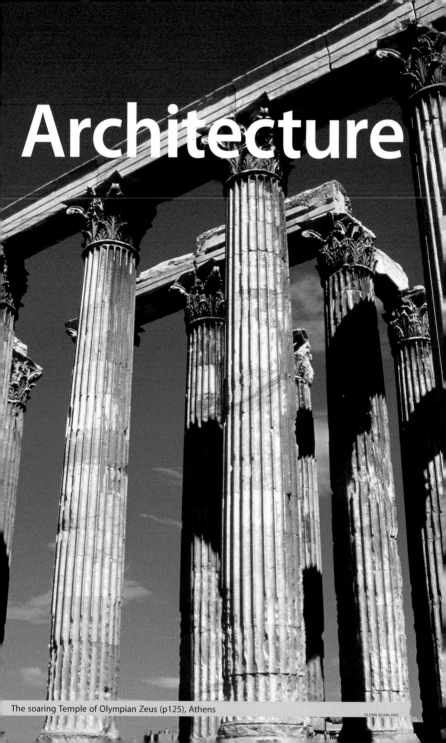

Architecture

The soaring Temple of Olympian Zeus (p125), Athens

GLENN BEANLAND

There's no denying it: Greece contains the world's natural library of architectural reference. Here you'll find classical temples that have inspired entire civilisations. Indeed, Greek temple styles are renowned as international symbols of democracy and have spawned major architectural movements such as the Italian Renaissance and the British Greek Revival – but forget those humbug copycats, Greece has the real thing. It's also an exciting time for modern Greece. Visitors can track the country's transition from fugly modern high-rise to exciting modern hi-tech, and heritage gurus are restoring neoclassical glamour with sassy retrofits. Much of Greece is moving forward, including its past.

MINOAN MAGNIFICENCE

Most of our knowledge of Greek architecture proper begins at around 2000 BC with the Minoans, who were based on Crete but whose influence spread throughout the Aegean to include the Cyclades. Minoan architects are famous for having constructed technologically advanced, labyrinthine palace complexes. The famous site at **Knossos** (see below) is one of the largest. Usually characterised as 'palaces', these sites were in fact multifunctional settlements that were the primary residences of royalty and priests, but housed some plebs, too. Minoan townships dotted the rural landscape, along with some grand residential villas that were microversions of the palaces up the road, complete with multilevel abodes, shrines, storage facilities and workshops. Large Minoan villages, such as those of **Gournia** (p506) and **Palekastro** (p508) on Crete, also included internal networks of paved roads that extended throughout the countryside to link the settlements with the palaces. More Minoan palace-era sophistication exists at **Phaestos** (p471), **Malia** (p471) and **Ancient Zakros** (p508) on Crete, and at the Minoan outpost of **Ancient Akrotiri** (p437) in the south of Santorini.

However, several gigantic volcanic eruptions rocked the region in the mid-15th century BC, causing geological ripple-effects that at the very least caused big chunks of palace to fall to the ground. The Minoans resolutely rebuilt their crumbling palaces on an even grander scale, only to have more natural disasters wipe them out again. The latter effected an architectural chasm that was filled by the emerging Mycenaean rivals on mainland Greece.

GRANDEUR OF KNOSSOS

The elaborate palace complex at **Knossos** (p469) was originally formed largely as an administrative settlement surrounding the main palace, which comprised the main buildings arranged around a large central courtyard (1250 sq metres). Over time, the entire settlement was rebuilt and extended. Long, raised causeways formed main corridors; narrow labyrinthine chambers flanked the palace walls. The multilevel palace comprised luxurious living spaces, banquet and reception halls, and shrines and ceremonial rooms for religious events. There were even designated areas for celebrating bull contests – this meandering floor plan of enigmatic labyrinthine corridors, together with the graphic ritual importance of bulls, inspired the myth of the labyrinth and the Minotaur. The compound featured strategically placed interior light wells, sophisticated ventilation systems, aqueducts, freshwater irrigation wells, and bathrooms with extensive plumbing and drainage systems. The ground levels consisted mostly of workshops, cylindrical grain silos, and magazines.

Minoan fresco depicting the *Boxing Children*, National Archaeological Museum (p127), Athens
JOHN ELK III

MYCENAEAN ENGINEERING

The Mycenaeans had a fierce reputation as spectacular structural engineers and expert builders of massive masonry. These rich warmongering people roamed most of southern mainland Greece, picking off the choice vantage points for their large and austere palaces, which were fenced within formidable citadels. Usually built to a compact and orderly plan, the citadels' enclosing fortified Cyclopean stone walls were on average an unbreachable 3m (10ft) to 7m (25ft) thick – it was believed for a time, of course, that only the legendary race of giants could have lifted such monumental blocks of stone. The famous Lion Gate at the citadel of **Ancient Mycenae** (p184) is the oldest monumental gate in Europe, and is dominated by the triangular-shaped sculpture above that's designed to protect the lintel from the weight of the wall. The immense royal beehive tomb of the **Treasury of Atreus** (aka Tomb of Agamemnon) at Mycenae was constructed using tapered limestone blocks weighing up to 120 tonnes. The palace at **Tiryns** (p192) has stupendous corbel-vaulted galleries and is riddled with secret passageways; and the incredibly well-preserved **Nestor's Palace** (p224), near modern Pylos, also illustrates the Mycenaeans' structural expertise. At their zenith, the Mycenaeans had constructed over 300 of these supersized citadels throughout mainland Greece and the Aegean, and ultimately overran the remaining Minoan palaces on Crete.

ARCHAIC ANARCHY

When the notorious, warmongering Dorian tribes bounded across the Greek plains in about 1000 BC, they carried with them a penchant for iron weaponry. Fortunately, however, their great light-bulb moment came during the Archaic period (from about the 8th century BC), when they put their strong iron metallurgy skills to good use and developed a Hellenic architectural vision for temples. Doric masons now used iron rods cased in lead to support monumental limestone drums for columns (instead of the traditional use of timber). Architects designed temples that were now not only reinforced masonry, but also featured terracotta roof tiles and stone guttering. This guttering had a clever outer decorative band *(sima)* that was covered in elaborately sculptured reliefs forming spouts that allowed rainwater to drain away.

Odeon of Herodes Atticus (p122), Athens

MUST-SEE THEATRES

- Epidavros (p193)
- Delphi (p243)
- Odeon of Herodes Atticus (p122)
- Theatre of Dionysos (p121)
- Theatre of Dodoni (p341)
- Argos (p183)

Almost three millennia later, only very goat-grazed ruins remain of these once-grand Archaic temples; hardcore architecture buffs can muse over the **Sanctuary of Poseidon** (p182) in Ancient Isthmia or the first **Temple of Apollo** (p180) in Ancient Corinth.

CLASSIC COMPOSITIONS

The classical age (5th to 4th centuries BC) is when most Greek architectural clichés converge. This is when temples became characterised by the famous orders of columns, particularly the Doric, Ionic and Corinthian. Doric columns feature austere cushion capitals, fluted shafts and no bases. The classical temple style is also underpinned by the architects' refined knack for mathematics and aesthetics. The monument with the biggest reputation for this noble geometric intellect is the mother of all Doric structures, the 5th-century-BC **Parthenon** (p120), whose blueprints are attributed to master architects Iktinos and Kallicrates. The Parthenon emerged as the ultimate in architectural bling: a gleaming, solid marble crown. To this day, it's probably *the* most obsessively photographed jewel in all of Greece.

In the meantime, the Greek colonies of the Asia Minor coast were creating their own Ionic order, designing a column base in several tiers and adding more flutes. This more graceful order's capital received an ornamented necking, and Iktinos fused elements of its design in the Parthenon. This order is used on the Acropolis' **Temple of Athena Nike** (p119) and the **Erechtheion** (p121), where the famous Caryatids regally stand.

Towards the tail end of the classical period, the Corinthian column was in limited vogue. Featuring a single or double row of ornate leafy scrolls (usually the very sculptural acanthus), the order was subsequently adopted by the Romans and used only on Corinthian temples in Athens. The **Temple of Olympian Zeus** (p125), completed during Emperor Hadrian's reign, is a grand, imposing structure. Another temple design, the graceful, circular temple *tholos* (dome) style, was used for the great **Sanctuary of Athena** (p243) at Delphi.

The Greek theatre design is also a hallmark of the classical period. The original classical theatre design had a round stage to accommodate the traditional circular dance. The small structure called a *skene* (scene building) in the background was used as dressing-hut and stage backdrop. The semicircle of steeply banked stone benches seated many thousands, but the perfect acoustics meant every spectator could monitor every syllable uttered on the stage below. It's thought this auditory marvel may have been aided by the limestone used to construct the seats, which helped to reflect the high-frequency sounds from the stage. The seats were also usually hollowed out so that spectators could draw back their feet to allow others to pass. While Hadrian was still kicking, parts of some theatres were renovated and roofed to create an odeum (music hall), which sometimes shortened the stage into a semicircle. Most ancient Greek theatres are still used for summer festivals, music concerts and plays. See the boxed text (opposite) for a list of must-see theatres.

HELLENISTIC CITIZENS

In the twilight years of the classical age (from about the late 4th century BC), cosmopolitan folks started to take a very individualistic approach to life, becoming rather weary of focusing so much on temples. They cast their gaze towards a more decadent urban style for their civic and domestic sites. The Hellenistic architects reflected this new wave by responding to calls for new designs for palaces and private homes. Wealthy citizens, dignitaries and political heavyweights of antiquity (think Cleopatra) lavishly remodelled their abodes; many homes featured painted stonework and were redesigned with peristyled (column-surrounded) courtyards in marble, and striking mosaics were displayed as status symbols (read *more* bling). The best Hellenistic ancient home displays are the **grand houses at Delos** (p397).

BYZANTINE ZEAL

Church-building was particularly expressive during the Byzantine era in Greece (from around AD 700). The Byzantine church design has the perfect symbiotic relationship between structural form and function. The original Greek Byzantine model features a distinctive cross-shape – essentially a central dome supported by four arches on piers and flanked by vaults, with smaller domes at the four corners and three apses to the east. Theologian architects opted for spectacular devotional mosaics and frescoes instead of carvings for the stylistic religious interiors, which are vivid microcosmic portrayals. Symbolically, working down from the dome (which is always representative of Christ in heaven), images of the Virgin are shown in the apse (symbolising the point between heaven and earth), with the walls decorated in images of saints or apostles, representing the descent to earth (the nave). In Athens, the very appealing 12th-century

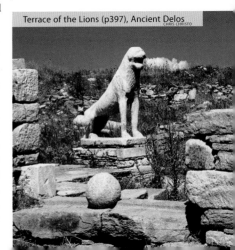
Terrace of the Lions (p397), Ancient Delos
CHRIS CHRISTO

TOP FIVE PROVINCIAL ORIGINALS

- See the medieval, labyrinthine vaulted island village of **Pyrgi** (p610) in Chios, for its unique Genoese designs of intricate, geometric grey-and-white facades

- Gaze at the slate mansions of the **Zagorohoria** (p342) – schist-slab roofs, stone walls and fortified courtyards

- Watch out for the lovely but paranoid semiruined hamlet of **Vathia** (p213) in Mani, for its startling meerkat-esque stone tower houses with round turrets as sentry posts

- Squint at the volcanic-rock hewn village of **Oia** (p434) in Santorini – dazzlingly whitewashed (and we mean really white) island streetscapes and homes

- Discover the strangely attractive wooden-framed houses of **Lefkada Town** (p689); lower floors panelled in wood; the upper floors lined in painted sheet metal or corrugated iron

Streetscape nestled in niches hewn into the volcanic rock at Oia (p434), Santorini
CHRISTOPHER GROENHOUT

Church of Agios Eleftherios (p126) incorporates fragments of a classical frieze in Pentelic marble. The charming 11th-century **Church of Kapnikarea** (p126) sits stranded, smack bang in the middle of downtown Athens – its interior flooring is of coloured marble and the external brickwork, which alternates with stone, is set in patterns. Thessaloniki's 8th-century **Church of Agia Sofia** (p287), with its 30m-high dome, is a humble version of its namesake in İstanbul.

There are numerous Byzantine chapels in **Kastoria** (p320), many of which were originally private chapels attached to enchanting 17th- and 18th-century *arhontika* (mansions once owned by *arhons,* wealthy bourgeoisie merchants).

Several Byzantine monastic sites have made it to the Unesco World Heritage register, including the *katholikon* (main churches) of **Agios Loukas** (p248), significant for their late-Byzantine multidomed style, and the 11th-century **Moni Dafniou** (p126), northwest of Athens, which stands on the site of an ancient Sanctuary of Apollo.

Byzantine Monemvasia (p205), Peloponnese
GEORGE TSAFOS

FRANKISH KEEPS & VENETIAN STRONGHOLDS

After the sack of Constantinople by the Crusaders in 1204, much of Greece became the fiefdoms of Western aristocrats. The Villehardouin family punctuated the Peloponnesian landscape with Frankish castles, eg at **Kalamata** (p216) and at **Mystras** (p204), where they also built a palace that ended up a court of the Byzantine imperial family for two centuries. When the Venetians dropped by to seize a few coastal enclaves, they built the impenetrable 16th-century **Koules Venetian fortress** (p464) in Iraklio, the very sturdy fortress at **Methoni** (p221), and the imposing 18th-century **Palamidi fortress** (p187) at Nafplio. The rambling defence at **Acrocorinth** (p180) is studded with imposing gateways, and the rock-nest protecting the enchanting Byzantine village at **Monemvasia** (p205) commands spectacular ocean views.

OTTOMAN OFFERINGS

Interestingly, remarkably few monuments are left to catalogue after four centuries of Ottoman Turkish rule (16th to 19th centuries). Though many mosques and their minarets have sadly crumbled or are in serious disrepair, lucky for us some terrific Ottoman-Turkish examples survive. These include the prominent pink-domed **Mosque of Süleyman** (p520) in Rhodes' Old Town, which still bears many legacies of its Ottoman past, as does the walled quarter of Ioannina and its restored **Fetiye Cami** (Victory Mosque; p338). The **Fethiye Mosque** (p136) and **Turkish Baths** (p130) are two of Athens' few surviving Ottoman reminders, and the architect for the 16th-century **Koursoum Tzami** (p270) in Trikala also designed the Blue Mosque in İstanbul. The Turkish quarter of **Varousi** (p270) in Trikala, and the streets of **Thessaloniki** (p282), and **Didymotiho** (p331), near the Turkish border, showcase superb Turkish-designed homes with stained-glass windows, wooden overhangs on buttresses, decorated plasterwork and painted woodwork.

Greeks are becoming acutely aware that their 400-year-long Ottoman dossier is worth preserving. One good restoration job is the 18-domed **Imaret** (p308) in Kavala, which incorporates a mosque, college and hammam (Turkish bath).

NEOCLASSICAL SPLENDOUR

Regarded by experts as the most beautiful neoclassical building worldwide, the 1885 **Athens Academy** (p127) reflects Greece's post-Independence yearnings for grand and geometric forms,

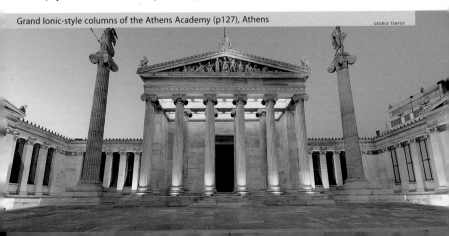

Grand Ionic-style columns of the Athens Academy (p127), Athens

GEORGE TSAFOS

Acropolis Museum (p122), Athens
GEORGE TSAFOS

and Hellenistic detail. Renowned Danish architect Theophile Hansen drew inspiration from the Erechtheion to design the Academy's Ionic-style column entrance (guarded over by Apollo and Athena). The great interior oblong hall is lined with marble seating, and Austrian painter Christian Griepenkerl was commissioned to decorate its elaborate ceiling and wall paintings. In a similar vein, the Doric columns of the Temple of Hephaestus influenced Theophile's solid marble **National Library** (p127), while Christian Hansen (Theophile's brother) was responsible for the handsome but more sedate **Athens University** (p127), with its clean lines.

Meticulously restored neoclassical mansions house notable museums, such as the acclaimed **Benaki Museum** (p128) and the Ernst Ziller–built **Numismatic Museum** (p130), which contains beautiful frescoes and mosaic floors.

Many provincial towns also display beautiful domestic adaptations of neoclassicism. In Symi, the harbour at **Gialos** (p545) is flanked by colourful neoclassical facades (still striking even if a little derelict) and **Nafplio** (p186) is also embellished with neoclassical buildings.

MODERN IDEAS

Athens today is embracing a sophisticated look-both-ways architectural aesthetic by showcasing its vast collection of antiquities and archaeological heritage in evolutionary buildings (see the boxed text, below), and by beautifying landscapes for pedestrian zones to improve the urban environment. Examples include the well-designed facelift of the historic centre, including its spectacular floodlighting (designed by the renowned Pierre Bideau) of the **ancient promenade** (p122), and the cutting-edge spaces emerging from once-drab and derelict industrial zones, such as the **Technopolis** (p138) gasworks arts complex in Gazi.

BEST FUTURISTIC ATHENS

- **Acropolis Museum** (p122) This new space houses Greece's antiquities. Designed by Bernard Tschumi, the museum features an internal glass cella (inner room) mirroring the Parthenon with the same number of columns (clad in steel) and a glass floor overlooking excavated ruins in situ.

- **Stavros Niarchos Foundation's Cultural Park** The Pritzker Prize–winning architect Renzo Piano is designing the SNFCP. Plans include new venues for the National Library of Greece, the National Opera and the National Ballet School, to be set amid natural surroundings that will also feature an agora and a canal linking the park (at the old horse-racing tracks in Faliro) with the sea. Completion is due in 2015.

- **Planetarium** (p133) This is the world's largest digital hemispherical dome, providing 360-degree 3D virtual rides through the galaxy.

- **Athens Olympic Complex** (OAKA; p132) Notable for Spanish architect Santiago Calavrata's striking ultramodern glass-and-steel roof, which is suspended by cables from large arches.

Athens & Attica
Αθήνα & Αττική

Ancient and modern, with equal measures of grunge and grace, bustling Athens is a heady mix of history and edginess, lively cafes and alfresco dining, chaos and downright fun.

The magnificent Acropolis rising majestically above the sprawling metropolis has stood witness to the city's many transformations. Over a decade of radical urban renewal Athens has reinvented itself. Post-Olympics Athens is conspicuously wealthier, more sophisticated and cosmopolitan. The shift is evident in the stylish new restaurants, shops and hip hotels, and in the emerging artsy-industrial neighbourhoods and entertainment precincts.

The car-free historic centre is an open-air museum, yet the city's cultural and social life takes place around these ancient monuments, reconciling past and present. Beyond its fascinating ancient ruins and museums, Athens has a rich cultural calendar of festivals and a burgeoning contemporary arts scene. Its seasonal social life gives it an exciting energy.

Athens remains a city of contradictions, as trying as it is seductive, as quirky and villagelike as it is urbane. Despite its work-in-progress facelift, the city will always have a gritty side, though its architectural hotchpotch and run-down areas become undeniably more palatable when the sun sets and the city lights up, bringing on its renowned nightlife.

Athens used to be a love-it-or-hate-it place. These days it's hard to not concede it's come a long way and be enamoured of its intoxicating mix of history, bustling streetlife, cafes and late-night dining culture. Athens is a city to experience, not just to visit.

HIGHLIGHTS

- **Ancient Splendour** Climbing to the awe-inspiring Acropolis (p118)
- **Historic Trails** Promenading around the streets of Athens' historic centre (p122)
- **Greek Treasures** Viewing the superb antiquities at the National Archaeological Museum (p127)
- **Ancient Stage** Catching an Athens Festival (p137) show at the Odeon of Herodes Atticus
- **Feast for the Eyes** Dining in Thisio or Plaka (p144), with a view of the floodlit Acropolis
- **Magic Nights** Enjoying summer nightlife, lively bars, glamorous beach clubs and moonlight cinema (p148)
- **Museum Masterpieces** Admiring the Parthenon sculptures in the new Acropolis Museum (p122)

- National Archaeological ★ Museum
- Plaka
- Thisio ★ ★★ Acropolis
- Odeon of ★
- Herodes Atticus ★ Acropolis Museum

- POPULATION: ATHENS 3.7 MILLION; ATTICA 4 MILLION
- AREA: 3808 SQ KM

ATHENS AΘHNA

HISTORY

Early History

The early history of Athens is inextricably interwoven with mythology, making it impossible to disentangle fact from fiction. What is known is that the hill-top site of the Acropolis, with two abundant springs, drew some of Greece's earliest Neolithic settlers. When a peaceful agricultural existence gave way to the war-orientated city-states, the Acropolis provided an ideal defensive position.

By 1400 BC the Acropolis had become a powerful Mycenaean city. It survived the Dorian assault in 1200 BC but didn't escape the dark age that enveloped Greece for the next 400 years. Little is known of this period.

After its emergence from the dark age in the 8th century BC, a period of peace followed, during which Athens became the artistic centre of Greece, excelling in ceramics. The geometric vase designs from the dark age evolved into a narrative style, depicting scenes from everyday life and mythology (known as the Proto-Attic style).

By the 6th century BC, Athens was ruled by aristocrats and generals. Labourers and peasants had no rights until Solon, the harbinger of Athenian democracy, became *arhon* (chief magistrate) in 594 BC and improved the lot of the poor, with reforms such as the annulment of debts and the implementation of trial by jury. Continuing unrest over the reforms created the pretext for the tyrant Peisistratos, formerly head of the military, to seize power in 560 BC.

Peisistratos built up a formidable navy and extended the boundaries of Athenian influence. A patron of the arts, he inaugurated the Festival of the Great Dionysia, the precursor of Attic drama, and commissioned many splendid sacred and secular buildings – most of which were destroyed by the Persians.

Peisistratos was succeeded by his tyrant son Hippias in 528 BC. Athens managed to rid itself of this oppressor in 510 BC with the help of Sparta. Hippias went to Persia and returned with Darius 20 years later, only to be defeated at the Battle of Marathon.

Athens' Golden Age

After Athens finally repulsed the Persian Empire at the battles of Salamis and Plataea (again, with the help of Sparta), its power knew no bounds.

In 477 BC Athens established a confederacy on the sacred island of Delos and demanded tributes from the surrounding islands to protect them from the Persians. It was little more than a standover racket because the Persians were no longer much of a threat. The treasury was moved to Athens in 461 BC and Pericles (ruler from 461 BC to 429 BC) used the money to transform the city. This period has become known as Athens' golden age, the pinnacle of the classical era.

Most of the monuments on the Acropolis today date from this period. Drama and literature flourished in the form of the tragedies written by such luminaries as Aeschylus, Sophocles and Euripides. The sculptors Pheidias and Myron and the historians Herodotus, Thucydides and Xenophon also lived during this time.

Rivalry with Sparta

Sparta did not let Athens revel in its newfound glory. The jockeying for power between the two led to the Peloponnesian Wars (see p39) in 431 BC, which dragged on until 404 BC, when Sparta gained the upper hand. Athens was never to return to its former glory. The 4th century BC did, however, produce three of the West's greatest orators and philosophers: Socrates, Plato and Aristotle. The degeneracy into which Athens had fallen was

---

GODS & MYTHS

Athena, the city's patron deity, dominates Athens' mythology and the city's great monuments are dedicated to the goddess. As the myth goes, Athena won this honour in a battle with Poseidon. After Kekrops, a Phoenician, founded a city on a huge rock near the sea, the gods of Olympus proclaimed that it should be named after the deity who could produce the most valuable legacy for mortals. Athena (goddess of wisdom, among other things) produced an olive tree, symbol of peace and prosperity. Poseidon (god of the sea) struck a rock with his trident and a horse sprang forth, symbolising the qualities of strength and fortitude. The gods judged that Athena's gift would better serve the citizens of Athens than the arts of war personified by Poseidon's effort.

perhaps epitomised by the ignominious death sentence passed on Socrates for the crime of corrupting the young with his speeches.

In 338 BC Athens, along with the other city-states of Greece, was conquered by Philip II of Macedon. After Philip's assassination, his son Alexander the Great, a cultured young man, favoured Athens over other city-states. After Alexander's untimely death, Athens passed in quick succession through the hands of his generals.

Roman & Byzantine Rule

The Romans defeated the Macedonians and in 186 BC attacked Athens after they sided against them in a botched rebellion in Asia Minor. They destroyed the city walls and took its precious sculptures to Rome. During three centuries of peace under Roman rule known as the 'Pax Romana', Athens continued to be a major seat of learning and the Romans adopted Hellenistic culture. Many wealthy young Romans attended Athens' schools and anybody who was anybody in Rome at the time spoke Greek. The Roman emperors, particularly Hadrian, graced Athens with many grand buildings. Christianity became the official religion of Athens and worship of the pagan Greek gods was outlawed.

After the subdivision of the Roman Empire into east and west, Athens remained an important cultural and intellectual centre until Emperor Justinian closed its schools of philosophy in 529. The city declined into an outpost of the Byzantine Empire.

Between 1200 and 1450, Athens was continually invaded – by the Franks, Catalans, Florentines and Venetians, all opportunists preoccupied with grabbing principalities from the crumbling Byzantine Empire.

Ottoman Rule & Independence

Athens was captured by the Turks in 1456, and nearly 400 years of Ottoman rule followed. The Acropolis became the home of the Turkish governor, the Parthenon was converted into a mosque and the Erechtheion was used as a harem.

On 25 March 1821 the Greeks launched the War of Independence (declaring independence in 1822). Fierce fighting broke out in the streets of Athens, which changed hands several times. The Western powers eventually stepped in and destroyed the Turkish-Egyptian fleet in the famous Bay of Navarino in October 1927.

Initially, the city of Nafplio was named Greece's capital. After elected president Ioannis Kapodistrias was assassinated in 1831, Britain, France and Russia again intervened, declaring Greece a monarchy. To avoid taking sides, the throne was given to 17-year-old Prince Otto of Bavaria, who transferred his court to Athens – which became the Greek capital in 1834.

At the time, Athens was little more than a sleepy village of about 6000 residents, many having fled after the 1827 siege. Bavarian architects created a city of imposing neoclassical buildings, tree-lined boulevards and squares. The best surviving examples are on Leoforos Vasilissis Sofias and Panepistimiou, though sadly many of these building were demolished. Otto was overthrown in 1862 after a period of discontent, during which there were power struggles and military and external interventions, including British and French occupation of Piraeus aimed at quashing 'the Great Idea', Greece's doomed expansionist goal. The new imposed sovereign was Danish Prince William, crowned Prince George in 1863.

The 20th Century

Athens grew steadily throughout the latter half of the 19th and early 20th centuries, and enjoyed a brief heyday as the 'Paris of the eastern Mediterranean'. This ended abruptly in 1923 with the Treaty of Lausanne, which resulted in nearly a million Greek refugees from Turkey descending on Athens.

Athens suffered appallingly during the German occupation of WWII, during which time more Athenians died from starvation than were killed by the enemy. This suffering was perpetuated in the bitter civil war that followed.

The industrialisation program launched during the 1950s, with the help of US aid, brought another population boom, as people from the islands and mainland villages moved to Athens in search of work.

The colonels' junta (1967–74; see p50), with characteristic insensitivity, tore down many of the old Turkish houses of Plaka and the neoclassical buildings of King Otto's time, but failed to tackle the chronic infrastructure problems resulting from such rapid and unplanned growth of the 1950s. The elected governments that followed didn't do much better, and by the end of the 1980s the city had gained a sorry reputation as one of the most traffic-clogged, polluted and dysfunctional in Europe.

The turning point came in the 1990s, with politicians finally accepting the need for radical solutions. Authorities embarked on an ambitious program to drag the city into the 21st century. The 2004 Olympics deadline fast-tracked projects, such as the expansion of road and underground metro networks and the construction of a new international airport, and forced changes across the public and private sectors. As Athens absorbed more than 600,000 migrants, legal and illegal, the city's social fabric was also changing, presenting a new set of challenges.

Post-Olympics Athens

After a frantic, suspense-filled period of construction and doomsaying, the 2004 Olympic Games were an overwhelming success. The Olympics legacy was a more attractive, cleaner, greener and more efficient capital, after billions of euros were poured into major infrastructure and beautification projects, ranging from removing ugly billboards to revamping the city's parks and squares. The Games' other legacy was a newfound pride and optimism, buoyed by a decade of booming economic growth.

But the optimism and fiscal good times were short-lived: the global financial crisis, political malaise and widespread disenchantment with the country's governance combined to darken Athens' mood. The extraordinary December 2008 riots, sparked by the police shooting of a teenaged boy in Exarhia, were a black mark in Athens history, the worst social unrest in decades.

ORIENTATION
City Centre

Athens' historic centre and most major sites are located within walking distance of Plateia Syntagmatos (Syntagma Sq). The city's two major landmarks, the Acropolis and Lykavittos Hill, can be seen from just about anywhere and are useful for getting one's bearings. Major streets are generally signposted in English.

Downtown Athens is a city of distinct neighbourhoods, each with its own individual character.

SYNTAGMA ΣΥΝΤΑΓΜΑ

Plateia Syntagmatos (translated as Constitution Sq) is the heart of modern Athens, dominated by the Parliament (p132) and surrounded by major hotels, the CBD, shopping precincts and the National Gardens (p132). With pleasant shady benches, a fountain, cafes and the Syntagma metro station, the square is a popular meeting place and a focal point for public rallies and civic events. The changing of the guard ceremony outside the Parliament is a popular spectacle.

PLAKA ΠΛΑΚΑ

South of Syntagma, the old Turkish quarter in Plaka is virtually all that existed when Athens was declared capital of Greece. Its paved, narrow streets nestle into the northeastern slope of the Acropolis and pass by many of the city's ancient sites.

Plaka is touristy in the extreme, but it is still the most atmospheric part of Athens. The main streets, Kydathineon and Adrianou, are packed solid with restaurants and souvenir shops, but elsewhere you can find a peaceful oasis in virtually car-free streets with restored neoclassical mansions.

The quaint labyrinthine Anafiotika quarter above Plaka is a narrow maze of whitewashed, island-style houses built by stonemasons from the island of Anafi, brought in to build the king's palace.

MONASTIRAKI ΜΟΝΑΣΤΗΡΑΚΙ

Centred on busy Plateia Monastirakiou (Monastiraki Sq), the area just west of Syntagma is the city's grungier but nonetheless atmospheric market district. The famous Athens flea market (p151) is southwest of the square, while the central market (Varvakios Agora; p144) is to the north on Athinas.

PSYRRI ΨΥΡΡΗ

The once clapped-out neighbourhood of Psyrri (psee-ree), just north of Monastiraki, has morphed into a busy entertainment precinct, with bars, restaurants, theatres and art galleries. Slick warehouse conversions and restored neoclassical houses compete with a hotchpotch of quirky stores, bakeries, workshops and dilapidated buildings. Psyrri comes alive after dusk and is a good place for live Greek music at one of the tavernas. Of late, it has lost its hip edge, and the bordering streets are rife with junkies and the city's seedier elements.

THISIO ΘΗΣΕΙΟ

Thisio's remarkable transformation began in the late 1990s, when the former traffic-clogged, noisy thoroughfare of Apostolou Pavlou was turned into one of the most serene parts of the city. It's now a lovely green pedestrian promenade under the Acropolis, a heritage trail with its share of cafes and youth-filled bars.

KOLONAKI ΚΟΛΩΝΑΚΙ

Kolonaki, east of Syntagma, is undeniably chic. Tucked beneath Lykavittos Hill, it has long been the favoured address of Athenian socialites. Its streets are full of classy boutiques and private art galleries, as well as dozens of cafes, trendy restaurants and upscale apartment buildings. Plateia Kolonakiou (Kolonaki Sq) and the cafes along Milioni are prime positions for people-watching and fashion-victim–spotting.

Imposing Leoforos Vasilissis Sofias is lined with neoclassical buildings housing museums, embassies and government offices.

MAKRYGIANNI & KOUKAKI
ΜΑΚΡΥΓΙΑΝΝΗ & ΚΟΥΚΑΚΙ

The quiet residential neighbourhoods south of the Acropolis, around the new Acropolis Museum, are refreshingly untouristy.

Makrygianni, between Filopappou Hill and Leoforos Syngrou, has a few upmarket hotels and restaurants, and boasts the city's first gay precincts (between Stratigou Makrygianni and Leoforos Syngrou; see boxed text, p151). Further south, the low-key residential district of Koukaki, which runs along the foothills of the Acropolis, has some excellent neighbourhood eateries.

AROUND OMONIA ΟΜΟΝΟΙΑ

The commercial district around Omonia was once one of the city's smarter areas, but despite ongoing efforts to clean it up, it is still seedy, especially at night, when the city's less desirable elements congregate in the middle of the square (or, rather, giant roundabout). A quasi-Chinatown and ethnic quarter has evolved in the streets behind Omonia and west of Plateia Eleftherias (Koumoundourou), rife with hostels, squats and makeshift mosques for the city's increasing refugee and illegal-immigrant population. It makes a confronting backdrop for the trendy bars and boutique hotels that have sprouted in the area.

The area to the northwest of Plateia Omonias (Omonia Sq) probably rates as the sleaziest part of Athens, particularly the streets around Plateia Vathis – notorious for prostitutes and junkies.

EXARHIA ΕΞΑΡΧΕΙΑ

Next to the National Archaeological Museum, the Athens Polytechnio (Technical University) is the symbol of democratic struggle. It led the infamous student sit-in of 1973, in opposition to the junta, and continues to be the hot spot of political resistance. Exarhia, the bohemian graffiti-covered neighbourhood squashed between the Polytechnio and Strefi Hill, is a lively spot popular with students, artists and left-wing intellectuals. It has many good-value restaurants, cafes and bars, and alternative book, comic, music and clothing stores (as well as a strong presence of anarchists and riot police).

GAZI ΓΚΑΖΙ

Gazi's revival started with the transformation of the historic gasworks into a cultural centre. The red neon-lit chimney stacks illuminate the surrounding streets, packed with bars and restaurants. Gazi is one of the burgeoning gay-friendly neighbourhoods of Athens, with a host of gay bars and clubs.

With Gazi almost reaching saturation point, the new hip area is heading towards Keramikos and nearby Metaxourghio, as well as along busy Pireos, which now boasts one of the fanciest restaurants in Athens (see Varoulko, p146), a boutique hotel, the Benaki Museum's contemporary wing (p128) and some of the city's biggest nightclubs.

METS & PANGRATI ΜΕΤΣ & ΠΑΓΚΡΑΤΙ

To the east of the Acropolis, opposite the Zappeio Gardens, is the district of Mets, which is characterised by some delightful old Turkish houses. Mets runs behind the imposing old Olympic Stadium, built into Ardettos Hill. Leoforos Vasileos Konstantinou leads to the National Art Gallery (p130), while to the east is Pangrati, a pleasant residential neighbourhood with interesting music clubs, cafes and restaurants.

Outer Athens
GLYFADA ΓΛΥΦΑΔΑ

Once Attica's principal beach-resort town, these days Glyfada (off Map p108), 12km southeast of Athens, is a chic seaside suburb popular with expats. In summer Athenians descend on Glyfada, drawn by its beaches, bars and restaurants – and sea breezes. Glyfada marks the beginning of a stretch of coastline known as the Apollo Coast (and the

Athens Riviera), which has a string of fine beaches and upmarket resorts running south to Cape Sounion.

KIFISIA ΚΗΦΙΣΙΑ

Leafy Kifisia (off Map p108) was once a cool northern retreat where rich Athenians had their villas. The rich and famous still monopolise this elite suburb, whose lovely tree-lined streets, mansions and gardens couldn't be further from the hustle and bustle of downtown Athens. Kifisia has some of the city's best shopping, fine restaurants and most chic hotels in town. It is the last stop on metro line 1.

Maps

The free map handed out by the tourist office is fine for central Athens. To seriously explore beyond the centre, buy a copy of the Athens-Piraeus street directory (in Greek), available at most bookshops and stationery stores.

INFORMATION
Bookshops

Anavasi (Map pp112–13; ☎ 210 321 8104; www .anavasi.gr; Stoa Arsakiou, Panepistimiou) Travel bookstore with extensive range of Greece maps, and walking and activity guides.

Compendium (Map pp110–11; ☎ 210 322 1248; Navarhou Nikodimou 5, cnr Nikis, Plaka) Specialises in books in English, and has a popular secondhand section.

Eleftheroudakis Syntagma (Map pp112–13; ☎ 210 331 4180; Panepistimiou 17); Plaka (Map pp110–11; ☎ 210 322 9388; Nikis 20) The seven-floor Panepistimiou store is the biggest bookshop in Athens, with a level dedicated to English-language books.

Road Editions (Map pp112–13; ☎ 210 361 3242; www .road.gr; Solonos 71, Exarhia) Wide range of travel literature and all the Road Editions maps.

Emergency

Athens central police station (Map pp114–15; ☎ 210 770 5711/17; Leoforos Alexandras 173, Ambelokipi)
ELPA road assistance (☎ 10400)
Police (☎ 100)
Tourist police (Map p116; ☎ 24hr 171, 210 920 0724; Veïkou 43-45, Koukaki; ☺ 8am-10pm)
Visitor emergency assistance (☎ 112) Toll-free 24-hour service in English.

Internet Access

Most hotels have lobby and in-room internet access and are increasingly installing wi-fi. There are free wireless hot spots at Syntagma, Thisio, Gazi, Plateia Kotzia and the port of Piraeus

(with more neighbourhoods coming online). Internet cafes charge €2 to €4 per hour.

Bits & Bytes Internet Café (Map pp110–11; ☎ 210 382 2545; Kapnikareas 19, Monastiraki; per hr €2.50; ☺ 24hr)
Cyberzone (Map pp112–13; ☎ 210 520 3939; Satovrianidou 7, Omonia; per hr €2; ☺ 24hr) Cheaper rates of €1.50 per hour apply between midnight and 8am.
Ivis Internet (Map pp110–11; Mitropoleos 3, Syntagma; per hr €3; ☺ 24hr)
Public (Map pp110–11; ☎ 210 324 6210; Karageorgi Servias 1, Syntagma; ☺ 9am-9pm Mon-Sat) Free internet on the third floor.

Internet Resources

www.breathtakingathens.gr Official visitor site of the Athens Tourism and Economic Development Agency, with handy what's on listings.
www.culture.gr Ministry of Culture guide to museums, archaeological sites and cultural events.
www.elculture.gr Informative bilingual arts and culture guide, including theatre, music and cinema listings.

Laundry

Laundromat (Map p116; ☎ 210 923 5811; Veïkou 3a, Makrygianni; wash per 10kg €5, dry €2; ☺ 8am-10pm) Underneath Athens Studios.

Left Luggage

Most hotels will store luggage free for guests, although many do no more than pile the bags in a hallway. You'll find luggage storage facilities at the airport and at the metro stations at Omonia, Monastiraki and Piraeus.

Pacific Travel Luggage Storage (Map pp110–11; ☎ 210 324 1007; Nikis 26, Syntagma; per day €2; ☺ 8am-8pm Mon-Sat)

Media

Athens News (www.athensnews.gr) Published every Friday; provides entertainment listings.
Athens Plus (www.ekathimerini.com) Comprehensive weekly English news and entertainment newspaper; published on Friday by *Kathimerini* and available online.
Insider (www.insider-magazine.gr) Monthly glossy magazine aimed at visitors and foreigners living in Greece.
Kathimerini (www.ekathimerini.com) The *International Herald Tribune* publishes an eight-page English-language edition of this Greek daily, with news, arts, cinema listings and daily ferry schedules.
Odyssey (www.odyssey.gr) Bimonthly Greek diaspora magazine; handy annual summer guide to Athens.

Medical Services

Ambulance/First-Aid Advice (☎ 166)
Duty Doctors & Hospitals (☎ 1434, in Greek) Published in *Kathimerini*.

Pharmacies (☎ 1434, in Greek) Check pharmacy windows for notice of nearest duty pharmacy. There is a 24-hour pharmacy at the airport.

SOS Doctors (☎ 1016, 210 821 1888; ☽ 24hr) Pay service with English-speaking doctors.

Money

Major banks have branches around Syntagma and there are ATMs all over the city. Standard bank opening hours are 8am to 2.30pm Monday to Thursday and 8am to 2pm on Friday, though some banks open until 8pm weekdays and on Saturday morning.

Eurochange Syntagma (Map pp110-11; ☎ 210 331 2462; Karageorgi Servias 2; ☽ 9am-9pm); Omonia (Map pp112-13; ☎ 210 552 2314; Kotopoulou 1); Monastiraki (Map pp110-11 ; ☎ 210 322 2657; Areos 1) Exchanges travellers cheques and arranges money transfers.

National Bank of Greece (Map pp110-11; ☎ 210 334 0500; cnr Karageorgi Servias & Stadiou, Syntagma) Has a 24-hour automatic exchange machine.

Post

Athens central post office (Map pp112-13; www.elta .gr; Eolou 100, Omonia; ☽ 7.30am-8pm Mon-Fri, 7.30am-2pm Sat) Unless specified otherwise, all poste restante is sent here.

Parcel post office (Map pp110-11; Nikis 33, Syntagma; ☽ 7.30am-2pm Mon-Fri) Parcels weighing over 2kg must be taken here, unwrapped, for inspection.

Syntagma post office (Map pp110-11; Plateia Syntagmatos, Syntagma; ☽ 7.30am-8pm Mon-Fri, 7.30am-2pm Sat)

Telephone

Public phones all over Athens allow international calls. Phonecards are available at kiosks.

Toilets

Public toilets are relatively scarce in Athens and keep inconsistent hours. There are 24-hour portable, self-cleaning pay toilets (€0.50) around the centre. Fast-food outlets and big hotels are also handy.

Tourist Information

EOT (Greek National Tourist Organisation; www.gnto.gr) Syntagma (Map pp110-11; ☎ 210 331 0392; Leoforos Vasilissis Amalias 26a; ☽ 9am-7pm Mon-Fri, 10am-4pm Sat & Sun); Airport (☎ 210 353 0445-7; Arrivals Hall; ☽ 9am-7pm Mon-Fri, 10am-4pm Sat & Sun) Has a handy free map of Athens and public transport information. You can also pick up a free copy of the glossy Athens & Attica booklet.

Tourist police (Map p116; ☎ 24hr 171, 210 920 0724; Veïkou 43-45, Koukaki; ☽ 8am-10pm) General tourist information and emergency help.

DANGERS & ANNOYANCES

Athens has its fair share of the problems found in all major cities but is one of Europe's safest capitals. Violent street crime remains rare, but travellers should be alert to the traps listed here. The streets northwest and southwest of Omonia have become markedly seedier, with the increasing presence of prostitutes, junkies and mostly illegal immigrants, and should be avoided at night.

Pickpockets

The favourite hunting grounds for pickpockets are the metro system, particularly the Piraeus–Kifisia line, and the crowded streets around Omonia, Athinas and the Monastiraki flea market.

Scams

BAR SCAMS

Unsuspecting travellers have been taken in by the various bar scams in central Athens, particularly around Syntagma.

One scam runs something like this: friendly Greek approaches solo male traveller; friendly Greek then reveals that he, too, is from out of town or does the old 'I have a cousin in Australia' routine and suggests they go to a bar for a drink. Before they know it women appear, more drinks are ordered and the conman disappears, leaving the traveller to pay an exorbitant bill. The smiles disappear and the atmosphere turns threatening.

Other bars lure intoxicated males with talk of sex and present them with outrageous bills.

TAXI TOUTS

Some taxi drivers work in league with overpriced, low-grade hotels around Omonia, though it's not widespread. The scam involves taxi drivers picking up late-night arrivals and persuading them that the hotel they want to go to is full – even if they have a booking. The taxi driver will pretend to phone the hotel, announce that it's full and suggest an alternative. Ask to speak to the hotel yourself, or simply insist on going to your hotel.

(Continued on page 117)

ATHENS & ATTICA

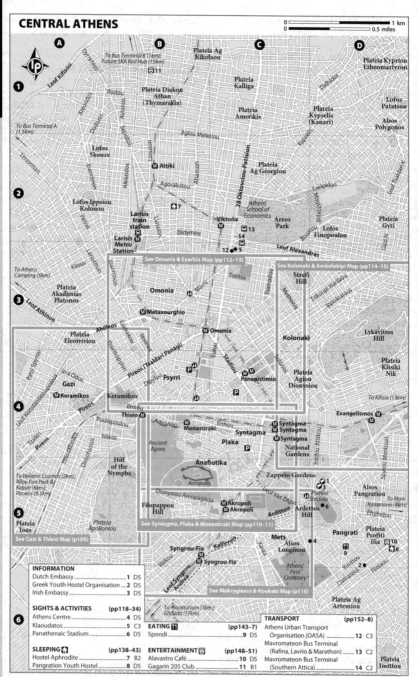

CENTRAL ATHENS

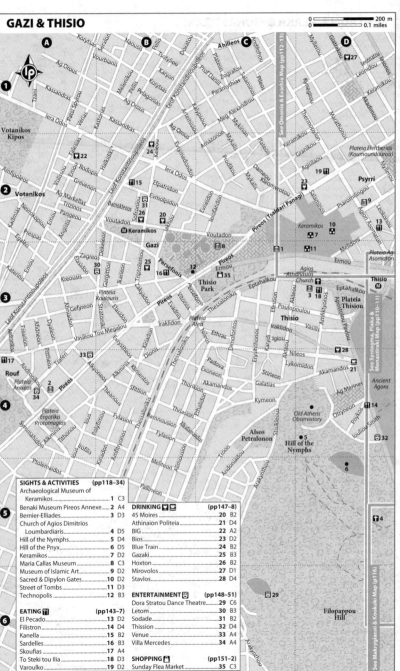

GAZI & THISIO

0 — 200 m
0 — 0.1 miles

SYNTAGMA, PLAKA & MONASTIRAKI

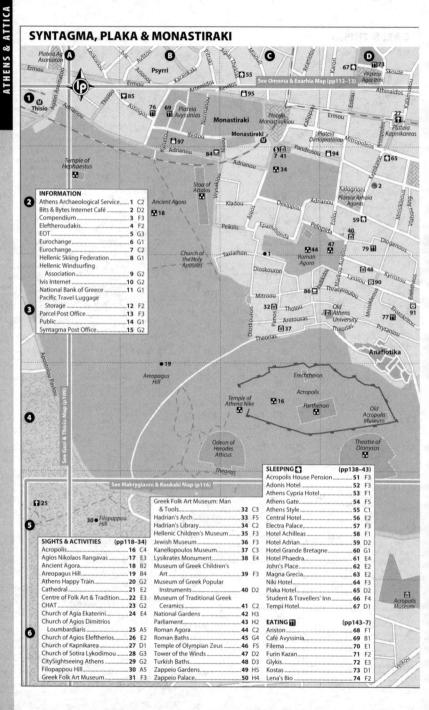

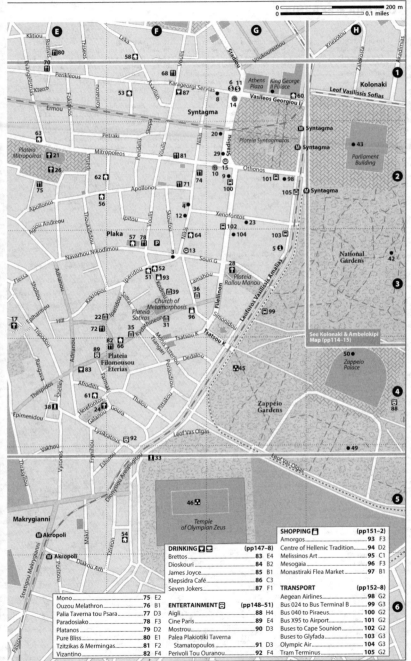

0 _____ 200 m
0 _____ 0.1 miles

OMONIA & EXARHIA

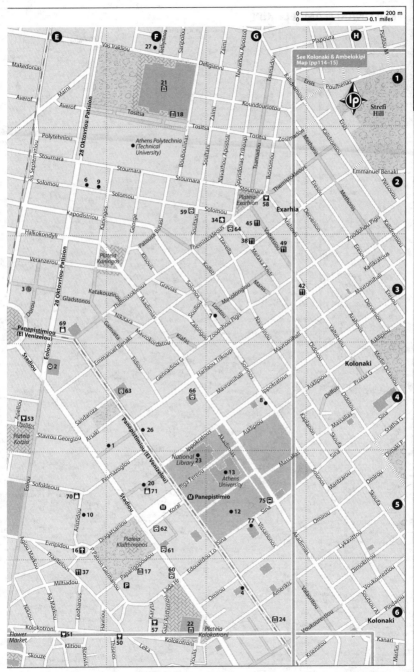

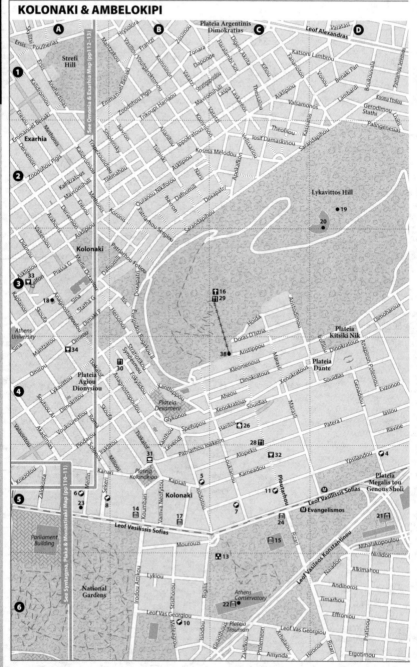

KOLONAKI & AMBELOKIPI

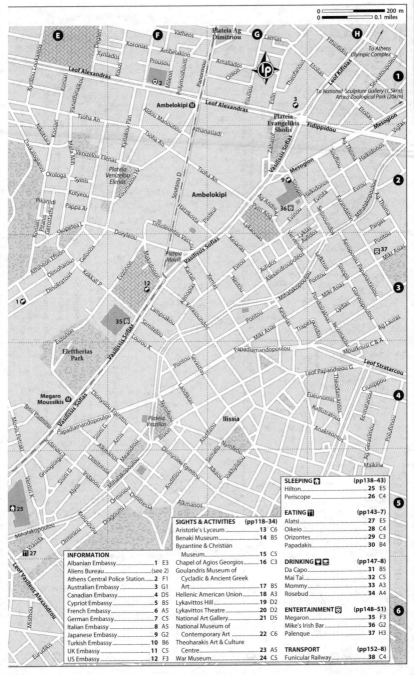

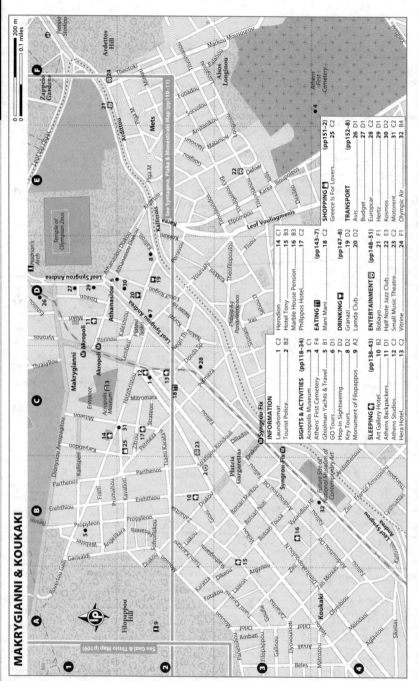

MAKRYGIANNI & KOUKAKI

ATHENS & ATTICA

(Continued from page 107)

TRAVEL AGENTS

Some travel agents in the Plaka/Syntagma area employ touts to promote 'cheap' packages to the islands. These touts hang out at the bus and metro stops, hoping to find naive new arrivals, take them back to the agency and pressure them into buying outrageously overpriced packages. You will always be able to negotiate a better deal when you get to the island of your choice. If you are worried that everywhere will be full, select a place from the pages of this guide and make your own booking.

Slippery Surfaces

Many of Athens' pavements and other surfaces underfoot are made of marble and can become incredibly slippery, especially when wet, so tread carefully and wear sensible shoes.

Adulterated Drinks

Some bars and clubs in Athens serve what are locally known as *bombes*, adulterated drinks that have been diluted with cheap illegal imports or methanol-based spirit substitutes. They can leave you feeling decidedly worse for wear the next day. To avoid the risk, drink beer and other alcoholic drinks that are bottled, ensure that you ask for a drink with a distinctive taste or name your brand.

Taxi Drive rs

Athenian taxi drivers have an awful reputation and it is certainly not entirely undeserved – most locals and tourists alike will have horror rip-off stories to report. While the standards of the city's taxis and their drivers' manners have improved dramatically overall, it can still be a bit of a toss-up whether you get polite, efficient and honest service or one of the nasty ones. Beware: the friendly ones can be the worst offenders.

Most (but not all) rip-offs involve taxis picked up late at night from the ranks at the airport, train stations, bus terminals and particularly the port of Piraeus. Some drivers don't like to bother with the meter and demand whatever they think they can get away with – and refuse to take you if you insist on using the meter. Only negotiate a set fare if you have some idea of the cost; you are better off getting the driver's details to report them to the tourist police, then finding another taxi. At Piraeus, avoid the drivers at the port exit asking if you need a taxi – it's better to hail one off the street further away.

ATHENS IN...

Two Days

Start by climbing the glorious **Acropolis** (p118), winding down through the **Ancient Agora** (p123). Stop at a **cafe** (p147) along Adrianou before exploring **Plaka** (p104) and the **Monastiraki flea market** (p151). Head to the new **Acropolis Museum** (p122) for lunch and the Parthenon masterpieces. Amble around the grand promenade, then up to **Filopappou Hill** (p131) and the cafes of **Thisio** (p104), before dinner at a restaurant with an Acropolis view.

On day two, watch the **changing of the guard** (p132) at Syntagma before heading through the gardens to the **Panathenaic Stadium** (p126) and the **Temple of Olympian Zeus** (p125). Take a trolleybus to the **National Archaeological Museum** (p127) and spend the afternoon exploring downtown Athens or revisiting Plaka. Catch a show at the historic **Odeon of Herodes Atticus** (p122), or head to **Gazi** (p105) for dinner and nightlife.

Four Days

If you've got a couple more days, you can add the following activities to your itinerary.

On the third day, head to the **Benaki Museum** (p128) and nearby **Byzantine & Christian Museum** (p128) before lunch and shopping in **Kolonaki** (p105). Take the *teleferik* (funicular railway) up to **Lykavittos Hill** (p131) for panoramic views. Have dinner in **Exarhia** (p144) and catch a movie by moonlight at **Aigli** (p149), Athens' oldest outdoor cinema. Alternatively, enjoy live music at a **taverna** (p149) in Psyrri or, in winter, at a **rembetika club** (p149).

On the fourth day, explore the **central market** (p144) and the **Keramikos site** (p124), stopping for lunch in Thisio. Take the tram along the coast and walk or swim at a **beach** (p133), or take a trip along the coast to the **Temple of Poseidon** (p162). If you've stayed in the centre all day, dine at **Mikrolimano harbour** (p161) or experience summer nightlife at Athens' **beach bars** (p150).

In extreme cases, drivers have accelerated meters or switch them to night rate (tariff 2 lights up) during the day. Some will also often add their tip to the price they quote. Check the extra charges for airport pick-ups and tolls, which are set and must be displayed in every taxi.

The best way to protect yourself is to record the taxi's number plates and ask for a receipt – they are obligated to provide one and most have electronic receipt machines installed (though many do not work). If you do have a dispute, call the police (☎ 100), insist the driver takes you to the local police station to sort it out, or take the driver and taxi's registration number and report them to the tourist police. A pilot taxi complaint service (☎ 1019) was also in operation at the time of research.

SIGHTS
Acropolis

The **Acropolis** (High City; Map p119; ☎ 210 321 0219; adult/concession €12/6; ☒ 8.30am-8pm Apr-Oct, 8am-5pm Nov-Mar; ☒) is the most important ancient site in the Western world. Crowned by the Parthenon, it stands sentinel over Athens, visible from almost everywhere within the city. Its monuments of Pentelic marble gleam white in the midday sun and gradually take on a honey hue as the sun sinks, while at night they stand brilliantly illuminated above the city. A glimpse of this magnificent sight cannot fail to lift your spirits.

Inspiring as these monuments are, they are but faded remnants of Pericles' city. Pericles spared no expense – only the best materials, architects, sculptors and artists were good enough for a city dedicated to the cult of Athena. The city was a showcase of lavishly coloured colossal buildings and of gargantuan statues, some of bronze, others of marble plated with gold and encrusted with precious stones.

There are several approaches to the site. The main approach from Plaka is along the path that is a continuation of Dioskouron. From the south, you can walk along Dionysiou Areopagitou to the path just beyond the Odeon of Herodes Atticus to get to the main entrance, or you can go through the Theatre of Dionysos entrance near the Akropoli metro station, and wind your way up from there. Anyone carrying a backpack or large bag (including camera bags) must enter from the main entrance and leave bags at the cloakroom.

Arrive as early as possible, or go late in the afternoon, as it gets incredibly crowded. Wear shoes with rubber soles – the paths around the site are uneven and slippery. People in wheelchairs can access the site via a cage lift rising vertically up the rock face on the northern side. Those needing assistance should present at the main entrance.

The Acropolis admission includes entry to other sites (see boxed text, p121).

HISTORY

The Acropolis was first inhabited in Neolithic times. The first temples were built during the Mycenaean era in homage to the goddess Athena. People lived on the Acropolis until the late 6th century BC, but in 510 BC the Delphic oracle declared that it should be the province of the gods.

After all the buildings on the Acropolis were reduced to ashes by the Persians on the eve of the Battle of Salamis (480 BC), Pericles set about his ambitious rebuilding program. He transformed the Acropolis into a city of temples, which has come to be regarded as the zenith of classical Greek achievement.

Ravages inflicted upon them during the years of foreign occupation, pilfering by foreign archaeologists, inept renovations following Independence, visitors' footsteps, earthquakes and, more recently, acid rain and pollution have all taken their toll on the surviving monuments. The worst blow was in 1687 when the Venetians attacked the Turks, opening fire on the Acropolis and causing an explosion in the Parthenon, where the Turks were storing gunpowder, damaging all the buildings.

Major restoration programs are continuing and many of the original sculptures have been moved to the Acropolis Museum and replaced with casts. The Acropolis became World Heritage–listed site in 1987.

BEULÉ GATE & MONUMENT OF AGRIPPA

Once inside the site, a little way along the path on your left you will see the Beulé Gate, named after the French archaeologist Ernest Beulé, who uncovered it in 1852. The 8m pedestal on the left, halfway up the zigzag ramp leading to the Propylaia, was once topped by the Monument of Agrippa, a bronze statue of the Roman general riding a chariot erected in 27 BC to commemorate victory in the Panathenaic Games.

PROPYLAIA

The Propylaia formed the monumental entrance to the Acropolis. Built by Mnesicles between 437 BC and 432 BC, its architectural brilliance ranks with that of the Parthenon. It consists of a central hall with two wings on either side. Each section had a gate, and in ancient times these five gates were the only entrances to the 'upper city'. The middle gate (which was the largest) opened onto the Panathenaic Way. The imposing western portico of the Propylaia consisted of six double columns, Doric on the outside and Ionic on the inside. The fourth column along has been restored. The ceiling of the central hall was painted with gold stars on a dark-blue background. The northern wing was used as a *pinakothiki* (art gallery) and the southern wing was the antechamber to the Temple of Athena Nike.

The Propylaia is aligned with the Parthenon – the earliest example of a building designed in relation to another. It remained intact until the 13th century, when various occupiers started adding to it. It was badly damaged in the 17th century when a lightning strike set off an explosion in a Turkish gunpowder store. Archaeologist Heinrich Schliemann paid for the removal of one of its appendages – a Frankish tower – in the 19th century. Reconstruction took place between 1909 and 1917, and again after WWII.

TEMPLE OF ATHENA NIKE

The exquisitely proportioned small Temple of Athena Nike stands on a platform perched atop the steep southwest edge of the Acropolis, to the right of the Propylaia. The temple was dismantled piece by piece in 2003 in a controversial move to restore it offsite and was undergoing a painstaking reassembly at the time of research.

Designed by Kallicrates, the temple was built of Pentelic marble between 427 BC and 424 BC. The building is almost square, with four graceful Ionic columns at either end. Only fragments remain of the frieze, which had scenes from mythology, the Battle of Plataea (479 BC) and Athenians fighting Boeotians and Persians. Parts of the frieze are in the Acropolis Museum (p122), as are some relief sculptures, including the beauti-

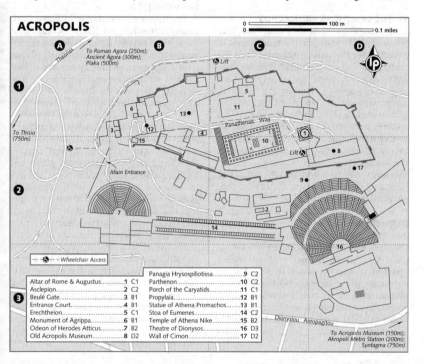

ACROPOLIS

Altar of Rome & Augustus............**1** C1	Panagia Hrysospiliotissa............**9** C2
Asclepion..........................**2** C2	Parthenon........................**10** C2
Beulé Gate.........................**3** B1	Porch of the Caryatids.............**11** C1
Entrance Court.....................**4** B1	Propylaia.........................**12** B1
Erechtheion........................**5** C1	Statue of Athena Promachos........**13** B1
Monument of Agrippa................**6** B1	Stoa of Eumenes...................**14** C2
Odeon of Herodes Atticus...........**7** B2	Temple of Athena Nike.............**15** B2
Old Acropolis Museum...............**8** D2	Theatre of Dionysos...............**16** D3
	Wall of Cimon....................**17** D2

PANATHENAIC PROCESSION

The biggest event in ancient Athens was the Panathenaic procession, the climax of the Panathenaia Festival held to venerate the goddess Athena. Colourful scenes of the procession are depicted in the 160m Parthenon frieze in the new Acropolis Museum. The Panathenaic Way, which cuts across the middle of the Acropolis, was the route taken by the Panathenaic procession.

There were actually two festivals: the Lesser Panathenaic Festival took place annually on Athena's birthday, but the Great Panathenaic Festival was held on every fourth anniversary of the goddess's birth.

The Great Panathenaic Festival began with dancing, followed by athletic, dramatic and musical contests. On the final day, the Panathenaic procession began at Keramikos, led by men carrying animals sacrificed to Athena, followed by maidens carrying rhytons (horn-shaped drinking vessels) and musicians playing a fanfare for the girls of noble birth who held aloft the sacred *peplos* (a glorious saffron-coloured shawl). The *peplos* was placed on the statue of Athena Polias in the Erechtheion in the festival's grand finale.

ful depiction of Athena Nike fastening her sandal. The temple housed a wooden statue of Athena.

This is the third time the temple has been dismantled. The Turks took it apart in 1686 and put a huge cannon on the platform. It was carefully reconstructed between 1836 and 1842, but was taken apart again 60 years later because the platform was crumbling.

STATUE OF ATHENA PROMACHOS

Continuing ahead along the Panathenaic Way you will see, to your left, the foundations of pedestals for the statues that once lined the path, including one that held Pheidias' 9m-high statue of Athena Promachos (*promachos* means 'champion'). Symbolising Athenian invincibility against the Persians, the helmeted goddess held a shield in her left hand and a spear in her right. The statue was carted off to Constantinople by Emperor Theodosius in AD 426. By 1204 it had lost its spear, so the hand appeared to be gesturing. This led the inhabitants to believe that the statue had beckoned the Crusaders to the city, so they smashed it to pieces.

PARTHENON

The Parthenon is the monument that more than any other epitomises the glory of ancient Greece. *Parthenon* means 'virgin's apartment' and it is dedicated to Athena Parthenos, the goddess embodying the power and prestige of the city. The largest Doric temple ever completed in Greece, and the only one built completely of Pentelic marble (apart from its wooden roof), it took 15 years to complete.

Built on the highest part of the Acropolis, the Parthenon had a dual purpose – to house the great statue of Athena commissioned by Pericles, and to serve as the new treasury. It was built on the site of at least four earlier temples dedicated to Athena. It was designed by Iktinos and Kallicrates to be the pre-eminent monument of the Acropolis and was completed in time for the Great Panathenaic Festival of 438 BC.

The temple consisted of eight fluted Doric columns at either end and 17 on each side. To achieve perfect form, its lines were ingeniously curved to create an optical illusion – the foundations are slightly concave and the columns are slightly convex to make both look straight. Supervised by Pheidias, the sculptors Agoracritos and Alcamenes worked on the architectural sculptures of the Parthenon, including the pediments, frieze and metopes, which were brightly coloured and gilded.

The metopes on the eastern side depicted the Olympian gods fighting the giants and on the western side they showed Theseus leading the Athenian youths into battle against the Amazons. The southern metopes illustrated the contest of the Lapiths and Centaurs at a marriage feast, while the northern ones depicted the sack of Troy.

Much of the frieze, depicting the Panathenaic procession (see boxed text, above), was damaged in the explosion of 1687 or later defaced by the Christians, but the greatest existing part (over 75m) consists of the controversial Parthenon Marbles, now in the British Museum in London. The British government continues to ignore campaigns for its return.

The ceiling of the Parthenon, like that of the Propylaia, was painted blue and gilded with stars. At the eastern end was the holy cella (inner room of a temple), into which only a few privileged initiates could enter.

Here stood the statue for which the temple was built – the Athena Polias (Athena of the City), considered one of the wonders of the ancient world. Designed by Pheidias and completed in 432 BC, it was gold plated over an inner wooden frame and stood almost 12m high on its pedestal. The face, hands and feet were made of ivory, and the eyes were fashioned from jewels. Clad in a long gold dress with the head of Medusa carved in ivory on her breast, the goddess held a statuette of Nike (the goddess of victory) in her right hand, and in her left a spear with a serpent at its base. On top of her helmet was a sphinx with griffins in relief at either side.

In AD 426 the statue was taken to Constantinople, where it disappeared. There is a Roman copy (the Athena Varvakeion) in the National Archaeological Museum (p127).

ERECHTHEION
Although the Parthenon was the most impressive monument of the Acropolis, it was more of a showpiece than a sanctuary. That role fell to the Erechtheion, built on the part of the Acropolis held most sacred, where Poseidon struck the ground with his trident, and where Athena produced the olive tree (see boxed text, p102). Named after Erichthonius, a mythical king of Athens, the temple housed the cults of Athena, Poseidon and Erichthonius.

The Erechtheion is immediately recognisable by the six larger-than-life maiden columns that support its southern portico, the **Caryatids** (so called because they were modelled on women from Karyai, modern-day Karyes, in Lakonia). Those you see are plaster casts. The originals (except for one removed by Lord Elgin, and now in the British Museum) are in the Acropolis Museum (p122).

The Erechtheion was part of Pericles' plan, but the project was postponed after the outbreak of the Peloponnesian Wars. Work did not start until 421 BC, eight years after his death, and was completed around 406 BC.

Architecturally, it is the most unusual monument of the Acropolis, a supreme example of Ionic architecture ingeniously built on several levels to counteract the uneven bedrock. The main temple is divided into two cellae – one

dedicated to Athena, the other to Poseidon – representing a reconciliation of the two deities after their contest. In Athena's cella stood an olive-wood statue of Athena Polias holding a shield on which was a gorgon's head. It was this statue on which the sacred *peplos* (a glorious saffron-coloured shawl) was placed at the culmination of the Great Panathenaic Festival.

The northern porch consists of six Ionic columns; on the floor are the fissures supposedly left by the thunderbolt sent by Zeus to kill King Erechtheus. To the south of here was the **Cecropion** – King Cecrops' burial place.

The Erechtheion was the last public building erected on the Acropolis in antiquity, except for a small temple of Rome and Augustus.

OLD ACROPOLIS MUSEUM
With the treasures of the Acropolis safely ensconced in the new Acropolis Museum, plans for the old museum include an exhibition about the 30-year restoration program, as well as engravings, photographs and artefacts found on the slopes of the Sacred Rock.

Southern Slope of the Acropolis
THEATRE OF DIONYSOS
The importance of theatre in the Athenian city-state can be gauged from the dimensions of the enormous **Theatre of Dionysos** (Map p119; ☎ 210 322 4625; Dionysiou Areopagitou; admission €2, free with Acropolis Pass; ☉ 8am-8pm Apr-Oct, 8am-5pm Nov-Mar) on the southeastern slope of the Acropolis.

The first theatre on this site was a timber structure erected sometime during the 6th century BC, after the tyrant Peisistratos

---

SIX FOR THE PRICE OF ONE

The €12 Acropolis admission includes entry to Athens' main ancient sites: Ancient Agora, Roman Agora, Keramikos, the Temple of Olympian Zeus and the Theatre of Dionysos. The ticket is valid for four days; otherwise individual site fees apply, though this is not strictly enforced. The same opening hours (8.30am to 8pm April to October, 8am to 5pm November to March) apply for all of these sites, but it pays to double-check as summer opening hours come into effect at different times from year to year. There is free entrance to the sites on the first Sunday of the month (except for July and August) and on certain days of the year.

ANCIENT PROMENADE

The once traffic-choked streets around Athens' historic centre have been transformed into a spectacular 3km pedestrian promenade connecting the city's most significant ancient sites. Locals and tourists alike come out in force for an evening *volta* (walk) along the stunning heritage trail – one of Europe's longest pedestrian precincts – under the floodlit Acropolis.

The grand promenade starts at Dionysiou Areopagitou, opposite the Temple of Olympian Zeus, and continues along the southern foothills of the Acropolis, all the way to the Ancient Agora, branching off from Thisio to Keramikos and Gazi, and north along Adrianou to Monastiraki and Plaka.

introduced the Festival of the Great Dionysia. Everyone attended the contests, where men clad in goatskins sang and danced, followed by feasting and revelry.

During the golden age in the 5th century BC, the annual festival was one of the major events. Politicians would sponsor dramas by writers such as Aeschylus, Sophocles and Euripides, with some light relief provided by the bawdy comedies of Aristophanes. People came from all over Attica, with their expenses met by the state.

The theatre was reconstructed in stone and marble by Lycurgus between 342 BC and 326 BC, with a seating capacity of 17,000 spread over 64 tiers, of which about 20 survive. Apart from the front row, the seats were built of Piraeus limestone and were occupied by ordinary citizens, although women were confined to the back rows. The front row's 67 thrones, built of Pentelic marble, were reserved for festival officials and important priests. The grandest was reserved for the Priest of Dionysos, who sat shaded from the sun under a canopy. His seat can be identified by well-preserved lion-claw feet at either side. In Roman times, the theatre was also used for state events and ceremonies, as well as for performances.

The reliefs at the rear of the stage, mostly of headless figures, depict the exploits of Dionysos and date from the 2nd century BC. The two hefty, hunched-up guys who have managed to keep their heads are *selini*, worshippers of the mythical Selinos, the debauched father of the satyrs, whose favourite pastime was charging up mountains with his oversized phallus in lecherous pursuit of nymphs.

ASCLEPION & STOA OF EUMENES

Directly above the Theatre of Dionysos, wooden steps lead up to a pathway. On the left at the top of the steps is the Asclepion, which was built around a sacred spring. The worship of Asclepius, the physician son of Apollo, began in Epidavros and was introduced to Athens in 429 BC at a time when plague was sweeping the city.

Beneath the Asclepion is the Stoa of Eumenes, a colonnade built by Eumenes II, King of Pergamum (197–159 BC), as a shelter and promenade for theatre audiences.

ODEON OF HERODES ATTICUS

The path continues west from the Asclepion to the Odeon of Herodes Atticus, built in AD 161 by wealthy Roman Herodes Atticus in memory of his wife Regilla. It was excavated in 1857–58 and completely restored between 1950 and 1961. Performances of drama, music and dance are held here during the Athens Festival (p137). The theatre is only open to the public during performances.

PANAGIA HRYSOSPILIOTISSA

Above the Theatre of Dionysos, an indistinct rock-strewn path leads to a grotto in the cliff face. In 320 BC Thrasyllos turned the grotto into a temple dedicated to Dionysos. The tiny Panagia Hrysospiliotissa (Chapel of Our Lady of the Cavern) is now a poignant little place with old pictures and icons on the walls. Above the chapel are two Ionic columns, the remains of Thrasyllos' temple. It was closed to visitors at the time of research.

Acropolis Museum

The long-awaited **Acropolis Museum** (Map p116; ☎ 210 900 0901; www.theacropolismuseum.gr; Dionysiou Areopagitou 15, Akropoli; ☒ 8am-8pm Tue-Sun; admission €5; ♿) opened with much fanfare in 2009 in the southern foothills of the Acropolis. Ten times larger than the former on-site museum, the imposing modernist building brings together the surviving treasures of the Acropolis, including items held in other museums or storage, as well as pieces returned from foreign museums. While the collection covers the Archaic and Roman periods, the emphasis is on the Acropolis of the 5th century BC, considered the apotheosis of Greece's artistic achievement.

At the entrance you can see the ruins of an ancient Athenian neighbourhood, which have been cleverly incorporated into the museum design after being uncovered during excavations.

Finds from the slopes of the Acropolis are on display in the first gallery, which has an ascending glass floor that emulates the climb up to the sacred hill, while allowing glimpses of the ruins below. Exhibits include painted vases and votive offerings from the sanctuaries where gods were worshipped, and more recent objects found in excavations of the settlement, including two clay statues of Nike at the entrance.

Bathed in natural light, the 1st-floor Archaic Gallery is a veritable forest of statues, mostly votive offerings to Athena, including stunning examples of 6th-century *kore* (maiden) statues of young women in draped clothing and elaborate braids, usually carrying a pomegranate, wreath or bird. Most were recovered from a pit on the Acropolis, where the Athenians buried them after the Battle of Salamis.

The 570 BC youth bearing a calf is one of the rare male statues found. There are also bronze figurines and finds from temples predating the Parthenon, which were destroyed by the Persians, including pedimental sculptures from earlier temples, such as Heracles slaying the Lernaian Hydra and a lioness devouring a bull.

The museum's crowning glory is the top-floor Parthenon Gallery, a glass atrium built in alignment with the temple, and a virtual replica of the cella of the Parthenon, which can be seen from the gallery. It showcases the temple's sculptures, metopes and 160m frieze, which for the first time in more than 200 years is shown in sequence as one narrative about the Panathenaic procession (see boxed text, p120). The procession starts at the southwest corner of the temple, with two groups splitting off and meeting on the east side for the delivery of the *peplos* to Athena. Interspersed between the golden-hued originals are stark white plaster replicas of the missing pieces – the controversial Parthenon Marbles hacked off by Lord Elgin in 1801 and later sold to the British Museum (more than half the frieze is in Britain). The sight makes a compelling case for their reunification.

Other highlights include five Caryatids, the maiden columns that held up the Erechtheion (the sixth is in the British Museum), and a giant floral *akrotirion* that once crowned the southern ridge of the Parthenon pediment.

Designed by US-based architect Bernard Tschumi, with Greek architect Michael Photiadis, the €130 million museum cleverly showcases layers of history, floating above the ruins and with the Acropolis visible above, allowing visitors to see the masterpieces in context.

The restaurant has superb views (and is surprisingly good value) and there's a fine museum shop.

Ancient Agora

The heart of ancient Athens was the **Agora** (Market; Map p124; ☎ 210 321 0185; Adrianou; adult/concession €4/2, free with Acropolis pass; ☺ 8.30am-8pm Apr-Oct, 8am-5.30pm Nov-Mar), the lively, crowded focal point of administrative, commercial, political and social activity. Socrates spent a lot of time here expounding his philosophy, and in AD 49 St Paul spent his days here winning converts to Christianity.

First developed in the 6th century BC, the site was devastated by the Persians in 480 BC, but a new Agora was built in its place almost immediately. It was flourishing by Pericles' time and continued to do so until AD 267, when it was destroyed by the Herulians, a Gothic tribe from Scandinavia. The Turks built a residential quarter on the site, but this was demolished by archaeologists after Independence and later excavated to classical and, in parts, Neolithic levels. If they'd had their way, the archaeologists would have also knocked down the whole of Plaka.

The main monuments are the Temple of Hephaestus, the Stoa of Attalos and the Church of the Holy Apostles.

There are a number of entrances, but the most convenient is the northern entrance from Adrianou.

STOA OF ATTALOS

The **Agora Museum**, in the reconstructed Stoa of Attalos, is a good place to start to make sense of

---

VIRTUAL AGORA

Get a fascinating glimpse of life in the Ancient Agora with an interactive virtual-reality trip at Hellenic Cosmos (p133). The 45-minute show at the high-tech Tholos dome theatre spans various periods of history, from classical to Roman times, giving unique insight into the cultural and political life of ancient Athens.

ANCIENT AGORA

```
0 ────────────── 100 m
0 ────────────── 0.1 miles
```

Agora Museum.............................(see 11)
Altar of the Twelve Gods...............**1** C1
Church of the Holy Apostles.........**2** D2
Entrance......................................**3** C1
Metroön......................................**4** C2
Middle Stoa................................**5** C2
Mosaic showing reconstruction of
     Agora......................................**6** C1
New Bouleuterion........................**7** C1
Odeon of Agrippa.......................**8** C2
Plan of Site................................**9** B2
Sewer..**10** C2
Stoa of Attalos..........................**11** D1
Stoa of Basileios.......................**12** C1
Stoa of the Giants.....................**13** C1
Stoa of Zeus Eleutherios............**14** C1
Stoa Poikile...............................**15** C1
Temple of Apollo........................**16** C1
Temple of Ares...........................**17** C1
Temple of Hephaestus................**18** B1
Tholos.......................................**19** C2

the site. The museum has a model of the Agora
as well as a collection of finds from the site.

The first-ever shopping arcade, the original
stoa was built by King Attalos II of Pergamum
(159–138 BC), two storeys high with two aisles
housing expensive shops. People also gathered
here to watch the Panathenaic procession.

It was authentically reconstructed between
1953 and 1956 by the American School of
Archaeology, but the facade was left in natural
Pentelic marble (it was originally painted red
and blue). The stoa has a series of 45 columns
that are Doric on the ground floor and Ionic
on the upper gallery.

TEMPLE OF HEPHAESTUS

The best-preserved Doric temple in Greece,
this **temple** on the western edge of the Agora
was dedicated to Hephaestus, god of the
forge, and surrounded by foundries and metalwork shops. It was one of the first buildings
of Pericles' rebuilding program. Built in 449
BC by Iktinos, one of the architects of the
Parthenon, it has 34 columns and a frieze on
the eastern side depicting nine of the Twelve
Labours of Heracles. In AD 1300 it was converted into the Church of Agios Georgios.
The last service was held in 1834 in honour
of King Otto's arrival in Athens.

To the northeast of the temple are the
foundations of the **Stoa of Zeus Eleutherios**, one
of the places where Socrates expounded his
philosophy. Further north are the founda-
tions of the **Stoa of Basileios** and the **Stoa Poikile**
(Painted Stoa). The Stoa Poikile was so called

because of its murals, which were painted by
the leading artists of the day and depicted
mythological and historical battles.

To the southeast of the Temple of
Hephaestus was the **New Bouleuterion** (Council
House), where the Senate (originally created
by Solon) met, while the heads of government
met to the south at the circular **Tholos**.

CHURCH OF THE HOLY APOSTLES

This charming little church, near the southern entrance, was built in the early 10th
century to commemorate St Paul's teaching
in the Agora. Between 1954 and 1957 it was
stripped of its 19th-century additions and restored to its original form. It contains some
fine Byzantine frescoes.

Keramikos

The city's cemetery from the 12th century
BC to Roman times was **Keramikos** (Map p109;
☎ 210 346 3552; Ermou 148, Keramikos; adult/concession
incl museum €2/1, free with Acropolis pass; ☻ 8.30am-8pm
Apr-Oct, 8am-5.30pm Nov-Mar). Discovered in 1861
during the construction of Pireos street, it is
one of the most green and tranquil ancient
sites in Athens.

SACRED & DIPYLON GATES

Once inside, head for the small knoll ahead to
the right, where you'll find a plan of the site
(Map p109). A path leads down to the right
from the knoll to the remains of the **city wall**
built by Themistocles in 479 BC, and rebuilt
by Konon in 394 BC. The wall is broken by

the foundations of two gates. Tiny signs mark each one.

The first, the Sacred Gate, spanned the Sacred Way and was the one by which pilgrims from Eleusis entered the city during the annual Eleusian procession. The second, the Dipylon Gate, to the northeast of the Sacred Gate, was the city's main entrance and where the Panathenaic procession began. It was also where the city's prostitutes gathered to offer their services to jaded travellers.

From a platform outside the Dipylon Gate, Pericles gave his famous speech extolling the virtues of Athens and honouring those who died in the first year of the Peloponnesian Wars.

Between the Sacred and Dipylon Gates are the foundations of the **Pompeion**, used as a dressing room for participants in the Panathenaic procession.

STREET OF TOMBS
Leading off the Sacred Way to the left as you head away from the city is the Street of Tombs (Map p109). This avenue was reserved for the tombs of Athens' most prominent citizens. The surviving stelae are now in the National Archaeological Museum (p127), and what you see are mostly replicas. The astonishing array of funerary monuments, and their bas reliefs, warrant more than a cursory examination.

Ordinary citizens were buried in the areas bordering the Street of Tombs. One well-preserved stele (up the stone steps on the northern side) shows a little girl with her pet dog. The site's largest stele is that of sisters Demetria and Pamphile.

ARCHAEOLOGICAL MUSEUM OF KERAMIKOS
The small Keramikos museum (Map p109) was established by its benefactor, Gustav Oberlaender, a German-American stocking manufacturer. It contains stelae and sculptures from the site, as well as a good collection of vases and terracotta figurines.

Roman Athens
TOWER OF THE WINDS & ROMAN AGORA
Entrance to the **Roman Agora** (Map pp110–11; ☎ 210 324 5220; cnr Pelopida & Eolou; adult/concession €2/1, free with Acropolis pass; ☉ 8.30am-8pm Apr-Oct, 8am-5.30pm Nov-Mar) is through the well-preserved **Gate of Athena Archegetis**, which is flanked by four Doric columns. It was erected sometime during the 1st century AD and financed by Julius Caesar.

The rest of the Roman Agora is hard to make sense of. To the right of the entrance are the foundations of a 1st-century public latrine. In the southeast area are the foundations of a propylon and a row of shops.

The well-preserved Tower of the Winds was built in the 1st century BC by a Syrian astronomer named Andronicus. The octagonal monument of Pentelic marble is an ingenious construction that functioned as a sundial, weather vane, water clock and compass. Each side represents a point of the compass, and has a relief of a figure floating through the air, which depicts the wind associated with that particular point. Beneath each of the reliefs are the faint markings of sundials. The weather vane, which disappeared long ago, was a bronze Triton that revolved on top of the tower. The Turks allowed dervishes to use the tower.

HADRIAN'S ARCH
The Roman emperor Hadrian had a great affection for Athens. Although he did his fair share of spiriting its classical artwork to Rome, he also embellished the city with many monuments influenced by classical architecture. Grandiose as these monuments are, they lack the refinement and artistic flair of their classical predecessors.

Hadrian's Arch (Map pp110–11) is a lofty monument of Pentelic marble that stands where busy Leoforos Vasilissis Olgas and Leoforos Vasilissis Amalias meet. It was erected by Hadrian in AD 132, probably to commemorate the consecration of the Temple of Olympian Zeus (below). The inscriptions show that it was also intended as a dividing point between the ancient and Roman city. The northwest frieze bears the inscription 'This is Athens, the Ancient city of Theseus', while the southeast frieze states 'This is the city of Hadrian, and not of Theseus'.

TEMPLE OF OLYMPIAN ZEUS
This is the largest **temple** (Map pp110–11; ☎ 210 922 6330; adult/concession €2/1, free with Acropolis pass; ☉ 8.30am-8pm Apr-Oct, 8am-5.30pm Nov-Mar) in Greece. The temple was begun in the 6th century BC by Peisistratos, but was abandoned for lack of funds. Various other leaders had stabs at completing it, but it was left for Hadrian to complete the work in AD 131. It took more than 700 years to build.

The temple is impressive for the sheer size of its 104 Corinthian columns (17m high with a base diameter of 1.7m), of which 15 remain – the fallen column was blown down in a gale in 1852. Hadrian put a colossal statue of Zeus in the cella and, in typically immodest fashion, placed an equally large one of himself next to it.

HADRIAN'S LIBRARY

To the north of the Roman Agora is this vast 2nd-century-AD library (Map pp110–11), the largest structure erected by Hadrian. It included a cloistered courtyard bordered by 100 columns and there was a pool in the centre. As well as books, the building housed music and lecture rooms and a theatre.

ROMAN BATHS

Excavation work to create a ventilation shaft for the metro uncovered the well-preserved ruins of a large Roman bath complex (Map pp110–11). The baths, which extend into the National Gardens, were established near the Ilissos river after the Herulian raids in the 3rd century AD; they were destroyed and repaired again in the 5th or 6th century.

PANATHENAIC STADIUM

The Panathenaic Stadium (Map p108), which lies between two pine-covered hills between the neighbourhoods of Mets and Pangrati, was originally built in the 4th century BC as a venue for the Panathenaic athletic contests. A thousand wild animals are said to have been slaughtered in the arena at Hadrian's inauguration in AD 120. The seats were rebuilt in Pentelic marble by Herodes Atticus.

After hundreds of years of disuse, the stadium was completely restored in 1895 by wealthy Greek benefactor Georgios Averof to host the first modern Olympic Games the following year. It is a faithful replica of the original Panathenaic Stadium, comprising seats of Pentelic marble for 70,000 spectators, a running track and a central area for field events. It made a stunning backdrop to the archery competition and the marathon finish during the 2004 Olympics. It is occasionally used for concerts and public events, and the annual Athens marathon finishes here.

Byzantine Athens

Byzantine architecture in Athens is fairly thin on the ground. By the time of the split in the Roman Empire, Athens had shrunk to little more than a provincial town. The most

important Byzantine building is the World Heritage–listed, 11th-century Moni Dafniou at Dafni, 10km northwest of Athens, which has been closed since it was damaged in the 1999 earthquake.

The 12th-century **Church of Agios Eleftherios** (Little Metropolis; Map pp110-11; Plateia Mitropoleos, Plaka) is considered one of the city's finest. It is built partly of Pentelic marble and decorated with an external frieze of symbolic beasts in bas relief. It was originally dedicated to the Panagia Gorgoepikoos (meaning 'Virgin swift to answer prayers') and was once the city's cathedral, but now stands in the shadows of the much larger new **cathedral** (Map pp110–11).

The small 11th-century **Church of Kapnikarea** (Map pp110-11; Ermou, Monastiraki; ☺ 8am-2pm Tue, Thu & Fri) stands smack in the middle of the Ermou shopping strip. It was saved from the bulldozers and restored by Athens University. Its dome is supported by four large Roman columns.

The 11th-century **Church of Agii Theodori** (Map pp112-13; Syntagma), behind Plateia Klafthmonos, has a tiled dome and walls decorated with a pretty terracotta frieze of animals and plants.

The lovely 11th-century **Agios Nikolaos Rangavas** (Map pp110-11; Plaka) was part of the palace of the Rangavas family, who counted among them Michael I, emperor of Byzantium. The church bell was the first installed in Athens after liberation from the Turks (who banned them), and was the first to ring in 1833 to announce the freedom of Athens.

The unique 11th-century **Church of Sotira Lykodimou** (Map pp110-11; Plateia Rallou Manou), now the Russian Orthodox Cathedral, is the only octagonal Byzantine church and has an imposing dome.

One of the oldest churches in Athens is the 10th-century **Church of the Holy Apostles** (p124) in the Ancient Agora. Other churches worth seeing are the 11th- to 12th-century **Church of Agia Ekaterini** (Map pp110–11), in Plaka near the choregic Lysikrates Monument, and the 15th-century **Church of Agios Dimitrios Loumbardiaris** (p132) on Filopappou Hill. Most of these sites don't open set hours.

The lovely Byzantine monastery, **Moni Kaisarianis** (p133), is also worth a visit.

Neoclassical Athens

Athens boasts a large number of fine neoclassical buildings dating from the period after Independence. Foremost are the celebrated neoclassical trilogy on Panepistimiou, halfway between Omonia and Syntagma.

The centrepiece is the splendid **Athens University** (Map pp112–13), designed by the Danish architect Christian Hansen and completed in 1864. It still serves as the university's administrative headquarters. Next door, the **Athens Academy** (Map pp112–13) was designed by Hansen's brother, Theophile, and completed in 1885. The Ionian-style entrance mimics the eastern entrance to the Erechtheion. Neither is open to the public.

The trilogy is completed by the **National Library** (Map pp112-13; ☎ 210 338 2541; www.nlg.gr; Panepistimiou 32, Syntagma; admission free; ☧ 9am-8pm Mon-Thu, 9am-2pm Fri & Sat). Its main feature is the corridor leading to the reading room, which is flanked by a row of Doric columns influenced by the Temple of Hephaestus (p124) in the Ancient Agora.

Museums & Galleries
NATIONAL ARCHAEOLOGICAL MUSEUM

One of the world's most important museums, the **National Archaeological Museum** (Map pp112-13; ☎ 210 821 7717; www.namuseum.gr; 28 Oktovriou-Patision 44; adult/concession €7/3; ☧ 1.30-8pm Mon, 8.30am-8pm Tue-Sun Apr-Oct, 8.30am-3pm Nov-Mar) houses the finest collection of Greek antiquities. Treasures include exquisite sculptures, pottery, jewellery, frescoes and artefacts found throughout Greece, dating from the Neolithic era to classical periods.

Housed in an imposing 19th-century neoclassical building, the museum has been totally overhauled since it was damaged in the 1999 earthquake. The final galleries opened in 2009, bringing to light previously unseen collections. The exhibits are displayed largely thematically and are beautifully presented.

With 10,000 sq metres of exhibition space, it could take several visits to appreciate the museum's vast holdings, but it is possible to see the highlights in a half-day.

Ahead of you as you enter the museum is the **prehistoric collection**, showcasing some of the most important pieces of Mycenaean, Neolithic and Cycladic art.

The fabulous collection of **Mycenaean antiquities** (Gallery 4) is the museum's *tour de force*. The first cabinet holds the celebrated **Mask of Agamemnon**, unearthed at Mycenae by Heinrich Schliemann, along with key finds from Grave Circle A, including bronze daggers with intricate representations of the hunt. The exquisite **Vaphio gold cups**, with scenes of men taming wild bulls, are regarded as among the finest surviving examples of Mycenaean art. They were found in a *tholos* (Mycenaean tomb shaped like a beehive) at Vaphio, near Sparta.

The **Cycladic collection** in Gallery 6 includes the superb figurines of the 3rd and 2nd centuries BC that inspired artists such as Picasso.

Backtrack and enter the galleries to the left of the entrance, which house the oldest and most significant pieces of the **sculpture collection**. Galleries 7 to 13 exhibit fine examples of Archaic *kouroi* (male statues) dating from the 7th century BC to 480 BC, including the colossal 600 BC **Sounion Kouros** (Room 8), found at the Temple of Poseidon in Sounion. Made of Naxian marble, the statue was a votive offering to Poseidon and stood before his temple.

Gallery 15 is dominated by the 460 BC bronze **statue of Zeus or Poseidon**, found in the sea off Evia, which depicts one of the gods (no one really knows which one) with his arms outstretched and holding a thunderbolt or trident in his right hand.

In Gallery 21 you will see the striking 2nd-century-BC **statue of a horse and young rider**, recovered from a shipwreck off Cape Artemision in Evia. Opposite the horse is the lesser-known **statue of Aphrodite**, showing a demure nude Aphrodite struggling to hold her draped gown over her private parts.

From Gallery 21, head left and up the stairs to the museum's other big crowd-puller, the spectacular **Minoan frescoes** from Santorini (Thira). The frescoes – the *Boxing Children,* the *Spring* wall painting showing red lilies and a pair of swallows kissing in mid-air, and the *Antelopes* – were uncovered in the prehistoric settlement of Akrotiri (p437), which was buried by a volcanic eruption in the late 16th century BC. The Thira Gallery also has videos showing the 1926 volcanic eruption, the Akrotiri excavation and preservation work.

Also on the 1st floor is the superb **pottery collection**, which traces the development of pottery from the Bronze Age through the Protogeometric and Geometric periods, to the emergence of the famous Attic black-figured pottery of the 6th century BC, and the red-figured pottery from the late 5th to early 4th centuries BC. Other uniquely Athenian vessels are the Attic White Lekythoi, the slender vases depicting scenes at tombs.

In the centre of Gallery 56 are six **Panathenaic amphorae**, presented to the winners of the Panathenaic Games. Each amphora contained oil from the sacred olive trees of Athens and victors might have received up to 140 of them. They are painted with scenes from the relevant sport (in this case wrestling) on one side and an armed Athena Promachos on the other.

Also on the 1st floor are several recently opened galleries exhibiting **Hellenistic pottery**, the **Cypriot antiquities collection** and a stunning array of **gold jewellery**, including intricate wreaths, as well as new galleries showcasing the Vlastos-Serpieris and Stathatos private collections. The **terracotta collection** includes 2nd-century-BC winged figurines of Nike and Eros and theatre masks. The two-room **Egyptian gallery** presents the best of the museum's significant collection, including mummies, Fayum portraits and bronze figurines.

Heading back to the ground floor, turn right into Gallery 36 for the **bronze collection**. The larger-than-life-sized, 2nd-century-BC statue of the **Lady of Kalymnon** in Gallery 39, wearing a long draped tunic, was found in bad shape by a fisherman off the island of Kalymno in 1994.

Many of the smaller bronzes are masterpieces from the leading bronzesmithing workshops of ancient Greece. The 200 BC statue of **Athena Varvakeion** is the most famous copy – much reduced in size – of the statue of Athena Polias by Pheidias that once stood in the Parthenon.

There's a basement gift shop and cafe with a pleasant garden courtyard.

The museum is a 10-minute walk from Viktoria metro station, or catch trolley-bus 2, 4, 5, 9 or 11 from outside St Denis Cathedral on Panepistimiou and get off at the Polytechnio stop.

BENAKI MUSEUM

Greece's finest private **museum** (Map pp114-15; ☎ 210 367 1000; www.benaki.gr; Koumbari 1, cnr Leoforos Vasilissis Sofias, Kolonaki; adult/concession €6/3, free Thu; ☻ 9am-5pm Mon, Wed, Fri & Sat, 9am-midnight Thu, 9am-3pm Sun) contains the vast collection of Antonis Benakis, accumulated during 35 years of avid collecting in Europe and Asia. In 1931 he turned the family house into a museum and presented it to the Greek nation. The collection includes Bronze Age finds from Mycenae and Thessaly; works by El Greco; ecclesiastical furniture brought from Asia Minor; pottery, copper, silver and woodwork from Egypt, Asia Minor and Mesopotamia; and a stunning collection of Greek regional costumes.

The museum has expanded into several branches to house its vast and diverse collections and is a major player in the city's arts

scene. The **Benaki Museum Pireos Annexe** (Map p109; ☎ 210 345 3111; www.benaki.gr; Pireos 138, cnr Andronikou, Rouf; ☻ 10am-6pm Wed, Thu & Sun, 10am-10pm Fri & Sat) hosts regular visual arts, cultural and historical exhibitions as well as major international shows. The impressive former industrial building has a cafe and excellent gift store.

The **Museum of Islamic Art** (Map p109; ☎ 210 325 1311; www.benaki.gr; cnr Agion Asomaton & Dipylou, Keramikos; adult/concession €5/3, free Thu; ☻ 9am-3pm Tue & Thu-Sun, 9am-9pm Wed) showcases one of the world's most significant collections of Islamic art, the bulk of which was assembled by Antonis Benakis in the 19th century. Housed in two restored neoclassical mansions near Keramikos, the museum exhibits more than 8000 items covering the 12th to 19th centuries, including weavings, carvings, prayer carpets, tiles and ceramics. On the 3rd floor is a 17th-century reception room with an inlaid marble floor from a Cairo mansion. A very pleasant rooftop cafe overlooks Keramikos and you can see part of the Themistoklean wall in the basement.

GOULANDRIS MUSEUM OF CYCLADIC & ANCIENT GREEK ART

This private **museum** (Map pp114-15; ☎ 210 722 8321; www.cycladic.gr; cnr Leoforos Vasilissis Sofias & Neofytou Douka, Kolonaki; adult/concession €7/3.50; ☻ 10am-5pm Mon, Wed, Fri & Sat, 10am-8pm Thu, 11am-5pm Sun; 🔾) houses a collection of Cycladic art second in importance only to that displayed at the National Archaeological Museum (p127). The 1st-floor Cycladic collection, dating from 3000 BC to 2000 BC, includes the marble figurines with folded arms that inspired many 20th-century artists with their simplicity and purity of form. The rest of the museum features Greek art dating from 2000 BC to the 4th century AD, while the 4th-floor exhibition, Scenes from Daily Life in Antiquity, includes artefacts and films depicting life in ancient Greece.

The adjacent 19th-century mansion is used for temporary art exhibitions.

BYZANTINE & CHRISTIAN MUSEUM

This outstanding **museum** (Map pp114-15; ☎ 210 721 1027; www.culture.gr; Leoforos Vasilissis Sofias 22; adult/concession €4/2; ☻ 8.30am-7.30pm Tue-Sun May-Sep, 8.30am-3pm Tue-Sun Oct-Apr; 🔾) presents a priceless collection of Christian art, dating from the 3rd to 20th centuries. Thematic snapshots of the Byzantine and post-Byzantine world – a part of Greek history that is often ignored in favour of its ancient past – are exceptionally

ART RENAISSANCE *Victoria Kyriakopoulos*

The contemporary arts scene in Athens is flourishing, with a proliferation of private galleries and art spaces, and major international arts events.

'In the last five years Athens has developed a very international arts scene,' says artist Angelo Plessas, now based in Athens after four years in New York.

'If you are a Greek artist you don't need to move abroad to Berlin or London or a big metropolitan city any more. Everything has changed. We have the Biennial, the Museum of Contemporary Art, we have the big collections here.

'It's not as big as New York or London, but the good galleries and museums here are bringing a lot of international big names so you can get a snapshot of what is happening universally. Artists who come here from abroad comment that Athens is fresh and lots of things are happening all the time. I believe Athens could become the Berlin of the south.'

Plessas is exhilarated by the city's new creative energy and, like many artists of his generation, has established an international career, showing in galleries abroad and online in the cutting-edge neen art scene.

'It's not an easy place, but Athens has a good energy and that's the most important thing for an artist. People here are passionate and that's good in terms of creativity and discussion. The thing with Athens is that you either love it or hate it. If you want things politically correct and everything to be in order then you will hate it. If you want to explore more unpredictable things, the city has this energy, this craziness.'

Art Events

- **Art-Athina** (www.art-athina.gr) International contemporary art fair held in May.

- **Athens Biennial** (www.athensbiennial.org) Held every two years in various venues from June to October.

- **ReMap** (www.remap.org) Parallel event to the Biennial, exhibiting in abandoned buildings around Keramikos and Metaxourghio.

Art Galleries

- **AMP** (Map pp112-13; ☎ 210 325 1881; www.a-m-p.gr; Epikourou 26, cnr Korinis, Psyrri; ⏱ noon-7pm Mon-Fri, noon-4pm Sat)

- **Bernier-Elliades** (Map p109; ☎ 210 341 3935; Eptahalkou 11, Thisio; ⏱ 10.30am-8pm Tue-Fri, noon-4pm Sat)

- **Breeder** (Map pp112-13; ☎ 210 331 7527; www.thebreedersystem.com; Iasonos 45, Metaxourghio; ⏱ noon-8pm Tue-Fri, noon-5pm Sat)

- **Rebecca Camhi Gallery** (Map pp112-13; ☎ 210 523 3049; www.rebeccacamhi.com; Leonidou 9, Metaxourghio; ⏱ by appointment)

You can find a full list of galleries and art spaces at www.athensartmap.net; alternatively, pick up an *Athens Contemporary Art Map* at galleries and cafes around town.

presented in the expansive multilevel underground galleries (the final galleries opened in 2009). The collection includes icons, frescoes, sculptures, textiles, manuscripts, vestments and mosaics. The museum is housed in the grounds of the former Villa Ilissia, an urban oasis recently transformed into a culture park, with an open-air amphitheatre, outdoor exhibitions and ancient ruins, including the Peisistratos aqueduct and the adjacent site of **Aristotle's Lyceum**.

KANELLOPOULOS MUSEUM

This excellent **museum** (Map pp110-11; ☎ 210 321 2313; Theorias 12, cnr Panos, Plaka), in a 19th-century mansion on the northern slope of the Acropolis, houses the Kanellopoulos family's extensive collection, donated to the state in 1976. The collection includes jewellery, clay-and-stone vases and figurines, weapons, Byzantine icons, bronzes and objets d'art. It was due to reopen in 2009 after a major refurbishment.

NATIONAL ART GALLERY

Greece's premier **art gallery** (Map pp114-15; ☎ 210 723 5857; Leoforos Vasileos Konstantinou 50; adult/concession €6/5; ☺ 9am-3pm Mon & Wed-Sat, 10am-2pm Sun; ☖) presents a rich collection of Greek art spanning four centuries from the post-Byzantine period. A new wing housing its permanent collection explores the key art movements chronologically. The 1st floor hosts works from the post-Byzantine period, the gallery's prized El Greco paintings, including *The Crucifixion* and *Symphony of the Angels*, and works from the Ionian period until 1900. On the 2nd floor are works by leading 20th-century artists, including Parthenis, Moralis, Maleas and Lytras. The gallery also has works by European masters, including paintings by Picasso, and hosts major international exhibitions.

The gallery's significant sculpture collection is now housed at the **National Sculpture Gallery** (off Map pp114-15; ☎ 210 770 9855; Army Park, Katehaki; adult/concession €6/3; ☺ 9am-3pm Mon & Wed-Sat, 10am-3pm Sun).

NATIONAL MUSEUM OF CONTEMPORARY ART

Periodic exhibitions and exhibitions of contemporary art from this museum's significant Greek and international collections are on show at its temporary gallery at the **Athens Conservatory** (Map pp114-15; ☎ 210 924 2111; www .emst.gr; Leoforos Vas Georgiou B 17-19, enter from Rigilis; admission €3; ☺ 11am-7pm Tue, Wed & Fri-Sun, 11am-10pm Thu). Exhibitions include paintings, installations, photography, video and new media, as well as experimental architecture. The museum will eventually move to the old Fix brewery on Leoforos Syngrou.

NUMISMATIC MUSEUM

This magnificent neoclassical mansion is worth a visit, even if you have little interest in coins. The **museum** (Map pp112-13; ☎ 210 364 3774; Panepistimiou 12, Syntagma; adult/concession €3/2; ☺ 8.30am-8pm Tue-Sun) comprises 400,000 coins from ancient Greek, Hellenic, Roman and Byzantine times. The building was once the home of the celebrated archaeologist Heinrich Schliemann. The lovely shady cafe in the gardens is a little oasis.

GREEK FOLK ART MUSEUM

An excellent collection of secular and religious folk art, mainly from the 18th and 19th centuries, is housed in this **museum** (Map pp110-11; ☎ 210 322 9031; Kydathineon 17, Plaka; admission €2,

free Sun; ☺ 9am-2.30pm Tue-Sun). The 1st floor has embroidery, pottery, weaving and puppets, while the 2nd floor has a reconstructed traditional village house with paintings by the primitive artist Theophilos. Greek traditional costumes are displayed on the upper levels.

The museum has an **annexe** (Greek Folk Art Museum: Man & Tools; Map pp110-11; ☎ 210 321 4972; Panos 22, Plaka; admission €2; ☺ 9am-2.30pm Tue-Sun) dedicated to men and tools, and a fine exhibition of ceramics at the **Museum of Traditional Greek Ceramics** (Map pp110-11; ☎ 210 324 2066; Areos 1, Monastiraki; admission €2; ☺ 9am-2.30pm Tue-Sun) at the old mosque.

NATIONAL HISTORICAL MUSEUM

Specialising in memorabilia from the War of Independence, this **museum** (Map pp112-13; ☎ 210 323 7617; Stadiou 13, Syntagma; adult/concession €3/1, free Sun; ☺ 9am-2pm Tue-Sun) has Byron's helmet and sword, a series of paintings depicting events leading up to the war, Byzantine and medieval exhibits, and a collection of photographs and royal portraits.

The museum is housed in the old Parliament building at Plateia Kolokotroni, where Prime Minister Theodoros Deligiannis was assassinated on the steps in 1905.

CITY OF ATHENS MUSEUM

Housed in two interconnected historic buildings, including the palace where King Otto lived between 1830 and 1846, this **museum** (Map pp112-13; ☎ 210 323 1397; Paparigopoulou 7, Syntagma; adult/concession €3/2; ☺ 9am-4pm Mon & Wed-Fri, 10am-3pm Sat & Sun) contains an extensive collection of royal furniture, antiques, paintings and personal mementos, as well as a model of 1842 Athens and a massive painting showing Athens before the Venetian destruction in 1687. The 2nd-floor gallery hosts temporary exhibitions.

JEWISH MUSEUM

This **museum** (Map pp110-11; ☎ 210 322 5582; Nikis 39, Plaka; adult/concession €5/2; ☺ 9am-2.30pm Mon-Fri, 10am-2pm Sun) traces the history of the Jewish community in Greece back to the 3rd century BC through an impressive collection of religious and folk art, and documents. It includes a reconstruction of a synagogue.

TURKISH BATHS

The beautifully refurbished 17th-century **bathhouse** (Map pp110-11; ☎ 210 324 4340; Kyrristou 8,

FREE MUSEUMS

Athens has some interesting free museums. The **Museum of Greek Popular Instruments** (Map pp110-11; ☎ 210 325 4119; Diogenous 1-3, Plaka; ☽ 10am-2pm Tue & Thu-Sun, noon-6pm Wed) has displays and recordings of a wide selection of traditional instruments, including those of the great masters of Greek music, as well as costumes worn during festivals. Concerts are held in the courtyard on weeknights in summer. A restored *hammam* in the gift store is one of the few surviving private Turkish baths in Athens.

The most significant collection of Greek inscriptions can be seen at the **Epigraphical Museum** (Map pp112-13; ☎ 210 821 7637; Tositsa 1; ☽ 8.30am-3pm Tue-Sun), a veritable library of stone tablets next to the National Archaeological Museum.

The **War Museum** (Map pp114-15; ☎ 210 725 2975; Rizari 2, cnr Leoforos Vasilissis Sofias; ☽ 9am-2pm Tue-Sun) is a relic of the junta years and an architectural statement of the times. All periods from the Mycenaean to the present day are covered, and displays include weapons, maps, armour and models.

The **Centre of Folk Art & Tradition** (Map pp110-11; ☎ 210 324 3987; Hatzimihali Angelikis 6, Plaka; ☽ 9am-1pm & 5-9pm Tue-Fri, 9am-1pm Sat & Sun) is worth seeing for the stunning Plaka mansion as much as for its interesting periodic exhibitions.

The **Maria Callas Museum** (Map p109; ☎ 210 346 1589; Technopolis, Pireos 100, Gazi; ☽ 10am-3pm Mon-Fri) is dedicated to the revered opera diva and includes letters and unpublished photographs, as well as personal mementos, books and videos. It is located on the 2nd floor of the Sikelianos building in the superbly converted Athens gasworks complex, which also hosts multimedia exhibitions, concerts and special events.

Plaka; admission €2; ☽ 9am-2.30pm Wed-Mon) is the only surviving public bathhouse in Athens and one of the few remnants of Ottoman times. A helpful free audio tour takes you back to the bathhouse days.

THEOHARAKIS ART & CULTURE CENTRE

This new **art and culture centre** (Map pp114-15; ☎ 210 361 1206; www.thf.gr; Leoforos Vasilissis Sofias 9, Kolonaki; adult/concession €6/3; ☽ 10am-6pm Mon, Wed & Fri-Sun, 10am-10pm Thu) has three levels of exhibition space featuring local and international artists, a theatre, an art shop and a pleasant cafe. Music performances are held between September and May.

Hills of Athens

The Athens basin is surrounded by mountains, bounded to the north by Mt Parnitha, the northeast by Mt Pendeli, the west by Mt Egaleo and the east by Mt Ymittos. Downtown Athens is dominated by the much smaller hills of Lykavittos (277m) and the Acropolis (156m).

LYKAVITTOS HILL

The name Lykavittos means 'Hill of Wolves' and derives from ancient times when the hill was surrounded by countryside and its pine-covered slopes were inhabited by wolves. Today, the hill (Map pp114-15) rises out of a sea of concrete to offer the finest panoramas in

Athens. The dreaded *nefos* (pollution haze) permitting, there are panoramic views of the city, the Attic basin, the surrounding mountains, and the islands of Salamina and Aegina. A path leads to the summit from the top of Loukianou. Alternatively, you can take the **funicular railway** (Map pp114-15; ☎ 210 721 0701; return €6; ☽ 9am-3am, half-hourly), referred to as the '*teleferik*', from the top of Ploutarhou in Kolonaki.

Perched on the summit is the little **Chapel of Agios Georgios** (Map pp114–15), floodlit like a beacon over the city at night. The summit cafe and upmarket restaurant (see Orizontes, p147) have spectacular views. The open-air **Lykavittos Theatre** (Map pp114–15), northeast of the summit, is used for concerts in summer.

WEST OF THE ACROPOLIS

Filopappou Hill (Map pp110–11), also called the Hill of the Muses, is identifiable to the southwest of the Acropolis by the **Monument of Filopappos** (Map p116) at its summit. The monument was built between 114 and 116 in honour of Julius Antiochus Filopappos, who was a prominent Roman consul and administrator.

The pine-clad slopes are a pleasant place for a stroll, and offer good views of the plain and mountains of Attica and of the Saronic Gulf, and some of the best vantage points for photographing the Acropolis. There are small paths all over the hill, but the paved path to the top starts near the *periptero* (street kiosk) on Dionysiou Areopagitou. After 250m, the path passes the **Church of Agios Dimitrios Loumbardiaris** (Map pp110–11), which contains some fine frescoes.

North of here is the rocky **Hill of the Pnyx** (Map p109), the meeting place of the Democratic Assembly in the 5th century BC, where the great orators Aristides, Demosthenes, Pericles and Themistocles addressed assemblies. The less visited site offers great views over Athens and a peaceful walk.

Continuing northwest is the **Hill of the Nymphs** (Map p109), on which stands the **old Athens observatory** built in 1842.

Areopagus Hill (Map pp110–11) is a rocky outcrop below the Acropolis overlooking the Ancient Agora, a popular place for lovers and tourists to take in the views. According to mythology, it was here that Ares was tried by the council of the gods for the murder of Halirrhothios, son of Poseidon. The council accepted his defence of justifiable deicide (the act of killing a god) on the grounds that he was protecting his daughter, Alcippe, from unwanted advances.

The hill became the place where murder, treason and corruption trials were heard before the Council of the Areopagus. In AD 51, St Paul delivered his famous 'Sermon to an Unknown God' from this hill and gained his first Athenian convert, Dionysos, who became patron saint of the city.

To get to the top, you can climb the worn, slippery marble steps cut into the rock (opposite the main entrance to the Acropolis), or you can take the recently added stairs.

Parks & Gardens

The area around Syntagma and the historic centre is surprisingly green, but the rest of Athens is sadly lacking in parks and green spaces. The best walks are around the base of the Acropolis and around Filopappou Hill and the Hill of the Pnyx.

NATIONAL GARDENS

A delightful, shady refuge during summer, the **National Gardens** (Map pp110-11; entrances on Leoforos Vasilissis Sofias & Leoforos Vasilissis Amalias, Syntagma; 7am-dusk) were formerly the royal gardens designed by Queen Amalia. There's also a large children's **playground**, a duck pond and a shady cafe.

ZAPPEIO GARDENS

Between the National Gardens and the old Olympic stadium are the **Zappeio Gardens** (Map pp110-11; entrances on Leoforos Vasilissis Amalias & Leoforos Vasilissis Olgas), laid out in a network of wide walkways around the grand **Zappeio Palace** (www.zappeion.gr). The palace was built in the 1870s for the forerunner of the modern Olympics, with money donated by the wealthy Greek-Romanian benefactor Konstantinos Zappas. The Zappeio hosts conferences, events and exhibitions, and there's a pleasant cafe, restaurant and open-air cinema next door.

Other Attractions
PARLIAMENT

Designed by the Bavarian architect Von Gartner and built between 1836 and 1842, Greece's Parliament (Map pp110–11) was originally the royal palace. It was from the palace balcony that the syntagma (constitution) was declared on 3 September 1843. In 1935 the palace became the seat of the Greek parliament. The royal family moved to a new palace, which became the presidential palace upon the abolition of the monarchy in 1974. Only the library is open to the public, though exhibitions are held in the Eleftherios Venizelos Hall.

The war memorial in the forecourt, known as the **Tomb of the Unknown Soldier**, is guarded by the city's famous statuesque *evzones,* the presidential guards whose uniform of short kilts and pom-pom shoes is based on the attire worn by the klephts (the mountain fighters of the War of Independence). The changing of the guard takes place every hour, while every Sunday at 11am the *evzones* perform an extended **changing of the guard ceremony** in full ceremonial dress, accompanied by a military band.

ATHENS OLYMPIC COMPLEX

Crowned by the striking glass-and-steel roof designed by Spanish architect Santiago Calatrava, the showpiece **Athens Olympic Complex** (Map p163; ☎ 210 683 4777; www.oaka.com.gr; Marousi) is where the main action took place in 2004. The vast stadium complex includes the futuristic, shimmering Wall of Nations. The main stadium hosts major soccer games, sporting events and concerts. There are guided site tours for groups (minimum 15 people; per person €3) but independent travellers can wander around the site. Take metro line 1 (Irini stop).

MONI KAISARIANIS

Nestled on the slopes of Mt Hymettos, 5km from the city, the 11th-century **Moni Kaisarianis** (Monastery of Kaisariani; Map p163; ☎ 210 723 6619; Mt Hymettos; admission €2; ⊗ 8.30am-2.45pm Tue-Sun, grounds Tue-Sun 8.30am-sunset) is a peaceful sanctuary. The walled complex has a central court surrounded by the kitchen and dining rooms, the monks' cells and the bathhouse. The domed *katholikon* (main church) is built in cruciform style. The church was built on the foundations of an ancient temple, and its dome is supported by four columns from the ancient temple. Most of the well-preserved frescoes date back to the 17th and 18th centuries. On weekends the complex can be swarming with picnickers

Take bus 224 from Plateia Kaningos (at the north end of Akadimias) to the terminus. From here it's about 30 minutes' walk to the monastery – or just get a taxi. The site was due to reopen in 2009 after renovations.

ATHENS' FIRST CEMETERY

This **cemetery** (Map p116; Anapafseos, Trivonianou, Mets; ⊗ 7.30am-sunset), the resting place of many famous Greeks and philhellenes, is a fascinating and peaceful place to explore.

Most of the tombstones and mausoleums are lavish in the extreme. Some are kitsch and sentimental; others are works of art created by the foremost 19th-century Greek sculptors, such as Halepas' *Sleeping Maiden* on the tomb of a young girl.

Among the cemetery's famous residents is the archaeologist Heinrich Schliemann (1822–90), whose mausoleum is decorated with scenes from the Trojan War.

HELLENIC COSMOS

To put ruins and museums into perspective, take a virtual-reality trip to ancient Greece at the futuristic **Foundation for the Hellenic World** (off Map p108; ☎ 212 254 0000; www.hellenic-cosmos.gr; Pireos 254, Tavros; adult €6-10, child €3.90-8, day pass €15; ⊗ 9am-4pm Mon-Fri, 10am-3pm Sun Jun-Sep, closed for 2 weeks mid-Aug; 🖳 ♿), about 2km from the city centre. The **Tholos virtual-reality theatre** takes you on an interactive tour of the Ancient Agora or allows you to get a feel for life in ancient Athens. The **Kivotos time machine** has 3D floor-to-ceiling screens with a live guide taking you through ancient Olympia and Miletus.

Take bus 049 or 914 from Omonia. From October until May call ahead or check the website for opening hours.

PLANETARIUM

Athens boasts the world's largest and most technologically advanced digital **Planetarium** (off Map p108; ☎ 210 946 9600; www.eugenfound.edu.gr; Leoforos Syngrou 387, Palio Faliro; adult €6-8, concession €4-5; ⊗ 5.30-8.30pm Wed-Fri, 10.30am-8.30pm Sat & Sun, closed mid-July–late Aug). The 280-seat planetarium, with a 950-sq-metre hemispherical dome, offers 3D virtual trips to the galaxy, as well as IMAX movies and other high-tech shows. There is simultaneous narration in English (€1). The planetarium is part of the Eugenides Foundation, a progressive scientific and educational institution.

Take the metro to Syngrou-Fix then bus 550 or B2 to the Onassio stop, and take the underpass across the road. Enter from Penteli.

Beaches

Athens is the only coastal European capital with beaches within easy distance of the city centre, along the coast towards Glyfada (p105). This is where Athenians cool off and where much of the summer nightlife takes place.

The better beaches are privately run and charge admission (between €4 and €15 per adult). They're usually open between 8am and dusk, May to October (later during heatwaves), and have sun beds and umbrellas (additional charge in some places), changing rooms, children's playgrounds and cafes.

The flashiest and most exclusive summer playground is **Astir Beach** (☎ 210 890 1621; www.astir-beach.com; admission Mon-Fri €15, Sat & Sun €25; ⊗ 8am-9pm), with water sports, shops and restaurants. You can even book online.

The following can be reached by tram and then buses from Glyfada or Voula:

Akti Tou Iliou (☎ 210 985 5169; Alimo; adult/child Mon-Fri €6/3, Sat & Sun €8/4; ⊗ 8am-8pm)

Asteras Beach (☎ 210 894 1620; www.balux-septem.com; Glyfada; adult/child Mon-Fri €6/3, Sat & Sun €7/3; ⊗ 10am-7pm)

Yabanaki (☎ 210 897 2414; www.yabanaki.gr; Varkiza; adult/child Mon-Fri €7/4.50, Sat & Sun €8/4.50; ⊗ 8am-8pm)

There are free beaches at Palio Faliro (Edem), Kavouri and Glyfada.

There is also good (free) swimming at Shinias, Marathon and Vravrona in the north, though these take much longer to get to and are best reached by car.

You can swim year-round at **Limni Vouliagmenis** (Map p163; ☎ 210 896 2239; Leoforos Vouliagmenis; adult/child €8/5; ☺ 7am-8pm), a part-saltwater/part-springwater lake whose temperature usually doesn't fall below 20°C and which is known for its therapeutic mineral qualities. It is set dramatically against a huge jutting cliff, just off the coast, and has a quaint old-world atmosphere thanks to the regular clientele of elderly citizens dressed in bathing caps and towelling gowns.

ACTIVITIES
Diving

Aegean Dive Centre (☎ 210 894 5409; www.adc.gr; Zamanou 53, cnr Pandoras, Glyfada; PADI certification from €390, day/night dives €35/100) organises dives between Vouliagmeni and Cape Sounion. Prices include diving equipment.

Popular with seasoned divers, the new **Planet Blue Dive Centre** (☎ 22920 26446; www.planetblue.gr; Velpex Factory, Lavrio; PADI certification from €300, dives €35-80) caters for all levels at sites around Cape Sounion. Prices include diving equipment.

Golf

Athens' only golf course is the international-standard, 18-hole **Glyfada Golf Club** (☎ 210 894 6820; www.athensgolfclub.com; off Konstantinos Karamanli, Glyfada; 9-/18-hole green fees €42/55). Clubs and buggies are available for hire. Bookings are required for weekends and public holidays.

Skiing

The closest ski resorts to Athens are at Mt Parnassos (p246) in the northwest and Kalavryta (p175) in the Peloponnese. The season usually lasts from mid-January to late March. Day excursions to Parnassos and Kalavryta from Athens are organised by **Trekking Hellas** (Map pp112-13; ☎ 210 331 0323; www.trekking.gr; Rethymnou 12, Exarhia) and **Klaoudatos** (Map p108; ☎ 210 578 1880; www.klaou datos.gr).

WALKING TOUR

This walk takes in most of the main sites in Athens. It involves just over one hour's walking, but can take up to four hours allowing for lingering at various sites and a few detours.

The walk begins at the fountain in the middle of the square at Syntagma. The square has been a favourite place for protests ever since the rally that led to the granting of a constitution on 3 September 1843, declared by King Otto from the balcony of the royal palace. In 1944 the first round of the civil war began here after police opened fire on a communist rally, while in 1954 it was the location of the first demonstration demanding the *enosis* (union) of Cyprus with Greece.

Standing facing the metro station, to your left is the historic **Hotel Grande Bretagne** (**1**; p142), the grandest of Athens' hotels. Built in 1862 as a 60-room mansion for visiting dignitaries, it was converted into a hotel in 1872 and became the place where the crowned heads of Europe and eminent politicians stayed. The Nazis made it their headquarters during WWII, and in 1944 the hotel was the scene of an attempt to blow up Winston Churchill.

To the left of the metro entrance you can see a section of the **ancient cemetery** and the **Peisistratos aqueduct** (**2**), which was unearthed during metro excavations.

Take the metro underpass to go across to the Parliament, stopping en route at the upper hall of **Syntagma metro station** (**3**), showpiece of the city's swish metro system. Glass cases at the southern end of the hall display finds uncovered during construction, while the western wall has been preserved like a trench at an archaeological dig.

The underpass emerges to the right of the former royal palace, now the **Parliament** (**4**; p132). In front of the Parliament, you will see the much-photographed *evzones*, the presidential guards. They stand sentinel under the striking Tomb of the Unknown Soldier, which depicts a slain soldier and has inscriptions with excerpts of Pericles' epitaph. Time your visit to catch the **changing of the guard** (**5**; p132), every hour on the hour.

Walk through the lush **National Gardens** (**6**; p132) and exit to the **Zappeio Palace** (**7**; p132), which was used as the Olympic village in the second modern Olympics in Athens. Follow the path past the playground and go left until you see the crossing to the **Panathenaic Stadium** (**8**; p126), where the first Olympic Games were held in 1896.

Crossing back towards the Zappeio, walk along the periphery of the gardens and cross over the tramlines when you get close to the entrance to the striking **Temple of Olympian Zeus** (**9**; p125), the largest temple ever built. Heading towards Plaka, on the corner ahead of you, teetering on the edge of the traffic, is **Hadrian's Arch**

(**10**; p125), the ornate gateway erected to mark the boundary of Hadrian's Athens.

Cross over Leoforos Vasilissis Amalias and head right towards Lysikratous, where you will make a left turn into Plaka. Ahead on your right you will see the ruins of a Roman monument in the forecourt of the 11th- to 12th-century **Church of Agia Ekaterini (11)**.

Continuing ahead you will reach the choregic **Lysikrates Monument (12)**. This monument was built in 334 BC to commemorate a win in a choral festival. The reliefs on the monument depict the battle between Dionysos and the Tyrrhenian pirates, whom the god had transformed into dolphins. It is the earliest known monument using Corinthian capitals externally. It stands in what was once part of the **Street of Tripods** (**13**; Modern Tripodon), where winners of ancient dramatic and choral contests dedicated their tripod trophies to Dionysos. In the 18th century the monument was incorporated into the library of a French Capuchin convent, in which Lord Byron stayed in 1810–11 and wrote *Childe Harold*. The convent was destroyed by fire in 1890.

Facing the monument, turn left and then right into Epimenidou. At the top of the steps, turn right into Stratonos, which skirts the Acropolis. Just ahead you will see the **Church of St George of the Rock (14)**, which marks the entry to the **Anafiotika quarter (15)**. The picturesque maze of little whitewashed houses is the legacy of stonemasons from the small Cycladic island of Anafi, who were brought in to build the king's palace after Independence. It's a peaceful spot, with brightly painted olive-oil cans brimming with flowers bedecking the walls of the tiny gardens in summer.

Following the narrow path that winds around the houses, hand-painted signs pointing to the Acropolis lead you to the tiny **Church of Agios Simeon (16)**. It looks like a dead end but persevere and you will emerge at the Acropolis

WALK FACTS

Start Syntagma
Finish Syntagma
Duration One to four hours

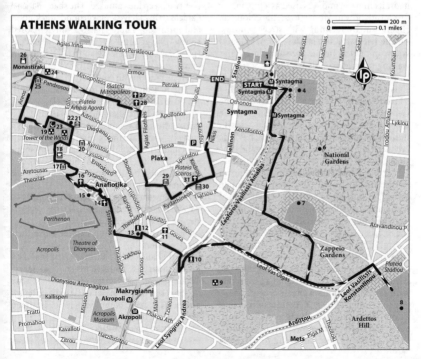

ATHENS WALKING TOUR

road. Turn right and then left into Prytaniou, veering right after 50m into Tholou. The yellow-ochre building at No 5 is the **old Athens University (17)**, built by the Venetians. The Turks used it as public offices and it housed Athens University from 1837 to 1841.

A few metres along, turn right on Klepsidras down some narrow steps that lead to the little **Klepsidra Café (18**; Thrasyvoulou 9), where you can have a rest stop or continue down to the ruins of the **Roman Agora (19**; p125).

To the right of the Tower of the Winds on Kyrristou are the **Turkish Baths (20**; p130), while the **Museum of Greek Popular Instruments (21**; p131), just ahead on Diogenous, has one of the only remaining private *hammams* (Turkish baths) in its gift store. As you turn onto Pelopida you will see the **Gate of the Muslim seminary (22)**, built in 1721 and destroyed in a fire in 1911, and the **Fethiye Mosque (23)**, on the site of the Agora.

Follow the road around the Agora, then turn right into Peikilis and right again into Areos. Ahead on your right are the ruins of **Hadrian's Library (24**; p126). Next to them is the **Museum of Traditional Greek Ceramics (25**; p130), housed in the 1759 Mosque of Tzistarakis. After Independence it lost its minaret and was used as a prison.

You are now in Monastiraki, the colourful, chaotic square teeming with street vendors. To the left is the **flea market (26**; p151), and you won't fail to notice the souvlaki aromas wafting from Mitropoleos.

Turn right at the mosque into Pandrosou. This relic of the old Turkish bazaar is full of souvenir shops. The street is named after King Cecrops' daughter, Pandrosos, who was the first priestess of Athens. Pandrosou leads to the **Athens Cathedral (27)**. The cathedral has little architectural merit, but next to it stands the smaller, more historically significant, 12th-century **Church of Agios Eleftherios (28**; p126), known as the Little Metropolis. Just past this church, turn right into Agias Filotheis, which is lined with buildings belonging to the Greek Church. The mansion with the elaborate gold doors is the residence of the Archbishop of Greece.

Emerging at Adrianou, walk ahead and turn left at Hatzimihali Angelikis, where you can visit the free **Centre of Folk Art & Tradition (29**; p131), worth seeing to check out a beautifully maintained Plaka mansion.

Cut through to busy Kydathineon's Plateia Filomousou Eterias, which is packed with cafes and outdoor tavernas. Turn left and a little way along you will come to the **Greek**

Folk Art Museum (30; p130), opposite the **Church of Metamorphosis (31)**.

Continue along Kydathineon and turn left into Nikis, heading all the way to Ermou, where you can turn left into Athens' main shopping drag, or right to return to Syntagma.

COURSES

If you are serious about learning Greek, several places offer intensive courses for beginners and various proficiency levels. Most of the places listed below run three- to 10-week immersion courses (from €400 to €600) as well as conversation, business and grammar courses.

Athens Centre (Map p108; ☎ 210 701 2268; www.athenscentre.gr; Arhimidous 48, Mets)

Hellenic American Union (Map pp114-15; ☎ 210 368 0900; www.hau.gr; Massalias 22, Kolonaki)

Hellenic Cultural Centre (Map pp112-13; ☎ /fax 210 523 8149; www.hcc.edu.gr; Halkokondyli 50, Omonia)

For information on language courses on the islands, see p715.

ATHENS FOR CHILDREN

Athens is short on playgrounds but there is plenty to keep kids amused. The shady **National Gardens** (p132) have a playground, duck pond and mini zoo. There is also a fully enclosed shady playground in the **Zappeio Gardens** (p132). At the **War Museum** (p131), kids can climb into the cockpit of a WWII plane and other aircraft in the courtyard.

The **Hellenic Children's Museum** (Map pp110-11; ☎ 210 331 2995; Kydathineon 14, Plaka; admission free; ⏲ 10am-2pm Tue-Fri, 10am-3pm Sat & Sun) is more of a play centre, with a games room and a number of 'exhibits' – such as a mock-up of a metro tunnel – for children to explore, as well as workshops ranging from baking to bubble-making. Parents must be on hand to supervise their children at all times.

The **Museum of Greek Children's Art** (Map pp110-11; ☎ 210 331 2621; Kodrou 9, Plaka; admission free; ⏲ 10am-2pm Tue-Sat, 11am-2pm Sun, closed Aug) has a room set aside where children can let loose their creative energy.

Further afield, the enormous **Allou Fun Park & Kidom** (off Map p108; ☎ 210 425 6999; cnr Leoforos Kifisou & Petrou Rali, Renti; admission free, rides €2-4; ⏲ 5pm-1am Mon-Fri, 11am-1am Sat & Sun) is Athens' biggest amusement park complex. Kidom is aimed at younger children.

The **Attica Zoological Park** (off Map pp114-15; ☎ 210 663 4724; www.atticapark.gr; Yalou, Spata; adult/3-12yr €14/10;

(☼ 9am-sunset) has an expanding collection of big cats, birds, reptiles and other animals, including a monkey forest and Cheetahland, where you can walk through a tunnel. The 19-hectare site is near the airport. Take bus 319 from Doukissis Plakentias metro station.

You can always escape the heat and amuse the kids with a virtual-reality tour of ancient Greece at the **Hellenic Cosmos** (p133), or explore the universe at the impressive **Planetarium** (p133).

TOURS

Athens Sightseeing Public Bus Line (Bus Route 400; tickets €5) stops at 20 key sites, such as the Acropolis, National Archaeological Museum and Panathenaic Stadium. Buses run half-hourly between 7.30am and 9pm from June to September, half-hourly between 9am and 6pm in October and May, and hourly between 10am and 4pm from November to April. Tickets can only be purchased on board. Tickets are valid for 24 hours and can be used on all public transport, excluding airport services.

CitySightseeing Athens (Map pp110-11; ☎ 210 922 0604; www.city-sightseeing.com; adult/concession €18/8; ☼ every 30min 9am-6pm; ᕧ) has open-top double-decker buses cruising around town on a 90-minute circuit. You can get on and off at 15 stops on a 24-hour ticket.

Athens Happy Train (Map pp110-11; ☎ 210 725 5400; adult/concession €6/4; ☼ 9am-midnight) runs minitrain tours, with stops at Monastiraki and the Acropolis. The tours take one hour if you don't get off – or you can get on and off over five hours. Trains leave from the top of Ermou every 30 minutes and go as far as the Panathenaic Stadium.

Four main companies run almost identical and pricey air-conditioned city coach tours around Athens, as well as excursions to nearby sights:

CHAT (Map pp110-11; ☎ 210 323 0827; www.chatours .gr; Xenofontos 9, Syntagma)
GO Tours (Map p116; ☎ 210 921 9555; www.gotours.gr; Athanasiou Diakou 20, Makrygianni)
Hop In Sightseeing (Map p116; ☎ 210 428 5500; www.hopin.com; Syngrou 19, Makrygianni) Offers a hop-on/hop-off city tour option.
Key Tours (Map p116; ☎ 210 923 3166/266; www .keytours.com; Kaliroïs 4, Makrygianni)

Tours include a half-day sightseeing tour of Athens (from €52), usually doing little more than pointing out all the major sights and stopping at the Acropolis; and an 'Athens by Night' tour (€60), which includes a taverna dinner

in Plaka with a folk-dancing show. They also run half-day trips to Ancient Corinth (€56) and Cape Sounion (€40); day tours to Delphi (including lunch €96), the Corinth Canal, Mycenae, Nafplio and Epidavros (similar prices); and pricey cruises to Aegina, Poros and Hydra (including lunch €98). Hotels act as booking agents for at least one company and often offer substantial discounts.

Trekking Hellas (Map pp112-13; ☎ 210 331 0323; www .trekking.gr; Rethymnou 12, Exarhia) runs activities ranging from Athens walking tours (€22) to two-hour bike tours (€35).

If you're game, you can hire a bike (though even experienced riders might find the roads a challenge) or join a bike tour with **Acropolis Bikes** (Map pp112-13; ☎ 210 324 5793; www.acropolis-bikes.gr; Aristidou 10-12, Omonia; €10, per 4hr/day €10/15).

FESTIVALS & EVENTS
Hellenic Festival

Greece's premier cultural festivals, held annually under the auspices of the **Hellenic Festival** (www.greekfestival.gr) from late May to October, feature a top line-up of local and international music, dance and theatre.

Major shows in the **Athens Festival** take place at the superb Odeon of Herodes Atticus (p122), one of the world's most historic venues, with the floodlit Acropolis as a backdrop. Patrons sit on cushions on the worn marble seats that Athenians have been entertained on for centuries. The festival, which has been going strong for more than 50 years, presents a diverse program of international standing, ranging from ancient theatre and classical music to contemporary dance. Events are also held in various modern theatres and venues around town.

The **Epidavros Festival** presents local and international productions of ancient Greek drama at the famous Epidavros ancient theatre (p193) in the Peloponnese, about two hours west of Athens. Performances are held every Friday and Saturday night during July and August.

The **Musical July** festival takes place at the lovely 3rd-century-BC Ancient Epidavros Little Theatre, set among the olive groves and pine trees in the seaside village of Epidavros. Performances are held on Friday and Saturday and range from Greek music to classical offerings. The theatre is a 15-minute walk from the port.

The festival program should be available from the beginning of February on the festival website and at the **festival box office** (Map pp112-13; ☎ 210 327 2000; arcade, Panepistimiou 39, Syntagma; ⊙ 8.30am-4pm Mon-Fri, 9am-2pm Sat). Tickets can be booked online or by phone and can also be purchased on the day of the performance at the theatre box offices, but queues can be very long. There are half-price student discounts for most performances on production of an ISIC.

Special KTEL buses to Epidavros (return €20) depart from bus terminal A (p153) on Friday and Saturday, returning after the show. Tickets can be bought a day ahead at the ticket booth in the forecourt of the church of Agiou Konstantinou (Map pp112–13).

You can also take a **dinner cruise** (adult/concession from €55/30) to a show at Ancient Epidavros Little Theatre or Epidavros. Coaches leave from Syntagma and Plateia Klafthmonos around 5pm. Ancient Epidavros Little Theatre is a short walk from the port, while the Epidavros ancient theatre is a 15-minute bus ride away. Supper is served on the return leg. Book through the festival box office.

Rockwave Festival

The annual international **Rockwave Festival** (☎ 210 882 0426; www.rockwavefestival.gr) has been growing in stature and popularity, and rock fans can expect to see some of the world's top acts – the 2009 line-up ranged from Moby, Placebo and Mötley Crüe to local artist Konstantino Bita. Rockwave is held at Terra Vibe, a huge parkland venue on the outskirts of Athens in Malakassa, at the 37th kilometre on the Athens–Lamia Hwy. Tickets are available online from www.ticketpro.gr or from **Ticket House** (Map pp112-13; ☎ 210 360 8366; www.tickethouse.gr; Panepistimiou 42, Syntagma). Special buses are organised and there is also a cheap camp site for ticketholders.

August Moon Festival

Every August on the night of the full moon, musical performances are held at key historic venues, including the Acropolis, the Roman Agora and other sites around Greece. Details are normally announced at the last minute.

Other Festivals & Events

A range of festivals and cultural events take place during summer at the **Technopolis** (Map p109; ☎ 210 346 7322; Gazi), the former gasworks complex turned cultural centre.

The six-day **European Jazz Festival** at the end of May/early June and the two-week **International Dance Festival** in July come under the auspices of the **City of Athens** (☎ 195; www.cityofathens.gr), which also organises free concerts and music and dance performances across the city.

The three-day international **Synch Electronic Music & Digital Arts Festival** (☎ 210 628 6287; www.synch.gr) is held in July at Technopolis and other venues around town. In June, **European Music Day** (www.musicday.gr) is a five-day affair with free concerts and events in various squares around town.

Greece's leading artists and international acts can be seen during two summer festivals held at stunning venues in former quarries: the **Vyronas Festival** (☎ 210 760 9340; www.festival byrona.gr, in Greek) held at the Theatro Vrahon in the suburb of Vyronas; and the **Petras Festival** (☎ 210 506 5400; Petroupoli) in western Athens. Programs and tickets for both are available from Metropolis Music stores (p152), Public (p106) and ticket agencies (see boxed text, below).

Summer concerts are also held at the Lykavittos Theatre (p131) and the Panathenaic Stadium (p126).

The annual **Athens International Film Festival** (☎ 210 606 1413; www.aiff.gr) is held in September.

SLEEPING

The standard of accommodation in Athens has continued to improve markedly since the 2004 Olympics. Prices have skyrocketed accordingly, but the level of service is not always in line with what you might expect.

Athens is a noisy city that sleeps late, so we've mostly selected hotels in quiet areas, pedestrian precincts or side streets. Prices

---

WHAT'S ON IN ATHENS

For comprehensive events listings in English, with links to online ticket sales points, try the following:

▪ www.elculture.gr (arts and culture listings)

▪ www.breathtakingathens.gr (Athens Tourism site)

▪ www.tickethouse.gr (Rockwave and other festivals)

▪ www.tickethour.com (also has sports matches)

▪ www.ticketservices.gr (range of events)

quoted here are for the high season, but most places offer considerable discounts, especially in the low season and online.

Most of the top city hotels are around Syntagma. Plaka is the most popular place for travellers and has a choice of accommodation across the price spectrum. There are also some good pensions and midrange hotels south of the Acropolis, around the quiet neighbourhoods of Makrygianni and Koukaki.

Around Monastiraki and Omonia, many run-down hotels have been upgraded and some turned into hip boutique hotels, but there is still a general seediness that detracts from the area, especially at night. Omonia also has a plethora of largely unattractive accommodation, mostly characterless modern C-class places or cheap bordellos, where you won't get a wink of sleep.

The best rooms in Athens fill up quickly in July and August, so it's wise to book ahead to avoid a fruitless walk in the heat. You can get good deals online.

Budget
CAMPING

There are no camping grounds in central Athens. The EOT's *Camping in Greece* booklet and www.travelling.gr/camping/athens list sites in the Attica region. Most camp sites in the Athens area offer basic facilities and are not generally up to European standards.

Athens Camping (off Map p108; ☎ 210 581 4114; www.campingathens.com.gr; Leoforos Athinon 198, Haidari; camp sites per adult/tent €7/5; ☺ year-round) This unattractive place, 7km west of the city centre on the road to Corinth, is the nearest camping ground to Athens. It has reasonable facilities.

There are better camp sites further afield, at Shinias (p164) and Cape Sounion (p162).

HOSTELS

Hostel Aphrodite (Map p108; ☎ 210 881 0589; www.hostelaphrodite.com; Einardou 12, Stathmo Larisis; dm €14-16, s/d/tr without bathroom €17/23/35; ✖ ▦ ☎) It's not central, but this well-run hostel is a good budget option and the lively bar is a popular traveller meeting spot. It has clean, good-sized dorms, some with en-suite bathrooms, as well as double rooms with and without private bathrooms – many with balconies. It's a 10-minute walk from the Larisis train and metro stations or five minutes from Viktoria.

Athens Easy Access Hostel (Map pp112-13; ☎ 210 524 3211; www.athenseasyaccess.com; Satovrianidou 26,

Omonia; dm €14-18, d/tr/q per person €25/23/18, incl breakfast; ✖ ▦ ☎) Right behind Plateia Omonias, this friendly backpacker hotel has been newly renovated with a smart fit-out and has a range of doubles and dorm accommodation. The breakfast room becomes a popular happy-hour bar with cheap beer and meals. There's free wi-fi, an internet centre and laundry.

Pangration Youth Hostel (Map p108; ☎ 210 751 9530; www.athens-yhostel.com; Damareos 75, Pangrati; dm €15; ☎) The dorms are basic and dated, but it's a cheery enough place in a safe residential neighbourhood. Welcoming owner Yiannis is something of a philosopher, and guests add jokes and words of wisdom to the noticeboards. Hot showers are coin-operated (€0.50, seven minutes); there's a communal kitchen, TV room and laundry. Take trolleybus 2 or 11 from Syntagma to the Filolaou stop on Frinis.

Athens Backpackers (Map p116; ☎ 210 922 4044; www.backpackers.gr; Makri 12, Makrygianni; dm incl breakfast €17-25; ✖ ▦) The popular rooftop bar with cheap drinks and Acropolis views is a major drawcard of this modern and friendly Australian-run backpacker favourite, right near the Acropolis metro. There's a barbecue in the courtyard, a well-stocked kitchen, and a busy social scene with film nights and bar crawls. The six-bed dorms with en-suite bathrooms and lockers have bedding but towels cost €2. The same management runs dorms and well-priced modern studios nearby (see boxed text, p142).

Student & Travellers' Inn (Map pp110-11; ☎ 210 324 4808; www.studenttravellersinn.com; Kydathineon 16, Plaka; dm €18, d/tr without bathroom €65/81, s/d/tr with bathroom €55/65/90; ✖ ▦ ☎) Its location in the heart of Plaka makes this long-established hostel popular with visitors of all ages. It's a friendly place with a pleasant, shady courtyard with large-screen TV, free wi-fi and a helpful travel service. There's a mix of dorms and basic rooms, some with private bathroom and air-conditioning, though shared bathrooms are run-down and complaints about cleanliness common.

Athens Style (Map pp110-11; ☎ 210 322 5010; www.athenstyle.com; Agias Theklas 10, Psyrri; dm €20-24, s/d €51/68, studios €90-124; ✖ ▦) The newest hostel in town, this bright and arty place has tasteful, well-equipped studios and hostel beds in a handy location within walking distance of the metro, major sights, restaurants and nightlife. Each dorm has lockers. Artists have painted murals in the reception and some of the rooms, and there's a cool basement lounge with art exhibitions, pool table, home cinema and internet corner. The small rooftop bar is ideal for evening drinks under the Acropolis. It produces a weekly arts and culture guide.

HOTELS
Plaka & Syntagma
John's Place (Map pp110-11; ☎ 210 322 9719; Patroou 5, Plaka; s/d/tr without bathroom €30/50/60; ✹) For basic budget accommodation, this small, old-style, family-run place is in a handy location just west of Syntagma. The owners are friendly and the timber staircase, old doors and high ceilings give it some charm. The furniture and bathrooms have been updated, and each room has a hand basin, but it's much as it has been for years. Some rooms have air-conditioning, but all bathrooms are basic and shared.

Acropolis House Pension (Map pp110-11; ☎ 210 322 2344; www.acropolishouse.gr; Kodrou 6-8, Plaka; d €59-65, s/d/tr incl breakfast €72.50/87/113.50; ✹ ☎) This atmospheric family-run pension is in a beautifully preserved, 19th-century house, which retains many original features and has lovely painted walls. There are discounts for stays of three days or more. Some rooms have bathrooms across the hall.

Adonis Hotel (Map pp110-11; ☎ 210 324 9737; www.hotel-adonis.gr; Kodrou 3, Plaka; s/d incl breakfast €60/85; ✹ ▯) This comfortable, if bland, pension on a quiet pedestrian street in Plaka is a decent budget base if you're out sightseeing all day. The rooms are basic and clean and come with TV, though the bathrooms are small. There are great views of the Acropolis from the 4th-floor rooms and from the rooftop bar where breakfast is served. Credit-card payments are not accepted.

Hotel Phaedra (Map pp110-11; ☎ 210 323 8461; www.hotelphaedra.com; Herefontos 16, Plaka; s €65, d €65-80, tr €95; ✹ ▯) Many of the rooms at this small, family-run hotel have balconies overlooking a church or the Acropolis. The hotel had an Olympics makeover and is tastefully furnished, though room sizes vary from small to snug. Some rooms have private bathrooms across the hall. A great rooftop terrace, friendly staff and a good location make this one of the better deals in Plaka.

Monastiraki & Thisio
Tempi Hotel (Map pp110-11; ☎ 210 321 3175; www.tempihotel.gr; Eolou 29, Monastiraki; s/d without bathroom €40/55, d/tr with bathroom €64/78; ✹ ☎ &) Location and affordability are the strengths of this older, family-run place on pedestrian Eolou, with front balconies overlooking the church and flower market on Plateia Agia Irini, and side views of the Acropolis. Basic rooms have satellite TV, but the bathrooms are primitive and the top-floor rooms are small and quite a hike. There is a communal kitchen and free wi-fi.

Koukaki
Marble House Pension (Map p116; ☎ 210 923 4058, 210 922 8294; www.marblehouse.gr; Zini 35a; d/tr without bathroom €40/53, s/d/tr with bathroom €35/45/59; ✹) This pension in a quiet cul-de-sac is one of Athens' best value budget hotels, though it is a fair walk from the tourist drag (but close to the metro). Rooms have been artfully updated, with wrought-iron beds and furniture. All rooms have a fridge and ceiling fans and some have air-con (€9 extra). Breakfast costs an extra €5.

Hotel Tony (Map p116; ☎ 210 923 0561; www.hoteltony.gr; Zaharitsa 26; s/d/tr €45/65/75; ✹ ☎) This clean, well-maintained pension has been upgraded, with all but one of the rooms having en-suite bathrooms. Air-con costs €9 extra and hot water can be patchy. All rooms have fridges, TV and air-con. Tony also has roomy, well-equipped studio apartments nearby, which are similarly priced and excellent for families or longer stays.

Around Omonia
Hotel Exarchion (Map pp112-13; ☎ 210 380 0731; www.exarchion.com; Themistokleous 55, Exarhia; s/d/tr incl breakfast €50/65/80; ✹ ▯) Right in the heart of bohemian Exarhia, this characterless but comfortable 1960s high-rise hotel offers reasonably priced accommodation, with updated, well-equipped rooms. There's a rooftop cafe-bar and plenty of dining and entertainment options at your doorstep. It's a 10-minute walk from Omonia metro station.

Midrange
PLAKA & SYNTAGMA
Athens Cypria Hotel (Map pp110-11; ☎ 210 323 8034; www.athenscypria.com; Diomias 5, Syntagma; s/d €94/130; ✹ ▯) Tucked in a side street off Ermou, this small, family-friendly hotel is a little characterless, but it is modern and comfortable, with good facilities and a very handy location. There are family rooms (€230 including breakfast) and discounts for children. There are small balconies but no great view.

Plaka Hotel (Map pp110-11; ☎ 210 322 2096; www.plakahotel.gr; Kapnikareas 7, cnr Mitropoleos, Plaka; s/d/tr €109/135/145; ✹ ☎) It's hard to beat the

Acropolis views from the rooftop garden at this refurbished hotel, which you also enjoy from the top-floor rooms. Rooms have light timber furniture and floors, and satellite TV, though the bathrooms are on the small side.

Niki Hotel (Map pp110-11; ☎ 210 322 0913; www.nikihotel .gr; Nikis 27, Syntagma; s/d/q incl breakfast €110/117/240; ✄ 💻) This small hotel bordering Plaka has undergone one of the more stylish makeovers in the area, with a contemporary design and furnishings. The rooms are well appointed and there is a two-level suite for families, with balconies offering Acropolis views.

Hotel Achilleas (Map pp110-11; ☎ 210 323 3197; www.achilleashotel.gr; Leka 21, Syntagma; s/d/tr incl breakfast €110/135/159; ✄ 💻) From the sleek lobby with marble checkerboard floors, to the well-appointed rooms, the conveniently located Achilleas has been tastefully renovated. The comfortable rooms are large and airy, and those on the top floor open onto garden balconies. There are large family rooms (€175).

Central Hotel (Map pp110-11; ☎ 210 323 4357; www .centralhotel.gr; Apollonos 21, Plaka; s/d/tr incl buffet breakfast from €111/136/185; ✄ 💻) This stylish hotel has been tastefully decorated in light, contemporary tones. It has comfortable rooms with all the mod cons and decent bathrooms. There is a lovely roof terrace with Acropolis views, a small spa and sun lounges. Central is in a handy location between Syntagma and Plaka.

Hotel Adrian (Map pp110-11; ☎ 210 322 1553; www .douros-hotels.com; Adrianou 74, Plaka; s/d/tr incl buffet breakfast €115/140/159, s/d with view €130/155; ✄ 🛜) This small hotel right in the heart of Plaka serves breakfast on a lovely shady terrace with Acropolis views. The refurbished, well-equipped rooms are pleasant enough and have free tea and coffee. The 3rd-floor rooms are the best, with large balconies overlooking the square.

MONASTIRAKI & THISIO

Hotel Attalos (Map pp112-13; ☎ 210 321 2801; www .attaloshotel.com; Athinas 29, Psyrri; s/d/tr €76/94/110; ✄ 💻 🛜) Though decor has never been its strong point, this nonetheless comfortable and reliable hotel had an Olympic makeover. It's very central and close to the metro, but its best feature remains the rooftop bar that offers wonderful views of the Acropolis by night. Rooms at the back have Acropolis views from the balconies. There's free internet access.

Hotel Cecil (Map pp112-13; ☎ 210 321 7909; www.cecil .gr; Athinas 39, Monastiraki; s/d/tr incl breakfast €80/115/150; ✄ 🛜) This charming old hotel on busy

Athinas has beautiful high, moulded ceilings, polished timber floors and an original cage-style lift. The simple rooms are tastefully furnished, but don't have fridges. Two connecting rooms with a shared bathroom are ideal for families or friends.

Magna Grecia (Map pp110-11; ☎ 210 324 0314; www .magnagreciahotel.com; Mitropoleos 54, Monastiraki; incl breakfast s €120, d €150-180; ✄ 💻 🛜) This intimate boutique hotel, in a historic building opposite the cathedral, has great Acropolis views from the front rooms and rooftop terrace. Twelve individually decorated rooms with murals are named after Greek islands, and offer excellent amenities, including comfortable mattresses, DVD players and minibars.

MAKRYGIANNI & KOUKAKI

Art Gallery Hotel (Map p116; ☎ 210 923 8376; www.art galleryhotel.gr; Erehthiou 5, Koukaki; s/d/tr/q €70/100/120/140; ✄ 🛜) This charming, family-run place is full of personal touches and works by an artist who once had her studio upstairs. Some rooms are a little small but all have been refurbished. Original furniture from the '60s has been retained in the communal areas. You can have a generous breakfast (€7) on the balcony with Acropolis views. There are a few cheaper rooms with shared bathrooms. Wi-fi is free.

Philippos Hotel (Map p116; ☎ 210 922 3611; www .philipposhotel.com; Mitseon 3, Makrygianni; s/d incl breakfast €107/140; ✄ 🛜) This friendly, small hotel close to the new Acropolis Museum had a smart Olympics makeover. Rooms are small but well appointed and have free wi-fi. The small double on the roof has a private terrace.

Athens Gate (Map pp110-11; ☎ 210 923 8302; www .athensgate.gr; Leoforos Syngrou 10, Makrygianni; s/d incl breakfast €130/145; ✄ 💻) With stunning views over the Temple of Olympian Zeus from the spacious front rooms, and a handy (if busy) location, this totally refurbished hotel is great value compared with some of the similarly priced offerings. The stylish rooms are immaculate and have all the mod cons, staff are friendly and breakfast is served on the superb rooftop terrace with a choice of 360-degree Athens views.

AROUND OMONIA

our pick **Fresh Hotel** (Map pp112-13; ☎ 210 524 8511; www.freshhotel.gr; Sofokleous 26, cnr Klisthenous, Omonia; s/d/ste incl buffet breakfast from €115/130/350; ✄ 🛜 ▣) The first of the hip hotels to open in the gritty Omonia area, this is a cool place as long as you're happy to ignore the working girls

STUDIOS & APARTMENTS

For longer stays or if you're travelling with the family, a furnished studio or apartment may offer better value than some of the budget hotels.

In Psyrri, Athens Style (p139) has well-equipped studios (€90 to €125) on the upper level, with kitchenettes, flat-screen TVs, stylish modern bathrooms and great balconies with Acropolis views.

Near the Acropolis, there are comfortable, modern studio apartments in two buildings at **Athens Studios** (Map p116; ☎ 210 923 5811; www.athensstudios.gr; Veïkou 3a, Makrygianni; apt €60-100; ☞).

For a comfortable home away from home, there are four superbly renovated, spacious apartments at **EP16** (Map pp112-13; ☎ 6976484135; www.boutiqueathens.com; Epikourou 16, Psyrri; apt €90-110, min 3-night stay; ⚅ ☞), above a gem of an old garlic store. A spiral staircase (no lift) leads up to apartments decked out in contemporary designer furniture, with large kitchens and Aesop toiletries in the marble bathrooms. The massive roof garden with Acropolis views has sunbeds, a barbecue and a stocked-up beer fridge. The only downside is the location, in the seedy outskirts of Psyrri.

hovering in the streets below after hours. Once inside the candy-coloured reception, the seediness gives way to chic design and brightly coloured rooms and suites with all the mod cons. The fantastic rooftop – with pool, bar and restaurant with Acropolis views – couldn't be further from the world below.

our pick **Baby Grand Hotel** (Map pp112-13; ☎ 210 325 0900; www.classicalhotels.com; Athinas 65, Omonia; s/d incl buffet breakfast €120/130; 🖳 ☞) Orang-utans hanging in the restaurant downstairs and the reception desk created out of two Mini Coopers set the tone for this fun, revamped hotel. There's original graffiti art in the corridors and rooms, and iPod docking stations. Individually decked-out rooms have designer furniture, and anything from chandeliers to faux animal skins.

Top End

Hera Hotel (Map p116; ☎ 210 923 6682; www.hera hotel.gr; Falirou 9, Makrygianni; s/d incl breakfast €130/160, ste from €250; ⚅ 🖳) This elegant boutique hotel, a short walk from the Acropolis and Plaka, was totally rebuilt but the formal interior design is in keeping with the lovely neoclassical facade. There's lots of brass and timber, and stylish classic furnishings with a modern edge. The rooftop garden, restaurant and bar have spectacular views.

Hilton (Map pp114-15; ☎ 210 728 1000; www.athens .hilton.com; Leoforos Vasilissis Sofias 46, Ilissia; r/ste from €144/364; 🅿 ⚅ 🖳 ☞ 🍸) Popular with business travellers, this vast concrete edifice looks more like a 1950s housing project than a luxury hotel, but inside no expense has been spared. It has lashings of marble and bronze, enormous chandeliers and somewhat giddy

designer carpets. The fine Milos restaurant is downstairs and there is a lovely pool. Internet rates (€11 per hour) are a bit rich.

Herodion (Map p116; ☎ 210 923 6832; www.herodion .com; Rovertou Galli 4, Makrygianni; s/d incl breakfast €152/182; ⚅ 🖳 ☞ ♿) This elegant four-star hotel is geared towards the well-heeled traveller. The rooms are small but well appointed, with super-comfortable beds. There is a lovely atrium restaurant, laptops in the foyer and free wi-fi. There are unbeatable Acropolis views from the rooftop spa and lounge.

our pick **Periscope** (Map pp114-15; ☎ 210 729 7200; www.periscope.gr; Haritos 22, Kolonaki; r €195-225, ste from €325 incl breakfast; ⚅ ☞) Right in chic Kolonaki overlooking Lykavittos, Periscope is a smart boutique hotel with industrial decor. There are clever gadgets and design features, including the lobby slide show, the sea-level measure on the stairs, travelling TVs, aerial shots of the city on the ceilings and Korres toiletries. The penthouse's private rooftop spa has sensational views.

Electra Palace (Map pp110-11; ☎ 210 337 0000; www.electrahotels.gr; Navarhou Nikodimou 18, Plaka; d/ste incl breakfast from €220/560; 🅿 ⚅ 🖳 🍸) Plaka's smartest hotel is one for the romantics. You can have breakfast under the Acropolis on your balcony in the front rooms (from €325), and dinner in the rooftop restaurant. Completely refurbished in classic style, the rooms are well appointed. There is an indoor swimming pool and gym as well as a rooftop pool with Acropolis views.

Hotel Grande Bretagne (Map pp110-11; ☎ 210 333 0000; www.grandebretagne.gr; Vasileos Georgiou 1, Syntagma; r/ste from €280/420; 🅿 ⚅ 🖳) If you are wealthy or aspire to the best, the place to stay in Athens is – and always has been – the Hotel Grande Bretagne, right on the square in Syntagma. Built in 1862 to accommodate visiting heads of state, it ranks among the grand hotels of the world. No other hotel in Athens can boast such a rich history. Though completely renovated, it still retains an old-world grandeur. There is a divine spa, and the rooftop restaurant and bar are a treat.

EATING

Athens has a vibrant restaurant scene and a delightful culture of casual, convivial alfresco dining. Getting together to eat, drink and talk is the main source of entertainment for Greeks, so you are spoilt for choice.

The city's culinary offerings have come a long way in the past decade, with a renaissance in Greek cuisine and the arrival of a diverse crop of ethnic and international-style restaurants. A new generation of chefs has found inspiration in Greece's regional cuisine and produce, while grandma's cooking has entered the kitchens of the city's finest restaurants. Trendy Nuevo-Greek restaurants compete alongside traditional tavernas, *ouzeries* (places that serve ouzo and light snacks) and quaint old-style *mayireia* (cook houses).

Having said that, some places put more effort into decor and attitude than into the food, charging more for average taverna fare. You may well find your most memorable meals served with minimum ambience.

It's hard to resist one meal in atmospheric Plaka, but the food is generally overpriced and nothing to rave about. Better places are scattered around the city. Gazi has many modern tavernas, while old-style eateries downtown cater to city workers. In Monastiraki, the end of Mitropoleos is a souvlaki hub, with musicians adding to the area's at times festive atmosphere. *Mezedhopoleia* (restaurants specialising in mezedhes) and fancier restaurants can be found around Adrianou, along the rail line to Thisio and in Psyrri. Exarhia's popular *ouzeries* and tavernas cater largely to locals, while chic Kolonaki has some of the best finedining options.

We've stuck largely to downtown Athens and Greek cuisine. Unless stated otherwise, all the restaurants listed here are open daily for lunch and dinner.

Budget
PLAKA & SYNTAGMA
Paradosiako (Map pp110-11; ☎ 210 321 4121; Voulis 44a, Plaka; mains €4-10) For great traditional fare, you can't beat this inconspicuous, no-frills taverna on the periphery of Plaka, with a few tables on the pavement. There's a basic menu but it's best to choose from the daily specials, which include fresh and delicious seafood. It fills up quickly with locals, so get there early.

Doris (Map pp112-13; ☎ 210 323 2671; Praxitelous 30, Syntagma; mains €4.20-8.80; 🕙 8.30am-6.30pm Mon-Sat) This Athens institution started as a *galaktopoleio* (dairy store) in 1947 and became a traditional *mayireio* catering to city workers. Pink walls aside, the classic marble tables, historical photos and old-style waiters give it a yesteryear ambience. Choose from the trays of daily specials (the stewed chickpeas are excellent), as the printed English menu only has the basics, and finish off with the renowned *loukoumadhes* (ball-shaped doughnuts served with honey and cinnamon).

our pick Filema (Map pp110-11; ☎ 210 325 0222; Romvis 16, Syntagma; mezedhes €4.50-12; 🕙 Mon-Sat) This popular *mezedhopoleio* has two shopfronts and fills tables on both sides of this narrow street, which is a busy commercial area by day but a peaceful spot when the shops close. It has a great range of mezedhes such as plump *keftedhes* (small tasty rissoles) and grilled sardines.

Vizantino (Map pp110-11; ☎ 210 322 7368; Kydathineon 18, Plaka; specials €5-9.50) Despite the touts, this place is recommended. It's touristy in the extreme, but is the best of the restaurants around Plateia Filomousou Eterias. Go for the daily specials.

Glykis (Map pp110-11; ☎ 210 322 3925; Angelou Geronta 2, Plaka; seafood mezedhes €5.50-6) In a quiet corner of Plaka, this casual *mezedhopoleio* with a shady courtyard is mostly frequented by students and locals. It has a tasty selection of mezedhes, including traditional dishes such as *briam* (oven-baked vegetable casserole) and cuttlefish in wine.

Lena's Bio (Map pp110-11; ☎ 210 324 1360; Nikis 11, Syntagma; salads €6-10; 🕙 8am-6pm Mon-Fri, 8am-4pm Sat) A wholesome option with a delicious range of organic meals, snacks and juices – if you can snag a table.

Platanos (Map pp110-11; ☎ 210 321 8734; Diogenous 4, Plaka; mains €6.20-12.50; 🕙 noon-4.30pm & 6.30pm-midnight Mon-Sat) This age-old Plaka taverna, with an antiquated menu in several badly translated languages, is in a pleasant village-style square away from the main tourist drag. There are tables under a giant plane tree and reliable home-style fare, such as chicken with okra. No credit cards.

Pure Bliss (Map p110-11; ☎ 210 325 0360; Romvis 24a, Syntagma; salads €7-9; ⏰ 10am-1am Mon-Sat, 5-9pm Sun) One of the few places in Athens where you can get organic coffee, exotic teas and soy products. There's a range of healthy salads, juices, smoothies and mostly organic food and wine (including organic cocktails).

MONASTIRAKI & OMONIA

Diporto Agoras (Map pp112-13; ☎ 210 321 1463; cnr Theatrou & Sokratous, Omonia; ⏰ 8am-6pm Mon-Sat, closed 1-20 Aug) This quirky old taverna is one of the dining gems of Athens. There's no signage, only two doors leading to a rustic cellar where there's no menu, just a few dishes that haven't changed in years. The house speciality is *revythia* (chick peas), usually followed by grilled fish and washed down with wine from one of the giant barrels lining the wall. The often erratic service is part of the appeal.

The streets around the colourful and bustling **Varvakios Agora** (Athens central market; Map pp112-13; Athinas, Omonia; ⏰ Mon-Sat) are a sensory delight. The meat and fish market is in the historic building on the eastern side, and the fruit and vegetable market is across the road. The meat market might sound like a strange place to go for a meal, but the market tavernas – such as **Papandreou** (☎ 213 008 2297; Aristogitonos 1; ⏰ 24hr) – are an Athenian institution, turning out huge quantities of tasty, traditional fare. The clientele ranges from hungry market workers to elegant couples emerging from nightclubs at 5am in search of a bowl of hangover-busting *patsas* (tripe soup).

PSYRRI

Ivis (Map pp112-13; ☎ 210 323 2554; Navarhou Apostoli 19; mezedhes €4-10) This cosy corner *mezedhopoleio*, with its bright, artful decor, has a small but delicious range of simple, freshly cooked mezedhes. Ask for the daily offerings as there's only a rough Greek hand-written menu – the potato salad and refreshing beetroot with yoghurt are winners. There's a good ouzo selection to wash it down.

Taverna tou Psyrri (Map pp112-13; ☎ 210 321 4923; Eshylou 12; mains €6.50-9) This cheerful place just off Plateia Iroön turns out decent, no-frills, traditional taverna food, from reliable grills to

mayirefta (ready-cooked meals; on display in the back). It's been around for years and has some original character, from the barrels in the basement wall to the colourful murals of androgynous women.

Telis (Map pp112-13; ☎ 210 324 2775; Evripidou 86; pork chops with chips €7; ⏰ 8am-2am Mon-Sat) You can't get more basic than this fluoro-lit, bare-walled, paper-tablecloth *psistaria* (restaurant serving grilled food). Telis has been slaving over the flame grill, cooking his famous pork chops, since 1978. There's nothing else on the menu – just meat and chips and Greek salad, washed down with rough house wine or beer.

EXARHIA

Kimatothrafstis (Map pp112-13; ☎ 213 030 8274; Harilaou Trikoupi 49; small/large plate €3/6; ⏰ 8am-11pm) With riot police outside Pasok headquarters across the road adding a distinctive Exarhia ambience, this impressive newcomer dishes out a range of home-style Greek cooking and alternative fare. It's a great-value, bright and casual modern *mayireio* with communal tables. Choose from the buffet of the day's offerings. Plates come in two sizes – big or small.

Rozalia (Map pp112-13; ☎ 210 330 2933; Valtetsiou 58; mains €4.50-11) An old-style Exarhia favourite on a lively pedestrian strip, this family-run taverna has a standard menu of grills and home-style fare such as *pastitsio* (layers of buttery macaroni and seasoned minced lamb). The large courtyard garden is popular in summer, when fans spraying water help keep you cool. They also run the adjacent Achilleas.

Food Company (Map pp112-13; ☎ 210 380 5004; Emmanuel Benaki 63-65; dishes €5.50-9.50; ⏰ 10am-2am) This place is recommended for its range of healthy salads, wholesome dishes, and hot and cold pasta and noodle dishes.

Midrange

PLAKA & SYNTAGMA

our pick **Tzitzikas & Mermingas** (Map p110-11; ☎ 210 324 7607; Mitropoleos 12-14, Syntagma; mezedhes €5.90-9.90) This bright, cheery, modern *mezedhopoleio* isn't in the most atmospheric of locations, but it dishes out a great range of delicious and creative mezedhes. There are walls of shelves lined with Greek products and the theme extends playfully to the toilets.

Palia Taverna tou Psara (Map p110-11; ☎ 210 321 8734; Erehtheos 16, Plaka; seafood dishes €11.50-26)

STREET FOOD

From vendors selling *koulouria* (fresh pretzel-style bread) and grilled corn or chestnuts, to the raft of fast-food offerings, there's no shortage of snacks on the run.

You can't go wrong with local *tiropites* (cheese pies) and their various permutations. **Ariston** (Map pp110-11; ☎ 210 322 7626; Voulis 10, Syntagma; pies €1.10-1.70; ☟ 10am-4pm Mon-Fri) has been around since 1910, serving the best range of tasty, freshly baked pies with all manner of fillings.

However, Greece's favourite tasty snack is the souvlaki, packing more punch for €2 than anything else. You can't miss the smells wafting from the souvlaki hub at Monastiraki, but you'll find one of the best souvlaki joints in Athens nearby at tiny **Kostas** (Map pp110-11; ☎ 210 323 2971; Plateia Agia Irini 2, Monastiraki; souvlaki €2; ☟ 5am-5pm). This old-style virtual wall joint, in a pleasant square opposite Agia Irini church, churns out tasty, freshly made pork souvlakia and kebabs, with its signature spicy tomato sauce.

Hidden away from the main hustle and bustle of Plaka, this taverna is a cut above the rest, which is why they fill the tables on the street, the terrace and the place next door. There is a choice of mezedhes but it is known as the best seafood taverna in Plaka (top fresh fish €62 per kilogram).

Mono (Map pp110-11; ☎ 210 322 6711; Paleologou Venizelou 4, Plaka; mains €12-22; ☟ Mon-Sat) This classy taverna, on the outskirts of Plaka near the cathedral, is one of the new breed of restaurants serving refined contemporary Greek cuisine, not just the same old stuff in a nicer setting. Decor is subtle Greek chic, there's a lovely courtyard, and the presentation and ambience are top-rate, even if it doesn't have the picturesque setting of nearby eateries. Try the pork with rosemary mezes.

Furin Kazan (Map pp110-11; ☎ 210 322 9170; Apollonos 2, Syntagma; sushi €18-22; ☟ 1-5pm & 7-11.30pm Mon-Fri, 5-11.30pm Sat & Sun) One of the best Japanese eateries in town, this place has been refurbished but remains a casual restaurant with a good selection of rice and noodle dishes (€7 to €8), and fresh sashimi and sushi.

MAKRYGIANNI & THISIO

Filistron (Map p109; ☎ 210 346 7554; Apostolou Pavlou 23, Thisio; mezedhes €7.50-15; ☟ Tue-Sun) It's wise to book a prized table on the rooftop terrace of this excellent *mezedhopoleio*, which enjoys breathtaking Acropolis and Lykavittos views. Specialising in regional cuisine, it has a great range of tasty mezedhes – try the grilled vegetables with haloumi or the Mytiline onions stuffed with rice and mince – and an extensive Greek wine list.

To Steki tou Ilia (Map p109; ☎ 210 345 8052; Eptahalkou 5, Thisio; chops per portion/kg €9/30; ☟ 8pm-

late) You'll often see people waiting for a table at this *psistaria*, famous for its tasty grilled lamb chops. With tables on the quiet pedestrian strip opposite the church, it's a no-frills place with barrel wine and simple offerings of dips, chips and salads. For those who don't eat lamb, there are pork chops, too.

ourpick Mani Mani (Map p116; ☎ 210 921 8180; Falirou 10, Makrygianni; mains €9.50-17; ☟ closed Jul & Aug) Forgo a view and head upstairs to the relaxing dining rooms of this delightful modern restaurant, which specialises in regional cuisine from Mani in the Peloponnese. The ravioli with Swiss chard, chervil and cheese, and the tangy Mani sausage with orange are standouts. It's great value and almost all starters and mains can be ordered as half-serves (at half-price), allowing you to try a range of dishes.

PSYRRI & MONASTIRAKI

ourpick Café Avyssinia (Map pp110-11; ☎ 210 321 7407; Kynetou 7, Monastiraki; mezedhes €4.50-16.50; ☟ noon-1am Tue-Sat, noon-7pm Sun) Hidden away on grungy Plateia Avyssinias, in the middle of the flea market, this bohemian *mezedhopoleio* gets top marks for atmosphere, food and friendly service. It specialises in regional Greek cuisine, from warm fava to eggplants baked with tomato and cheese, and has a great selection of ouzo, *raki* (Cretan firewater) and *tsipouro* (distilled spirit similar to ouzo but usually stronger). There is often acoustic live music, from Manos Hatzidakis to *rembetika* (blues). There are fantastic Acropolis views from the window seats upstairs.

Ouzou Melathron (Map pp110-11; ☎ 210 324 0716; Filipou 10, cnr Astingos, Monastiraki; seafood mezedhes €6.60-18.04) The famous *ouzerie* chain from Thessaloniki has been a hit since it opened in downtown Athens. It's a fun place serving tasty mezedhes from an oversized menu with a good dose of whimsy (such as the transvestite lamb, which is actually chicken), including the odd-numbered prices.

OMONIA & EXARHIA

Hell's Kitchen (Map pp112-13; ☎ 210 524 1555; Kleisthenous 13, Omonia; mains €9.50-15.95; noon-midnight Tue-Sat, noon-6pm Sun & Mon) Behind the Town Hall, this friendly, contemporary cafe is a great place to lunch on wholesome burgers, pastas and salads (and coffees are reasonably priced). The pavement tables are on a garden deck and in the evenings it livens up with mojito-sipping patrons watching the area's seedier elements parade by.

our pick Yiantes (Map pp112-13; ☎ 210 330 1369; Valtetsiou 44, Exarhia; mains €10-17) This modern taverna set in a lovely garden courtyard is next to an open-air cinema. It is upmarket for Exarhia, but the food is superb and made with largely organic produce. There are interesting greens such as *almirikia*, the fish is perfectly grilled, and the mussels and calamari with saffron are memorable.

Arheon Gefsis (Map pp112-13; ☎ 210 523 9661; Kodratou 22, Metaxourghio; mains €10-20; Tue-Sat) This gimmicky but fun place turns the clock back 2500 years to ancient Greece. The waiters dress in flowing robes and there are no glasses – the ancients used earthenware cups and spoons instead of forks. The menu derives from ancient times; roast meats and fish dominate, served with purées of peas or chickpeas and vegetables.

GAZI & ROUF

our pick Skoufias (Map p109; ☎ 210 341 2252; Vasiliou tou Megalou 50, Rouf; mains €5-9; 9pm-late) This gem of a taverna near the railway line is a little off the beaten track but is worth seeking out. There are tables outside opposite the church. The menu has Cretan influences and an eclectic selection of regional Greek cuisine, including many dishes you are unlikely to find in any tourist joint, from superb rooster with ouzo to lamb *tsigariasto* (braised) with *horta* (wild greens), and potato salad with orange. The house wine works a treat.

Kanella (Map p109; ☎ 210 347 6320; Leoforos Konstantinoupoleos 70, Gazi; dishes €7-10.50; noon-late) Homemade village-style bread, retro mismatched crockery and brown-paper tablecloths set the tone for this trendy taverna

opposite the train line serving regional Greek cuisine. There are daily one-pot and oven-baked specials such as lemon lamb with potatoes, and an excellent zucchini and avocado salad. The house wine is a little rough.

Sardelles (Map p109; ☎ 210 347 8050; Persefonis 15, Gazi; fish dishes €9-15.50) This modern fish taverna specialises in simply cooked seafood mezedhes. It's a friendly place with tables outside, opposite the illuminated gasworks, excellent service and nice touches such as the fishmonger paper tablecloths and souvenir pots of basil. Try the grilled *thrapsalo* (squid) and excellent *taramasalata* (a thick purée of fish roe, potato, oil and lemon juice). Meat eaters should venture next door to its meat counterpart, Butcher Shop.

KOLONAKI & PANGRATI

our pick Oikeio (Map pp114-15; ☎ 210 725 9216; Ploutarhou 15, Kolonaki; specials €7-13; 1pm-2.30am Mon-Sat) With excellent home-style cooking, this modern taverna lives up to its name (meaning 'homey'). Oikeio is cosy on the inside and the tables on the pavement allow you to people-watch without the normal Kolonaki bill. There are pastas, salads and more international food, but try the *mayirefta* specials like the excellent stuffed zucchini.

our pick Alatsi (Map pp114-15; ☎ 210 721 0501; Vrasida 13, Ilissia; mains €12-16.50) Cretan food is in, and just behind the Hilton, Alatsi represents the new breed of trendy upscale restaurants, serving traditional Cretan cuisine, such as *gamopilafo* (wedding pilaf) with lamb or rare *stamnagathi* (wild greens), to fashionable Athenians. The food and service are excellent.

Top End

There are plenty of upmarket, blow-the-budget dining options in Athens. Reservations are essential.

Papadakis (Map pp114-15; ☎ 210 360 8621; Fokylidou 15, Kolonaki; mains €18-38; Mon-Sat) In the foothills of Lykavittos, this understatedly chic restaurant specialises in seafood, with creative dishes such as stewed octopus with honey and sweet wine, delicious *salatouri* (fish salad) with small fish, and sea salad (a type of green seaweed/sea asparagus).

our pick Varoulko (Map p109; ☎ 210 522 8400; Pireos 80, Gazi; mains €20-35; dinner from 8pm Mon-Sat) For a magical Greek dining experience, you can't beat the winning combination of Acropolis views and delicious seafood by Lefteris Lazarou, the only Greek Michelin-rated chef. Lazarou specialises in fish and seafood creations, though there are also meat dishes on the menu. The service is faultless and the wine list enviable. The restaurant has a superb rooftop terrace.

Orizontes (Map pp114-15; ☎ 210 722 7065; Lykavittos Hill; dishes €23-38) For a special night out, you can take the *teleferik* up to the peak of Lykavittos and watch the sun set over Athens. The menu at this upmarket restaurant is Mediterranean/international and the food and service are excellent, as is the wine list.

Spondi (Map p108; ☎ 210 752 0658; Pironos 5, Pangrati; mains €30-50; ☯ 8pm-late) Spondi is consistently voted Athens' best restaurant, and the accolades are totally deserved. It offers Mediterranean haute cuisine, with heavy French influences, in a relaxed, classy setting in a charming old house in Pangrati. There is a range of set dinner and wine menus, and the restaurant has a lovely garden terrace draped in bougainvillea in summer. This is a special-occasion place.

Another good option to seek out is the modern Plous Podilatou (p161), where you can dine by the Mikrolimano harbour in Piraeus.

DRINKING
Cafes

Athens seems to have more cafes per capita than virtually any other city, inevitably packed with Athenians, prompting many a visitor to wonder if anyone ever works in this city. More recently, the burning question has been why it has Europe's most expensive coffee (between €3 and €5). One explanation is that you actually hire the chair, not just pay for coffee, as people sit on a coffee for hours.

You won't have trouble finding a cafe anywhere in town. In Kolonaki, **Da Capo** (Map pp114-15; Tsakalof 1) on the main square is known for excellent coffee and people-watching. It's self-serve if you can find a table.

Another cafe-thick area is Adrianou, along the Ancient Agora, where you'll find students and young people filling the shady tables at **Dioskouri** (Map pp110-11; Adrianou 39). Further along the pedestrian promenade along Apostolou Pavlou, you'll get great Acropolis views from **Athinaion Politeia** (Map p109; Akamandos 1).

Bars

In Athens the line between cafe and bar is often blurred, as you can drink just about anywhere and any time. Some bars are also restaurants that become clubs late at night. Many bars don't get busy until after 11pm and open till late.

Every neighbourhood has its fair share of bars. In typical Athens fashion, 'hot spots' quickly become saturated and lose their appeal, and the action moves on to the next big boom area. In 2009 authorities were forced to crack down on the incursion of bars and cafes onto pavements and public spaces in areas such as Psyrri and Gazi.

That won't stop patrons spilling out into the streets at Gazi trailblazer **Gazaki** (Map p109; Triptolemou 31), which has a great rooftop bar. If you can't stand the crowds at hip **Hoxton** (Map p109; Voutadon 42), you can get some fresh air on the terrace of rock bar **45 Moires** (Map p109; Iakhou 18, cnr Voutadon), overlooking Gazi's neon-lit chimney stacks.

Psyrri's bars come and go but a couple of staples are mainstream **Fidelio** (Map pp112-13; Ogygou 2), which has a retractable roof, and long-time favourite Lilliputian warren **Thirio** (Map pp112-13; Lepeniotou 1). **Soul** (Map pp112-13; Evripidou 65) attracts a cool young crowd and has a dance club upstairs.

Funky bars have also popped up in obscure alleys and formerly deserted streets in downtown Athens. **Bartessera** (Map pp112-13; Kolokotroni 25) is a cool bar at the end of a narrow arcade, with great music. A safe downtown bet for 30-somethings and great cocktails is **Toy** (Map pp112-13; Karytsi 10), near the cluster of bars around Plateia Karytsi, or the lively **Seven Jokers** (Map pp110-11; Voulis 7). With tables overlooking Plateia Kotzia, **Higgs** (Map pp112-13; Efpolidos 4) is an old *kafeneio* (coffee house) morphed into an alternative bar that cranks up the music at night and is occasionally known to bring out the barbecue.

An alternative, multi-use, all-day bar with an arts focus, **Booze** (Map pp112-13; Kolokotroni 57) has gallery spaces in the basement and a nightclub upstairs. In an industrial Bauhaus building near Gazi, the avante garde **Bios** (Map p109; Pireos 84) is a multilevel warren with a bar, live performances, art and new media exhibitions, a basement club, a tiny art-house cinema and a roof garden.

Kolonaki has two main drinking haunts. In the strip of bars at the top end of Skoufa, **Rosebud** (Map pp114-15; Omirou 60, cnr Skoufa) is a good start, while **Mommy** (Map pp114-15; Delfon 4), in a side street, is popular for English-speaking locals and its weekly '80s night. Or you can join the crowds squeezing into the tiny bars on Haritos, or around the corner at the less snooty **Mai Tai** (Map pp114-15; Ploutarhou 18).

Exarhia is a good bet for youthful, lively bars. **Wunderbar** (Map pp112-13; Themistokleous 80), on Plateia Exarhion, is a decent place to start, while the cheap bar precinct on nearby Mesolongiou is popular with students and anarchists.

In Thisio, the multizoned **Stavlos** (Map p109; Iraklidon 10) is a veteran of the string of cafes and bars along Iraklidon's pedestrian precinct. It plays mainly alternative music inside and more mellow sounds in the garden.

You won't find any happening bars in Plaka, but **Brettos** (Map pp110-11; Kydathineon 41) is a delightful old bar and distillery, with a stunning wall of colourful bottles and huge barrels. You can sample shots of Brettos' home brand of ouzo, brandy and other spirits, as well as the family wine.

At Monastiraki's **James Joyce** (Map pp110-11; ☎ 210 323 5055; Astingos 12; mains €9-14) Irish pub you'll find free-flowing Guinness, decent pub food, live music and plenty of travellers and expats.

ENTERTAINMENT

English-language entertainment information appears daily in the *Kathimerini* supplement in the *International Herald Tribune*, while *Athens News* and *Athens Plus* also have entertainment listings.

You can also check out www.elculture.gr and other entertainment websites (see boxed text, p138) for events and concerts around town.

Cinemas

Athenians are avid cinema-goers. Most cinemas show recent releases in English (they don't dub them), but art-house foreign films have Greek subtitles. In summer Athenians prefer outdoor cinemas (see boxed text, opposite). Admission costs €7 to €8.

The following cinemas are in central Athens:

Apollon & Attikon (Map pp112-13; ☎ 210 323 6811; Stadiou 19, Syntagma)

Astor (Map pp112-13; ☎ 210 323 1297; Stadiou 28, Syntagma)

Asty (Map pp112-13; ☎ 210 322 1925; Koraï 4, Syntagma)

Ideal (Map pp112-13; ☎ 210 382 6720; Panepistimiou 46)

Classical Music & Opera

In summer the main cultural activity takes place at the historic Odeon of Herodes Atticus

and other venues under the auspices of the Hellenic Festival (p137).

Megaron (Athens Concert Hall; Map pp114-15; ☎ 210 728 2333; www.megaron.gr; Kokkali 1, cnr Leoforos Vasilissis Sofias, Ilissia; ☯ box office 10am-6pm Mon-Fri, 10am-2pm Sat) The city's state-of-the-art concert hall presents a rich winter program of operas and concerts featuring world-class international and Greek performers.

The **Greek National Opera** (Ethniki Lyriki Skini; ☎ 210 360 0180; www.nationalopera.gr) season runs from November to June. Performances are usually held at the **Olympia Theatre** (Map pp112-13; ☎ 210 361 2461; Akadimias 59, Exarhia) or the Odeon of Herodes Atticus in summer.

Theatre

Athens has more theatres than any city in Europe but, as you'd expect, most performances are in Greek. Theatre buffs may enjoy a performance of an old favourite if they know the play well enough.

National Theatre (Map pp112-13; ☎ 210 522 3243; www.n-t.gr; Agiou Konstantinou 22-24, Omonia) The recently refurbished theatre is one of the city's finest neoclassical buildings. Performances of contemporary plays and ancient theatre take place on the main stage and in venues around town. In summer, plays are performed in ancient theatres across Greece, such as at Epidavros (p193).

Greek Folk Dancing

Dora Stratou Dance Theatre (Map p109; ☎ 210 921 4650; www.grdance.org; Filopappou Hill; adult/concession €15/10; ☯ performances 9.30pm Tue-Sat, 8.15pm Sun May-Sep) Every summer the Dora Stratou company performs its repertoire of folk dances from all over Greece at its open-air theatre on the western side of Filopappou Hill. Formed to preserve the country's folk culture, it has gained an international reputation for authenticity and professionalism. It also runs folk-dancing workshops in summer. The theatre is signposted from the western end of Dionysiou Areopagitou. Take trolleybus 22 from Syntagma and get off at Agios Ioannis.

Live Music
ROCK

Athens has a healthy rock-music scene and is a regular stop on most European touring schedules. In summer check Rockwave (p138) and other festival schedules.

Gagarin 205 Club (Map p108; Liosion 205) The Gagarin 205 Club is primarily a rock venue, with gigs on Friday and Saturday nights featuring leading rock and underground music bands. Tickets are available from **Ticket House** (Map pp112-13; ☎ 210 360 8366; www.tickethouse.gr; Panepistimiou 42, Syntagma).

AN Club (Map pp112-13; ☎ 210 330 5056; Solomou 13-15, Exarhia) The small AN Club hosts lesser-known international bands, as well as interesting local bands.

Mike's Irish Bar (Map pp114-15; ☎ 210 777 6797; www.mikesirishbar.gr; Sinopis 6, Ambelokipi; ☿ 8pm-4am) A long-time favourite of the city's expatriate community, Mike's has live music most nights from 11.30pm.

JAZZ & WORLD MUSIC

You can hear an eclectic range of music in small clubs around Athens. Cover charges vary depending on the performances. Note that they are normally closed during July and August.

Half Note Jazz Club (Map p116; ☎ 210 921 3310; Trivonianou 17, Mets) The stylish Half Note, opposite the Athens cemetery, is the city's principal and most serious jazz venue. It hosts an interesting array of international names.

our pick Alavastro Café (Map p108; ☎ 210 756 0102; Damareos 78, Pangrati) The Alavastro features an eclectic mix of modern jazz, ethnic and quality Greek music in a casual and intimate venue.

Small Music Theatre (Map p116; ☎ 210 924 5644; Veïkou 33, Koukaki) This small venue hosts an interesting assortment of bands, often jazz and fusion.

Palenque (Map pp114-15; ☎ 210 775 2360; www .palenque.gr; Farandaton 41, Ambelokipi; ☿ 9.30pm-late) A slice of Havana in Athens, Palenque presents regular live music, with artists from around the world, salsa parties and flamenco shows.

GREEK MUSIC
Rembetika Clubs

Athens is where you can see some of the best *rembetika* (Greek blues) in intimate, evocative venues. Most close down from May to September, so in summer try the live music tavernas around Psyrri and Plaka (below). Most sets include a combination of *rembetika* and *laïka* (urban popular music). Performances start at around 11.30pm; most places do not have a cover charge, but drinks can be expensive.

our pick Stoa Athanaton (Map pp112-13; ☎ 210 321 4362; Sofokleous 19, Omonia; ☿ 3-6pm & midnight-6am Mon-Sat, closed Jun-Sep) The almost legendary Stoa Athanaton occupies a hall above the central meat market. It is a popular venue, with classic *rembetika* and *laïka* from a respected band of musicians – often starting from mid-afternoon. Access is by a lift in the arcade.

Perivoli Tou Ouranou (Map pp110-11; ☎ 210 323 5517; Lysikratous 19, Plaka; ☿ 9pm-late Thu-Sun, closed Jul-Sep) A favourite Plaka music haunt in a rustic old-style venue where you can have dinner and listen to authentic *laïka* and *rembetika* by leading exponents.

Kavouras (Map pp112-13; ☎ 210 381 0202; Themistokleous 64, Exarhia; ☿ 11pm-late, closed Jul & Aug) Above Exarhia's popular souvlaki joint, this lively club usually has a decent line-up of musicians playing *rembetika* and *laïka* until dawn.

Live Music Tavernas

If you want to hear some music over dinner, many tavernas around Plaka and Psyrri have live music in the evenings, playing traditional *laïka* and *rembetika*.

Palea Plakiotiki Taverna Stamatopoulos (Map pp110-11; ☎ 210 322 8722; Lyssiou 26, Plaka; ☿ 7pm-2am Mon-Sat, 11am-2am Sun) A Plaka institution, this place has reasonable food and live music

---

SUMMER CINEMA

One of the delights of balmy summer nights in Athens is the enduring tradition of open-air cinema, where you can watch the latest Hollywood or art-house flick under moonlight. Many refurbished original outdoor cinemas are still operating in gardens and on rooftops around Athens, with modern sound systems.

The most historic outdoor cinema is **Aigli** (Map pp110-11; ☎ 210 336 9369) in the verdant Zappeio Gardens, where you can watch a movie in style with a glass of wine.

Try to nab a seat with Acropolis views (seats on the right) on the rooftop of Plaka's **Cine Paris** (Map pp110-11; ☎ 210 322 0721; Kydathineon 22), or meander around the foothills of the Acropolis to **Thission** (Map p109; ☎ 210 342 0864; Apostolou Pavlou 7, Thisio).

nightly. It's popular with locals and can get extremely busy later in the evening, so you'll need to get in early to get a table.

Mostrou (Map pp110-11; ☎ 210 322 5558; Mnisikleous 22, cnr Lyssiou, Plaka; ⏰ 9pm-late Thu-Sun) Mostrou has a full-sized stage and dance floor and is popular with locals. In summer, there's more sedate live music on the terrace.

Psyrri has a tradition of merry Sunday afternoons, but you'll find live music most nights at many of the tavernas, including **Paliogramofono** (Map pp112-13; ☎ 210 323 1409; Navarhou Apostoli 8), which has decent food.

There is also live music most nights and on weekends at Café Avyssinia (p145).

Nightclubs

Athens is renowned for its nightlife, with vibrant bars and dance clubs to suit all types and musical tastes, from the latest dance beats to indie pop rock, plus the classic Greek *bouzoukia* or *skyladika* (literally 'dog houses', a playful term for second-rate places with crooning singers). Admission to some clubs ranges from €10 Monday to Thursday to €15 on Friday and Saturday nights. The admission price usually includes one drink. Clubs generally get busy around midnight. The majority of the top clubs close in summer or move to outdoor venues by the beach.

ourpick Venue (Map p109; ☎ 210 341 1410; www .venue-club.com; Pireos 130, Rouf; admission €10-15; ⏰ midnight-late Fri & Sat) Arguably the city's biggest dance club, this new venue puts on the biggest dance parties with the world's biggest DJs. It has a three-stage dance floor and an energetic crowd.

Letom (Map p109; ☎ 6992240000; Dekeleon 26, Gazi) Late-night clubbers flock to the dance parties at this trendy club in Gazi, with its giant mirrorball elephant, top line-up of international and local DJs, and gay-friendly, hip young crowd.

El Pecado (Map p109; ☎ 210 324 4049; Tournavitou 11, Psyrri; admission €10; ⏰ 9pm-late, closed Jun-Sep) This winter club has an almost theme-park party feel – they literally ring a church bell to fire up the 30-something crowd. It's a good bet if you want to dance the night away. In summer it moves beachside to Glyfada.

Villa Mercedes (Map p109; ☎ 210 342 2886; Tzaferi 11, cnr Andronikou; ⏰ from 9.30pm) For an ultraswanky evening you could have dinner at this unashamedly pretentious but undeniably chic club

and stay on for a cocktail and dance. The restaurant is well regarded and there's pleasant outdoor seating. Bookings recommended.

SUMMER CLUBS

Athens has some great open-air urban venues, but in summer much of the city's serious nightlife moves to glamorous, massive seafront clubs. Many clubs are on the tram route, which runs 24 hours on weekends. If you book for dinner you don't pay for entry; otherwise admission at most places can range from €10 to €20, and usually includes one drink. Glam up to ensure you get in the door.

Akrotiri (☎ 210 985 9147; Vasileos Georgiou B 5, Agios Kosmas; ⏰ 10pm-5am) One of the city's top beach clubs, this massive venue has a capacity for 3000, with bars, a restaurant and lounges over different levels. It hosts great party nights with top resident and visiting DJs, and pool parties during the day.

Balux (☎ 210 894 1620; Leoforos Poseidonos 58, Glyfada; ⏰ 10pm-late) This glamorous club right on the beach must be seen to be believed, with its poolside lounges and four-poster beds with flowing nets. There's a restaurant and a top line-up of local and guest DJs.

Vitrine (Map p116; ☎ 210 924 2444; Markou Mousourou 1, Mets; ⏰ 10pm-late) A firm favourite when it comes to downtown nightspots. The name of this venue may keep changing but the superb Acropolis and city views afforded from the top never do.

Bobayo (Map p116; ☎ 210 921 9397; Ardittou 1, Zappeio; ⏰ 10pm-late Tue-Sun) Formerly called On the Road because it's literally on a traffic island in the middle of two busy roads, this colourfully lit garden is a relaxed bar where you can sip cocktails, dine and dance.

If you're spruced up and happy to make the trek, head to the dreamy all-time classic summer club/restaurant **Island** (☎ 210 965 3563; Varkiza, 27th km, Athens-Sounion road), with superb island decor and a seaside location, or head 3km further along to the massive new summer home of Venue (left).

Sport

The 2004 Olympics left a legacy of world-class sports stadiums, and Athens has begun attracting some major international and European sporting and athletic events. The most popular sports are soccer and basket-

GAY & LESBIAN ATHENS

Athens' gay and lesbian scene has gained prominence in recent years, with a new breed of gay and gay-friendly clubs opening around town, predominantly in and around Gazi, Psyrri and Metaxourghio. The Athens Pride march, held in June, has been an annual event since 2005, with celebrations centred on Plateia Klafthmonos. Gazi has the closest thing to a gay village, but for the most part the gay scene is relatively low-key.

The best place to start the night in Gazi is **Blue Train** (Map p109; ☎ 210 346 0677; www.bluetrain .gr; Leoforos Konstantinoupoleos, Gazi), along the railway line, which has a club upstairs. **Sodade** (Map p109; ☎ 210 346 8657; www.sodade.gr; Triptolemou 10, Gazi) attracts a young clubbing crowd, while **BIG** (Map p109; ☎ 6946282845; Falesias 12, Gazi) is the hub of Athens' lively bear scene.

All-day hang-out **Magaze** (Map pp112-13; ☎ 210 324 3740; Eolou 33, Monastiraki) has Acropolis views from the pavement tables and becomes a lively bar after sunset.

Athens' more established gay bars and clubs are located around Makrygianni, including the veteran **Granazi** (Map p116; ☎ 210 924 4185; Lembesi 20, Makrygianni) and the busy, three-level **Lamda Club** (Map p116; ☎ 210 942 4202; Lembesi 15, cnr Leoforos Syngrou, Makrygianni).

The cafe-bar-restaurant **Mirovolos** (Map p109; ☎ 210 522 8806; Giatrakou 12, Metaxourghio) is a popular lesbian haunt.

Limanakia, below the rocky coves near Varkiza, is a popular gay beach. Take the tram or A2/E2 express bus to Glyfada, then take bus 115 or 116 to the Limnakia B stop.

Check out www.athensinfoguide.com/gay or the limited English information at www.gay.gr, or look for a copy of the *Greek Gay Guide* booklet at *periptera* (street kiosks) around town.

ball. Sports fans should contact local clubs or sporting bodies directly for match information, or check the English-language press or www.sportingreece.com.

SOCCER

Greece's top teams are Athens-based Panathinaikos and AEK, and Piraeus-based Olympiakos, all three of which are in the European Champions League.

Generally, tickets to major games can be bought on the day at the venue. Big games take place at the Olympic Stadium in Marousi and the Karaiskaki Stadium in Piraeus, the country's best soccer stadium. Information on Greek soccer and fixtures can be found on club websites or www.greeksoccer.com. Some match tickets can be bought online at www.tickethour.gr.

BASKETBALL

The biggest basketball games in Athens take place at the **Peace & Friendship Stadium** (Map p160; ☎ 210 489 3000; Ethnarhou Makariou) in Palio Faliro.

Basketball receives little prematch publicity, so you'll need to ask a local or check the website of the **Hellenic Basketball Association** (www.esa ke.gr).

ATHLETICS

The annual **Athens Marathon** (www.athensclassic marathon.gr) is held on the first Sunday in November and finishes at the historic marble Panathenaic Stadium (p126). More than 3000 runners from around the world tackle the 42km event, following the historic route run by Pheidippides in 490 BC from the battlefield at Marathon to Athens to deliver the news of victory against the Persians (before collapsing and dying from exhaustion).

SHOPPING

Downtown Athens is one big bustling shopping hub, with an eclectic mix of stores and specialist shopping strips. The main central shopping street is Ermou, the pedestrian mall lined with mainstream fashion stores running from Syntagma to Monastiraki.

Top-brand international designers and jewellers are located around Syntagma, from the Attica department store past pedestrian Voukourestiou to the fashion boutiques of Kolonaki. Plaka and Monastiraki are rife with souvenir stores and streetwear. The big department stores are found on Stadiou, stretching from Syntagma to Omonia. Kifisia and Glyfada also have excellent high-end shopping opportunities.

Flea Markets

Athens' traditional Monastiraki Flea Market (Map pp110–11) has a festive atmosphere. The permanent antiques, furniture and collectables stores have plenty to sift through and are open all week, while the streets around the station and Adrianou fill with vendors selling mostly jewellery, handicrafts and bric-a-brac.

The big Sunday Flea Market (Map p109) takes place at the end of Ermou, towards Gazi, where traders peddle their stuff from the crack of dawn and you can find some bargains, interesting collectables and kitsch delights among the junk. This is the place to test your haggling skills. It winds up around 2pm.

Speciality Foods

You can find a delectable array of food at the colourful central market (p144).

Mesogaia (Map pp110-11; ☎ 210 322 9146; cnr Nikis & Kydathineon, Plaka) This small shop boasts a wonderful array of the finest produce from around the country, including delicious cheeses, herbs, honey, jams, olive oil and wine.

To Pantopoleion (Map pp112-13; ☎ 210 323 4612; Sofokleous 1, Omonia) This expansive store sells traditional food products from all over Greece, from Santorini capers to boutique olive oils and Cretan rusks. There are jars of sweets and goodies for edible souvenirs, and a large range of Greek wines and spirits.

Traditional Handicrafts & Souvenirs

Amorgos (Map pp110-11; ☎ 210 324 3836; www.amorgosart .gr; Kodrou 3, Plaka; ☼ 11am-3pm & 6-8pm Mon-Fri, 11am-3pm Sat) This charming store is crammed with Greek folk art, trinkets, ceramics, embroidery and woodcarved furniture made by the owner, while his wife and daughter run the store.

Centre of Hellenic Tradition (Map pp110-11; ☎ 210 321 3023; Pandrosou 36, Plaka; ☼ 10am-7.30pm) Upstairs from the arcade are great examples of traditional ceramics, sculptures and handicrafts from all parts of Greece. There is also a great *ouzerie* and a gallery on the 1st floor.

Melissinos Art (Map pp110-11; ☎ 210 321 9247; www .melissinos-art.com; Agias Theklas 2, Psyrri; ☼ 10am-8pm Mon-Sat, 10am-6pm Sun) Artist Pantelis Melissinos continues the sandal-making tradition of his famous poet/sandal-maker father Stavros, whose past customers include the Beatles, Rudolph Nureyev, Sophia Loren and Jackie Onassis. It's the best place for authentic handmade leather sandals based on ancient Greek styles (€25 to €29); they can also be made to order.

Greece Is For Lovers (Map p116; ☎ 210 924 5064; www.greeceisforlovers.com; Karyatidon 13a, Makrygianni; ☼ 10am-6pm Mon-Fri, 11am-3pm Sat) A fun place for a cheeky designer play on the concept

of Greek kitsch, from Corinthian column dumb-bells to crocheted iPod covers and Aphrodite bust candles. Look for the giant Grecian sandal skateboard.

Music

Metropolis Music (Map pp112-13; ☎ 210 383 0804; Panepistimiou 64, Omonia) This major music store is well stocked with Greek and international CDs and has extensive specialist sections. There's a dedicated Greek music store a few doors down. Metropolis sells tickets to concerts around town.

Xylouris (Map pp112-13; ☎ 210 322 2711; www.xilouris .gr; arcade, Panepistimiou 39, Panepistimio) This music treasure trove is run by the son and widow of the Cretan legend Nikos Xylouris. Georgios is a font of music knowledge and can guide you through the comprehensive range of traditional and contemporary Greek music, including select and rare recordings, and eclectic world music. Traditional Greek music is also available from their specialist new store in the Museum of Greek Popular Instruments (p131).

GETTING THERE & AWAY

Air

Athens is served by **Eleftherios Venizelos International Airport** (Map p163; ☎ 210 353 0000; www .aia.gr) at Spata, 27km east of Athens.

The state-of-the-art airport, named in honour of the country's leading 20th-century politician, has all the standard facilities, great shopping and a transit hotel. If you have time to kill, it is worth visiting the small archaeological museum on the 1st floor above the check-in hall. The airport website has real-time flight information.

See p155 for information on public transport to/from the airport.

DOMESTIC FLIGHTS

The majority of domestic flights are operated by **Olympic Air** (Map p116; ☎ 801 144 444, 210 926 9111; www.olympicairlines.com; Leoforos Syngrou 96, Makrygianni). Olympic takes bookings online and also has branch offices at **Syntagma** (Map pp110-11; ☎ 210 926 4444; Filellinon 15) and **Omonia** (Map pp112-13; ☎ 210 926 7218; Kotopoulou 1).

Olympic Air has several daily flights to Thessaloniki, Iraklio, Mykonos, Santorini, Rhodes and all Greek airports. Average one-way fares range from €76 to €120, but vary dramatically depending on the season you're travelling, so check for specials and book in advance if you can.

Aegean Airlines (☎ reservations 801 112 0000, 210 626 1000; www.aegeanair.com) competes with Olympic on the most popular domestic routes. Aegean has the best early-bird specials and bookings can be made online. Aegean has daily flights to Thessaloniki, Iraklio, Rhodes, Mykonos, Santorini and Hania, as well as several flights weekly to key destinations around Greece. There's an office in **Syntagma** (Map pp110–11; ☎ 210 331 5522; Othonos 15).

Athens Airways (☎ 8018014000; www.athensairways .com) has daily flights to several destinations on the mainland and the islands, including Crete, Mykonos, Rhodes, Santorini, Chios and Zakynthos.

For more information, see also Island Hopping (p746).

INTERNATIONAL FLIGHTS

For information on international services from Athens, see p725.

Boat

Most ferry, hydrofoil and high-speed catamaran services to the islands leave from Athens' massive port at Piraeus (p158). Piraeus is the busiest port in Greece, with a bewildering array of departures and destinations, including daily services to all the island groups, except the Ionians and the Sporades. The departure points for ferry destinations are shown on Map p160.

There are also ferry and high-speed services for Evia and the Cyclades from the smaller ports at Rafina (p164) and Lavrio (p164).

You can check the daily schedules in the *International Herald Tribune* or search and buy tickets online. For contact details see the Getting There & Away sections for each island; for specific information about services see Island Hopping (p743).

Note that there are two departure points for Crete at Piraeus port. Ferries for Iraklio leave from the western end of Akti Kondyli, but ferries for other Cretan ports occasionally dock there as well. Ferries for Rethymno leave from Akti Miaouli, so check where to find your boat when you buy your ticket.

Most hydrofoil and high-speed catamaran services from Piraeus to the Saronic Gulf Islands, the Peloponnese and a growing range of destinations in the Cyclades are run by **Hellenic Seaways** (Map p160; ☎ 210

419 9000; www.hellenicseaways.gr; cnr Akti Kondyli & Elotikou, Great Harbour). Other operators include **Aegean Speedlines** (☎ 210 969 0950; www.aegeansp eedlines.gr).

For information contact the **Piraeus Port Authority** (☎ 1441; www.olp.gr).

TICKETS

Agents selling ferry tickets are thick on the ground around Plateia Karaïskaki in Piraeus and at the Rafina and Lavrio ports. You can also normally purchase tickets at ticket booths located on the quay, next to each ferry. Contrary to what some agents might tell you, it costs no more to buy tickets at the boat.

Bus

Athens has two intercity (IC) KTEL bus terminals. Terminal A, 7km northwest of Omonia, has departures to the Peloponnese, the Ionians and western Greece. Terminal B, 5km north of Omonia, caters to central and northern Greece, and to Evia. The EOT office (p107) has IC bus schedules.

TERMINAL A

Terminal A (off Map p108; ☎ 210 512 4910; Kifisou 100) is not a good introduction to Athens – particularly if you arrive after midnight when there is no public transport. See p155 for details of fares, and p117 for information on taxi rip-offs. From the terminal, bus 051 goes to central Athens (junction of Zinonos and Menandrou, near Omonia) every 15 minutes from 5am to midnight. A taxi to Syntagma should cost no more than €8.

TERMINAL B

Terminal B (off Map p108; (☎ 210 831 7153; Liosion 260, Kato Patisia) is less chaotic and much easier to handle than Terminal A, although again there is no public transport from midnight to 5am. The terminal is on Gousiou, a side street off Liosion 260. Take bus 024 from outside the main gate of the National Gardens (Map pp110–11) on Leoforos Vasilissis Amalias and ask to get off at Praktoria KTEL. A taxi from Syntagma should cost no more than €8.

MAVROMATEON TERMINAL

Buses for destinations in southern Attica leave from the **Mavromateon terminal** (Map p108; ☎ 210 880 8000; cnr Leoforos Alexandras & 28 Oktovriou-Patision, Pedion Areos), about 250m north of the National

Archaeological Museum. Buses to Rafina, Lavrio and Marathon leave from the northern section of the Mavromateon terminal (just 150m to the north).

Car & Motorcycle

Getting in and out of Athens is now significantly easier thanks to the new Attiki Odos (Attiki Rd) and the upgraded National Rd (Ethniki Odos), as well as various ring roads around the city.

The top end of Leoforos Syngrou, near the Temple of Olympian Zeus, is lined with car-rental firms. Local companies tend to offer better deals than the multinationals, so it pays to do the rounds to get the best price. The average price you can expect to pay for a small car for a day is €50, much less for three or more days.

Athens Airport Car Rentals (☎ 210 965 2590; www .athensairport-car-rentals.com; Spata; from €33)

Avis (Map p116; ☎ 210 322 4951; Leoforos Vasilissis Amalias 48, Makrygianni; per day from €46)

Budget (Map p116; ☎ 210 921 4771; Leoforos Syngrou 8, Makrygianni; per day from €40)

Europcar (Map p116; ☎ 210 924 8810; Leoforos Syngrou 43, Makrygianni; per day from €45)

Hertz (Map p116; ☎ 210 922 0102; Leoforos Syngrou 12, Makrygianni; per day from €90)

Kosmos (Map p116; ☎ 210 923 4695; www.kosmos -carrental.com; Leoforos Syngrou 9; per day from €42)

You can rent mopeds and motorcycles if you have a licence and the steely nerves required to take on Athens' traffic. **Motorent** (Map p116; ☎ 210 923 4939; www.motorent.gr; Rovertou Galli 1, Makrygianni) has a choice of machines from 50cc to 250cc (high-season prices start at €15.50 per day).

Train

Intercity trains to central and northern Greece depart from the central Larisis train station (Map p108), located about 1km northwest of Plateia Omonias (metro line 2). See p728 for information on international train services.

KEY BUS SERVICES FROM ATHENS

Key Bus Destinations from Terminal A

Destination	Duration	Fare	Frequency
Corfu*	9½hr	€47.50	3 daily
Epidavros	2½hr	€10.60	2 daily
Igoumenitsa	7½hr	€40.40	4 daily
Kalavryta	3hr	€15.10	2 daily
Lefkada	5½hr	€30.50	4 daily
Nafplio	2½hr	€11.80	hourly
Olympia	5½hr	€26.90	2 daily
Patra	3hr	€17	half-hourly
Zakynthos*	6hr	€30.70	4 daily

*includes ferry ticket

Key Bus Destinations from Terminal B

Destination	Duration	Fare	Frequency
Agios Konstantinos	2½hr	€14.70	hourly
Delphi	3hr	€13.60	6 daily
Halkida	1¼hr	€6.20	half-hourly
Karpenisi	4½hr	€22.50	3 daily
Paralia Kymis	4½hr	€13.80	2 daily
Trikala	4½hr	€24	8 daily
Volos	4½hr	€24.70	12 daily

Key Bus Services from Mavromateon Terminal

Destination	Duration	Fare	Frequency
Cape Sounion (coastal road)	1½hr	€5.20	hourly
Lavrio port	1½hr	€4.40	half-hourly
Marathon	1¼hr	€3.40	hourly
Rafina port	1hr	€2.20	half-hourly

For the Peloponnese, take the suburban rail to Kiato and change for other OSE services there. A new rail hub (SKA) is going to be located about 20km north of the city.

OSE (☎ 1110; www.ose.gr; ☺ 24hr) offices at **Omonia** (Map pp112-13; ☎ 210 529 7005; Karolou 1; ☺ 8am-3pm Mon-Fri) and **Syntagma** (Map pp112-13; ☎ 210 362 4405; Sina 6; ☺ 8am-3pm Mon-Sat) handle advance bookings.

GETTING AROUND
To/From the Airport
Getting to and from the airport has never been easier or faster since the metro and suburban rail began operating. The cheapest alternative is the bus, though it takes longer. You can also opt to take the suburban train to Piraeus.

BUS
Express buses operate 24 hours between the airport and the city centre, Piraeus and KTEL bus terminals.

Bus X92 operates between the airport and the suburb of Kifisia (about 45 minutes), departing every 45 minutes to one hour all day.

Bus X93 operates between the airport and the Terminal B (Kifisos) bus station (about 60 minutes), departing every 30 minutes all day.

Bus X94 operates between the airport and Ethniki Amyna metro station (about 25 minutes), departing every 10 minutes from 7.30am to 11.30pm.

Bus X95 operates 24 hours between the airport and Syntagma, departing every 30 minutes. The journey takes about an hour, depending on traffic. The Syntagma bus stop is on Othonos.

Bus X96 runs 24 hours between the airport and Plateia Karaïskaki in Piraeus (90 minutes), with services every 20 minutes.

Bus X97 operates between the airport and Dafni metro station (about one hour), departing every 30 minutes all day.

Tickets (€3.20) are not valid for other forms of public transport.

METRO
The metro airport service from Monastiraki is not express, so you can pick it up at any station along line 3. Just check that it is the airport train (displayed on the train and platform screen). Otherwise you can take any train to the Doukissis Plakentias metro station, where you can connect to the airport train.

Trains run every 30 minutes, leaving Monastiraki between 5.50am and midnight, and the airport between 5.30am and 11.30pm.

The metro airport ticket costs €6 per adult one way or €10 return (but the return is only valid for 48 hours). Note that the fare for two or more passengers works out at €5 each, so purchase tickets together (this is also the case with the suburban rail). The airport ticket is valid for all forms of public transport for 90 minutes. If you are still in transit before the 90 minutes is up, revalidate your ticket on the final mode of transport to show you are still on the same journey.

SUBURBAN RAIL
You can take the suburban rail from the central Athens (Larisis) station then change trains for the airport at Ano Liosia, or from Nerantziotissa, on the metro line 1 (connection from Doukissis Plakentias metro station). Trains to the airport run from 6am to midnight, while trains from the airport to Athens run from 5.30am to 11.30pm. The trip takes 38 minutes and trains run every 15 minutes from Nerantziotissa. The suburban rail has the same pricing as the metro but the return ticket is valid for a month.

Suburban rail services also go from the airport to Piraeus (change trains at Nerantziotissa) and Kiato in the Peloponnese (via Corinth).

TAXI
Unfortunately, catching a taxi from the airport can often involve an argument about the fare (see p117 for the full rundown).

Check that the meter is set to the correct tariff. You will also have to pay a €3.40 airport surcharge and a €2.70 toll for using the toll road, as well as €0.35 for each piece of luggage over 10kg. Fares vary depending on traffic, but expect to pay from €25 to €30 from the airport to the city centre, and €30 to Piraeus. Most drivers will add the tip, so it can be worth checking the breakdown before adding any extra. Both trips should take no longer than an hour. If you have any problems, do not hesitate to threaten to involve the police.

TRAINS FOR PELOPONNESE

Destination	Duration	Fare	Frequency
Corinth (suburban rail)	1hr 20min	€6	13 daily
Kiato (suburban rail)	1hr 40min	€8	13 daily
Kiato-Diakofto*	1¾hr	€4.90	2 daily
Kiato-Diakofto (IC)	2½hr	€4.40	2 daily
Diakofto-Kalavryta*	1hr 5min	€9.50	3-5 daily
Kiato-Patra	2hr	€6.90	5 daily
Kiato-Patra (IC)	1hr 40min	€6.90	4 daily
Kiato-Pyrgos (IC)	3hr 20min	€11	3 daily
Pyrgos-Olympia	30min	€1	2 daily

*from Kiato, you can change to slow or intercity (IC) services

TRAINS FOR NORTHERN GREECE & EVIA

Destination	Duration	Fare	Frequency
Alexandroupoli	12hr 20min	€49	2 daily
Alexandroupoli (IC)	10hr 5min	€71	2 daily
Halkida	1½hr	€5	17 daily
Thessaloniki	6hr	€28	5 daily
Thessaloniki (IC)	5hr	€36	4 daily
Thessaloniki (IC Express)	4hr 20min	€48	2 daily
Volos (IC)	4hr 40min	€28.20	1 daily

Car & Motorcycle

While the metro, the Attiki Odos and a new network of ring roads have helped ease Athens' notorious traffic congestion, it can still be a nightmarish city to drive in. Heavy traffic, confusing signposting, impatient drivers and one-way streets in the city centre make driving a challenge.

Drivers have a cavalier attitude towards road laws and parking restrictions. Athens' kerbs and car parks are insufficient for the number of cars in the city (more than two million in Attica), prompting Athenians to develop ruthless and creative parking techniques. Contrary to what you will see, parking is actually illegal alongside kerbs marked with yellow lines, on pavements and in pedestrian malls. There are now paid parking areas, with tickets available from kiosks.

For details of rental agencies in Athens, see p154.

Public Transport

Athens has an extensive and inexpensive integrated public transport network of buses, metro, trolleybuses and tram.

Athens Urban Transport Organisation (OASA; ☎ 185; www.oasa.gr; Metsovou 15, Exarhia/Mouseio; ⏰ 6.30am-11.30pm Mon-Fri, 7.30am-10.30pm Sat & Sun) can assist with most inquiries. Transport maps can be downloaded from its website and are also available at the airport, at train stations and from the organisation's head office near the National Archaeological Museum.

A €1 ticket can be used on the entire Athens urban transport network, including the suburban rail (except airport services), and is valid for 90 minutes. There is also a daily €3 ticket valid for 24 hours, and a weekly €10 ticket with the same restrictions on airport travel. There's also a new €15 tourist ticket (see the boxed text, p158).

Children under six travel free. People under 18 and over 65 travel at half-fare.

Plain-clothed inspectors make spot checks and issue on-the-spot fines to passengers travelling without a validated ticket. Penalties average €30 to €72 or up to 60 times the ticket price.

BUS & TROLLEYBUS

Blue-and-white local express buses, regular buses and electric trolleybuses operate every 15 minutes from 5am until midnight. Buses run 24 hours between the centre and Piraeus – every 20 minutes from 6am until midnight and hourly at other times. The free OASA map shows most of the routes.

Tickets for buses and trolleybuses (€1) can be purchased at transport kiosks or

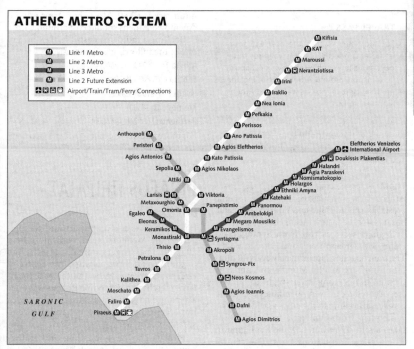

ATHENS METRO SYSTEM

Legend:
- Line 1 Metro
- Line 2 Metro
- Line 3 Metro
- Line 2 Future Extension
- Airport/Train/Tram/Ferry Connections

Kifisia
KAT
Maroussi
Nerantziotissa
Irini
Iraklio
Nea Ionia
Pefkakia
Perissos
Anthoupoli
Ano Patissia
Peristeri
Agios Eleftherios
Eleftherios Venizelos International Airport
Agios Antonios
Kato Patissia
Doukissis Plakentias
Sepolia
Agios Nikolaos
Halandri
Agia Paraskevi
Attiki
Nomismatokopio
Holargos
Larisis
Viktoria
Ethniki Amyna
Metaxourghio
Katehaki
Panepistimio
Panormou
Egaleo
Omonia
Ambelokipi
Eleonas
Megaro Mousikis
Keramikos
Evangelismos
Monastiraki
Syntagma
Thisio
Akropoli
Petralona
Syngrou-Fix
Tavros
Neos Kosmos
Kalithea
Agios Ioannis
Moschato
Faliro
Dafni
SARONIC GULF
Piraeus
Agios Dimitrios

most *periptera* (street kiosks) and must be validated on board.

METRO

The expanding and efficient **metro** (www.ametro. gr) system has transformed travel around central Athens, making it quick and easy to get around. The stations are an attraction in their own right, displaying finds from the excavation works and contemporary art. Trains and stations can be stifling in summer as limited (or no) air-conditioning was installed. All have wheelchair access.

Tickets must be validated at the machines at platform entrances. Trains operate between 5am and just after midnight. They run every three minutes during peak periods, dropping to every 10 minutes at other times.

Line 1 (Green)

The old Kifisia–Piraeus line has transfer stations at Omonia and Attiki for line 2; Monastiraki is the transfer station for line 3. Nerantziotissa connects with the suburban rail. The hourly all-night bus service (bus 500) follows this route, with bus stops located outside the train stations.

Line 2 (Red)

Line 2 runs from Agios Antonios in the northwest to Agios Dimitrios in the southeast (check the boards so you don't confuse your saints). Attiki and Omonia connect with line 1, while Syntagma connects with line 3.

Line 3 (Blue)

Line 3 runs northeast from Egaleo to Doukissis Plakentias, with the airport train continuing from there. Monastiraki is the transfer station for line 1 and Syntagma is the transfer station for line 2.

SUBURBAN RAIL

A fast and comfortable **suburban rail** (☎ 1110; www.trainose.com; 24hr) connects Athens with the airport, Piraeus, the outer regions and the northern Peloponnese. It connects to the metro at Larisis, Doukissis Plakentias and Nerantziotissa stations, and spans from the airport to Kiato (1¾ hours, €10). The

> **TRAVEL PASS**
>
> For short-stay visitors, the new €15 tourist ticket is good value. It is valid for three days and allows unlimited travel on all public transport around Athens, including the metro airport service, as well as the Athens Sightseeing bus.

network will eventually span 281km, connecting Athens to Thiva, Lavrio, Rafina and Halkida.

TRAM

Athens' **tram** (www.tramsa.gr) makes for a scenic coastal journey to Faliro and Voula, via Glyfada, but it is not the fastest means of transport.

Regular services run from Syntagma to Faliro, Syntagma to Voula and Faliro to Voula. The tram operates approximately every 10 minutes from 5am to 1am Monday to Thursday, then 24 hours from Friday night to Sunday (services reduce to every 40 minutes), servicing revellers travelling to the city's seaside clubs.

The trip from Syntagma to Faliro (SEF) takes about 45 minutes, while Syntagma to Voula takes around one hour. The central terminus is on Leoforos Vasilissis Amalias, opposite the National Gardens. There are ticket vending machines on platforms.

A tram extension to Piraeus is expected to be completed in 2010.

Taxi

If you see an Athenian standing on the road bellowing and waving their arms, chances are they are trying to get a taxi at rush hour. Despite the large number of yellow taxis on the streets, it can be tricky getting one.

Hailing a taxi often involves standing on the pavement and shouting your destination. If a taxi is going your way the driver may stop even if there are already passengers inside. The fare is not shared: each person is charged the fare on the meter (note where it is at when you get in).

Make sure the meter is switched on when you get in. The flag fall is €1.05, with a €0.95 surcharge from ports and train and bus stations, and a €3.40 surcharge from the airport. After that, the day rate (tariff 1 on the meter) is €0.60 per kilometre. The night rate (tariff 2 on the meter) increases to €1.05 per kilometre between midnight and 5am. Baggage is charged at a rate of €0.35 per item over 10kg. The minimum fare is €2.80. Most short trips around downtown Athens should cost around €4.

Booking a radio taxi costs €1.70 extra. Try one of the following companies:

Athina 1 (☎ 210 921 2800)
Enotita (☎ 801 115 1000)
Ikaros (☎ 210 515 2800)
Kosmos (☎ 18300)
Parthenon (☎ 210 532 3000)

For more information about Athens' taxi drivers, see p117.

PIRAEUS ΠΕΙΡΑΙΑΣ

pop 175,697

Piraeus is Greece's main port and the biggest in the Mediterranean, with more than 20 million passengers annually. It is the hub of the Aegean ferry network, the centre of Greece's maritime trade and the base for its large merchant navy. While Piraeus was once a separate city, nowadays it virtually melds imperceptibly into the expanded urban sprawl of Athens.

Piraeus can be as bustling and traffic-congested as Athens. Its waterfront was tarted up before the Olympics, creating a tree-lined promenade along the ancient walls surrounding the harbour.

Central Piraeus is not a place where many visitors linger; most come only to catch a ferry from the intimidating expanse of terminals. Beyond its facade of smart new shipping offices, banks and grand public buildings, much of Piraeus is an interesting hotchpotch of rejuvenated pedestrian precincts, shopping strips, restaurants and cafes, and more grungy industrial and run-down areas.

The most attractive part is the eastern quarter around Zea Marina, and the lovely, albeit touristy, Mikrolimano harbour, lined with restaurants, bars and nightclubs. The charming residential neighbourhood of Kastella, on the hill above Mikrolimano, and the swanky seaview apartment blocks around Freatida are where the money is.

HISTORY

Piraeus has been the port of Athens since classical times, when Themistocles transferred his Athenian fleet from the exposed port of Phaleron (modern Faliro) to the security of

Piraeus. After his victory over the Persians at the Battle of Salamis in 480 BC, Themistocles fortified Piraeus' three natural harbours. In 445 BC Pericles extended these fortifying walls to Athens and Phaleron. The Long Walls, as they were known, were destroyed as one of the peace conditions imposed by the Spartans at the end of the Peloponnesian Wars, but were rebuilt in 394 BC.

Piraeus was a flourishing commercial centre during the classical age, but by Roman times it had been overtaken by Rhodes, Delos and Alexandria. During medieval and Turkish times, Piraeus diminished into a tiny fishing village, and by the time Greece became independent it was home to fewer than 20 people.

Its resurgence began in 1834 when Athens became the capital of independent Greece, and by the beginning of the 20th century it had superseded the island of Syros as Greece's principal port. In 1923 its population swelled with the arrival of 100,000 Greek refugees from Turkey. The Piraeus that evolved from this influx had a seedy but somewhat romantic appeal with its bordellos, hashish dens and *rembetika* music – as vividly portrayed in the film *Never on a Sunday* (1960).

ORIENTATION

Piraeus is 10km southwest of central Athens. The largest of its three harbours is the Great Harbour on the western side of the Piraeus peninsula, which is the departure point for all ferry, hydrofoil and catamaran services. Zea Marina and the picturesque Mikrolimano, on the eastern side, are for private yachts.

The metro and train lines from Athens terminate at the northeastern corner of the Great Harbour on Akti Kalimassioti. Most ferry departure points are a short walk over the new footbridge from here. A left turn out of the metro station leads after 250m to Plateia Karaïskaki, the terminus for buses to the airport. A block to the right is the suburban rail station.

INFORMATION

There are lots of places to change money along the Great Harbour, as well as plenty of ATMs. There are luggage lockers at the metro station (€3 for 24 hours). There is a free wi-fi hot spot around the port.

Bits & Bytes Internet (☎ 210 412 1615; Iroon Polytehniou 2; per hr €3; ☾ 8am-10pm)

Emporiki Bank (cnr Antistaseos & Makras Stoas) Has a 24-hour automatic exchange machine.

National Bank of Greece (cnr Antistaseos & Tsamadou) Near Emporiki Bank.

Post office (cnr Tsamadou & Filonos; ☾ 7.30am-8pm Mon-Fri, 7.30am-2pm Sat)

SIGHTS

The **Piraeus Archaeological Museum** (☎ 210 452 1598; Harilaou Trikoupi 31; adult/concession €3/2; ☾ 8.30am-8pm Tue-Sun, 2-8pm Mon, closes 3pm in winter) contains some important finds from classical and Roman times. These include some fine tomb reliefs dating from the 4th to 2nd centuries BC. The star attraction is the magnificent statue of Apollo, the *Piraeus Kouros*, the oldest larger-than-life, hollow bronze statue yet found. It dates from about 520 BC and was discovered in Piraeus, buried in rubble, in 1959.

The **Hellenic Maritime Museum** (☎ 210 451 6264; Akti Themistokleous, Plateia Freatidas, Zea Marina; adult/concession €3/1.50; ☾ 9am-2pm) brings Greece's maritime history to life, with models of ancient and modern ships, seascapes by leading 19th- and 20th-century Greek painters, guns, flags and maps, as well as part of a submarine on the museum grounds.

There is also a small **Museum of the Electric Railway** (☎ 210 414 7552; admission free; ☾ 9am-2pm & 5-8pm) in the metro station at the end of the platform.

SLEEPING

If you're catching an early ferry or don't want to stay downtown, there are hotels around the Great Harbour, but many are shabby and aimed more towards accommodating sailors and clandestine liaisons than tourists. The better hotels are geared for the business market. Don't attempt to sleep out – Piraeus is probably one of the most dangerous places in Greece to do so.

Pireaus Dream Hotel (☎ 210 411 0555; www .pireausdreamhotel.com; Filonos 79-81; s/d/tr incl breakfast €45/55/65; ☒ ☐) With quiet rooms starting on the 4th floor, this renovated hotel about 500m from the station has good facilities, including laptop and PlayStation rental, and serves a big American breakfast.

Hotel Triton (☎ 210 417 3457; www.htriton.gr; Tsamadou 8; s/d/tr incl breakfast €55/70/80; ☒ ☐) This refurbished hotel with sleek executive-style rooms is a treat compared to the usual run-down joints in Piraeus. Some rooms overlook the colourful market square.

ATHENS & ATTICA

PIRAEUS

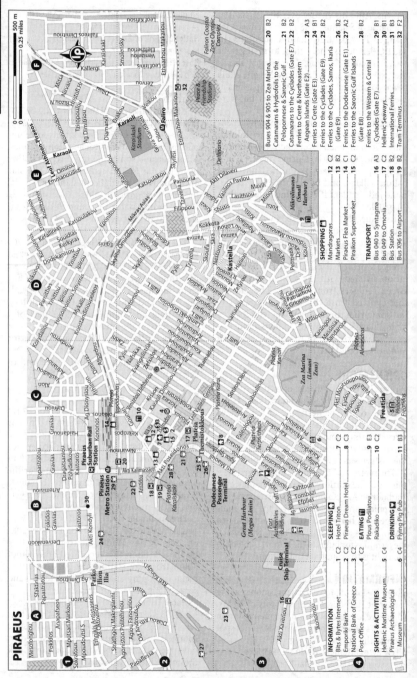

INFORMATION	
Bits & Bytes Internet.................1	C2
Emporiki Bank........................2	C2
National Bank of Greece...........3	C2
Post Office............................4	C2

SIGHTS & ACTIVITIES	
Hellenic Maritime Museum.........5	C4
Piraeus Archaeological	
Museum.............................6	C4

SLEEPING	
Hotel Triton..........................7	C2
Piraeus Dream Hotel................8	C3

EATING	
Plous Podilatou.....................9	E3
Rakadiko.............................10	C2

DRINKING	
Flying Pig Pub......................11	B3

SHOPPING	
Mandragoras.......................12	C2
Markets..............................13	B2
Piraeus Flea Market...............14	C1
Piraikon Supermarket.............15	C2

TRANSPORT	
Bus 040 to Syntagma.............16	A3
Bus 049 to Omonia................17	C2
Bus Station.........................18	B2
Bus X96 to Airport.................19	B2
Buses 904 & 905 to Zea Marina...20	B2
Catamarans & Hydrofoils to the	
Peloponnese & Saronic Gulf......21	B2
Catamarans to the Cyclades (Gate E7)...22	B2
Ferries to Crete & Northeastern	
Aegean Islands (Gate E2)........23	A3
Ferries to Crete (Gate E3).......24	B1
Ferries to the Cyclades (Gate E9)...25	B2
Ferries to the Cyclades, Samos, Ikaria	
(Gate E9)...........................26	B2
Ferries to the Dodecanese (Gate E1)...27	A2
Ferries to the Saronic Gulf Islands	
(Gate E8)...........................28	B2
Ferries to the Western & Central	
Cyclades (Gate E7)................29	B1
Hellenic Seaways..................30	B1
International Ferries...............31	B3
Tram Terminus.....................32	F2

EATING & DRINKING

The waterfront around the Great Harbour is lined with cafes, restaurants and fast-food places, but the better restaurants are in the backstreets or further afield at the Mikrolimano harbour and Zea Marina, as well as along the waterfront promenade at Freatida.

Rakadiko (☎ 210 417 8470; Stoa Kouvelou, Karaoli Dimitriou 5; mezedhes €4-10; ☿ 11am-midnight Tue Sun) Down this arcade you are transported to a village square of bygone days. The menu has mezedhes from all over Greece, produce is brought in daily from Crete and the two cooks from Ikaria are always looking out for interesting recipes from the islands. There is live *rembetika* music on Friday and Saturday nights and also on Sunday afternoons.

Plous Podilatou (☎ 210 413 7910; www.plous -podilatou.gr; Akti Koumoundourou 42; mains €12-20) Dining by the Mikrolimano harbour is a delight, and the food at this slick, modern restaurant will not disappoint. The year-round sibling of pioneering Nuevo-Greek restaurant Kitrino Podilato has a Mediterranean menu, with an emphasis on well-prepared fresh fish and seafood.

Flying Pig Pub (☎ 210 429 5344; Filonos 31; ☿ 9am-1am) Run by a friendly Greek-Australian, the Flying Pig Pub is a popular bar with a large range of beers. The Pig also serves decent food, including a very generous English breakfast.

SHOPPING

Piraeus is a large commercial centre with excellent shopping, concentrated around the pedestrian strip along Sotiros Dios.

Piraeus Flea Market (cnr Alipedou & Skylitsi Omiridou; ☿ 7am-4pm Sun) This bustling Sunday market rivals its famous counterpart in Athens, with stalls flogging almost anything and nearby stores selling jewellery, ceramics and antiques. The market is near Plateia Ippodamias, behind the metro station. Antique hunters are better off scouring the stores in the streets around the market.

Mandragoras (☎ 210 417 2961; Gounari 14; ☿ 8am-4pm Mon, Wed & Sat, 8am-8pm Tue, Thu & Fri) In the heart of the central food market, this is a superb delicatessen with a fine selection of gourmet delights, from cheeses and ready-made mezedhes to spices, olive oils and preserved foods to take home.

You can also stock up on supplies before a ferry trip, in the area just inland from Akti Poseidonos. The **markets** (☿ 6am-4pm Mon-Fri) are on Dimosthenous, or try **Piraikon Supermarket** (Ippokratous 1; ☿ 8am-8pm Mon-Fri, 8am-4pm Sat) opposite the markets.

GETTING THERE & AWAY
Bus

Buses 040 and 049 run 24 hours between Piraeus and central Athens; they run every 20 minutes from 6am until midnight and then hourly. Bus 040 runs between Akti Xaveriou in Piraeus and Filellinon in Athens. Bus 049 runs between Plateia Themistokleous in Piraeus and Omonia in Athens.

The X96 Piraeus–Athens Airport Express bus leaves from the southwestern corner of Plateia Karaïskaki.

See p153 for information on bus services to the rest of Greece.

Metro & Suburban Rail

The metro is the fastest and easiest way to get from Piraeus to central Athens. The station is at the northern end of Akti Kalimassioti. Travellers should take extra care as the section between Piraeus and Monastiraki is notorious for pickpockets.

Piraeus is also connected to the suburban rail, whose terminus is located opposite the metro station. To get to the airport or the Peloponnese, change trains at Nerantziotissa.

GETTING AROUND

The port is massive and a free bus between the ferry terminal gates and passenger terminals runs regularly from the metro station.

Piraeus has its own network of buses. The services likely to interest travellers are buses 904 and 905 between Zea Marina and the metro station.

ATTICA ATTIKH

Greater Athens and Piraeus account for the bulk of the population of the prefecture of Attica. The plain of Attica is an agricultural and wine-growing region, with several large population centres. It has some fine beaches, particularly along the Apollo Coast and at Shinias, near Marathon.

Until the 7th century, Attica was home to a number of smaller kingdoms, such as those at Eleusis (Elefsina), Ramnous and Brauron

(Vravrona). The remains of these cities continue to be among the region's main attractions, although they pale alongside the superb Temple of Poseidon at Cape Sounion.

Many of these places can be reached by regular city buses; others can be reached by KTEL services from the Mavromateon bus terminal (p153).

CAPE SOUNION ΑΚΡΩΤΗΡΙΟ ΣΟΥΝΙΟ
Temple of Poseidon Ναός του Ποσειδώνα

The ancient Greeks knew how to choose a site for a temple. Nowhere is this more evident than at Cape Sounion, 70km south of Athens, where the **Temple of Poseidon** (☎ 22920 39363; adult/concession €4/2; ☒ 8am-8pm) stands on a craggy spur that plunges 65m down into the sea. Built in 444 BC at the same time as the Parthenon, it is constructed of local marble from Agrilesa and its slender columns – of which 16 remain – are Doric. It is thought that the temple was built by Iktinos, the architect of the Temple of Hephaestus in Athens' Ancient Agora.

The temple looks gleaming white when viewed from the sea and is discernible from a long distance. It gave great comfort to sailors in ancient times; they knew they were nearly home when they saw it. The views from the temple are equally impressive. On a clear day you can see Kea, Kythnos and Serifos to the southeast, and Aegina and the Peloponnese to the west. The site also contains scanty remains of a propylaeum, a fortified tower and, to the northeast, a 6th-century temple to Athena.

Try to visit early in the morning before the tourist buses arrive – or head there for the sunset – if you wish to indulge the sentiments of Byron's lines from *Don Juan*: 'Place me on Sunium's marbled steep, Where nothing save the waves and I, May hear our mutual murmurs sweep…'. Byron was so taken by Sounion that he carved his name on one of the columns – sadly many others have followed suit.

There are a couple of tavernas just below the site if you want to combine a visit with lunch and a swim.

You can take either the inland or the more scenic coastal bus to Cape Sounion from Athens. Coastal buses (€5.70, 1½ hours) leave Athens hourly, on the half-hour, from the Mavromateon bus terminal. These buses also stop on Filellinon, on the corner of

Xenofontos, 10 minutes later, but by this time they're usually very crowded.

ELEFSINA (ELEUSIS) ΕΛΕΥΣΙΝΑ

The ruins of **Ancient Eleusis** (☎ 210 554 6019; adult/concession €3/2; ☒ 8.30am-3pm Tue-Sun) lie surrounded by oil refineries and factories beside the industrial town of Elefsina, 22km west of Athens.

It's hard to imagine Eleusis in ancient times, but nestled on the slopes of a low hill close to the shore of the Saronic Gulf, it was built around the **Sanctuary of Demeter**. The site dates back to Mycenaean times, when the cult of Demeter, one of the most important cults in ancient Greece, began. By classical times it was celebrated with a huge annual festival, which attracted thousands of pilgrims wanting to be initiated into the Eleusinian mysteries. They walked in procession from the Acropolis to Eleusis along the Sacred Way, which was lined with statues and votive monuments. Initiates were sworn to secrecy on punishment of death, and during the 1400 years that the sanctuary functioned, its secrets were never divulged. It was closed by the Roman emperor Theodosius in the 4th century AD.

The site's **museum** helps make some sense of the scattered ruins, with models of the old city.

From Athens, take bus A16 or B16 from Plateia Eleftherias (Koumoundourou), north of Monastiraki. Buses run every 20 minutes and take about 30 minutes in reasonable traffic.

MARATHON & AROUND
Marathon Μαραθώνας

The plain surrounding the unremarkable, small town of Marathon, 42km northeast of Athens, is the site of one of the most celebrated battles in world history. In 490 BC an army of 9000 Greeks and 1000 Plataeans defeated the 25,000-strong Persian army, proving that the Persians were not invincible. The Greeks were indebted to the ingenious tactics of Miltiades, who altered the conventional battle formation so that there were fewer soldiers in the centre, but more in the wings. This lulled the Persians into thinking that the Greeks were going to be a pushover. They broke through in the centre but were then ambushed by the soldiers in the wings. At the end of the day, 6000 Persians and only 192 Greeks lay dead. The story goes that after the battle a runner was sent to Athens to announce the victory.

After shouting *'Enikesame!'* ('We won!') he collapsed and died. This is the origin of today's marathon race.

Four kilometres before the town of Marathon, 350m from the Athens–Marathon road, is the 10m-high tumulus or burial mound that is the **Marathon tomb** (☎ 22940 55462; site & museum €3; ⏰ 8.30am-3pm Tue-Sun Jun-Oct). In ancient Greece, the bodies of those who died in battle were returned to their families for private burial, but as a sign of honour the 192 men who fell at Marathon were cremated and buried in this collective tomb. The site has a model of the battle and historical information.

Nearer to the town is the excellent Marathon **museum** (☎ 22940 55155; admission incl site €3; ⏰ 8.30am-3pm), which has local dis-coveries from various periods, including Neolithic pottery from the Cave of Pan and finds from the Tomb of the Athenians. New finds from the area include several well-preserved, larger-than-life statues from an Egyptian sanctuary. Next to the museum is one of the area's prehistoric grave circle sites, which has been preserved under a hangarlike shelter, with raised platforms and walkways. There is another hangar containing an early Helladic cemetery site on the way to the museum.

About 8km west of Marathon is **Lake Marathon**, a massive dam that was Athens' sole source of water until 1956. The dam wall, completed in 1926, is faced with the famous Pentelic marble that was used to build the Parthenon.

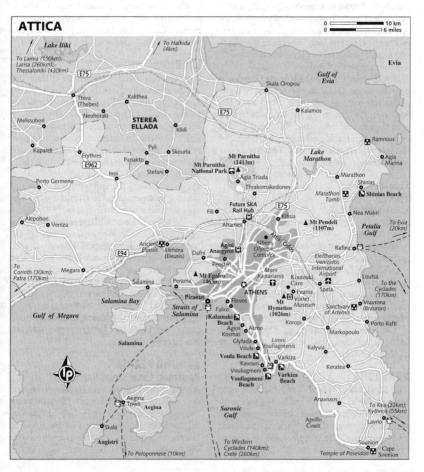

It's an awesome sight, standing over 50m high and stretching for more than 300m.

Hourly (half-hourly in the afternoon) buses depart from Athens' Mavromateon terminal to Marathon (€3.40, 1¼ hours). The tomb and the museum are within a short walking distance of bus stops (tell the driver where you want to get off). There are no bus services to Lake Marathon.

Ramnous Ραμνούς

The ruins of the Ramnous **ancient port** (☎ 22940 63477; admission €2; ☼ 8.30am-3pm) are about 10km northeast of Marathon. It's an evocative, overgrown and secluded site, standing on a picturesque plateau overlooking the sea. Among the ruins are the remains of the Doric **Temple of Nemesis** (435 BC), which once contained a huge statue of the goddess. Nemesis was the goddess of retribution and mother of Helen of Troy. There are also ruins of a smaller 6th-century temple dedicated to Themis, goddess of justice.

Another section of the site leads 1km down a picturesque track to the relatively well-preserved fortress on the clifftop near the sea, with the remains of the city, a temple, a gymnasium and a theatre. Ramnous is well off the beaten track, and consequently one of the least spoilt ancient sites. You need your own transport to get here.

Shinias Σχοινιάς

The long, sandy, pine-fringed beach at Shinias, southeast of Marathon, is the best in this part of Attica and very popular at weekends.

Ramnous Camping (☎ 22940 55855; www.ramnous .gr; Leoforos Marathonas 174, Nea Makri; camp sites per adult/ tent €7.50/7; ☼ Apr-Oct), about 1km from Shinias Beach, is the most pleasant camping ground in Attica, with sites nestled in shrubbery and trees. There's a minimarket, bar/restaurant, playground, laundry and tents for hire.

The bus to Marathon stops at the entrance to the camp site and within walking distance of Shinias Beach.

VRAVRONA ΒΡΑΥΡΩΝΑ

The **Sanctuary of Artemis** (☎ 22990 27020; adult/ concession €3/1.50; ☼ 8.30am-3pm Tue-Sun) was a re-vered site for worshippers of the goddess of the hunt, protector of women in childbirth and newborns. The temple is one of several monuments from this Neolithic settlement.

The museum (temporarily closed at the time of research) houses exceptional finds from the sanctuary and excavations in the area.

From Athens, take the metro to Ethniki Amyna, then bus 304 to Loutsa. It's a 10-minute taxi ride from there, with a nice stretch of beach on the way.

RAFINA ΡΑΦΗΝΑ

Rafina, on Attica's east coast, is Athens' main fishing port and the second-most important port for passenger ferries. The port is far smaller than Piraeus and less confusing – and fares are about 20% cheaper – but it does take an hour on the bus to get here.

Rafina port police (☎ 22940 22300) occupies a kiosk near the quay.

There are frequent buses between Athens and Rafina from the Mavromateon bus ter-minal (€2.20, one hour) between 5.45am and 10.30pm.

LAVRIO ΛΑΥΡΙΟ

Lavrio, an industrial town on the coast 60km southeast of Athens, is the port for ferries to Kea and Kythnos and high-season catamarans to the western Cyclades. It is scheduled to become a major container port, with a rail link to Athens. In antiquity, it was an impor-tant mining town. The silver mines funded the great classical building boom in Athens and helped build the fleet that defeated the Persians. Some of the underground shafts and mining galleries are still visible. Lavrio has also become a windsurfing spot.

The town has a small **Archaeological Museum** (☎ 22920 22817; Sepieri; admission €2; ☼ 10am-3pm Tue-Sun) as well as a **Mineralogical Museum** (☎ 22930 26270; Iroon Polytehniou; admission €1.20; ☼ 10am-noon Wed, Sat & Sun).

Lavrio had many fish tavernas and *ouzeries*, as well as a great fish market.

Buses to Lavrio (€5.20, 1½ hours) run every 30 minutes from the Mavromateon terminal in Athens. **Lavrio Port Authority** (☎ 22920 25249) has ferry information.

AROUND PEANIA
Koutouki Cave Σπηλιά Κουτούκι

Although the facilities here are run-down, this two-million-year-old **cave** (☎ 210 664 2910; www .culture.gr; adult/concession €5/3; ☼ 9.30am-2.45pm Mon-Fri, 10am-2.15pm Sat & Sun) is one of the finest in Greece, covering 3300 sq metres and contain-ing stalagmites and stalactites. It is well lit and guided tours end with a quirky sound-and-light finale with classical music.

The cave is best visited by car. Buses 125 and 308 from outside Athens' Ethniki Amyna metro station can take you as far as Peania, but it's a further 4.5km to the cave.

Vorres Museum Μουσείο Βορρέ

This impressive, private modern art and folk **museum** (☎ 210 664 2520; www.culture.gr; Parodos Diadohou Konstantinou 4, Peania; adult/child €5/2.50; ☒ 10am-2pm Sat & Sun year-round, daily in Aug, by appointment Sep-Jul) is on the lovely 2.5-hectare estate that is the home of Ion Vorres. Vorres migrated to Canada as a young man but built his home here in 1963 and began collecting art (housed in a modern gallery), furniture, artefacts, textiles and historic objects from around Greece to preserve the national heritage.

Take bus 308 to Koropi-Peania from Athens' Ethniki Amyna metro station.

MT PARNITHA ΠΑΡΝΗΘΑ

The densely forested **Mt Parnitha National Park** (www.parnitha-ng.gr), about 25km north of Athens, is the highest mountain range sur-rounding the city and serves as the 'lungs' of Athens. Tragically, more than 4200 hectares of century-old fir and pine forest was razed in the devastating six-day fires of 2007. The state has tripled the area designated as national park and launched a major re-forestation program, but it will take decades to recover.

Mt Parnitha comprises a number of smaller peaks, the highest of which is Karavola at 1413m – high enough to get snow in winter. The park is crisscrossed by numerous walking trails, is a popular hiking and mountain-biking destination and has two shelters for hikers. Trails are marked on the Road Editions trekking map of the area. There are many caves and wildlife, including red deer.

Most visitors access the park by cable car from the outer Athens suburb of Thrakomakedones, which drops you below the incongruous **Regency Casino Mont Parnes** (☎ 210 242 1234; www.regencycasinos.gr; ☒ 24hr). The casino runs a free bus service from various locations in Athens, including outside the Hilton. You can get to the cable car station on bus 714 from the south end of Aharnon, near Plateia Omonias.

Peloponnese
Πελοπόννησος

The Peloponnese (pel-o-*pon*-ih-sos) is the stuff that legends are made of. Numerous myths were born and borne out here – it is where many Greek gods or heroes strutted their stuff (and aired their bodies). Today this region is far from a fable. It boasts historical sites, with classical temples, Mycenaean palaces, Byzantine cities, and Frankish and Venetian fortresses. You can rub shoulders with the ghost of Agamemnon at Mycenae, mighty redoubt of a once-great civilisation, or flex your muscles at Ancient Olympia, spiritual home of the Olympics. You can cite Oedipus in the Theatre of Epidavros or be entranced by Mystras, where the Byzantine civilisation died in the 14th century. Greece's first capital, Nafplio, is today a cosmopolitan and romantic city; captivating, too, is the Venetian stronghold of Monemvasia.

The region's natural playground truly mesmerises, with lofty, snowcapped mountains, lush gorges, valleys of citrus groves and vineyards, cypress trees, streams and sun-speckled beaches. Spring is a perfect time for do-it-yourself explorations. Hike in the wildflower-covered mountains of Arkadia, or in the rugged Mani, which bristles with fortified tower houses. Summer is a beach bum's delight: the beaches of Messinia are among Greece's finest. Winter brings snow to the higher ground and a chance to launch yourself down Mt Helmos on skis. For centuries Greeks have fought hard against invaders of their Peloponnese paradise; today foreigners are far from repelled (ask the permanent influx of Brits). *Filoxenia* (hospitality) is as strong here as anywhere in the country. The locals claim to have the best of everything to give. And that's no myth.

HIGHLIGHTS

- **Historical Havens** Soaking up the past and present of Nafplio (p186) and Monemvasia (p205)
- **Ancient Wonders** Marvelling at the sanctuary of Ancient Olympia (p227) – birthplace of the Olympic Games
- **Wild Wanderings** Walking in the remote and rugged Mani (p209)
- **Mountain Delights** Hiking to the monasteries of Lousios Gorge (p197) and discovering the delights of charming mountain-top villages of Stemnitsa (p196), Dimitsana (p197), Karitena (p196) and Andritsena (p230)
- **Magic Moments** Meandering through the magical Mystras (p202), a World Heritage–listed site
- **Mythical Moments** Exploring the citadels of Mycenae (p184), Tiryns (p192) and the theatre of Epidavros (p192)

- POPULATION: 1 MILLION
- AREA: 21,439 SQ KM

History

Since ancient times the Peloponnese has played a major role in Greek history. When the Minoan civilisation declined after 1450 BC, the focus of power in the ancient Aegean world moved from Crete to the hill-fortress palaces of Mycenae and Tiryns in the Peloponnese. As elsewhere in Greece, the 400 years following the Dorian conquests in the 12th century BC are known as the Dark Ages. When the region emerged from darkness in the 7th century BC, Athens' arch rival, Sparta, had surpassed Mycenae as the most powerful city in the Peloponnese. The period of peace and prosperity under Roman rule (146 BC to around AD 250) was shattered by a series of invasions by Goths, Avars and Slavs.

The Byzantines were slow to make inroads into the Peloponnese, only becoming firmly established during the 9th century. In 1204, after the fall of Constantinople to the Crusaders, the Frankish Crusader chiefs William de Champlitte and Geoffrey de Villehardouin divided the region into 12 fiefs, which they parcelled out to various barons of France, Flanders and Burgundy. These fiefs were overseen by De Villehardouin, the self-appointed Prince of Morea, as the region was called in medieval times, perhaps because mulberry trees grow so well in the area (*mouria* means mulberry tree).

The Byzantines gradually won back the Morea and, although the empire as a whole was now in terminal decline, a glorious renaissance took place in the area, centred on Mystras (see p203), which became the region's seat of government.

The Morea fell to the Turks in 1460 and hundreds of years of power struggles between the Turks and Venetians followed. The Venetians had long coveted the Morea and succeeded in establishing profitable trading ports at Methoni, Pylos, Koroni and Monemvasia.

The Greek War of Independence supposedly began in the Peloponnese, when Bishop Germanos of Patra raised the flag of revolt near Kalavryta on 25 March 1821. The Egyptian army, under the leadership of Ibrahim Pasha, brutally restored Turkish rule in 1825.

In 1827 the Triple Alliance of Great Britain, France and Russia, moved by Greek suffering and the activities of philhellenes (Byron's death in 1824 was particularly influential), came to the rescue of the Greeks by destroying the Turkish-Egyptian fleet at the Battle of Navarino, ending Turkish domination of the area.

The Peloponnese became part of the independent state of Greece, and Nafplio (in Argolis) became the first national capital. Ioannis Kapodistrias, Greece's first president, was assassinated on the steps of Nafplio's Church of St Spyridon in October 1831, and the new king, Otto, moved the capital to Athens in 1834.

Like the rest of Greece, the Peloponnese suffered badly during WWII; part of this history is vividly and tragically illustrated in the mountain town of Kalavryta, where nearly all males aged over 15 were massacred (see p175).

The civil war (1944–49) brought widespread destruction and, in the 1950s, many villagers migrated to Athens, Australia, Canada, South Africa and the USA.

ACHAÏA AXAÏA

Overseas visitors are slowly discovering the delights of Achaïa. The spectacular region hides a string of coastal resorts, some high and ski-able mountain country (reached via a fantastic rack-and-pinion railway) and a burgeoning capital: the bustling, cosmopolitan city of Patra.

Achaïa owes its name to the Achaeans, an Indo-European branch of migrants who settled on mainland Greece and established what is more commonly known as the Mycenaean civilisation. When the Dorians arrived, the Achaeans were pushed into this northwestern corner of the Peloponnese, displacing the original Ionians.

Legend has it that the Achaeans founded 12 cities, which later developed into the powerful Achaean Federation that survived until Roman times. Principal among these cities were the ports of Patra and Egio (on the coast of the Gulf of Corinth).

PATRA ΠΑΤΡΑ
pop 167,600

The largest city in the Peloponnese and Achaïa's capital, Patra is named after King Patreas, who ruled Achaïa around 1100 BC. Despite an eventful 3000 years of history, Patra is often dismissed by travellers; many pass straight through, boarding or disembarking

PELOPONNESE

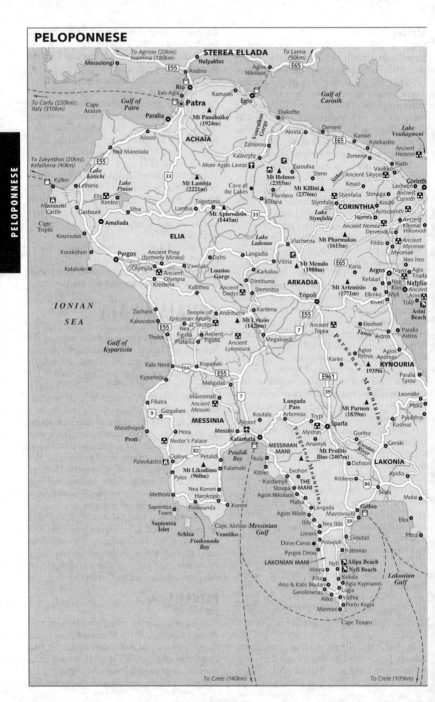

PELOPONNESE

from boats that sail between here, Italy and the Ionian Islands.

Yet those who do stay a night or two will find a cosmopolitan city with a vibrant cafe and clubbing scene (helped by the presence of Patra's 40,000 university students), some interesting sites, good shopping, and a busy arts and culture community.

At first sight, Patra is not beautiful – the cityscape is dominated by a large port, bland 1950s concrete tenements that squat between the few surviving 19th-century neoclassical buildings and traffic-snarled streets. But the city also has attractive squares and architectural landmarks, such as the Apollon Theatre, plus the impressive, shiny Rio–Andirio suspension bridge, linking the city with western continental Greece.

Orientation

Rebuilt with wide, arcaded streets and large squares after its destruction by the Turks during the War of Independence, Patra has a simple modern grid system. The waterfront is known as Iroön Polytehniou at the north end, Othonos Amalias in the middle and Akti Dimeon to the south. The bus and train stations and agencies selling ferry tickets are on Iroön Polytehniou and Othonos Amalias. The main pedestrian thoroughfare is Agiou Nikolaou and the principle square is Plateia Georgiou.

Information

BOOKSHOPS

Newstand (☎ 2610 273 092; Agiou Andreou 77) A small selection of novels, as well as international newspapers and magazines.

EMERGENCY

First Aid Centre (☎ 2610 277 386; cnr Karolou & Agiou Dionysiou; ☽ 8am-8pm)
Tourist police (☎ 2610 695 191; 4th fl, Gounari 52, cnr Ypsilandou; ☽ 7.30am-9pm)

INTERNET ACCESS

Info Center (☎ 2610 461 740/1; www.infocenterpatras .gr; Othonos Amalias 6; per 20min free; ☽ 8am-10pm)
Netp@rk (Gerokostopoulou 36a; per hr €2; ☽ 24hr)
Plazanet@Internet (Gerokostopoulou 28; per hr €2.10; ☽ 9am-midnight)

INTERNET RESOURCES

www.infocenterpatras.gr An excellent website for information on the city.

PELOPONNESE

MYTHOLOGY MADE PELOPONNEASY

If you are interested in treading the real landscape of Greek mythology, the Peloponnese is home to a great many of its fabled places.

It takes some getting used to seeing so many road signs to places of legend, such as Mycenae (p184), Tiryns (p192) and Nestor's Palace (p224); homes to Homer's heroes and villains in the 'Iliad', and places of real historical as well as mythological interest.

If you want to find the entrance to the Underworld, try exploring along the Styx River in northeastern Arkadia, known to modern Greeks as the Mavroneri River. Or perhaps you'd prefer to see Aphrodite's birthplace, off a magnificent spot on the remote island of Kythira (p231).

Even the territory itself is named after a mythical figure – Pelops – who, according to legend, became king of Elia after sneakily defeating the previous king Oimanaos in a chariot race (by nobbling his chariot wheels) and to whom subsequent rulers from the area were desperate to prove a blood line.

Gods and demigods sported here, too, including Pan, who sexually harassed nymphs in bucolic Arkadia, and Hercules, who worked as a kind of supernatural pest controller, ridding the country around Argos of the many-headed Hydra and strangling the fearsome Nemean Lion at Nemea. According to the ancient Greek writer Plutarch, even Zeus himself celebrated here, after beating his father Cronos at wrestling, by holding the first ever Olympics at Ancient Olympia (p227).

LAUNDRY
Skafi Laundrette (☎ 2610 620 119; Zaïmi 49; per load €8; ⏰ 9am-2.30pm Mon-Sat, 5.30-8.30pm Tue, Thu & Fri) Will wash and dry a load.

LEFT LUGGAGE
Train station (per 8hr €2, per 24hr €3; ⏰ 5am-3am) Has large lockers.

MONEY
National Bank of Greece (Plateia Trion Symachon; ⏰ 8am-2.30pm Mon-Thu, 8am-2pm Fri) Opposite the train station.

POST
Post office (cnr Zaïmi & Mezonos; ⏰ 7.30am-8pm Mon-Fri, 7.30am-2pm Sat & Sun)

TOURIST INFORMATION
Info Center (☎ 2610 461 740/1; www.infocenterpatras .gr; Othonos Amalias 6; ⏰ 8am-10pm) This is one of the best-organised information offices in Greece, run by the city of Patra (rather than the EOT; Greek National Tourist Organisation). It's stocked with maps, lists and brochures on local sites plus information on everything, including transport and hotels. The delightful English-speaking staff is eager to please. There's even free 20-minute internet access and free bike hire.

Sights & Activities
The city's wonderful old **kastro** (fortress; admission free; ⏰ 8.30am-3pm Tue-Sun) stands on the site of the acropolis of ancient Patrai. The Romans were the first to build a fort here around AD 550, but the present structure is of Frankish origin, remodelled many times over the centuries by the Byzantines, Venetians and Turks. It was in use as a defensive position until WWII. Set in an attractive pencil-pine park, it is reached by climbing the 190-plus steps at the southeastern end of Agiou Nikolaou. Great views of the Ionian islands of Zakynthos and Kefallonia are the reward.

The long-awaited, space-aged **Archaeological Museum of Patras** (☎ 2610 220 829; cnr Amerikis & Patras-Athens National Rd; admission free; ⏰ 8.30am-3pm Tue-Sun) opened in July 2009. Its shiny metallic domes and contemporary buildings make up the country's second-largest museum. Its collections – across three themed halls – feature objects from prehistoric to Roman times (including extraordinary mosaics, sarcophagi and jewellery) from Patra and surrounds; many pieces haven't been exhibited for decades. The museum also includes a particulary significant collection of Mycenaean swords. At the time of research, the entrance was free, but there are plans to introduce admission fees in 2010.

Seating 5500 people, the **Church of Agios Andreas** (Agiou Andreou) is one of the largest in the Balkans. It houses religious icons and paintings, plus St Andreas' skull, along with part of the cross he was crucified on.

The **hammam** (Turkish baths; ☎ 2610 274 267; Boukaouri 29; ⏰ 9am-9pm Mon-Sat) is a privately

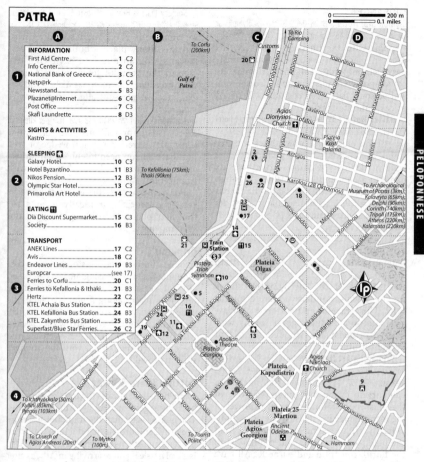

PATRA

0 — 200 m
0 — 0.1 miles

INFORMATION	
First Aid Centre	**1** C2
Info Center	**2** C2
National Bank of Greece	**3** C3
Netp@rk	**4** C4
Newsstand	**5** B3
Plazanet@Internet	**6** C4
Post Office	**7** C3
Skafi Laundrette	**8** D3

SIGHTS & ACTIVITIES	
Kastro	**9** D4

SLEEPING	
Galaxy Hotel	**10** C3
Hotel Byzantino	**11** B3
Nikos Pension	**12** B3
Olympic Star Hotel	**13** C3
Primarolia Art Hotel	**14** C2

EATING	
Dia Discount Supermarket	**15** C3
Society	**16** B3

TRANSPORT	
ANEK Lines	**17** C2
Avis	**18** C2
Endeavor Lines	**19** B3
Europcar	(see 17)
Ferries to Corfu	**20** C1
Ferries to Kefallonia & Ithaki	**21** B3
Hertz	**22** C2
KTEL Achaia Bus Station	**23** B3
KTEL Kefallonia Bus Station	**24** B3
KTEL Zakynthos Bus Station	**25** B3
Superfast/Blue Star Ferries	**26** C2

PELOPONNESE

run venture, but you can scrub up here as the Turks (AD 1500) did before you.

Festivals & Events

Patra's citizens party hard during the annual **Patras Carnival** (www.carnivalpatras.gr). This program (whose dates change annually) features a host of minor events leading up to a wild weekend of costume parades, colourful floats and celebrations in late February or early March. The event draws big crowds, so hotel reservations are essential if you want to stay overnight.

The **Patras International Festival** (www.info centerpatras.gr) runs from June to September and features a range of music and other acts with visiting international performers.

Sleeping

There are a couple of budget choices, but stretching yourself to a slightly higher budget pays dividends with a few plush choices.

BUDGET

Rio Camping (☎ 2610 991 585; camp sites per person/tent/car €6/6/4) The nearest camping ground is several kilometres north at the popular Rio Beach. Bus 6 leaves every hour from outside the train station.

Nikos Pension (☎ 2610 623 757; cnr Patreos & Agiou Andreou; s/d with shared bathroom €23/33, with private bathroom €28/38; ✷) Don't judge this centrally located, '60s-style place by its flaking shutters. Inside, Nikos runs a tight ship with clean rooms on several floors and a pleasant roof terrace.

MIDRANGE

Olympic Star Hotel (☎ 2610 622 939; www.olympicstar
.gr; Agiou Nikolaou 46; s/d incl breakfast €65/90; ⚄ ▣)
Popular with the business traveller, this
modern place has a slight try-hard business feel, but with a solid performance. Its
contemporary rooms feature hydro showers
and personal flat-screen computers. Reduced
prices without breakfast.

Galaxy Hotel (☎ 2610 275 981; www.galaxyhotel
.com.gr; Agiou Nikolaou 9; s/d/tr incl breakfast €68/88/108;
⚄ ⚆) This orange and brown, black and grey
(think contemporary retro) joint does some
good marketing – even the carpet bears its
name in a contemporary design. Although
its makeover in the mid-noughties has
worn off a bit, it's still reasonably sleek. Its
efficient service ensures its popularity with
business travellers.

TOP END

Hotel Byzantino (☎ 2610 243 000; www.byzantino
-hotel.gr; Riga Fereou 106; s/d/tr incl breakfast
€90/110/130; ⚔ ⚄ ▣) The Byzantino shows
up the town's standard concrete mono-
liths. This graceful and restored neoclassical building features good rooms with
large iron bedsteads, wooden floors and
period furniture.

Primarolia Art Hotel (☎ 2610 624 900; www.art
hotel.gr; Othonos Amalias 33; s incl breakfast €99, d incl
breakfast €129-157; ⚄ ⚆) Follow your mood: you
can curl up in the shell room, 'veg out' in
the mushroom room or dream of travel in
the map room. This stylish place oozes individuality, with sleeping spaces ranging from
the bold, contemporary and minimalist to
the florid, romantic and baroque. All have
TV with international channels, fax, minibar
and safe. There's even an in-house sauna.

Eating

To do frappé (Greek-style iced coffee) with
the best of 'em, head along Agiou Nikolaou.
For good eating options head southeast to
Trion Navarhon.

Mythos (☎ 2610 329 984; cnr Trion Navarhon & Riga
Fereou; mains €8-14; ☾ dinner) Flowers, petunias
and shrubs create an oasis outside this eatery; Mediterranean antiques, lamps and
other surprises adorn the inside (thanks to
the female owner-decorator). But it's not all
frills. Flavoursome dishes abound. Try the
mythos pie (containing chicken, feta and
fresh vegetables) and chocolate soufflé.

Society (Taratsa Bistrot; ☎ 2610 622 677; Riga Fereou
96 & Drakopoulou 2; mains €8-18; ☾ dinner) OK, so
we could be in NYC, and it's hardly Greek.
But this funky place – both bar and restaurant – on an *aire libre*–style roof terrace in the heart of town, offers a great
vibe, excellent international dishes and social 'cred'. A pleasant alternative if you're
mousaka'd out.

Ichthyóskala (☎ 2610 333 778; fish per kilogram
€50-60) This unpretentious place offers few
trimmings, save for a lemon wedge or two.
But that's all you need to enhance fresh fish
eaten alfresco. It's about 1km southwest
from central Patra.

For self-caterers, **Dia Discount supermarket** (Agiou Andreou 29) is ideally located for
travellers planning to buy provisions and
keep moving.

Drinking

Around sunset Patra transforms into a cosmopolitan, sharp-dressing, buzzy, cafe-lined
city. Sit, see and be seen at any one of the
dozens of places along Agiou Nikolaou, the
wide pedestrianised street leading to the port.
Radinou is a short, lively, narrow alley packed
with bars (some with DJs) that open late into
the night and quickly fill with the younger
student crowd.

Getting There & Away

Many first-time visitors to Greece assume the
best way to get from Patra to Athens is by bus.
The bus is faster than the train, but it's more
expensive and drops you off a long way from
the centre of Athens at Terminal A (p153). This
is a real hassle if you're arriving in Athens after
midnight, when there are no connecting buses
to the city centre, leaving newcomers at the
mercy of the Terminal A taxi drivers.

The train takes you close to the Athens
city centre, with easy connections to the
metro system. If you arrive after midnight,
you're within easy walking distance of
good accommodation.

BOAT

Domestic

Patra is the departure point for ferry serv-
ices to Kefallonia and Ithaki – operated by
Strintzis Lines (☎ 2610 240 000); and Corfu –
provided by **ANEK Lines** (☎ 2610 226 053; Othonos
Amalias 25) and **Minoan Lines** (☎ 2610 426 000; Iroön
Polytehniou 50).

International

Patra is Greece's main port for ferry services to Italy – Ancona, Bari, Brindisi and Venice. All departures to Italy leave at midnight. (Be sure to check as this schedule changes.) Most of these ferries stop at Igoumenitsa and Corfu. Note: under no circumstances are you permitted a free stopover on Corfu.

Superfast/Blue Star Ferries (☎ 2610 622 500; Othonos Amalias 12) runs trips to Ancona and Bari; and **Agoudimos Lines** (☎ 2610 461 800; Iroön Politechniou 36, Gate 7) heads to Bari. **Minoan Lines** (☎ 2610 426 000; Iroön Polytehniou 50) and **ANEK Lines** (☎ 2610 226 053; Othonos Amalias 25) have ferries to Ancona and Venice. **Endeavor Lines** (☎ 2610 622 676; www.endeavor-lines.com/en/schedules; cnr Pantanassis & Othonas Amalias) services Brindisi.

BUS

The main **KTEL Achaia bus station** (☎ 2610 623 886; Othonos Amalias) has buses to Athens (€17, three hours, every half-hour) via Corinth Isthmus (€11.30, 1½ hours); to Pyrgos (€8.80, two hours, 10 daily); Ioannina (€20.90, 4½ hours, at least two daily); Kalavryta (€7.50, two hours, at least two daily); Kalamata (€20, four hours, two daily) and Thessaloniki (€40, seven hours, four daily).

Buses to the Ionian islands of Lefkada (€14.50, two weekly, three hours) and Kefallonia leave from the **KTEL Kefallonia bus station** (☎ 2610 274 938, 2610 277 854; cnr Othonos Amalias & Gerokostopoulou). Services to Kefallonia travel by ferry to Poros (€18, three hours) and continue by road to Argostoli (€21, one hour). Also departing from here are buses to Amfissa (for Delphi; €12, three hours, two daily Monday to Saturday, one on Sunday). Four daily buses to Zakynthos (including ferry; €15, 3½ hours, three on Sunday) leave from the **KTEL Zakynthos bus station** (☎ 2610 220 129; Othonos Amalias 48).

Conveniently, they also travel via the port of Kyllini (€6.80, 1¼ hours). Note: the schedules change seasonally.

TRAIN

For Athens, there are at least seven trains daily from Patra to Kiato (where you change for the *proastiako*, the smart new Athens suburban rail service); five are normal trains (€3.70, 2½ hours) and two are intercity (IC; express) services (€6.90, 2½ hours). All trains between Patra and Corinth or Patra and Kiato stop at Diakofto (normal trains €2.30, one hour; IC €4.90, 45 minutes). Note: on arrival in Athens you can use your *proastiako* ticket for 1½ hours on the metro, but to do this you *must* validate the ticket or you will be fined.

There are also several daily services to Pyrgos (normal/IC €3.70/6.30, 1½ to three hours). For Olympia, change trains at Pyrgos. There are regular daily services to Kyparissia (normal/IC €5.10/9.80, three hours) and Kalamata (normal/IC €6.60/11.30, five hours).

Getting Around

Local buses leave from Plateia Georgiou.

Recommended car-hire outlets:

Avis (☎ 2610 275 547; 28 Oktovriou 16)
Europcar (☎ 2610 226 053; Othonos Amalias 25) In the ANEK Lines office.
Hertz (☎ 2610 220 990; Karolou 2)

DIAKOFTO ΔΙΑΚΟΦΤΟ
pop 2290

Diakofto (dih-ah-kof-*to*), 55km east of Patra and 80km northwest of Corinth, is a serene village, tucked between steep mountains and the sea, amid lemon and olive groves. There is a small **beach** on the eastern side of town; the holidaying hordes flock here in summer.

PELOPONNESE

GAUGING THE RAILWAY: TRAIN LINES IN THE PELOPONNESE

At the time of research the train lines in the Peloponnese were being upgraded from a narrow to standard gauge. Normally, there are two main routes: Athens to Kalamata (via the centre – Corinth and Tripoli, with another line from Argos to Nafplio) and Athens to Kalamata (via the west coast – Patra and Pyrgos, with another line from Patra to Olympia). At the time of publication services to Corinth and Tripoli (and Argos and Nafplio) were suspended; these lines were still being worked on. In many cases bus-replacement services were operating, but we suggest that it is more convenient to use the KTEL buses in these instances.

Meanwhile, a new service, the *proastiako* (Athens suburban rail service), was operating between Kiato and Athens (and Athens airport). It will eventually link Athens to Patra in the Peloponnese.

DIAKOFTO–KALAVRYTA RAILWAY

One of the unmissable journeys to make in the Peloponnese is aboard the tiny, unique **train** (☎ in Diakofto 26910 43228) running along the railway from Diakofto to Kalavryta. It takes travellers on an unforgettable ride through the dramatic **Vouraïkos Gorge**. The train climbs over 700m in 22.5km, using a rack-and-pinion (cog) system for traction on the steep sections, effectively clamping itself to the notched girder you can see running between the rails. Built by an Italian company between 1885 and 1895, the railway was a remarkable feat of engineering for its time, with only a handful of equivalents around the world (most notably in the Swiss Alps). Between 2007 and 2009 the trains were off the tracks as the entire rails and cog sections were completely replaced, and four new modern trains were constructed to replace the former carriages.

The opening section of the journey is fairly sedate, the ascent beginning in earnest about 5km south of Diakofto. The section from here to Zahlorou is spectacular as the line switches back and forth across the gorge. As the gorge narrows, the train disappears into a long curving tunnel (there are seven tunnels in total) and emerges clinging to a narrow ledge that seems to overhang the river, at its most dramatic when swollen by spring snowmelt from the surrounding mountains. South of the charming village of Zahlorou, the line follows the river beneath a leafy canopy of plane trees, before meandering through open country for the final run to Kalavryta.

The journey takes just over an hour, stopping en route at Zahlorou. At the time of research, a fare cost €9.50/19 one way/return. A good website to check its status (run by a passionate trainspotter) is www.odontotos.com.

The original steam engines that first plied the route were replaced in the early 1960s by diesel cars, but the old engines can still be seen outside Diakofto and Kalavryta stations.

The main reason for visiting is to board the unique rack-and-pinion train service along the Vouraïkos Gorge as far as Kalavryta (see the boxed text, above).

Orientation & Information

Diakofto's layout is simple. The train station is in the middle of the village. To reach the waterfront and beach, cross the railway track and walk down the road for 1km.

There is no EOT (Greek National Tourist Organisation) or tourist police. The National Bank of Greece and the **post office** (7.30am-2pm Mon-Fri) are on the main street that leads inland from the station.

Sleeping & Eating

Hotel Chris-Paul (☎ 26910 41715/855; www.chrispaul-hotel.gr; s/d/tr €35/65/78; P 🕮 🖭) This modernish, plain place has friendly management and is a block from the platform – prime position for train travellers. Most rooms have balconies overlooking the garden and pool. Breakfast is €5.

Hotel Lemonies (☎ 26910 41229/820; fax 26910 43710; s/d/tr €36/48/57; P 🕮) This simple, pleasant place has kind owners and basic but spacious, comfortable rooms – with fridge and TV. It's 500m north of the train station on the road leading to the beach.

Breakfast is €6. There's a steep set of stairs to rooms.

Hotel Panorama (☎ 26910 41614; www.greecepanorama.gr; s/d/tr incl breakfast €50/60/80; 🕮) This unpretentious '70s place is located in the northeasternmost part of village, right in front of the beach. Rooms are plain but perfectly adequate (note, there is no lift). It can be noisy in summer, thanks to the taverna below, but delightful the rest of the year.

Costas (☎ 26910 43228; mains €6-10; 🕒 lunch & dinner) This popular *psistaria* (restaurant serving char-grilled food), near the National Bank, is a good eating choice. The friendly Greek-Australian owners offer taverna-style dishes alongside usual grilled meats. It's known for its dolmadhes (vine leaves stuffed with rice and sometimes meat; €7).

Opposite the train station, a small supermarket has good picnic supplies for walkers. Ten minutes walk away, the beach strip has a couple of good seaside tavernas worth checking out.

Getting There & Away
BUS
Trains are the most convenient way to get to Diakofto. Patra–Athens buses bypass the village on New National Rd.

TRAIN
Diakofto is on the main Corinth–Patra line; there are frequent trains in both directions (€7).

The refurbished **Diakofto–Kalavryta Railway** (☎ 26910 43228) has departures daily along the rack-and-pinion line to Kalavryta to a changing schedule via Zahlorou. See opposite.

ZAHLOROU ΖΑΧΛΩΡΟΥ
pop 50
The picturesque and unspoilt settlement of Zahlorou, the halfway stop on the Diakofto–Kalavryta train line, straddles both sides of the river and the railway line. Some people take the train to this point and walk back to Diakofto – the walk takes up to four hours.

Sights
MONI MEGALOU SPILEOU
ΜΟΝΗ ΜΕΓΑΛΟΥ ΣΠΗΛΑΙΟΥ
A steep path leads up from Zahlorou to the **Moni Megalou Spileou** (Monastery of the Great Cavern; admission free). The original monastery was destroyed in 1934 when gunpowder stored during the War of Independence exploded. The new monastery houses illuminated gospels and relics, and the miraculous icon of the Virgin Mary, which, like numerous icons in Greece, is said to have been painted by St Luke. It was supposedly discovered in the nearby cavern by St Theodore and St Simeon in 362. The 3km-long walk takes about an hour.

Sleeping & Eating
Taverna Oneiro (☎ 26920 23772; www.villa-oneiro .gr; apt/villa from €80/100) For something more upmarket, and on the hill behind the platform, try this taverna, which has eight plush new 'villas' aside its taverna and older apartments nearby. Check for opening months, however.

Of the two budget sleeping options right on the platform, **Zachlorou** (☎ 26920 22789; www .zachlorou.gr; r from €30) is the preferred option over the sootier **Hotel Romantzo** (☎ 26920 22758; r €40). However, both have 3rd-class prices, so don't expect luxury accommodation.

Getting There & Away
All Diakofto–Kalavryta trains stop at Zahlorou. You can drive to Zahlorou on a narrow road leading off the Diakofto–Kalavryta road. The turn-off is 7.5km north of Kalavryta.

KALAVRYTA ΚΑΛΑΒΡΥΤΑ
pop 1747
Perched 756m above sea level, Kalavryta (kah-lah-vrih-tah) is a delightful resort town with fresh mountain air, gushing springs and a tree-shaded square. The town is especially popular among Athenians, who arrive in numbers on weekends and during the winter ski season. As such, prices can be a bit higher here compared with other villages and locals tend to be a little tourist wary (some might say weary).

Two relatively recent historical events have assured the town of Kalavryta a place in the hearts of all Greeks. First, despite plenty of evidence that fighting had already begun elsewhere, the official version of the War of Independence states that the revolt against the Turks began here on 25 March 1821, when Bishop Germanos of Patra raised the Greek flag at Moni Agias Lavras, 6km from Kalavryta. Second, on 13 December 1943, in one of the worst atrocities of WWII, the Nazis set fire to the town and massacred nearly all its male inhabitants over the age of 15 (498 people), as punishment for resistance activity. The hands of the old cathedral clock stand eternally at 2.34, the time the massacre began. The event is solemnly and movingly recorded in the old schoolhouse, now a museum (below) dedicated to the memory of those killed both in this event and in the region (about 700 people in total).

Orientation & Information
The train station is on the northern edge of town, opposite the museum. To the right of the museum is Syngrou/25 Martiou, a pedestrian precinct. To the left of the museum is Konstantinou.

The central square, Plateia Kalavrytou is two blocks up from the train station. The bus station is on Kapota.

There is no tourist office. The websites www.kalavrita.gr (in Greek) and www.kala vrita-ski.gr have good local information.
National Bank of Greece (25 Martiou) Just before Plateia Kalavrytou.
Post office (🕑 7.30am-2pm Mon-Fri) Behind Plateia Kalavrytou.

Sights
MUSEUM OF THE KALAVRYTA HOLOCAUST
This extraordinary **museum** (☎ 26920 23646; 1-3 Syngrou; admission €3; 🕑 10am-5pm Tue-Sun Jun-Sep,

PELOPONNESE

9am-4pm Tue-Sun Oct-May) should be a compulsory first stop for all visitors to this village. It is a most powerful tribute to the memory of the estimated 700 people killed by the German army in the region during WWII, especially those who died in the 13 December 1943 slaughter. It's a dignified, understated, yet extremely evocative account of the struggle between the occupying forces and partisan fighters in the area, and the events running up to the massacre; an atrocity reported to be partly put in motion by the partisans' execution of a group of German prisoners.

Whatever you do, don't pass by the videos on continuous loop dotted throughout the exhibition. These are the accounts of surviving villagers who escaped death in the slaughter or, after being locked with their mothers in the schoolhouse (the museum building), apparently to be burned alive, only to escape; they were left to bury the dead. The wall covered with pictures of the dead Kalavryta villagers is an especially striking memorial.

MARTYRS' MONUMENT

A huge white cross on a cypress-covered hillside just east of town marks the site of the 1943 massacre. Beneath this imposing monument is a poignant little shrine to the victims. It is signposted off Konstantinou.

Sleeping

Lodges are dotted outside the village; the village itself has few hotel options. Peak period here is the ski season (November to April), when reservations are essential. Bookings are also required on weekends throughout the year, when Athenians come to enjoy the cool mountain air. Prices are slashed by as much as 50% at other times.

The cheapest option is the domatia (private rooms) on the streets behind the train station.

Hotel Filoxenia (☎ 26920 22422; www.hotelfiloxenia .gr; Ethnikis Andistasis 10; s/d/tr incl breakfast €92/121/137; 🛇 🛜) Kind of like an old-fashioned ski lodge – old, brown and a bit daggy, but comfortable and friendly. Rooms have a minibar, safe, hairdryer, TV and balcony.

Hotel Kynaitha (☎ 26920 22609; www.kynaitha.gr; Ethnikis Andistasis 11; s/d/tr/ste incl breakfast €95/115/145/190; 🛇) Modern and comfortable with spacious and attractively furnished rooms boasting minibar, hairdryer and TV, plus gleaming white bathrooms and posh toiletries.

Hotel Helmos (☎ 26920 29222; www.hotelhelmos .gr; Plateia Eleftherias 1; s/d/tr €120/160/180; 🛇 🛜) Housed in one of the village's stunning original buildings, this renovated option has all the creature comforts in contemporary surrounds. Prices are slashed on weekdays and in low season; reservations are essential in winter.

Eating

Most places to eat are on 25 Martiou; head from top to bottom and go where the Greeks go. Even out of ski season Kalavryta is one of *the* weekend places for Athenians, so it has an abundance of trendy bars and cafes throughout.

Ellinikon (☎ 26920 23502; snacks €1.50-4) This terrific bakery is near the petrol station on the road out of town towards Patra and Klitoria. It has ideal picnic fare: wonderful bread, minipizzas and dozens of types of sweet pastries.

Gri Gri Café (25 Martiou; snacks €2-4) Opposite the museum you'll find this good (less fashion-conscious) family-run spot. Recommended for its sweet or savoury homemade snacks, such as cheese pie, baklava and tasty *crèma* (sweet, set custard).

Lixoudies (☎ 26920 24470; Syngrou 6; mains €6-10; 🛇 lunch) Away from the crowds and opposite the bus station, you come here for the food, not the street outlook. This is a friendly place with good-quality traditional taverna grills. It's also popular with the locals.

Getting There & Around

The newly refurbished rack-and-pinion train to/from Diakofto via Zahlorou (see the boxed text, p174) runs to a changing timetable.

There are buses to Patra (€7, two hours, five daily), Athens (€15.10, three hours, at least one to two daily) and Klitoria (€2.60, one to three daily).

Most of the attractions are out of town, so it's very handy to have your own transport.

Kalavryta's **taxi rank** (☎ 26920 22127) is in front of the train station.

AROUND KALAVRYTA
Moni Agias Lavras Μονή Αγίας Λαύρας

The original 10th-century **monastery** (🛇 10am-1pm & 3-4pm winter, 4-5pm summer only) was burnt by the Nazis. The new monastery has a small museum where the banner standard is displayed along with other monastic memorabilia. Buses heading south from Kalavryta to Klitoria can drop you a short walk from the monastery, or take a taxi from Kalavryta (one way around €10).

Cave of the Lakes Σπήλαιο των Λιμνών

The remarkable **Cave of the Lakes** (☎ 26920 31001; www.kastriacave.gr; adult/child €9/4.50; ♥ 9am-5.30pm Mon-Fri, 9am-6.30pm Sat & Sun Jul & Aug; 9am-4.30pm Mon-Fri, 9am-5.30pm Sat & Sun Sep-Jun) lies 16.5km south of Kalavryta near the village of Kastria. The cave features in Greek mythology and is mentioned in the writings of the ancient traveller Pausanias (p206), but its whereabouts remained unknown in modern times until 1964, when locals noticed water pouring from the roof of a smaller, lower cave after heavy rain and decided to investigate. They found themselves in a large bat-filled cavern at the start of a winding 2km-long cave carved out by a subterranean river.

The cavern is now reached by an artificial entrance, which is the starting point for a 500m boardwalk that snakes up the riverbed. You must go with a guide (Greek-speaking) on the 35-minute tour. The ornate stalactites are mere sideshows alongside the lakes themselves. The lakes are a series of 13 stone basins formed by mineral deposits over the millennia. In summer the waters dry up to reveal a curious lacework of walls, some up to 3m high.

Getting to the cave is difficult without your own transport. A taxi from Kalavryta costs about €35 return.

Trout Farms & Restaurants

A pleasant afternoon's eating can be had in the tiny village of **Planitero**, about 20km south of Kalavryta (6km north of the village of Klitoria), where half a dozen **trout restaurants** and several **trout farms** line the banks of the tree-lined Aroanios River. Several restaurants have outdoor seating areas built out over the river; most are under the shade of the plane trees themselves.

You can't really go wrong choosing a restaurant. They offer similar fare at similar prices – it's fun to cruise the area (all are within a 500m radius) to find an ambience that suits you. A trout of your choice costs around €7 to €9.

The turn-off to Planitero is signposted to the left about 4km short of Klitoria.

Activities

With 12 runs and seven lifts (two chairlifts), the **Ski Centre** (☎ 26920 24451; www.kalavrita-ski.gr; ♥ 9am-4pm Dec-Apr), elevation 1700m to 2340m, is 14km east of Kalavryta on Mt Helmos (2355m). It has a cafeteria and first-aid centre but no overnight accommodation. It also rents skis and snowboard equipment (€20 to €25 for boots and skis or snowboard). In Kalavryta try **Ski Time Center** (☎ 2692 022030; Agiou Alexiou) for ski hire.

There is no public transport to the ski centre from Kalavryta. A taxi costs about €25 return. The season lasts from December to April, snow permitting.

For rafting or hiking opportunities along the Ladonas River, see the boxed text, p197.

CORINTHIA ΚΟΡΙΝΘΙΑ

Corinthia has disappointingly little to show for all its rich and tumultuous history (something it owes largely to its strategic position adjoining the Corinth Isthmus). Throughout time several empires have wrestled for dominance over the Peloponnese here; the Romans constructed a vast wall across the isthmus, many centuries later the Turks overran it and pretty much everyone else has attempted to carve a canal across it (like most large-scale civil engineering projects the schedule slipped a little bit behind: about 2600 years, in fact).

The Corinthia region was once dominated by the mighty, ancient city of Corinth; this makes a fascinating visit. Several minor sites in the pretty hinterland west of Corinth are worth a detour if you have time or your own transport.

CORINTH ΚΟΡΙΝΘΟΣ

pop 29,787

Modern Corinth (*ko*-rin-thoss), located 6km west of the Corinth Canal, is the administrative capital of Corinthia prefecture. The town was built here after the old town was destroyed by an earthquake in 1858. The new town was wrecked by another, equally violent and damaging, earthquake in 1928 and badly damaged again in 1981.

The rather plain, modern town is dominated by cold concrete edifices, built to withstand future earthquakes. But it has a fairly pleasant harbour, a thriving stretch

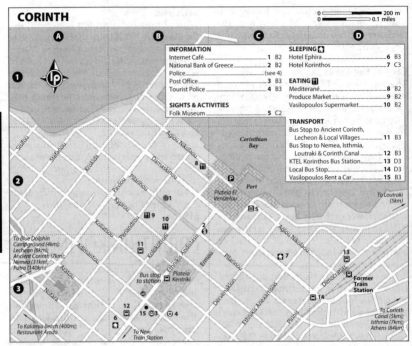

INFORMATION			SLEEPING		
Internet Café	1	B2	Hotel Ephira	6	B3
National Bank of Greece	2	B2	Hotel Korinthos	7	C3
Police		(see 4)			
Post Office	3	B3	EATING		
Tourist Police	4	B3	Mediterané	8	B2
			Produce Market	9	B2
SIGHTS & ACTIVITIES			Vasilopoulos Supermarket	10	B2
Folk Museum	5	C2			
			TRANSPORT		
			Bus Stop to Ancient Corinth,		
			Lecheon & Local Villages	11	B3
			Bus Stop to Nemea, Isthmia,		
			Loutraki & Corinth Canal	12	B3
			KTEL Korinthos Bus Station	13	D3
			Local Bus Stop	14	D3
			Vasilopoulos Rent a Car	15	B3

of cafe-lined beachfront and helpful, friendly locals.

Orientation & Information

Corinth is laid out on a grid of wide streets stretching back from the waterfront. Social activity clusters in the cafe-lined pedestrian Pilarinou, and the nearby Kalamia Beach, 1km west of the port. The main square by the harbour is the recently renovated Plateia El Venizelou, by no means the social centre. Administrative activity is along Ethnikis Andistasis.

There is no EOT in Corinth.

Internet Café (☎ 27410 25570; Pilarinou 70; per hr €3; ☺ 8.30am-10.30pm Mon-Sat)

National Bank of Greece (Ethnikis Andistasis) Has ATM.

Police (☎ 27410 81100; Ermou 51, Plateia Kentriki) In the same building as the tourist police.

Post office (Adimantou 33; ☺ 7.30am-2pm Mon-Fri)

Tourist police (☎ 27410 23282; Ermou 51, Plateia Kentriki; ☺ 8am-2pm)

Sights & Activities

To the south of the wharf, the **Folk Museum** (☎ 27410 25352; Ermou 1; admission €1.50; ☺ 8.30am-

1.30pm Tue-Sun) focuses on bridal and festive costumes from the past three centuries from the islands and the mainland. There is also metalwork, embroidery, gold and silver objects, and carvings, both secular and ecclesiastical.

If you're spending time in town, it's worth heading for **Kalamia Beach**, an attractive strip of sand fronted by a fashionable and thriving row of cafes and restaurants, 1km due west of the port.

Tours

In summer, **Periandros** (☎ 27410 30800, 6942013685; www.corinthcanal.com/cruises.html) offers visitors tours (around seven per week) through the Corinth Canal (p181) on its boat *Canal Vista*.

Sleeping

Blue Dolphin Campground (☎ 27410 25766/7; www.camping-blue-dolphin.gr; camp sites per adult/tent/car €6.50/5/3.50; ☺ Apr-Oct; ☒) About 4km west of town beyond the ruins of the ancient port of Lecheon is this well-organised camping ground. It has its own stretch of

Gulf of Corinth pebble beach. Buses from Corinth to Lecheon can drop you there; staff will pick you up from the bus or train stations.

Hotel Korinthos (☎ 27410 26701/2/3; www.korinthos hotel.gr; Damaskinou 26; s/d/tr €40/65/75; ☒) In general, it's like the rest of Corinth – it has definitely seen better days. The dated rooms have balconies and those at the back have views over the Gulf of Corinth. But management is very friendly and there's also a roof garden.

Hotel Ephira (☎ 27410 22434/4021; www.ephira hotel.gr; Ethnikis Andistasis 52; s/d/tr €50/70/80; ☒) This may be Corinth's smartest and most professional hotel. Indeed, it's comfortably furnished, with a few blemishes. The more spacious suites on the 6th floor are a notch more upmarket (€180). Breakfast costs €5.

Eating

There are limited dining options in town. Most of the evening action takes place in the cafes along Kalamia Beach, which is also a good place to sunbathe or sip a drink during the day. The cafes along Pilarinou are popular with younger locals.

Restaurant Arodo (☎ 27410 71500; Kalamia Beach; fish per kilogram €40-60, mains €8-16; ☽ lunch & dinner) This restaurant has model ships inside and views of real ones in the Gulf beyond. In line with all things marine, fish dishes are the catch here, although all dishes are good. It's a great place to kick back for the afternoon or evening, especially on the outdoor deck area.

Mediterané (☎ 27410 73232-5; Agiou Nikolaou 29; mains €8-18; ☽ lunch & dinner) This new, large but light and airy barnlike place serves up the lot – from smaller tasters, traditional dishes and steaks. It looks dangerously like it might cater to groups, but to date, many are pleased with this new addition.

For self-caterers, **Vasilopoulos supermarket** (☎ 27410 85281; Kolokotroni 8; ☽ 8am-9pm Mon-Fri, 8am-6pm Sat) is the best of the supermarkets around town. The **Produce Market** (cnr Kyprou & Periandrou) is the main market for fruit and veg, meat, cheese and other foods.

Getting There & Away
BUS

Buses to Athens (€7.50, 1½ hours) leave every hour from the **KTEL Korinthos bus station**

> ### CORINTH ISTHMUS (PELOPONNESE) KTEL BUS STATION: GATEWAY TO THE PELOPONNESE
>
> Although it's plonked on a main road on the Peloponnese side of the Corinth Canal, the **Corinth Isthmus (Peloponnese) KTEL bus station** (☎ 27410 83000, 27410 73987) is the spot to change for buses south to the rest of the Peloponnese. No formal timetables are available; all buses from Athens heading to the Peloponnese stop here.

(☎ 27410 75424; Dimocratias 4). This is also the departure point for buses to Ancient Corinth (€1.40, 20 minutes, hourly), Lecheon (€1.40, 15 minutes, half-hourly) and Nemea (€4.80, one hour, six daily). You can catch the bus to Nemea from the corner of Aratou and Ethnikis Andistasis and the other buses from the corner of Kolokotroni and Koliatsou.

Buses to the train station and the *proastiako* depart from Plateia Kentriki (about €1, 20 minutes).

Buses to Isthmia (€1.40, 15 minutes, four daily) and Loutraki (€1.70, 10 minutes, every half-hour) depart from the local bus stops Aratou and Ethnikis Andistasis.

All buses to other regions in the Peloponnese can be caught from the KTEL bus station on the Peloponnese side of the Corinth Canal (see the boxed text, above). To get there from Corinth, catch one of the frequent local buses to Loutraki.

CAR

There are several car-hire outlets around the city centre, including **Vasilopoulos Rent a Car** (☎ 27410 25573; Adimantou 39).

TRAIN

Seven trains daily head along the north coast to Diakofto (€7, 1½ hours) and Patra (normal/IC €5.70/8.90). Four trains run daily to Pyrgos (€13, four hours). For Olympia you must change to the local train at Patra.

At the time of research the inland line to Tripoli was under repair and replacement buses were in service. Alternatively, take the KTEL buses from the Corinth Canal (see the boxed text, above).

The handy *proastiako* train service runs between Corinth and Athens airport (€10, one hour, eight daily).

ANCIENT CORINTH & ACROCORINTH
ΑΡΧΑΙΑ ΚΟΡΙΝΘΟΣ & ΑΚΡΟΚΟΡΙΝΘΟΣ

Ancient Corinth was an affluent and powerful city during its first golden age, when Greek merchants made a mint from their control of trade on both sides of the isthmus and, centuries later, when the Romans rebuilt it anew (but only after first trashing the place in revenge for resisting its rule a few decades earlier). Earthquakes and centuries of pillage left little standing of Ancient Corinth, except for remnants of once-grand buildings, located 7km southwest of the modern city. Thanks to paths, on-site descriptions and a lovely site museum (which is divided into Classical and Roman periods), this wondrous ancient city makes a fascinating visit.

Surrounding the site is the village of Ancient Corinth. Towering 575m above is the Acrocorinth, a massive and much more physically imposing limestone outcrop. It commands dramatic views across the surrounding valleys and hills and is well worth perusing if you have time. Stout shoes are a sensible precaution on the uneven ground.

Most visitors come on whirlwind guided tours, but there's enough here to warrant an overnight stay. With a choice of restaurants and tavernas, it's also a better alternative to staying in modern Corinth.

History

During the 6th century BC Corinth was one of ancient Greece's richest cities, thanks to its strategic position on the Corinth Isthmus. Its twin ports, one on the Aegean Sea (Kenchreai, near Kechries) and one on the Ionian side (Lecheon) enabled it to trade throughout the Mediterranean. It survived the Peloponnesian Wars and flourished under Macedonian rule, but it was sacked by the Roman consul Mummius in 146 BC for rebelling against Roman rule. In 44 BC Julius Caesar began rebuilding the city and it again became a prosperous port.

During Roman times, when Corinthians weren't clinching business deals, they were paying homage to the goddess of love, Aphrodite, in a temple dedicated to her (which meant partying with the temple's sacred prostitutes, both male and female). St Paul – perturbed by the Corinthians' wicked ways – spent 18 mostly fruitless months preaching here.

Sights
ANCIENT CORINTH

The **ruins** (☎ 27410 31207; site & museum adult/concession €6/3; ☉ 8am-8pm Apr-Oct, 8am-3pm Nov-Mar) lie right in the centre of the modern village. Thanks to the area's compact size (although excavations are ongoing), and the excellent signs in English, complete with diagrams, a visit here is enjoyable and fascinating.

The remains are mostly from Roman times. An exception is the prominent 5th-century-BC Doric **Temple of Apollo**. To the south of this temple is a huge **agora** (forum) bounded on its southern side by the foundations of a **stoa** (long colonnaded building). This was built to accommodate the bigwigs summoned here in 337 BC by Philip II to sign oaths of allegiance to Macedon. In the middle of the central row of shops is a **bema**, a marble podium from which Roman officials addressed the people.

At the eastern end of the *agora* are the remains of the **Julian Basilica**. To the north is the **Lower Peirene fountain** – the Upper Peirene fountain is on Acrocorinth. According to mythology, Peirene wept so much when her son Kenchrias was killed by Artemis that the gods, rather than let all the precious water go to waste, turned her into a fountain (actually, it's a spring). The water tanks, or cisterns, are concealed in a fountain house with a six-arched facade.

West of the fountain, steps lead to the **Lecheon road**, once the main thoroughfare to the port of Lecheon. On the east side of the road is the **Peribolos of Apollo**, a courtyard flanked by Ionic columns, some of which have been restored. Nearby is a **public latrine**, where some seats remain.

South of the museum is **Temple E** (also known as Temple of Octavia; Pausanias describes it as being dedicated to Octavia, sister of Augustus). Several columns remain.

The site's **museum** has three main rooms: the first two exhibit fine Greek and Roman statues, mosaics, figurines, reliefs and friezes. The third room, the museum's latest addition, houses the finds of excavations at the nearby Sanctuary of Asklepios, a temple from the 5th century BC. Some interesting pieces include grave markers and votive genitalia from the 4th century BC.

Opposite the site entrance is the **ancient theatre**, constructed in the 5th century BC for up to 15,000 spectators, and altered vari-

THE WINE ROAD

The Nemea region, in the rolling hills southwest of Corinth, is one of Greece's premier wine-producing areas, famous for its full-bodied reds, produced from the local *agiorgitiko* grape. Look out also for wine made from *roditis*, a local variety of white grape.

Nemea has been known for its fine wines since Mycenaean times, when nearby Phlius supplied the wine for the royal court at Mycenae. Until recent times production took place behind closed doors, but growers are waking up to the tourist potential of winery tours and tastings and are marketing their wine region. About half a dozen wineries provide tastings for visitors (usually free, some by appointment). They include **Skouras** (☎ 27510 23688; www.skouraswines.com; ☽ 9am-3pm) northwest of Argos, **Ktima Palivou** (☎ 27460 24190; www.palivos.gr; ☽ 10am-6pm) in Ancient Nemea (with a good selection of Cabernet Sauvignon) and **Lafkioti** (☎ 27460 31244; www .lafkiotis.gr; ☽ 11am-3pm) in Ancient Kleonai, 3km east of Ancient Nemea.

North of Nemea and further up into some pretty hill country you'll find **Gaia Wines** (☎ 21080 55642/3, 27460 22057; www.gaia-wines.gr; Koutsi; ☽ tastings 9am-4pm), which produces unfiltered wines ranging from inexpensive vins de pays to pricier *appellation d'origine contrôlée* (AOC) varieties.

A bit further along the road is the dramatically located **Domaine Helios** (☎ 27460 20360; www .semeliwines.com), which produces various varieties of reds, whites and a rosé.

ous times, and the **odeion** (indoor theatre), a Roman construction from the 1st century AD. You view both sites from the road.

ACROCORINTH

The sheer bulk of limestone known as **Acrocorinth** (admission free; ☽ 8am-3pm) was one of the finest natural fortifications in ancient Greece and it remains an impressive ruin to this day, commanding wonderful views over the surrounding region.

The original fortress was built in ancient times, but it has been modified many times over the years by a string of invaders. The ruins are a medley of imposing Roman, Byzantine, Frankish, Venetian and Turkish ramparts, harbouring remains of Byzantine chapels, Turkish houses and mosques.

On the higher of Acrocorinth's two summits is the **Temple of Aphrodite** where the sacred courtesans (exactly how these differed from the less holy variety isn't clear), who so raised the ire of St Paul, catered to the desires of the insatiable Corinthians. Little remains of the temple, but the views are tremendous.

It's a bit of a (do-able) 4km uphill hike to the fortress and there's no bus. If you're lucky, you can grab a lift or take a village taxi.

Sleeping & Eating

There are several places in the village advertising rooms to rent.

Rooms to Rent Tasos (☎ 27410 31225; s/d €30/45, tr €55-60; ✖) In the village centre, on the road

into town from Corinth, and above Taverna O Tasos, are these basic, but clean and convenient, rooms.

Marinos Rooms (☎ 27410 31209; fax 27410 31994; s/d/tr incl breakfast €45/60/75; **P**) The 1980s-style glass facade glosses over any flaws of this slightly overpriced place, but it has simple rooms and a pretty and shady garden. Also operates an on-site taverna in summer, and gets booked out in June with archaeology students.

Taverna Dionysos (☎ 27410 31579; mains €8-15) This is the pick of the tavernas in town, as much for its more upmarket decor as for its freshly cooked fare. In high season, however, it brings out the more familiar Greek favourites.

CORINTH CANAL
ΔΙΩΡΥΓΑ ΤΗΣ ΚΟΡΙΝΘΟΟΥ

The concept of cutting a canal through the Corinth Isthmus to link the Ionian and Aegean Seas was first proposed by Periander, tyrant of Ancient Corinth at the end of the 7th century BC. The magnitude of the task defeated him, so he opted instead to build a *diolkos* (paved slipway) across which sailors dragged small ships on rollers, a method used until the 13th century.

In the intervening years many leaders, including Alexander the Great and Caligula, toyed with the canal idea, but it was Nero who actually began digging in AD 67. In true megalomaniac fashion, he struck the first blow himself, using a golden pickaxe. He then left it to 6000 Jewish prisoners to

PELOPONNESE

do the hard work. The project was soon halted by invasions by the Gauls. It was not until the 19th century (1883–93) that a French engineering company completed the canal.

The Corinth Canal, cut through solid rock, is over 6km long and 23m wide. The vertical sides rise 90m above the water. The canal did much to elevate Piraeus' status as a major Mediterranean port. It's an impressive sight, particularly when a ship is passing through. Corinth-based Periandros (p178) offers cruises through the canal.

Getting There & Away

The easiest way to get to the canal is by the Loutraki bus from modern Corinth (p179) to the canal bridge. Any bus or train between Corinth and Athens will pass over the bridge.

ISTHMIA/KYRAS VRYSI
ΙΣΘΜΙΑ/ΚΥΡΑΣ ΒΡΥΣΗ

Near the village of modern Isthmia and 8km east of Corinth at the southeastern end of the Corinth Canal is the present-day village of Kyras Vrysi. It was formerly the site of the biennial Isthmian Games – one of four events that made up the Panhellenic Games circuit along with the games at Delphi, Nemea and Olympia.

The first recorded games at Isthmia were staged in 582 BC, organised by the city of Corinth in honour of Poseidon, god of the sea, who had long been associated with the site. Corinth continued to host the games until its destruction by Rome in 146 BC.

The **Isthmia Museum and (archaelogical) site** (☎ 27410 37244; admission free; ✆ 8.30am-3pm Tue-Sun) are located in Kyras Vrysi. The site and museum were closed for renovation at the time of research.

Another reason to visit Isthmia is for its **submersible bridge**, one of two crossing the canal (the other is near Loutraki). You can cross this wooden and metal bridge in a car or on foot. It gives an excellent perspective of the canal plus, if you're lucky enough to see a ship pass over the submerged bridge, the canal banks near the bridge are great viewing points.

ANCIENT NEMEA ΑΡΧΑΙΑ ΝΕΜΕΑ

Lying on the northeastern edge of modern Nemea, **Ancient Nemea** (☎ 27460 22739; site,

museum & stadium adult/concession €4/2, site & museum adult/concession €3/2; ✆ museum 8.30am-3pm, museum closed Mon morning) is 31km southwest of Corinth. According to mythology it was around here that Hercules carried out the first of his labours – the slaying of the lion that had been sent by Hera to destroy Nemea. The lion became the constellation Leo (each of the 12 labours is related to a sign of the zodiac).

Like Olympia, Nemea was not a city but a sanctuary and venue for the biennial Nemean Games, held in honour of Zeus. These games were hosted by the nearby city of Kleonai, and they became one of the great Panhellenic festivals. Three original columns of the 4th-century-BC Doric **Temple of Zeus** survive, and have been joined by two more columns reassembled by an American team. Other ruins include a **bathhouse**, probably used by athletes to oil up pre-competition, and a **hostelry**.

The site's **museum** has two models of the ancient site – the first shows what it would have looked like in 573 BC, the second in AD 500 – and explanations in English. The jewel, literally, is the collection of **Gold of Aidonia**, exquisite gold rings, seals and beads from the site of Aidonia, near Nemea.

The **stadium** (☎ 27460 22739; stadium only adult/concession €2/1; ✆ 8.30am-3pm) is 500m back along the road, and was once connected to the sanctuary by a sacred road. The athletes' starting line is still in place, together with the distance markers. Look out for ancient 'graffiti' in the tunnel used by athletes (note: the tunnel is slightly hidden).

Getting There & Away

Buses from Corinth (€4.80, one hour, six daily) will stop outside the site on the way to modern Nemea, a busy agricultural service town about 4km northwest of the site. There are also buses to Nemea from Argos (€3, one hour, two weekly on Monday and Thursday; note – schedule changes).

ARGOLIS ΑΡΓΟΛΙΔΑ

The Argolis Peninsula, which separates the Saronic and Argolic Gulfs, is a veritable treasure trove for archaeology buffs, history lovers and those after a fascinating frolic. The town of

Argos, from which the region takes its name, is thought to be the longest continually inhabited town in Greece. Argolis was the seat of power of the Mycenaean empire that ruled Greece from 1600 to 1100 BC. Its citadels, Mycenae and Tiryns, are two of the region's major attractions, along with the famous Theatre of Epidavros. The delightful old Venetian town of Nafplio makes a perfect base from which to explore.

ARGOS ΑΡΓΟΣ
pop 24,239

The ancient town of Argos stretches back an astonishing 6000 years. Today most vestiges of its past glory lie buried beneath the existing modern town. Argos is overshadowed by its nearest neighbour, Nafplio; Argos itself is mainly used by visitors as a transport hub for buses.

However, it's an extremely pleasant, bustling town; it's worth stopping for a quick look at the town's museum, as well as the ruins and fortress out of town. If you're really penny pinching, this is a far less expensive option than Nafplio from which to explore the region.

Orientation & Information

Argos' showpiece and focal point is its grand central square, Plateia Agiou Petrou, with its art-nouveau street lights, citrus and palm trees, and the impressive Church of Agios Petros. Beyond, Argos deteriorates into a fairly typical working town.

The main bus station, KTEL, is just south of the central square on Kapodistriou, while the train station is on the southeastern edge of town by the road to Nafplio.

An Alpha Bank is on the central square. There is no tourist office or tourist police.

Netp@rk (Mistakopoulou 1; per hr €2) Travellers can check email here.

Police (☎ 100) If you need them, this is the regular police.

Post office (◷ 7.30am-2pm Mon-Fri) Clearly signposted on Kapodistriou, southeast of the central square, Plateia Agiou Petrou.

Sights
ARCHAEOLOGICAL MUSEUM OF ARGOS

The **archaeological museum** (☎ 27510 68819; Plateia Agiou Petrou; adult/concession €2/1; ◷ 8.30am-3pm Tue-Sun), on the edge of the central square spans three floors and includes a pretty garden. The collection includes some outstanding and complete Roman mosaics and sculptures, and bronze objects from the Mycenaean tombs. Highlights include the statuette of a goddess, the mosaic

of the four seasons in the courtyard, a suit of 8th-century-BC bronze armour, and some fine Neolithic, Mycenaean and Geometric pottery; including some outstanding Argive grey and brown vases dating to before 1600 BC.

ROMAN RUINS & FORTRESS OF LARISSA

Impressive **Roman ruins** (admission free; ◷ 8.30am-3pm) straddle both sides of a road (Tripolis). To get there from the central square, head south along Danaou for about 500m and then turn right onto Theatrou, which joins the road (Tripolis) opposite the star attraction: the enormous **theatre**, which could seat up to 20,000 people (more than at Epidavros). It dates from Classical times but was greatly modified by the Romans. Nearby are the remains of a 1st-century-AD **odeion** and **Roman baths**. Opposite is the **Ancient Agora**. The complex has been given a new lease of life – signage now provides clear diagrams and contextualises the setting.

It is a 45-minute hard slog by footpath from the theatre up to the **Fortress of Larissa**, which is a conglomeration of Byzantine, Frankish, Venetian and Turkish architecture, standing on the foundations of the city's principal ancient citadel. There is also a road to the top of the fortress, signposted from the centre of town.

Sleeping & Eating

Hotel Apollon (☎ 27510 68065; www.argolidaonline .gr/apollon-hotel, in Greek; Papaflessa 13; s/d/tr €30/40/55; ❀) The best budget choice, tucked away on a quiet side street behind the central square. Although basic, the rooms come with TV.

Hotel Mycenae (☎ 27510 68332; mycenae@otenet .gr; Plateia Agiou Petrou 10; s/d incl breakfast €30/60; ❀) Situated on the central square, the 1970s-style Hotel Mycenae has large, comfortable, pastel-coloured rooms. 'Student' rates and rooms available.

Hotel Morfeas (☎ 27510 68317; www.hotel-morfeas .gr; Danaou 2, cnr Plateia Agiou Petrou; s incl breakfast €45, d incl breakfast €50-70; ❀ 🖳) Smart, if ever so slightly tired, Morfeas provides a few little toiletries and other trimmings, especially for business visitors.

Argos is in the midst of experiencing an explosion of cool cafes around the main square and beyond. **Restaurant Aigli** (☎ 27510 67266; Plateia Agiou Petrou 6; mains €6-11) is a more traditional experience, offering mezedhes (appetisers), burgers and traditional meals. With outdoor seating opposite the church in the central square, this is perfect for people-watching.

There are several supermarkets around the town centre or try to catch the Wednesday or Saturday market on Tsokri.

Getting There & Around

BUS

Just south of the central square, **KTEL Argolis** (☎ 27510 67324; Kapodistriou 8) has bus services to Nafplio (€1.40, 30 minutes, half-hourly), Mycenae (€1.50, 30 minutes, three daily) and Nemea (€3, one hour, two weekly on Monday and Thursday).

There are also bus services to Athens between 5.30am and 8.30pm (€11, two hours, six daily) via Corinth Canal (€4.70, 50 minutes), and to Tripoli (€5, one hour, four daily except Sunday).

Services south to Astros (€2.70, one hour) and Leonidio (€7, 2¼ hours) are operated by KTEL Arkadia. Ask at the cafe **Sweet Corner** (☎ 27510 23162; Theatrou 40). There are three services a day (Sunday, only two) on this route.

CAR

Car hire is available from **Aspida** (☎ 27510 68033; www.aspida-carrental.com; Tripoleos 51).

TRAIN

At the time of research, the Kalamata–Corinth railway line was closed due to track work (see boxed text, p173).

MYCENAE ΜΥΚΗΝΕΣ

pop 450

The modern village of Mycenae (mih-*kee*-nes), 12km north of Argos and just east of the main Argos–Corinth road, is geared towards the hordes of package tourists that visit Ancient Mycenae and has little to recommend it other than its proximity to the ancient site, 2km to the north. There is accommodation along its main road. There's an ATM in the main street.

Sights

ANCIENT MYCENAE

In the barren foothills of Mt Agios Ilias (750m) and Mt Zara (600m) stand the sombre and mighty ruins of **Ancient Mycenae** (☎ 27510 76585; citadel, Treasury of Atreus & museum €8; ☘ site 8am-8pm summer, 8.30am-3pm winter). For 400 years (1600–1200 BC) this vestige of a kingdom

was the most powerful in Greece, holding sway over the Argolid (the modern-day prefecture of Argolis) and influencing the other Mycenaean kingdoms.

History & Mythology

World Heritage–listed Mycenae is synonymous with the names Homer and Schliemann. In the 9th century BC Homer told in his epic poems, the 'Iliad' and the 'Odyssey', of 'well-built Mycenae, rich in gold'. These poems were, until the 19th century, regarded as no more than gripping and beautiful legends. But in the 1870s the amateur archaeologist Heinrich Schliemann (1822–90), despite derision from professional archaeologists, struck gold, first at Troy then at Mycenae. (Although, owing to doubts about the provenance of some of his information and even allegations that he falsified some finds to fit his theories, his reputation has since suffered.)

In Mycenae, myth and history are inextricably linked. According to Homer, the city of Mycenae was founded by Perseus, the son of Danae and Zeus. Perseus' greatest heroic deed was the killing of the hideous snake-haired Medusa, whose looks literally petrified the beholder. Eventually, the dynasty of Perseus was overthrown by Pelops, a son of Tantalus. The Mycenaean Royal House of Atreus was probably descended from Pelops, although myth and history are so intertwined, and the genealogical line so complex, that no one really knows. Whatever the bloodlines, by Agamemnon's time the Royal House of Atreus was the most powerful of the Achaeans (Homer's name for the Greeks). It eventually came to a sticky end, fulfilling the curse that had been cast because of Pelops' misdeeds.

The historical facts are that Mycenae was first settled by Neolithic people in the 6th millennium BC. Between 2100 and 1900 BC, during the Old Bronze Age, Greece was invaded by people of Indo-European stock who had crossed Anatolia via Troy to Greece. The invaders brought an advanced culture to then-primitive Mycenae and other mainland settlements. This new civilisation is now referred to as the Mycenaean, named after its most powerful kingdom. The other kingdoms included Pylos, Tiryns, Corinth and Argos, all in the Peloponnese. Evidence of Mycenaean civilisation has also been found at Thiva (Thebes) and Athens.

The city of Mycenae consisted of a fortified citadel and surrounding settlement. Due to the sheer size of the citadel walls (13m high and 7m thick), formed by stone blocks weighing 6 tonnes in places, the Ancient Greeks believed they must have been built by a Cyclops, one of the giants described in the 'Odyssey'.

Archaeological evidence indicates that the palaces of the Mycenaean kingdoms declined some time around 1200 BC and the palace itself was set ablaze around 1100 BC. Whether the destruction was the work of outsiders or due to internal division between the various Mycenaean kingdoms remains unresolved.

Exploring the Site

Before exploring the site, it's a good idea to head to the impressive **museum** (admission incl site fee of €8; ☉ noon-8pm Mon, 8am-7.30pm Tue-Sun). It has good English explanations and contains numerous impressive finds from the digs, including pottery, weaponry and jewellery. On display are the important early clay tablets inscribed in Linear B, an early form of written language first unearthed in Knossos and a sign of the kingdom's wealth and power –

not to mention the highly organised nature of its administration.

The lavish gold jewellery exhibits on display, including the gold funeral mask once thought to have been that of Agamemnon, are in fact copies (the originals can be found at the National Archaeological Museum (p127) in Athens.

Entry to the **Citadel of Mycenae** is through the dramatic **Lion Gate**, solidly constructed of massive stone blocks, over which rear two large lionesses. This motif is believed to have been the insignia of the Royal House of Atreus.

Inside the citadel, you will find **Grave Circle A** on the right as you enter. This was the royal cemetery and contained six grave shafts. Five shafts were excavated by Schliemann between 1874 and 1876, uncovering the famous and magnificent gold treasures, including a well-preserved gold death mask. Fervently, he sent a telegram to the Greek king stating, 'I have gazed upon the face of Agamemnon'. The mask turned out to be that of an unknown king who had died some 300 years before Agamemnon.

PELOPONNESE

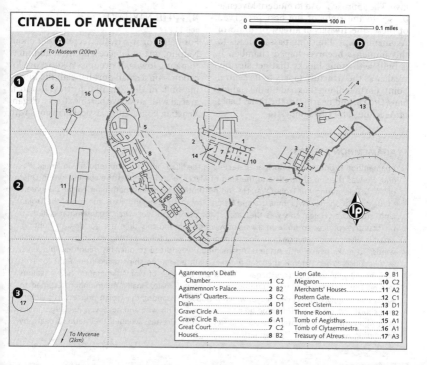

CITADEL OF MYCENAE

0   100 m
0   0.1 miles

To Museum (200m)

To Mycenae (2km)

Agamemnon's Death Chamber.........................**1** C2		Lion Gate.................................**9** B1
Agamemnon's Palace...............**2** B2		Megaron................................**10** C2
Artisans' Quarters....................**3** C2		Merchants' Houses.................**11** A2
Drain...**4** D1		Postern Gate..........................**12** C1
Grave Circle A..........................**5** B1		Secret Cistern........................**13** D1
Grave Circle B..........................**6** A1		Throne Room..........................**14** B2
Great Court...............................**7** C2		Tomb of Aegisthus.................**15** A1
Houses......................................**8** B2		Tomb of Clytaemnestra...........**16** A1
		Treasury of Atreus..................**17** A3

To the south of Grave Circle A are the remains of a group of houses. In one was discovered the famous **Warrior Vase**, regarded by Schliemann as one of his greatest discoveries because it offered a glimpse of what Mycenae's legendary warriors looked like.

The main path leads up to **Agamemnon's Palace**, centred on the **Great Court**. The rooms to the north were the private royal apartments. One of these rooms is believed to be the chamber in which Agamemnon was murdered. Access to the **throne room**, west of the Great Court, would originally have been via a large staircase. On the southeastern side of the palace is the **megaron** (reception hall).

On the northern boundary of the citadel is the **Postern Gate** through which, it is said, Orestes escaped after murdering his mother. In the far northeastern corner of the citadel is the **secret cistern**, which can be explored by torchlight, but take care – the steps are slippery.

Until the late 15th century BC the Mycenaeans put their royal dead into shaft graves. They then devised a new form of burial – the *tholos* tomb, shaped like a beehive. The approach road to modern Mycenae passes to the right of the best preserved of these, the **Treasury of Atreus**, or tomb of Agamemnon. A 40m-long passage leads to this immense beehive-shaped chamber. It is built with stone blocks that get steadily smaller as the structure tapers to its central point. Further along the road on the right is **Grave Circle B**, and nearby are the **tholos tombs** of Aegisthus and Clytaemnestra.

Sleeping & Eating

Camping Atreus (☎ 27510 76221; atreus@otenet.gr; camp sites per adult/tent €6/3.50; ☻ May-Oct; Ⓟ ☎) A well-equipped, shady camping ground on the edge of town on the main road from Fihtio. The friendly owner, Pandelis, speaks English.

Hotel Klitemnistra (☎ 27510 76451; d/tr incl breakfast €45/55; ☒ ☎) This place has clean, comfortable rooms, some with great balconies overlooking pretty rolling hills. The friendly Australian-Greek owners can suggest walks in the area. Book ahead in summer.

Any of the town tavernas serve a standard grill (mains €8 to €15), although you may have to compete with tourist groups en masse.

Getting There & Away

Three daily buses head to Mycenae from Nafplio (€2.60, one hour) and Argos (€1.60, 30 minutes). The buses stop in the village and at the ancient site.

Other bus services, such as Athens–Nafplio, stop at the village of Fihtio on the main road, leaving you 3km from the village.

NAFPLIO ΝΑΥΠΛΙΟ
pop 13,822

For better or worse, the secret is out about Nafplio, one of Greece's prettiest and most romantic towns. It occupies a knockout location – on a small port beneath the towering bulk of the Palamidi fortress – and is graced with attractive narrow streets, elegant Venetian houses, neoclassical mansions with

---

AGAMEMNON AFFAIRS

Agamemnon is one of the principal characters in the 'Iliad' and crops up regularly in Greek legend. He was the son of Atreus and the king of Mycenae and was later the commander-in-chief of the Greeks during the Trojan War. He and his brother, Menelaus, both married the daughters of the King of Sparta, Clytaemnestra and Helen. According to legend, Paris, the son of the Trojan king, stole away Helen; this was the catalyst for the Trojan War when Agamemnon called on his country's princes to unite in a war of revenge. Around this time the goddess of hunting, Artemis, also sought revenge from Agamemnon and stalled the departing war ships with adverse winds. To make peace with Artemis, Agamemnon was forced to offer his daughter, Iphigenia, as a sacrifice. When Artemis then set the seas right again, the ships sailed from Aulis for Troy and the 10-year siege of Troy began. During the last year of war Agamemnon had a jealous quarrel with Achilles over the attentions of a captive female. Finally, Agamemnon returned to Argolis victorious with his war spoils, which included Cassandra, the Trojan princess. His victory was shortlived; on his return home he was murdered by his wife and her lover, Aegisthus. Years later Agamemnon's daughter, Electra, and her brother, Orestes, avenged their father's death by murdering Aegisthus and Clytaemnestra.

flower-bedecked balconies, and interesting museums. Both overseas visitors and week-ending Athenians flock to this lively, up-wardly mobile place that is jammed with quayside cafes, posh boutiques and many comfortable hotels and guest houses (it does get somewhat overcrowded in high season and holidays).

The town, 12km southeast of Argos on the Argolic Gulf, was the first capital of Greece after Independence (between 1833 and 1834) and has been a major port since the Bronze Age. So strategic was its position that it had three fortresses – the massive principal fortress of Palamidi, the smaller Akronafplia and the diminutive Bourtzi on an islet west of the old town.

With good bus connections and services, the town is an ideal base from which to explore many nearby ancient sites.

Orientation

The old town occupies a narrow promontory with the Akronafplia fortress on the southern side and the promenades of Bouboulinas and Akti Miaouli on the north side.

The principal streets of the old town are Amalias, Vasileos Konstantinou, Staïkopoulou and Kapodistriou. The old town's central square is Plateia Syntagmatos, at the western end of Vasileos Konstantinou.

The KTEL bus station can be found on Syngrou, which is the street separating the old town from the new.

The main streets of the new town – easterly continuations of Staïkopoulou – are 25 Martiou and further on, Argou.

Information

BOOKSHOPS

Odyssey (☎ 27520 23430; Plateia Syntagmatos) Stocks international newspapers, maps, and a small selection of novels in English, French and German.

EMERGENCY

Hospital (☎ 27520 98100; cnr Asklipiou & Kolokotroni)
Tourist police (☎ 27520 98728/9; Eleftheriou 2)

INTERNET ACCESS

Internet places are rare in Nafplio; most hotels offer wi-fi.

Echorama (☎ 27520 26050; Alexandrou 9; per hr €3; ☻ 10am-9pm) A CD shop in the heart of the old town with a few internet terminals and fast connections.

Extreme Net Pl@ce (per hr €10; ☻ 8am-6am) Behind Marinopoulos supermarket (p191) and popular among night owls for its games.

LAUNDRY

Bubbles (☎ 27520 29260; Asklipiou 61; per load up to 5kg €9; ☻ 8am-9pm Mon-Fri, 8am-3pm Sat) This pricey place next to the army barracks east of the centre has the monopoly on suds – it's the only one in town.

MONEY

All the major banks have branches in town; the following banks have ATMs.
Alpha Bank (Amalias) At the western end of the street.
National Bank of Greece (Plateia Syntagmatos)

POST

Post office (cnr Syngrou & Sidiras Merarhias; ☻ 7.30am-2pm Mon-Fri)

TOURIST INFORMATION

Municipal tourist office (☎ 27520 24444; 25 Martiou 4; ☻ 9am-1pm & 4-8pm) Not the strongest aspect of the town's services.
Staikos Travel ☎ 27520 27950; www.staikostravel.gr; Bouboulinas 50; ☻ 8.30am-2pm & 5.30-9pm, closed Sun winter) A helpful source, as well as an efficient service for all travel services.

Sights & Activities

PALAMIDI FORTRESS

This vast and spectacular **citadel** (☎ 27520 28036; adult/concession €4/2; ☻ 8am-7pm summer, 8am-3pm winter) stands on a 216m-high outcrop of rock with excellent views down onto the sea and surrounding land. It was built by the Venetians between 1711 and 1714, and is regarded as a masterpiece of military architecture. Within its walls stands a series of independent bastions, strategically located across the hill. The most important, and best preserved, is the western **Agios Andreas Bastion**, which stands at the top of the steps from town. It was the home of the garrison commander, and it is named after the tiny church in the interior courtyard. There are wonderful views over the Akronafplia and the old town from the bastion walls.

The **Miltiades Bastion**, to the northeast, is the largest of the bastions. It was used as a prison for condemned criminals from 1840 to 1920. War of Independence hero Theodoros Kolokotronis spent several years here after being condemned for treason.

There are two main approaches to the fortress. You can go via the road (taxis cost about

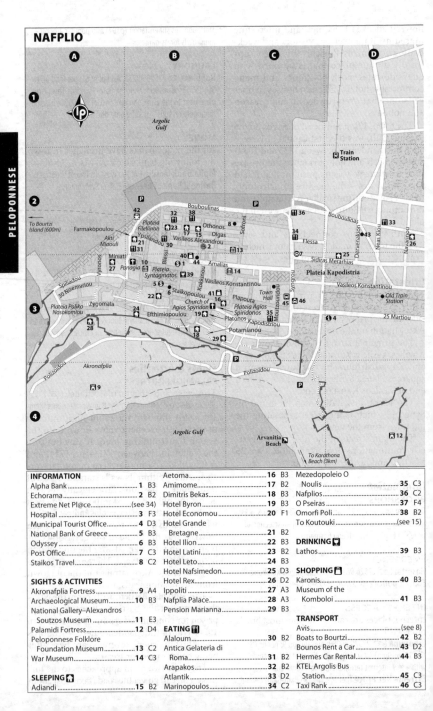

NAFPLIO

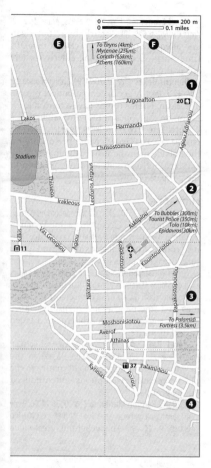

€8 one way) or the energetic can tackle the seemingly endless steps that begin southeast of the bus station. The exact number of steps is an issue of much conjecture. Locals claim that there are 999 steps, which has prompted many travellers to conduct independent counts. Most report a considerably lower figure; locals respond that the 999 steps are to the Church of Agios Andreas. Whatever the number, climb early and take water.

AKRONAFPLIA FORTRESS
Rising above the old part of town, the **Akronafplia fortress** is the oldest of Nafplio's three castles, although there's much less to see here than at the other two forts. The lower sections of the walls date back to the Bronze Age.

Until the arrival of the Venetians, the town was restricted to within its walls. The Turks called it İç Kale (meaning 'inner castle'). It was used as a political prison from 1936 to 1956.

There's a lift up to the fortress from Plateia Poliko Nosokomiou at the western edge of town – look for the flags at the entrance of the tunnel leading to the lift. It heads up to a flash hotel complex (see Nafplia Palace, p191) from where you can access the fortress. The old gateway to the fortress, crowned with a fine Venetian lion emblem, is at the top of Potamianou, the stepped street that heads uphill off Plateia Agios Spiridonos.

BOURTZI
The island fortress of Bourtzi lies about 600m west of the town's port. Most of the existing structure was built by the Venetians. Boats (€4 return per person) to the island leave from the northeastern end of Akti Miaouli.

MUSEUMS
Nafplio's award-winning **Peloponnese Folklore Foundation Museum** (☎ 27520 28947; Vasileos Alexandrou 1; adult/concession €4/2; ☻ 9am-3pm & 6-9pm Mon & Wed-Sat, 9.30am-3pm Sun, closed Tue mornings) is a beautifully arranged collection of folk costumes and household items from Nafplio's former times. Not to be missed. There's also a gift shop on the ground floor.

An arm of the Athens National Gallery, beautiful **National Gallery – Alexandros Soutzos Museum** (☎ 27520 21915; Sidiras Merarhias 23; adult/concession €3/2, admission free Mon; ☻ 10am-3pm Mon, Thu & Sat, 10am-3pm & 5-8pm Wed & Fri; 10am-2pm Sun) is housed in a stunningly restored neoclassical building and displays works on the 1821 Greek War of Independence, including paintings of Greek painters Vryzakis and Tsokos, considered the most important painters of the postwar years. The paintings, a few sculptures and artefacts are divided according to themes: battles, dying heroes, victorious sea battles, consequences of war in everyday life and ideology of the Free State.

The **war museum** (Amalias 22; admission free; ☻ 9am-2pm Tue-Sun) traces Greece's military history from the War of Independence onwards through a collection of photographs, paintings, uniforms and assorted weaponry.

Overlooking Plateia Syntagmatos and opened in 2009 following seven years of renovations, the **Archaeological Museum** (Plateia Syntagmatos; ☉ 8.30am-3pm Tue-Sun; adult/concession €2/1) has fine exhibits on show over two light and airy floors. The oldest exhibits, fire middens, date from 32,000 BC. Another highlight is the only bronze armour in existence from near Mycenae, dating from the 12th to 13th centuries BC.

BEACHES

Arvanitia Beach is a small pebble beach just 10 minutes' walk south of town, tucked beside the Akronafplia fortress. If you're feeling energetic, you can follow a path east around the coast for about an hour (roughly 3km) to sandy **Karathona Beach**, at the far side of the Palamidi fortress. The walk is extremely pretty, as would be the beach if it weren't for the litter.

Festivals & Events

Nafplio hosts a **classical music festival** (www .nafplionfestival.gr) to changing dates between late May and July featuring Greek and international performers. The Palamidi fortress is one of the concert venues.

The town is also a good base for visits to Epidavros for performances at the famous theatre during the Epidavros Festival (see p194) in July and August, part of the larger cultural Hellenic Festival.

Sleeping

BUDGET

The old town is the most interesting place to be, although budget accommodation is limited.

Hotel Economou (☎ 27520 23955; Argonafton 22; dm/s €10/20, d €25-30) A fairly basic but clean and adequate place to stay, caught in a '70s time warp. The welcoming elderly owners speak English.

Dimitris Bekas (☎ 27520 24594; Efthimiopoulou 26; s/d/tr €23/29/40) A good, central budget option. The clean, homey rooms have a top-value location on the slopes of the Akronafplia.

Hotel Leto (☎ 27520 28093; www.leto-hotel.com; Zigomala 28; s/d/tr €45/60/90) More personality on the outside than the inside (the interiors are c 1980s) but it's in an attractive position in the old part of town.

MIDRANGE

Hotel Byron (☎ 27520 22351; www.byronhotel.gr; Platonos 2; d €60-80, tr €90; ✷) Occupying a fine Venetian building, the Byron is a reliable favourite, with neat rooms, iron bedsteads and period furniture. Breakfast costs €5.

Hotel Nafsimedon (☎ 27520 25060; www.nafsim edon.gr; Sidiras Merarhias 9; s €60-70, d €82-120, tr €105-140, incl breakfast; ✷) These unpretentious lodgings in a fine neoclassical mansion feature antique rugs, timber floorboards and faded period furniture.

Hotel Rex (☎ 27520 26907; www.rex-hotel.gr; Bouboulinas 21; s €70, d €80, tr €110) Based in the new town, this is a modern alternative to the older Venetian-style options. Often booked out by groups.

our pick **Pension Marianna** (☎ 27520 24256; www .pensionmarianna.gr; Potamianou 9; s €70, d €85, tr €100, incl breakfast; P ✷ ☎) This delightful, great-value

---

BOUTIQUE HOTELS

Nafplio's boutique-hotel industry has exploded over the past few years. These renovated former mansions cater to the moneyed Athenians and weekend out-of-towners. Most hotels have four to eight (often cramped) rooms with contemporary, period or kitsch furnishings. Prices include cable TV. Note: all have steep internal stairs. We've found that with time, hotel interiors are not always being maintained to their standards. Among the plethora of boutique hotels on offer, the following are worth considering (it's a coincidence that many begin with *alpha* – A):

Aetoma (☎ 27520 27373; www.nafplionhotel.com; Plateia Agios Spiridonos 2; d incl breakfast €90-110, tr €130; ☎) Small, but comfortable, with dark, heavy and stylish furnishings.

Adiandi (☎ 27520 22073; www.hotel-adiandi.com; Othonos 31; r incl breakfast €110-120; ✷ ☎) Rooms in this fun and upmarket place are quirkily decorated with artistic door bedheads and contemporary decor. A funky cafe-cum-breakfast room is downstairs.

Amimone (☎ 27520 99477; www.amymone.gr; Othonos 39; s €65-75, d €80-90, incl breakfast; ▯ ☎) Owned by the proprietor of Adiandi, this place has colourful rooms with more traditional touches such as wrought iron bedsteads.

Hotel Latini (☎ 27520 96470; www.latinihotel.gr; s/d/ste incl breakfast €75/90/140; ☎) Overlooking the pretty Plateia Agiou Nikolaou, with sunny, airy rooms and great views.

abode – a bright yellow icon – is the pick of Nafplio. The warm and welcoming owner-hosts, the Zotos brothers, epitomise Greek *filoxenia* and serve up more than just delicious breakfasts in a cheerful dining area. Clean and comfortable rooms (all different, and some smaller than others) open onto terraces where you can feast on the view from your hill-top position. Heights come at a (small) cost – several flights of stairs. Parking is available on the road behind leading up to the fortress. Rates are €5 less per person without breakfast.

Hotel Ilion (☎ 27520 25114; www.ilionhotel.gr; Kapodistriou 4; d incl breakfast €90-180) In-your-face elaborate rococco-style decor with your very own frescoes and fiddly bits.

TOP END

Ippoliti (☎ 27520 96088; www.ippoliti.gr; Miniati; r €120-180; 🐾) The 19 rooms in this new and discretely luxurious place are decked out in tasteful muted Tuscan furnishings with neoclassical touches. There are even glass-screened fireplaces in the rooms (extra cost). It has the feel of a boutique pension with hotel services, including a gym.

Hotel Grande Bretagne (☎ 27520 96200; www .grandebretagne.com.gr; Plateia Filellinon; s/d incl breakfast €130/180; 🐾) Nafplion elegance – this is a plush, traditionally styled period hotel and right in the heart of the waterfront cafe action.

Nafplia Palace (☎ 27520 70800; www.nafplion hotels.gr; Akronafplia; d/bungalows/villas from €390/580/1300; 🅿 🐾 🖥 🛜 🐾) This provides the ultimate take-no-prisoners luxury stakes. It offers ultramodern, uberchic villas, with personal butlers, hi-tech audiovisuals and mini swimming pools.

Eating

Surprisingly, although full of reasonable eateries, Nafplio won't blow your culinary mind. The streets of the old town are filled with dozens of restaurants, all serving hearty taverna fare. The tourist eateries along Staïkopoulou offer some authentic and reasonably priced taverna dishes for lunch and dinner, but the alleyways hide some excellent surprises.

Mezedopoleio O Noulis (☎ 27520 25541; Moutzouridou 22; mezedhes €3-10; ✆ 10am-4pm Mon-Sat Oct-Apr, 10am-3pm & 7-11pm May-Sep) This modest place serves a faultlessly fresh range of mezedhes. The tasting plate of 10 different morsels is a tasty meal in itself (€7.50).

Omorfi Poli (☎ 27520 29452; Bouboulinas 75; mains €6-16; ✆ dinner) This pleasant restaurant's professional chef whips up Greek and Italian dishes. The mezedhes (€5) have a slight non-Greek twist – there's mushroom risotto plus Greek favourites including *saganaki* (grilled cheese) and grilled sardines. Our favourite main is the delicious *mousakas* (layers of eggplant or zucchini, minced meat and potatoes topped with cheese sauce) baked in its own ceramic dishes (piping hot in every sense, and a steal at €7). Bonuses include the friendly service and good wine list (€17 to €47).

our pick **Antica Gelateria di Roma** (☎ 27520 23520; www.anticagelateria.gr; cnr Farmakopoulou & Komninou) 'Bongiorno – this is an Italian gelati shop!' announces Italian gelati *maestro* and *maestra* Marcello and Claudia Raffo as you enter their premises. That's just in case you didn't see and smell (and we'll bet, soon taste) the smorgasbord of the best (yes, best) traditional gelati outside Italy. And don't say we didn't warn you!

Some taverna options also recommended:

Nafplios (☎ 27520 97999; cnr Bouboubilas & Syngrou; mains €6-11; ✆ lunch & dinner) One of the most genuine places around, this unpretentious place overlooks the car park. Hearty dishes – all traditional – are on display in large pans.

Arapakos (☎ 27520 27675; Bouboulinas 81; mains €7-12, fish per kilogram €30-80; ✆ lunch & dinner) If you're feeling fishy, hook onto this upmarket morsel for quality seafood.

Alaloum (☎ 27520 29883; Papanikolaou 10; mains €7-13; ✆ lunch & dinner) In a lovely spot on a square, and serves up Greek Mediterranean fare.

O Pseiras (☎ 27520 24117; Porou 5; mains €8-12; ✆ dinner Wed-Mon) This no-nonsense taverna will get you out of your comfort zone (it's in the Prania region, east of town), with reasonable fare and occasional live music (often to accommodate tourist groups).

To Koutouki (✆ 27520 24477; Olgas 44, mains €8-18; ✆ dinner) Good for quality grills, pastas and mezedhes. Not on the waterfront, but is reliable and has a pleasant outdoor setting in summer.

Self-caterers will find a choice of supermarkets in Nafplio's new town, including **Marinopoulos** (cnr Syngrou & Flessa) and **Atlantik** (Bouboulinas 24).

Drinking

Despite being simply jammed with cafes and bars, there still doesn't seem to be enough of them in town to hold the throngs of trendy party animals who flock to Nafplio in summer. Most options are on Bouboulinas – just cruise along until you find an image (and the latest decor) to your taste and a musical volume you can handle.

An alternative to the homogenous trendy drinking hole, **Lathos** (Vasileos Konstantinou 3; 7pm-late Wed-Mon) is a quirky place that's jam-packed with remote-controlled junkyard automata from moving tables to an armclanging cymbal. Depending on his mood, the philosophical owner/DJ plays a haphazard mix of musical beats – perfect for jiving with your surroundings.

Shopping

The alleyways of Nafplio's old town between Plateia Syntagmatos and the war museum offer boutique-style clothing, jewellery and accessories, plus inevitable tourist paraphernalia. For your daily shopping needs, plus pharmacies and shoe shops (Imelda Marcos, eat your heart out), head to Argous St.

Karonis (27520 24446; www.karoniswineshop.gr; Amalias 5) Wine enthusiasts can find a fine selection of wines from all over the country, especially Nemean reds and spirits.

Museum of the Komboloi (27520 21618; www.komboloi.gr; Staïkopoulou 25; adult/concession €3/free; 9.30am-9pm Mon-Thu & Sun, to 9.30pm Fri & Sat) This shop – with a private museum above – sells *komboloï* (worry beads), evil-eye charms and amulets.

The Peloponnese Folklore Foundation Museum (p189) houses an attractive gift shop (ground floor), with a range of items, including books, from Greece and around the world.

Getting There & Away

The **KTEL Argolis bus station** (27520 27323; Syngrou 8) has buses to Athens (€12, 2½ hours, hourly) via the Corinth Isthmus (Peloponnese) KTEL bus station (near Corinth; €6, 1½ hours), Argos (€1.40, 30 minutes, half-hourly), Tolo (€1.40, 15 minutes, hourly), Epidavros (€2.60, 45 minutes, four daily), Mycenae (€2.60, one hour, two daily), Kranidi (€7, two hours, four daily except Sunday) and Galatas (€7.40, two hours, two daily Monday to Friday). Other destinations include Tripoli (€6, 1½ hours, two daily Monday to Saturday, one on Sunday). Note: weekend schedules are often reduced.

Getting Around

For taxis call 27520 24120 or head to the rank on Syngrou.

Car-hire agencies include the following:
Avis (27520 24160/1; www.carrental-greece.gr; Bouboulinas 51)
Bounos Rent a car (27520 24390; www.bounos-carrental.com; Dervenakion 7)
Hermes Car Rental (27520 25308; www.hermestravel.gr; Amalias 7)

TIRYNS ΤΙΡΥΝΘΑ

Situated 4km from Nafplio, just to the east of the Nafplio–Argos road, is the impressive acropolis of **Tiryns** (27520 22657; adult/concession €3/2; 8am-8pm summer, 8am-3pm winter), an important and underrated Mycenaean acropolis and the apogee of Mycenaean architectural achievement, especially its massive walls. In parts, they are 7m thick and, according to mythology, were built by the Cyclops.

Tiryns shares equal billing on the World Heritage list with Mycenae, although Tiryn's setting is less awe-inspiring. The layout of some of the ruins is easy to make out, and there are few crowds. As yet, the site has no signs or descriptions; it's worth buying a guidebook, such as *Tiryns* (by Dr Alkestis Papademetriou; €7) at the ticket office. While further excavations continue, visitors are limited to exploring the Upper and Lower Citadels plus (a more recent opening), a large area where water was stored in ancient times.

Any Nafplio–Argos bus can drop you outside the site.

EPIDAVROS ΕΠΙΔΑΥΡΟΣ

In its day **Epidavros** (27530 22009; adult/concession €6/3; 8am-7.30pm summer, 7.30am-5pm winter), 30km east of Nafplio, was famed and revered as far away as Rome as a place of miraculous healing. Visitors came great distances to this sanctuary of Asclepius (god of medicine) to seek a cure for their ailments.

Today visitors are more likely to flock to the site for its amazingly well-preserved theatre, which remains a venue during the Hellenic Festival (p137) for Classical Greek theatre (along with other more modern plays, opera and music), first performed here up to 2000 years ago. The site occupies a glorious setting amid pine-clad hills. Not surprisingly, Epidavros is a protected under the World Heritage listings.

If visiting Epidavros on your own by car, do not be confused by the sign to P Epidavros (Paleia Epidavros) – this means Ancient Epidavros. To confuse matters more, the so-called 'small theatre' used for some festival performances is located here; the 'large theatre' referred to on festival programs is at the main site (see below), signed as Theatre of Edipavros.

History

Legend has it that Asclepius was the son of Apollo and Coronis. While giving birth to Asclepius, Coronis was struck by a thunder bolt and killed. Apollo took his son to Mt Pelion where the physician Chiron instructed the boy in the healing arts.

Apollo was worshipped at Epidavros in Mycenaean and Archaic times, but by the 4th century BC he had been superseded by his son. Epidavros became acknowledged as the birthplace of Asclepius. Although the afflicted worshipped Asclepius at sanctuaries throughout Greece, the two most important were at Epidavros and on the island of Kos. The fame of the sanctuary spread, and when a plague raged in Rome, Livy and Ovid came to Epidavros to seek help.

It is believed that licks from snakes were one of the curative practices at the sanctuary. Asclepius is normally shown with a serpent, which – by renewing its skin – symbolises rejuvenation. Other treatments provided at the sanctuary involved diet instruction, herbal medicines and occasionally even surgery. The sanctuary also served as an entertainment venue and every four years, during the Festival of Asclepieia, Epidavros hosted dramas and athletic competitions.

Sights

THEATRE OF EPIDAVROS

Today it's the 3rd-century theatre, not the sanctuary, that pulls the crowds to Epidavros. It is one of the best-preserved Classical Greek structures, renowned for its amazing acoustics; a coin dropped in the centre can be heard from the highest seat. Built of limestone, the theatre seats up to 14,000 people. Its entrance is flanked by restored **Corinthian pilasters**. It's used for performances of Ancient Greek drama during the annual Hellenic Festival (p137).

SANCTUARY

The ruins of the sanctuary are less crowded than the theatre. In the south is the huge **katagogeion**, a hostelry for pilgrims and patients. To the west is the large **banquet hall** in which

the Romans built an **odeum**. It was here that the Festival of Asclepieia took place. Opposite is the **stadium**, venue for the festival's athletic competitions. This is one of several areas under reconstruction; at the time of research one side was completed.

To the north are the foundations of the **Temple of Asclepius** (covered by earth at the time of research for impending excavations) and next to them is the **abaton**. The therapies practised here seemed to have depended on the influence of the mind upon the body. It is believed that patients were given a pep talk by a priest on the powers of Asclepius, then put to sleep in the *abaton* to dream of a visitation by the god. The dream would hold the key to the healing process.

East is the **Sanctuary of Egyptian Gods**, which indicates that the cult of Asclepius was an adaptation of the cult of Imhotep, worshipped in Egypt for his healing powers. To the west of the Temple of Asclepius are the remains of the **tholos** (built 360–320 BC); the function of which is unknown.

Set among the green foothills of Mt Arahneo, the air redolent with herbs and pine trees, it's easy to see how the sanctuary would have had a beneficial effect upon the ailing. Considering the state of Greece's current health system, perhaps the centre should be resurrected.

At the time of research, some of the buildings, including the *tholos* and *abaton*, were in the process of being partially reconstructed. This entails adding sections of columns and, in some places, recreating parts of ruins in their entirety. Depending on your point of view, this controversial practice enhances a sense of place, helping visitors to visualise, or destroys your romantic notion of what ruins should look like. In any case, archaeologists have deliberately used different coloured stone to clearly distinguish what is new and what is not.

MUSEUM

The museum, between the sanctuary and the theatre, houses statues, stone inscriptions recording miraculous cures, surgical instruments, votive offerings and partial reconstructions of the sanctuary's once-elaborate *tholos*. There's not much in the way of written information but some of

PELOPONNESE

the statuary and the chunks of marble do hint at the sanctuary's former status. After the theatre, the *tholos* is considered to have been the site's most impressive building and fragments of beautiful, intricately carved reliefs from its ceiling are also displayed. Most of the statues are copies (the real ones are in the National Archaeological Museum in Athens).

Festivals & Events

The Epidavros Theatre is the venue for performances staged (with both modern theatre and Ancient Greek dramas) during the annual **Epidavros Festival** in July and August (to a changing program); part of the larger cultural Hellenic Festival. Tickets can be bought in Epidavros at the **site office** (☎ 27530 22026; www.greekfestival.gr; 9am-2pm & 5-8pm Mon-Thu, 9.30am-9.30pm Fri & Sat), or from the Hellenic Festival box office (p138) in Athens. Prices vary according to seating, and student discounts are available. There are special bus services available from Athens and Nafplio.

Sleeping & Eating

Hotel Avaton (☎ 27530 22178; fax 27530 23059; r €55; P) If you're planning an early-morning visit to the site, this small, clean and modern hotel is the best accommodation option, just 1km away, at the junction of the road to Kranidi and to the site of Epidavros.

There is a choice of restaurants on the main street of Ligourio, several kilometres from Epidavros.

Getting There & Away

There are buses from Nafplio to Epidavros (€2.60, 45 minutes, three to four daily) and two buses daily to Athens from nearby Ligourio (€12, 2½ hours).

SOUTHWEST ARGOLIS

Very few travellers take the time to venture down to the southwestern heel of the Argolis peninsula, centred on the agricultural service town of **Kranidi**, located 90km southeast of Nafplio. The region is famous for its pomegranates, which appreciate the mild winter temperatures around here. These spectacular ruby-red fruits ripen in November.

The small resorts of **Porto Heli**, 4km south of Kranidi, and **Ermioni**, 4km east of Kranidi, are both popular weekend escapes for Athenians. For travellers, they offer convenient connections to the Saronic Gulf islands of Hydra and Spetses.

The **Frachthi Cave**, overlooking Kilada Bay 7km north of Kranidi, rates among the most important early sites in Europe. Excavations around here have revealed a history of continuous occupation from Upper Paleolithic to Late Neolithic times (25,000–3000 BC). Note: it's not advisable to visit the cave – the area is full of large, unfilled holes, the unfortunate legacy of poorly completed excavations. The cave is floodlit at night, creating a spectacular backdrop for diners at the fish restaurants at **Kilada**, on the southern side of the bay.

About 1km west of the village of Didyma, don't miss the **Didyma Caves** (admission free), two extraordinary sinkholes, caves that collapsed thousands of years ago leaving large craterlike holes. One hides a sensational surprise – a tiny Byzantine church – constructed under a crevice. The caves are well signposted.

Getting There & Away

BOAT

Hydrofoils change each season; at the time of research **Hellenic Seaways** (☎ 27540 31514) were running the show. Normally, regular hydrofoils depart from Porto Heli to Piraeus via Spetses and Hydra, and from Ermioni to Piraeus via Hydra.

BUS

There are **bus services** (☎ 2754 21237) between Kranidi and Nafplio (€7, two hours, four daily except Sunday), and local buses from Kranidi to Ermioni (€1.40, 10 minutes, two daily) and Porto Heli (€1.40, 10 minutes, three daily).

ARKADIA ΑΡΚΑΔΙΑ

The picturesque rural prefecture of Arkadia occupies much of the central Peloponnese. Its name evokes images of grassy meadows, forested mountains, gurgling streams and shady grottoes and thankfully, despite the tragic bushfires in 2007, this is largely still the case. It was a favourite haunt of Pan, who played his pipes, guarded herds and frolicked with nymphs in this sunny, bucolic idyll.

Almost encircled by mountain ranges, Arkadia was remote enough in ancient times to remain largely untouched by the battles and intrigues of the rest of Greece, and was the only region of the Peloponnese not conquered by the Dorians. The region – dotted with crumbling medieval villages, remote monasteries and Frankish castles – is popular among outdoor-loving visitors. It also has 100km or so of rugged and unspoilt coastline on the Argolic Gulf, running south from the pretty town of Kiveri to Leonidio.

TRIPOLI ΤΡΙΠΟΛΗ

pop 25,520

The violent recent history of Arkadia's capital, Tripoli (*tree*-po-lee), is in stark contrast with its peaceful rural surroundings. In 1821, during the War of Independence, the town was captured by Kolokotronis and its 10,000 Turkish inhabitants massacred. The Turks retook the town three years later and burnt it to the ground before withdrawing in 1828.

Tripoli itself is not a place where tourists tend to linger, but it's a major transport hub for the Peloponnese and hard to avoid if you're relying on public transport.

Orientation

Tripoli can seem a little bit confusing at first. The streets radiate out from the central square, Plateia Vasileos Georgiou, like an erratic spider's web. The main streets are Washington, which runs south from Plateia Vasileos Georgiou to Kalamata; Ethnikis Andistasis, which runs north from the square and becomes the road to Kalavryta; and Vasileos Georgiou, which runs east from the square to Plateia Kolokotroni. El Venizelou runs east from Plateia Kolokotroni, leading you to the Corinth road.

The KTEL Arkadia bus station is 1km west of Plateia Koloktroni, along the Argos–Corinth road and just beyond an AB Supermarket. The city's other bus 'station' is opposite the train station, about a 10-minute walk away, at the southeastern end of Lagopati, the street that runs behind the KTEL Arkadia bus station.

Information

Tripoli has branches of all the major banks on Plateia Koloktroni and Plateia Vasileos Georgiou.

Memories Lounge Net Café (☎ 2710 235600; Dareiotou 10; per hr €2; ☼ 8am-late)

Police (☎ 2710 230540; OHE Ave) Out on the western edge of town, between the train station and the KTEL Arkadia bus station.

Post office (cnr D Plapouta & Nikitara; ☼ 7.30am-8pm Mon-Fri)

Sights
ARCHAEOLOGICAL MUSEUM

The city's **Archaeological Museum** (☎ 2710 242148; Evangelistrias 2; adult/concession €2/1; ☼ 8.30am-3pm Tue-Sun) is clearly signposted off Vasileos Georgiou, behind Hotel Alex, and is well worth dropping into. It houses relics from the surrounding ancient sites of Megalopoli, Gortys, Lykosoura, Mantinea and Paliokastro, including some important prehistoric finds, such as Neolithic fertility figures and ornate storage jars, plus sculptures from Herodus Atticus. The little votive offerings from Arkadian shrines in the area are also interesting.

Sleeping & Eating

Hotel Alex (☎ 2710 223465; Vasileos Georgiou A26; s/d/tr €50/80/90; ☒ ℗) Centrally positioned, simple, spacious rooms with TV represent good value.

Hotel Anaktoricon (☎ 2710 222545; www .anaktorikon.gr; Ethnikis Andistasis 48; s/d/tr €80/102/127; ℗ ☒ ☐) The pick of places in town for comfort and plush furnishings, this friendly, family-run boutique-style hotel is beyond the town hall.

Kouros (☎ 2710 223534; Dareiotou 18; mains €5-13; ☼ lunch & dinner) Ask locals and they all recommend this tasteful, central taverna. Dishes err on the traditional.

Taverna Piterou (☎ 2710 222058; Kalavrytou 11a; mains €6-9; ☼ lunch & dinner) This bustling taverna, said to be the oldest in Tripoli, nestles under the shade of vine trellises on Kalavrytou (the northern extension of Ethnikis Andistasis), beyond the park with the old steam train. The huge selection of tasty mains and accompanying side dishes include rabbit *stifadho* (sweet stew cooked with tomato and onions), beef stew, codfish and even braids of lamb's intestines.

Getting There & Away
BUS

The **KTEL Arkadia bus station** (☎ 2710 222560; Plateia Kolokotroni) is the main bus terminal, 1km west from the city centre. There are 13 buses daily to Athens (€13.50, 2¼ hours) via Corinth Isthmus (€7.30, one hour). There are also two buses daily west to Olympia (€11.10, three hours) and Pyrgos (€12.80, 3½ hours), and three east to Argos (€5, one hour) and Nafplio

(€6, 1½ hours). Buses also head to Kalavryta (€9, 2¼ hours, one daily) and Patra (€13, 3½ hours, two daily).

Regional services include buses to Megalopoli (€3, 40 minutes, seven daily) and Stemnitsa (€3.70, one hour, once daily Monday to Friday). There are also two daily services (one on Sunday) to Dimitsana (€5.80, 1½ hours), Andritsena (€7, 1½ hours) via Karitena (€4.70), and Leonidio (€8, 2½ hours).

The **bus stop** (☎ 2710 242086) on Lagopati handles departures to Sparta (€4.90, one hour, 10 daily), Kalamata (€7.20, two hours, nine daily, fewer on weekends).

TRAIN

Tripoli lies on the line that runs between Corinth and Kalamata. At the time of research, this line was under repair. See p173 for more information.

MEGALOPOLI ΜΕΓΑΛΟΠΟΛΗ
pop 5114

Despite its name, there's little left of Megalopoli (Great City) that reflects its former grandeur. It was founded in 371 BC as the capital of a united Arkadia and was nestled in a leafy valley; now the ruins lie near an enormous smoke-spewing power station that's fuelled by the coal strip–mined surrounding plains.

Despite its magnificent ancient theatre (now closed), the town merely acts as a transport hub on the main route from Tripoli to Kalamata and Pyrgos. The KTEL bus station is one block from the square. There are bus services to Athens (€16.40, three hours, eight daily) via Tripoli (€3, 40 minutes) and Kalamata (€4.40, one hour), as well as to Andritsena (€4.10, 1¼ hours, two daily) via Karitena.

CENTRAL ARKADIA

The area to the west of Tripoli is a tangle of medieval villages, precipitous ravines and narrow winding roads, woven into valleys of dense vegetation beneath the slopes of the Menalon Mountains. This is the heart of the Arkadia prefecture, and you'll find it's an area with some of the most breathtaking scenery in the Peloponnese. The region is high above sea level and nights can be chilly, even in summer. Snow is common in winter.

Your own transport is highly recommended here, but the three most important villages – Karitena, Stemnitsa and Dimitsana – are within reach of Tripoli by public transport.

Karitena Καρίταινα
pop 271

High above the Megalopoli–Andritsena road is the splendid medieval village of Karitena (kar-eet-eh-nah). A stepped path leads from the central square to the 13th-century **Frankish castle**, perched atop a massive rock. The castle was captured by Greek forces under Kolokotronis early in the War of Independence and became a key stronghold as the war unfolded.

Before the advent of the euro, Karitena was known as the home of the wonderful arched stone bridge over the Alfios River that adorned the old 5000 drachma note. The old bridge now sits beneath a large modern concrete bridge.

SLEEPING & EATING

Vrenthi Rooms (☎ 27910 31650; d/tr €50/65) As one of the few places to stay, this attractive stone hotel could charge a bomb, but it doesn't and is good value. The nearby Café Vrenthi doubles as reception for the rooms.

Stavrodromi (☎ 27910 31284; mains €6-10) Stavrodromi means crossroads, the location of this reliable option – serving warm, filling meals – if the village taverna is closed. It's down the hill at the junction (own transport recommended).

GETTING THERE & AWAY

There are two buses daily (one on Sunday) between Tripoli and Karitena (via Megalopoli; €5.30, one hour). One bus continues to Andritsena (€2.30) – check the schedule at Café Vrenthi or Café Toledo. (Note: some buses arrive/depart from the crossroads, from where it's an arduous walk to the village.)

Stemnitsa Στεμνίτσα
pop 412

Stemnitsa (stem-*nee*-tsah), 16km north of Karitena, is a striking and beautiful village of stone houses and Byzantine churches. There are several monasteries in the area along the riverbank to the site of **Ancient Gortys**. The area is an excellent gateway for walks in the Lousios Gorge (see the boxed text, opposite).

GORGE YOURSELF

Hiking

Hiking is a popular activity in these magnificent surroundings. There are some wonderful walks along the Lousios Gorge; the most accessible departure points are from Stemnitsa (opposite) or Dimitsana (below). Walks vary from one hour to long (and hilly) day hikes, where you can hike the entire length of the gorge, taking in monasteries including Prodomou and New and Old Philosophou. Other walks extend beyond the gorge to mountain villages. A range of walks are outlined in the excellent publication *Walker's Map of the River Lousios Valley* (€4.50), available at the Open-Air Water Power Museum (p198) in Dimitsana.

Rafting & Kayaking

Based in the village of Dimitsana, **Trekking Hellas of Arcadia** (☎ 27910 25978, 6974459753; www .trekkinghellas.gr) offers various activities, including white-water rafting (€50 to €80) on the nearby Lousios and Alfios Rivers, hiking along the gorge (€20 to €50) and river trekking (€45). Minimum rates apply.

No longer in the gorge, but further north on the Ladonas River, 20km south of Klitoria (and best accessed from Klitoria), **Eco Action** (☎ 6976510597, in Athens 210 331 7866; www.ecoaction.gr) offers a choice of rafting or kayaking (both €45 to €50) on the beautiful Ladonas River. Mountain-biking trips are also available. Its riverside base camp is 7.5km from the pretty, mountaintop village of **Dafni**. You will normally join a group to make up numbers.

Behind the base camp, **Ladonas** (☎ 6972849530; www.dafneos.gr; d/tr €70/80) offers comfortable self-contained stone cottages, with the river about 100m away. At the time of research, a hotel was being constructed in Dafni. From Dafni you can also visit the **Ladonas Dam**.

Caution: river activities must not be taken lightly. Fatal accidents can and do occur.

The town boasts a small **folk art museum**, but check the sign for its irregular opening times. There are an incredible 40 churches in and around the hills vicinity. Ask around for the keys to the central ones.

SLEEPING & EATING

There are domatia signs around the village. Ask at the bakery or some of the cafes for options and directions.

Sarakiniotis Rooms (☎ 27950 81441; www .sarakiniotis.gr; s/d/tr €40/50/65) Among the town's few options for the budget traveller are these basic, slightly dark rooms.

ourpick Mpelleiko (☎ 6976607967; www.mpel leiko.gr; s/d/tr incl breakfast €80/95/110) Superior in design and lofty location, this superbly renovated house is perched behind the village and is by far the most original of all sleeping options. The friendly, hospitable English-speaking owner has converted her family home (dating from 1650) into a guest house in artistic and tasteful contemporary Greek style. You can even sleep in the former 'donkey basement'. The breakfasts – serving homemade produce – and the breakfast room are especially tasteful. For directions, enquire at the jam shop

at the southern end of town; look for the 'B&B' sign.

Hotel Trikolonion (☎ in Athens 210 688 9249; www.countryclub.gr; d incl breakfast €150; 🖳) A member of the Country Club group, the large, stone-hewn Trikolonion offers a more predictable luxurious, lodge-style experience. The rooms feature dark-wood furnishings, muted colours and heavy fabrics. Rates soar on Friday and Saturday.

I Stemnitsa (☎ 27950 81371; mains €3.50-13; 🕑 lunch & dinner) It may be the only taverna open year-round, but you could do worse. Tables are under giant brollies and good, honest (if slighly repetitive) dishes are on offer. The local butcher owns the establishment, so expect quality, hearty meat cuts.

GETTING THERE & AWAY

There is one bus each weekday to/from Stemnitsa and Tripoli (€4, one hour). The bus to Tripoli heads to Dimitsana. Times change seasonally.

Dimitsana Δημητσάνα
pop 230

Built amphitheatrically on two hills at the beginning of the Lousios Gorge, Dimitsana (dih-mi-*tsah*-nah), 11km north of Stemnitsa, is a delightful medieval village. This small place played a significant role in the country's struggle for self-determination. Its Greek school, founded in 1764, was an important spawning ground for the ideas leading to the uprisings against the Turks. Its students included Bishop Germanos of Patra and Patriarch Gregory V, who was hanged by the Turks in retaliation for the massacre in Tripoli. The village also had a number of gunpowder factories and a branch of the secret Filiki Eteria (Friendly Society) where Greeks met to discuss the revolution.

It's a sleepy village in low season, but on weekends and during summer the town springs to life as eager hikers and out-of-towners enjoy its ambience and surrounding walks.

SIGHTS
Open-Air Water Power Museum
It may sound of marginal interest but this excellent little **museum** (☎ 27950 31630; www .piop.gr; adult/concession €3/1.50; ☉ 10am-6pm Wed-Mon summer, 10am-5pm Wed-Mon winter) offers an illuminating insight into the region's preindustrial past. It occupies the old Agios Yiannis mill complex 1.5km south of town (signposted), where a spring-fed stream once supplied power for a succession of mills spread down the hillside. A flour mill, a gunpowder mill and a fulling tub (for treating wool) have been restored to working order. There's also an old leather factory. A new hall will hold temporary exhibitions.

The intelligent and imaginative explanations and subtitled videos (both in English) explain the processes of gunpowder and leather production.

Four kilometres southwest from Dimitsana, along the winding road, is Zatouna village. Be sure to stop for a drink at the quirky **Kafeneio To Kentron** (☎ 27950 31361; ☉ 8am-10pm), almost a museum in itself, thanks to the previous proprietor, the current owner's grandfather, who was both a barber and avid collector (you'll see what we mean).

SLEEPING & EATING
You'll see several signs for domatia in the middle of town (Plateia Agias Kyriakis).

Tsiapas Rooms to Rent (☎ 27950 31583; d €50-60) These great-value so-clean-you-could-eat-off-the-floor type rooms also boast fridges

and hotplates. The communal living room has a fireplace – perfect for a cold evening. Signposted off Plateia Agias Kyriakis.

Koutsenis Village (☎ 27950 31445; www.koustenis village.gr; r incl breakfast €70-90; ☒) These brand new modern stone rooms won't be to everyone's taste – they are in a complex and are 1km south out of town, near the water museum – but they are well-run, clean and pleasant and afford great views down the gorge.

Hotel Dimitsana (☎ 27950 31518; www.hoteldimitsana .gr; s/d/tr incl breakfast €100/130/150; P) Situated 1km south of the village on the road to Stemnitsa, this place is like a giant ski lodge, with puffy sofas, rich fabrics and an open fire. The comfortably appointed rooms have wonderful views over the Lousios Valley.

There is little to distinguish the village's tavernas – all serve reasonable, if similar, fare, such as rooster in red wine and *fasoladha* (bean soup).

GETTING THERE & AWAY
There are buses from Tripoli to Dimitsana (€6, 1½ hours, two daily) and one daily (except weekends) from Dimitsana to Tripoli.

KYNOURIA ΚΥΝΟΥΡΙΑ
Kynouria is the coastal region of Arkadia. It covers a narrow strip of territory that stretches south from the tiny village of Kiveri, 41km east of Tripoli, to Kosmas, perched high in the Parnonas Mountains. Much of the land is incredibly rugged, with a narrow coastal plain and very little fertile ground.

In ancient times the region was contested by Argos and Sparta – the Argives held sway in the north and the Spartans controlled the south. The easiest access is from Argos.

Kiveri to Leonidio Κιβέρι προς Λεωνίδιο
No more than a blip on the map, Kiveri is just south of where the main roads east from Tripoli and south from Argos meet. From here, the road hugs the coast for most of the 64km south to Leonidio, curving above a succession of tiny pebble-beached villages.

The first town of consequence is **Astros**, perched in the hills 28km south of Argos. The main attraction around here is the **Villa of Herodes Atticus**, in the hills 4.5km from the turn-off to Tripoli (or 2.5km from central Astros). It was built in the 2nd century AD for the wealthy Roman founder of the celebrated

Odeon of Herodes Atticus (p122) in Athens. This was his modest country retreat, spread out over a small plateau with views over the Argolic Gulf. Recent excavations have uncovered a stunning spread of more than 10,000 sq metres of mosaics. At the time of research they were being excavated and were fenced off. Apart from some magnificent coastal scenery, there's very little to see between Astros and the minor resort of **Paralia Tyrou**, 29km further south.

Leonidio Λεωνίδιο

pop 3224

Leonidio, 76km south of Argos, has a dramatic setting at the mouth of the Badron Gorge. Its tiny Plateia 25 Martiou is an archetypal, unspoilt, whitewashed Greek village square. Some of the older people around here still speak Tsakonika – a highly distinctive dialect dating back to the time of ancient Sparta.

There are some pleasant beaches to be found at the nearby seaside villages of **Plaka** and **Poulithra**. Plaka, 5km from Leonidio and the town's port, is no more than a cluster of buildings around a small square. The fertile alluvial river flats between Leonidio and the coast are intensively farmed.

Leonidio is famous for its Tsakonian aubergines; each summer the town holds an annual **Aubergine Festival**.

SLEEPING & EATING

There are apartments for rent in town, but most people head for the beach at Plaka, where there are several domatia.

Hotel Dionysos (☎ 27570 23455, 6970804050; s/d/tr €35/45/50) Plaka's only hotel, opposite the port, is a good spot to unwind and do nothing for a few days.

Fishermen's Tavern (☎ 27570 22815; fish per kilogram €30-50; 🕐 lunch & dinner Apr-Oct) The most modest (and the least contrived) of Plaka's eateries is this small place with a cosy terrace. Net the daily catch of Nikos, the understated son of the owner and also a fisherman.

GETTING THERE & AWAY

There are buses up and down the coast to/from Argos (€7, 2¼ hours, three daily) and Tripoli (€8, 2½ hours, two daily). In summer, there are two buses between Plaka and Leonidio (€0.80, 10 minutes). The KTEL bus station is at the **Café Bar 2Porto** (☎ 27570 22255; Thiporto).

South of Leonidio

The road south from Leonidio over the Parnonas Mountains to the village of Geraki in Lakonia, 48km away, is one of the most scenic in the Peloponnese. For the first 12km, the road snakes west up the **Badron Gorge**, climbing slowly away from the river until at times the water is no more than a speck of silver far below. The road then leaves the Badron and climbs rapidly towards Kosmas on dramatic hairpin bends (that make the Monaco circuit seem like an airstrip).

Just before the top of the climb, there's a sealed road to the left leading to **Moni Panagias Elonis**, a remarkable little monastery perched precariously on the mountainside. Visitors are welcome provided they are suitably dressed.

It's another 14km from the monastery to the peaceful, beautiful mountain village of **Kosmas**. There are several sleeping options here, including **Filinouda Studios** (☎ 27570 31463; Central Sq, Kosmas; s/d/tr €55/60/85), where you can watch the village world go by from one of these five studios (with cooking facilities), housed in a beautiful stone building. All share a pleasant communal living area with open fireplace. Ask at the shop next door (no English is spoken). Even if you don't stay overnight, it's worth trying the town speciality (goat) at a taverna beneath the huge plane trees in the square.

After Kosmas the road descends – more gently this time – to the village of **Geraki**. A brief pause is warranted to visit the quaint churches and to see the locals at play in the busy square. From here you can head 40km west to Sparta, or continue south through Skala, Molai and Sikia, also in Lakonia, to Monemvasia.

There is no public transport between Leonidio and Kosmas.

LAKONIA ΛΑΚΩΝΙΑ

The region of Lakonia occupies almost identical boundaries to the powerful mountainskirted kingdom ruled by King Menelaus in Mycenaean times. It is home to legends, including the city of Sparta and the spectacular ruins of Mystras, the Byzantine Empire's last stronghold.

Dominating the landscape are two massive mountain ranges, the Taÿgetos Mountains in the west and the Parnonas Mountains in the east. These taper away to create the central and eastern fingers of the Peloponnese.

Between them lies the fertile valley of the Evrotas River, famous for its olives and oranges. The valley has been a focal point of human settlement since Neolithic times, and the location of the original Mycenaean Sparta, home of King Menelaus and his wife Helen, possessor of the 'face that launched a thousand ships'. It was the abduction of Helen by Paris, the prince of Troy, that sparked the Trojan Wars of Homer's 'Iliad'.

The site of this Mycenaean city has yet to be confirmed, but it is thought to have been at Pellana, 27km north of modern-day Sparta. The city was re-established in its present location by the Dorians at the start of the 1st millennium BC. Unfortunately, this ancient city lies beneath the modern town, leaving little to explore. The disappointment is more than compensated for, however, by the glorious Byzantine churches and monasteries at Mystras, just to the west in the foothills of the Taÿgetos Mountains. Another evocative place is the medieval fortress town of Monemvasia, in the southeast.

English speakers can thank the Lakonians for the word 'laconic' (terse or concise).

SPARTA ΣΠΑΡΤΗ
pop 14,817

The gridlike streets of modern Sparta (*spar-tee*) are in line with its ancient precursor's image of discipline (see The Spartans, p37), although fortunately, not deprivation. It is an easy-going, if unremarkable, town that lies at the heart of the Evrotas Valley, surrounded by olive and citrus groves, while the Taÿgetos Mountains, snowcapped until early June, provide a stunning backdrop to the west.

The town was refounded in 1834 on the orders of King Otto, who had just made the decision to move his court from Nafplio to Athens.

Mindful of history, Otto and his court felt that since Athens was to be rebuilt to reflect its former glory, so too should Sparta. There's a pleasant enough square and a fascinating oil museum, and a few ruins attesting to its ancient pre-eminence. Most visitors head to the nearby site of Mystras, but it's worth spending at least a few hours here.

Orientation

Sparta's layout is as ordered as its ancient troops. With two main roads, Paleologou runs north–south through the town and Lykourgou east–west, intersecting in the middle of town. The central square, Plateia Kentriki, is a block southwest of the intersection. The main bus station is at the eastern end of Lykourgou.

Information

Cosmos Club Internet Café (☎ 27310 21500; Paleologou 34; per hr €2; ⏰ 8am-11pm) For internet; the sign actually says 'Hellas Net'.

Laikos Books (☎ 27310 23687; Paleologou 62) Good for maps and foreign newspapers.

National Bank of Greece (cnr Paleologou & Dioskouron) Has ATM.

Post office (Archidamou 10; ⏰ 7.30am-2pm Mon-Fri)

Tourist police (☎ 27310 89580; Theodoritou 20)

Sights

EXPLORING ANCIENT SPARTA

'If the city of the Lacedaemonians were destroyed, and only its temples and the foundations of its buildings left, remote posterity would greatly doubt whether their power were ever equal to their renown.'

Thucydides, *The Histories*

A wander around ancient Sparta's meagre ruins bears testimony to the accuracy of Thucydides' prophecy. Head north along Paleologou to the **King Leonidas statue**, which stands belligerently in front of a soccer stadium. West of the stadium, signs point the way to the southern gate of the **acropolis**.

Signs point left (west) through olive groves to the 2nd- or 3rd-century-BC **ancient theatre**, the site's most discernible ruin. You'll find a reconstructed plan of the theatre at the Restaurant Elysse (p202).

The main cobbled path leads north to the acropolis (some of which is fenced off), passing the **Byzantine Church of Christ the Saviour** on the way to the hill-top **Sanctuary of Athena Halkioitou**. Some of the most important finds in the town's archaeological museum were unearthed here. Alternatively, you can see and approach the theatre from here. There are impressive views of the snowcapped Taÿgetos Mountains.

The history of the **Sanctuary of Artemis Orthia**, on the northeastern side of town, is more in-

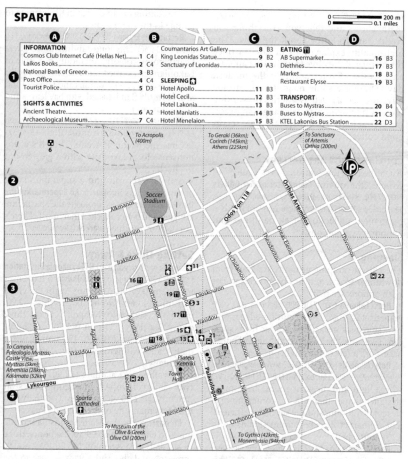

PELOPONNESE

teresting than the site. Like most of the deities in Greek mythology, the goddess Artemis had many aspects, one of which was Artemis Orthia. In the earliest times this aspect of the goddess was honoured through human sacrifice. The Spartans gave this activity away for the slightly less gruesome business of flogging young boys in honour of the goddess. The museum houses a collection of clay masks used during ritual dances. The sanctuary is signposted at the junction of Odos Ton 118 and Orthias Artemidos. One of the other remaining remnants of ancient Sparta is the **sanctuary of Leonidas**, although in reality its provenance and purpose in ancient Sparta is unknown.

ARCHAEOLOGICAL MUSEUM

Sparta's **archaeological museum** (☎ 27310 28575; cnr Lykourgou & Agiou Nikonos; adult/concession €2/1; ☻ 8.30am-3pm Tue-Sun) sits in a beautiful park setting with a fountain and an orange grove. Its artefacts are from Sparta's illustrious past, including votive sickles that Spartan boys dedicated to Artemis Orthia, heads and torsos of various deities, a statue of the great King Leonidas, and masks and grave stelae. Mosaics from Hellenistic and Roman Sparta are also on show.

MUSEUM OF THE OLIVE & GREEK OLIVE OIL

This stunningly designed **museum** (☎ 27310 89315; www.piop.gr; Othonos Amalias 129; adult/concession

€3/1.50; 🕙 10am-6pm 1 Mar-15 Oct, 10am-5pm 16 Oct-18 Feb) shows and tells you everything you could want to know about the olive. The high-quality explanations in English trace the history of the olive from its first appearance in the Mediterranean to the modern day. There are some magnificent antique olive presses, as well as a series of working models that demonstrate changes in pressing technology. The downstairs cafe serves good coffee.

COUMANTARIOS ART GALLERY

An annex of the National Art Gallery of Athens, the quaint **Coumantarios Art Gallery** (☎ 27310 81557; Paleologou 123; admission free; 🕙 9am-3pm Wed-Sat & Mon, 10am-2pm Sun) holds a permanent collection of 40 paintings and temporary exhibitions.

Sleeping

The closest camping grounds are 2km from downtown Sparta, or near Mystras village. For both options see p205.

Hotel Lakonia (☎ 27310 28954; Paleologou 89; s/d/tr incl breakfast €45/65/85) The 32 cutting-edge rooms best suit sleek geeks, and are far from spartan. Two-tone chairs, spot lighting and portal access are a few of the mod cons.

Hotel Maniatis (☎ 27310 22665; www.maniatishotel.gr; Paleologou 72-76; s/d/tr incl breakfast €89/113/147; ✹ 🛜) These light and pleasant rooms have more designer shapes than a NYC contemporary-design exhibition, and the service is efficient. The upmarket Zeys restaurant (mains €6 to €15) is attached.

Hotel Menelaion (☎ 27310 22161-5; www.menelaion .com; Paleologou 91; s/d/tr €97/130/162; ✹ 🖳 🛜) This place has one of the town's finest neoclassical facades and, following a renovation in 2009, some pretty swish and glitzy rooms. Breakfast costs €9.

Also recommended:

Hotel Apollo (☎ 27310 22491/2/3; fax 27310 23936; Thermopylon 84; s/d/tr €35/45/60) A reasonable accommodation option.

Hotel Cecil (☎ 27310 24980; ktza78@otenet.gr; Paleologou 125; s/d €40/55; ✹ 🛜) The small, family-run Cecil is personable, spruce and a little dated. Worth it only if you prefer smaller places. Breakfast costs €5.

Eating

Most of the larger hotels have restaurants. There are other eateries along Paleologou, but no stand-out star. Spartans clearly eat at home

before coming out in droves in the evening to lounge in the town's cafes.

Restaurant Elysse (☎ 27310 29896; Paleologou 113; mains €5.50-9.50) This longstanding place offers hearty home cooking, including a couple of Lakonian specialities, such as *bardouniotiko* (chicken cooked with onions and feta, €7) and *arni horiatiki* (lamb baked with bay leaves and cinnamon, €7).

Diethnes (☎ 27310 28636; Paleologou 105; mains €7-9) It's been going for more than 45 years (as has the decor, it seems), but it's a no-nonsense local favourite with a garden out the back.

Self-caterers will find a superabundance of supermarkets in Sparta. **AB Supermarket** (cnr Thermopylon & Gortsologlou), opposite the Sparta Inn, is bigger and better-stocked than most. There's also a fresh-produce **market** (Kleomvrotou).

Getting There & Away

Sparta's well-organised **KTEL Lakonia bus station** (☎ 27310 26441; cnr Lykourgou & Thivronos) has buses to Athens (€17.60, 3¼ hours, eight daily) via Corinth (€11.60, two hours), Gythio (€3.90, one hour, six daily), Neapoli (€12.80, three hours, six daily), Tripoli (€4.70, one hour, four daily), Geraki (€3.60, 45 minutes, three daily) and Monemvasia (€9, two hours, three daily).

Travelling to Kalamata (€2.90, one hour, two daily) involves changing buses at Artemisia (€2.90, 40 minutes, two daily) on the Messinian side of the Langada Pass.

Departures to the Mani peninsula include buses to Gerolimenas (€9.30, 2¼ hours, three to six daily) via Areopoli (€6.20, two hours, three to six daily) and a 9am service to the Diros Caves (€7); the return times change.

There are also buses to Mystras (€1.40, 30 minutes, 10 daily). You can catch these on their way out to Mystras at the stop next to the OTE building on Lykourgou, or at the stop on Leonidou.

MYSTRAS ΜΥΣΤΡΑΣ

The captivating ruins of churches, libraries, strongholds and palaces in the fortress town of Mystras (miss-*trahss*), a World Heritage–listed site, spill from a spur of the Taÿgetos Mountains 7km west of Sparta. The site is among the most important, historically speaking, in the Peloponnese. This is where the Byzantine Empire's richly artistic and intellectual culture made its last stand before an invading Ottoman army, almost 1000 years after its foundation.

Note: most facilities for the traveller are in Mystras village, a kilometre or so below the ancient site of Mystras.

History

The Frankish leader Guillaume de Villehardouin built the fortress in 1249. When the Byzantines won back the Morea from the Franks, Emperor Michael VIII Paleologus made Mystras its capital and seat of government. Settlers from the surrounding plains began to move here, seeking refuge from the invading Slavs. From this time, until Dimitrios surrendered to the Turks in 1460, a despot of Morea (usually a son or brother of the ruling Byzantine emperor) lived and reigned at Mystras.

While the empire plunged into decline elsewhere, Mystras enjoyed a renaissance under the despots. Gemistos Plethon (1355–1452) founded a school of humanistic philosophy here and his enlightened ideas, including the revival of the teachings of Plato and Pythagoras, attracted intellectuals from all corners of Byzantium. After the Turks occupied Mystras, Plethon's pupils moved to Rome and Florence, where they made a significant contribution to the Italian Renaissance. Art and architecture also flourished, as seen in the splendid buildings and frescoes of the town.

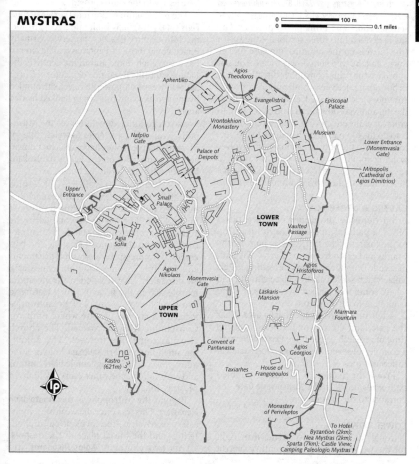

Mystras declined under Turkish rule, but thrived again after the Venetians captured it in 1687 and developed a flourishing silk industry, the population swelling to 40,000. The Turks recaptured it in 1715 and from then on it was downhill all the way; the Russians burnt it in 1770, the Albanians in 1780 and Ibrahim Pasha torched what was left in 1825. By the time of independence it was a largely abandoned ruin. Much restoration has taken place since the 1950s (and continues to this day) and in 1989 it was declared a World Heritage site.

Sights

EXPLORING THE SITE

At least half a day is needed to do justice to the **ruins of Mystras** (☎ 27310 83377; adult/concession €5/3; ☉ 8am-7.30pm summer, 8.30am-3pm winter). Wear sensible shoes and bring plenty of water. The site is divided into three sections – the *kastro* (the fortress on the summit), the *hora* (upper town) and the *kato hora* (lower town). You can approach the ruins from either direction – top to bottom or vice versa (both options are quite strenuous). If you have transport and start at the top and walk down, you'll need to return to your car at the end of your visit. An alternative is to do the top half first, then drive to the bottom, and do the bottom section (this involves walking uphill; you can use the same ticket to re-enter). If you catch a taxi from Sparta, it's best to head to the top and wander downhill.

KASTRO & UPPER TOWN

From opposite the upper entrance ticket office, a path (signposted '*kastro*') leads up to the fortress. The fortress was built by the Franks and extended by the Turks. The path descends from the ticket office leading to **Agia Sofia**, which served as the palace church, and where some frescoes survive. Steps descend from here to a T-junction.

A left turn leads to the **Nafplio Gate**. Near the gate, and closed for restoration at the time of research, is the huge **Palace of Despots**, a complex of several buildings constructed at different times.

From the palace, a winding, cobbled path leads down to the **Monemvasia Gate**, the entrance to the lower town.

LOWER TOWN

Through the Monemvasia Gate, turn right for the well-preserved, 14th-century **Convent of Pantanassa**. This features a beautifully ornate stone-carved facade and is still maintained by nuns, Mystras' only inhabitants. It's an elaborate, perfectly proportioned building – never overstated. Exquisite, richly coloured, 15th-century frescoes are among the finest examples of late-Byzantine art. Look out for the tiny stamped silver and gold votive offerings beneath the large icon of the Virgin. You'll find images of eyes, ears, legs, arms, breasts and even houses stamped onto these small tablets, depending on the (usually health-related) problems the faithful are hoping for supernatural help with. There is a wonderful view of the pancake-flat and densely cultivated plain of Lakonia from the columned terrace on the northern facade. The nuns ask that, before entering, you cover bare legs with the cloths provided.

The path continues down to the **Monastery of Perivleptos** (☉ summer), built into a rock. Inside, the 14th-century frescoes, preserved virtually intact, equal those of Pantanassa. The church has a very high dome and in the centre is the Pantokrator (the Byzantine depiction of Christ as the universal, all-powerful ruler), surrounded by the apostles, and the Virgin flanked by two angels.

As you continue down towards the Mitropolis, you will pass **Agios Georgios**, one of Mystras' many private chapels. Further down, and above the path on the left, is the **Laskaris Mansion**, a typical Byzantine house.

The **Mitropolis** (Cathedral of Agios Dimitrios) is a complex of buildings enclosed by a high wall. The original church was built in the 1200s, but was greatly altered in the 15th century. The church stands in an attractive courtyard surrounded by stoae and balconies. Its impressive ecclesiastical ornaments and furniture include a marble iconostasis, an intricately carved wooden throne and a marble slab in the floor in which features a two-headed eagle (symbol of Byzantium) – located exactly on the site where Emperor Constantine XI was crowned. The church also has some fine frescoes. The adjoining small but modern **museum** houses some quirky pieces, including female hair, buttons and embroidery, and other everyday items of Mystras' inhabitants.

Beyond the Mitropolis is the **Vrontokhion Monastery**. This was once the wealthiest monastery of Mystras, the focus of cultural activities and the burial place of the despots. Of its two churches, **Agios Theodoros** and

Aphentiko, the latter is the most impressive, with striking frescoes.

Outside the lower entrance to Mystras is a *kantina* (mobile cafe) selling snacks and drinks.

Sleeping & Eating

Hotel Byzantion (☎ 27310 83309; www.byzantionhotel .gr; s/d/tr incl breakfast €45/60/70; ❄ ☐ ☎) In the centre of the modern village of Nea Mystras is this small, appealing option, an alternative to sleeping in Sparta. There's a delightful garden and the bright rooms have balconies offering arresting valley or mountain views. It's about 1km from the site.

There are two camping options: **Camping Paleologio Mystras** (☎ 27310 22724; fax 27310 25256; camp sites per adult/tent/car €7/4/4; ☯ year-round; ☎) 2km west of Sparta and approximately 4km from Mystras village, and **Castle View** (☎ 27310 83303; www.castleview.gr; camp sites per adult/tent/car €6/4/4, 2-person bungalow €30, ☯ Apr-Oct; ☎) about 1km before Nea Mystras village and set in olive trees; buses will stop outside either if you ask.

There are also several domatia around the village, along with a couple of cafes and tavernas.

Getting There & Away

Frequent buses go to Mystras from Sparta (€1.40, 30 minutes, 10 daily). A radio taxi from Sparta to Mystras' lower entrance (Xenia Restaurant) costs around €9 to €10, or slightly more to the upper entrance. A cheaper option is to take a **taxi** (☎ 27310 25300) from Mystra but these can be elusive.

LANGADA PASS
ΟΡΕΙΝΗ ΔΙΑΒΑΣΗ ΛΑΓΚΑΔΑ

The 59km Sparta–Kalamata road is one of the most stunning routes in Greece, crossing the Taÿgetos Mountains by way of the Langada Pass.

The climb begins in earnest at the village of **Trypi**, 9km west of Sparta, where the road enters the dramatic **Langada Gorge**. To the north of this gorge is the site where the ancient Spartans left babies too weak or deformed to become good soldiers to die (see boxed text, p37).

From Trypi, the road follows the course of the Langada River before climbing sharply through a series of hairpin bends to emerge in a sheltered valley. This is a good spot to stop

for a stroll among the plane trees along the river bank. The road then climbs steeply once more, to the high point of 1524m – crossing the boundary from Lakonia into Messinia on the way. You can stop overnight here. The descent to Kalamata is equally dramatic.

Travelling this route by bus involves changing buses at Artemisia, the closest Messinian settlement to the summit.

Sleeping & Eating

Pandoheio Canadas (☎ 27210 21436; s/d/tr €20/28/29) This small guest house, 22km from Sparta, is perched on the upper slopes of the Taÿgetos Mountains at an altitude of 1250m. The rooms are basic but offer great mountain views. The restaurant is a major attraction, turning out delicious homemade treats such as pork sausages.

Hotel Taÿgetos (☎ 27210 99236; fax 27210 98198; s/d/tr €30/40/50) The Taÿgetos has a superb location at the very top of the Langada Pass. It also boasts a good restaurant with specialities such as roasted goat, rooster with red wine and rabbit *stifadho*. It's 24km from Sparta.

MONEMVASIA & GEFYRA
ΜΟΝΕΜΒΑΣΙΑ & ΓΕΦΥΡΑ

Vast, imposing, spectacular Monemvasia (mo-nem-vah-*see*-ah or mo-nem-*vah*-see-ah) is the Greek equivalent to France's Mont St-Michel. This perfect fortress is an iceberglike slab of rock moored off the coast, with sheer cliffs rising hundreds of feet from the sea, and a single highly defendable causeway.

These days Monemvasia incorporates both the rock, whose medieval village is enclosed within the walls of the rock's *kastro*, plus the modern mainland village of Gefyra just across the causeway. In summer, both places brim with visitors. Fortunately, the extraordinary visual impact of the medieval village in particular – and the delights of exploring it – override the effects of mass tourism. The staunch communist poet Yiannis Ritsos was born here and only seven people are permanent residents.

From Gefyra, you can see little of the fortress. But cross the causeway and follow the road that curves around the side of the rock and you will come to the official entrance, a narrow tunnel in a massive fortifying wall. The tunnel is L-shaped, so the magical town

---

PEREGRINATIONS OF PAUSANIAS

Lonely Planet and its competitors were beaten to publishing guidebooks by nearly 20 centuries. The traveller and geographer Pausanias (2nd century AD) wrote what is believed to be the first – and most definitive – 'guidebook' for tourists. His work, Description of Greece (sometimes known as Tour or Itinerary of Greece), is a series of 10 books in which he describes most of Greece as seen at the time (between 143 and 161), covering the regions of Attica, Beotia, Phocis and Ozolian Locris plus the regions that make up much of the Peloponnese – Corinthia, Lakonia, Messinia, Elia, Achaïa, Arkadia. Classical Greek scholars, historians and archaeologists regard it as an extremely important historical work for its insight into places, people, monuments and sites, as well as associated facts and legends. Pausanias is believed to be from Lydia in Asia Minor and travelled extensively throughout Greece, Macedonia, Italy and parts of Africa and Asia.

---

is concealed until you emerge, blinking, on the other side.

History

The rock island of Monemvasia was part of the mainland until it was cut off by an earthquake in AD 375. Its name means 'single entry' (*moni* – single, *emvasia* – entry), as there is only one way to the medieval town.

During the 6th century barbarian incursions forced inhabitants of the surrounding area to retreat to this natural rock fortress. By the 13th century it had become the principal commercial centre of Byzantine Morea – complementing Mystras, the spiritual centre. It was famous throughout Europe for its highly praised Malvasia-grape wine.

The Franks, Venetians and Turks all invaded in the following centuries. During the War of Independence its Turkish inhabitants were massacred after their surrender, following a three-month siege.

Orientation & Information

All the practicalities are located in Gefyra. The main street is 23 Iouliou, which runs south around the coast from the causeway, while Spartis runs north up the coast and becomes the road to Molai. Malvasia Travel, just before the causeway in Geyfra, acts as the bus stop. The National Bank of Greece, with an ATM, and **post office** (7.30am-2pm Mon-Fri) are opposite. The **police** (27320 61210; Spartis 137) are in one of the few buildings in town with a street number.

Sights

KASTRO – MEDIEVAL TOWN

> You can find everything you want in this city – except water.
> *18th-century Turkish traveller*

The narrow, cobbled main street is lined with souvenir shops and tavernas, flanked by winding stairways that weave between a complex network of stone houses with walled gardens and courtyards. The main street leads to the central square and the **Cathedral of Christ in Chains**, dating from the 13th century. Opposite is the **Church of Agios Pavlos**, built in 956. Further along the main street is the **Church of Myrtidiotissa**, virtually in ruins, but still with a small altar and a defiantly flickering candle. Overlooking the sea is the recently restored, whitewashed 16th-century **Church of Panagia Hrysafitissa**.

The path to the **fortress** and the **upper town** is signposted up the steps to the left of the central square. The upper town is now a vast and fascinating jumbled ruin, except for the **Church of Agia Sofia**, which perches on the edge of a sheer cliff.

MONEMVASIA ARCHAEOLOGICAL MUSEUM

This small **museum** (27320 61403; admission free; 8.30am-3pm Tue-Sun winter, 8am-8pm Tue-Sun summer) displays a detailed map of Monemvasia, useful for orientating yourself. It also houses finds unearthed in the course of excavations and building around the old town. The star turn is the **templon** (chancel screen) from an 11th-century church near the sea gate. Other pieces of note include a marble door frame from the Church of Agia Sofia and plenty of fine ceramics.

Sleeping

There's no truly budget accommodation in the *kastro* itself but considering where you are, some places offer excellent value (where else in the world can you sleep at or near a World Heritage site?). Prices are far from rock solid; they alter drastically depending on good ol' supply and demand. The hotels are nearly identical – boutique in manner, stylishly furnished in timber and muted materials throughout.

A pocket torch and sensible shoes are good options for those staying on the cobbled, dimly lit *kastro*.

If the *kastro* doesn't give you the urge to splurge, there are cheaper hotels and numerous domatia in Gefyra.

Hotel Akrogiali (☎ 27320 61360; Gefyra; s/d with shower €40/45) This basic but spotless hotel, next to the National Bank of Greece on Spartis, has the cheapest rooms in town.

Malvasia Hotel (☎ 27320 61160/3007; malvasia @otenet.gr; Monemvasia; s incl breakfast €45-65, d incl breakfast €65-120; ⚡) Easily the best value on Monemvasia (if you can believe its prices).

Hotel Byzantino (☎ 27320 61254/351; Monemvasia; s/d/tr €60/100/120; ⚡) Also great value; rooms are a notch smarter than Malvasia Hotel. Try to get a room with sea-facing balconies. Breakfast costs €5.

our pick Monopati Rooms & Apartments (☎ 27320 61772; www.byzantine-escapade.com; Monemvasia; apt €70-85, 'little house' €110-140) These delightful stone options ooze personality, as do the hospitable owners. Stylish decor fills the apartments' quirky spaces. Rates vary according to the number of people staying and are slightly higher in Easter, July and August. Breakfast – which can be served where you like it, when you like it – costs €6.

Hotel Lazareto (☎ 27320 61991; www.lazareto.gr; Monemvasia; s €135, d €160-205; ⚡) Located outside the fortress walls, past the causeway and occupying the handsome stone buildings of a former quarantine hospital, the Lazareto is the most luxurious choice. The furnishings in the well-equipped rooms are stylishly muted. But watch your head – the door frames are for little people. Breakfast is extra.

Ardamis (☎ 27320 61887; www.ardamis.gr; Monemvasia; d €140-160, 4-person r €250-450) Especially popular among Greek clients, rooms here blend old with modern (some weird mood lighting goes on here – to highlight the architectural spaces). The owners are welcoming and quaint garden spaces provide a change from the sea view.

Eating

Taverna Trata (☎ 27320 62084; Gefyra; fish per kilogram €45-55) On the right immediately after you cross the causeway back to Gefyra. The hanging gulls and model yachts point to a nautical theme – seafood is the go here.

Three tavernas sit cheek to cheek in Monemvasia's old town: **Matoula** (☎ 27320 61660), **Marianthi** (☎ 2732 61371) and **To Kanoni** (☎ 27320 61387). You can't really go wrong with any – choose between them for dish type (all traditional Greek) or ambience. Mains are around €8 to €13.

Self-caterers will find most things at the Lefkakis supermarket just past the post office in Gefyra.

Getting There & Away

Buses leave from outside **Malvasia Travel** (☎ 27320 61752), just over the causeway in Geyfra; Malvasia also sells tickets. There are buses to Athens (€27, six hours, four daily) via Sparta (€9, 2½ hours), Tripoli and Corinth Isthmus.

Getting Around

The medieval *kastro* of Monemvasia is inaccessible to cars and motorcycles, but these can cross the causeway. Parking is available along the narrow road skirting the rock, outside the old town. It's sometimes easier to park in Gefyra than risk the tight squeeze.

A **shuttle bus** (🕐 8am-midnight Jun-Sep, Christmas & Easter) ferries visitors between Geyfra and the *kastro*.

Car hire is available from **Kypros Rent a Car** (☎ 27320 61383; www.kypros-rentacar.gr, houtris@otenet .gr). Turn right at the street after the National Bank of Greece.

NEAPOLI ΝΕΑΠΟΛΗ
pop 2727

Neapoli (neh-*ah*-po-lih), 42km south of Monemvasia, lies close to the southern tip of the eastern prong of the Peloponnese. It's a functioning, if uninspiring, town, in spite of its location on a huge horseshoe bay. Most foreign travellers visit Neapoli to catch a ferry to the island of Kythira, clearly visible across the bay.

The western flank of the bay is formed by the small island of **Elafonisi**, renowned for its white beaches and visiting loggerhead turtles (*Caretta caretta*), not to mention sun-loving nudists. Regular ferries make the 10-minute trip (per person/car €1/10) from a small port several kilometres west of Neapoli.

Hotel Aivali (☎ 27340 22287; Akti Voion 164; s/d €50/60; ❄ ☃) is a small family hotel, ideally located right on the seafront, close to the ferry dock for Kythira. Like all the hotels in town, it's booked out from mid-July to August.

There are numerous lively *ouzeries* (places that serve ouzo and appetisers) along the waterfront, serving the local speciality: delicious grilled octopus.

There are daily ferries from Neapoli to Diakofti on Kythira. Tickets are sold at **Vatika Bay Shipping Agency** (☎ 27340 24004), 350m before the small bridge. (Leave plenty of time to find the place and buy the ticket.) See also Island Hopping (p758) for more details.

KTEL (☎ 27340 23222) has buses from Neapoli to Athens (€33, three daily) via Sparta (€12.80, three hours, three daily) and Molai (€6, 1¼ hours). Molai is the place to change buses for Monemvasia.

Rent a Moto Elafonisos (☎ 27340 61377) might be a useful point of call if you want to see Elafonisi once there.

GYTHIO ΓΥΘΕΙΟ
pop 4489

Once the port of ancient Sparta, Gythio (*yee-thih-o*) is the gateway to the Lakonian Mani. This attractive fishing town's bustling waterfront has pastel-coloured, 19th-century buildings, behind which crumbling old Turkish houses and scruffy streets cling to a steep, wooded hill.

Orientation

Gythio is easy to get around. Most restaurants and cafes are along the seafront on Akti Vasileos Pavlou. The bus station is at the northeastern end, past the small triangular park known as the Perivolaki (meaning 'tree-filled'). Behind this is the main square, Plateia Panagiotou Venetzanaki.

The local shopping area, and the main approach to/from town is Ermou. The square at the southwestern end of Akti Vasileos Pavlou is Plateia Mavromihali, hub of the old quarter of Marathonisi. The ferry quay is situated opposite this square. Beyond it the waterfront road becomes Kranais, which leads south to the road to Areopoli. A causeway leads out to Marathonisi Islet at the southern edge of town.

Information

EOT (☎ /fax 27330 24484; Vasileos Georgiou 20; ☿ 8am-2.30pm Mon-Fri) This is the information equivalent of Monty Python's famous cheese-free cheese shop: remarkably information-free, even by EOT's lamentable standards.

Hassanakos Bookstore (☎ 27330 22064; Akti Vasileos Pavlou 39) Also stocks international newspapers.

Internet Jolly Café (cnr Dirou & Grigoraki; per hr €2.50) One block from the bus station.

Kostas Vretto's Antiquities Shop (Vassileos Pavlou 25) Not official information per se, but this philosopher-poet-man-of-the-world is well worth a visit.

Police (☎ 27330 22100; Akti Vasileos Pavlou)

Post office (cnr Ermou & Arheou Theatrou; ☿ 7.30am-2pm Mon-Fri)

Sights & Activities
MARATHONISI ISLET

According to mythology, tranquil pine-shaded Marathonisi is ancient Cranae, where Paris (prince of Troy) and Helen (wife of Menelaus) consummated the affair that sparked the Trojan Wars. The 18th-century **Tzanetakis Grigorakis tower** at the centre of the island houses a small **Museum of Mani History** (adult/concession €2/1; ☿ 8am-2.30pm), which relates Maniot history through the eyes of European travellers who visited the region between the 15th and 19th centuries. Upstairs, the architecturally minded will find an absorbing collection of plans of the castle and Maniot towers.

ANCIENT THEATRE

Gythio's small but well-preserved **ancient theatre** is next to an army camp on the northern edge of town. It's signposted off Ermou, along Arheou Theatrou. (Turn right after the post office.) You can scramble up the hill behind the theatre to get to the **ancient acropolis**, now heavily overgrown. Most of ancient Gythio lies beneath the nearby Lakonian Gulf.

BEACHES

There's safe swimming along the 6km of sandy beaches that extend from the village of **Mavrovouni**, 2km south of Gythio.

Sleeping

There are many domatia signs along the waterfront. Taxis to/from Mavrovouni and Gythio cost €5.

Camping Meltemi (☎ 27330 23260; www.camping meltemi.gr; Mavrovouni beach; camp sites per adult/tent/car €6/5/4, bungalows €40-55; ☿ Apr-Oct) Very well organised and the pick of the three camping grounds at Mavrovouni. Three kilometres southwest of Gythio, it's right behind the beach and sites are set among 3000 well-tended olive trees.

The bungalows include kitchen, air-con and TV. Buses to Areopoli stop outside.

Xenia Karlaftis Rooms to Rent (☎ 27330 22719, 27230 22991; s €25, d & tr €40) Ideally situated opposite Marathonisi, this friendly place offers basic but clean rooms. A communal kitchen area has a fridge and small stove for making tea and coffee.

Saga Pension (☎ 27330 23220; Kranais; d €50; 🕮) This is a good-value saga-free, comfortable place with balconies. It's 150m from the port, overlooking Marathonisi Islet. The upmarket Saga Restaurant is below (mains €9 to €15, fish per kilogram €45 to €70).

Matina's (☎ 27330 22518; d/tr €60/65) A clean and comfortable abode in a great location in a house-cum-hotel, right in the heart of town. Owner Matina speaks no English but is welcoming.

Alkion Apartments (☎ 27330 23112; fax 27330 29041; Mavrovouni beach; d €80; 🕮) If you want a beach setting, these smart and modern apartments are the best value at Mavrovouni and are equipped with small kitchenettes. There are larger and slightly more expensive options for families.

Eating

Seafood is the obvious choice, and the waterfront is lined with numerous fish tavernas, especially on Kranais, where tourists walk the gauntlet of waiters touting for custom.

Taverna Petakou (☎ 27330 22889; mains €3-7) This no-frills place is a local favourite. The day's menu is written down in an exercise book in Greek. It may include a hearty fish soup, which comes with a large chunk of bread on the side. Beside the stadium on Xanthaki.

Poulikakos Restaurant-Grill (☎ 27330 22792; mains €6-14, fish per kilogram €35-55) You know the deal: Greek favourites for lovers of traditional cuisine. Decor is basic, helpings are gargantuan, quality is good – and prices are reasonable.

Taverna O Potis (☎ 27330 23245; mains €6.50-16; ⌚ closed Thu) This ship-shape place has a spotless kitchen and generous helpings that locals flock aboard for. The house red is a bit like a massive ocean swell, but the taverna is well worth the walk to the far end of the promenade, opposite Marathonisi Islet.

For self-catering, we recommended supermarkets **Kourtakis** (Irakleos), around the corner from the bus station, and **Karagiannis** (cnr Vasileos Georgiou & Orestou).

Getting There & Away

BOAT

LANE Lines has one weekly summertime ferry to Crete via Kythira and Antikythira. Check the ever-changing schedule with **Rozakis Travel** (☎ 27330 22207; rosakigy@otenet .gr), on the waterfront at Pavlou 5. See also Island Hopping (p758).

BUS

The **KTEL Lakonia bus station** (☎ 27330 22228; Evrikleos) is found northwest along the waterfront near Jande Café. Services run north to Athens (€21.40, 4½ hours, six daily) or via Sparta (€3.90, one hour) and Tripoli; and south to Areopoli (€2.40, 30 minutes, four daily), Gerolimenas (€5.40, 1¼ hours, three daily), the Diros Caves (€3.30, one hour, one daily) and Vathia (€5.90, 1½ hours, three weekly).

Helpful George will explain the best way to see the Mani from Gythio (return) in one day. Getting to Kalamata can be fiddly; it involves taking onward connections from either Itilo (€3.40, 45 minutes) or Sparta. There are only two buses daily (5am and 1pm) except Sunday to Itilo (the 1pm bus may require a change at Areopoli).

Getting Around

For car hire, contact **Rozakis Travel** (☎ 27330 22207; rosakigy@otenet.gr). Mopeds and scooters are available from **Moto Makis** (☎ 27330 25111; Kranais). The town **taxi rank** (☎ 27330 23400) is opposite the bus station.

THE MANI H ΜΑΝΗ

The Mani, the region covering the central peninsula in the south of the Peloponnese, is a wild, rugged place; and Greeks from elsewhere will tell you, so are its people. Such was the formidable reputation of the inhabitants of the remote inner Mani that many would-be occupiers opted in the end to leave them alone.

For centuries the Maniots were a law unto themselves, renowned for their fierce independence, resentment of attempts to govern them and for their bitter, spectacularly murderous internal feuds. Dotted around the territory – particularly in the inner Mani – you'll find bizarre tower settlements that were built as refuges during clan wars from the 17th century onwards.

Thankfully these feuds, some of which took entire armies to halt, are long forgotten and the Maniots are as friendly and hospitable as Greeks elsewhere. The architecture lives on, however, and the buildings – there's a mini construction boom going on – must adhere to stone exteriors.

It's worth including this region in your itinerary. The steep tumbling skirts of the Taÿgetos Mountains (threaded with wonderful walking trails) and the tiny coves and ports nestling beside them make for some memorably dramatic scenery. As well as the towers, there are magnificent churches, and caves.

The Mani is generally divided into the Messinian Mani (or outer Mani) and the Lakonian (or inner) Mani. The Messinian Mani starts southeast of Kalamata and runs south between the coast and the Taÿgetos Mountains, while the Lakonian Mani covers the rest of the peninsula south of Itilo.

Anyone visiting the region should definitely arm themselves with a copy of Patrick Leigh Fermor's *Mani,* a vivid and erudite account of the area (he loved the region so much he settled here). Keen explorers should ask at local shops for *Inside The Mani: A Walking Guide* by Mat Dean, and *The Mani* by Bob Barrow and Mat Dean. The books are full of walking and information gems about the region's villages, towers and churches. Also worth reading is *Deep into Mani* by Eliopoulis and Greenhold.

History

The people of the Mani regard themselves as direct descendants of the Spartans. After the decline of Sparta, citizens loyal to the principles of Lycurgus (founder of Sparta's constitution) chose to withdraw to the mountains rather than serve under foreign masters. Later, refugees from occupying powers joined these people, who became known as Maniots, from the Greek word 'mania'.

The Maniots claim they are the only Greeks not to have succumbed to foreign invasions. This may be somewhat exaggerated but the Maniots have always enjoyed a certain autonomy and a distinctive lifestyle. Until independence the Maniots lived in clans led by chieftains. Fertile land was so scarce that it was fiercely fought over. Blood feuds were a way of life and families constructed towers as refuges.

The Turks failed to subdue the Maniots, who eagerly participated in the War of Independence. But, after 1834, although reluctant to relinquish their independence, they became part of the new kingdom.

LAKONIAN MANI

Grey rock, mottled with defiant clumps of green scrub, characterises the Scottish-like mountains of inner Mani. Cultivatable land is at a premium, and supports little more than a few stunted olives and figs. The wild flowers that cloak the valleys in spring exhibit nature's resilience by sprouting from the rocks.

The indented coast's sheer cliffs plunge into the sea, and rocky outcrops shelter pebbled beaches. This wild and barren landscape is broken only by austere and imposing stone towers, many now being restored, still standing sentinel over the region.

With your own vehicle you can explore the Mani by the loop road that runs down the west coast from the main town, Areopoli, to Gerolimenas, and return via the east coast (or vice versa). Public transport exists, although is limited.

Areopoli Αρεόπολη
pop 774

Areopoli (ah-reh-*o*-po-lih), capital of the Mani, is aptly named after Ares, the god of war. Dominating the main square, Plateia Athanaton, is a statue of Petrobey Mavromihalis, who proclaimed the Maniot insurrection against the Turks. Konstantinos and Georgios Mavromihalis (1765–1848), who assassinated Kapodistrias, belonged to the same family. The town retains many other reminders of its rumbustious past.

ORIENTATION & INFORMATION

The town is split into two parts: the new upper town, around Plateia Athanaton, and the old lower town, around Plateia 17 Martiou. The two squares are linked by a 'main' lane (formerly Kapetan Matapan but no longer officially referred to). There is no tourist office or tourist police.

Invincible Mani (☎ 27330 53670; Plateia Athanaton) Has an excellent selection of maps and books on the region.

National Bank of Greece (Petrobey Mavromihali; ☒ 8am-1pm Mon-Thu, 8am-1.30pm Fri Aug, 8am-1pm Tue & Thu Sep-Jul) The only bank in town; has an ATM.

Post office (Petrobey Mavromihali; ☒ 7.30am-2pm Mon-Fri) At the northern edge of town.

SIGHTS & ACTIVITIES

There are some fine examples of Maniot architecture to be found in the narrow alleyways surrounding Plateia 17 Martiou.

They start with the 18th-century **Church of Taxiarhes** on the southern side of the square. Its four-storey bell tower marks it as the most important of the town's many churches. Look out for the extremely well-preserved relief carvings above the main door. The much older **Church of Agios Ioannis**, on the southern edge of the old town, contains a series of frescoes relating the life of Jesus. It was built by the Mavromihalis family.

There are numerous examples of tower houses – some in poor condition; others have been converted into smart accommodation. The **Mavromihalis Tower** (Tzani Tzanaki), south of Plateia 17 Martiou, was once the mightiest tower in town, but now it stands sadly derelict.

In the southern end of town (ask for directions), the **Religious Museum** (www.culture.gr; admission free) – off the visitor radar due to lack of signage and promotion – is a must-see. Housed in a restored tower, the Pikoulakis Tower, it houses exquisite Byzantine pieces from Mani churches, including superb manuscripts and jewellery.

There is some fabulous walking in the area; experienced hikers should have no problem with compasses and equipment.

SLEEPING

Budget

Tsimova Rooms (☎ 27330 51301; s/d/apt €40/60/80) You might have to battle your way through the cuddly toys and photos in this homey place, a renovated tower located behind the Church of Taxiarhes. Not to forget the weaponry collection of the elderly ex-partisan owner, ranging from daggers to cast-iron cannons. Rooms are rather overpriced.

Hotel Kouris (☎ 27330 51340; fax 27330 51331; Plateia Athanaton; s/d €50/60) Out of place against the Maniot towers, this concrete block is characterless, but a useful fallback.

Midrange & Top End

Hotel Trapela (☎ 27330 52690; www.trapela.gr; s/d/tr €50/70/80; ❄) This small 12-room place is promoted as a 'new traditional' hotel, as indeed it is. The comfortable wood and stone rooms have tasteful muted colours and the design is along Maniot lines.

Hotel Petrounis (☎ 27330 51151; www.petrounis.gr; d €65-70, tr €90; ❄ ⊛) This recently opened renovated place offers a slightly jumbled blend of Maniot and modern, but is pleasantly velvety and very central. The friendly owner speaks good English.

our pick Londas Pension (☎ 27330 51360; www.londas.com; d/tr incl breakfast €80/110) This 200-year-old tower is the undisputed king of the castle: stylish whitewashed rooms tastefully decorated in an antique and modern fusion. Signposted right at the Church of Taxiarhes.

EATING

To Katoi (☎ 27330 51201; mains €7-10; ❄ dinner Mon-Fri, lunch & dinner Sat & Sun) This cosy place is recommended for its daily specials (not on the menu). It's in a lovely location near the Church of Taxiarhes.

Nicola's Corner Taverna (☎ 27330 51366; Plateia Athanaton; mains €8-10) Ignore the menu – this popular spot on the central square displays a good choice of tasty taverna staples that change daily. Don't miss the handmade maccaroni with fried local cheese.

For self-caterers, the small Koilakos supermarket is near Plateia Athanaton.

GETTING THERE & AWAY

The **bus station** (☎ 27330 51229; Plateia Athanaton) is a few doors left of Europa Grill. There are buses to Gythio (€2.80, 30 minutes, four daily), which proceed to Athens (€23.80). There are bus services to Itilo (€1.40, 20 minutes, three daily Monday to Saturday, no service Sunday) via Limeni, to Gerolimenas (€3.30, 45 minutes, three daily), the Diros Caves (€1.40, 15 minutes, one daily; returns at 12.45pm), Lagia (€3.30, 40 minutes, one to two daily) and Vathia (€3.80, one hour, two weekly).

Limeni Λιμένι

The tiny village of Limeni is 3km north of Areopoli on the southern flank of beautiful **Limeni Bay**.

High on the hill, on the south side of Limeni Bay is **Limeni Village** (☎ 27330 51111/2; www.limenivillage.gr; s/d/tr incl breakfast €80/120/140; ⓟ ❄ ⊛), a complex of replica Maniot towers with spectacular vistas of the bay, hills and village. Restaurant attached.

In a glorious location set out over water, **Takis** (☎ 27330 51327; fish per kilogram €55-65; ❄ lunch & dinner) lures in diners; it's *the* place for fish in the area.

Itilo & Nea Itilo Οίτυλο & Νέο Οίτυλο
pop 331

Itilo (*eet*-ih-lo), 11km north of Areopoli, was the medieval capital of the Mani. To travel between Lakonian and Messinian Mani, you must change buses at Itilo.

The village is a tranquil backwater, but shows signs of recent renovation, and is perched on the northern edge of a deep ravine traditionally regarded as the border between outer and inner Mani. Above the ravine is the massive 17th-century **Castle of Kelefa**, from which the Turks attempted to constrain the Maniots. It's on a hill above the road from Nea Itilo. Nearby, the **Monastery of Dekoulou** has colourful frescoes in its church.

Nea Itilo, 4km away, lies at the back of secluded Limeni Bay.

There are three buses daily except Sunday to Areopoli (€1.40, 20 minutes) and Kalamata (€4, 2¼ hours). Areopoli–Itilo buses go via Nea Itilo and Limeni.

Diros Caves Σπήλαιο Διρού

These extraordinary **caves** (☎ 27330 52222; adult/concession incl tour €12/7; ☉ 8.30am-5.30pm Jun-Sep, 8.30am-3pm Oct-May) are 11km south of Areopoli, near the village of **Pyrgos Dirou** – notable for its towers (signposted to the right off the road down to the caves).

The natural entrance to the caves is on the beach and locals like to believe the legend that they extend as far north as Sparta (speleologists have so far estimated the caves to be 14km; tourists enter to 1.5km). They were inhabited in Neolithic times, but were abandoned after an earthquake in 4 BC and weren't rediscovered until 1895. Systematic exploration began in 1949. The caves are famous for their stalactites and stalagmites, which have fittingly poetic names such as the Palm Forest, Crystal Lily and the Three Wise Men.

Unfortunately, the half-hour guided tour through the caves is disappointingly brief – it covers only the lake section, and bypasses the most spectacular formations of the dry area.

The nearby **Neolithic Museum of Diros** (☎ 27330 52223; adult/concession €2/1; ☉ 8.30am-3pm Tue-Sun) houses items found in an adjoining Neolithic cave, the **Alepotrypa Cave**. Entrance to the museum includes entrance to this cave. This was used to store crops, and housed workshops, living areas and formal burial grounds. The inhabitants died as a result of the earthquake

of 4 BC, after which the cave was sealed by boulders.

Pyrgos Dirou to Gerolimenas
Πύργος Διρού προς Γερολιμένας

Journeying south down Mani's west coast from Pyrgos Dirou to Gerolimenas, the barren mountain landscape is broken only by deserted settlements with mighty towers. A right turn 9km south of Pyrgos Dirou leads down to the **Bay of Mezapos**, sheltered to the east by the frying pan–shaped Tigani peninsula. The ruins on the peninsula are those of the **Castle of Maina**, built by the Frankish leader Guillaume de Villehardouin in 1248, and subsequently adapted by the Byzantines.

Kita, 13km south of Pyrgos Dirou, bristles with the ruins of war towers and fortified houses. It was the setting for the last great interfamily feud recorded in the Mani, which erupted in 1870 and required the intervention of the army, complete with artillery, to force a truce.

Gerolimenas Γερολιμένας
pop 55

Gerolimenas (yeh-ro-lih-*meh*-nahss) is a tranquil fishing village built around a small, sheltered bay at the southwestern tip of the peninsula. It's the perfect place for scenic seclusion.

SLEEPING & EATING

Hotel Akrogiali (☎ 27330 54204; www.gerolimenas-hotels.com; s €25-30, d €50-80, tr €70-120, 2-/3-/4-person apt €80/100/120; ☒) The Akrogiali has a great setting overlooking the bay on the western edge of town. It offers various sleeping options, from OK doubles in the traditional hotel building and squishier rooms in a newer stone wing, and apartments nearby. Breakfast costs €6.

Hotel Akrotenaritis (☎ 27330 54205; s €60-65, d €75-80, tr €85; ☒) The rough-looking exterior doesn't reflect the cosy inside of this ski lodge–style place with its wooden features, marble floors and smart fixtures. There are cheaper and perfectly pleasant rooms in an older building nearby (singles €25 to €30, doubles €40).

our pick Hotel Kirimai (☎ 27330 54288; www.kyrimai.gr; d €110-260, ste €300; ⓟ ☒ ☒) The luxurious Kirimai is one of Greece's most swish hospitality experiences. It sits in an idyllic setting at the far southern end of the harbour. The stone-floored, timber-beamed rooms are individually finished with decor-magazine flair. Its restaurant is open to nonguests. It's worth splurging here; the restaurant's head chef was Greek Chef of the Year 2006 and the menu changes regularly (mains €15 to €25).

Xenonas Laula (☎ 27330 54271; www.gerolimenas .net; d/tr/ste €120/120/250) The new kid on the very small block, the seven rooms in this boutique-style place have a rustic chic decor and relaxed ambience.

There is a small supermarket on the promenade, and a couple of cafes and tavernas.

GETTING THERE & AWAY
There are three buses daily from Gerolimenas to Areopoli (€3.30, 45 minutes) – and on to Athens (€27), Gythio (€5.40, 1¼ hours) and Sparta (€9.30, 2¼ hours). The bus stop is outside Hotel Akrotenaritis; tickets are bought on board.

Gerolimenas to Porto Kagio
Γερολιμένας προς Πόρτο Κάγιο
South of Gerolimenas, the road continues 4km to the small village of Alika, where it divides. One road leads across the mountains to the east coast, and the other goes south to Vathia and Porto Kagio. The southern road follows the coast, passing pebbly beaches. It then climbs steeply inland to **Vathia**, the most dramatic of the traditional Mani villages, comprising a cluster of closely packed tower houses perched on a rocky spur.

A turn-off to the right 9km south of Alika leads to **Marmari**, with its two sandy beaches, while the main road cuts across the peninsula to the tiny east-coast fishing village of **Porto Kagio**, set on a perfect horseshoe bay. The village's three competing accommodation options are in as remote a place you'll find anywhere on the Peloponnese.

There's a wonderful walk to one of Europe's southernmost points, **Cape Tenaro** (or Cape Matapan), whose beautiful lighthouse has been recently restored. The cape has been an important location for millenia and was first mentioned by Homer in his 'Iliad'. Follow the signs from Porto Kagio; from the car park it's a 45-minute walk.

Akroteri Domatia (☎ 27330 52013; www.porto -kagio.com; Porto Kagio; d €70-80, tr €80-100) is the type of place you'll book into spontaneously. Its large rooms with balconies overlook the bay, glorious bay. Owner Nikos also runs boat trips.

But Arkoleri Domatia's (former) monopoly is no longer rock-solid. Enter **Hotel Psamathous** (☎ 27330 52033; www.portokale.gr; Porto Kagio; d/tr incl breakfast €70/90; ❄), a Flinstones-style (modern Maniot) place owned by the crowd at Porto Taverna. Set back from the waterfront, it has stone-platform beds, mezzanines and a nearly-but-not-quite-there designer touch. And **Porto Kale** (☎ 6938 872159; Porto Kagio; d €80-90, tr €110-120), which has a clean and stylish range of rooms.

Your next-hardest decision is which of the three fish waterfront tavernas to eat at. Prices are much the same for all (mains €7 to €17, fish per kilogram €40 to €70).

East Coast
The east coast is even more rugged and barren than the west. The main town is **Lagia**, 12km northeast of the Alika turn-off. Perched some 400m above sea level, it was once the chief town of the southeastern Mani. Some of its towers are now derelict (although many are being renovated); it remains a formidable-looking place, especially when approached from Alika.

From Lagia, the road winds down with spectacular views of the little fishing harbour of **Agios Kyprianos** – a short diversion from the main road. The next village is **Kokala**, a busy place with two pebbled beaches. The best beach is further north at **Nyfi**, where a turn-off to the right leads to sheltered **Alipa Beach**. Continuing north, a turn-off beyond Flomohori descends to **Kotronas**, while the main road cuts back across the peninsula to Areopoli.

There are a couple of seasonal hotels in Kokala and Kotronas, but nothing worth stopping for.

Public transport is limited – there's a bus service between Areopoli and Lagia (€3.30, 40 minutes, one to two daily).

MESSINIAN MANI
The Messinian Mani, or outer Mani, lies to the north of its Lakonian counterpart, sandwiched between the Taÿgetos Mountains and the west coast of the Mani peninsula. Kalamata lies at the northern end of the peninsula. The rugged coast is scattered with small coves and beaches, and backed by mountains that remain snowcapped until late May. There are glorious views and hiking opportunities.

Stoupa Στούπα
pop 625

The former fishing village of Stoupa, 10km south of Kardamyli, is a resort village teetering on the verge of overdevelopment, and billed as a place for discriminating (mainly British) package tourists. Although not as picturesque as Kardamyli, it does have two lovely sandy beaches.

Celebrated author Nikos Kazantzakis lived here for a while and based the protagonist of his novel *Zorba the Greek* on Alexis Zorbas, a coal mine supervisor in Pastrova, near Stoupa. Useful for walkers is *Walks in the Stoupa Area* by Lance Chilton, available from travel agencies.

ORIENTATION & INFORMATION
Stoupa is 1km west of the main Areopoli–Kalamata road, connected by roads both north and south of town. Both roads lead to the larger of Stoupa's main beaches – a crescent of golden sand.

Stoupa's amenities have yet to catch up with its development. There is no tourist office, but most travel agencies will reliably change money and organise car hire. Recommended agencies include **Zorbas** (☎ 27210-77735; www .zorbas.de) along the waterfront and **Thomeas Travel** (☎ 27210 77689; www.thomeastravel.gr). On the coast road behind the main beach, **Katerina's supermarket** (☎ 27210 77777) doubles as the post office; it also changes money and sells phonecards.

SLEEPING & EATING
Stoupa's growing band of pensions and custom-built domatia tend to be block booked by package-tour operators. Travel agencies may be able to help you.

Hotel Apartments Maistreli (☎ 27210 77595; maistreli@otenet.gr; 2-/4-person studio €60/100; ✸) The Maistreli is comfortable, clean and about 100m back from the beach.

Hotel Lefktron (☎ 27210 77322; info@lefktron-hotel .gr; s/d incl breakfast €87/104; ✸ ☎) Signposted off the southern approach road to Stoupa, this is a comfortable modern hotel 150m from the beach. The rooms have fridge and air-con, satellite TV and balconies.

Dolcini (☎ 27210 78234) Chocaholics will love this pastry shop – it's almost worth coming to Stoupa for this place alone.

our pick **Voula's Yesterday & Today** (☎ 27210 77535; mains €4.50-12.50; ✷ dinner) Voula in her

words, 'cooks from her heart'. She serves up traditional foods from a bygone era and contemporary dishes. The menu includes lamb in the oven (€10), smoked pork with pesto and mozarella (€12.50), and homemade pies (from €4.50), as well as other sweet and savoury treats.

Taverna Akrogiali (☎ 27210 77335; mains €7-12; ✷ breakfast, lunch & dinner) This taverna has a top location at the southern end of the beach, and an extensive menu that's strong on seafood (platters for €12) and good local dishes.

There are supermarkets on the main road behind Stoupa.

GETTING THERE & AWAY
Stoupa is on the main Itilo–Kalamata bus route. Three to four buses head daily to Itilo (40 minutes) and Kalamata (1¼ hours, 20 minutes). There are bus stops at the junctions of both the southern and northern approach roads, but the buses don't go into town.

Kardamyli Καρδαμύλη
pop 400

It's easy to see why Kardamyli (kahr-dah-*mee*-lih) was one of the seven cities offered to Achilles by Agamemnon. This tiny village has one of the prettiest settings in the Peloponnese, nestled between the blue waters of the Messinian Gulf and the Taÿgetos Mountains. The **Vyros Gorge**, which emerges just north of town, runs to the foot of **Mt Profitis Ilias** (2407m), the highest peak of the Taÿgetos. Today the gorge and surrounding areas are very popular with hikers. Visitor numbers can swell to around 4000 in summer.

ORIENTATION & INFORMATION
Kardamyli is on the main Areopoli–Kalamata road. The central square, Plateia 25 Martiou 1821, lies at the northern end of the main thoroughfare.

Kardamyli's main pebble-and-stone beach is off the road to Kalamata; turn left beyond the bridge on the northern edge of town. The road up to Old (or Upper) Kardamyli is on the right before the bridge. The **post office** (✷ 7.30am-2pm Mon-Fri) is on the main strip.

The useful website at www.kardamili -greece.com can also provide some information.

ACTIVITIES

Hiking has become Kardamyli's biggest drawcard. The hills behind the village are criss-crossed with an extensive network of colour-coded walking trails. Many guest houses in the village can supply you with route maps (of varying detail and quality). Most of the hikes around here are strenuous, so strong footwear is essential to support your ankles on the often relentlessly rough ground, particularly if you venture into the boulder-strewn gorge itself. You will also need to carry plenty of drinking water.

Many of the walking trails pass through the mountain village of **Exohorio**, which is perched on the edge of the Vyros Gorge at an altitude of 450m. For nonwalkers the village is also accessible by road, and it's a good place to get into a spot of more gentle exploration. The turn-off to Exohorio is 3km south of Kardamyli.

For those who don't want to go it alone, **2407 Mountain Activities** (☎ 27210 73752; www.2407m .com) offers a range of activities including hiking (€25 to €40 per person; minimum four) and mountain-bike trips (€25 to €40; minimum two) in and around the Taÿgetos Mountains, venturing into 'secret' forested and rocky regions. The owners have cleaned old paths and are proud to have a 'traveller, not tourist attitude' towards locals. They don't enter villages en masse, for example, and prefer to stick to their secret locations. The office is half way along the main street.

SLEEPING

There are plenty of domatia signs along the main road. The street down to the sea opposite the pharmacy is a good place to look. Prices are considerably less outside high season.

Olympia Koumounakou Rooms (☎ 27210 73623/21026; s/d €30/35) Olympia loves her budget travellers (as they do her) and offers clean, comfortable rooms and a communal kitchen. It's on the road before the pharmacy. At the time of research, some apartments were being constructed next door by a family member and will be worth checking out.

Volvere Studios (Stratis Bravakos Rooms) (☎ 27210 73326; d/tr €45/65) Volvere, directly opposite Olympia's, is also great value for spotless studio apartments with kitchen facilities.

Hotel Vardia (☎ 27210 73777; www.vardia-hotel.gr; studio €85, apt €120-170) March into this top choice: a relaxing and stylish stone place (near a former sentry tower and situated high behind the village), whose 18 rooms have exceptional views of the Messinian Gulf. For those with transport, it's worth tackling the hill. Entrance is south of town: turn at the bookshop.

Kalamitsi Hotel (☎ 27210 73131; www.kalamitsi -hotel.gr; d/ste €110/160) Situated 1km south of town, the Kalamitsi is a lovely, modern, stone-built hotel with serene, well-appointed rooms (family bungalows also available €220). Within its tree-shaded grounds, paths lead to a secluded pebbly beach. Home-cooked dinners (set menu €20, guests only) and fresh buffet breakfasts (€10) are also available.

Elies (☎ 27210 73140, 6974722819; www.elieshotel.gr; 2-person apt €120, 4-person apt €140-170, 6-person apt €220; ⊠) This tasteful provincial-style complex of stone maisonettes, situated 1km north of the village, has stylish interiors. It's set in an olive grove (which turns into a car park during high season – the only let-down). Attached, but at a discreet distance, is a popular weekend lunch restaurant (see below).

EATING

There's no shortage of excellent eating options in and around Kardamyli.

Elies (☎ 27210 73140, 6974722819; mains €6.50-10; ⊙ lunch) Location, location. Right by the beach, 1km north of town, and nestled in olive groves. It's got a Mediterranean provincial in-a-private-garden feel with top-quality nosh to boot. Think lemon lamb casserole (€7). Worth an afternoon in your itinerary.

O Perivoulis (☎ 27210 73713; mains €6.50-10) What it lacks in seaside (it's in the village) it makes up for with a pretty garden, friendly Australian-Greek owners and excellent taverna dishes.

Taverna Dioskouri (☎ 27210 73236; mains €7.50-11.50) A safe, nothing-over-the-top option, except for the friendly owner and the clifftop view – it overlooks the ocean from the hillside just south of town.

There are two supermarkets side by side at the northern edge of the village.

GETTING THERE & AROUND

Kardamyli is on the main bus route from Itilo to Kalamata (€3.10, one hour, four daily). The bus stops at the central square at the northern end of the main thoroughfare, and at the bookshop at the southern end.

Only one daily bus heads to Exohorio (€1.40; runs to changing times) nearby; most travellers prefer to take a taxi (around €10).

MESSINIA ΜΕΣΣΗΝΙΑ

The beaches in the southwestern corner of the Peloponnese are extremely pleasant, and while villages such as Finikounda and Koroni have felt the weight of package tourism, the old Venetian towns of Pylos and Methoni still remain delightful hideaways.

Messinia's boundaries were established in 371 BC following the defeat of Sparta by the Thebans at the Battle of Leuctra. The defeat ended almost 350 years of Spartan domination of the Peloponnese – during which time Messinian exiles founded the city of Messinia in Sicily – and meant the Messinians were left free to develop their kingdom in the region stretching west from the Taÿgetos Mountains. Their capital was ancient Messini, about 25km northwest of Kalamata on the slopes of Mt Ithomi.

KALAMATA ΚΑΛΑΜΑΤΑ
pop 49,154

Kalamata is Messinia's capital and the second-largest city in the Peloponnese. Compared to its more peaceful surrounds, it is a less-inspiring destination for visitors, but both museum lovers and shoppers will be sated. Built on the site of ancient Pharai, the city takes its modern name from a miracle-working icon of the Virgin Mary known as *kalo mata* (good eye). It was discovered in the stables of the Ottoman aga (governor), who converted to Christianity as a result of the miracles it was believed to have performed. The icon now resides inside the city's oversized cathedral, the Church of Ypapantis.

In front of the *kastro* is the small, but attractive, old town, which was almost totally destroyed by the Turks during the War of Independence and rebuilt by French engineers in the 1830s. On 14 September 1986 Kalamata was devastated by an earthquake; 20 people died, hundreds were injured and more than 10,000 homes were destroyed.

Orientation

The lively waterfront along Navarinou is a long, hot walk from the *kastro*, which is situated above the old town. The main streets linking the two areas are Faron and Aristomenous. The city centre is situated around the central square on Aristomenous.

The KTEL Messinia bus station is on the northern edge of town on Artemidos, while local buses leave from Plateia 23 Martiou – bus 1 goes to the waterfront. The train station is on Frantzi, west of the central square. At the southern end of Aristomenous is the leafy OSE park, home to a collection of old steam locomotives and carriages.

Information

There are branches of all the major banks. The National Bank of Greece has a branch on Aristomenous, at the central square, and another on the waterfront on the corner of Akrita and Navarinou.

Diktyo Internet Café (☎ 27210 97282; Nedontos 75; per hr €2; ☉ 6.30am-midnight)

EOT (☎ 27210 86868; Polyvriou 5; ☉ 7.30am-3pm Mon-Fri) Barely ever open, but given the paucity of information on offer, no great shame.

Launderette (☎ 27210 95978; Methonis 3; per load wash & dry €8; ☉ 9am-2pm & 6-9pm Mon-Fri, to 2pm Sat)

Port post office (Navarinou; ☉ 7.30am-2pm Mon-Fri) Opposite the port.

Post office (Olgas; ☉ 7.30am-2pm Mon-Fri)

Tourist police (☎ 27210 44680; Messinis; ☉ 8am-9pm Mon-Fri)

Sights
KASTRO

Looming over the town is the 13th-century **kastro** (admission free; ☉ 8am-2pm Mon-Fri, 9am-3pm Sat & Sun). Remarkably, it survived the 1986 earthquake. The entry gate is its most impressive feature. There's not much else to see, but there are good views from the battlements.

BENAKION ARCHAEOLOGICAL MUSEUM

This **museum** (☎ 27210 26209; Papazoglou 6) was about to reopen at the time of research after a period of renovation. Based on the excitement, we suggest it's well worth checking out. It's just north of Plateia 23 Martiou, signposted off Ypapantis.

HISTORICAL & FOLKLORE MUSEUM OF KALAMATA

This eggshell-blue building holds an exquisite **collection** (☎ 27210 28449; Ioannou 12, cnr Kyriakou; adult/concession €2/1; ☉ 9am-1pm Tue-Sat, 10am-1pm Sun) of local artefacts – from tools and looms to household items and clothes – that offer a thorough insight into Kalamata's bygone

era. All the items have been donated by local people; the museum is run by volunteers with support from the Association for the Spread of Education. The compact exhibitions are spread over two floors. It's a professional place and well worth supporting in any event.

MILITARY MUSEUM
Keen military buffs may enjoy the **Military Museum** (☎ 27210 21219; Mitropolitou Meletiou 10; admission free; 9am-2pm Tue-Sat,11am-2pm Sun). The displays span a broad chronological sweep from the Turkish occupation (depicted in grisly paintings) to the 21st century. National servicemen take guided tours (English speakers are supposedly available). Unfortunately, all signage is in Greek.

Festivals & Events
Held in July each year to changing dates, the **Kalamata International Dance Festival** draws crowds for its quality performances of traditional music and dance. Venues include the amphitheatre of the *kastro*. Tickets range between €12 and €25. See www.kalamata dancefestival.gr for more information.

Sleeping

The waterfront east of Faron is lined with characterless C-class (two-star) hotels that are best avoided.

Hotel Nevada (☎ 27210 81811; www.hotelnevada.gr; Santa Rosa 9; s/d €30/50) This 20-plus-year-old place has had a makeover. It has simple, spacious and clean rooms, outfitted in modern Greek style. It's not located by the beach, but in a quieter street nearby. Depending on demand, we're not convinced the prices will remain as stated. If they do, they're good value.

Hotel Haikos (☎ 27210 88902; www.haikos.com; Navarino 115; s/d/tr €70/105/125) One of the best choices of the slightly daggy, modern(ish) two-star hotels along the beachfront. It has motel-style trimmings, such as hair dryers and bar fridges. Rooms at the front can catch the street noise. Breakfast is €6 extra. Prices are significantly less outside high season.

Hotel Rex (☎ 27210 94440; www.rexhotel.gr; Aristomenous 26; s/d/tr/ste incl breakfast €97/138/172/245; ⊠ ⊑) The Rex stands unchallenged as the best address (with the slowest lift) in Kalamata. It occupies a fine neoclassical building, and offers travellers comfortable – if slightly cramped – modern rooms with all the facilities, including satellite TV.

Eating

I Milopetra (☎ 27210 98950; snacks €3.50-10; ☺ lunch & dinner) A cosmopolitan, contemporary and upmarket cafe with an olive theme, in a handy location near Plateia 23 Martiou in the old town. Serves gourmet snacks and olive-based products.

Routsi's (☎ 27210 80830; Navarino 127; mains €7-10) A favourite among expats, this eatery serves traditional food at very reasonable prices.

The Marina is the best place for seafood and other tavernas at a varying range of styles and prices.

Self-caterers should visit the large **food market** (Nedontos) across the bridge from the KTEL Messinia bus station. Kalamata is noted for its olives, olive oil and figs (see the boxed text, right). There are also dozens of supermarkets around town. **AB** (Kritis 13) is the biggest and the best.

Getting There & Away

AIR

Olympic Air runs a flight between Kalamata and Thessaloniki (€80, three weekly), but not Athens.

KALAMATA OLIVES

Kalamata gives its name to the prized Kalamata olive, a plump, purple-black variety that is found in delicatessens around the world and is also grown extensively (although not exclusively) in neighbouring Lakonia. The region's reliable winter rains and hot summers make for perfect olive-growing conditions.

The Kalamata tree is distinguished from the common olive (grown for oil) by the size of its leaves. Like its fruit, the leaves of the Kalamata are twice the size of other varieties and a darker shade of green.

Unlike other varieties, Kalamata olives can't be picked green. They ripen in late November and must be hand-picked to avoid bruising. You can buy and sample these famous olives at the markets in Kalamata.

BOAT

A weekly ferry service operated by LANE Lines runs from Kalamata to Crete, via Kythira. Contact **SMAN Travel/Maniatis** (☎ 27210 20704; smantrv@otenet.gr; Psaron), by the port, for the schedule. For more detailed information about getting to the Greek islands from Kalamata, see Island Hopping (p758).

BUS

KTEL Messinia bus station (☎ 27210 28581; Artemidos) has buses to Athens (€20, 4½ hours, 13 daily) via Tripoli (€7.20, 1¼ hours) and Corinth Isthmus (€15, 2½ hours), Kyparissia (€6, 1¼ hours, four daily) and Patra (€20.30, four hours, two daily) via Pyrgos (€14, two hours).

Heading west, there are buses to Koroni (€4.20, 1½ hours, eight daily), Pylos (€4.20, 1¼ hours, five daily), Methoni (€5, 1½ hours, five daily) and Finikounda (€6.30, 1¾ hours, three daily). Heading east across the Langada Pass to Sparta (€2.40, 45 minutes, two daily) involves changing buses at Artemisia. There are also three buses to the Messinian Mani, travelling as far as Itilo (€6.60, 2¼ hours). Two of these head via Kardamyli (€3.40, one hour, weekdays only) and Stoupa (€4, 1¼ hours). Weekend services for all routes are greatly reduced or nonexistent.

TRAIN

Kalamata is the end of the line for the Peloponnese railway (see the boxed text, p173). Four trains depart daily on the west-coast line to Corinth (€17.60), Pyrgos (normal/IC €3.70/6.90) and Patra (normal/IC €6.60/11.30, five hours).

Getting Around
TO/FROM THE AIRPORT
Kalamata's airport is 10.5km west of the city near Messini. There is no airport shuttle bus. A taxi costs about €15 to €20.

BUS
Local buses leave from the KTEL Messinia bus station. The most useful service is bus 1, which goes south to the seafront and then east along Navarinou as far as the Filoxenia Hotel. Buy tickets (€1) from kiosks or the driver.

CAR & MOTORCYCLE
Kalamata is a good place to rent a vehicle, due to hot competition between the agencies at the waterfront end of Faron. Recommended options:

Alpha Rent a Bike (☎ 27210 93423; www.alphabike .gr; Vyronos 143) Rents a range of bikes from 50cc to 500cc.
Avis (☎ 27210 20352; Kesari 2)
Hertz (☎ 27210 88268; www.hertz.gr; cnr Methonis & Kanari 88)
Verga Rent a Car (☎ 27210 95190; Faron 202)

MAVROMATI (ANCIENT MESSINI)
ΜΑΥΡΟΜΑΤΙ (ΑΡΧΑΙΑ ΜΕΣΣΗΝΗ)
pop 388
The fascinating ruins of Ancient Messini lie scattered across a small valley below the pretty village of Mavromati, 25km northwest of Kalamata. The village takes its name from the fountain in the central square; the water gushes from a hole in the rock that looks like a black eye (*mavro mati* in Greek).

History
Ancient Messini was founded in 371 BC after the Theban general Epaminondas defeated Sparta at the Battle of Leuctra, freeing the Messinians from almost 350 years of Spartan rule.

Built on the site of an earlier stronghold, the new Messinian capital was one of a string of defensive positions designed to keep watch over Sparta. Epaminondas himself helped to plan the fortifications, which were based on a massive wall that stretched 9km around the surrounding ridges and completely enclosed the town.

Apart from its defensive potential, Ancient Messini was also favoured by the gods. According to local myth, Zeus was born here – not Crete – and raised by the nymphs Neda and Ithomi, who bathed him in the same spring that gives the modern village its name.

Sights
EXPLORING THE SITE
The best views of this beautiful site are from Mavromati's central square, and it's worth briefly examining the layout before heading down for a closer look. Access is by a road near the museum, about 300m northwest of the square.

The **museum** (☎ 27210 51201; adult/concession €2/1; ⓨ 8.30am-3pm Tue-Sun) houses a small and interesting collection of finds from the site, mainly statues recovered from the *asklepion*. They include two statues assumed to be of Machaon and Podaleiros, the sons of Asclepius. They are thought to be the work of the sculptor Damophon, who specialised in oversized statues of gods and heroes, and was responsible for many of the statues that once adorned Ancient Messini.

Before heading down to the site, it's worth continuing another 800m along the road past the museum to view the celebrated **Arcadian Gate**. This unusual circular gate guarded the ancient route to Megalopoli – now the modern road north to Meligalas and Zerbisia – which runs through the gate. Running uphill from the gate is the finest surviving section of the mighty defensive wall built by Epaminondas. It remains impressive, studded with small, square forts, and is well worth the gentle uphill walk from the village.

The **site** (admission free) itself remained unexplored until recent times, and is still emerging from the valley floor as ongoing excavations are taking place. One of the most impressive areas is the **asklepion** complex that lay at the heart of the ancient city. This extensive complex was centred on a **Doric temple** that once housed a golden statue of Ithomi. The modern awning west of the temple protects the **artemision**, where fragments of an enormous statue of Artemis Orthia were found. The structures to the east of the *asklepion* include the **ekklesiasterion**, which once acted as an assembly hall.

The site's main path leads downhill from the *asklepion* to the imposing **stadium**, which is surrounded by the ruins of an enormous **gymnasium**.

Sleeping & Eating

Likourgos Rooms (☎ 27240 51297; d/tr €55/70) This is a spacious and comfortable modern option whose front rooms afford glimpses of the ruins. The helpful owner speaks some English.

Besides a couple of local *kafeneia* (coffee houses), Taverna Ithomi is the only eatery in town (mains €6 to €12).

Getting There & Away

There are two buses to Mavromati (€2.20, one hour, weekdays only) from Kalamata, one in the early morning, the other in the afternoon, to a changing schedule. Check at the taverna.

KORONI ΚΟΡΩΝΗ

pop 1668

Koroni (ko-*ro*-nih) is a lovely Venetian port town, 43km southwest of Kalamata, situated on Messinia Bay. Medieval mansions and churches line the town's quaint, narrow and winding streets. These lead to a promontory, on which perches an extensive castle.

Orientation & Information

Buses will drop you in the central square outside the Church of Agios Dimitrios, one block back from the harbour. The main street (formal name Perikli Ralli, but few know it) runs east from the square, one block back from the sea.

There is no tourist office, but the large town map on the cathedral wall shows the location of both banks and the **post office** (⏱ 7.30am-2pm Mon-Fri), all of which are nearby. There are no tourist police.

Sights & Activities

Much of the old castle is occupied by the **Timios Prodromos Convent**. Note the castle's impressive Gothic entrance. The small promontory beyond the castle is a tranquil place for a stroll, with lovely views over the Messinian Gulf to the Taÿgetos Mountains.

Koroni's main attraction is **Zaga Beach**, a long sweep of golden sand just south of the town. It takes about 20 minutes to walk to

Zaga Beach – you can cut through the castle or go via the road. Ask locals for directions.

Koroni also sees loggerhead turtles, which lay their eggs near Zaga. For more information regarding this endangered species, see p707.

Sleeping & Eating

Accommodation is a bit limited in Koroni. Most of the rooms are spread around a cluster of domatia by the sea, at the eastern end of the main street. There are more domatia overlooking Zaga Beach, but they are often block booked in summer.

Camping Koroni (☎ 27250 22119; www.koroni camping.com; camp sites per adult/tent/car €8/5/4; 🐕) Located only 200m from Koroni, near the beach and with good facilities.

Hotel Diana (☎ /fax 27250 22312; www.dianahotel -koroni.gr; s/d €30/50; 🐕) This place is blessed (or otherwise) with Byzantine gold-plated bar stools, icons and the like. Rooms are not quite as glossy, if adequate. It's off the central square almost on the seafront. Breakfast is €5 per person.

Sofotel (☎ 27250 22230; www.koroni-holidays. com; d €65) Koroni's new hotel in town, the prices are good (if they last). Modern – in an orange-and-cream-hued kind of way – and 12 rooms have creature comforts, some with balconies.

Zagas Apartments (☎ 27250 22722; 6973754036; Zaga Beach; 2-/4-/6-person apt €65/80/120; 🐕 🅿) Personable apartments with kitchen facilities and balconies and views over Zaga Beach.

Eleas Yi (mains €6-13) We admit the outlook isn't what you'd expect – it's next to the supermarket on the way into town – and overlooks olive trees rather than a marine vista. It's recommended overwhelmingly by local people for its taverna cuisine, which speaks volumes.

Getting There & Away

There are seven buses daily to Kalamata (€4.30, 1½ hours) and one to Athens (€24.10). Tickets can be bought from Elite pastry shop on the main square.

FINIKOUNDA ΦOINIKOYNTA

pop 560

A former fishing village, Finikounda, midway between Koroni and Methoni, is now something of a seasonal minipackage-tour resort; it's popular for **windsurfing**. Thankfully it lacks high-rises, but the main road cuts a swath behind the village. Its pleasant **beaches** stretch either side of the village.

All the shops and facilities – these days rather tourist-focussed – are around the port. The bus stop is outside Hotel Finikountas, 100m from the port. The village's commercial website is www.finikounda.com.

Sleeping & Eating

There are domatia signs throughout the village and numerous camp sites along the main road.

Hotel Finikounda (☎ 27230 71208; fax 27230 71018; s €40, d €50-60; ⊠) It lacks a seafront position, but the neat rooms, with pine bedheads, and balconies, make it a good-value option.

Akti Studios (☎ 27230 71316; r €65; P ⊠) This small, family-run place has nine comfortable studios with kitchen facilities. It's set back from the beach road about 250m east of the port. The rooms have balconies with beach views.

Oinoysses (☎ 27230 71446; mains €6.50-10; ⊠ Apr-Oct) A lovely place to while away your eating time. This attractive place perched out over the sand at the village's eastern end, serves excellent and very fresh daily specials such as octopus salad, plus a range of grills.

Elena Taverna (☎ 27230 71235; mains €8-14) Position, position, position. With a prime spot on the headland overlooking the port at the western end of town, it's the perfect spot to enjoy superlative filleted grilled sardines and the like, with a view to match.

Getting There & Away

There are buses to Kalamata (€6, 1¾ hours, around three daily), one via Koroni, the others via Methoni (€2) and Pylos (€2.50).

METHONI ΜΕΘΩΝΗ
pop 1169

Methoni (meh-*tho*-nih), 12km south of Pylos, was another of the seven cities offered to Achilles by Agamemnon. Homer described it as 'rich in vines'. Today it's a pretty seaside town with a popular sandy beach, next to which crouches a sturdy 15th-century Venetian fortress.

Orientation & Information

The road from Pylos forks on the edge of town to create Methoni's two main streets, which then run parallel through town to the fortress. As you come from Pylos, the fork

to the right is the main shopping street. It has numerous shops, *kafeneia*, a National Bank of Greece (and ATE Bank ATM) and a nearby supermarket. The left fork leads directly to the fortress car park, passing the **post office** (⊠ 7.30am-2pm Mon-Fri) on the way. Turn left at the fortress end of either street onto Miaouli, which leads to Methoni Beach. The small square by the beach is surrounded by fairly characterless hotels and several seafood restaurants.

There is no tourist office or tourist police. The regular **police** (☎ 27230 31203) are signposted near the post office.

Sights

FORTRESS

This splendid **kastro** (admission free; ⊠ 8am-7pm May-Sep, to 3pm Oct-Apr), a great example of military architecture, is vast and romantic. Within the walls are a Turkish bath, a cathedral, a house, a cistern, parapets and underground passages. See how many Lion of St Mark insignias you can spot.

This vast fortification is built on a promontory south of the modern town and is surrounded on three sides by the sea and separated from the mainland by a moat. The medieval port town, which was located within the fortress walls, was the Venetians' first and their longest-held possession in the Peloponnese. It was also a stopover point for pilgrims en route to the Holy Land. During medieval times the twin fortresses of Methoni and Koroni were known as 'the Eyes of the Serene Republic'.

A short causeway leads from the fortress to the diminutive octagonal **Bourtzi castle** on an adjacent islet.

Sleeping & Eating

Hotel Achilles (☎ /fax 27230 31819; www.achilleshotel .gr; s/d €55/70; ⊠ year-round; ⊠) The smartest of a range of small family hotels in town, with 13 comfortable modern rooms, all with balcony and views. There's a light, airy dining area, too. Breakfast costs €6.

ourpick Apartments Melina (☎ 27230 31505; www.geocities.com/messinias; studio €65-75, 2-/3-/4-person apt €75/85/90; 6-person 'villa' €120) Immaculate, spacious apartments right across from the beach, with a trim garden of vines, roses and palms, and friendly English-speaking owners.

O Nikos (☎ 27230 31282; Miaouli; mains €5-11; ⊠ year-round) 'Good, clean, cheap and with big helpings' is the local boast of this quaint and unpretentious place. A reliable bet.

Taverna Klimatari (☎ 27230 31544; Miaouli; mains €6-13; ☺ Apr-Oct) Locals are in agreement: this is the place to head for traditional dishes. It's in an old home – with seating on the front porch or in a courtyard. Typical choices include onion pie, stuffed zucchini flowers and cod fish with spinach.

Getting There & Away

Buses depart from Methoni from the fork at the Pylos end of town where the two main streets meet. Bus services depart for Pylos (€1.50, 15 minutes, six daily), Kalamata (€5.50, 1½ hours, six daily) and Finikounda (€2, 15 minutes, one to two daily). Unbelievably, there is no bus between Methoni and Koroni; you must change at Finikounda – if the timetable works, that is. The bus to Kalamata stops at Harakopio, 4.5km from Koroni. For bus information call ☎ 27230 22230.

PYLOS ΠΥΛΟΣ
pop 2104

Pylos (*pee*-loss), on the coast 51km southwest of Kalamata, presides over the southern end of an immense bay. With its huge natural harbour almost enclosed by the Sfaktiria Islet, a delightful tree-shaded central square, two castles and surrounding pine-covered hills, Pylos is one of the most picturesque towns in the Peloponnese.

From the bay on 20 October 1827, the British, French and Russian fleets, under the command of Admiral Codrington, fired at point-blank range on Ibrahim Pasha's combined Turkish, Egyptian and Tunisian fleet, sinking 53 ships and killing 6000 men, with negligible losses on the Allies' side.

The attack was known as the Battle of Navarino (which is the town's former name) and was decisive in the War of Independence, but it was not meant to have been a battle at all. The Allied fleet wanted to achieve no more than to persuade Ibrahim Pasha and his fleet to leave, but things got somewhat out of hand. George IV, on hearing the news, described it as a 'deplorable misunderstanding'.

Orientation & Information

Everything of importance is within a few minutes' walk of the central square, Plateia Trion Navarhon (Sq of the Three Admirals), down by the seafront.

The KTEL Messinia bus station is on the inland side of the square. Nileos runs uphill from the bus station.

There is no tourist office. The National Bank of Greece and ATE Bank (with ATM) are on the square.

Internet P@ndigit@l (Episkopou 17; per hr €2.50; ☺ 8am-2pm & 5-9pm Mon-Sat) Cutting-edge services.

Police station (☎ 27230 23733/2316) On the central square.

Post office (Nileos; ☺ 7.30am-2pm Mon-Fri)

Sights & Activities
CASTLES

There are castles on each side of Navarino Bay. The more accessible of them is the **Neo Kastro** (☎ 27230 22010; adult/concession €3/2; ☺ 8.30am-3pm Tue-Sun), on the hill top at the southern edge of town, off the road to Methoni. It was built by the Turks in 1573 and later used as a launching pad for the invasion of Crete. It remains in good condition, especially the formidable surrounding walls. Within its walls are a citadel, a mosque converted into a church and a courtyard surrounded by dungeons (used as a prison until the 1900s). The site's museum exhibits a collection of pictures of the Battle of Navarino, donated by René Puaux (1878–1937). He bequeathed his collection of porcelain, engravings and lithographs on condition that it be exhibited at Pylos, near the battle's location. The road to Methoni from the central square goes past the castle. Allow a couple of hours for relaxed exploration.

For coverage of the ancient Paleokastro, the other castle that is 6km north of Pylos, see p224.

BOAT TOURS

Club Boats (☎ 27230 23155, 6972263565) in the kiosk on the quay runs boat tours around the Bay of Navarino and to Sfaktiria Islet. The price depends on the number of passengers, but reckon on about €10 per person (minimum €70 for the tour). On the trip around the island, stops can be made at memorials to admirals of the Allied ships. Napoleon's nephew and British casualties are also buried here. If conditions are still, boats pause to see silt-covered wrecks of sunken Turkish ships, still discernible in the clear waters.

BIRDWATCHING & THE GIAVOLA LAGOON

The best – and most accessible – birdwatching site in the Peloponnese is the **Gialova Lagoon**. Between September and March the lagoon is home to up to 20,000 assorted waterbirds, while many others pause here on their spring migration between Africa and Eastern Europe.

The Hellenic Ornithological Society has recorded 265 of around 400 species found in Greece, including 10 species of duck and eight types of heron. Waders descend in their thousands, along with flamingos and glossy ibis. Birds of prey include the internationally threatened species, the imperial eagle, plus osprey, peregrine falcon and harriers.

The lagoon and associated wetlands cover 700 hectares at the northern end of Navarino Bay, separated from the bay by a narrow spit of land leading out to Koryphasion Hill. They are fed by two freshwater streams that flow into the reed beds on the northern and eastern flanks of the lagoon and empty into Navarino Bay, below Koryphasion Hill.

The wetlands and surrounding coastal habitats were declared a protected area in 1997. The old pump house, former nerve centre of an ill-considered drainage scheme, has been converted into an information centre and is the starting point for two walking trails that guide visitors through a range of habitats.

Sleeping

Rooms to Rent Stavroula Milona (☎ 27230 22724; d without bathroom €30) This creaky place (with wobbly floors) is charming. The small, basic rooms are clean and comfortable. There's a communal kitchen and TV lounge. It's on the seafront, south of Hotel Miramare, above Café-Bar En Plo (the bar's nightly music may bother some).

Hotel Nilefs (☎ 27230 22518; fax 27230 22575; Rene Pyot, s/d/tr incl breakfast €45/65/78; 🕑 Apr-Oct; 🖭) This good-value place run by a pleasant woman (no English spoken) offers a spic 'n' span experience. The neat rooms have balconies. It's just back from the seafront on the castle side of the square.

Hotel Karalís (☎ 27230 22970; hotel_karalis@yahoo.gr; Paralia, s/d incl breakfast €110/120) It's hard not to like this hotel for the setting alone – under the castle walls, clinging to a cliff over the water. This formerly dated place had a makeover in 2008 and the spruced-up version provides comfortable lodgings. Lower low-season prices make it better value, however.

Eating

There are plenty of tavernas with standard favourites and seafood.

Koukos (☎ 27230 22950; mains €5-10) A plain, unpretentious and good-ol'-fashioned taverna serving massive portions of grills and oven-baked dishes, to a changing menu. Locals enjoy Koukos for its hearty meals and atmosphere.

Restaurant Grigoris (☎ 27230 22621; mains €5-14) A great alternative to the central square options. Forget the menu – round off your appetite with the chef's stove-top displays. In summer there's a shady garden. On a quiet spot one street north of, and parallel to, the harbour.

There is a supermarket on the central square.

Getting There & Away

From the **KTEL Messinia bus station** (☎ 27230 22230) there are bus services to Kalamata (€4.30, 1¼ hours, eight daily), Kyparissia (€5.20, 1¼ hours, four daily) via Nestor's Palace (€1.80, 30 minutes, four services Saturday and two on Sunday), and Hora (€2, 35 minutes), Methoni (€1.40, 20 minutes, five daily) and Finikounda (€1.80, 30 minutes, three services daily Monday to Saturday, none on Sunday). There are two daily buses to Athens (€24.20, five hours). For Patra, there's one connection per day at Kyparissia. Services are reduced, if existent, on weekends.

GIALOVA ΓΙΑΛΟΒΑ
pop 260

The village of Gialova lies 8km north of Pylos on the northeastern edge of Navarino Bay. It boasts a fine sandy beach and safe swimming in the sheltered waters of the bay. The Gialova Lagoon is a prime birdwatching site in winter (see boxed text, above).

Sleeping & Eating

Camping Erodios (☎ 27230 28240; www.erodioss.gr; camp sites per adult/tent/car €7/6/4, 2-/4-bed cabins €65/75; ☎) This great camping nest is northwest of the village on the road leading out to the Gialova Lagoon and Paleokastro. It has a good stretch of beach on Navarino Bay and great facilities.

Hotel-Restaurant Zoe (☎ 27230 22025; www .hotelzoe.com; s/d/tr incl breakfast €58/70/110; ☎ ☎) This formerly small family-run place on the seafront near the pier is morphing into a complex of rooms and apartments (located in a resort-like section behind). We like the hotel rooms with the small front balcony, although they're potentially noisy if Zoe's outdoor taverna rocks on.

Elia (☎ 6946006875; mains €6-14) Gourmet Greek might well describe the dishes served at this contemporary Mediterranean eatery. The stuffed bream and octopus can only be outdone by the ambience, with its trendy designer lights and flower boxes.

Getting There & Away

There are four buses a day south to Pylos (€1.40, 15 minutes) and five north to Kyparissia via Nestor's Palace and Hora. A taxi between Gaivola and Pylos costs around €8.

AROUND GIALOVA
Paleokastro

The ruins of this ancient castle lie 5km west of Gialova on rugged **Koryphasion Hill**, a formidable natural defensive position overlooking the northern entrance to Navarino Bay.

The road out to the castle is signposted on the northern edge of the village. It crosses the narrow spit of land that separates Navarino Bay from the Gialova Lagoon, and finishes at a car park at the southern end of the hill. Signs point to the beginning of a rough track that snakes up the steep hillside to the castle entrance.

The castle was built by the Franks at the end of the 13th century, and sits on the site of the acropolis of Ancient Pylos. It was occupied in 1381 by Spanish mercenaries from Navarra, after whom the bay is named.

The car park is also the starting point for another track that skirts around the base of Koryphasion Hill to **Voidokilia Beach**. This beautiful, sandy horseshoe bay is presumed to be Homer's 'sandy Pylos', where Telemachus

was warmly welcomed when he came to ask wise old King Nestor the whereabouts of his long-lost father, Odysseus, King of Ithaca. There's another path up to the castle from the southern side of the beach that passes Nestor's Cave. According to mythology, this is the cave where Hermes hid the cattle he stole from Apollo. This small cave boasts a few stalactites.

Voidokilia Beach can also be approached via road from the village of **Petrohori**, 6km north of Gialova off the road to Hora.

Nestor's Palace

So called because it is believed to have been the court of the mythical hero Nestor, who took part in the voyage of the Argonauts and fought in the Trojan War, **Nestor's Palace** (☎ 27630 31437; site only adult/concession €3/2, site & museum adult/concession €4/2; ☎ 8.30am-3pm, museum closed Mon) is the best preserved of all Mycenaean palaces. Originally a two-storey building, the palace's walls stand 1m high, giving a good idea of the layout of a Mycenaean palace complex. The main palace, in the middle, was a building of many rooms. The largest room, the **throne room**, was where the king dealt with state business. In the centre was a large, circular hearth surrounded by four ornate columns that supported a 1st-floor balcony. Some of the fine frescoes discovered here are housed in the museum in the nearby village of Hora (below). Surrounding the throne is the **sentry box**, **pantry**, **waiting room**, a **vestibule** and, most fascinating, a **bathroom** with a terracotta tub still in place.

The most important finds were 1200 or so Linear B script tablets, the first discovered on the mainland. Some are in Hora's museum. The site was excavated later than the other Mycenaean sites, between 1952 and 1965. An excellent guidebook by Carl Blegen, who led the excavations, is sold at the site.

Nestor's Palace is 17km north of modern Pylos. Buses from Pylos to Kyparissia go via Nestor's Palace (€1.40, 30 minutes).

Hora Χώρα

Hora's fascinating little **archaeological museum** (☎ 27632 31358; museum only adult/concession €2/1, museum & site adult/concession €4/2; ☎ 8.30am-3pm Tue-Sun), 4km northeast of Nestor's Palace, houses finds from the site and other Mycenaean artefacts from Messinia.

The prize pieces are the incomplete frescos from the throne rooms at Nestor's Palace and the Linear B tablets (even if the tablets are copies).

Buses from Pylos to Kyparissia stop at Hora.

ELIA ΗΛΙΑ

Most people come to Elia for one reason: to visit the historically important and impressive site of Ancient Olympia, birthplace of the Olympic Games, in the region's western prefecture. Elia is otherwise largely an agricultural area.

Ancient Elia took its name from the mythical King Helios. Its capital was the city of Elis, now a forgotten ruin on the road from Gastouni to Lake Pinios. When the Franks arrived, they made Andravida the capital of their principate of Morea. Pyrgos is the dull modern capital.

THOLOS TO PYRGOS
ΘΟΛΟΣ ΠΡΟΣ ΠΥΡΓΟΣ

Heading north into Elia from Messinia, the mountains to the east give way to populated plains fringed by golden-sand beaches. Elia's coastline has one of the longest stretches of beaches, even if interspersed here and there by pebbled shores and rocky outcrops. Unfortunately, behind the beaches, buildings are increasingly impeding potentially pretty views. Among the best southern beaches are **Tholos**, **Kakovatos** and **Kouroutas**. There is seaside accommodation available in each village, but most of it is in uninspiring concrete buildings.

A sign outside Tholos points to the mountain village of **Nea Figalia**, 14km inland. From here, it's a further 21km to reach the tranquil and overgrown site of **Ancient Figalia**, set high above the Neda River. Laurel, cypress and citrus trees are clustered around the ruins of this ancient Arkadian marketplace, with remnants of towers, a small acropolis and a temple to Dionysos, the wine pourer. Some of the city walls (formerly around 4.5km long) still remain and you can see these from the road. Few people come here so wandering around here at your leisure is pleasurable, if hot in summer (bring plenty of water). A road leads about 19km east from Nea Figalia to Andritsena.

PYRGOS ΠΥΡΓΟΣ
pop 23,274

Pyrgos, the capital of Elia prefecture, 98km southwest of Patra and 24km from Olympia, is a busy service town with little of interest to the visitor, except for a plethora of clothes shops. But you'll probably end up here: all forms of public transport, including buses and trains to Olympia, pass through the town. The train and bus stations are about 400m apart, the former at the northern edge of town on Ypsilantou, and the modern, well-organised bus station on the other side of the train tracks northwest of the station.

You'd only stay here if absolutely necessary (Olympia is a more pleasant option), but if you need to stay overnight, there are several modernish and slightly overpriced hotels that lack personality and cater to business visitors, on the streets leading into town, off Ypsilantou.

Getting There & Away
BUS
There are up to 16 buses each day servicing Olympia (€1.90, 30 minutes), as well as eight daily to Athens (€24.90, four hours), nine daily to Patra (€8.80, two hours), and two daily to Andritsena (€5.50, two hours), Kyllini (€5.80, one hour, two daily), Kyparissia (€5.50, 1¼ hours) and Kalamata (€11.40, two hours, four daily). The schedule is reduced on weekends.

TRAIN
Heading north, there are six trains daily to Corinth (normal/IC €6.70/13, 4¾/3½ hours) via Patra; heading south, there are five trains daily to Kyparissia (normal/IC €2.30/5, 1¼ hours), which continue to Kalamata (normal/IC €7/3.70, 3¼ hours). There are also trains daily on the branch line to Olympia (€1, 40 minutes).

AROUND PYRGOS
Nemea's wine country is not the only region of the Peloponnese to produce a decent drop (for details see the boxed text, p529). The **Mercouri Estate** (☎ 26210 41601; www.mercouri.gr; ☷ tastings 9am-2pm Mon-Sat), 1km north of Korakohori village and about 15km from Pyrgos, is another worthwhile winery. This handsome estate produces a dry white Foloi, and a prize-winning rich red, its flagship Domaine

Mercouri. It also runs tours of the grounds (reservations recommended).

OLYMPIA ΟΛΥΜΠΙΑ
pop 1000

With countless overpriced souvenir shops and eateries, the modern village of Olympia (o-lim-*bee*-ah) panders unashamedly to the hundreds of thousands of tourists who continually pour through here on their way to Ancient Olympia. Despite this, the town is far from kitsch. Only 500m south of the well-kept leafy streets over the Kladeos River is Ancient Olympia. Although the site's surrounds were tragically burnt in the 2007 bushfires, rendering it devoid of trees, Ancient Olympia survived, thanks to efforts of locals and firefighters; it remains one of the most luxuriantly green, beautiful and historically important sites to be consumed.

Orientation

The main street, Praxitelous Kondyli, runs through town and leads to the Ancient Olympia site. The bus stop for Pyrgos and Tripoli is one block before the church as you enter Olympia from Pyrgos, and the train station is close to the town centre near the end of Douma St.

Information

Cafe Zeus (Praxitelous Kondyli) One of several cafes with wi-fi access.

EOT Olympia (☎ 26240-22262; www.eot.gr; Praxitelous Kondyli; ☙ 9am-3pm Mon-Fri May-Sep) Helpful tourist office but unfortunately only open on weekdays. Bus, train and ferry schedules (from Kyllini and Patra) are posted on the window.

National Bank of Greece (cnr Praxitelous Kondyli & Stefanopoulou) One of four banks in town.

Post office (Pierre Coubertin 3; ☙ 7.30am-2pm Mon-Fri)

Tourist police (☎ 26240 22550; Spiliopoulou 5)

Sights

Four museums focus on Ancient Olympia and Olympia (and Olympics) mania. The Archaeological Museum of Olympia (right) and Museum of the History of the Olympic Games in Antiquity (right) are not to be missed; the other two are only worth it if you have time to kill or interest to satisfy. And this is before you even hit the Olympic site itself.

You can buy a joint ticket for both the Olympic site and for the Archaeological Museum – highly recommended. Note: entrance times change yearly and seasonally; check with the tourist office on arrival.

MUSEUM OF THE HISTORY OF THE OLYMPIC GAMES IN ANTIQUITY

This **museum** (admission free; ☙ 1.30-8pm Mon, 8am-8pm Tue-Sun Apr-Oct, 10.30am-5pm Mon, 8.30am-5pm Tue-Sun Nov-Mar), opened in 2004 (after the Athens Olympics), is a beautifully presented space depicting the history of all things athletic, as well as the Nemean, Panathenaic and, of course, Olympic Games. The sculptures, mosaics and other displays all pay tribute to athletes and athleticism. Women – and their involvement (or lack of) – is also acknowledged.

MUSEUM OF THE HISTORY OF EXCAVATIONS IN OLYMPIA

Next to the Museum of the History of the Olympic Games, and housed in a small historic building, this **museum** (admission free; ☙ 1.30-8pm Mon, 8am-8pm Tue-Sun Apr-Oct, 10.30am-5pm Mon, 8.30am-5pm Tue-Sun Nov-Mar) will appeal more to archaeology and history buffs. It displays items relating to the site's German excavations in the 19th century.

ARCHAEOLOGICAL MUSEUM OF OLYMPIA

This superb **museum** (☎ /fax 26240 22742; adult/concession €6/3, incl site visit €9/5; ☙ 1.30-8pm Mon, 8am-8pm Tue-Sun Apr-Oct, 10.30am-5pm Mon, 8.30am-3pm Tue-Sun Nov-Mar) – Ancient Olympia's archaeological site museum – about 200m north of the sanctuary's ticket kiosk, is a great place to start or end your visit to the site of Ancient Olympia.

There is a scale site model, and the reassembly of the pediments and metopes from the Temple of Zeus are spectacular (despite not being complete). The **eastern pediment** depicts the chariot race between Pelops and Oinomaos, the **western pediment** shows the fight between the Centaurs and Lapiths, and the **metopes** depict the Twelve Labours of Hercules.

Don't miss the 4th-century Parian marble statue of **Hermes of Praxiteles**, a masterpiece of classical sculpture from the Temple of Hera. Hermes was charged with taking the infant Dionysos to Mt Nysa.

You'll also find intriguing collections of tiny, but beautifully crafted, votive offerings

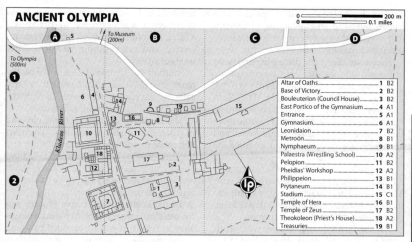

ANCIENT OLYMPIA

Altar of Oaths	**1** B2
Base of Victory	**2** B2
Bouleuterion (Council House)	**3** B2
East Portico of the Gymnasium	**4** A1
Entrance	**5** A1
Gymnasium	**6** A1
Leonidaion	**7** B2
Metroön	**8** B1
Nymphaeum	**9** B1
Palaestra (Wrestling School)	**10** A2
Pelopion	**11** B2
Pheidias' Workshop	**12** A2
Philippeion	**13** B1
Prytaneum	**14** B1
Stadium	**15** C1
Temple of Hera	**16** B2
Temple of Zeus	**17** B2
Theokoleon (Priest's House)	**18** A2
Treasuries	**19** B1

discovered on the site, and the sculptured **Head of Hera**.

MODERN MUSEUM OF THE OLYMPIC GAMES

Only real Olympic devotees or avid collectors will enjoy this **museum** (☎ 26240 22544; adult/concession €2/free; ☉ 8am-3.30pm), owned by the Olympic Academy. It houses a collection of commemorative paraphernalia of all the modern Olympics to date, including photos, posters, coins, stamps and Olympic torches. It's two blocks west of Praxitelous Kondyli, opposite the junction of Agerinai and Kosmopoulou.

SITE OF ANCIENT OLYMPIA

The Olympics were undoubtedly the Ancient World's biggest sporting event. During the games warring states briefly halted their squabbles, corporate sponsors vied to outdo each other, and victorious competitors won great fame and considerable fortune. You could say much the same about the modern-day equivalent, the main difference being that back then only men could compete and they did most of it *sans* underpants. Held every four years until their abolition by killjoy Emperor Theodosius I in AD 394, the games lasted at least 1000 years. The World Heritage–listed site of **Ancient Olympia** (☎ 26240 22517; adult/concession €6/3, site & archaeological museum €9/5; ☉ 8am-8pm Apr-Oct, 8.30am-3pm Nov-Mar) is still a recognisable complex of temples, priests' dwellings and public buildings. The site contains excellent explanatory boards, with depictions of what the buildings would have looked like, along with a plan and description in English.

History & Mythology

The origins of Olympia date back to Mycenaean times. The Great Goddess, identified as Rea, was worshipped here in the 1st millennium BC. By the Classical era Rea had been superseded by her son Zeus. A small regional festival, which probably included athletic events, began in the 11th century BC.

The first official quadrennial Olympic Games were declared in 776 BC by King Iphitos of Elis. By 676 BC they were open to all Greek males and reached the height of their prestige in 576 BC. The games were held in honour of Zeus, popularly acclaimed as their founder, and took place around the first full moon in August.

The athletic festival lasted five days and included wrestling, chariot and horse racing, the pentathlon (wrestling, discus and javelin throwing, long jump and running), and the *pancratium* (a vicious form of fisticuffs).

Originally only Greek-born males were allowed to participate, but later Romans were permitted. Slaves and women were not allowed to enter the sanctuary as participants or spectators. Women trying to sneak in were thrown from a nearby rock.

The event served purposes besides athletic competition. Writers, poets and historians read their works to large audiences, and the citizens of various city-states got together.

Traders clinched business deals and city-state leaders talked in an atmosphere of festivity that was conducive to resolving differences through discussion, rather than battle.

The games continued during the first years of Roman rule. By this time, however, their importance had declined and, thanks to Nero, they had become less sporting. In AD 67 Nero entered the chariot race with 10 horses, ordering that other competitors could have no more than four. Despite this advantage he fell and abandoned the race, yet was still declared the winner by the judges.

The games were held for the last time in AD 394, before they were banned by Emperor Theodosius I as part of a purge of pagan festivals. In AD 426 Theodosius II decreed that the temples of Olympia be destroyed.

The modern Olympic Games were instituted in 1896 and, other than during WWI and WWII, have been held every four years in different cities around the world ever since, including (to much celebration in Greece) the 2004 Athens Olympics. The Olympic flame is lit at the ancient site and carried by runners to the city where the games are held.

Exploring the Site

Ancient Olympia is signposted from the modern village. The entrance is beyond the bridge over the Kladeos River. Thanks to Theodosius II and various earthquakes, little remains of the magnificent buildings of Ancient Olympia, but enough exists to sustain an absorbing visit in an idyllic, leafy setting; allow a minimum of half a day. A visit to the archaeological museum (p226) beforehand will help with visualising the ancient buildings. The first ruin encountered is the **gymnasium**, which dates from the 2nd century BC. South of here is the partly restored **palaestra** (wrestling school), where contestants practised and trained. The next building was the **theokoleon** (priests' house). Behind it is **Pheidias' workshop**, where the gargantuan ivory-and-gold Statue of Zeus, one of the Seven Wonders of the Ancient World, was sculpted. The workshop was identified by archaeologists after the discovery of tools and moulds. Beyond the *theokoleon* is the **leonidaion**, an elaborate structure that accommodated dignitaries.

The **altis**, or **Sacred Precinct of Zeus**, lies east of the path. Its most important building was the immense 5th-century Doric **Temple of Zeus**, which enshrined Pheidias' statue, later removed to Constantinople by Theodosius II (where it was destroyed by fire in AD 475). One column has been restored and re-erected, and helps you put into perspective its sheer size.

South of the Temple of Zeus is the **bouleuterion** (council house), containing the **altar of oaths**, where competitors swore to obey the rules decreed by the Olympic Senate.

The **stadium** lies to the east of the *altis* and is entered through an archway. The start and finish lines of the 120m sprint track and the judges' seats still survive. The stadium could seat at least 45,000 spectators. Slaves and women spectators had to be content to watch from the Hill of Cronos.

To the north of the Temple of Zeus was the **pelopion**, a small, wooded hillock with an altar to Pelops. It was surrounded by a wall containing the remains of its Doric portico. Many artefacts, now displayed in the museum, were found on the hillock.

Further north is the 6th-century Doric **Temple of Hera**, the site's most intact structure. Hera was worshipped along with Rea until the two were superseded by Zeus.

To the east of this temple is the **nymphaeum**, erected by the wealthy Roman banker Herodes Atticus in AD 156–60. Typical of buildings financed by Roman benefactors, it was grandiose, consisting of a semicircular building with Doric columns flanked at each side by a circular temple. The building contained statues of Herodes Atticus and his family. Despite its elaborate appearance, the nymphaeum had a practical purpose; it was a fountain house supplying Olympia with fresh spring water.

Beyond the nymphaeum and up a flight of stone steps, a row of 12 **treasuries** stretched to the stadium, each erected by a city-state for use as a storehouse and marking the northern boundaries of the *altis*.

At the bottom of these steps are the scant remains of the 5th-century-BC **metroön**, a temple dedicated to Rea, the mother of the gods. Apparently the ancients worshipped Rea in this temple with orgies.

The foundations of the **philippeion**, west of the Temple of Hera, are the remains of a circular construction with Ionic columns built by Philip of Macedon to commemorate the Battle of Chaironeia (338 BC), where he defeated a combined army of Athenians and

Thebans. The building contained statues of Philip and his family.

North of the *philippeion* was the **prytaneum**, the magistrate's residence. Here, winning athletes were entertained and feasted.

Sleeping

Camping Diana (☎ 26240 22314; fax 26240 22425; camp sites per adult/tent/car €8/6/5; ☯ year-round; ☲) A well-run place, with delightful owners and luxuriant tree canopy; clearly signposted 250m west of the village.

Hotel Hermes (☎ 26240 22577; fax 26240 22040; s/d/tr inc breakfast €30/35/45; ☷) This friendly, family-run budget option has basic, but spotless, rooms with linoleum floors. It's after the BP petrol station on the right-hand side as you enter town from the south.

Pension Posidon (☎ 26240 22567; Stefanopoulou 9; s/d/tr €35/40/45) A helpful couple run this centrally located place, whose simple, bright and airy rooms have balconies. Breakfast costs €5.

Hotel Kronio (☎ 26240 22188; www.hotelkronio.gr; Tsoureka 1, s €46, d/tr incl breakfast €56/72; ☷ ▯ ☷) In 2008 this place had a makeover. Its contemporary look and bright and airy rooms make it one of the best-value options around. The helpful multilingual owner adds to the package.

Hotel Pelops (☎/fax 26240 22543; www .hotelpelops.gr; Varela 2; s/d/tr/ste incl breakfast €48/60/84/110; ☒ ☷ ▯ ☷) Opposite the church, this is among the town's best contenders, with comfortable rooms. The friendly Greek-Australian owners provide friendly service and a buffet breakfast fit for an athlete. On offer each night is the Pelops Platter, a massive dish of gourmet mezedhes.

Best Western Hotel Europa International (☎ 26240 22650; www.hoteleuropa.gr; s/d/tr €90/130/150; ☲ ☷ ▯ ☷ ☷) It may have a franchise name and is popular with groups, but this family-owned hotel (1km west of town) wins the gold medal for its large, luxurious rooms with balcony vistas. A bar, restaurant (see right), swimming pool, and a decent poolside taverna (under the shade of olive trees) add value to its winning streak.

Eating

There are no outstanding favourites among Olympia's restaurants; with so many one-off customers passing through, they lack incentive to strive for excellence. You're better off heading to the outer villages, including Floka, 1.5km north and Ancient Pissa (for-

merly Miraka and renamed after the 2007 bushfires). To get to Ancient Pissa, take the national road and follow the signs.

No name takeaway (snacks €1.50; ☯ 7am-3pm) This nondescript blink-and-you'll-miss-it takeaway joint has been here for 20 years, and with good reason. Owner Takis makes the best *tyropita* (cheese pie) and other homemade treats in the Pelops – some would say, Greece.

Mithos (☎ 26243 00369; mains €6-8; ☯ lunch & dinner) A locally recommended place off the tourist drag. The place to get your chops around some good-quality grills. Enough said.

O Thea (☎ 26240 23264; Floka; mains €6-12; ☯ dinner Apr-Oct) It's worth the effort to venture uphill (even on foot) to the small village of Floka, 1.5km north of Olympia, for hearty traditional taverna fare. Enjoy the grills, zucchini balls and views of Floka from the large terrace. That is, if the locals don't beat you to it. It's open irregularly outside high season.

Taverna Bacchus (☎ 26240 22298; www.bacchus tavern.gr; Ancient Pissa; mains €7-12; ☯ lunch & dinner; ☐ ☷ ☷) The god of wine, Bacchus, has extended his portfolio to include delectable delights with fresh ingredients in this smart stone taverna in nearby Ancient Pissa. It errs on an international, rather than local, ambience, but the food is good. Rather overpriced accommodation is on-site (per room including breakfast €90).

Best Western Hotel Europa International (☎ 26240 22650; mains €10-15; ☯ lunch & dinner) Familiar Greek dishes and vegies (from the family farm) and grilled meats deserves a laurel or two. The taverna is set under olive trees and vines (open June to September).

Self-caterers will find a good supermarket near the Shell petrol station.

Getting There & Away

BUS

There is no direct service from Olympia to Athens. Eight or so of the 16 buses (reduced schedule on Sunday) go via Pyrgos (€1.90, 30 minutes) and allow time to connect for services to Athens (see p225). From Olympia, there are also buses east to Tripoli (€11.10, three hours, at least two daily) and to Dimitsana (€6.50, 2½ hours) on Monday and Friday; on all other days, it goes to Karkalou, about 5km from Dimitsana. From here you could try your luck for a lift, or take a taxi. For these services, buy your ticket in advance from the small KTEL Arkadia outlet situated on the main street, one block before the church.

TRAIN
Train services from Olympia head to Pyrgos only – there are five local departures daily (€1, 30 minutes). From Pyrgos, you can catch connections to other destinations. Note: to get to Athens, you take the train from Pyrgos (via Diakofto) and change to the *proastiako* at Kiato.

ANDRITSENA ΑΝΔΡΙΤΣΑΙΝΑ
pop 575
The village of Andritsena, situated 65km southeast of Pyrgos, hovers on a hillside overlooking the valley of the Alfios River. Crumbling stone houses, some with rickety wooden balconies, flank the village's narrow cobbled streets and a stream gushes and bubbles its way through the central square, Plateia Agnostopoulou. Keep an eye out for the fountain emerging from the trunk of a huge plane tree. Andritsena makes an appealing base from which to visit the magnificent Temple of Epicurean Apollo at Vasses, a World Heritage–listed site, located some 14km away from the village.

Information
An ATE Bank ATM and the **post office** (🕙 7.30am-2pm Mon-Fri) are near the central square.

Sights
NIKOLOPOULOS ANDRITSENA LIBRARY
You don't need to be a reader to appreciate the stunning legacy of Nikolopoulos at this **library** (☎ 26260 22242; admission free; 🕙 8.30am-3pm Tue-Sat). In 1838 he donated 4000 rare books – then one of Europe's largest private collections, including a book from 1502 and a 1657 Bible with rare binding – to his father's home town to establish a school. The nearby village of Stemnitsa donated another 4000 books and today the collection is on display, along with manuscripts from Greece's 1821 independence movement. Don't miss the short explanatory video in English. The library is housed above the town's lending library behind Hotel Theoxenia.

FOLK MUSEUM
This much advertised, but rarely open **Folk Museum** (🕙 11am-2pm & 6-8pm) contains a quaint collection of local items from furniture to traditional clothing.

TEMPLE OF EPICUREAN APOLLO AT VASSES
Situated 14km from Andritsena, on a wild, isolated spot overlooking rugged mountains and hills, the World Heritage–listed Vasses with its **Temple of Epicurean Apollo** (☎ 26260 22275; adult/concession €3/2; 🕙 8am-8pm), is one of Greece's most romantic and atmospheric archaeological sites. The road from Andritsena climbs along a mountain ridge, taking you through increasingly dramatic scenery, until you arrive at the temple, which stands at an altitude of 1200m.

The striking and well-preserved temple is robbed of some of its splendour and immediate visual impact by the giant (and semipermanent) steel-girded tent enclosing it, as it undergoes a superslow restoration program, but it's magnificent all the same.

The temple was built in 420 BC by the people of nearby Figalia, who dedicated it to Apollo Epicurus (the Helper) for delivering them from the plague. Designed by Iktinos, the architect of the Parthenon, the temple combines Doric and Ionic columns and a single Corinthian column – the earliest example of this order.

No public buses run to Vasses. You could try to arrange a group to share a taxi.

Sleeping & Eating
Epikourios Apollon (☎ 26260 22840; Plateia Agnostopoulou; s/d/tr incl breakfast €50/70/85; 🕙 year-round) This guest-house-cum-hotel has well-equipped, warm and cheerful rooms overlooking the central square or the valley behind.

For eating, try any of the half a dozen casual tavernas and grill places spread along the main street.

Getting There & Away
There are buses to Pyrgos (around €5.50, 1½ hours, two daily except Sunday), and to Athens (around €20.50, two hours, two daily) via Karitena, Megalopoli, Tripoli and Corinth Isthmus.

KYLLINI ΚΥΛΛΗΝΗ
The port of Kyllini (kih-*lee*-nih), 78km southwest of Patra, warrants a mention merely as the jumping-off point for ferries to Kefallonia

and Zakynthos. Most people arrive on buses from Patra to board the ferries. See Island Hopping (p758) for more information.

There are three to seven buses daily to Kyllini (€6.80, 1¼ hours) from the KTEL Zakynthos bus station in Patra (some have connecting ferries), as well as two daily from Pyrgos (€5.80, one hour). Note: there are no buses from Kyllini to Patra. You can, however, catch buses from Lethena, 16km from Kyllini. A **taxi** (☎ 6973535678) to Lethena costs €13, and to Patra €60.

KYTHIRA & ANTIKYTHIRA

KYTHIRA ΚΥΘΗΡΑ
pop 3334

The island of Kythira (*kee*-thih-rah), 12km south of Neapoli, is perfect for people who want to experience a genuine, functioning and unspoilt island.

Some 30km long and 18km wide, Kythira dangles off the tip of the Peloponnese's Lakonian peninsula, between the Aegean and Ionian Seas. The largely barren landscape is dominated by a rocky plateau that covers most of the island, and the population is spread among more than 40 villages that capitalise on small pockets of agriculturally viable land. The villages are linked by narrow, winding lanes, often flanked by ancient dry-stone walls.

Although Kythira is (officially) part of the Ionian Islands, some of the houses, especially those in the island's main town, Hora, are more Cycladic in looks, with whitewashed walls and blue shutters. (And, although Ionian, we've included it in this chapter because most people visit the island from the Peloponnese.) Mythology suggests that Aphrodite was born in Kythira. She's meant to have risen from the foam where Zeus had thrown Cronos' sex organ after castrating him. The goddess of love then re-emerged near Pafos in Cyprus, so both islands haggle over her birthplace.

Tourism remains very low-key on Kythira for most of the year, until July and August, when the island goes mad. Descending visitors include the Kythiran diaspora returning from abroad (especially Australia) to visit family and friends (who themselves have returned after leaving the island several decades ago). Accommodation is virtually impossible to find during this time, and restaurants are flat out catering for the crowds. For the remaining 10 months of the year, Kythira is a wonderfully peaceful island with some fine, uncrowded beaches. The best times to visit Kythira are in late spring and around September/October.

Few people venture to the tiny island of Antikythira, the most remote island in the Ionians, 38km southeast of Kythira; it has become a bit of a forgotten outpost, although some ferries stop there on the way to/from Crete.

For information on Kythira, refer the commercial websites: www.kythira.gr, www.kithera.gr, www.kythira.info and www.visitkythera.gr. Definitely pick up a copy of the informative community newspaper *Kythera*, published in English and available in travel agencies, hotels and some shops. Keen walkers should seek out a copy of *Kythira on Foot: 32 Carefully Selected Walking Routes* (€10) by Frank van Weerde (a long-time resident of Kythira).

GETTING THERE & AWAY
Air

In high season there are daily flights between Kythira and Athens (€52 to €70, 40 minutes). The airport is 10km east of Potamos, and **Olympic Air** (☎ 27360 33362) is on the central square in Potamos. Book also at **Kythira Travel** (☎ 27360 31390) in Hora.

Boat

The island's main connection is between Diakofti and Neapoli in the Peloponnese. Tickets are sold at the port just before departure, or at **Kythira Travel** (☎ in Hora 27360 31390, in Potamos 27360 31848) in Hora and Potamos.

LANE Lines calls at the southern port of Diakofti on its weekly schedule between Piraeus, Kythira, Antikythira, Crete and Gythio (Peloponnese). Information and tickets are available from the helpful staff at **Porfyra Travel** (☎ /fax 27360 31888; www.kythira.info) in Livadi (north of Hora).

GETTING AROUND

Occasional buses may operate during August. There are taxis, but the best way to see the island is with your own transport. **Drakakis Tours** (☎ 27360 31160, 6944840497; www.drakistours.gr; Livadi) rents a range of cars, including vans and 4WD. **Panayotis Rent A Car** (☎ 27360 31600; www.panayotis-rent-a-car.gr) on Kapsali's waterfront rents cars and mopeds. Both will arrange pick-up from the port or the airport.

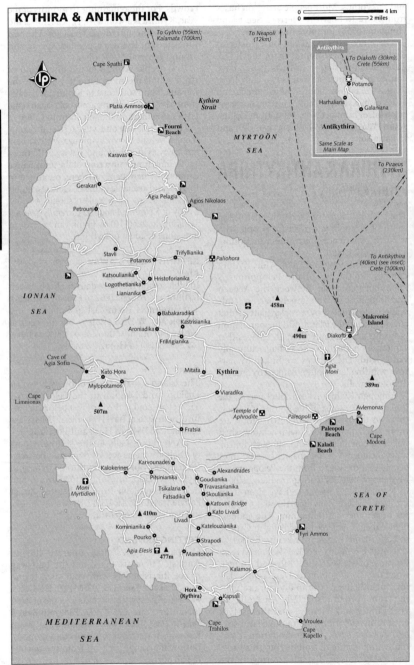

KYTHIRA & ANTIKYTHIRA

PELOPONNESE

Hora Χώρα
pop 267

Hora (or Kythira), the island's capital, is a pretty village of Cycladic-style white, blue-shuttered houses, perched on a long, slender ridge stretching north from an impressive 13th-century Venetian *kastro*. The central square, planted with hibiscus, bougainvillea and palms, is Plateia Dimitriou Staï. The main street, Spyridonos Staï, runs south from the central square to the *kastro*.

INFORMATION

Branches of the National Bank of Greece and ATE Bank, both with ATMs, are on the central square.

Fos Fanari (☎ 27360 31644; ⌚ 8am-late) This cafe-bar offers free wi-fi to clients.

Internet Service (Kodak shop, Spyridonos Staï; per hr €5; ⌚ 9am-2pm & 6-9pm Mon-Sat) Travellers can check email here.

Police station (☎ 27360 31206) Near the *kastro*.

Polyredo (☎ 27360 39000; per hr €4) The island's best internet place is based in Livadi, just north of Hora.

Post office (⌚ 7.30am-2pm Mon-Fri) On the central square.

SIGHTS

Hora's Venetian **kastro** (admission free; ⌚ 8am-7pm), built in the 13th century, is at the southern end of town. If you walk to its southern extremity, passing the Church of Panagia, you will come to a sheer cliff – from here there's a stunning view of Kapsali and, on a good day, of Antikythira.

Call in to **Stavros** (☎ 27360 31857), a shop north of the square (opposite the turn-off to Kapsali) and pick up some of the local produce, including some of Greece's best honey.

At the time of research, the town's archaeological museum, north of the central square, was closed due to damage from the earth tremor in January 2006.

SLEEPING& EATING

Castello Rooms (☎ 27360 31069; www.castelloapts -kythera.gr; d/tr €45/55; ❄) The seven comfortable rooms represent the best deal in town, if not the island. Set back from the main street, this place is surrounded by a well-tended garden full of flowers, vegetables and fruit trees. The rooms have TV and some have kitchen facilities. It's signposted at the southern end of Spiridonos Staï.

Hotel Margarita (☎ 27360 31711; www.hotel -margarita.com; off Spyridonos Staï; s/d incl breakfast €70/110; ❄) This white-walled, blue-shuttered and generally charming hotel offers atmospheric rooms (all with TV and telephone) in a renovated 19th-century mansion, featuring B&W marble floors and a quirky old spiral staircase. The whitewashed terrace affords fantastic port views.

Zorba's (☎ 27360 31655; ⌚ dinner) The pick of the bunch for the town's meals, and highly recommended by locals.

Kapsali Καψάλι
pop 34

The scenic village of Kapsali, 2km south of Hora, served as Hora's port in Venetian times. It features twin sandy bays and a curving waterfront; this looks striking viewed from Hora's castle. Restaurants and cafes line the beach, and safe **sheltered swimming** is Kapsali's trademark. However, it can get crowded in high season.

Offshore you can see the stark rock island known as **Avgo** (Egg) or **Itra** (Cooking pot), rearing above the water. Locals say that when the wind blows in a certain direction clouds always gather and sit just above the rock, making it look like a steaming cooking pot.

Kapsali goes into hibernation in winter, coming to life between April and October. There's a small supermarket, and the Kytherian Gallery sells international newspapers as well as souvenirs.

Panayotis at **Moto Rent** (☎ 27360 31600), on the waterfront, rents canoes and pedal boats as well as cars, mopeds and bicycles. **Kaptain Spiros** (☎ 6974022079) takes daily boat cruises on his glass-bottomed boat (from €12 per person), including to Itra, where you can swim.

SLEEPING & EATING

Aphrodite Apartments (☎ 27360 31328; afrodite@aias.gr; d/tr/q €70/75/90) These no-nonsense, no-frills but perfectly pleasant apartments on the road and facing the sea, are run by a friendly, English-speaking local. Great value, and prices plummet outside August.

Spitia Vassilis (☎ 27360 31125; www.kythira bungalowsvasili.gr; d/tr/q €80/95/100) This attractive green-and-white complex of studios has the perfect setting – away from the hordes and overlooking Kapsali Beach. The spacious rooms feature that rustic-painted-timber-floor look and good bay views. It is on the right as you approach Kapsali from Hora. No English spoken.

El Sol Hotel (☎ 27360 31766; www.elsolhotels.gr; d/tr/ studio incl breakfast €120/140/150 🅿 🕸 🖭) Signposted off the Hora–Kapsali road is this luxurious resort-style, Cycladic-looking option, with a view of Kapsali and Hora's *kastro*. Management's promo line is 'If Zeus went on holidays, you'd surely have him as a room mate'. If they could throw him in, too, we'd say it's great value; at this stage, save your pennies (and energy) until the cheaper rates outside high season.

Hydragogio (☎ 27360 31065; mains €5-12, fish per kilogram €20-70) Occupying a great spot overlooking the beach at the far end by the rocks, and specialising in fresh fish and traditional Greek fare (with a good vegetarian range), this is the place to go for a good feed, and to feel you're really on holiday.

Potamos Ποταμός
pop 680

Potamos, 10km southwest of Agia Pelagia, is the island's commercial hub. The National Bank of Greece (with ATM) is on the central square and the **post office** (🕘 7.30am-2pm Mon-Fri) is just north of the central square.

Its Sunday morning **flea market** seems to attract just about everyone on the island.

There are a couple of decent places to look out for. Popular with locals, **Taverna Panaretos** (☎ 27360 34290; mains €7-14; 🕘 lunch & dinner year-round) is a natural – it uses home-grown everything, from oil to vegies and cheese. Want to try wild goat with olive oil and oregano (€9.50) or eggplant on coals (€4)? Naturally.

The island's hip and happenin' place, **Kafe Astikon** (☎ 27360 33141; 🕘 7am-late; 🛜), offers a mix of retro designer mixed with 1930s French. Add in great music – from traditional Greek to Latin and rock, plus wireless connection, and you'll not care what you're there for. Except that it's got great drinks of the top-shelf variety and all manner of snacks.

Mylopotamos Μυλοπόταμος
pop 70

Mylopotamos is a quaint village nestled in a small valley, 12km southwest of Potamos. Its central square is flanked by a charming church and the authentically traditional **Kafeneio O Platanos** (☎ 27360 33397), which in summer becomes a restaurant with an outdoor setting

in the square. It's worth a stroll to the **Neraïda** (water nymph) waterfall, with luxuriant greenery and mature, shady trees. As you reach the church, take the right fork and follow the signs to an unpaved road leading down to the falls. (Alternatively, you can head there on foot – follow the signs after the church.)

To reach the abandoned **kastro** of Mylopotamos, take the left fork after the *kafeneio* and follow the old faded sign for **Kato Hora** (Lower Village) and then the modern signs to the Cave of Agia Sofia. The road leads to the centre of Kato Hora, from where a portal leads into the spooky *kastro*, with derelict houses and well-preserved little churches (locked).

Several fabulous walks start in Mylopotamos – refer to *Kythira on Foot: 32 Carefully Selected Walking Routes* (see p231). The most picturesque and challenging walk heads along a gorge where there are the ruins of former flour mills. You pass waterfalls and swimming holes along the way.

The staff at Kafeneio O Platanos (left) is happy to help you with sleeping options.

Agia Pelagia Αγία Πελαγία
pop 280

Kythira's northern port of Agia Pelagia is a simple, friendly waterfront village, although sadly, this is on the verge of being ruined by modern buildings, as are the sand-and-pebble beaches either side of the quay. Nevertheless, it's pleasant for relaxing, and **Red Beach**, south of the headland, is a good swimming spot.

A good sleeping option is the **Hotel Pelagia Aphrodite** (☎ 27360 33926/7; www.pelagia-aphrodite.com; s/d/tr €75/90/120; 🕘 Apr-Oct; 🅿 🕸). This Greek-Australian-run hotel is modern and spotless with large, airy rooms, most with balconies overlooking the sea. Its perfect location is on a small headland on the southern edge of the village. Breakfast is €7.

our pick Kaleris (☎ 27360 33461; mains €5.50-12; 🕘 dinner) might inspire you to ask what is a place like this doing in a place like this? Agia Pelagia is all the better for it. Owner-chef Yiannis pushes the culinary boundaries, giving Greek cuisine a refreshing new twist. Thankfully, he hasn't lost sight of his roots – he uses the best of local products. So fresh, in fact, that his delectable parcels of feta cheese drizzled with local thyme-infused honey (€6), *vrechtoladea* (traditional rusks; €5) and home-made beef tortellini (€8) simply walk out the door. See also Stirring Traditions, opposite.

Around Kythira

If you have transport, a spin round the island is rewarding. The monasteries of **Agia Moni** and **Agia Elesis** are mountain refuges with superb views. **Moni Myrtidion** is a beautiful monastery surrounded by trees. From Hora, drive northeast to **Avlemonas**, via **Paleopoli** with its wide, pebbled beach. Archaeologists spent years searching for evidence of a temple at Aphrodite's birthplace at Avlemonas. Here, you must stay on the ball: see if you can spot the blink-or-you'll-miss **kofinidia** – two small rock protrusions – these are the mythological (or otherwise) sex organs of Cronos, after Zeus had tossed them into the sea foam. Don't bypass the spectacularly situated ruins of the Byzantine capital of **Paliohora**, in the island's northeast, fun for exploring.

In **Kato Livadi**, don't miss the small but stunning collection of artworks of Kythira in the **Museum of Byzantine and post-Byzantine art on Kythira** (☎ 27360 31731; ☒ 8.30am-2.30pm; adult/ concession €2/1; closed Mon). Just north of Kato Livadi make a detour to see the architecturally anomalous **Katouni Bridge**, a British-built legacy of Kythira's time as part of the British Protectorate in the 19th century. In the far north of the island the village of **Karavas** is verdant, very attractive and close to both Agia Pelagia and the reasonable beach at **Platia Ammos**. Beachcombers should seek out **Kaladi Beach**, near Paleopoli. **Fyri Ammos**, closer to Hora, is another good beach – but hard to access.

EATING

Skandia (☎ 27360 33700; Paleopolis; mains €7-10; ☒ lunch & dinner Apr-Oct, Fri-Sun Nov-Mar) Among one of the most pleasant places to eat on the island, mainly because of its setting: away from the madding crowds, under shady elm trees, in a homey environment. Its fish is priced per kilogram; lobster with spaghetti is a fave (but watch the wallet – lobster weighs in at a hefty €85 per kilogram).

STIRRING TRADITIONS

Yiannis Prineas, 31, left Athens and returned to Agia Pelagia, on the island of Kythira to run his family restaurant, Kaleris (opposite), started by his grandfather in 1956. Yiannis is pushing the boundaries of traditional Greek cuisine, producing fine Greek dishes with a gourmet twist (think *mousakas* – usually baked layers of eggplant or zucchini – with mushrooms, and feta in cheese parcels drizzled with thyme-infused honey and sesame seeds). The result has convinced the most hardened of traditional taverna-goers – locals and visitors – that there's more to Greek food than Mama-style home cooking (as good as this may be) and a full stomach.

What is your aim? My basic vision is Greek and traditional Greek-Mediterranean but I'm trying to make modern dishes with local products. I want to make my experiences (working in five-star hotels in gourmet restaurants in Athens) into something a bit more modern with how people view traditional cuisine.

Most of the Greeks love food because it's an enjoying time [sic]…but many of the Greeks, they are not so focussed. They don't understand the flavours – they eat with beers and cigarettes. Many are hard workers – builders and farmers – and food is to fill their stomach. They do not take a menu and review it.

A lot of our food is 'Mama's food'. Mama's food is lovely, but…

Have you succeeded in changing people's views about traditional Greek food? I have changed some people and I have seen people change on their own. When they find the difference, they start to appreciate it and their minds start to work: food is not only to fill the stomach! Even if they don't like my dishes, I like this, because [at least] they have an opinion.

What is your secret? Every day is a new day. Every day is a new space for creativity. You have to be 'inside' of the food. If you are inside you do not do mistakes… You can make the best food even with not so many things [ingredients]. It's the process: how you prepare and how you cook. I change the menu every week. Here in Kythira we are in the heart of the Mediterranean with excellent cheese, vegetables, meats (sheep, goats and chickens) – our materials [ingredients] are good.

PELOPONNESE

Varkoula (☎ 27360 34224; Platia Ammos; mains €7-12, fish per kilogram €40-75; ☽ lunch & dinner daily May-Oct, Fri & Sat Nov-Mar) At this *varkoula* ('little boat') you can enjoy freshly cooked fish to the tunes of the bouzouki-strumming owner and his cardiologist guitar-playing friend. Athena's famous fried bread with cheese is a real heart stopper. It's a beat away from Karavas, in the island's north. As it's a decent drive north, ring ahead first to confirm opening hours – these can be irregular.

Estiatorion Pierros (☎ 27360 31014; Livadi; mains €10-12, fish per kilogram €35-60; ☽ lunch & dinner) Since 1933 this family-run and long-standing favourite has served no-nonsense Greek staples. Visit the kitchen to view the daily offerings – there's no menu. On the main road through Livadi.

Sotiris (☎ 27360 33722; Avlemonas; fish per kilogram €30-75; ☽ lunch & dinner daily Apr-Oct, Fri-Sun Nov-Mar) This popular fish taverna in pretty Avlemonas has good lobster and fish soup (fish and lobster are priced per kilogram).

Psarotaverna H Manolis (☎ 27360 33748; Diakofti; fish & lobster per kilogram €45-70; ☽ lunch & dinner) A star among Diakofti's uninspiring port setting. Locals head here for the excellent fresh fish and seasonal offerings.

ANTIKYTHIRA ΑΝΤΙΚΥΘΗΡΑ
pop 20

The tiny island of Antikythira, 38km southeast of Kythira, is the most remote island in the Ionians. It has only one settlement (Potamos), one doctor, one police officer, one telephone and a monastery. It has no post office or bank. The only accommodation option is 10 basic rooms in two purpose-built blocks, open in summer only. Potamos has a *kafeneio*-cum-taverna.

Getting There & Away

The ferry company **ANEN Lines** (www.anen.gr) calls at Antikythira on its route between Kythira and Kissamos on Crete. This is not an island for tourists on a tight schedule and will probably only appeal to those who really like isolation. For information and tickets, contact **Porfyra Travel** (☎ /fax 27360 31888; porfyra@otenet.gr) in Livadi on Kythira.

Central Greece
Κεντρική Ελλάδα

First-time visitors to Central Greece are often surprised by its rugged and diverse landscape, ranging from rocky sea cliffs and hidden bays to inland river valleys and olive groves, all punctuated with dramatic reminders of Greek history and mythology, oracles and muses, warriors and centaurs.

The ruins at Delphi, where Alexander the Great sought the advice of the famous oracle, remain one of Greece's most inspiring archaeological sites and are also the starting point for hikes that retrace ancient footpaths that overlook the Corinthian Gulf.

In the northern region of Thessaly, the surrounding flatlands and hills suddenly give way to breathtaking outcroppings of rocky towers, the sheer monastery-topped cliffs of Meteora. These spectacular columns of rock are not only a mecca for Greek Orthodox pilgrims, but also home to world-class rock climbing. Away to the west, river-rafting and hiking opportunities abound in the South Pindos mountain range, its high alpine meadows perfect for breezy summer hikes.

Facing the northern Aegean Sea lies the Pelion Peninsula, criss-crossed with historic cobblestone paths that link lush mountain hamlets with coves and beaches that rival the best islands, but without the crowds. According to Greek mythology, it was in nearby Volos that Jason and the Argonauts set sail in search of the Golden Fleece, in a boat made from timbers of the Pelion forests.

It is no coincidence that this dramatic landscape was the setting for heroic struggles among gods and mortals, or that a resilient and good-natured people endure and thrive here still.

HIGHLIGHTS

- **Together at Last** Joining the evening crowd for outdoor summer cinema in Volos (p261)
- **Riverside Dining** Feasting on fresh trout from mountain streams near Karpenisi (p253)
- **Go with the Flow** White-water river rafting in the Tria Potamia area (p271)
- **Walk this Way** Following the cobblestone trails to the sea on the Pelion Peninsula (p262)
- **Don't Look Down** Climbing the monastery-topped rock pinnacles at Meteora (p275)
- **Historical Meditation** Catching the last light of day at the Sanctuary of Athena (p243), in Ancient Delphi
- **End of the Road** Spotting Dalmatian pelicans skimming over Klisova Lagoon (p250)

- ★ Meteora
- ★ Tria Potamia
- ★ Volos
- ★ Pelion Peninsula
- ★ Karpenisi
- ★ Ancient Delphi
- ★ Klisova Lagoon

- POPULATION: 1.9 MILLION
- AREA: 37,042 SQ KM

CENTRAL GREECE

STEREA ELLADA
ΣΤΕΡΕΑ ΕΛΛΑΔΑ

Greek mythology and history seem to mingle in the rugged and scenic landscape of Sterea Ellada. On the slopes of Mt Parnassos, overlooking the Gulf of Corinth, sits Delphi, regarded by the ancient Greeks as the centre of the world. Beyond Delphi, the lands stretch east to Attica, where legendary King Oedipus met his fate, and west to Messolongi, where British bard Lord Byron died of fever during the Greek War of Independence. In fact, the region acquired the name Sterea Ellada (Mainland Greece) in 1827, as part of the newly formed Greek state.

Sterea Ellada is bordered by the narrow gulfs of Corinth and Patra in the south, and Epiros to the north. Much of this mountainous region is known as the Agrafa or 'Unrecorded', so named during the *Tourkokratia* (Turkish occupation), when the hard-to-reach mountain villages were written off for tax purposes as uncollectable. Today, these same mountains are prized for their beauty, and explored by hikers and river rafters alike.

THIVA (THEBES) ΘHBA
pop 22,400

Thiva, the birthplace of Hercules and Dionysos, was a powerful city-state in 400 BC during Greece's golden age, occupying a strategic position between northern Greece and the Peloponnese. The tragic fate of its royal dynasty, centred on the myth of Oedipus, rivalled that of ancient Mycenae. Although present-day Thiva has few vestiges of its past glory, the tragic fate of its royal dynasty, centred on the myth of Oedipus, rivalled that of ancient Mycenae.

After the Trojan War in the 12th century BC, Thiva became the dominant city of the Boeotia region. In 371 BC the city was victorious in battle against once-invincible Sparta. Thiva's glorious run ended abruptly in 335 BC, when it was sacked by Alexander the Great for rebelling against Macedonian control and siding with Persia. Alexander spared the temples, but not 6000 Thebans who died in the bloody battle. Another 30,000 were taken prisoner.

In keeping with its history, Thiva has an impressive **Archaeological Museum** (☎ 22620 27913;

admission €2; ⊙ 8am-2.30pm Tue-Sat) which includes jewellery found in the Mycenaean palaces, terracotta masks and decorated sarcophagi. However, the museum has been closed for renovations since 2007, and is not scheduled to reopen until 2011.

Sleeping & Eating

Hotel Niovi (☎ 22620 29888; www.hotelniovi.gr; Epaminonda 63; s/d incl breakfast €43/55; ❄ ☐ ⊚) This welcoming lodging manages to be both homey and modern, with flower pots adorning the marble interior stairs, satellite TV and free wi-fi. The hotel is adjacent to the *plateia* (square) and DIA supermarket, and a 10-minute stroll from the archaeological museum.

Dionysos Restaurant (☎ 22620 24445; mains €4-7.50) Welcoming proprietor Kypriotakis boasts of his oven-ready dishes made 'in the old Greek way', such as lamb in lemon sauce, and *pastitsio* (buttery macaroni and lamb).

Ladhokola (☎ 22620 28400; mains €5-8.50) Just opposite, on the square, this snappy eatery serves tasty grilled shrimp, chops and souvlakia (cubes of meat on skewers).

Getting There & Away

Buses operate to Athens (€7.40, 1½ hours, hourly) from Thiva's central **bus station** (☎ 22620 27512), 500m south of Plateia Agios Kalotinis. The bus stop (no phone) for Livadia and Delphi (€4.80, 50 minutes, five daily) is near the Shell petrol station and train station.

Trains from **Thiva station** (☎ 22620 27531), 100m north of the museum, depart for Athens (normal/intercity [IC] express €3.50/9.20, 75/60 minutes, 13 daily), and Thessaloniki (normal/IC express €12.60/33, four/5½ hours, 10 daily).

AROUND THIVA

The well-preserved 4th-century **Fortress of Eleftherae**, guarding the Kaza Pass over Mt Kythairon, stands between Athens and Thiva. According to mythology, baby Oedipus was left to perish on this mountain bordering ancient Attica before being rescued by a shepherd. History buffs can also inspect the **ruins** near Erythres, where the Battle of Plataea (479 BC) took place, marking the end of the Persian Wars. A road branching off to Porto Germeno leads to 4th-century-BC **Aigosthena**, with the best-preserved fortress walls in all Greece.

CENTRAL GREECE

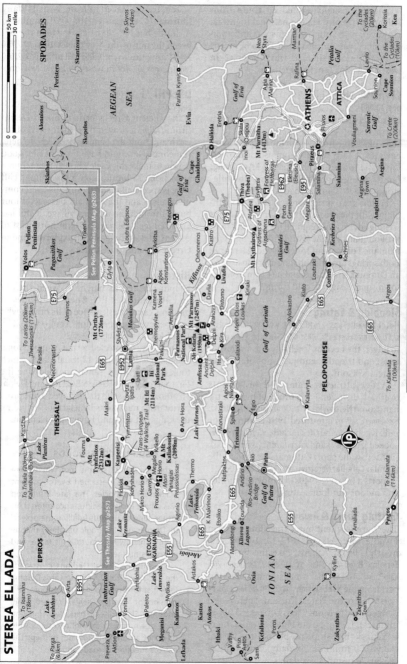

STEREA ELLADA

Thiva is usually visited en route from Athens to Delphi, via the national highway. However, with your own transport and a yen for history, you can also reach Thiva by means of a scenic mountain road, which begins 2km west of Elefsina (ancient Eleusis).

LIVADIA ΛΙΒΑΔΕΙΑ
pop 20,980

Livadia is on the Athens–Delphi road, 45km northwest of Thiva. The town flanks both sides of a gorge from which the Erkynas River emerges. A 14th-century Frankish castle overlooks the town, and the shaded **Kryes springs** (cold springs) grant Livadia worthwhile-stopover status on the road to Delphi.

Livadia's two springs are associated in mythology with the oracle of Trophonios. Pilgrims seeking advice were required to first drink from the Fountain of Lethe (Forgetfulness) and then from the Fountain of Mnemosyne (Memory). Both springs are still bubbling away, just above an Ottoman-era bridge, and just 1km from the town square, signed 'cold spring'.

Sleeping & Eating
Hotel Levadia (☎ 22610 23611; www.levadiahotel.gr; s/d/tr incl breakfast €55/70/85; ✷) Should you need to linger, the Levadia is reliably old-fashioned, clean and friendly, and just opposite central Plateia Kotsoni.

A few attractive cafes and restaurants overlook the river. For a touch of history, try handsome **Neromylos** (☎ 22610 26928; mains €6-12; ✷ dinner), set in a restored 19th-century flour mill. Kitchen favourites include *kleftiko* (slow-cooked lamb, €9) and *karydopita* (walnut pie). Just across the short Ottoman-era bridge, the popular **Café-Bar Nerotrivi** (☎ 69716 33838; snacks €2-5) sports a massive 1940s-era movie projector and indoor-outdoor seating.

Getting There & Away
There are frequent buses travelling between Livadia and Athens (€11.10, two hours, hourly). From Athens, take the bus from **Terminal B** (off Map p108; ☎ 210 831 7173; Liosion 260, Kato Patisia). In Livadia, Athens-bound buses depart from the **KTEL-station** (☎ 22610 28336), 1.5km northwest of the Plateia Kotsoni. There is also daily service to Moni Osios Loukas (€3.30, 30 minutes). Just opposite Hotel Levadia, there is a kiosk–bus stop (no phone) for Delphi (€3.90, 50 minutes, six daily) and Amfissa (€5.80, 70 minutes, six daily).

Ten trains travel to/from Athens daily (normal/IC express €4/10, 95/75 minutes). A shuttle bus (€1.20) makes the 6km run between the out-of-the-way **train station** (☎ 22610 28046) and the town's **OSE rail office** (☎ 22610 28661; Filonos 30), 400m west of Plateia Kotsoni.

DELPHI ΔΕΛΦΟΙ
pop 2500

If the ancient Greeks hadn't chosen Delphi (from *Delphis*, or womb) as their navel of the earth and built the Sanctuary of Apollo here, someone else would have thought of a good reason to make this eagle's nest village a tourist attraction. Its location on a precipitous cliff edge is spectacular and, despite its overt commercialism and the constant passage of tour buses through the modern village, it still has a special feel. Delphi is 178km northwest of Athens and is the base for exploring one of Greece's major tourist sites.

History
Delphi reached its height between the 6th and 4th centuries BC, when multitudes of pilgrims came to ask advice of its oracle, who was believed to speak for Apollo (see The Delphic Oracle, p243).

Delphi was protected by the Amphictyonic League, a federation of 12 tribal-states, which took control of the sanctuary following the First Sacred War (595–586 BC), making Delphi an autonomous state that enjoyed great prosperity from numerous benefactors, including the kings of Lydia and Egypt, and Hadrian.

THE OEDIPUS CROSSROADS

A traveller can still see the spot 'where three roads meet', as described by the ancient playwright Sophocles. This fateful junction was where proud Oedipus encountered his father, King Laius, thus fulfilling the powerful Delphic oracle's tragic prophecy that he would unknowingly murder his father and marry his mother.

To find the actual Oedipus crossroads (heading west from Livadia towards Delphi), look first for the road sign to Distomo, and 1km on for a sign to Davlia. Proceed uphill another 1.5km to the car park (P) on the right. Look down and to the right to see visible traces of an ancient crossing, perhaps the narrow meeting of roads and fate.

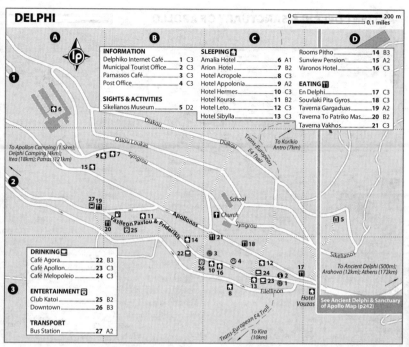

DELPHI

INFORMATION		
Delphiko Internet Café	1	C3
Municipal Tourist Office	2	C3
Parnassos Café	3	C3
Post Office	4	C3

SIGHTS & ACTIVITIES		
Sikelianos Museum	5	D2

SLEEPING		
Amalia Hotel	6	A1
Arion Hotel	7	B2
Hotel Acropole	8	C3
Hotel Appolonia	9	A2
Hotel Hermes	10	C3
Hotel Kouras	11	B2
Hotel Leto	12	C3
Hotel Sibylla	13	C3

Rooms Pitho	14	B3
Sunview Pension	15	A2
Varonos Hotel	16	A2

EATING		
En Delphi	17	C3
Souvlaki Pita Gyros	18	C3
Taverna Gargaduas	19	A2
Taverna To Patriko Mas	20	B2
Taverna Vakhos	21	C3

DRINKING		
Café Agora	22	B3
Café Apollon	23	C3
Café Melopoleio	24	C3

ENTERTAINMENT		
Club Katoi	25	B2
Downtown	26	B3

TRANSPORT		
Bus Station	27	A2

See Ancient Delphi & Sanctuary of Apollo Map (p242)

CENTRAL GREECE

The sanctuary survived fire (548 BC) and earthquake (373 BC), and in the 3rd century BC, it was conquered by the Aetolians, and then by the Romans in 191 BC. Although the Roman Sulla plundered the sanctuary in 86 BC, other emperors, fascinated by its reputation, kept the rituals at Delphi alive, well into the 2nd century AD, when the oracle's influence began to dwindle. The sanctuary was finally abolished by the Byzantine emperor Theodosius in the late 4th century AD. By the 7th century, a new village, Kastri, had appeared over the ancient site. Much of what is known about Delphi today comes from the notes of 2nd-century-AD Athenian geographer Pausanius.

Orientation & Information

Almost everything you'll need in Delphi is on Vasileon Pavlou & Friderikis. Delphi's other through roads are Apollonos, which runs north of and parallel to Vasileon Pavlou & Friderikis, and Filellinon, which runs south and parallel to the main drag. Four steep stairways transverse all three roads.

The small bus station is on Vasileon Pavlou & Friderikis next to Taverna Gargaduas on the Itea side of town. The **post office** (Map p241; 7.30am-2pm) and three bank ATMs are also on this street.

You'll find helpful information at the **municipal tourist office** (Map p241; ☎ 22650 82900; 7.30am-2.30pm Mon-Fri, 8am-2pm Sat), toward the Arahova end of Vasileon Pavlou & Friderikis. There are internet facilities at nearby **Delphiko Internet Café** (Map p241; per hr €3; 6.30am-1am) and **Parnassos Café** (Map p241; per hr €3; 7.30am-midnight).

Ancient Delphi (comprising the Archaeological Museum and site) is 500m along the pine-shaded main road toward Arahova.

Sights
ANCIENT DELPHI

Of all the archaeological sites in Greece, **Ancient Delphi** (Map p242; www.culture.gr) is the one with the most potent 'spirit of place'. Built on the slopes of Mt Parnassos, overlooking the Gulf of Corinth and extending into a valley of cypress and olive trees, this World Heritage

lonelyplanet.com

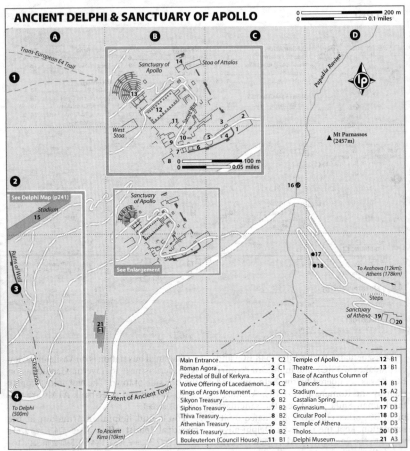

ANCIENT DELPHI & SANCTUARY OF APOLLO

Main Entrance	1	C2	Temple of Apollo	12	B1
Roman Agora	2	C1	Theatre	13	B1
Pedestal of Bull of Kerkyra	3	C1	Base of Acanthus Column of		
Votive Offering of Lacedaemon	4	C2	Dancers	14	B1
Kings of Argos Monument	5	C2	Stadium	15	A2
Sikyon Treasury	6	B2	Castalian Spring	16	C2
Siphnos Treasury	7	B2	Gymnasium	17	D3
Thiva Treasury	8	B2	Circular Pool	18	D3
Athenian Treasury	9	B2	Temple of Athena	19	D3
Knidos Treasury	10	B2	Tholos	20	D3
Bouleuterion (Council House)	11	B1	Delphi Museum	21	A3

site's allure lies both in its stunning setting and its inspiring ruins. The ancient Greeks regarded Delphi as the centre of the world; according to mythology, Zeus released two eagles at opposite ends of the world and they met here. In summer, visit the site early to avoid the crowds and the heat.

Sanctuary of Apollo

The Sanctuary of Apollo is on the left of the main road as you walk toward Arahova. Just to the right of the entrance, notice the brickwork of the **Roman agora** (Map p242).

From the main entrance, the steps on your right lead to the **Sacred Way**, which winds gradually up to the foundations of the Doric Temple of Apollo. Entering the site, you pass several

stone bases. The first is the pedestal which held the **statue** (Map p242) of a bull dedicated by the city of Corfu (Kerkyra). Just beyond it, on the right, are the remains of the **Votive Offering of Lacedaemon** (Map p242), commemorating a battle victory. The next two semicircular structures on either side of the Sacred Way were erected by the Argives (people of Argos). To their right stood the **Kings of Argos Monument** (Map p242).

In ancient times the Sacred Way was lined with treasuries and statues (Map p242) given by grateful city-states – Athens, Sikyon, Siphnos, Knidos and Thiva (Thebes) – all in thanks to Apollo. To the north of the reconstructed **Athenian Treasury** (Map p242) are the foundations of the **bouleuterion** (council house; Map p242).

The 4th-century-BC **Temple of Apollo** (Map p242) dominated the entire sanctuary with a statue of Apollo and a hearth where an eternal flame burned. On the temple vestibule were inscriptions of Greek philosophers, such as 'Know Thyself' and 'Nothing in Excess'.

Above the temple is the well-preserved 4th-century-BC **theatre** (Map p242), which was restored by the Pergamenon kings in the 1st century BC, yielding magnificent views from the top row. Plays were performed here during the Pythian Festival, held, like the Olympic Games, every four years. From the theatre the path continues to the **stadium** (Map p242), the best-preserved in all of Greece. Check out the sprinters' etched-stone starting blocks at the eastern end; on occasion, stadium access is limited because of possible rockslides.

From the Sanctuary of Apollo, the paved path towards Arahova runs parallel to the main road and leads to the **Castalian Spring** (Map p242) on the left, where pilgrims cleansed themselves before consulting the oracle.

Between the Castalian Spring and the Sanctuary of Athena, you will find the remains of an ancient **gymnasium** (Map p242). Two running tracks occupied an upper terrace here; on a lower terrace, boxers and wrestlers practised their art and then cooled off in the large, spring-fed **circular pool** (Map p242), which is still visible among the ruins.

Sanctuary of Athena

Opposite the Castalian Spring is the Sanctuary of Athena, the site of the 4th-century-BC **tholos** (rotunda; Map p242; admission free), the most striking of Delphi's monuments. This graceful circular structure comprised 20 columns on a three-stepped podium – three of its columns were re-erected in the 1940s. The white portions of each column are the original marble; the darker portions are new material. To its west, the foundations of the Temple of Athena are all that remain of a rectangular structure which was heavily damaged by the same rock slides and earthquake that leveled much of the *tholos*.

Delphi Museum

From around the 8th century BC, Ancient Delphi managed to amass a considerable treasure trove, much of it reflected in its magnificent **museum** (Map p242; ☎ 22650 82312; www.culture .gr/war/index_en.jsp; adult site or museum €6, adult/student site & museum €9/5, free Sun Nov-Mar; ☺ 8am-7.45pm Tue-Sun, 1.30-7.45pm Mon Apr-Oct, 8.30am-2.45pm Nov-Mar).

Upon entering the museum, in room 5 you'll first notice the **Sphinx of the Naxians**, dating from 560 BC. Also residing here are well-preserved parts of the **frieze** from the Siphnian treasury, which depicts not only the battle between the gods and the giants, but also the Judgment of Paris (far left corner as you enter), who was called upon to decide which goddess was most beautiful (he chose Aphrodite). In room 3 are two fine examples of 6th-century-BC **kouroi** (young men), the 'twins of Argos'.

In the rooms to the left are fragments of **metopes** (figures within the frieze) from the Athenian treasury depicting the Labours of Hercules, the Exploits of Theseus and the **Battle of the Amazons** (room 7). Further

---

THE DELPHIC ORACLE

The Delphic oracle, the most powerful in Greece, sat on a tripod at the entrance to a chasm that emitted intoxicating vapours. A popular story proposes that the earliest oracles were young women who regularly ran off with their advice-seeking pilgrims, leaving the post temporarily vacant. Hence it became customary for the appointed seer (Pythia) to be at least 50 years of age.

When she was consulted for divine advice, the priestess inhaled the fumes and entered a trance. Her inspired, if somewhat vague, answers were translated into verse by a priest. In fact, the oracle's reputation for infallibility may have rested with the often ambiguous or cryptic answers. Wars were fought, marriages sealed and journeys begun on the strength of the oracle's visions.

Legend holds that one oracle suffered for her vagueness, whether vapour-induced or not. When Alexander the Great visited, hoping to hear a prophecy that he would soon conquer the ancient world, the oracle refused direct comment, instead asking that he return later. Enraged, he dragged her by the hair out of the chamber until she screamed, 'Let go of me; you're unbeatable'. He quickly dropped her, saying 'I have my answer'.

on you can't miss the tall **Acanthus Column of Dancers** (room 11), with three women dancing around its top. Next to it is the **omphalos**, a sculpted cone that once stood at what was considered the centre of the world. In the end room is the celebrated life-size **Bronze Charioteer**, which commemorates a victory in the Pythian Games of 478 or 474 BC.

SIKELIANOS MUSEUM

Fans of Greek drama should head to the intimate **Sikelianos Museum** (Delphic Festivals Museum; Map p241; ☎ 22650 82731; admission €1; ☺ 9am-3pm Thu-Mon) in a classic mansion overlooking Delphi, dedicated to Greek poet Angelos Sikelianos and his American-born wife Eva Palmer, who together in the late 1920s established Delphi as a European centre for drama and the arts, with masks, costumes and photos on display. The town and museum sponsor a 10-day ancient drama festival every July.

Activities

Two popular **day hikes**, both part of the Trans-European E4 trail, start and end at Delphi. The first connects two ancient sites, the Temple of Apollo and **Korikio Antro**, a sacred mountain cave-shrine for Pan and Dionysos. Many hikers first hire a taxi in Arahova (p247) as far as Kalyvia (€25), hike to the cave (500m), and return to Delphi via a well-marked path within four hours. Along the way, there are awesome views of Delphi, the Amfissa plain and Galaxidi.

A second hike meanders through the shady olives groves that stretch from Delphi to **Ancient Kirra** on the Gulf of Corinth, and takes four to five hours. After lunch or a swim, return by bus (€2) to Delphi. The E4 trailhead is marked 100m east of the Hotel Acropole.

Tours

English-language tours of Delphi are offered by **Georgia Hasioti** (☎ 69449 43511, 22550 82722) who also speaks Japanese, French and Italian; **Penny Kolomvotsos** (☎ 69446 44427) who also speaks German; and **Electra Togia** (☎ 69378 13215); who also speaks Italian and Spanish.

Sleeping

Accommodation is plentiful and high quality in Delphi, but it's advisable to book ahead in peak season (April–May and July–September) and on public holidays.

BUDGET

Hotel Sibylla (Map p241; ☎ 22650 82335; www .sibylla-hotel.gr; Vasileon Pavlou & Friderikis 9; s/d/tr from €24/30/40; ❄ ☎) An excellent budget choice, cosy Sibylla has very helpful staff along with simple and spotless rooms, all with adjustable ceiling fans rather than air-con, and several with views to the Corinthian Gulf.

Sunview Pension (Map p241; ☎ 22650 82349; dkal@ otenet.gr; Apollonos 84; s/d/tr incl breakfast from €25/35/50; P ❄ 🖳 ☎) This active pension commands a stunning location in upper Delphi, with brightly painted rooms and friendly family owners who treat it like their own home, which it happens to be.

Hotel Kouros (Map p241; ☎ 22650 82473; www.kouros hotel.com.gr; Vasileon Pavlou & Friderikis 58; s/d/tr incl breakfast €35/45/60; ❄ ☎) The comfortable Kouros is managed by the welcoming Asimina, who gets credit for the room artwork, and for arranging breakfast on the verandah.

Rooms Pitho (Map p241; ☎ 22650 82850; www .pithorooms.gr; Vasileon Pavlou & Friderikis 40a; s/d/tr/q incl breakfast €35/45/65/70; ❄ ☎) Gift shop below, small hotel above, Pitho's modern rooms, excellent service and location make it a top budget choice in Delphi.

A free shuttle cart runs hourly between Delphi and two excellent camping grounds. The closest, **Apollon Camping** (off Map p241; ☎ 22650 82762; www.apolloncamping.gr; camp sites per person/tent €7.50/4; P 🖳 ☎ 🖳), is 2km west of modern Delphi, and boasts first-rate facilities including restaurant, minimarket and barbecue. **Delphi Camping** (off Map p241; ☎ 22650 82209; www .delphicamping.com; camp sites per person/tent €6.50/4.50; P 🖳 ☎ 🖳), 4.5km from Delphi toward Itea, is similar, with views of the Gulf.

A recommended option is **Arion Hotel** (Map p241; ☎ 22650 82097; www.hotel-arion.gr; Syngrou; s/d/tr/q incl breakfast €30/45/60/75; ❄ ☎), offering comfort and value, plus a quiet back rooms with views.

MIDRANGE

Varonos Hotel (Map p241; ☎ 22650 82345; www.hotel -varonos.gr; Vasileon Pavlou & Friderikis 25; s/d/tr/ste incl breakfast €42/62/70/120; ❄ 🖳 ☎ ᕕ) The lobby of the charming Varonos is filled with potted plants and homey antiques, giving it a lived-in feel. A suite sleeps four to six people with room to spare, and there's wheelchair access too.

Hotel Hermes (Map p241; ☎ 22650 82318; www .hermeshotel.gr; Vasileon Pavlou & Friderikis 27; s/d/ste incl breakfast €45/50/80; 🐾 🖳 🛜) The welcoming and family-run Hermes is in the heart of Delphi. Most of the large wood-shuttered rooms have balconies facing the gulf. Service is excellent, and the views from the breakfast lounge are splendid.

Hotel Leto (Map p241; ☎ 22650 82302; Apollonos 15; www.leto-delphi.gr; s/d/tr incl breakfast from €45/60/75; 🐾 🐾 🖳 🛜) If the traditional Greek motif is getting you down, head to these smartly decorated digs, with nonsmoking rooms, modern decor throughout, plus free wi-fi.

Hotel Acropole (Map p241; ☎ 22650 82675; www .delphi.com.gr; Filellinon 13; s/d/tr incl breakfast €64/79/98; 🐾 🖳 🛜) On the quieter street below the main drag, Acropole's sharp rooms have soft beds, reading lamps, and wood and marble fittings. Top-floor rooms have great views to the gulf. A large lobby bar doubles as breakfast central.

TOP END

Hotel Appolonia (Map p241; ☎ 22650 82919; www .apollonia.gr; Syngrou; s/d/tr/ste incl breakfast €80/120/160/220; 🅿 🐾 🖳 🛜) The swank Appolonia has an intimate feel to it, tucked away on Delphi's upper Syngrou street. Rooms are quite modern with elegant dark-wood furnishings, carpet, large basin-sink bathrooms and balcony views over all Delphi.

Also recommended is **Amalia Hotel** (Map p241; ☎ 22650 82101; www.amaliahotels.com; s/d/ste incl breakfast from €110/150/180; 🅿 🐾 🛜 🕹). It's posh and rambling, but don't trip over the tour buses.

Eating

Eating in Delphi can find you waiting in crowded restaurants for so-so food. Try these worthy exceptions.

Taverna Gargaduas (Map p241; ☎ 22650 82488; mains €4-9) Easily the local favourite for grilled meats and good value as well. The house summer speciality is *provatina* (slow-roasted lamb, €7.50). You can also tuck into a combo of pasta, souvlaki, salad and seasonal fruit for a modest €10. Next to the bus station.

ourpick Taverna Vakhos (Map p241; ☎ 22650 83186; Apollonos 31; mains €4.50-11) Take the steps above the National Bank to this excellent family taverna featuring traditional local fare. You could make a meal of appetisers alone, like stuffed zucchini flowers or goat cheese with lemon, followed by *kouneli stifadho* (rabbit stew) or lamb in lemon sauce (both €8.20). Choose from an all-Greek wine list to wash it down.

Taverna To Patriko Mas (Map p241; ☎ 22650 82150; Vasileon Pavlou & Friderikis; mains €6-12) Set in a 19th-century stone building, this swank taverna is decidedly upscale, and the food keeps its end of the bargain. You'll find generous mezedhes and salads, great grills including a vegie souvlaki, along with a fine all-Greek wine list.

Other good eateries:

Souvlaki Pita Gyros (Map p241; ☎ 69393 10801; Apollonos; mains €2-6) Cheap, fast, fresh, go. Opposite Hotel Leto.

En Delphi (Map p241; ☎ 22650 82230; Apollonos; mains €6-10) Tour groups lurk, but there's well-prepared Greek standards, plus tree-shaded outdoor tables.

Drinking & Entertainment

There are plenty of cafe-bars along Vasileon Pavlou & Friderikis.

Café Melopoleio (Map p241; ☎ 22650 83247; snacks €1.50-4; ⏰ 7am-11pm; 🛜) Stop by for excellent coffee, fresh juices, flaky breakfast *pites* (pies) and free wi-fi.

Café Agora (Map p241; ☎ 22650 83116; Vasileon Pavlou & Friderikis; breakfast & snacks €2-10; 🛜) Great verandah views and pizza.

Café Apollon (Map p241; ☎ 22650 82842; Vasileon Pavlou & Friderikis; ⏰ 7am-10pm) For the cheapest coffee, worst English and no internet now or ever, try this charming place next to Hotel Sibylla.

While the rest of Delphi sleeps, two mainstreet clubs provide plenty of DJ dancing into the wee hours. **Club Katoi** (Map p241; ☎ 69325 26578; admission €6) is opposite the BP petrol station, and nearby **Downtown** (Map p241; ☎ 69465 02043; Vasileon Pavlou & Friderikis; admission €6) is next door to the Hermes Hotel.

Getting There & Away

BUS

Buses depart from the **bus station** (Map p241; ☎ 22650 82317; Vasileon Pavlou & Friderikis) at the Itea end of town. Note: travellers to Kalambaka/ Meteora should find better connections via Lamia and Trikala, rather than Larisa, especially with the 10am Delphi departure.

AROUND DELPHI

Olive groves and clear skies mark the road south from Delphi, which stretches 18km to the Gulf of Corinth where it branches east to **Kira** (2km). This was ancient Kirra, the port of Delphi, now a quiet suburb of the market town of **Itea**, with a long sand-and-pebble beach, very clean sea and good beachside camping.

BUSES FROM DELPHI

Destination	Duration	Fare	Frequency
Amfissa	30min	€1.90	6-7 daily
Arahova	20min	€1.40	6-7 daily
Athens	3hr	€13.60	6-7 daily
Galaxidi	45min	€3.20	3-4 daily
Itea	30min	€1.70	3 daily
Lamia	2hr	€8.20	2 daily
Larisa	3½hr	€19.60	1 daily
Livadia	55min	€3.80	6-7 daily
Nafpaktos	2½hr	€9.70	3 daily
Patra	4hr	€12.10	1 daily
Thessaloniki	5hr	€32	1 daily
Thiva	1¼hr	€7.10	6-7 daily
Trikala	4½hr	€13.80	2 daily

The town of **Amfissa** sits in the foothills 20km northwest of Delphi on the road to Lamia. Sacked in 338 BC by Phillip of Macedon, it's better known today among Greeks for its marvellous green olives, a beautiful and well-preserved Byzantine church, **Agios Sotiras** (Church of the Saviour), and the excellent **Archaeological Museum** (☎ 22650 23344; admission €2; ◷ 8am-2.30pm Tue-Sat) featuring a collection of early pre-coin money.

Heading west from Delphi toward Amfissa and Itea, the beautiful 19th-century convent of **Moni Profiti Ilia** (☎ 22650 82002; ◷ 8am-noon & 4-7pm) rests on a hillside overlooking the Gulf of Corinth. The turn-off is marked with a small cross and '3km' sign.

North of Delphi, at the unique **Amfikaia Farm Hotel** (☎ 22340 48860; www.amfikaia.gr; s/d/f incl breakfast from €45/55/70), guests can dig in, for real, at this comfortable agro-tourism lodging. There are ducks to feed, horses to groom, and good bikes to test the nearby trails. Breakfast is likely to be something you've picked, plucked or poked.

MT PARNASSOS ΠΑΡΝΑΣΣΟΣ ΟΡΟΣ

Established in 1938, **Parnassos National Park** (www.routes.gr), to the north of Delphi and Arahova, has three peaks over 2300m: Liakoura (2456m) the highest, Gerondovrachos (2396m) and Tsarkos (2416m). Kouvelos (1882m) is a popular rock-climbing face. Mt Parnassos is also part of the very elaborate Trans-European E4 international footpath (*orivatiko monopati*) from Gibraltar to Sweden, also known as the European Ramblers Path. See the **European Ramblers Association** (www.era-ewv-ferp.org) website for more information.

Between 800m and 1800m, the slopes of Parnassos support Kefallonian fir, spruce and juniper, interspersed with yellow-flowered shrubs, plum trees and the rare purple-flowered *Daphne jasminea*. Above the tree line are meadows of fescue grass. Spring flowers including crocuses, squills, tulips, orchids and irises sprout from the limestone rocks. Greece's most common mammals – foxes, hares, squirrels and jackals – may be seen, as well as vultures, passerines and hawks.

Activities

HIKING

The most popular ascent on Parnassos is to **Liakoura Peak**. The route begins at the Parnassos refuge (1990m), 20km north of Arahova and 25km south of Amfiklia. For information, contact well-regarded local guide **Stathis Samartzis** (☎ 22670 31525, 6932566206), or the **Greek Alpine Club** (☎ 21032 12429).

SKIING

The **Parnassos Ski Centre** (☎ 22340 22694; www.parnassos-ski.gr/en; ◷ Nov-May) handles ski and snowboard operations for the most popular slope on the mountain, **Kelaria** (1950m). At last count, there were 13 lifts covering more than 20 ski runs and alpine trails. The centre is 24km from Arahova and 17km from Amfiklia. There are complete holiday facilities with accommodation, restaurants, hip cafes, babysitting services, a safety network and medical centre, along with ski and snowboarding schools. Adjacent to Kelaria are the steeper slopes of **Fterolakkas** (six lifts), popular with extreme skiers.

CENTRAL GREECE

For more information, see www.snow report.gr, or contact the DETPA municipal tourist office (below) in nearby Arahova. For ski instruction, find the reliable **Papos & Baldoumis** (☎ 22670 31552, 6944567678; www.skisc hool.gr).

Getting There & Away

There is public transport on winter weekends between Arahova and the ski centre on Parnassos, free with the price of a lift ticket. A taxi from Delphi runs about €40.

ARAHOVA ΑΡΑΧΩΒΑ
pop 4100

Arahova (ah-*ra*-ho-vah), only 12km from Delphi, rests on a rocky spur of Mt Parnassos at an altitude of 960m. This rugged mountain town is primarily a winter resort for skiers, and for Greeks it is very much the place to be during the skiing season. Prices in winter reflect this trend and some restaurants close in summer.

The main street and stepped alleyways of Arahova are flanked by shops selling embroidery, hand-woven bags and *flokati* (shaggy woollen rugs) and various other souvenirs. The town is also noted for its cheese, honey, *hilopites* (fettuccine-style pasta) and red wine.

Orientation & Information

The town's main thoroughfare is Delphon, which snakes its way through three squares: Pappaioannou, the central Lakka and Xenias. Delphon doubles as the main Athens–Delphi road, and the police are constantly reminding locals not to double-park. The bus station is opposite Plateia Xenias.

The **DETPA municipal tourist office** (☎ 22670 31630; detpa@arahova.gr; 9am-9pm), near the clock tower, can help with accommodation and visiting Mt Parnassos. The **post office** (Plateia Xenias) is near four bank ATMs, and the entire village is a wi-fi hotspot.

Festivals & Events

The **Festival of Agios Georgios** is held in town around 23 April (if this date falls during Lent, the festival is postponed until the following Easter Tuesday). It's a joyous three-day celebration with virtually the entire village in costume, dancing and singing, a tug-of-war contest, and, on the last day, feasting on roasted lamb, all compliments of the town.

Sleeping

Room prices in Arahova jump about 50% on winter weekends and holidays, from November to April.

Hotel Likoria (☎ 22670 31180; www.likoria .gr, in Greek; s/d/tr incl breakfast from €55/75/100; P X 🖳 🛜) Off the main road, 250m northwest of Plateia Xenias, the low-key Likoria feels more like a country inn. Rooms are quite traditional, with carpeting, huge soft beds and shuttered doors opening to large balconies. The friendly English-speaking staff is a plus.

Pension Nostos (☎ 22670 31385; www.nostosp.gr; d/tr incl breakfast €75/105) This handsome chalet-style lodging overlooking Delphi and Mt Parnassos sports swank bathrooms, a worthy breakfast and lobby photos of some famous visitors: the Beatles slept here in 1967.

Other recommendations:

Pension Ro (☎ 22670 29180; www.arahova-ro.gr; s/d/tr/q incl breakfast from €30/40/50/70; P X 🖳) Clean and woodsy, on Plateia Xenias.

Pension Petrino (☎ 22670 31384; fax 22670 32663; s/d from €30/45; X 🖳) Persian carpets, near Plateia Xenias.

Pension Alexandros (☎ 22670 32884; www .alexandrosgr.com; r €60-90; P X 🛜) Upscale mansion, antiques and murals, behind Plateia Lakka.

Eating

our pick **Taverna Karathanasi** (☎ 22670 31456; mains €4-8.50) Look for the sign in Greek opposite the church steps, to find this outstanding and friendly eatery with well-prepared grills, soups, salads and *mayirefta* (ready-cooked) standards such as 'lamb in the pan' (€8) or baked chicken (€7).

Taverna Panagiota (☎ 22670 32735; mains €5-12) Unless you drive here, it's a mere 263 steps up to this cosy taverna, behind Agios Georgios church. Tasty traditional Greek oven dishes fill the tables, and in winter there's always a fire going.

Taverna Agnandio (☎ 22670 32114; mains €6-10) This handsome and traditional Greek eatery, just east of Plateia Lakka, serves a daily selection of oven-ready dishes, tasty lamb and chicken grills, along with the family's own red house wine, poured from the jug.

Other recommendations:

To Yefira Taverna (The Bridge; ☎ 22670 31917; mains €4-7) By the clock tower, with good *pites* and spaghetti.

Taverna To Kalderimi (☎ 22670 31418; mains €6-11; closed mid-Jul–mid-Aug) Popular meaty stews, sauces and mezedhes.

Getting There & Away

The six daily buses that run between Athens and Delphi (€13.60, 2½ hours) stop at Arahova's Plateia Xenias. There are hourly local buses to Delphi (€1.40, 20 minutes).

LIVADIA TO DELPHI

Moni Osios Loukas Μονή Οσίου Λουκά

Moni Osios Loukas (Monastery of St Luke; ☎ 22670 22797; admission €3; ☽ 8am-6pm) is 23km southeast of Arahova, between the villages of Distomo and Kyriaki. Its principal church contains some of Greece's finest Byzantine frescoes. Modest dress is required (no shorts).

The monastery is dedicated to a local hermit who was canonised for his healing and prophetic powers. The monastic complex includes two churches. The interior of the larger **Agios Loukas** is a glorious symphony of marble and mosaics. There are also icons by Michael Damaskinos, the 16th-century Cretan painter.

In the main body of the church, the light is partially blocked by the ornate marble window decorations, creating striking contrasts of light and shade. Walk around the corner to find several fine frescoes which brighten up the crypt where St Luke is buried.

Nearby, the smaller **Agia Panagia** (Church of the Virgin Mary), built in the 10th century, has a colourful but less impressive interior as none of its original frescoes have survived.

This World Heritage–listed monastery is in an idyllic setting, with breathtaking vistas from its terrace, where **Café-Bar Yannis** sells local sweets and coffee – in case you're one of those people who can't go anywhere outside hissing distance of an espresso machine.

GETTING THERE & AWAY

From Livadia, three buses reach Moni Osios Loukas each day (€3.20, 30 minutes). From Delphi, you can take the Livadia/Athens bus only as far as the Distomo crossing (€2.50, 35 minutes, hourly), then walk or hitch the 2km to Distomo.

Taxis will get you to the monastery from Distomo (€25 return), Livadia (€30 return) or Delphi (€40 return); in all cases, the taxi will wait an hour at the monastery.

Distomo Δίστομο

pop 3820

Distomo is remembered throughout Greece for the massacre of 10 June 1944, when Nazi troops killed 218 villagers in a door-to-door

reprisal for a guerrilla ambush in nearby Steiri. In 1966, the German government erected a dramatic white-marble **war memorial**, with inscriptions in both Greek and German.

GALAXIDI ΓΑΛΛΑΞΙΔΙ

pop 3030

Easily the prettiest of the low-key resorts on the Gulf of Corinth, Galaxidi is graced with narrow cobblestone streets and two small harbours, and makes a pleasant base from which to visit Delphi. The town is reasonably tranquil except during summer and holiday weekends, when its charm is tested by carloads of Athenians. Galaxidi's most prosperous period was between 1830 and 1910 when it was a major centre for building caïques (small boats).

Orientation & Information

Galaxidi's central square is Plateia Iroön (aka Manousakia), from where the main street of Nikolaou Mama leads to the larger of Galaxidi's two harbours. Kammenoi leads to the smaller harbour of Hirolakas. The post office and a bank are on Nikolaou Mama. A forested headland, opposite the waterfront, is fringed by a 1.5km walking path and pebbled coves popular with swimmers.

You can access the internet for free at cafebar **To Kafeneio** (☎ 22650 41315; Akti Oianthis 55; desserts €2.50-4.50), open from morning till late.

Sights

The excellent **Nautical Historical Museum** (☎ 22650 41795; Plateia Manousakia; adult/child €5/1; ☽ 10.10am-1.30pm & 5.30-8.30pm Jun-Sep, 10.10am-4pm Oct-May) documents Greece's maritime history and Galaxidi's unique ship-building lore, and includes several splendid ship figureheads.

The carved-wood iconostasis in the **Church of Agios Nikolaos** is one of Greece's finest. Follow the English signs for the museums and church.

The little 13th-century **Moni Metamorfosis** stands amid olive groves and cypress trees, 7km inland from Galaxidi. From this vantage point there are terrific views down to the Gulf of Corinth. To reach it, go under the flyover and take the road opposite.

Sleeping

In summer, several of the waterfront cafes have rooms to let, though they're often pricey, given the noisy location.

ourpick Hotel Ganimede (☎ 22650 41328; 69371 54567; www.ganimede.gr; Nik Gourgouris 20; s/d/tr €35/58/65; ❄ ▢ ☎) This delightful courtyard hotel in a 19th-century captain's house offers pastel-shaded rooms with wood-panelled ceilings and period furniture. Owner Chrisoula Papalexi's homemade breakfasts (€9) include jams, cheeses, fresh-squeezed juices and breads from the nearby family bakery. The captain's original living room is a split-level suite that sleeps five (€170 with breakfast). There are also three modern apartments (from €58), each with kitchen.

To Spitaki (☎ 22650 41257, 6977512238; d/f incl breakfast from €95/140; ❄ P ▢) Its name meaning 'little house' in Greek, this converted 1850s stone *ouzerie* (ouzo bar) is one of three adjacent properties, each complete with kitchen and flower garden, and halfway between the port and main square. Owner Stella stocks each kitchen with tasty breakfast basics.

Other recommendations:

Pension Votsalo (☎ 22650 42292, 6972555488; Plateia Hirolaka; d/tr €40/50; ❄ P ▢) Three unique rooms, each with its own colour scheme, on the bay.

Hotel Galaxa (☎ 22650 41620; fax 22650 42053; old harbour; s/d/f €65/75/110; P ❄) Family-sized rooms, garden terrace, and 100m to harbour swimming.

Eating

Albatross (☎ 22650 42233; Konstadinou Satha 36; mains €4-9; ❄ 8am-midnight) You could write the menu of this sweet six-table taverna, near the Church of Agios Nikolaos, on the back of a postcard, but the generous offerings of mezedhes (*taramasalata* and tzatziki) along with a few oven-ready dishes such as *bakaliaro* (baked cod) or roasted pork are always tasty and cheap.

Ouzeri Orea Ellas (☎ 22650 42016; Akti Oianthis 79; mains €5-8) Look for the model yacht inside this well-regarded waterfront taverna, popular for fresh seafood and traditional *mousakas*, *soupia krasati* (cuttlefish) and *kokoras krasatos* (rooster in wine).

Taverna Anamnisis Apo Ta Limania (Memories of the Port, ☎ 22650 42003; mains €5-12) This down-to-earth port standby is better known by the owner's name, Kavouras, who hauls in the fresh catch each day. Standouts include seafood risotto and *garidhes* (prawns).

Porto Restaurant (☎ 22650 41182; mains €6-10) On the corner opposite the waterfront *plateia*, this family eatery serves up well-prepared *mayirefta* dishes such as vegie *mousakas*, lamb with pasta and baked cod.

Other options around the port:

Art Cafe Liotrivi (☎ 22650 41781; old harbour; mains €4-10; ❄ daily Jul & Aug, Fri & Sat Sep-Jun) Half museum and half taverna, simple olives to shrimp flambé.

Taverna Tasso (☎ 22650 41291; Akti Oianthis 69; mains €4-12) Usually packed for mezedhes and lobster.

Taverna Maritsa (☎ 22650 42000; Akti Oianthis 71; mains €8-15) First-rate kitchen in upscale atmosphere.

Shopping

You can browse for jewellery, icons and handmade pottery at the good-looking **Ostria** (☎ 22650 41206), 100m past the port kiosk. Owners Katarina and Petros run a nearby studio **workshop** (☎ 22650 41063), open to summer visitors.

Getting There & Away

The **bus station** (☎ 22650 42087) is on Plateia Manousakia. There are buses to Delphi (€3.20, 45 minutes, five daily), Patra (€9, 1¾ hours, two to three daily) and Athens (€16.80, 3½ hours, four daily).

NAFPAKTOS ΝΑΥΠΑΚΤΟΣ
pop 16,200

West of Galaxidi, the coastal highway winds in and out of a number of seaside towns and villages, including picturesque **Monastiraki**, 12km before the bustling market town of Nafpaktos. Opposite the village of Spilia, look for **Trizonia**, the only inhabited island in the Gulf of Corinth.

Nafpaktos spreads out from a handsome circular-walled harbour, dotted with plane trees, trendy cafes, a good **swimming beach** (Psani) and a well-preserved fortress and Venetian **kastro** (castle), the latter protected by a series of five terraced stone walls built by a succession of conquerors (Doric, Roman, Byzantine, Venetian and Turk). Nafpaktos was known as Lepanto in medieval times, and it was here on 7 October 1571 that the naval battle of Lepanto took place between the Ottoman Empire and the combined navies of the Vatican, Spain and Venice. The decisive victory over the Turks temporarily ended their naval domination of the Mediterranean. Look for a small bronze statue of battle hero **Miguel de Cervantes**, below the harbour seawall.

Information

Hobby Club (☎ 26340 22288; per hr €1; ❄ 9am-2am) Check email at this place opposite Psani Beach.

Nafpaktos Tourist Information (☎ 26340 38533; Tzavela St; ❄ 10am-1.30pm & 6-9pm) Opposite the old

BUSES FROM NAFPAKTOS

Station	Destination	Duration	Fare	Frequency
KTEL Nafpaktos	Agrinio	1½hr	€7.80	2 daily Mon-Fri
KTEL Nafpaktos	Astakos	2½hr	€6.10	1 daily Mon-Fri
KTEL Nafpaktos	Athens via Andirio-Rio	3hr	€18.60	2 daily
KTEL Nafpaktos	Delphi	3hr	€9.70	4 daily
KTEL Nafpaktos	Lamia	3½hr	€13.10	2 daily
KTEL Nafpaktos	Messolongi	50min	€4.40	3 daily Mon-Fri
KTEL Nafpaktos	Patra	30min	€3	8 daily Mon-Fri
KTEL Nafpaktos	Thessaloniki	6hr	€34.70	2 daily
KTEL Fokida	Athens via Delphi & Thiva	5hr	€23.30	4 daily
KTEL Fokida	Galaxidi	1¼hr	€6.60	4 daily
KTEL Fokida	Itea	1¾hr	€8.10	4 daily

harbour, and next to several bank ATMs, recognisable by a cluster of trendy wi-fi cafe-bars.

Sleeping & Eating

Camping Dounis Beach (☎ 26340 31665; fax 26340 31131; camp sites per adult/tent €8/4.50) Towards the Rio–Andirio bridge, this simple beach site is clean and quiet, with a minimarket and taverna.

Hotel Regina (☎ 26340 21555; fax 26340 21556; Psani Beach; s/d/tr from €40/50/70; ⚋ 🖳) The Regina represents a great deal for families, with handsome two-room studios, all with kitchenettes and balconies, 100m west of the harbour square.

Hotel Akti (☎ 26340 28464; www.akti.gr; Grimbovo Beach; s €40-55, d €50-80, ste €110-140; 🅿 ⚋ 🖳) The Akti's exterior looks like a pastel colour chart with balconies. Inside this very welcoming lodging you'll find area rugs, antiques galore and rooms that are high, wide and comfortable. Sharp top-floor suites sleep four to six.

Among several decent waterfront eateries, head first to **Taverna O Stavros** (☎ 26340 27473; Grimbovo Beach; mains €4-9), excellent *spanakopita* (spinach pie), oven-ready dishes such as *youvetsi* (baked meat in tomato sauce) or *yemista* (stuffed vegetables), along with baked or grilled fresh fish.

Getting There & Away

Nafpaktos has two bus stations. The **KTEL Nafpaktos station** (☎ 26340 27224; cnr Manassi & Botsari) is behind the large Church of Agios Dimitrios. The **KTEL Fokida station** (☎ 26340 27241; cnr Kefalourisou & Asklipiou) is 400m further east.

The striking Rio–Andirio suspension bridge, completed in 2004 by a French con-

sortium, now connects mainland Andirio and Rio on the Peloponnese, a crossing formerly only made by ferry. Despite the steep toll (€11.70 each way), getting to places such as Patra couldn't be easier.

MESSOLONGI ΜΕΣΟΛΟΓΓΙ
pop 12,580

From a distance, Messolongi's flat landscape lacks the siren's irresistible draw. The town skirts the motionless Klisova Lagoon, the largest natural wetland in Greece, a favourite winter stopover for thousands of migrating birds and an important breeding ground for the endangered Dalmatian pelican – not to mention a pilgrimage site for photographers and birdwatchers. The town centre is anything but motionless, with the pedestrian lanes around the central square lined with lively bars and tavernas.

History

During the War of Independence (1821–30), Britain's philhellenic bard Lord Byron arrived in Messolongi with the intention of organising the troops and supporting the Greek war effort. After months of vain attempts, Byron contracted a fever and died on 19 April 1824, his immediate aims unfulfilled.

But Byron's death was not in vain – it spurred international forces to hasten the end of the War of Independence, making him, to this day, a Greek national hero. Many men bear the name Byron (Vyronas in Greek) and most Greek towns have a street named after him.

In the spring of 1826, under the helm of Egyptian general Ibrahim, Messolongi was captured by the Turks. Their year-long siege

CENTRAL GREECE

drove 9000 men, women and children to escape on the night of 22 April 1826 through what is now called the Gate of Exodus. Many took refuge on nearby Mt Zygos, only to be caught or killed by an Albanian mercenary force. A smaller group remained behind to detonate explosives as the Turks approached. This tragic exodus was immortalised in Dionysios Solomos' epic poem 'I Eleftheri Poliorkimeni' ('The Free Besieged').

Orientation & Information

Messolongi is the capital of the prefecture of Etolo-Akarnania. The central square, Plateia Markou Botsari, is dominated by the town hall on its eastern side. Several of the surrounding cafes have free wi-fi, and **Virtual Reality Internet Cafe** (26310 26058; Razikotsika 4; per hr €2; ☻ 24hr) is just north of the square.

Sights

Just beyond the Gate of Exodus is the **Garden of the Heroes** (☻ 8am-8pm), translated incorrectly as 'Heroes' Tombs' on the road sign. This memorial garden was established by the first governor of Greece following independence, Yiannis Kapodistrias, who issued the following decree:

> …within these walls of the city of Messolongi lie the bones of those brave men, who fell bravely while defending the city…it is our duty to gather together, with reverence, the holy remains of these men and to lay them to rest in a memorial where our country may, each year, repay its debt of gratitude.

You will find the Greek text of this decree on the marble slab to the right as you enter the garden. A **statue of Lord Byron** features prominently in the garden. When Byron died, the Greeks were heartbroken at the loss of a British nobleman who had given his life for their freedom. At the end of a national 21-day mourning period, Byron's embalmed body was returned to England, but his heart was kept by the Greeks and is buried beneath the statue. The English authorities at the time refused Byron's burial at Westminster Abbey. Today, the monument is marked by two flags, one Greek and one British.

The **Museum of History & Art** (☎ 26310 22134; Plateia Markou Botsari; admission free; ☻ 9am-1.30pm

& 4-7pm), is dedicated to the revolution and features a collection of Byron memorabilia and paintings.

Sleeping & Eating

Hotel Avra (☎ 26310 22284; hotelayram@panafonet.gr; Harilaou Trikoupi; s/d €28/45; ☒) The Avra is tidy and comfortable; rear-facing rooms avoid the evening din of the adjacent central Plateia Markou Botsari.

Taverna Filoxenos (☎ 26310 28008; Razikotsika 7; mains €5-9) One of the best kitchens along pedestrian-friendly Razikotsika, this handsome eatery serves lagoon-speared *heli* (grilled eel), plus fine mezedhes.

Ouzerie Dimitroukas (☎ 26310 23237; Razikotsika 11; mains €5-9) Next door to Filoxenos, this reliable place is also popular for Messolongi's speciality – look for the eels hanging in the window.

Getting There & Away

The **KTEL Messolongi station** (☎ 26310 22371; Mavrokordatou 5) is just off the central Plateia Markou Botsari. There are regular buses to Athens via Rio–Andirio (€21, 3½ hours, 12 daily), Patra (€5, one hour, nine daily), Agrinio (€3.30, 35 minutes, hourly), Nafpaktos (€5, 50 minutes, three daily), Amfissa (€12, three hours, twice daily) and Mytikas (€8, 1½ hours, once daily).

AROUND MESSOLONGI

Tourlida Τουρλίδα

You can drive, walk or cycle across the surreal **Klisova Lagoon** via the 5km-long causeway to visit the sandy hamlet of Tourlida, with **Alikes Taverna** (☎ 26310 24327; mains €5-8), worth a stop for excellent grilled eel, and clean and breezy **Domatia Iliovasilema** (☎ 26310 51408, 69779 28335; d/tr/q €40/50/60; ☐ ☒) making staying overnight easy.

Northwest to Mytikas & Astakos

Μύτικας & Αστακός

Of the scattered seaside villages facing the Ionian Sea, only Astakos and Mytikas merit a second look. In summer, it's a lovely coastal drive, and a lone bus makes daily runs from Messolongi.

A sleepy charmer on the Ionian coastline (63km from Messolongi) the pebbly shore of **Mytikas** is lined with palm trees, houses, a few domatia (rooms in a private house) plus a scattering of tavernas. You can take a local caïque to the isolated islets of **Kalamos**

CENTRAL GREECE

(€3 return, 15 minutes, twice daily) looming over Mytikas, or **Kastos**, tucked away on the other side. Enquire at **Taverna Limani** (☎ 26460 81271) near the dock. If the owner-captain-cook isn't mending a fishing net, he'll probably take you over on demand. And if you decide the outside world can wait a day, scan the beach for **Kohili Rooms** (☎ 26460 81356; s/d €40/60; ⌘). **Camping Ionion** (☎ /fax 26460 81110; camp sites per adult/tent €6/5; ⌕ May-Oct) is 500m south of village.

Astakos, 14km south, lacks Mytikas' cosiness, but it's a convenient stepping stone for access to the Ionian Islands via the daily ferry to Ithaki (Piso Aetos) and Kefallonia (Sami) in summer. For details see Island Hopping (p746). A few cafes, domatia and tavernas line the small waterfront, but best-in-show goes to **Poseidon Palace** (☎ 26460 41661; mains €4-7.50), where cook-proprietor George modestly claims, 'Have everything, simple souvlaki, great fish, what you like'. A kids' menu is a bonus.

KARPENISI ΚΑΡΠΕΝΗΣΙ
pop 9390

Karpenisi, the low-key capital of the mountainous prefecture of Evritania, lies in the well-wooded foothills of Mt Tymfristos, or Velouchi (2312m), between Lamia and Lake Kremasta. Not surprisingly, the town has an alpine-village feel to it, with chalet-style lodgings mixed in among its churches, tavernas and bakeries. Today, opportunities abound for hiking, rafting, skiing and mountain biking to steep villages and historical monasteries. Pick up Anavasi Map No 2.4/2.5, *Mountains of Evritania,* for detailed routes.

Karpenisi lies in the heart of mainland Greece, reachable from Trikala to the north, Lamia to the east, or Agrinio to the southwest via a spectacular if tortuous mountain route. Perhaps the most interesting approach, however winds north from Nafpaktos through the town of Thermo in the hills above Lake Trihonida, Greece's largest natural lake, then past the dramatic village of Prousos.

Orientation

The thoroughfares of Zinopoulou, Athanasiou Karpenisioti and Spyridonos Georgiou Tsitsara run downhill from Plateia Markos Botsaris; Ethnikis Andistasis runs northwest from it.

Information
EMERGENCY
Hospital (☎ 22370 80680; Ethnikis Antistasis 9)
Police (☎ 22370 23666; Pavlou Bakogianni 2)

INTERNET ACCESS
Cinema Café (☎ 69797 27467; cnr Evritanon & Neraida; wi-fi free; ⌕ 8am-3am)
Phoenix Internet Café (☎ 22370 23696; Kosma Aitolou; per hr €2; ⌕ 11am-3am)

LAUNDRY
Ariston Laundry (☎ 22370 22887; Athanasiou Karpenisioti 25)

MONEY
Six of the banks around the central square have ATMs.

POST
Post office (cnr Agiou Nikolaou & Athanasiou Karpenisiotou; ⌕ 7.30am-1.30pm)

TOURIST INFORMATION
Tourist office (☎ /fax 22370 21016; www.karpenissi.gr; Markou Botsari 5; ⌕ 9am-2pm & 5-8pm Mon-Fri, 10am-2pm & 5-8pm Sat, 10am-2pm Sun) Can provide local maps and help with accommodation and destinations around Karpenisi; 100m down the cobbled lane below the *plateia*.

Activities

The Karpenisi **ski centre** (☎ 22370 23506; www .snowreport.gr/karpenissi) on Mt Tymfristos operates six lifts with 11 runs from November to March. Karpenisi is also a mecca for hikers, rafters, mountain bikers and rock climbers.

Three friendly competitors in town boast extreme-sports offerings including white-water rafting, snowboarding and canyoning. Prices average €30 to €40 per day, including equipment and transport.

The well-run **Trekking Hellas** (☎ 22370 25940; www.trekking.gr; Kosma Aitolou 1) organises hikes on the Trans-European E4 trail between Karpenisi and Krikello, along with canoeing, rock climbing, river hiking and mountain biking with jeep support. A day-long rafting trip on the Tavropos River for beginners runs to €25, and a two-day hike to the mountain village of Agrafa is €80, including meals.

Mountain Action (☎ 22370 22940, 6945323895; www .mountainaction.gr, in Greek; Oikonomou 9) specialises in exploring the nearby canyons of Evrytania, along with mountain-biking excursions and canoeing around peaceful Lake Kremasta.

F-Zein (☎ 22370 80150; Zinopoulou 61) offers graded rafting trips to three rivers: Aheloös (easy), Tavropos (moderate) and Krikelopotamos (advanced; white water).

For child-friendly horse riding near town (best viewed with drink in hand from the deck) check out the **Saloon Park** (☎ 22370 24606; riding per hr adult/child €20/10), a combination bar-restaurant and stable, 3km south of town. The unmistakable theme here is the American Old West, with a Jack Daniels–meets–ouzo ambience.

Sleeping

Hotel Galini (☎ 22370 22914; fax 22370 25623; Riga Fereou 3; s/d €25/40) The side-street Galini is a great budget choice, with simple rooms and friendly owners. From the *plateia*, walk 100m up Spyridonos Georgiou Tsitsara.

City Hotel Apollonion (☎ 22370 25001; www.hotel apollonion.gr; Athanasiou Karpenisioti 4; s/d/tr/ste incl breakfast from €50/60/70/120; 🖳 🛜) Rooms at the handsome Apollonion are mountain-modern, with carpeting and dark-wood touches, though bathrooms are smallish. Just 20m south of the central square.

Eating

Three Star Restaurant (☎ 22370 24800; Athanasiou Karpenisioti 35; mains €3.50-7; 🕒 8.30am-4am Wed-Mon) Karpenisi's cheapest eatery is a hit with the local night owls. Owner-cook Christos learned his craft in Brooklyn, New York. Choose from cholesterol-raising bacon-and-egg breakfasts (€4), pasta, hearty soups, or tuck into a generous plate of pork chops for just €6.

Taverna Panorama (☎ 22370 25976; Riga Fereou 18; mains €4-8) Roomy tables and a leafy outdoor terrace give Panorama a family feel, and there's a huge menu featuring plenty of grilled lamb or pork, plus a hearty goat and potato soup.

Taverna En Elladi (☎ 22370 22235; Kotsidou 4; mains €4.50-7.50) Look for the red-and-white tablecloths at this smart family-run taverna, just above the main square. There's always a hearty homemade soup of the day, along with excellent oven-ready dishes such as chicken in wine with pasta (€6.50), and a mountain speciality, *babaretsa,* a tasty cheese and corn flour appetiser (€3).

Entertainment

If you're in town during the busier winter months, catch some late-night, authentic live Greek music at **Notes Live** (☎ 69387 65562); Kosma Etolou 9; 🕒 Fri & Sat). Things don't get going until around midnight. And it's roughly the same at **Nefeles** (☎ 22370 25200), opposite Agiou Georgiou church.

Getting There & Away

BUS

Karpenisi's **KTEL bus station** (☎ 22370 80014) is 2.5km southeast of town. Buses run to Athens (€22.50, five hours, three daily), Lamia (€6.40, 1½ hours, five daily) and Agrinio (€9.70, 3½ hours, once daily).

AROUND KARPENISI

From Karpenisi, a scenic mountain road leads south for 34km towards the village of **Prousos**, and the 12th-century **Moni Panagias Proussiotissas** (☎ 22370 80705). Pilgrims flock here on 23 August for the **Feast of the Assumption**, to drink holy water from the spring and to step into the cavelike *katholikon* (principal church of a monastery), which claims a miracle working icon of the Virgin Mary.

Just 14km south of Karpenisi are the twin villages of **Megalo Horio** (Big Village) and **Mikro Horio** (Little Village), with traditional stone houses, including the central **Folklore Museum** (☎ 22370 41502; admission free; 🕒 10am-1pm Fri-Sun Sep-Jun, 10am-1pm & 6-8pm Fri-Sun Jul & Aug). The more scenic Megalo Horio is also the starting point for the all-day hike to **Mt Kaliakouda** (2098m) and back; enquire at the Karpenisi **tourist office** (☎ 22370 21016; www.karpenissi.gr). If you fancy something more level, you can take a satisfying stroll along the banks of the Karpenisiotis River on a footpath that begins opposite the village bus terminal.

Nearby riverside **Gavros** attracts Karpenisi families in search of a good meal in the countryside, or a stroll along the Karpenisiotis River.

With your own transport, you can visit the restored village of **Koryshades**, reached by a marked turn-off about 3km southwest of Karpenisi. The same scenic road continues another 20km southwest to the quaint village of **Fidakia**, with knock-out views of **Lake Kremasta**. A combination pension-taverna-cafe, the **Oihalia** (☎ 22370 24554) makes a good day-trip destination.

Sleeping & Eating

Pension Agrambeli (☎ 22370 41148; agrambeli@yahoo .gr; Gavros; s/d/f incl breakfast from €55/85/120; 🅿 🚉 🖳) This uniquely decorated mountain lodging in

CENTRAL GREECE

Gavros overlooks the river and Mt Talakondia. Each of the seven rooms varies in size and features, some with iron beds and area rugs, others with kitchens and fireplaces, all with fresh flowers.

Taverna To Spiti tou Psara (fisherman's house; ☎ 22370 41202; Gavros; mains €4-9) At this nearby and excellent riverside taverna, a house speciality is fresh *pestrofa* (grilled wild trout; €8). The handmade *pites* (€3), baked lamb and the owner's house-made wine justify a day trip from Karpenisi.

Taverna O Platanos (☎ 22370 25363; Prousos) This place overlooks the gorge and can provide a quick lunch of lamb souvlaki (€1.50) and Greek salad (€4).

Getting There & Away

BUS

Two local buses depart Karpenisi (on Monday and Friday only) for Megalo Horio, Mikro Horio and Gavros (€1.40, 25 minutes). A Friday bus continues to Prousos (€2.90, 50 minutes), but you'll need to stay overnight, or return by taxi.

TAXI

From Karpenisi's central *plateia* it's €14 to Gavros, Megalo Horio or Mikro Horio; to Prousos, about €30.

LAMIA ΛΑΜΙΑ

pop 47,650

Lamia is the capital of the prefecture of Fthiotida, built in the foothills of Mt Orthys at the western end of the Maliakos Gulf. Although midway between Delphi and Meteora, Lamia rarely figures on travellers' itineraries. But like many towns that are not dependent on tourism for their livelihood, Lamia is a vibrant and lively place year-round. It is famous for its *kokoretsi* (grilled lamb offal), *kourabiedes* (almond shortcake) and *xynogalo* (sour milk).

Orientation

Life in Lamia revolves around its rambling squares, two in particular. Plateia Eleftherias, with swank cafeterias, attracts a younger set, whereas Plateia Laou, shaded by large plane trees, kicks back with traditional *kafeneia* (coffee houses), bakeries and tavernas.

There's a bustling street market on Riga Fereou and its side streets every Saturday morning.

Information

Six banks, all with ATMs, encircle Plateia Parkou.

Battle Net (☎ 22310 67424; Rozaki Angeli 40; per hr €1) Internet access opposite Hotel Athina.

Police station (☎ 22310 22431; Patroklou)

Post office (Athanasiou Diakou) Opposite Plateia Parkou.

Sights

Lamia's **frourio** (fortress) is worth the hike just for the views. Within it is the **Archaeological Museum** (☎ 22310 29992; admission €2; ☺ 8.30am-3pm), which displays finds from Neolithic to Roman times, including some Hellenistic children's toys.

The original **Gorgopotamos Railway Bridge**, 7km south of Lamia, was blown up by a coalition of British and Greek guerrilla forces, on 25 November 1942, in order to delay the German advance, and is considered one of the greatest acts of sabotage of the time. The reconstructed bridge spans a deep ravine, with the replacement piers in stark contrast to the originals. The spectacular attack put the Greek underground on the map, and forced the Germans to divert resources away from the Russian front.

About 20km southeast of Lamia is the narrow pass of **Thermopylae**, where, in 480 BC, Leonidas and a band of 300 brave Spartans managed to temporarily halt the invading Persian army of Xerxes. A statue of Leonidas honours the heroic battle site where the Spartans ultimately perished against overwhelming odds.

Sleeping & Eating

Hotel Athina (☎ 22310 27700; lamiahotelathina@yahoo .gr; Rozaki Angeli 41; s/d/tr €40/50/60; P ❄ ☐ ☎) The 2008-renovated and family-managed Athina sports modern tile-floored rooms, large bathrooms, comfortable beds and, remarkably, its own parking. It's a short walk to Plateias Laou and Eleftherias.

Ouzerie Alaloum (☎ 22310 44470; Androutsou 24; mezedhes €2-5) You can nibble and sip your way through a meal at this prime people-watching spot, one of a cluster of inviting *ouzeries* 20m west of Plateia Laou, on a pedestrian lane.

Taverna Ilysia (☎ 22310 27006; Kalyva Bakogianni 10; mains €2.50-8) This large, no-frills taverna serves a huge range of tasty, oven-made, point-and-eat dishes, big salads included.

Fitilis Restaurant (☎ 22310 26761; Plateia Laou 6; mains €4.50-12) Upmarket Fitilis serves mostly classic *mayirefta* dishes, along with slow-cooked goat (€9), which sizzles over an open, antique wood oven. Vegie dishes are on hand, too (rice pilaf with leeks, €4.50).

Central Greece's proclivity for grilled meats reaches the point of deification in Lamia. The southern end of Plateia Laou is a vegetarian's nightmare, full of *psistarias* (restaurants serving grilled meat) with whole lambs, goats and pigs adorning the windows.

Getting There & Away
BUS
There are four long-distance bus terminals in Lamia, and one regional station.

From **Papakyriazi station** (☎ 22310 51345; cnr Satovriandou & Papakyriazi), buses depart for Athens (€18.40, three hours, hourly), Larissa (€9.60, 1½ hours, two daily) and Thessaloniki (€23.60, four hours, two daily, one on Saturday). The Athens-bound bus stops at Agios Konstantinos (€4.30, 50 minutes).

From **Agrafon station** (☎ 22310 22802; Agrafon 41), opposite Halliopouleio Sport Centre, buses go north to Trikala (€8.60, two hours, six daily) for Meteora and Kalambaka. Buses head south to Amfissa (€6.40, 1½ hours, three daily), Delphi (change in Amfissa; €8.20, two hours, three daily) and Patra (€16.90, three hours, four daily).

From **Markou Botsari station** (☎ 22310 28955; Markou Botsari 3) buses depart for Karpenisi (€6.40, 1¾ hours, five daily).

From the **KTEL Stelidos station** (☎ 22310 22627; Rozaki Angeli 69) you'll find buses for Volos (€11.50, two hours, two daily).

The **regional bus station** (☎ 22310 51347; Konstantinoupoleos) has buses for western Fthiotida province, including Ipati (€2, 40 minutes, four daily) and Pavliani (€3.90, 90 minutes, on Monday and Friday), both near Mt Iti National Park.

TRAIN
Lamia's main train station is 6km west of the town centre at Lianokladi. Train tickets should be purchased in Lamia from the **OSE ticket office** (☎ 22310 23201; Averof 28), where an OSE shuttle bus links up with the main Lianokladi train station.

Intercity trains run to Athens (€13, 2½ hours, six daily) and Thessaloniki (€27, three hours, six daily). Slower trains make both runs (Athens/Thessaloniki €10/22), and take an extra hour.

ITI NATIONAL PARK
ΕΘΝΙΚΟΣ ΔΡΥΜΟΣ ΟΙΤΗΣ
Iti is one of Greece's most beautiful but least developed national parks, a verdant region with forests of fir and black pine, meadows and snow-melt pools fringed by marsh orchids, and home to woodpeckers, eagles, deer and boar. According to mythology, Hercules built his own funeral pyre on Mt Iti, before joining his divine peers on Mt Olympus.

Trails are not uniformly well-marked, though a good day-hike begins clearly at Ipati and climbs to a refuge (Trapeza at 1850m) near the Pyrgos summit (2152m). Other popular day-hikes reach the villages of Kastania and Kapnohori. For information about hikes in Mt Iti, contact the **Hellenic Federation of Mountaineering** (☎ 210 364 5904; info@eooa.gr) in Athens. Also, check out Road Editions Map No 43, *Iti*, or Anavasi Map No 2.3, *Central Greece: Giona, Iti, Vardhousia*.

The bordering village of **Ipati**, located 22km west of Lamia and 8km south of the Karpenisi–Lamia road, has the remains of a fortress and is (along with Pavliani to the south) a starting point for hikes on Mt Iti. The hub of the village is the tree-shaded, central square Plateia Ainianon, flanked by traditional *kafeneia*.

The shady village of nearby **Loutra Ipatis**, is home to a summer sulphur spa. With your own transport, either village makes a good base for exploring the region. Try the immaculate **Hotel Alexakis** (☎ 22310 59380; alexakishotel@yahoo.com; Loutra Ipatis; s/d incl breakfast €35/40; P 🛇 🖵), and for reliable dinner fare and mezedhes, the modest **Ouzerie Eleni Karyampa** (☎ 22310 98335; Ipati; mains €4-7).

AGIOS KONSTANTINOS
ΑΓΙΟΣ ΚΩΝΣΤΑΝΤΙΝΟΣ
pop 2660
Agios Konstantinos, on the main Athens–Thessaloniki route, is one of the three mainland ports (along with Volos and Thessaloniki) that serve the islands of Skiathos, Skopelos and Alonnisos, which make up the northern Sporades.

With judicious use of buses between Athens and the port, you will not need to stay overnight before catching a Sporades-bound ferry or hydrofoil. However, if you get stranded, try the well-managed **Hotel Amfitryon** (☎ 22350 31702; fax 22350 32604; Eivoilou 10; s/d incl breakfast €45/65; P 🛇 🛜) between the

CENTRAL GREECE

port and central square. Several tavernas keep company with the ferry ticket offices, including the reliable **Taverna Kaltsas** (☎ 22350 33323; mains €5-9.50).

Getting There & Away
BOAT
Agios Konstantinos is a gateway to the northern Sporades isles of Skiathos, Skopelos and Alonnisos. For details see Island Hopping (p745).

BUS
From the **bus station** (☎ 22350 32223), next to the Galaxias supermarket about 200m south of the ferry landing, there are buses to Athens' Terminal B bus station (€14.20, 2½ hours, hourly), and buses to Lamia (€4.30, one hour, hourly), Thessaloniki (€27.50, four hours, two daily) and Patra (€20.50, 3½ hours, once daily).

THEOLOGOS ΘΕΟΛΟΓΟΣ
Halfway between Agios Konstantinos and Thiva, and roughly 125km north of Athens, this picturesque fishing village and Athenian beach getaway is home to a rare excavated example of an ancient Neolithic town, complete with detailed and colourful display boards. For information, visit the **Cornell Halai and East Lokris Project** (halai.arts.cornell.edu) website or contact the on-site archaeologist, Cornell University's **John Coleman** (☎ 69723 59601), or the site guard, English-speaking **Vlasis Charakliannis** (☎ 69484 61817), both of whom conduct impromptu tours for visitors. There are several tavernas, cafe-bars and domatia nearby.

THESSALY ΘΕΣΣΑΛΙΑ
The region of Thessaly occupies much of east-central Greece between the Pindos Mountains and the Aegean Sea. The fertile and river-fed Thessalian plain supported one of the earliest Neolithic settlements on the continent. Today, it boasts two of Greece's most extraordinary natural phenomena: the lofty monastery-capped rock pinnacles of Meteora, and the lush Pelion Peninsula, home to restored pensions, cobblestone trails and sheltered bays. The mountains and alpine meadows around Elati and Pertouli, west of Trikala, are destinations for hikers,

skiers and river rafters. And Volos, once ancient Iolkos, was the mythic home of Jason and his band of Argonauts.

LARISA ΛΑΡΙΣΑ
pop 140,820
Larisa is a major transport, military and service hub for the vast agricultural plain of Thessaly. Despite its workaday feel, it is a vibrant university town, as the bustling cafeterias around Plateia Makariou testify. Larisa has been inhabited for nearly 10,000 years, and its layered Byzantine and Ottoman past continues to unfold along its ancient riverside.

Perhaps because Larisa can heat up in the summertime, as any Greek will tell you, a 'Beach of Larisa' sign on the outskirts points toward Agiokampos, a mere 40km away.

Orientation
Larisa occupies the east bank of the Pinios River, which eventually flows through the Vale of Tembi to the Thermaikos Gulf. The train station is on the southern side of town and the main bus station is on the northern side.

A trio of squares (Laou, Ethnarhou Makariou, and Mihail Sapka) anchor the city's centre. The grand marble fountain on Plateia Ethnarhou Makariou gushes and splashes all day long and, come summer, half the town seems to cool down at Alkazar Park, across the river.

Information
There are ATMs at the train station and several banks around Plateia Mihail Sapka.
Hospital (☎ 24102 30031; Tsakalof 1)
Hotel Association of Larisa (☎ 24105 37161; Hotel Metropol, Rousvelt 14) Ask here for general information about the town.
K-Net (☎ 24105 39355; Rouzvelt 24; per hr €2; ⊙ 24hr) Internet access.
Municipal tourism office (☎ 24106 18189; fax 24105 37076; Ipirou 58; ⊙ 7am-2.30pm Mon-Fri)
Police station (☎ 24106 83137; Papanastasiou 86)
Post office (cnr Papanastasiou & Athanasiou Diakou)

Sights & Activities
Gaze at the ongoing archaeological excavation of a well-preserved 3rd-century-BC **ancient theatre** in the city centre, 100m north of Plateia Sarka. Nearby, the **acropolis** on Agios Ahillios Hill dates from the Neolithic Age (6000 BC).

The **Archaeological Museum** (☎ 24102 88515; 31 Avgoustou 2; admission free; ⊙ 8.30am-3pm Mon-Sat), op-

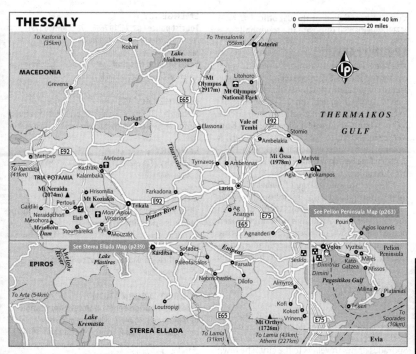

posite Plateia Laou, contains Neolithic finds and grave stelae from the region, housed in a handsome old mosque.

The **Municipal Art Gallery of Larisa** (Pinakothiki Katsigra; ☎ 24106 16266; cnr Papandreou & Kliou Patera; admission €3; ⏲ 10.30am-2pm & 6-9pm Mon-Sat) houses a superb private collection of contemporary Greek art that's second only to the National Art Gallery in Athens.

Sleeping & Eating

Hotel Metropol (☎ 24105 37161; www.hotelmetropol.gr; Rousvelt 14; s/d/f incl breakfast €50/70/85; P ⊠ ⚟ 🛜) Should you linger in Larisa, you'll find large and updated rooms decorated with the owner's paintings at this welcoming family-managed hotel, between Plateia Kentriki (Central Sq) and Ethnarhou Makariou.

Dozens of decent eateries are bunched together around Larisa's lively squares. Near Plateia Sarka, stop by **Magirio tis Yiayias** (☎ 24105 33351; Apollonos 9; mains €5-10). Translated as 'grandma's cookhouse', this charming restaurant seems half eatery and half grandma's antique stash. The menu (for kids too) ranges from grilled octopus and fresh squid to oven-cooked pasta with veal and a Greek salad for two.

Getting There & Away

BUS

Buses leave Larisa's **KTEL station** (☎ 24105 37777; cnr Georgiadou & Olympou) for Athens (€25, four hours, six daily), Lamia (€11.30, two hours, six daily), Thessaloniki (€13.50, two hours, 12 daily), Volos (€5, one hour, 12 daily) and Ioannina (€16.50, four hours, two daily).

From the branch **KTEL Trikalon station** (☎ 24106 10124; Iroön Polytehniou) near the junction with Gazi Anthimou, buses run regularly to/from Trikala (€5.70, one hour, hourly). Note: for Kalambaka, take one of the frequent Trikala buses, then change for Kalambaka.

TRAIN

Two IC trains pass daily through Larisa's **train station** (☎ 24105 90143; cnr 28 Octovriou & Iroön Politehniou) to/from Thessaloniki (€13, 80 minutes) and Athens (€27, 3½ hours, three daily). There are also hourly local trains to/from Thessaloniki (€6, two hours), Athens (€22, 4½ hours), and Volos (€2.90, 50 minutes).

You can buy tickets at the **OSE office** (☎ 24105 90239; Papakyriazi 35) opposite the town hall.

AROUND LARISA

The **Vale of Tembi**, a historical and dramatic gorge cut by the Pinios River between Mt Olympus and Mt Ossa, 25km northeast of Larisa, was sacred to Apollo in ancient times. Throughout history the valley has been a pathway into Greece for merchants and invaders, from Persian King Xerxes in 480 BC to the Germans in WWII. A small bridge connects the car park with 13th-century **Agia Paraskevi** church and 2km further on, the ruins of a **medieval fortress**.

The picturesque village of **Ambelakia**, 5km up a winding road from Tembi on the slopes of Mt Ossa, was a prosperous textile centre in the 18th century. Although only a few dozen of the original 600 mansions remain, walking the cobbled streets is a pleasure, and in summer, a welcome break from the heat of the valley 400m below.

VOLOS ΒΟΛΟΣ
pop 85,390

Volos is a large and bustling city on the northern shores of the Pagasitikos Gulf, and its function as the gateway to the Pelion Peninsula or the Sporades draws travellers to the city. The town has an inviting boardwalk lined with tavernas, *ouzeries*, small hotels, churches and cafes. The city is also home to the University of Thessaly, whose students liven up the Volos cafe scene.

Orientation

The waterfront street of Argonafton is, for half its length, a pedestrian zone; running parallel to it are the city's main thoroughfares of Iasonos, Dimitriados and Ermou. Ermou and its side streets make up another lively pedestrian precinct, anchored by the church at Plateia Agiou Nikolaou, populated by dozens of apparently devout skateboarders. Plateia Riga Fereou is at the northwestern end of the main waterfront area, near the train station. The bus station is 500m further along Grigoriou Lambraki, opposite the tourist information centre. Drivers dreaming of parking in the city centre should wake up and head for the car park at the quay (€1 per hour).

Information
BOOKSHOPS

Papasotiriou Books (☎ 24210 76210; Dimitriados 223) Has a good collection of English titles, newspapers and maps.

EMERGENCY
Tourist police (☎ 24210 76987; 28 Octovriou 179) Locals also refer to the street name for 28 Octovriou as Alexandras.
Volos General Hospital (☎ 24210 72421; Polymeri 134) Near the Archaeological Museum.

INTERNET ACCESS
Web (☎ 24210 30260; Iasonos 41; per hr €3; ⏰ 24hr) Internet shop. Many waterfront cafe-bars have free wi-fi.

LAUNDRY
Q-Laundry (☎ 24210 31216; Filelinon 5; ⏰ 8.30am-8.30pm Mon-Fri)

MONEY
There are several bank ATMs on Argonafton, Iasonos and Dimitriados.

POST
Post office (cnr Dimitriados & Agiou Nikolaou; ⏰ 7.30am-8pm)

TOURIST INFORMATION
Volos Information Centre & Hotels' Association of Magnesia (☎ 24210 30940; www.travel-pelion.gr; cnr Grigoriou Lambraki & Sekeri; ⏰ 8am-8pm; P 🖳) Just opposite the bus station. The helpful multilingual staff at this modern facility offer hotel information, town maps, and bus, train and ferry schedules along with helpful travel tips for the Pelion Peninsula and two fast internet computers free of charge.

Sights
The excellent **Archaeological Museum** (☎ 24210 25285; Athanasaki 1; admission €2; ⏰ 8am-8pm Tue-Sun, 1.30-8pm Mon) houses area finds from Dimini and Sesklo, along with an impressive collection of painted grave stelae from the nearby Hellenistic site of Dimitrias, including a mother-and-child image expressing *stenohoria* (sadness).

The superb **Makris Folk Art Centre** (☎ 24210 37119; Afendouli/Kitsou Makri 38; admission free; ⏰ 8.30am-12.30pm Mon-Fri, 10.30am-2pm Sun) is an intimate house-museum that also features 25 paintings by Theophilos Hatzimichael, mostly small murals that were carefully removed from buildings around the Pelion Peninsula, where the artist often traded his art for a warm meal. The museum is maintained by the University of Thessaly.

From 1926 until 1975, the Tsalapatas Rooftile and Brickworks was part of the cultural fabric of Volos. In 2006, the restored

CENTRAL GREECE

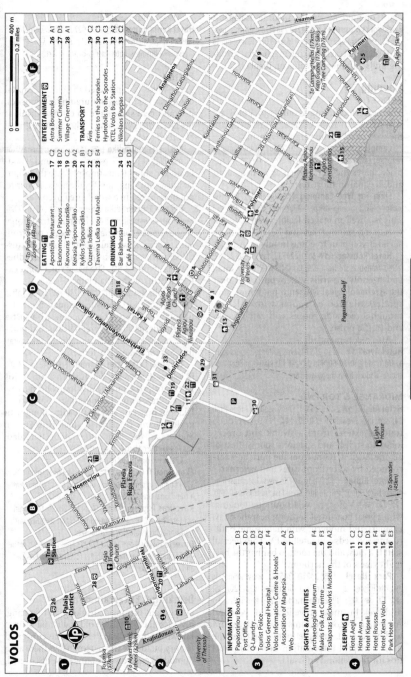

VOLOS

INFORMATION	
Papastiriou Books	1 D3
Post Office	2 D2
Q-Laundry	3 D3
Tourist Police	4 D2
Volos General Hospital	5 F4
Volos Information Centre & Hotels'	
Association of Magnesia	6 A2
Web	7 D3

SIGHTS & ACTIVITIES	
Archaeological Museum	8 F4
Makris Folk Art Centre	9 F3
Tsalapatas Brickworks Museum	10 A2

SLEEPING	
Hotel Aegli	11 C2
Hotel Avra	12 C2
Hotel Kipseli	13 D3
Hotel Roussas	14 F4
Hotel Xenia Volou	15 E4
Park Hotel	16 E3

EATING	
Apostolis Restaurant	17 C2
Ekonomou O Papous	18 D2
Kavouras Tsipouradiko	19 C2
Kerasia Tsipouradiko	20 A2
Kyklos Tsipouradiko	21 B1
Ouzerie Iolkos	22 C2
Taverna Lefka tou Manoli	23 E4

DRINKING	
Bar Balthassar	24 D2
Café Aroma	25 D3

ENTERTAINMENT	
Astra Bouzouki	26 A1
Summer Cinema	27 D3
Village Cinema	28 A1

TRANSPORT	
Avis	29 C2
Ferries to the Sporades	30 C3
Hydrofoils to the Sporades	31 C3
KTEL Volos Bus Station	32 A2
Nikolaos Pappas	33 C2

plant opened as the handsome **Tsalapatas Brickworks Museum** (☎ 24210 29844; old town; admission €3; 🕑 10am-6pm Wed-Mon 1 Mar-15 Oct, 10am-5pm 16 Oct-28 Feb) with brick-making machinery, grinding mills and massive kilns on display.

Sleeping
BUDGET
The nearest camping grounds to Volos are side by side at Kato Gatzea, 17km away, on the west coast of the Pelion Peninsula.

Camping Hellas (☎ 24230 22267; www.camping hellas.gr; camp sites per adult/tent €6/4; 🖳 🛜) This place shares the same beach as its neighbour and is equal in most respects.

Sikia Fig Tree Camping (☎ 24230 22279; www.camping-sikia.gr; camp sites per adult/tent €5.50/3.60; 🖳 🛜) This is a well-managed facility with a decent restaurant, minimarket and beach bar. Book ahead if you plan to come in July or August.

Hotel Roussas (☎ 24210 21732; fax 24210 22987; Iatrou Tzanou 1; s/d from €29/35; ❄ 🛜) This small and friendly no-frills waterfront hotel near the Archaeological Museum has simple and spotless tile-floored rooms with balcony, though street-side rooms will catch weekend traffic noise.

Also recommended:

Hotel Avra (☎ 24210 25370; avra@internet.gr; Solonos 3; s/d/tr/ste €40/50/60/80; ❄ 🖳) Updated budget choice, a block from the waterfront.

MIDRANGE & TOP END
Hotel Aegli (☎ 24210 24471; www.aegli.gr; Argonafton 24; s/d incl breakfast €60/80; ❄ 🛜) Art-deco touches extend from a swank and breezy lobby to stylish and spacious rooms. Best of all, the Aegli is 100m from the port, and surrounded by waterfront cafes and tavernas.

Hotel Kipseli (☎ 24210 22420; www.hotelkipseli.gr; Agiou Nikolaou 1; s/d/ste incl breakfast from €70/90/140; ❄ 🖳 🛜) Volos' newest boutique lodging, with a great boardwalk location near the quay, is smart and modern, with handsome bathrooms, soft beds and satellite TV. The cheerful staff is a plus, and the rooftop bar has the best night views of the harbour.

Park Hotel (☎ 24210 36511; www.amhotels.gr; Deligiorgi 2; s/d/tr incl breakfast €75/120/135; ❄ 🖳 🛜 🍸) The upmarket Park caters to midweek business travellers and weekend Athenian visitors. Rooms are modern and well-appointed, and the lobby bar faces the bay. A helpful information desk has travel tips for the Pelion Peninsula.

Also recommended:

Hotel Xenia Volou (☎ 24210 92700; www.domotel.gr; Plastira 1; s/d/ste from €95/130/185; 🅿 ❄ 🖳 🛜 🍸) Classy new business-hotel-meets-beach-resort.

Eating
Since Volos is considered the *ouzerie* capital of Greece (see The Tsipouradhika, opposite), it would be a shame not to eat and drink as the locals do. Typical mezedhes include grilled *ohtapodi* (octopus) and fried calamari.

Kyklos Tsipouradiko (☎ 24210 20872; Mikrasiaton 85; mezedhes €1.50-6) Flagstone floors and wood-beamed ceilings lend atmosphere to this popular university hang-out. Try the house favourite: potatoes baked in a wood-fired oven.

Kerasia Tsipouradiko (Cherry Tree; ☎ 24210 27920; Papakiriazi 40; mezedhes €2-4) Like most traditional *tsipouradhika (ouzerie)*, this one is open from 9am to 6pm. A typical round of *tsipouro* (distilled spirit similar to ouzo) and mezedhes plate is about €3.50. The basic rule: don't expect a drink without a plate!

Apostolis Restaurant (☎ 24210 26973; Argonafton 15; mains €2.50-6.50) Opposite the quay, this hole-in-the-wall eatery does wonders with just a few standards such as green beans and potatoes, or pork with leek, along with takeaway lunches for the nearby ferries.

Taverna Lefka tou Manoli (☎ 24210 28103; Fil Ioannou 4; mains €4-7.50) Just east of Agios Konstantinos Church, this long and narrow eatery serves up fine mezedhes, pork souvlaki and first-rate fish by the kilo, along with grilled *gavros* (marinated small fish, €6.50). Starters are excellent, too, and 'beeten salad' tastes better than it sounds.

Other good options:

Ekonomou O Papous (☎ 24210 34606; Anthimou Gazi 135) Charming shop with only one item for sale: *loukoumi*, a traditional Greek version of Turkish Delight.

Kavouras Tsipouradiko (☎ 24210 28520; Gatziagiri 8; mezedhes €2-4; 🕑 11am-6pm) Central stand-by with traditional hours and loyal customers.

Ouzerie Iolkos (☎ 24210 35227; Argonafton 32; mains €4-11) Basic and bustling, popular for seafood mezedhes and grilled mackerel.

Drinking & Entertainment
For a night of music, drinking and dancing, head for the revitalised old industrial district known as the Palaia. Between the converted factory buildings and narrow alleys there are a number of good dives waiting to be discovered.

THE TSIPOURADHIKA

Volos is famous throughout Greece for the quality and quantity (over 500) of its *ouzeries* and *tsipouradhika*. If you have not already come across one, an *ouzerie* (strictly speaking called a *tsipouradhiko*) is a type of small restaurant where you eat from various plates of mezedhes and drink tiny bottles of *tsipouro*, a distilled spirit that's similar to ouzo but is a bit stronger. You can dilute it with water if you prefer it weaker, or want it to last a little longer. When you've finished one round of mezedhes or *tsipouro*, you just keep ordering until you've had your fill or can't stand up. Try any one of these favourites in or near Volos:

- Kyklos Tsipouradiko (opposite)
- Kavouras Tsipouradiko (opposite)
- Kerasia Tsipouradiko (opposite)
- Taverna O Petros (p265)
- Ouzerie Vangelis (p269)

In the city centre, more music bars and *ouzeries* spread out from Agios Nikolaos church.

Café Aroma (☎ 24210 24568; waterfront; snacks €2-5) At the eastern edge of Argonafton, this breezy outdoor summer cafe puts gravel at your feet and a cold beer or dripping ice cream in your hand.

Astra Bouzoukia (☎ 24210 62182; Pagasson 68; drinks €2-5; ☽ Sep-May) In the Palaia district, Astra features live bouzouki music, drinks and dancing, but don't bother showing up before midnight. Come summer, Astra moves to breezier Alykes (same phone), 5km southwest.

Bar Balthassar (☎ 69449 65406; Oikonomaki 76; snacks €4-9) In the trendy heart of Volos' cafe district, Balthassar keeps its cool, a mellow beer-and-sausage hang-out that features fine Belgian ales and assorted planetary brews.

For movies, check out Volos' outdoor **summer cinema** (exoraistiki; ☎ 24210 29946; Dimitriados 263; admission €6, Tue €3.50) near the waterfront, or the **Village Cinema** (☎ 24210 94600; Giannitson 29; admission €6.50) in the old Palaia District.

Getting There & Away

BOAT

Volos is a gateway to the northern Sporades isles of Skiathos, Skopelos and Alonnisos. For details see Island Hopping (p763). Ferries arrive and depart from the far end of the dock; hydrofoils from the near end.

BUS

From the **KTEL Volos bus station** (☎ 24210 33254; cnr Zachou & Almyrou), opposite the tourist info centre, buses depart for Athens (€24.70, 4½ hours, 11 daily), Larisa (€5, one hour, 10 to 12 daily), Thessaloniki (€16.60, 2½ hours, nine daily), Trikala (€12.30, 2½ hours, four daily) and Ioannina (€21.60, 4½ hours, three daily).

TRAIN

The Volos **train station** (☎ 24210 24056; Papadiamanti) is about 200m northwest of Plateia Riga Fereou. There are 15 trains daily to Larisa (€2.90, one hour). Trains run to Athens (IC €28.20, five hours, two daily; normal €12.80, six hours, six daily) and Thessaloniki (IC €21.60, two hours, three daily; normal €12.90, three hours, three daily), both via Larisa.

Getting Around

Cars can be rented from **Nikolaos Pappas** (☎ 24210 70009; Iolkou 93b) and **Avis** (☎ 24210 22880; fax 24210 32360; Argonafton 41).

AROUND VOLOS

Just west of Volos are two major archaeological sites, both dating from early Greek civilisation in Thessaly. The first is **Dimini** (☎ 24210 85960; admission €2; ☽ 8.30am-2.30pm Tue-Sun), a late Neolithic site (4800–4500 BC) complete with traces of neatly arranged streets and houses. The second is **Sesklo** (☎ 24210 95172; admission €2; ☽ 8.30am-3pm Tue-Sun), with remains of the oldest acropolis in Greece (6000 BC). The architecture at both sites typifies the complex agrarian communities that could sustain much larger populations than those of their Palaeolithic hunter-gatherer ancestors.

PELION PENINSULA ΠΗΛΙΟΝ ΟΡΟΣ

The Pelion Peninsula lies to the east and south of Volos, a dramatic mountain range whose highest peak is Pourianos Stavros (1624m). The largely inaccessible eastern flank consists of high cliffs that plunge into the sea. The gentler western flank coils round the Pagasitikos Gulf. The interior is a green wonderland where trees heavy with fruit vie with wild olive groves and forests of horse chestnut, oak, walnut, eucalyptus and beech trees to reach the light of day. The villages tucked away in this profuse foliage are characterised by whitewashed, half-timbered houses with overhanging balconies, grey slate roofs and old winding footpaths.

Many lodgings in the Pelion are traditional *arhontika* (stone mansions), tastefully converted into pensions and reasonably priced. The peninsula has an enduring tradition of regional cooking, often flavoured with mountain herbs. Local specialities include *fasoladha* (bean soup), *kouneli stifadho*, *spetsofaï* (stewed pork sausages and peppers) and *tyropsomo* (cheese bread).

HISTORY
In mythology the Pelion was inhabited by *kentavri* (centaurs) – creatures, half-man and half-horse, who took delight in drinking wine, deflowering virgins and generally ripping up the countryside. Not all were random reprobates, however; Chiron, considered the wisest of the group, was renowned for his skill in medicine.

The Turkish occupation did not extend into the inaccessible central and eastern parts of the Pelion, and as a result the western coastal towns were abandoned in favour of mountain villages. In these remote settlements, culture and the economy flourished; silk and wool were exported to many places in Europe. The Orthodox Church at the time was instrumental

in maintaining *Kryfa Skolia* (Hidden Schools). Like many remote areas in Greece, the Pelion became a spawning ground for ideas that culminated in the War of Independence.

HIKING
The Pelion is a hiking mecca, and a centuries-old network of frequently restored *kalderimia* (cobbled mule pathways) connect most mountain and seaside villages. A detailed booklet in English, *Walks in the Pelion* by Lance Chilton, is available (with online updates) from **Marengo Publishers** (www.marengowalks .com/Pilionbk.html). The detailed Anavasi Map No 6.21, *Central Pelion* 1:25,000 is available in Volos bookshops and many *periptera* (kiosks). Both the Tsangarada tourist office (p267) and Mulberry Travel (p266) are up to date with conditions and routes.

GETTING THERE & AWAY
Buses to villages throughout the Pelion leave from the Volos bus station (see Buses from Volos to the Pelion Peninsula, below).

Northwest Pelion
VOLOS TO MAKRINITSA ΒΟΛΟΣ ΠΡΟΣ ΜΑΚΡΙΝΙΤΣΑ
Taking the northeastern route from Volos to Makrinitsa, the road climbs 6km to the village of **Ano Volos**, where you'll find the fascinating **Theophilos Museum** (☎ 24210 47340; Anakasia; admission free; 8am-2.30pm Mon-Fri), a converted mansion that was temporarily home to native artist Theophilos Hatzimichael (1866–1934), who wandered the Pelion region trading his artwork for food. The upstairs wall murals reflect local scenes and personal visions.

BUSES FROM VOLOS TO THE PELION PENINSULA

Destination	Duration	Fare	Frequency
Agios Ioannis	2hr	€5.40	2 daily
Kala Nera	50min	€1.60	12 daily
Makrinitsa (via Portaria)	45min	€1.40	10 daily
Milina (via Argalasti and Horto)	1½hr	€4.10	4 daily
Pinakates	1hr	€2.20	3 daily
Platanias	2hr	€5.80	2 daily
Pouri	1hr 45min	€4.50	2 daily
Trikeri	3hr	€6.80	1-2 daily
Tsangarada	1½hr	€4	2 daily
Vyzitsa (via Milies)	70min	€2.50	4-5 daily
Zagora (via Hania)	1½hr	€3.90	2 daily

PELION PENINSULA

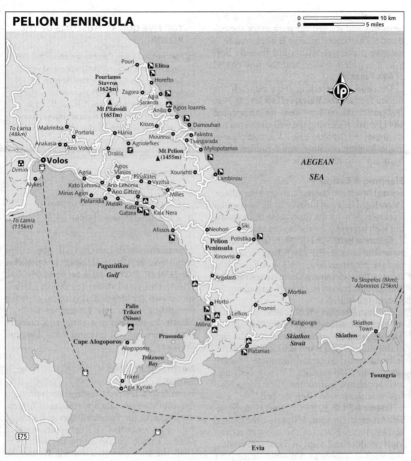

0 — 10 km
0 — 5 miles

Pouri
Elitsa
Horefto
Pourianos Stavros (1624m)
Zagora
Agia Saranda
Anilio
Agios Ioannis
Mt Pilassidi (1651m)
Kissos
Damouhari
To Larisa (48km)
Makrinitsa
Portaria
Hania
Mouressi
Fakistra
Anakasia
Agriolefkes
Tsangarada
Ano Volos
Drakia
Mt Pelion (1455m)
Mylopotamos
Volos
Dimini
Agria
Agios Vlasios
Xourichti
Alykes
Kato Lehonia
Pinakates
Vyzitsa
Lambinou
Minas Agios
Ano Lehonia
Ano Gatzea
Milies
To Lamia (115km)
Platanidia
Malaki
Kato Gatzea
Kala Nera
Afissos
Neohori
Siki
Pelion Peninsula
Potistika
Xinovrisi
Pagasitikos Gulf
Argalasti

AEGEAN SEA

To Skopelos (8km); Alonnisos (25km)
Mortias
Horto
Lefkos
Promiri
Palio Trikeri (Nisos)
Milina
Katigiorgis
Skiathos Town
Prasouda
Skiathos
Cape Alogoporos
Alogoporos
Skiathos Strait
Trikenou Bay
Platanias
Tsoungria
Trikeri
Agia Kyriaki
E75
Evia

CENTRAL GREECE

Portaria, 2km east of Makrinitsa, is 12km northeast of Volos. True to Pelion form, its *plateia* has a splendid old plane tree, and the little 13th-century **Church of Panagia of Portaria** has fine frescoes.

Head to the Portaria *plateia* to find the welcoming **Kritsa Restaurant & Hotel** (☎ 24280 99121; www.hotel-kritsa.gr; Portaria; mains €4-16; ℗ ✷ ☎), serving outstanding Pelion favourites such as slow-cooked 'lamb-in-the-jug,' or roasted wild greens with egg. Owner Eleni Karaïskou boasts of her 'from-the-mountain' menu, featuring local and mostly organic ingredients. Even her Greek coffee is made in a traditional brass *briki* (copper pot). Kritsa also doubles as a small hotel with eight pastel-shaded rooms (€40 to €55), each traditionally furnished with four-poster beds, lace curtains and woven rugs. The best part: you can wake up to an excellent breakfast downstairs, included in the room rate.

MAKRINITSA ΜΑΚΡΙΝΙΤΣΑ
pop 650

Clinging to a mountainside, Makrinitsa is aptly called the Balcony of Pelion. From a distance, the traditional houses give the impression that they are stacked on top of one another. Up close, the whitewashed structures are threaded with steep stairs crowded with geraniums, hydrangeas and roses. Further up, the path leads to more than 50 stone water fountains. It is one of the loveliest of the Pelion villages, and also the most visited.

The village is a pedestrian zone; a bus terminus and shaded car park mark the entrance. The central square is anchored by a massive plane tree with a kid-friendly hollow, a marble fountain and the tiny chapel of **Agia Panagia**.

Descend the winding steps beneath the square to reach the **Museum of Folk Art** (☎ 24280 99505; admission €2; ☉ 10am-4.30pm), set in a restored 1844 mansion. Among the well-displayed relics are an old *tsipouro* still, a Victrola phonograph 'talking machine' and a hidden water fountain built into a stone wall.

Sleeping & Eating

Several hotels are scattered around the village. Prices listed here can increase by 50% on winter weekends. Stop for the views at the main square, but look beyond it for the best eateries.

Kentavros Hotel (☎ 24280 99075; fax 24280 90085; r incl breakfast from €50; **P**) You'll have to squeeze past the geranium flowerpots as you climb the steps to the welcoming Kentavros, with large and spotless balconied rooms overlooking the *plateia* and hillsides.

Sisilianou Arhontiko (☎ 24280 99556; www.arhontiko -sisilianou.gr; d/tr incl breakfast from €80/100; **P** 🖳 🛜) This elegant 2007-rebuilt mansion is the pick of the village. Each room is unique and tastefully decorated in period furniture. Modern touches include satellite TV, soft beds and well-appointed bathrooms. Hint: room No 7 has mountain views from the bed.

Taverna A-B (☎ 24280 99355; mains €5-10; ☉ Tue-Sun) An excellent spot, 150m past the central square, the A-B makes the most of strictly local produce and meat in mountain favourites such as rabbit in red wine sauce (€8), lamb and zucchini casserole (€7), along with well-made appetisers and salads. The view from the verandah merits a glass of the house red by itself.

Other good options:

Arhontiko Repana (☎ 24280 99067; www.repana .gr, in Greek; s/d/tr incl breakfast from €40/70/90; **P**) Welcoming and woodsy, overlooking the *plateia*.

Taverna Apolafsi (☎ 24280 90085; ☉ Thu-Tue) Excellent grills, *mayirefta*.

Aeriko Café-bar (☎ 24280 99710; drinks €2-5; ☉ 10am-late) Halfway between Portaria and Makrinitsa.

MAKRINITSA TO HANIA

ΜΑΚΡΙΝΙΤΣΑ ΠΡΟΣ ΧΑΝΙΑ

Back on the main Volos–Zagora route, the road continues another 15km to the modern village of **Hania**, with views to both the

---

> **TOP FIVE QUIRKY MUSEUMS OF THE PELION**
>
> Part of the Pelion Peninsula's character derives from its rugged geography and virtual isolation. The region is well known for its unique art, cuisine and architecture. Much of that exceptional spirit is captured in a handful of small private museums, each one a minor revelation of the people and the land. Check out these gems:
>
> ■ Museum of the Olive (p268)
>
> ■ Serpentine Organic Garden (p267)
>
> ■ Theophilos Museum (p262)
>
> ■ Skolio tou Riga Museum (below)
>
> ■ Old Radio Museum (p269)

Aegean and the Pagastikos Gulf. About 3km uphill from here is the ski resort of **Agriolefkes** (☎ 24280 73719; lift day passes per weekday/weekend €11/18). This small resort (elevation 1350m) sports two ski lodges and is open, snowfall permitting, from late December to mid-March. In addition to a 5km cross-country track, there are two lifts and three downhill ski runs.

Northeast Pelion

ZAGORA ΖΑΓΟΡΑ

From Hania, the road zigzags down through chestnut trees to a junction leading to Zagora, the largest of the Pelion villages and a major fruit-growing centre – it's the apple capital of Greece. Until blight ruined the silk industry in 1850, the town exported fine silk around the continent. The successful Zagora Agricultural Cooperative was founded in 1916 and has been instrumental in promoting a sustainable agricultural economy in the village region, making the village much less dependent on tourism than its mountain neighbours.

Two War of Independence landmarks have their roots in Zagora. The **Skolio tou Riga Museum** (Hellinomouseion; ☎ 24260 23708; ☉ 9am-2pm & 6-8pm) is dedicated to revolutionary war hero Rigas Fereos, who learned his history lessons well from a lone priest who taught the children in secret, hidden from the disapproving Turks. Starting with just 48 schoolbooks in 1767, the fascinating **Library of Zagora** (☎ 24260 22591; www.vivlzagoras.gr, in Greek; ☉ Mon-Sat) is now home to one of Greece's largest collections of rare books and manuscripts.

For medical emergencies, contact the **Zagora Health Centre** (☎ 24260 22591), and for internet use, drop by **Java Internet Café** (☎ 24260 23452; Plateia Agia Kyriaki).

Sleeping & Eating

Villa Gayannis (☎ 24260 23391; www.villagayannis.gr; s/d/tr incl breakfast from €50/60/70; **P** 🖳) Also off Plateia Agios Georgios, this handsome villa is another good option.

Arhontiko Dhrakopoulou (☎ 24260 23566; fax 24260 23460; r incl breakfast €60) Don't expect to find room numbers at this homey lodging off Plateia Agios Georgios, managed by the local women's association. Instead, a local flower designates each of five simply furnished rooms.

Taverna O Petros (☎ 24260 23666; mains €4.50-7.50) Start out with a complimentary shot of local *tsipouro*, followed by a choice of good grills and *mousakas*.

Café Anemella (☎ 24260 23880) There's mellow music at this cafe whose name is Greek for silkworm – a reference to Zagora's agricultural roots.

AROUND ZAGORA

The laid-back village of **Pouri**, which spills down a steep mountainside to a small bay, is home to a few tavernas clustered beneath the church, and also the unlikely location of **Popotech Workshop** (☎ 69454 47878; www.artandcraft .gopelion.com) where Irish and Dutch transplants Gemma and Gary create unique jewellery, ceramics and found-metal sculpture. If this end-of-the-road village appeals, consider lingering at **Hiotis Theoharis Rooms** (☎ 24260 23168; 69388 10309; r incl breakfast €60; **P**) where English-speaking Vasiliki stocks a common kitchen with the family's homemade cheese.

Other picturesque villages adorn the road from Zagora to Tsangarada, one of the most scenically spectacular in the Pelion. The village of **Anilio** ('sunless' in Greek), rests in the shadow of a ridge of chestnut and walnut trees, a rich source for the **Anilion Women's Agricultural Group** (☎ 24260 31329; plateia) who make and sell traditional jams and pastries.

The flower-draped village of **Kissos** is built on steep terraces surrounding the 18th-century **Church of Agia Marina**, whose frescoes are considered the finest in the Pelion. An impressive old plane tree in the village square recently attracted a group of travellers who encircled its trunk in hopes of tapping a bit of its spiritual energy. When a curious taverna owner learned of their plan, she quickly commented, 'That's rubbish; I live under that tree for 10 years, and I have no energy left!'.

In Kissos, stop for lunch or dinner at **Taverna O Makris** (☎ 24260 31266), great for dolmadhes and *fasoladha*, or at **Taverna Klimataria** (☎ 24260 31214) for *hortopita* (pie made with wild greens) and potato cakes.

HOREFTO ΧΟΡΕΥΤΟ

Eight kilometres downhill from Zagora, Horefto is a low-key resort with palm trees and a long sandy beach. It's also the mythical home of Chiron, a roving centaur who healed the sick in the days when doctors still made house calls. The main beach is very decent, while isolated **Agia Saranda beach** fills a beautiful cove 2km south, with a simple domatia and taverna nearby.

Sleeping & Eating

Hotel Hagiati (☎ 24260 22405; www.pelion.com.gr/ hagiati.htm; s/d €40/50; **P** 🍴) Spacious tile-and-wood rooms, balconies and overhead fans make the reliable Hagiati good value. It's opposite the beach as you enter Horefto.

Maribou Hotel (☎ 24260 23710; www.marabouhotel .gr; s/d/ste €55/70/110; **P** 🍴 🖳) This comfortable hotel sits on a hillside 250m from the beach, visible from the verandah bar.

Taverna O Petros (☎ 24260 23585; mains €4-7) This reliable place serves up fine fish grills and a variety of vegie dishes (*ladhera* – fasting food; baked or stewed with plenty of olive oil), including the tasty local favourite, the *hortopita*.

Also recommended:

Domatia To Balkoni (☎ 24260 23260; s/d €50/60; 🍴 **P**) Palm trees, kitchenettes.

Taverna Ta Delfinia (24260 23585; mains €4-8) Popular for *mayirefta*.

AGIOS IOANNIS ΑΓΙΟΣ ΙΩΑΝΝΗΣ
pop 660

The once-sleepy port village of Agios Ioannis is now the busiest of the eastern coastal resorts, but there's still plenty of room. Small hotels, tavernas and pizzerias line the waterfront, and two sandy beaches lie just north (Plaka) and south (Papa Nero) of town, connected by a small wooden bridge.

Les Hirondelles Travel Agency (☎ 24260 31181; www.holidays-in-pelion.com.gr) arranges accommodation, car and motorbike rentals, and also organises hiking, boat, sea-kayaking and mountain-biking excursions.

Sleeping

You can expect the higher July and August rates quoted here to drop by at least 30% at other times.

Pension Katerina (☎ 24260 31159, 6945762183; s/d/f from €35/40/65; 🔆) A narrow lane off the waterfront opens to a cosy courtyard anchored by a lemon tree at this welcoming gem. Rooms are light, tidy and charming. Families will like the three apartments with kitchenettes.

Hotel Kelly (☎ 24260 31231; www.hotel-kelly.gr; s/d/tr incl breakfast €50/60/80; 🔆 P 🛜) Near the end of the waterfront, this modern Tuscan-red hotel has comfortable beach-side rooms, friendly service and the village's busiest lobby bar.

Anesis Hotel (☎ 24260 31123; www.hotelanesis.gr; s/d/tr incl breakfast €50/70/80; 🔆 🖳 🛜) Along with its appealing location away from the street, the comfortable Anesis sports spacious pastel-toned rooms, though bathrooms are smallish. Breakfast is served on a vine-shaded terrace overlooking the sea.

Sofokles Hotel (☎ 24260 31230; www.sofokleshotel.com; s/d incl breakfast from €65/100; P 🔆 🖳 🛜 🖳) The inviting and helpful Sofokles features smart, well-appointed rooms with wood and marble touches, small iron balconies and a vine-covered breakfast terrace opposite the beach.

Also recommended:

Camping ground (☎ 24260 31319; fax 24260 32159; camp sites per adult/tent €5/5) Got a 2009 makeover, south of the waterfront.

Hotel Kentrikon (☎ 24260 31232; www.bungalows-kentrikon.gr, in Greek; s/d/ste from €65/78/130; P 🔆 🖳 🛜 🖳) Nicely set back, excellent service.

Eating & Drinking

our pick Taverna Orea Ammoudia (☎ 24260 32126; mains €4-8) Spread out under a large plane tree at the end of Papa Nero beach, this efficient family taverna does excellent versions of oven-ready mains such as baked cod or chicken and potatoes, along with lamb grills and unusual salads such as *kritama* (tomatoes with sea herbs). A thatched bar serves up cool drinks and ice cream in summer.

Taverna Poseidonas (☎ 24260 31222; mains €4-8) The owners of Poseidonas are proud of their local reputation for serving only their own catch. In addition to the usual by-the-kilo offerings, you can sample oven-ready stand-bys such as *mousakas* and stuffed zucchini flowers (both €6) which change daily.

Taverna Akrogiali Apostolis (☎ 24260 31112; mains €5-10) Among the waterfront tavernas. Charming proprietor and host Apostolis serves up generous portions of taverna stand-bys such as lamb in lemon sauce, *vlita* (amaranth) and *spetsofaï* (sausage and pepper stew).

Also recommended:

Pizza Venezia (☎ 24260 31093; pizza €7-9) Snappy verandah pizzeria.

Lithos Bar (☎ 24260 32027) Open late for drinks, early for coffee.

DAMOUHARI & MOURESSI

ΝΤΑΜΟΥΧΑΡΗ & ΜΟΥΡΕΣΙ

Picturesque **Damouhari** is next to a rambling grove of olive trees that borders a pebble beach and protected cove that once shielded the hamlet from passing pirate ships. According to local lore, the village got its name from the expression *dos mou hari* (give me grace). The little church of **Agios Nikolaos** contains several fine frescoes. (Apostolis at the taverna next door keeps the key). Damouhari is also the starting point for a beautiful 4km **walk** to Fakistra Beach. Damouhari enjoyed brief fame from the 2008 movie, *Mama Mia!* (with Meryl Streep), which borrowed the secluded port for a couple of weeks of filming.

Nestled off the main road, 3km north of Tsangarada, is the mellow village of **Mouressi**, known for its cherries, chestnuts and *mouria* (mulberries). There are great views of the Aegean from the lime-tree shaded *plateia*.

Sleeping & Eating

Domatia Victoria (☎ 24260 49872; Damouhari; s/d €45/55; 🔆 🖳) One of two very decent domatia in Damouhari, this one has views of the bay.

our pick Old Silk Store (☎ 24260 49086, 6937156780; www.pelionet.gr; Mouressi; d from €65) This 19th-century neoclassical gem, with personality to spare, is a Mouressi landmark and features traditional-style rooms in a garden setting, with an available homemade breakfast of fresh-baked goodies and seasonal fruit (€10). British transplant Jill Sleeman runs the show, along with Mulberry Travel (same phone), which can take care of travel details, arrange cooking lessons, and organise guided walks in the Pelion, often accompanied by the resident donkey, Boy George.

Hotel Damouhari (☎ /fax 24260 49840; Damouhari; r from €85; **P** 🖭) You'll need to book well in advance for one of the quaint and creaky rooms – however, stop to check out the nautical antiques in the lobby, or to have a drink in the Kleopatra Miramar bar.

Taverna O Vangelis (☎ 24260 49609; Mouressi; mains €4-7.50) Hard-working cook, server and chatty host Vangelis has a loyal following for his good grills (pork chops, €6) and rich *spetsofaï* (€4.50).

Taverna Karagatsi (☎ 24260 49841; Damouhari; mains €4-9) Operated by the same family as at Hotel Damouhari, Karagatsi's flower-in-his-ear cook, Apostolis, serves up fine taverna standards, plus big Greek salads and tasty mezedhes such as *taramasalata,* all overlooking the tiny bay below.

Other good choices:

Taverna Bastounis (☎ 24260 49207; Damouhari; mains €4.50-8) Fresh fish always.

Taverna To Tavernaki (☎ 24260 49416; Mouressi; mains €5.50-9) Opposite the BP station.

TSANGARADA ΤΣΑΓΚΑΡΑΔΑ
pop 710

Tsangarada (tsang-ah-*rah*-dah), nestling in oak and plane forests, is a rambling and spread-out village comprising the four separate communities of Agio Taxiarhes, Agios Stefanos, Agia Kyriaki and Agia Paraskevi, the largest of the group and just north of the main Volos–Milies–Tsangarada road. The *plateia's* plane tree is said to be one of the largest and oldest in Greece. There is an ATM next to the post office, and next to that, a small **tourist office** (☎ 24260 48993; ❀ 10am-2pm) with maps and wi-fi.

Sights & Activities

ᴏᴜʀ ᴘɪᴄᴋ **Serpentine Organic Garden** (☎ 24260 49060; www.serpentin-garden.com; admission by donation) is a one-woman labour of love, the inspiration of Doris Schlepper, whose imagination has created a virtual museum of all things green and flowering, including rare trees and roses, along with sustainable vegie, berry and herb gardens. Doris offers one- to two-week bed-and-board volunteer internships, part of **World Wide Opportunities on Organic Farms** (WWOOF; www.wwoof.org) and opens to visitors by appointment.

Like much of the Pelion Peninsula, Tsangarada is prime **hiking** territory. Two relatively simple and unguided hikes begin nearby. From the square of **Agia Paraskevi**, it's two hours down to the small bay at Damouhari. And from the village of **Xourichti**, 4km south of Agia Paraskevi, a good cross-ridge path leads to the village of **Milies**, a hike of nearly three hours.

Sleeping & Eating

There are several domatia and roadside tavernas near Plateia Paraskevi and on the way to Mylopotamos.

Villa Ton Rodon (☎ 24260 49201; www.villatonrodon .gr, in english; Agia Paraskevi; s/d/tr incl breakfast €50/60/65; **P**) This tidy pension with balcony views is surrounded by the family fruit orchard, just 50m off the main road.

ᴏᴜʀ ᴘɪᴄᴋ **Lost Unicorn Hotel** (☎ 24260 49930; www .lostunicorn.com; Agia Paraskevi; s incl breakfast €60-70, d incl breakfast €90-110; **P** ⊠ 🖭) Persian carpets, slow-swirling fans and antique-outfitted rooms grace this elegant and well-appointed 19th-century mansion set in a beautiful glade. The Greek and English owners, Christos and Clare, keep things informal, and make a garden breakfast worthy of the scenery, complete with singing nightingales.

Taverna To Kalivi (☎ 24260 49578; mains €5-9) Look for the small wooden sign at the top of Plateia Taxiarhes to find this well-regarded old-fashioned taverna, known for meat stews, lamb grills with pasta, and wild greens in season.

MYLOPOTAMOS ΜΥΛΟΠΟΤΑΜΟΣ

Scenic Mylopotamos is divided by a rocky outcrop, with a natural tunnel connecting two small beautiful beaches. It's 7km along the road from Tsangarada's Agia Paraskevi.

Sleeping & Eating

Diakoumis Rooms (☎ 24260 49203; www.diakoumis.gr; s/ d/tr from €50/70/80; **P** ⊠ 🖭) Just 1km before the village and beach, genial owners Stathis and Athina have made the most of this dramatic cliff-side lodging. Light and airy stone-floored rooms have clear views of the bay and beyond, as well as four self-catering apartments (from €80).

Taverna Angelika (☎ 24260 49588; mains €5-9) This is a regular stop for many local Pelion residents who appreciate the good food and wine, not to mention the breezy view. Stuffed calamari, a generous Greek salad and plenty of local wine runs about €25 for two.

CENTRAL GREECE

CENTRAL GREECE

THE LITTLEST TRAIN

In 1895, a 13km railway line was built between Volos and Ano Lehonia. By 1903, the narrow-gauge line was extended to Milies, making the town a prosperous centre of commerce. **To Trenaki** (☎ 24210 24056; adult/child €12.90/8.50), the steam train that used to chug along this route, retired formally in 1971, but was revived in 1997 as a weekend and holiday tourist attraction. The popular four-carriage train leaves Ano Lehonia at 11am and returns around 5pm, leaving you time to stroll around Milies.

A restored Belgian coal-burning locomotive pulled the train when the route first reopened. But in 2000, a new diesel engine went into service after the train operators grew tired of following the smoke-belching original with a water tanker to put out the frequent grass fires started by airborne sparks. Despite the environmental upgrade, To Trenaki is still called *Moudzouris*, an affectionate term meaning 'the smudger'.

West-Central Pelion
VOLOS TO PINAKATES, VYZITSA & MILIES
ΒΟΛΟΣ ΠΡΟΣ ΠΙΝΑΚΑΤΕΣ, ΒΥΖΙΤΣΑ & ΜΗΛΙΕΣ

From Volos, the west-coast road heads south through the touristy villages of Agria and Ano Lehonia, where a branch road leads inland to Agios Vlasios, Pinakates, Vyzitsa and Milies, while the main road continues to neighbouring Kato Gatzea, Ano Gatzea and **Kala Nera**. After the tortuous and narrow roads of the eastern Pelion villages, this stretch of road is a blessing, and a great alternative to crowded Volos as a base for exploring the Pelion. The efficient **Hotel Nirvana** (☎ 24230 22205; www.hotel-restaurant-nirvana .com; d/tr incl breakfast from €50/60; 🍴 💻) is opposite the only decent beach on Kala Nera Bay.

Two nearby attractions merit a stop. The **Little Train of Pelion** begins its old-fashioned run at **Ano Lehonia** (see The Littlest Train, above). One of its quaint station stops is Ano Gatzea, home to the **Museum of the Olive** (☎ 24230 22009; www.mouseioelias.gr, in Greek; admission free; 🕗 8am-5pm), set in an old stone mansion with sparkling displays of tools, presses and storage vessels, plus a small shop.

PINAKATES ΠΙΝΑΚΑΤΕΣ
pop 100

An old plane tree anchors Plateia Agios Dimitrios, home to the church, two tavernas, a small fountain, ceramic shop and wood-oven bakery. Pristine Pinakates only acquired electricity in 1973, and from the looks of it, things haven't gotten out of hand.

Beautifully restored in 2007, **Hotel Ta Xelidonakia** (Little Swallows; ☎ 24230 86920; www.pinakates .com; d/tr incl breakfast €100/120; 🅿 💢 💻 📶 🔌) is a classic mansion that balances history and comfort in grand fashion. The verandah is anchored by a 3000L chestnut wine barrel.

Nearby **Taverna Drosia** (☎ 24230 86772; mains €4-8.50; 🕗 dinner) serves Pelion favourites such as baked goat and *spetsofaï*, with good local wine always on hand.

VYZITSA ΒΥΖΙΤΣΑ
pop 280

Between Pinakates and Milies, handsome Vyzitsa's cobbled pathways wind between traditional slate-roofed houses. To reach its shady central square and tavernas, walk up the cobbled path by Thetis Café.

Basic but comfortable, the old-fashioned **Thetis Hotel** (☎ 24230 86111; s/d incl breakfast from €35/45) is a stone pension, left of the car park, that's quiet and welcoming. The adjacent and rustic stone cafe serves breakfast on the terrace.

The well-managed **Hotel Stoikos** (☎ 24230 86406; www.stoikoshotel.com; s/d/tr from €50/70/90; 🅿 💢 📶) has a traditional look, especially with the beamed ceilings and stained glass of the spacious upper-floor rooms (great views). It's good value in pricey Vyzitsa.

A 50m path from the *plateia* leads to **Rooms Aphrodite Dimou** (☎ 24230 86484; info@aphrodete.gr; s/ d/tr incl breakfast from €60/80/100; 💻), a private lodging with just three rooms, but each light and well cared for by owner Aphrodite.

The pick of Vyzitsa's eateries is **Georgaras Restaurant** (☎ 24230 86359; mains €5-11), with a mountain menu featuring stews and rich sauces, including stuffed pork with orange sauce, and *kouneli* (rabbit in red-wine sauce).

MILIES ΜΗΛΙΕΣ
pop 640

Milies (mih-lih-*ess*) played a major role in the intellectual and cultural awakening that led to Greek independence. It was also the birthplace of Anthimos Gazis (1761–1828), who organised the revolutionary forces in Thessaly in 1821, and toured the mountain villages of the Pelion inspiring local resistance and leadership.

On the central square is **Agios Taxiarhes**, a church with beautiful 16th-century frescoes. Just 100m beyond the central square, **Milies Museum** (☎ 24230 86602; admission free; ☑ 10am-2.30pm & 6.30-9pm) houses a display of local crafts and costumes. Nearby **Library of Milies** (☎ 24230 86936; ☑ 8am-2pm) is home to hand-written books from the time of the War of Independence, but keeps things modern with free internet use for visitors.

Sleeping & Eating

O Palios Stathmos (Old Station; ☎ 24230 86425; www .paliosstathmos.com; s/d incl breakfast from €40/60) Nestled among a grove of plane trees, this comfortable pension recalls a bygone era, but only from the balconied rooms facing the narrow-gauge rail station.

Korbas Bakery (☎ 24230 86219; pies €1.50-4) Gastronomic highlights of Milies include the scrumptious *tyropsomo* and *eliopsomo* (olive bread) at this popular bakery on the main road.

Anna Na Ena Milo (☎ 24230 86889; snacks €2-4; ☑ 9am-10pm) The name of this cosy crêpe-and-jam cafe derives from a famous children's reader called *Anna Have an Apple*.

Taverna Panorama (☎ 24230 86128; mains €5-7) About 100m up from the central square (and nearly covered in climbing roses), this cosy grill serves up Pelion favourites such as zucchini pie, pork chops in wine, *spetsofaï* and *kouneli*.

South Pelion

SOUTH TO TRIKERI

The southern part of the Pelion has a wide-open feel to it, with sparsely forested hills and countless olive groves. Before heading inland after Kala Nera, the road skirts the little coastal fishing village of Afissos, winds upwards through to the attractive farming community of Argalasti, and then forks – the left fork continues inland, the right goes to the coastal resorts of Horto and Milina. From Milina the road branches southeast towards Platanias and southwest to Trikeri.

HORTO & MILINA ΧΟΡΤΟ & ΜΗΛΙΝΑ

Milina is the larger of these two coastal villages, and sees many package tourists. Both are on a

quiet part of the peninsula with pristine water and a few inviting pebble beaches. Resourceful George Fleris of **Milina Holidays** (☎ 24230 65020; www.milina-holidays.com) on the waterfront can help with accommodation, as well as arranging bike and boat rentals, plus day cruises to nearby Palio Trikeri (adult/child €37/20). Walks to inland mountain villages such as Promiri or Lefkos have lately benefitted from the community-based efforts of the 'Friends of the Kalderimi', dedicated to maintaining and restoring these historic cobblestone paths.

And if you're one of those people who think nostalgia isn't what it used to be, turn your dial to the **Old Radio Museum** (☎ 69703 74922; admission free; ☑ daily May 16-Sep 14, Sat & Sun Sep 15-May 15) in the village of **Lefkos**, 5km east of Milina, to check out one collector's pre-digital love affair with the original 'wireless'.

Look for the family-friendly bungalows at **Hotel Leda** (☎ 24230 65696; Horto; s/d/f from €40/50/80; P ♨ ⊚ ⊛) with beach bar and pool. **Ouzerie Vangelis** (☎ 24230 65465; Milina), one of a cluster of tavernas next to Milina's main jetty, is excellent for seafood mezedhes and *tsipouro*.

TRIKERI ΤΡΙΚΕΡΙ
pop 1180

There is an end-of-the-world feel about this part of the Pelion, as the road from Milina to Trikeri becomes more and more desolate. Donkeys outnumber cars in Trikeri, and the residents pride themselves on their tradition as seafarers, fighters against the Turks in the War of Independence, and upholders of traditional customs and dress. The week following Easter is one of constant revelry as dancing takes place every day and women try to outdo each other in their local costume finery.

AGIA KYRIAKI ΑΓΙΑ ΚΥΡΙΑΚΗ

This is the last stop on the Pelion Peninsula, a steep 2km drive off the main road, or a quick 1km walk down a cobblestone path. This fishing village sees few tourists, and the bright, orange-coloured boats are put to good use by a hard-working population of around 200. There is one hotel, **Agia Kyriaki Hotel** (☎ 69787 71831; s/d €35/40) and three fish tavernas in a row, facing the opposite shores of Evia.

PALIO TRIKERI ΠΑΛΙΟ ΤΡΙΚΕΡΙ

If you really must go that one step further to get away from it all, then head for this little island with a year-round population of 13, just off the coast; it's often called Nisos (Island) for short. To reach tiny Nisos from the fishing village of **Alogoporos**, a five-minute boat ride away, telephone Nikos at **Taverna Diavlos** (☎ 24230 55210, 6976851056) on Nisos. There are a couple of domatia at the taverna. Wild camping is possible as well, but the main activities on Palio Trikeri are explaining to locals why you're there, and then explaining to yourself why you're leaving.

PLATANIAS ΠΛΑΤΑΝΙΑΣ

Platanias (plah-tah-nih-*ahs*) was a popular resort until the hydrofoil service stopped in 2001, allowing it to return to its low-key roots. There's a good sand-and-pebble beach, a camping ground and a few tavernas and domatia.

From roughly early June through to the end of August, an excursion boat, the **Africana** (☎ 24230 71273), makes daily runs between Platanias and the island of Skiathos (adult/child one way €20/10). The 100-passenger boat departs Platanias at 9.30am and returns at 5.30pm.

TRIKALA ΤΡΙΚΑΛΑ
pop 50,340

The first thing you might notice about Trikala (*tree*-kah-lah) are the bicycles. Half the town, young and old, seems to be pedalling around, and in no particular hurry either. Every September the town declares a two-day holiday from cars, just to keep the free-wheeling spirit alive. Roughly half-way between Karditsa and Kalambaka, Trikala was once ancient Trikki, and home to Asclepius, the god of healing. A statue honouring the mythic doctor stands on a small bridge by the main square. Trikala is an attractive and bustling agricultural centre, and serves as a gateway to the South Pindos mountain resorts to the west.

Orientation

Bisecting the town is the Litheos River, really a landscaped channel with a narrow bridge separating the two squares – the plane-tree-shaded Plateia Iroön Polytehniou on the northeast bank, and rambling Plateia Riga Fereou on the southwest bank. Trikala's main thoroughfare, Asklipiou, begins here as a pedestrian precinct and then runs south 700m to the train station.

Information

Six banks with ATMs ring the squares on either side of the river. Most cafes offer free wi-fi around Plateia Riga Fereou.

Café Neo Kosmos (New World; ☎ 24310 72591; Vyronos 18; per hr €2; ☺ 8am-midnight) Has wi-fi and several fast internet computers.
Police station (☎ 24310 76100; Sidiras Merarhias)
Post office (Sarafi 13; ☺ 8am-8pm) Next to Plateia Riga Fereou.
Poulianiti Travel Services (☎ 24310 36140; gp travel@otenet.gr; Vyronos 37) Can help with accommodation, travel bookings and car hire.
Trekking Hellas (☎ 24310 87964; Vyronos 37) The office shares space with Poulianiti Travel Services and offers help with area tours, including rafting and hiking outings.

Sights

It is worth a wander up to the gardens surrounding the restored Byzantine **Fortress of Trikala**. An adjacent cafe-bar overlooks the town. Walk 400m up Sarafi from the central square and look for the sign pointing right. Just before the turn for the fortress are the remains of the **Sanctuary of Asclepius**. More interesting is the old Turkish quarter of **Varousi**, just east of the fortress. It's a fascinating area of narrow streets and fine old houses with overhanging balconies. At the corner of Anagiron and Virvou, peek at the fine murals within the 16th-century church of **Agioi Anargiri**. Another 200m up the hill from Varousi, you'll find the **Chapel of Profitis Ilias**.

On the other side of town is the **Koursoum Tzami**, built in the 16th century by Sinan Pasha, the same architect who built the Blue Mosque in İstanbul. The mosque was restored in the mid-1990s with EU funding. From Plateia Riga Fereou, follow the river for 350m south. The mosque is on your right.

Sleeping

Hotel Panellinion (☎ 24310 73545; www.hotel panellinion.com; Plateia Riga Fereou 2; s/d incl breakfast €40/60; ✲ �) Dating from 1914, this restored and spacious neoclassical hotel is just opposite the river and filled with traditional touches, though the classiest decorations occupy the high-ceilinged hallways.

Hotel Ntina (Dina; ☎ 24310 74777; www.ntinashotel.gr; cnr Asklipiou & Karanasiou; s/d/tr €40/50/60; ✲ ✲ ☐ ☰ ☰) This smart and airy business hotel's efficient charms include comfy beds, satellite TV and breakfast to order (€5). Top-floor rooms overlook the town and river.

Eating

The cafe life in Trikala is centred on the northern end of Asklipiou and across the river in the old Manavika district. For quick eats, head to Plateia Kitrilaki, where you'll find good €2 souvlakia plates.

Kebob Karthoutsos (☎ 24310 38084; Ioulietas Adam 5; mains €3-6) It's worth waiting for a table at this busy eatery near Plateia Riga Fereou, where a table full of lean pork souvlaki, *horta* (wild greens), feta and cold beer or local wine runs about €10 per head.

Taverna Palia Istoria (Old Story; ☎ 24310 77627; Ypsilanti 3; mains €3.50-8) This well-regarded alleyway eatery in the Manavika area puts a slight twist on tradition with the likes of *feta psiti* (baked feta with tomatoes, potatoes, ham and grilled onions), a bargain at €4.50, and pork chops with a sweet pepper sauce (€6.50).

Two snappy Manavika *tsipouradhika* worth a taste are **Taverna Diachroniko** (☎ 24310 21480; Ipsilanti; mains €3-7) and **Taverna To Diplo** (☎ 24310 72722; mains €3-7) next to Palia Istoria.

Drinking & Entertainment

On weekend nights, the idea in Trikala seems to be to tank up on coffee along Asklipiou until midnight, then cross the bridge to the humming Manavika district for mojitos, mezedhes and music. This three-block maze of narrow passageways and outdoor tables jumps with lamp-lit music bars, small *ouzerie*, and all-night cafes. For authentic Greek *rembetika* (blues), follow the locals to **Aparhes Bar** (☎ 24310 38486; Manavika; ☽ Fri & Sat), along the riverbank. At **1900 Coffee Store** (☎ 24310 28274; Ermou 11, Manavika), look for the old coffee roaster at the entrance and the post-1900 hissing espresso machine within.

Getting There & Away

BUS

Buses depart from Trikala's **KTEL bus station** (☎ 24310 73130; Rizargio), 5km south of town. A free shuttle runs from the **ticket office** (cnr Othonos & Garivaldi).

TRAIN

From Trikala **train station** (☎ 24310 27214) there are trains to Kalambaka (€1.30, 15 minutes, eight daily), Larisa (€4.60, one hour, two daily), Athens (IC €26, four hours, one daily; normal €11, five hours, one daily) and Thessaloniki (€11, 2½ hours, one daily).

AROUND TRIKALA

Pyli Πύλη

About 18km southwest of Trikala is the village of Pyli, 'gate' in Greek, opening to a spectacu-

BUSES FROM TRIKALA

Destination	Duration	Fare	Frequency
Athens	4½hr	€24	7 daily
Elati	1hr	€3	1-2 daily
Ioannina	2½hr	€13.10	2 daily
Kalambaka	30min	€1.90	hourly
Lamia	2hr	€8.60	7 daily
Larisa	1hr	€5.70	hourly
Neraidochori	1½hr	€4.50	1 daily
Pertouli	1¼hr	€4.30	1 daily
Thessaloniki	3hr	€16.50	6 daily
Volos	2¼hr	€12.30	4 daily

lar gorge and one of Greece's more inviting wilderness areas.

At the gorge's entrance is the 13th-century **Church of Porta Panagia**, with an impressive pair of mosaic icons and a marble iconostasis. To reach the church, cross the footbridge over the river and turn left.

The 16th-century **Moni Agiou Vissarion** stands on a slope of Mt Koziakas, 5km from Pyli. To get here, cross the bridge over the river and follow the sign uphill for 500m.

Elati & Around Ελάτη

With your own transport, you can explore the once-remote mountainous areas west and north of Elati, including the beautiful **Tria Potamia** (Three Rivers) area. A scenic half-day circular drive (via the Alexiou Bridge) brings you to Kalambaka. Forty-nine kilometres southwest of Elati, towards Arta, is the controversial **Mesohora Dam** (see A Fight for the River, p272). About 10km of this scenic road is unsealed, but is passable by 2WD.

From Pyli, the 40km road north to the village of **Neraidochori** climbs steadily through breathtaking alpine scenery, passing the villages of Elati and Pertouli. **Elati** is something of a hill station for Trikala and has grown into a thriving resort with 1000 beds. It was called Tierna before the Germans burned it to the ground for harbouring Greek resistance fighters in WWII. Smaller **Pertouli**, 10km up the road, has resisted Elati's expansion. The University of Thessaloniki maintains a forest research station there.

ACTIVITIES

Kayaking enthusiasts come to the beautiful Tria Potamia (Three Rivers) area, 30km north of Mesohora, to ride the waters of the Aheloös

CENTRAL GREECE

A FIGHT FOR THE RIVER

Conservationists, industrialists and villagers are still fighting over the government's construction of a 135m-high hydroelectric dam near Mesohora village on the upper Aheloös River in the South Pindos range, part of a larger plan to divert the water eastward to satisfy the agricultural needs of the plain of Thessaly. The government built the dam first, did the environmental studies second. As a result, the EU has declined to fund the project, Greek appellate courts have denied permits, and the finished dam sits empty.

If allowed to begin, the ecological effects would be felt as far south as the wetland wildlife sanctuaries around Messolongi, while the nearby village of Mesohora would be inundated. In Greek mythology, Aheloös is god of the river – his mother Tethys is crying now because, as one local put it, 'Her son is being cut into pieces for money and power'.

River. The popular sport attracts white-water jockeys from across Europe. **Hiking** trails criss-cross the region; a popular hiking path begins at the end of Pertouli and reaches a summit at Mt Neraida (2074m). For kayaking, canoeing or mountain-biking excursions, contact Thanasis Samouris, the Trikala representative of **Trekking Hellas** (☎ 2431087964, 6977451953; gptravel@ otenet). Half-day trips around Mt Koziakas begin at €20, and a full day of river rafting runs €50.

The small but popular **Pertouli Skiing Centre** (☎ 24340 91385; www.snowreport.gr/pertouli), on the slopes of Mt Koziakas (1340m), sports three lifts with four runs, including slalom and beginner slopes. Skis and snowboards can be hired (€10 to €15 per day).

SLEEPING & EATING

Most of Elati's hotels and tavernas are bunched up, probably to keep warm.

Hotel Koziakas (☎ 24340 71270; fax 24340 71106; Elati; s/d incl breakfast from €35/50) Try this rambling hotel for wood-beamed ambience and massively comfortable rooms. The lobby restaurant features boar chops and venison stew among its gamey offerings (€6 to €9).

Hotel Papanastasiou (☎ 24340 71280; fax 24340 71153; Elati; s/d/studio incl breakfast from €45/70/110) More woodsy rooms await at this place with a meaty taverna on the premises, specialising in grilled liver and other organ delicacies (€3 to €7).

Taverna To Limeri Tou Vassili (☎ 24340 91200; mains €6-10) Nestled on the right side of the road just before Pertouli, this welcoming taverna is known for wild mushrooms, traditional bean soup along with the ever-turning grilled meats.

METEORA ΜΕΤΕΩΡΑ

Meteora (meh-*teh*-o-rah) is an extraordinary place, and one of the most visited in all of Greece. The massive pinnacles of smooth rock are ancient and yet could be the setting for a futuristic science fiction tale. The monasteries atop them add to this strange and beautiful landscape.

Each monastery is built around a central courtyard surrounded by monks' cells, chapels and a refectory. In the centre of each courtyard is the *katholikon* (main church). Meteora is listed as a World Heritage Site.

An excellent map (available at the newsstand in Kalambaka) is the *Panoramic Map with Geology Meteora*. A detailed booklet and map in English, *The Footpaths of Meteora* by Andonis Kalogirou (Kritiki Publishers), is available from the same shop.

History

The name Meteora derives from the Greek adjective *meteoros*, which means 'suspended in the air'. The word 'meteor' is from the same root, and one look at this majestic feat of nature will convince you; see The Meteora: Geology of a Rock Forest, p276.

From the 11th century, hermit monks lived in the scattered caverns of Meteora. By the 14th century, the Byzantine power of the Roman Empire was on the wane and Turkish incursions into Greece were on the rise, so monks began to seek safe havens away from the bloodshed. The inaccessibility of the rocks of Meteora made them an ideal retreat.

The earliest monasteries were reached by climbing removable ladders. Later, windlasses were used so monks could be hauled up in nets. A story goes that when curious visitors asked how frequently the ropes were replaced, the monks' stock reply was 'when the Lord lets them break'.

These days, access to the monasteries is by steps that were hewn into the rocks in the 1920s, and by a convenient back road. Some windlasses can still be seen (you can have a good look at one at Agia Triada), but they are now used for hauling up provisions – and an occasional Greek Orthodox tourist-priest from abroad.

Sights
MONASTERIES

The monasteries are linked by asphalt roads, but it's possible to explore the area on foot on the old and once-secret *monopatia* (monk paths). Before setting out, decide on a route. If you start early, you can see several *mones* (monasteries), perhaps all, in one day. The main road surrounding the entire Meteora complex of rocks and monasteries is about 10km; with your own transport, you can easily visit them all. Every day, a bus (€1.20, 20 minutes) departs from Kalambaka and Kastraki at 9am, and returns at 1pm. That's enough time to explore three monasteries – Moni Megalou Meteorou, Moni Varlaam and Moni Agias Varvaras Rousanou. Perhaps the best route is to take the bus one way to the top and then work your way down and around on foot, finishing at either Moni Agiou Nikolaou on the Kastraki side, or at Moni Agia Triada on the Kalambaka side.

Walking and climbing around the rocks cans be thirsty work, but there are mobile canteens selling drinks and snacks at some monastery car parks. Also double-check opening hours; the monks are an independent lot, and no two monasteries keep exactly the same hours.

Entry to each monastery is €2, and dress codes apply: no bare shoulders are allowed, men must wear trousers and women must be covered to below the knee (baggy bottoms with elastic waistbands are generally provided).

Moni Agiou Nikolaou (Monastery of St Nikolaou Anapafsa; ☎ 24320 22375; ☽ 9am-3.30pm Sat-Thu Apr-Oct) is the nearest *moni* to Kastraki, just 2km from the village square to the steep steps leading to the *moni*. The monastery was built in the 15th century, and the exceptional frescoes in its *katholikon* were painted by the monk Theophanes Strelizas from Crete. Especially beautiful is the 1527 fresco *The Naming of Animals by Adam in Paradise*.

The best known of the monasteries, **Moni Megalou Meteorou** (Grand Meteora Monastery, Metamorphosis; ☎ 24320 22278; ☽ 9am-5pm Wed-Mon Apr-Oct, 9am-4pm Thu-Mon Nov-Mar) is an imposing form built on the highest rock in the valley, 613m above sea level. Founded by St

Athanasios in the 14th century, it became the richest and most powerful monastery thanks to the Serbian emperor Symeon Uros, who turned all his wealth over to the monastery and became a monk. Its *katholikon* has a magnificent 12-sided central dome. Its striking series of frescoes entitled *Martyrdom of Saints* depicts the graphic persecution of Christians by the Romans.

About 700m down from Moni Megalou, **Moni Varlaam** (☎ 24320 22277; ☽ 9am-4pm Wed-Mon Apr-Oct, Thu-Mon Nov-Mar) has a small museum, an original rope-basket (until the 1930s the method for hauling up provisions and monks), and fine late-Byzantine frescoes by Frangos Kastellanos. The mural *The Blessed Sisois at the Tomb of Alexander the Great* shows the great conqueror as a humble skeleton. Look just above the door, past the candles.

For a panoramic break, visit the rambling **Psaropetra** lookout, 300m east of the signposted fork northeast of Moni Varlaam.

Access to **Moni Agias Varvaras Rousanou** (☎ 24320 22649; ☽ 9am-6pm Thu-Tue Apr-Oct, 9am-4pm Nov-Mar) is via a small wooden bridge. The beautiful coloured-glass-illuminated *katholikon* is the highlight here, with superb frescoes of the *Resurrection* (on your left entering) and *Transfiguration* (on your right). The imposing steep structure of Rousanou is itself a stunning accomplishment, and is today home to an order of 15 nuns. If you're there near closing, listen for the call to vespers (see Harmony at Rousanou, p275).

Of all the monasteries, **Moni Agias Triados** (Holy Trinity Monastery; ☎ 24320 22220; ☽ 9am-5pm Fri-Wed Apr-Oct, 10am-3pm Nov-Mar) has the most remote feel about it, plus the longest approach. It was featured in the 1981 James Bond film *For Your Eyes Only*. The views here are extraordinary, and the small 17th-century *katholikon* is beautiful, in particular the *Judgement of Pilate* and the *Hospitality of Abraham*. A well-marked 1km *monopati* leads back to Kalambaka.

After the austere Moni Agias Triados, **Moni Agiou Stefanou** (☎ 24320 22279; ☽ 9am-1.30pm & 3.30-5.30pm Tue-Sun Apr-Oct, 9.30am-1pm & 3-5pm Nov-Mar) resembles a return to civilisation, with efficient nuns selling religious souvenirs and DVDs of Meteora. Among the exhibits in the museum is an exquisite embroidered picture of Christ on his *epitafios* (bier). The monastery is at the very end of the road, 1.5km beyond Agias Triados.

METEORA, KALAMBAKA & KASTRAKI

0 ———————— 500 m
0 ———————— 0.3 miles

INFORMATION
All Time Café..............................1 A5
Hollywood Café-Bar......................2 C6
Hospital....................................3 B6
Newsstand..................................4 B6
Post Office.................................5 C6
Tourist Information Office................6 B6
Tourist Police.............................7 B6

SIGHTS & ACTIVITIES
Adhrakhti..................................8 B5
Agios Andonios............................9 B5
Church of the Assumption of the
  Virgin Mary...........................10 C5
Doupiani Rock............................11 A4
Moni Agias Triados......................12 C5
Moni Agias Varvaras Rousanou........13 C4
Moni Agiou Nikolaou....................14 B3
Moni Agiou Stefanou....................15 D5
Moni Megalou Meteorou.................16 B3
Moni Varlaam.............................17 B3
Morning Market...................(see 41)
Psaropetra Lookout.....................18 C3

SLEEPING
Alsos House...............................19 C5
Boufidis Camping.........................20 A4
Doupiani House...........................21 A4
Guest House Elena........................22 C5
Hotel Kastraki...........................23 A5
Hotel Meteora............................24 B6
Hotel Tsikeli............................25 A5
Koka Roka Rooms & Taverna...........26 C5
Monastiri Guest House..................27 C6
Rooms Ziogas Vasiliki..................28 A5
Thalia Guest House......................29 B5
Vrachos Camping.........................30 A6

EATING
Champion Supermarket..................31 C6
Pizzaland.................................32 C6
Taverna Gardenia........................33 A5
Taverna Meteora Vavitsos..............34 A5
Taverna Panellinion.....................35 B6
Taverna Paradisos.......................36 B6
Taverna To Paramithi...................37 B6
Taverna Tou Zioga.......................38 A5

ENTERTAINMENT
ABG Café-Bar............................39 A5

TRANSPORT
Bus Stop..................................40 A5
Bus Stop for Meteora & Kastraki......41 B6
Central KTEL Bus Station...............42 B6
Hobby Shop...............................43 B6

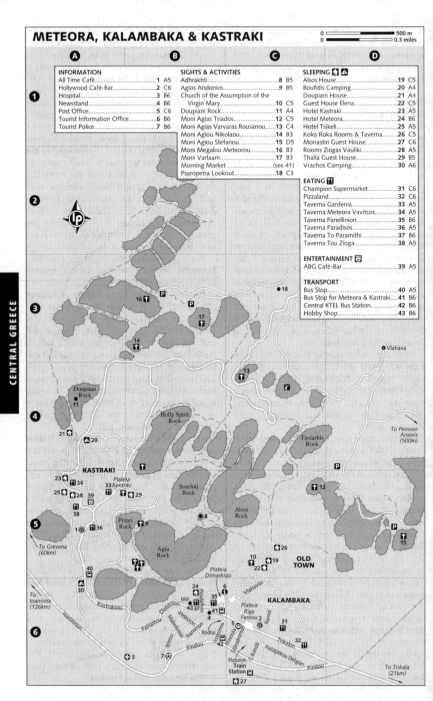

CENTRAL GREECE

HARMONY AT ROUSANOU *Michael Clark*

The monks and nuns who live atop the Meteora are gracious, but often appear solemn in contrast to the steady stream of pilgrims and tourists.

But not Siglitiki, one of the nuns who live, work and worship at Moni Agias Varvaras Rousanou (p273), one of the most striking of the monasteries. Her duties range from caring for the fine frescoes in the beautiful *katholikon* to managing a small museum shop. One woman asked Siglitiki if she would continue living at the convent for a long time. She laughed, saying, 'Yes, I hope so,' then, pointing up, quickly added, 'unless He decides otherwise!' Siglitiki chatted with one visiting family, pleased to see a teenage brother and sister. 'You don't often see children this age still travelling with their parents!' As dusk approached, she announced that it was time for *talando*, a word meaning harmony, but also describing a wooden board and mallet used to tap out an ancient rhythm that calls the faithful to prayer.

Siglitiki invited the daughter to grasp the mallet, and together they tapped out a silent measure in the air, careful not to strike the board, but smiling and laughing throughout. She paused to explain the word, 'something that moves in ta-lan-do, like harmony'.

As the family was leaving, she asked them to wait, returning quickly with a gift of *loukoumi*, a traditional Greek sweet flavoured with anise. Then she turned to tap out the *talando*. The visit was over, but a simple harmony lingered, evoking the spirit of the Meteora.

Activities

ROCK CLIMBING

Meteora has been a mecca for European rock climbers for several years. Climbers of various skill levels can choose routes from more than 100 peaks and towers with names such as the Tower of the Holy Ghost, the Great Saint, the Devil's Tower, the Corner of Madness and the Iron Edge.

There are about 700 routes in all, covering 120 sandstone towers of the Meteora. The style is clean or traditional face climbing, and rates III or IV on the UIAA international scale. Best times weather-wise are mid-March to mid-June and mid-August to mid-November.

A typical climb averages three hours, and costs start from €40 per person, depending on routes and the degree of difficulty. Most climbs reach heights between 90m and 200m. A beginner's route takes about two hours on Doupiani Rock. (All equipment is included in prices, including harness, shoes and helmet.)

There are two excellent climbing guides in Kastraki, both friends and both experienced. Contact either licensed mountain guide **Lazaros Botelis** (☎ 24320 79165, 6948043655; meteora@nolimits .com.gr; Kastraki) or mountaineering instructor **Kostas Liolos** (☎ 6972457582; kliolios@kalampaka.com; Kalambaka). For detailed information and graded routes, check out www.kalampaka.com.

WALKING

The centre and heart of Meteora is considered the **Adhrakhti**, or obelisk, a striking column visible from anywhere in Kastraki. A 1km butt-kicker path up the gully will deposit you there in about 20 minutes from Kastraki's central square.

Nearby, on the east-facing side of the Pixari rock face, closer to Kastraki, look for the cave-chapel of **Agiou Andonios**. To the left of the chapel, in the hollows and cavities of the rock face, are the **Askitiria** (cave hermitages), complete with hanging ladders and nesting doves. The Askitiria were occupied until the early 20th century by solitary monks, and they remain a testament to the original spirit of Meteora.

KALAMBAKA ΚΑΛΑΜΠΑΚΑ
pop 8140

Kalambaka, the gateway to Meteora, is almost entirely modern, having been burned to the ground by the Nazis in WWII. It takes at least a day to see all of the monasteries of Meteora, so you'll need to spend the night either in Kalambaka or the village of Kastraki (p277).

Orientation

Plateia Dimarhiou is the main square in town, anchored by a large fountain. Kalambaka's other large square is Plateia Riga Fereou – Trikalon connects the two. The bus station is on Ikonomou.

Information

Six banks with ATMs surround the central Plateia Riga Fereou on Trikalon. There is also a currency-exchange window next to the post office.

THE METEORA: GEOLOGY OF A ROCK FOREST

The jutting pinnacles and cliffs of the Meteora were once sediments of an inland sea. About 10 million years ago vertical tectonic movements pushed the entire region out of the sea at a sloping angle. The same tectonic movements caused the flanking mountains to move closer, exerting extreme pressure on the hardened sedimentary deposits. The Meteora developed netlike fissures and cracks. The weathering and erosion that followed formed the towering outcrops of rock that now vault heavenwards. The rocks were conglomerates of many types: limestone, marble, serpentinite and metamorphic, interspersed with layers of sand and shale.

By the dawn of human civilisation, the rocks had weathered and eroded into fantastic shapes; the sandstone and shale washed away, isolating blocks of rock and cliffs. Where erosion was less extreme, caves and overhangs appeared in the rock face.

As early as the 11th century AD, these awesome natural caves had become the solitary abodes of hermit monks. Eventually, 24 monasteries were built on these pinnacles. Today, six are active religious sites, occupied by monks or nuns and visited by the faithful and curious alike.

Hollywood Café-bar (Map p274; ☎ 24320 24964; Trikalon 67; per hr €2; ☽ 9am-1am) Internet access.

Hospital (Map p274; ☎ 24320 22222; Pindou)

Newsstand (Map p274; ☎ 24320 24667; cnr Ioanninon & Patriarhou Dimitriou; ☽ 9am-8pm) Maps, books and international press.

Post office (Map p274; Trikalon 24; ☽ 7.30am-2pm Mon-Fri)

Tourist Information Office (Map p274; ☎ 24320 77734; Plateia Dimarhiou; ☽ 8am-9pm Mon-Fri, 10am-4pm Sat & Sun) Maps and town advice, opposite the fountain.

Tourist police (Map p274; ☎ 24320 76100; cnr Ipirou & Pindou)

Sights & Activities

First-time visitors to Kalambaka will be amazed at the vertical rocks that guard the northern edge of the town. Apart from the rocks, it's worth finding your way to the seventh-century Byzantine cathedral, the **Church of the Assumption of the Virgin Mary** (Map p274; admission €1.50; ☽ 9am-1pm & 3-5pm), a three-aisle basilica with superb frescoes dating to the 14th century. There is a bustling **morning market** (Map p274) every Friday, next to the fountain and bus stop.

Sleeping

Rooms are plentiful in Kalambaka, though it's best to avoid noisy Trikalon.

Koka Roka Rooms & Taverna (Map p274; ☎ 24320 24554; kokaroka@yahoo.com; Kanari 21; s/d €25/40; P ⬜ ☎) Fringed by mulberry trees in a tranquil spot below the rocks, family-run Koka Roka is an institution among travellers, with five clean and simple rooms over a small taverna with a fireplace where lamb is grilled. Generous breakfasts are available (€2 to €4.50).

ourpick Alsos House (Map p274; ☎ 24320 24097; www.alsoshouse.gr; Kanari 5; s/d/f incl breakfast €30/40/70; P ⬝ ⬝ ☎) Next to Koka Roka, the well-managed and very comfortable Alsos House has a well-stocked communal kitchen, laundry, wide views of the rocks, and owner Yiannis Karakantas is a wealth of information about the area.

Guest House Elena (Map p274; ☎ 24320 77789; www.elenaguesthouse.gr; Kanari 3; s/d/tr incl breakfast from €35/50/75; P ⬝ ⬜ ☎) Tastefully adorned with period furnishings, this inviting five-room bed and breakfast is immaculate. Three rooms include a Jacuzzi bath. English, Italian and French are spoken.

Monastiri Guest House (Map p274; ☎ 24320 23952; www.monastiri-guesthouse.gr; s/d/tr/ste incl breakfast €50/60/70/100; P ⬝ ⬝ ⬜ ☎) Opposite the railway station, this converted stone mansion is a delightful addition to Kalambaka, with colourful decorations, long poster-beds and light and airy bathrooms. The handsome wood-and-stone lobby sports a fireplace and bar.

Other good options:

Hotel Meteora (Map p274; ☎ 24320 22367; gekask@otenet.gr; Ploutarhou 14; s/d incl breakfast €25/30; P ⬝ ⬜) On a quiet cul-de-sac below the rocks.

Pension Arsenis (Off Map p274; ☎ 24320 23500; www.arsenis-meteora.gr; s/d/tr/f €30/40/48/55; P ⬝) Quiet hillside location, plus goat bells.

Eating

ourpick Taverna To Paramithi (Map p274; ☎ 24320 24441; Patriarhou Dimitriou 14; mains €4-9) Along with very good grills and fresh pasta, owner-cooks Makis and Eleni bring in fresh seafood daily from the coast. Roasted *gavros* (anchovies,

€5.50) are an unusual speciality, along with lamb ribs (€8.50) and *roka* (rocket lettuce) salad (€3.50). A few local musicians often end the night here, with guitar or bouzouki in hand (and possibly a glass of the tasty house wine).

Taverna Panellinion (Map p274; ☎ 24320 24735; Plateia Dimarhiou; mains €5-9) Panellinion serves first-rate mezedhes such as roasted feta, and fine versions of traditional dishes such as *pastitsio* (spaghetti and meat bake) and chicken in lemon sauce. Dishes always feature fresh local ingredients, resulting in a recent culinary award for this popular eatery opposite the fountain.

For quick eats and *gyros* (rotisserie-cooked meat skewers, usually served with pitta bread), roam the block south of Plateia Riga Fereou. The best pizza gets sliced at **Pizzaland** (Map p274; ☎ 24320 72135; Trikalon 93; pizza €7-9).

Self-caterers can opt for **Champion Supermarket** (Map p274; ☎ 24320 78503; ☼ 8am-8pm Mon-Sat), which is well-stocked with fresh produce and more.

Getting There & Away
BUS
Kalambaka's **Central KTEL bus station** (Map p274; ☎ 24320 22432; Ikonomou) is 50m down from the main square and fountain, and the arrival/departure point for Trikala bus connections. Note: travellers to Delphi should go via Lamia (not Larissa), taking the 9am bus, changing in Lamia to the 12.45pm Amfissa/Delphi bus, arriving by 3.30pm.

TRAIN
Trains depart from the Kalambaka **train station** (☎ 24320 22451). Trains to Thessaloniki and Volos change at Paliofarsalos.

Getting Around
Buses for Kastraki (€1.20) leave about every 45 minutes from the Plateia Dimarhiou fountain, and on weekends, two of these (8.20am and 1.20pm Saturday and Sunday) continue on to Moni Megalou Meteorou. But note that

TRAINS FROM KALAMBAKA

Destination	Duration	Fare	Frequency
Athens (normal/IC)	5½hr/ 4½hr	€14.60/ 24.30	2/2 daily
Thessaloniki (normal)	4hr	€12.10	3 daily
Volos	1½hr	€6	2 daily

BUSES FROM KALAMBAKA

Destination	Duration	Fare	Frequency
Athens	5hr	€25	7 daily
Ioannina	2½hr	€11.20	3 daily
Lamia	2hr	€10.50	7 daily
Metsovo	1½hr	€6.20	3 daily
Thessaloniki	3½hr	€17.50	6 daily
Trikala	30min	€1.90	hourly
Volos	2½hr	€14.20	4 daily

on weekdays the Meteora-bound buses depart from the KTEL station (9am and 1pm Monday to Friday).

Taxis (opposite the fountain) go to Kastraki (€3) and all the monasteries (for example, Moni Megalou Meteorou for €8). Some drivers speak English, German or French, and you arrange a taxi tour from about €20 per hour.

Bikes (€8) and motorcycles (€18) can be hired for the day from the **Hobby Shop** (Map p274; ☎ /fax 24320 25262; Patriarhou Dimitriou 28), near the newsstand.

KASTRAKI ΚΑΣΤΡΑΚΙ
pop 1200
The village of Kastraki is less than 2km from Kalambaka, but its impressive location right under the rocks gives it an otherworldly feel. If you want a base for exploring the Meteora monasteries, or for climbing the rocks themselves, Kastraki is a good choice.

Kastraki has an internet shop, **All Time Café** (Map p274; ☎ 24320 23930; per hr €3; ☼ 9am-2am), on the main road opposite Taverna Paradisos.

Sleeping
Vrachos Camping (Map p274; ☎ 24320 22293; www.campingmeteora.gr; camp sites per adult/tent €7/free; ⚡) This outstanding and well-shaded camping ground on the Kalambaka–Kastraki road features spotless toilet and shower blocks, a small market, a taverna and a barbecue for self-caterers.

Rooms Ziogas Vasiliki (Map p274; ☎ /fax 24320 24037; s/d/tr from €25/40/50; P ✗ ⚡) This friendly domatia is clean and airy, and there are great views from several rooms facing the rocks. Homemade breakfast, lunch or dinner is available upon request from the family owners.

Hotel Tsikeli (Map p274; ☎ 24320 22438; www.tsikelihotel.gr; s/d/tr incl breakfast €30/50/60; P ✗ ✗ ⚡) Two hundred metres past All Time Café, this welcoming lodging features simple pine- and marble-furnished rooms, large balconies and a grassy front garden. The rear-facing rooms are quieter, roughly half are nonsmoking.

Thalia Guest House (Map p274; ☎ 24320 23051; www .thaliarooms.gr; Kastraki; s/d €35/40; P ☒ ☒) Just three rooms, but the new and self-catering Thalia delivers a lot. Each room is sharp and comfortable, with balconies staring at the rocks. A modern shared kitchen is stocked by the genial French- and English-speaking hosts.

our pick Doupiani House (Map p274; ☎ 24320 75326; www.doupianihouse.com; s/d/tr incl breakfast €40/50/60; P ☒ ☐ ☜) Incomparably set just outside the village, 500m from the town square. The spotless and balconied rooms are tastefully furnished, and breakfast is served on a garden terrace overlooking the village and rocks. Hosts Thanasis and Toula are attentive and full of tips for exploring the village and monasteries.

Also recommended:

Boufidis Camping (Map p274; ☎ /fax 24320 24802; camp sites per adult/tent €6/3; ☐ ☜) More basic than Vrachos Camping, but location and pool bar redeem it.

Hotel Kastraki (Map p274; ☎ 24320 75336; fax 24320 75335; s/d incl breakfast from €40/50) Handsome lodging, often full with groups.

Eating

our pick Taverna Paradisos (Map p274; ☎ 24320 22723; mains €4-7.50) Look for outstanding traditional meals at the roomy Paradisos, along with spectacular views of the Meteora from the large terrace. Grilled lamb and *mousakas* are superb, along with tasty mezedhes and a choice of good Greek wines. A recent Greek cuisine award, noting the restaurant's fresh and traditional ingredients, is a source of pride to owner-cook Koula.

Taverna Gardenia (Map p274; ☎ 24320 22504; mains €4-8) Gardenia gets good marks locally for tasty taverna standards, such as lamb grills and stuffed tomatoes and peppers. Look for the patio shaded by two plane trees, just 20m south of the big church on the square.

Taverna Tou Zioga (Map p274; ☎ 24320 22286; mains €5-9) This indoor eatery is more upscale than most, but still reasonable, with *mayirefta* dishes, plus meaty standards such as souvlaki, grilled pork chops and Greek salad for a modest €4.50.

Taverna Meteora Vavitsos (Map p274; ☎ 24230 22285; mains €6-9) Just opposite Hotel Kastraki, this popular meat-and-more-meat taverna is set back in a leafy brick terrace, and features excellent lamb and pork grills, souvlakia and pasta dishes, always in hearty portions.

Entertainment

ABG Café-Bar (Map p274; ☎ 24320 75627; drinks & snacks €2-5) Kastraki's only nightspot is just past the turn-off to the Meteora. This combination jazz bar and gelateria has dark-red terrace walls, a mellow addition to low-key Kastraki.

Northern Greece
Βόρεια Ελλάδα

Greece's vast and varied north is unmatched for geographical, cultural and even gustatory diversity. Here, great stretches of mountains, lakes, forest and coastline remain to be discovered. Comprising terrain stretching from the azure Ionian Sea across the rugged Epirot mountains, through Macedonia's lakes and vineyards and across the Thracian plain to the Turkish border, the north offers something for everyone, from culture and urban sophistication to swimming, hiking and birdwatching.

The tangible reminders of a history both triumphant and traumatic remain scattered throughout northern Greece. Although the region has only been part of Greece since the Balkans were carved up in the 1912–13 Balkan Wars, it's hardly a young territory: Macedonians, Illyrians, Thracians and Romans all ruled in ancient times, while the Byzantines, Slavs and Turks later held sway for lengthy periods. Myriad monuments, fortresses, churches and mosques attest to their diverse influences.

Today, with the grand Egnatia Odos Hwy spanning the region completed, northern Greece is also getting easier – and quicker – to navigate. It's also becoming a pretty happening place. Thessaloniki, Greece's second city, offers outstanding eateries, nightlife and culture, while Epirot university town Ioannina is a lively spot close to the magnificent Pindos Mountains. Even fairly provincial Thracian cities such as Xanthi, Komotini and Alexandroupoli offer a piece of the action. And northern Greece even boasts great beaches – both for those seeking summer nightlife and for others seeking more secluded spots.

HIGHLIGHTS

- **Urban Explorations** Perusing the pretty upper town of Thessaloniki (p282) – Roman ruins, Byzantine churches and chic cafes
- **Liquid Refreshment** Indulging your inner connoisseur at a premium Macedonian winery (p300)
- **Med Magic** Soaking up the sun at Italian-influenced Parga (p350), on the Epirot Riviera
- **Divine Quest** Ascending into the clouds atop Mt Olympus (p311), ancient hang-out of Zeus and Co
- **Ottoman Flavours** Sampling Turkish sweets while visiting the mosques and museums of earthy Komotini (p326), in Thrace
- **Timeless Treasures** Breathing in the fresh mountain air amid the stone-and-slate villages of Zagorohoria (p342), up in Epiros' Pindos Mountains
- **Beach Safari** Camping in the remote sandy coves and islets of Halkidiki (p298)

- POPULATION: 3.12 MILLION
- AREA: 19,117 SQ KM

NORTHERN GREECE

MACEDONIA
ΜΑΚΕΔΟΝΙΑ

pop 2.4 million / area 33,785 sq km

Although for many foreigners the only thing that comes to mind with the word Macedonia (mah-keh-dho-*nee*-ah) is that boyish bygone conqueror, Alexander the Great, Greece's biggest province has much more to it. Yes, the capital of ancient Macedon at Pella and the gold-studded royal tombs of Vergina are definitely must-see attractions, but travellers will also want to check out Thessaloniki, Greece's sophisticated (and arguably, its coolest) second city, which boasts great eating, drinking and nightlife, the Halkidiki Peninsula's beaches, and forested Mt Olympus – home of the ancient gods and Greece's highest peak (2918m).

Divine Dionysian pleasures also await at Macedonia's renowned wineries, which offer tasting tours and some of Greece's best wines. The whole sprawling region combines plains, gentle lakes and forested mountains, creating unique microclimates and a rich soil abundant in wheat, sweet red peppers and ancient artefacts, too.

Indeed, Macedonia offers numerous off-the-beaten-track opportunities. In the northwest, brown bears amble through mountains that descend to the placid Prespa Lakes, home to pelicans, cormorants and serene medieval churches. Eastern Macedonian attractions include the palm-lined port of Kavala, crowned by a castle, and the isolated Byzantine-era monasteries of Mt Athos, set in tranquil wilderness on the third finger of the Halkidiki Peninsula.

History

Although human settlement in Macedonia goes back at least 700,000 years, it's best known for the powerful ancient Macedonian civilization that peaked with Alexander the Great (d 323 BC), whose conquests reached as far as India. Deemed barbarians by cultivated Athenians, the Macedonians had subjugated Greece under Alexander's father, Philip II, yet adopted Greek mores. Alexander and his generals spread the Greek culture and language widely, creating a Hellenistic society that would be absorbed by the Romans. Later, after the empire split into eastern and western halves in the 4th century AD, the society emerged as the Greek-speaking Byzantine Empire.

Thessaloniki became Byzantium's second city, a vital commercial, cultural and strategic centre on the crossroads of Balkan trade routes. However, 6th- and 7th-century-AD Slavic migrations brought new populations, and challenges for the empire, which was frequently at war with the medieval Bulgarian kingdom from the 9th century to the 11th century. In 1018, Emperor Basil II finally defeated Bulgarian Tsar Samuel, who had ruled much of the southern Balkans from his capital on western Macedonia's Mikri Prespa Lake.

After a short period of Serbian rule under Tsar Stefan Dusan in the 14th century, Macedonia and the Balkans were overrun by the Ottoman Turks. The Ottoman system distinguished subjects by religion, not race, something that would exacerbate the strife of the late 19th century, when myriad guerrilla movements arose to fight the Turks, pledging to annex Macedonia for Greece, Bulgaria or even an independent 'Macedonia for the Macedonians'; for a time in the very early 20th century, great powers such as Britain favoured the latter solution.

Ottoman atrocities against Macedonia's Christian populations caused the European great powers to enact a rather toothless monitoring mission (called the Mürzsteg Reform Programme, from 1902 to 1908), but it failed to stop the bloodshed. In the First Balkan War of 1912, Greece, Bulgaria and Serbia united to drive the Turks from Macedonia; however, the Bulgarians were unhappy with their share of the spoils, and declared war on their former allies in 1913 (the Second Balkan War). However, Bulgaria's defeat then resulted in the loss of its allotted portions of eastern Macedonia and Thrace, and thus, access to the Aegean. Greece emerged as the big winner, taking half of geographical Macedonia, with Serbia taking 38%. Bulgaria was left with just 13%, while newly-created Albania received a sliver of Macedonia around Ohrid and Prespa lakes.

In 1923, with the massive Greek-Turkish population exchanges, the Athens government chose to resettle many Anatolian Greek refugees in Macedonia, to the disadvantage of the indigenous (non-Greek) populations. A vigorous program for assimilating non-Greeks was already underway, primarily through the levers

MACEDONIA

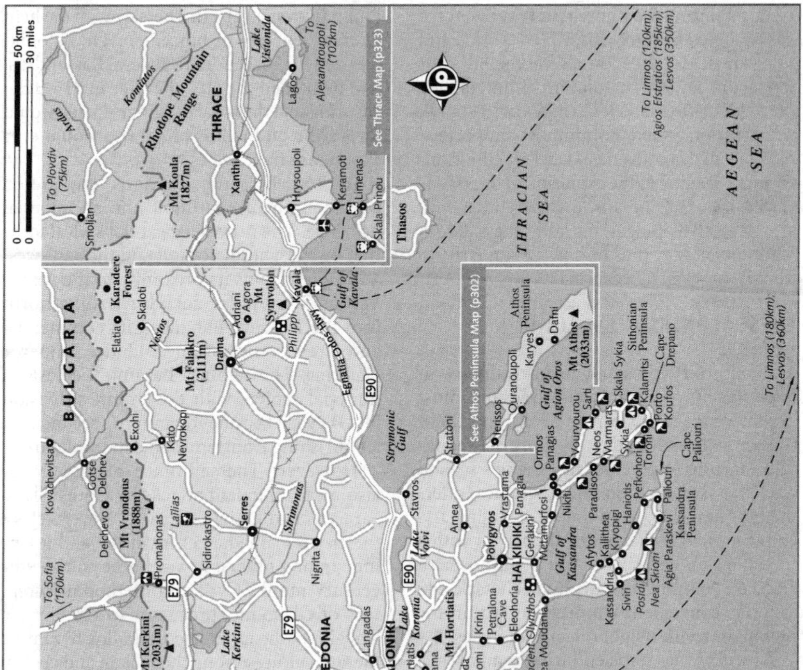
MACEDONIA
0 50 km
0 30 miles
FORMER YUGOSLAV REPUBLIC OF MACEDONIA
BULGARIA
ALBANIA
MACEDONIA
THRACE
THESSALY
EPIROS
HALKIDIKI
THRACIAN SEA
AEGEAN SEA
Strymonic Gulf
Thermaic Gulf
Gulf of Thessaloniki
Gulf of Kassandra
Gulf of Agion Oros
Gulf of Kavala
See Prespa Lakes Map (p318)
See Epiros Map (p335)
See Mt Olympus Map (p312)
See Athos Peninsula Map (p302)
See Thrace Map (p323)
To Tirana (100km)
To Skopje (105km)
To Skopje (90km); Belgrade (500km)
To Sofia (150km)
To Plovdiv (75km)
To Alexandroupoli (102km)
To Limnos (120km); Agios Efstratios (185km); Lesvos (350km)
To Limnos (180km); Lesvos (360km)
Rhodope Mountain Range
Mt Koula (1827m)
Mt Falakro (2111m)
Mt Symvolon
Mt Vrondous (1888m)
Mt Kerkini (2031m)
Mt Hortiatis
Mt Olympus (2918m)
Mt Athos (2033m)
Mt Voras (Kaïmaktsalan) (2151m)
Mt Vermio (320m)
Mt Vernon (1759m)
Mt Vitsi (2128m)
Mt Grammos (2520m)
Mt Smolikas (2637m)
Mt Gamila (2497m)
Mt Vasilitsa (2249m)
Lake Kerkini
Lake Doïrani
Lake Volvi
Lake Koronia
Lake Vegoritis
Lake Petron
Lake Himaditis
Lake Orestiada
Lake Aliakmonas
Lake Vistonida
Thessaloniki
Serres
Drama
Kavala
Xanthi
Kilkis
Polygyros
Katerini
Veria
Edessa
Florina
Kastoria
Kozani
Grevena
Larisa
Ioannina
Thasos
Athos Peninsula
Sithonian Peninsula
Kassandra Peninsula
Faros Beach & Potamos Beach
Egnatia Odos Hwy
NORTHERN GREECE

of education and the Church. In WWII, Greece was occupied by the Nazis, who deported and killed most of Macedonia's very significant Sephardic Jewish population. Immediately after, during the Greek Civil War (1944–49), authorities targeted 'communist supporters' – all too often, a convenient label for ethnic minorities – leading to the expulsion of thousands of (Slavic) Macedonians, many of them children, as well as Bulgarians and others. Greek Macedonia today thus bears little similarity to what it was even 60 years ago.

THESSALONIKI ΘΕΣΣΑΛΟΝΙΚΗ
pop 363,987

Thessaloniki (thess-ah-lo-nee-kih) is at once the hippest, most cultured and most expensive place to sleep and eat in northern Greece – though budget options are thankfully starting to emerge. As Greece's second city, Thessaloniki (also called Salonica) offers the best nightlife, shopping, fine dining and cultural events outside of Athens, but with a friendlier, less hectic vibe. And, being northern Greece's central transport hub, Thessaloniki also has convenient connections within the region and with neighbouring countries.

As with Athens, the enduring symbols of a glorious history are visible here. These include the White Tower, watching over the cafe-lined waterfront, erstwhile Ottoman *hammams* (Turkish baths)-turned-art-galleries, and lengthy Byzantine walls culminating at the Ano Poli (Upper Town), an enchanting neighbourhood of colourful old houses, where little Byzantine churches peek from winding alleyways. Thessaloniki's grand-scale structures include the 5th-century Church of Agios Dimitrios, the enormous Roman Rotunda, and Roman Emperor Galerius' 3rd-century palace ruins.

Thessaloniki is also a major college town, fleshed out by some 80,000 university students who enliven the city's innumerable cafes, restaurants and bars. Thessaloniki thus remains lively during the long months when the more touristy parts of Greece hibernate. And, though one could easily spend weeks here, Thessaloniki and its sites are compact enough for travellers with only a few days to spare.

History

Thessaloniki was named in honour of a woman who herself had been named to commemorate a military victory, that of her father, Philip II, over a tribe in Thessaly with the help of crack Thessalian horsemen. Thessaloniki married the Macedonian general Kassandros, and he named the city after her in 316 BC – ensuring that the royal daughter's name would forever be on the lips of all who would ever experience the city.

In 168 BC, the Romans conquered Macedon, incorporating it into an imperial province. The provincial capital's ideal location on the Thermaic Gulf and the east–west Via Egnatia, plus its proximity to the Axios/Vardar River valley corridor leading north into the Balkans, enhanced its commercial and strategic importance. Under Emperor Galerius, Thessaloniki became the eastern imperial capital; with the empire's division in AD 395, it became Byzantium's second city, a flourishing Constantinople in miniature.

However, Thessaloniki's attractiveness also meant frequent attacks by Goths, Slavs, Saracens and Latin Crusaders. Nevertheless, the city remained a centre of life and learning; among others, it was home to the 9th-century monks Cyril and Methodius (creators of Glagolitic, precursor to the Cyrillic alphabet), who expanded Orthodox Byzantine literary culture among the Balkan and central European Slavs, and the great 14th-century theologian, St Gregory Palamas.

In 1430, the Turks captured Thessaloniki, though it still remained a major city. After 1492, the shrewd Ottomans resettled Sephardic Jewish exiles fleeing the Spanish Inquisition, making Thessaloniki one of Europe's most important centres of Jewish life, education and commerce.

The 1821 War of Independence failed to dislodge the Ottomans from Thessaloniki and Macedonia in general. Throughout the 19th century, Thessaloniki thus became a lurid hub for diplomatic intrigue, secret societies and mutually antagonistic rebel groups and reform movements. Along with Greek liberation entities, these included the pro-Bulgarian Internal Macedonian Revolutionary Organisation (IMRO), which achieved notoriety for a terrorist bombing of the city's Ottoman Bank in 1895, and the Young Turks, who sought to introduce Western-style reforms to save the dwindling empire, and who successfully infiltrated the Ottoman military with their secret ideology. One notable Young Turk and Thessaloniki native, Mustafa Kemal, would become the

NORTHERN GREECE

founder of modern Turkey, and be deemed Atatürk (Father of the Turks).

The world wars were darkly decisive for Thessaloniki. The August 1917 fire burned most of it, and ethnic diversity shrank with the great population exchange of 1923 with Turkey and a smaller one with Bulgaria in 1926. And, in WWII, the occupying Nazis deported Thessaloniki's Jews to the concentration camps. The ensuing Greek Civil War led to the forced removal of other non-Greeks. Thessaloniki's character and complexity changed dramatically, the result today being a Hellenicised city built according to a French architect's 1920 avenue scheme.

Thessaloniki's next major innovation, the long-promised metro, is currently being built along Egnatia (and causing much traffic congestion). Peering into the trenches beside the sidewalk here reveals much older layers of Thessaloniki just beneath the surface. Archaeological items discovered in the metro dig will be displayed in a special museum to be housed in an old Ottoman structure nearby.

Orientation

Central Thessaloniki is bounded on the south by the sea and on the north by a sloping hill, site of the old Ano Poli, itself hemmed in by the Byzantine Walls. The cafe-lined waterfront avenue, Leoforos Nikis, runs west from the port to the White Tower (Lefkos Pyrgos) in the east; the new Office of Tourism Directorate is near this tower. Going from the water and Leoforos Nikis north (uphill), other principal streets also run parallel to the sea: first Mitropoleos, Tsimiski and, above them, the main thoroughfare Egnatia; north of this, other major east–west streets are Filippou and Agiou Dimitriou.

Thessaloniki's main squares include Plateia Eleftherias, near the port, and the grand Plateia Aristotelous, a popular meeting point that runs between Egnatia and Leoforos Nikis. Squares further east include Plateia Agias Sofias and Plateia Navarinou, just south of Egnatia.

Another prominent meeting point for locals is Kamara, the area around the Arch of Galerius on the northern side of Egnatia opposite Plateia Navarinou. Just east of Kamara, Egnatia intersects with Ethnikis Amynis; to the northeast of this intersection is the large Aristotle University, to the south-east, the HelExpo trade fair. After it crosses these facilities, Egnatia continues eastwards as Nea Egnatia. Taking Egnatia back westwards past Kamara and Plateia Aristotelous brings you to the cheap shopping/hotel district around Plateia Dimokratias. After this, Egnatia becomes Monastiriou and shortly passes the train station to the right, and continues towards the main bus station (3km further west).

Information

BOOKSHOPS

Bustart (☎ 2310 284 414; Grigoriou Palama 21) Sells art, design, photography and fashion books.

Travel Bookstore Traveller (☎ 2310 275 215; www .traveler.gr, in Greek; Proxenou Koromila 41) Hole-in-the-wall shop sells maps and Lonely Planet guides, among other travel titles.

EMERGENCY

Whenever closed, Thessaloniki pharmacies must display lists in the window stating which pharmacies in the vicinity should be open at that time.

Farmakeio Gouva-Peraki (☎ 2310 205 544; Agias Sofias 110, Ano Poli) Up in Ano Poli, this is a handy pharmacy with experienced staff.

Farmakeio Sofia Tympanidou (☎ 2310 522 155; Egnatia 17) Empathetic Kyria Sofia has long run this well-stocked pharmacy, and can often get hard-to-find medicines quickly.

First-Aid Centre (☎ 2310 530 530; Navarhou Koundourioti 10)

Ippokration (☎ 2310 837 921; Papanastasiou 50) Largest public hospital; 2km east of centre.

Port police (☎ 2310 531 504)

Tourist police (☎ 2310 554 871; 5th fl, Dodekanisou 4; ⏲ 7.30am-11pm)

INTERNET ACCESS

e-Global (cnr Egnatia & Iasonidou; per hr €2.50; ⏲ 24hr) Just as central, this place near Kamara is somewhat less boisterous than Web.

Web (☎ 2310 237 031; S Gonata 4, Plateia Navarinou; per hr €2.40; ⏲ 24hr) Big, central and well-equipped, but often packed with loud teenage gamers.

LAUNDRY

Bianca Laundrette (Panagias Dexias 3; per 6kg load €7; ⏲ 8am-8.30pm Tue, Thu & Fri, 8am-3pm Mon, Wed & Sat) In just two hours your clothes are washed, dried and folded at this no-nonsense laundromat powered by classic rock.

NORTHERN GREECE

NORTHERN GREECE

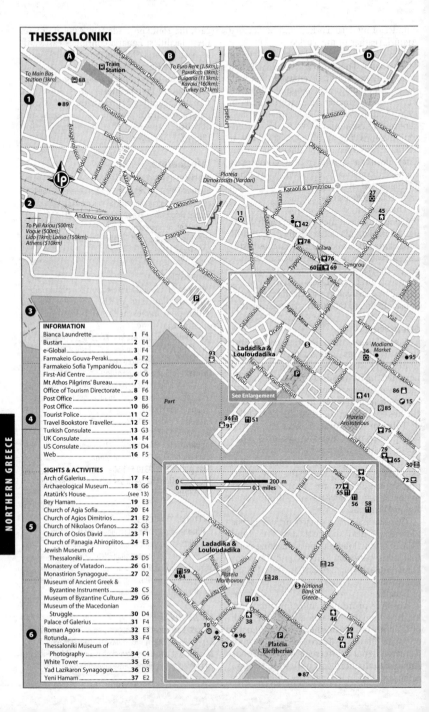

THESSALONIKI

INFORMATION
Bianca Laundrette	**1** F4
Bustart	**2** E4
e-Global	**3** F4
Farmakeio Gouva-Peraki	**4** F2
Farmakeio Sofia Tympanidou	**5** C2
First-Aid Centre	**6** C6
Mt Athos Pilgrims' Bureau	**7** F4
Office of Tourism Directorate	**8** F6
Post Office	**9** E3
Post Office	**10** B6
Tourist Police	**11** C2
Travel Bookstore Traveller	**12** E5
Turkish Consulate	**13** G3
UK Consulate	**14** F4
US Consulate	**15** D4
Web	**16** F5

SIGHTS & ACTIVITIES
Arch of Galerius	**17** F4
Archaeological Museum	**18** G6
Atatürk's House	(see 13)
Bey Hamam	**19** E3
Church of Agia Sofia	**20** E4
Church of Agios Dimitrios	**21** E2
Church of Nikolaos Orfanos	**22** G3
Church of Osios David	**23** F1
Church of Panagia Ahiropiitos	**24** E3
Jewish Museum of Thessaloniki	**25** D5
Monastery of Vlatadon	**26** G1
Monastirion Synagogue	**27** D2
Museum of Ancient Greek & Byzantine Instruments	**28** C5
Museum of Byzantine Culture	**29** G6
Museum of the Macedonian Struggle	**30** D4
Palace of Galerius	**31** F4
Roman Agora	**32** E3
Rotunda	**33** F4
Thessaloniki Museum of Photography	**34** C4
White Tower	**35** E6
Yad Lazikaron Synagogue	**36** D3
Yeni Hamam	**37** E2

0   200 m
0   0.1 miles

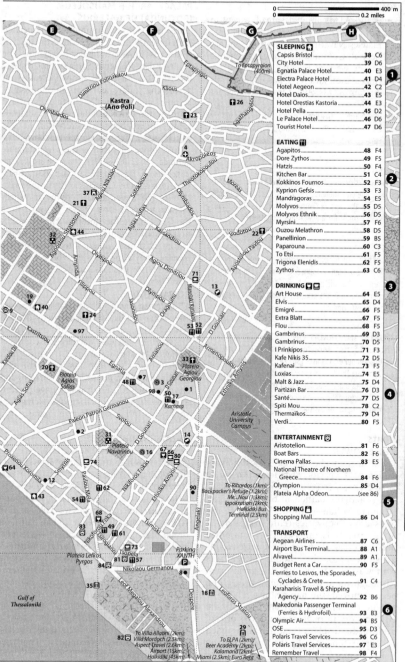

SLEEPING
Capsis Bristol	**38**	C6
City Hotel	**39**	D6
Egnatia Palace Hotel	**40**	E3
Electra Palace Hotel	**41**	D4
Hotel Aegeon	**42**	C2
Hotel Daios	**43**	D5
Hotel Orestias Kastoria	**44**	E3
Hotel Pella	**45**	D2
Le Palace Hotel	**46**	D6
Tourist Hotel	**47**	D6

EATING
Agapitos	**48**	F4
Dore Zythos	**49**	F5
Hatzis	**50**	F4
Kitchen Bar	**51**	C4
Kokkinos Fournos	**52**	F3
Kyprion Gefsis	**53**	F3
Mandragoras	**54**	E5
Molyvos	**55**	D5
Molyvos Ethnik	**56**	D5
Myrsini	**57**	F6
Ouzou Melathron	**58**	D5
Panellinion	**59**	B5
Paparouna	**60**	C3
To Etsi	**61**	F5
Trigona Elenidis	**62**	F5
Zythos	**63**	C6

DRINKING
Art House	**64**	E5
Elvis	**65**	D4
Emigré	**66**	F5
Extra Blatt	**67**	F5
Flou	**68**	F5
Gambrinus	**69**	D3
Gambrinus	**70**	D3
I Prinkipos	**71**	F3
Kafe Nikis 35	**72**	D5
Kafenai	**73**	F5
Loxias	**74**	E5
Malt & Jazz	**75**	D4
Partizan Bar	**76**	D3
Santé	**77**	D5
Spiti Mou	**78**	C2
Thermaïkos	**79**	D4
Verdi	**80**	F5

ENTERTAINMENT
Aristotelion	**81**	F6
Boat Bars	**82**	F6
Cinema Pallas	**83**	E5
National Theatre of Northern Greece	**84**	F6
Olympion	**85**	D4
Plateia Alpha Odeon	(see 86)	

SHOPPING
Shopping Mall	**86**	D4

TRANSPORT
Aegean Airlines	**87**	C6
Airport Bus Terminal	**88**	A1
Alvavel	**89**	A1
Budget Rent a Car	**90**	F5
Ferries to Lesvos, the Sporades, Cyclades & Crete	**91**	C4
Karaharissis Travel & Shipping Agency	**92**	B6
Makedonia Passenger Terminal (Ferries & Hydrofoil)	**93**	B3
Olympic Air	**94**	B5
OSE	**95**	D3
Polaris Travel Services	**96**	C6
Polaris Travel Services	**97**	E3
Remember Travel	**98**	F4

MONEY

Banks and ATMs are widespread, except in Ano Poli. Egnatia, Tsimiski, the port area and Plateies Navarinou and Aristotelous are well-served. Commission-hungry exchange offices line western Egnatia. The train station, bus station and ferry passenger terminals contain ATMs. Avoid travellers cheques if possible.

National Bank of Greece (Tsimiski 11) This historic structure is worth mentioning, mainly for its architectural grandeur.

PERMITS

Mt Athos Pilgrims Bureau (☎ Greek nationals 2310 252 575, foreign nationals 2310 252 578; pilgrimsbureau@ c-lab.gr; Egnatia 109; ☺ 9am-1pm Mon-Fri, 10am-noon Sat) Issues permits for the Mt Athos monasteries.

POST

Post office Aristotelous (Aristotelous 26; ☺ 7.30am-8pm Mon-Fri, 7.30am-2.15pm Sat, 9am-1.30pm Sun); Koundouriotou (Koundouriotou 6; ☺ 7.30am-2pm) The Koundouriotou branch is next to the port. The train station also has a post window.

TOURIST INFORMATION

Office of Tourism Directorate (☎ 2310 221 100; tour-the@otenet.gr; Tsimiski 136; ☺ 8am-8pm Mon-Fri, 8am-2pm Sat) The marvellously named new city tourism office occupies a grand building near the White Tower, replacing the former portside one. Friendly and well-informed staff provide assistance in English and German.

Sights

WHITE TOWER

The history of Thessaloniki's most famous landmark, the pacific **White Tower** (☎ 2310 267 832; Lefkos Pyrgos; admission free; ☺ 8.30am-3pm Tue-Sun), is actually bathed in blood. In 1826, Ottoman Sultan Mahmud II ordered the massacre of janizaries (elite troops made up of forcibly Islamicised Christian boys) deemed disloyal. After the Greek reconquest in 1913, the 'bloody tower' was whitewashed to expunge this grisly past. Although the tower's whitewash has long been removed, the name stuck. The tower's new interactive **museum** presents the city's history through several levels of cool multimedia displays (yes, it was designed by Apple), though sadly the former cafe up top is no more.

PALACE, ARCH & MAUSOLEUM (ROTUNDA) OF GALERIUS

Three major Roman monuments associated with the early-4th-century Emperor Galerius spill across Egnatia at Plateia Navarinou. The ruined **Palace of Galerius** (Plateia Navarinou; admission free; ☺ 8.30am-3pm Tue-Sun), sprawling east–west across the square, contains floor mosaics, columns and some walls. North of Egnatia at Kamara, the **Arch of Galerius** features sculpted soldiers in combat; it was erected in AD 303 to celebrate a victory over the Persians.

Just above the arch is the unmistakable **Rotunda** (☎ 2310 218 720; Plateia Agiou Georgiou; admission free; ☺ 8am-5pm Tue-Sun), a hulking brick structure built by Galerius as his future mausoleum (he never used it, dying in retirement in today's Serbia instead). Constantine the Great made the Rotunda Thessaloniki's first church (Agiou Georgiou), and later the Ottomans transformed it into a mosque; the minaret they added has now been restored. Some interior frescoes survive.

ROMAN AGORA

The **Roman Agora** (Plateia Dikastirion; admission free; ☺ 8am-3pm Tue-Sun) lies north of Plateia Aristotelous, across Egnatia on Plateia Dikastirion. Ancient Macedonian commercial activity, starting in the 3rd century BC, peaked under the Romans, when the area was buzzing with public affairs, services and shops. A helpful, English-language placard explains the site, which contains clustered shop walls and mosaic floor remnants.

BYZANTINE CHURCHES

Perhaps the grandest church in Greece, the enormous, 5th-century **Church of Agios Dimitrios** (☎ 2310 270 008; Agiou Dimitriou 97; admission free; ☺ 8am-10pm, crypt 8am-7.30pm Tue-Thu & Sun, 1.30-7.30pm Mon, 9-11pm Fri), honours Thessaloniki's patron saint. A Roman soldier, Dimitrios was killed around AD 303 on the site (then a Roman bath), on orders of Emperor Galerius, infamous for persecuting Christians. The martyrdom site is now an eerie underground **crypt**, open during the day and for the special Friday-night service (see Cryptical Envelopment, opposite). In 1980, the saint's relics were returned from Italy, and now occupy a silver reliquary inside.

The Ottomans made Agios Dimitrios a mosque, plastering over the wall frescoes. After the 1913 Greek reconquest, the plaster was removed, revealing Thessaloniki's fin-

CRYPTICAL ENVELOPMENT

Being a Christian in late-Roman Thessaloniki was extremely dangerous. Galerius (AD 250–311) made practising the new religion punishable by death – a stark reality that drove worshippers literally underground. One day in about the year AD 303, a young soldier named Dimitrios was caught preaching in a subterranean portico in the city *agora* (market). Dragged off to the baths, Dimitrios was speared to death as an example to others.

After the Eastern Roman Empire officially adopted Orthodox Christianity under Emperor Constantine the Great, Dimitrios became venerated as Thessaloniki's patron saint. Numerous miracles were credited to him, including sudden appearances to save the city whenever it fell under barbarian siege. Miraculous healing of the sick was especially associated with the crypt where Dimitrios was martyred, which lies beneath the enormous 5th-century church named after him (opposite).

During the Turkish occupation, however, the crypt was filled in and forgotten, only to be recovered after the Greek capture of Thessaloniki in 1912. The devastating fire of 1917 caused extensive damage to both church and crypt, necessitating much conservation work.

Open regularly to the public, the stone-and-brick crypt is mazelike and hauntingly lit, and displays archaeological finds from the ancient church. For a truly unearthly and uniquely Thessaloniki experience, descend into this other world of pungent incense and prayer at the special liturgy held here every Friday from 9pm to 11pm. People file in silently in ones and twos, heads down like members of some secret society, and take up places, freeform, in crumbling corners or in the darkness under stone archways that are soon reverberating with the deep intonations of Byzantine chants.

Observing a service in the underground crypt, one of the holiest places in Greece, also gives travellers the chance to experience, in some small way, religion as Thessaloniki's first Christians did, at a time when one's faith was constantly being tested by the all-too-real fear of being discovered and killed by the state. When the priest gathers parishioners around the site of the saint's martyrdom and speaks in soft tones of moral edification, this past reality really hits home.

The crypt liturgy also allows female travellers who wish they could visit Mt Athos a chance to experience modern Greece's unbroken tradition of ancient Orthodox spirituality first-hand. You don't have to be particularly religious to attend, so long as you dress and act quietly and respectfully (turn off your phone).

est church mosaics. While the 1917 fire was very damaging, five 8th-century mosaics have survived, spanning the altar.

The 8th-century **Church of Agia Sofia** (☉ 7am-1pm & 5-6.30pm), a not-so-small miniature of its İstanbul namesake, occupies Plateia Agias Sofias south of Egnatia. One of Thessaloniki's most important churches, it has a striking mosaic of the Ascension of Christ in the dome.

An even older Byzantine church, the 5th-century **Church of the Panagia Ahiropiitos** (☉ 7am-noon & 4.30-6.30pm) has a basilica form and notable surviving mosaics and frescoes. The name, meaning 'made without hands', refers to a miraculous 12th-century appearance of an icon of the Virgin.

Near Ano Poli's Byzantine Walls, the **Monastery of Vlatadon** (cnr Eptapyrgiou & Agathangelou; ☉ 7.30am-5pm & 5.30-8pm) has a leafy, secluded location and a small **museum** (☉ 10am-noon Sun), plus a gift shop. Nearby is the little 5th-century **Church of Osios David** (☉ 9am-noon & 4-6pm Mon-Sat), allegedly built to commemorate the baptism of the anti-Christian Galerius' daughter, Theodora, conducted secretly while her father was away on business. It contains well-preserved mosaics and rare 12th-century frescoes depicting the baptism of Christ.

A five-minute walk further east leads to the 4th-century **Church of Nikolaos Orfanos** (☎ 2310 213 627; Irodotou 20; ☉ 8.30am-2.30pm Tue-Sun), which has superb (though age-darkened) frescoes. To help preserve them, candles are only lit during Sunday-morning mass.

MUSEUMS

The **Archaeological Museum** (☎ 2310 830 538; Manoli Andronikou 6; admission €6, students free; ☉ 8.30am-8pm) showcases prehistoric, ancient Macedonian and Hellenistic finds. However, the most impressive exhibits, featuring finely worked gold objects discovered in the royal tombs at Vergina, have been returned to their

NORTHERN GREECE

rightful place, so to see them you'll have to go there. You can see the **Derveni Crater** (330–320 BC), a huge, ornate Hellenistic vase of bronze and tin. Used for mixing wine and water, and later as a funerary urn, it's marked by intricate relief carvings illustrating the life of Dionysos, with mythical figures, animals, vines and ivy branches. The **Derveni Treasure** contains Greece's oldest surviving papyrus piece (250–320 BC). The ground-floor exhibit, **Pre-Historic Thessaloniki**, boasts the Petralona Hoard – axes and chisels in an urn, abandoned by the artisan, in the Petralona Cave north of Halkidiki (see p298), plus daggers, pottery and tools from mound tombs dating from the Neolithic period to the late Bronze Age.

The snazzy **Museum of Byzantine Culture** (☎ 2310 868 570; www.mbp.gr; Leoforos Stratou 2; admission €4; 8am-8pm Tue-Sun, 1.30-8pm Mon) uses ambient lighting and features a running wall placard text explaining more than 3000 Byzantine objects, including frescoes, mosaics, embroidery, ceramics, inscriptions and icons from the early Christian period to the Fall of Constantinople (1453).

The **Museum of Ancient Greek & Byzantine Instruments** (☎ 2310 555 263; musbyzorga@otenet.gr; Katouni 12-14) displays instruments from antiquity to the 19th century, but was closed at the time of writing; consult the Office of Tourism Directorate in advance for news on this and the similarly shut **Museum of the Macedonian Struggle** (☎ 2310 229 778; Proxenou Koromila 23; admission free; 9am-2pm Tue-Fri, 10am-noon Sat), which recounts the Greek nationalist narrative of how heroic Hellenes wrested Macedonia from the clutches of both Turks *and* Bulgarians. Housed in Greece's one-time Ottoman consulate, the museum has hard-to-find maps, old firearms, photos, uniforms and more.

The hip **Thessaloniki Museum of Photography** (☎ 2310 566 716; www.thmphoto.gr; Warehouse A, Thessaloniki Port; 11am-7pm Tue-Fri, 11am-9pm Sat & Sun), in a former portside warehouse, displays historic and contemporary Greek photography, plus dynamic temporary exhibitions, and a waterfront cafe.

KASTRA (ANO POLI) & THE BYZANTINE WALLS

Homes in the Kastra (Castle), also called Ano Poli (Upper Town), largely survived the 1917 fire – although the fire had originated there, the wind swept the flames down towards the sea. It had been the 'Turkish quarter' during

Ottoman times, and contains Thessaloniki's most atmospheric urban architecture.

Here, timber-framed, pastel-painted houses with overhanging upper storeys are clustered on small winding streets. Ambling through Kastra's steep, winding lanes, marked by steps and tiny rivulets, is a great pleasure. Panoptic views of the city and the Thermaic Gulf can be had from the Byzantine walls above. Several important Byzantine churches are found here (see Walking Tour, opposite).

Kastra's walls were built by Emperor Theodosius (AD 379–475), who modelled them on his own great Constantinopolitan wall system. Rebuilt in the 14th century, the walls were strengthened with marble stones from the Jewish cemetery in 1821. It's possible to walk up them from opposite the university (Panepistimio Aristotelion) almost to the top.

Today the old quarter has also become a refuge for Thessaloniki's leftists. Slumbering cafes and expletive-rich displays of anarchist graffiti, spray-painted in several languages and colours on the walls are a part of what lend it its character.

OTTOMAN SITES

Despite (or, because of) more than 450 years of Ottoman rule in Thessaloniki, the Turkish heritage is practically nonexistent today. However, the few remaining sites are atmospheric and worth seeing.

Atatürk's House (☎ 2310 248 452; Apostolou Pavlou 75; admission free; 9am-5pm), located within the Turkish consulate grounds, was the birthplace of modern Turkey's illustrious founder, the dashing Mustafa Kemal, in 1881. Have your identity card or passport ready, the helpful staff will lead you through this faithfully restored house. Along with numerous original furnishings and memorabilia, you'll see other Atatürk paraphernalia such as dapper suits, white gloves and cane. Sporting!

A prison from Ottoman times until 1989, the **Eptapyrgion**, or Yediküle as it's called in Turkish (in both languages, it translates as 'Seven Towers'), is a grim reminder of Thessaloniki's penal past, recounted in *rembetika* (old Greek blues) songs, behind the Byzantine Walls.

Yeni Hamam (Aigli; cnr Kassandrou & Agiou Nikolaou), an atmospheric 17th-century Ottoman structure, has great acoustics – ideal grounds for seeing a concert.

Bey Hamam (Paradeisos Baths; cnr Egnatia & Plateia Dikastirion; admission free; ☺ 9am-9pm Mon-Fri, 8.30am-3pm Sat & Sun) is Thessaloniki's oldest Turkish bath (1444). The labyrinthine structure hosts art shows.

JEWISH SITES

Until WWII, when the occupying Nazis deported Thessaloniki's Jewish population, the city had been one of southeast Europe's most important centres of Jewish life. Today, there are several signs and symbols of this bygone heritage remaining, and a small, mostly elderly community that remains and clings to its traditions.

The **Jewish Museum of Thessaloniki** (☎ 2310 250 406; Agiou Mina 13; admission free; ☺ 11am-2pm Tue, Fri & Sun, 11am-2pm & 5-8pm Wed & Thu) traces Thessaloniki Judaism from 140 BC to the Sephardic immigrations following 1492, ending with the Holocaust. The museum also houses remains from Thessaloniki's large Jewish cemetery, vandalised in 1942 by the Nazis.

The only synagogue to have survived the Nazis is the **Monastirioton Synagogue** (☎ 2310 524 968; Syngrou 35); however, services are now held at the smaller **Yad Lazikaron** (☎ 2310 275 701; Vassiliou Irakliou 24), on Mitropolios opposite the Modiano Food Market in the former **Jewish district**.

Other Jewish sites remain east of the White Tower. Two 19th-century mansions here attest to the erstwhile wealth and prominence of Thessaloniki's Jews, the **Villa Allatini** (Olgas 98) and **Villa Mordoch** (Olgas 162). Incidentally, Olgas crosses Saadi Levi, named for the publisher of one of the city's 35 erstwhile Jewish newspapers.

Walking Tour

Excluding museums, Thessaloniki's main sites and attractions are doable in a day. Start at the top, head downwards, and go early (around 9am), as many churches close by noon. Sundays, Tuesdays and Saturdays are best; avoid Mondays, when most sites are closed.

Although bus 23 from Plateia Eleftheriou reaches the Kastra (get off at the Pyrgos Trigoniou or Agia Anargyi stops), save time by taking a taxi (€2.80 to €5). From the Kastra, get your bearings at the **viewing platform (1)**, and gaze out over the city you're about to conquer. The platform is at the easternmost

end of the walls surrounding the inner citadel or Eptapyrgio. Follow the walls west on the main road (also called Eptapyrgio); after Agathangelou, you'll see the leafy, relaxing **Monastery of Vlatadon (2**; p287) on the left. See the church here and, if open, the museum.

Returning to the entrance, continue east along Eptapyrgio, turning left on Sthenonos and down the stairs, veering right down along Dimitriou Poliorkitou. Further left, a narrow stairway doubles backwards, leading downwards; follow it and turn left again on Parodos Kassianis to the 5th-century **Church of Osios David (3**; p287), which contains rare 12th-century frescoes depicting the baptism of Christ, and holy water from an ancient spring.

From here, wander the labyrinthine Ano Poli eastwards along the small streets. The most direct route follows Fotiou across Akropolitis and straight on Krispou, then along Arolou, back up on Moreas, and a quick right on Amfitryonos before turning left on Irodotou to reach the 4th-century **Church of Nikolaos Orfanos (4**; p287), with its exquisite 14th-century frescoes. The friendly, English-speaking caretaker can explain the church's history and artwork.

Returning to Moreas, follow it south, crossing Olympiados to reach Kassandrou. Walk several blocks west along this large street, turning south on Agiou Nikolaou. On the right-hand side you'll see **Yeni Hamam (5**; opposite). This restored 17th-century Turkish bath, also called Aigli (like the nearby bus stop) is a voluminous, atmospheric structure that now hosts concerts.

Just below Yeni Hamam, the enormous **Church of Agios Dimitrios (6**; p286), occupies its own square. See the saint's relics, the 8th-century mosaics near the altar, and the otherworldly, subterranean crypt, where St Dimitrios was martyred (see Cryptical Envelopment; p287).

Next, continue south on Agnostou Stratiotou across Olympou, for the **Roman Agora (7**; p286). The entrance is marked, with a helpful explanatory board within. Next, retrace your steps to Agiou Dimitriou, and proceed east nine blocks to **Atatürk's House (8**; opposite), on your left, inside the Turkish consulate.

Across from the consulate, a block further east on Agiou Dimitriou, turn right on D Gounari for the **Rotunda (9**; p286). Gape at

NORTHERN GREECE

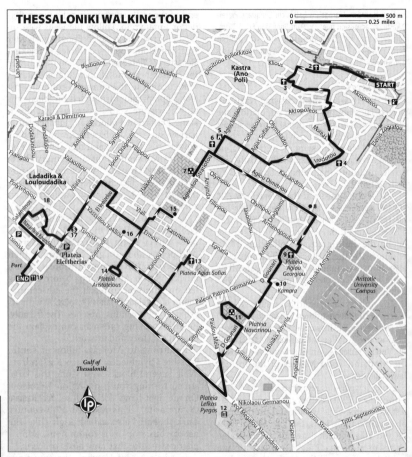

THESSALONIKI WALKING TOUR

NORTHERN GREECE

WALK FACTS

Start Kastra/Byzantine walls
Finish Port
Duration Three to four hours

its grandeur inside and inspect the ruins behind. Continue downhill to the photogenic, statue-studded **Arch of Galerius** (**10**; p286) at Kamara. Crossing Egnatia, continue straight downhill. Various Roman ruins run down the centre of this pedestrianised street/square, culminating at the **Palace of Galerius** (**11**; p286). It's worth exploring from within, though you can also just peer down on it from the railing above.

Continuing downhill, cross Tsimiski and, at Plateia Fanarioton, arc left down Pavlou Mela to reach the beloved **White Tower** (**12**; p286) and its hip new multimedia museum. Then continue west for a seaside stroll.

Leave the water by crossing Leoforos Nikis at the small traffic light at Agias Sofias. Either see the **Church of Agia Sofia** (**13**; p287) by walking straight until Plateia Agias Sofias, or proceed west on Tsimiski for window shopping on Thessaloniki's most fashion-conscious street. You'll soon hit Aristotelous, with its cafes, unique architecture and, on the south side, the large, lively **Plateia Aristotelous (14)**.

Continuing up Aristotelous on its western side, cross Egnatia for the atmospheric **Bey Hamam** (**15**; p289), a restored Turkish bath that hosts art and photography exhibitions. Then, returning to Aristotelous, proceed downhill, turning right on Vlali. Veer into **Modiano Market (16)**, full of fish on ice, trayloads of olives and cheese, hot-tempered butchers, and Greek grandmas arguing with vegetables.

Continue through Modiani, cross El Venizelou and turn left towards the water on the next street parallel to it, Ionos Dragoumi, through the Louloudadika district, where flower sellers once congregated, now containing clothes shops and a few bars and restaurants. Continue down Ionos Dragoumi and, at the Tsimiski intersection, you'll pass the splendid **National Bank of Greece (17)** building; after it, turn right onto Mitropoleos, immediately left on Katouni and right again on Aigyptou. Here begins the **Ladadika district (18)**, once comprising olive-oil warehouses and now home to atmospheric restaurants and cafes.

From here, the tour ends across Kountouriotou, at the port. Enter the gate and, on the eastern jetty, sink into the big, soft couches at the cool **Kitchen Bar (19**; p293) for a relaxing drink. Congratulations!

Festivals & Events

Major fairs and festivals occur at HelExpo during September and October. The **International Trade Fair** is followed by a **cultural festival**, which includes film screenings and musical performances, culminating with **St Dimitrios' Day** (26 October). Military parades follow on **Ohi Day** (28 October).

The **Thessaloniki International Film Festival** (☎ 2310 378 400; www.filmfestival.gr) occurs each November. Cinemas in various locations show 150 or so high-quality international films, ranging from experimental and obscure to well-known directors' works. The **Thessaloniki Documentary Festival** (www.filmfestival .gr) is in mid-March.

The **Office of Tourism Directorate** (☎ 2310 221 100; tour-the@otenet.gr; Tsimiski 136; ☉ 8am-8pm Mon-Fri, 8am-2pm Sat), near the White Tower, can provide more info on current cultural events.

Sleeping

Hotel rates and availability depend on Thessaloniki's convention and festival schedules. Autumn is especially busy; the **HelExpo** (www.helexpo.gr) website lists when fairs – which heighten accommodation demand, and prices – are held.

BUDGET

Decent budget accommodation is thankfully becoming more prevalent in Thessaloniki. Seedy budget hotels, however, remain in their traditional locale (the western stretch of Egnatia, near the train station), despite that expensive international chains have emerged even there. Thessaloniki remains a city priced for business travellers.

Backpacker's Refuge (☎ 6983433591; backpackers _refuge@hotmail.com; Botsari 84; dm per person €15; ☎) This snug, hostel-like flat comprises a two-bed and a four-bed dorm. It's run by the friendly Nina Delihristos and her brother, Grigoris, an ethnomusicologist and backpacker himself. The Refuge offers a shared kitchen, big bathroom with washing machine, and computer with wi-fi connection. Call, email or SMS ahead, as it's frequently booked and someone will have to meet you when you arrive, either at the Botsari bus stop (if taking bus 2 from the train station or bus 31 from the bus station), or the Laografiko Mouseio stop (if taking bus 78 from the airport). Grigoris also offers guided boat trips with camping on hidden islands near Halkidiki (see p299).

Hotel Orestias Kastoria (☎ 2310 276 517; www .okhotel.gr; Agnostou Stratiotou 14; s/d/tr €38/49/59; ☒ ☐) An old favourite near the Church of Agios Dimitrios, the Orestias Kastoria is a friendly, small place with cosy, clean rooms. Prices rise in September, when conventions are held.

Hotel Pella (☎ 2310 555 550; Ionos Dragoumi 63; s/d €40/50) A larger, port-area hotel, the Pella is less noisy than Egnatia hotels and has clean, well-maintained rooms and friendly staff.

Hotel Aegeon (☎ 2310 522 921; www.aegeon-hotel .gr; Egnatia 19; s/d €45/60; ☒ ☎) Recently renovated, this place in a historic building on Egnatia is surprisingly good value. The decent, clean rooms have low-key decor, bathrooms and most mod cons. It's a five- to 10-minute walk to the train station.

MIDRANGE

Tourist Hotel (☎ 2310 270 501; www.tourist hotel.gr; Mitropoleos 21; s/d/tr incl breakfast €55/70/90; ☒ ☐) At this classic place (built 1925), an old-school gated lift leads to rooms with all mod cons and decorated with elegance. Street noise is mitigated by the soundproof windows.

Le Palace Hotel (☎ 2310 257 400; www.lepalace .gr; Tsimiski 23; s/d incl breakfast €85/100; 🅿 🛜) At night gaze down from your little balcony at twinkling Tsimiski roaring by below (there's soundproofing). Le Palace has spacious, modern rooms with all mod cons. Valet parking costs €11 per 24 hours.

Egnatia Palace Hotel (☎ 2310 222 900; www.egnatia -hotel.gr; Egnatia 61; s/d/ste €90/115/145; 🅿 🛜) This four-star hotel above Plateia Aristotelous offers bright, modern rooms and suites with individual design and furnishings. The well-ness facilities include a heated pool, gym, *hammam*, sauna and massage room.

Electra Palace Hotel (☎ 2310 294 000; www.electra hotels.gr; Plateia Aristotelous 9; s/d €115/130; 🅿 🛜 🛗) Even if you come only to gaze out onto the harbour from the rooftop garden cafe, the appeal of this five-star city landmark that stands splendidly over Plateia Aristotelous is instantly apparent. Rooms are spacious and with all the expected amenities, including a mosaic-tiled indoor pool, rooftop outdoor pool and *hammam*.

City Hotel (☎ 2310 269 421; www.cityhotel.gr; Komninon 11; s/d €120/135; 🅿 🛜 🛗) A posh, recently renovated four-star business hotel near Plateia Eleftherias, this offers very professional service and some subdued elegance in its handsome rooms (some are wheelchair-friendly). Amenities include laundry services and parking. There's a big American-style breakfast and a spa centre.

TOP END

Daios (☎ 2310 250 200; www.daioshotels.com; Leoforos Nikis 59; s/d with sea view €170/225; 🅿 🛜 🛗) This White Tower boutique hotel has become a favourite among Greece's upper stratum. A keen sensitivity to light and shadow pervades the whole hotel, which has a contemporary, minimalist design. Suites have enormous, sound-proofed windows and wrap-around balconies (from some you only see water, not streets). The hotel's waterfront cafe is equally sophisticated and colour-rich. Staff is friendly and professional. Enter on the side street (2 Smyrnis).

Capsis Bristol (☎ 2310 521 321; www.capsishotel .gr; cnr Oplopiou & Katouni; s/d €192/250; 🅿 🛜) What was fated to become a stylish and friendly modern hotel was originally Thessaloniki's post office, in 1870. The Capsis Bristol's 16 rooms and four suites, decorated with ornate antiques, Persian rugs and artworks, suffuse

the hotel with an old-world charm befitting its location in historic Ladadika.

Eating

From quick and cheap souvlaki spots to fine dining, Thessaloniki has it all. In addition to the following, for Thessaloniki wine restaurants see Wineries of Northern Greece, p300. For sweets shops, see Sweet Indulgences, opposite). The website www.tavernoxoros.gr, in Greek, listing Thessaloniki eateries and locating them on the map, is a handy online resource.

Kyprion Gefsis (☎ 2310 202 800; Manou Kyriakou 5; grills €2-4) A popular place specialising in Cypriot pittas, the Kyprion Gefsis is a good and cheap pick near the Rotunda.

To Etsi (☎ 2310 222 469; Nikoforos Fokas 2; grills €2.50-4) This bawdily decorated, iconic eatery near the White Tower offers refreshingly light souvlaki and *soutzoukakia* (meat rissoles in tomato sauce) with vegetable dips, in Cypriot-style pitta bread. Look for the neon sign.

Me...Nou (☎ 2310 886 444; Petrou Sindika 25; mains €3-6) This inexpensive spot near the Backpacker's Refuge (p291) specialises in nourishing *mayirefta* (ready-cooked meals).

Ouzou Melathron (☎ 2310 275 016; Karypi 21; mezed-hes from €4.50, mains €6-11) This side-street *ouzerie* (ouzo bar) near Plateia Aristotelou is a bit touristy but still popular with locals. Occupy yourself with ouzo and mezedhes (appetisers), then dig into heartier fare such as lamb in sweet wine sauce.

Panellinion (☎ 2310 567 220; Salaminos 1; mains €6-10) This friendly taverna has traditional Ladadika decor, with its wooden floors and walls lined with olive-oil bottles and tins of produce. Panellinion's varied choices include a world of ouzos and cheeses to delicious seafood mezedhes; only organic vegetables are used.

our pick Myrsini (☎ 2310 228 300; Tsopela 2; mains €7-10) The only sad thing about Myrsini is that it's usually closed in July and August. Hearty portions of authentic and delicious Cretan dishes are served here, from rusks topped with tomato, Cretan olive oil and *dakos* (Cretan rusks) and flavourful wild *horta* (greens) to roast rabbit, pork and – crucially – *myzithro-pitakia* (flaky filo triangles with sweet sheep's milk cheese). Decor is simple, with worn wood floors and traditional accoutrements enhanced by Greek music.

Dore Zythos (☎ 2310 279 010; Tsirogianni 7; mains €7-12) Grab a table outside when the weather's warm and watch the White Tower across the way while savouring imaginative Mediterranean cuisine. Sister establishment Zythos (☎ 2310 540 284; Katouni 5; mains €8-12) in Ladadika has great architecture and equally fine food.

Kitchen Bar (☎ 2310 528 108; Warehouse B, Thessaloniki Port; mains €7-13) This perennial favourite offers both drinks and artfully prepared food, in a lofty, sumptuously decorated, renovated warehouse, with outdoors waterfront tables too. The salads and risotto are as bright as the flames in the open kitchen, where the chefs, like the style-conscious clientele, are always on display. However, if you wouldn't usually expect an omelette inside your chicken tortilla, say so.

Parakath (☎ 2310 653 705; Konstantinoupoleos 114; mains €8-13; ☽ dinner) Thessaloniki's only Pontian restaurant does rich, traditional pasta-based dishes with old Black Sea flair. Frenetic Pontian live-music performances occur on weekends (book ahead). It's out of the centre, so take a taxi.

Molyvos (☎ 2310 555 952; cnr Ionos Dragoumi & Kapodistriou; mains €8-15) Molyvos' refined setting elevates Greek cuisine to fine dining; nearby Molyvos Ethnik (☎ 2310 555 952; cnr Ionos Dragoumi and Papadopoulou; mains €6 to €10) is its freewheeling companion eatery, with high ceilings and polished mirrors, imaginative almost-fusion cuisine and Latin music.

Paparouna (☎ 2310 510852; www.paparouna.com; Syngrou 7; mains €8-16; ☽ 1pm-1am; ☎) Built a century ago as a bank, this lively restaurant is marked by lofty ceilings, great bursts of red (like the name, which means 'poppy') and checkerboard floor. The creative cuisine includes chicken with peppermint and honey, linguini with aromatic lemongrass and cherry tomatoes, and even organic Greek beer. It makes phenomenal desserts, too.

Miami (☎ 2310 447 996; Thetidos 18, Nea Krini; fish €12-18) Yes, it's expensive, but regular folks (as well as Greece's jet-set) hit this Kalamaria neighbourhood taverna on the water for Thessaloniki's best seafood. By taxi it's about a 20-minute ride, though public buses get there too.

Drinking

Thessaloniki's drinking scene ranges from vintage old-man *kafeneia* (traditional coffee houses) to pubs and thumping bars. Many stay open till 'late' – code for until no one's left standing'.

SWEET INDULGENCES

For a quick breakfast or sinful dessert, Thessaloniki's *zaharoplasteia* (patisseries) are hard to beat. Although classics such as baklava or chocolate profiterole are available throughout Greece, Thessaloniki's historic ties with the mores and populations of the Ottoman East have bequeathed it with an especially rich tradition of sweets – and a discerning local population to enjoy them. While tasty places are found everywhere, the following well-polished *zaharoplasteia* are particularly famous. Most prices are by the kilo (usually around €1 to €4 per piece).

Just above the Rotunda, the classic **Kokkinos Fournos** (Apostolou Pavlou 1, Rotunda) bakery does Thessaloniki's best *koulourakia vanilias* – crunchy, slightly sweet golden cookies perfect for dipping in Greek coffee.

Since 1908, when Thessaloniki was still Ottoman, local legend **Hatzis** (☎ 2310 968 400; Egnatia 119) has been replicating the tastes of old Constantinople. After Hatzis, you'll never ask for a simple 'baklava' again. The veritable symphony of sweets served here includes *vezir parmak* (*politika* syrup cake with cream filling), *hanoum bourek* (handmade pastry with raisins, peanuts and cream) and *malempi mastiha* (cream from milk and rice porridge, flavoured with *mastiha*, a sweet liquor from Chios, and served with rose syrup).

The posh **Agapitos** (☎ 2310 268 368; Egnatia 134) offers a taste of the Continent. Its cakes, fruit concoctions and profiteroles (chocolate pudding with a crunchy base and white cream) are excellent. Try the superlative *efrosini* chocolate cake, or smudge your fingers on the delicious mini-éclairs.

A veritable institution since 1960, **Trigona Elenidis** (☎ 2310 257 510; cnr D Gounari & Tsimiski) is a very rare thing in today's world: a shop specialising in only one product. Its sweet, flaky triangular cones filled with cool and unbelievably tasty cream are legendary; locals come out with 2kg boxes, but one large triangle will certainly fill you up.

NORTHERN GREECE

BEER ESSENTIALS

For beer lovers, the Greek preference for indistinguishably bland lagers can cause great consternation. In northern Greece, however, several watering holes are challenging the traditional orthodoxy of the Greek holy trinity of Heineken, Amstel and Mythos. Although you certainly pay for it – anywhere from €5 to €13 – at least the bottles are usually big.

The region's major city of Thessaloniki naturally has the best selection. **Extra Blatt** (☎ 2310 256 900; Svolou 46, Thessaloniki; beers €5-8; ⏰ 9am-2am), just off Plateia Navarinou, has numerous Belgian beers. Meanwhile, the Czech-run **Gambrinus** (cnr Valaoritou & Ionos Dragoumi, Thessaloniki; beers €3-5; ⏰ 9pm-late Mon-Sat) in the happening Syngrou district offers great and inexpensive, handcrafted Czech brews, accompanied by endless free popcorn and cooked snacks, like sausage with potatoes (€3). **Beer Academy** (☎ 2310 449 606; Mixalakopoulou 2, Kalamaria; beers €6-13; ⏰ 10am-3am), out in Kalamaria, has many (and pricey) world beers and full meals.

Further west in northern Greece, Ioannina (p337) boasts two great beer bars. Here, the student-packed **Presveia** (Embassy; ☎ 26510 26309; Karamanli 17, Ioannina; beers €4-11; ⏰ evening), offers around 100 different beers and good pub grub. The newer, spiffier **Jazz Beer House** (☎ 26510 27183; Pirsinella 1, Ioannina; ⏰ noon-late), located just inside an underpass opposite Piraeus Bank, cultivates a classic bistro look, with numerous great beers and wines.

Finally, over in Thrace's Alexandroupoli (p327), **Ginger Oil** (☎ 6977783524; cnr Dikastirion & Souliou, Alexandroupoli; ⏰ noon-3am), is a dark-lit, standing-room-only bar where 30 different beers are accompanied by vintage '60s and '70s rock.

Recently, a new bar hotspot has emerged around Syngrou/Valaoritou streets – the original 'hood' of pantyhose vendors, where the secret police also once ran safe houses. Here a bohemian feeling pervades and the commingled crowds spill out across the streets. In summer many city-centre nightclubs close and reopen in bigger spaces outdoors, on the airport road.

For speciality beer bars see Beer Essentials, above.

BARS

`our pick` **Spiti Mou** (cnr Egnatia & Leontos Sofou 26; ⏰ 1pm-late; 🛜) A new bar upstairs in a lofty old building in the Syngrou district, 'My House' (as the name means in Greek) was opened after its young owners realised their parties were becoming too big to fail. The relaxed feel is enhanced by eclectic music, well-worn decor and big couches spread out on a chequered floor. There's live music on Sundays, occasional costume parties and yes, even wi-fi. The entrance is unmarked, but is the doorway closest to Egnatia on Leontos Sofou.

Partizan Bar (☎ 2310 543 461; Valaoritou 29; ⏰ 8am-3am Mon-Thu, 8am-5am Fri & Sat, noon-3am Sun) Another Syngrou hotspot, this popular place has bohemian flair and gets packed with late-night revellers, from students to older folks.

Flou (☎ 2310 261 448; Nikoforou Foka 9; ⏰ 9pm-late Mon-Sat) What the French call 'Bobo' characterises this cosy bar on a White Tower sidestreet. Exuding neon and a *je ne sais quoi* eclectic retro decor, Flou gets packed on weekends with an early-30s crowd and plays a shameless selection of vintage pop.

Art House (☎ 2310 233 761; Vogatsikou 4; ⏰ 9pm-late) Up the old stairs and inside the door, enjoy the party at standing-room-only Art House, full of dark curves and Vulcan tints in the arches, mottled walls and worn wood floors. Music is funk and Eurohouse, the clientele mid-20s.

Santé (☎ 2310 510 088; Kapodistriou 3; ⏰ 9pm-late) This relaxed, stylish nightspot with Brazilian flair offers invigorating live music, like smokin' blues bands, on weekends.

Malt & Jazz (☎ 2310 278 876; Proxenou Koromila) Another live-music haven, Malt & Jazz has mainly jazz, but sometimes world music bands. Call after 8pm to check the schedule.

Elvis (☎ 2310 227 905; Leoforos Nikis 21) is a waterfront DJ bar that plays more interesting music than most of Nikis' bars; next door **Thermaïkos** (23 Leoforos Nikis) is a hipster stand-by that gets full and hypnotic late.

CAFES

`our pick` **Loxias** (☎ 2310 233 925; Isavron 7; ⏰ noon-2am) When in 2009 some miscreant stole the sound system at Loxias, Thessaloniki's first bookstore-*ouzerie*, charismatic owner Ioannis Kyprianidis just fired up the waiting piano instead. Educated Greeks have gravitated for years to this whimsical *steki* (hang-out), where they might discuss philosophy, politics or literature over ouzo and snacks. Loxias is decorated with wine casks, bursting bookshelves in the basement shop, and photos of Greek writers, Montenegrin princesses and the dervishes of old Hania. Romantics can duck the commotion on the back balcony's table for two, overlooking Roman ruins.

Kafenai (☎ 2310 220 310; cnr Ethnikis Amynis & Tsopela; 9am-2am) This new *kafeneio*, beside the Cretan restaurant Myrsini, impressively revives the spirit of old Salonica. With 1950s-style Greek decor, high ceilings supported by columns and low-key jazz, it's no wonder the place attracts local artists and musicians.

I Prinkipos (Apostolou Pavlou 22) This big studenty *kafeneio* beside the Turkish consulate is ideal for a Greek coffee and backgammon.

Kafe Nikis 35 (☎ 2310 230 449; Leoforos Nikis 35) More stylish than the adjacent waterfront places, this snug, friendly cafe just under street level is perfect for a Sunday-morning espresso. Get a window table and feel the dappled sunlight dancing through the blinds.

The last on Svolou's cafe row, **Verdi** (☎ 2310 236 803; cnr Svolou & Angelaki) has a spiffy woodtrim interior, cosy tables and a vaguely French attraction. Next door, **Émigré** (☎ 2310 262 282; Svolou 54) serves good espressos accompanied by crumbly cookies.

Entertainment

While packaged Greek pop and house music predominate, since 2009, live bands have been making a comeback in Thessaloniki (often, in the bars, opposite).

Lido (☎ 2310 539 055; Frixou 5, Sfageia; 9pm-late) Thessaloniki's big, mean disco machine, Lido pumps out R&B, house and more. Like most nightclubs, in summer it operates out on the airport road.

Pyli Axiou (☎ 2310 553 158; cnr Andreou Georgiou & Ermionis; 11pm-late) For a somewhat baser experience of contemporary Greek culture, visit Thessaloniki's most popular *bouzoukia* (club), and gape as ultrarich businessmen shower scantily-clad singers with flowers.

Vogue (☎ 2310 502 081; admission €5; 11pm-late) Just opposite Pyli Axiou, this is a trendy new nightclub playing the usual DJ-driven pop, R&B and house music.

Finally, for you partiers preferring an aqueous environment, take a booze cruise on one

of several **boat bars** (6pm-1am) moored on the waterfront south of the White Tower, in front of Alexander the Great's statue. Each boat has slightly different decorations and themes, with music ranging from pop to reggae to R&B. These cruisers leave every 20 minutes or so for a half-hour chug around the Thermaic Gulf; there's no admission charge and you can stay on board whether docked or adrift, for the whole evening if you wish – just keep drinking!

The **National Theatre of Northern Greece** (☎ 2310 288 000; Ethnikis Amynis 2) offers classical Greek drama and modern theatrical works. Additionally, the following cinemas operate:

Aristotelion (☎ 2310 262 051; Ethnikis Amynis 2)
Cinema Pallas (☎ 2310 278 515; Leoforos Nikis 73)
Olympion (☎ 2310 277 113; Plateia Aristotelous)
Plateia Alpha Odeon (☎ 2310 290 100; cnr Tsimiski & Plateia Aristotelous)

Shopping

West Egnatia has bargain-basement shopping, whereas Tsimiski offers high fashion (though not everything's expensive; women's shoes and jewellery are both affordable and good quality). International name-brand shops line Tsimiski, and fill the mall off it, below the US consulate.

Rihardos (☎ 2310 860 254; www.rihardos.gr, in Greek; Konstantinopoleos 27) Who knew there were so many different kinds of bouzouki? Rihardos, one of Greece's biggest purveyors of traditional instruments, has a huge array of Greek instruments, plus Western brand-name guitars (and Chinese knock-offs) in this and two other nearby shops. Friendly owner Rihardos and his English-speaking son, Joseph, explain everything about these unusual instruments. Take bus 31 from Egnatia east to the Faliro stop (five to 10 minutes); continue across the intersection with Paraskepoulos, turn left and Rihardos is facing you.

Getting There & Away

Thessaloniki is northern Greece's transport hub and gateway to the Balkans. Major European airlines and budget airlines fly regularly. Both planes and ferries serve some island groups.

AIR

Makedonia Airport (☎ 2310 473 212; www .thessalonikiairport.gr) is 16km southeast of town, and served by local bus 78. Internationally,

NORTHERN GREECE

Makedonia Airport serves a number of European destinations.

Olympic Air (☎ 2310 368 666; www.olympicairlines.com; Navarhou Koundourioti 1-3) is near the port, and **Aegean Airlines** (☎ 2310 280 050; www.aegeanair.com; Venizelou 2) is on Plateia Eleftherias.

Olympic Air operates more than 15 domestic routes, the most services go to Athens (€65 to €115, 55 minutes, seven daily). Aegean Airlines has 12 daily flights to Athens (€60 to €93). Travel agencies selling tickets are widespread; **Remember Travel** (☎ 2310 246 026; remembertravel@mail.gr; Egnatia 119), just off Kamara, sells tickets and has good postsale customer service. Another good all-purpose travel agency, further east, is **Aspect Travel** (☎ 2310 240 567; mail@aspect.ondsl.gr; Vasillis Olgas 283).

For island flights, see Island Hopping (p763).

BOAT

Thessaloniki's a major ferry and hydrofoil hub; see Island Hopping (p763).

Many port-area travel agencies sell tickets; try **Polaris Travel Services** (Agias Sofias ☎ 2310 278 613; Egnatia 81; ☼ 8am-8.30pm; Port ☎ 2310 548 655; polaris@otenet.gr; Navarhou Koundourioti 19; ☼ 8am-8.30pm) or **Karaharisis Travel & Shipping Agency** (☎ 2310 524 544; Navarhou Koundourioti 8; ☼ 8am-8.30pm).

BUS
Domestic

The **main bus station** (☎ 2310 595 408; Monastiriou 319), 3km west of centre, features different windows selling tickets to specific destinations, meaning the worker at one window cannot sell you a ticket for or give information about anything other than their specified destination. There's no general information booth and this enhances the station's unpleasant, stressful nature.

Note, however, that Halkidiki-bound buses leave from the **Halkidiki bus terminal** (☎ 2310 316 555; www.in-ktel.gr, in Greek), on Thessaloniki's eastern outskirts. To get there, take bus 2 or 31 to the Botsari stop from the train station, or from anywhere along Egnatia; at Botsari, bus 36 continues the final 10 minutes. With traffic, it's about one hour from the train station to the Halkidiki bus station.

International

OSE (☎ 2310 599 100; Aristotelous 26) runs buses to Sofia (€22, seven hours, two to four times daily) and Tirana (€31, twice daily). An office on the train station's eastern side sells tickets. Buses from the small **KTEL-Asprovalta station** (☎ 2310 536 260, Irinis 17) serve İstanbul (€45, 9½ hours, two daily).

For more buses to Tirana and other towns such as Korça (Korytsa) in Albania (€21, six hours, 9am, 7.30pm and 1.30am), visit **Alvavel** (☎ 2310 535 990; Giannitson 31) opposite the station.

TRAIN

Cheaper, often more comfortable and not always slower than the bus, the train goes

BUSES FROM THESSALONIKI'S MAIN BUS STATION

Destination	Duration	Fare	Frequency
Alexandroupoli	3¾hr	€26.50	8 daily
Athens	6¼hr	€35	10 daily
Drama	2hr	€12	13 daily
Edessa	2hr	€7.50	hourly
Florina	2¾hr	€14	6 daily
Ioannina	4¾hr	€28.50	6 daily
Kastoria	2½hr	€15.90	7 daily
Kavala	2¼hr	€13.30	15 daily
Komotini	2¾hr	€22.80	7 daily
Litohoro	1¼hr	€8	14 daily
Naoussa	1¼hr	€7.50	14 daily
Orestiada	5hr	€36	4 daily
Pella	45min	€3	every 45min
Serres	1¼hr	€7.40	every 30min
Veria	1hr	€6	every 45min
Volos	4hr	€13.30	7 daily
Xanthi	2½hr	€17	10 daily

everywhere in mainland Greece (except Kastoria, Halkidiki, Kavala and Epiros) and to all neighbouring countries (except Albania). Thessaloniki's **train station** (☎ 2310 599 421; Monastiriou) is also more central than the bus station. Get tickets at the station, or from **OSE** (☎ 2310 598 120; Aristotelous 18). The station's helpful information office provides printed timetables.

Trains are regular or intercity (IC or ICE). The latter are substantially more expensive, though not substantially faster. Prices below are for regular trains. Book in advance for Athens (especially for the cheapest trains). For any train, show up in advance to buy tickets since long lines are common.

Domestic

Ten regular trains daily serve Athens (€28, 6¾ hours) via Litohoro (€7, one hour), Larisa (€10, two hours, 12 daily) and Volos (€14, 4½ hours, 11 daily). The Athens intercity is more expensive (IC/ICE €36/48) but not significantly faster (5½ hours).

Some 14 daily trains service Veria (€3.20, one hour) and Edessa (€3.70, 1½ hours); of these, five continue to Amyndeo (for Kastoria bus connections) before terminating at Florina (€6, 2¾ hours), which has bus connections to the Prespa Lakes.

Thessaloniki–Thrace trains reach Orestiada (€16.40, 8½ hours, three daily), via Serres (€7.20, four hours, seven daily), Drama (€8, four hours, seven daily), Xanthi (€9, four hours, five daily), Komotini (€11, 4½ hours, five daily) and Alexandroupoli (€13.60, six hours, three daily).

Thessaloniki's train station has ill-kept toilets (downstairs), a National Bank of Greece, post office, ATMs, card phones, OTE (telephone office), kiosks, an old restaurant and some snazzy new sweets shops – plus an Orthodox chapel. Self-serve luggage storage lockers start from €3, or try the staffed luggage storage room (€3 per item per day) open until 10pm daily. For the latter, have your ongoing train ticket with you when depositing luggage.

International

One daily workhorse train plies the northern route through the ex–Yugoslav Republics of Macedonia, Serbia, Croatia and Slovenia, serving their respective capitals of Skopje (€13, 4½ hours), Belgrade (€32, 13 hours), Zagreb (€56.20, 20 hours) and finally Ljublana (€60, 24 hours). The 6.50pm train serves Skopje and Belgrade only. Departure times change seasonally, so double-check ahead.

Three daily trains serve Sofia (€17, six hours) via Kilkis in Greece and Blagoevgrad in Bulgaria. Two leave early (6.16am and 5.47am) and the third, which leaves at midnight, continues to Budapest.

Svilengrad and Plovdiv in Bulgarian Thrace are reached via the Thessaloniki–Thrace train route, departing daily at 11.44pm. A weekly, three-day train to Moscow usually runs in summer.

Trains to İstanbul (€30, two daily) transit in Alexandroupoli en route to Pythio, where you change trains before entering Turkey. A direct train, the *Filia Dostluk Express*, leaves at 8.35pm from Thessaloniki and returns from İstanbul at 8pm (11½ hours). A 2nd-class sleeper car costs €50, a 1st-class one €86.

Getting Around

TO/FROM THE AIRPORT

Bus 78 runs every 30 minutes from the airport west to the main bus station via the train station. From centre to airport by taxi costs €8 to €12.

BUS

Orange articulated buses operate within Thessaloniki, and blue-and-orange buses operate both within the centre and the suburbs. Happily, city buses now have electronic rolling signs listing the next destination, accompanied by a recording repeating the same in Greek and English. Bus 1 connects the bus station and the train station every 10 minutes; bus 31 goes every six minutes to Voulgari, bus 36 continues to the Halkidiki bus station. Major points on Egnatia such as Aristotelous, Agias Sofias and Kamara are served by many buses, such as the 10 and 14, from the train station.

Tickets are sold at *periptera* (street kiosks) for €0.50, or from on-board ticket machines (€0.60). If you buy the former, validate it on board. However, if you'll use the bus frequently, buy a 24-hour unlimited usage ticket (€2). Note the machine will not give change and doesn't accept bills.

Have change when boarding the bus, and buy a ticket immediately. Thessaloniki's ticket police combine the finesse of the amateur boxer with the efficiency of the Gestapo, and pounce at any sign of confusion – foreigners are especially easy targets. If they nab you, you'll pay €30 on the spot, or you can go with one of them to plead your case to the police.

CAR

The **ELPA** (Greek Automobile Club; ☎ 2310 426 319; Vasilissis Olgas 228), offering roadside assistance, is in Kalamaria. **Budget Rent a Car** (☎ 2310 229 519; Angelaki 15) and **Euro Rent** (☎ 2310 826 333; G Papandreou 5) are two biggies.

Finding parking on central streets is vexing; try the large parking lot by the ferry passenger terminal (per hour €2), or another one near the White Tower, Tsimiski and Office of Tourism Directorate; it's called Parking XANTH (Greek abbreviation for the nearby YMCA). Entrances are on both Tsimiski and around the corner on Nikolaou Germanou. Prices are €4.50 for the first hour, €3.50 for the second, and €2.50 per hour after that.

TAXI

Thessaloniki's blue-and-white taxis carry multiple passengers, and won't take you if you're not going in the same direction as pre-existing passengers. Stand in the direction you hope to go, flag one down, yell out your destination and anticipate the driver's upwards eyebrow roll of denial – good luck! The minimum fare is €2.80. Drivers work for five companies:

Alfa-Lefkos Pyrgos (☎ 2310 249 100)
Makedonia (☎ 2310 550 500)
Megas Alexandros (☎ 2310 866 866)
Omega (☎ 2310 511 855)
Thessaloniki (☎ 2310 551 525)

AROUND THESSALONIKI

While most tourists heading east from Thessaloniki flock immediately to the beaches of the Halkidiki Peninsula (right), even before entering it there are a few places worth visiting. Just 35km southeast of Thessaloniki, **Epanomi** is practically an urban suburb; however, it does have beaches and two 19th-century churches: the **Church of Agios Georgios** (1835), and the **Church of the Kimisis Theotokou** (1865), both with lavish icons. Most remarkable, however, is the **Domaine Gerovassiliou Winery**, situated amid vineyards overlooking the sea. Winery tours are recommended; see Wineries of Northern Greece, p300. Epanomi also offers a couple

of good fish tavernas near the water, such as Taverna tou Psilou and Agnanti.

Just 3km from Epanomi, the long, sandy **Faros Beach** and adjoining **Potamos Beach**, have clear waters and in summer organised activities, including beach volleyball and music, and some cafes. You can camp or get a private room close to the action at the well-maintained **Hotel Camping Akti Retzika** (☎ 6937456551; www.retzikas.gr; Potamos Beach; camp sites per person/tent €5/5, r from €35), which has extensive camping grounds, modern rooms, and a restaurant and snack bar.

Some 50km southeast of Thessaloniki on the main road is the stalagmite-rich **Petralona Cave** (☎ 23730 71671; admission €7; ◷ 9am). Discovered by Petralona village locals in 1959, it soon became famous when the skull of a prehistoric man (dubbed *Arhanthropos*; in Greek, the 'first' or 'original man') was found; scientists have since dated it as 700,000 years old, making *Arhanthropos* Europe's oldest known man. Numerous fossils have also been discovered here, some of extinct species, including lions, panthers, bears, rhinoceroses, elephants, bison, deer, numerous birds, bats and others. However, the most intriguing objects discovered, the so-called 'Petralonas Hoard', are kept at Thessaloniki's Archaeological Museum (p287). The ticket price includes a tour of the cave and the adjacent **anthropological museum**. Note that photos aren't allowed and the cave closes one hour before sunset.

HALKIDIKI ΧΑΛΚΙΔΙΚΗ

Immediately recognisable on maps for its three 'fingers' stretching into the North Aegean, the Halkidiki Peninsula has become all too famous for its tourist sprawl in summertime, when half of Thessaloniki descends for holidays. The first finger, Kassandra, has fared worst, filled with unimaginative villas, concrete and trinket shops. The second, Sithonia, remains somewhat less abused, and contains some truly magical beaches. Halkidiki's third finger has largely escaped the clutches of modern development – most of it comprises the monastic community of Mt Athos (Agion Oros), open only to male pilgrims and accessible only by boat.

In summer, budget accommodation in Halkidiki is nonexistent and traffic makes getting there exasperatingly slow. For campers, however, more than 30 high-quality and inexpensive camping grounds are available. Halkidiki has long, sandy beaches surrounded by aquamarine seas and pine forests, and scattered islets. It's best in September, when waters are warmest and the crowds are gone.

Kassandra Peninsula
Χερσόνησος Κασσάνδρας
The Kassandra Peninsula is what happens when Greek urbanites go on vacation and bring their motorcycles, concrete sidewalks and consumerism with them. It's not an oasis of tranquillity, but for nightlife it's great.

After entering Kassandra proper, built-up **Kallithea** has fleshed-out discos and bars, and a long, crowded beach. For reasonable self-catering domatia with air-conditioning (rooms €50), ask at Kallithea Market, beside the bus stop for Thessaloniki. **Manita Tours** (☎ 23740 24036) in the town centre does day trips, including a boat tour (€30) to beaches on the Sithonia Peninsula opposite.

Kassandra has good camping grounds, especially at **Posidi**, where the EOT (Greek National Tourist Organisation) runs **Camping Kalandra** (☎ 23740 41123; ⏰ May-Sep). **Camping Anemi Beach** (☎ 23740 71276; ⏰ May-Sep), with space for 115 tents, is at **Nea Skioni** on the quieter western shore.

For island camping on deserted isles between Kassandra and Sithonia, contact **Grigoris Delihristou** (☎ 6979773905; backpackers_refuge@hotmail.com) of the Backpacker's Refuge (p291) in Thessaloniki. For €100 per person, Greg takes small groups for four-day camping trips to these tiny islets surrounded by crystal-clear waters – luxuriate on the beach, swim or even go spear fishing. The price includes van and boat transport plus all food and drink – an astonishingly cheap adventure impossible to do independently.

GETTING THERE & AWAY
Thirteen buses daily go from Thessaloniki's **Halkidiki bus terminal** (☎ 23103 16555; www.in-ktel.gr, in Greek) to Kallithea (€7.60, 1½ hours) on the east coast; 10 go to Pefkohori (€10.20, two hours), also on the east coast, via Kryopigi and Haniotis; seven go to Paliouri (€11.10, two hours) on the southern tip.

Sithonian Peninsula Χερσόνησος Σιθωνίας
Sithonia has better beaches, more spectacular natural beauty and a more relaxed feel than Kassandra. The southern end and eastern coastline have beautiful beaches; outside high summer, they're yours.

The coast road loops around Sithonia, skirting wide bays, climbing into pine-forested hills and dipping down to the resorts.

WEST COAST
The west coast has long sandy beaches between **Nikiti** and **Paradisos**, notably **Kalogria Beach** and **Lagomandra Beach**. Beyond, **Neos Marmaras** is Sithonia's largest resort, with a crowded beach but many domatia.

From Neos Marmaras the road climbs into the hills, from which roads (some dirt) descend to more beaches and camping grounds. **Toroni** and **Porto Koufos**, two small southwestern resorts, offer relaxing beaches and a yacht harbour sheltered in a deep bay, with domatia and fish tavernas. Sithonia's relatively undeveloped southern tip is rocky, rugged and dramatic, with spectacular views of Mt Athos appearing as you rounding the southeastern tip.

Kalamitsi, with its gorgeous beach, has gotten overdeveloped, though it does have services such as boat rental at the **North Aegean Diving Centre** (☎ 23750 41338), which also does dives (€50) and courses (from €80).

Porto Camping (☎ 23750 41346; camp sites per adult/tent €3.80/4.50), on Kalamitsi's main beach, and the pricier **Camping Kalamitsi** (☎ 23750 41411; camp sites per adult/tent €6.50/7.20; ⏰ May-Sep), around the western headland, are both good. The best rooms are **O Giorgakis** (☎ 23750 41338; fax 23750 41013; studios €75), above the eponymous restaurant opposite the beach. The studios sleep five and are fully equipped. The quieter **Souzana Rooms** (☎ 23750 41786; apt €50) sits in a spacious garden and has good-sized apartments.

EAST COAST
Sarti, further up the coast, is a quiet resort with some nightlife, rooms and eating options, plus a very well-developed camping ground. Its long, sandy beach used to make it a place for escapists, though it's since been 'discovered'. There are great views of Mt Athos, also visible by boat excursions run by Sarti travel agents.

The large and very popular **Camping Armenistis** (☎ 23750 91487; www.armenistis.com.gr; per person/tent €7.20/6.30; ⏰ May-Oct), at Sarti, has a fantastic setting between forest and beach, and is outfitted with an astonishing range of services, from market, restaurant and crêperie to cinema, sports grounds and medical centre. Summer sees frequent concerts and DJ parties.

NORTHERN GREECE

WINERIES OF NORTHERN GREECE

Ever since the wine-inspired writings of Homer, Greece has been famous for its viticulture. Some of Greece's best wines are produced in the north. Here, conditions are ideal for grape cultivation, with arid yet fertile fields bounded by lakes, mountains and the sea, creating unique microclimates and cultivation zones. In Macedonia, endemic varietals are grown, along with more famous varietals such as Cabernet Sauvignon and Merlot. The most distinctive include *xinomavro*, a superlative dry red, rich in tannins and with high alcohol content. It's grown widely, and especially in Naoussa, Amyntaio, Pella and Velvendos, and in Halkidiki's vineyards.

Macedonian wineries run from small, family-size establishments to major producers with big export capacities. Both sorts now offer tasting tours (usually, with advance arrangements), often for free, with the opportunity to buy wine cheaper than in shops.

The renowned **Kir-Yianni Estate** (☎ 23320 51100; www.kiryianni.gr; Yianakohori village; ☯ 9am-5pm) near Naoussa, was established by Yiannis Boutaris, a living legend on the winemaking scene. Since the 1960s, this fourth-generation winemaker has helped shape the agricultural innovations and technological development that have enhanced Greek wine's reputation internationally. Yiannis helped revitalise whole tracts of territory near Naoussa, in vineyards on Mt Vermio (230m to 320m elevation) and the Amyntaio area south of Florina, near Lake Vegoritis.

Now, Yiannis' son, Stellios, is carrying on the family tradition. Speaking at a restored Ottoman-era tower overlooking the vineyards, Stellios says 'we are very proud of the progress we have made, and we have many plans for the future' – both for making better wine, and in offering more sophisticated tours. Visitors learn about Kir-Yianni's wine production, tour the facilities and sample several excellent wines while gazing out over the winery's lush vineyards – all for free.

Not far away, **Chateau Pigasos Winery** (☎ 23320 24740, 6937093658; chateaupegasuswine@hotmail .com; Polla Nera village) is a small boutique winery operated by winemaker Dimitris Markovitis and his sister Katerina, with vineyards in Polla Nera village, halfway between Naoussa and Edessa. Visitors to the winery, which produces Xinomavro, Chardonnay, Riesling and Cabernet Sauvignon, should arrange in advance to make sure someone is there. According to the cheerful Katerina, presenting samples of Chateau Pigasos wine along with select cheeses, 'we believe our wines are so good because we use only our own, carefully tended grapes and store the new wine in barrels 7m below the earth, for at least two years before being bottled'.

Haus Theodora (☎ 23750 94341; www.sarti-theodora .gr; apt €50), overlooking Sarti beach's northern end, offers brightly painted modern studios with spacious balconies.

Kivotos (☎ 23750 94143; mains €5-9) on the central waterfront offers great grilled fish on a table in the sand. Owner Daniel can help with finding rooms.

Between Sarti and Panagia the loop roads meet up and things get more interesting. Sithonia's best camping grounds and beaches are here. Rent a scooter to explore; 6km north of Sarti is a turn-off leading to **Kavourotrypes** (Crab Holes) – several small rocky coves great for swimming. Some 13km further north is popular **Vourvourou**, which has camping grounds and rooms for rent. Although it feels a bit packaged, the spacious **Hotel Vergos** (☎ 23750 91379; www.halkidiki .com/vergos; s/d/apt incl breakfast €58/63/105; 🖳) offers well-furnished rooms in a relaxed setting with a big lawn for kids.

A short dirt road from the centre leads to Vourvourou's best beach, **Karydi**. Backed by shady pine trees, this beach is an ideal mix of sand, rocks and solitude. Another sandy beach is at **Ormos Panagias**, 1km north.

GETTING THERE & AWAY

Buses leave from Thessaloniki's east-side **Halkidiki bus terminal** (☎ 23103 16555; www.in-ktel .gr, in Greek) for Neos Marmaras (€11.20, 2½ hours, seven daily), Sarti (€15.80, 3½ hours, five daily) and Vourvourou (€10.50, four daily). Most of the Sarti buses loop around the Sithonian Peninsula, enjoying coastal views.

Getting to Sithonia from Kassandra by bus requires changing at Nea Moudania, at the foot of Kassandra.

Athos Peninsula (Secular Athos)

Χερσόνησος Αθω

The third finger of Halkidiki is visited by both beachgoers, in the northerly stretches, and by

Visitors to western Macedonian wineries could lodge in Edessa (p315), Veria (p313), or in Naoussa – itself home to 22 wineries. Here, try the **Hotel Palea Poli** (☎ 23320 52520; www.paleapoli .gr; Vasileou Konstantinou 32, Naoussa; s/d €80/120), an exquisite boutique hotel with ornate traditional furnishings and a superior restaurant. The owners provide winery information.

Finally, eastern Macedonia's Halkidiki Peninsula boasts the truly remarkable **Domaine Gerovassiliou** (☎ 23920 44567; 6937307740; www.gerovassiliou.gr; Epanomi village). Just 25km southeast of Thessaloniki – accessible by city buses – the winery is the passion of Vangelis Gerovassiliou. Among other achievements, this French-educated oenologist saved an indigenous Greek varietal, *malagousia*, from extinction in 1976. A man who loves his work, and who looks after every detail, Vangelis affirms that 'we put great effort into everything we do here, as the visitor will understand not only when sampling the wines, but in enjoying our setting as well'.

Indeed, situated on a bluff overlooking the sea, Domaine Gerovassiliou is surrounded by sloping vineyards and herb gardens; on clear days, Mt Olympus itself rises from the horizon far across the water. See the fascinating museum of wine-related items, which include Mycenaean and Byzantine amphorae, antique cooper's tools, handmade wine-presses dating from the 18th to 20th centuries, wine bottles (16th–20th centuries), and an eclectic collection of ornate corkscrews from the same period.

If you haven't time to visit the wineries, sample some of their wine at any good Thessaloniki restaurant or bar. According to the Greek winemakers themselves, the city's best wine-restaurants include **Clochard** (☎ 2310 239 805; www.clochard.gr, in Greek; Proxenou Koromila 4; mains €10-17; ☯ noon-2am Mon-Sat), serving Greek and French cuisine, and **Mandragoras** (☎ 2310 285 372; cnr Mitropoleos & Pavlou Mela; mains €8-14), which, according to Stellios Boutaris, 'has the best wine list in Salonica'.

Finally, each March the **Thessaloniki International Wine Competition** presents hand-picked foreign experts and local producers to the public. It's sponsored by the **Wine Producers Association of Northern Greece** (www.wineroads.gr, in Greek).

religious pilgrims going to the isolated monastic community that takes up the mountainous southeastern part. There's no land entry allowed between the two sections.

At the northwestern, secular edge of the Athos Peninsula **Ierissos** has regular ferries to Athos' east-coast monasteries, while Ouranopoli on the southwestern coast is the port for ferries to the west-coast monasteries and their administrative centre, Karyes.

Secular Athos is visited by a few package tourists, but more so by Greek families. Here visit **Ammoliani**, a tiny island with fine beaches, domatia, camping and tavernas. Five to six daily ferries go there from **Trypiti** on the south coast.

OURANOUPOLI ΟΥΡΑΝΟΥΠΟΛΗ

Ouranoupoli is a low-key tourist village with good nearby beaches, and it's the jumping-off point for Athos' monastic community. Besides daily ferries for pilgrims, it has daily sightseeing **boat cruises** (per person €20; ☯ 10.30am) that circle the Athos Peninsula – giving females, who are banned from monastic Athos, a chance to see something. Alternatively, hiring a boat (€40) lets you visit the sandy, uninhabited **Drenia archipelago**, 1.9km offshore.

Sleeping

Ouranopoli Camping (☎ 23770 71171; camp sites per adult/tent €9/9; ☯ 20 May–30 Oct) A decent, though pricey camping ground; it's on Ouranopoli's northern beach side.

Xenios Zeus (☎ 23770 71274; www.ouranoupoli.com/zeus; s/d/tr €40/55/65; ☷) A friendly, family-run place on the main street, Xenios Zeus has clean and comfortable rooms, and will hold unnecessary luggage for monastery pilgrims. Members of the Britain-based Friends of Mt Athos (www .athosfriends.org) get a discount.

Lazaros Andonakis Rooms (☎ 23770 71366; s/d €45/55; ☷) This reasonable choice has airy, pine-furnished rooms, some with harbour views. To get there, continue 50m seaward from the Pilgrims' Office.

Mt Athos (Agion Oros) Αγιον Ορος

More than a millennium of unbroken spiritual activity has been taking place on the isolated southeastern part of Halkidiki's third finger, at the monasteries of Agion Oros (the Holy Mountain). A semi-autonomous monastic republic that still follows the Julian calendar, along with many other Byzantine edicts and mores, the Holy Mountain

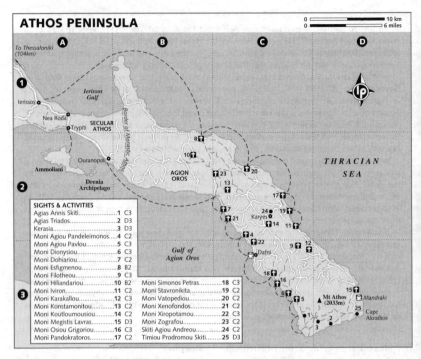

ATHOS PENINSULA

SIGHTS & ACTIVITIES	
Agias Annis Skiti	1 C3
Agias Triados	2 D3
Kerasia	3 D3
Moni Agiou Pandeleimonos	4 C2
Moni Agiou Pavlou	5 C3
Moni Dionysiou	6 C3
Moni Dohiariou	7 C2
Moni Esfigmenou	8 B2
Moni Filotheou	9 C3
Moni Hiliandariou	10 B2
Moni Iviron	11 C2
Moni Karakallou	12 C3
Moni Konstamonitou	13 C2
Moni Koutloumousiou	14 C2
Moni Megistis Lavras	15 D3
Moni Osiou Grigoriou	16 C3
Moni Pandokratoros	17 C2

Moni Simonos Petras	18 C3
Moni Stavronikita	19 C2
Moni Vatopediou	20 C2
Moni Xenofondos	21 C2
Moni Xiropotamou	22 C3
Moni Zografou	23 C2
Skiti Agiou Andreou	24 C2
Timiou Prodromou Skiti	25 D3

consists of 20 working monasteries and smaller *skites* (dependencies), with a few *very* old-school, remote mountain hermitages still inhabited by the odd ascetic. An enormous World Heritage Site that occupies most of the Athos Peninsula, Mt Athos is formally a part of the Greek state, though ecclesiastically it remains under the Orthodox Patriarchate of Constantinople (İstanbul).

Apocryphal legends say that the Virgin Mary herself visited Athos and blessed it; the Holy Mountain is considered the Garden of the Virgin, and it is dedicated exclusively to her – meaning there's no room for other women. Although frustrated Eurocrats in Brussels have contested this prohibition, they've proven no match for more than 1000 years of tradition and the gold-sealed *chrysobulls* (decrees) of Byzantine emperors, whose names are still invoked in prayers and whose edicts continue to be respected.

For men, visiting monastic Athos requires advance planning (see Getting the Permit, opposite). Visits are restricted to four days, though with special permission they can be extended – a worthwhile effort, if you have the time.

Experiencing the monasteries is wonderfully peaceful – and tiring. In many hosting monasteries, you follow the monks' lifestyle, eating and attending services (even at 3.30am) with them, and generally respecting the monasteries' customs. Walk in the still Athonite forests and down worn trails that connect the monasteries, and marvel at their architecture and art treasures, and perhaps enjoy the simple hospitality and anecdotes of the wise old monks over a Greek coffee or *raki* (Greek firewater).

HISTORY

Ever since Byzantine times, ascetics gravitated towards rugged, inaccessible Athos. Gradually, a loose community formed. Emperor Basil I's AD 885 chrysobull confirmed Athos' special status. In 943, the monastic territory's extent was officially mapped. Some 20 years later the Holy Mountain was formally dedicated, when Emperor Nikoforos II Fokas funded the Moni Megistis Lavras – the biggest, if not the first, monastery.

The monastic community flourished under imperial patronage and, as it expanded,

NORTHERN GREECE

sparked a reaction from conservative monks who feared old-school traditions were being diluted, and monasteries too commercially involved. Their grumblings prompted corrective imperial edicts, which reaffirmed prior ones; the most famous is that of Constantine IX Monomahos in 1060, which barred entry for women, female domestic animals, beardless persons and eunuchs. Today, women are still banned, hens are tolerated for their eggs, beards are no longer mandatory, and eunuchs are not readily available.

The 11th century was a glorious time for Athos, but destructive pillaging by pirates, Catalans and Crusaders (in 1204) followed. Nevertheless, the Holy Mountain was always reborn. Since founding and subsidising monasteries conferred considerable prestige on the donor, numerous Bulgarian, Russian and Serbian princes followed suit.

Athos submitted to Ottoman rule with Thessaloniki's capture in 1430, but managed to retain its semi-independent status. In 1542, the last Athonite monastery, Stavronikita, was founded. During the Greek War of Independence (1821–29), monasteries were plundered and libraries burned by Turkish troops. For more than 70 years following the 1917 Russian Revolution, Russian participation and patronage were drastically reduced.

Nowadays, 20 ruling monasteries and several dependencies and hermitages exist. Athos' modern constitution from 1924 was guaranteed in the 1975 Greek Constitution. Monks, regardless of origin, become Greek citizens, while the Holy Council *(Iera Synaxis)*, composed of one representative from each monastery, is responsible for internal administration. Although only 1600 monks currently live on Athos, their inordinate political influence is often breathlessly reported in the Greek media, as with a 2008 scandal over shady land-swaps involving monastery-owned land that resulted in the dismissal of one head monk and the sacking of a Greek government minister.

GETTING THE PERMIT

Plan ahead: advance booking of up to six months is usual in summer (though in winter it's easier). Only 10 non-Orthodox adult males and 100 Orthodox men may enter Mt Athos daily. Those under 18 must be accompanied by their father or, if visiting with a group leader or guardian, need written permission from their father.

Pilgrimage intention must be declared in writing, specifying your preferred visit dates. Send a passport copy to Thessaloniki-based **Mt Athos Pilgrims Bureau** (☎ 23102 52578; fax 23102 22424; pilgrimsbureau@c-lab.gr; Egnatia 109; 🕑 9am-2pm Mon-Fri, 10am-noon Sat), near Kamara. Start the permit process there. While you should double-check in advance, pilgrims can also book by email/fax, print out the confirmation email/fax and go directly to Ouranopoli. Clergymen need written permission from the **Ecumenical Patriarchate of Constantinople** (☎ in Turkey 90 212 5349037) to visit Athos.

With reservation secured and written/printed confirmation from the Mt Athos Pilgrims Bureau, go to Ouranopoli for the final permit *(diamonitirion)*.

ENTERING ATHOS

In Ouranopoli, the **Pilgrims' Office** (☎ 23770 71422; fax 23770 71450; 🕑 8.10am-2pm), is on the right-hand street just before a Jet Oil station. Look for the black-and-yellow Byzantine flag.

Officials will check your passport and booking confirmation, and issue a three-night (four-day) *diamonitirion*: students pay €10, Orthodox believers €25, and everyone else €30. Free entry is granted on a case-by-case basis to the poor, the sick and so on. Video cameras aren't allowed, but cameras are fine. Travellers with a vehicle can park at the lot (per day €7.50) on Ouranopoli's south side.

Alternatively, for east-coast Athonite monasteries, drive or take a bus from Thessaloniki directly to Ierissos: get your *diamonitirion* here (☎ 23770 71085; info@mtathosinfo.gr) before boarding the ferry.

From Ouranopoli, the first boat to Athos' main port of **Dafni** is the *Agia Anna,* which leaves at 8am and 11am Monday to Saturday, and 8.30am Sunday (€8). The *Axion Esti* leaves Ouranopoli at 9.45am (€6). The **ticket office** (☎ 23770 71248) is on the waterfront. Get your *diamonitirion* and your ferry ticket early, as queues are common.

The voyage takes two hours, with intermediate stops at several monasteries. In Dafni, a bus continues to the administrative capital of **Karyes** (€2.60). Alternatively, take a fast Ouranopoli–Dafni **water taxi** (☎ 6974060744), which will fit eight passengers (€140).

Once in Karyes, head to your chosen monastery. You stay free, but technically for one night only in each place. The *diamonitirion* can be extended in Karyes for another two

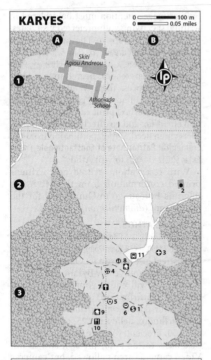

KARYES

0 — 100 m
0 — 0.05 miles

INFORMATION		
Agrotiki Bank	1	B3
Civil Administration Office	2	B2
Community Clinic	3	B3
OTE	4	B3
Police Station	5	B3
Post Office	6	B3

SIGHTS & ACTIVITIES		
Protaton	7	A3

SLEEPING ⌂		
Guest House	8	B3
Ilarion Guest House	9	A3

EATING 🍴		
Bakery	10	A3

TRANSPORT		
Bus & Taxi Stop	11	B3

days at the end. Try to book your monasteries in advance, especially in summer.

ORIENTATION & INFORMATION

Dafni has a port authority, police, customs, post office, shops for food and locally produced religious items, a cafe and card phones. All Greek mobile-phone networks operate.

For internet information on Athos, visit the detailed www.mountathos.gr, or the informative website of the British-based **Friends of Mt Athos** (www.athosfriends.org), whose members include no less than Prince Charles.

Karyes hosts the community's **Civil Administration Office** (☎ 23770 23314), **police station** (☎ 23770 23212), Agrotiki Bank, post office, OTE, **community clinic** (☎ 23770 23217), bus stop and rudimentary shops, including a bakery, and a public telephone. Athos' two nonmonastic guest houses, a nameless **guest house** (☎ 23770 23362) and the **Ilarion Guest House** (☎ 23770 23243), are here too.

The monastic community's northern part is thickly forested, while the south is dominated by the stark, soaring peak of Mt Athos (2033m). Since there's neither industry nor hunting, monastic Athos is practically a nature reserve. You won't find monks swimming around Athos' breathtaking, craggy coast, though you may hear tales of the occasional spear-fishing, scuba-diving ascetic.

Be aware that if you're staying in a monastery where pilgrims dine alongside the monks, the meal concludes when the simultaneous spiritually edifying reading ends – so eat up!

EXPLORING ATHOS

Monastic vehicles, local **taxis** (☎ 23370 23266) and boats operate, but walking is the best way to experience Athos' serenity. Paths pass through tranquil forests, where the only sounds are the rustling of leaves, chirping of birds and the occasional passing monk, rhythmically reciting his prayers.

Boat travel (around €2), allows great sea views. A caïque leaves Agias Annis Skiti daily at 9.45am for Dafni, serving intermediate west-coast monasteries or their *arsanas* (assigned landing areas) and returning every afternoon. A less-regular east-coast caïque travels three times weekly between Ierissos and Mandraki (the harbour for Moni Megistis Lavras). Another service around the south connects Mandraki and Agias Annis.

While in Karyes, visit the 10th-century **Protaton**, the basilican church opposite the Holy Epistasia. Its treasures include paintings by Panselinos, the master of the so-called 'Macedonian School' of ecclesiastical art.

Karyes to the Southeast Coast Monasteries & Mt Athos

For the grand tour of southeastern Athos, and perhaps a mountain hike, head northeast from Karyes by foot to the coastal **Moni Stavronikita** (☎ /fax 23770 23255; ☼ noon-2pm) or, just under it, **Moni Iviron** (☎ 23770 23643; fax 23770 23248; ☼ noon-2pm). The latter was founded by Georgian monks and contains a library of over 2000 manuscripts, including 100 rare Georgian-language parchments.

From Iviron, coastal paths or caïques access **Moni Filotheou** (☎ 23770 23256; fax 23770 23674). Filotheou is also accessible from Karyes, along a shady path with spring water (3½ hours). Beyond **Moni Karakallou** (☎ 23770 23225; fax 23770 23746) the Byzantine-era path becomes a road; from here it's a 5½-hour walk to Moni Megistis Lavras (alternatively, flag down a monastic vehicle).

Moni Megistis Lavras (☎ 23770 23754; fax 23770 23013) is Athos' biggest monastery and the only one never damaged by fire. Its treasures include frescoes by Theophanes of Crete and the tomb of St Athanasios, its founder.

A caïque leaves Megistis Lavras at 3pm for **Agias Annis Skiti** (☎ 23770 23320), a hermit's dwelling. Alternatively, take the wilderness path around the peninsula's southern tip; it passes **Timiou Prodromou Skiti**, then coastal **Agias Triados** (off the main track), then **Kerasia** and finally the hospitable **Agias Annis**. Kerasia or Agias Annis are good bases for climbing **Mt Athos** (2033m). The hike is not easy; inform someone that you're going, and don't hike alone. Take food and water and extra clothes, since it gets cold up there. There's a well with drinking water below the summit, at the chapel of **Panagia** (Virgin Mary). You can return to Dafni from Agias Annis by caïque.

Karyes to the Southwest Coast Monasteries

Alternatively, start west from Karyes towards the coast, site of spectacular clifftop monasteries such as Simonos Petras and Dionysiou. The first monastery, just west and then south of Karyes, is friendly **Moni Koutloumousiou** (☎ 23770 23226; fax 23770 23731). West of Koutloumousiou near the coast is **Moni Xiropotamou** (☎ 23770 23251; fax 23770 23733; ☼ 12.30-2.30pm), with comfortable, oil-lit guest rooms. Pilgrims here dine separately from the monks. The path southward accesses Dafni; follow the coastal path or take the daily caïque,

which leaves for Agias Annis at 12.30pm, calling at Simonos Petras, Osiou Grigoriou, Dionysiou and Agiou Pavlou. Alternatively, wooded paths in the peninsula's centre, accessible from Moni Koutlomousiou or Moni Filotheou, also reach Simonos Petras.

Spectacular **Moni Simonos Petras** (Simopetra; ☎ 23770 23254; fax 23770 23707; ☼ 1-3pm), fronted by wooden balconies jutting above a cliff, is Athos' most-photographed monastery. Here and at the other cliff monasteries, standing in the dark under a sky teeming with stars, with the sound of the sea below, is almost a religious experience in itself. From Simonos Petras the coastal path branches off the trail to the *arsanas* at a small shrine, leading to **Moni Osiou Grigoriou** (☎ 23770 23668; fax 23770 23671). This seafront monastery has a comfortable harbourside guest house.

The coastal path from here south climbs and descends three times before reaching the sublime **Moni Dionysiou** (☎ 23770 23687; fax 23770 23686), another cliff-hanging monastery especially ethereal at night. Dionysiou's *katholikon* (principal church) contains a very important wax-and-mastic icon of the Virgin and Child. Legend says that in AD 626, facing a grim combined Persian and Avar siege of Constantinople, the patriarch carried the icon round the walls and the city was miraculously saved. The icon is considered Athos' oldest, and though its features are no longer visible, the dark shape indeed resonates with a strange power in its ornate silver case.

After Dionysiou, the coastal path continues to **Moni Agiou Pavlou** (☎ 23770 23741; fax 23770 23355) and Agias Annis Skiti.

Karyes to the Northern Monasteries

The path north from Karyes towards Moni Vatopediou, Moni Xenofondos and Moni Konstamonitou, first passes the sprawling **Skiti Agiou Andreou** (☎ 23770 23810). Once home to Russian monks, it was largely abandoned during Soviet times but is currently being revitalised. Although it doesn't figure in the tourist guides, humble Agiou Andreou is actually at the very forefront of Mt Athos' current cultural and artistic endeavours. The *skiti* hosts projects by **Restaurateurs San Frontieres** (www.rsfturkey.org), a leading international organisation that has performed expert restoration work on more than 600 icons and 400 sq metres of wall paintings at a dozen Athonite monasteries, including Iviron, Stavronikita, Koutloumousiou and Dionysiou.

Agiou Andreou has a cultural centre, where artists, photographers, writers and musicians inspired by the Holy Mountain exhibit their works. Like-minded pilgrims or other art-lovers should definitely visit this unusual monastery.

After Agiou Andreou, continue to the coastal **Moni Pandokratoros** (☎ 23770 23880; fax 23770 23685), or take the long, lovely forest path to **Moni Vatopediou** (☎ 23770 41488; fax 23770 41462; ☻ 9am-1pm), further along the northeast coast. Although not exactly unorthodox, Vatopediou audaciously follows the modern Gregorian (Western) calendar. Vatopediou's sumptuous main church is a must-see, with a jaw-dropping collection of treasures.

From Vatopediou, a coastal path leads to **Moni Esfigmenou** (☎ 23770 23229). Further on is **Moni Hilandariou** (☎ 23770 23797; fax 23770 23108), a very hospitable and friendly Serbian monastery still recovering from a 2004 fire. The humble, pretty **Moni Konstamonitou** (☎ /fax 23770 23228) is worth visiting, but the Bulgarian **Moni Zografou** (☎ /fax 23770 23247) further north is more famous. Its name, meaning 'painter', comes from a miraculous icon not painted by human hands. The northernmost west-coast monastery, **Moni Dohiariou** (☎ /fax 23770 23245), slopes towards the sea and boasts remarkable architecture. These west-coast monasteries are served by the Ouranopoli–Dafni ferry.

Next on the coastal path is **Moni Xenofondos** (☎ 23770 23633; fax 23770 23631), first mentioned in 998, but probably dating to the 6th century. Its seafront position made it a target for pirates and it was frequently plundered. Nevertheless, Moni Xenofondos has impressive mid-Byzantine marble and wood-carved iconostases in its older, 10th-century *katholikon*; its newer one, completed in 1838, is Athos' largest.

Finally, **Moni Agiou Pandeleimonos** (☎ /fax 23770 23252; ☻ 10am-noon), a bit further on, is a friendly Russian monastery, closed at the time of writing. More than 1000 monks once inhabited this enormous facility.

GETTING THERE & AWAY

The bus to Ouranopoli leaves Thessaloniki's **Halkidiki bus terminal** (☎ 23103 16555; www.in-ktel.gr, in Greek) seven times daily (€10.70, 3½ hours). These buses also serve Ierissos (€9.30).

Taking the first bus (6.15am) from Thessaloniki cuts it close for organising your *diamonitirion* and ticket before the 9.45am boat; it's better to stay overnight in Ouranopoli. This lets you rest, buy extra food, and store unnecessary luggage.

The return ferry from Athos to Ouranopoli leaves Dafni at noon. There's a quick customs check, meant to prevent antiquities theft. The morning caïque from Agias Annis Skiti is timed to arrive in Dafni for the Ouranopoli-bound boat. The irregular east-coast caïque provides an alternative exit to Ierissos.

The last daily bus to Thessaloniki departs from Ouranopoli at 6.15pm, and Ierissos at 6.35pm.

KAVALA ΚΑΒΑΛΑ
pop 60,802

Palm-fronted Kavala, a port town crowned by a hill-top castle standing over a colourful old town, is a likeable place and Macedonia's easternmost major town. As an important ferry hub for the northeastern Aegean Islands, and especially Thasos, it sees many one-night visitors. However, Kavala itself deserves some further inspection; the grand aqueduct of Ottoman Sultan Süleyman the Magnificent (r 1520–66), a Byzantine fortress and the colourful old quarter of Panagia all repay a visit, while the harbour-front is lined with cafes and tavernas.

Modern Kavala was once ancient Neopolis, the port of Philippi. Its most famous modern resident was the Ottoman Pasha Mehmet Ali (1769–1849). The eventual founder of Egypt's last royal dynasty, Ali is infamous for ordering an Ottoman maritime assault during the Greek War of Independence that led to the slaughter of thousands on the remote island of Psara, an event still commemorated there every June (see p615). Somewhat ironically, Ali's former home has now been turned into an ultra-luxury boutique hotel.

Orientation

Kavala's focal point is Plateia Eleftherias, which has the helpful tourist information centre. The main thoroughfares, Eleftheriou Venizelou and Erythrou Stavrou, run west from here parallel with the waterfront (Ethnikis Andistasis). The old quarter, Panagia, stands at the harbour's southeastern side, above Plateia Eleftherias.

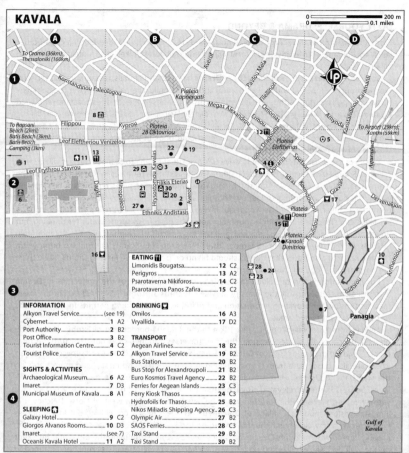

KAVALA

The bus station occupies the corner of Hrysostomou Kavalas and Filikis Eterias, near the Thasos hydrofoil quay. Public toilets stand near the hydrofoil departure point.

Information

ATM-equipped banks are widespread in the centre.

Alkyon Travel Service (☎ 25102 31096; alkyon-trv@ ticketcom.gr; Eleftheriou Venizelou 37; ⏰ 9am-6pm) This friendly travel agency in a central upstairs office books ferry tickets to the northeastern Aegean Islands (except Thasos) and train tickets, including the OSE overnight bus to İstanbul.

Cybernet (☎ 25102 30102; Erythrou Stavrou 64; per hr €2; ⏰ 6am-4am)

Port Authority (☎ 25102 23716; cnr Ethnikis Andistasis & Averof)

Post office (cnr Hrysostomou Kavalas & Erythrou Stavrou)

Tourist information centre (☎ 25102 31011; detaktic@otenet.gr; Plateia Eleftherias; ⏰ 8am-9pm Mon-Fri) Helpful, English- and German-speaking staff provide maps, plus transport and events information and hotel booking assistance.

Tourist police (☎ 25102 22246; Omonias 119)

Sights & Activities

The **Archaeological Museum** (☎ 25102 22335; Erythrou Stavrou 17; adult €2; ⏰ 8am-3pm Tue-Sun), on Ethnikis Andistasis' western end, displays sculpture, jewellery, grave stelae, terracotta figurines and vases from ancient Amphipolis, an Athenian colony west of Kavala that operated gold mines on nearby Mt Pangaeum. The **Municipal Museum of Kavala** (☎ 25102 22706; Filippou 4; admission

NORTHERN GREECE

DO IT YOURSELF: DRAMA & BEYOND

From Kavala, intrepid travellers can head northwards in Macedonia – and even try a cross-border jaunt to Bulgaria – to enjoy great local wines, tranquil forest hikes, and unusual traditional villages.

Some 36km from Kavala, the small city of **Drama** has midrange hotels, restaurants and services. Frequent buses connect it with Kavala, Xanthi and Thessaloniki. Drama's also on the Thessaloniki–Alexandroupoli train line. Although it lacks tourist attractions itself, the city does boast the renowned **Chateau Lazaridi Winery** (☎ 25210 82050; www.chateau-lazaridi.com; Agora village; ⌚ 9am-2pm Mon-Fri), 12km east in **Agora village** (near the slightly larger Adriani village). Tasting tours at Lazaridi's modern facilities are free, though large groups should book in advance (for more wineries, see Wineries of Northern Greece, p300).

Lovers of the great outdoors should drive 62km north of Drama to **Skaloti**, the last village with services. Some 10km further is **Elatia** (1600m), the base station for hikes in **Karadere Forest** (the name means 'Black Forest' in Turkish), a gorgeous wilderness of pines and rolling hills spilling across the border. According to Ioannis Kritoglu, a teacher from nearby Kato Nevrokopi and an enthusiastic hiker, 'Karadere has wonderful hiking trails, and the clean rivers are full of trout'.

Hikers can sleep free in multiple mountain huts that have fresh spring water for drinking, but no electricity or toilets. Trails are marked, and not too difficult (the highest point in the mountain range is 1814m). Even in summer, temperatures may drop significantly at night, so bring warm clothes. Kritoglu also notes that drivers should fill up on petrol before leaving Drama, since there are no petrol stations on this road north.

For more information on hiking in Karadere, visit the website of the prefecture of **Drama** (www.drama.gr). Also consult the forestry service's **Ioannis Aptoglu** (☎ 69428 41114), the main man responsible for providing information and maps, as well as issuing permits for special visits to the forest's protected areas.

Finally, from Kato Nevrokopi, it's just 10km to the Bulgaria-border post of **Exohi**. This recently opened, bear-friendly border crossing (the road traverses a tunnel, so as not to disturb our furry friends) leads to the sleepy town of **Gotse Delchev**, where accommodation and services are cheap (there are also buses here from Drama, leaving at 6pm Monday and Friday, and more buses on the way back to Drama). Here travellers can check out two remarkable nearby traditional villages. Some 25km east, elevated **Kovachevitsa** has idyllic guest houses and tasty restaurants, with sweeping views of the forested valley below. And, just 10km west of Gotse Delchev, the almost unvisited mountain village of **Delchevo** is the real deal – crumbling, but lovely homes with scarcely a few elderly inhabitants (including the keeper of the hamlet's one old-style cafe, a living legend who recounts Delchevo's 1960s heyday while strumming the old guitar he's kept on the wall ever since). Sleeping under the stars is utterly serene, but must be arranged in advance from Gotse Delchev; contact the **tourist information centre** (☎ in Bulgaria 359(0)75160125; tic.gdelchev@gmail.com; Ploshtad Makedoniya 2, Gotse Delchev).

free; ⌚ 8am-2pm Mon-Sat) displays contemporary Greek art. Its folk-art collection includes costumes, jewellery, handcrafts, household items and tools.

The narrow, tangled streets of the **Panagia quarter** are lined with pretty pastel houses, great for an evening stroll and atmospheric dining. The grandest of several well-preserved 18th-century buildings here is the **Imaret** (☎ 25102 20151; www.imaret.gr; Poulidou 6). This huge 18-domed structure overlooking the harbour was built in 1817 by Pasha Mehmet Ali as a hostel for Islamic theology students. Since being transformed into a very exclusive hotel,

the restored House of Mehmet Ali is no longer open for public viewing.

Rapsani Beach, 2km west, is popular in summer and good enough for swimming, though **Batis Beach** a bit further west is more popular with locals.

Sleeping

Kavala's hotels remain primarily staid, business-oriented and pricy. When various organised groups descend, the whole town can be inexplicably booked out. For a nominal fee (€1), the tourist information centre will be happy to telephone hotels and check availability – sometimes, getting you a slight discount in the process, and keeping you from having to wander aimlessly in the heat.

Batis Beach Camping (☎ 25102 45918; camp sites per adult/tent €6/4.90) This is a small, decent camping ground 3km west on the best Kavala-area beach.

Giorgos Alvanos Rooms (☎ 25102 21781; Anthemiou 35; s/d €20/30) Kavala's best budget option has simple rooms with shared bathrooms in a 300-year-old house up in Panagia. Rooms have refrigerators and sea views. It's a steep walk uphill to get here, so call in advance.

Galaxy Hotel (☎ 25102 24521; Eleftheriou Venizelou 27; s/d €40/50; ❄) Opposite the tourist information centre, the Galaxy is showing the ravages of time, offering ordinary, old-style rooms, and indifferent service, though it is central. Some rooms have port view.

Oceanis Kavala Hotel (☎ 25102 21981; Leoforos Erythrou Stavrou 32; s/d incl breakfast €68/82; ❄ 🖥) More expensive than the Galaxy but higher quality also, this big, business hotel one street back from the waterfront has comfortable, well-maintained modern rooms with balconies, a big cafe area and wi-fi.

Imaret (☎ 25106 20151; www.imaret.gr; Poulidou 6; s/d/ste incl breakfast €250/360/1500; ❄ 🖥 ⓦ) The world's your oyster at the Imaret, one of Greece's poshest hotels. It seeks to complement the original stone architecture devised by Pasha Mehmet Ali in the early 19th century with modern luxuries and elegant lighting. The huge rooms, with vaulted ceilings, harbour views and large fireplaces, are located around three inner courtyards. A Turkish *hammam* has been lavishly restored; there's a candle-lit indoor pool for essential-oil treatments, a reading room and even an orangerie.

Eating & Drinking
Panagia's elevated lanes and the eastern waterfront have good fish tavernas, while cafe-bars line the western waterfront.

Perigyros (☎ 25102 83440; cnr Erythmou Stavrou & Dagkli; souvlaki €2.60; ❄ 10am-2am) This busy, well-kept souvlaki joint beside Oceanis Kavala Hotel serves nourishing quick eats, salad, and heftier portions for cheap.

Limonidis Bougatsa (☎ 25108 32526; cnr Ionos Dragoumi & Megas Alexandrou; bougatsa €3.20; ❄ 6am-2pm) Behind the tourist information centre, this canopied outdoor *bougatsadhiko* (place where a *bougatsa*, cream pie, is served) is excellent for breakfast and espresso.

Psarotaverna Nikiforos (☎ 25102 28167; Plateia Karaoli 44; mains €6-9; ❄ 10am-1am) This handsomely appointed fish taverna serves good *ouzerie* fare; the adjoining cafe's popular with students.

Psarotaverna Panos Zafira (☎ 25102 27978; cnr Plateia Karaoli Dimitriou; fish €9-15; ❄ 10am-1am) Since 1965, this friendly place on the eastern waterfront has been serving fresh fish dishes, along with regular taverna fare.

Omilos (port; ❄ 10am-late) Watch the boats bob in the harbour from the draped blue-and-white-striped couches at this smooth cafe on the western port. The spacious central bar on the inside gets busy at night.

Vryallida (☎ 6948351600; Gravias 17; ❄ 8am-late) This hole-in-the-wall cafe approaching Panagia has a low-lit, relaxed ambience and brooding Greek music.

Getting There & Away
AIR
Kavala shares Alexander the Great Airport, near Hrysoupoli (29km), with Xanthi. **Olympic Air** (☎ 25102 23622; www.olympicairlines.com; Ethnikis Andistasis 8) does two daily Athens flights (€76), **Aegean Airlines** (☎ 25210 29000; Erythrou Stavrou 1) does one daily (€66). The few island flights all go via Athens or Thessaloniki.

BOAT
For timetables and prices for boats from Kavala to the northeastern Aegean Islands, see Island Hopping (p753).

Ferry tickets for Thasos are sold on the eastern waterfront's **ticket kiosk** (☎ 25930 24001; www.thassos-ferries.gr).

Euro Kosmos Travel Agency (☎ 25102 21960; www.eurokosmos.gr, in Greek; Erythrou Stavrou 1) near the bus station, **Nikos Miliadis Shipping Agency** (☎ 25102 26147; Karaoli-Dimitriou 36) or **Alkyon Travel Service** (☎ 25102 31096; alkyon-trv@ticketcom.gr; Eleftheriou Venizelou 37) all sell ferry tickets to the northeastern Aegean Islands.

From Kavala, hydrofoils serve Thasos only; for more information, see Island Hopping (p753). In Kavala, these hydrofoils berth at the port's western side, by the port police kiosk, which posts hydrofoil and ferry schedules. Buy tickets on boarding.

BUS
Domestic
The **bus station** (☎ 25102 22294; cnr Filikis Eterias & Hrysostomou Kavalas) serves Athens (€52, 8¾

hours, two daily), Xanthi (€5, one hour, half-hourly), Keramoti (€4.20, one hour, hourly), Serres (€8.40, two hours, four daily) and Thessaloniki (€13.30, 2¼hours, 15 daily). The *apothiki* (storeroom) keeps luggage cheaply.

Buses for Alexandroupoli (€10.95, two hours, seven daily) depart from the **bus station** (Hrysostomou 1) outside the small 7-Eleven snack bar opposite the KTEL office. Get tickets and information inside.

International
OSE buses from Thessaloniki via Drama leave Kavala for Turkey at 10pm daily (single €52).
Alkyon Travel Service (☎ 25102 31096; alkyon-trv@ ticketcom.gr; Eleftheriou Venizelou 37), from which buses also depart, has tickets.

Getting Around
Getting to or from the airport, taxi (€35) is the only option. **Taxis** (☎ 25102 32001) wait near the bus station.
Alkyon Travel Service (☎ 25102 31096; alkyon-trv@ ticketcom.gr; Eleftheriou Venizelou 37) rents cars from €40 a day.

PELLA ΠΕΛΛΑ
The birthplace of Alexander the Great, **Pella** (☎ 23820 31160; admission €6; ☺ 8am-7.30pm Tue-Sun, noon-7.30pm Mon) spans the Thessaloniki–Edessa road, and features spectacular mosaics. Pella became Macedon's capital under King Archelaos (r 413–399 BC), though Vergina (Aigai), the former capital, remained the royal cemetery.

Created with naturally coloured, subtly contrasting stones, the mosaics depict mythological scenes. They were created for ancient houses and public buildings now destroyed. Some are in situ, others in the museum. Also on this (northern) side of the road are six re-erected columns and a courtyard decorated with a black-and-white geometric mosaic.

On the southern side is the **museum** (☺ 8am-7.30pm), admission is free with the Pella ticket. Room 1 has a wall reconstruction from an ancient house, and a circular table inlaid with intricate floral and abstract designs, which possibly belonged to Philip II. Room 2 houses more mosaics.

Getting There & Away
Thessaloniki–Pella buses go every 45 minutes from 6am to 10pm (€2.90, 40 minutes). To visit Pella and Vergina by bus in one day,

first see Pella, then take a Thessaloniki-bound bus to Halkidona and take a Vergina bus from there.

LITOHORO ΛΙΤΟΧΩΡΟ
pop 7011 / elev 305m
Relaxing Litohoro (lih-*to*-ho-ro) is the base for climbing or just admiring Olympus, though its winding, cobbled upper streets and lovely Macedonian-style wood-balconied houses make it appealing in its own right. The arrival here is dramatic: on the final eastern approach, the Enipeas River gorge parts, revealing the towering double peaks of Olympus. Booking ahead in summer is recommended.

Orientation
The main entry road from Thessaloniki or Katerini, Agiou Nikolaou, is also Litohoro's main thoroughfare; it leads to Plateia Eleftherias, the main square. For Prionia, where Olympus' main trail begins, go right on Ithakisiou, just before this *plateia*. To the left of the *plateia* is 28 Oktovriou, site of most shops.

The bus station is on Agiou Nikolaou, opposite the tourist information booth.

Information
Plateia Eleftheria hosts numerous ATMs.
EOS (Greek Alpine Club; ☎ 23520 84544; ☺ 9.30am-12.30pm & 6-8pm Mon-Sat Jun-Sep) Below the public parking lot; this office distributes pamphlets with general and hiking information on Olympus. Take Ithakisiou down from the square and turn left after 100m. The EOS also runs three mountain refuges.
GRNet (☎ 23520 82300; cnr Atanas & Koutrouba; per hr €2; ☺ 24hr) Internet access near the *plateia*.
Medical centre (☎ 23520 22222) Five kilometres away, at the Litohoro turn-off from the main coastal highway.
Police (☎ 23520 81100; cnr Ithakisiou & Agiou Nikolaou)
Post office (28 Oktovriou 11)
SEO (Association of Greek Climbers; ☎ 23520 84200; ☺ 6-10pm) This place is informative and runs an Olympus refuge; however, the EOS has more English speakers. Walk down Ithakiou, turn left and then left again.
Tourist information booth (Agiou Nikolaou) In a white building with wooden eaves, just before Ithakiou.
www.litohoro.gr Municipal website.

Sleeping & Eating
The nearby coast has well-served camping grounds (though the beaches are underwhelming and overcrowded). Litohoro's hotels have wonderful atmosphere.

NORTHERN GREECE

Olympios Zeus (☎ 23520 22115; Plaka Litohorou; camp sites per adult/tent €7/3.50) A good bet, though somewhat ramshackle.

Olympos Beach (☎ 23520 22112; www.olympos-beach .gr; Plaka Litohorou; camp sites per adult €7, tent €5-7) Like Olympios Zeus this place is decent, but livelier with its loud on-site Shark nightclub.

our pick Xenonas Papanikolaou (☎ 23520 81236; xenpap@otenet.gr; Nikolaou Episkopou Kitrous 1; s/d €45/50; ⊠ ▦) Solitude-seekers, head here first. This romantic guest house, set in a flowery garden up in the backstreets, is a world away from the tourist crowds on Litohoro's main street. Rooms feel more spacious than they actually are, and the tasteful decoration is enhanced by nice views of Litohoro's traditional terracotta rooftops. The cosy downstairs lounge has a fireplace and couches, and management is friendly and helpful. To get there from the square, take 28 Oktovriou uphill and turn left on Nikolaou Episkopou Kitrous.

Villa Pantheon (☎ 23520 83931; d/tr €55/70; ⊠) Outfitted with all mod cons and cursed as the 'white thing' blocking views of Mt Olympus, the Pantheon has comfortable, airy rooms.

Hotel Olympus Mediterranean (☎ 23520 81831; www.olympusmed.gr; Dionysou 5; d/tr incl breakfast €70/90, luxury ste €100; ⊠ ▦ ▣) A four-star hotel up in the backstreets, the Olympus Mediterranean occupies an imposing neoclassical building with ornate balconies, and has 20 luxurious rooms and three suites, plus an indoor pool, a mosaic-tiled Jacuzzi pool and sauna. Some rooms also have a fireplace and Jacuzzi.

Damaskinia (☎ 23520 81247; Vasileos Konstandinou 4; mains €6-8) A popular upper-town taverna, Damaskinia does tasty *mousakas* and *kokoretsi* (spit-roast lamb offal).

our pick Gastrodromio (☎ 23520 21300; Plateia Eleftherias; mains €7-13) If Gastrodromio was around in Olympian times, Zeus and Co would have eaten here. Litohoro's most delightfully inventive restaurant, the spacious, traditionally decorated Gastrodromio serves flavourful dishes such as octopus with peppercorn, cumin, garlic, hot pepper and wine, or rabbit cooked in wine and glazed with almonds, cinnamon and nutmeg. The wine list itself is 21 pages long.

Getting There & Away

From the **bus station** (☎ 23520 81271), buses serve Katerini (€2.10, 25 minutes, 13 daily), Thessaloniki (€8, 1¼ hours, 13 daily) and Athens (€28, 5½ hours, three daily via Katerini). Buses from Thessaloniki to Volos/ Athens leave you on the highway, where you catch a Katerini–Litohoro bus.

Litohoro's train station, 9km away, gets 10 daily trains on the Athens–Volos–Thessaloniki train line.

AROUND LITOHORO

Mt Olympus ΟΛΥΜΠΟΣ ΟΡΟΣ

Just as it did for the ancients, the cloud-covered lair of the Ancient Greek pantheon, awe-inspiring Mt Olympus fires the visitor's imagination today. Greece's highest mountain, Olympus also hosts around 1700 plant species, some rare and endemic. Its slopes are covered with thick forests of numerous different deciduous trees, conifers and pines. Bird life is equally varied. Olympus became Greece's first national park in 1937. Excepting the exertions of ancient deities, the first known mortals to reach Mytikas (2918m), Olympus' highest peak, were Litohoro local Christos Kakalos and Swissmen Frederic Boissonas and Daniel Baud-Bovy, in August 1913.

Although it's possible to drive up Olympus, most people come for the hike; consult the Litohoro-based hiking associations (opposite) for maps and current conditions.

Ancient Dion Δίον

Just north of Litohoro, **Ancient Dion** (Dion Archaeological Park; adult/student €6/2; ☽ 8am-8pm) was sacred for ancient Macedonians worshipping the Olympian gods and especially Zeus – before his epic eastern adventures, Alexander the Great even sacrificed here.

Originally, a fertility earth goddess was worshipped here. Later, other gods came into vogue, such as Asclepius, god of medicine. Dion's **Sanctuary to Isis**, the exotic Egyptian goddess, stands in a lush, low-lying area. Its votive statues were found virtually intact, with faint colour remaining. Copies stand in for the originals, now in the site's museum. A well-preserved **mosaic floor** from AD 200, depicts the Dionysos Triumphal Epiphany. During August's **Olympus Festival**, Dion's reconstructed **theatre** hosts performances.

The archaeological park ticket includes Dion's **museum** (☎ 23510 53206; ☽ 8am-7pm Tue-Fri, 10.30am-5pm Mon, 8.30am-3pm Sat & Sun), with its well-labelled collection of statues and other finds.

To get here, drive or catch a taxi from Litohoro (€9).

NORTHERN GREECE

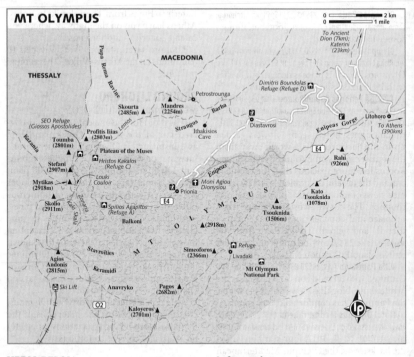

MT OLYMPUS

VERIA BEPOIA
pop 43,683

Seemingly a fairly uniform Greek town, Veria conceals a remarkable assortment of Byzantine-era churches, an old Jewish quarter, traditional Turkish houses and two worthwhile museums, plus good eating and nightlife. Seventy-five kilometres west of Thessaloniki on the Vergina road, Veria remains less visited by tourists than by Greek business travellers with local agriculture, wine and mineral water interests.

Orientation

The two main squares, Plateia Andoniou and Plateia Raktivan (1km apart), are linked by Venizelou and Mitropoleos. The conjunction of Venizelou and Mitropoleos Elias leads to the escarpment ridge along which Anixeos runs north–south. Within these major thoroughfares, the *pezodromos* (pedestrian street), Ellis, is a centre of nightlife cutting in from Kontogiorgaki, which has hotels, restaurants and shops. The bus station is one block east of Venizelou. The train station is 3km north on the old Thessaloniki road.

Information

ATM-equipped banks line Venizelou and Mitropoleos.

In-Spot (Elias 9; per hr €2; 24hr) Internet access.
Municipal Culture Office (cnr Pavlou Mela & Bizaniou) Tourism office.
Police (☎ 23310 22391; Mitropoleos)
Post office (Dionysiou Solomou 4)
Tourist information booth (cnr Anixeos & Plateia Elias; 9am-5pm)

Sights & Activities

Veria's evocative old Jewish quarter, **Barbouta**, is reached from Plateia Andoniou down Vasileos Konstandinou, old Veria's commercial street, flanked by shops and *kafeneia*. Halfway along on the right is a huge, ancient plane tree from which the Turks hanged Archbishop Arsenios in 1430, after taking Veria. Opposite is the dilapidated, 12th-century **cathedral**, whose decapitated minaret indicates the cathedral's Ottoman incarnation as a mosque.

The **Archaeological Museum** (☎ 23310 24972; Leoforos Anixeos 45; admission free; 8.30am-3pm Tue-Sun), at Anixeos' northern end, contains finds from the Vergina tombs and nearby Lefkadia. Funerary items, ancient vases, silver, gold and a lovely statue of 'Aphrodite taking off her sandals' also impress.

Up the hill across town, the **Byzantine Museum** (☎ 23310 25847; Thomaidou 26; admission €2; ☺ 8am-3pm Tue-Sun) is Veria's coolest museum. It presents priceless icons and other Byzantine antiquities, like 5th-century floor mosaics, marble epigraphy and ornate sarcophagi in a sumptuously lit, three-floor space complemented by explanatory wall placards. The helpful staff explain the exhibits, which illustrate daily life in ancient and Byzantine Veria.

Few of Veria's dozens of **Byzantine churches** are open; a good bet is the fresco-rich, 14th-century **Church of the Resurrection of Christ** (admission free; ☺ 8.30am-3.30pm Tue-Sun) in the centre.

In winter, **Mt Vermio**, 22km west, is a popular ski centre with eight slopes and three lifts – good for beginners.

Sleeping

Since Veria's largely a business destination, budget travellers are in for a world of pain.

Hotel Macedonia (☎ 23310 66902; Kontogiorgaki 50; s/d €50/72; **P** ✺) A quiet hotel with good, well-furnished rooms, the Macedonia also has a nice rooftop terrace. From Elias take Paster, which becomes Kontogiorgaki.

Hotel Villa Elia (☎ 23310 26800; eliaver@otenet.gr; Elias 16; s/d €55/70; ✺) Slightly louder but closer to the action is this business hotel with large, comfortable rooms.

Hotel En Eari (☎ 23310 75788; www.eneari.gr; Leoforos Anixeos 82; s/d/tr €85/110/143; **P** ✺ ☜) Sparkling new luxury hotel located near the Archaeological Museum with spacious rooms and well-lit cafe windows.

Eating & Drinking

Veria has numerous tasty eateries, and some buzzing bars on the *pezodromos*. Local specialities include oven-cooked *fasoladha* (bean soup) and *revani*, a sweet syrupy Turkish cake.

Zaharoplasteio Konstantinos (☎ 23310 70196; Elias 2; pites €2; ☺ 24hr) Visit this cheery central place for a morning coffee and *tyropita* (cheese pie), *bougatsa* (semonlina pudding) and other sweets.

Menou (☎ 23310 72788; Plateia Raktivan 14; mains €5-8) Try the *fasoladha* at this vegetarian-friendly joint, or the *imam baïldi* (baked eggplant with ground beef).

ourpick Vergiotiko (☎ 23310 74133; Thomaidou 2; mains €5-9; ☺ noon-midnight) This wonderful, grottolike traditional restaurant is literally carved from the town's old Byzantine walls, and has great ambience. Service is friendly, the portions hearty, the food fresh and inventive. Try the pork with aubergines, or pungent mushrooms. It's located up a hill, where the road forks left to Vergina or right to the Byzantine Museum.

To Katafygio (☎ 23310 27227; Kontogeorgaki 18; mains €5-9) This 'hide-out', as its name means in Greek, occupies a restored old building and serves game dishes such as quail, mushroom specialities, and more usual taverna fare.

Fournos (☎ 23310 29829; Ellis 14; ☺ 8.30pm-late) On the *pezodromos*, 100m down from the corner of Kontogiordaki, this cool, low-lit bar is marked by smooth wood and jazz (along with Greek music), and gets busy after midnight. Other popular bars are nearby too.

Getting There & Away

BUS
From the **bus station** (☎ 23310 22342; Trembesinas) buses serve Thessaloniki (€6, one hour, half-hourly), Athens (€31.50, 6½ hours, three daily), Edessa (€4.20, one hour, four daily), Naoussa (€1.80, 25 minutes, 22 daily) and Vergina (€1.40, 20 minutes, eight daily). Buses for Kastoria (€10.90, two hours, six daily) go from a **station** (☎ 23310 75170; Pierion 155), 2km west of town.

TRAIN
From the **train station** (☎ 23310 24444), north of town off the old Thessaloniki road, 14 daily trains traverse the line connecting Veria with Thessaloniki (€3.20, one hour) and Florina (€4, two hours).

Getting Around
Veria is walkable; there are also **taxis** (☎ 23310 63394).

VERGINA ΒΕΡΓΙΝΑ
pop 1246

Vergina (ver-*yee*-nah), 11km southeast of Veria, is the legendary burial site of the Macedonian kings, and their first capital (ancient Aigai). In 336 BC, at the wedding of his daughter Cleopatra, Philip II was assassinated here. At least the guests were already there.

NORTHERN GREECE

This World Heritage–listed site is also called the **Royal Tombs** (☎ 23310 92347; adult €8; ⏰ noon-7.30pm Mon, 8am-7.30pm Tue-Sun summer, 8.30am-3pm winter). A walkway through the interior of the major *tholos* (tumulose) leads to the four individual tombs. **Tomb I** is called Persephone's Tomb, after an intact mural depicting Hades' rape of Persephone. **Tomb II** probably belonged to Philip II. Intact until its discovery in 1977, the tomb yielded a gold larnax (ossuary) with bones. The 16-pointed star of the royal Macedonian family on the larnax lid, and damage to the skull identical with descriptions of an injury Philip sustained, pointed to its likely inhabitant. Philip's larnax and that of his presumed concubine or wife, plus some exquisite gold-leaf diadems, are displayed in the exhibition rooms. **Tomb III** was probably designated for Alexander IV, son of Alexander the Great, while the mysterious **Tomb IV** was looted in antiquity.

To see more of the site, continue 400m past the Royal Tombs to the ruins of an extensive **palatial complex**, summer residence of 3rd-century-BC king Antigonos Gonatas. The main attraction is a large Doric peristyle, surrounded by floors of pebble-mosaic; the most beautiful has a geometric floral design.

EDESSA ΕΔΕΣΣΑ
pop 16,000

Verdant Edessa (*edh*-eh-sah) is best known for its great waterfalls that keep the air moist and refreshing even on hot summer days. Its attractive, though dilapidated, old quarter, little streams, shaded parks and a Byzantine bridge are other sites in this town perched precariously on a ledge overlooking the seemingly endless agricultural plain below. Edessa's exciting recent improvements on the accommodation scene (see Sleeping, opposite) also make a further case for it as a good base for further forays into western Macedonia, such as tours of nearby wineries (see Wineries of Northern Greece, p300).

Until 1977, when Vergina's royal tombs were discovered, Edessa was thought to be the ancient Macedonian city of Aigai. With the government's Hellenisation project in Macedonia following the 1923 Greek-Turkish population exchanges, the town's long-existing Slavic name of Voden ('place of water') was replaced with the archaic name, Edessa.

Orientation

The central bus station occupies the corner of Filippou and Pavlou Mela. From there cross Filippou and follow Pavlou Mela to the T-junction; turning right puts you in the centre on Dimokratias. The train station, on Leoforos Nikis, is a 10-minute walk along 18 Oktovriou to the centre.

Edessa's waterfalls and the Varosi old quarter are well signposted. If lost, ask a local for the *kataraktes* (waterfalls).

Information

ATM-equipped banks line Dimokratias.
Police (☎ 23810 23333; Iroön Polytehniou)
Post office (Dimokratias 26)
Tourist information office (☎ 23810 23101; www .edessacity.gr; ⏰ 10am-8pm) This helpful office in a kiosk before the waterfalls provides maps of Edessa and nearby attractions.

Sights

Edessa's **waterfalls** emerge beyond the well-signposted park near the tourist office. The biggest thunders dramatically down a high cliff, filling the air with moisture. Enter the **observation deck** inside this waterfall and breathe in the mist from the crashing waters in front of your nose. Just before the observation deck is a small **cave** (admission €1), inside the cliff mass.

A winding path downwards accesses a second, less impressive waterfall. Further right, the **Water Museum** (adult €2; ⏰ 11am-4pm Wed-Mon) exhibits various water-industry equipment and a pretty, wild **aquarium**, with various species of fish, amphibians, snapping turtles, poisonous snakes and one cranky, cooped-up crocodile.

Along the escarpment ridge south lies **Varosi**, Edessa's old quarter, with cobbled streets, chapels and traditional houses. The colourful **Folkloric Museum** (adult €2; ⏰ 10am-5pm Tue-Sun) is here too. Turning the other way from the waterfalls through the park brings you to Edessa's very pretty **Byzantine bridge**, once part of the ancient Via Egnatia.

Activities

For outdoor activities, see **Giannis Hatziantoniou** (☎ 6944991075) who arranges hiking expeditions, cycling tours and GPS orienteering trips. **Tasos Privartitsanis** (☎ 6977248581) organises paragliding and hang-gliding trips. **George Mousios** (☎ 6973743127; 1-/2-hr rides €15/20) organises mountain horse riding.

NORTHERN GREECE

Sleeping

Varosi (☎ 23810 21865; www.varosi.gr, in Greek; Arhiereos Meletiou; s/d incl breakfast €55/70; P 🄿) This atmospheric pension is tucked away in the eponymous old quarter. It's a family-owned, restored traditional Macedonian wood-and-stone house, furnished with antique brass beds (though the mattresses can be rock-hard), fine linen and colourful embroidery. In winter, the lounge rooms are kept warm and cosy by log fires; in summer, there's a flower-filled balcony for relaxing over coffee.

Hagiati (☎ 23810 51500; www.hagiati.gr, in Greek; s/d incl breakfast €60/70; 🄿) This small guest house, around the corner before Varosi, has a nice open courtyard and peaceful setting. Fixtures are somewhat more modern, but it's still a nice choice.

our pick **Varosi Four Seasons** (☎ 23810 51440; 6983187397 www.varosi.gr; Arhiereos Meletiou; d incl breakfast from €70; P 🄿 🛜) Wow! The enterprising daughters of Anastasia Salahora (owner of the Varosi, above) have created Edessa's first boutique hotel – just down the road from mum. Of the 10 rooms, six have views of the great outstretched Edessa plain (as does the great outdoor verandah cafe). Rooms are pristine and sumptuously decorated, with a honeymoon feel, and service is friendly and attentive.

Eating

Raeti (☎ 23810 28769; 18 Oktovriou 20; mezedhes €3-5, mains €5.50-8) Try the well-prepared Macedonian fare, such as mezedhes and filling meat dishes, here.

Katarraktes Edessas (☎ 23810 27810; Kapetan Gareti-Perdika 1; mains €5-9) Publicly owned Katarraktes Edessas, before the falls, has both outdoor and indoor dining. The menu is standard but dependable.

Getting There & Around

From the **bus station** (☎ 23810 23511; Pavlou Mela 13) buses serve Thessaloniki (€7.50, two hours, hourly), Veria (€4.20, one hour, five daily) and Athens (€41.60, eight hours, three daily). Florina buses depart from another **station** (☎ 23810 29600), 30m away.

The **train station** (☎ 23810 23510; Leoforos Nikis) has trains to Thessaloniki (€3.70), Larisa (€6), Athens (€17), Kozani (€3) and Florina (€2.60).

Edessa is easily walkable; alternatively, take a **taxi** (☎ 23810 22904).

FLORINA ΦΛΩΡΙΝΑ

pop 15,555

Nestled between mountains in a verdant valley, Florina (flo-rih-nah) is famous throughout Greece for its sweet red peppers. It's also a small student town – visibly attested in the busy cafes on its central pedestrian street. In evenings, its river is a favourite place for leisurely strolls.

Florina is also the gateway to the Prespa Lakes to the west, and is about 40km south of Bitola, the first major city in the Former Yugoslav Republic of Macedonia (FYROM); the two have certain resemblances. Also, a small ski resort, Vigla, is located 15km west of Florina on the Prespes road.

Despite having only three small museums, Florina is important historically. It was the northernmost town occupied and subsequently annexed by Greek troops during the Balkan Wars of 1912–13, and near the front in subsequent wars. The issue of a (Slavic) Macedonian minority in Greece, which the government denies outright, has always been sensitive in Florina and nearby villages, where a significant percentage of the 'Greek' population speak the Macedonian language. Heavy, though subtle, pressure from Greek society, media and government has suppressed it, but if you have sharp ears and local awareness, you will still hear Macedonian spoken in Florina and environs, though mostly by older people.

Orientation

Florina is divided by a river, and curves below a forested peak on its western edge. The central street, Pavlou Mela, leads to the main square (Plateia Georgiou Modi). Pavlou Mela's western, pedestrianised half is lined with cafes.

From the bus station, head downhill on either of two roads hemming in the city park and cross Kastrisianaki to reach Pavlou Mela, or veer southwest onto Stefanou Dragoumi and after 300m find Plateia Georgiou Modi, marking the beginning of the pedestrianised half of Pavlou Mela. The river's just south.

From the train station, Pavlou Mela is close, running east from the southwestern edge of the park beside the station.

Information

ATM-equipped banks stand around the main square.

NORTHERN GREECE

InFlorina (☎ 23850 44144; www.inflorina.gr; Plateia Giorgiou Modi 13) A private agency with local tourism information.

Netville (☎ 23850 29494; Pavlou Mela; per hr €3; ☯ 10am-midnight) Internet cafe opposite, but slightly east of, Hotel Hellinis.

Police (☎ 23850 22222; Sangariou 24) The station is 500m west of Plateia Giorgiou Modi.

Post office (Kalergi 22) Left of Stefanou Dragoumi when approaching the bus station.

Sights

Florina's **Archaeological Museum** (☎ 23850 28206; Sidirodromikou Stathmou 3; admission €2; ☯ 8.30am-3pm Tue-Sun), near the train station, contains ancient finds, including objects from the Hellenistic City site on Agios Panteleimonos hill near Florina.

Straddling both riverbanks, **Old Florina** contains attractive Turkish houses and neo-classical mansions; one has been restored by the Society for the Friends of Art of Florina, and reincarnated as the **Museum of Modern Art** (☎ 23850 29444; Leoforos Eleftherias 103; admission free; ☯ 6-8pm Tue-Sat, 10am-1pm Sun). The museum's permanent collection of contemporary Greek art is complemented by frequent exhibitions. Walk down 25 Martiou, cross the bridge and turn right; the museum's 200m further.

The **Folk Museum** (Karavitou 2; admission free; ☯ 6-8pm Mon, Wed & Sat) near the courthouse keeps inconvenient hours, but has unique photographs and folk costumes.

Sleeping

Hotel Hellinis (☎ 23850 22671; hellinis@line.gr; Pavlou Mela 31; s/d €30/40; ☯) Florina's best budget option has clean, modern rooms and friendly staff that provide helpful local travel information. No Florina budget hotel has air-conditioning, but the Hellinis provides fans. The eclectic coffee bar has flower-painted walls, a working aquarium, paintings of schooners and the odd guitar. It's two minutes west of the train station and a three-minute walk down from the bus station.

Hotel Antigone (☎ 23850 23180; Arrianou 1; s/d incl breakfast €40/50) The faded Antigone is a little beyond the bus station, but well beyond its sell-by date, as indicated by the tattered rooms and old fixtures. Save a few euros by opting out of the lacklustre breakfast.

Hotel Lingos (☎ 23850 28322; www.hotel-lingos.gr; Tagmatarhou Naoum 1; s/d €70/90; P ☒ ☐) The Best Western–owned Lingos, just north of Plateia

Georgiou Modi, has all expected amenities for a four-star business hotel, such as dedicated PC phone ports, a roof garden, and the occasional Greek celebrity or political guest.

Eating & Drinking

Florina has simple tavernas, with cafes lining Pavlou Mela's pedestrian-only western half.

Prespes (☎ 23850 23973; Tyrnovou 12; mains €5-8; ☯ dinner) A no-nonsense central eatery, Prespes is strong on meats, served grilled or roasted.

Psarotaverna O Giorgos (☎ 23850 23622; Grevenon 16; fish €5-9; ☯ dinner Mon-Sat) Florina's only fish restaurant, this friendly hill-top place 500m west of the centre serves tasty golden fillets of Prespa carp and trout, plus fish from the Aegean; the owner, Giorgos Hasos, visits Thessaloniki's fish markets thrice weekly for fresh-off-the-boat seafood. It's open only for dinner, after 7pm in winter and after 9pm in summer.

To Varosi (☎ 23850 29191; Eleftherias 84; mains €6-8; ☯ Wed-Mon) Another good spot for grilled meats, about 200m west of the centre, on the riverbank.

Art Café (☎ 23850 26535; Pavlou Mela 106; ☯ 9am-2am) On the western end of Pavlou Mela, this outdoor place with many juices, ice cream, coffee and flowery retro couches, is one of the more colourful of several adjoining cafes.

Getting There & Away

BUS

Domestic

From the **bus station** (☎ 23850 22430) buses serve destinations including Athens (€45, nine hours, two daily) and Thessaloniki (€14, 2¾ hours, six daily).

For the Prespa Lakes, buses leave on Monday, Wednesday and Friday at 3pm to Agios Germanos (€4.80, 1½ hours); however, the bus continues to Psarades (€6) only on Wednesday. Buses from Florina return immediately, so you must stay over in Prespes. Out of school season, Florina–Prespes buses are infrequent.

For Kastoria, take a bus to Amyntaio (€3.80, 30 minutes, eight daily) and change there. However, Amyntaio has only three daily buses for the final one-hour leg to Kastoria, and only the 3pm bus (from Amyntaio) will get you there in time for same-day connections.

International

When school's in session, two buses daily go from Florina to the Macedonian border at Niki (€1.70, 30 minutes). For Albania, a weekly bus stops every Wednesday at the Greek border post at Krystallopigi (€6.10, one hour).

TAXI

A taxi to Bitola (40km) in the FYROM costs about €40 one way or €50 return; the latter includes two hours for shopping and sightseeing. Ask local taxi drivers, or arrange through your hotel.

TRAIN

Florina's **train station** (☎ 23850 22404) is where the Thessaloniki train line terminates; five daily trains ply this route. Major stops before Thessaloniki (€6, three hours) include Edessa (€2.60, 70 minutes) and Veria (€4, two hours).

PRESPA LAKES ΛΙΜΝΕΣ ΠΡΕΣΠΩΝ

Greek Macedonia's magical, mountainous northwest corner holds the twin treasures of lakes **Megali Prespa** and **Mikri Prespa** (Great Prespa and Small Prespa, collectively known as Prespes), separated by a narrow strip of land and partially divided between three countries. In the absence of foreign tourists, Prespes has retained its tranquil natural beauty, and boasts lovely traditional stone-house villages and significant Byzantine antiquities. The drive from Florina passes through thick forests with sweeping mountain views and the occasional bear-crossing sign.

Since the Balkan Wars in 1913, Mikri Prespa (43 sq km) has been largely Greece's, though the then-new state of Albania would later receive a tiny southwestern tip. Although small, Mikri Prespa is serene, lined with rustling reed beds hosting numerous bird species, including cormorants, Dalmatian pelicans, egrets, herons and ibises, making for great birdwatching (though not swimming).

A tectonic lake at least one million years old, Megali Prespa (850m) is one of Europe's oldest, feeding the equally old (but much larger) Lake Ohrid to the northwest through underground springs. The Balkan political intriguing of the 20th century led to Greece annexing 38 sq km of southeastern Megali Prespa, while a small southwestern piece was awarded to Albania. The majority of Megali Prespa (1000 sq km) further north belongs to the FYROM, and indeed the indigenous people around all sides of both lakes are Macedonian-speaking.

On the Greek side, much of the Megali Prespa shore is precipitous rock, rising dramatically from the chilly blue water. A few kilometres north across the Macedonian border, however, a sandy beach stretches 2km before the idyllic village of Dolno Dupeni; despite talk of reopening this long-dormant border crossing, ongoing political spats between Athens and Skopje make the possibility remote.

The whole 'microregion', as it's called by eager Eurocrats bent on multinational integration schemes, is still wild. In Greece, Prespes has been a national park for more than 30 years. And, around the northern section of Megali Prespa, national parks of the FYROM cover each of its mountainous banks (Galičica on the western, and Pelister on the eastern). Thus the whole area is a remarkably still haven for peace-seeking wildlife and human life alike.

As in Byzantine times, the whole Prespes region was a frontline battleground during the Balkan Wars of 1912–13, both world wars and the Greek Civil War, causing widespread suffering – the forced exile and emigration that resulted affected many thousands of local Macedonians and Greeks alike.

Agios Germanos Άγιος Γερμανός
pop 231

Polished Agios Germanos, filled with wonderful stone houses and notable Byzantine sites, is Prespes' main town and, though not on the lake, offers the most atmospheric accommodation. There's also good eating – and hill trails to walk it off.

ORIENTATION & INFORMATION

There's a bus stop, taxi and Prespes' only post office. There are no banks; change money at the post office.

Community clinic (☎ 23850 46284)

Information centre (☎ /fax 23850 51452; ⌚ 9.30am-3pm) On the road approaching the village, the national park information centre has interesting displays. Ask about free, guided birdwatching.

Police (☎ 23850 51202)

Steki (☎ 23850 51332; ⌚ 6-10pm Tue-Sat) In neighbouring Lemos, this friendly community centre has internet access.

PRESPA LAKES

NORTHERN GREECE

SIGHTS

Agios Athanasios and **Agios Germanos**, the village's two churches, are extraordinary works of ecclesiastic mid-Byzantine architecture. The latter, named after the village's patron saint, is a cosy, domed brick structure from the 11th century, which contains some vivid frescoes. An explanatory board provides background.

SLEEPING & EATING

Rooms Arhondiko (☎ 23850 46260; s/d €40/50; P) Another guest house with rustic charm, the Arhondiko has simple, clean rooms with balconies overlooking the water, and friendly service.

Agios Germanos Hostel (☎ 23850 51357; www.prespa .com.gr; s/d €40/60; P) Signposted just opposite Agios Germanos church, this restored old farmhouse offers wood-and-stone rooms and generous breakfasts.

To Petrino (☎ 23850 51344; s/d €45/60; P) The first hotel you'll see when entering town, To Petrino is an appealing traditional guest house with rustic furniture and wood beams. The hospitable owners provide local travel information.

To Tzaki (☎ 23850 51470; mains €5-9) After the Church of Agios Germanos, this garden taverna offers great spare ribs, sweet red Florina peppers in oil, *xinotyri* (sour cheese) and a flaky pie stuffed with nettles (not the stinging kind!) called *tsouknidopita*. The white dog and cat get along well enough to beg for scraps as a team.

GETTING THERE & AWAY

From Florina, buses depart at 3pm on Monday, Wednesday and Friday for Agios Germanos (€4.80, 1½ hours), returning to Florina immediately.

Psarades Ψαράδες
pop 158

Situated on a gusty promontory at the southern end of Lake Megali Prespa, Psarades is a lovely, slightly disoriented village of old stone houses, with a friendly, mostly elderly Macedonian population, many of whom know it by its Macedonian-language name, Nivitsi (a kind of small local fish). It's also the last Greek village before the aqueous trinational border, demarcated by a forlorn buoy.

Colourful caïques line Psarades' lakefront, where unique, endemic miniature cows spar in the grass. The village's upper streets (on the right-hand side of the main square) are totally authentic, filled with stone houses, jutting wood beams and drying blankets. You'll hear the Macedonian language spoken widely here. In Psarades, as elsewhere in Greek Prespa, carp is served in fillets.

ORIENTATION & INFORMATION

The road into Psarades ends at a lakefront car park. Past it, the square hosts a taverna, shops, restaurants and domatia. The village's houses fill the upper streets to the right. There's a card phone, and all Greek mobile phone networks work.

SIGHTS

A **boat trip** on Megali Prespa to the south side of the lake's three isolated **askitiria** (hermitages) begins with the 13th-century **Metamorfosi**, where scant remnants of original rich paintings, and two sections from the wood-carved *temblon* (votive screen) survive (the rest are now kept in Florina museum). The second hermitage, 15th-century **Mikri Analipsi**, and the equally old rock **Church of Panagia Eleousa**, tucked above a ravine, have beautiful frescoes. From the top of the stairs great views emerge of the lake and Albania opposite. More religious rock paintings visible opposite Psarades include **Panagia Vlahernitisa** (1455–56) and **Panagia Dexiokratousa** (1373).

Village fisherman can be approached, if one hasn't already approached you, to make the excursion. It's about €20 for a short tour to the rock paintings and one *askitiria*, or €25 for the full tour, with at least four people per boat. If you're solo, hope for €30.

In Psarades itself, see the **Church of Kimisis Theotokou** (1893), adorned with the double-headed eagle of Byzantium. An inscription refers to the village by its original Macedonian-language name, Nivitsi.

SLEEPING & EATING

Book ahead in summer.

To Hagiati (s/d €35/45) This restored little stone house with comfortable, traditional-style rooms is visible by its sign on the right when entering the village.

Rooms Arhondiko (☎ 23850 46260; s/d €35/50; **P**) Right on the lakefront, friendly owner Eleftheria offers clean, breezy rooms with balconies overlooking the water.

Five good tavernas line Psarades' elevated waterfront. Along with lake fish, they serve the local *fasoladha* speciality. **Akrolimnia** (☎ 23850 46260; mains €5-9), run by the owners of Rooms Arhondiko, does tasty fried trout or carp and draught wine.

GETTING THERE & AWAY

Rent a car in Florina or Kastoria; otherwise, three weekly buses go from Florina to Agios Germanos. Only the Wednesday bus continues to Psarades (€6); on the other days, take a **taxi** (☎ 23850 51247, 6942704496) from either Lemos or Agios Germanos. Approximate fares from Psarades are €20 to Lemos (to pick up the bus to Florina) and €50 direct to Florina or Kastoria.

Agios Ahillios Άγιος Αχίλειος

Mikri Prespa's island of Agios Ahillios may be small, but it has a big history. In the 10th century, it became the capital of Bulgarian Tsar Samuel, who had expanded his rule over much of the southern Balkans (much to the irritation of Constantinople). The grand, concave outer wall of his **Basilica of Agios Ahillios** stands on the island's eastern shore, with some half-toppled walls and columns, and a grand stone floor in front.

For a breathtaking view of the basilica with the lake and mountains behind it, ascend the facing hill that runs across the island's spine. **Birdwatching** is also good here, though devotees should explore the island's more hidden corners.

The island's name, Agios Ahillios, derives from that of the church, which itself derives from Samuel's invasion of Thessaly; while conquering Larissa in 983, he (rather rudely) 'borrowed' the sacred relics of 4th-century Saint Ahillios, an avid opponent of heretics who had miraculously coaxed oil to ooze from a rock to make his theological point. To celebrate his conquest, Samuel dedicated the new church to the abducted saint.

To reach Agios Ahillios from Agios Germanos, drive across the connecting strip between the two lakes and then turn immediately left; or, from Psarades, just keep going straight south instead of turning onto the interlake strip. After parking, walk across a 1km-long floating pontoon bridge to the island.

Off the bridge, the signposted path going slightly left hugs the east coast and leads to the Basilica of Agios Ahillios and other church ruins.

Alternatively, coming off the bridge, turn right for the island's only shop and taverna, which has rooms for rent from €25. Despite having been a medieval capital, Agios Ahillios is now sparsely inhabited, and it's full of ruined old stone houses. A **summer festival** every August, here and in other Prespes locations, features a headlining concert, with a big-name Greek singer. The amphitheatric basilica is then magically transformed into a stage, with audiences of up to 5000 watching from the hill above it, sometimes clutching candles.

KASTORIA ΚΑΣΤΟΡΙΑ
pop 16,218

Serene, wooded Kastoria (kah-sto-rih-*ah*) has an idyllic setting on the forested shores of placid Lake Orestiada, nestled between the mountains of Grammos and Vitsi. The town boasts more than 50 Byzantine and post-Byzantine churches, and several distinguished 17th- and 18th-century *arhontika* (mansions), once homes of the *arhons* – the town's leading citizens, mostly rich fur merchants.

Kastoria's erstwhile fur production trade, which made the town famous, ended when displaced Jewish furriers arrived; by the 19th century, the local *kastori* (beavers) were extinct. Nevertheless, the reputation remains, and Kastoria's furriers now work with fur imported from North America and Scandinavia. Huge fur warehouses line the entry road, while most shops sell furs.

NORTHERN GREECE

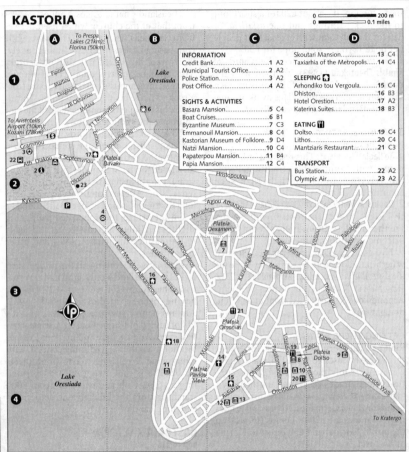

KASTORIA

INFORMATION	
Credit Bank	1 A2
Municipal Tourist Office	2 A2
Police Station	3 A2
Post Office	4 A2

SIGHTS & ACTIVITIES	
Basara Mansion	5 C4
Boat Cruises	6 B1
Byzantine Museum	7 C3
Emmanouil Mansion	8 C4
Kastorian Museum of Folklore	9 D4
Natzi Mansion	10 C4
Papaterpou Mansion	11 B4
Papia Mansion	12 C4

Skoutari Mansion	13 C4
Taxiarhia of the Metropolis	14 C4

SLEEPING	
Arhondiko tou Vergoula	15 C4
Dhiston	16 B3
Hotel Orestion	17 A2
Katerina Suites	18 B3

EATING	
Doltso	19 C4
Lithos	20 C4
Mantziaris Restaurant	21 C3

TRANSPORT	
Bus Station	22 A2
Olympic Air	23 A2

Orientation

The bus station is one block inland from the lake's southern side, on Athanasiou Diakou, where a park, the main taxi rank and a pay car park stand. Most services are at Kastoria's western end. The evocative old town with its *arhontika* and churches is on the eastern hill.

Information

Credit Bank (Grammou) Has ATMs.

Municipal tourist office (☎ /fax 24670 26777; www .kastoria.gr, in Greek; ☻ 8am-3pm Mon-Fri) Brochures, maps and information; in the lakeside park.

Police station (☎ 24670 83214; Grammou) Near the bus station.

Post office (Leoforos Megalou Alexandrou)

Sights & Activities

Kastoria's Byzantine churches were mainly originally chapels attached to *arhontika*. Most are locked; find a caretaker to enter.

External frescoes are visible, however, at some churches, such as **Taxiarhia of the Metropolis** (Plateia Pavlou Mela), south of Plateia Omonias, with its 13th-century fresco of the Madonna and Child above the entrance. It also contains the sacrosanct **tomb of Pavlos Melas**, the main military leader associated with the 1904–08 'Macedonian Struggle' in which Greek militants sought to annex the then-Ottoman region to Greece proper.

The **Byzantine Museum** (☎ 24670 26781; Plateia Dexamenis; admission free; ☻ 8.30am-3pm Tue-Sun) houses outstanding local icons.

Most *arhontika* occupy **Doltso**, southern Kastoria. Most significant are the **Emmanouil**, **Basara**, **Natzi**, **Skoutari**, **Papia** and **Papaterpou** mansions, named after the families that inhabited them.

One nice *arhontika* is now the must-see **Kastorian Museum of Folklore** (☎ 24670 28603; Kapetan Lazou; adult €2; ☽ 8.30am-2pm Tue-Sun). This 530-year-old house, formerly belonging to the wealthy Nerantzis Aïvazis family, is sumptuously furnished, displaying ornaments, kitchen utensils and tools.

Noon and evening **boat cruises** (€5, 1¼ hours) on Lake Orestiada start at the northside Psaradika Quay. Since the lake is not very clean, neither swimming nor fishing is recommended.

Festivals & Events

The **Nestorio River Festival** (www.riverparty.gr, in Greek), held in July on the wooded banks of the Nestorio River west of town, is a popular six-day event featuring famous Greek singers and ambient DJs. It draws around 10,000 young people, many of whom camp on the river. Along with the music, fun distractions include paintball, archery, sports and modern art. See the website for scheduled performances, camping and hotel accommodation options, and ticket vendors. If in Thessaloniki, try **Ticket House** (☎ 2310 253 630; cnr Ethnikis Amynis & Tsimiski).

During the festival, KTEL Kastoria runs special buses to Nestorio. There's organised, full-service camping, plus guest houses; the festival organisers can help book accommodation.

If you happen to be in Kastoria in winter, the local **Ragkountsaria Festival** (6–10 January), with likely pagan roots, features traditional dancing, costumed merrymaking and much eating and drinking.

The annual **International Fur Exhibition** (www.furfair.gr) draws big crowds. Check the website for dates and other information.

Sleeping

Kastoria is primarily a business destination, making prices high, but negotiable.

Hotel Orestion (☎ 24670 22257; Plateia Davaki 1; s/d €40/50; P ☒ ☐) This well-renovated business hotel has sleek modern rooms and the expected amenities, with deep couches and a tucked-away lounge bar.

Dhiston (☎ 24670 22250; Leoforos Megalou Alexandrou 91; d/tr €60/75) Upstairs from one of Kastoria's oldest cafes, these spacious suites have great

lake views. The French- and English-speaking manager provides maps and information.

Katerina Suites (☎ 24670 24645; Leoforos Megalou Alexandrou 127; s/d €60/80) These four suites with lake views can accommodate up to five people each. Suites are clean, modern and spacious; book ahead.

Arhondiko tou Vergoula (☎ 24670 23415; sfinas@ otenet.gr; Aidistras 14; d/tr incl breakfast €75/100; ☽) This restored 150-year-old mansion in a quiet quarter has lovely lake views, and is decorated with pieces from the owners' Asian adventures, giving it an exotic feel. Rooms are breezy and well maintained. It also has a cosy breakfast/dinner salon.

Eating

our pick **Kratergo** (☎ 24670 22981; Orestion 19, Psaradika; mains €6-9; ☽ 8pm-2am) This north-side lakefront taverna is worth the 20-minute drive. Featuring well-prepared Greek specialities, it has a great feel about it, with impressive stone arches, ambient lighting and lake views. Wistful *rembetika* plays on in the background.

Mantziaris Restaurant (☎ 24670 29492; Valala 8; mains €6-9) Unpretentious Mantziaris serves *mayirefta* and made-to-order grills.

Lithos (☎ 24670 26760; Orestiados 51; mains €6-10) The traditional wood-and-stone decor here matches the hearty taverna fare; the few innovations include 'Lithos aubergines' (herb-laced fried mushrooms).

Doltso (☎ 24670 24670; Plateia Doltso; mains €7-10) Housed in a rather imposing restored *arhontika*, Doltso's menu is standard, though the speciality, meatballs in *makalo* sauce (onion, garlic, flour and tomato), is unusual and excellent.

Getting There & Away

Kastoria's **Aristotelis airport** (☎ 24670 42515), 10km south, offers flights to Athens (€120, four weekly). **Olympic Air** (☎ 24670 22275; www.olympicairlines.com; Leoforos Megalou Alexandrou 15) is centrally located.

From Kastoria's **bus station** (☎ 24670 83455; Athanasiou Diakou) buses depart for Thessaloniki (€15.90, 2½ hours, seven daily), Ioannina (€16.30, 3½ hours, two daily), Konitsa (€12.10, 2½ hours, two daily), Athens (€41.60, nine hours, three daily) and Veria (€10.30, two hours, two daily). For Florina (€3.20, 30 minutes, eight daily), take a bus to Amyntaio and wait for a connecting bus.

Taxis (☎ 24670 82100) are also available.

NORTHERN GREECE

THRACE ΘΡΑΚΗ

pop 363,300 / area 6129 sq km

Diverse, dusty and still somewhat mysterious, Thrace (thr-*aaa*-kih) is one of Greece's most striking but least-visited areas. Once home to a powerful, non-Greek ancient Thracian civilisation, the region in more modern times has been dramatically affected by other neighbouring peoples, such as Bulgarians and Turks (the cumulative geographical entity of Thrace is indeed shared with Bulgaria and Turkey).

Thrace and its peoples have always lived from agriculture, still visibly attested by its tobacco crops, rolling wheat fields and vivid plains of sunflowers. The relative lack of tourism has preserved its character. The visible Turkish minority, with its own traditions of language, culture and cooking, has roots in Ottoman times. The landscape is dotted with mosque minarets and little villages of Turkish-style, red-roofed houses, and the traditional sweet shops are among Greece's best.

Other attractions in this sparsely inhabited province include unique expanses of wilderness. In the north, the rolling Rhodopi Mountains form the border with Bulgaria, full of pristine forests and animal life, while Thrace's eastern stretches nearer to Turkey host significant migratory bird populations at the Dadia Forest Reserve and the Evros Delta on the Aegean coast. The largest town, Alexandroupoli, is also the jumping-off point for ferries to Samothraki (p632).

Thrace may be a hinterland, but as Greece's only land border with Turkey, it's a strategic one. Around 30,000 Greek soldiers are stationed here. However, the only Greek warriors you'll see are the ones socialising in cafes along with university students called up to serve at various far-flung faculties. Since there's still little tourism, local communities appreciate the economic boost these twin armies provide.

History

What is known about the ancient Thracians comes from Greek sources; few inscribed records survive in their own, now lost language. Myth and supposition thus go into reconstructing this ancient civilisation, which had a reputation for warlike ways and mysterious religious practices. The most important, the cult of the Great Gods, began influencing Greek pagan religion after 1000

BC. At the Thracians' supreme temple on Samothraki, ancient Macedonian, Roman and Egyptian rulers were initiated into the cult. Secret rituals associated with Orpheus, the mythical, tragic Thracian father of music, also captivated society.

During the 7th century BC, powerful Greek city-states conquered the Thracian coast, and the Persians soon after. Athens prevailed after defeating Persia at the Battle of Plataea, but was ousted by Philip II of Macedon in 346 BC. With the Roman Empire's AD 395 division into western and eastern halves, Thrace, on the Via Egnatia trade route, became strategically significant. Eastern Thrace was called the 'breadbasket of Constantinople', an allusion to its significant wheat production.

Thrace was also a vital defensive zone for the Byzantine capital. However, its flatness left it vulnerable to marauding Goths, Huns, Vandals, Bulgars, Pechenegs, Cumans and even poorly behaved Latin Crusaders – probably why relatively few historic structures remain. Indeed, only the Ottoman Turks, who invaded in the mid-14th century, could enforce extended periods of peace and quiet.

Thrace's turbulent past was reawakened in the late 19th century. During the Russo-Turkish War of 1877, the Balkan Wars of 1912–13 and WWI up to the failed Greek invasion of Asia Minor in 1922, the territory changed hands frequently. The ancient Greek concept of hubris explains, as well as anything else, why the region's modern borders exist as they do; if not for various bombastic decisions on different sides, any of the three countries sharing Thrace could have taken more of it than they finally did.

What sets Greek Thrace apart is its Turkish minority. Along with the Greeks of Constantinople and Imvros (Gökçeada) and Tenedos (Bozcaada) islands, these Turks were exempt during the 1923 population exchanges mandated by the Lausanne Treaty – a treaty that the Greek government has increasingly begun to reference, self-defensively, when other issues of minority rights are invoked. However, while Turkey's Greek population has dwindled, the Turkish one in Greek Thrace is flourishing.

XANTHI ΞΑΝΘΗ
pop 45,118

The first important Thracian town when coming from Macedonia, atmospheric Xanthi

THRACE

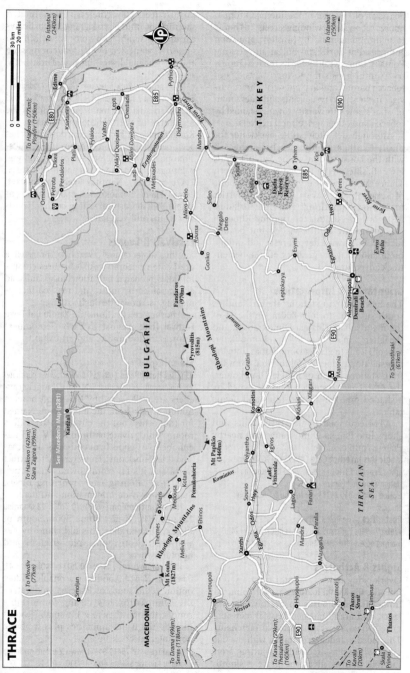

boasts an old quarter of traditional Ottoman houses set on steep, winding streets. It's home to an intriguing minority Muslim population comprised of Turks and Bulgarian-speaking Pomaks. Once wealthy for its tobacco industry, Xanthi boasts the former mansions of tobacco barons, and that old regal Thrace survives in the stylish restaurants and cafes found in what's now a university town sustained by tobacco and other agricultural exploits.

Although definitely still a backwater for most, Xanthi's importance has increased with the construction of the Egnatia Odos Hwy. Besides being the gateway to eastern Thrace, Xanthi lies near the Macedonian ports of Keramoti and Kavala, which have ferries to Thasos, Samothraki and other islands. Just north of Xanthi, the rippling Rhodopi Mountains are a little-visited but beautiful area filled with deep forests and unique mountain villages – great for off-the-beaten-track adventures.

Orientation & Information

The bus and train stations are on Xanthi's south side, the former 800m southeast of the main square (Plateia Dimokratias), and the latter 2km south of it. Dimokritou (later, Karaoli) leads to Plateia Dimokratias from the bus station, as does 28 Oktovriou, from the train station. North of Plateia Dimokratias, the Old Town occupies a hill crowned by a shaded pine forest with trails and picnic tables.

ATM-equipped banks, restaurants and shops line Plateia Dimokratias and nearby Plateia Antiko.

Magic Bus Internet Cafe (☎ 25410 26580; Anexarhou 2; per hr €1.40; 🕒 8am-2am) Between the bus station and Hotel Paris.

Police (☎ 25410 23333; cnr Nestou & Lykourgou Thrakis)

Post office (A Georgiou 16)

Web (Vasileos Konstantinou 63; per hr €2.40; 🕒 24hr) Internet access off Plateia Antiko.

Sights & Activities

Overlooking modern Xanthi from a serene hillside, **Old Xanthi** features pastel-coloured, timber-framed houses on narrow, winding lanes, and grand old neoclassical mansions once owned by wealthy tobacco merchants. This faded grandeur, combined with the bulbous, white-plastered bubbles jutting from humble homes, gives the place a slightly forlorn feel. Nevertheless, the animated shouting of little boys kicking footballs livens up Old Xanthi, also home to the Muslim minority, witnessed by the modern mosque and the satellite dishes tuned to Turkish TV stations.

The stately **Folk Museum** (Antika 5-7; admission free; 🕒 8.30am-2.30pm Wed-Fri & 10.30am-3pm Sat & Sun) stands in adjacent mansions, formerly the residences of the tobacco millionaires, the Kougioumtzoglu brothers. The downstairs has been beautifully restored, recreating a 1930s-atmosphere, while the original ceiling and wall paintings upstairs are lavish and imaginative.

On Saturday, Xanthi's lively **open market**, east of Plateia Dimokratias, maintains a venerable Balkan custom, selling clothes, jewellery, fruits and vegetables.

Festivals & Events

Xanthi's **winter carnival** (www.carnival-of-xanthi.gr), a pre-Lenten celebration that features colourful floats prepared by various local clubs, all accompanied by music and masked merry-making, is known throughout Greece.

Another celebration, the **Xanthi Old Town Festival** (late August to early September) features theatre, music and art exhibits.

Sleeping

our pick **Hotel Paris** (☎ 25410 20531; www.parishotel .gr; Dimokritou 12; s/d €30/40; 🔀 🖵) Budget travellers are well served by this small hotel, a minute's walk from the bus station. Named for the owner, not the city, the Paris offers rooms with private bathroom, TV and telephone, plus good firm beds and the occasional large balcony. However, there's street noise and it's far from downtown, though ideal for catching early-morning buses. Staff can provide information and maps.

Hotel Xanthippion (☎ 25410 77061; 28 Oktovriou 212; s/d €35/45; 🔀 🖵) Some 500m south of Plateia Dimokratias, this old stand-by has well-kept, clean rooms, plus friendly and helpful owners.

Hotel Dimokritos (☎ 25410 25111; 28 Oktovriou 41; s/d €40/58; 🔀 🖵) Another reasonable budget option 100m south of Plateia Dimokratias, the Dimokritos has clean, comfortable rooms, though they're a bit small. Rooms include the usual amenities plus a phone port internet hook-up.

Z Palace (☎ 25410 64414; www.z-palace.gr; Terma Georgiou Kondyli; s/d/ste €80/115/310; 🅿 🔀 🖵 🐾)

This five-star business hotel boasts an outdoor swimming pool, a fitness room, a children's hall, a French gourmet restaurant and a hair salon, hearkening back to the opulent days of the tobacco barons – though not in its decor, which though elegant is hardly traditional.

Eating & Drinking

Rose Family Zaharoplasteio (☎ 25410 75310; cnr Anaxarhou & Dimokritou; sweets €1-3; ☺ 8am-10pm) This friendly, bright cafe–sweet shop near the bus station, owned by Dimitris and Roula Triantafylidis (the name means rose) since 1960, has good cakes and coffees with seating.

our pick **Taverna To Perasma** (☎ 25410 78014; Ikoniou 16; mezedhes €2.50-4, mains €5-9) When you see a restaurant well away from the Old Town that's filled with merry locals, you know you're somewhere good. Off on a sidestreet not far from the bus station, To Perasma serves up huge portions of tasty mezedhes and Turkish-inspired Thracian delights. Try the roka salad with tomato and cucumber, *melitzanes* 'special' (oven-cooked aubergines topped with cheese), *sykoti krasato* (liver with wine) and *yiaourtlou kebab* (spicy beef kebabs with yoghurt on fried pitta strips with salsa); it'll cost about €20, and feed four.

Restaurant Palia Poli (☎ 25410 68685; Hasirtzoglou 7; mains €5-9) Most Old Town restaurants are unoriginal; however, the wood-and-brick Palia Poli, tucked discreetly into a side lane, is more inventive, offering quail, roast pork with plum sauce and orange duck.

Nedim (☎ 25410 25959; Basileos Konstantinou 35) The Xanthi branch of this Komotini-based classic Turkish sweet shop has a temptingly prominent setting in the centre – do give in to temptation.

Café Antica (☎ 25410 62193; Vasileos Konstantinou 86; ☺ 9am-2am) This voluminous, two-level, central cafe has a relaxed, traditional flavour, with long wooden rafters, soft couches and wall-bound antique implements. Try wine in summer, or one of the Antica's many hot chocolates in winter.

Getting There & Away

AIR

Xanthi shares Alexander the Great Airport with Kavala. It's 40km southwest of Xanthi, near Hrysoupoli. **Olympic Air** (☎ 25410 22944; www.olympicairlines.com; Michael Vogdou 4) is near Plateia Dimokratias.

BUS

From the **bus station** (☎ 25410 22684; Dimokritou 6) buses serve Komotini (€4.90, one hour, 14 daily), Thessaloniki (€17, 2½ hours, 10 daily) and Athens (€52, nine hours, one daily). Thessaloniki buses go via Kavala (€5, one hour). There aren't direct buses to Alexandroupoli (€8, one hour, 45 minutes); change at Komotini. Buses also serve Pomakohoria villages such as Thermes (€4, 1½ hours).

TRAIN

Xanthi's **train station** (☎ 25410 22581; Terma Kondyli) serves Komotini (€2, one hour, seven daily) and Alexandroupoli (€3.70, 1½ hours, seven daily). Other trains head west to Thessaloniki (€9, four hours, seven daily), with four of them continuing on to Athens (€30, 10 hours). Taxis to/from the train station cost €3 to €5.

Getting Around

No Olympic Air buses serve Hrysoupoli, only taxis (€35). Alternatively, take a Kavala-bound bus to Hrysoupoli, then a taxi 12km to the airport.

AROUND XANTHI

North of Xanthi, the fascinating, off-the-beaten-track **Pomakohoria** (Pomak villages) area lies tucked into the gentle folds of the Rhodopi Mountains, which form the border with Bulgaria. These 25 or so villages host a unique population of Bulgarian-speaking Muslims, the Pomaks, who spill across the borders and whose ethnic identity is a subject of some uncertainty (even to themselves). In Greece, they speak Greek, Bulgarian and Turkish and, along with the more confidently Turkish Turks of the region, are officially classified as 'Greek Muslims' by the government. During the Cold War, this border area was kept off-limits and tourists today are still rare.

Along with their lovely and unspoiled natural setting, some Pomak villages offer unique activities, such as the **hot mineral baths** of **Thermes**, 43km north of Xanthi. The main bath, in a building opposite the village church, costs money to enter; however, the other, outdoor, bath is free – from the tiny village shop-restaurant, it's about 100m to the right-hand side and below the main road. The baths are relaxing and therapeutic (various medical ailments are treated by professionals at the indoor one), so enjoy, but don't forget that since the Pomakohoria is a conservative area the baths are no place for debauchery, shouting or gleeful nudity.

Hill walking is wonderful here, though there are no marked trails. However, a 90-minute walk along the road to the remote hamlet of **Kidaris**, just across from Bulgaria, offers stunning mountain views and total serenity; indeed, since it's is now essentially uninhabited, you're unlikely to see anyone along the way.

Rustic country lunches of salad and spit-roasted goat or lamb (€7) are available in Thermes at the shop-restaurant, Kafe Psistaria O Kalemtzi. The owner, Kemal Kalemtzi, also provides simple rooms at **Enikiazomena Domatia Kalemtzi Kemal** (☎ 25540 22474, 6977597500; d €20) in an adjacent building. His son, Hassan, speaks English.

Getting There & Away
The Pomakohoria is accessible as a day trip from Xanthi, by car and even by bus (about 90 minutes). The bus for Thermes (€4.10 one way) leaves at 6.30am daily, and returns to Xanthi at 3.30pm. A later bus leaves Xanthi for Thermes at 2.10pm, but thus requires an overnight in Thermes.

KOMOTINI ΚΟΜΟΤΗΝΗ
pop 46,586
Komotini (ko-mo-tih-*nee*), 52km east of Xanthi, is the Rhodopi prefecture's provincial capital and central Thrace's biggest town. Despite its backwater nature, Komotini boasts several intriguing museums and historic buildings, and its prominent university population gives the town some measure of nightlife. These students, hailing from all over Greece, fill the cafes in the main square (Plateia Irinis).

This student body also dilutes the visibility of Komotini's Muslim presence; roughly half the population is Turkish – the largest percentage in any major Greek town. While Greeks and Turks cohabit the town amicably enough, they do generally live separate lives.

The main attractions of Komotini, built in the 4th century AD, stem from this mixed heritage, comprising Byzantine churches, Ottoman mosques and neoclassical mansions. So explore Komotini's street markets and characteristic old quarters, indulge in Turkish sweets and Greek bouzouki life – and

enjoy an authentic Thracian town in all its dusty splendour.

Orientation & Information
The train station is 1km southwest on Panagi Tsaldari. The bus station is a five-minute walk north-northeast to the oblong Plateia Irinis, centre of Komotini's little universe. This square is unmissable, and not only because of the unexpected playground in the form of a pirate ship that stands in the middle of it; most ATMs, hotels, eateries and cafes are here too. Komotini's main attractions are all within walking distance.

Explorer Net Store (☎ 25310 32535; Nikolaou Zoidi 52; per hr €2; ☻ 24hr) Central internet cafe.

Hospital (☎ 25310 24601; Sismanoglou 45) It's 900m southeast of Plateia Irinis.

Police (☎ 25310 34444)

Sights
Sparse remains of Komotini's 4th-century AD **Byzantine Fortress**, built by Emperor Theodosius, lie near Plateia Irinis. Only the ruins of one out of 16 original towers survive. Nearby, the **Church of the Assumption of Mary** (Ekklisia Kimisis Theotokou), built in 1800 on the site of an earlier Byzantine shrine, contains 16th-century icons and wood carvings.

Thracian archaeological finds are displayed at the classy **Archaeological Museum** (☎ 25310 22411; Simeonidi 4; admission free; ☻ 8.30am-5pm). The collection, accompanied by informative English-language wall texts detailing ancient Thracian history, also contains Roman coins, clay figurines, delicate gold wreaths and Byzantine glazed ceramics. The helpful staff will guide you and provide a detailed map showing the major archaeological sites in Thrace and Eastern Macedonia.

Valuable post-Byzantine icons are displayed at the **Ecclesiastic Museum** (Imaret; ☎ 25310 34177; Xenofontos 8; admission €3; ☻ 10.30am-1.30pm Tue-Sun, 5-8pm Wed-Fri). The museum occupies Komotini's most unique building, an early Ottoman almshouse (*ptohokomeio* in Greek), occupying an enclosed courtyard. The structure's brickwork and design resemble a Byzantine church; indeed, it was built around 1363 by Gazi Ervinoz Bey, the Ottoman conqueror of Byzantine Komotini. Besides the marvellous icons, occasional surprises such as 500-year-old printed gospels, silver ceremonial crosses, gold embroidery and 18th-century Hebrew scrolls are kept.

Just behind Plateia Irinis Komotini's relaxing **Turkish quarter** begins, lined with quaint old houses, barber shops and tea-houses. Sights include the **Clock Tower** (Orologio), built in 1884, **Yeni Camii** ('New Mosque' in Turkish) and **Eski Camii**. The latter mosque, dating from 1608, still operates, despite the flowers growing out of its roof.

Sleeping

Komotini remains a business destination, and so somewhat expensive. Midrange hotels are classy and close to the action.

Orpheus Hotel (☎ 25310 37180; orfhotel@otenet.gr; Parassiou 1; s/d/tr €40/50/60; ✖) With its prominent location at the entrance to the *plateia* and its big windows, you can't miss the Orpheus. The hotel has nicely restored and soundproofed modern rooms. Management is welcoming and friendly.

Hotel Astoria (☎ 25310 22707; www.astoriakomotini .gr; Plateia Irinis 28; d €57; ✖ ▢) More elegant than the Orpheus, but easier to miss, the Astoria is concealed by the square's side cafes. Its modern rooms have attractive, understated decor and amenities, plus small balconies overlooking the square.

Eating & Drinking

our pick **Nedim** (☎ 25310 22036; cnr Leoforosoros Orfeos & Syntagmatos Kriton; sweets €2-4) This emporium of traditional sweets has been serving perhaps the best baklava this side of İstanbul since 1950. Try *saray kataïfi*, a delicate golden treat of the Ottoman palace, and *samali*, a sweet cake with almonds, flavoured by aromatic Chios mastic. Thirty-five kinds of traditional sweets on display for sale include the monstrous *soutzouk loukoumi* – thick Turkish delight dusted with confectioner's sugar, and shaped like a giant, curling sausage. Delicious!

To Sokaki tis Lakokolas (☎ 25310 81800; Parasiou 5; mains €5-7; ✖ noon-midnight) In an underpass opposite Emboriki Bank, this lively taverna has simple, nourishing grills and salads, and attentive service. Try the *yiaourtlou kebab*.

Ta Aderfia (☎ 25310 20201; Orfeos 33; mains €5-7) An unassuming, old-school taverna west of the square, Ta Aderfia is a good local lunch spot, when more than 30 kinds of *mayirefta* are on offer; the selection narrows by dinnertime.

Cafes and bars line Plateia Irinis; **Café Bel Air** (Plateia Irinis 55; ✖ 10am-3am) is a student favourite.

The nearby **Rock Bar** (Plateia Irinis 18; ✖ 11am-3am Sep-May) is a cosy upstairs hole-in-the-wall playing rock, blues, jazz and funk – an antidote to the prevailing candy-pop of other cafes. The friendly owners can provide info on fun local activities.

For Greek nightlife in all its scantily dressed licentiousness, visit the **Ihodromio** (Parasiou 4; ✖ 9pm-4am), a loud *bouzoukia* (nightclub where bouzouki is played) where businessmen and students meet over mezedhes, lusty dancing and some seriously overpriced cocktails.

Getting There & Away
BUS

From Komotini's **bus station** (☎ 25310 22912) buses serve Xanthi (€4.90, one hour, nine daily) and Alexandroupoli (€5.70, one hour, 14 daily). Going west, buses reach Kavala (€9.40, 1½ hours), Thessaloniki (€22.80, 2½ hours, 10 daily) and Athens (€60, 8¾ hours, one daily).

TRAIN

From the **train station** (☎ 25310 22650) six trains daily go east to Alexandroupoli (€2.70, one hour) and seven go west to Thessaloniki (€11, 4½ hours), via Xanthi (€2, 30 minutes). A train to İstanbul via Pythio leaves daily at 11.30am (€40, 16 hours).

Getting Around

Komotini sprawls, but is walkable. There are **taxis** (☎ 25310 37777) and **Evros Car Rental** (☎ 25310 32905; evroscar@hol.gr; Tountzas 1) hires cars (from €40) and Jeeps (€60).

ALEXANDROUPOLI ΑΛΕΞΑΝΔΡΟΥΠΟΛΗ
pop 49,176

Alexandroupoli (ah-lex-an-*dhroo*-po-lih) is eastern Thrace's largest town, and the most appealing. The axis of travel in four directions, this port gets a steady stream of visitors heading to or from Turkey, Bulgaria, elsewhere in northern Greece, and in summer for ferries to Samothraki. Alexandroupoli itself has two marvellous museums, a pretty if somewhat kitsch lighthouse, some good seafood restaurants and elementary nightlife.

Orientation

Alexandroupoli's simple grid system of streets was created by Russians in 1878 during the Russo-Turkish War. The main streets run east–west, parallel with the waterfront. Its eastern

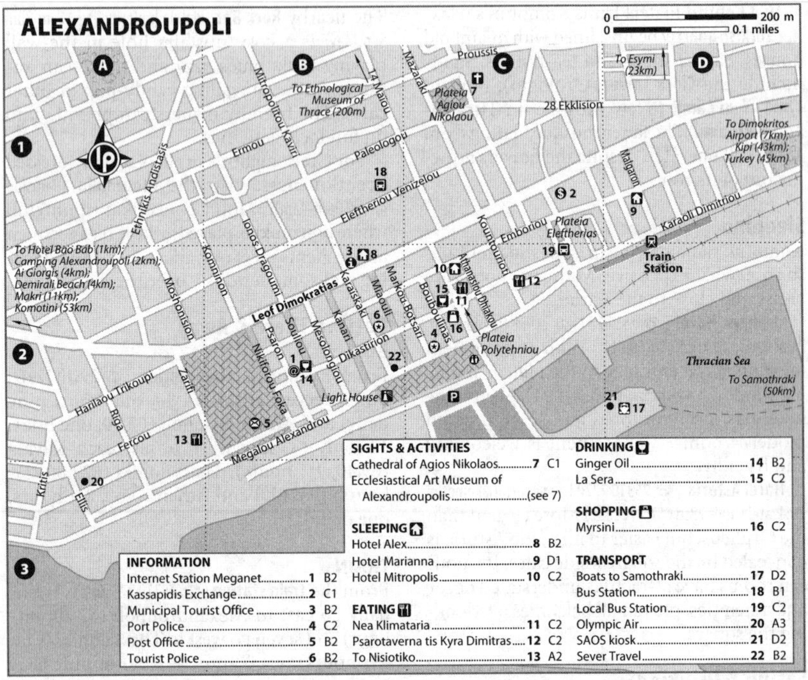

end is called Karaoli Dimitriou, the western, Megalou Alexandrou. The main squares are Plateia Eleftherias and Plateia Polytehniou, both one block north of Karaoli Dimitriou.

Alexandroupoli's train station is on the waterfront south of Plateia Eleftherias, beside the local bus station, 100m east of the port, where boats leave for Samothraki. The main bus station is five blocks inland.

Information

ATM-equipped banks stretch along Leoforos Dimokratias.

Internet Station Meganet (☎ 25510 33639; cnr Dikastirion & Psaron; per hr €2.40; 🕒 24hr) Internet access.

Kassapidis Exchange (☎ 25510 80910; Leoforos Dimokratias 209; 🕒 8am-9.30pm Mon-Sat, 10am-2pm Sun) Changes 87 currencies, including Balkan ones, and does Western Union money transfers.

Municipal tourist office (☎ 25510 64184; Leoforos Dimokratias 306; 🕒 7.30am-3pm) The helpful staff provide maps, plus accommodation and transport information.

Port police (☎ 25512 26468; cnr Megalou Alexandrou & Markou Botsari)

Post office (cnr Nikiforou Foka & Megalou Alexandrou)

Tourist police (☎ 25510 37424; Karaïskaki 6)

Sights & Activities

The **Ethnological Museum of Thrace** (☎ 25510 36663; www.emthrace.com; 14 Maiou 63; adult €3; 🕒 10am-2pm & 6-9pm Tue-Sat, 10am-2pm Sun), housed in a mansion built in 1899, faithfully displays Thracian traditional customs. Each room is devoted to a specific topic, ranging from traditional costumes and musical instruments to oil presses, a dye-room and sweet-making equipment. The accompanying texts explain, among other things, how many silkworms it takes to make 25g of silk and which Greek sweet is made by slamming the ingredients against a wall. If you are travelling further in Thrace, the friendly staff can outline the most interesting sites. There's a small back courtyard cafe.

Priceless icons, many brought by refugees from Asia Minor and Turkish Thrace, are exhibited at the **Ecclesiastical Art Museum of Alexandroupoli** (☎ 25510 26359; Plateia Agiou Nikolaou; adult €3; 🕒 9am-2pm Tue-Fri, 10am-2pm Sat). The museum also contains early printed Greek books and is adjacent to the **Cathedral of Agios Nikolaos** (Plateia Agiou Nikolaou); which boasts a miracle-working 13th-century icon of the

NORTHERN GREECE

Panagia Trifotissa, brought from Aenos (Enez in Turkish) across the Evros River. The story goes that by praying before the icon, villagers whose eyes had been damaged by the glare of sunlight reflected on the salt marshes around Aenos had their vision restored.

Since swimming isn't good in Alexandroupoli itself, head 4km west to **Demirali Beach**, preferred by locals. This sandy beach with clear waters hosts a famous local restaurant, Ai Giorgis (right).

Sleeping

Camping Alexandroupoli (☎ 25510 26055; Leoforos Makris; camp sites per adult/tent €5/4.50) This large camping ground (2km west) is clean, well-run and has good facilities. Take local bus 7 from Plateia Eleftherias.

Hotel Mitropolis (☎ 25510 26443; Athanasiou Dhiakou; s/d/tr €30/40/50; 🔀) This dated budget hotel is close to the water and good restaurants and cafes, though fixtures are old and service is hit-or-miss.

Hotel Alex (☎ 25510 26302; Leoforos Dimokratias 294; s/d/tr €35/40/50; 🔀) Up on the main street, this decent budget option has good, though cramped, rooms and the necessary amenities. Front-facing rooms get street noise.

Hotel Bao Bab (☎ 25510 34823; Alexandroupoli-Komotini Hwy; s/d/tr €40/60/70; P 🔀 🖳) Just 1km west of town, this lavish waterfront hotel has large, comfortable rooms. There's decent swimming on the sandy, shallow beach. Adding in the excellent restaurant and lounge bar, this is likely the Alexandroupoli area's best value for money.

Hotel Marianna (☎ 25510 81456; fax 25510 81455; Malgaron 11; s/d €45/60) This friendly downtown hotel has small, though clean and fresh-smelling, rooms and a colourful breakfast area. Hospitable owners Georgios Hrysohoidis and his Italian wife Patricia cumulatively speak English, Italian, French, Spanish, German and Greek.

Eating

Nea Klimataria (☎ 25510 26288; Plateia Polytehniou; mains €5-8) This heavy-duty, popular place on the square is not setting records, but it does have tasty prepared dishes, good roast chicken and big salads.

our pick Psarotaverna tis Kyra Dimitras (☎ 25510 34434; cnr Kountourioti & Dikastirion; fish €6-11) Venerable old Kyra Dimitra is still running the show at

this seafood restaurant, in the family since 1915. Choose from the daily catch, set out on ice at the front; *tsipoura* (sea bream) is tasty and only €20 per kilo, while a plateful of small crunchy fish makes for a scrumptious lunch. In summer, the amiable Kyra Dimitra might surprise you with a plate of complementary watermelon.

Ai Giorgis (☎ 25510 71777; Demirali Beach; fish €7-10; ⏰ 10am-1am) On Demirali Beach, 4km west, this waterfront taverna is a local favourite, with smooth wood floors and candle-lit tables. Everything is good, from the varied salads and stuffed mushrooms to fish dishes.

To Nisiotiko (☎ 25510 20990; Zarifi 1; fish €8-14) This west-side waterfront fish taverna has ambience, with eclectic decor, but prices are steep.

Drinking

Alexandroupoli's cool nightspots change with the whims of its students. Leoforos Dimokratias has trendy bars, while cafes line the waterfront. For a unique Alexandroupoli beer bar, see Beer Essentials, p294.

La Sera (☎ 25510 38765; Plateia Polytehniou; ⏰ 10am-3am) This smooth bar near the water is lit by little red candles, and is popular with both students and the older set.

Shopping

Myrsini (☎ 25510 31205; www.silkyhouse.gr; Plateia Polytehniou) This family-run business sells Soufli silk originals, from silk table runners (€15 to €100) and ornate raw silk scarves (€20) to enormous silk spreads embellished with a Byzantine double-headed eagle and floral motifs (€807).

Getting There & Away

AIR

Alexandroupoli's Dimokritos Airport is 7km east of town near Loutra.

Olympic Air (☎ 25510 26361; www.olympicairlines .com; cnr Ellis & Koletti) is downtown; **Aegean Airlines** (☎ 25510 89150; www.aegeanair.com) is at the airport. Both offer four daily flights to/from Athens (€75, 55 minutes). For information on flights from Alexandroupoli to Crete, see Island Hopping (p745).

BOAT

Alexandroupoli is a major ferry port for Samothraki; however, at the time of writing, the longstanding ferry line to the northeastern

Aegean Islands and Dodecanese wasn't running. For information on ferries and hydrofoils from Alexandroupoli to Samothraki, see Island Hopping (p745). Get tickets from the portside SAOS kiosk, or from travel agencies such as **Sever Travel** (☎ 25510 22555; sever1@otenet. gr; Megalou Alexandrou 24).

BUS

Domestic

From Alexandroupoli's **bus station** (☎ 25510 26479; Eleftheriou Venizelou 36) frequent buses ply the northeastern line to Feres (€2.30), Soufli (€5.50, 1½ hours), Didymotiho (€7.30, 1½ hours) and Orestiada (€9.50, two hours). Another bus terminates at Kipi on the Turkish border (€3.50, five daily).

One daily bus serves Athens (€61, 10 hours), and nine serve Thessaloniki (€26.50, 3¾ hours). Buses to Kavala (€13.50, two hours) go via Komotini (€5.70, 70 minutes, 14 daily) and Xanthi (€9.50, 1¾ hours).

International

An OSE bus to İstanbul leaves at 8.30am (€15, six hours) Tuesday to Sunday.

TRAIN

Domestic

From the **train station** (☎ 25510 26395) six daily trains serve Thessaloniki (€9, seven hours); one continues to Athens (€49, 14 hours). Trains also run northeast to Dikea (€5.10, 2½ hours, seven daily) via Pythio (€3.70), Didymotiho (€3.70), Orestiada (€4.30, three daily) and Kastanies (€4.70), where there's a Turkish border crossing.

International

Going to Bulgaria from Alexandroupoli, a daily train leaves at 5.30am for Svilengrad (€7, four hours), with connections to Plovdiv and Sofia.

For Turkey, a direct train with sleeper cars to İstanbul leaves nightly at 1am (€38, seven hours). Two trains originating in Thessaloniki also pass through en route to İstanbul.

Getting Around

Only the camping ground or beaches require a bus or taxi. For the airport, take a Loutra-bound bus from Plateia Eleftherias, or a **taxi** (☎ 25510 28358) for about €8.

EVROS DELTA ΔΕΛΤΑ ΕΒΡΟΥ

The Evros Delta (20km southeast of Alexandroupoli) is one of Europe's most important wetlands, comprising 188 sq km of coastal lakes, lagoons, interior rivers, sand dunes, swamps and reed beds. This environment makes it ideal for birdlife, and thus birdwatchers. More than 330 varieties, including several endangered species, can be seen. More than 200,000 migrating waterfowl winter here.

The **Evros Delta visitor centre** (☎ /fax 25510 61000; evroswet@hol.gr; Loutra; ⏰ 8am-4pm) arranges birdwatching trips. The delta's western segment is always open, though motorised transport is restricted along the southern littoral. Visiting the delta's most fascinating part, the eastern section, near Turkey, requires a permit from the Greek police and army.

The visitor centre arranges permits for free: fax or email them 12 to 14 days ahead with your name and surname (as on your passport), your passport number and date of expiry, plus your date of birth. The centre also provides maps, and conducts guided tours (€10 per person) and minibus and boat trips around the delta.

ALEXANDROUPOLI TO SOUFLI
ΑΛΕΞΑΝΔΡΟΥΠΟΛΗ ΠΡΟΣ ΣΟΥΦΛΙ

Two routes lead from Alexandroupoli northwards to Didymotiho, the western one and the main eastern one, which hugs the Turkish border. The western route passes through tranquil, unvisited villages such as Esymi, Megalo Derio and Mikro Derio; some 10km west of the latter is Roussa, site of **megalithic Thracian tombs** from the 9th century BC, decorated with mysterious rock carvings.

There are two eastern roads; the 'new' one heading straight north, and the old one that runs with the train line and the Evros River along the Turkish border. This part of Thrace is all rolling hills, punctuated by storks' nests on phone poles and great fields of wheat and sunflowers. Although the occasional sign prohibits photography, there's no hassle from the military. The following destinations have frequent bus connections, and some have train connections, with Alexandroupoli.

Following the river route 29km northeast of Alexandroupoli, **Feres** boasts Thrace's most impressive Byzantine church. Built by

Byzantine royal Isaac Komnenos in 1152 as a miniature of Constantinople's great Agia Sofia, the **Church of Panagia Kosmosotira** survives miraculously intact and is signposted. Feres also has a small **tourist information centre** (☎ 25550 24310).

Beyond Feres, little **Tyhero** might be nondescript, but it does have the area's most unique lodgings: the family-friendly **Thrassa Eco-Tourism Guesthouse** (☎ 25540 20080, 6946462350; www.thrassa .gr; s/d/ste €45/65/95; P ⛽ 🛜). Built on an 800m-long lake, it has big, breezy rooms and numerous hanging plants and vines. Friendly owner Sofia Hajisavva (also a tennis coach) organises sports, boat and pony rides for kids, who can also scamper about on the lawns and look for ducks, fish and turtles. The only drawback is the mosquitoes, but all the rooms and buildings have screens.

If arriving here on one of the frequent north–south buses passing along the river road, ask for Tyhero's Gymnasio stop, from where the guest house is 200m opposite. While the guest house has a cafe, for food visit the village, where several tavernas converge: **O Thomas** (☎ 25540 41259; Tyhero centre; mains €5-8) is an old favourite and can also deliver to Thrassa.

Further north on the main road (a total of 30km from Feres), a left-hand turnoff leading west 7km culminates at the birdwatcher's promised land: **Dadia Forest Reserve**, on one of Europe's two main bird migration routes and home to 36 of the 38 known species of European raptors (birds of prey), some rare. The park includes a protected inner zone (73 sq km) and a buffer zone (352 sq km). It takes 1000kg of meat a week to keep the birds satiated (most deposited from slaughterhouses). Almost as entertaining as watching the birds frolic on their carrion through long-lens telescopes is observing the more zealous birdwatchers argue about which bird it is they're actually seeing.

While there's usually activity, the best time is May, before migration begins, or in July, when baby vultures hop curiously out of their nests. Your starting point on-site is the **Ecotourist Centre** (☎ 25540 32209; dadia@otenet .gr; 🕙 10am-4pm Dec-Jan, 9am-7pm Mar-May & Sep-Nov, 8.30am-8.30pm Jun-Aug), which has detailed bilingual wall displays, an educational film and minibus service to an Alamo-like bird hide (€3). Alternatively, hike for one hour up the trail – it's marked orange on the way up and

yellow coming down. The hide offers binoculars, telescopes and a tripod for photography buffs. Those desiring even more information may also seek out the itinerant World Wildlife Foundation scientist (her office adjoins the Ecotourist Centre).

You can sleep at the adjoining **Ecotourist Hostel of Dadia** (☎ 25540 32263; dadia@otenet.gr; s/d/tr €30/43/50). These simple but clean rooms with bathrooms are named after different ferocious fowls. A cafe's next door. For eating, return 1km to Dadia village where the **Traditional Family Taverna** (☎ 25540 32481; mains €4-6) near the church serves Greek fare.

Soufli, 38km north of Alexandroupoli, is most famous for its silk. The area's prevalence of mulberry trees, upon which silkworms feed, have made it a centre for the silk industry since Alexander the Great's time. However, the industry suffered several blows in the past century; the creation of modern Turkey in 1923 cut some farmers off from their former lands and, more recently, numerous mulberry trees have been sacrificed for crop space. While small-scale production continues, there's talk of cheap Chinese imports being passed off as Soufli-made: try to ensure you're buying the real thing.

Although Soufli's **silk museum** (☎ 25510 23700; Eleftheriou Venizelou 73) remained closed at time of writing, several private silk museums/shops have opened, best of all the **Art of Silk Museum** (☎ 25540 22371; www.silkmuseum.gr; Vasilis Georgiou 199; 🕙 9.30am-8.30pm, 🔦), which occupies a restored silk-producing mansion and includes a tempting entrance shop. The displays present the history of Soufli silk production, and are enhanced by state-of-the-art technology, such as videos and interactive, multilingual audio guides.

Koukouli Inn (☎ 25540 22400; fax 25540 22441; Olorou 14; s/d incl breakfast €45/55), built in 1850 for harvesting and screening silkworm cocoons, offers atmospheric accommodation. It's opposite town hall.

Soufli also has ATMs and services – and perhaps Greece's smallest old-school bus station.

DIDYMOTIHO ΔΙΔΥΜΟΤΕΙΧΟ
pop 8700
Rough-and-tumble Didymotiho (dih-dih-*mo*-tih-ho), a military outpost just beyond Soufli, has significant historical ruins. Aside from

them, however, it's fairly sleepy, as opposed to a place where you would want to sleep, thus making it better for a day trip or drive-by from Orestiada (below) than an overnight stay. Didymotiho has ATM-equipped banks, pharmacies and a small, central **Tourism information centre** (☎ 25530 22222).

The town's name derives from its once-magnificent double walls (*didymo* 'twin', *tihos* 'wall'), the remains of which stand proudly in its upper town. Founded in the late 8th century as a hinterland fort for Constantinople, Didymotiho became an important Byzantine town, and was the birthplace of numerous eminent figures. In 1341, Byzantine Emperor John Kantakouzenis was crowned here. When Turkish Sultan Murad I conquered in 1361, Didymotiho briefly became his capital, before being relocated in 1365 to Adrianople (modern Edirne, Turkey).

Didymotiho's *plateia* is marked by a huge, pyramid-roofed mosque, ordained by Murad and finished in 1368 by his son Bayezit – thus, **Bayezit's Mosque**. It was Europe's first, and the biggest the Ottomans would build there. Today it lies in forlorn disrepair, its minaret topless, windows smashed and walls crumbling.

A steep walk from the main square passes Ottoman-style timber-framed houses and winds into the upper town. Near the **Church of Agios Athanasios**, well-preserved sections of Didymotiho's **Byzantine walls**, and strange catacomb-like side structures remain.

If you're thirsty, stop for lemonade at the iconic Café Samantha, which has impressive views over Didymotiho's traditional roofs as far as the river. Kindly old Leftheris, the owner, can point out the symbol of Byzantine noble Tarhaniotis, engraved in the wall above his cafe's garden.

Getting There & Away

From Didymotiho the main road continues 20km to Orestiada, Evros' last major town. However, if you hug the river on the old road (or are travelling by train), it's around 35km between them.

Buses run hourly from Orestiada (€1.70, 20 minutes).

ORESTIADA ΟΡΕΣΤΙΑΔΑ
pop 25,000

Orestiada is the largest town beyond Alexandroupoli, with reasonable amounts of shopping, social life and services. It's a good base for day trips to Didymotiho, plus totally unvisited villages and other historic sites. Orestiada's also the jumping-off point for Bulgarian Thrace or nearby Edirne in Turkey. It's also just south of Kastanies village, with its popular summer music festival.

Orestiada was built in 1923, during the population exchanges between Greece and Turkey. Unlike most of the ragged refugees, however, the dignified residents of the new Orestiada chose to leave their homes on the Turkish side of the river together and resettle in an organised way. Like other border towns, Orestiada has a robust military presence, though actual uniformed soldiers are less noticeable than are the suited businessmen on army-related contracts.

Orientation & Information

From Orestiada's train station walk uphill on Vasileos Konstantinou; the intersection with Anthanasiou Pantazidou reaches the central square. Turn left on Pantazidou for the Hotel Elektra, cafes, restaurants and post office; turn right for the tourist information and Web internet cafe. ATM-equipped banks hug the main square. Shops are on Konstantinopoleos, parallel with Pantazidou opposite the square. The bus station's also nearby; follow Vasileos Konstantinou for two blocks, and turn right on Adrianoupoleos.

Hatzigiannis Tours (☎ 25520 25666; cnr Konstantinopoleos & Emmanouel Riga) Sells plane, boat and train tickets.

Post office (☎ 25520 22435; Athanasiou Pantazidou)

Web (☎ 25520 25012; Athanasiou Pantazidou 64; per hr €2; 🕑 24hr) Internet access.

Sights & Activities

Orestiada's humble **Folk Museum** (☎ 25520 28080; Agion Theodoron 87; 🕑 11am-1pm & 7-9pm Tue-Sat) has traditional Thracian furnishings and costumes, old weaponry and, intriguingly, a fragment from the original Lausanne Treaty, which stipulated the Greek–Turkish population exchange.

The **Metropolitan Church of the Saints Theodoros** (cnr Konstantinopoleos & Orfeas), west of the *plateia*, is an old and unusual red-brick structure that contains some nice icons.

Almost 3km from Orestiada on the Didymotiho road, **Cataract Water Park** (☎ 25520 28922) has various pools and slides for keeping cool in summer and Mojito, a popular disco – plus a licentious new *bouzoukia*.

Sleeping

our pick Hotel Elektra (☎ 25520 23540; www.hotel
-electra.gr; Athanasiou Pantazidou 52; s/d €38/50;
P ⊠ ≋) The bright B-class Elektra is a
friendly and well-kept hotel in a restored
neoclassical mansion. The lobby decor
may be a bit gauche, but considering the
cheap attic singles (€25), the Elektra offers
Orestiada's best value for money. Helpful
owner Ismini Diamanti can assist with local
trip planning.

Hotel Alexandros (☎ 25520 27000; Vasileos
Konstantinou 10; s/d/tr €45/58/65; ⊠) Fancier (and
pricier) than the Elektra, the Alexandros has
good-sized balconies and airy rooms near
the train station.

Eating & Drinking

Taverna Petinos (☎ 25520 22071; Lohagou Diamandi 3;
mains €4-7) has simple taverna fare in a friendly,
hospitable setting, while the popular **Safran**
(☎ 25520 29088; Vasileos Konstantinou; mains €5-7), just
down from the Hotel Elektra, does more international cuisine.

Orestiada's cafes line Emmanouel Riga,
between Konstantinopoleos and Athanasiou
Pantazidou, and work from early morning
until midnight or later. Popular places include
Café Café, Bel Air and Social.

Getting There & Around

From Orestiada's **bus station** (☎ 25520 22550),
hourly buses serve Didymotiho (€1.70, 20
minutes), many continuing to Alexandroupoli
(€9.50, 1¼ hours). Change in Alexandroupoli for buses to Komotini, Xanthi and
Thessaloniki.

Buses also go northwards to Dikea (€5.20,
four daily) and the Bulgarian border at
Ormenio (€5.30, two daily). The Turkish border crossing at Kastanies is served six times
daily (€1.50).

From the **train station** (☎ 25520 22328) trains
head south to Alexandroupoli (€4.30, three
hours, seven daily) via Pythio, Didymotiho,
Soufli and Feres; five continue from
Alexandroupoli west to Komotini (€6.30, four
hours, seven daily), Xanthi (€7.40, 4½ hours,
seven daily), Thessaloniki (€16.40, 8½ hours)
and Athens (€52, 15 hours).

Trains also go from Orestiada northwards
to Dikea (€1, 35 minutes, seven daily), with
four continuing another 10 minutes to
Ormenio. The train that leaves Orestiada at
8.07am continues to Svilengrad, Bulgaria.

Get around Orestiada by walking or catching a **taxi** (☎ 25520 25025).

AROUND ORESTIADA

Some 18km southeast on the old road,
running parallel with the Evros River and
the train line, the **Byzantine castle of Pythio**
stands solemnly atop a tall bluff. Built above
Pythio village, which has attractive traditional
Thracian brick-and-wood houses, the castle has a commanding view out over the
Thracian plain and the river's dark tree line.
Built in 1347 by Byzantine Emperor John
Kantakouzenos, during a turbulent period of
civil wars and Turkish invasions, this castle is
Thrace's best surviving example of Byzantine
defensive architecture. Renovations continue,
so you might find it's closed when you visit.
Even if you can't sneak in, nevertheless you
can get near enough to appreciate the castle's
grandeur.

If you're hankering for pheasant, venison
or wild boar, rustic **Pendalofos** 35km northwest of Orestiada, has a game restaurant,
Evrothirama (☎ 25560 61202; mains €7-10). It's open
only on weekends, and is well off the beaten
track, so call or ask Ismini at Hotel Elektra
(left) to help book. She can assist with planning west Evros day trips also.

One such trip involves driving west
through Valtos to reach **Mikri Doxipara**, where
recent excavations of a 1st-century-AD
Roman tomb have unearthed five interred
funerary carts with horses and harnesses.
From here, turn north to Pendalofos for
lunch and then to **Petrota**, the last Greek
village in the northwestern corner before
the Bulgarian border, with vineyards and
traditional stone houses. The road continues eastward along the border through
Ormenio and Dikea, before heading south
back to Orestiada.

Some 19km north of Orestiada near
Kastanies, the **Ardas River Festival** (☎ 25520
81140; www.ardas.gr) occurs each July, drawing
several thousand young people. The festival attracts top Greek singers, Turkish and
Bulgarian groups, and DJs both Greek and
foreign. Besides music, there's beach volleyball, minisoccer, motocross, theatrical performances and water-park trips.

Kastanies is also Greece's northernmost
Turkish border crossing; evocative **Edirne**
(Adrianoupolis in Greek) is just 9km
beyond it.

NORTHERN GREECE

Finally, just 4km from Orestiada, in the village of **Lepti**, **Apiso Ranch** (☎ 6977817820; Lepti village; ☺ 9am-9pm) offers horse riding along the Thracian plain.

EPIROS ΗΠΕΙΡΟΣ

pop 352,400 / area 9203 sq km

Northern Greece's most spectacular sights are surely those of Epiros, a place that will (literally) take your breath away. The lofty Pindos Mountain range, that comprises most of it, has for thousands of years been safeguarding civilisations and confounding invaders. Bisecting the Pindos is the stunning 12km-long Vikos Gorge – probably the world's deepest – and now a national park filled with leafy forests, waterfalls and ice-cold mountain lakes, and surrounded by immaculate traditional stone-and-slate villages, the Zagorohoria.

South of these mountains, the provincial capital of Ioannina is a fun, studenty city with history and ambience, set along a placid lake decorated with an island. To the west lies the Ionian Sea, where several alluring coastal spots include long sandy beaches punctuated by archaeological sites. As with the Ionian Islands just opposite, centuries of Venetian rule have given the Epirot coast an Italian flavour, especially at the micro-resort of Parga. For those continuing to Italy itself, international ferries operate from Igoumenitsa, a bit further north.

Getting to Epiros can be an event in itself. The main road, whether it be from Kozani in Macedonia or from Kalambaka in Thessaly, winds up over the Pindos Mountains – except when it cuts straight through them, inside the massive tunnels created for the Egnatia Odos cross-country highway, a spectacular feat of modern engineering that cannot fail to impress.

History

When the Dorians invaded Greece (1100–1000 BC), three main Greek-speaking tribes emerged in Epiros: the Thesproti, the Chaones and the Molossi. The last won out and, showing savvy, married their princess Olympias to the powerful Macedonian king, Philip II. However, this created conflict with Rome, a rising power. The most famous Molossi ruler, King Pyrrhus (319–272 BC),

defeated the Romans at Ausculum, but at a very heavy price; the event gave birth to a concept, the 'Pyrrhic victory', that remains with us today.

When the Roman Empire split in AD 395, Epiros became the westernmost province of the Byzantine (Eastern) Empire. Later, it was a vital stronghold of Hellenism after Latin Crusaders overthrew the Byzantine Empire in 1204; refugees from noble Byzantine families escaped to Ioannina and the mountains, establishing a key Byzantine successor state there.

Although the empire was partially restored in 1261, stubbornly independent lords continued their infighting. In the 14th century, Stefan Dušan's expanding Serbian empire briefly took over, but in 1430 the Ottoman Turks conquered for good. When they invaded Constantinople 22 years later, the phenomenon of eminent Greek refugees fleeing to Epiros' mountain fastnesses was repeated.

Although the Turks allowed Epiros considerable autonomy, it wasn't enough for Ali Pasha. In 1778, the Turks made this Albanian lord pasha of Ioannina; however, the flamboyant Ali had bigger ambitions and proceeded to seize much of Albania and western Greece before being killed by Ottoman troops in 1822. Nevertheless, Ali Pasha had continuously worn down and distracted the Turks, tacitly assisting the Greek revolutionaries in 1821.

Epiros was engulfed in the Balkan Wars of 1912–13, when the newly created Albanian state got a northern piece of it. In 1940, Mussolini's invasion of Greece was repelled in Epiros, which became a stronghold for the communist resistance fighting the brutal Nazi occupation; however the communists were thereupon defeated in the Greek Civil War (1944–49).

METSOVO ΜΕΤΣΟΒΟ

pop 3195 / elev 1156m

South of the magnificent Katara Pass, and east of the Zagorohoria region, idyllic Metsovo (*met*-so-vo) clings to a mountainside at 1156m. The village attracts skiers in winter, and those seeking to escape the lowland heat in summer. In any season, the village is especially well known for its traditional architecture, local cheeses and hospitable locals – mostly Vlachs, historically a nomadic sheep-herding people who speak the Arromanian language. Closely related to Romanian, the language ultimately derives from Latin.

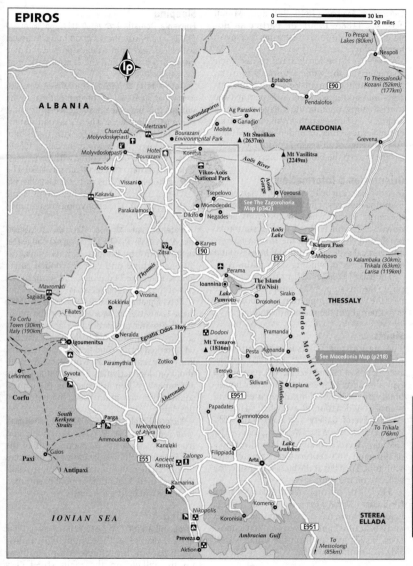

EPIROS

The Vlachs, some believe, descended from ancient Roman soldiers sent to guard the mountain passes.

Metsovo's wealth, manifest in its churches and restored stone mansions, attests to its unique history; in Ottoman times, the canny Metsovite shepherds were given extensive privileges in return for guarding the Katara Pass (1705m), the only route across the Pindos Mountains. However, in 1795 Ali Pasha abolished Metsovo's privileges, and in 1854 Ottoman troops caused considerable damage.

Nevertheless, many locals became wealthy through commerce, industry and other non-sheep-related enterprises. Local luminaries

Georgios Averof (1815–99) and Mihail Tositsas (1885–1950) in particular donated heavily towards restoring Metsovo's former glory.

Nowadays, the locals have turned their characteristic shrewdness towards tourism, transforming old mansions and stone cottages into boutique hotels and opening twee tourist shops, making the village perhaps a bit precious. However, the fresh mountain air and majestic setting are undeniably appealing, and the range of all-season outdoor activities is sure to keep the blood flowing.

Orientation & Information

Metsovo lies 1km below the main Kalambaka–Ioannina highway. The main thoroughfare to the central square, where the bus stops, heads downwards and is lined with restaurants, hotels and shops, giving the town a narrow and vertical aspect. Traditional houses stand around a maze of winding stone pathways.

The **police** (☎ 26560 41233) are on the right opposite the bus stop. ATM-equipped banks are near the *plateia*; turning from it, the post office is to the right of the main thoroughfare.

Sights

The signposted Tositsas mansion hosts Metsovo's **folk museum** (☎ 26560 41084; adult/student €3/2; ⏰ 9am-1.30pm & 4-6pm Fri-Wed), recreating a typical wealthy 19th-century Metsovite household, with handcrafted furniture, artefacts and utensils. Guided tours go every half an hour.

The **Averof Gallery** (☎ 26560 41210; adult/student €3/2; ⏰ 10am-6.30pm Wed-Mon), financed by Georgios Averof's children, exhibits the works of 19th- and 20th-century Greek painters and sculptors. Turn left at the *plateia's* far side; the gallery's on the right.

The 14th-century **Moni Agiou Nikolaou** (⏰ 8.30am-1.30pm & 4-6pm), occupying a gorge below Metsovo, has post-Byzantine frescoes and a beautiful hand-carved wooden iconostasis. It's signposted from the square's west side (a 30-minute walk).

Activities

Approaching from Kalambaka, Metsovo's **ski centre** (☎ 26560 41211; ⏰ 9.30am-3.45pm) is on the right-hand (north) side of the highway, just before the Metsovo turn-off. The centre has an 82-seat ski lift, two downhill runs and a 5km cross-country run, plus a nourishing taverna. Rent skis in Metsovo.

Sleeping

Filoxenia Domatia (☎ 26560 41332; jsp@hol.gr; s/d €35/50) The Filoxenia is a good budget choice, with clean and comfortable domatia and nice views. It's just behind the central park area, near the art gallery.

Hotel Asteri (☎ 26560 42222; 693274089; www.asteri metsovo.com; s/d €38/50) Set prominently atop the village, this big place has 40 cheerful rooms, some with fireplaces. There's a good restaurant, plus a homey lounge with traditional rugs and low couches, where the delightful old owners will sip Greek coffee with you.

Hotel Galaxias (☎ 26560 41202; s/d €40/50) The closest hotel to the bus stop, the Galaxias offers large, traditionally furnished rooms (some with fireplaces). The eponymous restaurant's here too.

Hotel Bitouni (☎ 26560 41217; www.hotelbitouni .com; d/ste €50/80; ℗ 🖳) There's a ski-lodge feel to the family-run Bitouni, with its sauna, traditional fixtures and carved wooden coffee tables. There are 24 doubles, and seven suites; two of the latter have Jacuzzis.

Hotel Egnatia (☎ 26560 41900; fax 26560 41485; Tositsa 19; d/studios incl breakfast €60/80) The renovated Egnatia offers doubles and spacious studios with handsome bathrooms. The hotel's marked by its wood fixtures and friendly, knowledgeable owner, who provides info about outdoor activities. The mountain views are superb. When approaching the central square from the main road, the hotel's on the right.

Victoria Hotel (☎ 26560 41771; www.victoriahotel .gr, in Greek; d from €60; 🖭) The hospitable and friendly Victoria has 37 rooms with all the mods cons, including Jacuzzis and fireplaces in some. The restaurant serves local specialities, and there's an outdoor pool in summer. Find it 900m before the centre.

Eating

Tyrokomika Pigi (☎ 26560 42163; Varonou Mihail Tositsa 17; cheeses €3-6) Visit kindly old Dimitris Boumbas in his cheese shop, midway up the village on the main street. Try the *metsovona*, one of several local hard cheese specialities.

To Koutouki tou Nikola (☎ 26560 41732; mains €7-10) This wonderful family-run restaurant just beneath the post office cooks up hearty traditional dishes, from *pites* (pies) to traditional roast lamb and *gida vrasti* (boiled goat soup).

Restaurant Galaxias (☎ 26560 41202; mains €8-12)
This hotel restaurant is surprisingly good. Local
specials include leek meatballs or spicy sausage,
accompanied by local red wine (Katoyi). The
rustic scene is enhanced by a log fire in winter
and an ivy-covered balcony in summer.

Paradosiako (mains €8-11) Another traditional
place, and especially strong on meats, the
Paradosiako is located opposite the Hotel
Bitouni. There are also good mezedhes and
vegetarian options.

Getting There & Away

Direct buses leave for Ioannina daily at
6.30am, 10.15am, 3pm and 4.30pm (€7, 1½
hours) and for Trikala at 8am and 2pm (€11,
3½ hours). For a Thessaloniki bus (€22), go to

the main road and wave down the bus coming
from Ioannina.

IOANNINA ΙΩΑΝΝΙΝΑ
pop 61,629

The Epirot capital and gateway to the Vikos-
Aoös National Park, hip Ioannina (ih-o-*ah*-nih-
nah or *yah*-nih-nah) is a bustling commercial
and cultural centre, and home to 20,000 university students who energise the local nightlife.
Ioannina's set on the placid (though polluted)
Lake Pamvotis and faces sheer mountains. This
idyllic setting is further enhanced by an evocative old quarter (the Kastro), interspersed with
narrow lanes and architectural wonders from
Byzantine and Ottoman times. The city also has
excellent restaurants, bars and cafes.

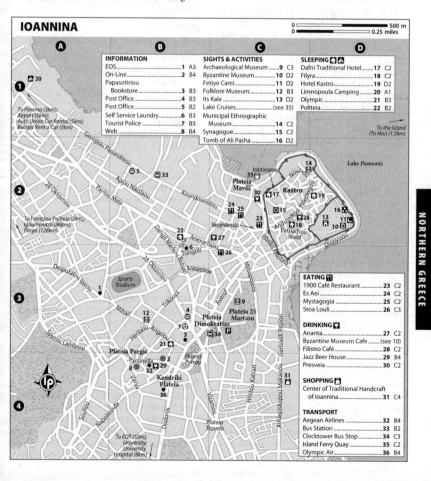

History

Founded in the early 6th century by the great Byzantine Emperor Justinian, Ioannina became an important commercial and cultural outpost. In 1082, however, it was raided by the Normans during the first stages of an East–West antagonism that peaked in 1204, when Latin Crusaders sacked Constantinople and dismembered the Byzantine Empire. Numerous illustrious Greek families fled to Epiros, where an important Byzantine successor state developed under nobleman Michael I Komnenos Doukas. The Greeks remained in control until the Serbs arrived in the early 14th century, followed briefly by more Latins and finally by the Ottomans, who conquered in 1430.

However, things were not terrible during Ottoman times for Ioannina, which enjoyed special privileges and became a leading cultural and artistic centre. Important new schools were founded, skilled craftsmen created intricate silver and gold jewellery and, through the 16th and 17th centuries, the 'Epirot School' of religious painting blossomed.

As Ottoman power ebbed in the late 18th century, crafty opportunists such as Albanian warlord Ali Pasha (1741–1822) seized their opportunity. In 1789, the morally reprehensible yet oddly charismatic Ali made Ioannina the capital of his personal fiefdom, one which would encompass much of Albania and western Greece. Despite a penchant for cruelty that sickened that philhellene, Lord Byron, Ali enforced law and order, and Ioannina flourished. Nevertheless, in 1822, trapped at the Agios Pandeleimon monastery on the Island (To Nisi) in Lake Pamvotis, the octogenarian Ali was finally liquidated by some very irritated Ottomans, who paraded his severed head around İstanbul.

Although Ottoman rule returned to Ioannina, it would become increasingly tenuous, and during the Balkan Wars of 1912–13, Ioannina was captured by the Greek army. The city's ethnic character changed dramatically over the next 30 years; in 1923, with the mandated Greek–Turkish population exchanges, Muslim Turks were replaced with Anatolian Greek refugees, while in 1943 the occupying Germans deported most of Ioannina's centuries-old Jewish population to concentration camps.

Orientation

Ioannina is large, though walkable; parking, however, is tough. There's a municipal car park (€2) off the main square, Plateia Pyrrou. Ioannina's new bus station is on Georgiou Papandreou, a five-minute walk to the old town (the Kastro), where the majority of Ioannina's historic sites are located. Though essentially residential, the Kastro has Ioannina's most atmospheric accommodation choices. The airport is 5km northwest of town.

Information

BOOKSHOPS

Papasotiriou Bookstore (☎ 26510 64000; Mihail Angelou 6) English-language books, maps and Lonely Planet guides.

EMERGENCY

Tourist police (☎ 26510 65938; 28 Oktovriou 11)

INTERNET ACCESS

On-Line (☎ 26510 72512; Pyrsinella 4; per hr €2; ⓧ 9am-6am)
Web (☎ 26510 26813; Pyrsinella 21; per hr €2.30; ⓧ 24hr)

LAUNDRY

Self Service Laundry (☎ 26510 25542; Tsirigoti 3; full wash €8; ⓧ 9.30am-2.30pm & 6-9pm Mon-Fri, 9.30am-2.30pm Sat)

MEDICAL SERVICES

University Hospital (☎ 26510 99111) Eight kilometres south, inside the university campus.

MONEY

Plateia Pyrrou and Averof's southern end host the major banks/ATMs.

POST

Post office Georgiou Papandreou (Georgiou Papandreou); Octovriou (28 Oktovriou 3)

TOURIST INFORMATION

EOS (Greek Alpine Club; ☎ 26510 22138; Despotatou Ipirou 2; ⓧ 7-9pm Mon-Fri)
EOT (☎ 26510 41142; fax 26510 49139; Dodonis 39; ⓧ 7.30am-2.30pm Mon-Fri) Provides general information and hiking updates for the Zagorohoria and Vikos Gorge.

Sights

The Kastro's sublime **Its Kale** (Inner Citadel; ⓧ 8am-5pm & 8-10pm Tue-Sun) rises from a long bluff overlooking lake and mountain. The relaxing Its Kale contains the **Tomb of Ali Pasha** and the restored **Fetiye Cami** (Victory Mosque), originally built in 1611 to reassert Ottoman dominance, following a failed Greek uprising that caused Christians to be expelled from the citadel.

The adjacent **Byzantine Museum** (☎ 26510 25989; Its Kale; admission €3; ☉ 8am-5pm Tue-Sun), housed in two nearby buildings (including Ali Pasha's former palace) presents early Christian and Byzantine art, pottery, coins and silverware, and even post-Byzantine icons and manuscripts. The priceless treasures include early printed Greek books from Venice and ornate silver jewellery boxes with cloisonné enamel. Textual accompaniments give a fascinating overview of Ioannina's history from the 4th to the 17th century.

The **Municipal Ethnographic Museum** (☎ 26510 26356; adult/student €3/1.50; ☉ 8am-8pm) is at the Kastro's northern end in the Aslan Pasha Mosque (1619). Local costumes and period photographs are displayed, as are tapestries and prayer shawls from the **synagogue** (loustinianou 16) of Ioannina's once significant Jewish community. See similar items, including embroidery and cooking utensils, at the **Folklore Museum** (☎ 26510 23566; Mihail Angelou 42-44; adult/student €2/1; ☉ 9am-2pm Tue, Thu & Fri, 9am-2pm & 5.30-8pm Wed & Sat).

The **Archaeological Museum** (☎ 26510 33357; Plateia 25 Martiou 6), containing finds from Dodoni, Vitsa and Efira, still remained closed for renovations at the time of writing.

Activities

The relaxing, one-hour **lake cruise** (☎ 6944470280; tickets €5; ☉ 10am-midnight Mon-Sun summer, Sat & Sun winter) departs from near the Island ferry quay. Since swimming is not advisable, this is the only way to experience the lake.

Serious hikers should first get the map (Anavasi Mountain Editions; *Pindus-Zagori* 1:50,000), available for €8 from local *periptera* (street kiosks) or at Papasotiriou Bookstore (opposite), and then get apprised with current conditions at the EOT or EOS (see opposite).

Sleeping

Perama, 10 minutes by bus around the lake, has cheap domatia. Most Ioannina hotels are near the noisy central *plateia*; for tranquillity and atmosphere, stay inside the Kastro.

Limnopoula Camping (☎ 26510 25265; Kanari 10; camp sites per adult/tent €8/4; ☉ Apr-Oct) A breezy lakeside camping ground 2km northwest, Limnopoula has fine facilities, including a kitchen, laundry and nearby restaurant, though note again that swimming is not advisable.

Filyra (☎ 26510 83560, 6932601240; Andronikou Paleologou 18; s/d €45/55) This flower-bedecked boutique hotel inside the Kastro has five spacious self-catering suites on a quiet side street, and friendly and helpful owners.

our pick **Dafni Traditional Hotel** (☎ 26510 83560, 6932601240; loustinianou 12; s/d €45/65) This remarkable new traditional guest house is actually built into the inside of the Kastro's enormous outer walls. Rooms combine traditional and modern amenities, and there's one grand, well-decorated family room (€90). Reception is at the Filyra.

Hotel Kastro (☎ 26510 22866; Andronikou Paleologou 57; s/d €75/90; P) This restored Kastro mansion overlooking Its Kale has great atmosphere: antique brass beds, stained-glass windows and a tranquil courtyard create a feeling of romantic seclusion. Service is friendly and prompt.

Olympic (☎ 26510 22233; www.hotelolymp.gr, in Greek; Melanidhis 2; s/d €90/110; P ⊠ ⌨) Book ahead for this, Ioannina's poshest hotel. Rooms have amenities and great lake views, and there's even a red carpet; shame then that there's little seclusion or tradition in this noisy central spot.

Politeia (☎ 26510 22235; www.etip.gr; Anexartisias 109; s/d/ste incl breakfast €90/110/170; P ⊠ ⌨) This central place set around a quiet inner courtyard and cafe offers studios with kitchenette and all mod cons. Rooms are tastefully decorated and painted in soft tones.

Eating

Most of Ioannina's best places only open for dinner.

Mystagogia (☎ 26510 34571; Koundouriotou 44; mains €6; ☉ dinner) A popular late-night *tsipouradhiko* (place serving *tsipoura* – an ouzo-like spirit – and light snacks), the studenty Mystagogia has nourishing mezedhes and good beef *keftedhes* (meatballs).

Stoa Louli (☎ 26510 71322; Anexartisias 78; mains €7-12) The Stoa Louli has seen many incarnations since being built in 1875; first it was an inn, later a trade centre for Jewish leather merchants, and even an Ottoman Bank. This tastefully lit place, fronted by grand arches, serves an alluring range of Greek favourites with a contemporary twist.

Es Aei (☎ 26510 34571; Koundouriotou 50; mains €8-12) This favourite haunt of local and foreign gastronomes combines an Ottoman flair with a unique, glass-roofed courtyard dining room. Its inventive dishes include mezedhes made from organic ingredients and Ioannina specials including grilled pork sausages.

1900 Café Restaurant (☎ 26510 33131; Neoptolemou 9; mains €10-15; ☒ dinner Sep-Jun) If you want to wow a date – or simply enjoy a really good Italian meal – this is the place to come. Genial owner Miltos Miltiadis provides a warm welcome at this restored, two-floor mansion, a living lesson in style with thick-painted crimson walls, Latin music, worn wood floors and soft light. Everything is good, from the penne and parmesan to portobello mushrooms with *mavrodafni* (dessert wine) sauce.

Drinking

For Ioannina's excellent speciality beer bars see Beer Essentials, p294.

Frontzou Politeia (☎ 26510 21011; Lofos Agias Triadas; ☒ 9am-3am) Find superlative views of the city, lake and mountain opposite at this relaxed cafe 2km up on Ioannina's western hill. Lean back in the plush, colourful couches and enjoy a cool coffee drink on a warm summer morning, or a mixed one by night.

Filistro Café (☎ 26510 72429; Andronikou Paleologou 20) For a splendid spot of tea or afternoon liqueur, drop in to this classic, vividly painted Kastro cafe.

Ananta (☎ 26510 26261; cnr Anexartisias & Stoa Labei; ☒ 9pm-3am) With its shadows and a long bar set under an upward-curving, bare stone ceiling, the Ananta smacks of a Franciscan monastery – albeit one powered by rock music and alcohol.

Byzantine Museum Cafe (☎ 26510 64206; Its Kale; ☒ 9pm-midnight) Up atop Its Kale, this busy place with outdoor seating offers everything from coffees to waffles with ice cream and other snacks.

Shopping

Ioannina has been known for its silverwork since the 17th century; the **Center of Traditional Handcraft of Ioannina** (☎ 26510 45221; www.kepavi.gr; Arhiepiskopou Makariou 1; ☒ 9.30am-2.30pm & 5.30-8.30pm), near the lake, brings together scores of artisans, whom you can watch as they work. The centre also has a large shop selling everything from inexpensive earrings and necklaces to elaborate and expensive silver dining sets. Everything is locally produced.

Getting There & Away

AIR

Olympic Air (☎ 26510 26518; www.olympicairlines.com; Kendriki Plateia) has two daily Athens flights

(€99). **Aegean Airlines** (☎ 26510 64444; www.aegeanair. com; Pyrsinella 11) has one Athens flight daily (€65). Flight times change seasonally.

BUS
Domestic

From Ioannina's **bus station** (☎ 26510 26286; Georgiou Papandreou) buses serve Igoumenitsa (€8.80, 1¼ hours, eight daily), Athens (€35.20, 6½ hours, nine daily), Konitsa (€5.60, 1¼ hours, seven daily), Thessaloniki (€28.50, 4¾ hours, six daily), Volos (€21.60, 4½ hours, three daily) and Metsovo (€5.30, one hour, four daily). There are two buses daily to Trikala (€13.10, 2¼ hours) and Kozani (€20, 2½ hours), and one daily in summer to Parga (€11, 1½ hours). Buses also serve Arta (€6.40, 1¼ hours, seven daily) and Patra (€20.40, 3½ hours, two daily), along with services to Preveza (€9.30, two hours, six daily) and Dodoni.

International

From Ioannina buses reach the border post of Kakavia (€5.60, one hour, nine daily) for Albania.

Getting Around

Ioannina airport is 5km northwest on the Perama road; take Bus 7 (every 20 minutes, from the clock tower).

Budget Rent a Car (☎ /fax 26510 43901; Dodonis 109) is at the airport, as is **Auto Union Car Rental** (☎ /fax 25610 67751; Dodonis 66), which offers good deals.

Taxis (☎ 26510 46777) wait near Plateia Pyrrou and the lake.

AROUND IOANNINA
The Island Το Νησί

Ioannina's closest getaway, the Island (To Nisi) lies just opposite in Lake Pamvotis. The Island's whitewashed village, built in the 17th century by refugees from Peloponnesian Mani, has around 300 permanent residents (among them four school kids). Several important monasteries decorated with very unusual frescoes are found here, plus a couple of good fish tavernas. The old, white-plastered houses have lovely flower gardens and shutters, and silver shops also exist.

The Island was most notably the place where the last act unfolded in the long saga of Ali Pasha, the Albanian warlord who ruled Ioannina in the late 18th and early 19th centuries. Ali's fickle allegiances and brazen challenge to Ottoman authority caused the Sultan to take out the 'Lion of Ioannina' in 1822. Perfidiously assured of a pardon, the elderly Ali Pasha withdrew with his guard to **Moni Pandeleïmonos** on the Island – only to be trapped and liquidated by Ottoman troops.

The hole in the floorboard where the fatal bullet passed through is still visible in the **Ali Pasha Museum** (adult €1; ☻ 8am-10pm summer, 9am-9pm winter), in a building inside the monastery. There's a printed narrative (in English) of the heady events of Ali's last days, as well as various personal effects and etchings of the portly pasha in full repose, sitting fat and happy with his consort, beards and hookah. To get there, walk up the hill from the ferry dock into town and take the main street left; the monastery is signposted.

Also see **Moni Filanthropinon**, on the Island's western side. Built in the 13th century by the Filanthropini, a leading Constantinopolitan family who fled the rampaging Crusaders in 1204, the monastery boasts unusual 16th-century frescoes of pagan Greek philosophers, including Plato, Aristotle and Plutarch, alongside more suitably Christian personalities. The expressiveness and pathos of these paintings, characteristic of the 'Epirot School' of art, has aroused great interest from art historians. Moni Filanthropinon was also a 'secret school' for Christians during the centuries of Ottoman Muslim domination.

For eating on the Island, try **Gripos** (☎ 26510 81081; mains €6-8), on the left of the ferry dock, or **Propodes** (☎ 26510 81214; fish €4-6), located on the path to Moni Pandeleïmonos. Both specialise in lake fish and other local creatures. You should not miss Propodes: its eye-catching tanks outside, reminiscent of a Chinese market, are filled with wriggling eels, hopping frogs and crayfish waiting for the kettle. Both are good, though Propodes is slightly cheaper and has a relaxing location under an awning above the water; go for the golden carp fillet (€6).

GETTING THERE & AWAY

Ioannina's ferry dock is below the Kastro in Ioannina. Boats to the Island (€1.30, 10 minutes) go between 7am and 11.30pm in summer, and between 7am and 10pm in winter. In summer, the boat goes every 15 minutes, in winter, only hourly.

Perama Cave Σπήλαιο Περάματος

Four kilometres from Ioannina, **Perama Cave** (☎ 26510 81521; www.spilaio-perama.gr; adult/student €6/3; ☻ 8am-8pm) is one of Greece's largest and most impressive caves, loaded with white stalactites. Locals hiding from the Nazis discovered it in 1940; later, it was explored by speleologists Ioannis and Anna Petroñilos. The enormous 1100m-long cave has three storeys of chambers and passageways. There's an hour-long tour.

Buses 8 and 16 from near Ioannina's clocktower run every 20 minutes to Perama, 250m south of the cave.

Dodoni Δωδώνη

The colossal, 3rd-century-BC **Theatre of Dodoni** (☎ 26510 82287; adult €2; ☻ 8am-5pm), 21km southwest of Ioannina, is Epiros' most important ancient site. An earth goddess had been worshipped at this valley spot from around 2000 BC. The oracle she spoke through was reputedly Greece's oldest, and the one most venerated (before the Delphic oracle took precedence in the 6th century BC). By the 13th century BC, Zeus was speaking through the rustling of leaves from a sacred oak tree to worshippers at the site. Around 500 BC a temple was built in his honour, though today only its foundations and a few columns remain.

Under King Pyrrhus, however, things took a dramatic turn and a theatre was erected. Now restored, the Theatre of Dodoni hosts Ioannina's **Festival of Ancient Drama** in July. On its north side, a gate leads to the **acropolis**, where remnants of its once-substantial walls remain. The foundations of the **bouleuterion** (council house) and a small **Temple of Aphrodite** lie east of the theatre. Nearby are the scant remains of the **Sanctuary of Zeus**, where once stood the top god's sacred oak and oracle.

Later, in the 6th century, a Byzantine basilica was built over the site's Sanctuary of Hercules.

GETTING THERE & AWAY

Buses from Ioannina leave at 6.30am and 4.30pm daily, except for Thursday and Sunday, returning at 7.30am and 5.30pm. One other bus, on Sunday, leaves at 6pm and returns at 6.45pm.

A taxi from Ioannina costs around €35 return plus €3 per hour for waiting.

NORTHERN GREECE

THE ZAGOROHORIA ΤΑ ΖΑΓΟΡΟΧΩΡΙΑ

A cluster of 46 providentially preserved mountain hamlets, the Zagorohoria takes its name from an old Slavonic term, *za Gora* (behind the mountain), and the Greek word for villages (*horia*). Tucked into the Pindos range, these villages conceal inexhaustible local legends and boast marvellous houses, ranging from humble cottages of stone and slate to grand, fortified mansions made of the same hardy materials. These remote villages were once connected by paths and old stone bridges. Today, you'll see the bridges arching over riverbeds and valleys, though paved roads now connect the villages.

Although time and emigration have left some villages mostly uninhabited, shed no tears: the rise of boutique and environmental tourism has led savvy locals to prosper by converting the Zagorohoria's *arhontika* and smaller traditional homes into lovely and unique *xenones* (guest houses); indeed, their growing popularity with Greek and foreign tourists has also made them quite expensive.

The Zagorohoria's fascinating history is bound up with the dismemberment of Byzantium by the Latin Crusaders in 1204, and the subsequent Turkish capture of Constantinople in 1453; in both cases, numerous important Greek families fled the capital for the mountain fastnesses of Epiros, where Greek culture and traditions could be safeguarded.

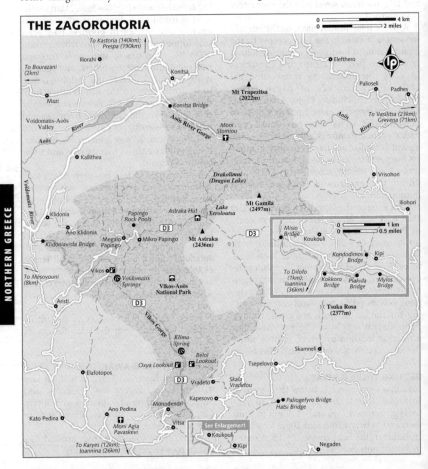

In Ottoman times, the Zagorohoria also received privileges and autonomy for guarding the mountain passes. This, together with the remittances and gifts sent from the large Epirot diaspora abroad, funded the upkeep of the villages and their great churches, in whose lavish decorations we can appreciate what the holy shrines of Byzantium would have looked like in their prime.

Vikos-Aoös National Park
Εθνικός Δρυμός Βίκου Αώου
The Zagorohoria's literal and figurative centrepiece, the Vikos-Aoös National Park, bursts with pristine rivers and forests, flowering meadows, and shimmering lakes reflecting jagged mountains and endless blue sky. Almost one-third of Greece's flora (some endemic) lives here, along with endemic fish, foxes and chamois, rare hawks, river otters and brown bears. The park's major Tymfi Massif, part of the north Pindos Mountains, contains numerous ear-popping peaks including **Mt Trapezitsa** (2022m), **Mt Astraka** (2436m) and **Mt Gamila** (2497m). The 12km-long Vikos Gorge passing beneath them may be the world's deepest.

While most people you encounter will be fellow hikers or their local hosts, you can still find seminomadic Vlach and Sarakatsani shepherds, taking their flocks up to high grazing ground in summer and returning to the valleys in autumn.

Dilofo & Negades Δίλοφο & Νεγάδες
From Ioannina, the first Zagorohoria village is enchanting **Dilofo**, 5.7km northeast of Asprangeli (32km from Ioannina total). Unlike the larger and more visited villages, tiny Dilofo has only recently awoken from its slumber and thus remains still and unchanged. Its jumbled slate-roofed houses tucked into a mountainside are highly evocative, and there's a great view across the valley to Koukouli.

This view is part of the explanation for the enormous, 13.5m-high **Loumidi Mansion**, visible on the left-hand side when entering Dilofo. The story goes that after a young woman from Koukouli was wedded to a Dilofo man, she became so homesick that she wanted to return to her village. The father of the groom instead ordered the erection of a house tall enough for the woman to see her parents' house across the valley – and so it was.

Dilofo's small *plateia* features an enormous, 400-year-old plane tree, a card telephone and taverna. There are limited, though excellent, accommodation options, and the setting is undeniably tranquil.

In Dilofo's upper part, the **Church of Kimisis Theotokou** (Dormition of the Virgin), has an intricate, hand-carved wooden iconostasis and nice icons. It's open for Sunday liturgy, or find village doctor Giorgos Triandafilidis, who has the key.

Although few know it, Dilofo is also an entry point for hiking the Vikos Gorge (left); starting here rather than in Monodendri makes the route even longer.

A nice excursion 13km east is **Negades**, a stone-housed village with little tourism. The 20-minute drive involves superb views of

---

HIKING THE ZAGOROHORIA: THE GRAND TOUR

To see the Zagorohoria at its most spectacular, get off the roads and into nature. You don't necessarily need a guide, but get updated on conditions from the EOT or EOS (p338) in Ioannina first. Also essential is the *Pindus-Zagori* 1:50,000 map from **Anavasi Mountain Edition** (www .mountains.gr; €8), available in Ioannina, Monodendri, Papingo and in some guest houses in other villages too, or on the Anavasi website. Armed with this information and tough hiking boots, a compass, sunscreen, sticks and water, you're good to go.

Along with numerous day hikes, a three-day 'grand tour' is possible, sleeping in guest houses and mountain huts along the way.

One such hike goes from Monodendri to Tsepelovo. From Monodendri the trail leads through the stunning Vikos Gorge to the **Papingo villages** (6½ hours). From here it's another three hours to the **Astraka Hut** (☎ 6973223100; dm €10; ☺ May-Oct), at 1950m. There's no phone or electricity, but the 52-bed hut is always open and has a warden, generator power and food.

From here it's a 30-minute hike to the sublime **Drakolimni** (Dragon Lake), though returning takes 45 minutes. From Drakolimni, the spectacular ascent to **Mt Gamila** is a tougher hike, and takes four hours. Another five hours from Gamila brings you finally to Tsepelovo. Alternatively, from Gamila hike up to **Vrisohori**, along the Aoös River, with crystal-clear mountain springs.

delicate stone bridges spanning densely wooded valleys and imposing cliffsides.

Negades' impressive post-Byzantine **Church of Agios Georgios** (1792) is sumptuously decorated with exquisite icons and a gilded, hand-carved wood iconostasis, and lined with wall-to-wall frescoes, including rare paintings of pagan philosophers Aristotle and Plutarch. Don't leave without seeing the church's back section, where women were sent behind a grill to observe the service. The persuasive frescoes here, apparently created for purposes of moral edification, include a depiction of Judas being devoured by a sea monster, and a scrawny devil apparently riding and beating a bedded husband and wife who were too lazy to get up for church.

Since the church isn't always open, plan in advance with Giorgos Kontaxis at the EOT in Ioannina, or at his Dilofo guest house, the Arhontiko Dilofo (see opposite).

Monodendri, Vitsa & Ano Pedina
Μονοδένδρι, Βίτσα & Άνω Πεδινά

Thirty-eight kilometres north of Ioannina, **Monodendri** is Zagorohoria's main settlement, close to the Vikos Gorge. It's signposted right off the main Ioannina–Konitsa road near Karyes. Hikers, sightseers and week-ending couples have made Monodendri one of the most-visited villages, though it's still reasonably relaxing.

Agia Paraskevi Monastery here has spectacular gorge views. According to legend, local lord Mihalis Voevodas Therianos founded the church in 1413 to thank God for healing his daughter of an incurable illness. The church's frescoes partially date to the 15th century. A second Monodendri church, the cross-domed **Church of Agios Minas** near the square, dates from the early 17th century (as do some frescoes inside).

South of Monodendri, **Vitsa**, is less visited and more aesthetically pleasing. In Byzantine times, it was a major settlement called Vizitsini. Vitsa also has a cross-domed church built concurrently with Monodendri's Agios Minas, the **Church of Agios Nikolaos**.

Most intriguingly, between Monodendri and Vitsa lie remnants of an **ancient Molossi settlement** (9th century to 4th century BC). Ancient Epiros was ruled by the Molossi and King Pyrrhos. Parts of ancient houses and graves from here are in Ioannina's (temporarily closed) Archaeological Museum.

From Vitsa, drive 7.2km west-northwest to reach **Ano Pedina**, more touristy but a good base for exploring the central Zagorohoria. The village has many guest houses, some quite striking.

Aristi to the Papingo Villages

Driving up the vertiginous, ribboning northern road to **Megalo Papingo** and **Mikro Papingo** offers some breathtaking views. If coming from Vitsa or Ano Pedina, the secondary road will join the main road running up from Ioannina. After heading west through **Kato Pedina**, follow the main road northwards until it branches after 4.1km; take the right branch to Papingo.

Aristi, the last village before Papingo, features the lovely **Monastery of Panagia Spiliotissa** (1665), a narrow arched church lined with frescoes, located on the side of a boulder by the Voïdomatis River. The monastery's philanthropy helped build schools in Zagorohoria during the Ottoman centuries.

After Aristi, the paved road hugs the river and opens onto increasingly spectacular views. It's all white-knuckle driving as you ascend a tight succession of 15 hairpin turns up to the ledge where the Papingo villages nestle under the looming hulk of Mt Astraka. Look right to see superlative views of the Vikos Gorge.

Megalo (Big) Papingo features enormous stone formations known as 'towers'. It's also quite touristy, whereas Mikro (Small) Papingo is quieter. In the latter's old schoolhouse, there's a **WWF information centre** (⏰ 10.30am-5.30pm) with an excellent exhibition on local wildlife and fauna.

The Papingo villages have wonderfully refreshing **rock pools**, good for a revitalising dip on a hot day of hiking. They're reached via a 300m path from a bend in the road connecting the two villages.

Vikos Gorge Χαράδρα του Βίκου

Bisecting the Zagorohoria is the 12km-long, 900m-deep Vikos Gorge; according to the *Guinness Book of World Records*, it is the world's deepest, though gorge lobbyists elsewhere contest the claim. In either case, Vikos is a truly awe-inspiring work of nature.

The gorge begins near Monodendri (1090m) in the south and runs north until the Papingo villages. You can start from either end, but if you want to return to where you started, you'll have to arrange transport back via the long road route.

The Ioannina EOT or EOS (p338) advises on current weather conditions and provides maps and other information. You'll need water, stout walking boots and some endurance; the hike takes around 6½ hours.

Starting from Monodendri, walk to the 15th-century **Agia Paraskevi Monastery** for a spectacular view over the gorge. You can descend here, on a steep, marked path. From there, it's a four-hour walk to the end, from where a right-hand trail leads to Mikro Papingo (2½ hours). The larger Megalo Papingo is a further 2km west, but the track splits into two at the base of the climb. The **Klima Spring**, about halfway along the gorge, is the only water source.

You can also terminate your hike at **Vikos**, south of the Papingo villages, where the owner of the *kafeneio* on the square will drive you back to Monodendri for €40 (a taxi would cost double). Located 5km northeast of Aristi, Vikos has accommodation and excellent views.

Stunning gorge views can be enjoyed from the **Oxya Lookout**, 5km on a good dirt road beyond Monodendri. Opposite on the eastern side, there's another jaw-dropping peer into the abyss at **Beloi Lookout**. To get there, drive 9km on a winding road or go to **Vradeto** from the signposted turn-off near Kapesovo, and then hike 1.5km along a marked trail at the end of the dirt road; you can also drive, but it's bumpy. Vradeto enjoys a striking position along striated limestone cliffs. The Beloi Lookout is accessible on foot via a vertiginous rock stairway, the **Skala Vradetou**, signposted outside **Tsepelovo**, itself a relaxing base for hill walking and hiking to northern Zagorohoria sites such as the Drakolimni (Dragon Lake). It has a post office, card phone, and good accommodation and eating options.

Activities

In Kato Pedina, the new, full-service **Compass Adventures** (☎ 26530 71770; 6978845232; info@compass adventures.gr; Kato Pedina) organises hiking, skiing and mountain-biking forays into the Pindos Mountains. In winter, Compass operates a ski school and trips for off-piste skiing on virgin terrain.

Similarly, in Aristi try rafting, kayaking, hiking and even archery and paintball with **Rafting Athletic Center** (☎ 26530 41888; 6942015143; info@rafting-athletic-center.gr; Aristi).

Sleeping

Prices are steadily getting higher, even as Zagori guest houses continue to proliferate, though they drop in spring and fall.

Arhontiko Zarkada (☎ 2653071305; www.monodendri .com; Monodendri; s/d €40/60) These clean, snug rooms have balconies with gorge views. Some rooms have spa baths for nursing bruised hikers back to health.

Xenonas Mikro Papingo 1700 (☎ 26530 41179; Mikro Papingo; s/d €45/60) The 1700 has five handsomely appointed rooms. It's a lovely choice with real character.

Xenos Vikos (☎ 26530 71370; Monodendri; d €50-70; ☯ Mar-Dec) Only 400m from the Vikos Gorge, next to the lower village square, this relaxed but lively *xenonas* has a leafy breakfast courtyard, plus communal kitchen and lounge.

Xenonas Dias (☎ 26530 41257; Mikro Papingo; s/d €50/70) This rustic pension with 12 rooms and a tasty restaurant will appeal to solitude-seekers in the quiet Mikro Papingo village.

Porfyron (☎ 26530 71579; Ano Pedina; s/d €55/70) A 19th-century mansion converted into an inn, the red-painted Porfyron has considerable rustic charm, with antique furnishings and soft-coloured walls complementing the classic, wood-panelled ceilings. The ground-floor doubles have spiral staircases leading down to en suites. Owners Rita and Yannis provide local information and, if your room is one with a fireplace, will happily get you the wood.

Papaevangelou (George's Place; ☎ 26530 41135; Megalo Papingo; s/d/tr/studio €60/75/90/110) Nice stone rooms and spectacular views, along with hearty homemade breakfasts, are available here. At the central square, turn left on the unpaved road. The hotel is situated on the right.

Hotel Agriogido (☎ 26530 42055, 6945364484; georgio@papingo.gr; Megalo Papingo; s/d/tr incl breakfast €60/80/100) A relaxing guest house in a restored old Zagori dwelling. When entering Megalo Papingo, you'll see it on the left.

our pick **Arhontiko Dilofo** (☎ 26530 22455, 6978417715; www.dilofo.com; Dilofo; d incl breakfast from €65) One of the most wonderful guest houses in all of Zagorohoria, this 475-year-old restored mansion in placid Dilofo is ideal for anyone seeking total peace and natural harmony. Rooms feature traditional carpets, furnishings and ornate painted window shutters that, when closed, give you a feeling of being inside the warm hold of a grand seafaring vessel.

The Arhontiko has a lovely enclosed garden and scenic views over the village's cluttered slate rooftops. The friendly and immensely knowledgeable owner, Giorgos Kontaxis, happily speaks of the gold pipes, secret letters and other centuries-old mementos he discovered while renovating the mansion, inhabited since 1633. Greek, English, German and Italian are spoken here.

Primula (☎ 26530 71133; Ano Pedina; d from €70) Another restored 19th-century mansion in Ano Pedina centre, the romantic Primula has a captivating assortment of differently appointed rooms; the walls of some are stone, while others are well painted in mottled pastel tones. Billowing drapes add to the charm.

Mikri Arktos (Little Bear; ☎ 26530 81128; kittasth@otenet.gr; Tsepelovo; d from €75) This cosy guest house on Tsepelovo's *plateia* is named after owner Thomas Kittas' favourite constellation, one of many visible in the perfectly clear mountain sky at night. It's a friendly place where you can doze off in the shade of a plane tree, try the specials at the downstairs taverna, or cook in the kitchenettes in each of the unique and vividly painted rooms.

To Arhontiko tis Aristis (☎ 26530 42210, 6945676261; www.arhontiko-aristis.gr, in Greek; Aristi; s/d/tr €100/120/140) This new place in Aristi offers spectacular views and is built of solid stone, with lovely wood floors. The baths are very modern and there are other unexpected modern touches such as a billiards table.

Eating

Edesma (☎ 26530 81088; Tsepelovo; pites €3-6) Come here for *pites* or *mayirefta*, right in Tsepelovo.

O Dionysos (☎ 26530 71366; Monodendri; pites €5-6) Along upper Monodendri's main street, this is a good spot for a tasty *fakopita* (lentil pie) or other traditional Epirot pies.

Sopotseli (☎ 26530 22629; Dilofo; €5-7) This relaxing taverna along Dilofo's square serves up hearty portions of grilled Greek meats and fresh salads.

Ta Soudena (☎ 26530 71209; Ano Pedina; mains €5-8) A popular taverna at the entrance to Ano Pedina, Ta Soudena offers Greek vegetable mezedhes, *pites* and grilled meats.

Restaurant H Tsoumanis (☎ 26530 42170; Vikos; mains €6-9) Gorge yourself near the gorge at this iconic taverna in Vikos; wild boar, goat and other mountain creatures are recommended.

Spiros Tsoumanis (☎ 26530 12108; Megalo Papingo; mains €8-13) This hearty country grill at the end of Megalo Papingo specialises in local *pites* and roast lamb *sti gastra* (chickpea stew), with fresh-from-the-garden *horta* (wild greens) salads.

Getting There & Away

From Ioannina, buses serve Dilofo (€3.50), continuing to Tsepelovo (€4.10, 1½ hours, 5.30am and 3.15pm Monday, Wednesday and Friday). Other buses serve Megalo and Mikro Papingo (€4.90, two hours, 5am and 3pm Monday, Wednesday and Friday, with the Wednesday bus hitting Vikos in summer) and Monodendri (€3.10, one hour, 6am and 3pm Monday, Wednesday and Friday). All buses return to Ioannina immediately. On weekends, take a taxi: Ioannina–Monodendri fares are approximately €30 to €45, though you can negotiate.

KONITSA ΚΟΝΙΤΣΑ
pop 2871

Carved amphitheatrically into a hillside under endless blue skies, Konitsa (*ko*-nit-sah) is a lively mountain market town in its own right, and one not without its share of rugged individuals. Kayakers, hikers and river explorers circle their wagons at night here, and Greek hunters too use Konitsa as a sort of cowboy depot. The town's only a few kilometres southwest of the Mertziani border crossing with Albania.

From Ioannina, Konitsa is 64km north on the national road; past it, the old road arcs northeast on a magnificent route between the Grammas and Smolikas Mountains, to Kastoria in western Macedonia. However, with the completion of the Egnatia Odos Hwy, this road is suffering from a lack of upkeep, and can be dangerous, especially at night.

Orientation & Information

Coming from Ioannina, Konitsa is on the right-hand side of the national road, and sprawls up from it for some 2km. Konitsa's central square has pharmacies, a post office and ATM-equipped banks. The bus station is a short walk downhill from here. There's also a small hospital for first aid.

For tourist information, try Yiannis Mourehidis at To Dendro Guesthouse, for more than 30 years the independent traveller's first port of call in Konitsa.

Activities

Just outside Konitsa begins a gorgeous 4.5km hike along the Aoös River Gorge to **Moni Stomiou**, founded in the 15th century but relocated here in 1774 from its original location on Mt Trapezitsa. Start at the beginning of the town, where the river is straddled by the impressive **Konitsa Bridge**. This 20m-high, 40m-long single-arched stone structure was built in 1870 by a local master craftsman, using money pooled from the then-Ottoman town's Christian and Muslim citizens.

After the bridge, follow the river's turquoise waters along a signposted trail. The first third is a drivable dirt road, but it soon becomes a narrow path between the water and a steep bank, and then barrels gradually upwards through dense vegetation. The last 1.5km is wider, but steep. The monastery might be open; even if it's not, the hike is worthwhile for the tremendous views over the Aoös River canyon. Spring water is available.

Sleeping & Eating

To Dendro Guesthouse (☎ 26550 22055; d/tr €40/55; **P**) A moustachioed man clad in leather and answering to the name 'Johnny Dendro', who trims his hedges with a hunting knife, Yiannis Mourehidis has been a Konitsa legend for more than 30 years, and offers clean and comfortable rooms. The charismatic Yiannis can organise trips to Albania and kayaking adventures, and also runs a spirited taverna. Entering town, look for the UN-like display of flags on the last bend of the road before the main square.

Kougias Hotel (☎ 26550 23830; www.kougias.gr; s/d €45/60) Right on the square, the friendly though reserved Kougias is a good bet. Rooms are well done, with an upper floor of attic doubles offering excellent views. Try the owner's award-winning Cabernet Sauvignon.

Grand Hotel Dendro (☎ 26550 29365; www.grandhotel dentro.gr; d/tr/ste €60/75/100; **P** **☒**) A different ambience pervades this, the upmarket sister hotel of To Dendro Guesthouse, which seeks to merge the traditional with the luxurious. The attic suites, with hydromassage showers, spacious living rooms and fireplace, are reminiscent of a superior ski lodge, while soft lighting and pastel colours lend a newlywed feel to the doubles. Excellent home-cooked Greek fare is served in the formal dining room.

Konitsa Mountain Hotel (☎ 26550 29390; www .konitsahotel.gr; s/d/tr/ste incl breakfast €70/90/120/150; **P** **☒**) High up the hill behind town, this supe-rior place offers spacious rooms and combines smooth marble, beautifully seasoned wood floors and, of course, breathtaking mountain views. Some rooms have large Jacuzzis and fireplaces. The hotel also has a sauna, Turkish baths and a gym. Friendly owners Babis and Georgia, and their English-speaking son Apostolis, can advise about local activities. To get here, follow the road behind the centre uphill for 2km or take a taxi from the *plateia* (about €2).

To Dendro Restaurant (☎ 26550 22055; mains €5-8) Greek hunters and veteran travellers alike know that this, the taverna of innkeeper Yiannis Mourehidis, is the best place in town for wild boar in wine, pot-roasted lamb and delicious lake trout. Kick back with a beer and listen to Yiannis' stories about life in the Konitsa wilds, but whatever you do don't leave without trying the delectable hot grilled feta with chilli and tomato special.

Getting There & Away

From the **bus station** (☎ 26550 22214) buses serve Ioannina (€5.10, two hours, seven daily); change here for other destinations.

Buses reach the Albanian border at Mertziani (€1.30, 30 minutes, three daily) and go to Bourazani (€1.20, 30 minutes, four daily). The Petrina Horia villages of Molista and Ganadio have twice-weekly buses (€2.30, 30 minutes). If there are passengers, an afternoon bus leaves three times weekly for Kastoria (€14, four hours).

AROUND KONITSA

Bourazani Μπουραζάνι

The **Bourazani Environmental Park** (☎ 26550 61283; www.bourazani.gr; adult/child €10/6; ☺ from sunset), 14km west of Konitsa, educates about Epiros' wild things. It occupies a whole mountain close to the Albanian border, and includes a conference hall for environmental education and feeding areas for boar, deer, kri-kri and moufflon. Watch animals feeding at dusk via a bus tour from the adjacent **Hotel Bourazani** (☎ 26550 61283; bourazani@otenet.gr; s/d/tr/ste €80/105/120; **P** **☒**), a good family spot that combines a hunting lodge ethos with a recreational centre (it has a pool, and tennis and basketball courts). The hotel's restaurant grills up the Environmental Park's unluckier inhabitants.

Molista & Ganadio Μόλιστα & Γαναδιό

To see some wonderful and totally unvisited traditional villages amid lush forests, head north of Konitsa to the Petrina Horia (Stone Villages) of **Molista** and **Ganadio**. Molista is quiet, with only a few elderly year-round inhabitants. The village's stone architecture and cobblestone streets are aesthetically soothing and it also has the large **Church of Agios Nikolaos kai Taxiarhes** (St Nicholas and the Archangels), created in 1864 on the site of a much older one. The church has a large belfry and an opulent wood-carved iconostasis, with fine detail work illustrating Biblical tales such as Adam, Eve, and the serpent in the Garden of Eden. Its impressive icons are at least 130 years old. However, locals keep the previous church's icon collection under lock and key; no-one knows how old they are, as the villagers are still waiting for the Ministry of Culture to send an expert.

Molista has a humble but lovely guest house, the **Arhontiko tis Serafi** (☎ 26550 24090, 6945691216; s/d/tr €50/60/70), run by the good-natured Vangelis Serafis. The rooms aren't spectacular but they are intimate, with some nice touches, antiques and the occasional vividly painted wall motif. There's central heating in the winter, and some rooms have fireplaces; however, you pay for the wood (about €10 per night). The hotel's ceiling was hand-carved in 1912. Downstairs, between stone arches, the *arhontiko* has a cosy restaurant specialising in homemade Epirot food such as *lahanopita* (vegetable pie) and grilled meats.

Nearby **Ganadio** has even more impressive stonework, but no accommodation. The village is more than 450 years old, and taking a leisurely stroll along its cluttered, old stone houses and flower gardens in the warm summer evening shadows is a real pleasure.

Ganadio also has a cafe where the elderly locals keep loose, and the grand **Church of Agii Taxiarhes** (Church of the Holy Archangels, 1870) opposite. It's not likely to be open, so ask someone in the cafe to find charismatic local priest Ioannis, who will be glad to show you around and, if you're lucky, have you over for a crisp distilled beverage on his patio. The stone church has unusual blue-painted walls, and its eclectic decor testifies to the contributions of local artisans and the Epirot diaspora: the hand-carved wood iconostasis was made in Gjirokastër (Argyrokastro in Greek) in Albania, while ornaments from Bucharest, Russian icons and lavish wall murals attest to diaspora funding.

The Petrina Hora are never crowded, though the summer **panigyria** (festivals) on 15 and 20 of August, celebrating saint's days with music, dancing and traditional food and drink, liven things up in Ganadio. Nevertheless, if you're going in spring or autumn you'll have the place to yourself, and there are plenty of wonderful local walks to enjoy.

Getting There & Away
From Konitsa's **bus station** (☎ 26550 22214) there are buses to Bourazani (€1.20, 30 minutes, four daily) and to Molista and Ganadio (€2.30, two weekly).

It's better to drive to Molista or Ganadio than take the bus. From the entrance to Konitsa, head north on the national road (towards Kastoria) for 17.2km; a sign reading 'traditional stone villages' will appear. Turn right here and follow the next sign to Molista (2km).

PREVEZA ΠΡΕΒΕΖΑ
pop 17,724
Set on a peninsula between the Ionian Sea and the Ambracian Gulf, Preveza (*preh-veh-zah*) is a small fishing and commercial port beautified by yachts in the harbour and painted houses in its narrow backstreets. However, despite its small student population and some holidaying Greeks, Preveza is more a waystation for nearby beach resorts and a destination for business travellers than anything else. Nevertheless, it's an attractive town with friendly locals, and worth visiting for a relaxing seafood lunch and for a wander through the old streets.

Orientation & Information
From the bus station, 2km north of centre, the major thoroughfare is Leoforos Irinis; the main sights are between it and the water, hemmed in by the (closed) Venetian Castle of Agios Andreas on the north. Ethnikis Andistasis, roughly parallel with Leoforos Irinis and two blocks up from the waterfront, holds banks, ATMs and shops. The street's prominent clocktower marks the centre; restaurants line the nearby alleys, while the waterfront has cafes.

An underwater car tunnel (€3) linking Preveza with Aktion to the south starts about 2.5km west of Preveza centre; there are no passenger ferries between Preveza and Aktion.
NetcaféAscot (☎ 26820 27746; Balkou 6; per hr €3; ⌚ 9.30am-2am)

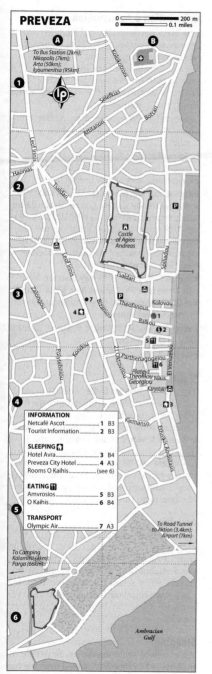

PREVEZA

INFORMATION
Netcafé Ascot.........................1 B3
Tourist Information..................2 B3

SLEEPING
Hotel Avra.............................3 B4
Preveza City Hotel...................4 A3
Rooms O Kaihis..................(see 6)

EATING
Amvrosios..............................5 B3
O Kaihis.................................6 B4

TRANSPORT
Olympic Air............................7 A3

Tourist information (☎ 26820 21078; www.preveza .gr, in Greek; Balkou) Opposite NetcaféAscot.

Sleeping

Camping Kalamitsi (☎ 26820 22192; Kalamitsi; camp sites per adult/tent €6/4; ⌘) Preveza's best camping ground, 4km along the main Preveza–Parga road, has 116 grassed sites with ample shade, a large pool, restaurant, and good services.

Rooms O Kaihis (☎ 26820 24866; Parthenagogiou 7; s/d €20/30) Above the taverna of the same name, this new place is the best budget destination in town, with simple but clean rooms near the waterfront.

Hotel Avra (☎ 26820 21230; www.hotelavra.net, in Greek; Eleftheriou Venizelou 19; s/d €40/60; P ⌘ ⌘) Avra prides itself on location and has clean, airy rooms, though it's no longer the town's most luxurious. Those with balconies over-looking the harbour have good views, but also street noise. There's free parking in the municipal lot opposite.

Preveza City Hotel (☎ 26820 89500; Leofors Irinis 69; s/d €50/80; P) This business hotel up on noisy Leoforos Irinis has standard business rooms with all the expected amenities. Service is brisk though friendly.

Eating

O Kaihis (☎ 26820 24866; Parthenagogiou 7; fish €5-9) This friendly fish taverna on a side street near the water, prepares excellent fresh fish dishes and more standard taverna fare. The friendly owner, who also rents rooms (see above), can provide good local travel tips.

Amvrosios (☎ 26820 27192; Grigoriou tou Pemptou 9; fish €7-11) Another good fish taverna spilling out onto a flowering side lane by the waterfront, this is a popular lunch spot with a good selection of fish dishes.

Getting There & Away
AIR

Five flights weekly serve Athens (€95, one hour). **Olympic Air** (☎ 26820 28343; www.olympic airlines.com; Leoforos Irinis 37) has an office. Preveza airport, 7km south of the town, is sometimes called Lefkada or Aktion. Olympic Air oper-ates an airport bus (€1.55). An airport taxi is €10. For more domestic flight services, see also Island Hopping (p758).

BUS

From the **bus station** (☎ 26820 22213) buses serve Ioannina (€8.70, two hours, eight daily),

Parga (€6.10, two hours, five daily), Igoumenitsa (€8.50, 2½ hours, two daily), Thessaloniki (€39, eight hours, one daily) and Athens (€32, six hours, five daily).

AROUND PREVEZA

Nikopolis Νικόπολη

In 31 BC Octavian (later, Emperor Augustus) defeated Mark Antony and Cleopatra in the famous naval Battle of Actium (present-day Aktion). To celebrate, he built **Nikopolis** (City of Victory; ☎ 26820 41336; adult €2; ⏱ 8.30am-3pm). Octavian forcibly resettled people here from surrounding towns and villages. In the 5th and 6th centuries AD, Nikopolis was plundered by Vandals and Goths, but was rebuilt by Byzantine Emperor Justinian. It was sacked again by the Bulgarians in the 11th century, and that was it.

The original **Roman walls** barely survive, though the **Byzantine walls** and a **theatre** are better preserved. Remnants of a **Temple of Ares**, a **Temple of Poseidon**, an **aqueduct**, **Roman baths** and a restored **Roman odeum** also exist. The enormous site sprawls across the Preveza–Arta road; Preveza–Arta buses stop here.

The site's **Archaeological Museum** (☎ 26820 41336; adult €4; ⏱ 8.30am-3pm) has ancient exhibits, while other finds are displayed in Ioannina's (currently closed) Archaeological Museum.

PARGA ΠΑΡΓΑ

pop 2432

The microresort of Parga is essentially a pretty old village of white-plastered houses stacked on winding, flowery streets, in the fold of a bay crowned by a Venetian castle. On both sides of the town, long sandy beaches stretch, and in high season its waterfront bars get busy with Greeks and Italian and other foreigners. Out of high season, primarily Northern European package tourists visit. Nevertheless, in any season it's still possible to find moments of seclusion and authenticity amid Parga's narrow back streets and little chapels.

A former Venetian possession, Parga resembles the similarly Italian-influenced Ionian Islands opposite, and indeed makes a good base for excursions to two of them, Paxi and Antipaxi, along with the mysterious Nekromanteio of Afyra. With its good outlying beaches and even a nice one right in town, Parga is also good for families with small kids.

Orientation & Information

The main north–south road from Preveza to Igoumenitsa passes by Parga at its top; from where the bus stops on the east side of town, Spyrou Livada descends into the centre. A second road further west also leads into the centre; it connects to the 2km-long Valtos Beach just southwest.

Several ATM-equipped banks are available in Parga, which also has a small medical centre.

Dr Spiros Radiotis (☎ 26840 32450; 6944162261; Alexandrou Baga 1) On call 24 hours a day for medical emergencies; his office is beside Emporiki Trapeza.

International Travel Services (ITS; ☎ 26840 31833; www.parga.net; Spyrou Livada 4) Just down from the bus station, this very experienced and helpful starting point at the village entrance can find accommodation, book local tours, arrange travel tickets, provide general information and even sells international newspapers and magazines. A Budget Rent a Car office is within ITS.

Parga.net (☎ 26840 32177; www.parga.net; Anexartisias 17; per hr €3; ⏱ 8.30am-1.30pm & 5.30-11.30pm May-Oct) An internet cafe; also visit the Parga.net website itself for useful information.

Police (☎ 26840 31222; Alexandrou Baga 18) The tourist police are located here too.

Post office (Alexandrou Baga 18)

Sights

The cliff-top **Venetian Castle** (To Kastro) marks Parga's western edge, and separates the town from Valtos Beach. Attesting to the 400-year Venetian presence in Epiros, the castle offers superb views of the coastline and town from its ramparts. The renovated central area has a **cafe** (☎ 26840 31150; ⏱ 11am-late) in the former French armoury. Since the ramparts are partially unfenced, it's not a place for small children to go running around.

Activities

Visits to the Nekromanteio of Afyra (€42), cruises on the Aherondas River (€25), day trips to Albania or Paxi and Antipaxi (€20) are available from ITS (above), the helpful travel agency across from the bus stop. ITS can inform you about local hill walks and even organise a one-day beginner's dive course for €35.

Sleeping

An excellent accommodation-finder for all budgets is ITS (above), located near the bus

PARGA

INFORMATION	
Dr Spiros Radiotis	**1** B2
International Travel Services	**2** C1
Parga.net	**3** C3
Police	**4** B1
Post Office	**5** B1

SIGHTS & ACTIVITIES	
Venetian Castle	**6** A3

SLEEPING	
Acropol	**7** B2
Hotel Paradise	**8** B2
San Nectarios Hotel	**9** C2

EATING	
Castello Restaurant	(see 7)
O Arkoudas	**10** C3
Peradzada	**11** C3
Taverna to Souli	**12** C3

DRINKING	
Antico	**13** B2
Sugar Bar	**14** C3

TRANSPORT	
Budget Rent a Car	(see 2)
Bus Station	**15** C1
Europcar	**16** B2
Excursion Boats to Paxi	**17** C3
Water Taxis	**18** C3

stop. Simple domatia are on Gaki Zeri, a narrow street with a view over Valtos Beach.

Enjoy Lihnos Beach Camping (☎ 26840 31371; www .enjoy-lichnos.net; Lihnos Beach; camp sites per adult/tent €5/4, d €55) This shady spot on a clean, sandy beach has a supermarket and restaurant; studios are also available.

Valtos Camping (☎ 26840 31287; Valtos Beach; camp sites per adult/tent €6/4) This camping ground set amid orange trees at Valtos Beach, 2km west of Parga centre, has a restaurant. The 15-minute walk from Parga centre is steep, though you can also drive.

Hotel Paradise (☎ 26840 31229; Spyrou Livada 23; s/d €50/65; ⌘ 🖳 🕮) The friendly, central Hotel Paradise has a lovely courtyard pool and downstairs bar. Rooms are airy and clean, with all mod cons. A Europcar, bike rental and National Bank of Greece are all nearby.

ourpick Acropol (☎ 26840 31239; www.pargatravel .com; Agion Apostolon 4; s/d €60/90; ⌘) The refined Acropol, built in 1884, is tucked midway up among Parga's little laneways. The 10 luxurious rooms have king-sized beds, hydromassage showers and handmade Italian

furniture. Some of the small balconies have views of the Kastro. The Acropol is signposted from all over in town, so even if you can't see this hidden gem, you can't miss it. The Acropol also hosts the discerning Castello Restaurant.

Utopia Studios (☎ 26840 31133; www.utopia.com. gr; Agiou Athanasiou; d/tr €60/100; ☼ May-Oct; ⌘ 🕮) These five spacious, sea-view apartments give the relaxing sense of being in a real house. The wood furnishings have an understated elegance, and the balconies are large and relaxing. Some of the bathrooms feature large hydromassage baths. There's a wi-fi hotspot too.

San Nectarios Hotel (☎ 26840 31150; www.san -nectarios.gr; Agias Marinas 2; d/tr €70/90; 🕮) The first hotel you find when entering Parga, the San Nectarios' enviable hill-top location offers splendid views of the town, sea and castle. The rooms are clean and come with all amenities.

Bella Vista Studios & Apartments (☎ 26840 3145, 26840 31833; Lihnos Beach; studio/apt €80/100; ⌘ 🕮) Above Lihnos Beach, these very modern studios and apartments are set around an inviting pool amid citrus trees. The 16 rooms are all recently renovated and kitchens are well equipped. The apartments sleep up to five and all the upper rooms have large balconies overlooking the beach and the olive-clad hills. You can walk downhill to the beach in five minutes; the management also offers deep discounts on weekly car hire.

Eating & Drinking

Taverna to Souli (☎ 26840 31658; Anexartisias 45; mezedhes €4-6, mains €6-9) This relaxing place does great mezedhes, with a focus on local treats such as *feta Souli* (grilled feta cheese with tomatoes and herbs). Try the *kleftiko* (oven-baked lamb or goat) for a filling main course.

Peradzada (☎ 26840 31683; waterfront; mains €5-10) A bit more authentic than most waterfront restaurants, the new Peradzada specialises in hearty portions of traditional Greek cooking.

ourpick O Arkoudas (☎ 26840 32553; Grigoriou Lambraki; fish €6-9) Down on the waterfront strip, 'The Bear', as it's called in Greek, is a friendly place that serves up a tasty variety of fresh fish dishes.

Castello Restaurant (☎ 26840 31833; Hotel Acropol, Agion Apostolon 4; mains €8-12) A creative fusion of French, Italian and Greek cuisine is prepared with style at the Castello. It has an elegant, relaxed feel – probably the only place in town where you can hear classic Miles Davis tracks playing during dinner, and definitely the only one whose wine cellar is visible through a glass panel beneath your feet.

Sugar Bar (www.sugarbar.gr; waterfront; ☒ 10am-late) While it might at first seem indistinguishable from the other cafes wrapped along the waterfront, laid-back Sugar has substance as well as style, serving 106 different cocktails; the loyal following, like the music, is both Greek and international.

Antico (☎ 26840 32713; Anexartasies 4; ☒ 10am-3am) You can't stop the rock at this cosy little bar tucked in an upper side street, its walls lined with guitar posters. The friendly bartender is dedicated to a playlist strong on '70s and '80s classic rock, with an occasional dip into the '60s back catalogue.

Getting There & Away

BUS

From the **bus station** (☎ 26840 31218) buses serve Igoumenitsa (€5.20, one hour, five daily), Preveza (€6.10, two hours, four daily), Thessaloniki (€39, seven hours, one daily) and Athens (€35.30, seven hours, three daily).

CAR

Hire a car (from €40 per day) at **Europcar** (☎ 26840 32777; Spyrou Livada 19) or Budget Rent a Car, located at **ITS** (☎ 26840 31833; www.parga .net; Spyrou Livada 4).

WATER TAXI

Water taxis go to Voltos Beach (€4, from 9.30am to 6pm), Lihnos Beach (€7, from 11am to 5pm) and Sarakiniko (€8, from 10am).

AROUND PARGA

Nekromanteio of Afyra

Νεκρομαντείο της Αφύρας

The ancients feared it as the gate of Hades, god of the underworld; for visitors today the **Nekromanteio of Afyra** (☎ 26840 41206; adult €2; ☒ 8.30am-3pm) is just the labyrinthine ruin at the end of a beautiful boat ride down the coast and up the Aherondas River.

To ancient Greeks, the Nekromanteio was an oracle: pilgrims made offerings of milk, honey and the blood of sacrificed animals in order to communicate with the spirits of the dead. The remnants of the structure were only discovered in 1958, and with them also the ruined monastery of **Agios Ioannis Prodromos** and a **graveyard**. The eerie underground vault is probably the place into which confused ancient visitors were lowered by windlass, thinking that they were entering the realm of Hades itself.

Parga travel agents offer a Nekromanteio day trip, which costs about €40. Otherwise, drive south towards Mesopotamos (19km), and watch for the Nekromanteio sign. The site is 1km off the main road.

IGOUMENITSA ΗΓΟΥΜΕΝΙΤΣΑ

pop 9104

Igoumenitsa (ih-goo-meh-*nit*-sah) is the end of the line for northwestern Greece, a busy, characterless port town 86km from Ioannina. It's where you take the ferry to Italy or Corfu. Although Igoumenitsa is no tourist destination, the completion of the Egnatia Odos Hwy, linking Igoumenitsa with İstanbul, will enhance its stature as a leading cargo port.

Information

Ethnikis Andistasis hosts currency-exchange machines and major-bank ATMs. The new port has more exchange booths. An EOT booth is outside the new port's arrivals area.

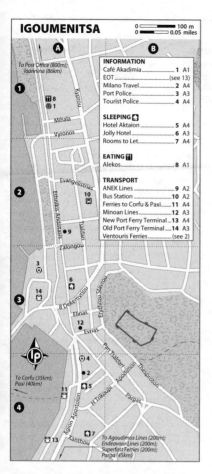

IGOUMENITSA

INFORMATION
Café Akadimia	1 A1
EOT	(see 13)
Milano Travel	2 A4
Port Police	3 A3
Tourist Police	4 A4

SLEEPING
Hotel Aktaion	5 A4
Jolly Hotel	6 A3
Rooms to Let	7 A4

EATING
Alekos	8 A1

TRANSPORT
ANEK Lines	9 A2
Bus Station	10 A2
Ferries to Corfu & Paxi	11 A4
Minoan Lines	12 A2
New Port Ferry Terminal	13 A4
Old Port Ferry Terminal	14 A3
Ventouris Ferries	(see 2)

Café Akadimia (☎ 26650 29233; Ethnikis Andistasis 80; per hr €2.50; ☒ 8am-2am) Internet access.

Milano Travel (☎ 26650 23565; milantvl@otenet.gr; Agion Apostolon 11b)

Port police (☎ 26650 22707) Beside the old port ferry terminal.

Post office (☎ 26650 22209; Tzavelenas 2) Eight hundred metres north of town.

Tourist Police (☎ 26650 22222; Agion Apostolon 5) Both the tourist and regular police are together on the main road near the port.

Sleeping & Eating

Igoumenitsa's identity as a merely functional town has rubbed off on its limited accommodation and eating options, but you probably won't stay long enough to let it depress you.

Rooms to Let (☎ 26650 23612; Xanthou 12; s/d €30/40) Proximity to the ferry is the selling point for these plain, drab rooms.

Hotel Aktaion (☎ /fax 26650 22707; Agion Apostolon 17; s/d €40/50) and **Jolly Hotel** (☎ 26650 23971; jollyigm@otenet.gr; Ethnikis Andistasis 44; s/d incl breakfast €55/65; ☐) are both waterfront C-class hotels with uninspiring yet quiet rooms; the latter offers better services.

The humble **Alekos** (☎ 26650 23708; Ethnikis Andistasis 84; mains €4.50-7) taverna serves *mayirefta* and grilled meat.

Getting There & Away
BOAT

Igoumenitsa is a major ferry hub for Piraeus, Corfu and Italy (and vital for those wishing to take a vehicle between the two countries).

Ferries for Italy and Corfu leave from three adjacent but separate quays on the Ethnikis Andistasis waterfront. Ferries for Ancona and Venice (in Italy) depart from the new, southern port; those for Brindisi and Bari (in Italy) use the old port by the shipping offices; and ferries for Corfu (Kerkyra) and Paxi go from just north of the new port.

Domestic

For details on ferries and hydrofoils from Igoumenitsa to the rest of Greece, see Island Hopping (p751). An **English-speaking operator** (☎ 26650 99460) can be reached for questions about Igoumenitsa–Corfu ferries. Book tickets at portside agencies or through the ferry companies' offices/websites.

Agoudimos Lines (☎ 26650 21175; www.agoudimos-lines.com; Agion Apostolon 147)

ANEK Lines (☎ 26650 22104; www.anek.gr; Revis Travel Tourism & Shipping, Ethnikis Andistasis 34)

Endeavor Lines (☎ 26650 26833, 26650 26833; www.endeavor-lines.com/en/schedules; Eleni Pantazi General Tourism Agency, Ioniou Pelagous)

Minoan Lines (☎ 26650 22952; www.minoan.gr; Ethnikis Andistasis 58a)

Superfast Ferries (☎ 26650 29200; www.superfast.com; Pitoulis & Co Ltd, Agion Apostolon 147)

Ventouris Ferries (☎ 26650 23565; www.ventouris.gr; Milano Travel, Agion Apostolon 11b)

International

For Italian services, you can usually just show up in Igoumenitsa and buy an onward deck-class passenger ticket, though you'll want to book ahead for car tickets or sleeping cabins. Be at the port two hours before departure,

BOATS FROM IGOUMENITSA TO ITALY

Destination	Port	Duration	Fare	Frequency
Ancona)	Igoumenitsa	14-15hr	€49-79	3-4 daily
Bari	Igoumenitsa	8½-10½hr	€60-70	2-3 daily
Brindisi	Igoumenitsa	6-9½hr	€58-65	3-4 daily
Venice	Igoumenitsa	23hr	€49-79	1-3 daily*
* except Wednesday				

and check in at the shipping agent's office for your boarding pass. On-board 'camping' is allowable on certain services for those with campervans. Vehicle prices for Bari and Brindisi start from €50, while the longer trip to Ancona/Venice is around €140.

For details of services to Italy from Igoumenitsa, see the boxed text, above.

BUS

The **bus station** (☎ 26650 22309; Kyprou 29), two blocks behind the waterfront, serves Ioannina (€8.20, two hours, nine daily), Parga (€5.20, one hour, four daily), Athens (€32.60, eight hours, five daily), Preveza (€8.50, 2½ hours, two daily) and Thessaloniki (€30.20, eight hours, one daily). These buses are less frequent out of summer.

Saronic Gulf Islands
Νησιά του Σαρωνικού

The Saronic Gulf Islands offer a fast track to the Greek island dream.

They may lack the romantic image of the hazy Cyclades or the far-flung Dodecanese, yet the main islands of the group have enough allure to satisfy anyone's expectations and they all have facilities aplenty. There is a reassuring sense of accessibility about the Saronics and collectively the islands seem to merge the best of Greece's mainland attractions with all that is the best of island life. Yet the islands are also remarkably distinctive. You can ring the changes as you island-hop between classical heritage, resort beaches, stylish architecture, a sense of island escapism and top-class Greek cuisine.

The most accessible islands, Aegina and Angistri, are just under an hour by ferry from Piraeus. Aegina is almost an Athenian suburb, yet this lively bustling place has more than its fair share of cultural sights. Twenty minutes to the east of Aegina lies pine-clad Angistri, a typical holiday island but one with reassuring corners of tranquility, even in high season.

Further south is Poros, only a few hundred metres across the water from the Peloponnese and with several decent beaches and a peaceful forested hinterland. Next comes the Saronic showpiece, Hydra, where a tiered jigsaw of pastel-hued houses rises from a harbourside that is always frothing with fashionable life. Deepest south of all is pine-scented Spetses, only minutes away from the mainland yet entirely part of the Aegean Island world.

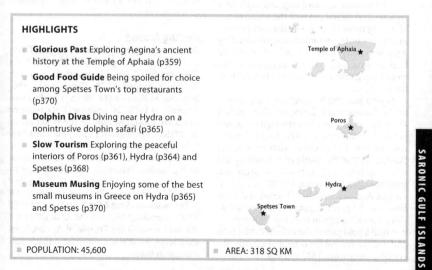

HIGHLIGHTS

- **Glorious Past** Exploring Aegina's ancient history at the Temple of Aphaia (p359)

- **Good Food Guide** Being spoiled for choice among Spetses Town's top restaurants (p370)

- **Dolphin Divas** Diving near Hydra on a nonintrusive dolphin safari (p365)

- **Slow Tourism** Exploring the peaceful interiors of Poros (p361), Hydra (p364) and Spetses (p368)

- **Museum Musing** Enjoying some of the best small museums in Greece on Hydra (p365) and Spetses (p370)

Temple of Aphaia ★

Poros ★

Hydra ★

Spetses Town ★

- **POPULATION: 45,600**
- **AREA: 318 SQ KM**

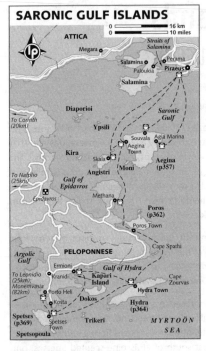

SARONIC GULF ISLANDS

AEGINA ΑΙΓΙΝΑ

pop 13,500

Beyond its bustling port, Aegina (*eh*-yi-nah) has the seductive, easygoing character of a typical Greek island but with the added bonus of having more than its fair share of prestigious ancient sites and museums. Weekending Athenians sharpen the mix and visitors should bear in mind that, even in winter, fast ferries from Piraeus are often fully booked prior to the weekend.

Aegina was the leading maritime power of the Saronic Gulf during the 7th century BC, when it grew wealthy through trade and political ascendancy. The island made a major contribution to the Greek victory over the Persian fleet at the Battle of Salamis in 480 BC. Despite this solidarity with the Athenian state, it was invaded in 459 BC out of jealousy of Aegina's wealth and status and of its liaison with Sparta. Aegina never regained its glory days although in the early 19th century it played a bold part in the defeat of the Turks and was the temporary capital of a partly liberated Greece from 1827 to 1829.

Today the island plays a more mundane role as Athens' island suburb and Greece's main producer of pistachio nuts. Past glory lingers, however, not least at the splendid ruin of the 5th-century Temple of Aphaia. There are modest beaches too and an enjoyable taverna and nightlife scene.

Getting There & Away

Aegina's main port is Aegina Town, which has links to Piraeus, Angistri, Poros and Methana, in the Peloponnese. There are no direct ferries from Aegina and Angistri to Hydra and Spetses or to mainland Ermioni and Porto Heli. For these destinations you need to connect with fast ferries at Piraeus or Poros. The smaller Aegina ports of Agia Marina and Souvala have links with Piraeus in the high season only. You should always check details close to the date of your planned trip. For details see Island Hopping (p744).

A local small ferry, the distinctive blue and yellow *Agistri Express,* which is owned by the Angistri community, makes several trips daily to and from Aegina to Angistri's main port of Skala (€5, 20 minutes) and then on to neighbouring Mylos (€5.20, 25 minutes). It leaves from midway along the Aegina harbour front and timetables are displayed there.

Another option between Aegina and Angistri is the **water taxi service** (☎ 22970 91387, 6972229720). It costs €40 one way, regardless of numbers.

Getting Around

Buses run frequently between Aegina Town and Agia Marina (€1.70, 30 minutes) via Paleohora (€1.40, 15 minutes) and the Temple of Aphaia (€1.70, 25 minutes). Other buses go to Perdika (€1.40, 15 minutes) and Souvala (€1.40, 20 minutes). Departure times are displayed outside the ticket office on Plateia Ethnegersias and you must buy tickets at the booth.

There are numerous car and motorcycle hiring outfits. Prices start at around €30 to €40 a day for a car and €15 to €25 a day for a 50cc machine. Bicycles are about €8 a day. **Sklavenas Rent A Car** Aegina Town (☎ 22970 22892; Kazantzaki 5); Agia Marina (☎ 22970 32871), on the road towards the Temple of Apollo, hires cars, jeeps, scooters, motorbikes, quads and mountain bikes.

SARONIC GULF ISLANDS

AEGINA TOWN
pop 7410

Aegina Town replicates some of the vibrancy of downtown Athens with its gritty charm and decidedly Greek edge. The town is the capital and main port of the island, and its long harbour front buzzes with life. The two-lane harbour-front road is a bit of a speedway, so take care when crossing.

The waterside promenade that runs the length of the harbour makes for a pleasant open stroll, but canopied cafes overwhelm its inland counterpart. Narrow lanes strike inland from the harbour front, across parallel streets that are crammed with shops of every kind. A few 19th-century neoclassical buildings survive and Ancient Greece is represented by the impressive ruins of the Temple of Apollo just to the north of the ferry quays.

Orientation

The large outer quay, with its little church of St Nikolaos, is where the bigger ferries dock. The smaller inner quay is where hydrofoils dock. Crossing the road from the end of either quay and then bearing left leads to Plateia Ethnegersias where the bus terminal and post office are located. This road then continues past the Temple of Apollo, where it becomes single-lane, and on towards the north coast. Turning right from the end of the quays leads along the busy harbour front for about 500m to the Church of Panagytsa and then on to Perdika or Agia Marina.

AEGINA & ANGISTRI

Information

Aegina does not have an official tourist office, but you can find some useful information at www.aegina greece.com.

There is a line of ferry ticket offices at the exit to the main quay and an information board listing accommodation options with a telephone handset for direct contact.

Alpha Bank and the Bank of Piraeus are located opposite the end of the hydrofoil quay. The National Bank of Greece is about 300m to the right of the ferry quays. All the banks have ATMs.

Kalezis Bookshop (☎ 22970 25956; ☒ from May) Midway along the harbour front; has a selection of foreign newspapers and books.

Perla Laundry (☎ 22970 23497; Mitropoleos 23; 7am-1.30pm & 5-9pm; 2kg wash & dry/wash only €5/3) Also does pick up and delivery.

Port police (☎ 22970 22328) At the entrance to the ferry quays.

Post office (Plateia Ethnegersias; ☒ 7.30am-2pm Mon-Fri)

Tourist police (☎ 22970 27777; Leonardou Lada) A short distance up a lane opposite the hydrofoil dock.

Sights

The intriguing remains of the **Temple of Apollo** (☎ 22970 22637; adult/concession €3/2; ☒ 8.30am-3pm Tue-Sun) stand on the hill of Coloni, northwest of the port. The ruined walls, pavements, cisterns and broken pillars in honey-coloured stone are lorded over by a solitary surviving column, all that's left of a 5th-century-BC temple that was once part of an ancient acropolis. Just below is the informative **Sanctuary Museum** (☒ 8.30am-3pm Tue-Sun), where you buy tickets and which displays artefacts from the temple. Information is in Greek, English and German.

Festivals & Events

Fistiki means pistachio nut and the three-day **Aegina Fistiki Fest** (www.aeginafistikifest.gr) was inaugurated in 2009 to promote Aegina's famous pistachio through events such as live-music concerts, visual-arts events, trade fairs and culinary contests. It is hoped to stage the festival in mid September each year, at the end of the pistachio harvesting period.

Sleeping

Aegina has a reasonable selection of hotels and rooms, but it's advisable to book ahead, especially at weekends. Some of the more basic hotels are not the best value and can be overpriced.

Marianna Studios (☎ 22970 25650, 6945869465; www.aeginarooms.com/mariannastudios; 16-18 Kiverniou St; s/d/tr €35/40/45; ☒) These simple, very basic rooms are an excellent budget option. The tiny entrance hides a sizeable courtyard and some rooms overlook a quiet, leafy garden. The welcome is very friendly.

Electra Domatia (☎ 22970 26715, 6938726441; www.aegina-electra.gr; Leonardou Lada 25; s/d €45/50; ☒). There are no scenic views from this small pension, but rooms are impeccable and comfy and are in a quiet corner of town. It outclasses nearby hotels by a long way. Head up Leonardou Lada, opposite the ferry quays.

Aeginitiko Archontiko (☎ 22970 24968; www.aeginitikoarchontiko.gr; cnr Ag Nikolaou & Thomaiados; s/d/tr/ste €60/70/80/120; ☒) This old Aegina mansion retains period features that hark back to the glory days of 19th-century Greece's first years of independence. The splendid breakfast costs about €10 per person.

our pick Rastoni (☎ 22970 27039; www.rastoni.gr; Metriti 31; s/d/tr €85/80/110; P ☒ ☐ ☎) Each of the spacious rooms at this handsome boutique hotel has individual decor reflecting Asian and African themes. There's a lovely garden with views to the Temple of Apollo. The hotel is in a quiet area a few minutes walking distance from the harbour front. There are discounts for several days' stay. Breakfast is €5.

Eating

The inland side of the harbour front is packed with cafes and restaurants. They make for lazy world-watching, but are not particularly good value, unless you hit the local unvarnished *ouzeries* (a place serving ouzo and light snacks) scattered throughout. Local pistachio nuts are on sale everywhere, priced from €6 for 500g.

Babis (☎ 22970 23594; mains €5-12) Located at the far end of the harbour front, the cool, stylish decor of this inventive restaurant complements its creative cuisine, which includes its resilient signature dish, chicken with pistachio and unsalted *anthotyro* (dry white cheese).

Tsias (☎ 22970 23529; Dimokratias 47; mains €6-7.50) Street-side Greek eating at its best. Try shrimps with tomatoes and feta, or crab salad for under €5, followed by pork fillet. There are also simple fish dishes for under €10.

Mezedopoleio to Steki (☎ 22970 23910; Pan Irioti 45; dishes €6-12) Tucked in behind the noisy mid-harbour fish market is this vibrant place.

Together with its immediate neighbour, I Agora, it's always packed with people tucking into hell-fired octopus or sardines, plus other classic mezedhes.

Drinking & Entertainment

Music bars and cafes along the harbour front have luxurious seating in competing colours.

Heaven (☎ 22970 28872; Dimokratias) Soft sofas and upbeat decor feature in this popular music bar–cafe.

Yes! (☎ 22970 28306; Dimokratias) Easy-listening daytime sounds and sharper spins from local and visiting DJs at night give Yes! its edge for a younger crowd.

Avli (☎ 22970 26438; Pan Irioti 17) Avli mixes '60s and Latin music and plays Greek sounds when Athenian weekenders hit town.

AROUND AEGINA
Temple of Aphaia

The impressive **Temple of Aphaia** (☎ 22970 32398; adult/concession/under 18yr €4/2/free; ⏰ 8am-7.30pm Apr-Oct, 8.30am-5pm Nov-Mar) celebrates a local deity of pre-Hellenic times and is the major ancient site of the Saronic Gulf Islands. It was built in 480 BC, soon after the Battle of Salamis.

The temple's pediments were decorated with splendid Trojan War sculptures, most of which were robbed in the 19th century and now decorate Munich's Glyptothek. The remains of the temple stand proudly on a pine-covered hill with far-reaching views over the Saronic Gulf. There are interpretive panels in Greek and English.

Aphaia is 10km east of Aegina Town. Buses to Agia Marina stop at the site (€1.70, 20 minutes). A taxi from Aegina Town costs about €12 one way. If relying on buses it should be remembered that there might be several hours between services. It can be a hot hill top.

Paleohora Παλαιοχώρα

This enchanting site has had several of its old churches and chapels renovated recently and is a haven of peace. The ancient town of Paleohora was Aegina's capital from the 9th century and throughout the medieval period and was abandoned finally only during the 1820s. Over 30 surviving churches and chapels punctuate the rocky heights of the original citadel, and several have been carefully refurbished in recent years. Many are open to visitors and are linked by a network of

---

FLYING FREE

Yiannis Pouloupolous, the director of the **Hellenic Wildlife Hospital** (EKPAZ; see p360) on Aegina is larger than life. He needs boundless energy to maintain his lifelong commitment to wounded wild animals, which began when he was a veterinary student and nurtured injured small birds in his student flat. Yiannis has never stopped caring for wild creatures. Now he devotes virtually every waking hour to the wildlife hospital in the rugged hills of central Aegina. Here, Yiannis and his many devoted colleagues and volunteer helpers have had many successes, not least the release of rehabilitated eagles into the wilds of Crete and northern Greece.

At the EKPAZ base there are scores of creatures, many of them protected species and most of them the victims of humankind's desire to hunt and kill with guns. 'Why do they shoot such magnificent beings?' is Yiannis' eternal question.

Here you see the rarest of creatures – Eleonora's falcons (down to single figures in some countries), their wings half shot away; imperial eagles, Egyptian vultures, white storks, herons and waders, with smashed legs, some even blinded, disabled griffon vultures grumping and gossiping in one compound. These are all Yiannis' 'chickens'. 'They are all family,' he says. 'We are all one, surely.'

It is illegal to shoot protected species, but education, persuasion and example are probably the only ways, albeit painfully slow, to stop the destruction of wild creatures for sport. The brutal fact is that to point a gun at birds such as eagles, vultures, storks and swans means an inevitable cheap triumph for the shooter. Such slow, stately creatures do not twist and turn. Once fixed in the sights they are easy meat for just about anyone who can squeeze a trigger. As Yiannis drolly puts it: 'To shoot a wild bird is no achievement, no triumph. Perhaps they should try video games instead.'

Until they do, Yiannis Pouloupolous and his small army of colleagues and volunteers will continue their work in the hills of Aegina.

paths. The site is 6.5km east of Aegina Town near the enormous modern church of **Moni Agiou Nektariou**. Buses from Aegina Town to Agia Marina stop at the turn-off to Paleohora (€1.40, 10 minutes). A taxi is €8 one way.

Christos Capralos Museum

From 1963 until 1993, the acclaimed sculptor Christos Capralos (1909–93) lived and worked on Aegina during the summer months. Today, many of his works are on display at the **Christos Capralos Museum** (☎ 22970 22001; Livadi; admission €2; ☷ 9am-2.30pm & 5-8pm Tue-Sun Jun-Oct, 10am-4pm Fri-Sun Nov-May) in his one-time home and studio on the coast near Livadi, 1.5km north of Aegina Town. At first glance the monumental works, especially those in eucalyptus wood, may seem harsh and discomfiting, but their fluidity and power are exhilarating. The *Crucifixion Tableau* is superb. In a separate gallery is the 40m-long *Pindus Frieze*, a powerful memorial to the Battle of Pindus, in which the Greek Army beat back an Italian advance in WWII.

Hellenic Wildlife Hospital

The oldest and largest wildlife rehabilitation centre in Greece and Southern Europe, the **Hellenic Wildlife Hospital** (Elliniko Kentro Perithalpsis Agrion Zoön; ☎ 22970 28367, 6973318845; www.ekpaz .gr; ☷ 10am-7pm) each year treats and cares for anything from 3000 to 4500 wounded and disabled wild animals (see boxed text, p359). You can visit the hospital, which lies amidst rugged hills about 10km southeast of Aegina Town and 1km east of Pahia Rahi on the road to Mt Oros. Admission is free, but donations are appreciated. It is best to phone ahead to ask if a visit is possible. If you want a more hands-on commitment, the centre welcomes volunteers for whom accommodation is supplied. Potential volunteers should be aware that the work is hard and unglamorous, albeit hugely rewarding.

Perdika Πέρδικα

The fishing village of Perdika lies about 9km south of town on the southern tip of the west coast. Perdika's harbour inlet is very shallow and swimming is not much fun. Instead, catch one of the regular caïques (€4) from the harbour to the little island of Moni, a few minutes away. Moni is a nature reserve and has a magic tree-lined beach and summertime cafe.

There are a couple of hotels and a few rooms in Perdika. **Villa Rodanthos** (☎ 22970 61400; www .villarodanthos.gr; s/d €45/65; ☒ ☐) is a gem of a place, not least because of its charming owner. Each room has its own colourful decor and is equipped with a kitchen. It is about 100m along the right-hand branch road that starts opposite the bus stop at the edge of town.

Tavernas line the raised harbour-front terrace and dish up Greek staples for about €6 to €10. It all buzzes with life in summer and the tavernas mix it with some swaggering late-night music bars. A smart newcomer is Muzik, the ideal place for Perdika sunsets and relaxing sounds.

Buses run every couple of hours to Perdika from Aegina Town (€1.40, 30 minutes). A taxi is €10 one way.

Beaches

Beaches are not Aegina's strongest points. The east-coast town of **Agia Marina** is the island's main package resort. It has a shallow-water beach that is ideal for families, but it's backed by a fairly crowded main drag and it gets very busy in summer.

There are a couple of sandy beaches by the roadside between Aegina Town and Perdika, such as the pleasant **Marathonas** where the taverna **Ammos** (☎ 22970 28160; Marathonas; mains €5.50-12) offers excellent local dishes with an international flair.

ANGISTRI ΑΓΚΙΣΤΡΙ

pop 700

Angistri lies a few kilometres off the west coast of Aegina and offers a rewarding day trip or a worthwhile longer escape from the mainstream; better so out of high season.

The port of **Skala** is a resort village crammed with small hotels and apartment blocks, tavernas and cafes. Its beach, the best on the island, all but disappears beneath sun loungers and grilling flesh in July and August; but life, in general, still ticks along gently. Angistri's other port of **Mylos** (Megalochori) has a more appealing traditional character.

Orientation & Information

There is a board on Skala's ferry quay that lists accommodation options, with phone numbers. A right turn from the quay leads to the small harbour beach and then along a paved walkway to a church on a low headland. Beyond here lies the long, but narrow, main beach. A kilometre further west takes you to Mylos, with rooms and tavernas, but no beach. Turning left from the quay at Skala takes you south in about half an hour to the pebbly and clothing-optional **Halikadha Beach**.

There is a branch of Emboriki Bank with ATM in Skala's main street.

Sleeping & Eating

Angistri has many sleeping places, but booking ahead is advised, especially in August and at summer weekends.

Alkyoni Inn (☎ 22970 91378; www.alkyoni.com; s/d/tr €40/50/60; 😊) The welcoming Alkyoni Inn is a 10-minute stroll southeast of the ferry quay. Its seafront rooms and apartments have great views. Other rooms back onto the road. The Alkyoni has a popular taverna (mains €4.50 to €12) with well-prepared fish and meat dishes at reasonable prices.

Rosy's Little Village (☎ 22970 91610; www.rosyslittlevillage.com; s/d/tr €50/70/90; 😊 😊) A complex of Cubist-style buildings that step gently down to the sea, a short way to the east of Skala's ferry quay. Rosy's is full of light and colour. Free sunbeds and free mountain bikes enhance things even more and there's a weekly picnic and a live-music evening in summer. Breakfasts are €6.50 and there's a restaurant serving lunch and dinner with emphasis on organic sources. Mains are about €6.50 to €10. Check the website for information on various cultural courses that are available.

Two good local tavernas are **Gialos** (☎ 6977787785), just outside Skala on the Mylos road, and **Kafeses** (☎ 22970 91357), overlooking Mylos harbour. Both offer local specialities. In Skala, **Pizzeria Avli** (☎ 22970 91573) has above-ordinary pizzas.

Getting There & Away

Angistri is well-served by ferries, especially in summer, with several fast hydrofoils running each day to Angistri from Piraeus via Aegina and a car ferry running several days a week from Piraeus via Aegina. For details see Island Hopping (p746). The local ferry, Agistri Express, runs to and from Aegina several times a day (see p356).

The **water taxi service** (☎ 22970 91387, 6972229720) costs €40 one way between Aegina and Angistri, regardless of numbers.

Getting Around

Several buses a day run from 6.30am to about 9pm during the summer months from Skala and Mylos to the little village of Limenaria and to Dhragonera Beach. It's worth hiring a moped (€15) or sturdy mountain bike (€10) to explore the island's coastline road. Good hire outfits are **Kostas Bike Hire** (☎ 22970 91021; Skala) and **Takis Rent A Bike & Bicycles** (☎ 22970 91001; Mylos).

You can also follow tracks from Metohi overland through cool pine forest to reach the west-coast beach of Dhragonera. Take a compass with you; the tracks divide often and route finding can be frustrating.

POROS ΠΟΡΟΣ

pop 4500

Poros is a popular holiday island, yet it has a refreshing sense of remoteness in its sparsely populated and forested interior. The island is separated from the mountainous Peloponnese by a narrow sea channel, and the picturesque surroundings make the main settlement of Poros Town seem more like a lakeside resort in the Swiss Alps than a Greek island port. The mainland town of Galatas lies on the opposite shore.

Poros is in fact made up of two 'almost' islands: tiny Sferia, which is occupied mainly by the town of Poros, and the much larger and mainly forested Kalavria, which has the island's beaches and its larger seasonal hotels scattered along its southern shore. An isthmus, cut by a narrow canal and spanned by a road bridge, connects the two islands.

Getting There & Away

There are numerous daily ferries from Piraeus to Poros in summer and about four daily in winter. Fast ferries continue south to Hydra, Spetses, Ermioni and Porto Heli. Conventional ferries connect Aegina to Poros and on to Methana on the mainland. For details see Island Hopping (p758).

Caïques shuttle constantly between Poros and Galatas (€0.80, five minutes) on the mainland. They leave from the quay opposite Plateia Iroön in Poros Town. Hydrofoils dock about 50m north of here and car ferries to Galatas leave from the dock several hundred metres north again, on the road to Kalavria.

Getting Around

A bus operates May to October every half hour from 7am until midnight on a route that starts near the main ferry dock on Plateia Iroön in Poros Town. It crosses to Kalavria and goes east along the south coast as far as Moni Zoödohou Pigis (€1.50, 10 minutes), then turns around and heads west as far as Neorion Beach (€1.50, 15 minutes).

Some of the caïques operating between Poros and Galatas switch to ferrying tourists to beaches during summer. Operators stand on the harbour front and call out destinations.

There are several places on the road to Kalavria offering bikes for hire, both motorised and pedal-powered. Bikes start at €8 per day, and mopeds and scooters are €15 to €20.

POROS TOWN
pop 4102

Poros Town is a pleasant place where whitewashed houses with red-tiled roofs look out across the narrow channel towards the shapely mountains of the Peloponnese. Fast ferries and sizeable conventional ferries glide through the channel to dock on the harbour front, and smaller vessels scurry to and fro between the island and the mainland town of Galatas. Behind the harbour front a rocky bluff rises steeply to a crowning clock tower.

The town is also a useful base from which to explore the ancient sites of the adjacent Peloponnese.

Orientation

The main ferry dock is at the western end of the town's long harbour front.

Across the road from the main ferry dock is the small triangular-shaped 'square' of Plateia Iroön. To either side of the *plateia* the road is lined with cafes, tavernas and tourist shops. The island bus leaves from next to the kiosk at the eastern end of Plateia Iroön. Steps lead up from the inner corner of the *plateia* to the attractive lanes and squares of the upper town and to the clock tower and cathedral. A short distance south of Plateia Iroön is Plateia Karamis, set back from the harbour-front road and boasting a small war memorial.

A left turn from the dock leads north along the extended harbour front and on to the Kalavria road.

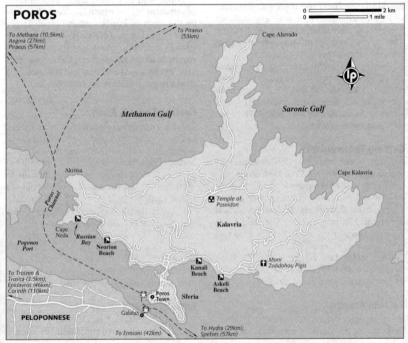

Information

Poros doesn't have a tourist office, but you can find useful information at www.poros.gr.

Alpha Bank (Plateia Iroön) Has an ATM.

Bank Emporiki (Plateia Iroön) Has an ATM.

Family Tours (☎ 22980 25900; www.familytours.gr) On the harbour front. Sells ferry tickets and arranges accommodation, car hire, tours and cruises.

Marinos Tours (☎ 22980 23423; www.marinostours.gr) On the harbour front. Arranges hydrofoil tickets and other services.

National Bank of Greece (Papadopoulou) About 100m north of Plateia Iroön; has an ATM.

Post office (☎ 22980 22274; Tombazi; ⏲ 7.30am-2pm Mon-Fri) Next to Seven Brothers Hotel.

Suzi's Laundrette Service (Papadopoulou; 5kg wash & dry €12; ⏲ 8am-2pm & 6-9pm Mon-Sat May-Oct, 9am-2pm Mon-Sat Nov-Apr) Next to the National Bank of Greece.

Tourist police (☎ 22980 22462/22256; Dimosthenous 10) Behind the Poros high school.

Sleeping

Georgia Mellou Rooms (☎ 22980 22309, 6937850705; Plateia Georgiou; s/d/tr €35/45/55; ⚛) Tucked away at the heart of the old town, next to the cathedral and high above the harbour front, these simple, old-fashioned rooms are a decent budget option. The owner is charming and there are great views from the west-side rooms.

Seven Brothers Hotel (☎ 22980 23412; www.7brothers.gr; Plateia Iroön; s/d/tr €55/65/75; ⚛ 🖥) Conveniently close to the hydrofoil dock, this modern hotel has bright, comfy rooms with small balconies and tea- and coffee-making facilities.

Hotel Manessi (☎ 22980 22273/25857; www.manessi.com; Paralia; s/d €70/80; ⚛ 🛜) Well-placed at the mid-point of the harbour front, the recently renovated Manessi is a central option. The business-style rooms are comfy and immaculate.

Eating

There's not much haute cuisine on Poros, but there are traditional tavernas with character to match the cooking.

Taverna Karavolos (☎ 22980 26158; mains €5-7.80; ⏲ 7pm-late) Karavolos means 'big snail' in Greek and snails are a speciality of the house here, served in a thick tomato sauce (€6). Classic Greek meat dishes and some fish dishes are also on the oft-changing menu. Head north from the cathedral for about 100m, then go left and down broad steps towards the harbour.

Taverna Rota (☎ 22980 25627; Plateia Iroön; mains €5-15) Located on the edge of Plateia Iroön, this longstanding, family-run taverna dishes up breakfast (€4.50 to €7), traditional dishes, a range of salads, pasta and pizzas. The fish soup (€6) is excellent and they make their own flavoursome bread. The mixed seafood platter for two costs €25.

Dimitris Family Taverna (☎ 22980 23709; mains €4.50-20) The owners of this cheerful, family-run place have a butcher's business. Cuts of pork, lamb and chicken are of the finest quality, yet vegetarians can still mix and match a selection of nonmeat dishes. To get here, head north from the cathedral for 20m, turn right and then left for 100m.

AROUND POROS

Poros has several good beaches. **Kanali Beach**, on Kalavria 1km east of the bridge, is pebbly. **Askeli Beach** is about 500m to the east and has a long sandy stretch. The **Hotel New Aegli** (☎ 22980 22372/23200; www.newaegli.com; s/d/st €70/80/120; ⚛ 🛜 ⚛) is a decent resort-style hotel on Askeli Beach, with all the expected amenities, and even weekend Greek music and dancing. **Neorion Beach**, 3km west of the bridge, has water skiing and banana-boat and air-chair rides. The best beach is at **Russian Bay**, 1.5km past Neorion.

The 18th-century **Moni Zoödohou Pigis**, on Kalavria, has a beautiful gilded iconostasis from Asia Minor. The monastery is well signposted, 4km east of Poros Town.

From the road below the monastery you can head inland to the 6th-century **Temple of Poseidon**. There's very little left of this temple, but the walk is worthwhile and there are superb views of the Saronic Gulf and the Peloponnese. From the ruins you can continue along the road and go back to the bridge onto Sferia. It's about 6km in total.

PELOPONNESIAN MAINLAND

The Peloponnesian mainland opposite Poros can be explored conveniently from the island, with caïques running constantly between Poros and Galatas (see Getting There & Away, p361).

The ruins of ancient **Troizen**, legendary birthplace of Theseus, lie in the hills near the modern village of Trizina, 7.5km west of Galatas. There are buses to Trizina (€1.40, 15 minutes) from Galatas, leaving a walk of about 1.5km to the site.

The inspiring ancient theatre of **Epidavros** (p192) can be reached from Galatas. Your own transport is the most convenient way of getting there. Otherwise a couple of buses depart daily from Galatas (€8, two hours) and can drop you off at the ancient site, but you should check the return times and ongoing connections.

HYDRA ΥΔΡΑ

pop 2900

Hydra (*ee-dhr-ah*) is still the catwalk queen of the Saronics. Details matter here, such as the absence of ugly overhead power lines from the town and of cars and scooters from the streets. The island has long attracted throngs of tourists, cruise passengers and yacht crews, and the occasional celebrity on their way to hidden holiday homes among the tiers of picturesque buildings that rise above the harbour. Beyond the town, there are corners of lovely wilderness, accessible to those willing to hike – usually uphill.

Inflated prices sometimes go with the Hydra experience, but there are affordable gems among the sleeping and eating options and there are serene corners outside the harbour area and the main tributary streets.

History

Hydra experienced the light hand of an overstretched Ottoman Empire. Consequently the island prospered mightily after enterprising Greeks from the Peloponnese settled here to escape the more repressive Turkish regime of the mainland. Hydra was ever barren and waterless, so the new settlers began building boats and took to the thin line between maritime commerce and piracy with enthusiasm. By the 19th century, Hydra was a maritime power, earning itself the ambivalent sobriquet of 'Little England'. Wealthy shipping merchants built most of the town's grand old mansions and Hydra supplied 130 ships for a blockade of the Turks during the Greek War of Independence. The island bred such leaders as Georgios Koundouriotis, who was president of Greece's national assembly from 1822 to 1827, and Admiral Andreas Miaoulis, who commanded the Greek fleet. Streets and squares all over Greece are named after these two champions.

Getting There & Away

At the time of writing only fast ferries linked Hydra with Poros, Piraeus and Spetses, and Ermioni and Porto Heli on the mainland. For details see Island Hopping (p751). You can buy tickets from **Idreoniki Travel** (☎ 22980 54007; www.hydreoniki.gr), opposite the ferry dock.

Getting Around

In summer, there are caïques from Hydra Town to the island's beaches. There are also **water taxis** (☎ 22980 53690), which will take you anywhere you like; examples are Kamini (€11) and Vlyhos (€15).

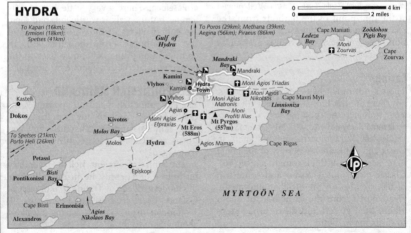

The donkey owners clustered around the port charge around €16 to transport your bags to your hotel.

HYDRA TOWN

pop 2526

Hydra Town's red-roofed houses with their pastel-painted walls form a pretty amphitheatre behind the harbour, where the cobbled quayside is a colourful throng of ambling pedestrians, mules and donkeys. The mules and donkeys are the main means of heavy transport; they load the air with a reassuring bouquet of genuine earthiness. Fast ferries with imperious beaked bows glide frequently through the harbour gaps and smart yachts come and go alongside the quay in an absolute froth of bad rope management. Behind the harbour, steep steps and alleyways paved with multicoloured stone lead ever upwards to the rock-studded slopes of old Hydra. The harbour front and the streets leading inland are crammed with cafes and craft and souvenir shops.

Information

There is no tourist office on Hydra but a useful website is www.hydradirect.com.

There is an ATM at Saitis Tours on the harbour front. The **post office** (☎ 7.30am-2pm Mon-Fri) is opposite the fish market on a small side street that runs between the Bank Emporiki and the National Bank of Greece, both of which have ATMs. The **tourist police** (☎ 22980 52205; Votsi; ☎ mid-May–Sep) can be found sharing an office with the regular police.

You can check email at the **Flamingo Internet Café** (☎ 22980 53485; Tombazi; per 30min €3; ☎ 8.30am-late).

There are loos of last resort alongside the fish market.

Sights & Activities

Hydra's star cultural attraction is the handsome **Lazaros Koundouriotis Historical Mansion** (☎ 22980 52421; nhmuseum@tee.gr; adult/concession €4/2; ☎ 9am-4pm Tue-Sun), an ochre-coloured building sitting high above the harbour. It was the home of one of the major players in the Greek independence struggle and is a fine example of late-18th-century traditional architecture. The main reception rooms of the 2nd floor have been restored to their full. The mansion is quite a steep hike up steps from the southwest corner of the harbour.

On the eastern arm of the harbour is the **Historical Archives Museum of Hydra** (☎ 22980 52355; www.iamy.gr; adult/child €5/3; ☎ 9am-4pm & 7.30-9.30pm Jul-Oct, 9am-4pm Nov-Jun). It houses a collection of portraits and naval oddments, with an emphasis on the island's role in the War of Independence.

The **Ecclesiastical Museum** (☎ 22980 54071; admission €2; ☎ 10am-5pm Tue-Sun Apr-Oct) is housed in the peaceful complex of the Monastery of the Assumption of the Virgin Mary on the harbour front. It contains a collection of icons and assorted religious paraphernalia.

Kallianos Diving Center (☎ 27540 31095; www.kallianosdivingcenter.gr) is based at the private island of Kapari. Activities include a two-dive outing for €80 with full equipment supplied, or €125 with instructor. There's a monthly diving-with-dolphins trip starting at €200, with a 50% refund if the dolphins don't turn up. PADI courses are also available. The centre does pick-up and return to Hydra, and non-divers can also take the trip to Kapari (€15).

Festivals & Events

Hydriots celebrate their contribution to the War of Independence in late June by staging an exuberant mock battle in Hydra harbour during the **Miaoulia Festival**, held in honour of Admiral Miaoulis. Much carousing, feasting and fireworks accompany it. **Easter** is also celebrated in colourful fashion.

Sleeping

Accommodation in Hydra is of a generally high standard. You pay accordingly, but there are also some very reasonably priced places of quality. The prices shown are for high season, which in Hydra means weekends as well as July and August. Most owners will meet you at the harbour if pre-arranged and will organise luggage transfer.

BUDGET & MIDRANGE

Pension Erofili (☎ /fax 22980 54049; www.pensionerofili.gr; Tombazi; s/d/tr €45/55/65; ☎) Tucked away in the inner town, these pleasant, unassuming rooms are a decent budget deal for Hydra. The young family owners add a friendly sparkle. It also has a large studio room with private kitchen. During July and August you can get breakfast for €7.

Bahia (☎ 22980 52257, 6977462852; Oikonomou; s/d €55/60; ☎) These decent rooms are above a clothes and jewellery shop called Alexander. They have cooking facilities.

Glaros (☎ 22980 53679, 6940748446; s/d €50/60; ❄) These simple, well-kept rooms are in a very convenient position down an alleyway just back from the harbour front.

Pension Loulos (☎ 22980 52411/6972699381; s/d/tr €50/60/70; ❄) A grand old house brimming with seagoing history and tradition. Loulos' eponymous owner was a noted sea captain and his rooms have old-fashioned charm, but with every amenity including tea- and coffee-making facilities. Most have glorious views. The roof terrace is sunset heaven. The pension is a few minutes inland on the slopes above Tombazi.

our pick **Nereids** (☎ 22980 52875; www.nereids -hydra.com; Tombazi; s/d €60/65; ❄ 🤖). These lovely rooms represent exceptional value and quality. They are spacious, peaceful and have beautiful decor and open views to Hydra's rocky heights. Nereids is a few minutes' walk up Tombazi from the harbour, but it's worth it.

Pension Alkionides (☎ 22980 54055; www .alkionidespension.com; off Oikonomou; d/tr €60/75, ste €100-120; ❄) The Alkionides is in a peaceful cul-de-sac and has a pretty courtyard. Rooms are smart, though some are quite small, and they have tea- and coffee-making facilities.

TOP END

Hotel Leto (☎ 22980 53385; www.letohydra.gr; off Miaouli; s €123-137, d €160-180, tr €197-220; ❄ 🖥 🤖 ♿) Stylish, modernist decor, spacious rooms and a relaxing atmosphere make Leto one of Hydra's classiest hotels. The price ranges depend on such variables as room size, balconies and floor location. There's one fully equipped room for disabled use. Buffet breakfast is included and there's a fitness studio, sauna and bar.

Angelica Hotel (☎ 22980 53202; www.angelica.gr; Miaouli; s €130-160, d €150-180, tr €220; ❄ 🤖) An attractive boutique hotel in a quiet location, the Angelica has comfortable, luxurious rooms, all individually themed and named after Greek gods. There's a minipool and Jacuzzi and relaxing public areas.

Hotel Orloff (☎ 22980 52564; www.orloff.gr; Rafalia; s/d incl breakfast €160/200; ❄ 🤖) There's a marvellous sense of historic Hydra without stuffiness at this beautiful, old mansion. A Russian admiral of the 18th century gave his name to the original house. The comfortable rooms have elegant furnishings and there's a lovely garden in which buffet breakfast is served. It's family-run and the welcome is warm.

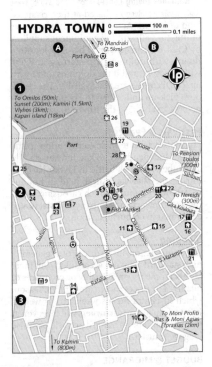

HYDRA TOWN

Eating

You'll pay extra for basic coffee at some of the harbour-front cafes, but lively people-watching comes with it.

Creperie Mikro Café (☎ 22980 52335; Oikonomou; meals €3-7.20; ⏰ 10am-1am) A handy budget option, just inland from the harbour, this little place offers sandwiches and hamburgers as well as crepes.

Isalos Café (☎ 22980 53845; snacks €3.50-7) A good bet right by the ferry dock, Isalos offers decent snacks and drinks at reasonable prices.

ourpick Taverna Gitoniko (Manolis & Christina; ☎ 22980 53615; Spilios Haramis; mains €4-9) Greek atmosphere with Greek courtesy is the tone at this long-established place that is better known by the first names of its owners, a sure sign of continuity and family tradition. Classic Greek favourites, such as zucchini balls, spinach pies and dolmadhes are tops, as is the local lamb. The family was in the process of building a new taverna on Tombazi, which should be open by the time you read this.

Paradosiako (☎ 22980 54155; Tombazi; mains €7-15) This little streetside *mezedhopoleio* (restaurant specialising in mezedhes) is traditional Greek personified. Classic pies come in cheese, beef, shrimp and vegie varieties and favourite mezedhes are plentiful. A bottle of decent wine starts at about €12, but the house wine at €7 is just fine.

Bratsera (☎ 22980 52794; Tombazi; mains €9-20; ⏰ 1-4pm & 8-11pm Apr-Oct) The in-house restaurant by the pool of the Bratsera Hotel makes imaginative use of fresh local ingredients and sources the best cuts of meat. There's even fresh salmon when available. The wine list is equally selective.

Sunset (☎ 22980 52067; mains €9-22) Famed by name alone for its splendid location a short distance to the west of the harbour, the Sunset throws in live Greek music in summer to accompany such longstanding favourite starters as mackerel salad. Local fish are well prepared with mains such as grilled sea bream marinated in herbs, and meat and pasta dishes are also done with flair.

There's a supermarket, fruit shop and fish market just inland, mid-harbour side. O Fournos is an aroma-rich bakery next to the Pirate club across the alleyway.

Drinking & Entertainment

Hydra's harbour front revs up at night, when daytime cafes become hot music bars. Most bars are at the far end of the harbour, where places like **Pirate** (☎ 22980 52711) and **Saronikos** (☎ 22980 52589) keep going until dawn. Most play lounge sounds by day; at night Pirate plays rock, while Saronikos goes more for Greek pop.

Notionally closing in the 'early hours', the definitely red-hot **Red** (☎ 6974421398) has been known to keep things rocking for days at a time. It plays exuberant Greek sounds but also whatever suits the crowd.

A few blocks inland from the harbour front the more chilled **Amalou** (☎ 6977461357; Tombazi) does a lively line in cocktails and smoothies to a Latin rhythm. About 100m beyond the western edge of the harbour is the waterside **Omilos** (☎ 22980 53800), a chic daytime cafe and night-time dance venue.

AROUND HYDRA

Hydra's stony, arid interior, now with some regenerating pine woods, makes a robust but peaceful contrast to the clamour of the quayside.

An unbeatable Hydra experience is the long haul up to **Moni Profiti Ilias**, but you need to be fit and willing. Starting up Mialou from the harbour, it's a tough hour or more through relentless zigzags and pine trees. Just follow your nose and the occasional timely sign. You can visit the **Moni Agias Efpraxias** just before reaching Profiti Ilias itself. The latter is a wonderful complex of central church within a rectangular walled compound. Inside are beautiful icons and serenity; it's worth the hike.

Other paths lead to **Mt Eros** (588m), the island's highest point, and also along the island spine to east and west, but you need advanced route-finding skills or reliable walking directions from knowledgeable locals. A useful map for walkers is the *Hydra* map in the Anavasi Central Aegean series (www.mount ains.gr).

Hydra's shortcoming – or blessing – is its lack of appealing beaches to draw the crowds. There are a few strands all the same. **Kamini**, about a 1.5km walk along the coastal path from the port, has rocks and a very small pebble beach. **Vlyhos**, a 1.5km walk further on from Kamini, is an attractive village offering a slightly larger pebble beach, two tavernas and a ruined 19th-century stone bridge.

A path leads east from the port to the reasonable pebble beach at **Mandraki**, 2.5km away. **Bisti Bay**, 8km away on the south-western side of the island, has a decent pebble beach.

SARONIC GULF ISLANDS

SPETSES ΣΠΕΤΣΕΣ

pop 4000

Spetses is only a few kilometres across the sea from the mainland Peloponnese, but there is a stronger sense of island Greece here than in other Saronic Gulf destinations. The novelist John Fowles used the island as the setting for his powerful book *The Magus* (1965). His portrayal of lascivious heat and pine-scented seduction probably sent many a northern European hotfooting it to the beautiful south on their first Greek-island idyll.

Long before Fowles' day, Spetses, like Hydra, grew wealthy from shipbuilding. Island captains busted the British blockade during the Napoleonic Wars and refitted their ships to join the Greek fleet during the War of Independence. In the process they immortalised one local woman, albeit from a Hydriot family, the formidable Laskarina Bouboulina, ship's commander and fearless fighter (see p370).

The island's forests of Aleppo pine, a legacy of the far-sighted and wealthy philanthropist Sotirios Anargyrios, have been devastated by fires several times in the past 20 years. Many trees survive, however, and burnt areas are slowly recovering. Anargyrios was born on Spetses in 1848 and emigrated to the USA, returning in 1914 as a very rich man. He bought two-thirds of the then largely barren island and planted the pines that stand today. Anargyrios also financed the Spetses road network and commissioned many of Spetses Town's grand buildings.

Getting There & Away

At the time of writing only fast ferries linked Spetses with Hydra, Poros and Piraeus, and Ermioni and Porto Heli on the mainland. For details see Island Hopping (p762).

Ferry tickets can be bought at **Bardakos Tours** (☎ 22980 73141, Dapia Harbour) and at **Mimoza Travel** (☎ 22980 75170), a few metres to the left of the ferry quay.

In summer, there are caïques from the harbour to Kosta on the mainland (€4 per person). The larger car ferry, Katerina Star, costs €1 per person.

Getting Around

Spetses has two bus routes that start over the Easter period, then continue, depending on demand, until the end of May. From June to September there are three or four buses daily. The routes are from Plateia Agiou Mama in Spetses Town to Agii Anargyri (€3, 40 minutes), travelling via Agia Marina and Xylokeriza. All departure times are displayed on a board by the bus stop. There are also hourly buses in summer (every two hours in winter) to Ligoneri (€1.40). They leave from in front of the Hotel Possidonion, the monumental old building (being renovated at the time of writing) on the seafront just to the northwest of Dapia Harbour.

Only locally owned vehicles are allowed on Spetses. There are not too many of these, although the number is increasing. Hundreds of noisy scooters and motorbikes more than make up for it. There are motorbike-hire shops everywhere; rental is around €16 to €25 per day.

For quieter pedal power, there are sturdy bikes for hire (€6 per day) to suit all ages, including baby seats, from the excellent **Bike Center** (☎ 22980 74143; 9.30am-9.30pm) behind the fish market.

Water taxis (☎ 22980 72072; Dapia Harbour) leave from the quay opposite the Bardakos Tours office. Fares are displayed on a board. One-way fares are €16 to the Old Harbour, €30 to Agia Marina, €63 to Agii Anargyri, €45 to mainland Porto Heli, and €20 to Kosta. A round trip of the island costs €80. Fares are per trip, not per person. Add 50% to the price from midnight to 6am.

SPETSES TOWN

pop 3550

Spetses Town lies on the northeast coast of the island. It straggles a lengthy waterfront and its houses rise steeply from behind the main Dapia Harbour.

There's evidence of an early Helladic settlement near the Old Harbour (Palio Limani) and at Dapia. Roman and Byzantine remains have been found in the area behind Moni Agios Nikolaos, halfway between the two.

From the 10th century Spetses is thought to have been uninhabited for almost 600 years, until the arrival of Albanian refugees fleeing the fighting between Turks and Venetians in the 16th century.

The Dapia district has a few impressive *arhontika* (old mansions). The main part of town is given over to chic tourist shops and cafes. There are some rich ironies, not least the

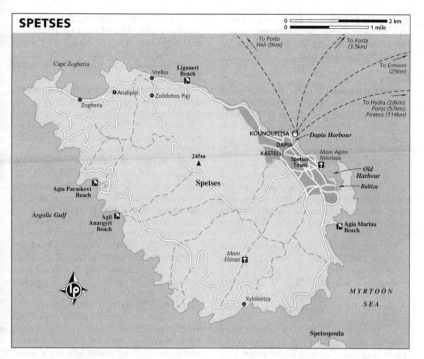

SPETSES

To Porto Heli (9km)
To Kosta (3.5km)
To Ermioni (25km)
To Hydra (28km); Poros (57km); Piraeus (114km)

Cape Zogheria
Vrellas
Ligoneri Beach
Analipsis
Zoödohos Pigí
Zogheria
KOUNOUPITSA
DAPIA
Dapia Harbour
KASTELI
Moni Agios Nikolaos
Spetses Town
Old Harbour
Baltiza
245m
Spetses
Agia Paraskevi Beach
Agia Marina Beach
Argolic Gulf
Agii Anargyri Beach
Moni Elonas
MYRTOÖN SEA
Xylokeriza
Spetsopoula

juxtaposition of the cheerfully whiffy fish market with fashion shops selling such fragrant lines as Danoff, Clink, Zulu and Trussardi.

The town is awash with noisy motorbikes, scooters and quad bikes. Take great care at sharp corners.

A kilometre or so along the eastern harbour front takes you to the attractive Old Harbour (Palio Limani), the Church of Agios Nikolaos, and Baltiza yacht anchorage and boatbuilding area.

Orientation

At Dapia Harbour the quay serves both ferries and hydrofoils. A left turn at the end of the quay, facing in, leads east through Plateia Limenarhiou and along the harbour-front road of Sotiriou Anargyriou, past the town beach and Plateia Agiou Mama. Beyond here, the seafront road continues to the Old Harbour and on to Baltiza.

From the inner left-hand corner of Plateia Limenarhiou a narrow lane leads left to Plateia Orologiou (Clocktower Sq), which is enclosed by cafes, tavernas and shops and is overlooked by its namesake clock tower.

The narrow 'Main Street' climbs directly inland from the back of Plateia Limenarhiou.

From the north side of the harbour a road leads through the harbour-front Kounoupitsa area to become the road that runs northwest to Ligoneri.

Information

There is no tourist office on Spetses. A useful website is www.spetsesdirect.com.

Alpha Bank at Dapia Harbour has an ATM and there are others outside Alasia Travel on the waterfront and the Bank of Piraeus at the entrance to Plateia Orologiou. There are ATMs just up to the right along the harbour terrace.

The **port police** (☎ 22980 72245), **tourist police** (☎ 22980 73100; ☺ mid-May–Sep) and OTE (telephone office) all share the same building just beyond the Dapia Harbour upper terrace.

1800 Net Café (☎ 22980 29498; near Hotel Possidonion; per hr €3; ☺ 9am-midnight; ☎) Wi-fi is free to customers.

Mimoza Travel (☎ 22980 75170; mimoza-kent@aig .forthnet.gr) On the harbour front just past Plateia Limenarhiou; can help with accommodation and other services.

Newsagent (☎ 22980 73028; Main St) Impressive selection of newspapers and magazines in numerous languages.

Post office (⏲ 7.30am-2pm Mon-Fri) On the street running behind the seafront hotels.

Sights

The **Spetses museum** (☎ 22980 72994; adult/concession €3/2; ⏲ 8.30am-2.30pm Tue-Sun) is housed in the old mansion of Hatzigiannis Mexis (1754–1844), a shipowner who became the island's first governor. The collections on view are not extensive, but are fascinating. They include traditional costumes, folkloric items and portraits of the island's founding fathers. Most have Greek and English annotations. To reach the museum, go straight up from the top left-hand corner of Plateia Orologiou, turn left at the junction and then right, then follow the signposts.

The mansion of Spetses' famous daughter, the 19th-century seagoer Laskarina Bouboulina, has been converted into **Bouboulina's Museum** (☎ 22980 72416; www .bouboulinamuseum-spetses.gr; adult/concession/child €5/3/1; ⏲ 10am-9pm Mar-Oct). Times may vary. Entry is via a 40-minute guided tour, which run every 45 minutes. Billboards around town advertise the starting times of tours and in which language. To reach the museum, turn left at the end of the line of cafes on the Dapia Harbour terrace.

There's an impressive **statue** of Bouboulina on the harbour front opposite the Hotel Possidonion. For more details about Bouboulina, see A Female Force (p44).

The **Old Harbour** (Palio Limani), which is about a 1.5km stroll from Dapia, is usually filled with a jumble of commercial vessels. A bit further on is **Baltiza**, a sheltered inlet crammed with all types of craft, from half-built caïques to working fishing boats, minor-league private cruisers and yachts.

Sleeping

Spetses has a decent mix of sleeping options and most places offer discounts outside August.

Klimis Hotel (☎ 22980 72334; klimishotel@hol.gr; s/d/tr €40/65/80; 🅿) Serviceable rooms at this standard waterfront hotel are as cheap as you'll get in Spetses. The ground floor sports a cafe-bar and patisserie.

Hotel Kamelia (☎ 6939095513; s/d €50/55; ⏲ Apr-Sep; 🅿) These fresh, airy rooms are good value. The hotel is tucked away from the busy sea-

front. Head along the lane to the right of the kiosk in Plateia Agiou Mama for 100m, then bear right before a little bridge. In another 100m or so, go right along a narrow lane to a quiet square, where the Kamelia lies drenched in bougainvillea.

Villa Christina Hotel (☎ 22980 72218; www.villa christinahotel.com; s/d/tr incl breakfast €50/70/85; 🅿) Located about 200m uphill on the main road inland from the harbour, these well-kept rooms are tucked away from the worst traffic noise. There's a lovely garden area.

Villa Marina (☎ 22980 72646; www.villamarina spetses.com; off Plateia Agiou Mama; s/d €60/75; 🅿) Under new ownership, this handy hotel was being refurbished at the time of writing. It's just to the right of Plateia Agiou Mama. All rooms have refrigerators and there is a well-equipped communal kitchen downstairs.

Kastro (☎ 22980 75319; www.kastro-margarita.com; s/d/tr/apt incl breakfast €90/100/120/200; 🅿 🖥) These studios and apartments are in a choice position close to the centre, yet within a private and quiet complex. Decor and furnishings combine traditional style with modern amenities and there are attractive public areas. There are discounts in low season. Head west along the harbour front for several hundred metres and Kastro is along a short lane to the left.

Nissia (☎ 22980 75000; www.nissia.gr; studio incl breakfast €270-365; ⏲ Apr-Oct; 🅿 🖥 🛜 🖥) Nissia is an exclusive oasis of peace and quiet in stylish surroundings. Studios are arranged around a spacious courtyard, complete with swimming pool and soothing greenery. It's about 300m northwest of Dapia Harbour. The hotel has a restaurant (mains €8 to €26).

Eating

Cockatoo (☎ 22980 74085; mains €1.50-7; ⏲ noon-midnight) At this budget base, you can get a souvlaki for €2, a Greek salad for €5 or a takeaway chicken for €12. Head left from the top of Plateia Limenarhiou, and then right.

Taverna O Lazaros (☎ 22980 72600; mains €5-9) A hike of about 400m up Main St from the harbour sharpens your appetite for Greek standards at this very local taverna where the goat in lemon sauce is still the favourite and the house retsina complements it all. Open evenings only.

our pick **Akrogialia** (☎ 22980 74749; Kounoupitsa; mains €9-17; ⏲ 9am-midnight) This excellent restaurant is on the Kounoupitsa harbour front and matches its great food with friendly service and

---

PEDAL POWER

Spetses' circular coast road can be enjoyed astride motorbike or scooter, but it cries out for a cycle – an antidote to all that fine Greek food. The road is satisfyingly sinuous and scenic and the circuit hugs the coast for 26km. Which way to go is definitely arguable. Locals advise anti-clockwise to get some hefty climbs behind you, but going clockwise leaves some well-earned freewheeling at the end of the trip. Why not do it twice, both ways, and get really fit and virtu-ous? You can bounce off all of the island's beaches on the way.

The interior of the island is crisscrossed with quieter roads and woodland tracks and you can veer off for some more strenuous uphill off-roading into the lovely wooded hills of the island. (But take a decent map and compass with you.)

Bike Center (☎ 22980 74143; ⊙ 9.30am-9.30pm) behind the fish market hires out bikes for €6 per day.

---

a bright setting. There are tasty options such as oven-baked *melitzana rolos* (eggplant with cream cheese and walnuts). Fish is by the kilo but you can enjoy a terrific fish risotto for €17 or settle for a choice steak; all accompanied by a thoughtful and classy selection of Greek wines. Breakfast, coffee and lunch are also available.

To Nero tis Agapis (☎ 22980 74009; Kounoupitsa; mains €12-19) The sweetly named 'Water of Life' is a sister restaurant to Tarsanas (below) but offers meat as well as fish dishes. The cray-fish tagliatelle is worth every bite, as is the *zarzuela* (fish stew). Meat-eaters can settle for pork fillet in a cream sauce, and there's a selection of creative salads. It's located about 1km northwest of Dapia Harbour.

Tarsanas (☎ 22980 74490; Old Harbour; mains €17-26) A hugely popular *psarotaverna* (fish taverna), this family-run place deals almost exclusively in fish dishes using fresh local fish when avail-able. It can be pricey, but the fish soup at €6 alone is a delight and other starters such as anchovies marinated with lemon start at about €4.50. For mains try the Tarsanas special: a seafood *saganaki* (fried cheese) for €17.

Self-caterers will find everything they need at **Kritikos Supermarket** (☎ 22980 74361; Kentriki Agora), next to the fish market on the harbour front. The entrance is along a covered pas-sageway. There's also a fruit and vegetable shop next to the newsagents in Main St.

Drinking & Entertainment

Bar Spetsa (☎ 22980 74131; ⊙ 8pm-late) One of life's great little bars, this Spetses institu-tion never loses its integrity and its easygo-ing atmosphere. The music is guaranteed to stir memories for just about everyone with a soul. The bar is 50m beyond Plateia Agiou Mama on the road to the right of the kiosk.

Balconi Wine Bar (☎ 22980 72594; Sotiriou Anargyriou; ⊙ 10.30am-3am May-Oct, 7pm-3am Nov-Apr) Paying stylish homage to cocktails, wine and well-sourced whisky, this smart place next to the seafront Stelios Hotel features classical music by day and subtle jazz riffs by night.

Music and dance venues are concentrated at the Old Harbour–Baltiza area and include Fortezza and Mourayo, which play Greek pop, Tsitsiano for traditional Greek and the big dance venue Baltiza, which may have a cover charge.

AROUND SPETSES

Spetses' coastline is speckled with numerous coves with small, pine-shaded beaches. The beach at **Ligoneri**, about 2.5km west of town, is easily reached by bus. The long, pebbly **Agia Paraskevi** and the sandier **Agii Anargyri** on the southwest coast have good, albeit crowded, beaches; both have water sports of every de-scription. **Agia Marina**, about 2km southeast of Spetses Town, is a small resort with a beach that gets crowded.

A surfaced road skirts the entire coastline, so a scooter is the ideal way to explore the is-land. Or for a healthy alternative take a bicycle (see boxed text, above).

Cyclades Κυκλάδες

The Cyclades (kih-*klah*-dhez) lie at the deep blue heart of the Aegean and are so named because they form a *kyklos* (circle) around the island of Delos, the most compelling ancient site in the Aegean. The circle is not entirely symmetrical, but the symbolism is what matters. During archaic times Delos was the sacred equivalent of the Vatican and commercially was the treasure house, or Wall Street, of the Greek world.

Today, the Cyclades are the symbol of what dream islands should be: white cubist houses, golden beaches, olive groves, pine forests, herb-strewn mountain slopes and terraced valleys. Throw in a dash of hedonism and a vivid culture, and the Greek island dream can become reality.

Other realities are more down to earth, at least for native islanders, who have often struggled for a living through centuries of deprivation. Beneath the tourism gloss, many still raise livestock and grow food on reluctant soil, or chase a diminishing supply of fish from seas that are regularly rough and dangerous. Winters are often grey, bleak and unforgiving.

The Cyclades range from big fertile Naxos, with its craggy mountains and landlocked valleys, to the tiny outliers of Donousa and Koufinissi, where the sea dominates, with attitude, on every side. The beaches of Mykonos and Ios are awash with sun-lounger society and raucous diversions; their main towns seethe with commercialism. Iconic islands such as Santorini are world destinations for the fashion conscious and the cruise-ship aficionado. Other islands, such as Andros, Amorgos and Sifnos, have kept tourism to a more sedate scale, while tiny retreats such as Iraklia and Anafi are remote jewels in the Cycladean circle.

HIGHLIGHTS

- **Ancient Glories** Exploring the wonderful archaeological sites of Delos (p395) and Ancient Thira (p436)
- **Cycladic Cuisine** Being spoiled for choice by modern Greek cuisine on Mykonos (p386) and Paros (p397)
- **Off Track** Veering off to the remoter islands of the Little Cyclades (p414) and Anafi (p438)
- **Night Play** Partying until dawn on Mykonos (p386) and Ios (p423)
- **Sunset Serenade** Viewing spectacular sunsets from Fira and Oia on Santorini (p427)
- **High Life** Hiking through the mountains of Naxos (p406) and Andros (p374)

- ★ Andros
- ★ Mykonos
- Delos
- Paros ★
- Naxos ★
- Little Cyclades
- ★ Ios
- Santorini (Ancient Thira)
- ★ Anafi

- POPULATION: 109,814
- AREA: 2429 SQ KM

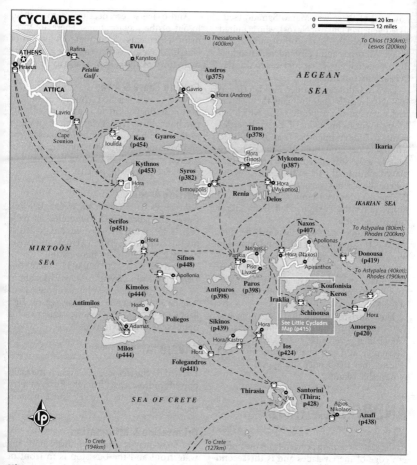

History

The Cyclades are said to have been inhabited since at least 7000 BC. Around 3000 BC there emerged a cohesive Cycladic civilisation that was bound together by seagoing commerce and exchange. During the Early Cycladic period (3000–2000 BC) the tiny but distinctive Cycladic marble figurines, mainly stylised representations of the naked female form, were sculpted.

In the Middle Cycladic period (2000–1500 BC) many of the islands were occupied by the Minoans – at Akrotiri, on Santorini, a Minoan town has been excavated. At the beginning of the Late Cycladic period (1500–1100 BC) the archipelago came under the influence of the Mycenaeans, who were followed by the Dorians in the 8th century BC.

By the middle of the 5th century BC the islands were members of a fully fledged Athenian empire. In the Hellenistic era (323–146 BC) they were controlled by Egypt's Ptolemaic dynasties and then by the Macedonians. In 146 BC the islands became a Roman province and lucrative trade links were established with many parts of the Mediterranean.

The division of the Roman Empire in AD 395 resulted in the Cyclades being ruled from Byzantium (Constantinople), but after the fall of Byzantium in 1204, they came under a Venetian governance that doled out the islands to opportunistic aristocrats. The most powerful of these was Marco Sanudo (self-styled Venetian Duke of Naxos), who acquired Naxos, Paros, Ios, Santorini, Anafi, Sifnos, Milos, Amorgos and Folegandros, introducing a Venetian gloss that survives to this day in island architecture.

The Cyclades came under Turkish rule in 1537. Neglected by the Ottomans, they became backwaters prone to pirate raids, which led to frequent relocation of coastal settlements to hidden inland sites and, finally, to wholesale depopulation. In 1563 only five islands were still inhabited. The Cyclades played a minimal part in the Greek War of Independence, but became havens for people fleeing from other islands where insurrections against the Turks had led to massacres and persecution.

Italian forces occupied the Cyclades during WWII. After the war the islands emerged more economically deprived than ever. Many islanders lived in deep poverty; many more gave up the struggle and headed to the mainland, or to America and Australia, in search of work.

The tourism boom that began in the 1970s revived the fortunes of the Cyclades. The challenge remains, however, of finding alternative and sustainable economies that will not mar the beauty and appeal of these remarkable islands.

ANDROS ΑΝΔΡΟΣ

pop 10,112

Andros sits dreaming peacefully on the northern edge of the Cyclades and is the second largest of the group, after Naxos. It makes for a rewarding escape for those who want a less tourist-oriented world.

Satisfyingly remote in places, Andros is a mix of bare mountains and green valleys where tall cypresses, like green tapers, rise above smaller trees. Neoclassical mansions and Venetian tower-houses contrast with the rough unpainted stonework of farm buildings and patterned dovecotes. Handsome stone walls, made up of large slabs with smaller boulders packed between them, lock the sometimes friable hill slopes in place. A network of footpaths, many of them stepped and cobbled, is also maintained, and the island has a fascinating archaeological and cultural heritage.

Andros has several beaches, many of them in out-of-the way locations. There are three main settlements: the unpretentious port of Gavrio, the resort of Batsi and the handsome main town of Hora, known also as Andros.

Getting There & Away

Andros is best reached from the mainland port of Rafina, 66km away and a reasonable two hours by ferry. Regular ferries run south to the neighbouring islands of Tinos, Syros and Mykonos, from where onward links to the rest of the archipelago can be made. For details see Island Hopping (p746).

Getting Around

Nine buses daily (fewer on weekends) link Gavrio and Hora (€3.80, 55 minutes) via Batsi (€2.10, 15 minutes). Schedules are posted at the bus stops in Gavrio and Hora; otherwise, call ☎ 22820 22316 for information.

A **taxi** (☎ Gavrio 22820 71171, Batsi 22820 41081, Hora 22820 22171) from Gavrio to Batsi costs about €8 and to Hora, €30. Car hire is about €35 in August and about €25 in the low season. **Euro Rent A Car** (☎ 22820 72440; www.rentacareuro.com) is opposite the Gavrio ferry quay.

GAVRIO ΓΑΥΡΙΟ

pop 798

Located on the west coast, Gavrio is the main port of Andros. Apart from the flurry of ferry arrivals, it is pretty low key and can seem touch drab.

Orientation & Information

The ferry quay is situated midway along the waterfront and the bus stop is in front of it. The post office is 150m to the left as you leave the ferry quay. There's an ATM outside Kyklades Travel and there's a bank with ATM on the middle of the waterfront.

Kyklades Travel (☎ 22820 72363; lasia@otenet .gr) A helpful office opposite the ferry quay with another office about 50m to the right next to the Agricultural Bank of Greece. They sell ferry tickets and can arrange accommodation.

Port police (☎ 22820 71213) Located on the waterfront.

Sleeping & Eating

Andros Camping (☎ 22820 71444; www.campingandros .gr; adult/child/tent €6.50/3/3; **P** **☛**) Located about 400m behind the harbour front, this pleasant camping site is shaded by trees. You can rent a small tent for €6 or a large one for €10.

ANDROS

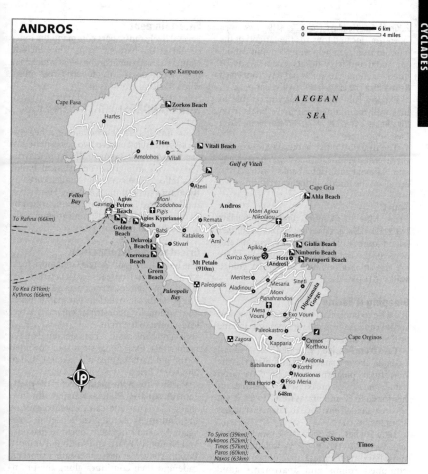

```
0 ————————— 6 km
0 ————————— 4 miles
```

Cape Kampanos

Cape Fasa

Hartes

Zorkos Beach

AEGEAN

SEA

▲ 716m
Amolohos   Vitali

Vitali Beach

Gulf of Vitali

Ateni

Fellos Bay

Gavrio   Agios Petros Beach

Moni Zoödohou Pigis

Andros

Moni Agiou Nikolaou

Cape Gria

Ahla Beach

To Rafina (66km)

Agios Kyprianos Beach

Golden Beach

Batsi

Delavoia Beach

Remata

Katakilos

Arni

Stenies

Gialia Beach

Nimborio Beach

Paraporti Beach

Apikia

To Kea (31km); Kythnos (66km)

Anerousa Beach

Green Beach

Stivari

Mt Petalo (910m)

Sariza Spring

Hora (Andros)

Paleopolis

Menites

Mesaria

Aladinou

Sineti

Moni Panahrandou

Dipotamata Gorge

Paleopolis Bay

Mesa Vouni

Exo Vouni

Paleokastro

Cape Orginos

Zagora

Kapparia

Ormos Korthiou

Batsilianos

Aidonia

Korthi

Mousionas

Pera Horio

Piso Meria

648m

To Syros (39km);
Mykonos (52km);
Tinos (57km);
Paros (60km);
Naxos (63km)

Cape Steno

Tinos

Ostria Studios (☎ 22820 71551; www.ostria
-studios.gr; s/d/apt €60/70/85; P ⟨P⟩ ⟨❄⟩ ⟨▯⟩) Rooms at
this well-located place, located about 300m
along the Batsi road, are getting a bit worn,
but they are spacious, have cooking facilities
and stand in a pleasant terraced complex.

To Konaki (☎ 22820 71733; mains €5-14) Located
about 50m to the left of the ferry quay, To
Konaki has a healthy selection of fish, meat
and vegetarian dishes with a local flavour.
The cod in garlic sauce is a speciality.

Sails (☎ 22820 71333; mains €7-22) An excellent
ouzerie (place that serves ouzo and light
snacks) and *psarotaverna* (fish tavern), Sails
usually has some good locally caught fish.
You'll pay about €22 for a decent-sized sea

bream. There are chicken and pork dishes
as well.

BATSI ΜΠΑΤΣΙ
pop 971

Easy-going yet upbeat, Batsi is the island's
main resort. It has a small yacht marina that
brings a bit of seaborne colour in summer.
The resort lies 7km south of Gavrio on the
inner curve of a handsome bay. A sandy
beach on the north side merges eventually
with a harbour front promenade backed by a
colourful swath of cafes, tavernas and shops.
There's a dusty car park across the road from
the beach and a smaller one at the far end of
the harbour front.

CYCLADES

Greek Sun Holidays (☎ 22820 41198; www.andros -greece.com), located towards the far end of the harbour front, can help with accommodation, car rental and ferry tickets. Scooters can be hired for about €16 to €24 per day from **Dino's Rent-a-Bike** (☎ 22820 42169), by the car park.

During July and August you're able to hire well-maintained self-drive boats from **Riva Boats** (☎ 22820 24412, 6974460330) in Hora (see opposite).

The tiny post office is tucked away beside the taverna opposite the bus stop. The taxi rank and National and Alpha banks (with ATMs) are all on the middle of the waterfront.

Tours

From May to October, **Greek Sun Holidays** (☎ 22820 41198; greeksun@travelling.gr) organises island tours (€20) that take in Paleopolis and some of the island's loveliest villages. There are also small-group half- or full-day guided walks (€18).

Sleeping & Eating

It's wise to book accommodation well ahead for July and August and for weekends in June and September.

Cavo D'ora Pension (☎ 22820 41766; s/d €25/45) Located above a snack bar and pizzeria, the handful of pleasant rooms here are good value. You can get breakfast for €5.50, mezedhes for €6 to €7 and pizzas for €7 to €9. It's at the tree-shaded entrance to town, just across from the beach.

Likio Studios (☎ 22820 41050; www.likiostudios .gr; s/d/apt €64/80/130; [P] [X]) A welcoming atmosphere makes these spacious and well-equipped rooms and apartments amid a peaceful flower-filled garden a great choice. It is about 150m inland from Dino's Rent-a-Bike.

Oti Kalo (☎ 22820 41287; mains €5-9) The name means 'everything good', and it's no idle boast. Specialising in the Andros speciality, *froutalia* (spicy sausage and potato omelette), while other mains include meat and fish as well as pasta.

Stamatis Taverna (☎ 22820 41283; mains €6.50-16) A well-run taverna on the terrace above the harbour, offering a great choice of starters such as *pikandiko* (feta, tomato, green pepper, oregano and spices cooked in a pot). For €7 you can enjoy a fish or vegetable soup and they have a fine touch with local dishes also.

Entertainment

Several lively music bars command the inner corner of the harbour front. They include Nameless, Aqua and Kimbo, all of which play mainstream disco with modern Greek music when the local crowd is in.

HORA (ANDROS) ΧΩΡΑ (ΑΝΔΡΟΣ)
pop 1508

Hora unfolds its charms along a narrow, rocky peninsula between two bays on the east coast of Andros, 35km southeast of Gavrio. The town's numerous neoclassical buildings reflect Venetian origins underscored by Byzantine and Ottoman accents. Hora's cultural pedigree is even more distinguished by its Museum of Modern Art and an impressive archaeological museum.

Orientation & Information

The bus station is on Plateia Goulandri, from where a narrow lane leads past a taxi rank, beside the spacious town square, to a T-junction. The post office is to the left. The marble-paved and notionally pedestrianised main street leads down to the right.

Several banks with ATMs are found on the main street. Occasional steps lead down left to the old harbour area of Plakoura, and to Nimborio Beach.

Further down the main street is the pretty central square, Plateia Kaïri, with tree-shaded tavernas and cafes watched over by the Andros Archaeological Museum. Steps again descend from here, north to Plakoura and Nimborio Beach and south to Paraporti Beach. The street passes beneath a short arcade and then continues along the promontory, bends left, then right and ends at Plateia Riva – a big, airy square with crumbling balustrades and a giant bronze statue of a sailor.

Sights & Activities

Hora has two outstanding museums; both were donated to the state by Basil and Elise Goulandris, of the wealthy ship-owning Andriot family. The **Andros Archaeological Museum** (☎ 22820 23664; Plateia Kaïri; adult/child/student €3/2/free; ⏰ 8.30am-3pm Tue-Sun) contains impressive finds from the settlements of Zagora and Paleopolis (9th to 8th century BC) on Andros' east coast, as well as items of the Roman, Byzantine and early Christian periods. They include a spellbinding marble copy of the 4th-century bronze **Hermes of Andros** by Praxiteles.

The **Museum of Contemporary Art** (☎ 22820 22444; www.moca-andros.gr; adult/student €6/3 Jun-Sep, €3/1.50 Oct-May; ☺ 10am-2pm & 6-8pm Wed-Sat & Mon, 10am-2pm Sun Jun-Sep, 10am-2pm Sat-Mon Oct-May) has earned Andros a reputation in the international art world. The main gallery features the work of prominent Greek artists, but each year during the summer months the gallery stages an exhibition of works by one of the world's great artists. To date there have been exhibitions featuring original works by Picasso, Matisse, Braque, Toulouse-Lautrec and Miro, a remarkable achievement for a modest Greek island. To reach the gallery, head down the steps from Plateia Kaïri towards the old harbour.

The huge **bronze statue** of a sailor that stands in Plateia Riva celebrates Hora's great seagoing traditions, although it looks more Russian triumphalist than Andriot in its scale and style. The ruins of a **Venetian fortress** stand on an island that is linked to the tip of the headland by the worn remnants of a steeply arched bridge.

A great option is to hire a self-drive boat and head out to some of the west and north coasts' glorious beaches, most of which are difficult to reach by road. **Riva Boats** (☎ 22820 24412, 6974460330; Nimborio) has superb 4.5m Norwegian-built open boats with 20HP outboards, life raft and anchor, and even a mobile phone. Hire per boat for a minimum of one day is about €90 and no licence is necessary. Riva can also arrange by phone for boats to be hired from Batsi.

Scooters and motorbikes can be hired from Riva Boats and through Karaoulanis Rooms (see below) for €15 to €18 per day.

Sleeping & Eating

Karaoulanis Rooms (☎ 22820 24412, 6974460330; www.androsrooms.gr; d/apt €50/100) This tall, old house is right down by the harbour and has bright and pleasant rooms. There are good discount prices in low season. Greek, English and French are spoken by family members. Check here also for scooter and boat hire.

Karaoulanis Studios-Apartments (☎ 22820 24412, 6974460330; www.androsrooms.gr; d €50-60, apt €100) In 2009 the same family opened stylish new apartments on the outskirts of Hora that command splendid views across the wooded slopes to the south of town.

Alcioni Inn (☎ 22820 24522, 6973403934; alcioni@hellastourism.gr; ☎ Nimborio; d €70-80) These comfortable self-catering rooms are in the midst of the main Nimborio beachfront, below and to the north of Hora.

Niki (☎ /fax 22820 29155; xenonaw.nik@g.mail.com; s/d/tr €70/90/100; ☒) Open-beamed ceilings and wooden galleries enhance the traditional style and modernised facilities of this handsome old house on Hora's main street. There's a ground-floor cafe with a large veranda where you can relax and get breakfast for about €8.

Ermis (☎ 22820 22233; Plateia Kaïri) A pleasant little cafe and pastry shop on Plateia Kaïri.

Nonna's (☎ 22820 23577; Plakoura; mains €5-10) Authentic mezedhes and main dishes of fresh fish from the family's own boat are the order of the day at this popular little taverna at the old harbour. Sea bream, monkfish and red mullet are just a few of the fish dishes available. Vegetarians have a decent choice too, from salads to zucchini pie.

Palinorio (☎ 22820 22881; Nimborio; mains €5.50-8.50; ☺ 11am-2am) Fish is priced by the kilo at this long-established and reliable restaurant on the waterfront at the edge of Nimborio Beach. Lobster dishes are especially well prepared. Traditional Greek dishes and pasta dishes are also available.

AROUND ANDROS

Between Gavrio and Paleopolis Bay are several pleasant beaches, including **Agios Kyprianos**, where there's a little church and a taverna close by; **Delavoia**, one half of which is naturist, **Anerousa** and **Green**.

Paleopolis, 7km south of Batsi on the coast road, is the site of Ancient Andros, where the Hermes of Andros was found. The small but intriguing **Archaeological Museum of Paleopolis** (☎ 22829 41985; admission free; ☺ 8.30am-3pm Tue-Sun) displays and interprets finds from the area.

If you have transport, a worthwhile trip is to head down the west coast of the island before turning northeast at Batsilianos through a charming landscape of fields and cypresses to reach **Ormos Korthiou**, a bayside village that lacks only a decent beach to give it full resort status. Head north from here along a lovely coastal road that climbs and turns through raw hills and wooded valleys for 20km to reach Hora.

CYCLADES

From Hora you can continue north on a lovely scenic route through the high hills of central Andros before descending through switchbacks to Batsi.

TINOS ΤΗΝΟΣ

pop 8614

Hora, the port of Tinos, is a focus of Orthodox devotion that climaxes, with fervour, during festivals at the imposing Church of Panagia Evangelistria, home to the sacred icon of the Megalochari, the Holy Virgin. The icon is one of Greece's most famous and is said to have been found in 1822 on land where the church now stands. Healing powers were accorded to the icon, thus leading to mass pilgrimage and a commercial future for Tinos. Religion still takes centre stage in Hora, although the town rattles and hums around it all like a typical island port should.

Beyond all this, Tinos survives as an island of great natural beauty. Its landscape of rugged hills is dotted with over 40 villages that protrude like marble outcrops from the brindled slopes. Scattered across the countryside are countless ornate dovecotes, legacy of Venetian influence. There is a strong artistic tradition on Tinos, not least in the sculptors' village of Pyrgos in the north of the island where the island's marble quarries are located.

Getting There & Away

Tinos is well served by ferries and there are regular connections to the mainland ports of Rafina and Piraeus as well as to the neighbouring islands of Syros and Andros and south to Mykonos and beyond. For details see Island Hopping (p763).

There are two ferry departure quays in Hora, known locally as 'ports'. The Outer Port is the main dock for conventional and larger fast ferries. It is about 300m to the north of the main harbour. The Middle Port, where smaller, fast ferries dock, is at the north end of the town's main harbour. When you buy a ferry ticket it's essential to check which of these two ports your ferry is leaving from. Allow at least 20 minutes to walk from the centre of Hora to the Outer Port.

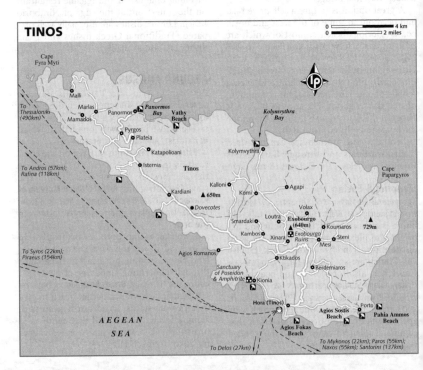

Getting Around

From June to September there are frequent buses from Hora (Tinos) to Porto and Kionia (€1.40, 10 minutes) and several daily to Panormos (€4, one hour) via Kambos (€1.40, 15 minutes) and Pyrgos (€3.30, 50 minutes). Buses leave from the bus station on the Hora harbour front opposite the bus ticket office, which is next to the Poseidon Hotel. You buy tickets on the bus.

Motorcycles (per day €15 to €20) and cars (minimum per weekday €44; on weekends €60) can be hired from a number of outfits along the waterfront at Hora. Rates drop out of season. **Vidalis Rent a Car & Bike** (☎ 22830 25670; Trion Ierarhon 2) is a reliable firm.

HORA (TINOS) ΧΩΡΑ (ΤΗΝΟΣ)
pop 4934

Hora, also known as Tinos, is the island's capital and port. The harbour front is lined with cafes and hotels and the narrow streets behind are full of restaurants and tavernas. The streets leading up to the Church of Panagia Evangelistria are lined with shops and stalls crammed with souvenirs and religious ware.

Orientation & Information

There are two ferry departure quays, the locations of which visitors definitely need to know (see opposite).

The uphill street of Leoforos Megaloharis, straight ahead from the middle of the main waterfront, is the route pilgrims take to the church. The narrower shopping street of Evangelistria, also leading to the church, is to its right.

The post office is at the southeastern end of the harbour front, just past the bus station, and the National Bank of Greece (with ATM) is 50m left of Hotel Posidonion.

Malliaris Travel (☎ 22830 24241; fax 22830 24243; malliaris@thn.forthnet.gr; Paralia) On the waterfront near Hotel Posidonion; sells ferry tickets.

Port police (☎ 22830 22348; Kionion) Just up from Windmills Travel.

Symposion (☎ 22830 24368; Evangelistria 13) A pleasant cafe-restaurant with internet access (€3 for 30 minutes).

Windmills Travel & Tourism (☎ 22830 23398; www.windmillstravel.com; Kionion 2) Just across the way from the Outer Port ferry quay, Windmills is very helpful, and staff can arrange accommodation, car hire and much more.

Sights

The neoclassical **Church of Panagia Evangelistria** (Church of the Annunciation; ✆ 8am-8pm) is built of marble from the island's Panormos quarries. The complex lies within a pleasant courtyard flanked by cool arcades. Inside the main building, the acclaimed icon of the Holy Virgin is draped with gold, silver, jewels and pearls, and is surrounded by gifts from supplicants. A hanging garden of chandeliers and lampholders fills the roof space.

Set into the surface of the street on one side of Leoforos Megaloharis is a rubberised strip, complete with side lights. This is used by pilgrims, who may be seen at any time of year heading for the church on their hands and knees, pushing long candles before them. The final approach is up carpeted steps.

Within the church complex, several **museums** house religious artefacts, icons and secular artworks.

The small **archaeological museum** (☎ 22830 22670; Leoforos Megaloharis; admission €2; ✆ 8am-3pm Tue-Sun), on the right-hand side of the street as you descend from the church, has a collection that includes impressive clay *pithoi* (Minoan storage jars), grave reliefs and sculptures.

Sleeping

Hora should be avoided on 25 March (Annunciation), 15 August (Feast of the Assumption) and 15 November (Advent). If not booked into a hotel months ahead, you'll have to join the roofless devotees who sleep on the streets at these times.

BUDGET

Camping Tinos (☎ 22830 22344; www.camping.gr/tinos; camp sites per adult/child/tent €7/4/4, bungalows with/without bathroom €28/20) A well-equipped site with good facilities. South of the town near Agios Fokas, it's about a five-minute walk from the Middle Port. A minibus meets ferries.

Nikoleta (☎ 22830 24719; nikoleta@thn.forthnet.gr; Kapodistriou 11; s/d without air-con €25/30, s/d with air-con €40/50, ste €55; ✖) Some distance inland from the south end of town, but its spotless, uncluttered rooms are exceptional value and come with a charming welcome. There is a lovely garden area.

Faros (☎ 22830 22712, 6932800525; s/d/tr €35/50/80; ✖) This is a handy place for the Outer Port ferry quay. The rooms are colourful and quirky, but some are rather small. The small outside courtyard is filled with leafy colour.

CYCLADES

MIDRANGE

Oceanis (☎ 22830 22452; oceanis@mail.gr; Akti G Drosou; s/d/tr €35/50/70; ☒) Rooms are not overly large at this modern, well-run hotel, but they are clean and well equipped. It even has some genuine, if very small, single rooms. There's a lift to all floors. Breakfast costs €5.

Hotel Posidonion (☎ 22830 23123; www.poseidonio .gr; Paralia 4; s/d/tr €60/70/85; ☒) A convenient midwaterfront position makes this long-established hotel with decent, comfortable rooms a popular choice. Communal lounges overlooking the harbour front are a pleasant feature.

Altana Hotel (☎ 22830 25102; www.altanahotel.gr; s/d €85/100, ste €145-195; ☒ ☒ ☒ ☒) Located about 700m to the north of town, this charming boutique hotel has a modernist Cycladean style, all snowy white walls and cool interiors incorporating distinctive Tinian motifs. Altana is an ideal base from which to explore the island, and its young family owners are courteous and friendly. Full breakfast is included.

Eating

Malamatenia (☎ 22830 24240; G Gagou; mains €6.50-12) A local favourite, Malamatenia is just up from To Koutouki and has specialities such as shrimps in a wine and tomato sauce with feta cheese, and *youvetsi*, beef in tomato sauce cooked in a clay pot, with pasta.

To Koutouki tis Elenis (☎ 22830 24857; G Gagou 5; mains €7-18) This cosy little place on the narrow lane that veers off from the bottom of Evangelistria has such worthwhile dishes as chicken in lemon sauce, fresh cuttlefish and fish soup.

Pallada Taverna (☎ 22830 23516; Plateia Palladas; mains €7.50-11) Excellent Greek dishes are on offer here with some particularly fine items such as fresh squid stuffed with rice, and zucchini balls with anise and cheese. Local wines from the barrel are persuasive and the house retsina is more than fine.

Metaxy Mas (☎ 22830 25945; Plateia Palladas; mains €8-20) Modern Mediterranean cuisine is the rule at this stylish restaurant where starters such as Tinian artichokes, aubergine soufflé and *louza* (local smoked ham) smooth the way to mains of chicken, pork and veal or specialities such as cuttlefish with spinach.

our pick Symposion (☎ 22830 24368; Evangelistria 13; mains €9-18) A pretty staircase leads to this elegant cafe-restaurant. It does breakfasts

(€4 to €13), crêpes and sandwiches (€3.50 to €8.50), as well as pasta dishes, mixed plates, and main dishes such as grilled sea bass with piquant local greens.

Drinking & Entertainment

Café Piazza (☎ 22830 23483) A busy, gossipy place at the inner end of the line of cafe-bars on the Tinos harbour front. It has a deep terrace and a cosy inside area.

Koursaros (☎ 22830 23963; ☽ 8am-3am) This long-established bar spins an engaging mix of rock, funk and jazz. It's at the far end of the line of harbour-front cafe-bars.

In the back lanes opposite the Middle Port there's a clutch of music and dance bars such as Village Club, Volto and Sibylla, glowing with candy-coloured light and churning out clubby standards and Greek pop as a counterbalance to all that sacred song.

AROUND TINOS

Outside Hora's conspicuous religiosity and down-to-earth commercialism, the countryside of Tinos is a revelation in itself, a glorious mix of wild hill tops crowned with crags, unspoiled villages, fine beaches and fascinating architecture that includes picturesque dovecotes.

At **Porto**, 6km east of Hora, there's a pleasant, uncrowded beach facing Mykonos, while about a kilometre further on is the even lovelier **Pahia Ammos Beach**.

Kionia, 3km northwest of Hora, has several small beaches. Near the largest are the scant remains of the 4th-century-BC **Sanctuary of Poseidon & Amphitrite**, a once enormous complex that drew pilgrims in much the same way as the present Church of Panagia Evangelistria does today.

About 12km north of Hora on the north coast is **Kolymvythra Bay**, where there are two sandy beaches, the smaller with sun loungers, umbrellas and a seasonal cafe; the larger backed by reed beds.

On the north coast, 28km northwest of Hora, is the seaside village of **Panormos**, from where the distinctive green marble, quarried in nearby **Marlas**, was once exported. The waterfront at Panormos is lined with tavernas.

Pyrgos, on the way to Panormos, is a handsome village where even the cemetery is a feast of carved marble. Many of the houses have attractive fanlights. During the late 19th and early 20th centuries Pyrgos was the centre of a remarkable tradition of sculpture sustained by the supply of excellent local marble.

Just across the road from the car park at the entrance to Pyrgos is the **Museum House of Yannoulis Halepas** (adult/child €5/2.50; 🕙 10.30am-2.30pm & 5-8pm Apr–mid-Oct). It's a fascinating place, where the sculptor's humble rooms and workshop, with their striated plaster walls and slate floors, have been preserved. An adjoining gallery has splendid examples of the work of local sculptors. Outstanding are *Girl on a Rock* by Georgios Vamvakis; *Hamlet* by Loukas Doukas; and a copy of the superb *Fisherman* sculpture by Dimitrios Filippolis.

About 6km directly north of Hora is the tiny village of **Volax**, a scribble of white houses at the heart of an amphitheatre of low hills studded with thousands of dark-coloured boulders. Behind the doorways, Volax really is old Greece. There's a small **folklore museum** (ask at the nearest house for the key), an attractive Catholic chapel and a small outdoor theatre. There are a couple of tavernas, including the recommended **Rokos** (☎ 22830 41989; mains €6-9), serving reliable Greek favourites.

The ruins of the Venetian fortress of **Exobourgo** lie 2km south of Volax, on top of a mighty 640m rock outcrop.

SYROS ΣΥΡΟΣ

pop 20,220

Syros is an authentic merging of traditional and modern Greece. It is one of the smallest islands of the Cyclades (its outline bears a quirky resemblance to the British mainland), yet it has the highest population and is the legal and administrative centre of the entire archipelago; the ferry hub of the northern islands; and home to Ermoupolis, the largest and handsomest of all Cycladic towns. If you break the lightest of laws anywhere in the Cyclades, you may end up at court in Syros. Go under your own steam instead and discover one of the most endearing islands in the Aegean, with several attractive beaches, great eating options and the best of everyday Greek life.

History

Excavations of an Early Cycladic fortified settlement and burial ground at Kastri in the island's northeast date from the Neolithic period (2800–2300 BC).

During the medieval period Syros had an overwhelmingly Roman Catholic population. Capuchin monks and Jesuits settled on the island during the 17th and 18th centuries, and such was the Catholic influence that France was called upon by Syros to help it during Turkish rule. Later Turkish influence was benevolent and minimal and Syros busied itself with shipping and commerce.

During the War of Independence thousands of refugees from islands ravaged by the Turks fled to Syros. They brought with them an infusion of Greek Orthodoxy and a fresh commercial drive that made Syros the commercial, naval and cultural centre of Greece during the 19th century. This position was lost to Piraeus in the 20th century. The island's industrial mainstay of shipbuilding has declined, but Syros still has textile manufacturing, a thriving horticultural sector, a sizable administrative and service sector and a small but healthy tourism industry. There is still a local Catholic population.

Getting There & Away

With Syros being of such administrative and social importance there are ferry connections to the mainland ports of Piraeus and Rafina, to neighbouring islands and even to such far-flung destinations as Folegandros. For details see Island Hopping (p762).

Getting Around

About nine buses per day run a circular route from Ermoupolis to Galissas (€1.40, 20 minutes), Vari (€1.40, 30 minutes) and Kini (€1.70, 35 minutes). They leave Ermoupolis every half-hour from June to September and every hour the rest of the year, with alternating clockwise and anticlockwise routes. All of these buses will eventually get you to where you want to go, but it's always worth checking which route is quickest.

There is a bus from Ermoupolis bus station to Ano Syros at 10.30am every morning except Sunday (€1.30, 15 minutes). **Taxis** (☎ 22810 86222) charge €4 to Ano Syros from the port.

A free bus runs along the length of the entire harbour front between car parking at the north and south ends of town about every half-hour from around 7am until late evening. It does not run after 2pm Saturday or on Sunday.

Cars can be hired per day from about €40 and scooters per day from €15 at numerous hire outlets on the waterfront.

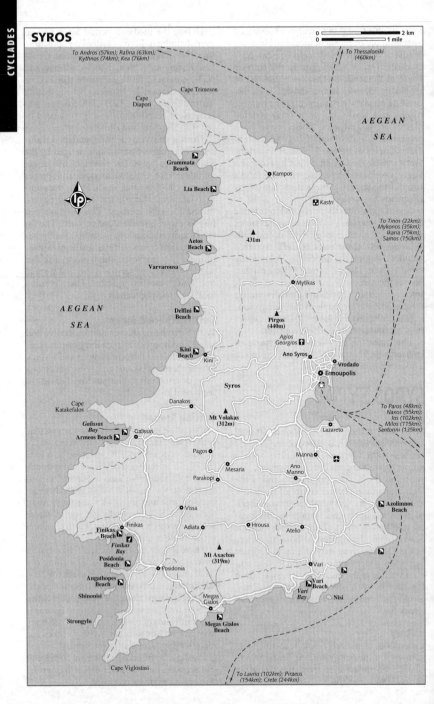

SYROS

0 — 2 km
0 — 1 mile

To Andros (57km); Rafina (63km); Kythnos (74km); Kea (76km)

To Thessaloniki (460km)

Cape Trimeson

Cape Diapori

AEGEAN SEA

Grammata Beach

Kampos

Lia Beach

Kastri

To Tinos (22km); Mykonos (35km); Ikaria (75km); Samos (150km)

Aetos Beach

431m

Varvarousa

Mytikas

AEGEAN SEA

Delfini Beach

Pirgos (440m)

Agios Georgios

Kini Beach

Kini

Ano Syros

Vrodado

Ermoupolis

Syros

To Paros (48km); Naxos (55km); Ios (102km); Milos (115km); Santorini (135km)

Cape Katakefalos

Danakos

Mt Volakas (312m)

Lazareto

Galissas Bay

Galissas

Armeos Beach

Pagos

Manna

Mesaria

Ano Manno

Parakopi

Vissa

Adiata

Hrousa

Atelio

Azolimnos Beach

Finikas

Finikas Beach

Finikas Bay

Posidonia Beach

Mt Axachas (319m)

Vari

Vari Beach

Angathopes Beach

Posidonia

Vari Bay

Nisi

Shinonisi

Megas Gialos

Strongylo

Megas Gialos Beach

Cape Viglostasi

To Lavrio (102km); Piraeus (154km); Crete (244km)

ERMOUPOLIS ΕΡΜΟΥΠΟΛΗ
pop 13,000

Ermoupolis grew out of the refugee town that sprang up during the Greek War of Independence. The refugees were Greek Orthodox and, after some early antagonism, lived in harmony with the original Catholic majority. In 1826 the town was named formally after Hermes, the god of commerce. Ermoupolis is a lively and likeable place, full of paved stairways, restored neoclassical mansions and handsome public buildings, and has a busy shopping scene.

The Catholic settlement of Ano Syros and the Greek Orthodox settlement of Vrodado lie to the northwest and northeast and both spill down from high hill tops, with even taller hills rising behind.

Orientation

The main ferry quay is at the southwestern end of the port. The bus station is on the waterfront, just along from the main ferry quay.

To reach the central square, Plateia Miaouli, walk northeast from the ferry quay for about 200m, and then turn left into El Venizelou for another 100m. There are three sets of public toilets: at the eastern end of the port, off Antiparou and on Akti Papagou near the ferry quay.

Information

There is an information booth run by the Syros Hotels' Association on the waterfront, about 100m northeast of the main ferry quay; opening times are not guaranteed. The website www.syros.com has a reasonable amount of information.

Alpha Bank (El Venizelou) Has an ATM.

Enjoy Your Holidays (☎ 22810 87070; Akti Papagou 2) Opposite the bus station. Sells ferry tickets and can advise on accommodation.

Eurobank (Akti Ethnikis Andistasis) Has an ATM.

Hospital (☎ 22810 96500; Papandreos)

InSpot (☎ 22810 85330; Akti Papagou; internet per hr €3.40; ۞ 24hr) Fast connections but often monopolised by game fans.

Piraeus Bank (Akti Petrou Ralli) Has an ATM.

Police station (☎ 22810 82610; Plateia Vardaka) Beside the Apollon Theatre.

Port police (☎ 22810 82690/88888; Plateia Laïkis Kyriarchias) On the eastern side of the port.

Post office (Protopapadaki) Western Union money transfer.

Teamwork Holidays (☎ 28810 83400; www.team-work.gr; Akti Papagou 18) Just across from the main ferry quay. Sells ferry tickets and can arrange accommodation, excursions and car hire.

Sights

The great square of **Plateia Miaouli** is the finest urban space in the Cyclades and is worthy of Athens. Once the sea reached as far as here, but today the square is well inland and is flanked by palm trees and lined along its south side by cafes and bars. The north side of the square is dominated by the dignified neoclassical **town hall**. The small **archaeological museum** (☎ 22810 88487; Benaki; admission €3; ۞ 8.30am-3pm Tue-Sun) at the rear, founded in 1834 and one of the oldest in Greece, houses a tiny collection of ceramic and marble vases, grave stelae and some very fine Cycladic figurines.

The **Industrial Museum of Ermoupolis** (☎ 22810 84764; Papandreos; adult/concession €2.50/1.50, free Wed; ۞ 10am-2pm & 6-9pm Thu-Sun, 10am-2pm Mon & Wed Apr-Sep, 10am-2pm & 5.30-7.30pm Mon, Wed, Sat & Sun, 10-2pm Fri Oct-Mar) is about a kilometre from the centre of town. It celebrates Syros' industrial and shipbuilding traditions and occupies old factory buildings. There are over 300 items on display.

Ano Syros, originally a medieval settlement, has narrow alleyways and whitewashed houses. It is a fascinating place to wander around and has views of neighbouring islands. Be wise and catch the bus up to the settlement. From the bus terminus, head into the steeply rising alleyways and search out the finest of the Catholic churches, the 13th-century **Agios Georgios** cathedral, with its star-fretted barrel roof and baroque capitals. Follow your nose down from the church, past stunning viewpoints to reach the main street.

Activities

Cyclades Sailing (☎ 22810 82501; csail@otenet.gr) can organise yachting charters, as can **Nomikos Sailing** (☎ 22810 88527); call direct or book through Teamwork Holidays (left).

You can also book a day **coach trip** (adult/child €20/7) around the island on Tuesday, Thursday and Saturday through Teamwork Holidays.

Sleeping

Ermoupolis has a reasonably broad selection of rooms, with most budget options clustered above the waterfront near where the ferry docks. Most places are open all year.

CYCLADES

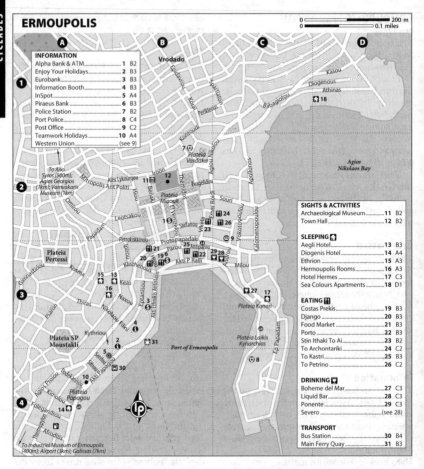

ERMOUPOLIS

INFORMATION
Alpha Bank & ATM	**1** B2
Enjoy Your Holidays	**2** B3
Eurobank	**3** B3
Information Booth	**4** B3
InSpot	**5** A4
Piraeus Bank	**6** B3
Police Station	**7** B2
Port Police	**8** C4
Post Office	**9** C2
Teamwork Holidays	**10** A4
Western Union	(see 9)

SIGHTS & ACTIVITIES
Archaeological Museum	**11** B2
Town Hall	**12** B2

SLEEPING
Aegli Hotel	**13** B3
Diogenis Hotel	**14** A4
Ethrion	**15** A3
Hermoupolis Rooms	**16** A3
Hotel Hermes	**17** C3
Sea Colours Apartments	**18** D1

EATING
Costas Prekis	**19** B3
Django	**20** B3
Food Market	**21** B3
Porto	**22** B3
Stin Ithaki To Ai	**23** B3
To Archontariki	**24** C2
To Kastri	**25** B3
To Petrino	**26** C2

DRINKING
Boheme del Mar	**27** C3
Liquid Bar	**28** C3
Ponente	**29** C3
Severo	(see 28)

TRANSPORT
Bus Station	**30** B4
Main Ferry Quay	**31** B3

Hermoupolis Rooms (☎ 22810 87475; Naxou; s/d/tr €35/50/70; ❄) Clean, well-kept rooms tucked away in narrow Naxou, a short climb up from the waterfront. Front rooms open on to tiny, bougainvillea-cloaked balconies.

Ethrion (☎ 22810 89066; www.ethrion.gr; Kosma 24; s €50, d €60-75; ❄ 🖵 🛜) Close to the harbour front and centre of town yet in a quiet area, Ethrion has comfortable rooms, several having balconies with views over the town. The price range indicates rooms with or without balconies and sea views.

Diogenis Hotel (☎ 22810 86301-5; www.diogenishotel .gr; s/d €73/99; ❄ 🛜) Business-class quality is the rule at this well-run, child-friendly waterfront hotel. Breakfast is an extra €10, but is filling. There's a pleasant cafe on the ground floor.

Aegli Hotel (☎ 22810 79279; hotegli@otenet.gr; Klisthenous 14; s/d/tr incl breakfast €83/105/130; ❄ 🖵 🛜) Located in a quiet side street, yet very close to the centre, this attractive hotel has an air of exclusivity. Rooms are comfortable, and upper-floor balconies at the front have great views over the port. There's a roof garden.

Also recommended:

Hotel Hermes (☎ 22810 83011; fax 22810 87412; Plateia Kanari; s/d/tr incl buffet breakfast €65/100/ 120; ❄ 🛜) The Hermes is a long-established hotel in a fine position on the eastern side of the waterfront.

Sea Colours Apartments (☎ 22810 81181/83400; Athinas; s/d €50/66, apt €72; ❄) These pleasant apartments overlook Agios Nikolaos Bay at the north end of town.

Eating

Standard restaurants and cafes throng the waterfront, especially along Akti Petrou Ralli and on the southern edge of Plateia Miaouli. In quieter corners, however, there are several fine tavernas and restaurants.

Django (☎ 22810 82801; Hiou; snacks from €2.50) This useful little streetside crêperie and snack bar is right at the heart of bustling Hiou and is up and running in the mornings before most cafes. It dishes out sandwiches and hot and cold drinks as well, and has voluptuous tubs of some seriously wicked ice cream.

To Kastri (☎ 22810 83140; Antiparou 13; mains €5-6; ⏲ 9am-5pm) Sentiment should never influence the stomach, but this unique eating place deserves support, and the food's great anyway. It's run by an association of local women who cook up a storm of traditional island dishes. They sell an attractive cookery book (with Greek and English editions).

Porto (☎ 22810 81178; Akti Petrou Ralli 48; mains €5-8) The place with the brightly painted tables and chairs midwaterfront, Porto is a classic little *ouzerie* offering a range of seafood dishes including crab and tuna salads, mussels and shrimps. Snails figure also and the pumpkin pie is rich. They do pork and veal dishes as well.

To Petrino (☎ 22810 87427; Stefanou 9; mains €5-17) Swaths of bougainvillea bedeck the pleasant little enclave of Stefanou, and at its heart is the popular To Petrino serving dishes such as small pork chops with mustard sauce, and squid stuffed with feta.

Stin Ithaki to Ai (☎ 22810 82060; Stefanou 1; mains €5.50-8) Try the *flogeres* (pie stuffed with cheese and ham) or main dishes such as *tsoukalaki* (veal baked in a pot with mushrooms and potatoes and a light cheese sauce).

To Archontariki (☎ 22810 81744; Emm Roidi 8; mains €6-18) Classic Greek dishes go well with a fine selection of regional wines, including Santorini vintages, at this long-established restaurant. Starters, such as spinach with mushrooms and leek pie, lead on to inventive mains of veal with plums or prawn tails in ouzo.

The best place to buy fresh produce is at the small but well-stocked morning **food market** (Hiou; ⏲ 7am-1pm).

Also on Hiou is **Costas Prekis** (☎ 22810 87556; Hiou 4) a shop with a fine selection of traditional products, including snails, capers, local cheeses, sauces, pasta, jams, dried figs and liqueurs.

ELEFTHERIA *Des Hannigan*

There is a distinctive type of young, modern Greek. Confident, wise, stylish, focused, thoughtful, fearless. And just a little bit scary. They have attitude, in the best sense of the word. On Syros there is Eleftheria Thymianou. She does not let me off with anything. 'That's a great name,' I say. 'Eleftheria equals "freedom". What do they call you for short?' I get the full weight of Greek history in my face. 'No one shortens my name,' she says. 'That name means something…'

Entertainment

Music bars are clustered along the waterfront on Akti Petrou Ralli. They play mostly lounge music by day and a mix of house, funk and modern Greek music by night. They draw a great local crowd and rock into the early hours.

Heading up the young scene is **Boheme del Mar** (☎ 22810 83354), with the also lively **Liquid Bar** (☎ 22810 82284) about 60m to the northwest. Next door to Liquid is **Severo** (☎ 22810 88243), which has a great racy atmosphere and good DJs, while new kid on the block **Ponente** (☎ 6944918748) is a very chilled lounge with all the right sounds.

GALISSAS ΓΑΛΗΣΣΑΣ
pop 120

When Ermoupolis becomes too metro for you, head west on a short bus ride to Galissas, a small resort with one of the best beaches on Syros, several bars and restaurants and some great places to stay. The main bus stop is at an intersection behind the beach.

Sleeping

Two Hearts Camping (☎ 22810 42052; www.twohearts -camping.com; camp sites per adult/child/tent €8/4/4) Set in a pistachio orchard about 400m from the village and beach, this popular camping ground has good facilities. It also rents a range of fixed accommodation from wooden 'tents' to bungalows from €12 to €20 per person. A minibus meets ferries in high season.

Oasis (☎ 22810 42357, 6948274933; freri_stefania@ hotmail.com; s/d/studios €30/45/55; 🅿 🛜) A genuine 'oasis', this lovely little farm has bright and airy rooms, and the welcome is charming. It's about 400m back from the village, set amid olive trees and vines. Follow signs from the main bus stop intersection in the village.

Hotel Benois (☎ 22810 42833; www.benois.gr; s/d/tr incl breakfast €70/90/110, apt €150; ☒ ☐ ☎ ☒) A well-run hotel, the Benois has pleasant, spick-and-span rooms. It's close to the beach at the northern entrance to the village.

Eating & Drinking

Socrates (☎ 22810 43284; mains €4.50-9) Eat beneath a leafy canopy on the garden terrace at this well-run place with traditional dishes including *youvetsi* (choice pieces of lamb in a tomato sauce, baked with pasta).

Iliovasilema (☎ 22810 43325; mains €5-12) A good local eatery where fish such as black bream is by the kilo, but where there are reasonably priced seafood starters and fish soup.

Savvas (☎ 22810 42998; mains €6-10) Next door to Iliovasilema, Savvas is distinguished by locally sourced ingredients and authentic Syran cuisine; signature dishes include pork in honey and aniseed.

Also recommended is the Green Dollars Bar on the beach road, for daytime snacks and music while you drink. Rock and reggae are favourites from 10am to 4am.

AROUND SYROS

The beaches south of Galissas all have domatia (rooms, usually in a private home) and some have hotels. Some beaches are narrow, roadside strips of dullish sand, but they're not too busy. They include **Finikas**, **Posidonia** and **Angathopes**. Back on the main road and on the south coast proper, the town of **Megas Gialos** has a couple of roadside beaches.

The pleasant **Vari Bay**, further east, has a sandy beach with some development, including a couple of hotels and a beachfront taverna.

Kini Beach, out on its own on the west coast, north of Galissas, has a long stretch of beach and is developing into a popular resort with standard modern hotels, apartments, cafes and tavernas.

MYKONOS ΜΥΚΟΝΟΣ

pop 9660

Mykonos is the great glamour island of the Cyclades and happily flaunts its camp and fashionable reputation with style. Beneath the gloss and glitter, however, this is a charming and hugely entertaining place where the sometimes frantic mix of good-time holidaymakers, cruise-ship crowds, pos-turing fashionistas and preening celebrities is magically subdued by the cubist charms of Mykonos town, a traditional Cycladic maze. Local people have had 40 years to get a grip on tourism and have not lost their Greek identity in doing so.

Be prepared, however, for the oiled-up lounger lifestyle of the island's packed main beaches, the jostling street scenes and the relentless, yet sometimes forlorn, partying. That said, there's still a handful of off-track beaches worth fighting for. Plus, the stylish bars, restaurants and shops have great appeal, and you can still find a quieter pulse amid the labyrinthine old town. Add to all this the archaeological splendour of the nearby island of Delos, and Mykonos really does live up to its reputation as a fabulous destination.

Getting There & Away

Mykonos is well served by air connections to Athens, Thessaloniki and Santorini. There are also direct Easyjet flights to London from about May to mid September.

With Mykonos being such a major tourist destination, ferry connections to the mainland ports of Piraeus and Rafina are very good, as are connections to neighbouring islands. Links south to that other popular destination, Santorini, and to points between are also excellent.

Mykonos has two ferry quays: the Old Port, 400m north of town, where some conventional ferries and smaller fast ferries dock, and the New Port, 2km north of town, where the bigger fast ferries and some conventional ferries dock. There is no hard-and-fast rule, and when buying outgoing tickets you should always double-check which quay your ferry leaves from.

For further details see Island Hopping (p756).

Getting Around

TO/FROM THE AIRPORT

Buses from the southern bus station serve Mykonos' airport (€1.40), which is 3km southeast of the town centre. Make sure you arrange an airport transfer with your accommodation (expect to pay around €6) or take a **taxi** (☎ 22890 22400, airport 22890 23700).

BOAT

Caïque (little boat) services leave Hora (Mykonos) for Super Paradise, Agrari and Elia

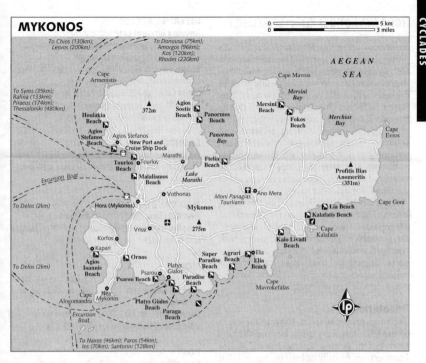

MYKONOS

0   5 km
0   3 miles

To Chios (130km);
Lesvos (200km)

To Donousa (75km);
Amorgos (96km);
Kos (120km);
Rhodes (220km)

Cape
Armenistis

*AEGEAN
SEA*

Cape Mavros

To Syros (35km);
Rafina (133km);
Piraeus (174km);
Thessaloniki (480km)

372m

Agios
Sostis
Beach

Panormos
Beach

Mersini
Beach

*Mersini
Bay*

*Merchias
Bay*

Cape
Evros

Houlakia
Beach

Agios
Stefanos
Beach

Agios Stefanos
New Port and
Cruise Ship Dock

*Panormos
Bay*

Fokos
Beach

Marathi

Tourlos Beach

Tourlos

Ftelia
Beach

Excursion Boat

Malaliamos
Beach

*Lake
Marathi*

Profitis Ilias
Anomeritis
(351m)

Moni Panagias
Tourlianis

Ano Mera

To Delos (2km)

Vothonas

Hora (Mykonos)

Mykonos

Cape Goni

Lia Beach

Kalafatis Beach

Vrissi

275m

Cape
Kalafatis

Kalo Livadi
Beach

Korfos

Kapari

Ornos

Super
Paradise
Beach

Agrari
Beach

Elia

Elia
Beach

To Delos (2km)

Agios
Ioannis
Beach

Psarou
Platys
Gialos

Psarou Beach

Paradise
Beach

Cape
Mavrokefalas

Cape
Alogomandra

Nea
Mykonos

Platys Gialos
Beach

Paraga
Beach

Excursion
Boat

To Naxos (46km); Paros (54km);
Ios (70km); Santorini (128km)

Beaches (June to September only) and from Platys Gialos to Paradise (€7), Super Paradise (€8), Agrari (€7) and Elia (€7) Beaches.

BUS

The Mykonos bus network (☎ 22890 26797; www .ktelmykonos.gr) has two main bus stations and a pick-up point at the New Port. The **northern bus station** (Remezzo) is behind the OTE office and has frequent departures to Agios Stefanos via Tourlos (€1.40), and services to Ano Mera, (€1.40), Elia Beach (€1.70) and Kalafatis Beach (€1.90). Trips range from 20 minutes to 40 minutes. There are two buses daily to Kalo Livadi Beach (€1.50). Buses for the New Port, Tourlos and Agios Stefanos stop at the Old Port. The **southern bus station** (Fabrika Sq [Plateia Yialos]) serves Agios Ioannis Beach (€1.40), Ornos, (€1.40), Platys Gialos (€1.40), Paraga (€1.40) and Paradise Beach (€1.40). Trips range from 15 minutes to 40 minutes.

Bus tickets are sold at machines, street kiosks, minimarkets and tourist shops. You must buy a ticket before boarding (buy return tickets if required), validate the ticket on the bus and hang on to it. From 12.15am to 6am all prices are €1.70.

CAR & MOTORCYCLE

For cars, expect to pay (depending on model) from about €45 per day, plus insurances, in high season; €35 in low season. For scooters it starts at €20 to €40 (ATVs) in high season; €15 to €30 in low season. Reliable hire agencies are the Mykonos Accommodation Centre (p388) and **OK Rent A Car** (☎ 22890 23761; Agio Stefanos). There are several car- and motorcycle-hire firms around the southern bus station in Hora.

TAXI

If you're after a **taxi** (☎ 22400 23700/22400), you'll find them at Hora's Taxi Sq (Plateia Manto Mavrogenous) and by the bus stations and ports. The minimum fare is €3, but there's a charge of €0.30 for each item of luggage. Fares from Hora to beaches: Agios Stefanos €8.50, Ornos €8, Platys Gialos €8.70, Paradise €9, Kalafatis €14.70 and Elia €14.70. Add €1.50 for phone booking.

HORA (MYKONOS) ΧΩΡΑ (ΜΥΚΟΝΟΣ)
pop 6467

Hora (also known as Mykonos), the island's port and capital, is a warren of narrow alleyways that wriggle between white-walled buildings, their stone surfaces webbed with white paint. In the heart of the Little Venice area (Venetia), tiny flower-bedecked churches jostle with trendy boutiques, and there's a deluge of bougainvillea around every corner. Without question, you will soon pass the same junction twice. It's entertaining at first, but can become frustrating as throngs of equally lost people, fast moving locals and disdainful Mykonos veterans add to the stress. For quick-fix navigation, familiarise yourself with main junctions and the three main streets of Matogianni, Enoplon Dynameon and Mitropoleos, which form a horseshoe behind the waterfront. The streets are crowded with chic fashion salons, cool galleries, jangling jewellers, languid and loud music bars, brightly painted houses and torrents of crimson flowers – plus a catwalk cast of thousands.

Orientation

The town proper is about 400m to the south of the Old Port ferry quay, beyond the tiny town beach. A busy square, Plateia Manto Mavrogenous (usually called Taxi Sq), is 100m beyond the beach and on the edge of Hora. East of Taxi Sq, the busy waterfront leads towards the Little Venice neighbourhood and the town's iconic hill-top row of windmills. South of Taxi Sq and the waterfront, the busy streets of Matogianni, Zouganelli and Mavrogenous lead into the heart of Hora.

The northern bus station is 200m south of the Old Port ferry quay, on the way into town. The southern bus station is on Fabrika Sq, on the southern edge of town. The quay from where boats leave for Delos is at the western end of the waterfront.

Information
BOOKSHOPS
International Press (☎ 22890 23316; Kambani 5) Numerous international newspapers, although editions are a day late. Also a wide range of magazines and books.

EMERGENCY
Police station (☎ 22890 22716) On the road to the airport.
Port police (☎ 22890 22218; Akti Kambani) Midway along the waterfront.
Tourist police (☎ 22890 22482) At the airport.

INTERNET ACCESS
Angelo's Internet Café (☎ 22890 79138; Xenias; per hr €4; ◷ 10am-midnight) On the road between the windmills and the southern bus station.
Bolero Bar (☎ 6936322484; Malamatenias; ☞) Free internet for customers. Consoles and wi-fi.
Stairs Café (☎ 22890 26904; Plateia Manto Mavrogenous; ☞) Free internet for customers until 10.30pm. Consoles and wi-fi.

LAUNDRY
White Mykonos (☎ 22890 27600, 6977352531; Xenias; ◷ 9.30am-2pm & 5-9pm Mon-Fri) Machine wash and dry up to 5kg €10.

MEDICAL SERVICES
First Aid Clinic (☎ 22890 22274; Agiou Ioannou)
Hospital (☎ 22890 23994) Located about 1km along the road to Ano Mera.

MONEY
Several banks by the Old Port quay have ATMs. Eurobank has ATMs at Taxi Sq and Fabrika Sq.
Eurochange (☎ /fax 22890 27024; Plateia Manto Mavrogenous) Money exchange office in Taxi Sq.

POST
Post office (☎ 22890 22238; Laka) In the southern part of town.

TOURIST INFORMATION
Tourist Information Office (☎ 22890 25250; www .mykonos.gr; Plateia Karaoli Dimitriou; ◷ 9am-9pm Jul & Aug, 10am-5pm Easter-Jun, Sep & Oct) This office is run by the municipality and was launched in 2007.

TRAVEL AGENCIES
Delia Travel (☎ 22890 22322; travel@delia.gr; Akti Kambani) Halfway along the inner waterfront. Sells ferry tickets and tickets for Delos. It's also the French Consulate.
Mykonos Accommodation Centre (☎ 22890 23408; www.mykonos-accommodation.com; 1st fl, Enoplon Dynameon 10) Well organised and very helpful for a range of information. Can also arrange midrange, top-end and gay-friendly accommodation.
Sea & Sky (☎ 22890 22853; Akti Kambani) Information and ferry tickets.
Windmills Travel (☎ 22890 26555; www. windmillstravel.com; Xenias) By the southern bus station on Fabrika Sq, this is another helpful office for all types of information, including gay-related. Also sells ferry tickets.

HORA (MYKONOS)

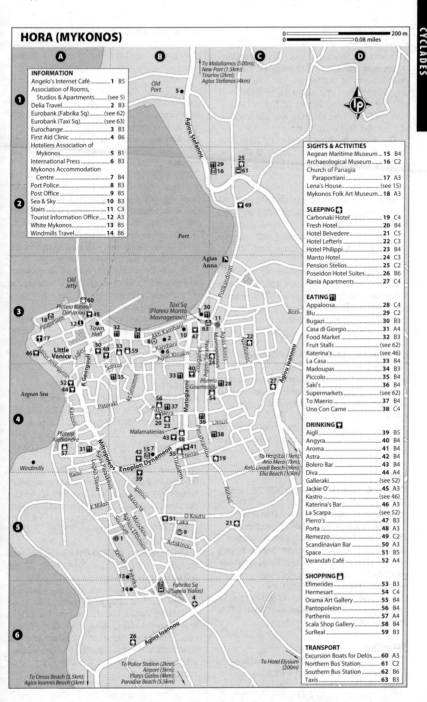

0   200 m
0   0.08 miles

INFORMATION
Angelo's Internet Café 1 B5
Association of Rooms,
   Studios & Apartments ......(see 5)
Delia Travel................................. 2 B3
Eurobank (Fabrika Sq)........ (see 62)
Eurobank (Taxi Sq).............. (see 63)
Eurochange................................. 3 B3
First Aid Clinic 4 B6
Hoteliers Association of
   Mykonos.................................. 5 B1
International Press 6 B3
Mykonos Accommodation
   Centre 7 B4
Port Police 8 B3
Post Office 9 B5
Sea & Sky 10 B3
Stairs 11 C3
Tourist Information Office........ 12 A3
White Mykonos........................ 13 B5
Windmills Travel...................... 14 B6

SIGHTS & ACTIVITIES
Aegean Maritime Museum 15 B4
Archaeological Museum........ 16 C2
Church of Panagia
   Paraportiani 17 A3
Lena's House.......................(see 15)
Mykonos Folk Art Museum ... 18 A3

SLEEPING
Carbonaki Hotel 19 C4
Fresh Hotel 20 B4
Hotel Belvedere...................... 21 C5
Hotel Lefteris 22 C3
Hotel Philippi.......................... 23 B4
Manto Hotel 24 C3
Pension Stelios........................ 25 C2
Poseidon Hotel Suites............ 26 B6
Rania Apartments................... 27 C4

EATING
Appaloosa................................ 28 C4
Blu.. 29 C2
Bugazi..................................... 30 B3
Casa di Giorgio 31 A4
Food Market........................... 32 B3
Fruit Stalls ....(see 62)
Katerina's ....(see 46)
La Casa 33 B4
Madoupas................................ 34 B3
Piccolo..................................... 35 B4
Saki's 36 B4
Supermarkets.....................(see 62)
To Maerio 37 B4
Uno Con Carne 38 C4

DRINKING
Aigli 39 B5
Angyra.................................... 40 B4
Aroma...................................... 41 B4
Astra 42 B4
Bolero Bar 43 B4
Diva 44 A4
Galleraki...............................(see 52)
Jackie O'.................................. 45 A3
Kastro ....(see 46)
Katerina's Bar 46 A3
La Scarpa ....(see 52)
Pierro's 47 B3
Porta.. 48 A3
Remezzo.................................. 49 C2
Scandinavian Bar.................... 50 A3
Space 51 B5
Verandah Café 52 A4

SHOPPING
Efimerides............................... 53 B3
Hermesart................................ 54 C4
Orama Art Gallery 55 B4
Pantopoleion........................... 56 B4
Parthenis................................. 57 A4
Scala Shop Gallery.................. 58 B4
SurReal 59 B3

TRANSPORT
Excursion Boats for Delos....... 60 A3
Northern Bus Station.............. 61 C2
Southern Bus Station 62 B6
Taxis.. 63 B3

Sights

MUSEUMS

Mykonos has five museums. The **archaeological museum** (☎ 22890 22325; adult/concession €2/1; ☑ 8.30am-3pm Tue-Sat, 10am-3pm Sun) houses pottery from Delos and some grave stelae and jewellery from the island of Renia (Delos' necropolis). Chief exhibits include a statue of Hercules in Parian marble.

The **Aegean Maritime Museum** (☎ 22890 22700; Tria Pigadia; adult/concession €4/1.50; ☑ 10.30am-1pm & 6.30-9pm Apr-Oct) has a fascinating collection of nautical paraphernalia, including ships' models.

Next door, **Lena's House** (☎ 22890 22390; Tria Pigadia; admission €2; ☑ 6.30-9.30pm Mon-Sat, 7-9pm Sun Apr-Oct) is a charming late-19th-century, middle-class Mykonian house (with furnishings intact). It takes its name from its last owner, Lena Skrivanou.

The **Mykonos Folk Art Museum** (☎ 6932178330; Paraportianis; admission free; ☑ 5.30-8.30pm Mon-Sat, 6.30-8.30pm Sun Apr-Oct), housed in an 18th-century sea captain's house, features a large collection of furnishings and other artefacts, including old musical instruments.

CHURCH OF PANAGIA PARAPORTIANI

Mykonos' most famous church is the rock-like **Panagia Paraportiani** (admission free, donations appreciated; ☑ variable, usually open mornings). A rugged, rocky little building beyond Delos ferry quay on the way to Little Venice, it comprises four small chapels plus another on an upper storey that is reached by an outside staircase.

Tours

Mykonos Accommodation Centre (MAC; ☎ 22890 23408; www.mykonos-accommodation.com; 1st fl, Enoplon Dynameon 10) Organises guided tours to Delos (return €15, 30 minutes; see p395). The MAC also runs tours to Tinos (adult/child €58/38), as well as a Mykonos bus tour (adult/child €33/22), island cruise (adult/child €58/33) and a wine and culture tour (adult/child €29/21), and can arrange private charter, including gay-only, boat cruises.

Windmills Travel (☎ 22890 23877; www.windmillstravel.com; Plateia Yialos) The booking agent for snorkelling (€25 for 30 minutes) and island cruises (€50 to €60, four weekly).

Sleeping

There are scores of sleeping options in Mykonos, but if you arrive without a reservation between July and September and you find reasonably priced accommodation, grab it – 'budget' in Mykonos is relative to the generally high prices and this is reflected in the listings.

Otherwise, check out the local accommodation organisations – when you get off at the town ferry quay, you will see a low building with numbered offices. Number 1 is the **Hoteliers Association of Mykonos** (☎ 22890 24540; www.mha.gr; Old Port; ☑ 8am-4pm). The association also has a desk at Mykonos Airport (☎ 22890 25770; ☑ 9am-10pm) and will book a room on the spot, but does not accept telephone bookings prior to your arrival. Number 2 is the **Association of Rooms, Studios & Apartments** (☎ 22890 24860, fax 22890 26860; ☑ 9am-5pm Apr-Oct). If you choose domatia from the owners who meet ferries check their exact location and ask if they charge for transport (some do).

If you plan to stay in Hora and want somewhere quiet, think carefully before settling for domatia on the main streets – bar noise until dawn is inevitable.

Some places only advertise doubles, but single occupancy may be negotiable. During late July and early August some hotels will only accept a minimum of three-night stays.

BUDGET

Manto Hotel (☎ 22890 22330; www.manto-mykonos.gr; Agias Anna; s/d/tr incl breakfast €75/100/125; ☒) Buried in the heart of town and close to the action, Manto is a decent budget option (for Mykonos), with well-kept rooms and a pleasant breakfast room.

Pension Stelios (☎ 22890 24641, 6944273556; s/d/tr €90/100/130) Fairly basic but clean and quiet, Stelios has a hillside location just above the northern bus station about five minutes from Taxi Sq. There are great views over Hora from some of the small balconies. Flights of steps lead to the pension.

Hotel Lefteris (☎ 22890 27117; www.lefterishotel.gr; Apollonos 9; s/d €90/115, studios €190-240; ☒) A colourful entranceway sets the tone for this welcoming international meeting place for all ages. Tucked away from the crowds, close to Taxi Sq, the Lefteris has simple but bright and comfy rooms, most with fans or aircon. There is a communal kitchen and the roof terrace is a great place to relax. Studios are well equipped and the hotel has other rooms nearby.

MIDRANGE

Hotel Philippi (☎ 22890 22294; chriko@otenet.gr; Kalogera 25; s/d €90/125; ⚡ ☎) A pleasant garden full of trees, flowers and shrubs makes this a good choice in the heart of Hora. There's an appealing ambience in the bright, clean rooms that open onto a railed veranda overlooking the garden. Rooms have tea- and coffee-making facilities.

Rania Apartments (☎ 22890 28272/3; www.rania -mykonos.gr; Leondiou Boni 2; s €105, d €135-195, tr €210-220, q €255-285, apt €365; ⚡ ☎) A great location high above the harbour means a bit of an uphill walk from town, but the apartments are easily accessed from Agiou Ioannou, the 'ring road'. In a lovely garden setting, the accommodation is charming and well appointed. Facilities include hot plate and coffeemaker.

Poseidon Hotel-Suites (☎ 22890 22437; www.poseidon hotelmykonos.gr; Agiou Ioannou; s €110-141, d 130-166, tr/ste 186/319; ⚡ ⚡ ☎ ⚡) One of the best locations in Mykonos, the Poseidon is located overlooking the sea and is within a few minutes' walk along the shore to Windmill Hill. Standard rooms are more than adequate and the newer suites are plush and overlook the attractive pool area.

our pick **Carbonaki Hotel** (☎ 22890 24124/22461; www.carbonaki.gr; 23 Panahrantou St; s/d/tr/q €120/160/200/240; ⚡ ☎) This family-run boutique hotel, right on the edge of central Mykonos, has a delightful ambience and charming owners. Rooms are comfortable and bright and there are relaxing public balconies dotted round the pleasant central courtyards. A Jacuzzi and small sauna were being added at time of research. Breakfast is €10.

Fresh Hotel (☎ 22890 24670; www.marioshotel -mykonos.com; Kalogera 31; s/d incl breakfast €130/170; ⚡ ⚡ ☎) Previously Mario's Hotel, the gay-friendly Fresh is located right in the heart of town and is handy for all the action. There's a pleasant central garden, an attractive breakfast room and bar, and a Jacuzzi. Rooms have wooden floors and furnishings are a pleasant mix of old and new.

TOP END

Hotel Elysium (☎ 22890 23952; www.elysiumhotel .com; s €260-340, d €310-400, tr €480-560; ⚡ Apr-Oct; ⚡ ⚡ ⚡ ⚡) Located high above the main town in the School of Fine Arts area, this stylish gay hotel (although nongays are also welcome) has cool decor and good-sized comfortable rooms. There are plenty of special trimmings, including personal computers in suites and deluxe rooms, and a spa and massage service.

Hotel Belvedere (☎ 22890 25122; www.belvedere hotel.com; Rohari; d €280-2000; ⚡ ⚡ ⚡ ☎ ⚡) It's all billowing drapes and white linen amid the modernist landscape and furnishings of this leading Mykonos hotel. The Belvedere has had a major refurbishment in recent years. Jacuzzis, massage therapy, a fitness studio, and music and movie facilities seal the deal. Within the complex is the Matsuhisa Restaurant, under the aegis of the noted Japanese chef, Nobu Matsuhisa; and the Belvedere Restaurant, recently renovated and with a menu created by the equally noted Australian-Greek chef, George Calombaris.

Eating

High prices don't necessarily reflect high quality in many Mykonos eateries. There are, however, excellent good-value restaurants of all kinds.

BUDGET

Piccolo (☎ 22890 22208; Drakopoulou 18; snacks €3.90-7.80) There are no linen-draped tables at this little food outlet, but the food is first class and ranges from crisp salads to a great selection of sandwich fillings that include Mykonian prosciutto, *manouri* (soft cheese), smoked local ham, smoked eel and crab.

Madoupas (☎ 22890 22224; mains €7-12) Walk into Madoupas of a Sunday morning and all of local Mykonos is there. This is the place for morning coffee or for big helpings of good Greek standards for as little as €7. The evening menu has a broader choice.

There's also a cluster of cheap fast-food outlets and crêperies around town:

Bugazi (☎ 22890 24066; snacks €4.60-6.70) Good selection of crêpes, just off the edge of Taxi Sq.

Saki's (☎ 22890 24848; Agion Saranta) A popular place with locals, Saki's dishes out kebabs and souvlaki for €2.50, and other budget fillers for €5 to €7.

There are supermarkets and fruit stalls, particularly around the southern bus station area, and there's a food and fish market on the waterfront where Mykonos' famous pelicans hang out.

MIDRANGE & TOP END

La Casa (☎ 22890 24994; Matogianni 8; mains €9.90-18.90) The classic La Casa has a strong Greek basis with Italian, Arabic and Lebanese influences. Starters of smoked cheeses with mushrooms and inventive salads – including a Mykonian special with *louza* (local smoked ham), local prosciutto cheeses and rocket – lead on to mains such as pork fillet with mustard, *pleurotus* mushrooms and tarragon.

ourpick Katerina's (☎ 22890 23084; Agion Anargyron; mains €11-25) The famous Katerina's Bar, whose eponymous matriarch was celebrated in the 1950s as Greece's first female boat skipper at age 18, has now branched out with its own small restaurant. There's a thoughtful and creative menu of crisp salads and starters such as prawn *saganaki* (skillet-fried) or wild Porcini mushrooms. Mains include fresh sea bass or mixed seafood plate for two (€50) or vegetarian options. The balcony view is to die for, of course, as is the 'Chocolate from Heaven' sweet.

Blu (☎ 22890 22955; mains €12-24) Just along from the Old Port on the way into town, this stylish place has an attractive terrace with a great view of the harbour. A subtle menu includes such starters as sautéed mushrooms in sweet wine and cumin sauce, and mains of veal fillet in Marsala wine with dark rice. Fish is by the kilo and the wine list is well chosen. The adjoining Blu-Blu cafe has internet.

To Maereio (☎ 22890 28825; Kalogera 16; dishes €14-21) A small, but selective menu of Mykonian favourites keeps this cosy little place popular. The mainly meat and poultry dishes can be preceded by salad mixes that include apple and pear, yoghurt and a balsamic vinegar sauce.

Uno Con Carne (☎ 6944479712; Panachra; mains €19-98) Recently opened as Mykonos' major place for meateaters, this big, stylish space knows how to prepare the best steaks, from prime Chateaubriand and South American Pichana 'Black Angus' to Tyson T-bone and mouth-melting 'proper' hamburger. Starters of scampi tartare or gazpacho prepare for the main feast and you can cool the palate later with sorbet or ice cream. Lamb and chicken dishes also feature.

Also recommended:

Appaloosa (☎ 22890 27086; Mavrogenous 1, Plateia Goumeniou; mains €8.50-29) International cuisine with Mexican and Indonesian influences. A hot line in tequila and cocktails goes with cool music.

Casa di Giorgio (☎ 6932561998; Mitropoleos; mains €12-22) A good range of pizzas and pastas, as well as meat and seafood dishes, served on a big terrace.

Drinking

Hora's Little Venice quarter is not exactly the Grand Canal, but it does offer the Mediterranean at your feet as well as rosy sunsets, windmill views, glowing candles and a swath of colourful bars. The music meanders through smooth soul and easy listening, but can ear crunch you at times with shattering decibel rivalries.

A good spot is **Galleraki** (☎ 22890 27188), which turns out superb cocktails. Nearby, it's the sunset view at **Verandah Café** (☎ 22890 27400), while **La Scarpa** (☎ 22890 23294) lets you lean back from the sea on its cosy cushions. Further north, **Katerina's Bar** (☎ 22890 23084; Agion Anargyron) has a cool balcony and eases you into the evening's action with relaxing sounds.

Deeper into town, the relentlessly stylish **Aroma** (☎ 22890 27148; Enoplon Dynameon; ☾ breakfast-late) sits on a strategic corner, providing the evening catwalk view. It's open for breakfast and coffee as well. Just across the way, down an alleyway is **Bolero Bar** (☎ 6936322484; Malamatenias) a longstanding favourite, frequented in its time by such stellar celebs as Keith Richards.

Further down Enoplon Dynameon is **Astra** (☎ 22890 24767), where the decor is modernist Mykonos at its best, and where some of Athens' top DJs feed the ambience with rock, funk, house and drum'n'bass. Just across from Astra, cocktail-cool **Aigli** (☎ 22890 27265) has another useful terrace for people watching. Matogianni has a couple of music bars, including **Angyra** (☎ 22890 24273), which sticks with easy listening and mainstream.

Scandinavian Bar (☎ 22890 22669; Ioanni Voinovich 9) is mainstream mayhem with ground-floor bars and a space upstairs for close-quarters moving to retro dance hits.

For big action into the dawn, **Space** (☎ 22890 24100; Laka) is the place. The night builds superbly through a mix of techno, house and progressive, and the bar-top dancing fires up the late-night action. **Remezzo** (☎ 22890 24100; Polykandrioti) is run by the Space team but features lounge and dance for a more relaxing scene. Entry is around €20 to each of the clubs.

GAY BARS

Mykonos is one of the world's great gay-friendly destinations. Gay life is less overt here, but Hora has many gay-centric clubs and hang-outs from where the late-night crowds spill out onto the streets.

Kastro (☎ 22890 23072; Agion Anargyron) With a leaning towards stylish classical sounds, this is a good place to start the night on cocktails as the sun sets on Little Venice.

Jackie O' (☎ 22890 79167; www.jackieomykonos.com; Plateia Karaoli Dimitriou) Hottest gay bar in Mykonos in 2009, Jacki O' seems set to hold centre stage for some time yet. Straight-friendly and with a fabulous vibe revved up by fabulous shows.

Diva (☎ 22890 27271; K Georgouli) A great up-beat atmosphere makes this a Mykonos favourite with a mixed crowd and a loyal lesbian core.

Porta (☎ 22890 27807; Ioanni Voinovich) Head downstairs into Porta's cruisey ambience where things get crowded and cosy towards midnight.

Pierro's (☎ 22890 22177; Agias Kiriakis) Long-standing last stop for the nightwatch, where things round off with a backdrop of heavy-beat house and superbly over-the-top drag action in upstairs Ikaros. Can take over the outdoors, also.

Shopping

Style and art venues vie for attention throughout Hora's streets and include authentic Lacoste, Dolce & Gabbana, Naf Naf, Diesel and Body Shop. Clothes hanging apart, there are some stand-out venues worth seeking out.

Scala Shop Gallery (☎ 22890 26992; www.scalagallery.gr; Matogianni 48) Scala is one of the more stylish galleries of Mykonos. It stages changing displays of fine art and also sells contemporary jewellery and ceramics. The owner, Dimitris Rousounelos, is an accomplished writer on Mykonos traditions. His book, *Tastes of Sacrifice*, on sale at the gallery, gives a trenchant and evocative view of Mykonian life beyond the gloss of fashionable tourism.

Parthenis (☎ 22890 23089; Plateia Alefkandra) Featuring the distinctive couture – in black-and-white only – of Athens designer and long-time Mykonos resident Dimitris Parthenis.

Hermesart (☎ 22890 24652; Plateia Goumenio) There's some quirky and appealing art at this small gallery, with smaller pieces at affordable prices.

Orama Art Gallery (☎ 22890 26339; Fournakia) Just off Enoplon Dynameon, Orama shows the highly original work of Louis Orosko and Dorlies Schapitz.

Pantopoleion (☎ 22890 22078; Kalogera 24) A genuine all-organic grocery with products covering just about every need from fresh fruit and vegetables, cheese, pasta and bread to herbal cosmetics and even organic cleaning products and books on all things organic.

For original gift ideas try **Efimerides** (☎ 22890 79180; Drakopoulou 4) with its selection of objets d'art, while opposite is **SurReal** (☎ 22890 28323; Drakopoulou 1), which specialises in leaflike leatherware.

AROUND MYKONOS
Beaches

Mykonos has a good number of beaches and most have golden sand in attractive locations. They're not big enough, though, that you'll escape from the crowds, and they're extremely popular and busy, especially from June onwards. Don't expect seclusion, although there can be a distinct sense of *exclusion* as various cliques commandeer the sun loungers, while segregation zones of style and sheer snobbery dominate at some locations.

You need to be a party person for the likes of Paradise and Super Paradise. It can all get very claustrophobic, but it's heaven for the gregarious. Most beaches have a varied clientele, and attitudes to toplessness and nudity also vary, but what's accepted at each beach is obvious when you get there.

An excellent guide to island beaches and their specific or mixed clientele can be found on the beaches link of www.mykonos-accommodation.com.

The nearest beaches to Hora (Mykonos), which are also the island's least glamorous beaches, are **Malaliamos**; the tiny and crowded **Tourlos**, 2km to the north; and **Agios Stefanos**, 4km. About 3.5km south of Hora is the packed and noisy **Ornos**, from where you can hop onto boats for other beaches. Just west is **Agios Ioannis**. The sizable package-holiday resort of **Platys Gialos** is 4km from Hora on the southwest coast. All of the above beaches are family orientated.

Platys Gialos is the caïque jumping-off point for the glitzier beaches to the east, such as Paradise and Super Paradise.

Approximately a kilometre south of Platys Gialos you'll find the pleasant **Paraga Beach**, which has a small gay section. About 2km east of here is the famous **Paradise**, which is not a recognised gay beach, but has a lively younger scene. **Super Paradise** (aka **Plintri** or **Super P**) has a fully gay section. Mixed and gay-friendly **Elia** is the last caïque stop, and a few minutes' walk from here is the small and pleasant **Agrari**. Nudity is fairly commonplace on all of these beaches.

North-coast beaches can be exposed to the *meltemi* (northeasterly wind), but **Panormos** and **Agios Sostis** are fairly sheltered and becoming more popular. Both have a mix of gay and nongay devotees.

For out-of-the-way beaching you need to head for the likes of **Lia** on the southeast coast, or the smaller **Fokos** and **Mersini** on the east coast, but you'll need tough wheels and undercarriage to get there.

ACTIVITIES

Dive Adventures (☎ 22890 26539; www.diveadventures .gr; Paradise Beach) offers a full range of diving courses with multilingual instructors. Two introductory dives cost €130; snorkelling costs €30. There are various dive packages starting with a five-dive deal for €225 and PADI certification courses are available.

On a great location at Kalafatis Beach, **Planet Windsailing** (☎ 22890 72345; www.pezi-huber. com) has a one-hour or one-day windsurfing for €26 or €60, respectively, or a three-hour beginner's course for €75.

Also at Kalafatis, the **Kalafati Dive Center** (☎ 22890 71677; www.mykonos-diving.com) has the full range of diving courses including a 10-boat-dive deal with tank and weights for €290 and with full gear for €390. A single boat dive with tank and weights costs €45, or with all equipment €60. A 'discover scuba diving' session is €45. There's a 10% discount for prepaid bookings.

SLEEPING

Mykonos Camping (☎ 22890 24578; www.mycamp.gr; camp sites per adult/child/tent €10/5/5, bungalows per person €15-30, apt €180-235) This budget option is by the pleasant Paraga Beach (a 10-minute walk from Platys Gialos). Total peace and privacy cannot be guaranteed but facilities are reasonable and there are also bungalows and apartments that sleep two to six people.

Twins Apartments (☎ 22890 26241; www.twins-mykonos. com; d/tr/q €130/145/160; ❄) Located close to Ornos beach, these bright, spacious apartments are ideal for families and have cooking facilities.

Princess of Mykonos (☎ 22890 23806; www.princess ofmykonos.gr; s €200, d €220-280, tr €245-320 incl breakfast; P ❄ ☐ ☜) Sea-view rooms are the most expensive at this swish hotel, which merges traditional island style with Art Deco touches. The hotel is above the often busy Agios Stefanos beach.

EATING

our pick **Christos** (☎ 22890 26850; Agios Ioannis Beach; mains €6-18) Fisherman, chef and sculptor Christos runs his beachside eatery with unassuming style. It's right on the 'Shirley Valentine' shoreline, but Christos really is authentic Mykonos, where the best fish and seafood, not least unbeatable *astakos* (crawfish or spiny lobster), is prepared with skill.

Tasos Trattoria (☎ 22890 23002; Paraga Beach; mains €9-19) Central to Paraga Beach, this popular taverna does terrific fish, chicken, pork and veal dishes and a great mix of vegie options.

ENTERTAINMENT

Cavo Paradiso (☎ 22890 27205; www.cavoparadiso.gr) When dawn gleams just over the horizon, hard-core bar-hopper s move from Hora (Mykonos) to Cavo Paradiso, the megaclub that's been blasting at Paradise Beach since 1993 and has featured top international DJs ever since, including house legends David Morales and Louie Vega.

Ano Mera Ανω Μέρα
pop 1310

The village of Ano Mera, 7km east of Hora, is the island's only inland settlement and is worth a passing visit as an antidote to Hora and the beaches. It's a fairly unassuming place with a big central square flanked on three sides by tavernas offering standard fare. There's a big car park adjoining the main square.

The 6th-century **Moni Panagias Tourlianis** (☎ 22890 71249; ☼ 9am-1pm & 2-7.30pm) has a fine, multistage, marble bell tower with elegant carvings and 16th-century icons painted by members of the Cretan School, but pride of place goes to an exquisite wooden iconostasis carved in Florence in the late 1700s.

DELOS ΔΗΛΟΣ

The Cyclades fulfil their collective name *(kyklos)* by encircling the sacred island of **Delos** (☎ 22890 22259; museum & sites adult/concession €5/3; ⏲ 8.30am-3pm Tue-Sun), but Mykonos clutches the island jealously to its heart. Delos has no permanent population and is a soothing contrast to the relentless liveliness of modern Mykonos, although in high summer you share it all with fellow visitors. The island is one of the most important archaeological sites in Greece and the most important in the Cyclades. It lies a few kilometres off the west coast of Mykonos.

Delos still hides its secrets and every now and then fresh discoveries are made. In recent years a gold workshop was uncovered alongside the Street of the Lions.

History

Delos won early acclaim as the mythical birthplace of the twins Apollo and Artemis and was first inhabited in the 3rd millennium BC. From the 8th century BC it became a shrine to Apollo, and the oldest temples on the island date from this era. The dominant Athenians had full control of Delos – and thus the Aegean – by the 5th century BC.

In 478 BC Athens established an alliance known as the Delian League, which kept its treasury on Delos. A cynical decree ensured that no one could be born or die on Delos, thus strengthening Athens' control over the island by expelling the native population.

Delos reached the height of its power in Hellenistic times, becoming one of the three most important religious centres in Greece and a flourishing centre of commerce. Many of its inhabitants were wealthy merchants, mariners and bankers from as far away as Egypt and Syria. They built temples to their homeland gods, but Apollo remained the principal deity.

The Romans made Delos a free port in 167 BC. This brought even greater prosperity, due largely to a lucrative slave market that sold up to 10,000 people a day. During the following century, as ancient religions lost relevance and trade routes shifted, Delos began a long, painful decline. By the 3rd century AD there was only a small Christian settlement on the island, and in the following centuries the ancient site was looted of many of its antiquities. It was not until the Renaissance that its antiquarian value was recognised.

Getting There & Away

Boats for Delos (return €15, 30 minutes) leave Hora (Mykonos) about six times a day from about 9am in high season with the last outward boat about 12.50pm. Departure and return times are posted on the ticket kiosk at the entrance to the Old Jetty at the south end of the harbour. There are fewer boats outside July and August. There are no boats on Monday when the site is closed. Boats return from the island between 11am and 3pm. When buying tickets establish which boat is available for your return, especially later in the day. In Hora (Mykonos), **Delia Travel** (☎ 22890 22322; travel@delia.gr; Akti Kambani) and the **Mykonos Accommodation Centre** (☎ 22890 23408; www.mykonos-accommodation.com; 1st fl, Enoplon Dynameon 10) sell tickets. You pay an entrance fee of €3 at a kiosk on the island.

The Mykonos Accommodation Centre organises guided tours to Delos at 10am every day except Monday, between May and September (adult/child €40/31, three hours). They include boat transfers from and to the Old Jetty, and admission to the site and museum. Tours are in English, French, German and Italian, and in Spanish and Russian on request.

A boat departs for Delos from Platys Gialos on Mykonos' (€14, 30 minutes) at 10.15am daily.

ANCIENT DELOS

The quay where excursion boats dock is south of the tranquil Sacred Harbour. Many of the most significant finds from Delos are in the National Archaeological Museum (p127) in Athens, but the site **museum** still has an interesting collection, including the lions from the Terrace of the Lions (those on the terrace itself are plaster-cast replicas).

Overnight stays on Delos are forbidden and boat schedules allow a maximum of about six or seven hours there. Bring water and food, as the cafeteria's offerings are poor value for money. Wear a hat and sensible shoes.

ANCIENT DELOS

0 ————————— 200 m
0 ————————— 0.1 miles

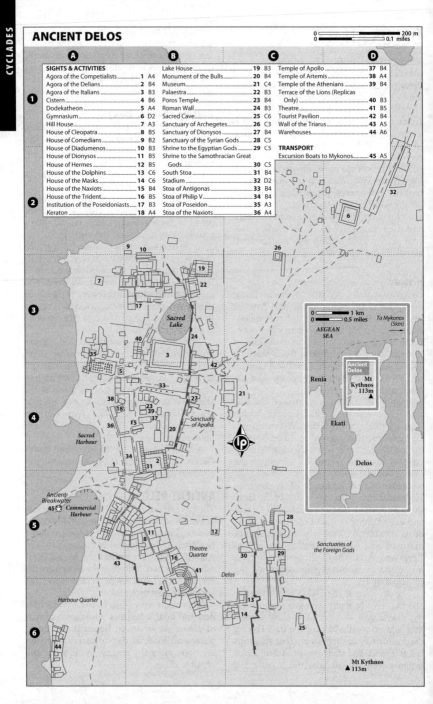

SIGHTS & ACTIVITIES		
Agora of the Competialists	1	A4
Agora of the Delians	2	B4
Agora of the Italians	3	B3
Cistern	4	B6
Dodekatheon	5	A4
Gymnasium	6	D2
Hill House	7	A3
House of Cleopatra	8	B5
House of Comedians	9	B2
House of Diadumenos	10	B3
House of Dionysos	11	B5
House of Hermes	12	B5
House of the Dolphins	13	C6
House of the Masks	14	C6
House of the Naxiots	15	B4
House of the Trident	16	B5
Institution of the Poseidoniasts	17	B3
Keraton	18	A4

Lake House	19	B3
Monument of the Bulls	20	B4
Museum	21	C4
Palaestra	22	B3
Poros Temple	23	B4
Roman Wall	24	B3
Sacred Cave	25	C6
Sanctuary of Archegetes	26	C3
Sanctuary of Dionysos	27	B4
Sanctuary of the Syrian Gods	28	C5
Shrine to the Egyptian Gods	29	C5
Shrine to the Samothracian Great Gods	30	C5
South Stoa	31	B4
Stadium	32	D2
Stoa of Antigonas	33	B4
Stoa of Philip V	34	B4
Stoa of Poseidon	35	A3
Stoa of the Naxiots	36	A4

Temple of Apollo	37	B4
Temple of Artemis	38	A4
Temple of the Athenians	39	B4
Terrace of the Lions (Replicas Only)	40	B3
Theatre	41	B5
Tourist Pavilion	42	B4
Wall of the Triarus	43	A5
Warehouses	44	A6

TRANSPORT		
Excursion Boats to Mykonos	45	A5

Exploring the Site

The following is an outline of some significant archaeological remains on the site. For further details, a guidebook from the ticket office is advisable, or take a guided tour.

The rock-encrusted **Mt Kythnos** (113m) rises elegantly to the southeast of the harbour. It's worth the steep climb, even in the heat; on clear days there are terrific views of the surrounding islands from its summit.

The path to Mt Kythnos is reached by walking through the **Theatre Quarter**, where Delos' wealthiest inhabitants once built their houses. These houses surrounded peristyle courtyards, with colourful mosaics (a status symbol) being the most striking feature of each house.

The most lavish dwellings were the **House of Dionysos**, named after the mosaic depicting the wine god riding a panther, and the **House of Cleopatra**, where headless statues of the owners were found. The **House of the Trident** was one of the grandest. The **House of the Masks**, probably an actors' hostelry, has another mosaic of Dionysos resplendently astride a panther. The **House of the Dolphins** has another exceptional mosaic.

The **theatre** dates from 300 BC and had a large **cistern**, the remains of which can be seen. It supplied much of the town with water. The houses of the wealthy had their own cisterns – essential as Delos was almost as parched and barren then as it is today.

Descending from Mt Kythnos, explore the **Sanctuaries of the Foreign Gods**. Here, at the **Shrine to the Samothracian Great Gods**, the Kabeiroi (the twins Dardanos and Aeton) were worshipped. At the **Sanctuary of the Syrian Gods** there are the remains of a theatre where an audience watched ritual orgies. There is also the **Shrine to the Egyptian Gods**, where Egyptian deities including Serapis and Isis were worshipped.

The **Sanctuary of Apollo**, to the northeast of the harbour, is the site of the much-photographed **Terrace of the Lions**. These proud beasts, carved from marble, were offerings from the people of Naxos, presented to Delos in the 7th century BC to guard the sacred area. To the northeast is the **Sacred Lake** (dry since it was drained in 1925 to prevent malarial mosquitoes breeding) where, according to legend, Leto gave birth to Apollo and Artemis.

PAROS ΠΑΡΟΣ

pop 13,000

Paros has a friendly, welcoming face. Its rolling hills are less formidable than the genuine mountains of neighbouring Naxos, and their slopes rise smoothly to the central high point of Mt Profitis Ilias (770m). White marble made Paros prosperous from the Early Cycladic period onwards – most famously, the *Venus de Milo* was carved from Parian marble, as was Napoleon's tomb.

Busy Parikia is the main town and port. The other major settlement, Naousa, on the north coast, is a lively resort with a still-active fishing harbour. On the east coast is the engaging little port and low-key resort of Piso Livadi, while deep at the heart of Paros is the peaceful mountain village of Lefkes.

The smaller island of Antiparos, 1km southwest of Paros, is easily reached by car ferry or excursion boat.

Getting There & Away

Paros is the main ferry hub for onward travel to other islands in the Aegean. It is thus well served by regular ferries from Piraeus and by connections to and from most of the other islands of the eastern Cyclades, and also Thessaloniki, Crete and the Dodecanese. For details see Island Hopping (p757).

Getting Around

BOAT

Water taxis leave from the quay for beaches around Parikia. Tickets range from €8 to €15 and are available on board.

BUS

About 12 buses daily link Parikia and Naousa (€1.40) directly, and there are seven buses daily from Parikia to Naousa via Dryos, Hrysi Akti, Marpissa, Marmara, Prodromos, Lefkes, Kostos and Marathi. There are 10 buses to Pounta (for Antiparos; €1.40) and six to Aliki (via the airport; €1.40).

CAR, MOTORCYCLE & BICYCLE

There are rental outlets along the waterfront in Parikia and all around the island. A good outfit is **Acropolis** (☎ 22840 21830). Minimum hire per day in August for a car is about €45; for a motorbike it's €20.

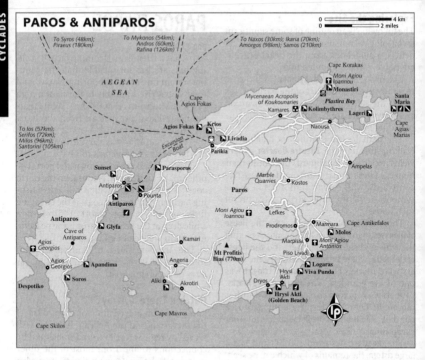

PAROS & ANTIPAROS

0 — 4 km
0 — 2 miles

To Syros (48km);
Piraeus (180km)

To Mykonos (54km);
Andros (60km);
Rafina (126km)

To Naxos (30km); Ikaria (70km);
Amorgos (98km); Samos (210km)

Cape Korakas

Moni Agiou
Ioannou

Monastiri

Santa
Maria

AEGEAN
SEA

Cape
Agios Fokas

Mycenaean Acropolis
of Koukounaries
Kamares

Plastira Bay
Kolimbythres

Lageri

To Ios (57km);
Serifos (72km);
Milos (96km);
Santorini (105km)

Agios Fokas

Krios
Livadia

Naousa

Cape
Agias
Marias

Excursion
Boat

Parikia

Sunset

Parasporos

Marathi

Ampelas

Antiparos

Pounta

Marble
Quarries

Kostos

Paros

Antiparos

Antiparos

Glyfa

Moni Agiou
Ioannou

Lefkes

Cave of
Antiparos

Kamari

Prodromos

Marmara

Cape Antikefalos

Molos

Agios
Georgios

Angeria

Marpissa

Moni Agiou
Antonios

Agios
Georgios

Apandima

Mt Profitis
Ilias (770m)

Piso Livadi

Soros

Aliki

Akrotiri

Dryos

Logaras
Viva Punda

Despotiko

Hrysi
Akti

Hrysi Akti
(Golden Beach)

Cape Mavros

Cape Skilos

TAXI
Taxis (☎ 22840 21500) gather beside the roundabout in Parikia. Fixed fares: airport €12, Naousa €10, Pounta €8, Lefkes €10 and Piso Livadi €13. Add €1 if going from the port. There are extra charges of €2 if you book ahead more than 20 minutes beforehand, €3 if less than 20 minutes. Each piece of luggage is charged €0.30.

PARIKIA ΠΑΡΟΙΚΙΑ
pop 4522
Parikia is a lively, colourful place full of the comings and goings of a typical island port but enhanced by a labyrinthine old town, 13th-century Venetian *kastro* (fort) and a long, straggling waterfront crammed with tavernas, bars and cafes.

Orientation
The busy hub of Parikia is the windmill roundabout, where you come off the ferry quay. The large main square, Plateia Mavrogenous, refurbished in 2007–08, is straight ahead from the windmill. The busy road to the left (east) leads along the water-front to the beach at Livadia. The road to the right (south) follows the waterfront past a long line of cafes and tavernas and on towards Pounta (for Antiparos) and the south of the island.

Agora (Market St) is the main commercial thoroughfare running southwest from Plateia Mavrogenous through the narrow and pedestrianised streets of the old town and up into the area known as Kastro, where the Venetian *kastro* once stood.

The bus station is 50m to the right of the quay (looking inland) and the post office is 400m to the left.

A free, green by nature, green in colour bus – powered by electricity – runs around Parikia at regular intervals from early morning until late evening all year; a laudable energy-saving strategy by the local authority, it is reportedly well-used by locals at all times.

Information
BOOKSHOPS
Newsstand (Ekatondapylianis) A great selection of newspapers, magazines and books in all languages.

EMERGENCY
Police station (☎ 22840 23333; Plateia Mavrogenous)
Port police (☎ 22840 21240) Back from the northern waterfront, near the post office.

INTERNET ACCESS
Wired Café (☎ 22840 22003; Agora; per hr €3.50; ☾ 10.30am-2pm & 6-11pm Mon-Sat, 6-11pm Sun) Reliable internet access in a relaxed atmosphere. Also has webcam and connections for laptop computers, and digital-picture transfer.

INTERNET RESOURCES
Parosweb (www.parosweb.com)

LAUNDRY
Ostria Laundry (☎ 22840 21969, 6949079176; per wash & dry per 5kg around €12; ☾ 9am-9pm Mon-Sat, 10am-2pm Sun Jun-Sep, 9am-2pm & 5.30-8.30pm Oct-May) The average load is ready in one hour at this efficient place.

MEDICAL SERVICES
Health Centre (☎ 22840 22500; Prombona; ☾ 9am-1.30pm Mon-Fri) Also has a dentist.

MONEY
The following banks all have ATMs.
Alpha Bank (Ekatondapylianis)
Commercial Bank of Greece (Plateia Mavrogenous)
Eurobank (Ekatondapylianis)
National Bank of Greece (Plateia Mavrogenous)

POST
Post office (☎ 22840 21236) Located 400m east of the ferry quay.

TOURIST INFORMATION
In high season, kiosks on the quay give out information on domatia and hotels (see Rooms Association, right).

TRAVEL AGENCIES
Santorineos Travel Services (☎ 22840 24245) On the waterfront, just to the southwest of the windmill roundabout. Sells ferry tickets and can advise on accommodation and tours, and has a luggage store (€1 per hour). Other services include bureau de change, FedEx (dispatch only) and MoneyGram (international money transfers).

Sights
The **Panagia Ekatondapyliani** (☎ 22840 21243; Plateia Ekatondapyliani; ☾ 7.30am-9.30pm Easter-Sep, 8am-1pm & 4-9pm Oct-Easter), which dates from AD 326, is one of the most splendid churches in the Cyclades. The building is three distinct churches: Agios

Nikolaos, the largest, with superb columns of Parian marble and a carved iconostasis, is in the east of the compound; the others are the Church of Our Lady and the Baptistery. The name translates as Our Lady of the Hundred Gates, but this is a wishful rounding-up of a still-impressive number of doorways. The **Byzantine Museum** (admission €1.50; ☾ 9.30am-2pm & 6-9pm), within the compound, has a collection of icons and other artefacts.

Next to a school and behind the Panagia Ekatondapyliani, the **Archaeological Museum** (☎ 22840 21231; admission €2; ☾ 8.30am-2.45pm Tue-Sun) is a cool escape from the heat and hustle of town. It harbours some marvellous pieces, including a 5th-century Nike on the point of alighting and a 6th-century Gorgon also barely in touch with the sullen earth. Earlier examples of splendid pottery include the bosky *Fat Lady of Saliagos*, while a major exhibit is a fragment slab of the 4th-century **Parian Chronicle**, which lists the most outstanding artistic achievements of ancient Greece. It was discovered in the 17th century and, rather typically, two other slabs ended up in the Ashmolean Museum, in Oxford, England.

North along the waterfront there is a fenced **ancient cemetery** dating from the 7th century BC; it was excavated in 1983. Roman graves, burial pots and sarcophagi are floodlit at night.

The **Frankish kastro** was built by Marco Sanudo, Duke of Naxos, in AD 1260, on the remains of a temple to Athena. Not much of the *kastro* remains, save for a large wall that is a jigsaw of unpainted column bases and dressed blocks.

Tours
Santorineos Travel Services (☎ 22840 24245) can book bus tours of Paros (€32), boat trips to Mykonos and Delos (€40), and boats to Santorini (including a bus tour of the island, €55).

Sleeping
In August the **Rooms Association** (☎ 22840 22722, after hrs 22840 22220), located on the quay, has information on domatia; otherwise, owners meet ferries. The **Hotel Association** (☎ 22840 51207) has information about hotels on Paros and Antiparos. All camping grounds have minibuses that meet ferries.

BUDGET
Koula Camping (☎ 22840 22801; www.campingkoula.gr; camp sites per adult/child/tent €8/3/4; ☾ Apr-Oct; **P** 🛜)

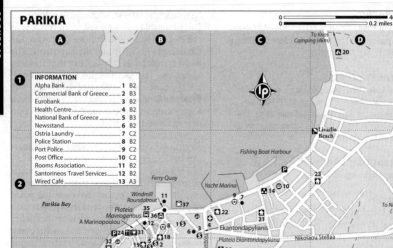

PARIKIA

INFORMATION
Alpha Bank	1	B2
Commercial Bank of Greece	2	B3
Eurobank	3	B2
Health Centre	4	B2
National Bank of Greece	5	B3
Newsstand	6	B2
Ostria Laundry	7	C2
Police Station	8	B2
Port Police	9	C2
Post Office	10	C2
Rooms Association	11	B2
Santorineos Travel Services	12	B2
Wired Café	13	A3

SIGHTS & ACTIVITIES
Ancient Cemetery	14	C2
Archaeological Museum	15	C3
Byzantine Museum	(see 16)	
Panagia Ekatondapyliani	16	C3
Santorineos Travel Services	(see 12)	

SLEEPING
Angie's Studios	17	B3
Captain Manoli's Hotel	18	B2
Hotel Argonauta	19	B3
Koula Camping	20	D1
Pension Rena	21	C2
Rooms Mike	22	B2
Sofia Pension	23	D2

EATING
Albatross	24	B2
Apollon	25	B3
Argonauta Taverna	(see 19)	
Happy Green Cows	26	B3
Idea	27	B3
Levantis	28	B3
Micro Café	29	B3
Taverna Mira	30	A3

DRINKING
Ellinadiko (Island)	31	B2
Evinos	32	A3
Pebbles Jazz Bar	33	A3
Pirate	34	A3
Simple Cafe	(see 32)	

TRANSPORT
Bus Station	35	B2
Taxi Stand	36	B2
Water Taxi to Beaches & Excursion Boats to Antiparos	37	B2

Koula is a pleasant, shaded little site behind the beach at the north end of the Parikia waterfront and only minutes from the centre. Two-person bungalow tents are €20; three-person €25.

Krios Camping (☎ 22840 21705; www.krios-camping. gr; camp sites per adult/child/tent €8/4/3; ☒ Jun-Sep; ⓟ ▢ ⬤ ⬤) This site is on the north shore of Parikia Bay about 4km from the port, but there's a water taxi across the bay to Parikia every 10 minutes for €4 per person (return). You can rent bungalow tents for €25. There's an on-site restaurant (dishes from €4 to €8).

Pension Rena (☎ 22840 22220; www.cycladesnet. gr/rena; s/d/tr €35/45/55; ☒ ⬤) One of the best choices in town, these immaculate rooms are excellent value, and there's a friendly welcome. The rooms are in a quiet but handy location just back from the waterfront. Air-con is €5 extra. The owners also have good apartments to rent in Naousa.

Rooms Mike (☎ 22840 22856; www.roomsmike .com; s/d/tr €35/45/60; ☒) A long-standing favourite in sight of the ferry quay, you'll never be short of chat and advice at Mike's place. There's a shared kitchen and a roof terrace. Mike also has well-maintained and well-equipped studios (€55) elsewhere in town. Enquire for details. Credit cards are accepted.

Captain Manoli's Hotel (☎ 22840 21244; www .paroswelcome.com; s/d/tr €50/60/72; ☒) Hidden away at the centre of town are these decent rooms that are clean and brightly decorated. Check prices for July and August when there is a minimum-stay requirement.

MIDRANGE

our pick Sofia Pension (☎ 22840 22085; www.sofiapension-paros.com; s/d/tr €65/75/90; P ✿ 💻 📶) Set in a garden full of greenery and flowers lovingly tended, this delightful place has immaculate rooms with individual decor. The owners are charming. Breakfast is available for €8.

Hotel Argonauta (☎ 22840 21440; www.argonauta.gr; Plateia Mavrogenous; s/d/tr €65/85/95; ✿ 📶) A long-established, family-run hotel with a central location overlooking Plateia Mavrogenous, the Argonauta has a welcoming atmosphere and has been recently refurbished. The furnishings have attractive traditional touches and the rooms are spotless and comfy and have double-glazing.

Angie's Studios (☎ 22840 23909/6977; www.angies-studios.gr; Makedonias; d/tr €80/90; 🕑 Apr-Oct; P ✿) A garden glowing with bougainvillea surrounds these handsome studios. They are in a very quiet area that's about a level 500m from the ferry dock. The studios are big and extremely well kept and each has its own kitchen. There are generous discounts in the low season.

Eating

Micro Café (☎ 22840 24674; Agora; snacks €4-5) This great gathering spot for locals and visitors alike is bright and cheerful and lies at the heart of Kastro. It does breakfasts for €4, as well as coffee and snacks, sandwiches, fresh fruit and vegetarian juices. There are drinks and music into the early hours.

Parasporos Restaurant (☎ 6947183732; Parasporos Beach; mains €5-10) The owner of Micro Café also runs this restaurant on Parosporos Beach, 2km south of town. The emphasis at both venues is on vegetarian food.

Albatross (☎ 22840 21848; D Vasiliou; mains €5-15) Albatross is a local favourite not least because of its excellent fish dishes. The fisherman's salad for €15 is a sure bet, or savour cuttlefish with spinach in an unfussy setting on the waterfront.

Taverna Mira (☎ 22840 22592; mains €5.80-10.80) One of the best eateries along Parikia's fairly relentless southern strip of cafes, bars and tavernas, Mira's is known for its *arni lemonato* (lamb in lemon sauce) and *kleftiko* (lamb baked in a clay pot with feta cheese and wine). Vegetarians also have a good choice of combinations.

Idea (☎ 22840 21038; mains €7-9.50) For a peaceful alternative to the often traffic-logged waterfront, this relaxed cafe-bar is opposite Panagia Ekatondapyliani and shares some of its tranquillity. It does crêpes, omelettes and heftier dishes such as pork cooked in beer and honey with rice. Breakfasts are €5 to €8.

our pick Levantis (☎ 22840 23613; Kastro; dishes €9-15) A courtyard garden setting enhances dining at this long-established restaurant at the heart of the Kastro area. There is a truly splendid cuisine with imaginative starters such as fennel and pear salad with mixed greens, croutons and Parmesan shavings, while mains include honey-spiced lamb with apples, prunes and almonds. Lovely desserts, such as honey and almond truffles covered in bitter cocoa, round things off with a flourish. Excellent house wine is underpinned with a good choice of Greek vintages.

Happy Green Cows (☎ 22840 24691; dishes €12-23; 🕑 7pm-midnight) Camp decor and upbeat service goes with the quirky name (inspired by a surreal dream, apparently) of this little eatery that is a vegetarian's delight. It's a touch pricey, but worth it for the often saucily named dishes. Dishes include sweetcorn croquettes in a lemon and yoghurt sauce or marinated artichokes in olive oil with fresh herbs topped with Parmesan cheese.

Also recommended:

Argonauta Taverna (☎ 22840 23303; mains €4.50-9) Attached to the hotel of the same name and offering sturdy Greek standards.

Apollon (☎ 22840 21875; Agora; mains €9-24) A long-established restaurant in Kastro.

Drinking

our pick Pebbles Jazz Bar (☎ 22840 22283; 📶) Heading down through Kastro in the late evening you'd think Pebbles' sunset backdrop was a vast painting. Perched above the seafront, this chilled place has lounge music by day and jazz in the evenings, with a classical climax for the sunset and occasional live performers during July and August. Pebbles has an adjacent *mezedhopoleio* (restaurant specialising in mezedhes) open from 9am to 1am, with breakfast from €4.50 to €7 and a great selection of mezedhes for €7 to €8, as well as omelettes and salads.

Pirate (☎ 6974315991) Ultracool corner of Parikia, Pirate is an ideal refuge, lulled by hazy jazz and blues beats to combat all that brilliant Cycladean light. It's just off the far end of Market St beyond Micro Café.

OFF THE BEATEN TRACK

Athens may think it has the acropolis *par excellence*, but Paros has its own little Mycenaean acropolis at **Koukounaries** near Naousa, where you won't mix it with too many fellow admirers. This is a grand site atop a gnarly little hill of boisterous sandstone boulders and buttresses, smoothed over and frozen into Dalí-esque shapes. Over 35,000 pieces of broken pottery have been found at the site. Signs point the way from the main Naousa road to parking at the base of the hill, but fade thereafter. Be warned: good footwear and careful footwork are essential to negotiate the initial rocky slabs, which are water-polished in places. At the top of the slabs you bear right towards a distinctive curved pillar just below the skyline. Follow your nose thereafter to the top of the hill and the scattered roots of buildings, unadorned and simple. The views are classic.

Ellinadiko (☎ 22840 25046) Also known as 'Island', this popular local bar with foot-stomping Greek music and late-night dancing is in an alleyway between Plateia Mavrogenous and the seafront.

There are more bars along the southern waterfront, including the popular **Evinos** (☎ 22840 23026) and **Salon D'Or** (☎ 22840 22176).

NAOUSA ΝΑΟΥΣΑ
pop 2865

Fast stealing some of the glitz and glamour of Mykonos, Naousa has transformed itself from a quiet fishing village into a popular tourist resort. Located on the shores of the large Plastira Bay on the north coast of Paros, there are good beaches nearby, and the town has several excellent restaurants and a growing number of stylish beachside cafes and bars. Behind the waterfront is a maze of narrow whitewashed streets, peppered with fish and flower motifs and with a mix of smart boutiques and souvenir shops.

Orientation & Information

The bus from Parikia terminates some way up from the main square just in from the waterfront, where a dried-up riverbed serves as a road leading south and inland. The main street of Naousa lies on the left of the riverbed. If arriving by car, be warned: parking in certain areas is banned from June to September. Signs may not be clear, but the €35 fines are painfully so. There's parking by the harbour and along the sides of the riverbed road, with a larger car park at the top end of the riverbed road.

Naousa Information (☎ 22840 52158; ⏱ 10am-midnight Jul & Aug, 11am-1pm & 6-10pm mid-Jun–Jul) can find you accommodation and is based in a booth by the main square.

The post office is a tedious uphill walk from the main square. There are several banks with ATMs around the main square.

For internet access, try **Jamnet3** (☎ 22840 52203; per hr €2.50; ⏱ 10am-1am), just by the entrance to the main square.

Sights & Activities

Naousa's **Byzantine museum** (admission €1.80; ⏱ 10am-1pm & 6-9pm Aug) is housed in the blue-domed church, about 200m uphill from the central square on the main road to Parikia. A small **folklore museum** (☎ 22840 52284; admission €1.80; ⏱ 9am-1pm & 6-9pm), which focuses on regional costumes, can be reached by heading inland from the main square to another blue-domed church. Turn right behind the church.

The best beaches in the area are **Kolymbythres** and **Monastiri**, which has some good snorkelling and a clubbing venue. Low-key **Lageri** is also worth seeking out. **Santa Maria**, on the other side of the eastern headland, is good for windsurfing. They can all be reached by road, but caïques go from Naousa to each of them during July and August.

Kokou Riding Centre (☎ 22840 51818; www.kokou. gr) has morning (€45), evening (€30) and one-hour (€25) horse rides, and can arrange pickup from Naousa's main square for a small charge. The rides explore the surrounding countryside and coast.

Sleeping

There are two camping grounds, both with minibuses that meet ferries. Visit the Naousa Information booth for help with finding accommodation.

Surfing Beach (☎ 22840 52491; fax 22840 51937; info@surfbeach.gr; camp sites per adult/child/tent €7.50/3.60/4) A fairly large site, but with reasonable facilities and a good location at

Santa Maria. The site has a windsurfing and water-skiing school.

Young Inn (☎ 6976415232; www.young-inn.com; dm €9-20, d & tr €66; **P** 🔁 🖳) This well-run place caters for a young, international clientele and organises events and outings. Scooter hire can be arranged. Breakfasts start at €3. It's located to the east of the harbour, behind Naousa's cathedral.

Hotel Stella (☎ 22840 51317; www.hotelstella.gr; s/d €55/75 🔁 🖳) Deep in the heart of the old town and within a leafy, colourful garden, the Stella has decent rooms and good facilities. It's best reached by heading up the main street, turning left at the National Bank, going beneath an archway and then turning right and up past a small church.

Hotel Galini (☎ 22840 53382; www.hotelgaliniparos. com; s/d/tr €60/70/85; 🔁 🛜) Opposite the blue-domed local church (Byzantine museum), on the main road into town from Parikia, this little hotel has comfortable, recently updated rooms. Be certain that this is our recommended hotel. There is a similarly named establishment elsewhere in town.

ourpick Katerina's Rooms (☎ 22840 51642; www.katerinastudios.gr; s/d/tr/studio €60/75/90/120; 🔁) Unbeatable views make these immaculate rooms (complete with tea- and coffee-making facilities) an excellent choice. You need to hike uphill a touch, but it's all worth it.

Sunset Studios and Apartments (☎ 22840 51733; www.paros.biz; d/tr €85/102, apt €180-216; **P** 🔁 🛜) Tucked away on the hill above the centre of Naousa and a few minutes stroll from the harbour are these peaceful rooms and apartments enhanced by a leafy garden and a warm welcome.

Eating & Drinking

Moshonas (☎ 22840 51623; dishes €4.50-9) An unbeatable location right at the edge of the harbour makes this family-run *ouzerie* and fish restaurant a favourite with locals and visitors alike. Fish is by the kilo but there are mains fish dishes at reasonable prices and you'll likely see the family's own caïques tie up and deliver the fresh octopus that will soon be on your plate.

Glafkos (☎ 22840 52100; mains €6-12) There's a great take on seafood at this beachside eatery, with subtle dishes such as shrimps and *manouri*, and scallops in a cream sauce.

Perivolaria (☎ 22840 51598; dishes €7-19) Reliable Greek and international cuisine, pastas and wood-fired pizzas are the style at this long-established restaurant where there's a lovely garden setting. Try the *pastourmali* (pastrami and cheese pie, a mix of meat, tomatoes, feta and *manouri*). Perivolaria is reached along the river road from the main square.

Christos (☎ 22840 51442; dishes €10-29; 🕑 7pm-1am Apr-Oct) A leafy canopy of vines adds style to the lovely courtyard dining area of Christos, which is enhanced even more by the paintings that line the walls. The food matches the attentive service and is modern Mediterranean with flair, all backed by a superb wine list. Head up the main street and it's on the left after about 50m.

Beyond the harbour, there's a beachfront line of cafes and music bars with cool lounge decor worthy of Mykonos. Places like **Fotis** (☎ 6938735017) and **Briki** (☎ 22840 52652) spill out onto little beaches and play a mix of classical strands by day and jazzier, funkier sounds by night.

AROUND PAROS

Lefkes Λεύκες
pop 494

Lovely Lefkes clings to a natural amphitheatre amid hills whose summits are dotted with old windmills. Siesta is taken seriously here and the village has a general air of serenity. It lies 9km southeast of Parikia, high among the hills, and was capital of Paros during the Middle Ages. The village's main attractions are its pristine alleyways and buildings. The **Cathedral of Agia Triada** is an impressive building, shaded by olive trees.

From the central square, a signpost points to a well-preserved Byzantine path, which leads (in 3km) to the village of **Prodromos**. At the edge of the village, keep left at a junction (signposted) with a wider track. Sections of the route retain their original paving.

Down on the southeast coast is the attractive harbour and low-key resort of **Piso Livadi**, where there is a pleasant beach. **Perantinos Travel & Tourism** (☎ 22840 41135; perantin@otenet.gr) can arrange accommodation, car hire and boat trips to other islands, and also arranges money exchange. There is an ATM next to Perantinos.

Beaches

There is a fair scattering of beaches around the island's coastline, including a good one at **Krios**, accessible by water taxi (return €4) from

Parikia. Paros' top beach, **Hrysi Akti** (Golden Beach), on the southeast coast, is hardly spectacular, but it has good sand and several tavernas, and is popular with windsurfers.

There is a decent enough beach at **Aliki** on the south coast.

SIGHTS & ACTIVITIES

The straits between Paros and Antiparos are especially suited to windsurfing and the spectacular sport of kiteboarding – effectively windsurfing in midair.

Down the coast at Pounta, **Eurodivers Club** (☎ 22840 92071; www.eurodivers.gr) has an impressive range of diving courses and dives for all levels and interests. A PADI open-water certification course costs €410, all inclusive.

Paros Kite Pro Center (☎ 22840 92229; www.paroskite-procenter.com), well run by the same team as Eurodivers Club, has a range of courses. These include an introductory one-hour kiteboarding session for €45, while more intensive courses start at €190 for four to six hours.

At Golden Beach, **Aegean Diving College** (☎ 22840 43347, 6932289649; www.aegeandiving.gr) offers a range of dives of archaeological and ecological interest led by scientists and experienced professional divers. A 'discover scuba' dive costs €80, and PADI open-water certification is €450.

Octopus Sea Trips (☎ 6932757123; www.octopuseatrips.com), based at Golden Beach and affiliated with Aegean Diving College, runs marine environmental courses and activities with snorkelling and diving for families and children.

Fanatic Fun Centre (☎ 6938307671; www.fanatic-paros.com; Hrysi Akti) runs catamaran sailing, water-skiing and windsurfing. One-hour windsurfing instruction costs €23 and a two-hour kiteboarding course is €75.

SLEEPING & EATING

Piso Livadi, which has a sunny magic of its own, has a number of modern rooms and apartments and a few decent tavernas.

ᴏᴜʀ ᴘɪᴄᴋ Anna's Studios (☎ 22840 41320; www.annasinn.com; Piso Livadi; s/d/tr/ste/apt €43/57/65/65/95; ⛄ ⌨) Anna's bright and spacious studios, just inland from the harbour, are unbeatable value, right down to the exquisite decorative embroidery pieces by Anna's mother. The family also has well-kept rooms right on the harbour front, but without the seclusion of the studios. There are tea- and coffee-making facilities.

Halaris Taverna (☎ 22840 43257; mains €5-9) Right on the Piso Livadi waterfront, Halaris is one of the best tavernas on Paros and specialises in fresh fish from the family's boat as well as traditional meat and vegetable dishes. A fish plate costs €10. The cod croquettes, shrimp pies and tomato croquettes are peerless. Add in the local wine and cheerful service and it doesn't get better than this.

Thea (☎ 22840 91220, 6945751015; Pounta; dishes €9-18) The location of this great restaurant, near the Antiparos ferry quay at Pounta, may be unassuming but the views across the channel are marvellous. There are rich aromas of old Greece and Asia Minor in the air, and the food is superb. Mains include Cappadocian lamb with apricots, and beef with quinces, rice and plums. There are over 400 different vintages kept in a wine room–cum–bar, which even has a glass floor with bottles nestling beneath your feet. The music collection is every bit as fine.

ENTERTAINMENT

Punda Beach Club (☎ 22840 41717; www.pundabeach.gr; Viva Punda) For the ultragregarious this all-day clubbing venue, on the east coast south of Piso Livadi, is the place to head for. It's a huge complex with swimming pools, bars, restaurants, a gym, live music shows and a relentlessly crowded beach scene.

ANTIPAROS
ΑΝΤΙΠΑΡΟΣ

pop 1037

Change down several gears for Antiparos, a laid-back and lovely island, which is rightly proud of its distinctiveness and independence from Paros; you forget this at your peril in front of local people. The main village and port (also called Antiparos) is a relaxed place. There's a touristy gloss round the waterfront and main streets, but the village runs deep inland to quiet squares and alleyways that give way suddenly to open fields.

ORIENTATION & INFORMATION

Go right from the ferry quay along the waterfront. The main street, Agora, heads inland just by the Anargyros Restaurant. Halfway up the main street are an Emporiki Bank and

National Bank of Greece, next to each other and both with ATMs. The post office is also here. The central square is reached by turning left at the top of the main street and then right, behind Smiles Cafe.

To reach the *kastro*, another Venetian creation, go under the stone arch that leads north off the central square.

The rest of the island runs to the south of the main settlement through quiet countryside. There are several decent beaches, especially at Glyfa and Soros on the east coast.

Nautica Café (☎ 22840 61323; internet per hr €2; ▣ ⊛) is a busy waterfront cafe with internet access and free wi-fi for customers.

There are several tour and travel agencies, including **Cave Travel** (☎ 22840 61376) and **Oliaris Tours** (☎ 22840 61231; oliaros@par.forthnet.gr). **Blue Island Divers** (☎ 22840 61493; www.blueisland-divers.gr) can also arrange accommodation and car hire.

SIGHTS & ACTIVITIES

Despite previous looting of stalactites and stalagmites, the **Cave of Antiparos** (admission €3.50; ⊛ 10.45am-3.45pm summer) is still awe-inspiring. It is 8km south of the port. Follow the coast road south until you reach a signed turn-off into the hills. From the port there are hourly buses to the cave (one way €5), and there are cave tours every hour.

On the main pedestrian thoroughfare of town, with a gear and clothes shop attached, is the helpful **Blue Island Divers** (☎ 22840 61493; www.blueisland-divers.gr) which has a wide range of dive options. The owners have a great knowledge of the Antiparos scene. Accommodation and car rental can also be arranged. A four-day PADI open-water course is €350 and an advanced course is €270. A 'discover scuba diving' day session is €50. Trips can be tailored to suit individual wishes.

TOURS

MS Thiella (☎ 22840 61028) runs tours around the island daily, stopping at several beaches. The price (adult/child €45/25) covers barbecue and drinks; you can book at local travel agencies.

SLEEPING

Camping Antiparos (☎ 22840 61221; camp sites per adult/child/tent €6/4/4) This pleasant beachside camping ground is planted with bamboo 'compartments' and cedars and is 1.5km north of the port. It has a minimarket, bar

and restaurant. A site bus picks up from the port.

Anarghyros (☎ 22840 61204; mak@par.forthnet.gr; s/d €40/55; ⊠) There's good value at this well-kept, family-run hotel on the waterfront, where rooms are a decent size and come with tea- and coffee-making facilities. Attached to the hotel is a decent restaurant offering standard Greek dishes from €5 to €9.

Hotel Mantalena (☎ 22840 61206; www.hotelmantalena.gr; s/d/tr €50/65/75; ⊠ ▣ ⊛) The Mantalena has bright, clean rooms and is located a short distance to the north of the main harbour quay. There's a pleasant terrace and the building is set back from the harbour road. You get a decent breakfast for €6.

EATING & DRINKING

The waterfront and main street of Antiparos have several cafes and tavernas serving Greek staples and fish dishes. You'll also find supermarkets and a bakery in the main street.

Yannis Place (☎ 22840 61469; mains €5-8) Halfway up the main street is this bright place with a little streetside terrace, ideal for people watching. Breakfast is €6 to €8, and it does omelettes, toasties, crêpes and pastas, as well as smoothies and ice cream for post-midday, and cocktails for the evening gear change.

Maki's (☎ 22840 61616; dishes €5.50-12) Seafood is the speciality at this harbour-front taverna. It's generally excellent, from the prawn souvlaki with calamari to lobster (by the kilo when available).

Yam Bar Restaurant and Cocktail Bar (dishes €6-9; ⊛ 8pm-4am mid-Jun–mid-Sep) You can enjoy salads and cold plates of chicken or pasta at this relaxing spot with views of the sea. Sounds are a general mix that includes Latin, house and occasional jazz. It's signposted left off the top end of Market St.

Soul Sugar is along to the right from the top of the main street. It plays funk, disco and house into the small hours, and serves great cocktails.

GETTING THERE & AWAY

In summer, frequent excursion boats depart for Antiparos from Parikia. There is also a half-hourly car ferry that runs from Pounta on the west coast of Paros to Antiparos (one way €1, per scooter €1.80, per car €6, 10 minutes); the first ferry departs from Pounta about 7.15am and the last boat returning to Pounta leaves Antiparos at about 12.30am.

GETTING AROUND

The only bus service on Antiparos runs, in summer, to the cave in the centre of the island (see p405; €5). The bus continues to Soros and Agios Georgios.

Cars, scooters and bicycles can be hired from **Aggelos** (☎ 22840 61626/61027), the first office as you come from the ferry quay. Cars start at €42 per day in high season, scooters are €15 per day and bicycles are €5 per day.

NAXOS ΝΑΞΟΣ

pop 18,188

It was on Naxos that an ungrateful Theseus is said to have abandoned Ariadne after she helped him escape the Cretan labyrinth. In keeping with even mythic soap opera, she didn't pine long, and was soon entwined with Dionysos, the god of wine and ecstasy and the island's favourite deity. Naxian wine has long been considered a fine antidote for a broken heart.

The island was a cultural centre of classical Greece and of Byzantium. Venetian and Frankish influences have also left their mark.

Naxos is more fertile than most of the other islands and produces olives, grapes, figs, citrus fruit, corn and potatoes. Mt Zeus (1004m; also known as Mt Zas or Zefs) is the Cyclades' highest peak and is the central focus of the island's mountainous interior, in which you find enchanting villages such as Halki and Apiranthos. There are numerous fine beaches and the island is a great place to explore on foot, as many old paths between villages, churches and other sights still survive. There are walking guides and maps available from local bookshops.

Getting There & Away

Like Paros, Naxos is something of a ferry hub of the Cyclades, with a similar number of conventional and fast ferries making regular calls to and from Piraeus, and weekly links to and from the mainland ports of Thessaloniki and Lavrio and eastward to the Dodecanese. There is a daily flight to and from Athens. There are daily connections to the other main Cycladic islands in summer. For details see Island Hopping (p756).

Getting Around

TO/FROM THE AIRPORT

The airport is 3km south of Hora. There is no shuttle bus, but buses to Agios Prokopios Beach and Agia Anna pass close by. A taxi costs €12 to €15 depending on the time of day and if booked.

BUS

Frequent buses run from Hora to Agia Anna (€1.80). Five buses daily serve Filoti (€2) via Halki (€1.80); four serve Apiranthos (€3) via Filoti and Halki; and at least three serve Apollonas (€5), Pyrgaki (€2.50) and Melanes (€1.80). There are less frequent departures to other villages.

Buses leave from the end of the ferry quay in Hora; timetables are posted outside the **bus information office** (☎ 22850 22291; www.naxos destinations.com), diagonally left and across the road from the bus stop. You have to buy tickets from the office.

CAR & MOTORCYCLE

August rates for hire cars range from about €45 to €55 per day, and motorcycles from about €18. **Rental Center** (☎ 22850 23395; Plateia Evripeou) is a good bet.

HORA (NAXOS) ΧΩΡΑ (ΝΑΞΟΣ)

pop 6533

Busy Hora, on the west coast of Naxos, is the island's port and capital. It's a large town, divided into two historic neighbourhoods – Bourgos, where the Greeks lived, and the hill-top Kastro, where the Venetian Catholics lived.

Orientation

The ferry quay is at the northern end of the waterfront, with the bus station at its inland end. The broad waterfront, Protopapadaki, known universally as Paralia, leads off to the south from the ferry quay and is lined with cafes, tavernas and shops on its inland side. Behind Paralia, narrow alleyways twist and turn beneath archways as they seem to vanish into the old town area of Bourgos and climb into the Kastro.

A northerly turn at the end of the ferry quay leads to a causeway over to Palatia Islet and the unfinished **Temple of Apollo**, Naxos' most famous landmark, known as the Portara. There is not much else to see at

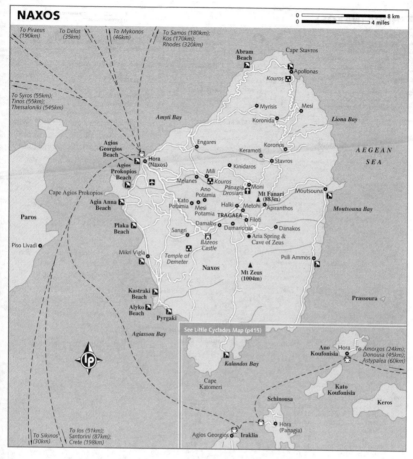

NAXOS

0 — 8 km
0 — 4 miles

To Piraeus (190km)
To Delos (35km)
To Mykonos (46km)
To Samos (180km); Kos (170km); Rhodes (320km)

Abram Beach

Cape Stavros

Apollonas

Kouros

To Syros (55km); Tinos (55km); Thessaloniki (545km)

Amyti Bay

Myrisis

Mesi

Liona Bay

Koronida

Engares

Keramoti

Koronos

AEGEAN SEA

Agios Georgios Beach

Hora (Naxos)

Stavros

Agios Prokopios Beach

Kinidaros

Mili

Cape Agios Prokopios

Melanes

Kouros

Panagia Drosiani

Moni

Mt Fanari (883m)

Moutsouna

Ano Potamia

Agia Anna Beach

Kato Potamia

Mesi Potamia

Halki

Metohi

Apiranthos

Moutsouna Bay

Paros

TRAGAEA

Filoti

Plaka Beach

Damalas

Damarionas

Danakos

Sangri

Aria Spring & Cave of Zeus

Piso Livadi

Bazeos Castle

Mikri Vigla

Temple of Demeter

Naxos

Psili Ammos

Mt Zeus (1004m)

Kastraki Beach

Prassoura

Alyko Beach

Pyrgaki

Agiassou Bay

See Little Cyclades Map (p415)

Ano Koufonisia

Hora

To Amorgos (24km); Donousa (45km); Astypalea (60km)

Kalandos Bay

Kato Koufonisia

Cape Katomeri

Schinousa

Keros

To Sikinos (30km)
To Ios (51km); Santorini (87km); Crete (198km)

Agios Georgios

Iraklia

Hora (Panagia)

the temple other than the two columns and their crowning lintel surrounded by fallen masonry, but it makes for a romantic spot, especially at sunset.

There are a few swimming spots along the waterfront promenade below the temple. Southwest of the town is the pleasant, but busy, beach of Agios Georgios.

Information
BOOKSHOPS
Zoom (☎ 22850 23675; Paralia) A large, well-stocked newsagent and bookshop that has most international newspapers the day after publication.

EMERGENCY
Police station (☎ 22850 22100; Paparrigopoulou) Southeast of Plateia Protodikiou.

Port police (☎ 22850 22300) Just south of the quay.

INTERNET ACCESS
Grotta Tours (☎ 22850 25782; Paralia; per hr €3)
Rental Center (☎ 22850 23395; Plateia Evripeou; per hr €3)
Zas Travel (☎ 22850 23330; fax 22850 23419; Paralia; per hr €4)

LAUNDRY
To Ariston (☎ 22850 26750; 5kg wash & dry €10; ⏲ 8am-2pm & 5.30-9pm Mon, Tue, Thu & Fri, 8am-2pm Wed & Sat)

MEDICAL SERVICES
Hospital (☎ 22853 60500; Prantouna) New hospital opened in 2009.

CYCLADES

HORA (NAXOS)

0 _____ 200 m
0 _____ 0.1 miles

A **B** **C** **D**

INFORMATION
Agricultural Bank of Greece 1 C4
Alpha Bank 2 B5
Bus Information Office 3 B3
Grotta Tours 4 B3
Hospital 5 D5
Information Booth 6 B3
National Bank of Greece 7 C4
Naxos Tours 8 C4

OTE 9 B5
Port Police 10 B3
Post Office 11 B6
Rental Center 12 C5
To Ariston 13 C5
Town Hall 14 B6
Zas Travel 15 B3
Zoom 16 C4

SIGHTS & ACTIVITIES
Archaeological Museum 17 C4
Della Rocca-Barozzi Venetian
Museum 18 C3

Mitropolis Museum 19 C3
Naos Silver Gallery 20 C4
Roman Catholic Cathedral 21 C4

SLEEPING
Chateau Zevgoli 22 C3
Despina's Rooms 23 C3
Hotel Anixis 24 C3
Hotel Glaros 25 B6
Hotel Grotta 26 D2
Pension Irene I 27 D5
Pension Irene II 28 D6
Pension Sofi 29 C3

EATING
Bakery .... (see 16)
East West Asian
  Restaurant 30 C6
Irini's 31 B3
Lucullus 32 B3
Meltemi 33 B6
Meze 2 .... 34 B3
O Apostolis 35 C3
Picasso Mexican Bistro 36 C6
Vidalis Supermarket 37 D3
Zoom Minimarket 38 C4

DRINKING
Jam 39 C5
Jazz-Blues Café 40 B3
On the Rocks 41 C5

ENTERTAINMENT
Abyss 42 C3
Cine Astra 43 D6
Della Rocca-Barozzi
  Venetian Museum .... (see 18)
Ocean 44 B5

SHOPPING
Antico Veneziano .... (see 17)
Kiriakos Tziblakis 45 C5
Naksia 46 C5
Takis' Shop 47 B3

TRANSPORT
Bus Station 48 B3
Ferries to Mykonos, Paros,
  Piraeus, Ios & Santorini 49 B3
Ferry to Little Cyclades &
  Amorgos 50 B4

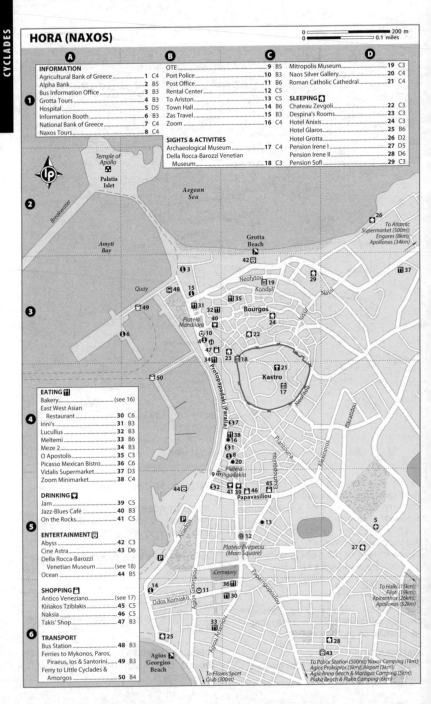

Temple of
Apollo

Palatia
Islet

Breakwater

Aegean
Sea

Amyti
Bay

Quay

Grotta
Beach

Neofytou

Kondyli

Bourgos

Platela
Mandilara

Kastro

Nassi

Protopapadaki (Paralia)

Pranouna

Plateia
Pigadakia

Papavasiliou

Plateia Evirpeou
(Main Square)

Arkadiou

Agiou Giourgiou

Odos Komiakis

Cemetery

Agiou Arsenia

Papatrigopoulou

Aleximeros

Mikraatidou

Agios
Georgios
Beach

To Atlantic
Supermarket (500m);
Engares (8km);
Apollonas (34km)

To Halki (15km);
Filoti (19km);
Apiranthos (26km);
Apollonas (52km)

To Police Station (500m); Naxos Camping (1km);
Agios Prokopios (3km); Airport (3km);
Agia Anna Beach & Maragas Camping (5km);
Plaka Beach & Plaka Camping (6km)

To Flisvos Sport
Club (300m)

MONEY

All the following banks have ATMs:
Agricultural Bank of Greece (Paralia)
Alpha Bank (cnr Paralia & Papavasiliou)
National Bank of Greece (Paralia)

POST

Post office (Agios Giorgiou) Go past the OTE, across Papavasiliou, and left at the forked road.

TELEPHONE

OTE (telecommunications office; Paralia) Has several phone kiosks in an alleyway.

TRAVEL AGENCIES

There is no official tourist information office on Naxos. Travel agencies can deal with most queries. Naxos Tours and Zas Travel both sell ferry tickets and organise accommodation, tours and rental cars.
Grotta Tours (☎ 22850 25782; Paralia)
Naxos Tours (☎ 22850 22095; www.naxostours.net; Paralia)
Zas Travel (☎ 22850 23330; zas-travel@nax.forthnet .gr; Paralia)

Sights

To see the Bourgos area, head into the winding backstreets behind the northern end of Paralia. The most alluring part of Hora is the residential **Kastro**. Marco Sanudo made the town the capital of his duchy in 1207, and several Venetian mansions survive. Take a stroll around the Kastro during siesta to experience its hushed, timeless atmosphere.

A short distance behind the northern end of the waterfront are several churches and chapels, and the **Mitropolis Museum** (☎ 22850 24151; Kondyli; admission free; 8.30am-3pm). The museum features fragments of a Mycenaean city of the 13th to 11th centuries BC that was abandoned because of the threat of flooding by the sea. It's a haunting place where glass panels underfoot reveal ancient foundations and larger areas of excavated buildings.

The **archaeological museum** (☎ 22850 22725; admission €3; 8.30am-3pm Tue-Sun) is in the Kastro, housed in the former Jesuit school where novelist Nikos Kazantzakis was briefly a pupil. The contents include Hellenistic and Roman terracotta figurines and some early Cycladic figurines.

Close by, the **Della Rocca-Barozzi Venetian Museum** (☎ 22850 22387; guided tours adult/student €5/3; 10am-3pm & 7-10pm end May–mid-Sep), a hand-

some old tower house of the 13th century, is within the Kastro ramparts (by the northwest gate). There are changing art exhibitions in the vaults. Tours are multilingual. The museum also runs tours (adult/student €15/10) of the Kastro at 11am Tuesday to Sunday; tours last just over two hours. Evening concerts and other events are staged in the grounds of the museum (see p411). The **Roman Catholic cathedral** (6.30pm-8.30pm), also in the Kastro, is worth visiting too.

Activities

Flisvos Sport Club (☎ 22850 24308; www.flisvos-sportclub. com; Agios Georgios) has a range of windsurfing options, starting with a beginner's course of six hours for €150, or a five-hour Hobie Cat sailing course for €95. The club also organises walking trips and hires out mountain bikes at a per-week rate of €60.

Naxos Horse Riding (☎ 6948809142) organises daily horse rides (10am to 1pm and 5pm to 8pm) inland and on beaches (per person €48). You can book a ride up until 6pm the day before and can arrange pick-up and return, to and from the stables. Beginners, young children and advanced riders are catered for. Bookings can also be made at the **Naos Silver Gallery** (☎ 22850 24130; Pigadakia).

Tours

There are frequent excursion boats to Mykonos (adult/child €45/23), Delos (€45) Santorini (adult/child €55/30), Paros and Naousa (adult/child €20/10) and Iraklia and Koufonissi (adult/child €40/20); book through travel agents (see left).

Sleeping

Hora has plenty of good accommodation options. If you settle for an offer at the port from a persistent accommodation hawker, establish with certainty the true distance of the rooms from the centre of town. In high season there may be booths on the quay dispensing information about hotels and domatia.

BUDGET

Despina's Rooms (☎ 22850 22356; fax 22850 22179; Kastro; s/d €40/50;) These decent rooms are tucked away in the Kastro and some have sea views. Rooms on the roof terrace are popular despite their small size. There's a communal kitchen.

Hotel Anixis (☎ 22850 22932; www.hotel-anixis.gr; s/d/tr €50/60/75; ❄ ❐) Tucked away in a quiet location in Kastro, this pleasant hotel, in a garden setting, has bright and well-kept rooms and there are great views to the sea. Breakfast is €5.

Pension Irene I (☎ 22850 23169; www.irene pension-naxos.com; s/d €50/60; ❄ ❐) This long-standing favourite is a bit of a hike from the ferry dock but is in a quiet side street and has clean, comfortable rooms.

There are several camping grounds near Hora, and all have good facilities. Minibuses meet the ferries. The sites are all handy to good beaches and there's an approximate price per person of €9.

Camping Maragas (☎ 22850 24552; www.maragas camping.gr) At Agia Anna Beach, south of Hora.

Naxos Camping (☎ 22850 23500; www.naxos -camping.gr; ❐) About 1km south of Agios Georgios Beach. The camping ground closest to town.

Plaka Camping (☎ 22850 42700; www.plakacamping .gr; ❐) At Plaka Beach, 6km south of town.

MIDRANGE

Pension Irene II (☎ 22850 23169; www.irenepension -naxos.com; s/d €60/70; ❄ ❐ ❐ ❐) Bright, clean rooms and a swimming pool have made this well-run place popular with a younger set.

Pension Sofi (☎ 22850 25593; www.pensionsofi.gr; s/d/tr €65/70/90; ❄) Hospitality is the rule at this family-run place. It's just a short distance inland from the port and is framed by one of the biggest bougainvilleas you're likely to see. Rooms are clean and well equipped and include cooking facilities.

Hotel Glaros (☎ 22850 23101; www.hotelglaros .com; Agios Georgios; s incl breakfast €65, d incl breakfast €85-95; ❄ ❐ ❐) The attractive decor of Hotel Glaros captures the colours of sea and sky. Service is efficient and thoughtful and the rooms are bright and clean. The hotel is only a few steps away from the beach. The owners also have attractive studios nearby (€65 to €100).

our pick **Hotel Grotta** (☎ 22850 22215; www.hotel grotta.gr; Grotta; s/d incl breakfast €70/85; ❐ ❄ ❐ ❐) Located on high ground to the east of the ferry quay, this fine modern hotel has comfortable and immaculate rooms, great sea views from the front, spacious public areas and a Jacuzzi. It's made even better by the cheerful, attentive atmosphere.

Chateau Zevgoli (☎ 22850 26123; www.apollon hotel-naxos.gr; Kastro; s/d/ste €75/90/120; ❄ ❐) Tucked away at the heart of Kastro is this long-established hotel. It has a leafy garden setting to go with the traditional Naxian style of rooms and furnishings.

Eating

Naxian cuisine cherishes such local specialities as *kefalotyri* (a hard cheese made from sheep's milk), honey, *kitron* (a liqueur made from the leaves of the citron tree – see p412), *raki* (Greek firewater, smoother than *tsipouro*, Greece's main firewater), ouzo and fine white wine.

Meze 2 (☎ 22850 26401; Paralia; mains €3-9) The emphasis at this popular *mezedhopoleio* is on fish, and even the local fishermen eat here. Superb seafood is prepared and served by family members in an atmosphere that is never less than sociable. There is another Meze at Plaka Beach.

Meltemi (☎ 22850 22654; Komiakis; mains €5.50-14) Top dishes at this family-run taverna are lamb flavoured with fresh lemon juice and oregano, and *exohiko*, tender pieces of baked meat with Gruyere cheese and vegetables. They also do three-course fixed menus for €10 to €12.50, all served with courtesy and good humour on a leafy terrace that makes up for an otherwise dull street scene.

O Apostolis (☎ 22850 26777; Old Market; mains €5.50-17) Right at the heart of the labyrinthine Old Market area of Bourgos, Apostolis serves up rewarding dishes such as mussels in garlic butter and parsley, and *bekri mezes*, a popular Cretan dish of casseroled beef. The *kleftiko*, lamb wrapped in filo pastry with sautéed vegetables and feta cheese is particularly good.

Irini's (☎ 22850 26780; Paralia; mains €6-9.50) The real deal at this pleasant taverna is the terrific selection of dishes such as codfish croquettes and shrimp *saganaki* – from which you can construct a very satisfying meal.

Lucullus (☎ 22850 22569; Old Market St; mains €6.50-18) One hundred years' service and still going strong, this famous restaurant has starters such as mushroom pie, while mains include *lemonato*, tender veal in a fresh lemon juice and white wine sauce. The fisherman's pasta mixes shrimps, tomatoes, garlic and dill.

Also recommended:

East West Asian Restaurant (☎ 22850 24641; Odos Komiakis; dishes €5.60-13) Thai, Chinese and Indian favourites.

Picasso Mexican Bistro (☎ 22850 25408; Agiou Arseniou; dishes €5.25-12.75; ❄ 7pm-late) The fajitas at this great Tex-Mex place are world class. Also at Picasso on the Beach, Plaka Beach.

Near the Zoom newsagent and bookshop is the town's best bakery. Next door is the Zoom Minimarket. The cheapest supermarkets are Atlantic and Vidalis, both a little way out of town on the ring road.

Drinking

The seafront Paralia has a good mix of music cafe-bars interspersed with shops and offices, all ideal for people watching.

our pick **On the Rocks** (☎ 22850 29224; Pigadikia; 🖳 🛜) The place to go for character and cocktails. Enjoy Havana cigars or a *sheesha* (water pipe) with a wide selection of flavours from apple to mango, peach or pistachio. Or go for Cuban-style daiquiris or tequila. It all goes with sounds that vary between funk, house and electronic. Occasional live performances and karaoke stir the mix.

Jazz-Blues Café (☎ 22850 22006; Old Market St) A cosy little evening and late-night cafe-bar that plays what it says it does, just where the narrow, almost tunneled alleyways start to wriggle up into Kastro.

Jam (Pigadakia) A huge playlist with rock and standard favourites is the background to this long-established music bar. There's a matching list of cocktails.

Entertainment

CINEMAS

Cine Astra (☎ 22850 25381; Andreas Papandreou; adult/child €8/5) About a five-minute walk from the main square, it shows newly released mainstream films and has a bar. Sessions are at 9pm and 11pm.

NIGHTCLUBS

Abyss (Grotta; admission €12; 🕙 11.30pm-3am May–mid-Sep, 11.30pm-late Fri & Sat mid-Sep–Apr) Previously known as Super Island, this place had something of a makeover inside and out, but plays much the same sounds with house and modern Greek at the fore.

Ocean (☎ 22850 26766; Seafront; admission €12; 🕙 11.30pm-3am May–mid-Sep, 11.30pm-late Fri & Sat mid-Sep–Apr) A sizeable space features house and some modern Greek music, and runs special nights with guest DJs.

SUNSET CONCERTS

Della Rocca-Barozzi Venetian Museum (☎ 22850 22387; Kastro; events admission €15-20; 🕙 8pm Wed-Sun Apr-Oct) Special evening cultural events are held at the museum, and comprise traditional music and dance concerts, and classical and contemporary music recitals. Prices depend on seat position.

Shopping

Takis' Shop (☎ 22850 23045; Plateia Mandilara) Among the splendid wines here are such fine names as Lazaridis from northern Greece, Tslepos from the Peloponnese and Manousakis from Crete – all masterful vintages. You can also find Vallindras *kitron* (see p412) and ouzo here. Incorporated is Takis' jewellery shop, where fine individual pieces from some of Greece's most famous designers often reflect ancient designs and the imagery of the sea.

Kiriakos Tziblakis (☎ 22859 22230; Papavasiliou) A fascinating cavelike place crammed with traditional produce and goods, from pots and brushes to herbs, spices, wine, *raki* and olive oil.

Naksia (☎ 22850 23660; Plateia Pigadakia) For a remarkable collection of candles try this colourful shop tucked away in a cul-de-sac off the Plateia.

Antico Veneziano (☎ 22850 26206; Kastro) Deep within Kastro is this upmarket antique store and gallery that makes for a fascinating visit.

AROUND NAXOS

Beaches

Conveniently located just south of the town's waterfront is **Agios Georgios**, Naxos' town beach. It's backed by hotels and tavernas at the town end and can get very crowded, but it runs for some way to the south and its shallow waters mean the beach is safe for youngsters.

The next beach south of Agios Georgios is **Agios Prokopios**, in a sheltered bay to the south of the headland of Cape Mougkri. It merges with **Agia Anna**, a stretch of shining white sand, quite narrow but long enough to feel uncrowded towards its southern end. Development is fairly solid at Prokopios and the northern end of Agia Anna.

Sandy beaches continue down as far as **Pyrgaki** and include **Plaka**, **Kastraki** and **Alyko**.

One of the best of the southern beaches is **Mikri Vigla** – its name translates as 'little lookout', a watching place for pirates, and is a reference to the headland, all golden granite slabs and boulders, that divides the beach into two. The settlement here is a little scattered and is punctuated by half-finished buildings in places, but there's a sense of escapism and open space.

Near the beach at Ágios Prokopios is **Villa Adriana** (☎ 22850 42804; www.adrianahotel.com; s/d/tr/apt €75/85/90/120; P ✗ 🛜 🅿), a well-appointed hotel with excellent service and bright, comfortable rooms.

A great 'away from it all' option is **Oasis Studios** (☎ 22850 75494; www.oasisnaxos.gr; d/tr/apt €87/100/116; P ✗ 🅿 🅿) at Mikri Vigla, 20km south of Hora. It is close to the beach and has lovely big rooms with kitchens. The owner and staff are very helpful and there's an outside terrace with a swimming pool and bar that encourages sociability.

The beachside **Taverna Liofago** (☎ 22850 75214, 6937137737; dishes €4.50-9) has a dreamy beach location. It has been in business for decades and favours a variety of dishes with special Naxian flavour. The *keftedhakia* (meatballs) are a speciality.

South of Mikri Vigla, at Kastraki, is one of the best restaurants on the island, **Axiotissa** (☎ 22850 75107), noted for its sourcing of organic food and for its traditional dishes with added Anatolian flair.

Tragaea Τραγαία

The Tragaea region is a vast plain of olive groves and unspoilt villages, couched beneath the central mountains.

MT ZEUS

Filoti, on the slopes of **Mt Zeus** (1004m), is the region's largest village. It has an ATM booth just down from the main bus stop. On the outskirts of the village (coming from Hora), an asphalt road leads off right to the isolated hamlets of **Damarionas** and **Damalas**.

From Filoti, you can also reach the **Cave of Zeus (Zas)**, a large, natural cavern at the foot of a cliff on the slopes of Mt Zeus. There's a junction signposted Aria Spring and Zas Cave, about 800m south of Filoti. If travelling by bus, ask to be dropped off here. The side road ends in 1.2km. From the road-end parking, follow a walled path past the **Aria Spring & Cave of Zeus**, a fountain and picnic area, and on to a rough track uphill to reach the cave. The path leads on from here steeply to the summit of Zas. It's quite a stiff hike of about 3km. A good way to return to Filoti, taking another 4km, is to follow the path that leads north from the summit. This is not a mere stroll, so be fit and come equipped with good footwear, water and sunscreen. A longer, but less strenuous, route up Mt Zeus starts from the little chapel

of Aghia Marina on the road to Danakos. Ask to be let off the Apiranthos bus at the Danakos junction about 6km beyond Filoti.

HALKI ΛΛΚΕΙΟ

One of Naxos' finest experiences is a visit to the historic village of Halki, which lies at the heart of the Tragaea, about 20 minutes' drive from Naxos town. Halki is a vivid reflection of historic Naxos and is full of the handsome facades of old villas and tower houses, legacy of a rich past as the one-time centre of Naxian commerce.

The main road skirts Halki. There is some roadside parking but you may find more at the schoolyard at the north end of the village and on a piece of rough ground just beyond the school. Lanes lead off the main road to the beautiful little square at the heart of the village.

Since the late 19th century Halki has had strong connections with the production of **kitron**, a unique liqueur. The citron (*Citrus medica*) was introduced to the Mediterranean area in about 300 BC and thrived on Naxos for centuries. The fruit is barely edible in its raw state, but its rind is very flavoursome when preserved in syrup as a *glika koutaliou* (spoon sweet). *Kitroraki*, a *raki*, can be distilled from grape skins and citron leaves, and by the late 19th century the preserved fruit and a sweet version of *kitroraki*, known as *kitron*, were being exported in large amounts from Naxos.

The **Vallindras Distillery** (☎ 22850 31220; ⏲ 10am-11pm Jul-Aug, 10am-6pm May-Jun & Sep-Oct) in Halki's main square, distils *kitron* the old-fashioned way. There are free tours of the old distillery's atmospheric rooms, which still contain ancient jars and copper stills. *Kitron* tastings round off the trip and a selection of the distillery's products are on sale. To arrange a tour during the period November to April you need to phone ☎ 22850 22534 or ☎ 6942551161.

Another Halki institution is the world-class ceramics shop **L'Olivier** and its nearby gallery (see boxed text, opposite).

There are sleeping possibilities in Halki and Filoti, but you are best to ask around locally.

Near the L'Olivier gallery is the fascinating shop **Era** (☎ 22859 31009; eraproducts@mail .gr) where marmalade, jam and spoon desserts are made using the best ingredients.

ART OF THE AEGEAN: L'OLIVIER, NAXOS *Des Hannigan*

The first time I walked into **L'Olivier** (☎ 22850 32829; www.fish-olive-creations.com; Halki), a ceramics gallery and shop in the little village of Halki on Naxos, it was late evening, early summer. The velvety dusk of the Tragaea, the mountain basin of Naxos, had settled like a veil on Halki's little village square. Young owls hooted from marble ledges on the facades of old Naxian mansions. Inside L'Olivier it was as if a sunset glow lingered. Even the artificial lighting was subtly deployed. Everywhere I looked were pieces of stoneware ceramics and jewellery that took my breath away.

Each piece of work reflected the ancient Mediterranean themes of fish and olive that are at the heart of the work of Naxian potter Katharina Bolesch and her partner, artist and craftsman Alexander Reichardt. Three-dimensional ceramic olives framed the edges of shining plates or tumbled down the side of elegant jugs and bowls. Grapes too, hung in little ceramic bunches. Painted shoals of fish darted across platters and swam around bowls and dishes. Silver and ceramic fish jewellery extended the theme. Those first impressions have never faded. Each time I walk into L'Olivier now, the world lights up.

Katharina Bolesch was partly brought up on Naxos and is rooted in the island's landscape and culture. Alex Reichardt is entirely of the Mediterranean. His life among the islands and his long experience as a diver inspire his painted fish motifs, his silver and ceramic fish jewellery, and his work in wood and marble. These two outstanding artists are based in a tiny Cycladean village, yet their fame is international and their work has been exhibited in such major galleries and museums as the Academy of Athens, the Goulandris Natural History Museum, Greece's Cretaquarium, the UN Headquarters in New York and the Design Museum of Helsinki.

President of the Goulandris Natural History Museum, Mrs Niki Goulandris, is a longstanding patron. She speaks enthusiastically of the work of Bolesch and Reichardt and places it within the traditions of classical Greek and Cycladic art while recognising its modern context. 'Their work represents boldness and commitment to tradition,' she says. 'Their motifs are emphatically the symbols of the Greek land and sea.'

In spite of such a high profile, the work of Bolesch and Reichardt remains entirely accessible and affordable. L'Olivier is a cornucopia of beautiful yet functional work that includes jewellery, tiles and dishes, large jugs and bowls of luminous beauty, fine artefacts in olive wood, and olive products such as oil and soap.

In 2006 Bolesch and Reichardt opened a separate gallery and workshop just around the corner from their shop. Here they stage exhibitions by accomplished artists in a building that has been designed with great style and that fits perfectly amid Halki's traditional Naxian facades and the serene beauty of the Tragaea. (Poor-quality imitations of Katharina Bolesch's work are sold elsewhere on Naxos, so be warned.)

In Halki's central square, **Yianni's Taverna** (☎ 22850 31214; dishes €5.50-7.50) is noted for its good local meat dishes and fresh salads with *myzithra* (sheep's-milk cheese). Do not miss **Glikia Zoi** (Sweet Life; ☎ 22850 31602), directly opposite the L'Olivier gallery. Here Christina Falierou works her magic in a traditional cafe setting, making delicious cakes and sweets to go with coffee or drinks. Also of interest is **Penelope** (☎ 6979299951), a shop where you'll find some splendid handwoven textiles and embroidery work.

Halki is spreading its cultural wings even further with the inception of an annual music, arts and literary festival, the **Axia Festival** (Aug/Sep), which will feature international musicians,

artists and writers. The festival is nonprofit and is organised by the L'Olivier gallery.

An alternative scenic route from Hora to Halki is along the road that passes **Ano Potamia**. It's here that you'll find **Taverna Pigi** (☎ 22850 32292; mains €5-22), known for good local cooking, enjoyed with the serene music of the gurgling spring that the taverna is named after.

Panagia Drosiani Παναγία Δροσιανή

The **Panagia Drosiani** (☼ 10am-7pm May–mid-Oct) just below **Moni**, 2.5km north of Halki, is one of the oldest and most revered churches in Greece. It has a warren of cavelike chapels, and several of the frescoes date back to the 7th century. Donations are appreciated.

Sangri Σαγκρί

The handsome towerlike building of **Bazeos Castle** (☎ 22850 31402; 10am-5pm & 6-9pm) stands prominently in the landscape about 2km east of the village of Sangri. The castle was built in its original form as the Monastery of Timios Stavros (True Cross) during the 17th century, but monks abandoned the site in the early 19th century. It was later bought by the Bazeos family, whose modern descendants have refurbished the building and its late-medieval rooms with great skill and imagination. The castle now functions as a cultural centre and stages art exhibitions and the annual **Naxos Festival** during July and August, when concerts, plays and literary readings are held. The price of admission to these varies.

About 1.5km south of Sangri is the impressive **Temple of Demeter** (Dimitra's Temple; ☎ 22850 22725; 8.30am-3pm Tue-Sun). The ruins and reconstructions are not large, but they are historically fascinating. There is a site **museum** with some fine reconstructions of temple features. Signs point the way from Sangri.

Apiranthos Απείρανθος

Apiranthos is an atmospheric mountain village of unadorned stone houses, marble-paved streets and alleyways that scramble up the slopes of Mt Fanari (883m). Its inhabitants are descendants of refugees who fled Crete to escape Turkish repression; they retain a strong individuality and a rich dialect, and the village has always been noted for its spirited politics and populism. There is an impressive trio of museums.

On the main road, to the right of the start of the village's main street, is the **museum of natural history** (admission €3; 8.30am-2pm Tue-Sun). The **geology museum** (admission €3; 8.30am-2pm Tue-Sun) and the **archaeology museum** (admission free; 8.30am-2pm Tue-Sun) are part-way along the main street. The latter has a marvellous collection of small Cycladian artefacts. The museums are notionally open from 7pm to 10pm in summer, but all the opening times stated here are 'flexible', in keeping with an admirable local spirit of independence.

There are a number of tavernas and *kafeneia* (coffee houses) in the village.

There is parking at the entrance to Apiranthos, on the main Hora–Apollonas road.

Moutsouna Μουτσούνα

pop 74

The road from Apiranthos to Moutsouna descends in an exhilarating series of S-bends through awe-inspiring mountain scenery. Formerly a busy port that shipped out the emery mined in the region, Moutsouna is now a quiet place, although there is some development. Seven kilometres south of the village is a good beach at **Psili Ammos**.

There are a few pensions and tavernas, mainly in Moutsouna, but some are scattered along the coast road.

Apollonas Απόλλωνας

pop 107

Tavernas line the waterfront adjoining a reasonable beach at Apollonas, on the north coast, but the main attraction here is a giant 7th-century-BC **kouros** (male statue of the Archaic period), which lies in an ancient quarry in the hillside above the village. It is signposted to the left as you approach Apollonas on the main inland road from Hora. This 10.5m statue may have been abandoned before being finished, because weaknesses in the stone caused cracking. Apollonas has several domatia and tavernas.

With your own transport you can return to Hora via the west-coast road, passing through wild and sparsely populated country with awe-inspiring sea views. Several tracks branch down to secluded beaches, such as **Abram**.

LITTLE CYCLADES
ΜΙΚΡΕΣ ΚΥΚΛΑΔΕΣ

Step off the already slow-paced world of the larger Cycladic islands and head, with time to spare, for the chain of small islands between Naxos and Amorgos. Only four – Donousa, Ano Koufonisia, Iraklia and Schinousa – have permanent populations. All were densely populated in antiquity, as shown by the large number of ancient graves found on the islands. During the Middle Ages, only wild goats and even wilder pirates inhabited the islands. Post Independence, intrepid souls from Naxos and Amorgos recolonised. Now, the islands welcome growing numbers of independent-minded tourists.

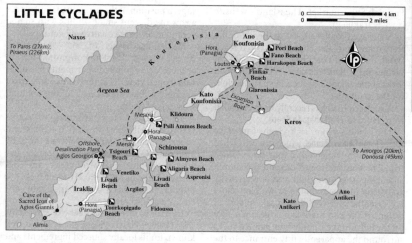

LITTLE CYCLADES

Donousa is the northernmost of the group and the furthest from Naxos. The others are clustered near the southeast coast of Naxos. Each has a public telephone and post agency and there are ATMs on all islands except Iraklia, although you should still bring a decent amount of ready cash with you.

Getting There & Away

There are daily connections to and from Naxos to the Little Cyclades but services can be disrupted when sea conditions are poor; make sure you have plenty of time before committing yourself – these islands are not meant for last-minute visits or for one-night tick lists. In recent years the big Blue Star car ferries have established a regular schedule from Piraeus via Naxos to all of the Little Cyclades islands and on to Amorgos and Astypalea and back.

The sturdy little ferry **Express Skopelitis** (☎ 22850 71256/519; Katapola, Amorgos) runs from Naxos (daily in summer, four days a week in winter) to the Little Cyclades and Amorgos. It's a defining Cycladic experience but bad weather can blow the schedule. Most seating is open deck so, when it's windy, brace yourself for some real rocking and rolling. In rough weather you'll know what's coming when the crew starts dishing out the *see-through* sick bags. If you're on deck, work out exactly which side of the boat is protected from wind and sea on each section between islands and stay there, or that bracing sea air may become a bracing Aegean Sea deluge. Regardless of sea conditions, locals, the crew and this writer

head straight below for the comfy saloon and bar where they become engulfed in cigarette smoke and gossip. The choice is yours…

For details see Island Hopping (Iraklia p752, Schinousa p760, Koufonisia p754 and Donousa p750).

IRAKLIA ΗΡΑΚΛΕΙΑ
pop 115

Iraklia (ir-a-*klee*-a) is only 19 sq km in area, a little Aegean gem dozing in the sun. Dump the party gear and spurn the nightlife, the 'sightseeing' and the dreary souvenirs. Instead, brace yourself for a serene and quiet life and Iraklia will not disappoint. Only in July and August will you have to share the idyll with like-minded others.

The island now has the distinction of having the first offshore **desalination plant** in Greece. *And* it's driven by solar panels and windpower. You pass it as you enter the harbour. Raise a cheer for sustainability.

The port and main village of Iraklia is Agios Georgios. It has an attractive cove-like harbour, complete with a sandy beach. Turn right at the end of the ferry quay, and then go up left for a well-supplied general store, Perigiali Supermarket. Further uphill is a smaller store and *kafeneio* (coffee house) called Melissa's, which is also the ferry ticket office, postal agency and perennial gossip shop. There are card phones outside Perigiali Supermarket and Melissa's and there is an ATM just up from the harbour. A medical centre is located next to

Perigiali Supermarket. The island's website is www.iraklia.gr.

A surfaced road leads off to the left of the ferry quay, and after about 1km you'll reach **Livadi**, the island's best beach. A steep 2.5km further on is **Hora (Panagia)**. Where the road forks at the village entrance, keep to the right for the main street.

A surfaced road has recently been extended from Hora to **Tourkopigado Beach**.

The island's major 'sight' is the **Cave of the Sacred Icon of Agios Giannis**, which can be reached on foot from Panagia in a four-hour return trip. The path starts just beyond the church at a signpost on the right and is very rocky and steep in places; boots or walking shoes are essential and you should take plenty of water. At the site there is a large open cave on the left. On the right, white-painted rocks surround the apparently tiny entrance to the main sequence of caves. A torch is useful and the initial scramble along a low-roofed tunnel is worth it, leading as it does to caves full of stalactites and stalagmites. On 28 August, the eve of the death of John the Baptist, crowds of local people assemble at the cave and crawl inside to hold a candle-lit service.

Beyond the cave the path leads to the beach at **Alimia**, which is also served by boat from Agios Georgios in summer, offering a shortcut to the cave.

During July and August, a local boat ferries people to island beaches and also runs day trips to nearby Schinousa. Enquire at Perigiali Supermarket.

Sleeping & Eating

Domatia and tavernas are concentrated in and around Agios Georgios, although a few open on the beach at Livadi in summer. Domatia owners meet the boats, but in high season it's advisable to book.

Anna's Place (☎ 22850 71145; s €40, d €50-70, tr €85; ❂) Located on high ground above the port, these lovely, airy rooms have stylish furnishings and the front balconies have sweeping views. There's a big communal kitchen and outside eating area.

Agnadema/Dimitri's (☎ /fax 22850 71484, 6978048789; studio/d €40/50; ❂) There's a great choice at this peaceful, family-owned property on the hillside above Agios Georgios harbour. Agnadema's rooms are big, bright and immaculate. Agnadema means 'great view', an understatement considering the

superb position of the property. Dimitri's are a row of adjacent small studios with shared verandah and are equally well equipped.

Maistrali Apartments (☎ 2285071807; nickmaistrali @in.gr; d/tr €40/60; ❂) The communal terrace at these well-equipped apartments has unrivalled open views to Ios and the south. There are only a few rooms, so booking for high season is advised.

There are a few tavernas in Agios Georgios. All serve fresh fish dishes and other Greek standards. **Maïstrali** (☎ 22850 71807; dishes €3.80-7) has a pleasant terrace and also has rooms and fairly creaky internet access. **Perigiali** (☎ 22850 71118; dishes €4-7), a popular place, has a large marble table encircling an old pine tree.

In Hora, **Taverna to Steki** (☎ 22850 71579; dishes €4-8) is a classic village eatery and is well known for its locally sourced ingredients and traditional food.

SCHINOUSA ΣΧΙΝΟΥΣΑ
pop 206

Schinousa (skih-*noo*-sah) lies a mere 2km across the sea from Iraklia and is similar in nature – slow-paced and endearing. It has a number of beaches, although not all are attractive, and down-to-earth Hora (Panagia) on the breezy crest of the island has sweeping views of the sea.

Ferries dock at the fishing harbour of Mersini. Hora is a hot 1km uphill (domatia owners are always around to meet ferries with transport).

Paralos Travel (☎ 22850 71160; fax 22850 71957) is halfway along the main street. It sells ferry tickets and also doubles as the post office. **Grispos Travel** (☎ 22850 29329), at the far end of the village, sells ferry tickets.

There's a public telephone in the main square and an ATM next to Deli restaurant. A reasonably useful website is www.schinousa.gr.

On the way down to Tsigouri beach is a little **folk museum** that features a reconstructed bread oven. Opening hours go with the flow of island life.

Dirt tracks lead from Hora to beaches around the coast. The nearest are **Tsigouri** and **Livadi**, both uncrowded outside August. Haul a little further to decent beaches at **Almyros** and **Aligaria**. With the exception of Tsigouri, there are no shops or tavernas at the beaches, so take food and water.

Sleeping

There are a few rooms down at Mersini, but if you want to see the rest of the island you're much better off staying in Hora.

Anna Domatia (☎ 22850 71161; Hora; s/d/tr €40/45/50; ✦) Well-kept, good-sized rooms, just behind the main street on the west side of the village, make Anna's a good-value choice. For an extra €5 you can get a room with a kitchen.

Iliovasilema (☎ 22850 71948; iliovasilema@schinousa .gr; Hora; s €45, d €55-60, tr €60-65; ✦ ⊚) Ideally located on the western outskirts of the village, looking south over the island, this bright, clean place has good-sized rooms and most of the balconies have fine views.

Galini (☎ 22850 71983, 21046 29448; s/d/tr €50/50/60) Most rooms at this well-positioned pension have fabulous views. It stands right at the far end of town in its own grounds. Rooms are bright and clean and pleasantly quaint. There's no air conditioning, but there are sturdy ceiling fans.

Eating

Akbar (☎ 22850 72001; dishes €3-6.50) A colourful little cafe in the main street, Akbar has mezes and fresh salads, as well as breakfast for about €7.

Loza (☎ 22850 71864; dishes €4.50-9.50) Just opposite Akbar and a local rendezvous for breakfasts (€7.50) as well as salads and pizzas. It's also a bakery and makes pastries, including baklava and walnut pie.

our pick **Deli Restaurant and Sweet Bar** (☎ 22850 74278; mains €7.50-9) The outstanding Deli is run by the same creative team that once ran Margarita's down the road. Excellent Greek cuisine, with a strong local basis, features starters such as millefeuille eggplant with fresh tomatoes and local soft cheese, or fava beans with onions and olive oil. Mains include chicken with herbs and lemon, and small pieces of local pork with peppers in a wine sauce. Vegetarians can enjoy a plate of the day. They also do breakfast for €6. The upper floor houses the restaurant, the ground floor is a very cool cafe-bar and downstairs there's a sweet section. The wine list is trim but excellent with some fine Macedonian vintages.

KOUFONISIA ΚΟΥΦΟΝΗΣΙΑ

pop 366

The islands of **Ano Koufonisia** and **Kato Koufinisia** face each other across blue waters. It's Ano Koufonisia that's populated. Its excellent beaches make it one of the most visited islands of the Little Cyclades, and modernisation has taken hold. New hotels and studios are springing up, and a marina with capacity for 50 yachts is due to be completed 'any time now'. Koufinisia's substantial fishing fleet still sustains a thriving local community outside the summer season.

A caïque ride away, Kato Koufonisia has some beautiful beaches and a lovely church. Archaeological digs on **Keros**, the rocky, bull-backed mountain of an island that looms over Koufonisia to the south, have uncovered over 100 Early Cycladic figurines, including the famous harpist and flautist now on display in Athens' National Archaeological Museum (p127). Important finds in recent years seem to confirm that Keros was a Cycladian site of major importance.

Orientation & Information

Koufonisia's only settlement spreads out behind the ferry quay. On one side of the quay is the planned yacht marina; on the other side is a wide bay filled with moored fishing boats. A large beach of flat, hard sand gives a great sense of space to the waterfront. Its inner edge is used as a road and everyone uses it as a football pitch. The older part of town, the *hora*, sprawls along a low hill above the harbour and is one long main street, often strewn with fallen leaves of bougainvillea.

There are a couple of supermarkets along the road that leads inland from the beach to link with the main street, and there's a ticket agency halfway along the main street. The post office is along the first road that leads sharply left as you reach the road leading inland. There is an ATM outside the post office.

Sights

BEACHES

An easy walk along the sandy coast road to the east of the port leads in a couple of kilometres to **Finikas**, **Harakopou** and **Fano** beaches. All tend to become swamped with grilling bodies in July and August and nudity becomes more overt the further you go.

Beyond Fano a path leads to several rocky swimming places, then continues to the great bay at **Pori**, where a long crescent of sand slides effortlessly into the ultimate Greek-island-dream sea. Pori can also be reached by an inland road from Hora.

CYCLADES

Tours

Koufonissia Tours (☎ 22850 71671; www.koufonissiatours
.gr), based at Villa Ostria hotel (see below), organises caïque trips to Keros, Kato Koufonisia
and to other islands of the Little Cyclades.
Bike hire is also available.

Sleeping

Independent camping is not permitted on
Koufonisia. There is a good selection of domatia and hotels, and Koufonissia Tours organises accommodation on the island.

Lefteris Rooms (☎ 22850 71458; d/tr €40/45) Right
behind the town beach and above Lefteris
restaurant are these simple but colourful
rooms, with the ones at the back being the
most peaceful.

Anna's Rooms (☎ 22850 71061, 6974527838; s/d/tr/q
€50/60/70/80; ❄) In a quiet location at Loutro
on the west side of the port, these big, bright
rooms are a great choice and the welcome is
charming. Rooms overlook the old harbour
and are set amid colourful gardens. Each
room has tea- and coffee-making facilities.

Ermis (☎ 22850 71693; fax 22850 74214; s/d €55/70;
❄) In a quiet, leafy location behind the post
office, these spacious rooms have attractive
decor and generous balconies at the front.

our pick **Alkyonides Studios** (☎ 22850 74170; www
.alkionides.gr; d/tr/q incl breakfast €70/75/80) Taking the
high ground on Koufinisia are these well-
located studios above Loutro's little harbour.
The name 'Alkyonides' is proudly displayed
on an old boat, just one of a few eccentric
touches. The spacious, bright rooms have fans
rather than air conditioning, a plus as far as
some are concerned. Breakfast is included (the
egg layers are just down the road). Don't be
put off by the rocky road approach or the odd
abandoned car. A path leads down to Loutro
in a few minutes.

Villa Ostria (☎ 22850 71671; www.koufonissiatours.gr;
s/d/tr incl breakfast €70/85/90; ❄ 🛜) A stylish, small
hotel, Villa Ostria stands on the high ground
above the beach and has a charming garden
area. Rooms are smart and comfortable and
have fridges.

Eating

Kalamia Café (☎ 22850 74444; snacks €3-5.50; 💻 🛜) A
great gathering point and net-browsing venue.
Link-up is free to customers and there's a
bar-top screen if you don't have your own
kit. They do a range of breakfast fare from
€3.50 to €6.

Karnagio (☎ 22850 71694; mains €4-10) Don't miss
this little *ouzerie* at Loutro where the tables
skirt the harbour. It operates out of a tiny
building. Prawn *saganaki* and seafood platters
at €10 for small, €20 for large, go well with
the ambience.

Lefteris (☎ 22850 71458; dishes €4.50-8) Lefteris
dishes up reasonably priced Greek standards
to huge numbers of visitors in high summer.
Its vast terrace looks out over the town beach
and it's open for breakfast and lunch also.

Capetan Nikolas (☎ 22850 71690; mains €4.50-11)
One of the best seafood places on the islands,
this happy, family-run restaurant overlooks
the little harbour at Loutro. Shrimp salad for
€6.50 is a good bet while locally caught fish,
such as red mullet and sea bream, are a speciality and are priced by the kilo.

Drinking

Scholeio (☎ 22850 71837; 🕕 6pm-3.30am) A little
island bar and crêperie that goes well with
the island's laid-back ambience. Scholeio
does a great line in cocktails and other
drinks, and plays jazz, blues, rock and other
choice sounds. It's right at the western end
of the village's main street above Loutro.
The owners are accomplished photographers
and often have exhibitions of their work
on show.

Sorokos (☎ 22850 71704; 🕕 4pm-3am) Drinks
and snacks and hot sounds that range from
early-hours lounge music to harder vibes at
night make this a popular hangout beyond
the town beach.

DONOUSA ΔΟΝΟΥΣΑ
pop 110

Donousa is the out-on-a-limb island where
you stop bothering about which day it might
be. In late July and August the island can
be swamped by holidaymaking Greeks and
sun-seeking north Europeans, but out of
season be prepared to linger – and be rewarded for it.

Agios Stavros is Donousa's main settlement
and port, a cluster of functional buildings
round a handsome church, overlooking a
small bay. Little has changed here over the
years, but water shortage – on an island that
was once always well supplied – has resulted
in recent pipe-laying to houses from a new
storage tank for imported water. New surfaced walkways have been a welcome side-
effect. The town also has a good **beach**, which

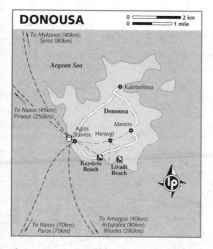

DONOUSA

0 — 2 km
0 — 1 mile

To Mykonos (40km);
Syros (80km)

Aegean Sea

Kalotaritissa

To Naxos (45km);
Piraeus (250km)

Donousa

Mersini

Agios
Stavros   Haravgi

Kendros   Livadi
Beach   Beach

To Amorgos (40km);
Astypalea (80km);
Rhodes (280km)

To Naxos (70km);
Paros (75km)

also serves as a thoroughfare for infrequent vehicles and foot traffic to a clutch of homes, rental rooms and a taverna across the bay.

Roussos Travel (☎ 22850 51648) on the waterfront is the ticket agency for the local ferry *Express Skopelitis*.

Sigalis Travel (☎ 22850 51570, 6942269219) in the To Iliovasilema restaurant complex (see right) sells tickets for Blue Star ferries.

There is an ATM outside Roussos Travel (it's sometimes hidden behind a blue shutter for protection from blown sand). But be sure to bring sufficient cash in high season. There is a public telephone up a steep hill above the waterfront; it's hidden behind a tree. You can get telecards at the souvenir shop just up from the quay-end of the beach.

There is a **medical centre** (☎ 22850 51506) and postal agency just below the church.

Kendros, situated 1.25km to the southeast of Agios Stavros, along a rather ugly bulldozed track, is a sandy and secluded beach with a seasonal taverna. **Livadi**, a dusty 1km hike further east, sees even fewer visitors. Both Kendros and Livadi are popular with naturists. Bulldozed, unsurfaced roads have marred Donousa in places, but there are still paths and tracks that lead into the hills to timeless little hamlets such as **Mersini**.

Sleeping & Eating

Most rooms on the island are fairly basic but are well kept, clean and in good locations. You should book ahead for stays in July and August, and even early September.

Prasinos Studios (☎ 22850 51579; d €40-60, apt €80) In a lofty position on the high ground on the far side of the beach, this pleasant complex has a mix of well-kept rooms.

To Iliovasilema (☎ 22850 51570; d/tr/studios €45/50/55; 🖥) Reasonable rooms, some with kitchens, overlook the beach. There's a popular restaurant with a fine terrace and a good selection of food (dishes €4.50 to €20).

Capetan Giorgis (☎ 22850 51867; mains €4.50-9) Sturdy traditional food is on the menu at the Capetan's, where the terrace, just above the harbour, has good views across the bay.

There are a couple of food shops that have a reasonable selection of goods in July and August.

The hub of village life is Kafeneio To Kyma by the quay, where things liven up late into the night in summer.

AMORGOS ΑΜΟΡΓΟΣ

pop 1873

Amorgos (ah-mor-ghoss) lies well to the southeast of the main Cycladic group; this lovely island rises from the sea in a long dragon's back of craggy mountains that is 30km from tip to toe and 822m at its highest point. The island's southeast coast is unrelentingly steep and boasts an extraordinary monastery embedded in a huge cliff. The northern half of the opposite coast is equally spectacular, but relents a little at the narrow inlet where the main port and town of Katapola lies.

Amorgos' other port town, Aegiali, lies at the island's northern end and is more appealing as a resort. It has a good beach and is encircled by rugged mountains. The enchanting Hora (also known as Amorgos) nestles high in the mountains above Katapola.

There's plenty of scope for beaching, but Amorgos is much more about archaeology and the outdoor world – there's great walking, scuba diving and a burgeoning rock-climbing scene, although currently the latter is for the very experienced rather than the passing thrillseeker.

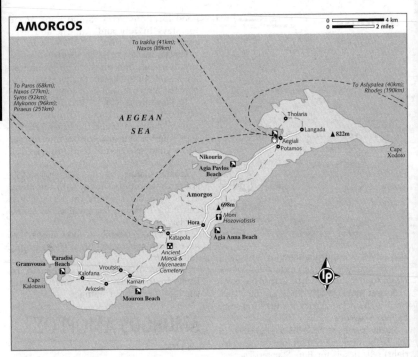

AMORGOS

Getting There & Away

Connections between Amorgos and Naxos are very good with the small ferry, *Express Skopelitis*, running each day and connecting the Little Cyclades and Amorgos. The big Blue Star ferries also run to and from Piraeus and continue to Astypalea and to Rhodes while other ferries link from Piraeus via Folegandros and Santorini. For details see Island Hopping (p745).

Getting Around

Regular buses go from Katapola to Hora (€1.40, 15 minutes), Moni Hozoviotissis (€1.60, 15 minutes) and Agia Anna Beach (€1.50, 20 minutes), and less-frequent services go to Aegiali (€2.40, 30 minutes). However, there are fewer services on weekends. There are also buses from Aegiali to the picturesque village of Langada. Schedules are posted on bus windscreens.

Cars and motorcycles are available for hire from the travel agencies **N Synodinos** (☎ 22850 71201; synodinos@nax.forthnet.gr; Katapola) and **Aegialis Tours** (☎ 22850 73107; fax 22850 73394; www.amorgos-aegialis.com; Aegiali).

KATAPOLA ΚΑΤΑΠΟΛΑ
pop 130

The island's principal port, Katapola, straggles round the curving shoreline of a dramatic bay in the most verdant part of the island. The fascinating and extensive remains of the ancient city of **Minoa**, as well as a **Mycenaean cemetery**, lie above the port and can be reached by a steep, surfaced road. Amorgos has also yielded many Cycladic finds; the largest figurine in the National Archaeological Museum (p127) in Athens was found in the vicinity of Katapola.

Orientation & Information

Boats dock right on the waterfront. The bus station is to the left along the main waterfront, on the eastern shore of the bay.

A bank (with ATM) is midwaterfront and there's an ATM next to N Synodinos. There is a postal agency next to the Hotel Minoa on the central square.

Hotel Minoa (☎ 22850 71480; 🕒 9am-2pm & 7-10pm; internet per hr €5)

N Synodinos (☎ 22850 71201; synodinos@nax.forth
net.gr) Sells ferry tickets and has money exchange and car
hire (per day in high season €45).
Port police (☎ 22850 71259) On the central square.

Sleeping & Eating

Domatia owners usually meet ferries and
are among the most restrained and polite in
the Cyclades.

Diosmarini (☎ 22850 71636; www.diosmarini.com;
d/tr/apt €50/70/100) On the northern shores
of the bay and about 1km from the ferry
quay, Diosmarini is a good option away from
the main port. It has big rooms in a handsome and modern Cycladic-style building.
There are airy views from most balconies.

Pension Sofia (☎ 22850 71494; www.pensionsofia.gr;
d/tr €55/80; ⊠) The charming, family-run Sofia
stands amid gardens and little meadows in
a quiet area of town. Rooms are fresh and
colourful. The same family has well-equipped
studios and apartments elsewhere in the area
(€120 to €150).

Eleni's Rooms (☎ 22850 71628; roomseleni@gmail
.com; s/d/tr €60/65/75) An unbeatable position
to the west of the ferry quay makes these
unfussy but bright and airy rooms an excellent choice. The rooms rise through
several levels and offer unbeatable views.
You can even hop down in seconds for a
morning swim at an adjoining beach.

Mouragio (☎ 22850 71011; dishes €4.50-9) Down
to earth and nearly always packed by mid-
evening, Mouragio specialises in seafood. It's
on the main waterfront near the ferry quay.
Shellfish are by the kilo but reasonable dishes
include fish soup.

Elichryson (☎ 22850 71517; dishes €5-8.50; ⊠ 8am-
10pm) Ideal for breakfast (€3.50 to €8), the
pleasant Elichryson cafe is just back from the
main waterfront.

Vitsentzos (☎ 22850 71518; dishes €5.50-9) A fine
traditional restaurant with exposed stonework
and a varnished wooden floor in its interior,
Vitsentzos also has a leisurely terrace overlooking the bay. Food is classic Greek with
modern influences. Seafood is by the kilo.

Drinking

Moon Bar (☎ 22850 71598) On the northern waterfront, this is the place to reflect on all that is
well with the world with reassuring views to
the sea and great background sounds that
range from classical through blues, rock and
funk into the early hours. Breakfasts are €5.

Le Grand Bleu (☎ 22850 71633) Still keeping alive
the spirit of the iconic film *The Big Blue*, this
popular bar plays rock, reggae and modern
Greek music on the northern waterfront.

HORA ΧΩΡΑ
pop 416

The old capital of Hora sparkles like a snow-
drift across its rocky ridge. It stands 400m
above sea level and is capped by a 13th-century
kastro atop a prominent rock pinnacle. Old
windmills stand like sentinels on surrounding
cliffs. There's a distinct veneer of sophistication, not least in the handful of trendy bars
and shops that enhance Hora's appeal without
eroding its timelessness.

The bus stop is on a small square at the edge
of town. The post office is on the main square,
reached by a pedestrian lane from the bus
stop. The island's **police station** (☎ 22850 71210)
is halfway along the main street.

Hora's **archaeology museum** (⊠ 9am-1pm & 6-
8.30pm Tue-Sun) is on the main pedestrian thoroughfare, near Café Bar Zygós.

Sleeping & Eating

Hora has a handful of pleasant pensions.

Pension Ilias (☎ 22850 71277; s/d/tr/apt €45/55/65/80)
Tucked away amid a jumble of traditional
houses just down from the bus stop is
this unpretentious, family-run place with
decent rooms.

View To Big Blue (☎ 22850 71814, 6932248867; s/d
€50/70) At the top end of the village is this attractive place in its own little garden. Rooms
are very bright and comfy.

Café Bar Zygós (☎ 22850 71155; snacks €3-8; ⊠ 8am-
3am) Right at the cool, colourful heart of Hora,
Zygos is open for breakfast, sandwiches, baguettes, salads and cold plates as well as coffee,
cakes, candied fruit and ice cream – all to
lounge sounds by day, and dance music with
cocktails at night. A speciality is a selection of
distinctive mushroom dishes.

Keep heading up the winding main street
to reach **Tsagaradiko** (☎ 6937281226; dishes €3-8),
a great little *ouzerie* with tables on a lovely
small square.

MONI HOZOVIOTISSIS ΜΟΝΗ
ΧΟΖΟΒΙΩΤΙΣΣΗΣ

Amorgos is defined by this iconic **monastery**
(⊠ 8am-1pm & 5-7pm), a dazzling white building embedded in an awesome cliff face high
above the sea. It lies on the precipitous east

coast below Hora. The monastery contains a miraculous icon that was found in the sea below the cliff. It got there (allegedly unaided) from Asia Minor, Cyprus or Jerusalem – depending on which legend you're told. A few monks still live here and short tours, which usually end with a pleasant chat with one of the monks, take place sporadically, usually when a reasonable number of visitors have gathered at the door of the monastery. The tour is free but donations are appreciated.

Out of respect, modest dress is essential: long trousers for men; a long skirt or dress for women, who should also cover their shoulders. Wraps are no longer available at the entrance, so make sure you are prepared.

AEGIALI ΑΙΓΙΑΛΗ
pop 232

Aegiali is Amorgos' second port and has more of a resort style, not least because of the fine sweep of sand that lines the inner edge of the bay on which the village stands. Steep slopes and impressive crags lie above the main village.

Efficient **Amorgos Travel** (☎ 22850 73401; www.amorgostravel.gr), above the central supermarket on the waterfront, can help with a host of travel needs including ferry tickets, accommodation and island tours. Check it out for diving and walking possibilities also. Long-established **Aegialis Tours** (☎ 22850 73107; www.aegialistours.com) sells ferry tickets, and can organise accommodation, tours and vehicle hire.

There's a postal agency about 100m uphill from Aegialis Tours.

Tours

Ask at travel agencies about a daily bus outing (€25) around the island that leaves at 9.30am and returns at 4.30pm, with stops at Agia Pavlos, Moni Hozoviotissis and Hora. Boat trips around the island (€30) and to the Little Cyclades (€40) can also be arranged.

Sleeping

As is the case in Katapola, domatia owners meet the ferries.

Aegiali Camping (☎ 22850 73500; www.aegiali camping.gr; camp sites per adult/child/tent €5.50/2.70/3.50) Good facilities and a pleasantly shaded location on the road behind the beach makes

this camping ground an attractive proposition. You can rent a tent for €6.30.

Pension Askas (☎ 22850 73333; www.askas pension.gr; d €60-70, tr €65-75; 🔀 🛜) Next to Aegiali Camping is this decent pension in a garden setting, with clean, attractive rooms.

Lakki Village (☎ 22850 73505; www.lakkivillage.gr; s/d/tr incl breakfast €85/95/105, apt incl breakfast €110-145; 🔀 🖳 🛋) This attractive, well-kept complex ambles inland from the beachfront through lovely gardens and water features. Rooms are in Cycladic-style buildings and have colourful traditional furnishings. Top-priced apartments sleep four people.

Eating

Restaurant Lakki (☎ 22850 73253; mains €3.50-8) A beach and garden setting makes the restaurant of Lakki Village a relaxing place to enjoy well-prepared Greek dishes.

To Koralli (☎ 22850 73217; dishes €4-12.50) Up a flight of steps at the eastern end of the waterfront, To Koralli has an airy view that goes with excellent Greek cuisine. Treat yourself to a platter of shrimps, octopus and squid, and small fish or meat dishes such as veal with eggplant, cheese, tomatoes and peppers.

Askas Taverna (☎ 22850 73333; mains €4.50-7) Adjoining Aegiali Camping and Pension Askas, this taverna offers good helpings of Greek standards. They stage *rembetika* (Greek blues) music evenings four times a week in July and August.

our pick **To Limani** (☎ 22850 73269; dishes €4.50-9) Traditional fare prepared with home-grown produce makes Limani a popular place. Local dishes include baked goat and, for fish lovers, fish soup, while vegetarians can enjoy fava beans with stuffed eggplant. For dessert the home-made orange pie is superb. There's a hugely popular Thai food night every Friday except during August. The owners also have beautiful rooms, studios and apartments (from €80 to €115) high above the bay in the village of Potamos.

AROUND AMORGOS

On the east coast, south of Moni Hozoviotissis, is **Agia Anna Beach**, the nearest beach to both Katapola and Hora. Don't get excited; the car park is bigger than any of the little pebbly beaches strung out along the rocky shoreline, and all the beaches fill up quickly. Next to the car park on the cliff-top there's a small cantina selling food and drinks.

The lovely villages of **Langada** and **Tholaria** nestle amid the craggy slopes above Aegiali. The views from both are worth the trip alone. The two are linked to each other, and to Aegiali, by a signposted circular path that takes about four hours (Greek time). Regular buses run between the villages and Aegiali.

In Langada the **Pagali Hotel** (☎ 22850 73310; www.pagalihotel-amorgos.com; d/ste €75/95; ❄ 🖤) is tucked away in the lower village and has superb views. The spacious rooms and studios are fronted by an almost Alpine-like terrace, where there's a long, narrow pitch of earth used for the nightly game of *bales*, the Amorgan version of *boules*, played with balls roughly carved out of olive wood. The hotel is a good contact point for alternative holidays that include experiencing the owners' organic farm, yoga and meditation sessions, art workshops, walking and rock climbing on the neighbouring crags.

The adjoining **Nico's Taverna** (☎ 22850 73310; mains €6-8) is run by the same family that owns the Pagali Hotel. Nico's makes a strong play for sustainability, with organic ingredients from the family's own farm, including olive oil, home-made wine and cheeses. Vegetarians should be in their element, but local goat dishes are also superb.

Special-Interest-Holidays (SP.IN; ☎ 6939820828; www.amorgos.dial.pipex.com), based at Langada, organises walking holidays with very experienced and knowledgeable guides.

IOS ΙΟΣ

pop 1900

Ios is slowly shedding its image as the party capital of the Cyclades. It has always been as traditional in landscape and cultural terms as any other island in the group, and Greek life goes on sturdily beyond the wall-to-wall bars and nightclubs of Hora and the beach scene. The opening of the recently excavated Bronze Age site of Skarkos (see p424) has enhanced the island's appeal and there is evidence that families and older holidaymakers are heading for Ios in increasing numbers. There's still hard partying, though, and you need some stamina to survive the late-night action in the centre of Hora.

Getting There & Away

Ios lies conveniently on the Mikonos–Santorini ferry axis and has regular connections with Pireaus. For details see Island Hopping (p752).

Getting Around

In summer crowded buses run between Ormos, Hora and Mylopotas Beach about every 15 minutes (€1.40). From June to August private excursion buses go to Manganari Beach (one way €3) and Agia Theodoti Beach (one way €2.50). Buses leave at 11am and return at 4.30pm.

Caïques travelling from Ormos to Manganari cost €12 per person for a return trip (departing 11am daily). Ormos and Hora both have car and motorcycle hire that can be booked through the Plakiotis Travel Agency (p424) and Acteon Travel (below).

HORA, ORMOS & MYLOPOTAS
ΧΩΡΑ, ΟΡΜΟΣ & ΜΥΛΟΠΟΤΑΣ

Ios has three population centres, all very close together on the west coast: the port, Ormos; the capital, Hora (also known as the 'village'; population 1656), 2km inland by road from the port; and Mylopotas (population 73), the beach 2km downhill from Hora.

Orientation

The bus terminal in Ormos is straight ahead from the ferry quay on Plateia Emirou. If you don't mind the heat, it's possible to walk from the port to Hora by heading up left from Plateia Emirou, then right up a stepped path after about 100m. It's about 1.2km.

In Hora the main landmark is the big cathedral opposite the bus stop, on the other side of the dusty car park and play area. Plateia Valeta is the central square.

There are public toilets uphill behind the main square.

The road straight ahead from the bus stop leads to Mylopotas Beach.

Information

There's an ATM right by the information kiosks at the ferry quay. In Hora, the National Bank of Greece, behind the church, and the Commercial Bank, nearby, both have ATMs.

The post office in Hora is a block behind the main road (town-hall side).

Acteon Travel (☎ 22860 91343; www.acteon.gr) On the square near the quay, and in Hora and Mylopotas. Internet is €4 per hour.

CYCLADES

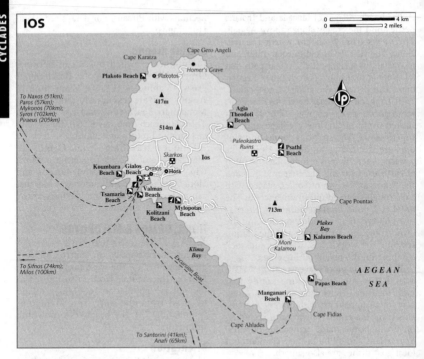

IOS

0 — 4 km
0 — 2 miles

To Naxos (51km);
Paros (57km);
Mykonos (70km);
Syros (102km);
Piraeus (205km)

Cape Karatza

Cape Gero Angeli

Homer's Grave

Plakoto Beach · Plakotos

▲ 417m

Agia
Theodoti
Beach

514m ▲

Paleokastro
Ruins

Psathi
Beach

Skarkos

Ios

Koumbara
Beach
Gialos
Beach
Ormos
Hora

Tsamaria
Beach
Valmas
Beach

Kolitzani
Beach
Mylopotas
Beach

▲ 713m

Cape Pountas

Plakes
Bay
Kalamos Beach

Klima
Bay

Moni
Kalamou

Excursion Boat

To Sifnos (74km);
Milos (100km)

A E G E A N

S E A

Papas Beach

Manganari
Beach

Cape Fidias

To Santorini (41km);
Anafi (65km)

Cape Ahlades

Doubleclick Internet (☎ 22860 92155; Hora; per hr
€4) A well-equipped place with good connection.
Hospital (☎ 22860 91227) On the way to Gialos, 250m
northwest of the quay; there are several doctors in Hora.
Plakiotis Travel Agency (☎ 22860 91221; plaktr2@
otenet.gr) On the Ormos waterfront.
Port police (☎ 22860 91264) At the southern end of
the Ormos waterfront, just before Ios Camping.

Sights

Hora is a lovely Cycladic village with a labyrinth of narrow lanes and cubist houses. It's
at its most charming during daylight hours
when the bars are shut and it recaptures the
atmosphere of other island towns.

Ios can rightly celebrate a cultural triumph in its award-winning archaeological
site of **Skarkos** (the Snail). This early-to-late
Bronze Age settlement crowns a low hill in
the plain just to the north of Hora. The site
was not yet open to the public at the time
of writing but was scheduled to open mid-
summer 2009. There is likely to be an entrance fee. Walled terraces surrounding the
settlement have been restored and the low
ruins of several Cycladic-style buildings of

the period are exposed. A visitor centre is
part of the development. The site lies on the
lower ground to the north of Hora.

Finds from Skarkos are displayed at the
excellent **archaeological museum** (Hora; admission €2,
EU students free; ⏰ 8.30am-3pm Tue-Sun) in the town
hall by the bus stop in Hora. There are also
exhibits from island excavations in general.

At the time of writing a remarkable **art gallery** was under construction on the summit
of the highest hill behind Hora. It's being
built to house the works of the radical artist
Yiannis Gaitis, who had a house on Ios, and
his wife, the sculptor Gabriella Simosi. The
works of other artists will also be exhibited.
The building comprises several huge gallery
spaces worthy of European capitals. Fingers
crossed it will be completed soon.

Activities

Banana rides (€12), canoe hire (per hour €15)
and mountain-bike hire (per day €15) are all
available at **Yialos Watersports** (☎ 22860 92463,
6944926625; ralfburgstahler@hotmail.com; Gialos Beach). You
can also hire windsurfing equipment (per half-
day €30) or take a tube ride (€14 to €17).

HOMER'S GRAVE RIDDLE

Homer is said to have died on the island of Ios because of the distress brought on by his inability to solve a riddle posed by fishermen that 'what they caught they discarded and what they could not catch, they kept'. Ios has long laid claim to being the site of 'Homer's Grave' although Homer would have puzzled himself to death over why a major surfaced road (for Ios) should now wind its way through empty hills for 12km to end a few hundred metres from his – alleged – last resting place, a rather forlorn little mausoleum that looks decidely post-Homeric. The views are worth it, however. Sikinos, Naxos, Iraklia and Schinousa make for a nicely balanced crescent of islands across the sea. Homer would have appreciated the symmetry (if not the fishermen's fleas…).

Mylopotas Water Sports Center (☎ 22860 91622; www.ios-sports.gr; Mylopotas) has snorkelling and windsurfing gear, pedal boats (per hour €15) and canoes (single/double per hour €15/20) for hire. Waterskiing (per 15 minutes €30), banana rides (€12 to €15) and sailing (per hour/day €25/70) are also available. Beach volleyball and soccer rental is from €3 to €15. There is also a speedboat taxi available for hire.

New Dive Diving Centre (☎ 22860 92340; www.ios -sports.gr; Mylopotas) runs a PADI 'discover scuba diving' session (€65), plus more intensive PADI courses from €290 to €795. Speciality courses range from deep diving to underwater photography, fish identification and underwater navigation (€250 to €350). There are also daily diving and snorkelling trips, with shore dives (from €25).

Windsurfing (per hour/day €15/40) is on offer at **Meltemi Water Sports** (☎ 22860 91680; www .meltemiwatersports.com; Mylopotas) at the beach opposite Far Out Camping. Laser sailboats (per hour/day €30/65) are available for hire, as are canoes and pedalos. Tube rides cost from €15 to €30. Meltemi runs a similar scene at Manganari Beach and has a water taxi from Mylopotas to other beaches.

Sleeping

ORMOS

The port has several good sleeping options, reasonable eating places, a couple of handy beaches and regular bus connections to Hora and other beaches.

Ios Camping (☎ 22860 92035; fax 22860 92101; camp sites per person €8; ⚑) Tucked away on the west side of Ormos, this site has good facilities, including a restaurant in high season. Head all the way round the waterfront.

Golden Sun Hotel (☎ 22860 91110; www.iosgolden sun.com; s/d/tr incl breakfast €70/80/90; P ⚑ ⬚) The road from Gialos to Hora may not seem ideal sleeping territory, but this pleasant family-run hotel is located just up from the port and lies well down from the road. It overlooks open fields towards the sea. The good-sized rooms are well cared for.

Hotel Poseidon (☎ 22860 91091; www.poseidon hotelios.gr; s/d/tr €71/88/112; ⚑ ⚑) A very pleasant family-run hotel that lifts you high above the bustle and noise of the port, the Poseidon has terrific views from its front balconies. A flight of steps leads up to the hotel where rooms are immaculate and well equipped and there's a pleasant swimming pool.

GIALOS BEACH

Hotel Helena (☎ 22860 91276; www.hotelhelena.gr; s/d/tr/apt €50/70/90/120; ⚑ ⬚ ⬚ ⚑) Set a short way back from the midpoint of the beach is this quiet and well-run place. It has a cool patio, kindly owners and bright, clean rooms.

To Corali (☎ 22860 91272; www.coralihotel.com; d/tr incl breakfast €95/105, apt €120; P ⚑ ⬚ ⬚) These sparkling rooms are in a good position right opposite the beach and are attached to the restaurant of the same name. There's a colourful garden at the rear and the owners create a happy atmosphere.

HORA

Francesco's (☎ 22860 91223; www.francescos.net; dm €15, s €40-45, d €50-60; ⬚) Long established and very well run, the famous Francesco's has clean dormitories and rooms, and is in an enviable position with great views of the bay. It's away from the centre but is a lively meeting place for the younger international set. There's a busy bar and terrace and a big aprés-beach Jacuzzi. Francescos is reached by going up right from the cathedral for about 30m and then going left along Odos Scholarhiou for a couple of hundred metres.

Skala Hotel (☎ 22860 92027; skalahtl@otenet.gr; d/tr €85/100, apt €90-160; ⚑ ⬚ ⚑) A short hike uphill from the centre of town takes you well above the action zone to this well-situated hotel with great views over Hora. Good-sized rooms are bright and half of them have kitchenettes. Guests also have access to the pool and Jacuzzi.

MYLOPOTAS

Purple Pig Stars Camping & Bungalows (☎ 22860 91302; www.purplepigstars.com; camp sites per person €9, dm/d €20/45; 🐾) This pleasant camping ground is right at the entrance to the beach and has a relaxing tempo while being close to the action. It's shaded by trees.

Far Out Camping, Village Hotel & Beach Club (☎ 22860 91468; www.faroutclub.com; camp sites per adult/child €12/6, bungalows €12-22, studio €90; 🖵 🐾) There's plenty of action here, backed by wall-to-wall facilities. Meltemi Water Sports (see p425) is just across the road, and a diving centre has been established in recent years. There's a bar, restaurant and four swimming pools. The 'bungalows' range from small tent-sized affairs to neat little 'roundhouses' with double and single beds. The studios are in a separate location and have all mod cons.

Paradise Rooms (☎ 22860 91621; parios11@otenet.gr; s/d €55/65; 🐾) The family-run rooms here are about halfway along the beachfront, and the beautiful garden is looked after with love and skill. Breakfast costs €3 to €4.

ourpick Hotel Nissos Ios (☎ 22860 91610; www .nissosios-hotel.com; s/d/tr €60/75/90; 🐾 🖵) This excellent place has bright and fresh rooms, and wall murals add a colourful touch. Each room has tea- and coffee-making facilities. The welcome is good-natured, and the beach is just across the road. There's an outdoor Jacuzzi. In front of the hotel is the Bamboo Restaurant & Pizzeria (opposite).

Paradise Apartments (☎ 22860 91621; apt €90-140; 🐾 🐾) These apartments are located a short distance away from Paradise Rooms, and are run by a member of the same family. They're located in a secluded setting and have a lovely pool and big patio. At both Paradise accommodations, guests can get a 50% reduction at Mylopotas Water Sports Center (p425).

Eating

ORMOS

Peri Anemon (☎ 22860 92501; mains €5-10) A pleasant little cafe-taverna in the square next to Akteon Travel on the Ormos harbourfront, where you can get snacks and Greek standards.

GIALOS BEACH

To Corali (☎ 22860 91272; dishes €5-9) Mouthwatering wood-fired pizzas are list-toppers at this well-run eatery that's right by the beach and in front of the hotel of the same name. You can sit out at tables on the beach. It does pastas and salads as well, and it's a great spot for coffee, drinks and ice cream.

HORA

Porky's (☎ 22860 91143; snacks €2-4.50) Fuel up with toasties, salads, crêpes and hamburgers at this relentless Ios survivor, just off the main square.

Ali Baba's (☎ 22860 91558; dishes €7-12) Another great Ios favourite. this is the place for Thai dishes, including *pad thai* (thin rice noodles stir-fried with dried shrimp, bean sprouts, tofu and egg) cooked by authentic Thai chefs. The service is very upbeat and there's a garden courtyard. It's on the same street as the Emporiki bank.

Lord Byron (☎ 22860 92125; dishes €7-14) Near the main square, this long-standing favourite is relaxing and intimate, and the food is a great fusion of Greek and Italian. Dishes range from shrimp cooked in a tomato sauce with feta and ouzo, to penne with a wild mushroom and cream sauce – and it all comes in generous helpings.

Pomodoro (☎ 22860 91387; dishes €8-14) Spread over two floors, Pomodoro is just off the main square above Disco 69. There's a fabulous roof garden with panoramic views. Big helpings are the order of the day and authentic wood-fired pizzas are just part of its excellent, modern Italian and Mediterranean menu.

ourpick Pithari (☎ 22860 92440; mains €9-17) A longstanding local favourite located alongside the cathedral, Pithari has an excellent menu of traditional Greek cuisine given a modern twist. Shrimps flambé vie with filo pastry pies of feta cheese with honey and sesame seeds. They also do lunch, with pastas and other well-sourced local dishes.

There are also *gyros* (meat slivers cooked on a vertical rotisserie; usually eaten with pitta bread) stands where you can get a cheap bite.

MYLOPOTAS

Harmony (☎ 22860 91613; dishes €4-12) Few places take chill-out to the honed level of this great bar. Hammocks, deckchairs and discerning sounds set the pace and kids are well looked after here. It's just along the northern arm of

Mylopotas beach. There's live music too, and Tex-Mex food is the main attraction.

Drakos Taverna (☎ 22860 91281; dishes €4.50-9) Enjoy reasonably priced fish dishes (although some species are by the kilogram) at this popular taverna that overlooks the sea at the southern end of the beach.

Bamboo Restaurant & Pizzeria (☎ 22860 91648; dishes €6.50-8.50) Run by a member of the same family that operates Hotel Nissos Ios (opposite), this pleasant place does a good line in traditional *mousakas* and pizzas, plus a range of other Greek dishes. Breakfasts are €4.50 to €7.50.

Entertainment

Nightlife on Ios is a blitz. No one signs up for an early night in Hora's tiny main square, where it gets so crowded by midnight that you won't be able to fall down, even if you want to. Be young and carefree – but (women especially) also be careful. For a marginally quieter life there are some less full-on venues around.

Slammer Bar (☎ 22860 92119; Main Sq, Hora) Hammers out house, rock and Latin, as well as multiple tequila shots; head-banging in every sense.

Superfly (☎ 22860 92259; Main Sq, Hora) Plays funky house tunes.

Disco 69 (☎ 22860 91064; Main Sq, Hora) Hardcore drinking – and hard-core T-shirts – to a background of disco and current hits.

Other central venues are Blue Note, Flames Bar, Red Bull and Liquid.

Outside the centre of Hora are equally popular bars and some bigger dance clubs. **Ios Club** (☎ 22860 91410) Head here for a cocktail and watch the sun set to classical, Latin and jazz music from a great terrace with sweeping views. It's along the pathway by Sweet Irish Dream.

Orange Bar (☎ 22860 91814) A more easy-paced music bar playing rock, indie and Brit-pop just outside the war zone.

Scorpion's is a late-night dance-to-trance and progressive venue with laser shows. A great favourite is Kandi featuring top Norwegian guest DJs, while Aftershock goes for sensation with raunchy dancers and house, trance and Greek hits.

AROUND IOS

Travellers are lured to Ios by its nightlife, but also by its beaches. Vying with Mylopotas as one of the best is **Manganari**, a long swath of

fine white sand on the south coast, reached by bus or by caïque in summer (see Getting Around, p423).

From Ormos, it's a 10-minute walk past the little church of Agia Irini for **Valmas Beach**. A 1.3km walk northwest of Ormos, **Koumbara** is the official clothes-optional beach. **Tsamaria**, nearby, is nice and sheltered when it's windy elsewhere.

Agia Theodoti, **Psathi** and **Kalamos Beaches**, all on the northeast coast, are more remote. Psathi is a good windsurfing venue.

On Cape Gero Angeli, near Plakoto Beach at the northernmost tip of the island and 12km from Hora, is the alleged site of **Homer's Grave** (see boxed text, p425).

Moni Kalamou, on the way to Manganari and Kalamos Beaches, stages a huge **religious festival** in late August and a **festival of music and dance** in September.

SANTORINI (THIRA)
ΣΑΝΤΟΡΙΝΗ (ΘΗΡΑ)

pop 13,670

Santorini will take your breath away. Even the most jaded traveller succumbs to the spectacle of this surreal landscape, relic of what was probably the biggest eruption in recorded history. You do share the experience with hordes of other visitors, but the island somehow manages to cope with it all.

The caldera and its vast curtain of multicoloured cliffs is truly awesome. If you want to experience the full dramatic impact it's worth arriving by a slower ferry with open decks, rather than by enclosed catamaran or hydrofoil.

Santorini is famous for its spectacular sunsets. The village of Oia on the northern tip of the island is a hugely popular sunset-viewing site because there is an uninterrupted view of the sun as it finally sinks below the horizon.

Santorini is not all about the caldera, however. The east side of the island has black-sand beaches at popular resorts such as Kamari and Perissa and although the famous archaeological site of Akrotiri is closed for the forseeable future, Ancient Thira above Kamari is a major site.

The island's main port, Athinios, stands on a cramped shelf of land at the base of Sphinxlike cliffs and is a scene of marvellous chaos that always seems to work itself out when ferries arrive. Buses (and taxis) meet all ferries and then cart passengers through an ever-rising series of S-bends to the capital, Fira, which fringes the edge of the cliffs like a snowy cornice.

History

Minor eruptions have been the norm in Greece's earthquake record, but Santorini has bucked the trend – with attitude – throughout history. Eruptions here were genuinely earth-shattering, and so wrenching that they changed the shape of the island several times.

Dorians, Venetians and Turks occupied Santorini, as they did all other Cycladic islands, but its most influential early inhabitants were Minoans. They came from Crete some time between 2000 BC and 1600 BC, and the settlement at Akrotiri (p437) dates from the peak years of their great civilisation.

The island was circular then and was called Strongili (Round One). Thousands of years ago a colossal volcanic eruption caused the centre of Strongili to sink, leaving a caldera with towering cliffs along the east side – now one of the world's most dramatic sights. The latest theory, based on carbon dating of olive-oil samples from Akrotiri, places the event 10 years either side of 1613 BC.

Santorini was recolonised during the 3rd century BC but for the next 2000 years sporadic volcanic activity created further physical changes that included the formation of the volcanic islands of Palia and Nea Kameni at the centre of the caldera. As recently as 1956 a major earthquake devastated Oia and Fira, yet by the 1970s the islanders had embraced tourism as tourists embraced the island and today Santorini is a world destination of truly spectacular appeal.

Getting There & Away

There are several flights a day to and from Athens, Thessaloniki, Crete, Mykonos and Rhodes. There are also a good number of ferries a day to and from Piraeus and to and from many of Santorini's neighbouring islands. There are daily ferries to Crete and about four ferries a week go to Rhodes and Kos in the Dodecanese. For details see Island Hopping (p760).

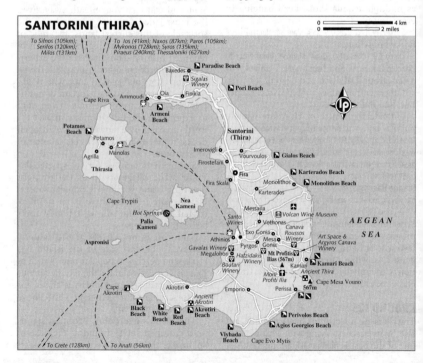

SANTORINI (THIRA)

0 — 4 km
0 — 2 miles

Getting Around

TO/FROM THE AIRPORT

There are frequent bus connections in summer between Fira's bus station and the airport, located southwest of Monolithos Beach. Enthusiastic hotel and domatia staff meet flights, and some also return guests to the airport. A taxi to the airport costs €12.

BUS

In summer buses leave Fira every half-hour for Oia (€1.40), Monolithos (€1.40), Kamari (€1.40) and Perissa (€2). There are less-frequent buses to Exo Gonia (€1.40), Perivolos (€2) and Vlyhada (€2.20). In summer the last regular bus to Fira from Oia leaves at 11.00pm.

Buses leave Fira, Kamari and Perissa for the port of Athinios (€2, 30 minutes) an hour and a half before most ferry departures. Buses for Fira meet all ferries, even late at night. It is wise to check port departures well in advance.

CABLE CAR & DONKEY

A **cable car** (☎ 22860 22977; M Nomikou; ☺ every 20min 7am-10pm, to 9pm winter) hums smoothly between Fira and the small port below, known as Fira Skala, from where volcanic island cruises leave. One-way cable car tickets cost €4 per adult, and €2 per child; luggage is €2. You can make a more leisurely, and aromatic, upward trip by donkey (€5).

CAR & MOTORCYCLE

A car is the best way to explore the island during high season, when buses are intolerably overcrowded and you're lucky to get on one at all. Be very patient and cautious when driving – the narrow roads, especially in Fira, can be a nightmare. Note that Oia has no petrol station, the nearest being just outside Fira.

Two very good local hire outfits are **Damigos Rent a Car** (☎ 22860 22048, 6979968192) and, for scooters, **Zerbakis** (☎ 22860 33329, 6944531992).

TAXI

Fira's **taxi stand** (☎ 22860 23951/2555) is in Dekigala just round the corner from the bus station. A taxi from the port of Athinios to Fira costs €12, and a trip from Fira to Oia is also €12. Both cost €13 if you book ahead. If you miss the last bus from Oia to Fira, three or four people can bargain for a shared taxi for about €12. A taxi to Kamari is €10, to Perissa €15 and to Ancient Thira €22 one way.

FIRA ΦΗΡΑ

pop 2113

A multitude of fellow admirers cannot diminish the impact of Fira's stupendous landscape. Views from the edge of the caldera over the multicoloured cliffs are breathtaking, and at night the caldera edge is a frozen cascade of lights that eclipses the displays of the gold shops in the streets behind.

CYCLADES

Orientation

The busy heart of Fira is Plateia Theotokopoulou (Central Sq). It's a fairly crowded, chaotic place; the main road, 25 Martiou, intersects the square as part of a one-way system that just manages to keep the nonstop traffic flow going. The bus station is on Mitropoleos, 150m south of Plateia Theotokopoulou. Between 25 Martiou and the caldera is the essence of Fira, a network of pedestrianised alleyways, the main ones running parallel to 25 Martiou. Erythrou Stavrou is the main commercial thoroughfare.

A block west of Erythrou Stavrou is Ypapantis, whose southern section is known also as Gold St because of its many jewellers. It runs along the edge of the caldera and has superb panoramic views until the shops intrude. Below the edge of the caldera is the paved walkway of Agiou Mina, which heads north and merges eventually with the clifftop walkway that continues north past the pretty villages of Firostefani and Imerovigli. Keep going and you'll reach Oia; but it's a long, hot 8km.

Information

Fira doesn't have an EOT (Greek National Tourist Organisation) or tourist police. It's best to seek out the smaller travel agents in the town, where you'll receive helpful service.

Toilets are north of Plateia Theotokopoulou near the port police building. You may need to brace yourself (they're of squat vintage). Bring your own paper – but not to read.

BOOKSHOPS

Books & Style (☎ 22860 24510; Dekigala) An excellent range of books in various languages. There's a great selection of volumes on Greece as well as travel guides, children's books and novels.

EMERGENCY

Hospital (☎ 22860 22237) On the road to Kamari. A new hospital at Karterados was under construction at the time of writing.
Police station (☎ 22860 22649; Karterados) About 2km from Fira.
Port police (☎ 22860 22239; 25 Martiou) North of the square.

INTERNET ACCESS

PC World (☎ 22860 25551; Plateia Theotokopoulou; per hr €1.90; 9am-9pm) A good range of services.

LAUNDRY

AD the Laundry Station (☎ 22860 23533; average load wash & dry €10; 9am-9pm)

MONEY

There are numerous ATMs scattered around town.
Alpha Bank (Plateia Theotokopoulou) Represents American Express and has an ATM.
National Bank of Greece (Dekigala) South of Plateia Theotokopoulou, on the caldera side of the road. Has an ATM.

POST

Post office (Dekigala)

TRAVEL AGENCIES

Aegean Pearl (☎ 22860 22170; www.aptravel.gr; Danezi) An excellent, helpful agency that sells all travel tickets and can help with accommodation, car hire and excursions.
Pelican Tours & Travel (☎ 22860 22220; fax 22860 22570; Plateia Theotokopoulou) Sells ferry tickets and can book accommodation and excursions.

Sights & Activities

MUSEUMS

Near the bus station, the **Museum of Prehistoric Thera** (☎ 22860 23217; Mitropoleos; admission €3; 8.30am-8pm Tue-Sun Apr-Sep, 8.30am-3pm Tue-Sun Oct-Mar) houses extraordinary finds that were excavated from Akrotiri (where, to date, only 5% of the area has been excavated). Most impressive is the glowing gold ibex figurine, measuring around 10cm in length and dating from the 17th century BC.

The **Archaeological Museum** (☎ 22860 22217; M Nomikou; adult/EU student/non-EU student €3/free/2; 8.30am-3pm Tue-Sun), near the cable-car station, houses finds from Akrotiri and Ancient Thira, some Cycladic figurines, and Hellenistic and Roman sculptures.

Megaron Gyzi Museum (☎ 22860 22244; Agiou Ioannou; adult/student €3.50/2; 10.30am-1pm & 5-8pm Mon-Sat, 10.30am-4.30pm Sun May-Oct) has local memorabilia, including fascinating photographs of Fira before and immediately after the 1956 earthquake.

Petros M Nomikos Conference Centre (☎ 22860 23016; adult/child €4/free; 10am-7pm May-Oct) The centre is run by the Thera Foundation (www.therafoundation.org) and hosts major conferences but also stages the fascinating Wall Paintings of Thera exhibition, a collection of three-dimensional life-size reproductions of the finest Akrotiri wall paintings. There's

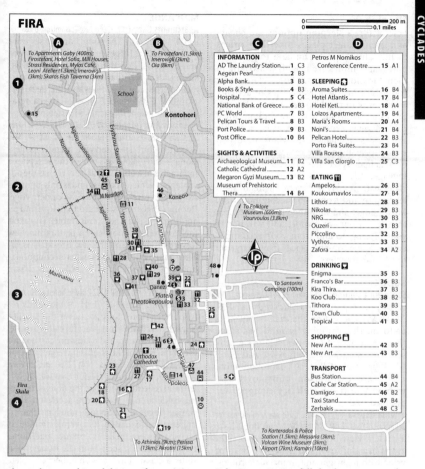

FIRA

INFORMATION	
AD The Laundry Station......1	C3
Aegean Pearl.....................2	B3
Alpha Bank.......................3	B3
Books & Style...................4	B3
Hospital............................5	C4
National Bank of Greece.....6	B3
PC World..........................7	B3
Pelican Tours & Travel.......8	B3
Port Police........................9	B3
Post Office......................10	B4

SIGHTS & ACTIVITIES	
Archaeological Museum....11	B2
Catholic Cathedral...........12	A2
Megaron Gyzi Museum......13	B2
Museum of Prehistoric Thera......14	B4

Petros M Nomikos	
Conference Centre........15	A1

SLEEPING	
Aroma Suites...................16	B4
Hotel Atlantis..................17	B4
Hotel Keti.......................18	A4
Loizos Apartments............19	B4
Maria's Rooms.................20	A4
Noni's.............................21	B4
Pelican Hotel...................22	B3
Porto Fira Suites..............23	B4
Villa Roussa....................24	B3
Villa San Giorgio.............25	C3

EATING	
Ampelos.........................26	B3
Koukoumavlos.................27	B4
Lithos.............................28	B3
Nikolas...........................29	B3
NRG...............................30	B3
Ouzeri............................31	B3
Piccolino.........................32	B3
Vythos...........................33	B3
Zafora............................34	A2

DRINKING	
Enigma...........................35	B3
Franco's Bar....................36	B3
Kira Thira........................37	B3
Koo Club.........................38	B2
Tithora...........................39	B3
Town Club.......................40	B3
Tropical..........................41	B3

SHOPPING	
New Art..........................42	B3
New Art..........................43	B3

TRANSPORT	
Bus Station......................44	B4
Cable Car Station.............45	A2
Damigos.........................46	B2
Taxi Stand.......................47	B4
Zerbakis.........................48	C3

also a photographic exhibition of excavations at Akrotiri.

Located on the eastern tip of the island, the **Folklore Museum of Santorini** (☎ 22860 22792; adult/child €3/free; ☼ 10am-2pm & 6-8pm Apr-Oct) houses an intriguing collection that casts light on Santorini's traditions and history. The museum is in a lovely setting and a major feature is an ancient *canava*, a sizeable cave excavated from the volcanic earth.

Tours

Tour companies operate various trips to and fro across the caldera. A tour to the volcanic island of Nea Kameni is €13, to the volcano and hot springs (including swimming) of

Palia Kameni, €18, full-day boat tours to the volcanic islets Thirassia and Oia, €25, sunset boat tour €35 and a bus tour including wine tasting €25. Book at travel agencies.

The *Bella Aurora,* an exact copy of an 18th-century schooner, scoots around the caldera every afternoon on a sunset buffet dinner tour (€45, from May to October), stopping for sightseeing on Nea Kameni and for ouzo on Thirasia. Most travel agencies sell tickets.

Courses

If you fancy a professional photography course based on Santorini, contact **Greek Island Workshops** (www.glennsteiner.com). It's run by top professional Glenn Steiner.

Sleeping

Few of Fira's sleeping options are cheap, and even budget places hike their prices in July and August. Domatia touts at the port reach impressive heights of hysteria in their bids for attention. Some claim their rooms are in town, when they're actually a long way out; ask to see a map showing the exact location. If you're looking for a caldera view, expect to pay at least double the prices of elsewhere. Many hotels in Fira, especially on the caldera rim, cannot be reached by vehicle. If you have heavy luggage, this is worth remembering, especially as there may be several flights of steps leading to and from your accommodation. Most budget and midrange places offer free transfer to port or airport and will porter your luggage to and from your accommodation. Some top-end places may charge up to €15 for transfers.

BUDGET

Santorini Camping (☎ 22860 22944; www.santorini camping.gr; camp sites per adult/child/tent €10/6/5; 🅿 🖳 🛒) Located on the eastern outskirts of town, this camping ground has some shade and decent facilities. There's a self-service restaurant, minimarket and pool. It's 400m east of Plateia Theotokopoulou. There are two-person bungalows also with air-con (€70), with one equipped for disabled use.

Villa Roussa (☎ 22860 23220; www.villaroussa.gr; Dekigala; s/d €55/75; 🅿 🎮 🛜 🛒) You don't have a caldera view but this small hotel is right at the heart of town and is hard to beat for value with its bright and immaculate rooms. It even has a swimming pool.

Villa San Giorgio (☎ 22860 23516; www.sangiorgio villa.gr; s/d/tr €60/70/85; 🎮 🛜) Not a scenic location but very close to the centre of Fira and an excellent option with its decent rooms and friendly owners.

Hotel Sofia (☎ 22860 22802; Firostefani; s/d €60/75; 🎮 🛒) These fresh, comfy rooms at the heart of Firostefani are a pleasant alternative to the bustle of Fira. Fira's centre is about 1.5km south, along a lovely caldera-edge walkway. Breakfast is €8.

Maria's Rooms (☎ 22860 25143; 6973254461; Agiou Mina; d €70; 🎮) A handful of charming rooms open onto a shared terrace that has unbeatable caldera and sunset views. Rooms are small but immaculate, and blissfully peaceful.

MIDRANGE

Apartments Gaby (☎ 22860 22057; Nomikou; d €65-95, tr €110, apt €120; 🎮) The rooms on the series of roof terraces at this excellent place guarantee sunset views, and there's a quiet and reassuring local feel that transcends Fira's surface gloss. Gaby is just beyond the Petros M Nomikos Conference Centre on the caldera-edge path where it reaches Firostefani.

Loizos Apartments (☎ 22860 24046; www.loizos .gr; s €75, d €85-95, tr/apt €110/140; 🅿 🎮 🖳 🛜 🛒) Recently refurbished and with friendly, professional service, Loizos is one of the best places in Fira. It's in a quiet cul-de-sac, yet has the advantage of vehicular access and is only minutes from the centre of town and the caldera edge. Rooms range from standard to deluxe and all are bright, clean and comfortable. Those on the front upper floor have a panoramic view towards Kamari and the sea. Breakfast is €7. The same owners have cheaper accommodation (single/double €55/65) at Messaria, 2.5km southeast of Fira.

Hotel Keti (☎ 22860 22324; www.hotelketi.gr; Agiou Mina; d €90-120, tr/ste €117/140; 🎮 🛜) Recently refurbished, Hotel Keti is one of the smaller 'sunset view' hotels in a peaceful caldera niche. Its attractive traditional rooms are carved into the cliffs. Half of the rooms have Jacuzzis.

OUR PICK **Aroma Suites** (☎ 22860 24112; www .aromasuites.gr; Agiou Mina; s €120, d €140-160; 🎮 🛜) In an excellent location at the quieter end of the caldera edge, and more accessible than similar places, this boutique hotel has charming service to match its overall ambience. Stylish, modern facilities enhance traditional caldera interiors, such as in the honeymoon suite: a classic Fira cave chamber, complete with Jacuzzi.

Also recommended:

Pelican Hotel (☎ 22860 23113; www.pelican.gr; Danezi; s/d/tr incl breakfast €70/80/100; 🎮 🖳 🛜) There's no caldera view, but rooms are comfy and well appointed at this longstanding hotel only metres from the centre of town.

Nonis (☎ 22860 24112; s/d €120/140) Run by the owners of Aroma Suites, Noni's has similar rooms with terrace Jacuzzi and superb caldera views.

TOP END

Hotel Atlantis (☎ 22860 22232; www.atlantishotel .gr; Mitropoleos; s/d incl breakfast €195-300; 🅿 🎮 🛒) The Atlantis is a handsome old building that overlooks the southern end of Ypapantis with dignity. It's full of cool, relaxing lounges and terraces, and the bright and airy bedrooms in the front have caldera views. The price range indicates views and window or balcony options.

Mill Houses (☎ 22860 27117; www.millhouses.gr; Firostefani; ste incl breakfast €210-410; ✸ ✺ ⬜) Located on the side of the caldera at Firostefani, these superb studios and suites are full of light and Cycladic colour. The creative decor and stylish furnishings go with first-class facilities and service. A sunset view is inevitable.

Porto Fira Suites (☎ 22860 22849; www.portofira.gr; Agiou Mina; 2-/3-/4-person ste incl breakfast €274/336/376; ✸ ✺ ⬀) This top-rated Fira hotel merges tradition with luxury and modern conveniences. Rooms are individually furnished and have huge stone-based beds and Jacuzzis. There's a cafe-bar and restaurant and breakfasts are lush affairs.

Strass Residences (☎ 22860 33765; www.thestrass.com; Firostefani; ste incl breakfast €280-420; ✸ ✺) They even manage palm trees round the pool at this exclusive little enclave of three luxury studios, all in glorious white. It feels as if the rest of the world is miles away, but Fira is just down the road.

Eating

Tourist-trap eateries, often with overpriced, indifferent food, are still an unfortunate feature of summertime Fira. In some places singles, and even families with young children, may find themselves unwelcome in the face of pushy owners desperate to keep tables full and their turnover brisk. However, there are excellent exceptions.

BUDGET

There are numerous fast-food outlets and cafes in Fira. Plateia Theotokopoulou has a few cafe-bars where the terraces are great for seeing all human life pass by.

Vythos (☎ 22860 22285) A local favourite, located at the start of the *plateia*.

Mylos Café (☎ 22860 25640; Firostefani; ⬜ ⬀) On the caldera edge in Firostefani, this stylish and relaxing venue is located in a converted windmill and is the ideal place for relaxing drinks and light snacks. It has a unique circular internet area (per hour €3.50) on the top floor and the cafe is a wi-fi hotspot.

Piccolino (☎ 22860 22595; Danezi; snacks €1-2.30) A snack bar and takeaway that dishes out a terrific range of sandwiches, wraps and other snacks, as well as hot and cold drinks.

NRG (☎ 22860 24997; Erythrou Stavrou; dishes €2.20-6.20) Still one of the best places to stop for a snack at the heart of Fira, this popular little crêperie offers crêpes, sandwiches, tortillas and an ever-popular Indian curry (€5), as well a range of ice cream, coffee and smoothies.

Nikolas (☎ 22860 24550; Erythrou Stavrou; dishes €6-9) The traditional Nikolas just keeps on flying the flag for the village taverna, at the heart of Fira. No-nonsense service dishes out grilled calamari, cuttlefish in a wine sauce and beef stew with onions.

Ouzeri (☎ 6945849921; Fabrika Shopping Centre; dishes €6.50-13.50) Fish dishes are especially good at this central *mezedhopoleio* and include prawn *saganaki* and a seafood platter of mixed fish. Starters such as artichoke *saganaki* ring the changes, as do meat dishes that include *youvetsi* (veal in tomato sauce with pasta) and pork fillet in a mustard sauce. Vegetarians can enjoy Dakos salads and a variety of nonmeat starters.

You'll also find several *gyros* stands in and around Fira's main square.

MIDRANGE

Lithos (☎ 22860 24421; Agiou Mina; mains €7-19.50) Amid a swath of eateries on the caldera edge, Lithos stands out for its well-prepared dishes and attentive service. Choose from persuasive starters such as fava with cheese and cherry tomatoes. Salads are crisp and fresh and mains cover poultry, meat, fish and shellfish dishes.

Zafora (☎ 22860 23203; cnr Nomikou & M Nomikou; mains €8.50-22.50) Sturdy Greek classics come with stunning caldera views at this big restaurant near the cable-car station. The pork tenderloin marinated in red wine, ginger, honey and soy sauce is a favourite and there are fish dishes, pasta and crêpes also on offer and breakfasts at €4.50 to €8.50.

Ampelos (☎ 22860 25554; Fabrika Shopping Centre; mains €10-26) There's plenty of space in this central Fira restaurant with its 2nd-floor terrace with a view. Try the grilled shrimp in a red pepper sauce with rice or the mussels *saganaki* or settle for a selection of such starters as stuffed mushrooms with dill, garlic and parsley in white wine and the speciality pie of green onion, dill, pine nuts and Parmesan cheese. There's a pleasing house wine or excellent Santorini and mainland reds and whites for up to €50 or so a bottle.

ourpick Koukoumavlos (☎ 22860 23807; mains €25-35) Discreet in location and outstanding for cuisine, the terrace of this fine restaurant has good views, while the interior has retained the vaulted style of its original Fira mansion. An uncrowded menu lists such certainties as lobster and monkfish terrine, or Santorini fava and smoked trout and salmon in a mandarin sauce with roasted almonds. Meat dishes are equally subtle and the wine list likewise. Look for the wooden doorway down to the right of the Hotel Atlantis.

Drinking

Drinks prices can be cranked up in Fira, even for beer, never mind the stellar cocktail prices. You're often paying for the view, so don't glaze over too early.

Kira Thira (☎ 22860 22770; Erythrou Stavrou) This bar is comfortable with itself; unsurprisingly as it's the oldest bar in Fira and one of the best. Smooth jazz, ethnic sounds and occasional live music fill out the background beneath the barrel roof.

Tropical (☎ 22860 23089; Marinatou) Nicely perched just before the caldera edge Tropical draws a vibrant crowd with its seductive mix of rock, soul and occasional jazz, plus unbeatable balcony views that are still there into the early hours.

Franco's Bar (☎ 22860 24428; Marinatou) Check your cuffs for this deeply stylish and ultimate sunset venue where music means classical sounds only. Expensive cocktails match the sheer elegance and impeccable musical taste.

Entertainment

After midnight Erythrou Stavrou fires up the clubbing caldera of Fira.

Koo Club (☎ 22860 22025; Erythrou Stavrou) Several bars with variable moods rise through the levels here. Sounds are soft house, trance and Greek hits, and you're never alone.

Town Club (☎ 22860 22820; Erythrou Stavrou) Still clinging defiantly to stylish kitsch, Town Club has faux-Classical facades, in lilac, to go with its gleaming whiteout interior. Modern Greek music and mainstream are just right for this upbeat place.

Tithora (☎ 22860 23519; off Danezi) Fira's big rock venue 'underneath the arches', where you can bliss out to big sounds.

Enigma (☎ 22860 22466; Erythrou Stavrou) A full-on dance venue when it gets going, this is the catwalk clientele's favourite spot amid coolness and floaty drapes. House and mainstream hits fit the style.

Shopping

So much shopping, so little time for the flood of cruise-ship passengers who forage happily through Fira's glitzy retail zones. You can get everything from Armani and Versace to Timberland and Reef – at rather glitzy prices, too.

Fira's jewellery and gold shops are legion. The merchandise gleams and sparkles, though prices may dull the gleam in your eye.

New Art (☎ 22860 23770; Erythrou Stavrou & Fabrika Shopping Centre) Forget the standard painted-on T-shirts. If you want quality to take back home, the subtle colours and motifs of designer Werner Hampel's Ts have real style.

Leoni Atelier (☎ 22860 23770; Firostefani) For art lovers, the studio and gallery of the internationally acclaimed artist, Leoni Schmiedel, is a worthwhile visit. Here, the artist creates her nuanced and multilayered collages that are inspired by Santorini's geology, natural elements and intense colours. The studio is reached by heading north past the windmill in Firostefani and then by following signs to the left.

AROUND SANTORINI

Oia Οία

pop 763

The village of Oia (ee-ah), known locally as Pano Meria, reflects the renaissance of Santorini after the devastating earthquake of 1956. Restoration work and upmarket tourism have transformed Oia into one of the loveliest villages in the Cyclades. Efforts are under way to introduce schemes that will ease the serious overcrowding; the price Oia pays in high summer for its attractiveness. Built on a steep slope of the caldera, many of its dwellings nestle in niches hewn into the volcanic rock. Oia, believe it or not, gets more sunset time than Fira, and its narrow passageways get very crowded in the evenings.

ORIENTATION & INFORMATION

From the bus terminal, head left and uphill to reach the rather stark central square and the main street, Nikolaou Nomikou, which skirts the caldera.

Atlantis Books (☎ 22860 72346; www.atlantisbooks
.org; Nikolaou Nomikou) A fascinating and well-stocked
little bookshop run with flair and enthusiasm by an
international group of young people. Cultural events are
sometimes staged here.

ATMs On Main St, outside Karvounis Tours, and also by the
bus terminus.

Karvounis Tours (☎ 22860 71290; www.idogreece
.com; Nikolaou Nomikou) For obtaining information, booking hotels, renting cars and bikes, and making international calls. It's also a wedding specialist.

SIGHTS & ACTIVITIES

The **maritime museum** (☎ 22860 71156; adult/stu-
dent €3/1.50; ✆ 10am-2pm & 5-8pm Wed-Mon) is located along a narrow lane that leads off right
from Nikolaou Nomikou. It's housed in an
old mansion and has endearing displays on
Santorini's maritime history.

Ammoudi, a tiny port with good tavernas and
colourful fishing boats, lies 300 steps below
Oia at the base of blood-red cliffs. It can also
be reached by road. In summer, boats and
tours go from Ammoudi to Thirasia daily;
check with travel agencies in Fira (p430) for
departure times.

SLEEPING

Oia Youth Hostel (☎ 22860 71465; www.santorinihostel
.gr; dm incl breakfast €17; ✆ May–mid-Oct; 🖥) One of
the cleanest and best-run hostels you'll hope
to find. It has better facilities than some hotels.
There's a small bar and a lovely rooftop terrace with great views. Internet is €2 per hour.
To find the hostel, keep straight on from the
bus terminus for about 100m.

Chelidonia (☎ 22860 71287; www.chelidonia.com;
Nikolaou Nomikou; studios €155, apt €170-205, ste €220-230;
🅿 🖥) Traditional cliffside dwellings that have
been in the owner's family for generations
offer a grand mix of old and new at Chelidonia.
Buried beneath the rubble of the 1956 earthquake, the rooms have been lovingly restored.
Modern facilities are nicely balanced by the
occasional fine piece of traditional furniture
and each unit has a kitchenette. Some places
are reached by several flights of steps.

Perivolas (☎ 22860 71308; www.perivolas.gr; ste
€505-1590; 🅿 🖥 🛜 🐾 🅰) Ultimate caldera-
edge accommodation at over-the-edge prices.
This is one of Greece's most renowned hotels, however, and features beautiful rooms
with vaulted ceilings, individual terraces and
kitchenettes. Breakfast, of rare quality, is included. There's a Wellness Studio, bar and

restaurant and the infinity pool has graced
the cover of *Condé Nast Traveller* magazine.
You know where you're at…

EATING & DRINKING

Thomas Grill (☎ 22860 71769; €7-15) Tucked into
the alleyway that leads up from the bus terminus, this Oia institution serves down-to-earth
Greek favourites, including its noted signature
dish, stuffed pork.

218 degrees (☎ 22860 71801; dishes €8-15) Opened
in 2009 and little sister to Oia's top restaurant,
1800, a great caldera-edge location at this styl-
sih place enhances such dishes as steamed
mussels with ouzo, fresh tomatoes and herbs.
It's open all day for breakfast, lunch, coffee
and drinks.

Nectar (☎ 22860 71504; €8-18) Quality cuisine, creative salads and main dishes such
as chicken with figs, plus some seriously
fine wines, ensure a rewarding meal at this
bright eatery.

Skala (☎ 22860 71362; Nikolaou Nomikou; dishes €8-19)
Watch life pass up and down to Ammouda
from the high ground of Skala's lovely terrace. Subtle international touches enhance the
traditional Greek dishes here, such as rabbit
stifadho (sweet stew cooked with tomato and
onions) and chicken fillet stuffed with mushrooms. The mezes are special. Try the cheese
pies with added onion and pine nuts.

Ambrosia (☎ 22860 71504; www.ambrosia-nectar.com;
mains €24-31) A top Oia restaurant, Ambrosia
presents a swath of handsome dishes from
starters of Santorini fava purée with grilled
octopus and caramelised onions to lobster
veloute, sautéed crawfish and cream of sea
urchin, or millefeuille of veal fillet layered
and roasted with tomatoes and goat's cheese
and smoked aubergine purée. The wine list
matches it all.

Megalahori Μεγαλωχωρί
pop 457

Signposts on the main road to Perissa and
Akrotiri indicate the 'traditional settlement'
of Megalohori village amid what at first seems
a fairly dull landscape. Turn off, however, to
parking at the entrance to the village and then
descend gently on foot into an older Santorini,
passing unvarnished old houses and beneath a
church belltower that straddles the street. At
the heart of Megalahori are a pleasant little
square and a handsome church with a little
pebble-surfaced enclave and war memorial.

SANTORINI WINES

Santorini's lauded wines are its crisp, clear dry whites, such as the delectable Assyrtico, and the amber-coloured, unfortified dessert wine Vinsanto. Most local vineyards hold tastings and tours.

A worthwhile visit is to **Santo Wines** (☎ 22860 22596; www.santowines.gr; Pyrgos) where you can sample a range of wines and browse a shop full of choice vintages as well as local products including fava, tomatoes, capers and preserves.

One of the most entertaining venues is the **Volcan Wine Museum** (☎ 22860 31322; www.volcan wines.gr; admission €5; ⏰ noon-8pm), housed in a traditional *canava* (winery) on the way to Kamari. It has interesting displays, including a 17th-century wooden winepress. Admission includes an audio guide and three wine tastings. On Friday night from May to October there's a festival night (€48), which includes a visit to the museum, three tastings, free buffet, free wine, live music and traditional costume dances, and even plate breaking.

There's also the Art Space gallery-winery outside Kamari – see below.

The following wineries should be contacted before visiting:

Boutari (☎ 22860 81011; www.boutari.gr; Megalohori)

Canava Roussos (☎ 22860 31278; www.canavaroussos.gr; Mesa Gonia)

Hatzidakis (☎ 22860 32552; www.hatzidakiswines.gr; Pyrgos Kallistis)

Sigalas (☎ 22860 71644; www.sigalas-wine.com; Oia)

There are a few cafes and tavernas and the signposted **Gavalas Winery** is worth a visit for its traditional ambience.

Kamari Καμάρι
pop 1351

Kamari is 10km from Fira and is Santorini's best-developed resort. It has a long beach of black sand, with the rugged limestone cliffs of Cape Mesa Vouno framing its southern end with the ancient site of Ancient Thira on its summit. The beachfront road is dense with restaurants and bars. Things get very busy in high season. Other less appealing but quieter beaches lie to the north at **Monolithos**.

Lisos Tours (☎ 22860 33765; lisostours@san.forthnet .gr) is especially helpful and has an office on the main road into Kamari, and another just inland from the centre of the beach. It sells ferry tickets and can organise accommodation and car hire. All kinds of tours can be arranged and there's internet access and a bureau de change.

The unmissable gallery **Art Space** (☎ 22860 32774; Exo Gonia) is just outside Kamari. It is located in **Argyro's Canava**, one of the oldest wineries on the island. The atmospheric old wine caverns are hung with superb artworks while sculptures transform lost corners and niches. The collection is curated by the owner and features some of Greece's finest modern artists. Winemaking is still in the owner's blood, and part of the complex is given over to producing some stellar vintages. A tasting of Vinsanto greatly enhances the whole experience.

SLEEPING
Anna's Rooms (☎ 22860 22765; s/d €25/35) Unbeatable budget deals can be had at these straightforward rooms. One group of rooms is behind Lisos Tours at the back of town; the other is behind Lisos Tours in the village.

Hotel Matina (☎ 22860 31491; www.hotel-matina .com; s/d/tr/ste incl breakfast €108/116/144/192; ❄ 🖳 🔊) A very well-run independent hotel, the Matina has spacious, brightly decorated rooms and is set back from the road in quiet grounds.

ourpick Aegean View Hotel (☎ 22860 32790; www.aegeanview-santorini.com; studio/apt €130/150; 🅿 ❄ 🖳 🔊 🔊) Tucked below the limestone cliffs high above Kamari, this outstanding hotel has spacious studios and apartments superbly laid out and with first-class facilities, including small kitchen areas. There's a lift to some rooms.

EATING
Amalthia (☎ 22860 32780; dishes €3.50-12) A long-established local favourite, Amalthia is a couple of blocks inland at the southern end of town, and there's a lovely garden area and a terrace with barbecue. There are well-prepared Greek dishes (the lamb is particularly good) and a range of pastas.

Mistral (☎ 22860 32108; mains €5.50-14) Seafood is what this classic *psarotaverna* is all about. Fish plates for two are about €30 and the likes of bream and red mullet are by the kilo.

our pick Mario No 1 (☎ 22860 32000; Agia Paraskevi, Monolithos; dishes €6.50-12) Right on the beach at Monolithos, near the airport, is this outstanding restaurant, one of Santorini's best. Fish is by the kilo and you can select shellfish from a display. There's a great list of mezedhes such as mussels' *saganaki* or sweet red peppers stuffed with feta, garlic, tomato and parsley. Meat dishes include roast lamb with rosemary and proper *mousaka*.

Ancient Thira Αρχαία Θήρα

First settled by the Dorians in the 9th century BC, **Ancient Thira** (admission €4; ⏰ 8am-2.30pm Tue-Sun) consists of Hellenistic, Roman and Byzantine ruins and is an atmospheric and rewarding site to visit. The ruins include temples, houses with mosaics, an *agora* (market), a theatre and a gymnasium. There are splendid views from the site. With the current closure of Ancient Akrotiri, this site more than makes up for it.

From March to October **Ancient Thira Tours** (☎ 22860 32474; Kamari) runs a bus every hour from 9am until 2pm, except on Monday, from Kamari to the site. If driving, take the surfaced but narrow, winding road from Kamari for just over 1km. From Perissa, on the other side of the mountain, a hot hike up a dusty path on sometimes rocky, difficult ground takes over an hour to the site.

Ancient Akrotiri Αρχαίο Ακρωτήρι

Excavations at **Akrotiri** (☎ 22860 81366), the Minoan outpost that was buried during the catastrophic eruption of 1650 BC, began in 1967 and have uncovered an ancient city beneath the volcanic ash. Buildings, some three storeys high, date back to the late 16th century BC. Outstanding finds are the stunning frescoes and ceramics, many of which are now on display at the Museum of Prehistoric Thera (p430) in Fira.

At the time of writing the site was closed indefinitely, pending ongoing negotiations over remedial construction work – one visitor was killed and several others injured when a section of the roof collapsed during the summer of 2005. You may find that there is a degree of confusion locally about whether or not the site is open. Check the 'archaeological sites' section of www.culture.gr and check thoroughly on arrival at Santorini before making a bus or taxi journey to what may still be a closed site. You can experience some of the rich value of the site at the archaeological museum (p430) and the Petros M Nomikos Conference Centre (p430) both in Fira.

Beaches

At times Santorini's black-sand beaches become so hot that a sun lounger or mat is essential. The best beaches are on the east and south coasts.

One of the main beaches is the long stretch at **Perissa**, a popular destination in summer. **Perivolos** and **Agios Georgios**, further south, are more relaxed. **Red Beach**, near Ancient Akrotiri, has high red cliffs and smooth, hand-sized pebbles submerged under clear water. **Vlyhada**, also on the south coast, is a pleasant venue. On the north coast near Oia, **Paradise** and **Pori** are both worth a stop.

Based at Perissa and **Akrotiri Beach** is the **Santorini Dive Centre** (☎ 22860 83190; www.divecenter .gr), offering a good range of courses including 'discover scuba diving' for €55, half-day snorkelling for €40 and an open-water diving course for €380.

SLEEPING & EATING

The main concentration of rooms can be found in and around Perissa.

Youth Hostel Anna (☎ 22860 82182; www.hostel world.com; dm €12-15, d €25; ⏰ May-Sep; P ✂ 🖵) A well-managed and popular hostel, Anna's is on the busy roadside at the entrance to Perissa and about five minutes from the beach. The private rooms are in a separate building. You can book excursions and boat tickets here, there's money exchange, and credit cards are accepted. A minibus picks up guests from the ferry port.

Stelio's Place (☎ 22860 81860; www.steliosplace .com; d/tr/q €70/90/120; ⏰ year-round; P ✂ 🛜 🖵) In a great position set back from the main drag but barely a minute from the beach, and with immaculate, well-appointed rooms, Stelio's is great value. Prices can drop below half in the low season.

Hotel Drossos (☎ 22860 81639; www.familydrossos .gr; s/d/tr incl breakfast €102/112/153; P ✂ 🖵 🛜 🖵) Behind the simple facade of this fine hotel lies a lovely complex of rooms and studios with stylish decor and furnishings.

CYCLADES

There's reliable Greek food on offer at **God's Garden** (☎ 22860 83027; dishes €4.50-11), a decent taverna with fish dishes starting at about €6.

Most beaches have a range of tavernas and cafes.

THIRASIA & VOLCANIC ISLETS
ΘΗΡΑΣΙΑ & ΗΦΑΙΣΤΕΙΑΚΕΣ ΝΗΣΙΔΕΣ

Unspoilt Thirasia (pop 158) was separated from Santorini by an eruption in 236 BC. The cliff-top *hora*, **Manolas**, has tavernas and domatia. It's an attractive place, noticeably more relaxed and reflective than Fira could ever be.

The unpopulated islets of **Palia Kameni** and **Nea Kameni** are still volcanically active and can be visited on various boat excursions from Fira Skala and Athinios (see Tours, p431). A day's excursion taking in Nea Kameni, the **hot springs** on Palia Kameni, Thirasia and Oia is about €28.

ANAFI ΑΝΑΦΗ

pop 272

Anafi is the escape clause of Santorini, an island perched on a distant horizon somewhere between yesterday's dream and a modern-day holiday delight; a slow-paced traditional lifestyle and striking Cycladic landscapes are the marks of this endearing island. There are few other visitors outside high summer, although Anafi is growing in popularity.

Orientation & Information

The island's small port is **Agios Nikolaos**. From here, the main village, **Hora**, is a 10-minute bus ride up a winding road, or a 1km hike up a less winding but steep walkway. In summer a bus runs every two hours from about 9am to 11pm and usually meets boats. Hora's main pedestrian thoroughfare leads uphill from the first bus stop and has most of the domatia, restaurants and minimarkets.

There is an ATM in a small kiosk just past a public telephone halfway along the harbour front, on the left.

There is a postal agency that opens occasionally, next to Panorama at the entrance to Hora.

You can buy ferry tickets at the **travel agency** (☎ 22860 61408) in Hora's main street next to Roussou minimarket or at a small office on the harbour front before ferries are due.

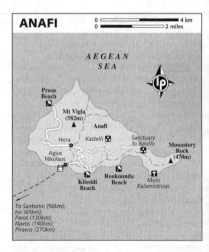

ANAFI 0 — 4 km / 0 — 2 miles

AEGEAN SEA

Prasa Beach
Mt Vigla (582m)
Anafi
Hora · Kastelli · Sanctuary to Apollo · Monastery Rock (470m)
Agios Nikolaos
Klissidi Beach · Roukounda Beach · Moni Kalamiotissas

To Santorini (56km);
Ios (65km);
Paros (130km);
Naxos (140km);
Piraeus (270km)

Sights

There are several lovely **beaches** near Agios Nikolaos. Palm-lined **Klissidi**, a 1.5km walk to the port, is the closest and most popular.

Anafi's main sight is the monastery of **Moni Kalamiotissas**, 9km by road from Hora or reached by a more appealing 6km walk along a path. It's in the extreme east of the island, near the meagre remains of a **sanctuary to Apollo** and below the summit of the 470m **Monastery Rock**, the highest rock formation in the Mediterranean Sea, outstripping even Gibraltar. The walk to the monastery is a rewarding expedition but it's a fairly tough trip in places and is a day's outing there and back. There is also a ruined Venetian *kastro* at **Kastelli**, east of Hora.

Sleeping

Domatia owners prefer long stays in high season, so if you're only staying one night you should take whatever you can get, or book ahead.

Apollon Village Hotel (☎ 22860 28739; www.apollon villa.gr; s/d/tr €48/65/75, studios €58-75; apt €70-125; 🅿 🛜) Rising in tiers above Klissidi Beach, these lovely individual rooms and studios, each named after an Olympian god and with glorious views, are outstanding value. Breakfast is €8 and the Blue Cafe-Bar is a cool stylish adjunct to the hotel with home-made sweets and pastries on offer.

Margarita's Rooms (☎ 22860 61237; anafi1@hotmail .com; s/d €50/60) Right by the beach and next to

Margarita's Café, these pleasant little rooms hark back to the beach life of quieter times.

Many of the rooms in Hora have good views across Anafi's rolling hills to the sea and to the great summit of Monastery Rock. The following recommended options are open all year and all charge about €45 for a double room:

Panorama (☎ 22860 61292)

Paradise (☎ 22860 61243)

Villa Gallini (☎ 22869 61279) In a particularly good location.

Eating

There are several tavernas in Hora, all of which are in the main street.

Liotrivi (☎ 22860 61209; mains €4-9) Great fish dishes (by the kilo), with the catch supplied from the family's boat; just about everything else, from eggs to vegetables and honey, comes from their garden.

Armenaki (☎ 22860 61234; mains €5-6.50) Good Greek traditional food at this great taverna is enhanced by an airy terrace and the pleasure of live bouzouki music on summer evenings.

Margarita's (☎ 22860 61237; Klissidi; mains €6-10.50) A sunny little terrace overlooking the bay at Klissidi makes for enjoyable eating here. Pork with mushrooms in a lemon sauce is a good option. Breakfasts are €2.50 to €5.

Getting There & Away

Anafi may be out on a limb and you can still face a challenge getting there out of season, but in summer the island has reasonable connections to Piraeus, Santorini, Sikinos, Folegandros, Naxos, Paros and even Syros. For details see Island Hopping (p746).

Getting Around

A small bus takes passengers from the port up to Hora. Caïques serve various beaches and nearby islands.

SIKINOS ΣΙΚΙΝΟΣ

pop 238

Lonely Sikinos (*see*-kee-noss) is another attractive escape from the clamour of Ios and Santorini, yet this lovely island is not much smaller than Santorini. It has a mainly empty landscape of terraced hills that sweep down to the sea. The main clusters of habitation are the port of **Alopronia**, and the linked inland villages of **Hora** and **Kastro**. The latter are reached by a 3.4km winding road that leads up from the port. There's a post office at the entrance to Kastro, and a National Bank of Greece ATM in the central square of Kastro. The medical centre is next door to the ATM. Ferry tickets can be bought in advance at **Koundouris Travel** (☎ 22860 51168, 6936621946). There is a petrol station outside Alopronia on the road to Kastro. You can hire scooters here for about €15 to €20.

Sights

Kastro, so named from an original Venetian fortress of the 13th century of which little physical sign remains, is a charming place, with winding alleyways between brilliant white houses. At its heart is the main square with a central war memorial surrounded by peaceful old buildings, one with ornate stone window-frames and sills long since whitewashed over. On one side is the **church of Pantanassa**. On the northern side of Kastro, the land falls sharply to the sea and the shells of old windmills punctuate the cliff edge. A flight of whitewashed steps leads up to the once-fortified church of **Moni Zoödohou Pigis** above the town.

To the west of Kastro, above steeply terraced fields and reached by an equally steep flight of steps, is the reclusive **Hora**, where numerous derelict houses are being renovated.

CYCLADES

From the saddle between Kastro and Hora, a surfaced road leads southwest to **Moni Episkopis** (admission free; �---- 6.30pm-8.30pm). The remains here are believed to be those of a 3rd-century-AD Roman mausoleum that was transformed into a church in the 7th century and then became the monastery Moni Episkopis 10 centuries later. From here you can climb to a little **church** and **ancient ruins** perched on a precipice to the south, from where the views are spectacular.

Caïques (about €6) run to good beaches at **Agios Georgios**, **Malta** – with ancient ruins on the hill above – and **Karra**. **Katergo**, a swimming place with interesting rocks, and **Agios Nikolaos Beach** are both within easy walking distance of Alopronia.

At the time of writing, a surfaced road was being laid to Agios Georgios and surrounding beaches. It is expected that buses will run to these beaches from Alopronia in summer.

Sleeping & Eating

There are several accommodation options at the port, but Hora is a more worthwhile place to stay.

Persephone's Rooms (☎ 22860 51229; Kastro; s/d/tr €40/60/70) Decent studio-type rooms on the outskirts of Kastro make for a good base on the island.

Lucas Rooms (☎ 22860 51076; www.diakopes.gr; Alopronia; d/studios €55/85; 🌊) Two good locations are on offer here and rooms are decent and clean; one set of rooms is on the hillside, 500m uphill from the port. The studios are on the far side of the bay from the ferry quay and have great views.

Kastro Studios (☎ 22860 51026/51283; Kastro; r €80; 🌊) There are only two places here but they are very new and quietly luxurious and have great views. They have cooking facilities.

Porto Sikinos (☎ 22860 51220; www.portosikinos.gr; Alopronia; s/d/tr incl breakfast €90/110/125; 🌊) Just up from the quay, the attractive rooms here rise in a series of terraces and have great balcony views. There's also a bar and restaurant.

Rock (☎ 22860 51186; Alopronia; dishes €2.60-8) High above the ferry quay is this seasonal cafe and pizza place, where you can also chill into the early hours (sometimes to live music). There are rooms here as well, with doubles priced at €40 to €60.

To Steki tou Garbi (Kastro; dishes €4-8) A good traditional grillhouse just around the corner from Koundouris Travel in Kastro.

To Iliovasilema (☎ 22860 51173; Kastro; mains €4.50-8) Outstanding views enhance a stop at this seasonal place, which dishes up standards as well as pizzas and pasta.

Lucas (☎ 22860 51076; Alopronia; dishes €6-13) Down at the port, this is the favourite taverna, offering Greek standards without frills and fish by the kilo.

Kastro Bar (☎ 22860 51026; Kastro) You'll find this little bar on the way to Moni Zoödohou Pigis. Coffee, drinks and ice cream are the mainstay and Greek music the style. Open morning until late.

There's a minimarket next to Lucas in Alopronia and another in Kastro.

Getting There & Around

For details of ferry services from Sikinos see Island Hopping (p761).

The local bus meets all ferry arrivals and runs between Alopronia and Hora/Kastro (€1.40, 20 minutes) every half-hour in August, but less frequently at other times of the year. A timetable is sometimes posted near the minimarket. It's wise to be in good time at the departure point.

FOLEGANDROS
ΦΟΛΕΓΑΝΔΡΟΣ

pop 662

Folegandros (fo-*leh*-gan-dross) sits elegantly on the southern edge of the Cycladics, a rocky ridge, barely 12km in length and just under 4km at its widest point. Much of the land is over 200m in height, the highest point being Agios Eleftherios at 414m.

The remoteness and ruggedness of Folegandros made it a place of exile for political prisoners from Roman times to the 20th century, and as late as the military dictatorship of 1967–74, yet today it is cherished by devotees of its beauty and character.

The capital is the concealed, cliff-top Hora, one of the most appealing villages in the Cyclades. Boats dock at the little harbour of Karavostasis, on the east coast. The only other settlement is Ano Meria, 4km northwest of Hora. There are several good beaches, but be prepared for strenuous walking to reach some of them.

CYCLADES

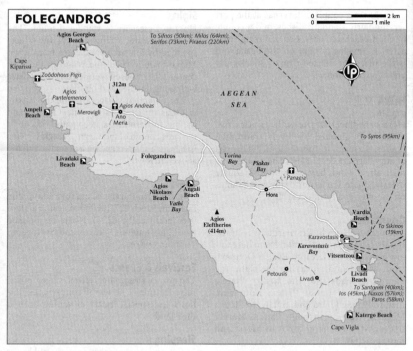

FOLEGANDROS

0 —————— 2 km
0 —————— 1 mile

Agios Georgios Beach

To Sifnos (50km); Milos (64km); Serifos (73km); Piraeus (220km)

Cape Kiparissi

Zoödohous Pigis

312m ▲

Agios Pantelemenos

AEGEAN SEA

Agios Andreas

Ampeli Beach

Merovigli

Ano Meria

To Syros (95km)

Livadaki Beach

Folegandros

Varina Bay

Piakas Bay

Panagia

Agios Nikolaos Beach

Angali Beach

Vathi Bay

Hora

Agios Eleftherios (414m)

Vardia Beach

To Sikinos (19km)

Karavostasis

Karavostasis Bay

Vitsentzou

Petousis

Livadi

Livadi Beach

To Santorini (40km); Ios (45km); Naxos (57km); Paros (58km)

Katergo Beach

Cape Vigla

Getting There & Away

Once poorly served by ferries, Folegandros at least in summer has good connections with Piraeus through the western Cyclades route. It even has connections to Santorini and as far as Amorgos during the summer. For details see Island Hopping (p750).

Getting Around

The local bus meets all ferry arrivals and takes passengers to Hora (€1.40). From Hora there are buses to the port one hour before all ferry departures. Buses from Hora run hourly in summer to Ano Meria (€0.80) and divert to Angali Beach. The bus stop for Ano Meria is located on the western edge of Hora.

There is a **taxi service** (☎ 22860 41048, 6944693957) on Folegandros.

You can hire cars for about €40 per day, and motorbikes from about €15 per day, from a number of outlets.

In summer, small boats ply regularly between beaches.

KARAVOSTASIS ΚΑΡΑΒΟΣΤΑΣΙΣ
pop 55

Folegandros' port is a sunny little place serviced by a sprinkling of domatia and tavernas, and with a pleasant pebble beach. Within a kilometre north and south of Karavostasis lies a series of other beaches, all enjoyable and easily reached by short walks. In high season, boats leave Karavostasis for beaches further afield.

Sleeping & Eating

Aeolos Beach Hotel (☎ 22860 41205; s/d/studios €50/55/80) Just across from the beach, this handy hotel has a pretty garden and clean straightforward rooms.

Vrahos (☎ 22860 41450; www.hotel-vrahos.gr; s incl breakfast €73, d incl breakfast €91-123, studios & apt €97-182; ✳ ▯ 🛜) In a great location at the far end of the beach, Vrahos rises through a series of terraces, and the front balconies have great views of the bay. Rooms have cool decor and there's an outdoor Jacuzzi, a bar and a breakfast area. Breakfast is €12.50.

CYCLADES

There are a couple of tavernas at the port serving fairly standard dishes, and a couple of good beachside bars. For enduring character, Evangelos is right on the beach and is the place for relaxed drinks, snacks and great conversation.

HORA ΧΩΡΑ
pop 316
Hora's medieval *kastro*, with its attractive main street flanked by lovely traditional houses, is a major feature of Hora, but the rest of the village is a delight also. The meandering main street winds happily from leafy square to leafy square. On its north side, Hora stands on the edge of a formidable cliff.

Orientation
The port to Hora bus turnaround is in the square called Plateia Pounta. From here follow a road to the left into Plateia Dounavi, from where an archway on the right, the Paraporti, leads into the *kastro*. Plateia Dounavi leads on to Plateia Kontarini, then to Plateia Piatsa and, finally, to Plateia Maraki. Keep on through Plateia Maraki to reach the bus stop for Ano Meria and most beaches.

Information
Folegandros does not have an official tourism office. A good source of information is www.folegandrosisland.com.

There's no bank, but there is an ATM on the far side of Plateia Dounavi, next to the community offices. The post office is on the port road, 200m downhill from the bus turnaround.

Travel agencies can exchange travellers cheques.

Diaplous Travel (☎ 22860 41158; www.diaploustravel.gr; Plateia Pounta) Helpful and efficient agency – sells ferry tickets, exchanges money and arranges accommodation, car and bike hire and boat excursions. Internet access per 15 minutes costs €1.

Maraki Travel (☎ 22860 41273; fax 22860 41149; Plateia Dounavi; ⏰ 10.30am-noon & 5-9pm) Sells ferry tickets and exchanges money.

Medical Centre (☎ 22860 41222; Plateia Pounta)

Police station (☎ 22860 41249) Straight on from Plateia Maraki.

Sottovento Tourism Office (☎ 22860 41444; www.folegandrosisland.com) On Plateia Pounta; doubles as the Italian consulate and is very helpful on all tourism matters, including accommodation, international and domestic flights and boat trips.

Sights
Hora is a pleasure to wander through. The medieval **kastro**, a tangle of narrow streets spanned by low archways, dates from when Marco Sanudo ruled the island in the 13th century. The houses' wooden balconies blaze with bougainvillea and hibiscus.

The extended village, outside the *kastro*, is just as attractive. From Plateia Pounta and the bus turnaround, a steep path leads up to the large church of the Virgin, **Panagia** (⏰ 6pm-8pm), which sits perched on a dramatic cliff top above the town.

Tours
Boat trips around the island (per adult/child including lunch €27/10) and to nearby Sikinos (per adult/child €22/11) can be booked through Diaplous Travel and Sottovento Tourism Office.

Festivals & Events
The annual **Folegandros Festival**, staged in late July, features a series of concerts, exhibitions and special meals, at venues around the island.

Sleeping
In July and August most domatia and hotels will be full, so book well in advance.

Evgenia (☎ 22860 41006; www.evgeniafol@yahoo.gr; s/d €60/70 ste €80-120; ⏾) These clean and well-kept rooms and studios are right at the entrance to Hora.

Pounta Accommodation (☎ 22860 41063; apt €80-90) Located about 1km from Hora, these are proper Folegandrian houses rather than studios or apartments and have great character within a superb setting.

Aegeo (☎ 22860 41468; aegeofol@hol.gr; s/d/tr €85/90/115; ⏾ 🖳 📶) Located on the outskirts of town, Aegeo captures the classic Cycladean style with its central courtyard area, all white and blue and draped with crimson bougainvillea. Rooms are immaculate and bright.

Hotel Polikandia (☎ 22860 41322; www.polikandia-folegandros.gr; s €85, d €95-120, ste €200; ⏾ 📶 🖲) A major makeover has transformed this always decent place into a colourful boutique hotel with lovely rooms encircling a gleaming pool. Decor and facilities are of high quality. It's just before the bus turnaround. Breakfast is €10. Bikes are offered free.

Anemomylos Apartments (☎ 22860 41309; www.anemomilosapartments.com; d €150-200; ⏾ 🖳 🖲 ♿)

A prime position on top of a cliff ensures awesome views from the seaward-facing rooms of this stylish complex and from its terraces. Rooms are elegant and fine antiques add to the ambience. Anemomylos is just up from the bus turnaround. One unit is equipped for use by those with disabilities.

Eating

Melissa (☎ 22860 41067; Plateia Kontarini; mains €5-9) Good food is matched by charming owners. The island speciality of *matsata* (handmade pasta) with meat of your choice is always worthwhile, as is the fish soup. Vegetarians will relish the stuffed cabbage. It also does good breakfasts.

Zefiros (☎ 22860 41556; dishes €5.50-9.50) A great *ouzerie* and *mezedhopoleio* with a challenging selection of ouzo varieties. There are mezedhes plates for two at €20, as well as mixed small plates, and dishes such as lamb in vine leaves and shrimp *saganaki*. Keep left beyond Plateia Kontarini.

ourpick Pounta (☎ 22860 41063; Plateia Pounta; dishes €6-13) In Pounta's garden setting there's an inescapable sense of an older Greece, and the courteous service underlines this. The traditional food is excellent, from breakfasts starting at €4.50, to evening meals of rabbit *stifadho* or artichoke casserole. It's all served on lovely crockery made by one of the owners, Lisbet Giouri; you can buy examples of her work.

Eva's Garden (☎ 22860 41110; mains €8-24) Opened in the past couple of years, Eva's brings an added flair to Folegandros cuisine. Starters include fava-bean purée with onion and parsley, while mains feature pork fillet in smoked cheese sauce or grilled marinated shrimps in a lime sauce with basmati rice. The wine list goes well with it all and includes Argiros vintages from Santorini. Keep right beyond Plateia Kontarini.

Also recommended:
Piatsa Restaurant (☎ 22860 41274; dishes €3-9.50)
Chic (☎ 22860 41515; dishes €4-9.50).

Drinking & Entertainment

Folegandros has some stylish cafe-bars such as **Caffé de Viaggiatori** (☎ 22860 41444), next door to Sottovento Tourism Office and offering Italian wines and finger food. Deeper into Hora is **To Mikro** (☎ 22860 41550), a good place for coffee, crêpes and cakes by day and cocktails at night.

At Hora's very own 'West End' is a clutch of colourful music bars starting with **Greco Café-Bar** (☎ 22860 41456), with a great mix of sounds from a stock of over 1000 CDs, all against a backdrop of vivid murals. Next door are **Avli Club** (☎ 22860 41100) for early evening lounge music and later rock, disco, Latin and Greek; and **Kolpo** (☎ 22860 41570) for reggae, world music and soul, and a hammock garden with scenic views.

A Folegandros local drink is *rakomelo* – heated *raki* with honey and cloves. One of the best bars to enjoy it and get into the spirit of things is Astarti, next to the Melissa taverna on Plateia Kontarini.

AROUND FOLEGANDROS
Ano Meria Ανω Μεριά
pop 291

The settlement of Ano Meria is a scattered community of small farms and dwellings that stretches for several kilometres. This is traditional island life where tourism makes no intrusive mark and life happily wanders off sideways.

The **folklore museum** (admission €1.50; ✆ 5pm-8pm) is on the eastern outskirts of the village. Ask the bus driver to drop you off nearby.

There are several very traditional tavernas in Ano Meria, including **I Synantisi** (☎ 22860 41208; dishes €4-8) and **Mimi's** (☎ 22860 41377; dishes €4). Things may get a touch fraught at busy periods.

Beaches

For **Livadi Beach**, 1.2km southeast of Karavostasis, follow the signs for Camping Livadi. Further round the coast on the southeastern tip of the island is **Katergo Beach**, best reached by boat from Karavostasis.

The sandy and pebbled **Angali** beach, on the coast opposite to Hora, is a popular spot, now with a surfaced road to it and a bus turnaround. There are some rooms here and two reasonable tavernas.

About 750m over the hill, by footpath, west of Angali is **Agios Nikolaos**, a nudist beach. **Livadaki** beach is over 2km further west again. It is best reached by another 1.5km hike from the bus stop near the church of Agios Andreas at Ano Meria. Boats connect these west-coast beaches in high season. **Agios Georgios** is north of Ano Meria and requires another demanding walk. Have tough footwear, sun protection and, because most beaches have no shops or tavernas, make sure you take food and water.

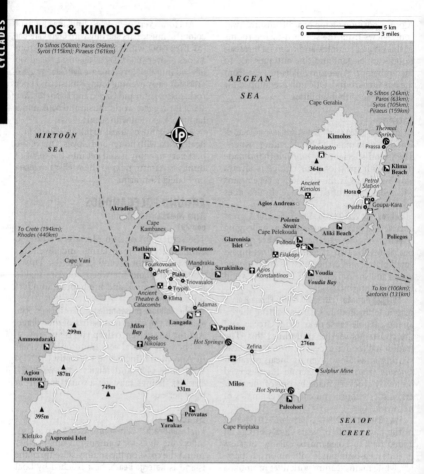

MILOS & KIMOLOS

In July and August, weather permitting, excursion boats make separate trips from Karavostasis to Katergo, Angali and Agios Nikolaos and from Angali to Livadaki beach.

MILOS ΜΗΛΟΣ

pop 4771

Milos (*mee*-loss) has a dramatic coastal landscape with colourful and surreal rock formations that reflect the island's volcanic origins. It also has hot springs, the most beaches of any Cycladic island and some compelling ancient sites.

The island has a fascinating history of mineral extraction dating from the Neolithic period when obsidian was an important material and was even exported to the Minoan world of Crete. Over the years sulphur and kaolin have been mined and today Milos is the biggest bentonite and perlite production and processing centre in the EU.

Filakopi, an ancient Minoan city in the island's northeast, was one of the earliest settlements in the Cyclades. During the Peloponnesian Wars, Milos was the only Cycladic island not to join the Athenian alliance. It paid dearly in 416 BC, when avenging Athenians massacred the adult males and enslaved the women and children.

The island's most celebrated export, the beautiful *Venus de Milo* (a 4th-century-BC statue of Aphrodite, found in an olive grove in 1820) is far away in the Louvre (allegedly having lost its arms on the way to Paris in the 19th century).

Getting There & Away
There are two flights weekly between Milos and Athens. These are often quite heavily booked ahead. Milos is on the same western-Cyclades ferry routes as its northern neighbour Serifos. For details see Island Hopping (p756).

Getting Around
There are no buses to the airport (south of Papikinou), so you'll need to take a **taxi** (☎ 22870 22219) for €7.65, plus €0.30 per piece of luggage, from Adamas. A taxi from Adamas to Plaka is €6.50; add €1 for evening trips. **Taxi Andriotis** (☎ 6942590951) is a friendly service.

Buses leave Adamas for Plaka and Trypiti every hour or so. Buses run to Pollonia (four daily), Paleohori (three daily), Provatas (three daily) and Achivadolimni (Milos) Camping (right), east of Adamas (three daily). All fares are €1.40.

Cars, motorcycles and mopeds can also be hired from places along the waterfront. A helpful outfit is **Giourgas Rent a Car** (☎ 22870 22352, 6937757066; giourgas@otenet.gr), reached by heading east from the ferry quay, going inland from where the waterfront road crosses a dry river bed and then turning right after several hundred metres.

ADAMAS ΑΔΑΜΑΣ
pop 1391

Plaka is the capital of Milos and the most appealing of all the settlements, but the pleasant, lively port of Adamas has most of the accommodation, shops and general services, plus a diverting waterfront scene.

Orientation
For the town centre, turn right from the arrival quay. The central square, with the bus stop, taxi rank and outdoor cafes, is at the end of this first stretch of waterfront, where the road curves inland. Just past the square is a road to the right that skirts the town beach.

Information
ATMs can be found along the main harbour front and in the main square. The post office is along the main road, 50m from the main square, on the right.

Internet Info (☎ 22870 23218; per 30min €1.50; ⏰ 9am-midnight) Located in the main street, just inland and on the right.
Municipal Tourist Office (☎ 22870 22445; www .milos-island.gr; ⏰ 8am-midnight mid-Jun–mid-Sep) Opposite the quay.
Police station (☎ 22870 21378) On the main square, next to the bus stop.
Port police (☎ 22870 22100) On the waterfront.
Terry's Travel Services (☎ 22870 22640; www .terrysmilostravel.com) Knowledgeable and helpful service goes with a great love of the island here. Help with accommodation, car hire, kayaking and sailing trips, diving and much more. Head left from the ferry quay, and, just past the bend in the road, go right up a lane.

Sights & Activities
The **Milos Mining Museum** (☎ 22870 22481; www .milosminingmuseum.gr; adult/concession €3/1.50; ⏰ 9am-2pm & 6-9pm Jul–mid-Sep, 8.30am-2.30pm Tue-Sat mid-Sep–Jun) is a must for mining enthusiasts; in fact, it's a must for everyone. It's about 600m east of the ferry quay.

Dive courses are offered by **Milos Diving Center** (☎ 22870 41296; www.milosdiving.gr), based at Pollonia. It's a member of the International Association for Handicapped Divers.

Kayak Milos (☎ 22870 23597; www.seakayakgreece .com) organises day trips for €60 per person, including picnic lunch. Longer expeditions and week-long packages are also available.

Tours
Around Milos Cruise (☎ 6944375799; tours €25; ⏰ May-Sep) Cruise on the wooden-hulled Captain Yiangos departing daily at 9am, stopping at beaches around the island and pausing at Kimolos for lunch. Return is about 6pm. Buy tickets on the waterfront.

Festivals & Events
The **Milos Festival**, a well-orchestrated event, is held in early July and features traditional dancing, cooking and jazz.

Sleeping
In summer, lists of available domatia are given out at the tourist office on the quay, but good options are thin on the ground – call ahead.

Achivadolimni (Milos) Camping (☎ 22870 31410; www.miloscamping.gr; Arhiva-dolimni; camp sites per adult/child/tent €7/4/4, bungalows €60-125; ⏰ 🛒) This camping ground has excellent facilities, including a restaurant, a bar and bike rental.

It's 4.5km east of Adamas; to get here, follow the signs along the waterfront from the central square or take the bus (see Getting Around, p445).

Hotel Delfini (☎ 22870 22001; fax 22870 22294; s/d €45/65; ⏰ Apr-Oct; ⋇) A pleasant, comfortable hotel with good rooms and facilities. Neighbouring hotels have rather stolen the view, but there's a lovely terrace and a warm ambience. It's to the west of the ferry quay and is tucked in behind the Lagada Beach Hotel.

Terry's Rooms (☎ 22870 22640; teristur@otenet .gr; d €50, apt €100-120; ⋇) A great option, these homely rooms are in a quiet location above the harbour and are a nice mix of traditional and modern. Follow directions for Terry's Travel Services (see p445).

Studios Helios (☎ 22870 22258; fax 22870 23974; heaton.theologitis@utanet.at; apt €90-100; ⏰ mid-May–mid-Oct; ⋇) In an unbeatable location, high above the port, are these stylish, beautifully furnished apartments for two or four people.

Portiani Hotel (☎ 22870 22940; www.portianimilos .com; s/d incl breakfast €110/135; Ⓟ ⋇) Right next to the square and busy waterfront, these well-appointed rooms manage to feel secluded. The upper balconies have great views. There's a lift to the upper floors. The buffet breakfast features local products.

Eating

I Milos (☎ 22870 22210; dishes €3.50-9) This likeable place is at the far end of the main square's line of waterfront cafes and tavernas. Breakfasts are €4.10 to €6.20. Lunch dishes include pizzas and pastas.

Taverna Barko (☎ 22870 22660; dishes €4.50-12) A classic *mezedhopoleio*. On the road to Plaka, near the outskirts of town, Barko serves local dishes such as Milos cheese pie and octopus in wine, as well as pastas.

Flisvos (☎ 22870 22275; dishes €5-9) Fish is by the kilogram at this busy waterfront taverna, to the east of the ferry quay. It serves good charcoal-grilled Greek specialities, salads are crisp and fresh, and the cheese and mushroom pies are mouth-melting.

Entertainment

Halfway up the first staircase along from the ferry quay are a couple of popular music bars including Ilori and Vipera Lebetina, playing disco, pop and Greek music during July and August.

Akri (☎ 22870 22064) Further uphill, opposite Villa Helios, Akri is in a beautiful location with a fine terrace overlooking the port. Music favours ethnic, funk and easy listening.

PLAKA & TRYPITI ΠΛΑΚΑ & ΤΡΥΠΗΤΗ

Plaka (population 877), 5km uphill from Adamas, is a typical Cycladic town with white houses and labyrinthine lanes. It merges with the settlement of Trypiti (population 489) to the south and rises above a sprawl of converging settlements, yet has a distinctive and engaging character.

Plaka is built on the site of Ancient Milos, which was destroyed by the Athenians and rebuilt by the Romans.

Sights & Activities

The **archaeology museum** (☎ 22870 21629; admission €3; ⏰ 8.30am-3pm Tue-Sun) is in Plaka, just downhill from the bus turnaround. It's in a handsome old building and contains some riveting exhibits, including a plaster cast of *Venus de Milo* that was made by Louvre craftsmen – as a sort of *Venus de Mea Culpa*, perhaps, considering the French 'appropriated' the original. Best of all is a perky little herd of tiny bull figurines from the Late Cycladic period.

The **Milos Folk & Arts Museum** (☎ 22870 21292; ⏰ 10am-2pm & 6-9pm Tue-Sat, 10am-2pm Sun & Mon) has fascinating exhibits, including traditional costumes, woven goods and embroidery. It's signposted from the bus turnaround in Plaka.

At the bus turnaround, go east for the path that climbs to the **Frankish Kastro**, built on the ancient acropolis and offering panoramic views of most of the island. The 13th-century church, **Thalassitras**, is inside the walls.

There are some Roman ruins near Trypiti, including Greece's only Christian **catacombs** (☎ 22870 21625; admission free; ⏰ 8am-7pm Tue-Sun). The site was closed for some time but has been skilfully renovated and was due to be open by 2010. Stay on the bus towards Trypiti and get off at a T-junction by a big signpost indicating the way. Follow the road down for about 500m to where a track (signed) goes off to the right. This leads to the rather forlorn, but somehow thrilling, spot where a farmer found the *Venus de Milo* in 1820; you can't miss the huge sign. A short way further along the track is the well-preserved **ancient theatre**, which hosts the **Milos Festival** every July. Back on the surfaced road, head downhill to reach the 1st-century catacombs.

Sleeping & Eating
All of the following places are located in Plaka.

Betty's Rooms (☎ 22870 21538; d €70) Forget Santorini; these rooms in a family house are at the bottom end of Plaka and have fantastic views.

Archondoula Karamitsou Studios (☎ 22870 23820; www.archondoula-studios.gr; ste €75-130) More great views are enjoyed at these traditional rooms, which are full of local craftwork and island antiques. Prices drop substantially outside August.

Windmill of Karamitsos (☎ 6945568086; kaliopekavalierou@yahoo.gr; r €170) A fascinating and unique sleeping experience can be had at this converted windmill that has a separate cooking and eating annexe. It's in a peaceful position on a hill top, of course, with great views.

ourpick **Archondoula** (☎ 22870 21384; dishes €5-15) All the family is involved at this great *mezedhopoleio*. The food is classic traditional across a range of favourites from fresh salads to beef with honey sauce and shrimps with cream sauce. It's just along the main street from the bus turnaround in Plaka.

Utopia Café (☎ 22870 23678) One of the best viewpoints in the Cyclades can be enjoyed from the cool terrace of Utopia, down the narrow alley opposite Archondoula.

AROUND MILOS
The village of **Klima**, below Trypiti and the catacombs, was the port of ancient Milos. It's a picturesque fishing village with a lovely little harbour. Whitewashed buildings, with coloured doors and balconies, have boathouses on the ground floor and living quarters above.

Plathiena is a fine sandy beach below Plaka, to the north. On the way to Plathiena you can visit the fishing villages of **Areti** and **Fourkovouni**.

At **Sarakiniko** are snow-white rock formations and natural terraces. **Pollonia**, on the north coast, is a fishing village-cum-resort with a beach and domatia. The boat to Kimolos departs here.

The beaches of **Provatas** and **Paleohori**, on the south coast, are long and sandy, and Paleohori has **hot springs**.

KIMOLOS ΚΙΜΩΛΟΣ
pop 769

Kimolos (Map p444) feels like a genuine step back in time. Perched off the northeast tip of Milos, it receives a steady trickle of visitors, especially day-trippers arriving from Pollonia. The boat docks at the port of **Psathi**, from where it's 1.5km to the pretty capital of **Hora**. The medieval **kastro**, embedded at the heart of Hora, is a mazelike joy. Albeit in ruins, there are surviving walls and restoration work is ongoing.

There's an ATM by the town hall in Hora.

Beaches can be reached by caïque from Psathi. At the centre of the island is the 364m-high cliff on which sits the fortress of **Paleokastro**.

There are domatia, tavernas, cafes and bars enough in Hora and Psathi. Domatia owners meet ferries. Expect to pay single/double rates of about €35/50.

The taverna **To Kyma** (☎ 22870 51001; dishes €5-12), on the beach at Psathi, is fine for Greek-standard meals.

There is one petrol station on Kimolos; it's about 200 metres to the north of Psathi.

Getting There & Away
Kimilos shares much the same regular ferry schedules as Milos. For details see Island Hopping (p754). A car ferry goes daily to and from Pollonia on Milos, departing from Kimolos at 8am, 10am, 1.15pm, 5.30pm and 10pm (€2, 20 minutes).

SIFNOS ΣΙΦΝΟΣ
pop 2900

Sifnos (*see*-fnoss) captivates the visitor with its hidden charms. It seems a barren place of heavy hills as you approach by sea, until the port of Kamares appears, as if by magic. Beyond the port and between the flanking slopes of rugged mountains lies an abundant landscape of terraced olive groves and almond trees, of oleanders and juniper and aromatic herbs covering the softer hillsides. The main settlement of Apollonia and the scenic village of Kastro have great appeal, and plenty of unspoiled paths link the island villages. Walking on Sifnos is particularly satisfying. The Anavasi map series *Topo 25/10.25 Aegean Cyclades/Sifnos* is useful for footpath details.

SIFNOS

0 — 4 km
0 — 2 miles

To Serifos (24km);
Kythnos (63km);
Paros (74km);
Piraeus (146km)

*AEGEAN
SEA*

Cape Heronisos

Heronisos

Agios Dimos

▲476m

Kamares
Bay

Sifnos

Kamares

Ano Petali

Artemonas

Kastro

Apollonia

Seralia

Kato Petali

Katavati

Exambelas

680m ▲

To Milos (50km);
Santorini (105km)

Moni
Profiti Ilia

Moni
Hrysopigis

Faros

Fasolou
Beach

Vathy

Platys Gialos

Hrysopigis
Beach

Vathy
Bay

▲201m

Platys
Gialos Bay

Cape Kondou

Kitriani

During the Archaic period (from about the 8th century BC) the island was very wealthy because of its gold and silver resources, but by the 5th century BC the mines were exhausted and Sifnos' fortunes were reversed. The island has a tradition of pottery making, basket weaving and cooking.

Getting There & Away

Sifnos is on the Piraeus–western-Cyclades ferry route and has good summer connections south to Serifos, Milos and Folegandros and with Santorini and Amorgos. For details see Island Hopping (p761).

Getting Around

Frequent buses link the island's main town, Apollonia, with Kamares (€1.20), with some services continuing on to Artemonas (€1.20), Kastro (€1.20), Vathy (€1.70), Faros (€1.30) and Platys Gialos (€1.70).

Taxis (☎ 22840 31347) hover around the port and Apollonia's main square. Fares from Kamares are €6 to Apollonia, €8 to Platys Gialos and €9 to Vathy. Cars can be hired from **Stavros Hotel** (☎ 22840 31641) in Kamares,

and from **Apollo Rent a Car** (☎ 22840 32237) in Apollonia, for €30 to €55.

KAMARES ΚΑΜΑΡΕΣ
pop 186

The port of Kamares (kah-*mah*-rez) always seems to have a holiday atmosphere, not least because of its large beach and the narrow, bustling beachside road with its waterfront cafes and tavernas and colourful mix of shops. The bus stop is by the tamarisk trees just past the inland end of the ferry quay.

Information

There are toilets near the tourist office, plus an ATM booth.

Municipal tourist office (☎ 22840 31977/31975; www.sifnos.gr) Opposite the bus stop is this very helpful and well-organised office. Opening times vary depending on boat arrivals. It sells ferry tickets and can find accommodation anywhere on the island. There's luggage storage (per item €1) and you can buy useful information sheets about the island as well as bus and boat timetables.

Sleeping & Eating

Domatia owners rarely meet boats and in high season it's best to book ahead.

Camping Makis (☎ 22840 32366, 6945946339; www.makiscamping.gr; camp sites per adult/child/tent €7/4/4, r from €55; ☼ Apr-Nov; P ⊠ ☎) This pleasant camping ground is just behind the beach. It has an outdoor cafe, a barbecue area, minimarket, a laundry, shaded sites and friendly owners.

Simeon (☎ 22840 31652; studios_simeon@hotmail.com; s/d/tr €50/70/80, apt €100-140; ☼ Apr-Oct; ⊠ ☎) From their little balconies, the small front rooms have stunning views down across the port and along the beach to soaring mountains beyond. Other rooms are not so blessed, but are bigger. You get here by going up steepish steps from the waterfront.

Stavros Hotel (☎ 22840 31641/33383; www.sifnostravel.com; s/d/tr €55/70/75; ⊠) Main street's Stavros has bright and comfy rooms of good size. Attached to the hotel is an information office that can arrange car hire and has a book exchange. The same family owns Hotel Kamari (☎ 22840 33383) on the outskirts of Kamares, on the road to Apollonia – rooms here are €40/50/55 per single/double/triple.

Hotel Afroditi (☎ 22840 31704; www.hotel-afroditi.gr; s/d/tr incl breakfast €70/91/114; P ⊠ ☎) The welcoming, family-run Afroditi is across the road from the beach. Rooms are a decent size and have been renovated recently. The breakfast is a definite plus. There are sea views to the front and mountain views to the rear.

Café Stavros (☎ 22840 33500; snacks €4-6) Overlooking the water halfway along the main street is this relaxing place, ideal for people watching. It does good breakfasts for about €5.

O Symos (☎ 22840 32353; dishes €4-8) Among a choice of waterfront tavernas, this popular place uses locally sourced ingredients in such appealing dishes as linguini and shrimps in saffron (€12) and *revythia* (chickpea) soup.

Another good eatery is the family-run **Posidonia** (☎ 22840 32362; dishes €3-8), where you can get breakfast for €6.

APOLLONIA ΑΠΟΛΛΩΝΙΑ
pop 1054

The 'capital' of Sifnos is situated on the edge of a plateau 5km uphill from the port.

The stop for buses to and from Kamares is on Apollonia's busy central square, where the post office and Museum of Popular Art are located. Because of congestion, all other buses pick up passengers about 50m further on, at a T-junction where the road to the right goes to Vathy and Platys Gialos and the road to the left goes to Artemonas and Kastro. Constant traffic seems to be the norm, but step away from the main road onto the pedestrian street behind the museum and Apollonia is transformed.

There is free parking at the big car park at the entrance to the village.

There is an ATM by the bus stop and at the Alpha Bank. The Piraeus Bank and National Bank of Greece (both with ATMs) are just around the corner from the Kamares stop on the road to Artemonas; the police station is another 50m beyond.

Internet Café 8 (☎ 22840 33734; per hr €4; ☼ 9am-1am) is about 150m along the road to Platys Gialos. The **bookshop** (☎ 22840 33523), just down from the bus stop, has newspapers and a good selection of books in various languages.

The quirky **Museum of Popular Art** (☎ 22840 31341; admission €1; ☼ 10am-2pm & 7.30-11.30pm Tue-Sun) on the central square contains a splendid confusion of old costumes, pots, textiles and photographs that could keep you going for hours.

Sleeping & Eating

Mrs Dina Rooms (☎ 22840 31125, 6945513318; s/d/tr/q €50/60/70/80; ☒) Laughter and flowers charac-

terise this pleasant little complex of rooms, located a couple of hundred metres along the road south towards Vathy and Platys Gialos. The rooms are well above the road and have views towards Kastro.

Gerontios Rooms (☎ 22840 31473; s/d/tr €50/60/70; ☒) There's another floral welcome here, high above the village centre with wide views to Kastro. From the post office head uphill and take the lane to the right of a small cafe.

Hotel Artemon (☎ 22840 31303; Artemonas; s/d/tr €55/70/84; ☒ ☒ ☎) In Artemonas, 2km uphill from Apollonia, is this old-style but very reasonable hotel that has enough rooms to make it a possible best bet in August if you're not booking ahead. Front rooms overlook the main road.

Veranda (☎ 22840 33969; snacks from €4; ☎) A cool corner in Apollonia, with wi-fi for customers, Veranda is next to the T-junction bus stop. Knotted white drapes dangle streetside from the eponymous veranda. It does breakfasts (€3.50 to €10), sandwiches and baguettes, ice cream and sweets and you can while the night away with drinks and lounge sounds.

Lempesis (☎ 22840 31303; Artemonas; mains €5.50-9) Part of the Hotel Artemon and run by the exuberant chef-owner, Artemon is a local favourite, not least for terrific baked meats and dishes like *revythia* soup, *exohiko* (lamb in pastry with cheese) and goat kid in lemon sauce. The house wine is very good indeed.

To Liotrivi (☎ 22840 31246; Artemonas; mains €6-9) Located in the pleasant square of Artemonas, this one-time olive press serves traditional Sifniot meat dishes such as rabbit with onions, while vegetarians can enjoy artichokes with potatoes, or *briam*, stewed vegetables.

Apostoli to Koutouki (☎ 22840 31186; dishes €8.50-12.50) Signature dishes such as beef baked in a clay pot with tomatoes, aubergine, cheese and wine complement fish dishes which are by the kilo at this long-established place on Apollonia's pedestrianised main street.

AROUND SIFNOS

Not to be missed is the walled cliff-top village of **Kastro**, 3km from Apollonia. The former capital, it is a magical place of buttressed alleyways and whitewashed houses. It has a small **archaeological museum** (☎ 22840 31022; admission free; ☼ 8.30am-3pm Tue-Sun).

Buses go to Kastro from Apollonia but you can walk there, mainly on old paved pathways. The start of the path is 20m to the right (Vathy road) from the T-junction in Apollonia. Go right down some steps and then through a tunnel beneath the road. A pleasant path circumnavigates Kastro and is especially scenic on its northern side. Midway round the northern side, above the glittering sea, is the charming little art workshop of **Maximos** (Panagiotis Fanariotis; ☎ 22840 33692), whose speciality is handmade jewellery in original gold and silver motifs. Prices for these lovely pieces start at about €6 and are far below the usual price charged for work of such high quality. There is also accommodation here (see below).

Platys Gialos, 6km south of Apollonia, has a big, generous beach, entirely backed by tavernas, domatia and shops. The bus terminates at the beach's southwestern end. The **Chrisopigi Travel Agency** (☎ 22840 71523; www.sifnoschrisopigi.gr) is a useful agency in Platys Gialos that sells ferry tickets, hires cars, books excursions and can find accommodation. **Vathy**, on the west coast, is an easy-going little village within the curved horns of an almost circular bay. **Faros** is a cosy little fishing hamlet with a couple of nice beaches nearby, including the little beach of **Fasolou**, reached up steps and over the headland from the bus stop.

Sleeping & Eating

KASTRO

Maximos (☎ 22840 33692; r €50) A tiny terrace with unbeatable sea views comes with this quirky little room beside Maximos' workshop, located on the northern side of Kastro.

Rafeletou Apartments (☎ 22840 31161, 69324 74001; d €60-77, tr €70-90, apt €105-120) For an authentic Kastro experience, these family-run apartments at the heart of the village are ideal.

ourpick To Astro (☎ 22840 31476; mains €5-9; ⊗ mid-Apr–Oct) Kastro's genuine 'star', as the name translates, certainly lives up to its appellation. Lovingly run by the owner-cook, it has tasty island dishes including eggplant and meatballs, octopus with olives, and lamb in traditional Sifniot style.

PLATYS GIALOS ΠΛΑΤΥΣ ΓΙΑΛΟΣ

Although there are plenty of sleeping places here, many cater for package tourists.

Angeliki Rooms (☎ 22840 71288; d/tr €55/70) A beachfront venue with pleasant rooms, near the quieter south end of the beach and just back from the bus terminus.

Hotel Efrosini (☎ 22840 71353; www.hotel-efrosini .gr; s/d/tr incl breakfast €65/95/117; 🅿 🛜) Right on the beach, this bright and well-kept hotel is one of the best on the Platys Gialos strip. The small balconies overlook a leafy courtyard.

Ariadne Restaurant (☎ 22840 71277; mains €6-16) You can tell from the well-kept and well-presented seating area that some care goes into this fine eatery. The lamb in red-wine sauce with herbs is a speciality. Fish is by the kilo, but you can settle for a seafood risotto for €16 or fish soup for €15.

VATHY ΒΑΘΥ

Areti Studios (☎ 22840 71191; d/apt €60/100; 🅿 🛜) Just in from the beach and amidst olive groves and a lovely garden, rooms here are clean and bright and some have cooking facilities. If you are driving, the approach is down a rough and at times very narrow track that goes off left just before the main road ends.

Vathy has a fair choice of beachfront tavernas, such as Oceanida and Manolis, offering reliable Greek dishes.

SERIFOS ΣΕΡΙΦΟΣ

pop 1414

Serifos (*seh*-ri-fohs) has a raw and rugged beauty that is softened by green folds in its rocky hills. The traditional *hora* is a dramatic scribble of white houses that crowns a high and rocky peak, 2km to the north of the port of Livadi. It catches your eye the minute the port comes in sight.

In Greek mythology, Serifos is where Perseus grew up and where the Cyclops were said to live. The island, in real time, was brutally exploited for iron ore during the 19th and 20th centuries and the rough remains of the industry survive (see boxed text, opposite).

There is some fine walking on Serifos and the Anavasi map series *Topo 25/10.26 Aegean Cyclades/Serifos* is useful.

Getting There & Away

Like Sifnos, Serifos is on the Piraeus–western-Cyclades route and has good summer connections south to Sifnos, Milos and Folegandros and even with Santorini and Amorgos. For details see Island Hopping (p760).

Getting Around

There are frequent buses between Livadi and Hora (€1.40, 15 minutes); a timetable is posted at the bus stop by the yacht quay. A taxi to Hora costs €6. Vehicles can be hired from Krinas Travel in Livadi.

LIVADI ΛIBAΔI
pop 537

The port town of Serifos is a fairly low-key place where, in spite of growing popularity, there's still a reassuring feeling that the modern world has not entirely taken over. Just over the headland that rises from the ferry quay lies the fine, tamarisk-fringed beach at **Livadakia**. A walk further south over the next headland, **Karavi Beach** is the unofficial clothes-optional beach.

Information

A useful website is www.e-serifos.com.

There is an Alpha Bank (with ATM) located on the waterfront and an ATM under the bakery sign opposite the yacht quay.

The post office is midway along the road that runs inland from opposite the bus stop and then bends sharply right.

Krinas Travel (☎ 22810 51488; www.serifos-travel. com) Just where the ferry quay joins the waterfront road, this helpful agency sells ferry tickets and organises car (per day €45) and scooter (per day €20) hire. It also has internet access at €2 per half-hour and a book exchange.

Port police (☎ 22810 51470) Up steps just beside Krinas Travel.

Sleeping & Eating

The best accommodation is on and behind Livadakia Beach, a few minutes hike from the quay. Most owners pick up at the port by arrangement.

Coralli Camping (☎ 22810 51500; www.coralli. gr; camp sites per adult/child/tent €7/3/6, bungalows s/d

€30/60; Ⓟ ⓦ ⓩ) In a great location just back from Livadaki Beach, this well-equipped camping ground is shaded by tall eucalyps. Bungalows have mountain or sea views. There's also a restaurant and a minimarket. A minibus meets all ferries.

Marieta Rooms (☎ 22810 51399; kamatso@otenet. gr; r/apt €45/90; ⓩ) The rooms at this modest place are small but bright and perfectly formed. Everything fits with ease and so will you. The apartment is, in turn, spacious. The rooms have a hot plate and welcome ceiling fans complement the air conditioning.

Medusa (☎ 22810 51128; rodolfosstamatakis@ yahoo.gr; s/d/tr €55/65/70; Ⓟ ⓩ) A great outlook is just one advantage of this immaculate place that stands above a lovely garden and has views of nearby Lividakia Bay and distant Sifnos. Rooms are big and comfy and each has a little hot plate and coffee-making facilities.

SERIFOS

0 — 4 km
0 — 2 miles

AEGEAN SEA

To Kythnos (52km); Piraeus (135km)

Sykamia Beach

Platys Gialos Bay

Moni Taxiarhon

Galani

Kendarhos

Panagia

Pirgos

Serifos

582m

Avessalos

Hora

502m

Koutalas

Ganema

Vagia

Megalo Livadi Beach

Ambeli Beach

Cape Katano

Livadi

Livadakia Beach

Karavi Beach

Agios Ioannis Beach

Psili Ammos Beach

Lia Beach

Vodi

To Paros (72km)

To Sifnos (24km); Kimolos (41km); Milos (55km); Ios (83km); Santorini (120km)

Alexandros-Vassilia (☎ 22810 51119; fax 22810 51903; d/tr/apt €80/96/125; 🛏) A rose-fragrant garden right on the beach makes this place a happy choice. Rooms are a good size and are clean and well equipped (apartments have cooking facilities). The garden taverna does sturdy Greek staples for €6 to €15 and toothsome dishes such as shrimps with pasta.

Yacht Club Serifos (☎ 22810 51888; breakfast €3.30-10.50, snacks & sandwiches €3.50-5.80; 🕑 7am-3am) Popular and always with a happy buzz, this waterfront cafe-bar plays lounge music by day and mainstream, rock, disco and funk late into the night.

Anemos Café (☎ 22810 51783; dishes €4-6) Views of the distant Hora from a sunny balcony overlooking the harbour make for a relaxed stop at this cafe at the inner end of the ferry dock. It's open early until late and does breakfast for about €7.

There are numerous tavernas along the waterfront.

Some recommended options:

Passaggio (☎ 22810 52212; mains €5.50-16) Traditional cuisine with international touches.

Stamatis (☎ 22810 51309; mains €5-11) A long-established taverna with decent food and good helpings.

Entertainment

Metalleio (☎ 22810 51755; 🕑 9pm-late) Tucked away on the road beyond the waterfront, Metalleio doubles as a decent restaurant and a very cool music venue featuring an eclectic array of sounds from around the world, including jazz, funk, Afro, Asian groove and Latin. The restaurant features mainly poultry and meat dishes (mains €5 to €12.50).

There are several music bars in the central waterfront area such as Shark and Edem that play mainly Greek sounds.

HORA ΧΩΡΑ

The *hora* of Serifos spills across the summit of a rocky hill above Livadi and is one of the most striking of the Cycladic capitals. Ancient steps lead up from Livadi, though they are fragmented by the snaking road that links the two. You can walk up, but in the heat of summer, going up by bus and then walking back down is wiser. There's a post office just up from the bus turnaround.

Just up from Hora's bus terminus, steps climb into the maze of Hora proper and lead to the charming main square, watched over by the imposing neoclassical town hall. From the square, narrow alleys and more steps lead ever upwards to the remnants of the ruined 15th-century **Venetian kastro**. Low walls enclose the highest part of the *kastro*, from where the views are spectacular. A small church occupies part of the summit.

Hora has a small **archaeological museum** (☎ 22810 51138; admission free; 🕑 8.30am-3pm Tue-Sun) displaying fragments of mainly Hellenic and Roman sculpture excavated from the *kastro*. Exhibits are sparse and the museum tiny, but it is a pleasure to visit. Panels in Greek and English spell out fascinating details, including the legend of Perseus.

There is a pleasant **walk** on a fine cobbled pathway that starts just above the archaeological museum and leads up the mountain to the little church of **Agios Georgios**. The views are superb.

Sleeping & Eating

I Apanemia (☎ 22810 51517, 6971891106; s/d €40/50; 🛏) You'll find excellent value at this good-natured, family-run place. The decent, well-equipped rooms (tea- and coffee-making facilities included) have front balcony views down towards the distant sea and side views towards Hora.

Karavomylos (☎ 22810 51261; dishes €4.50-14) Near the bus terminus, this is a local favourite offering mezedhes and local dishes. It does breakfast also (€3 to €9) and there's music in the bar and occasional live sessions of Greek traditional music, including *rembetika*. The famous *rakomelo*, a *raki* and honey drink, adds to the pleasure.

ourpick **Stou Stratou** (☎ 22810 52566; plates €5-18) The tradition of the *mezedhopoleio* is alive and well at this cafe-bar in the pretty main square. There are tasty mezedhes (€3 to €5) and choices such as a vegetarian plate or a mixed plate of Cretan smoked pork, ham, cheese, salami, stuffed vine leaves, feta, potato, tomatoes and egg, which will keep two people more than happy. Also available are breakfasts, ice creams, home-made cakes and cocktails. The menu is more like a little book and features the work of famous artists as well as excerpts from a number of writers.

AROUND SERIFOS

About 1.5 kilometres north of Livadi along a surfaced road is **Psili Ammos Beach**. A path from Hora heads north for about 4km to the pretty village of **Kendarhos** (aka Kallitsos), from where you can continue by a very windy road for another 3km to the 17th-century fortified **Moni Taxiarhon**, which has impressive 18th-century frescoes. The walk from the town to the monastery takes about two hours. You will need to take food and water, as there are no facilities in Kendarhos.

KYTHNOS ΚΥΘΝΟΣ

pop 1700

Kythnos is not high on the must-see list of foreign holidaymakers, but is a favourite of mainland Greeks and something of a weekend destination for 'gin palace' motorcruises also. Yet this is a Greek island of rare character, in spite of its rather dull port, and it has an easygoing lifestyle. The capital, Hora, is an endearing place and the very traditional village of Dryopida is rewarding.

Getting There & Away

Kythnos has reasonable connections with daily ferries to and from Piraeus and several ferries a week to Lavrio. Onward connections to islands to the south are fairly regular in summer. For details see Island Hopping (p754).

Getting Around

There are regular buses in high summer from Merihas to Dryopida (€1.40), continuing to Kanala (€2.50) or Hora (€1.40). Less regular services run to Loutra (€2.50). The buses supposedly meet the ferries, but usually they leave from the turn-off to Hora in Merihas. During term-time the only buses tend to be school buses.

Taxis (☎ 22810 32883, 6944 271609) are a better bet, except at siesta time. Hora is €8 and Dryopida €6.

A **taxi-boat** (☎ 6944906568) runs to and from local beaches in summer.

MERIHAS ΜΕΡΙΧΑΣ
pop 289

Merihas (*meh-ree-hass*) does not have a lot going for it other than a bit of waterfront life and a slightly grubby beach. But it's a reasonable base and has most of the island's accommodation options. There are better beaches within walking distance north of the quay (turn left facing inland) at **Episkopi** and **Apokrousi**.

Information

There's an Emboriki bank (with ATM) on the road above the Merihas waterfront, and an ATM just past the flight of steps as you come from the ferry quay.

Larentzakis Travel Agency (☎ 22810 32104, 6944906568) Sells ferry tickets, arranges accommodation and hires cars starting at about €35 a day in August. Scooters start at €20. They also run a taxi boat to beaches (price depending on numbers). It's up the flight of steps near Ostria Taverna that leads to the main road.

Port police (☎ 22810 32290) On the waterfront.

Thermia Travel (☎ 22810 32345) Attached to a neat little wine and food store, this is the place for efficient ferry ticketing and other tourism services.

Sleeping & Eating

Domatia owners usually meet boats and there are a number of signs along the waterfront advertising rooms. A lot of places block-book during the high season and there is some reluctance towards one-night stopovers. You should definitely book ahead for July and August.

Panayiota Larentzaki Rooms (☎ 22810 32268; s/d/tr €45/50/60; ❄) Serviceable, if a touch weary, these

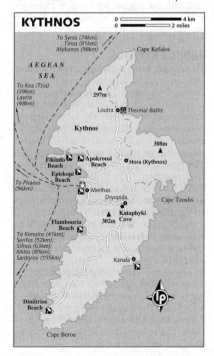

KYTHNOS

To Syros (74km);
Tinas (81km);
Mykonos (98km)

Cape Kefalos

AEGEAN
SEA

To Kea (Tzia)
(39km);
Lavrio
(48km)

297m

Loutra ● Thermal Baths

Kythnos

308m

Fikiado ● Apokrousi
Beach   Beach

Hora (Kythnos)

Episkopi
Beach

To Piraeus
(96km)

Merihas

Dryopida

Cape Tzoulis

Kataphyki
Flambouria   302m   Cave
Beach

To Kimolos (41km);
Serifos (52km);
Sifnos (63km);
Milos (85km);
Santorini (155km)

Kanala

Dimitrios
Beach

Cape Berou

0 ————— 4 km
0 ————— 2 miles

CYCLADES

rooms are a few metres up the road by the bridge. Cheerful Mrs P will probably find you first, as you wander uncertainly past her cafe.

Anna Gouma Rooms (☎ 22810 32105, 6949777884; s/d €50/60; 🔀) These pleasant, good-sized rooms are right across the bay from the ferry quay, and are away from the hubbub.

Studios Maria Gonidi (☎ 22810 32324; s/d/tr €50/60/70; 🔀) Over on the far side of the bay with lofty views, these are a top choice. Spacious, sparkling rooms have full self-catering facilities. During July and August there's little chance of securing short stays, however. Greek only spoken.

Café Vegera (☎ 22810 32636; snacks €4-6) Kythnos style jumps several scales at this cafe-bar that has a lovely waterside veranda. It beats Mykonos' Little Venice, and is without the hype and megahigh decibel count. Breakfast in the sun is €4 to €8.

Taverna to Kandouni (☎ 22810 32220; mains €6-14) On the southern bend of the waterfront, Kandouni is a popular family-run taverna specialising in grilled meat dishes.

Ostria (☎ 22810 32263; mains €6-15) Just along from the ferry quay, Ostria is the place for fish, with fish soup or a portion of anchovies as favourites. Seafood is generally by the kilo and they do meat dishes also.

AROUND KYTHNOS

The capital, **Hora** (also known as Kythnos or Messaria), is steadily taking on a distinctive charm, underpinned by its inherent Greek character. Small, colourful cafes and shops are growing in number. The long straggling main street, its surface decorated with painted motifs, makes for a pleasant stroll. The post office and the island's **police station** (☎ 22810 31201) are at the entrance to town coming from Merihas.

The resort of **Loutra** is 3km north of Hora on a windy bay and hangs on to its status through its surviving **thermal baths**.

From Hora there is a pleasant 5km-long walk south to **Dryopida**, a picturesque town of red-tiled roofs and winding streets clustered steeply on either side of a ravine. It is home to a remarkable cave called **Kataphyki** that extends for 600m. Much work has been carried out to make the cave accessible, but there was no access at the time of writing due to technical problems, although these may be resolved soon. You're best to cover the 5km back by road to Merihas by bus or taxi.

There are good beaches at **Flambouria** about 2.5km south of Merihas, and near **Kanala** on the southeast coast.

Sleeping & Eating

There are plenty of rooms and apartments in Loutra although they tend to be block-booked for stays of more than two days. In Dryopida some private houses let rooms in summer. Ask at shops and tavernas.

Filoxenia (☎ 22810 31644; www.filoxenia-kythnos.gr; d/tr/q €65/75/90; 🅿 🔀) One of the best bets in Hora, these attractive studios are just at the entrance to the main village and overlook a garden. Rooms are immaculate and have good facilities and there's a charming welcome.

There are several decent tavernas in Hora including Koursaros, To Steki and Mezzeria.

KEA (TZIA) ΚΕΑ (ΤΖΙΑ)

pop 2417

Kea is the most northerly island of the Cyclades and, being the island closest to Attica, attracts more mainland locals than foreign visitors. It

KEA (TZIA)

To Lavrio (31km)
To Andros (31km)

Agia Irini   Otzias
Vourkari
To Kythnos (39km); Korissia
Syros (76km)   Gialiskari Beach   Moni Panagias Kastrianis

Ioulida
Flea   Pera Meria   Cape Spathi
570m ▲

Astra
Ellinika
Kea
Piosses Beach

Koundouros   ▲ 450m
Havouna

AEGEAN
SEA

Cape Tamelos

0 — 4 km
0 — 2 miles

is an island that wears its many charms quietly. Between its bare hills, green valleys are filled with orchards, olive groves and almond and oak trees. The main settlements on the island are the port of Korissia, and the attractive capital, Ioulida, about 5km inland. There are several fine beaches and some excellent signposted footpaths. Local people use the name Tzia for their island.

Getting There & Away

The island's main connection to the mainland is through the port of Lavrio in southern Attica; there are no ferries from Piraeus to Kea. Connections onwards to other Cycladic islands are few. Boats are usually packed on Fridays and you should avoid the Sunday night ferry to Lavrio, unless you enjoy controlled rioting. If you plan a Sunday departure, make sure you get your ticket before Friday – and brace yourself for a bit of a mosh pit. For details see Island Hopping (p753).

Getting Around

In July and August there are, in theory, regular buses from Korissia to the villages of Vourkari, Otzias, Ioulida and Piosses although there may be irregularities in the schedules. A taxi (☎ 22880 21021/228) may be a better bet, to Ioulida (€6) especially. A taxi to Otzias is €5 and to Piosses, €20.

For motorcycle and car rental expect to pay, per day, €17 for a scooter and from €45 for a car. Try **Lion Cars** (☎ 22880 21898) located mid harbour front.

KORISSIA ΚΟΡΗΣΣΙΑ

pop 555

The port of Korissia (koh-ree-see-ah) is a fairly bland place, but there are enough tavernas and cafes to pass the time. The north-facing beach tends to catch the wind.

Information

There are ATMs on the waterfront and the Piraeus Bank, facing the beach, has an ATM. There is a small ferry ticket office next to the car-hire agency on the waterfront.

Internet Café (☎ 22880 22635; per hr €4; ☼ 10am-2.30pm & 5.30pm-midnight Mon-Fri, 10am-midnight Fri-Sun) Located just up an alleyway midway along the waterfront.

Tourist information office (☎ 22880 21500) The official tourist office, opposite the ferry quay, has lists of domatia in Greek, but not much more.

Sleeping & Eating

Domatia owners don't meet ferries. It's wise to book in high season and at weekends.

United Europe (☎ 22880 21362; uekeastudios@yahoo.gr; s/d/tr €40/60/70; ✘) Big, airy self-catering rooms make this quiet place an excellent option. All of the rooms are well kept and some have been refurbished in recent years. It's about 200m along the river road behind the beach.

Hotel Karthea (☎ 22880 21204; fax 22880 21417; s/d €65/85) Architectural blandness from a lost age defines the Karthea, but rooms are clean and comfortable and those at the rear overlook a quiet garden area. There's no lift to the several floors. In 1974, the deposed colonels of the Greek junta were said to have been imprisoned in the then newly opened hotel. You sleep with history…

Porto Kea Suites (☎ 22880 22870; www.portokea -suites.com; d €159, ste €197-338; P ✘ ▢ ▨) Korissia's top option, these rooms and suites are luxurious and their decor features white-painted stone walls and bright, stylish fittings. They all have small kitchen areas and there's an outside pool, a cafe and a restaurant.

Red Tractor Farm (☎ 22880 21346; www.red tractorfarm.com; d €90, studios €120-150; P ✘ ▢) Tucked away in the handsome hills of Kea alongside the owners' olive grove and vineyard is this lovely complex of buildings. The farm has received EU backing for its ecotourism achievements. Organic products are a feature and there are various seminars and activities.

Steki tou Strogili (☎ 22880 21025; 6976401015; mains €7-13) Popular with locals and in a pleasant setting above the main quay and next to the church, Strogili has a decent menu of traditional Greek favourites. Its selection of salads features a special version that includes chicken.

There are several tavernas along the waterfront, all dishing up fairly standard fare for about €5 to €11, with **Akri** (☎ 22880 21196) being one of the best.

Kea has more supermarkets than most islands. On Friday nights they get very busy as the weekender influx stocks up.

Drinking

There are traditional bars and cafes along the waterfront but for a more modern upbeat scene try Jamaica for mostly rock, or next door the bigger **Echo Club** (☎ 6947004625) goes for Greek sounds.

A ROSE BY ANY OTHER NAME

Piosses (or Pisses as once enunciated) has grown self-conscious of its unfortunate English slang connotations and is struggling to rechristen itself as Piosses. The Greek is, technically, Pioses. The form Piosses is now used on signposts and even the camping site uses this form. We see no reason why we should not help them with their semantic makeover!

IOULIDA ΙΟΥΛΙΔΑ
pop 700

Ioulida (ee-oo-lee-tha) is Kea's gem and has a distinctly cosmo feel at weekends. It's a pretty scramble of narrow alleyways and rising lanes that lies along the rim of a natural amphitheatre among the hills. It was once a substantial settlement of ancient Greece, but few relics remain and even the **Venetian kastro** has been incorporated into private houses. The houses have red-tiled roofs like those of Dryopida on Kythnos.

The bus turnaround is on a square just at the edge of town. Other than taxis and delivery vehicles there is no parking here. Cars should park in the car park, which is located below the square. From the car park follow steps up to a T-junction and turn right for the bus turnaround, from where an archway leads into the village. Beyond the archway, turn right and uphill along the main street and into the more interesting heart of Ioulida proper. The post office is partway up on the right.

There's a bank in the turnaround square but with no ATM. There's an ATM in the square by the town hall, halfway up the main street of Ioulida.

Sights

Ioulida's **archaeological museum** (☎ 22880 22079; adult/child €3/2; ☼ 8.30am-3pm Tue-Sun) is just before the post office on the main thoroughfare. It houses some intriguing artefacts, including some superb terracotta figurines, mostly from Agia Irini (right).

The famed **Kea Lion**, chiselled from slate in the 6th century BC, lies on the hillside beyond the last of the houses. Head uphill from the museum and keep going until abreast of the Kea Lion across a shallow valley. The path

then curves round past a cemetery and the lion, with its Mona Lisa smile, is ahead and is reached through a gate and down some steps. Continuing beyond the lion, the path leads in a few minutes to a big drinking fountain behind a huge plane tree. From just beyond here, a splendid path branches left and leads to the road just above Otzias in just over 3km. It's then 3km, unfortunately by road, to Korissia.

Sleeping & Eating

There are a few domatia in Ioulida, and several decent tavernas. Ask about rooms at tavernas.

Recommended eateries with good Greek dishes from about €4.50 to €9 (with lamb and fresh fish costing more):

Estiatorio I Piatsa (☎ 22880 22195) Just inside the archway.

Kalofagadon (☎ 22880 22118) On the main square.

AROUND KEA

The beach road from Korissia leads past **Gialiskari Beach** for 2.5km to where the waterfront quay at tiny **Vourkari** is lined with yachts and cafes. The **Marina Keas Gallery** (☎ 22880 21458) is set back midwaterfront among the cafes and restaurants; it stages changing exhibitions of world-class art works over the summer.

Just across the bay from Vourkari are the truncated remains of the Minoan site of **Agia Irini**, which lie rather forlornly behind rusting wire fences. Excavations during the 20th century indicated that there had been a settlement here since 3200 BC and that it functioned here for over 2000 years.

The road continues for another 3km to a fine sandy beach at **Otzias**. A surfaced road with rugged coastal views continues beyond here for another 5km to the 18th-century **Moni Panagias Kastrianis** (☎ 22880 24348).

Piosses is the island's best beach and is 8km southwest of Ioulida. A daily bus runs from and to Korissia in summer although hours are awkward. Piosses has a long and sandy beach that is backed by a verdant valley of orchards and olive groves, with rugged hills rising above. There's an extremely well-kept campsite here, **Piosses Camping** (☎ 22880 31302/4, fax 22880 31303; adult/child/tent €6/3/6; ☼ May-Sep) with a shop and cafe on site.

Crete Κρήτη

Crete is in many respects the culmination of the Greek experience. Its hospitable, spirited people maintain a proud sense of separateness, evident in everything from their haunting, violin-driven traditional music to their hearty, homegrown food and drink.

Everything about Crete is larger than life. Millions upon millions of olive trees produce some of the finest olive oil in Greece – and arguably, in the world – while the island is the mythical birthplace of Zeus himself, and site of the legendary Minoan civilisation; the much-visited Palace of Knossos is its most striking reminder. And, with their pretty pastel houses set on narrow stone lanes, the ancient Venetian ports of Hania and Rethymno are among Greece's most evocative towns. All in all, Crete bursts with the relics of millennia of culture, stretching from the prehistoric through Minoan, Byzantine, Venetian and Ottoman eras. Most visitors hang around the north-coast resorts, so it's easy to escape the crowds by heading for the south coast's numerous deserted beaches and inland rugged terrain trodden only by goats. Spectacular mountain ranges are dotted with thousands of caves and sliced by dramatic gorges that spill into the sea.

The northern coast features Crete's urban areas, and most of its package-tour resorts. Head south for off-the-beaten-track outdoors activities and pristine, peaceful beaches. The rugged interior, intermittently made up of mountains, agricultural plains and plateaus, hosts some of Crete's most authentic and down-to-earth villages, where you'll get a warm welcome from black-clad elders; such humble places often have the best (and cheapest) locally produced olive oil, honey, *raki* (Cretan firewater) and other superlative Cretan products.

HIGHLIGHTS

- **Time Out** Wandering the beautiful back lanes of Hania's Venetian Old Town (p483)
- **Minoan Magnificence** Visiting the grand, reconstructed Minoan palace at Knossos (p469)
- **Sylvan Idylls** Experiencing the haunted woodlands waterfalls and hermits' caves of offbeat Azogires village (p498)
- **Soldiering On** Taking the six-hour hike through Europe's longest gorge, Samaria (p491)
- **Back in Time** Exploring the ruined Venetian fortress of Spinalonga (p506), occupying its own islet in Crete's northeast
- **Beach Bliss** Swimming under a full moon at the south coast's remote Agios Pavlos and Triopetra beaches (p481)
- **Livin' Large** Kicking back amid the olive groves, beaches and big winds of lively Plakias (p479)

POPULATION: 540,045 | AREA: 8335 SQ KM

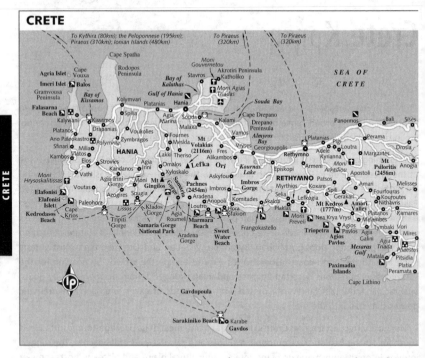

CRETE

To Kythira (80km); the Peloponnese (195km);
Piraeus (310km); Ionian Islands (480km)

To Piraeus (320km)

To Piraeus (320km)

History

Although it's been inhabited since Neolithic times (7000–3000 BC), Crete is most famous for its advanced Minoan civilisation. Traces of this still enigmatic society were only uncovered in the early 20th century, when British archaeologist Sir Arthur Evans discovered and then restored the palace at Knossos. Since no one knew what to call this lost race, Sir Arthur made an adjective of the mythical King Minos, the legendary former ruler of Knossos – and so emerged the name 'Minoans'.

Their actual name notwithstanding, we do know that the Minoans migrated to Crete in the 3rd millennium BC. These mysterious people were expert in metallurgy, making unprecedented artistic, engineering and cultural achievements during the Protopalatial period (3400–2100 BC); their most famous palaces (at Knossos, Phaestos, Malia and Zakros) were built then. Artistically, the frescoes discovered at Knossos have a naturalism lacking in contemporary Cycladic figurines, ancient Egyptian artwork and later Archaic sculpture. The Minoans also began producing their exquisite Kamares pottery and silverware, and

became a maritime power, trading with Egypt and Asia Minor.

Around 1700 BC, however, an earthquake destroyed the great palace complexes. Undeterred, the Minoans built bigger and better ones over the ruins, while settling more widely across Crete. Around 1450 BC, when the Minoan civilisation was in the ascendant, the palaces were mysteriously destroyed again, probably by a giant tsunami triggered by the massive volcanic eruption on Santorini (Thira). Knossos, the only palace saved, was finally burned down around 1400 BC.

Archaeological evidence shows that the Minoans lingered on for a few centuries in small, isolated settlements before disappearing as mysteriously as they had come. They were followed by the Mycenaeans, and the Dorians (around 1100 BC). By the 5th century BC, at the acme of classical Greek civilisation, Crete was divided into city-states. However, the island did not benefit particularly from the cultural glories of mainland Greece, and was bypassed by Persian invaders and the Macedonian conqueror Alexander the Great.

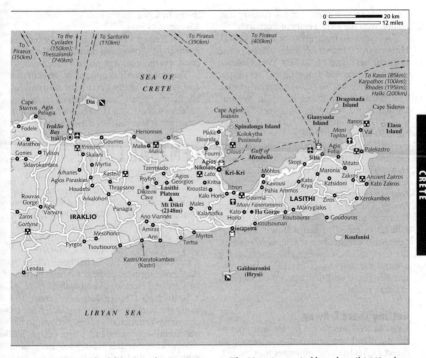

By 67 BC Crete had become the Roman province of Cyrenaica, with south-central Gortyna its capital; this province also included large chunks of North Africa. With the empire's division in AD 395 Crete, along with most of the Balkan Peninsula, fell under the jurisdiction of Greek-speaking Constantinople – the emerging Byzantine Empire. Things went more or less fine until AD 824, when Arabs appropriated the island, making it an emirate. Relatively little is known about this period.

In AD 961, however, the great Byzantine general and ill-fated emperor Nikiforas Fokas (AD 912–69) won the island back in the so-called 'expedition to Crete'. Fokas led approximately 300 ships and 50,000 men, taking the island following a nine-month siege of Iraklio (then called El Khandak by the Arabs). Crete flourished under Byzantine rule, but with the infamous Fourth Crusade of 1204 – when the Christian countries of the Latin West targeted Byzantium, instead of the Arabs – the maritime power of Venice received Crete as part of its 'payment' for supplying the Crusaders' fleet.

The Venetian period lasted until 1669, when Iraklio (then called Candia) became the last domino to fall after a 21-year Ottoman siege. Much of Crete's most impressive surviving architecture dates from this period, which also marked modern Crete's cultural peak (see the boxed text, p465). Turkish rule brought new administrative organisation, Islamic culture and Muslim settlers. Cretan resistance was strongest in the mountain strongholds, such as rugged Skafia in the southwest; here in 1770 the dashing Ioannis Daskalogiannis led the first notable rebellion. This and subsequent revolts were put down brutally, and it was only with the Ottoman Empire's disintegration in the late 19th century that Europe's great powers expedited Crete's sovereign aspirations.

Thus in 1898, with Russian and French consent, Crete became a British protectorate. However, the banner under which future Greek prime minister Eleftherios Venizelos and other Cretan rebels were fighting was *Enosis i Thanatos* (Unity or Death) – unity with Greece, not mere independence from Turkey. Yet it would take the Greek army's stunning successes in the Balkan Wars (1912–13) to turn

Crete's de facto inclusion in the country into reality, with the 1913 Treaty of Bucharest.

Crete suffered tremendously during WWII. Hitler wanted the strategically placed island as an air base, and on 20 May 1941 German parachutists started dropping in. Cretans put up resistance but were soon overwhelmed. The Battle of Crete, as it would become known, raged for 10 days between German and Allied troops from Britain, Australia, New Zealand and Greece. For two whole days the battle hung in the balance until the Germans captured Maleme airfield, near Hania. The Allied forces fought a valiant rearguard action, however, enabling the British Navy to evacuate 18,000 of the 32,000 Allied troops. The harsh German occupation lasted throughout WWII, with many mountain villages bombed or burnt down and their occupants executed en masse. Nevertheless, the Cretans (with foreign assistance) waged a significant resistance campaign that continually vexed and distracted their German military rulers.

Getting There & Away

Crete is well connected by air and boat to the mainland and, remarkably, international direct flights to Crete are sometimes cheaper than flying to the island from elsewhere in Greece – even from Greek carriers themselves. Aegean Airlines has direct scheduled flights from Iraklio to Milan, Rome and other European cities, while Olympic serves even more airports abroad.

If coming from a Western European country, it may be possible to score a cheap seat on a charter flight operating for package tourists without actually having to buy the rest of the package (accommodation, food, etc). However, you'll have to check with a travel agency in such a country to see if it's feasible.

European budget airlines are also starting to serve Crete in summer months. Iraklio, Sitia, Hania, Rethymno and Kissamos have ferry ports. The first three have airports also; Iraklio's being the largest. For more comprehensive information, see Island Hopping (p749).

Getting Around

A north-coast national highway runs from Kissamos in the west to Agios Nikolaos in the east, with an extension to Sitia planned.

Buses link the major northern towns from Kissamos to Sitia.

Less frequent buses operate between the north coast's towns and resorts and the south coast, via the inland mountain villages.

The wild south is spliced by mountains and gorges – many parts have no roads at all. Regular boats connect Paleohora on the southwest coast with Hora Sfakion, including settlements and beaches between them.

CENTRAL CRETE

Central Crete comprises the Iraklio prefecture, named after the island's burgeoning capital, and the Rethymno prefecture, named after its lovely Venetian port town. Along with its dynamic urban life and Venetian remnants, Iraklio's major attractions include the nearby Minoan sites of Knossos and Phaestos. However, the north coast east of Iraklio has been ruined by northern-European package tourism, particularly around Hersonisos and Malia.

Rethymno's more low-key resorts lie along the north coast nearby. Aside from its charming Venetian old town, Rethymno has a mountainous hinterland, where villages like Anogia cultivate the old-school machismo, moustaches and rugs of traditional Crete. The largely unspoilt southern coast boasts great beaches and the likeable, relaxed resort of Plakias.

IRAKLIO ΗΡΑΚΛΕΙΟ
pop 130,920

Iraklio (ee-*rah*-klee-oh), also called Heraklion, is Greece's fifth-largest city and the centre of Crete's economic and administrative life. It's a somewhat hectic place, full of the sounds of motorbikes throttling in unison at traffic lights while airplanes constantly thrust off into the sky in summer, over a long waterfront lined with the remnants of Venetian arsenals, fortresses and shrines.

Indeed, Iraklio does have some notable historic structures, though its traditional neighbourhoods suffered major bomb damage during WWII, robbing it of an architectural legacy comparable to that of Hania or Rethymno. Nevertheless, Iraklio is lively, with excellent eating, drinking and shopping. The best places lie off the interconnected pedestrianised stretches of the centre, where ongoing renovations continue to beautify things.

Iraklio hosts several worthwhile museums and, just south, the reconstructed Minoan palace at Knossos, one of Greece's most significant and most visited ancient sites. To the east of town, the Cretaquarium (p469) and an adjoining water park will keep kids happy. Further inland beyond Knossos, the Iraklio prefecture includes pretty traditional villages like Arhanes (p472). Full of olive trees and vineyards, this bucolic region is where Crete's best wines are produced.

History

Although Iraklio had always been populated, it didn't become the capital until AD 824, when Arabs arrived. Naming the city El Khandak (after its surrounding moat), the Arabs reputedly made it the Eastern Med's slave-trade capital. When the Byzantines recovered Crete in AD 961, they Hellenicised the name as 'Khandakos'. The Venetians added an Italian twist, calling the city Candia.

Venice used Crete, and its well-defended capital, to expand its maritime commercial empire. The fortifications it built were sufficiently strong to keep the Ottomans at bay for 21 years, even after the rest of Crete was lost; the Venetians finally surrendered Candia in 1669.

When Turkish control over Crete ended in 1898, Hania became the capital, and Candia was renamed Iraklio. However, because of its location, Iraklio became a hub of commerce and in 1971 once again became Crete's administrative centre.

Orientation

Iraklio is a work in progress, meaning some unfinished projects (like a lengthy pedestrian mall along the waterfront) may be completed soon. There are two main squares: Plateia Venizelou, also called Lion Sq after its famous landmark, Morosini Fountain, is most central, while the sprawling Plateia Eleftherias overlooks the harbour.

Many appealing sights are nestled around the pleasing, pedestrianised arc of Morosini Fountain down Handakos, and around Dedalou and Korai – the hub of Iraklio's lively cafe scene. The ferry port is 500m east of the old port. Iraklio's airport is 5km east of the centre.

From the bus station and port look towards the Hotel Megaron's parking lot; a concealed stone stairway here doubles back and up, accessing Epimenidou and the centre.

CRETE ONLINE

For information online, see www.interkriti .org, www.infocrete.com and www.explore crete.com.

Information

BOOKSHOPS

Planet International Bookshop (☎ 2810 289605; Handakos 73) Literature, history and travel books, including many recommended in this guide.

Road Editions (☎ 2810 344610; Handakos 29) Specialist travel bookshop with numerous maps, travel books and Lonely Planet guidebooks.

Vivliopoleion Filippos Athousakis (☎ 2810 229286; Epimenidou; ⏰ 8.30am-2.30pm & 5-9pm) Opposite Lato Boutique Hotel; sells books on Crete, plus Lonely Planet and other travel guides.

EMERGENCY

Tourist police (☎ 2810 397111; Halikarnassos; ⏰ 7am-10pm) No longer centrally located; now housed east with other police services in the new main station, (Astynomiko Megaron) in the Halikarnassos suburb, near the airport.

INTERNET ACCESS

In Spot Internet Cafe (☎ 2810 300225; Koraï 6; per hr €2.40, midnight-noon per hr €1.20; ⏰ 24hr)

INTERNET RESOURCES

www.heraklion-city.gr Official municipal website with useful information, such as phone numbers, opening hours and coming events.

LAUNDRY

Sweaty Iraklio is full of laundromats. Most charge €6 for wash and dry, and offer dry cleaning.

Inter Laundry (☎ 2810 343660; Mirabelou 25; ⏰ 9am-9pm)

Laundry Perfect (☎ 2810 220969; cnr Malikouti 32 & Idomeneos; ⏰ 9am-9pm Mon-Sat)

Laundry Washsalon (☎ 2810 280858; Handakos 18) Also offers left-luggage storage (per day €3).

Wash Center Laundry (☎ 2810 242766; Epimenidou 38; per load €7; ⏰ 8am-9pm)

LEFT LUGGAGE

Bus Station A Left Luggage Office (☎ 2810 246538; per day €2; ⏰ 6.30am-8pm)

Iraklio Airport Luggage Service (☎ 2810 397349; per day €2.50-5; ⏰ 24hr) Near the airport's local bus stop.

CRETE

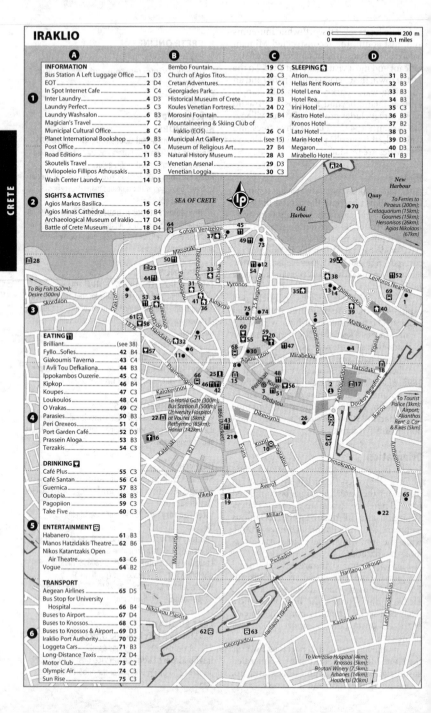

IRAKLIO

INFORMATION		
Bus Station A Left Luggage Office	1	D3
EOT	2	D4
In Spot Internet Cafe	3	C4
Inter Laundry	4	D3
Laundry Perfect	5	C3
Laundry Washsalon	6	B3
Magician's Travel	7	C2
Municipal Cultural Office	8	C4
Planet International Bookshop	9	B3
Post Office	10	C4
Road Editions	11	B3
Skoutelis Travel	12	C3
Vivliopoleio Fillipos Athousakis	13	D3
Wash Center Laundry	14	D3

SIGHTS & ACTIVITIES		
Agios Markos Basilica	15	C4
Agios Minas Cathedral	16	B4
Archaeological Museum of Iraklio	17	D4
Battle of Crete Museum	18	D4

Bembo Fountain	19	C5
Church of Agios Titos	20	C3
Cretan Adventures	21	C4
Georgiades Park	22	D5
Historical Museum of Crete	23	B3
Koules Venetian Fortress	24	D2
Morosini Fountain	25	B4
Mountaineering & Skiing Club of		
Iraklio (EOS)	26	C4
Municipal Art Gallery	(see	15)
Museum of Religious Art	27	B4
Natural History Museum	28	A3
Venetian Arsenal	29	D3
Venetian Loggia	30	C3

SLEEPING		
Atrion	31	B3
Hellas Rent Rooms	32	B3
Hotel Lena	33	B3
Hotel Rea	34	B3
Irini Hotel	35	C3
Kastro Hotel	36	B3
Kronos Hotel	37	B2
Lato Hotel	38	D3
Marin Hotel	39	D3
Megaron	40	D3
Mirabello Hotel	41	B3

EATING		
Brilliant	(see	38)
Fyllo...Sofies	42	B4
Giakoumis Taverna	43	C4
I Avli Tou Defkaliona	44	B3
Ippokambos Ouzerie	45	C2
Kipkop	46	B4
Koupes	47	C3
Loukoulos	48	C4
O Vrakas	49	C2
Parasies	50	B3
Peri Orexeos	51	C4
Port Garden Café	52	D3
Prassein Aloga	53	B3
Terzakis	54	C3

DRINKING		
Café Plus	55	C3
Café Santan	56	C4
Guernica	57	B3
Outopia	58	B3
Pagopiion	59	C3
Take Five	60	C3

ENTERTAINMENT		
Habanero	61	B3
Manos Hatzidakis Theatre	62	B6
Nikos Katantzakis Open		
Air Theatre	63	C6
Vogue	64	B2

TRANSPORT		
Aegean Airlines	65	D5
Bus Stop for University		
Hospital	66	B4
Buses to Airport	67	D4
Buses to Knossos	68	C3
Buses to Knossos & Airport	69	D3
Iraklio Port Authority	70	D2
Loggeta Cars	71	B3
Long-Distance Taxis	72	D4
Motor Club	73	C2
Olympic Air	74	C3
Sun Rise	75	C3

SEA OF CRETE

New Harbour

Old Harbour

Quay

To Ferries to Piraeus (200m); Cretaquarium (15km); Gournes (15km); Hersonisos (26km); Agios Nikolaos (67km)

To Big Fish (500m); Desire (500m)

To Hania Gate (300m); Bus Station B (500m); University Hospital at Voutes (5km); Rethymno (85km); Hania (142km)

To Tourist Police (3km); Airport; Alianthos Rent-a-Car & Bikes (5km)

To Venizelio Hospital (4km); Knossos (5km); Boutari Winery (7.5km); Arhanes (14km); Houdetsi (20km)

MEDICAL SERVICES

Iraklio's two hospitals are far from the centre and work alternate days – call first to find out where to go.

Venizelio Hospital (☎ 2810 368000) On the road to Knossos, 4km south of Iraklio.

University Hospital (☎ 2810 392111) At Voutes, 5km south of Iraklio (bus 11, ticket price €1.50), this is the best-equipped medical facility.

MONEY

Banks and ATMs line 25 Avgoustou, and are widespread throughout the centre.

POST

Post office (☎ 2810 234468; Plateia Daskalogianni; ⏱ 7.30am-8pm Mon-Fri, 7.30am-2pm Sat)

TOURIST INFORMATION

EOT (Greek National Tourist Organisation; ☎ 2810 246299; Xanthoudidou 1; ⏱ 8.30am-8.30pm Apr-Oct, 8.30am-3pm Nov-Mar) Opposite the archaeological museum.

TRAVEL AGENCIES

Magician's Travel (☎ 2810 301471; operation@ driveongreece.gr; Mitsotaki 1B) This helpful, patient travel agency near the waterfront can arrange and inform about all ferry and plane tickets.

Skoutelis Travel (☎ 2810 280808; www.skoutelis travel.gr; 25 Avgoustou 24) Airline and ferry bookings, excursions, accommodation help and car hire can all be arranged here.

Sights

ARCHAEOLOGICAL MUSEUM OF IRAKLIO

The outstanding Minoan collection makes Iraklio's **archaeological museum** (☎ 2810 279000; Xanthoudidou 2; admission €4, incl Knossos €10; ⏱ 8am-8pm Tue-Sun, 8am-1pm Mon Apr-Oct, 8am-3pm Tue-Sun, noon-3pm Mon late Oct-early Apr) second only to Athens' National Archaeological Museum. A €21-million restoration was unfinished at the time of writing (temporary entrance on Hatzidakis), meaning that a temporary exhibition of 400 (out of 15,000 total) artefacts is now exhibited, covering Neolithic until Roman times. Fear not, however – the collection's most valuable Minoan masterpieces are all displayed.

This treasure trove includes pottery, jewellery, figurines and sarcophagi, plus some famous frescoes. The most exciting Minoan finds come from the sites of Knossos, Phaestos, Malia, Zakros and Agia Triada.

The superlative Knossos frescoes include the **Procession fresco**, the **Griffin Fresco** (from the Throne Room), the **Dolphin Fresco** (from the Queen's Room) and the amazing **Bull-leaping Fresco**, which depicts a seemingly double-jointed acrobat somersaulting on the back of a charging bull.

Other frescoes include the lovely, restored **Prince of the Lilies**, along with two frescoes for the New Palace period – the priestess archaeologists have dubbed **La Parisienne**, and the **Saffron Gatherer**.

Also from Knossos are **Linear A and B tablets** (the latter have been translated as household or business accounts), an ivory statue of a **bull leaper**, and some exquisite **gold seals**.

From the Middle Minoan period, the most striking piece is the 20cm black-stone **Bull's Head**, a libation vessel. The bull's fine head of curls sprouts golden horns, and features extremely lifelike painted crystal eyes. Other fascinating contemporary exhibits include the tiny, glazed colour reliefs of Minoan houses from Knossos, called the **town mosaic**. Finds from a Knossos shrine include fine figurines of a bare-breasted **snake goddess**.

Among the treasures of Minoan jewellery is the beautiful **gold bee pendant** from Malia, depicting two bees dropping honey into a comb.

From Phaestos, the most prized find is the fascinating **Phaestos Disk**, a 16cm circular clay tablet inscribed with (still undeciphered) pictographic symbols.

Also displayed is the elaborate **Kamares pottery**, named after the sacred cave of Kamares where it was discovered; a superbly decorated vase from Phaestos with white sculpted flowers is here, too.

Finds from Zakros include the gorgeous **crystal rhyton** vase, discovered in over 300 fragments and painstakingly repaired, along with vessels decorated with floral and marine designs.

The most famous of Minoan sarcophagi, and one of Minoan art's greatest achievements, is the **sarcophagus of Agia Triada**, painted with floral and abstract designs and ritual scenes. Other significant Agia Triada finds include the **Harvester Vase**, of which only the top part remains, depicting young farm workers returning from olive picking. Another, the **Boxer Vase** shows Minoans indulging in two of their favourite pastimes – wrestling and bull-grappling. The **Chieftain Cup** depicts a more cryptic scene: a chief holding a staff and three men carrying animal skins.

Finds from Minoan cemeteries include two small clay models of groups of figures, found in a *tholos* (tomb shaped like a beehive). One depicts four male dancers in a circle, arms around one another's shoulders, possibly participants in a funerary ritual. The other shows two groups of three figures in a room flanked by two columns, with two large seated figures being offered libations by a smaller figure. Whether the large figures represent gods or departed mortals is unclear.

More insight into the inscrutable lifestyle of the Minoans can be gleaned from another exhibit, the elaborate **gaming board** decorated with ivory, crystal, glass, gold and silver, from Knossos' New Palace period.

HISTORICAL MUSEUM OF CRETE

The engrossing **Historical Museum** (☎ 2810 283219; www.historical-museum.gr; Sofokli Venizelou; admission €5; 9am-5pm Mon-Sat summer, 9am-3pm Mon-Sat winter) contains exhibits from Crete's Byzantine, Venetian and Turkish periods, displaying plans, charts, photographs, ceramics and maps. The 1st floor houses the only El Greco paintings in Crete – *View of Mt Sinai and the Monastery of St Catherine* (1570) and the tiny *Baptism of Christ*. Other rooms contain 13th- and 14th-century fresco fragments, coins, jewellery, liturgical ornaments and vestments, plus medieval pottery.

Highlights upstairs include the reconstructed **library of author Nikos Kazantzakis**, a **Battle of Crete** section and an outstanding **folklore collection**.

NATURAL HISTORY MUSEUM

Established by the University of Crete, the child-friendly **Natural History Museum** (☎ 2810 282740; www.nhmc.uoc.gr; Leoforos Venizelou; admission €3, adult accompanying child free; 10am-7pm Tue-Sun), in a restored former electricity building on the waterfront, has interactive appeal with a discovery centre for kids, complete with labs and excavation projects. Apart from the broader evolution of humankind, it explores the flora and fauna of Crete, the island's ecosystem and habitats, and its caves, coastline and mountains, plus Minoan life.

OTHER ATTRACTIONS

Iraklio burst out of its **city walls** long ago, but these massive fortifications, with seven bastions and four gates, still dwarf the concrete 20th-century structures around them.

Venetians built the defences between 1462 and 1562. You can follow them around the heart of the city for views of Iraklio's neighbourhoods, though it's not a particularly scenic trip.

The 16th-century **Koules Venetian fortress** (Iraklio Harbour; admission €2; 9am-6pm Tue-Sun), at the end of the Old Harbour's jetty, was called Rocca al Mare under the Venetians. It stopped the Turks for 22 years and then became a Turkish prison for Cretan rebels. The impressive exterior features reliefs of the Lion of St Mark. The interior has 26 overly restored rooms and good views from the top. The ground-level rooms are used as art galleries, while music and theatrical events are held in the upper level.

The long, vaulted arcades of the **Venetian Arsenal** are opposite the fortress.

Several other notable Venetian structures survive. Most famous is the **Morosini Fountain** (Lion Fountain) on Plateia Venizelou, which spurts water from four lions' jaws into eight ornate marble troughs. Built in 1629, the fountain was commissioned by Francesco Morosini, then governor of Crete. Its centrepiece marble statue of Poseidon with his trident was destroyed during the Turkish occupation. Opposite is the three-aisled, 13th-century **Agios Markos Basilica**. Frequently reconstructed, it's now the **Municipal Art Gallery** (☎ 2810 399228; 25 Avgoustou; admission free; 9am-1.30pm & 6-9pm Mon-Fri, 9am-1pm Sat). A little north is the attractively reconstructed 17th-century **Venetian Loggia**. A Venetian version of a gentleman's club where aristocrats came to drink and gossip, it's now the Town Hall.

The delightful **Bembo Fountain**, at the southern end of 1866, was built by the Venetians in the 16th century. The ornate hexagonal edifice adjacent was a pump house added by the Turks, and is now a *kafeneio* (coffee house).

The **Museum of Religious Art** (☎ 2810 288825; Monis Odigitrias; admission €2; 9.30am-7.30pm Mon-Sat Apr-Oct, 9.30am-3.30pm Nov-Mar) is in the former Church of Agia Ekaterini beside **Agios Minas Cathedral**. Its impressive collection of icons, frescoes and elaborate ecclesiastical vestments include six icons by Mihail Damaskinos, mentor of El Greco.

The **Church of Agios Titos** (Agiou Titou) was constructed after the Byzantine reconquest of Crete in AD 961, was converted to a Catholic church by Venetians, and then became an Ottoman mosque. It has been rebuilt twice

RENAISSANCE MEN OF VENETIAN CRETE

While many people have heard of a certain Cretan painter nicknamed El Greco, most visitors would be surprised to learn just how significant Cretan scholars and humanists were to the Italian Renaissance, and to early modern thought in general.

When the Turks conquered Constantinople in 1453, many Byzantine scholars took refuge in Venetian-held Crete, bringing with them priceless manuscripts and knowledge. The island became a way-station for intellectuals and ideas – at precisely the moment when a hunger for learning ancient Greek and Latin texts in the original was growing in Italy and other Western European countries. Indeed, wealthy Italian noblemen such as that great Florentine, Cosimo de' Medici, were funding whole Platonic 'academies', where aspiring scholars sat enraptured at the feet of learned Greek émigrés.

Further, the simultaneous invention of the printing press meant that ancient texts suddenly could be made widely available. And a Cretan typesetter and calligrapher, **Markos Mousouros** (1470–1517), designed the typeface in which Europeans would read many of the first printed Ancient Greek texts. His employer, Aldus Manutius, a Venetian publisher who revolutionised and popularised the study of Ancient Greek philosophy and literature, used the typeface based on Mousouros' own handwriting to print his editions of the Greek classics.

According to Dr George Karamanolis, professor of ancient philosophy at Crete's University of Rethymno, 'Cretan scholars and humanists played a considerable role in transmitting Greek texts and learning to Renaissance Italy'. The unique mixed culture on the Venetian-administered island, he says, meant that, 'cultural activity and scholarly life in Crete was quite similar to intellectual currents in Western Europe. Whole academies flourished, like the Accademia degli Stravaganti in Candia, while fiery contests of rhetorical oratory took place.'

One significant reason for the high level of Crete's intellectual life was the excellent education provided by the Catholic Venetians. Promising Cretan students were educated under church supervision, and this aided their travels. Dr Karamanolis, a noted expert on the subject, cites some of these prominent Cretans. **Maximos Margounios** (1549–1602), for example, was educated in Sitia by the learned Catholic bishop there, Gaspare Viviano. He later studied in Padua and finally lived in Venice, where he wrote on philosophy, rhetoric and theology, translating ancient and Byzantine texts. Margounios, who would have close collaboration with leading humanists in Italy, Germany and even England, was commended in a contemporary Venetian document as being 'very expert in Greek and Latin, with few equals in all Greece in erudition.'

According to Dr Karamanolis, Margounios 'retained close ties with humanist circles in his native Crete, and played an important role in assisting the projects of several European thinkers. Margounios' humanist peers considered his commentaries on philosophical texts by Aristotle and Porphyry very valuable.'

Another Cretan, **Frangiskos Portos** (1511–81), was a distinguished professor in the University of Geneva, 'appointed by Calvin himself'. The most beloved Cretan Renaissance man of all, however, was a poet. Over the four centuries of Venetian rule there was a unique and mutually influential fusion of Greek and Italian literature in Crete, at the same time as similar literary innovations elsewhere in Europe.

Vitsentzos Kornaros (1553–1617), a contemporary of Shakespeare, is today considered the father of Cretan poetry and one of Greece's greatest poets. Born into a Venetian-Cretan aristocratic family near Sitia, Kornaros penned Crete's national epic poem – the 'Erotokritos', a ballad dealing with traditional themes such as love, courage, bravery and friendship. A massive work, at 10,012 rhyming verses, the 'Erotokritos' was composed in the Cretan dialect, and in the traditional Byzantine dekapentasyllabic (15-syllable) verse style. It was meant to be sung as a *mantinadha* – Crete's traditional song style both then and now. Until quite recently, one could encounter elderly village women reciting the entire poem by heart while doing their work.

Today, Crete's Renaissance men are still obscure to all but specialists (and some proud Cretans). Yet their contributions, says Dr Karamanolis, enriched and expedited the progression of Western European thought tremendously. 'Without these Cretan humanists,' he attests, 'the Renaissance as we know it could not have unfolded as it did – we do owe them a debt of gratitude.'

after being destroyed by fire and then an earthquake.

The **Battle of Crete Museum** (☎ 2810 346554; cnr Doukos Beaufort & Hatzidaki; admission free; ☽ 8am-3pm) chronicles this historic battle.

Activities

Cretan Adventures (☎ 2810 332772; www.cretan-adventures.gr; 1st fl, Evans 10) is a well-regarded company run by two intrepid brothers, who organise hiking and trekking tours, mountain biking, plus specialist and extreme activities.

The **Mountaineering & Skiing Club of Iraklio** (EOS; ☎ 2810 227609; www.interkriti.org/orivatikos/orivat.html; Dikeosynis 53; ☽ 8.30pm-10.30pm) arranges weekend mountain climbing, cross-country walking and skiing excursions around Crete.

Iraklio for Children

Iraklio is surprisingly entertaining for kids. Aside from the lions spitting water, big buildings and motorcycles, there's the stuffed animals and interactive displays of the **Natural History Museum** (p464), plus the massive **Cretaquarium** (p469).

When the kids get museumed out, the waterfront **Port Garden Café** (☎ 2810 242411; Paraliaki Leoforo; ☽ 7am-late) opposite the Megaron Hotel has indoor and shady outdoor play areas, including jumping castles and swings. Kids can also run around in **Georgiades Park**, which has a shady cafe.

Festivals & Events

Iraklio's Summer Arts Festival happens at the **Nikos Kazantzakis Open Air Theatre** (☎ 2810 242977; Jesus Bastion; ☽ box office 9am-2.30pm & 6.30-9.30pm), near the moat of the Venetian walls, the nearby Manos Hatzidakis theatre and at the Koules fortress (p464). Check www.heraklion-city.gr for the program or consult the **Municipal Cultural Office** (☎ 2810 399211; Androgeiou 2; ☽ 8am-4pm) behind the Youth Centre cafe.

Sleeping

While the majority of Iraklio's larger and more established hotels operate year-round, most of the smaller, budget places close in the low season.

BUDGET

Hellas Rent Rooms (☎ 2810 288851; Handakos 24; dm/d/ tr without bathroom €12/30/42; ☽ Apr-Nov; ☎) Iraklio's de facto youth hostel is a relaxed place with a reception area and rooftop bar three flights

up. The rooms are somewhat stuffy, but have fans, wash basin and balconies. The shared bathrooms are basic but clean. Breakfast (€3) is available on the upstairs bar terrace.

Mirabello Hotel (☎ 2810 285052; www.mirabello-hotel.gr; Theotokopoulou 20; s/d without bathroom €35/45, d with bathroom €65; ☒) On a quiet and central side street, the relaxed Mirabello has spotless though somewhat cramped rooms, with TV, phone, balconies and upgraded bathrooms. Some share single-sex bathrooms.

Hotel Rea (☎ 2810 223638; www.hotelrea.gr; Kalimeraki 1; d with/without bathroom €40/30; ☽ Apr-Oct; ☎) Popular with backpackers and even families, this friendly, family-run budget place, in a lane parallel with pedestrianised Handakos, offers simple rooms with fans and sinks; some have private bathrooms, while others are shared. There's a small, basic communal kitchen. Family rooms go for €60.

Hotel Lena (☎ 2810 223280; www.lena-hotel.gr; Lahana 10; s/d with bathroom €45/60, without bathroom €35/50; ☽ year-round; ☒) On a quiet street, friendly Hotel Lena has 16 comfortable, airy rooms with phone, TV, fans and double-glazed windows. Most have private bathrooms but even shared bathrooms are pleasant and upgraded.

Kronos Hotel (☎ 2810 282240; www.kronoshotel.gr; Sofokli Venizelou 2; s/d €50/60; ☒ ▦) This well-maintained older waterfront hotel has comfortable rooms with double-glazed windows and balconies, phone and TV. Most are fridge-equipped; some have sea views.

MIDRANGE

Kastro Hotel (☎ 2810 284185; www.kastro-hotel.gr; Theotokopoulou 22; s incl breakfast from €50, d & tr incl breakfast €75-90; ☒ ▦) A refurbished, cheery B-class hotel in the back streets, the Kastro offers large rooms with fridge, TV, hairdryer and ISDN internet.

Irini Hotel (☎ 2810 229703; www.irini-hotel.com; Idomeneos 4; s/d incl breakfast €70/100; ☒) Close to the old harbour, this midsized (59-room) hotel has all mod cons in its airy rooms, with flowering balconies. Pay less by skipping breakfast.

Marin Hotel (☎ 2810 300018; www.marinhotel.gr; Doukos Beaufort 12; s incl breakfast €75, d incl breakfast €95-125; ☒ ▦) This refurbished hotel has front-facing rooms with great views of the harbour and fortress, some with big balconies. Rooms are attractive and well-appointed.

Atrion (☎ 2810 246000; www.atrion.gr; Hronaki 9; s/d incl breakfast €95/110; ☒ ▦) One of Iraklio's better hotels, the renovated Atrion has rooms tastefully deorated in neutral tones, the upper ones enjoying sea views and small balconies.

TOP END

Lato Hotel (☎ 2810 228103; www.lato.gr; Epimenidou 15; s/d €100/127, ste from €175; ✼ ☞) The full boutique experience awaits at the well-designed Lato, marked by its superior service. Overlooking the fortress, and a short walk from the bus and port, it's one of Iraklio's best hotels. The rooms' chic contemporary design is complemented by spectacular views, especially in the spacious suites; ascend to the atmospheric rooftop restaurant and bar for panoramic views. The Lato also boasts a spa centre, a beauty salon, and a fine-dining restaurant, Brilliant (right), downstairs.

Megaron (☎ 2810 305300; www.gdmmegaron.gr; Doukos Beaufort 9; s/d €190/215, ste from €247; Ⓟ ✼ ☞ ⊑) Iraklio's priciest place, this formerly derelict historic building, now transformed into a luxury hotel, has comfortable beds, Jacuzzis in the VIP suites and plasma-screen TVs. The rooftop restaurant and bar have fine harbour views, along with a unique glass-sided pool.

Eating

Many restaurants close on Sundays.

BUDGET

Giakoumis Taverna (☎ 2810 280277; Theodosaki 5-8; mayirefta €4-8; ✕ closed Sun) One of the best of the tavernas clustered around the 1866 market side streets, Giakoumis is always busy, and serves both vegetarian fare and meats hot off the grill. Cretan specialities dominate.

Ippokambos Ouzerie (☎ 2810 280240; Sofokli Venizelou 3; seafood mezedhes €5-9) At the edge of the tourist-driven waterfront dining strip, this is another local favourite with house specialities and fresh fish (try the baked cuttlefish).

O Vrakas (☎ 6977893973; Plateia 18 Anglon; seafood mezedhes €5-12) This small street-side *ouzerie* (place that serves ouzo and light snacks) grills fresh fish alfresco before you. It's a humble place, but very popular with locals.

Fyllo...Sofies (☎ 2810 284774; Plateia Venizelou 33; bougatsa €2.50; ✕ 5am-late; ☞) and the adjacent **Kipkop** (☎ 2810 242705; Plateia Venizelou 29) have always-packed tables sprawled out on the square, overlooking Morosini Fountain – the best spot for a breakfast *bougatsa* (creamy semolina pudding wrapped in a pastry envelope and baked). There's even wi-fi.

MIDRANGE

Koupes (☎ 6977259038; Agiou Titou 22; mezedhes €3-6.50) This student-frequented place serving powerful Cretan *raki* with appetisers (a *rakadhiko*) opposite the school does great mezedhes (appetisers).

Terzakis (☎ 2810 221444; Marineli 17; mezedhes €5-10) On a small square opposite Agios Dimitrios church, this excellent *ouzerie* has numerous mezedhes, *mayirefta* (ready-cooked meals) and grills. Try the sea-urchin salad or, if feeling really adventurous, ask if the kitchen has 'unmentionables': *ameletita* (fried sheep testicles).

I Avli tou Defkaliona (☎ 2810 244215; Prevelaki 10; meat dishes €6-10; ✕ dinner) This traditional taverna has simple decor, but is good for grills.

Parasies (☎ 2810 225009; Plateia Istorikou Mouseiou; grills €6.50-10) In the corner of the square next to the Historical Museum, this is a good lunch spot, with tasty grills.

Peri Orexeos (☎ 2810 222679; Koraï 10; mains €7-10) On the busy Koraï pedestrian strip, try excellent contemporary Greek food here, with creative takes like creamy chicken wrapped in *kataïfi* (angel-hair pastry), huge salads and solid Cretan cuisine.

TOP END

Brilliant (☎ 28103 34959; Lato Boutique Hotel, Epimenidou 15; mains €11-20) This upscale restaurant, part of the Lato Boutique Hotel, does fine Greek and international specialities, and has attentive and courteous service.

Prassein Aloga (☎ 2810 283429; Kydonias 21, cnr Handakos; mains €12-20) 'Mediterranean fusion' cuisine is served at this unassuming but inventive rustic-style cafe-restaurant. The menu constantly changes, and features unique dishes based on ancient Greek cuisine, like pork medallions with dried fruit on wild rice.

Loukoulos (☎ 2810 224435; Korai 5; mains €15-32) Loukoulos is as much about ambience as it is about food, served on fine china and accompanied by soft classical music. It does modern Greek and other Mediterranean dishes, but for the price they are not sufficiently special.

Drinking

ourpick Guernica (☎ 2810 282988; Apokoronou Kritis 2; ✕ 10am-late) The cool combination of traditional decor and eclectic contemporary music makes this Iraklio's hippest bar-cafe. The bar space wraps around a leafy terrace garden with tables. It's popular as a beer bar with students, and gets lively after midnight.

Pagopiion (☎ 2810 346028; www.icefacktory.gr; Plateia Agiou Titou; ☻ 10am-late) Once an ice factory, this popular cafe-bar-restaurant is marked by eccentric decorations and lighting that create a sort of Christmas-forest ambience.

Café Plus (Plateia Agiou Titou; ☻ 9am-2am) This big outdoor cafe at the nexus of Iraklio's pedestrianised zones is a relaxing place for a coffee or drink at night.

Outopia (Handakos; ☻ 9am-2am) This cafe on pedestrianised Handakos is a known emporium of chocolates (and other sweets) with impressively long lists of both beers and teas.

Also recommended are the lively **Take Five** (☎ 2810 226564; Akroleondos 7; ☻ 10am-late), a classic bar on a pedestrian street by El Greco Park, and **Café Santan** (☎ 6976 285869; Korai 13), which aspires to be 'oriental', with hookahs, sofas and belly dancing from 11pm.

Entertainment

Iraklio has big dance clubs along Leoforos Ikarou, just down from Plateia Eleftherias and along Epimenidou, though many close in summer. However, the revitalised waterfront west of the port houses some popular nightclubs, like Big Fish and Desire.

Vogue (☎ 6944577201; ☻ 10pm-6am) A bit more central, this is another waterfront place in an old building popular with Greeks; if you're foreign and look or act like you've stumbled out of a tacky package tour resort, you won't be let in.

Habanero (Handakos; ☻ 10pm-4am) This slick Latin music bar is fleshed out by lithe young Greek couples who actually know how to dance to this stuff.

Big Fish (☎ 2810 288011; cnr Makariou 17 & Venizelou; ☻ 10am-late) is housed in a restored old stone building. Desire is next door.

Getting There & Away

AIR

Iraklio's Nikos Kazantzakis Airport is Crete's biggest and gets many regular domestic, international and summertime charter flights. For details, see Island Hopping (p749).

Some operators:

Aegean Airlines (☎ 2810 344324; www.aegeanair.com)

Olympic Air (☎ 2810 244824; www.olympicairlines .com)

Sky Express (☎ 2810 223500; www.skyexpress.gr)

BOAT

For information on Iraklio's numerous ferry connections, see Island Hopping (p749). The portside **Iraklio Port Authority** (☎ 2810 244912) keeps ferry schedule information.

Ferry operators:

ANEK Lines Iraklio (☎ 2810 244912; www.anek.gr)

GA Ferries Iraklio (☎ 2810 222408; www.gaferries.gr)

LANE Lines (☎ 2810 346440; www.lane.gr)

Minoan Lines (☎ 2810 229624; www.minoan.gr)

BUS

Iraklio's main transport hub, **Bus Station A** (☎ 2810 246534; www.ktel-heraklio-lassithi.gr; Leoforos Nearhou), serves eastern and western Crete (including Knossos) from its waterfront location near the quay. **Bus Station B** (☎ 2810 255965), west of the city centre beyond Hania Gate, serves Phaestos, Agia Galini and Matala. See the boxed text, opposite, for more information. Most intercity (IC) services are reduced on weekends.

Airport bus 1 operates every 15 minutes between 6.30am and midnight (€0.90) and stops at Plateia Eleftherias.

Getting Around

Bus 1 serves the airport every 15 minutes between 6am and 1am. The bus terminal is near the Astoria Capsis Hotel on Plateia Eleftherias. An airport taxi costs €10 to €12; try **Ikarus Radio Taxi** (☎ 2810 211212).

Long-Distance Taxis (☎ 2810 210102) from Plateia Eleftherias, outside the Astoria Capsis Hotel and Bus Station B, are expensive but quick.

IRAKLIO'S WINE COUNTRY

Just south of Iraklio and Knossos, the fertile Peza region produces 70% of Cretan wines. The **Pezas Union of local producers** (☎ 2810 741945; www.pezaunion .gr; admission free; ☻ 9am-4pm Mon-Sat) has tastings, videos and a minimuseum. The state-of-the-art hilltop **Boutari Winery** (☎ 2810 731617; www.boutari.gr; Skalani; tour & tasting €4.50; ☻ 10am-6pm), about 8km from Iraklio, features a stunning tasting room and showroom overlooking the vineyard of the Fantaxometoho estate – and great wines.

IRAKLIO BUS SERVICES

From Bus Station A

Destination	Duration	Fare	Frequency
Agia Pelagia	45min	€3.20	3 daily
Agios Nikolaos	1½hr	€6.50	half-hourly
Arhanes	30min	€1.70	hourly
Hania	3hr	€10.50	18 daily
Hersonisos/Malia	45 min	€3.70	half-hourly
Ierapetra	2½hr	€10	8 daily
Knossos	20min	€1.30	3 hourly
Lasithi Plateau	2 hr	€4.70	1 daily
Milatos	1½hr	€4.70	2 daily
Rethymno	1¾hr	€6.30	18 daily
Sitia	3½hr	€13.10	5 daily

From Bus Station B

Destination	Duration	Fare	Frequency
Agia Galini	2 hr	€7.40	6 daily
Anogia	1 hr	€3.60	4 daily
Matala	2½ hr	€7.20	5 daily
Phaestos	1½ hr	€5.90	8 daily

Sample fares: Agios Nikolaos €60; Rethymno €70; Hania €100 to €120.

The airport has numerous car-hire companies, including **Alianthos Rent-a-Car & Bikes** (☎ 2810 390481, 6945449771; www.alianthos-group.com). Although not the cheapest, this island-wide agency commands a staggering 2500 cars and has flexible service and variety. Its other locations include Rethymno, Hania, Plakias and Agia Galini.

Some smaller local outlets:

Loggetta Cars (☎ 2810 289462; www.loggetta.gr; 25 Avgoustou 20)

Motor Club (☎ 2810 222408; www.motorclub.gr; Plateia 18 Anglon) Opposite the fortress; for motorcycles.

Sun Rise (☎ 2810 221609; 25 Avgoustou 46) Just off the pedestrian street.

CRETAQUARIUM

The massive **Cretaquarium** (☎ 2810 337788; www .cretaquarium.gr; adult/child over 4yr/under 4yr €8/6/free; ☯ 9am-9pm May–mid-Oct, 10am-5.30pm mid-Oct–Apr) at Gournes, 15km east of Iraklio, is the Eastern Mediterranean's largest aquarium. Several large tanks contain an amazing display of marine life, though really big fish are scarce. Interactive multimedia features and displays in several languages help explain things.

The north-coast buses (€1.70, 30 minutes) leaving from Iraklio's Bus Station A can drop you on the main road; from there it's a 10-minute walk. The turn-off to Kato Gouves is well signposted on the national road.

KNOSSOS ΚΝΩΣΣΟΣ

Crete's must-see historical attraction is the **Minoan Palace of Knossos** (☎ 2810 231940; admission €6; ☯ 8am-7pm Jun-Oct, 8am-3pm Nov-May), 5km south of Iraklio in Knossos (k-nos-*os*) village, and the capital of Minoan Crete.

Legendary home of King Minos' mythical Minotaur, Knossos was uncovered in the early 1900s by British archaeologist Sir Arthur Evans. Rival digger Heinrich Schliemann, discoverer of ancient Troy and Mycenae, had failed to win over the landowner, and Evans took the glory.

After 35 years and some £250,000 of his own money, Sir Arthur had excavated the site and accomplished partial reconstructions. His efforts proved controversial, with some archaeologists claiming that accuracy was sacrificed to imagination. However, for the casual visitor, the reconstructions are more than sufficient for visualising a real live Minoan palace.

History

Knossos' first palace (1900 BC) was destroyed by an earthquake around 1700 BC, and rebuilt with a grander and more

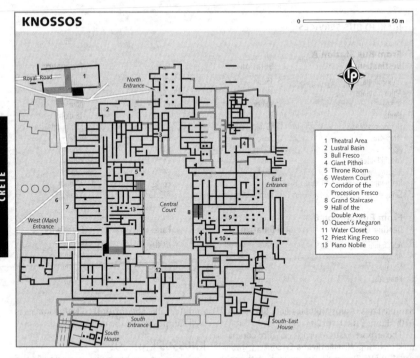

KNOSSOS

0 — 50 m

1 Theatral Area
2 Lustral Basin
3 Bull Fresco
4 Giant Pithoi
5 Throne Room
6 Western Court
7 Corridor of the Procession Fresco
8 Grand Staircase
9 Hall of the Double Axes
10 Queen's Megaron
11 Water Closet
12 Priest King Fresco
13 Piano Nobile

sophisticated design (Evans' reconstruction emulates the latter palace). It was partially destroyed again between 1500 and 1450 BC, then inhabited for another 50 years before finally burning down.

Knossos consisted of an immense palace, residences of officials and priests, the homes of ordinary people, and burial grounds. The palace comprised royal domestic quarters, public reception rooms, shrines, workshops, treasuries and storerooms, all built around a central court. Like all Minoan palaces, it was also the city hall, accommodating the bureaucracy.

Until 1997 visitors could enter the royal apartments, but the area was then cordoned off, before it disappeared altogether under the continual pounding of tourists' feet. Despite extensive ongoing repairs, it's unlikely to be reopened.

Exploring the Site

Evans' reconstruction brings to life the palace's most significant parts, including the reconstructed columns; painted deep brown-red with gold-trimmed black capitals, they taper gracefully at the bottom. Vibrant frescoes add another dramatic dimension to the palace. Additionally, the Minoans' highly sophisticated society is revealed by details like the advanced drainage system, the placement of light wells, and the organisation of space within rooms – meant to be cool in summer and warm in winter.

The palace complex entrance is across the **Western Court** and along the **Corridor of the Procession Fresco**, where a now-fragmentary fresco depicted a procession bearing gifts to the king. A copy, called the **Priest King Fresco**, is visible south of the Central Court.

Walking straight ahead from the Corridor of the Procession Fresco to the north entrance, you'll reach the **Theatral Area**. This series of steps may have been a theatre, or the place where important visitors arriving on the Royal Road were greeted.

The **Royal Road**, leading off to the west, was apparently Europe's first. It was flanked by workshops and ordinary residences. Sir Arthur surmised that the nearby **Lustral Basin** was where the Minoans performed ritual cleansings before religious ceremonies.

Entering the **Central Court** from the north, you pass the relief **Bull Fresco**, depicting a charging bull. Also in the palace's northern section, see the **Giant Pithoi**, large ceramic jars used for storing olive oil, wine and grain. Evans found over 100 *pithoi*, some 2m high. Ropes were required to move these heavy objects, thus warranting the raised patterns decorating the jars.

At the Central Court, once surrounded by the palace's high walls, the complex's most important rooms begin. From the northern end of the west side, steps descend to the **Throne Room**, fenced off but still visible. The centrepiece, a simple, beautifully proportioned throne, is flanked by the **Griffin Fresco** (the Minoans held these mythical beasts sacred). Possibly the room was a shrine and the throne used by a high priestess rather than a king. The Minoans worshipped their gods in small shrines, not great temples, and each palace had several.

On the 1st floor of the palace's west side is the section Evans called the **Piano Nobile** (the nobles' floor), believing that the reception and state rooms had been here. A room here displays copies of some frescoes found.

Returning to the Central Court, you'll see the impressive **Grand Staircase** leading from the palace's eastern side to the (now off-limits) royal apartments, which Evans called the **Domestic Quarter**. Within the royal apartments, the **Hall of the Double Axes** was the king's *megaron*, a spacious double room in which the ruler both slept and carried out certain court duties. There was a light well at one end and a balcony at the other to ensure air circulation. The room was named for the double axe marks on its light well, the sacred symbol of the Minoans.

A passage from here leads to the **Queen's Megaron**. Above the door is a copy of the **Dolphin Fresco**, one of the most exquisite Minoan artworks, and a blue floral design decorates the portal. Next to this room is the queen's bathroom, complete with terracotta bathtub and **water closet**, touted as the first ever to use the flush principle; water was poured down by hand.

Getting There & Away

Frequent buses from Iraklio's bus station (see p468) and from near Morosini Fountain serve Knossos. From the coastal road, occasional signs direct drivers. Since several free car parks exist close to the site, don't listen to touts advertising paid parking lots along the way.

OTHER MINOAN SITES

Besides Knossos, central Crete has other significant Minoan sites. Less reconstructed (and less flamboyant) than Knossos, they provide a somewhat different, more raw glimpse into Minoan life, without the architectural interpretations of Sir Arthur Evans. For this reason some archaeological purists prefer them to Knossos.

Malia Μάλια

Some 3km east of the package-tour sprawl of north-coast Malia, the **Minoan Palace of Malia** (☎ 28970 31597; admission €4; ☯ 8.30am-3pm Tue-Sun) is smaller than either Knossos or Phaestos. It once comprised a palace complex and a town built on this flat, fertile plain.

From the **West Court** (where the entrance is) walk to the southern end to see the eight circular pits probably used to store grain. East of these, the palace's former main entrance leads to the southern end of the **Central Court**. At the southwest corner stands the **Kernos Stone**, a disc with 34 holes around its edge; archaeologists still can't explain its original use.

The **Loggia**, north of the **Central Staircase** (at the north end of the palace's west side), was used for religious ceremonies.

The site's exhibition hall has reconstructions and interesting photos, including aerial shots. Half-hourly buses connect Malia with Iraklio (€3.70, one hour).

Phaestos Φαιστός

Conveniently, Crete's three other major archaeological sites lie near one other, forming a rough triangle 50km south of Iraklio.

Phaestos (☎ 28920 42315; adult/student €4/2, incl Agia Triada €6/3; ☯ 8am-7.30pm Jun-Oct, 8am-5pm Nov-Apr), 63km from Iraklio, was the second-most-important Minoan palace-city. Phaestos (*festos*) also enjoys the most awe-inspiring location, with panoramic views of the Mesara Plain and Mt Ida. The palace layout is identical to Knossos, with rooms arranged around a central court. And, like Knossos, most of Phaestos was built over an older palace destroyed in the late Middle Minoan period. However, unlike other Minoan sites, parts of this old palace have been excavated and its remnants are partially added on to the new palace.

CRETE

CRETE

AN ETHNO-ESCAPE

If you're doing the 'Minoan triangle' of sites south of Iraklio and want to see something equally edifying but a bit more modern, visit **Vori**. This unassuming village 4km east of Tymbaki boasts the private **Museum of Cretan Ethnology** (☎ 28920 91112, appointments 28920 91110; admission €3; ⏰ 10am-6pm Apr-Oct, by appointment winter). The exhibits, which cover rural life, war, customs, architecture, music, and the herbs, flora and fauna used in Crete's unique cuisine, provide fascinating insights into traditional Cretan culture. Beautiful weavings, furniture, woodcarvings and musical instruments are displayed too. It's well signposted from the main road.

Phaestos has its own distinctive attractiveness. There's an air of mystery about the desolate, unreconstructed ruins altogether lacking at Knossos. Also in contrast to Knossos, few frescoes remain here; Phaestos' palace walls were apparently mostly covered with white gypsum.

The new palace entrance is by the 15m-wide **Grand Staircase**. The stairs access the **Central Court**. North of here lie the palace complex's best-preserved sections, the reception rooms and private apartments. While excavations continue, it's known that the entrance here was marked by an imposing portal with half columns at either side, the lower parts of which are still in situ. Unlike the Minoan freestanding columns, however, they don't taper at the base. The celebrated Phaestos disc, now in Iraklio's archaeological museum (p463), was discovered in a building north of the palace.

There are eight daily buses from Iraklio to Phaestos (€5.90, 1½ hours), also stopping at the Gortyna site. Five daily buses also connect Phaestos with Agia Galini (€2.80, 25 minutes, five daily) and Matala (€1.80, 30 minutes, five daily).

Agia Triada Αγία Τριάδα

Pronounced ah-*yee*-ah trih-*ah*-dha, **Agia Triada** (☎ 28920 91564; admission €3, incl Phaestos €6; ⏰ 10am-4.30pm summer, 8.30am-3pm winter), 3km west of Phaestos, was a smaller but similarly designed palace, and possibly a royal summer villa, judging by the opulence of the objects

discovered here. North of the palace, the stoa (long, colonnaded building) of an erstwhile settlement has been unearthed. Iraklio's archaeological museum (p463) contains significant local finds, including a sarcophagus, two superlative frescoes and three vases.

The signposted right-hand turn to Agia Triada is about 500m past Phaestos on the Matala road. There's no public transport.

Gortyna Γόρτυνα

Sprawling across the road connecting Iraklio and Phaestos, on the Mesara plain, **Gortyna** (☎ 28920 31144; admission €4; ⏰ 8am-7.30pm, to 5pm winter) is a vast and intriguing site. Gortyna (pronounced *gor*-tih-nah) was inhabited from Minoan to Christian times, and became capital of Rome's Cyrenaica province.

The massive stone tablets inscribed with the wide-ranging **Laws of Gortyna** (5th century BC) comprise Gortyna's most significant exhibit. Fixed remains include the 2nd-century-AD **Praetorium**, once residence of the provincial governor; a **Nymphaeum**; and the **Temple of Pythian Apollo**. Finally, see the ruined 6th-century-AD **Basilica of Agios Titos**, dedicated to this protégé of St Paul and Crete's first bishop.

The ruins are 46km southwest of Iraklio and 15km from Phaestos. There's no public transport.

ARHANES ΑΡΧΑΝΕΣ
pop 4700

Pretty Arhanes, 14km south of Iraklio, is a restored traditional village with lovely old houses and excellent tavernas set around relaxing, leafy squares. Although Arhanes once boasted a Minoan palace, only ruins remain (signposted from the main road).

The **Archaeological Museum of Arhanes** (☎ 28107 52712; admission free; ⏰ 8.30am-3pm Wed-Mon) contains finds from regional archaeological excavations. The exhibits include *larnakes* (coffins) and musical instruments from Fourni, and an ornamental dagger from the Anemospilia temple.

Visit the site www.archanes.gr for online information.

Accommodation here includes **Neraidospilios** (☎ 6972720879; www.neraidospilios.gr; s/apt €40/70; 🅿 🅰) on the town outskirts. These superbly appointed, spacious studios and apartments overlook the mountains. Enquire with the owners, at Arhanes' Diahroniko cafe.

Hourly buses connect Iraklio with Arhanes (€1.70, 30 minutes).

ZAROS & AROUND ΖΑΡΟΣ
pop 2220

About 46km southwest of Iraklio, Zaros is a more rustic village, known for its spring water production. Nearby excavations indicate that this factor lured Minoans, and later Romans to settle here.

If you're driving, the Byzantine monasteries and other nearby villages are worth exploring. **Moni Agiou Nikolaou**, atop the verdant **Rouvas Gorge**, contains 14th-century paintings, while the nearby **Moni Agiou Andoniou Vrondisiou** boasts a 15th-century Venetian fountain and 14th-century frescoes.

Just outside Zaros, visit the lovely shady park at **Votomos** for its small lake, children's playground and excellent taverna-cafe, I **Limni** (☎ 28940 31338; trout per kilogram €22; ☽ 9am-late). From the lake, a path accesses both Moni Agiou Nikolaou (900m) and Rouvas Gorge (2.5km).

For overnights, try **Studios Keramos** (☎ /fax 28940 31352; Zaros; s/d incl breakfast €30/35; ☼), decorated with family heirlooms, antique beds and furniture – don't miss owner Katerina's home-cooked traditional Cretan breakfast. For eating, the main-street **Vengera** (☎ 28940 31730; Zaros; mains €4-6) serves home-cooked traditional Cretan food.

Two daily buses connect Zaros with Iraklio (€4.30, one hour).

MATALA ΜΑΤΑΛΑ
pop 100

Matala (*ma*-ta-la), on the south coast 11km southwest of Phaestos, was a groovy getaway in the early 1970s, when hippies would sleep around in the sandstone **caves** that pockmark the giant overhanging rock slab at water's edge. The caves, populated in earlier centuries, were never for particularly light sleepers – they were originally used as Roman tombs in the 1st century AD.

Matala's modern 'civilising' process of expansion has rather killed its initial escapist appeal, though it does still have its loyal returnees. It's a fairly ordinary, low-key vacation settlement nowadays, with domatia and tavernas, and a beautiful sandy **beach** below the caves. You can still clamber around freely in the caves, though they're normally

fenced off at night. There was no guard or entry charge at the time of writing. Matala also makes a convenient base for visiting Phaestos and Agia Triada.

Sleeping & Eating

Fantastic Rooms to Rent (☎ 28920 45362; s/d/tr €25/30/40, d/tr with kitchen €30/35; ℗ ☼) Around since the hippie heydays, the Fantastic has plain but comfortable rooms, many with kitchenette, phone, kettle and fridge.

Pension Andonios (☎ 28920 45123; d/tr €30/35; ℗ ☼) Run by the genial Antonis, this comfortable pension has attractively furnished rooms set around a lovely courtyard, many with kitchenette. The top rooms have balconies.

Hotel Zafiria (☎ 28920 45366, www.zafiria-matala .com; d incl breakfast €40; ℗ ☼ ☐ ☼) One of Matala's bigger places, the Zafiria has comfortable rooms with all mod cons. The balconies enjoy sea views, and there's a new pool beneath the cliffs.

Gianni's Taverna (☎ 28920 45719; mains €5-7.50) This no-frills place has inexpensive grills and other simple taverna fare.

Lions (☎ 28920 45108; specials €6-10) On the beach, this old standby has above-average food, with big trays of home-style dishes inside. It gets lively in the evening, when it doubles as a watering hole.

Getting There & Away

From Iraklio, five daily buses serve Matala (€7.20, 2½ hours). Buses also run between Matala and Phaestos (€1.80, 30 minutes).

RETHYMNO ΡΕΘΥΜΝΟ
pop 27,870

Delightful Rethymno (*reth*-im-no) is Crete's third largest town, noted for its picturesque old town running down to a lively harbour overlooked by a massive Venetian fortress. Although Rethymno is showing signs of urban sprawl, travellers seem to miss it (except when looking for parking), such is the attraction of the lovely old Venetian-Turkish quarter, with its maze of narrow streets, graceful woodbalconied houses and ornate Venetian monuments; minarets add an Ottoman flourish.

Rethymno has a softer, more feminine feel than Iraklio, partly due to architecture, but also because Rethymno's University of Crete

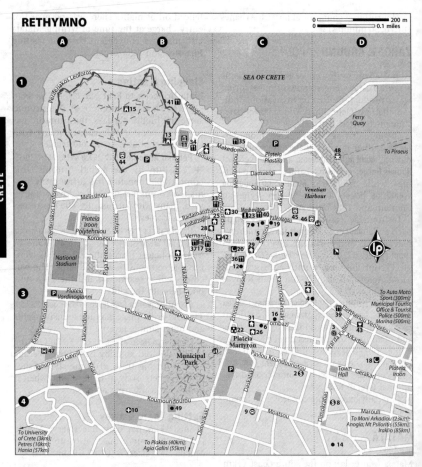

campus specialises in the humanities, which attracts more female students here than males. The full-time student population also keeps Rethymno lively in winter.

History

Rethymno's strategic position appealed to the Minoans, who settled here. The town was dubbed 'Rithymna' from the 4th century BC, when it was autonomous, issuing its own coinage. However, it waned in importance during Roman and Byzantine times.

Rethymno flourished again during Venetian rule (1210–1645), and its most important architecture dates from that period. The Ottomans ruled thereafter until 1897, when Russia became overseer of Rethymno dur-

ing the European Great Powers' occupation. The town's reputation as an artistic and intellectual centre grew from 1923, when the mandated population exchanges between Greece and Turkey brought many refugees from Constantinople.

Orientation

Rethymno's major sights and best sleeping and eating options are clustered near the harbour; a decent beach is on its eastern side.

The bus station, at the western end of Igoumenou Gavriil, is about 600m west of the Porto Guora (despite some discussions, it hadn't been relocated at the time of writing). If arriving by ferry, you'll see the old quarter opposite the quay.

Parking is very difficult around the old town in summer. Although a sign says parking isn't allowed in the giant lot by the quay, many seem to do so.

Information
BOOKSHOPS
Ilias Spondidakis bookshop (☎ 28310 54307; Souliou 43) Has English-language novels, books about Greece and Greek music.

Mediterraneo Editions (☎ 28310 50505; Paleologou 41; www.mediterraneo.gr; ☒ 8am-10pm) Friendly shop stocks foreign-language books, Lonely Planet and other guide books, and Anavasi hiking maps.

EMERGENCY
Tourist police (☎ 28310 28156; Delfini Bldg, Venizelou; ☒ 7am-2.30pm) At the municipal tourist office.

INTERNET ACCESS
Cybernet (Kallergi 44-46; per hr €3; ☒ 10am-5am)

LAUNDRY
Laundry Mat (☎ 28310 29722; Tombazi 45; wash & dry €9; ☒ 8.30am-2pm & 5.30-9pm Mon-Fri, 8.30am-2.15pm Sat) By the youth hostel.

LEFT LUGGAGE
KTEL (☎ 28310 22659; cnr Kefalogiannidon & Igoumenou Gavriil); €1.50 per day; ☒ 8am-6pm) Luggage service at the bus station.

MEDICAL SERVICES
Rethymno Hospital (☎ 28210 27491; Triandalydou 17; ☒ 24hr)

MONEY
Alpha Bank (Pavlou Koundouriotou 29)
National Bank of Greece (Dimokratias)

POST
Post office (☎ 28310 22302; Moatsou 21; ☒ 7am-7pm Mon-Fri)

TOURIST INFORMATION
Municipal Tourist Office (☎ 28310 29148; www.rethymno.gr; Delfini Bldg, Eleftheriou Venizelou; ☒ 8.30am-8.30pm Mon-Fri year-round, plus 9am-8.30pm Sat & Sun Mar-Nov)

TRAVEL AGENCIES
Alfa Odeon Holidays (☎ 28310 57610; www.odeontravel.gr; Paleologou 25) The helpful Manolis Chliaoutakis runs this full-service travel agency in the old town.
Ellotia Tours (☎ 28310 24533; www.rethymnoatcrete.com; Arkadiou 155; ☒ 9am-9pm Mar-Nov) Boat and plane tickets, currency exchange, car and bike hire and excursions can be arranged here.

Sights
Rethymno's 16th-century **fortress** (fortezza; ☎ 28310 28101; Paleokastro Hill; admission €3.10; ☒ 8am-8pm Jun-Oct) was originally an ancient acropolis. Although its massive walls once sheltered numerous buildings, only a church and a mosque survive. Nevertheless, there are many ruins to explore, and great views from the ramparts.

Once a prison, the small **archaeological museum** (☎ 28310 54668; admission €3; ☒ 8.30am-3pm Tue-Sun), near the fortress entrance, exhibits Neolithic tools, Minoan pottery excavated from nearby tombs, Mycenaean figurines and a 1st-century-AD relief of Aphrodite, plus an important coin collection.

Rethymno's **Historical & Folk Art Museum** (☎ 28310 23398; Vernardou 28-30; admission €3; ☼ 9.30am-2.30pm Mon-Sat), located in a historic Venetian building, documents traditional rural life, with its clothing, baskets, weavings and farm tools.

In the old quarter, the unmissable **Rimondi Fountain**, with its spouting lion heads and Corinthian capitals, attests to former Venetian rule, as does the 16th-century **Loggia** (now a museum shop). The well-preserved **Porto Guora** (Great Gate) is a remnant of the Venetian defensive wall.

Venetian and Turkish architecture is vividly displayed at the **Centre for Byzantine Art** (☎ 28210 50120; Ethnikis Antistaseos). This former mansion's terrace cafe offers great old-town views.

The nearby **Nerantzes Mosque**, converted from a Franciscan church in 1657, and, further east, the **Kara Musa Pasha Mosque**, with its vaulted fountain, are Rethymno's major remaining Ottoman structures. The latter now houses the **Hellenic Conservatory**, and makes an atmospheric concert venue.

Activities

The **Happy Walker** (☎ /fax 28310 52920; www.happy walker.com; Tombazi 56; ☼ 5pm-8.30pm) offers various countryside walks near Rethymno. More serious hikers should see **EOS** (Greek Mountaineering Club; ☎ 28310 57766; www.eos.rethymnon .com; Dimokratias 12) for detailed info on mountain climbing and other outdoors adventures in Rethymno prefecture.

The **Paradise Dive Centre** (☎ 28310 26317; www .diving-center.gr) runs diving activities and PADI courses for all levels. Its dive base is at Petres, 15 minutes west of Rethymno.

Festivals & Events

The annual **Renaissance Festival** (☎ 28310 51199; www.cultureguide.gr) is Rethymno's biggest event. Events primarily take place in the fortress's Erofili Theatre from July to September. The mid-July **Wine Festival** is held in the flower-filled municipal park, which is always good for a relaxing stroll. February sees fun **Winter Carnival** celebrations.

Sleeping
BUDGET

Rethymno Youth Hostel (☎ 28310 22848; www .yhrethymno.com; Tombazi 41; dm without bathroom €10, breakfast €2; ☐ ☎) This friendly, laid-back old-town hostel stays open year-round. It enjoys an enclosed, open location, with good bathrooms and a small bar.

Sea Front (☎ 28310 51981; www.forthnet.gr/elotia; Arkadiou 159; d €35-50; ☒) This waterfront pension has decent budget rooms with timber floors, plus studio apartments with sea views and ceiling fans further towards the beach.

Atelier (☎ 28310 24440; atelier@ret.forthnet.gr; Himaras 27; r €35-55) These clean and attractively refurbished rooms attached to Frosso Bora's pottery workshop represent great value. They're marked by Venetian architecture, like the exposed stone walls – along with flat-screen TVs, new bathrooms and kitchenettes.

Olga's Pension (☎ 28310 28665; Souliou 57; s/d/studio €40/45/65; ☒) On touristy but colourful Souliou, Olga's has a faded charm, with eclectic decor and terraces between the basic but colourful rooms. Most include fridge, TV, fan and a basic bathroom. Rates include breakfast, served downstairs in Souliou 55.

Byzantine Hotel (☎ 28310 55609; Vosporou 26; d incl breakfast from €50; ☒) Traditional ambience meets great value at this small hotel near the Porta Guora. The rooms in this historic structure feature carved timber furniture, and some have bathtubs. The back rooms overlook the old mosque and minaret.

Casa dei Delfini (☎ 28310 55120; kzaxa@reth.gr; Nikiforou Foka 66-68; studio €55-75, ste €80-140; ☒) Turkish and Venetian architectural features intermingle in this elegant pension, which includes an old stone trough and hammam ceiling in one of the studio bathrooms. The traditionally decorated rooms all feature kitchenettes; most impressive is the massive maisonette, with its large private terrace.

MIDRANGE & TOP END

our pick **Hotel Veneto** (☎ 28310 56634; www.veneto.gr; Epimenidou 4; studio/ste incl breakfast €125/145; ☒ ☎) For some of Rethymno's most beautiful aesthetic flourishes, visit the Veneto, which dates partially from the 14th century. The foyer's stunning pebble mosaic and a well-lit stone basin, where delicate flowers float, open onto a pretty back garden, where breakfast tables are set amidst verdure and a gurgling fountain. Rooms feature polished wood floors, iron beds, TV and kitchenettes. A subterranean, curving-stone chamber where monks once meditated is not the largest room, but is certainly the most striking. Out of high season, rates drop significantly.

Palazzo Rimondi (☎ 28310 51289; www.palazzo rimondi.com; cnr Xanthoulidou 21 & Trikoupi 16; d studio/ste incl breakfast €160/200; ❄ ⬛) This charming old-town Venetian mansion is a real treat, with its exquisite individually decorated studios with kitchenettes. There's a small splash pool in the breakfast courtyard.

Avli Lounge Apartments (☎ 28310 58250; www.avli .gr; cnr Xanthoudidou 22 & Radamanthyos; ste incl breakfast €210-250; ❄) Inconspicuously spread over two beautifully restored Venetian buildings in the old town, these singular suites feature ornate iron or wooden beds, antiques, exquisite furnishings and objets d'art.

Eating

The waterfront and Venetian harbour are, unsurprisingly, occupied by touristy places; head inland for better options.

Fanari (☎ 28310 54849; Kefalogiannidon 15; mezedhes €2.50-10) West of the Venetian harbour on the waterfront, this taverna serves good mezedhes, fresh fish and Cretan cuisine. Try the *bekri mezes* (pork with wine and peppers) or *apaki*, the local smoked-pork speciality, plus the homemade wine.

Taverna Kyria Maria (☎ 28310 29078; Moshovitou 20; Cretan dishes €4-6.50) Behind the Rimondi Fountain, this taverna has great home-style Greek cooking and outdoor seating, where bird cages hang from a leafy trellis.

Souliou 55 (☎ 28310 54896; Souliou 55; mayirefta €4-7) Known informally as 'Stella's Kitchen', this little place specialising in *mayirefta* is below Olga's Pension, run by Stella herself.

Samaria (☎ 28310 24681; Eleftheriou Venizelou; mayirefta €4-7) On the waterfront but still popular with locals, Samaria does good *mayirefta*, while the soups and grills are also excellent.

Thalassografia (☎ 28310 52569; Kefalogiannidon 33; mezedhes €4-9) With a breathtaking setting overlooking the sea, under the fortress, Thalassografia is a good place to sample mezedhes at sunset, though it's perhaps over-priced. The grilled sardines are excellent, as are the creamy mushrooms.

Lemonokipos (☎ 28310 57087; Ethnikis Antistaseos 100; mains €7-9) Dine among the lemon trees in the lovely courtyard of this old-town taverna. The traditional Cretan fare includes some unique twists, such as pork and vegetables flavoured with bitter orange leaves.

Castelvecchio (☎ 28310 55163; Himaras 29; mains €8-16; ❨ dinner Jul-Aug, dinner & lunch Sep-Jun) This welcoming family taverna on the fortress' edge

is friendly and does good Cretan specialities, like the *kleftiko* (oven-baked lamb).

Avli (☎ 28310 26213; www.avli.com; cnr Xanthoudidou 22 & Radamanthyos; mains €13.50-30) This delightful former Venetian villa is the place for a special night out. The Nuevo Cretan–style food is superb, the wine list excellent and you dine in a charming courtyard bursting with pots of herbs, bougainvillea canopies, fruit trees and works of art.

Also highly recommended are **Myrogdies Mezedopoleio** (☎ 28310 26083; Vernadou 32; mezedhes €4-6) and **Ousies** (☎ 28310 56643; Vernadou 20; mezedhes €4-7), two inexpensive *mezedhopoleia* (restaurants specialising in mezedhes and raki) with great summertime ambience, on Vernadou.

Drinking & Entertainment

Rethymno's nightlife is concentrated in the bars, clubs and discos around Nearhou and Salaminos, near the Venetian harbour, along with the waterfront bars off Plastira Sq. The indefatigable student population keeps Rethymno lively year-round.

Figaro (☎ 28310 29431; Vernadou 21; ❨ noon-late) Housed in an ingeniously restored old building, Figaro is an atmospheric 'art and music' all-day bar. It attracts everyone from the local intelligentsia and students to tourists drawn in by the subdued ambience and excellent music.

Living Room (☎ 28310 21386; www.livingroom-crete .gr; Venizelou 5; ❨ 9am-2am) This slick cafe-bar seems to have four waiters *per capita*, and exudes a Fashion-TV vibe in its ambient techno and eclectic modern decor. It's popular with students and other locals.

Rock Club Cafe (☎ 28310 31047; Petihaki 8; ❨ 9pm-dawn) One of Rethymno's classic hangouts, this club is popular with visitors and gets filled nightly in summer.

Fortezza Disco (Nearhou 20; ❨ 11pm-dawn) This big, flashy club gets busy late, and boasts three bars and a laser show.

Getting There & Away
BOAT

For information on ferries and high-speed boats from Rethymno, see Island Hopping (p749).

BUS

From the **bus station** (☎ 28310 22212; www.bus -service-crete-ktel.com; Igoumenou Gavriil), hourly buses run in summer to both Hania (€6.50, one hour) and Iraklio (€6.50, 1½ hours). Four daily buses serve Preveli (€4.10, 40 to 45 minutes), while seven go to Plakias (€4.10, one hour) – including an evening bus not usually listed on schedules, which goes via Preveli. Six buses a day serve Agia Galini (€5.60, 1½ hours), three serve Moni Arkadiou (€2.50, 30 minutes), and two go to both Anogia (€4.90, 50 minutes) and Omalos (€11.90, two hours). Daily buses serve Hora Sfakion via Vryses in summer. Low-season services are greatly reduced. Four buses serve Spili (€4, one hour).

Getting Around

Auto Moto Sport (☎ 28310 24858; www.automoto sport.com.gr; Sofokli Venizelou 48) has car hire and a great variety of motorbikes and motorcycles. It's a 10-minute walk from the Venetian harbour, eastwards along the coast road (Eleftheriou Venizelou) which becomes Sofokli Venizelou.

MONI ARKADIOU ΜΟΝΗ ΑΡΚΑΔΙΟΥ

The 16th-century **Moni Arkadiou** (Arkadi; ☎ 28310 83136; admission €2; ☻ 9am-7pm Apr-Oct) has deep significance for Cretans. This monastery, situated in the hills 23km southeast of Rethymno, was the site of an act of mass suicidal defiance that captured European public attention.

In November 1866 massive Ottoman forces arrived to crush island-wide revolts. Hundreds of Cretan men, women and children fled their villages to find shelter at Arkadiou. However, far from being a safe haven, the monastery was soon besieged by 2000 Turkish soldiers. Rather than surrender, the Cretans set light to stored gunpowder kegs, killing everyone, Turks included; one small girl miraculously survived, and lived to a ripe old age in a village nearby. A bust of this woman and one of the abbot who lit the gunpowder stand outside the monastery.

Arkadiou's most impressive building, its Venetian baroque church, has a striking facade marked by eight slender Corinthian columns and topped by an ornate triple-belled tower. Left of it is a small **museum**. The monastery's former windmill outside it has a macabre **ossuary**, containing skulls and bones of the 1866 fighters.

From Rethymno, three daily buses go to Moni Arkadiou (€2.50, 30 minutes).

ANOGIA ΑΝΩΓΕΙΑ
pop 2450

Memorable Anogia presides over the so-called 'Devil's Triangle' of macho mountain villages that occasionally get involved in armed standoffs with the police (usually, over illicit cannibis cultivation, but sometimes just due to perceived affronts to local honour), much to the excitement of the Athenian media. Perched aside **Mt Psiloritis**, 37km southwest of Iraklio, Anogia's known for its rebellious spirit and determination to express its undiluted Cretan character. Its famous 2000-guest **weddings** involve the entire village. It's also known for its stirring music and has spawned many of Crete's best known musicians.

Anogia's *kafeneia* (coffee shops) on the main square are frequented by black-shirted moustachioed men, the older ones often wearing traditional dress. The women stay home or flog the traditional blankets and other crafts that hang all over the village's shops. Indeed, Anogia is well known for its rugs and, if you know what you're looking for, you can sometimes come away with a nice one.

During WWII Anogia was a centre of resistance, and suffered heavily for it. The Nazis massacred all the local men in retaliation for their role in sheltering Allied troops and aiding in the kidnap of General Kreipe.

Anogia nowadays lives quite comfortably from its sheep-husbandry industry and tourism, the latter bolstered as much by curious Greeks as by foreign travellers in search of rustic authenticity. Don't refuse if a village man you don't even know offers to pay for your coffee – it could be considered impolite.

Anogia clings to a hillside, with the textile shops in the lower half and most accommodation and businesses above. There's an ATM-equipped bank and post office. The upper village's **Infocost** (☎ 28340 31808; per hr €3; ☻ 5pm-late) offers internet access.

Sleeping & Eating

Hotel Aristea (☎ 28340 31459; d incl breakfast €40; **P**) There are good views from this upper-village location. The simple but well-outfitted rooms have bathrooms and balconies. An excellent set of new studios is next door.

Ta Skalomata (☎ 28340 31316; grills €3-7) On the upper village's eastern edge, it serves great grills and Cretan dishes at reasonable prices. Zucchini with cheese and aubergine is very tasty, and do try the home-baked bread.

Getting There & Away

Four daily buses reach Anogia from Iraklio (€3.60, one hour), while two daily buses operate from Rethymno (€4.90, 1¼ hours).

PLAKIAS ΠΛΑΚΙΑΣ

pop 180

Some things in Crete never change, and Plakias is one of them. Set beside a long southcoast beach, between two immense wind tunnels – the gorges of Selia and Kourtaliotis – this unassuming resort is livened up in summer by a curious mix of Central European package tourists and the indomitable international legions quartered at the village's extraordinary youth hostel.

Plakias has good restaurants, plenty of accommodation, and offers local walks through olive groves and along cliffs overlooking the sea, some leading to sparkling hidden beaches. It's an excellent base for regional excursions, and the local olive oil is some of Crete's best. Plakias' massive summertime wind (and distance from Iraklio) has thankfully preserved it from overdevelopment, though parents should note that small children may not enjoy the flying sand and waves at this and other southcoast beaches.

Orientation & Information

Plakias' main street runs along the beach; another runs parallel to it one block in, while two streets perpendicular to the water lead further inland. Most services are near the waterfront, including the bus stop.

There are two ATMs on the central waterfront. The **post office** (☎ 28320 31212; ☀ 7am-2pm) stands on the first perpendicular street from the water, if coming from the east. Next door, the English-speaking **Dr Manolis Alexandrakis** (☎ 28320 31770) runs a small clinic and the adjacent pharmacy. There's a well-stocked **lending library**, 250m beyond the youth hostel on the left-hand dirt track.

Waterfront cafe-bars advertise wi-fi. **Ostraco Bar** (☎ 28320 31710; per hr €4; ☀ 9am-late) on the western waterfront has wi-fi and computers; so too **Youth Hostel Plakias** (☎ 28320 32118; per hr €3.60). At the time of writing, however, the only free wi-fi was at **On The Rocks**, a cafe above the western beach, 100m beyond the Ostraco.

Sleeping

Accommodation becomes cheaper the further you go inland from the waterfront. Along with a couple of resort-type hotels, domatia are abundant.

Youth Hostel Plakias (☎ 28320 32118; www.yhplak ias.com; dm incl breakfast €9.50; ☀ Apr-Oct; P ☐ ☎) This is a place where you come for three days and end up staying for three months, and where you make friends for life. It's one of the most unique hostels anywhere, as attested by the variety of ages and nationalities it attracts. Set around a green lawn amidst olive groves, about 500m from the waterfront, this purposefully lazy place has been led for 15 years by English manager Chris Bilson, who fosters an atmosphere of inclusiveness and good cheer, and who's constantly upgrading things. The hostel has eight-bed dorms (total capacity about 60) with fans, excellent toilets and showers (plus wash basins for clothes), while water, wine, beer and soft drinks are available.

Both roads perpendicular to the beach lead to the hostel, which is signposted in places. Book ahead if possible.

Ipokambos (☎ 28320 31525; amoutsos@otenet.gr; s/d €30/40; ☒ P) On the inland road parallel with the waterfront, this collection of spotless rooms with fridge and balconies is run by a very kind old couple. There's private parking behind.

Castello (☎ /fax 28320 31112; r/studio €35/45; ☒ P) This friendly place has cool, clean and fridge-equipped rooms, most with cooking facilities and big shady balconies. Two additional two-bedroom apartments are ideal for families (€50 to €60). Air-con costs an extra €5.

Flisvos Rooms (☎ 28320 31988; www.flisvos-plakias .gr; s/d €35/45; ☒) On the central-eastern waterfront, the Flisvos has tasteful rooms overlooking the sea, and friendly service.

Pension Thetis (☎ 28320 31430; thetisstudios@gmail .com; studio €45-70; ☒) A nice pick for families, these self-catering studios are set around a cool, leafy garden containing a small play park for kids. It's roughly opposite Ipokambos.

Eating

To Xehoristo (☎ 28320 31214; souvlaki €2.60) on the central-eastern waterfront is the local favourite for souvlaki (you must specify 'souvlaki *kalamaki*' when ordering, or you will be given *gyros* – the Greek version of doner kebab). The sound system plays traditional Cretan music, and the happy chefs sing along.

Nikos Souvlaki (☎ 28320 31921; mains €5-8) This bare-bones former souvlaki joint just up from the post office now serves sit-down meals instead, but it's still popular with the hostel crowd.

Taverna Manoussos (☎ 28320 31313; mains €5-9; ☺ 9am-1am) Cretan specialities are prepared at this friendly family-run taverna on the eastern side of the inland road parallel to the waterfront. The energetic, moustachioed owner, Manousos Christodoulakis, also rents simple rooms (double €30).

ourpick Taverna Plateia (☎ 28320 31560; Myrthios; mains €6-9; ☺ 9am-1am) Located in Myrthios village, just above Plakias, this long-time favourite run by the gracious Fredericos Kalogerakis and family enjoys sublime views of the sea far below. Try the wonderful *myzithropitakia* (sweet cheese pies) and octopus *stifadho* (octopus in tomato and wine sauce).

Taverna Christos (☎ 28320 31472; mains €7-10) Nestled amidst the more touristy western-waterfront tavernas, Christos has a romantic tamarisk-shaded terrace and does good Cretan dishes and fresh fish.

Drinking & Entertainment

Plakias' cafes line the waterfront, while the bars – few, but lively – are clustered along the western end.

Ostraco Bar (☎ 28320 31710; ☺ 9am-late) This old favourite on the western waterfront is a small upstairs bar, where gregarious drinking and dancing to the latest pop hits takes place. There's a nice outdoor balcony facing the water.

Joe's Bar (☺ 9am-late) Officially called Nufaro, at the time of writing this was the hostel crowd's local. Despite the dark, warehouse-like interior, it plays a good selection of rock and pop and service is friendly. It's on the central waterfront.

Getting There & Away

In summer seven daily buses come from Rethymno (€4.10, one hour), including an evening one via Preveli (usually not listed on Rethymno bus station's timetables). There are no buses eastward to Frangokastello and Hora Sfakion. The bus stop has a timetable.

Getting Around

Alianthos Rent-a-Car (☎ 28320 32033; www.alianthos -group.com) has Plakias' best selection of vehicles, and island-wide service; it's a block inland on Plakias' western side.

Easy Ride (☎ 28320 20052; www.easyride.gr), close to the post office, has mountain bikes, bicy-

cles, scooters and motorcycles for hire, as does nearby **Anso Travel** (☎ 28320 31712; www.ansotravel .com), which also offers guided walking tours.

AROUND PLAKIAS

Plakias is an excellent base for local activities, ranging from walks and beach adventures to traditional village exploration.

Some 2.5km west of Plakias on the coast, **Souda Beach** is an appealing sandy beach tucked within a lovely cove – often less windy than Plakias' main beach. There are umbrellas and a taverna behind, but it's more relaxed than the main one.

Also nice but more populated is **Damnoni Beach**, behind the striking stone headland that comprises Plakias Bay's eastern edge; further on, **One-Rock Beach** is an idyllic, clothing-optional sandy cove. A coastal path across the headland now allows a circular **coastal walk**, offering stunning sea views. Chris at Youth Hostel Plakias can inform about both the beach and walking trail.

The traditional villages of **Myrthios**, directly above Plakias, and the less visited **Selia**, a few kilometres further west, are two relaxing places for a stroll, with some eating, crafts shops and domatia.

Moni Preveli & Preveli Beach

Μονή Πρέβελη & Παραλία Πρεβελής

With a spectacular location high above the Libyan Sea, 14km east of Plakias and 35km from Rethymno, the well maintained and historic **Moni Preveli** (☎ 28320 31246; www.preveli .org; admission €2.50; ☺ 8am-7.30pm Jun-Oct) stands in tranquil isolation above one of Crete's most famous beaches. Like most Cretan monasteries, it was a centre of anti-Ottoman resistance, and was burned by the Turks during the 1866 onslaught.

History repeated itself after the Battle of Crete in 1941; after many Allied soldiers were sheltered here before being evacuated to Egypt, the Germans plundered the monastery. Preveli's **museum** contains a candelabra presented by grateful British soldiers after the war, along with valuable ecclesiastical objects.

Below the monastery lies the celebrated **Preveli Beach**, a highly photogenic stretch of sand also called Palm Beach (Paralia Finikodasous). It's at the mouth of the Kourtaliotis Gorge, from where the river Megalopotamos slices across it and empties into the Libyan Sea. The palm-lined riverbanks have freshwater pools good for a dip, while rugged cliffs begin where the sands end.

A steep path leads down to the beach (10 minutes) from a car park 1km before Moni Preveli. Alternatively, drive 5km down a signposted dirt road from a stone bridge just off the Moni Preveli main road. It ends at **Amoudi Beach**, from where you can walk west along a 500m track over the headland to reach Preveli.

In summer, four daily buses go from Rethymno to Preveli (€4.10, 40 to 45 minutes).

Spili Σπίλι
pop 640

A pretty mountain village with cobbled streets, rustic houses and plane trees, Spili (*spee*-lee) is 30km southeast of Rethymno, but much closer to Plakias and Preveli.

It has two ATMs and a post office, and its medical clinic also covers this part of southern Crete.

Spili's unique Venetian fountain spurts pure spring water from 19 lion heads. The village sees tourist buses during the day, but quietens down by evening. If you're looking for a bucolic inland base for operations, there are good sleeping and eating options here.

The bus stop is south of the square. Check email at Café Babis, near the fountain.

SLEEPING & EATING

Heracles Rooms (☎ /fax 28320 22411; heraclespapadakis@ hotmail.com; s/d €29/40; ❄) Has spotless, nicely furnished rooms with window screens, fridge and air-con, plus great mountain views.

Costas Inn (☎ 28320 22040; d incl breakfast €35) These well kept, pleasant rooms have ceiling fans and some amenities. Some offer a fridge.

Yianni's (☎ 28320 22707; mains €4-7) Past the fountain, Yianni's has a courtyard setting and excellent traditional cooking; try the delicious rabbit in wine, mountain snails and house red.

Panorama (☎ 28320 22555) This excellent traditional taverna, run by Pantelis Vasilakis and his wife Calliope, lies on the eastern outskirts. Try the homemade bread and Cretan specialities such as kid goat with *horta* (wild greens).

GETTING THERE & AWAY

From both Preveli and Plakias (following different roads) it's a little over 20km and a 30-minute drive from either place to Spili. There are four daily buses from Rethymno (€4, one hour).

AGIOS PAVLOS & TRIOPETRA
ΑΓΙΟΣ ΠΑΥΛΟΣ & ΤΡΙΟΠΕΤΡΑ

Idyllic, pristine and very remote, the beaches of Agios Pavlos and Triopetra have long been popular with yoga and meditation groups. However, if you're driving, they aren't particularly hard to access, via the village of Kato Saktouria (along the Spili–Agia Galini road), about 53km southeast of Rethymno. Surrounded by sand dunes and dramatic, red-rock cliffs, the coast here is certainly one of Crete's most beautiful places, ideal for escapists; the permanent local population is somewhere in the low single digits.

Agios Pavlos, the 'major' settlement, consists of a sandy cove overlooked by a few rooms, one shop, and tavernas. Better beaches are on the subsequent sandy coves, about a 10-minute walk over the western cliffs; like Plakias, strong summer winds are common.

These coves stretch west to the three giant rocks rising from the sea that give **Triopetra** its name. This junior settlement is populated by a single, though excellent, set of domatia and two tavernas above its placid sandy beach. From Agios Pavlos, it's a 3km drive along a paved road. Another 12km-long windy asphalt road from Akoumia village, west of Kato Saktouria on the Rethymno–Agia Galini road, also accesses Triopetra's westernmost beaches.

The all-encompassing silence at night and boundless starry sky, especially at Triopetra, add to the sensuous spirituality of the place, which even nonyogic visitors might appreciate. This is truly a magical spot, far from the distractions of the outside world, where you can experience southern Crete's desolate beauty at its most essential.

Sleeping & Eating

our pick **Taverna Pensione Pavlos** (☎ /fax 28310 25189, 6945998101; www.triopetra.com.gr; d/tr/q €35/37/45; P ❄) Some guests book three years in advance here. These simple rooms and terrace restaurant overlooking the sea remain the singular passion of owner Pavlos Kakogiannakis – now ably assisted by his kind, English-speaking son, Giorgos. The rooms are well maintained, with kitchenettes and sea-view balconies. The taverna serves local meat, home-grown organic produce, fish and lobster; since Pavlos is usually boating at dawn to check the nets, you'll only get fresher fish if you catch it yourself. It's best to 'reserve' a fish for dinner in the morning, before they're all taken. You'll encounter the taverna immediately after entering from Agios Pavlos.

Agios Pavlos Hotel & Taverna (☎ 28320 71104; www .agiospavloshotel.gr; d €40) This family-run place in Agios Pavlos is the area's main accommodation, and has a small shop selling basic supplies. The shady terrace, overlooking the beach, is bedecked with colourful hammocks and fruit drinks, creating an offbeat New-Age-meets-South-Seas kind of vibe.

The main building's simple rooms have small balconies overlooking the sea, plus rooms under the terrace below the taverna; it serves good Cretan food (*mayirefta* €5 to €8). The cafe-bar next door has internet.

Enquire at Agios Pavlos Hotel & Taverna about the large, self-contained studios on the facing cliff – the **Kavos Melissa complex** (r €45). A couple of slightly cheaper domatia exist higher above the beach, on the entry road.

AGIA GALINI ΑΓΙΑ ΓΑΛΗΝΗ
pop 1260

Further east of Agios Pavlos from the main road, the former fishing port of Agia Galini (*a-ya ga-lee-nee*) has lost much of its charm due to overdevelopment and package tourism. It's nothing like the rowdy north-coast party zones of Malia and Hersonisos; while both have large British contingents, Agia Galini is reserved more for the parents of the kids who flock to those places.

Agia Galini has a nice ambience at night, when the lights of its domatia, bars and tavernas flicker over the sea. It has a decent but crowded town beach (though boat excursions reach better beaches), and makes a convenient base for visiting Phaestos, Agia Triada, Agios Pavlos and Matala.

Orientation & Information

For information online, visit www.agia -galini.com. The bus station stands atop the entrance road, the post office is just past it. Agia Galini has ATMs and travel agencies with currency exchange, plus cafes with internet access, including **Hoi Polloi** (☎ 28320 91102; per hr €4; ◷ 9am-late).

Sleeping

Agia Galini Camping (☎ 28320 91386; camp sites per adult/tent €5/4; ⬛ ⬛) Next to the beach, 2.5km east of town, this well-run camping ground is shaded and has a pool, restaurant and minimarket.

Stohos Rooms & Taverna (☎ 28320 91433; www .stohos.gr; d incl breakfast €40-45; ⬛ ⬛) On the main beach, Stohos has self-catering apartments upstairs with big balconies, and huge studios downstairs ideal for families or groups. The excellent taverna serves *kleftiko* and other clay-oven Cretan specialities (€7 to €10).

Adonis (☎ 28320 91333; www.agia-galini.com; r €50-120; ⬛ ⬛ ⬛) This pool-equipped hotel spread over several buildings has light and clean rooms, studios and apartments, some with sea-view balconies.

Eating

Madame Hortense (☎ 28320 91351; dishes €6-13) Agia Galini's most atmospheric and elegant restaurant stands atop the three-level Zorbas complex, enjoying great harbour views. Cuisine is primarily Greek-Mediterranean.

Kostas (☎ 28320 91323; fish €6-27) Right on the beach at the eastern end, this established fish taverna decorated in classic blue and white is always packed with locals. It has numerous mezedhes, and pricey but excellent seafood.

Faros (☎ 28320 91346; fish €7-12) Inland from the harbour, this classic *psarotaverna* (fish tavern) prepares fresh fish (from €45 per kilogram) plus grills and *mayirefta*.

Getting There & Away

In summer, six daily buses serve Iraklio (€7.40, two hours), six to Rethymno (€5.60, 1½ hours) and five to Phaestos and Matala (€3, 40 to 45 minutes).

Daily summer boats from the harbour reach the beaches of Agios Georgios, Agiofarango and Preveli Beach (€4 to €30).

WESTERN CRETE

The west is the real Crete. Proud locals will tell you so, and they certainly can make a case for the claim. Hania, the prefecture's capital, is Crete's most beautiful and historic town, with a gorgeous old Venetian quarter at its core. The father of modern Greece, Eleftherios Venizelos, hailed from there, and the general area had spawned centuries of rebels against Venetian and Turkish rule long before him.

Also in the west, the spectacular Samaria Gorge is the most famous of several enormous canyons that stretch through rugged terrain into the Libyan Sea on the southern coast, where offbeat Hora Sfakion remains Crete's spiritual capital, obstinately upholding tradition across its stony village hinterland of Sfakia. The west also boasts Crete's most stunning beaches, while you can live large without much care (or cash) in quiet coastal villages like Paleohora and Sougia.

HANIA XANIA

pop 53,370

Hania (hahn-*yah*; also spelt Chania) is Crete's most evocative city, with its pretty Venetian quarter, criss-crossed by narrow lanes, culminating at a magnificent harbour. Remnants of Venetian and Turkish architecture abound, with old townhouses now restored, transformed into atmospheric restaurants and boutique hotels.

Although all this beauty means the Old Town is deluged with tourists in summer, it's still a great place to unwind. Excellent local handicrafts mean there's good shopping, too.

Crete's second biggest city, Hania is also the major transit point for hikers doing the Samaria Gorge, and is the main transport hub for all western destinations. While a few package-tourist resorts line the beaches west of town, they're much less noticeable than the Iraklio-area resorts.

History

Minoan Kydonia occupied the hill east of Hania's harbour, and was probably both a palace site and important town (as suggested by clay tablets with Linear B script discovered here). Although Kydonia was destroyed together with most other Minoan settlements in 1450 BC, it would flourish throughout Hellenistic, Roman and Byzantine times.

In the early 13th century Crete's new Venetian rulers renamed it La Canea. The massive fortifications they constructed were impressive but couldn't keep the Turks from invading, after a two-month siege, in 1645. When Ottoman rule ended in 1898, the great powers made Hania Crete's capital; Iraklio replaced it only in 1971.

German bombers did significant damage during WWII, but much of the Old Town survives.

Orientation

Hania's bus station is on Kydonias, two blocks southwest of Plateia 1866, from where the Old Harbour is a short walk north up Halidon.

Most accommodation lies in the Old Town's western half. Hania's headland separates the Venetian port from the modern town's crowded beach, Nea Hora. Koum Kapi, in the old Turkish quarter further east, has waterfront cafes; above it, on busy Leoforos Eleftherios Venizelos, is the Halepa district, once an upscale residential and consular district where Venizelos used to live (his home is now a museum).

Boats to Hania dock 7km southeast, at Souda.

Information

BOOKSHOPS

Mediterraneo Bookstore (☎ 28210 86904; Akti Koundourioti 57) Has English-language books on Crete, novels, and indispensable Anavasi hiking maps.

Pelekanakis (☎ 28210 92512; Halidon 98) Has maps and multilingual guidebooks.

EMERGENCY

Hania Hospital (☎ 28210 22000; Mournies) Somewhat chaotic modern hospital 5km south; take public bus or taxi (€8 to €10).

Tourist police (☎ 28210 73333; Kydonias 29; ⏰ 8am-2.30pm) By the Town Hall.

INTERNET ACCESS

Triple W (☎ 28210 93478; Valadinon & Halidon; per hr €2; ⏰ 24hr)

Vranas Internet (☎ 28210 58618; Agion Deka 10; per hr €2; ⏰ 9.30am-1am)

INTERNET RESOURCES

www.chania.gr Municipality website; has general info and cultural events calendar.

www.chania-guide.gr More online information.

LAUNDRY

Old Town Laundromat (☎ 28210 59414; Karaoli Dimitriou 38; wash & dry €7; 9am-2pm & 6-9pm Mon-Sat) Also does dry cleaning.

LEFT LUGGAGE

KTEL bus station (☎ 28210 93052; Kydonias 73-77; per day €1.50)

MONEY

Most banks are in the new city, but ATMs exist in the Old Town on Halidon.

HANIA

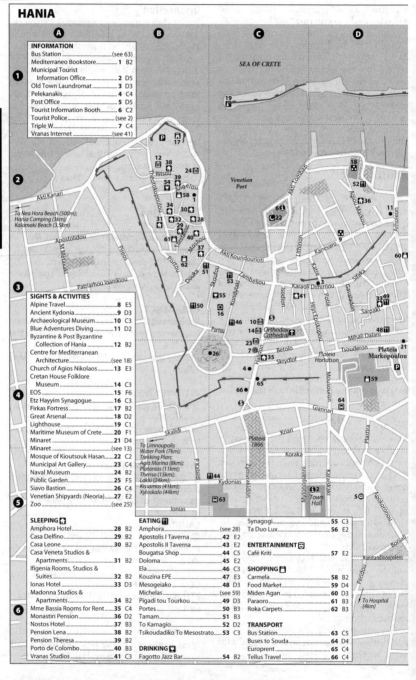

POST
Post office (☎ 28210 28445; Peridou 10; ⏰ 7.30am-8pm Mon-Fri, 7.30am-2pm Sat)

TOURIST INFORMATION & TRAVEL AGENCIES
Municipal Tourist Information Office (☎ 28210 36155; tourism@chania.gr; Kydonias 29; ⏰ 8am-2.30pm) Provides information and maps. The Old Harbour's information booth operates between noon and 2pm.
Tellus Travel (☎ 28210 91500; Halidon 108; www .tellustravel.gr; ⏰ 8am-11pm) Hires out cars, changes money, arranges air and boat tickets, accommodation and excursions.

Sights
MUSEUMS
Hania's **Archaeological Museum** (☎ 28210 90334; Halidon 30; admission €2, incl Byzantine collection €3; ⏰ 8.30am-3pm Tue-Sun), in the impressive 16th-century Venetian Church of San Francisco, is marked by a Turkish fountain attesting to its former incarnation as a mosque. Its collection of finds from western Crete dating from the Neolithic to the Roman era includes statues, vases, jewellery, three splendid floor mosaics and some impressive painted sarcophagi from Armeni's Late Minoan cemetery.

The **Naval Museum** (☎ 28210 91875; Akti Koundourioti; admission €3; ⏰ 9am-4pm), housed in the headland's Firkas Fortress (once a Turkish prison) exhibits model ships dating from the Bronze Age, naval instruments, paintings, photographs and Battle of Crete memorabilia. Similarly, the **Maritime Museum of Crete** (☎ 28210 91875; Akti Defkaliona; ⏰ 10am-3pm, 7-10.30pm), housed in the former Venetian shipyards, documents ancient and traditional shipbuilding.

The **Byzantine & Post Byzantine Collection of Hania** (☎ 28210 96046; Theotokopoulou; admission €2, incl Archaeological Museum €3; ⏰ 8.30am-3pm Tue-Sun), in the fortress' restored Church of San Salvatore, contains a fascinating collection of artefacts, icons, jewellery and coins, including a fine mosaic floor and a prized icon of St George slaying the dragon.

The **Cretan House Folklore Museum** (☎ 28210 90816; Halidon 46; admission €2; ⏰ 9.30am-3pm & 6-9pm) contains traditional crafts and implements, including weavings.

Some 1.5km away in the Halepa neighbourhood, the **Eleftherios Venizelos Residence & Museum** (☎ 28210 56008; Plateia Helena Venizelou; admission €2; ⏰ 10.30am-1.30pm & 6.30-9pm Mon-Fri,

CRETE

10.30am-1.30pm Sat & Sun) preserves the great statesman's home in splendid fashion, with original furnishings, maps and other information. Staff provide a guided tour. Take a public bus, or taxi (€3 to €6) to get there. Hours are reduced in winter.

OTHER ATTRACTIONS

Hania's massive **Venetian Fortifications** are impressive. Best preserved is the western wall, running from the **Firkas Fortress** to the **Siavo Bastion**. The bastion offers good views of the Old Town (enter through the Naval Museum).

The restored Venetian **lighthouse** at the entrance to the harbour is a 1.5km walk around the sea wall. On the inner harbour's eastern side, the prominent **Mosque of Kioutsouk Hasan** (also called Mosque of Janissaries) holds regular art exhibitions. Along the eastern waterfront, the hulking **Venetian Shipyards** (in Greek, 'neoria') languish, mostly unrepaired, though the easternmost portion is now the Maritime Museum. Although one can only gaze at these massive, somewhat Gothic-looking arched structures from without, their impressive size reaffirms La Serenissima's erstwhile maritime might.

The well-restored Venetian **Great Arsenal** houses the **Centre for Mediterranean Architecture**, which hosts regular events and exhibitions. Similarly, Hania's **Municipal Art Gallery** (☎ 28210 92294; www.pinakothiki-chania.gr; Halidon 98; ☺ 10am-2pm & 7-10pm Mon-Fri, 10am-2pm Sat; admission €2, Wed free) hosts exhibitions of modern Greek art.

The restored **Etz Hayyim Synagogue** (Parodos Kondylaki; ☎ 28210 86286; www.etz-hayyim-hania.org; ☺ 10am-8pm Tue-Fri, 5pm-8pm Sun, 10am-3pm & 5-8pm Mon) memorialises Hania's former Jewish population, victims of the Nazi occupation.

Just up from the eastern waterfront, the formerly Turkish **Splantzia quarter** is a relaxing spot, where the colourful, narrow streets and leafy squares now host boutique hotels, galleries, cafes and bars.

Here, on Daliani, stands one of Hania's two remaining **minarets**; the other, past a *kafeneio* on Plateia 1821, is quite memorably attached to the **Church of Agios Nikolaos** (Plateia 1821; ☺ 7am-noon & 4-7pm). Towering over the church's opposite end is a belltower. Strung along in the air across the centre of it all are flapping, intertwined flags of Greece and Byzantium, a cheery display of blues and yellows that seems to festively reassert the final victory of

Orthodoxy over both former occupiers, the schismatic Venetians and the infidel Turks.

The church's foundations were laid in 1205 by Venetians, but Franciscan monks (in 1320) can probably be credited with the massive structure's curving ceiling and array of stained-glass windows, which filter a beautiful, kaleidoscopic flood of colour across the floor in late afternoon. In 1645 the Ottoman's made the church into a mosque, but the Orthodox Church recovered it in 1918.

Finally, the **Ancient Kydonia** site east of the old harbour has few remains, though excavations continue.

Activities

EOS (☎ 28210 44647; www.eoshanion.gr; Tzanakaki 90), the Greek Mountaineering Association's local branch, gives info about serious treks and climbs in the Lefka Ori, mountain refuges and the Trans-European E4 trail. It runs weekend excursions.

Friendly, English-speaking **Manolis Mesarchakis** (☎ 69769 92921; mesarchas@yahoo.gr), an alpine ski instructor and hiker, provides valuable information and can help arrange guided trips for those hungry for outdoors challenges tougher than the Samaria Gorge (see also the boxed text, p493).

Trekking Plan (☎ 28210 60861; www.cycling.gr), 8km west in Agia Marina, organises treks to the Agia Irini and Imbros gorges, climbs of Mt Gingilos, mountain-bike tours, canyoning, rappelling, rock climbing and kayaking trips. **Alpine Travel** (☎ 28210 50939; www.alpine.gr; Boniali 11-19) also organises treks.

Blue Adventures Diving (☎ 28210 40608; www .blueadventuresdiving.gr; Arholeon 11) offers a PADI certification course (€370) and daily diving trips (two dives €80), including beginner dives. Snorkelling and cruise options are offered too. Some of the popular dives take place just 6km west of Hania and include sea cave visits where unique endemic pink coral can be seen and seals occasionally visit.

Hania for Children

The **public garden**, between Tzanakaki and Dimokratias, has a playground, a shady cafe, and a small **zoo** with two *kri-kri* (endemic Cretan wild goats). The giant water park **Limnoupolis** (☎ 28210 33246; Varypetro; day pass adult/child 6-12yr €17/12, afternoon pass €12/9; ☺ 10am-7pm) south of town is also entertaining. Buses leave regularly from the bus station (€1.70).

Tours

Boat excursions to the nearby **Agii Theodorou and Lazaretto islets,** and across the Gulf of Hania, leave from the harbour. The **M/S Irini** (☎ 28210 52001; cruises €15, sunset cruises €8, child under 7yr free) runs daily cruises on a lovely 1930s cruiser, including free snorkelling gear, and sunset cruises with complimentary fruit and *raki*. However, the advertised glass-bottomed boat tours aren't worth it.

Sleeping

Hania has evocative and memorable digs – you may linger longer than expected. However, if planning to visit out of high season, check ahead as many places may not operate year-round.

BUDGET

Hania Camping (☎ 28210 31138; camhania@otenet.gr; Agii Apostoli; caravan/camp sites per adult/child/tent €7/5/4; **P** **⊠**), 3km west of town on the beach, is shaded and has a restaurant, bar and minimarket and pool. Take a Kalamaki Beach bus (every 15 minutes) from the southeast corner of Plateia 1866.

Pension Theresa (☎/fax 28210 92798; Angelou 2; r €40-50; **⊠** **⊛**) Run by the kindly retired doctor Georgios Nikitas, this creaky old house with a steep spiral staircase and antique furniture oozes atmosphere. Some rooms have a view, though the best is from the rooftop terrace (which has a communal kitchen). Rooms have TV, air-con and lofts with an extra bed, though some are snug. It's small, so book ahead.

Monastiri Pension (☎/fax 28210 41032; Agiou Markou 18 & Kanevarou; d & tr €40-65; **⊠**) This older budget place has a stone arched entry and antique family furniture in the communal area. Bathrooms are a basic add-on, but rooms have fridge and some have air-con. The front rooms have sea-view balconies.

Vranas Studios (☎ 28210 58618; www.vranas.gr; Agion Deka 10; studio €40-70; **⊠** **⌨**) Vranas has spacious, immaculate self-catering studios with polished wooden floors, balconies, and all mod cons (plus an internet cafe attached).

Casa Veneta Studios & Apartments (☎ 28210 90007; www.casa-veneta.gr; Theotokopoulou 57; studio/apt €50/60; **☼** April-Oct; **⊛**) This old-town place has new, freshly painted self-catering rooms on three levels, and friendly service. Wi-fi works in the reception area. Prices drop in low season.

Pension Lena (☎ 28210 86860; lenachania@hotmail .com; Ritsou 5; s/d €35/55; **⊠**) This friendly pension in an old Turkish building has a cosy, old-world feel with scattered antiques; the front rooms are best.

Also recommended is **Mme Bassia Rooms for Rent** (☎/fax 28210 55087; Betolo 49; d/tr €50/65; **⊠**), with classy rooms in the Old Town and friendly service. Other hole-in-the-wall budget places can be found by pounding the pavement.

MIDRANGE

Ifigenia Rooms, Studios & Suites (☎ 28210 94357; www.ifigeniastudios.gr; Gamba 23 & Parodos Agelou; studio/ste €50/150; **⊠**) These six refurbished Old Town houses run from simple rooms to fancy suites with kitchenettes, Jacuzzis and views. Some bathrooms are very basic and the decor's a little contrived. A new suite for couples has Jacuzzi and rooftop terrace, though opening the heavy entrance hatch while standing on the spiral staircase below requires considerable dexterity.

Ionas Hotel (☎ 28210 55090; www.ionashotel.com; Sarpaki & Sorvolou; d incl breakfast €60-80, ste incl buffet breakfast €130; **⊠** **⊛**) This boutique hotel in the quiet but hip Splantzia quarter has a contemporary design. Rooms have all mod cons and there's a rooftop terrace.

Madonna Studios & Apartments (☎ 28210 94747; madonnastudios@yahoo.co.uk; Gamba 33; studio €70-110; **⊠**) This charming pension has five traditionally furnished studios with unique individual touches, set around a lovely flower-filled courtyard.

Nostos Hotel (☎ 28210 94743; www.nostos-hotel .com; Zambeliou 42-46; s/d/tr incl breakfast €60/80/120; **⊠**) A renovated 600-year-old Venetian building, the superlative Nostos has split-level self-catering rooms; balcony rooms have harbour views.

our pick **Hotel Doma** (☎ 28210 51772; www .hotel-doma.gr; Venizelos 124; s/d/tr/ste incl breakfast from €65/90/120/150; **☼** 1 Apr-31 Oct; **⊠**). If ever there was a place where one could retreat to write a mystery-suspense novel, this would be it. Long a refuge for famous writers, politicos and actors, the hotel's singularity lies in the original wood floors and furnishings, scattered antiquities, flowering back garden, and even a collection of exotic Asian headdresses. Although it's a 20-minute walk from the centre, public buses serve Halepa (it's at the Attika stop), and there's street parking behind. The

---

MEMORIES OF VENIZELOS

Few people can boast a family home like that of Rena and Ioanna Koutsoudakis. Built in the early 20th century as the Austro-Hungarian Empire's consulate, when Ottoman rule had just ended, it was later purchased by their family and leased to the British in August 1940, who reprised its diplomatic role. During WWII the building was reappropriated by the Germans (less subtly – a bomb in the garden blew out the windows). Then, in 1947, the Koutsoudakis' recovered it – promptly leasing it again to the British.

The Brits left in 1955, however, and the family home would become the Hotel Doma (p487), high in the Halepa district, overlooking the sea and the busy boulevard named after Eleftherios Venizelos, under whose stewardship Greece dramatically enlarged its northern and Aegean territories.

After the catastrophic Megali Idea ('Great Idea') led to the abrupt termination of 2000 years of Greek civilisation in Anatolia, Venizelos returned from a Parisian retirement to lead the Greek delegation that signed the 1923 Treaty of Lausanne, mandating the Greek-Turkish population exchanges. He later served as prime minister again, but died in Paris.

Venizelos experienced a second exile but spent many of his final years in Hania. Kyria Rena recalls Venizelos, then quite old, walking past on his morning constitutional. 'I was a little girl then,' she says, 'and my sister, who was then only two years old, would always rush to the window, at just the moment he would pass by every morning – we would wave excitedly and he would smile; he always waved back.'

She also recalls that one year, on Venizelos' name day, his political supporters promenaded past her house on the way to his home, 'carrying an enormous cake they had baked – of course, in the shape of Crete'.

Despite the partisanship that has chronically marked Greek politics, and other political factions' voluble opposition to Venizelos, when he died in 1936, at 72, there was a great outpouring of grief. In Hania, people hung black in their balconies. 'I remember that many men from the villages came in traditional dress, with knives on their belts, and my mother taking us to Agia Magdalini Church, where Venizelos was lying in state,' recalls Kyria Rena. 'When it was our turn to look in the coffin, she said to me, "Daughter, I want you to look very carefully, for this was a very great man. Look, and don't forget him!" That is a moment I have always remembered.'

---

front-facing rooms and breakfast hall enjoy sea views, while the top-floor suite has its own rooftop terrace, with kaleidoscopic views.

Porto de Colombo (☎ 28210 70945; colompo@otenet. gr; cnr Theofanous & Moshou; d/ste incl breakfast €90/115; 🖳) This Venetian mansion that became the French embassy and Venizelos' office is now a charming boutique hotel with 10 well-appointed rooms; the top suites enjoy fine harbour views.

TOP END

Amphora Hotel (☎ 28210 93224; www.amphora.gr; Parodos Theotokopoulou 20; d with view €140, ste €165; 🖳) This immaculately restored Venetian mansion boasts elegantly decorated rooms, the best being in the main wing, with harbour views. Rooms without a view are cheaper, though all could do with a fridge. Breakfast is €10 extra.

Casa Leone (☎ 28210 76762; www.casa-leone.com; Parodos Theotokopoulou 18; r incl breakfast €130-170; 🖳) This classy former Venetian residence offers

spacious, airy rooms, with balconies overlooking the harbour.

Casa Delfino (☎ 28210 93098; www.casadelfino.com; Theofanous 7; d & apt incl breakfast €200-325; 🖳) The famous Casa Delfino is Hania's most luxurious, housed in an elegant 17th-century Old Town mansion. Breakfast is in the splendid pebble-mosaic courtyard.

Eating

Avoid the mediocre, overpriced waterfront tavernas – the Old Town's back streets conceal some of Crete's finest and most atmospheric restaurants.

Bougatsa Shop (bougatsa €2; ⏰ 6am-2pm) Hania's most delicious *bougatsa*, made with Crete's sweet *myzithra* cheese, has been served since 1924 at this unassuming hole in the wall, opposite the bus station.

Mesogeiako (☎ 28210 59772; Daliani 36; mezedhes €3-6) Also in Splantzia, this trendy *mezedhopoleio* (restaurant specialising in mezedhes) does excellent Cretan appetisers with a twist. Try the pork meatballs with local *raki.*

Kouzina EPE (Daskalogianni 25; mayirefta €3-7; ☽ noon-8pm) This whimsical little place (the name roughly translates as 'Limited Liability Restaurant') at the edge of the Splantzia quarter serves nourishing and tasty *mayirefta.* Much beloved by locals, it's open only for lunch and early dinners.

Tsikoudadiko To Mesostrato (☎ 28210 72783; Zambeliou 31; mezedhes €4-7) There's great atmosphere within the walls of this 400-year-old roofless Venetian structure. The Tsikoudadiko is serenaded by roving musicians, while the crickets chirp in unison as if applauding from the foliage above. Try the snail, sweet red peppers, and fried mushrooms.

Michelas (☎ 28210 90026; mains €5-8; ☽ 10am-4pm Mon-Sat) Near the meat section of the food market (p490), Michelas is an old classic serving inexpensive and authentic Cretan fare.

To Karnagio (☎ 28210 53366; Plateia Katehaki 8; mains €5-10.50) Near the Great Arsenal, this popular outdoor place does good seafood (try the grilled cuttlefish) and classic Cretan dishes.

Doloma (☎ 28210 51196; Kalergon 8; mayirefta €5.50-7; ☽ Mon-Sat) Set amidst vines and foliage on an outdoor terrace, this harbourside place has excellent traditional specialities.

Tamam (☎ 28210 96080; Zambeliou 49; mains €5.50-8.50) Housed in old Turkish baths, Tamam (meaning 'OK' in Turkish) does excellent vegetarian specialities and eastern-influenced dishes. Try the house salad and the Beyendi chicken with creamy aubergine purée.

ourpick **Portes** (☎ 28210 76261; Portou 48; mains €6-9) Everyone visiting Hania must dine here at least once. Set along a quiet lane in the Old Town, this excellent little place run by affable Susanna from Limerick serves Cretan treats with flair. Try the divine *gavros* (marinated anchovies) or stuffed fish baked in paper, or the tasty meatballs with leek and tomato. The homemade bread is excellent too.

Ela (☎ 28210 74128; Kondylaki 47; mains €8-18; ☽ noon-1am) This 14th-century building was a soap factory, then a school, distillery and cheese-processing plant. Now Ela serves Cretan specialities like goat with artichokes, while musicians create ambience.

Pigadi tou Tourkou (☎ 28210 54547; Sarpaki 1-3; mains €10-17; ☽ dinner, closed Mon-Tue) This former steam bath includes the well for which it is named (Well of the Turk); the tantalising dishes have similar tastes of the orient, inspired by Crete, Morocco and the Middle East.

Apostolis I & II Taverna (☎ 28210 43470; Akti Enoseos; fish per kilogram up to €65) In the quieter eastern harbour, this two-building *psarotaverna* is well known for its seafood.

Also recommended is the excellent Amphora restaurant below the hotel of the same name.

Drinking & Entertainment

Clubs lie in Platanias and Agia Marina, 11km west of Hania, though the Old Town has lively bars. Sfrantzia's small streets hide hip new emerging favourites.

Synagogi (☎ 28210 96797; Skoufou 15) In a roofless Venetian building and former synagogue, this cool place with dark stone arches is a favourite of young locals.

Fagotto Jazz Bar (☎ 28210 71877; Angelou 16; ☽ 7pm-2am Jul-May) Down inside a restored Venetian building, this cool bar plays jazz and blues. Being indoors, however, it's busiest in winter.

The arty cafe-bar **Ta Duo Lux** (☎ 28210 52519; Sarpidona 8; ☽ 10am-late) is a favourite with the youths, while the rough-and-ready **Café Kriti**

MAGICAL MYZITHRA

People come to Crete just for its distinctive sweet cheese, *myzithra* (made from sheep's or goat's milk). Often hard to find elsewhere, it's the key ingredient in restaurants' *myzithropitakia* (sweet cheese pies) – crunchy, golden-brown triangles filled with the delicious cheese.

Myzithra is also used in *kalitsounies,* soft, circular breakfast pastries, their centres filled with the cheese and flecked with cinnamon. Find them at *zaharoplasteia* (sweet shops) and bakeries.

Local specialities use *myzithra* too. In the southwestern Sfakia area, the thin *Sfakiani pita,* filled with *myzithra* and topped with honey, is a dessert; however, travel just a bit further west, to Paleohora, and you will find your *myzithropitakia* will probably be made of the sour *xynomyzithra,* according to local custom. Whatever you do, don't leave Crete without partaking in this unique and appetising treat.

HANG ON TO YOUR HATS

One of the most dangerous night-time routes in the Hania area is the 10km road between the city and the popular Platanias resort, with its bars and clubs. Haris, a young Cretan man working as a security guard in Hania Hospital's emergency room, finds the sight of so many people with terrible injuries being rushed through every day very stressful.

'Every summer, we have many cases of emergencies, involving both Greeks and tourists, who are brought here after driving motorbikes while drunk,' says Haris. 'Just the other day, four English girls were brought here after crashing their bike while returning from the disco – two had severely broken legs.' Such mishaps, often perhaps avoidable, add to the burden of the already overworked health care system of this small city.

While it would seem like common sense not to jump on a motorbike when intoxicated, in Crete's summer heat it's no surprise that many motorcyclists don't wear their helmets. You won't be stopped by police for this but a helmet here, as anywhere, might mean the difference between life and death. As Haris remarks, 'In the worst of these emergency cases, the victim might fall into a coma or even die, because they didn't wear a helmet. Those are the saddest cases of all.'

So, when preparing to hit the open road on your Cretan vacation, it's a good idea to remember your helmet. And, if you've drunk too much, it won't kill you to spend €10 on a taxi.

(☎ 28210 58661; Kalergon 22; ☼ 8pm-late) has live traditional Cretan music.

Shopping

Zambeliou and Theotokopoulou have excellent shopping, with traditional artisans often plying their trade. Skrydlof is 'leather lane', and the central market is worth perusing. Hania's magnificent covered **food market** (☼ 9am-5pm Mon & Wed, 9am-8pm Tue, Thu & Fri, 9am-2pm Sat) has an excellent assortment of traditional Cretan food and drink, herbs, meats and veg; the market should be seen, even if you aren't buying.

Carmela (☎ 28210 90487; Angelou 7) This exquisite store features original jewellery designs, plus Carmela's unique ceramics using ancient techniques. It also has jewellery and ceramics by leading Greek artists.

Paraoro (☎ 28210 88990; Theotokopoulou 16) This functioning workshop features distinctive, decorative metal boats, and some unique ceramics.

Roka Carpets (☎ 28210 74736; Zambeliou 61) Observe master weaver Mihalis Manousakis at work on his 400-year-old loom, and know you're buying genuine, handwoven rugs and other items.

Miden Agan (☎ 28210 27068; www.midenaganshop.gr; Daskalogianni 70; ☼ 10am-3.30pm Mon & Wed, ☼ 10am-2.15pm & 6.15-10pm Tue & Thu-Sat) Unique 'house' wine and liquors, along with over 800 Greek wines, are sold at this smattering of foods shops, which also offers local gourmet delights.

Getting There & Away

AIR

Hania's airport (CHQ) is 14km east of town on the Akrotiri Peninsula. Flights only go to/from Athens and Thessaloniki. For flight details, see Island Hopping (p749).

BOAT

For information on ferries from Hania (serving Piraeus only), see Island Hopping (p749). The **port police** (☎ 28210 89240) can also provide ferry information.

Hania's main port is 7km southeast at Souda; frequent buses (€1.15) serve Hania, as do taxis (€8 to €10).

BUS

In summer, buses depart from Hania's **bus station** (KTEL; ☎ 28210 93052) during the week for numerous destinations. See the table, opposite.

Getting Around

Three daily buses serve the airport (€2.60, 20 minutes); taxis cost €18 to €20.

Local blue buses (☎ 28210 27044) meet incoming ferries at Souda port, leaving from outside Hania's food market (€1.30). Buses for western beaches leave from the main bus station.

Halidon has motorcycle-hire outlets, though Agia Marina firms offer competitive rates and can bring cars to Hania. The old town is largely pedestrianised, so find the free parking area near the Firkas Fortress (turn right off Skalidi where the big super-

BUS SERVICES FROM HANIA

Destination	Duration	Fare	Frequency
Elafonisi	2½hr	€9.60	1 daily
Falasarna	1½hr	€6.50	3 daily
Hora Sfakion	1hr 40min	€6.50	3 daily
Iraklio	2¾hr	€10.70	half-hourly
Kissamos	1hr	€4	13 daily
Moni Agias Triadas	30min	€2	2 daily
Omalos (for Samaria Gorge)	1hr	€5.90	3 daily
Paleohora	1hr 50min	€6.50	4 daily
Rethymno	1hr	€6	half-hourly
Sougia	1hr 50min	€6.10	2 daily
Stavros	30min	€1.80	3 daily

market car park is signposted, and continue to the waterfront).

You can hire cars from the following outfits:

Europrent (☎ 28210 27810; Halidon 87)

Tellus Travel (☎ 28210 91500; www.tellustravel.gr; Halidon 108) Also sells aeroplane tickets and runs excursions around the island.

AROUND HANIA

Northeast of Hania, the less visited **Akrotiri Peninsula** hosts the airport, port and a NATO base. Approximately 1500 British, Australian and New Zealand soldiers died here during the Battle of Crete; they are buried at Souda's **military cemetery**. Buses to Souda port leaving from outside the Hania food market pass this solemn place.

Near Akrotiri's northern tip, sandy **Stavros Beach** is good for a dip and famous as the dramatic backdrop for the final dancing scene in *Zorba the Greek*. From Hania, six daily buses serve Stavros beach (€2).

Straight south of Hania, the mountain village of **Theriso** was the site of a 1905 uprising against Crete's Royalist administration, through which Eleftherios Venizelos came to fame. Although the occasional taverna 'Greek night' with bussed-in package tourists can ruin the ambience, it's usually a peaceful place, and the drive passes through wonderful wooded territory. The road hugs the **Theriso Gorge**, good for hiking (check with Hania's EOS, p486).

The road from Hania to Crete's more famous Samaria Gorge (right) is truly spectacular. It heads through orange groves to Fournes, where you fork left to **Meskla**. The main road reaches **Lakki** (a total of 24km from Hania),

an unspoilt Lefka Ori (White Mountains) village with stunning views. Lakki was a centre of resistance against the Turks and later the Germans.

From Lakki, the road continues to **Omalos** and **Xyloskalo**, where the Samaria Gorge starts. Many hikers sleep in Omalos to ensure they'll get the earliest start possible. Here, the big, stone-built **Hotel Exari** (☎ 28210 67180; s/d €20/30) has well-furnished rooms with TV, bathtub and balconies. Owner Yiorgos can drive hikers to Samaria's trailhead and offers luggage delivery to Sougia for groups. Nearby, the **Hotel Gingilos** (☎ 28210 67181; s/d/tr €20/25/35) offers more sparse, but clean and large rooms (the triples are huge), with nice timber furniture and central balcony. Both hotels have tavernas.

The EOS-maintained **Kallergi Hut** (☎ 28210 33199; dm members/nonmembers €10/13), in the hills between Omalos and the Samaria Gorge, makes a good base for exploring Mt Gingilos and surrounding peaks.

SAMARIA GORGE ΦΑΡΑΓΓΙ ΤΗΣ ΣΑΜΑΡΙΑΣ

Although you'll have company (over 1000 people per day in summer), hiking the **Samaria Gorge** (☎ 28210 67179; admission €5; ☼ 6am-3pm May–mid-Oct), remains an experience to remember. Also remember to check climatic conditions in advance – many aspiring hikers have been disappointed when park officials close Samaria on exceptionally hot days.

At 16km, the Samaria (sah-mah-rih-*ah*) Gorge is supposedly Europe's longest. Beginning just below the Omalos Plateau, it's carved out by the river that flows between Avlimanakou (1857m) and Volakias (2116m) peaks. Samaria's width varies from 150m to

3m, and its containing cliffs reach 500m in height. Numerous wild flowers bloom in April and May.

Samaria also shelters endangered species like Crete's beloved wild goat, the *kri-kri*. Surviving in the wild only here, the islet of Dia, north of Iraklio, and on the eastern islet of Kri-Kri, near Agios Nikolaos, the *kri-kri* is shy and seldom seen. To save it from extinction, the gorge became a national park in 1962.

Hiking the Gorge

You can start early (before 8am) to avoid crowds, though even the first morning bus from Hania can be packed; sleeping in Omalos (p491) and getting an early lift from there allows you to get your toe on the line for the starting gun. Camping is forbidden, so time your trek (from 4½ to six hours) to finish by closing time (3pm).

Wear good hiking boots, and take sunscreen, sunglasses, hat and water bottle (springs with good water exist, though not the main stream). If it's too hard within the first hour, donkey-equipped park wardens can take you back. Look out for the elusive *kri-kri*, and for falling rocks; people have died from the latter (and from foolishly wandering off the main trail into the remote mountains).

You'll begin at **Xyloskalo**, named for the steep stone pathway flanked by wooden rails that enters the gorge, and finish at **Agia Roumeli** on the southern coast. In spring, wading through a stream is sometimes necessary; in summer, when the flow drops, the streambed rocks become stepping stones.

The gorge is wide for the first 6km, until the abandoned village of **Samaria**; its inhabitants were relocated when the gorge became a national park. Just south stands a small church dedicated to **Saint Maria of Egypt**, the gorge's namesake.

The going then narrows and becomes more dramatic until, at the 11km mark, the canyon walls shrink to only 3.5m apart – the famous **Iron Gates** (Sidiroportes). A rickety wooden pathway takes you 20m across the water to the other side. At 12.5km, the gorge ends north of almost abandoned **Old Agia Roumeli**. From here the final 2km hike to Agia Roumeli is less exciting, though most hikers will at that point just be anticipating the refreshing dip they'll take at this relaxed seaside village.

From Agia Roumeli, hikers must take a boat; most go to Sougia (and from there to

Hania by bus), though you can also reach Hora Sfakio, Loutro and Paleohora.

Agia Roumeli also has accommodation and eating, should you wish to stay over. **Farangi Restaurant** (☎ 28250 91225; mains €5-8.50) has excellent Cretan specials and rents simple but clean rooms (double/triple €30/35; air-conditioned) above, while **Gigilos Taverna & Rooms** (☎ 28250 91383; gigilos@mycosmos.gr; s/d/tr €30/35/45; ❄ 💻) on the beach has nicely furnished rooms with bathrooms, and a communal fridge. The taverna (mains €5 to €7) has a relaxing beachfront terrace.

Getting There & Away

Samaria Gorge excursions are organised by innumerable travel agencies and resorts across Crete. 'Samaria Gorge Long Way' is the regular trek from Omalos, while 'Samaria Gorge Easy Way' starts at Agia Roumeli, looping back at the Iron Gates. However, going independently, ideally from Hania or Omalos itself, is cheaper and allows more options.

Hania–Omalos buses to Xyloskalo (Omalos; €5.90, 1½ hours) leave from Hania at 6.15am, 7.30am, and 8.30am. A direct bus to Xyloskalo from Paleohora in the southwest (€5.50, 1½ hours) leaves at 6.15am.

When you finish the hike in Agia Roumeli, two daily afternoon boats to Hora Sfakion (€7.50, one hour, 3.45pm and 6pm) via Loutro (€7, 45 minutes) are timed to meet buses going back to Hania. A morning boat also runs from Paleohora to Hora Sfakion, via Agia Roumeli, if you end up sleeping over.

Alternatively, take the boat west to Paleohora (€14, 1½ hours) at 4.45pm, via Sougia (€8, 45 minutes). The **ticket office** (☎ 28250 91251) is on the port.

HORA SFAKION ΧΩΡΑ ΣΦΑΚΙΩΝ

pop 350

The more bullet holes you see in the passing road signs, the closer you are to Hora Sfakion (*ho-rah sfah-kee-on*). This eccentric, laid-back fishing port, a stopping-off point for returning Samaria Gorge hikers, is (along with Anogia) the island's most proudly 'Cretan' town. And, when surveying the barren moonscape of the surrounding territory (known as Sfakia), you do have to give the Sfakians credit; not only have they survived for time eternal in this inhospitable terrain, they also built a fighting force of extraordinary magnitude, keeping the Turks out for centuries.

EPIC ADVENTURES IN THE CRETAN WILDS

If you think Samaria is for wimps, head for the lesser-visited gorges south of Hania. They offer unparalleled opportunities for mountain treks, caving, rock climbing and even skiing in winter – though even seasoned pros will need local information and advice to ensure their safety and get the best from their experience.

The **Anavasi hiking maps**, marked with GPS coordinates, trails and other key details, are essential; most bookshops recommended in this guide sell them. Another book found mostly in Hania bookshops, *The Caves of Hania*, is recommended by local cavers.

Manolis Mesarchakis (p486), an alpine ski instructor and avid hiker from Hania, can help arrange hiking tours and cross-country ski tours (ski tours with three weeks' advance notice; €100) and advise serious outdoors adventurers. Hikers should also consult the **EOS** (p486) in Hania, which provides info, does weekend excursions and arranges stays in mountain refuges.

One of Manolis' favourite hikes is the 10-hour trek from Omalos to Sougia, via the **Trypiti Gorge**. This stunning canyon near Mt Gingilos, west of Samaria, sees few visitors – perfect for those seeking unspoilt nature. If you want to break the hike up into two days, there's a mountain hut along the way.

The sheer rock face of the **Klados Gorge**, running between and parallel to Trypiti and Samaria, 'offers exceptional rock climbing and rappelling', says Manolis. The outdoorsman also notes that 'Crete is a paradise for caving, with over 10,000 caves, including the deepest in Europe, at 1207m deep'.

Although few would expect sweltering Crete to be a ski destination, there's heavy snow in the high mountains, even until May. However, there are no resorts and no lifts, meaning you'll be doing old-school skiing on wild, unroped terrain. If you're capable of doing this stuff, you'll probably already know to bring your own equipment.

Indeed, after the rest of the island had fallen to the Ottomans, only Sfakia held out (possibly because there was nothing worth conquering in the rocky mountain region). National hero and insurrectionist Ioannis Daskalogiannis was born in the Sfakian village of Anopoli. To this day, the Sfakians cling fiercely to their local customs, culture and dialect; while most Cretans are content to simply assert that they are the best of the Greeks, Sfakia people consider themselves the best of the Cretans – and that's saying something.

Despite its small size, Hora Sfakion makes a relaxing and convenient base for western adventures, with some tasty seafood tavernas and rooms. It's also useful for catching boats further west, or south to Gavdos.

Orientation & Information

The ferry quay is at Hora Sfakion's eastern side, while water taxis leave from the western side; beyond the latter is the decent town beach.

On the eastern bluff, near the ferry ticket booth, a monument commemorates where the last British, Australian and New Zealand soldiers were evacuated after the WWII Battle of Crete. There are lovely views of the village wrapped up by its sheltering bay from here.

Buses leave from the square; if driving, park here, as vehicles aren't allowed on the waterfront promenade, where seafront tavernas and shops stretch under a long trellis that keeps the street shady. The **post office** (7am-2pm) is on the square. There are two ATMs.

Just in from the promenade's eastern side, Englishwoman Maxine Kolioveta owns a nameless, unmarked **souvenir shop** (6970414023; 9am-3pm). Among other unique gifts sold here, she does lovely, hand-etched cards, decorated with traditional Cretan motifs like violins and fishing boats.

Maxine also carries an engaging new book, *In Sfakia: Passing Time in the Wilds of Crete* (Lycabettus Press, 2008). Written by British linguist and long-time visitor Peter Trudgill, this easygoing narrative recounts the author's experiences with the proud Sfakians since the mid-1970s, and is very informative for local history. For those keen on Greek linguistics, a book consisting of about 200 pages of unique Sfakian dialect terms and phrases – some dating to Venetian, Byzantine and even Ancient Greek times – is sold here, too.

Sleeping & Eating

Hora Sfakion has a few hotels and domatia. Its waterfront tavernas are fairly similar, and specialise in fresh fish. Be sure to try the *Sfakiani pita* (sfakian pie) – a thin, circular pie with sweet *myzithra* cheese and flecked with honey.

Rooms Stavris (☎ 28250 91220; stavris@sfakia-crete .com; s/d €25/35; ✷) On the port's western side, this place has clean, basic rooms, most of them self-catering.

our pick Xenia Hotel (☎ 28250 91490, 6972120547; xenia-sfakion@otenet.gr; s/d €40/45; ✷) Friendly Giorgos Lykogiannakis' runs this excellent hotel, ideally set between the harbour and the beach on Sfakia's western side. All 17 of the spacious, airy rooms have sea-view balconies, and bathrooms are modern and well kept. Stairs lead down to the hotel's pebbled sunbathing patio; for swimmers, there's a ladder on the rocks below here, leading into the sea.

Getting There & Away

BOAT

For boat tickets, see the **booths** (☎ 28250 91221) in the car park and on the eastern bluff. In summer, a daily boat serves Paleohora (€11, three hours) via Loutro, Agia Roumeli and Sougia. Four additional boats reach Agia Roumeli (€7.50, one hour) via Loutro (€4, 15 minutes). Summertime boats (€12, 1½ hours) serve Gavdos Island on Friday, Saturday and Sunday at 11.30am.

Local fishermen run **water taxis** upon request to local destinations like Sweet Water Beach and Loutro, generally from the western harbour; enquire at the taverna below the Xenia Hotel.

BUS

Four daily buses connect Hora Sfakion with Hania (€6.50, two hours), the afternoon ones at 5.30pm and 7pm timed to meet incoming boats from Agia Roumeli. Two daily buses in summer serve Rethymno via Vryses (€6.50, one hour), and two more reach Frangokastello Beach (€1.50, 25 minutes). However, no buses serve Plakias or other points further east of this beach.

AROUND HORA SFAKION

A bit beyond town, the famous **Sweet Water Beach** (in Greek, Glyka Nera) has tranquil, lapping waters. Inexpensive taxi boats go there from Hora Sfakion.

Another relaxing escape is **Loutro**, a former fishing village west of town, and southern Crete's only natural port. There's no road, but boats heading west stop there. Merely a collection of white-and-blue domatia glittering around a tiny beach set against mountains, Loutro always maintains its happily isolated feel, even when busy in high summer. For overnights, try the **Blue House** (☎ 28250 91127; bluehouseloutro@chania-cci.gr; d from €45; ✷), with its spacious, well-appointed rooms with sea-facing verandas. The downstairs taverna serves excellent *mayirefta* (€5 to €8), including local specialities.

FRANGOKASTELLO ΦΡΑΓΚΟΚΑΣΤΕΛΛΟ
pop 150

One of Crete's best beaches lies just below the equally magnificent 14th-century fortress of **Frangokastello**, 15km east of Hora Sfakion. The Venetians built it to guard against pirates and feisty Sfakians, who rebelled from the beginning of the occupation. This history has generated a ghastly legend. On 17 May 1828, during the War of Independence, many Cretan fighters were killed here by the Turks. According to legend their ghosts – the *'drosoulites'* – march along the beach each year on the battle's anniversary.

The wide, packed white-sand **beach** beneath the fortress slopes gradually into shallow warm water, making it ideal for kids. On calm days it's delightful, but when the wind's up, flying sand will chase you off quickly. There is one shaded cafe on the beach, but it's otherwise placid.

A few domatia line the main road. **Oasis** (☎ / fax 28250 92136; www.oasisrooms.com), on the western side, offers spacious self-catering rooms set in a lovely garden, and its taverna does excellent Cretan dishes (€6 to €10).

Two daily buses from Hora Sfakion reach Frangokastello (€2).

ANOPOLI & INNER SFAKIA ΑΝΩΠΟΛΗ & ΜΕΣΑ ΣΦΑΚΙΑ

A zigzagging asphalt road winding northwest from Hora Sfakion leads, after 14km, to historic Anopoli (ah-*no*-po-lee). Now a tiny, sparsely settled village in Sfakia's stony interior, Anopoli was once prosperous and powerful, and the birthplace of revolutionary leader Ioannis Daskalogiannis. This dashing character, known for his bravery, even hobnobbed with Russian royalty and in 1770 organised the first Cretan insurrection against the Turks. However, the promised Russian reinforcements never came and Daskalogiannis surrendered himself to save his followers; he was skinned alive in Iraklio.

Today a white statue of Daskalogiannis stands conspicuously on Anopoli's square; here, the heartily recommended **Platanos** (☎ 28250 91169; www.anopolis-sfakia.com; mains €4-9) serves excellent local specialities like roast lamb, wild greens and, of course, *Sfakiani pita* (cheese pie with *myzithra* and honey). English-speaking owner Eva Kopasis, who also rents simple **rooms** (s/d €25/30; 🏠) year-round, is a proud Sfakian and provides information on local activities.

One such activity is the 1½-hour (3.5km-long) hike to the sea through the **Aradena Gorge**. The trail is signposted before the bridge leading to Aradena, on the road west from town. Alternatively, you can park in Anopoli and walk 3km to the trail head. The route is moderately difficult, ending at the lovely **Marmara Beach**. You can return to Anopoli, or go to nearby Loutro and return to Hora Sfakion by boat.

Nonhikers can drive on to **Aradena**, a small, undisturbed hamlet with a rather precarious wood-and-steel bridge that ripples as you cross it. There are great views into the gorge from here. At the end of the road lies the early Byzantine **Church of Agios Ioannis**; this whitewashed structure stands serene amidst the stones of Sfakia, but is unfortunately rarely open.

From here, a hiking path leads to the sea, forking either west to Agia Roumeli (via the Byzantine Church of Agios Pavlos, with stunning views), or east to Marmara Beach and Loutro. Before attempting such hikes, however, it's best to consult local experts (see the boxed text, p493).

If arriving by public transport, take the bus from Hora Sfakion to Anopoli at 4pm (€3, 30 minutes), which originates in Hania. The morning bus from Anopoli returns to Hora Sfakion at 6.30am, and then continues directly to Hania. Alternatively, taxis between the two cost €20.

For other forays into inner Sfakia, head north from Hora Sfakion on the main road that leads to Vryses. This breathtaking tour passes through the eastern Lefka Ori, with the stunning, 8km-long **Imbros Gorge** (admission €2) running parallel to the road on the western side. You'll soon reach the village of **Imbros**, which accesses this lesser-visited gorge; the trail ends at **Komitades** village. From here, it's a 5km walk to Hora Sfakion, or take a taxi (€20).

All Hania–Hora Sfakion buses can stop in Imbros.

SOUGIA ΣΟΥΓΙΑ
pop 110
Sougia (*soo*-yah), 67km south of Hania and on the ferry route between Hora Sfakion and Paleohora, is a tiny, laid-back beach resort with a curving sand-and-pebble beach. Archaeological remains on its eastern end, which prohibit development, have happily kept Sougia quiet. This sort-of resort has a few rooms, tavernas, lazy beach bars and two beach clubs. Campers and nudists accumulate towards the beach's eastern end.

Information
The bus stop is outside the Santa Irene Hotel, and there's an ATM. **Internet Lotos** (☎ 28230 51191; per hr €3) works from 7am until late.

Sleeping
Aretousa (☎ 28230 51178; fax 28230 51178; s/d/studio €35/40/45; 🏠) This lovely, modern pension on the Hania road has comfortable, well-equipped rooms, plus self-catering studios.

Captain George (☎ 28230 51133; g-gentek@otenet .gr; r/studio/tr €35/40/50; 🅿 🏠 💻) Attractive, good value rooms and studios in a lovely garden with a resident *kri-kri*. The owner runs taxi-boat trips to nearby Lissos and other beaches.

Arhontiko (☎ 28230 51200; r €40-50; 🏠) Behind the supermarket, Arhontiko has spacious, attractive new studios and apartments – good for longer stays.

Eating
Taverna Rembetiko (☎ 28230 51510; mezedhes €3-5) This popular place has good Cretan dishes, and great atmosphere with its traditional Greek music.

Polyfimos (☎ 28230 51343; mains €5-8; 🍴 dinner) Tucked off the Hania road behind the police station, ex-hippie Yianni makes his own oil, wine and *raki* and even makes dolmadhes (vine leaves stuffed with rice and sometimes meat) from the vines that cover the shady courtyard.

Getting There & Away

A daily bus operates between Hania and Sougia (€6.10, two hours), while morning boats leave Sougia for Agia Roumeli (€6.30, 1¾ hours), Loutro (€10, 1½ hours) and Hora Sfakion (€11, 1¾ hours). An evening boat at 5.15pm heads west to Paleohora (€7, one hour).

PALEOHORA ΠΑΛΑΙΟΧΩΡΑ

pop 2210

There' still a vaguely 1972 feel about Paleohora (pal-ee-o-*hor*-a), though its former hippie days are long over. This erstwhile fishing port is still a proud Cretan town, though, and an excellent place to enjoy authentic Cretan live music in summer. It has noticeable though low-key tourism, with two good beaches and accommodation ranging from camping grounds to small hotels. On summer evenings, tavernas fill the pretty pedestrianised streets and a couple of lively bars operate.

Although Paleohora gets a few European package tourists, including some families, it's probably Crete's most ambivalent resort. You might hear elderly domatia owners chattering in the back streets, asking rhetorically when the tourists will leave and give them back their peace and quiet. In fact, this relatively large town keeps awake during the winter, and is southwest Crete's unofficial capital.

Orientation & Information

Paleohora lies on a narrow peninsula, with a long sandy beach exposed to the wind on one side, and a sheltered pebbly beach on the other. The main street, Eleftheriou Venizelou, runs north–south. Three ATMs and a laundry are on the main drag. The post office is at Pahia Ammos Beach's northern end. Boats leave from the old harbour at the beach's southern end.

Erato Internet (☎ 28230 83010; Eleftheriou Venizelou; per hr €2)

Notos Rentals (☎ 28230 42110; www.notoscar.com; Eleftheriou Venizelou; per hr €2; ☺ 8am-10pm)

Tourist information office (☎ 28230 41507; ☺ 10am-1pm & 6-9pm Wed-Mon May-Oct)

Sights & Activities

From the elevated ruins of Paleohora's 13th-century **Venetian castle** there are great views of the sea and mountains. The castle's strategic location meant it was frequently attacked over the centuries, and little remains today.

From Paleohora, the E4 **coastal path** leads to Sougia (six hours), passing remnants of

ancient Lissos. Hiking the Samaria and Agia Irini Gorge from Paleohora is possible either through organised tours or the public bus service, returning by ferry.

Dolphin-watching trips (€16) and excursions to **Elafonisi Beach** (€7, one hour) are offered by travel agencies, like the friendly and helpful **Selino Travel** (☎ 28230 42272; selino2@otenet.gr) and **Tsiskakis Travel** (☎ 28230 42110; www.notoscar.com; Eleftheriou Venizelou). Both offer the usual travel agency services.

Sleeping

Most accommodation closes in the low season.

Camping Paleohora (☎ 28230 41120; camp sites per adult/tent €5/3; [P]) Some 1.5km northeast of town, this is a big but basic camping ground.

Camping Grammeno (☎ 6978388542; www.grammenocamping.gr; camp sites per adult/tent €6/4; [P]) This cheery place, 4km from Paleohora on the beach, has excellent facilities including kids' playground, communal kitchen and barbecue, all backed by a cedar forest.

ourpick Homestay Anonymous (☎ 28230 41509; www.anonymoushomestay.com; s/d/tr €19/23/28; ☒) There's excellent value at this small pension with clean, well-furnished rooms with exposed-stone wall decor. Friendly owner Manolis is a font of information on the area. Rooms can connect for families.

Oriental Bay Rooms (☎ 28230 41076; s/d/tr €30/35/38; ☒) These immaculate, beachfront rooms are well maintained and fridge-equipped. They have balconies with sea or mountain views.

Votsalo Rooms (☎ 28230 42369; votsalo@mail.gr; d/apt €35/40; ☒) Near Kyma Restaurant on Paleohora's pebble beach, it has simple but clean rooms with relaxing sea views.

Haris Studios (☎ 28230 42438; www.paleochoraholidays .com; d/apt €45/50; ☺ year-round; ☒) These studios, just around the port on the dramatic rocky seafront, are fairly basic, though the upper rooms are better and enjoy great views.

Eating

The only sad thing about eating in Paleohora and the surrounding area is that, unlike the rest of Crete, the *myzithra* cheese used here is not usually sweet – remember when ordering.

Grammeno (☎ 28230 41505; mains €4.50-11) Drive 5km west of Paleohora for no-nonsense Cretan specialities like braised rooster, various wild greens, lamb in vine leaves and tender roast goat.

CRETE

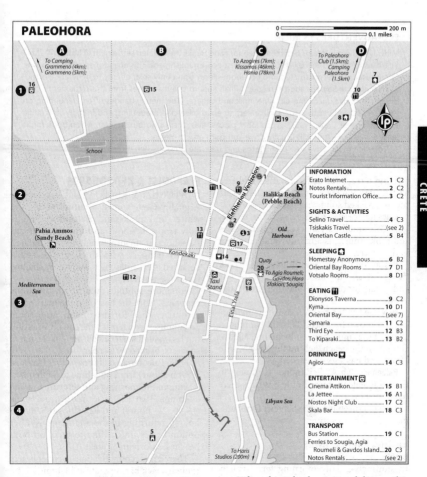

PALEOHORA

To Camping Grammeno (4km); Grammeno (5km);

To Azogires (7km); Kissamos (46km); Hania (78km)

To Paleohora Club (1.5km); Camping Paleohora (1.5km)

School

Halikia Beach (Pebble Beach)

Pahia Ammos (Sandy Beach)

Old Harbour

Kondekaki

Eleftheriou Venizelou

Quay

To Agia Roumeli; Gavdos; Hora Sfakion; Sougia

Mediterranean Sea

Taxi Stand

Enai Yiala

Libyan Sea

To Haris Studios (200m)

INFORMATION	
Erato Internet	**1** C2
Notos Rentals	**2** C2
Tourist Information Office	**3** C2

SIGHTS & ACTIVITIES	
Selino Travel	**4** C3
Tsiskakis Travel	(see 2)
Venetian Castle	**5** B4

SLEEPING	
Homestay Anonymous	**6** B2
Oriental Bay Rooms	**7** D1
Votsalo Rooms	**8** D1

EATING	
Dionysos Taverna	**9** C2
Kyma	**10** D1
Oriental Bay	(see 7)
Samaria	**11** C2
Third Eye	**12** B3
To Kiparaki	**13** B2

DRINKING	
Agios	**14** C3

ENTERTAINMENT	
Cinema Attikon	**15** B1
La Jettee	**16** A1
Nostos Night Club	**17** C2
Skala Bar	**18** C3

TRANSPORT	
Bus Station	**19** C1
Ferries to Sougia, Agia Roumeli & Gavdos Island	**20** C3
Notos Rentals	(see 2)

CRETE

Dionysos Taverna (☎ 28230 41243; mains €5-8) Excellent *mayirefta,* plus vegetarian dishes and grills, are served at this popular place.

Third Eye (☎ 28230 41234; mains €5-8) A local institution, the Third Eye, Crete's only vegetarian restaurant, has an eclectic menu of curries, salads, pastas and Greek and Asian dishes, plus live music weekly. Just inland from Pahia Ammos.

Oriental Bay (☎ 28230 41322; mains €5-9) This beachside taverna does good vegetarian dishes, like green beans and potatoes, plus meatier fare like 'rooster's kiss' (chicken fillet with bacon) and 'drunk cutlet' (pork chop in red wine).

our pick Samaria (☎ 28230 41572; mains €8-10; ☽ dinner) Housed in a roofless old stone build-

ing with ambient back courtyard dining, this traditional restaurant serves *mayirefta* and specialities like lamb *tsigatiasto,* and *stamnagkathi,* a kind of greens.

To Kiparaki (☎ 28230 42281; mains €8-11) There's excellent and fresh Asian-style food at this wee Dutch-run place, with but eight tables in a back garden.

Kyma (☎ 28230 41110; top fish per kilogram €40-65) Run by a fisherman, the Kyma is one of Paleohora's more trustworthy places for fresh and fairly priced fish. It has a relaxed beach setting, with tables under the trees.

Drinking & Entertainment

Skala Bar (☎ 28230 41671; www.skalabar.gr; port; ☽ 7am-5am; ☐) A portside classic that has a

---

ECO-ADVENTURES IN MILIA

Midway in the mountains between Paleohora and Hania, the isolated settlement of **Milia** (☎ 28220 51569; www.milia.gr; d from €60) is Crete's coolest eco-establishment. This abandoned village of stone farmhouses was reconstructed into eco-lodges, now using only solar energy to generate electricity. Needless to say, the food served at Milia's superb taverna comes from the settlement's own organic produce, including oil, wine, milk and cheese. (The menu changes often, depending on what's in season.) With a spectacular setting amid olive-clad mountains, and friendly staff, Milia is really one of Crete's most exceptional places. Alas, there's no bus, though if you book for at least a week the staff will usually drive you from and to Hania.

To reach Milia, drive just past **Vlatos** and take the drivable 3km dirt road up to it.

---

relaxing terrace for coffees, waffles and free wi-fi by day, while by night the small bar gets rockin', packed solid with partiers.

Agios (cnr Kondekaki & Eleftheriou Venizelou; ☒ 9am-3am) This small bar, marked by dark tones and funky music, is a friendly and fun place in the centre.

Nostos Night Club (btwn Eleftheriou Venizelou & the Old Harbour) Has an outdoor terrace bar and small indoor club playing Greek and Western music.

La Jettee (☒ 9am-2am) A favourite with tourists and known for its cocktails, the bar is open all day, but is most popular by night. La Jettee is right on the beach, behind the Villa Marise Hotel, and has a lovely garden.

Paleohora Club A slick indoor club next to Camping Paleohora; a shuttle bus runs there from the port.

Cinema Attikon (tickets €5) Screens films outdoors (10pm) in summer.

Getting There & Away
BOAT
In summer, a daily morning ferry usually goes to Hora Sfakion (€14, three hours), via Sougia (€7, 50 minutes), Agia Roumeli (€11, 1½ hours) and Loutro (€13, 2½ hours). Three weekly summer boats serve Gavdos (€15, 2½ hours).

BUS
From the **bus station** (☎ 28230 41914), six daily buses serve Hania (€6.50, two hours). A special early bus leaves at 6.15am for Omalos (€5.50, two hours) and the Samaria Gorge, also stopping at the Agia Irini Gorge (€4.50).

Getting Around
Notos Rentals (☎ 28230 42110; www.notoscar.com; Eleftheriou Venizelou) has cars, motorcycles and bicycles for hire.

ELAFONISI & KEDRODASOS
ΕΛΑΦΟΝΗΣΙ & ΚΕΔΡΟΔΑΣΟΣ
Arguably Crete's most beautiful beach, the white- and pink-sand **Elafonisi** is practically tropical. About an hour's drive from Paleohora, it unsurprisingly gets inundated by day-trippers who flock to the semi-detached islets, little coves, and warm, shallow turquoise waters.

For more solitude, hike about one hour eastwards from the beach on the marked E4 secondary road (or drive) and, after some greenhouses, you'll reach the equally beautiful but less visited **Kedrodasos Beach** – as the name suggests, backed by a cedar forest.

From Paleohora a daily boat serves Elafonisi (€7, one hour) from mid-June to September, leaving in the morning and returning in late afternoon. Two daily buses also go from Hania (€9.60, 2½ hours) and Kissamos (€5.90, 1¼ hours), returning in the afternoon. Neither option leaves much time to relax on both beaches, so driving is ideal.

There's no accommodation on either beach, though snack bars operate at Elafonisi.

AZOGIRES ΑΖΟΓΙΡΕΣ
pop 40
It's not known whether the hippies who once frolicked in this mountainside hamlet were sworn to secrecy, but it is surprising that more travellers haven't been turned on to Azogires. In an island full of storied eccentricities, this tranquil village 7km north of Paleohora stands out for its wooded, rock-pool waterfalls haunted by nereids, cave churches where hermits once meditated, and overall positive vibrations. No surprise then that Azogires, set above a stunning eponymous gorge, attracts the occasional foreign yoga and meditation group. If it's solitude you're after, this is the place.

The village also offers plenty of hill walks, tasty local products like olive oil and honey, memorable characters and limited but excellent sleeping and eating options. From Azogires, B-roads also continue to several destinations including Sougia, Omalos and Hania.

Information

Entering Azogires from the south, look left for **Alfa Restaurant** (☎ 28230 41620; Azogires Sq), the centre of local life. Here, American-born local Lakkis 'Lucky' Koukoutsakis can inform you about everything from the village's history to local activities, and also leads village tours. A free village map with all the local sights is available. There are no ATMs in Azogires.

Sights & Activities

Azogires' sights are all relatively close and connected by footpaths or roads. The side of the village west of the main road contains no less than six shrines, the two most revered being the **Holy Fathers' Cave**, accessible along a winding footpath northwest of the village, and **St John the Hermit's Cave**, somewhat closer, above Alpha Rooms. These mediaeval shrines have numerous colourful legends associated with them, and are still credited with miraculous occurrences.

Just across the main road from Alpha Rooms, a short path into the woods leads to a 1m-high **waterfall**, gushing behind deep **rock pools**. Here dazzling sunlight is reflected from the water's surface through a leafy canopy where immense green dragonflies flutter; it's not hard to see why locals have, since ancient times, believed exquisitely beautiful nereids inhabit the falls and can, on certain fatal nights, steal a man's soul. The rock pools make for great swimming by day and, apparently, by night – the place was used in the early 1970s as a sort of open-air disco by the itinerant hippies.

A footpath from here through the woods leads southeast to a lovely **old bridge**; cross it to reach the **Monastery of the Holy Fathers**, with its small **museum** of local ecclesiastical items and icons. Across a narrow road further east are the **Carved Caves of Ancient Azogires**, worth a peek.

You can hike the forested **Azogires Gorge** to Paleohora on shaded but rocky trails (three hours). The hike is moderately difficult, but the trail not well maintained, so enquire locally about current conditions.

The best way to see all the local sights, with some entertaining commentary along the way, is to take a circular **village walking tour** along shaded trails. The tour lasts three to four hours; groups should be between five and 15 people; the price, whatever you feel like paying. Tours are usually led from Alpha Restaurant (below) by the knowledgeable Lakkis 'Lucky' Koukoutsakis, who traces his family roots here to the year 1712; the 26-year-old Lucky's splendidly curving, pencil-thin Cretan moustache appears to date from the same era. This wry amateur historian enlivens his tours with remarkable vignettes about events during Turkish times and WWII, plus information on local customs and traditions, and all the legends surrounding Azogires' sacred sites.

Sleeping & Eating

Alfa Hotel (☎ /fax 28230 41620; alfacafeneion@aol .com; www.alfahotelazogires.blogspot.gr; Azogires; r from €25; P 🕃 🖳) Just up from the centre on the main road, the Alfa has clean, modern en suite rooms with balconies facing the far-off sea at Paleohora. Four of the eight rooms have air conditioning. There is a communal kitchen and a washing machine (€3 per load). A big hall is reserved for yoga and meditation groups; the terrace offers magnificent views of the mountains and sea. This tranquil, romantic place is ideal for alternative groups, including hill walkers and birdwatchers.

Alfa Restaurant (☎ 28230 41620; mains €4-6) Part coffee shop, part info centre, part restaurant, this place on the square does excellent local fare and makes a relaxing spot for a drink, too. Intriguing traditional implements and antiques line the walls, and local products like olive oil and honey are sold at very reasonable prices.

Getting There & Away

Azogires is about 15 minutes from Paleohora by car; taxis cost €10.

GAVDOS ISLAND ΝΙΣΙ ΓΑΥΔΟΣ
pop 100

Europe's most southerly point, Gavdos lies 65km south of Paleohora in the Libyan Sea. With but three tiny settlements and a smattering of rooms and tavernas, Gavdos is blissful, boasting several unspoilt beaches – some accessible only by boat. It attracts campers, nudists and free spirits seeking to peace out on balmy beaches under the stars.

Through the 1960s Gavdos had little water, electricity or phone lines. Water is now plentiful, but occasional power outages mean you should take a torch. When winds are too strong, boats won't risk the open-sea journey back to Crete, so always allow a little extra time just in case.

Sarakiniko Studios (☎ 28230 42182; www.gavdo studios.gr; d/tr studio incl breakfast €50/60), above Sarakiniko beach, has comfortable studios, plus new villas sleeping up to five (€80 to €100). Phone ahead for port pick-up or walk 20 minutes north from the port, Karabe.

Boat services to Gavdos vary seasonally, and can take between 1½ and five hours depending on the boat and other stops. The most direct route is from Hora Sfakion on Friday, Saturday and Sunday (€15, 1½ hours). From Paleohora, two weekly boats (increasing to three in high summer) run for €15, though they go via the other southern ports and Hora Sfakion, lengthening the trip.

Only some ferries take cars – enquire ahead if taking one.

Bike and car hire are available at Gavdos' port or in Sarakiniko, though insurance may not be included.

KISSAMOS ΚΙΣΣΑΜΟΣ
pop 3820

A sleepy tourist town sustained by agriculture, northwest-coast Kissamos is known primarily for its ferries to Kythira and the Peloponnese. However, it has a decent town beach, and fine beaches lie along the vast Kissamos Bay opposite. The superlative beaches at Falasarna and Gramvousa are also easily accessible from here.

In antiquity, Kissamos was the capital of an eponymous province. However, it later became called Kastelli, after a Venetian castle built here; the authorities intervened in 1966, ruling that confusion with Crete's other Kastelli (near Iraklio) meant the town should revert to its ancient name. Parts of the castle wall still survive.

Orientation & Information
The port is 3km west of town. In summer, a bus meets ferries; otherwise taxis cost €4 to €6. The bus station's on the main square, Plateia Tzanakaki; east lies the main commercial street, Skalidi, which has ATM-equipped banks. The post office is on the main through-road. Most tavernas and bars line the seafront promenade.

For online info see www.kissamos.net.

Sights & Activities
Archaeological Museum of Kissamos (☎ 28220 83308; Plateia Tzanakaki; admission free; ☼ 8.30am-3pm) Housed in a Venetian-Turkish building on the square, the museum displays local artefacts, including statues, jewellery, coins and an ancient villa's mosaic floor.

Strata Walking Tours (☎ 28220 24336; www.strata tours.com) Offers easy day trips (€40 including lunch) to full-on 15-day round trips (€895) to the south coast. It also runs jeep safaris to interesting off-road destinations (€40).

Sleeping
Bikakis Family (☎ 28220 22105; www.familybikakis.gr; Iroön Polemiston 1941; s/d/studio €20/25/30; ✖ 🖳) This well-run collection of self-catering rooms and studios has good views, and makes an excellent budget choice.

Thalassa (☎ 28220 31231; www.thalassa-apts. gr; Paralia Drapanias; studios €35-55; ✖ 🖳 📶) This isolated complex on the beach offers immaculate, breezy studios with all mod cons. A barbecue stands on the lawn and there's a small playground.

Eating
Kellari (☎ 28220 23883; mains €5-7) On the waterfront's eastern end, Kellari does excellent Cretan dishes, grills and fresh fish. Owned by the same family that runs Strata Walking Tours, it uses its own meat, wine, oil and other produce.

Papadakis (☎ 28220 22340; mains €6-11) One of Kissamos' oldest tavernas, this local favourite is well situated overlooking the beach and does great fish dishes.

Getting There & Away
BOAT
From Kissamos, ferries serve Kythira and Gythio; see Island Hopping (p749) for details.

BUS
From Kissamos' **bus station** (☎ 28220 22035), 14 daily buses serve Hania (€4, 40 minutes). In summer, two daily buses go to Falasarna (€3, 20 minutes), and one to Elafonisi (€5.90, 1¼ hours). One daily bus serves Paleohora (€6.50, 1¼ hours).

Getting Around

Moto Fun (☎ 28220 23440; www.motofun.info; Plateia Tzanakaki) has cars, bikes and mountain bikes for hire.

AROUND KISSAMOS

Some 16km west of Kissamos, **Falasarna** was a 4th-century-BC Greek city-state, though its mysterious place name possibly pre-dates the Greek language itself. Falasarna's long sandy beach is one of Crete's best, comprising several coves separated by rocky spits. Falasarna's end-of-the-world feel is accentuated by spectacular sunsets, when pink hues are reflected from the sand's fine coral.

Falasarna has no settlement, though a few domatia and tavernas stand behind the beach. You can drive, or else there are three buses daily from Kissamos (€3, 20 minutes), or three from Hania (€6.50, one hour).

North of Falasarna, the wild and remote **Gramvousa Peninsula** shelters the stunning **Balos Beach** on its western tip. From the idyllic sands here, you can gaze out at two islets: **Agria** (wild) and **Imeri** (tame).

A rough but drivable dirt road to Balos begins in **Kalyviani** village, and ends at a car park with a *kantina* (snack bar). A path leads down for 30 minutes to the sandy cliffs (the return takes 45 minutes).

West-bound buses from Kissamos leave you at the Kalyviani turn-off; from here it's a 2km walk to the beginning of the path, straight down Kalyviani's main street. The 3km walk to Balos is shadeless, so gear up and take water.

Summertime **boat tours** (☎ 28220 24344; www .gramvousa.com; adult/concession €25/15) go regularly from Kissamos. The morning boats stop at Imeri Gramvousa, crowned with a **Venetian castle**. The trip takes 55 minutes, departing at 10am, 10.15am and 1pm, returning at 5.45pm and 8pm.

EASTERN CRETE

If travelling east from Iraklio on the north-coast road is painful at first, close your eyes and think of England while passing the fish, chips and chlamydia of Hersonissos and Malia, the two package-tour ghettoes most infamous for foreign drunkenness and debauchery. Beyond this unfortunate stretch of road, however, Crete's less visited eastern expanse is actually quite intriguing. The fertile Lasithi Plateau, tucked into the Mt Dikti ranges, is atmospheric, offering cycling opportunities through tranquil villages to the Dikteon Cave – where Zeus himself was born. The eastern hinterland boasts the beautiful palm-forested beach of Vaï, and Minoan palace ruins at Zakros.

Eastern Crete also contains luxurious resorts around Elounda and Agios Nikolaos, frequented by the international jet set, though they also offer fun and excitement for mere mortals. Spinalonga, a former Venetian fortress with an intriguing history, lies on an islet near the former, while south-coast Ierapetra also has its own Venetian fortress and island getaway, Hrysi.

LASITHI PLATEAU ΟΡΟΠΕΔΙΟ ΛΑΣΙΘΙΟΥ

The tranquil Lasithi Plateau, 900m above sea level, contains pear and apple orchards, almond and other deciduous trees that change colour in fall. In the 17th century, some 20,000 metal windmills with white canvas sails were built here for irrigation purposes, but only 5000 still stand. Although few are still used, the windmills of Lasithi remain a distinctive and memorable sight as you arrive.

The area's relative inaccessibility allowed frequent revolts during Venetian and Turkish rule. After a 13th-century rebellion, the Venetians expelled the locals and destroyed their orchards; Lasithi lay abandoned for 200 years, until food shortages led the Venetians to cultivate this fertile area and build the irrigation trenches and wells still used today.

The largest of Lasithi's 20 villages, **Tzermiado** (population 750) is a bucolic place with two ATMs and a post office. Although tourists visiting the Dikteon Cave pass through, Tzermiado remains placid. Here **Restaurant Kourites** (☎ 28440 22054; mains €7-10) serves wood-oven specialities, like suckling pig with baked potatoes, plus vegetarian options, and offers rooms with balconies (single/double including breakfast €25/40) above the taverna. Free bicycle use is included. The same family also runs a lovely set of stone-built apartments in the abandoned upper village, **Argoulias** (☎ 28440 22754; www.argoulias.gr; d incl breakfast €60-80).

Nearby **Agios Georgios** (pronounced *agh*-ios ye-*or*-gios; population 554) is another relaxing spot; here **Hotel Maria** (☎ 28440 31774;

CRETE

s/d €20/25) has nicely decorated rooms with weavings and traditional furnishings (though beds are quite narrow). Maria's nourishing **Taverna Rea** (☎ 28440 31209; mains €4.50-8) is on the main street.

Psyhro, the closest village to the **Dikteon Cave** (adult/child €4/2; 🕑 8am-6pm Jun-Oct, 8am-2.30pm Nov-May), has tavernas and souvenir shops, but is prettier than Tzermiado. This cave was where Rhea hid the newborn Zeus from Cronos, his offspring-gobbling father. Excavated in 1900 by British archaeologist David Hogarth, the cave covers 2200 sq metres and features both stalactites and stalagmites. Numerous votives discovered here indicate cult worship; some are displayed in Iraklio's archaeological museum (p463).

Buses will drop you at Psyhro's far side; for the cave, walk 1km further uphill. It's a steep, 15-minute walk to the cave entrance. The fairly rough but shaded track on the right offers great views over the plateau; there's also a paved (but unshaded) trail next to Chalavro taverna, left of the car park. Alternatively, you can go by donkey (€10 or €15 return).

Opposite the cave, **Petros Taverna** (☎ 28440 31600; grills €6-9) has great views from the balcony. The owner also organises Mt Dikti hikes, including camping out under the stars.

Getting There & Away

From Iraklio, daily buses serve Tzermiado (€4.70, two hours), Agios Georgios (€5.10, two hours) and Psyhro. From Agios Nikolaos, buses to Lasithi only go on Sundays, though travel agencies run special cave tours.

AGIOS NIKOLAOS ΑΓΙΟΣ ΝΙΚΟΛΑΟΣ
pop 10,080

Pretty Agios Nikolaos (*ah*-yee-os nih-*ko*-laos), is Lasithi's capital, and enjoys a unique and photogenic setting around a curving harbour connecting to a small lake said to be once bottomless.

'Agios' has been a tourist draw since the 1960s, though infrastructure hasn't really changed since then; the narrow, one-way streets can be vexing for drivers in summer. The town, which boasts five beaches of varying sizes and reasonable nightlife, has always gone in cycles. Nowadays, Agios Nikolaos gets an intriguing mix of Western and Eastern European package tourists, plus some independents and families. With a mix of services, amenities and reasonable prices,

it is probably the north coast's best family holiday destination and serves as a good base for eastern explorations.

Orientation

The **bus station** (KTEL; ☎ 28410 22234) is 800m from the town's centre at Plateia Venizelou, though the action for tourists is centred around Voulismeni Lake. Most banks, ATMs, travel agencies and shops are on Koundourou and the parallel 28 Oktovriou.

Information

Anna Karteri Bookshop (☎ 28410 22272; Koundourou 5) Sells foreign-language maps and guidebooks.

Cafe Du Lac (☎ 28410 26837; 28 Oktovriou 17) At Du Lac Hotel. Offers free wi-fi and (pay) internet-equipped computers.

General Hospital (☎ 28410 66000; Knosou 3)

Municipal Tourist Office (☎ 28410 22357; www .agiosnikolaos.gr; 🕑 8am-9pm Apr-Nov) Provides info, changes money and assists with accommodation.

National Bank of Greece (Nikolaou Plastira)

PK's Internet Cafe (☎ 28410 28004; Akti Koundourou 1; per hr €2; 🕑 9am-2am)

Post office (☎ 28410 22062; 28 Oktovriou 9; 🕑 7.30am-2pm Mon-Fri)

Tourist police (☎ 28410 91408; Erythrou Stavrou 47; 🕑 7.30am-2.30pm Mon-Fri)

Sights & Activities

The **Archaeological Museum** (☎ 28410 24943; Paleologou Konstantinou 74; admission €4; 🕑 8.30am-3pm Tue-Sun) has Crete's second-most-significant Minoan collection, including clay coffins, ceramic musical instruments and gold from Mohlos. The chronologically organised exhibits run from the Neolithic finds on Mt Tragistalos, north of Kato Zakros, and early Minoan finds from Agia Fotia to finds from Malia and Mohlos. The highlight, the *Goddess of Myrtos* (2500 BC), is a clay jug found near Myrtos.

The **folk museum** (☎ 28410 25093; Paleologou Konstantinou 4; admission €3; 🕑 10am-2pm Tue-Sun), besides the tourist office, exhibits traditional handicrafts and costumes.

Within town, **Ammos Beach** and **Kytroplatia Beach** are small and crowded, though convenient for a quick dip. **Almyros Beach** (1km south), is also busy but much longer, with better sands. A taxi here costs €6, or walk (20 to 30 minutes) via a coastal path starting at Kitroplateia, passing the marina and then the stadium.

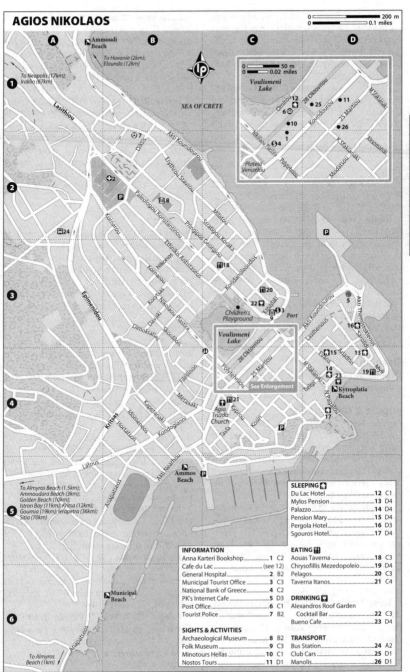

AGIOS NIKOLAOS

CRETE

Ammoudara Beach, 1.5km further south on the road towards Ierapetra, has tavernas and overpriced accommodation, but nothing else. Further towards Sitia, **Golden Beach** (Voulisma Beach) and **Istron Bay** boast long stretches of sand.

Agios Nikolaos' **Summer Cultural Festival** has almost daily events ranging from traditional Cretan music and theatre to literary readings, art exhibits and rock concerts. Some hotels and cafes have programs, while events are also advertised throughout town.

Tours

Minotours Hellas (☎ 28410 23222; www.minotours.gr; 28 Oktovriou 6) runs numerous tours, including to the Lasithi Plateau (€40) and Knossos (€40).

Nostos Tours (☎ 28410 22819; nostos@agn.forth net.gr; Roussou Koundourou 30; ☯ 8am-noon & 5-9pm) specialises in boat excursions, one being the four-hour boat trip to Spinalonga (€20), which includes a 30-minute swim on the Kolokytha Peninsula, and an on-board bar and restaurant. Nostos' full-day trip to Spinalonga (€25) includes a barbecue and two hours for swimming and sunbathing. Nostos also does full-day fishing trips in the Gulf of Mirabello (adult/child €30/20).

Sleeping

Depending on how locals think the season is going, bargaining is sometimes possible.

BUDGET & MIDRANGE

Pension Mary (☎ 28410 23760; Evans 13; s/d/tr €20/25/30; ✹) This friendly budget place has basic but clean rooms, most with private bathrooms, fridge and balconies with sea views. The upper room is cramped, though it has a terrace with barbecue. There's also a communal kitchen.

Pergola Hotel (☎ /fax 28410 28152; Sarolidi 20; r with view €35-40; ✹) This little place has simple, comfortable rooms with fridges. The pleasant veranda is good for a relaxed breakfast. Front rooms have balconies and sea views. The kindly old owners can do bus-station pick-ups and, though they're not sure what exactly it is, plan to have internet soon.

Mylos Pension (☎ 28410 23783; Sarolidi 24; d €40; ✹) This quaint pension is an extension of the friendly elderly owner's home. The small but clean rooms are basic, though the front ones have nice water views. All have fridge and TV. Air conditioning is €2 extra.

Du Lac Hotel (☎ 28410 22711; www.dulachotel.gr; 28 Oktovriou 17; s/d/studio €40/60/80; ✹ ☞) Well positioned beside the lake, this nice place has standard rooms and spacious, fully fitted-out studios, both with stylish furnishings and nice bathrooms. The hotel's popular cafe offers free wi-fi.

Sgouros Hotel (☎ 28410 28931; N Pagalou 3; www .sgourosgrouphotels.com; s/d/tr incl breakfast €50/68/75; ✹ ☞) Although not Agios' cheapest hotel, the recently renovated Sgouros represents great value. Well located overlooking Kitroplateia Beach, the hotel has 22 freshly painted, clean rooms with nice bathrooms, plus one suite and four interconnected family rooms.

TOP END

Palazzo (☎ 28410 25080; www.palazzo-apartments.gr; s/d/ste incl breakfast from €130/160/220; ✹ ▢) Opposite Kitroplateia Beach, these 10 snazzy apartments have mosaic-tiled floors and marble bathrooms, the front rooms with lovely balconies. But, considering the price, it would benefit from a more highbrow location.

Eating

Lakeside restaurants, and most on Kitroplateia, are touristy and overpriced. Locals prefer the small backstreet places.

our pick **Chrysofillis Mezedopoleio** (☎ 28410 22705; Kitroplateia; mezedhes €4-7) Reserving ahead at this excellent and fairly priced *mezedhopoleio* is not a bad idea. A newspaperlike menu explains Cretan terminology and outlines the specials: fresh mussels, barley pasta with prawns, fried rabbit, excellent *myzithropitakia,* and lively, light salads are just some. The balcony water view is complemented by a stylish interior; the classic old framed photos are for sale (€22 to €40).

Taverna Itanos (☎ 28410 25340; Kyprou 1; mayirefta €4-9) Locals frequent this no-nonsense taverna, known for its home-cooked *mayirefta,* such as goat with artichokes or lamb fricassee.

Aouas Taverna (☎ 28410 23231; Paleologou Konstantinou 44; mezedhes €5-9) This family-run place with a nice enclosed garden does tasty Cretan specialities such as herb pies and pickled bulbs, plus tasty grills.

Pelagos (☎ 28410 25737; Katehaki 10; fish €8-16) For fresh fish and seafood, this place, in a restored house with ambient garden, is very good – and also quite expensive. The mezedhes are excellent.

Drinking

Nightlife is quite active in summer – just follow your ears. Places popular with Greeks and tourists alike ring the lake, and extend towards the Kitroplateia.

Bueno Cafe (☎ 28410 24289; Kitroplateia; ☼ 8am-1am) One of several popular cafes right on the town beach, with a big array of cold coffees.

our pick **Alexandros Roof Garden Cocktail Bar** (☎ 28410 24309; cnr Kondylaki & Konstantinou; ☼ 12pm-late) With its hanging plants, soft trees and funky decor, this elevated cocktail bar is part Vegas, part Tahiti. It offers excellent views of the lake and town, lit up at night. The friendly Giorgos Halkadakis has been operating the place for 30 years, and plays an eclectic mix of popular music from five decades, for a similarly mixed Greek and international crowd.

Getting There & Away

BOAT

For ferry services from Agios Nikolaos, see Island Hopping (p749).

BUS

Agios Nikolaos' **bus station** (☎ 28410 22234) serves Elounda (€1.50, 20 minutes, 16 daily), Ierapetra (€3.50, one hour, eight daily), Iraklio (€6.50, half-hourly), Kritsa (€1.40, 15 minutes, 10 daily) and Sitia (€7.30, one hour, seven daily). Direct buses to Lasithi villages are only on Sundays, though run frequently from nearby Neapoli. To reach the bus station from downtown, walk (10 to 15 minutes) or take any local bus (€0.50, half-hourly), which stops precisely on the bridge, opposite the tourist info centre.

Note that to visit Elounda, you needn't start from the bus station; just go to the small **bus stop** opposite the tourist information centre. It displays timetables too.

Getting Around

You can hire cars from **Club Cars** (☎ 28410 25868; www.clubcars.net; 28 Oktovriou 30) from €40 per day; **Manolis** (☎ 28410 24940; 25 Martiou 12) has scooters, motorcycles, quad bikes and mountain bikes.

AROUND AGIOS NIKOLAOS

Elounda Ελούντα

pop 1660

Some 11km north of Agios Nikolaos on a gorgeous road overlooking the coast, Elounda (el-oon-da) is Crete's playground of the rich

and (sometimes, very) famous. It's arguable whether the resorts, which unsurprisingly possess helicopter pads and even occasional exotic luxuries like maple syrup, are worth the price of admission, though if you're staying here, cost is most likely not a concern.

While enjoying Elounda's resorts can offer unexpected glimpses into the poverty of the human condition, those more reticent to make the investment can also stay in the pretty waterfront town's cheaper hotels and rooms. The Elounda municipality allegedly receives more tax euros per capita than anywhere else in Greece, because of the resorts, though you wouldn't know it from the somewhat dated, faded signage on the tourist-oriented cafe-tavernas and shops.

Nevertheless, Elounda has a nice sandy beach with shallow, warm waters, and if you'd like to see Spinalonga, it's much cheaper to get one of the half-hourly boats from here than to go from Agios.

INFORMATION

Municipal Tourist Office (☎ 28410 42464; ☼ 8am-8pm Jun-Oct) On the square; gives general info and changes money.

SLEEPING & EATING

Hotel Aristea (☎ 28410 41300; www.aristeahotel.com; s/d/tr incl breakfast €35/45/55; ✷) This decent, central budget option has clean rooms, most with sea view, double-glazed windows and fridge.

Corali Studios (☎ /fax 28410 41712; studios from €70; ✷) About 800m from the clock tower on Elounda's northern side, these self-catering studios are set on lush lawns with a shaded patio. The affiliated Portobello Apartments (air-conditioned apartments €65 to €75) next door are also a solid bet.

Nikos (☎ 28410 41439; fish per kilogram €40-50) No-frills Nikos on the main street is a trustworthy pick for fresh fish and lobster, and good value.

Ferryman (☎ 28410 41230; fish €7-14) Featured in the TV series *Who Pays the Ferryman*, this waterfront place does excellent, though pricey fish, plus Cretan specialities.

GETTING THERE & AWAY

From Agios Nikolaos, 13 daily buses serve Elounda (€1.50, 20 minutes). Boats to Spinalonga leave every half-hour (adult/child €10/5).

CRETE

Spinalonga Island Νήσος Σπιναλόγκας

Spinalonga Island lies just north of the Kolokytha Peninsula. Its massive **fortress** (☎ 28410 41773; admission €2; ☺ 9am-6.30pm) was built in 1579 to protect Elounda Bay and the Gulf of Mirabello. The money-minded Venetians also harvested salt here, operating up to 45 saltworks at a time. From 1639 they rented the operations to locals, while maintaining monopoly control over production. The Greek state later did the same.

Remarkably, Spinalonga withstood Turkish sieges until 1715 – 46 years after Iraklio had fallen. The Turks used it for smuggling. After Crete joined Greece in 1913, the island became Europe's last leper colony; the final leper died here in 1953 and it's been uninhabited ever since. Locals still call it 'the island of the living dead'.

Spinalonga is fascinating to explore. After buying the entry ticket (€2), take the path going left through the tunnel and follow it clockwise around the outside of the structure until you've completed the circle. Various organised tours operate simultaneously, so you'll get free commentary in numerous European languages. More useful info is printed in various places, and you can purchase lovely copies of old Venetian maps of Crete and the area (€2 to €22). You'll pass numerous ruins of churches, fortress structures and residences, and the outer turrets offer spectacular views. The island has a small snack bar right of the ticket booth.

Ferries to Spinalonga depart half-hourly from Elounda (adults/children €10/5), giving you an hour to see the sights (though you can stay longer and return on a different boat). From Plaka, 5km north of Elounda, the price is half. From Agios Nikolaos, various companies offer basic tours and longer, day-trip excursions (from €20).

Kritsa & Around Κριτσά

pop 1614

Touristy Kritsa (krit-*sah*) enjoys a nice mountain setting and is renowned for its needlework and weaving. However, the overeager villagers physically pull you into their shops, and items are rather overpriced. It's 11km from Agios Nikolaos, and served by hourly buses (€1.50, 15 minutes).

One kilometre before Kritsa, the tiny, triple-aisled **Church of Panagia Kera** (☎ 28410 51525; admission €3; ☺ 8.30am-3pm) is a very signifi-

cant Byzantine shrine with priceless frescoes. And 4km north of Kritsa the 7th-century-BC Dorian city of **Lato** (admission €2; ☺ 8.30am-3pm Tue-Sun) is one of Crete's few non-Minoan ancient sites. Lato (lah-*to*), once a powerful city, sprawls over two acropolises in a lonely mountain setting, overlooking the Gulf of Mirabello. Worshipped here were Artemis and Apollo, children of Zeus by the goddess Leto – the city's namesake.

When facing the gulf, you'll see stairway remains of a **theatre**. Above it was the *prytaneion*, where Lato's rulers met. The stone circle behind the (fenced-off) central well was a threshing floor; columns beside it were from the stoa, which stood in the agora. Mosaic remains lie nearby. A right-hand path accesses the **Temple of Apollo**.

Lato gets no buses. From Kritsa, follow the (signposted) right-hand turn before Kritsa. Alternatively, enjoy the 4km walk through olive groves.

Another important site, Minoan **Gournia** (☎ 28410 24943; admission €3; ☺ 8.30am-3pm Tue-Sun), pronounced goor-*nyah*, is east of Kritsa on the coast road, 19km southeast of Agios Nikolaos. Ruins here date from 1550–1450 BC, and comprise a small palace and town. They include streets, stairways and houses, with 2m-high walls. Trade, domestic and agricultural implements discovered here indicate Gournia was fairly prosperous. Any bus east from Agios Nikolaos can drop you here.

MOHLOS ΜΟΧΛΟΣ

pop 90

Tranquil Mohlos (*moh*-los), renowned for its *psarotavernes,* lies down a 5km winding road off the Sitia–Agios Nikolaos highway. Now it's a chilled-out beach getaway with a few rooms, but from 3000 to 2000 BC it was a thriving Minoan town. The eponymous island now 200m offshore was joined to it in antiquity, and archaeologists still work in both places; an information board overlooking the harbour chronicles their finds.

While notable construction is ongoing, Mohlos' remoteness prevents it from ever being overrun. The small pebble-and-grey-sand beach has good swimming, but mind the currents between the island and the village.

Mohlos accommodation includes **Hotel Sofia** (☎ /fax 28430 94554; r €35-45; 🅿), above a tasty taverna. The smallish rooms have new furniture and bedding, plus fridge; the front ones boast sea-view balconies. **Kyma** (☎ 28430 94177; soik@in.gr; studio €35; 🐱), signposted on the western side, offers spotless self-contained studios. For eating, Cretans flock to **Ta Kochilia** (☎ 28430 94432; fish €4.50-10) with its excellent fresh fish. Sea-urchin salad, cuttlefish and sea bream are all great here.

Although Mohlos lacks direct buses, any Agios Nikolaos–Sitia bus can drop you at the turn-off, from where it's a 6km walk (or hitch) to Mohlos.

SITIA ΣΗΤΕΙΑ
pop 8240

Sitia (si-*tee*-ah), de facto capital of easternmost Crete, is a quiet seaside town but does boast an airport and Dodecanese-bound ferries. Here, agriculture and commerce supersede tourism, and most visitors are low-key Greeks.

Sitia's architecture, strung up a terraced hillside, mixes Venetian and newer structures. The pretty harbour-side promenade features tavernas and cafes, while a sandy beach skirts the eastern bay. Sitia is always laid back, and makes a good base for exploring nearby beaches and sights.

Orientation & Information

Plateia Iroon Polytehniou is Sitia's main square. The bus station is at the eastern end of Karamanli, behind the bay. Ferries dock 500m north of Plateia Agnostou. Several ATMs are available in the centre of town.

Akasti Travel (☎ 28430 29444; www.akasti.gr; Kornarou & Metaxaki 4) Does trips and provides info.

Java Internet Cafe (☎ 28430 22263; Kornarou 113; ⏱ 9am-late).

Post office (Dimokritou; ⏱ 7.30am-3pm) Heading inland, the first left off Venizelou.

Tourist office (☎ 28430 28300; Karamanli; ⏱ 9.30am-2.30pm & 5-8.30pm Mon-Fri, 9.30am-2.30pm Sat) Waterfront office offers maps.

Sights

Sitia's excellent **Archaeological Museum** (☎ 28430 23917; Piskokefalou; admission €2; ⏱ 8.30am-3pm Tue-Sun) exhibits local finds dating from Neolithic to Roman times. Significant Minoan items include the *Palekastro Kouros* – a statue painstakingly pieced together from fragments made of hippopotamus tusks and adorned with gold. Zakros palace finds include a wine press, a bronze saw and cult objects scorched by the conflagration that destroyed the palace. Most important are

the displayed Linear A tablets documenting administrative functions.

Sitia's towering **Venetian fort** (⏱ 8.30am-3pm), locally called *kazarma* (from 'casa di arma') is now only walls, and used as an open-air venue.

The **folklore museum** (☎ 28430 22861; Kapetan Sifinos 28; admission €2; ⏱ 10am-1pm Mon-Fri) displays local weavings.

Sleeping

Hotel Arhontiko (☎ 28430 28172; Kondylaki 16; d/studio without bathroom €30/35), occupying an uphill neoclassical building, has old-world ambience. This spotless guesthouse has shared bathrooms and garden.

El Greco Hotel (☎ 28430 23133; info@elgreco-sitia.gr; Arkadiou 13; s/d incl breakfast €30/40; 🐱) offers very clean and presentable rooms with fridge.

Apostolis (☎ 28430 28172; Kazantzaki 27; d/tr €40/47) These domatia have ceiling fans and relatively modern bathrooms. There's a communal balcony and fridge.

Hotel Flisvos (☎ 28430 27135; www.flisvos-sitia.com; Karamanli 4; s/d/tr incl breakfast €50/70/80; 🐱 💻) Along the southern waterfront, this modern hotel offers well-appointed rooms with all mod cons.

Eating

Taverna O Mihos (☎ 28430 22416; Kornarou 117; grills €5-8) In a traditional stone house behind the waterfront, O Mihos does great charcoal-grilled meats and Cretan fare. Eat on the beachfront terrace.

Sitia Beach (☎ 28430 22104; Karamanli 28; specials €5.50-9) Unexpectedly good pizza, plus home-style specials, are served at this beachfront place.

Balcony (☎ 28430 25084; Foundalidou 19; mains €10-19) Sitia's finest dining is upstairs in this well-decorated neoclassical building. The diverse range includes Cretan, Mexican and Asian-inspired dishes.

Getting There & Away
AIR

Sitia's **airport** (☎ 28430 24666) serves national destinations, with plans for international ones too. For domestic flight info, see Island Hopping (p749).

BOAT

Sitia's ferries primarily serve the Dodecanese. For ferry info, see Island Hopping (p749).

BUS

From Sitia's **bus station** (☎ 28430 22272), six daily buses serve Ierapetra (€5.40, 1½ hours), and seven go to Iraklio (€13.10, three hours) via Agios Nikolaos (€6.90, 1½ hours). Four buses go to Vaï (€3, 30 minutes), and two serve Kato Zakros via Palekastro and Zakros (€4.50, one hour) in summer only.

AROUND SITIA

Moni Toplou Μονή Τοπλού

The defences of the imposing fortesslike **Moni Toplou** (☎ 28430 61226; admission €2.50; ☾ 9am-6pm Apr-Oct), 18km east of Sitia, were tested by all from crusading knights to the Turks. The showpiece here is an 18th-century icon by Ioannis Kornaros, with 61 ornate miniature scenes inspired by an Orthodox prayer. More excellent icons, plus engravings, books, and Resistance-era military gear are exhibited in the monastery's **museum**. Ecclesiastical souvenirs, books on Crete, and the monastery's award-winning organic olive oil and wine are sold in the shop.

To reach Toplou, walk 3km from the Sitia–Palekastro road. Buses can stop at the junction.

Vaï Βάϊ

Europe's only 'natural' palm-forest beach is that of Vaï, 24km east of Sitia. Some say the palms sprouted from date pits spread by Roman legionaries kicking back after conquering Egypt. While closely related to the date, these palms are a separate, and unique, species. The inviting white sands here get packed in summer, though you can access a more secluded beach by clambering over a rocky outcrop behind the taverna. Also, 3km north the Minoan site of **Itanos** has good swimming nearby.

In summer, five daily buses operate from Sitia (€2.50, one hour) and stop at Palekastro. The beach car park charges €3; alternatively, park for free on the roadside 500m before Vaï.

Palekastro Παλαίκαστρο

pop 1080

Barren, agricultural Palekastro (pah-*leh*-kastro) lies on the road connecting Vaï Beach and the Zakros ruins, and itself has a promising site about 1km from town: Ancient Palekastro, where a major Minoan palace is possibly buried. The celebrated *Palekastro Kouros* in Sitia's Archaeological Museum (p507) was found there, and digging continues.

The **tourist office** (☎ 28430 61546; ☾ 9am-10pm Mon-Fri, 9am-1pm & 5.30-8pm Sat & Sun May-Oct) offers information. An ATM is adjacent. Digs include **Hotel Hellas** (☎ 28430 61240; hellas_h@otenet.gr; s/d €30/45; 🅿), offering simple rooms with fridge and good bathrooms; the downstairs **taverna** serves hearty, home-style cooking (mains €4 to €8).

Nearby, the nearly deserted **Kouremenos Beach** offers excellent windsurfing, while **Hiona Beach** has good *psarotavernes*. **Freak Surf Station** (☎ 28430 61116; www.freak-surf.com) on Kouremenos rents boards.

Also here, **Casa di Mare** (☎ 28430 25304; casadimare@hotmail.com; studio €40-60; 🅿 🖳) rents spacious, comfortable studios with stone floors and rustic-style decor, sleeping up to four. There's a small pool among the olive groves.

Five daily buses from Sitia stop at Palekastro en route to Vaï. Another two buses from Sitia to Palekastro (€2.20, 45 minutes) continue to Kato Zakros (€4.50).

KATO ZAKROS & ANCIENT ZAKROS

ΚΑΤΩ ΖΑΚΡΟΣ & ΑΡΧΑΙΑ ΖΑΚΡΟΣ

pop 790

Zakros (*zah*-kros), 37km southeast of Sitia, lies 7km from the Minoan Ancient Zakros site, and the beach settlement of Kato Zakros (*kah*-to *zah*-kros). This long pebbly beach, shaded by pines, with a few laid-back tavernas, is eternally peaceful; building is highly restricted since it's an archaeological zone. Local jaunts include the easy 8km walk from Zakros through a gorge dubbed the **Valley of the Dead**, after the cliffside **cave tombs**.

The gorge lies near the Minoan site, which is also the smallest of Crete's four palace complexes. The **Palace of Zakros** (☎ 28430 26897; Kato Zakros; admission €3; ☾ 8am-7.30pm Jul-Oct, 8.30am-3pm Nov-Jun) was a major Minoan port, doing commerce with Egypt, Syria, Anatolia and Cyprus. The palace comprised royal apartments, storerooms and workshops flanking a central courtyard.

Ancient Zakros occupied a low plain near the shore; however, rising water levels since have submerged parts of the palace – now literally living under a *helonokratia* (rule of turtles). While the ruins are sparse, the wildness and remoteness of the setting make it attractive.

Sleeping & Eating

Stella's Apartments (☎ /fax 28430 23739; www.stelapts.com; studio €40-80; 🅿 🖳) Nice studios with handmade wood furniture, surrounded by pines, 800m along the old road to Zakros. With barbecues, hammocks and helpful owners, they're perfect for longer stays.

Athena & Coral Rooms (d €40-50; 🕸) Athena has nice, stone-walled rooms, while neighbouring Coral has small but spotless rooms with a fridge and sea views from the communal balcony.

Akrogiali Taverna (☎ 28430 26893; www.ka tozakros.cretefamilyhotels.com) At this tasty taverna, Nikos Perakis arranges several good rooms, all on the beach except for Katerina Apartments (air-conditioned apartments €40 to €60). Opposite Stella's, this offers large, stone-built studios and maisonettes with superb views.

Restaurant Nikos Platanakis (☎ 28430 26887; specials €4.50-9) While Akrogiali does great fish, this friendly place offers tasty Greek staples like rabbit stew. The produce is fresh from the back garden.

Getting There & Away

Zakros has buses from Sitia via Palekastro (€4.50, one hour, two daily); in summer, these continue to Kato Zakros.

IERAPETRA ΙΕΡΑΠΕΤΡΑ
pop 11,680

Ierapetra (yeh-*rah*-pet-rah) on the south coast lives well enough from farming (as witnessed by the many bulbous greenhouses) to not particularly care about tourism. However, it was key as a Roman port for conquering Egypt, and the Venetians later built a (still standing) fortress on the harbour. Turkish quarter remnants attest to Ierapetra's Ottoman past.

This hot and dusty place offers a more authentic Cretan experience than the northeastern coast resorts. Tavernas and cafes line the waterfront, and nightlife is busy in summer. Local beaches are fairly good, and sandy, semitropical Gaïdouronisi Island (also called Hrysi) lies just opposite.

Orientation & Information

The east-side bus station is just back from the beachfront. ATMs line the main square.

City Netcafe (☎ 28420 23164; Kothri 6; per hr €3; 🕥 9am-late)

Post office (☎ 28420 22271; Vitsentzou Kornarou 7; 🕥 7.30am-2pm)

www.ierapetra.net Helpful website.

Sights & Activities

Ierapetra's humble **archaeological museum** (☎ 28420 28721; Adrianou (Dimokratias) 2; admission €2; 🕥 8.30am-3pm Tue-Sun) exhibits classical statuary and a superb 2nd-century-AD statue of Persephone. A *larnax* (clay coffin) from around 1300 BC, decorated with 12 vividly painted panels, is another highlight.

On the waterfront, the early Venetian 'Kales' **medieval fortress** (admission free; 🕥 8.30am-3pm Tue-Sun), was strengthened by Francesco Morosini in 1626. Although it's still closed for restoration, you can appreciate its structure from without.

Ierapetra's main **town beach** is near the harbour, while a second **beach** stretches east from Patriarhou Metaxaki. Both have coarse grey sand, but the main one is shadier.

Sleeping & Eating

Cretan Villa Hotel (☎ /fax 28420 28522; www.cretan-villa .com; Lakerda 16; d from €40; 🕸) This well-maintained 18th-century house has a great atmosphere, with traditionally furnished, fridge-equipped rooms and a peaceful courtyard. It's a five-minute walk from the bus.

Portego (☎ 28420 27733; Foniadaki 8; mezedhes €3-6) Excellent and inexpensive Cretan and Greek cuisine, like lamb in a clay pot with yoghurt, are served at this historic century-old house with a lovely courtyard for summer. The attached bar and *kafeneio* are good for drinks.

Oi Kalitehnes (☎ 28420 28547; Kyprou 26; mains €4-8) This unusual backstreet place does great-value organic food. Try the Egyptian owner's spicy falafel and kebabs.

Napoleon (☎ 28420 22410; Stratigou Samouil 26; mains €4.50-12) This respected waterfront establishment on Ierapetra's south side serves excellent fish and Greek and Cretan specialities.

Also recommended:

Coral Apartments (Lambraki; apt €45-60) These fully equipped apartments across town will satisfy families and self-caterers.

Coral Hotel (☎ 28420 22846; Katzonovatsi 12; d €30) This sister establishment to Ersi, in the quieter old town, is another good accommodation bet.

Ersi (☎ 28420 23208; Plateia Eleftherias 19; d €35; 🕸) This refurbished central hotel has snug rooms with fridge, TV and sea views.

Getting There & Away

Nine daily buses from Ierapetra's **bus station** (☎ 28420 28237; Lasthenous) serve Iraklio (€9.50, 2½ hours) via Agios Nikolaos (€3.30, one hour) and Gournia (about 25 minutes); seven go to Sitia (€5.40, 1½ hours) via Koutsounari (for camp sites); and seven to Myrtos (€1.80, 30 minutes).

AROUND IERAPETRA

Gaïdouronisi (Hrysi) Γαϊδουρονήσι (Χρυσή)

The tranquil Gaïdouronisi (Donkey Island), marketed as Hrysi (Golden Island), has nice sandy beaches, a taverna, and relaxing Lebanon cedars – the only such stand in Europe.

Regular **excursion boats** (€15 return) leave Ierapetra's port in the morning and return in the afternoon. Hrysi can get very crowded, but quiet spots are always available.

Myrtos Μύρτος

pop 440

Myrtos (*myr*-tos), 17km west of Ierapetra, is a fairly authentic coastal village popular with older European travellers. It hasn't been over-developed, thus preserving character. Myrtos makes a relaxing spot, with a decent beach and good eating options.

Prima Tours (☎ 28420 51035; www.sunbudget.net; internet per hr €3.50) offers internet access.

For overnight stays, try the west-side **Big Blue** (☎ 28420 51094; www.big-blue.gr; d/studio/apt €35/60/75; 🔀). You can choose between large, airy and pricey studios with sea views or cheaper ground-floor rooms. All are self-catering. **Cretan Rooms** (☎ 28420 51427; d €35), popular with independent travellers, offers traditional-styled rooms with balconies, fridges and shared kitchens.

Myrtos Taverna (☎ 28420 51227; mains €5-9), attached to an eponymous hotel, offers many mezedhes, including vegetarian dishes. The more touristy **Platanos** (☎ 28420 51363; mains €6-8), is set under a giant thatched umbrella below a plane tree.

Seven daily buses go from Ierapetra to Myrtos (€1.80, 30 minutes).

Dodecanese
Δωδεκάνησα

When the Greek Gods were doling out sandy coves, blankets of wildflowers and lofty views, the Dodecanese seem to have received more than their fair share. Add to this a rich culture heavily influenced by Italian rule, azure waters lapping at their shores, and a wealth of natural and historical sites, and it's not surprising that the Dodecanese beckon to so many.

Strung out along the coast of western Turkey and far from Athens, the Dodecanese maintain a certain air of separateness. Despite this degree of historical autonomy, outside forces have left heavy footprints across the islands' past. Here Christianity took root in Greece and the influences of consecutive invasions by the Egyptians, Crusaders, Turks and Italians are still seen in the islands' architecture and cuisine. The islands later became one of the final battlegrounds of WWII before formally becoming part of Greece in 1947. Only 26 of the 163 islands and islets are inhabited and most of these are quite literally a hop away from one another. Many are endowed with distinctive natural features like Kos' lengthy beaches, Nisyros' steaming volcano, or Karpathos' windswept coastline. Others have captivating sights, such as Rhodes' bustling old town, St John's Monastery on Patmos and countless castles, frescoed churches and archaeological ruins dotted across the map. While the bigger islands of Kos and Rhodes afford resort-style vacations, the smaller islands like Lipsi, Leros and Kalymnos offer quiet retreats and traditional island life. If you're a hiker, botanist, beachcomber, kitesurfer, archaeologist, historian or just someone longing for a sunlounge on a quiet beach, the Dodecanese won't disappoint.

DODECANESE

HIGHLIGHTS

- **Living it Up** Exploring the stylish nightlife and cafe scene in Rhodes Town (p523)
- **Other Worldly** Climbing inside the volcano on Nisyros (p554), with the steam rising around you
- **Stepping Back in Time** Staying in Olymbos after the tours have gone home and seeing traditional lifestyle still intact (p538), on Karpathos
- **Feeling the Rush** Cliff-diving and mountain-scaling on Kalymnos (p569)
- **Picture Perfect** Stepping into the postcard-perfect harbour scene on Symi (p543)
- **Kicking Back** Lounging on the long stretches of powder-soft beach on Kos (p562)
- **Royal Vista** Playing king at Pandeli Castle (p573), on Leros, with gob-smacking sunset views
- **Slowing Down** Immersing yourself in the quiet life on Lipsi (p580)
- **Mystical** Entering the cave where St John heard the voice of God on Patmos (p579)

★ Patmos
★ Lipsi
★ Leros
★ Kalymnos
★ Kos
Symi ★
★ Nisyros
Rhodes
★ Town
★ Olymbos

- POPULATION: 193,480
- AREA: 2714 SQ KM

History

The Dodecanese islands have been inhabited since pre-Minoan times, and by the Archaic period Rhodes and Kos had emerged as the dominant islands within the group. Distance from Athens gave the Dodecanese considerable autonomy and they were, for the most part, free to prosper unencumbered by subjugation to imperial Athens. Following Alexander the Great's death in 323 BC, Ptolemy I of Egypt ruled the Dodecanese.

The Dodecanese islanders were the first Greeks to become Christians. This was through the tireless efforts of St Paul, who made two journeys to the archipelago during the 1st century, and through St John, who was banished to Patmos where he had his revelation and added a chapter to the Bible.

The early Byzantine era saw the islands prosper, but by the 7th century AD they were plundered by a string of invaders. The Knights of St John of Jerusalem (Knights Hospitaller), arrived in the 14th century and eventually became rulers of almost all the Dodecanese, building mighty fortifications that were strong enough to withstand time but not sufficient to keep out the Turks in 1522.

The Turks were ousted by the Italians in 1912 during a tussle over possession of Libya. The Italians, inspired by Mussolini's vision of a vast Mediterranean empire, made Italian the official language of the Dodecanese and prohibited the practice of Orthodoxy. The Italians constructed grandiose public buildings in the Fascist style, which was the antithesis of archetypal Greek architecture. More beneficially, they excavated and restored many archaeological monuments.

After the Italian surrender of 1943, the islands (and particularly Leros) became a battleground for British and German forces, with much suffering inflicted upon the population. The Dodecanese were formally returned to Greece in 1947.

RHODES ΡΟΔΟΣ

Rhodes (*ro*-dos) is the jewel in the Dodecanese crown. It embraces you with its mild climate and charms you with the best of both worlds – the buzz of its beautiful, cultured capital and the tranquillity of its beaches and stunning scenery. It has worthwhile sights and quiet villages and offers plenty of places to get lost – from the labyrinthine back streets of the almost magical World Heritage–listed Old Town to the snaking mountain roads. Rhodes is also a great base for daytrips to surrounding islands and is very family-friendly. No wonder so many people make it their sole destination.

History

The Minoans and Mycenaeans were among the first to have outposts on the islands, but it wasn't until the Dorians arrived in 1100 BC that Rhodes began to exert power and influence. The Dorians settled in the cities of Kamiros, Ialysos and Lindos, and made each of them prosperous and autonomous states.

Rhodes continued to prosper until Roman times, switching alliances like a pendulum. It was allied to Athens in the Battle of Marathon (490 BC), in which the Persians were defeated, but had shifted to the Persian side by the time of the Battle of Salamis (480 BC). After the unexpected Athenian victory at Salamis, Rhodes hastily became an ally of Athens again, joining the Delian League in 477 BC. Following the disastrous Sicilian Expedition (416–412 BC), Rhodes revolted against Athens and formed an alliance with Sparta, which it aided in the Peloponnesian Wars.

In 408 BC the cities of Kamiros, Ialysos and Lindos consolidated their powers for mutual protection and expansion by co-founding the city of Rhodes. Rhodes became Athens' ally again, and together they defeated Sparta at the Battle of Knidos (394 BC). Rhodes then joined forces with Persia in a battle against Alexander the Great but, when Alexander proved invincible, quickly allied itself with him.

In 305 BC Antigonus, one of Ptolemy's rivals, sent his son, the formidable Demetrius Poliorketes (the Besieger of Cities), to conquer Rhodes. The city managed to repel Demetrius after a long siege. To celebrate this victory, the 32m-high bronze statue of Helios Apollo (Colossus of Rhodes), one of the Seven Wonders of the Ancient World, was built.

After the defeat of Demetrius, Rhodes knew no bounds. It built the biggest navy in the Aegean and its port became a principal Mediterranean trading centre. The arts also flourished. When Greece became the battleground upon which Roman generals fought for leadership of the empire, Rhodes allied

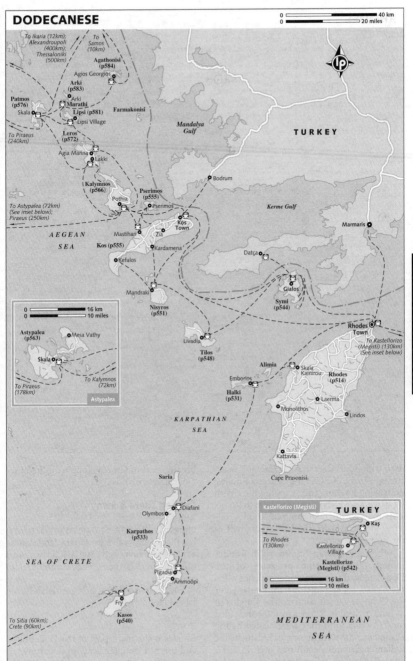

DODECANESE

0 — 40 km
0 — 20 miles

To Ikaria (12km);
Alexandroupoli
(400km);
Thessaloniki
(500km)

To
Samos
(10km)

Agathonisi
(p584)

Agios Georgios

Arki
(p583)

Arki

Patmos
(p576)

Skala

Marathi

Lipsi (p581)

Lipsi Village

Farmakonisi

Leros
(p572)

Agia Marina

Lakki

To Piraeus
(240km)

Kalymnos
(p566)

Pothia

To Astypalea (72km)
(See inset below);
Piraeus (250km)

Pserimos
(p555)

Pserimos

Mandalya
Gulf

T U R K E Y

Bodrum

Kerme Gulf

Marmaris

A E G E A N
S E A

Mastihari

Zia

Kos
Town

Kos (p555)

Kardamena

Kefalos

Datça

Mandraki

Nisyros
(p551)

Gialos

Symi
(p544)

Rhodes
Town

To Kastellorizo
(Megisti) (130km)
(See inset below)

Livadia

Tilos
(p548)

Alimia

Skala
Kamirou

Emborios

Halki
(p531)

Rhodes
(p514)

Monolithos

Laerma

Lindos

K A R P A T H I A N
S E A

Kattavia

Cape Prasonisi

Saria

Diafani

Olymbos

Karpathos
(p533)

S E A   O F   C R E T E

Pigadia

Ammoöpi

Fry

To Sitia (60km);
Crete (90km)

Kasos
(p540)

M E D I T E R R A N E A N
S E A

Astypalea inset

0 — 16 km
0 — 10 miles

Astypalea
(p563)

Mesa Vathy

Skala

To Piraeus
(178km)

To Kalymnos
(72km)

Astypalea

Kastellorizo inset

Kastellorizo (Megisti)

T U R K E Y

Kaş

To Rhodes
(130km)

Kastellorizo
Village

Kastellorizo
(Megisti) (p542)

0 — 16 km
0 — 10 miles

DODECANESE

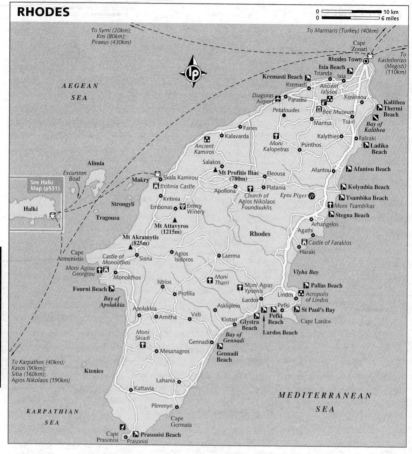

itself with Julius Caesar. After Caesar's assassination in 44 BC, Cassius besieged Rhodes, destroying its ships and stripping the city of its artworks, which were then taken to Rome. This marked the beginning of Rhodes' decline, and in AD 70 Rhodes became part of the Roman Empire.

When the Roman Empire split, Rhodes joined the Byzantine province of the Dodecanese. It was given independence when the Crusaders seized Constantinople. Later the Genoese gained control. The Knights of St John arrived in Rhodes in 1309 and ruled for 213 years until they were ousted by the Ottomans, who were in turn kicked out by the Italians nearly four centuries later. In 1947, after 35 years of Italian occupation, Rhodes became part of Greece along with the other Dodecanese islands.

Getting There & Away

AIR

Olympic Air (Map p517; ☎ 22410 24571; Ierou Lohou 9) has flights across Greece and the Dodecanese while **Aegean Airlines** (☎ 22410 98345; Diagoras airport) offers flights to Athens, Thessaloniki, Iraklio and Rome.

For more on flights between islands, see Island Hopping (p759).

BOAT

Rhodes is the main port of the Dodecanese and offers a complex array of departures to Piraeus, Sitia, Thessaloniki and many stops in between. **Dodekanisos Seaways** (Map p518; ☎ 22410 70590; Afstralias 3) runs daily catamarans up and down the Dodecanese. Tickets are available from the kiosk at the dock. In Rhodes Town you'll also find the Sea Star ticket booth for ferries to Tilos and the ANES ticket booth for long-distance ferries to Athens.

The EOT (p516) in Rhodes Town can provide you with current schedules. Tickets are available from at Skevos' Travel Agency (p516).

Two local ferries, the *Nissos Halki* and *Nikos Express*, run daily between Halki and Skala Kamirou on Rhodes (€10, approximately 30 minutes), including a daily car-carrying caïque.

Two local ferries, the *Nissos Halki* and *Nikos Express*, run daily between Halki and Skala Kamirou on Rhodes (€10, one hour).

See also Island Hopping (p759).

International
There is a daily catamaran from Rhodes' Commercial harbour to Marmaris, Turkey (50 minutes), departing at 8am and 4.30pm from June to September. In winter, sailings twice weekly at 2pm. Tickets cost €36 one way plus €15 Turkish port tax. Same-day return tickets are only €1 more. Open return tickets cost €46 plus €29 tax. There is also a passenger and car ferry service on this same route (car/passenger €95/49 including taxes, 1¼ hours), running four or five times a week in summer and less often in winter. Book online at rhodes.marmarisinfo.com or contact Triton Holidays (p516).

Getting Around
TO/FROM THE AIRPORT
The Diagoras airport is 16km southwest of Rhodes Town, near Paradisi. Buses depart regularly between the airport and Rhodes Town's Eastern Bus Terminal (Map p517) from 6.30am to 11.15pm (€2.20, 25 minutes). On Sunday, buses stop running at around 11.45am.

BICYCLE
A range of bicycles is available for hire at **Bicycle Centre** (Map p517; ☎ 22410 28315; Griva 39; per day €5).

BOAT
There are excursion boats to Lindos and Symi (€22 return) daily in summer, leaving Mandraki Harbour at 9am and return-ing at 6pm. An older boat heads to Diafani on Karpathos, departing at 8.30am from Mandraki Harbour and returning at 6pm. From Diafani, a bus will take you on to Olymbos. By tickets on board.

BUS
Rhodes Town has two island bus terminals, located a block away from one another, and each servicing half of the island. There is regular transport across the island all week, with fewer services on Saturday and only a few on Sunday. You can pick up schedules from the kiosks at either terminal or from the EOT office (p516). Unlimited travel tickets are available for one/two/three days (€10/15/25).

From the Eastern Bus Terminal (Map p517) there are regular services to the airport (€2.20), Kalithea Thermi (€2), Salakos (€4), Ancient Kamiros (€4.60) and Monolithos (€6). From the Western Bus Terminal (Map p517) there are services to Faliraki (€2), Tsambika Beach (€3), Stegna Beach (€3.50) and Lindos (€4.50).

CAR & MOTORCYCLE
There are numerous car- and motorcycle-hire outlets in Rhodes Town. Shop around and bargain because the competition is fierce. Agencies will usually deliver the car to you. You can also book through Triton Holidays (p516). The following agencies will deliver vehicles to you.

Drive Rent A Car (☎ 22410 68243/81011; www. driverentacar.gr; airport) Budget Rental Car outlet.

Etos Car Rental (☎ 22410 22511; www.etos.gr)

Orion Rent A Car (☎ 22410 22137)

TAXI
Rhodes Town's main taxi rank (Map p517) is east of Plateia Rimini. There are two zones on the island for taxi meters: Zone One is Rhodes Town and Zone Two (slightly higher) is everywhere else. Rates are double between midnight and 5am.

Taxis prefer to use set fare rates which are posted at the rank. Sample fares: airport €18, Lindos €43, Falaraki €15 and Kalithia €8. Ring a taxi on ☎ 22410 6800, 22410 27666 or 22410 64712 within Rhodes Town and on ☎ 22410 69600 from outside the city. For disabled-accessible taxis, call ☎ 22410 77079.

DODECANESE

RHODES TOWN

pop 56,130

The heart of Rhodes Town is the atmospheric Old Town, enclosed within massive walls and filled with winding passageways and alleys. Getting lost in this labyrinth of passages can easily be a highlight of your trip – you'll encounter quiet squares, children playing, out-of-the-way tavernas and gorgeous architecture. Visit early in the day or at dusk to see the sun reflected off the stonework and to avoid the crowds.

The New Town is mainly to the north. A few blocks are dominated by package tourism, while trendy cafes, name-brand shops, fine dining and a handful of sights take you to the more enjoyable neighbourhoods. This is also where you'll find the city's best beach.

Orientation

The Old Town is divided into three sectors: the Kollakio (Knights' Quarter), the Hora and the Jewish Quarter. The Kollakio contains most of the medieval historical sights while the Hora, often referred to as the Turkish Quarter, is primarily Rhodes Town's commercial sector with shops and restaurants. The Old Town is accessible by nine *pyles* (main gates) and two rampart-access portals and is a mesh of Byzantine, Turkish and Latin architecture. When on foot remember that, although the streets may look pedestrianised (and might not be much wider than your hips), mopeds and motorbikes zoom around the bends. If you've hired a car, don't try to drive in the Old Town – most streets are one-way and *very* narrow.

The commercial centre of the New Town lies north of the Old Town and is easily explored on foot. The Commercial Harbour (Kolona) is east of the Old Town. Excursion boats, small ferries, hydrofoils and private yachts use Mandraki Harbour, further north.

Information

INTERNET ACCESS

Mango Cafe Bar (Map p518; ☎ 22410 24877; www .mango.gr; Plateia Dorieos 3; per hr €5; ☽ 9.30am-midnight)

On The Spot Net (Map p518; ☎ 22410 34737; Perikleous 21; per hr €5; ☽ 8am-midnight) Comfortable surroundings in the Hotel Spot.

Walk Inn (Map p518; ☎ 22410 74293; Plateia Dorieos 1; per hr €2; ☽ 10am-11pm)

INTERNET RESOURCES

www.rhodesguide.com What's on, where to stay and where to hang out in Rhodes.

www.rodos.gr Upcoming events, links and background to Rhodes.

LAUNDRY

Wash House Star (Map p517; ☎ 22410 32007; Kosti Palama 4-6; per load €5; ☽ 8am-11pm, closed Sun) Have your clothes washed, dried and folded within two hours.

Washomatic (Map p518; ☎ 22410 76047; Platonos; per load €5; ☽ 8am-11pm Mon-Sat, summer only) Similar service in the Old Town.

MEDICAL SERVICES

Emergencies & ambulance (☎ 166)

General Hospital (Map p517; ☎ 22410 80000; Papalouka El Venizelou) Just northwest of the Old Town.

Krito Private Clinic (Map p517; ☎ 22410 30020; Ioannou Metaxa 3; ☽ 24hr)

MONEY

You'll find plenty of ATMs throughout Rhodes Town and at the following banks. You'll also find a handy ATM at the international ferry quay.

Alpha Credit Bank (Map p518; Plateia Kyprou)

Commercial Bank of Greece (Map p518; Plateia Symis)

National Bank of Greece New Town (Map p517; Plateia Kyprou); Old Town (Map p518; Plateia Mousiou)

POLICE

Port police (Map p517; ☎ 22410 22220; Mandrakiou)

Tourist police (Map p517; ☎ 22410 27423; ☽ 24hr) Next door to the EOT.

POST

Main post office (Map p517) On Mandraki Harbour.

TOURIST INFORMATION

EOT (Map p517; ☎ 22410 35226; www.ando.gr; cnr Makariou & Papagou; ☽ 8am-2.45pm Mon-Fri) Supplies brochures, city maps and the *Rodos News*, a free English-language newspaper.

TRAVEL AGENCIES

Charalampis Travel (Map p518; ☎ 22410 35934; ch_trav@otenet.gr; 1 Akti Saktouri) Books flights and boat tickets.

Skevos' Travel Agency (Map p517; ☎ 22410 22461; skeos@rho.forthnet.gr; 111 Amerikis) Books boat and flight tickets throughout Greece.

Triton Holidays (Map p517; ☎ 22410 21690; www.tri tondmc.gr; Plastira 9, Mandraki) Helpful staff book air and

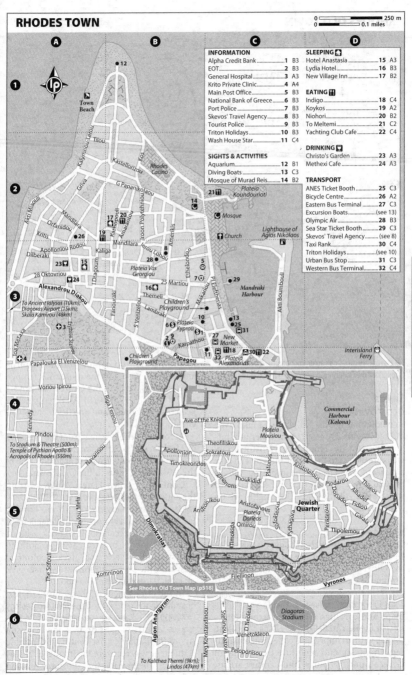

RHODES TOWN

INFORMATION		SLEEPING	
Alpha Credit Bank	**1** B3	Hotel Anastasia	**15** A3
EOT	**2** B3	Lydia Hotel	**16** B3
General Hospital	**3** A3	New Village Inn	**17** B2
Krito Private Clinic	**4** A4		
Main Post Office	**5** B3	EATING	
National Bank of Greece	**6** B3	Indigo	**18** C4
Port Police	**7** B3	Koykos	**19** A2
Skevos' Travel Agency	**8** B3	Niohori	**20** B2
Tourist Police	**9** B3	To Meltemi	**21** C2
Triton Holidays	**10** B3	Yachting Club Cafe	**22** C4
Wash House Star	**11** C4		
		DRINKING	
SIGHTS & ACTIVITIES		Christo's Garden	**23** A3
Aquarium	**12** B1	Methexi Cafe	**24** A3
Diving Boats	**13** C3		
Mosque of Murad Reis	**14** B2	TRANSPORT	
		ANES Ticket Booth	**25** C3
		Bicycle Centre	**26** A2
		Eastern Bus Terminal	**27** C3
		Excursion Boats	(see 13)
		Olympic Air	**28** B3
		Sea Star Ticket Booth	**29** C3
		Skevos' Travel Agency	(see 8)
		Taxi Rank	**30** C4
		Triton Holidays	(see 10)
		Urban Bus Stop	**31** C3
		Western Bus Terminal	**32** C4

See Rhodes Old Town Map (p518)

DODECANESE

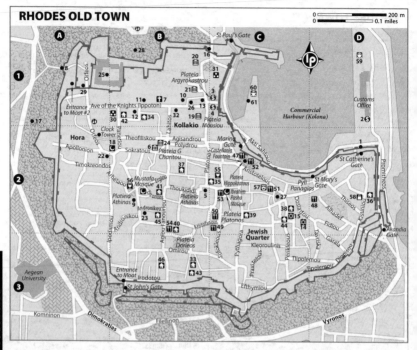

RHODES OLD TOWN

sea travel, hire cars, book accommodation and plan tours throughout the Dodecanese. They also sell tickets to Turkey.

Sights

OLD TOWN

In medieval times the Knights of St John lived in the Knights' Quarter, while other inhabitants lived in the Hora. The 12m-thick city walls are closed to the public but you can take a pleasant walk around the imposing walls of the Old Town via the wide and pedestrianised moat walk. All the Old Town sights are on Map p518.

Knights' Quarter

Begin your tour of the Knights' Quarter at **Liberty Gate**, crossing the small bridge into the Old Town. In a medieval building is the original site of the **Museum of Modern Art** (☎ 22410 23766; www.mgamuseum/gr; 2 Plateia Symis; 3 sites €3; ☉ 8am-2pm Tue-Sat). Inside you'll find maps and carvings. The main exhibition is now at the **New Art Gallery** (☎ 22410 43780; Plateia G Charitou) with an impressive collection of painting, engraving and sculpture from some of Greece's most popular 20th-century artists,

including Gaitis Giannis, Vasiliou Spiros and Katraki Vaso. For the museum's temporary exhibits, head to the **Centre of Modern Art** (☎ 22410 77071; 179 Socratous St). All three galleries keep the same hours and one ticket gains you entrance to all three.

Across the pebbled street from the Museum of Modern Greek Art, take in the remains of the 3rd-century-BC **Temple of Aphrodite**, one of the few ancient ruins in the Old Town.

Continuing down Plateia Argyrokastrou, the **Museum of the Decorative Arts** (☎ 22410 72674; Plateia Argyrokastrou; admission €2; ☉ 8.30am-2.40pm Tue-Sun) houses an eclectic array of artefacts from around the Dodecanese. It's chock-a-block with instruments, pottery, carvings, clothing and spinning wheels and gives a colourful view into the past. Captions are sparse; pick up explanatory notes at the door.

In the atmospheric 15th-century knights' hospital up the road is the **Museum of Archaeology** (☎ 22410 27657; Plateia Mousiou; admission €3; ☉ 8am-4pm Tue-Sun). Its biggest draw is the exquisite *Aphrodite Bathing*, a 1st-century-BC marble statue that was recovered from the local seabed. Many believe it is the cult statue missing from the nearby Temple of Aphrodite. The rest of the museum is filled with ancient statues and pottery found on Rhodes.

Wander up the **Avenue of the Knights** (Ippoton), once home to the knights themselves. They were divided into seven 'tongues' or languages, according to their place of origin – England, France, Germany, Italy, Aragon, Auvergne and Provence – and each was responsible for protecting a section of the bastion. The Grand Master, who was in charge, lived in the palace, and each tongue was under the auspices of a bailiff.

To this day the street exudes a noble and forbidding aura, despite modern offices now occupying most of the inns. Its lofty buildings stretch in a 600m-long unbroken wall of honey-coloured stone blocks, and its flat facade is punctuated by huge doorways and arched windows.

First on the right, if you begin at the eastern end of the Avenue of the Knights, is the 1519 **Inn of the Order of the Tongue of Italy**. Next door is the **Palace of Villiers de l'Isle Adam**; after Sultan Süleyman had taken the city, it was Villiers de l'Isle who had the humiliating task of arranging the knights' departure from the island. Next along is the **Inn of France**, the most ornate and distinctive of all the inns. On the opposite side of the street is the **Villaragut Building**, a knight's

home converted into an Ottoman Mansion in the 18th century. Closed for renovations at the time of writing, it now houses Byzantine antiques. Peek through the gate to see the Turkish garden.

Back on the right side is the **Chapelle Française** (Chapel of the Tongue of France), embellished with a statue of the Virgin and Child. Next door is the residence of the Chaplain of the Tongue of France. Across the alleyway is the **Inn of Provence**, with four coats of arms forming the shape of a cross, and opposite is the **Inn of Spain**.

Near the end of the avenue, **St John of the Collachio** was originally a knights' church with an underground passage linking it to the palace across the road. The Ottomans later turned it into a mosque and it was destroyed in 1856 when the gunpowder stored in the belltower exploded. Soon after, a neoclassical building was erected on the site and remains there today. Climb up to the viewing platform to also take in the ruins of the original transept and the underground gallery.

On the right is the truly magnificent 14th-century **Palace of the Grand Masters** (☎ 22410 23359; Ippoton; admission €6; ⏰ 8.30am-3pm Tue-Sun), which was severely damaged by the Turkish siege and then destroyed by an explosion in the mid-1800s. The Italians rebuilt the palace

---

THE KNIGHTS OF ST JOHN

As you travel through the Dodecanese, you'll quickly realise that the Knights of St John left behind a whole lot of castles. The knights were originally formed as the Knights Hospitaller, an organisation founded in Jerusalem in 1080 to provide care for poor and sick pilgrims on their way to the Holy Land. After the loss of Jerusalem in the First Crusade, the knights relocated to Rhodes (via Cyprus) in the early 14th century and managed to oust the ruling Genoese in 1309. The Knights of St John in Rhodes were supposedly a chivalrous Christian organisation but also established themselves as purveyors of legitimate and somewhat-less legitimate commercial activities – primarily piracy, and antipiracy against Ottoman shipping and pilgrims. This irked the Ottoman Sultan Süleyman the Magnificent (not a man you'd want to irk) and he set about dislodging the knights from the stronghold. Rhodes capitulated in 1523, after which the remaining knights relocated to Malta, where they continue to meet as the Sovereign Military Hospitaller Order of St John of Jerusalem, of Rhodes and of Malta.

---

following old plans for the exterior but introducing a grandiose, lavish interior. It was intended as a holiday home for Mussolini and King Emmanuel III but is open as a museum. Only 24 of the 158 rooms can be visited; inside you'll find antique furnishing, sculptures, frescoes and mosaic floors.

From the palace, walk through **D'Amboise Gate**, the most atmospheric of the gates which takes you across the moat. When the palace is open, you can also gain access to the walkway along the top of the wall from here, affording great views into the Old Town and across to the sea. Another option is to follow the peaceful **Moat Walkway**, which you can access next to **St Anthony's Gate**. It's a green oasis with lush lawns cushioned between trees and the old walls.

Hora

Bearing many legacies of its Ottoman past is the **Hora**. During Turkish times, churches were converted to mosques and many more Muslim houses of worship were built from scratch, although most are now dilapidated. The most important is the colourful, pink-domed **Mosque of Süleyman**, at the top of Sokratous. Built in 1522 to commemorate the Ottoman victory against the knights, it was renovated in 1808. For a bird's eye view of it, follow the footpath along the side of the neighbouring (and now defunct) clock tower.

Opposite is the 18th-century **Muslim Library** (Plateia Arionos; Sokratous; admission free; ☽ 9.30am-4pm Mon-Sat). Founded in 1794 by Turkish Rhodian Ahmed Hasuf, it houses a small number of Persian and Arabic manuscripts and a collection of Korans handwritten on parchment.

Continuing through the winding pedestrian streets will bring you to the municipal **Hammam Turkish Baths** (Plateia Arionis; admission €5; ☽ 10am-5pm Mon-Fri, 8am-5pm Sat). They are open to the public, with separate male and female baths. Warm yourself on the marble stones or opt for a massage. Lockers are available.

Jewish Quarter

The **Jewish Quarter** is an almost forgotten sector of Rhodes Old Town, where life continues at an unhurried pace and local residents live seemingly oblivious to the hubbub of the Hora no more than a few blocks away. This area of quiet streets and sometimes dilapidated houses was once home to a thriving Jewish community.

Built in 1577, **Kahal Shalom Synagogue** (Polydorou 5) is Greece's oldest synagogue and the only one surviving on Rhodes. The Jewish quarter once had six synagogues and, in the 1920s, a population of 4000. Have a look in at the **Jewish Synagogue Museum** (☎ 22410 22364; www.rhodes jewishmuseum.org; Dosiadou; ☽ 10am-3pm Sun-Fri, closed winter), in the old women's prayer rooms around the corner. Exhibits include lots of early 20th-century photos, intricately decorated documents and displays about the 1673 Jews deported from Rhodes to Auschwitz in 1944. Only 151 survived.

Close by is **Plateia Evreon Martyron** (Square of the Jewish Martyrs).

NEW TOWN

The **Acropolis of Rhodes** (off Map p517), southwest of the Old Town on Monte Smith, was the site of the ancient Hellenistic city of Rhodes. The hill is named after the English admiral Sir Sydney Smith, who watched for Napoleon's fleet from here in 1802. It has superb views.

The site is not well signposted but makes for an interesting wander. The restored 2nd-century-AD tree-lined **stadium** once staged competitions in preparation for the Olympic Games. Today, locals continue to use it for jogging. The adjacent **theatre** is a reconstruction of one used for lectures by the Rhodes School of Rhetoric. Steps above here lead to the **Temple of Pythian Apollo**, with four re-erected columns. A small exhibition between the stadium and the road details the history of the site and the reconstruction. This unenclosed site can be reached on city bus 5.

North of Mandraki, at the eastern end of G Papanikolaou, is the graceful **Mosque of Murad Reis** (Map p517). In its grounds are a Turkish cemetery and the Villa Cleobolus, where Lawrence Durrell lived in the 1940s, writing *Reflections on a Marine Venus*.

To get close-up to the underwater world of the Aegean, head to Rhodes' small **Aquarium** (Map p517; ☎ 22410 27308; www.hcmr.gr; Kos 1; admission adult/child €5/free; ⏰ 9am-8.30pm Apr-Oct, 9am-4.30pm Nov-Mar). The art deco building was constructed during the 1930s by the Italians as a biological research station. Walk through the sea cave to view a colourful array of molluscs, crabs, sea turtles and fish.

The town **beach** begins north of Mandraki and continues around the island's northernmost point and down the west side of the New Town. The best spots will depend on the prevailing winds but tend to be on the east side, where there's usually calmer water and more sand and facilities.

Activities

GREEK DANCING LESSONS

The **Nelly Dimoglou Dance Company** (Map p518; ☎ 22410 20157; deyappet@otenet.gr; Andronikou 7; admission per person/group €16/11; ⏰ May-Oct) gives lessons and stages lively performances (9.15pm on Monday, Wednesday and Friday) in folk dance theatre.

SCUBA DIVING

A number of diving schools operate out of Mandraki, all offering a range of courses, including a 'One Day Try Dive' for €40 to €50, and PADI certification. You can get information from their **boats** at Mandraki Harbour (Map p517).

Diving Centres (☎ 22410 23780)
Diving Med College (☎ 22410 61115; www.divemed college.com)

Scuba Diving Trident School (☎/fax 22410 29160)
Waterhoppers Diving Centre (☎/fax 22410 38146, 6972500971; www.waterhoppers.com)

Sleeping
BUDGET

During the summer, finding an affordable bed in the Old Town is very possible, particularly if you book ahead. In winter, most budget places shut down throughout the city so you'll definitely need to call ahead. While most of the New Town's hotels are modern and characterless, there are a few exceptions.

New Village Inn (Map p517; ☎ 2241034937, 6976475917; www.newvillageinn.gr; Konstantopedos 10; s/d €35/45) These village-style rooms in the New Town with very comfy mattresses are a home from home. All come with a ceiling fan and fridge. The tranquil interior courtyard and bar is overflowing with plants; you'd never guess that you're not near the hustle and bustle of downtown.

Hotel Isole (Map p518; ☎ 22410 20682, 6937580814; www.hotelisole.com; Evdoxou 35; s/d incl breakfast €30/50; 🅿 🖵) With its entrance under a stone archway in the narrow passages of the Old Town's backstreets, these seven rooms offer great value for money. Decorated in white and blue, they're a cool, quiet retreat. Chat with the multilingual owners at the small bar.

our pick **Hotel Anastasia** (Map p517; ☎ 22410 28007; www.anastasia-hotel.com; 28 Oktovriou 46; s/d/tr €38/52/55; 🅿 🖵) Tucked away off the main drag in the New Town, this Italian mansion has big open rooms with lots of light. The tiled floors and high ceilings give it stacks of character and the lush garden is a quiet place to sip a cocktail or coffee at the outdoor bar.

Pension Olympos (Map p518; ☎/fax 22410 33567; www.pension-olympos.com; Agiou Fanouriou 56; s/d/tr €40/55/60; 🅿) These pleasant rooms have a slight granny feel about them, with traditional artwork and comfy wrought-iron beds. The very private garden is a lovely place to relax. All rooms have a small fridge.

Continue your hunt for a bed at the following places:

Pension Eleni (Map p518; ☎ 22410 73282; www.eleni rooms.gr; Dimosthenous 25; s/d €35/65) Very simple but spotlessly clean rooms in the Jewish Quarter. Some rooms have a loft to sleep four and there's a small shared patio.
Mango Rooms (Map p518; ☎ 22410 24877; www.mango.gr; Plateia Dorieos 3; s/d/tr €46/58/68; ⏰ year-round; 🖵) Comfortable, well-maintained but basic rooms with ceiling fans and fridges. Rooftop terrace to relax on.

DODECANESE

Pink Elephant (Map p518; ☎ 22410 22469; www.pink elephantpension.com; Timakida 9; s/d €36/60; 🛜) Simple, fan-equipped rooms. Shared fridge, small courtyard and friendly owner.

MIDRANGE

Pension Andreas (Map p518; ☎ 22410 34156; fax 22410 74285; www.hotelandreas.com; Omirou 28d; s/d €55/60; 🕑year-round; 🛇 🖥 🛜) This small, rather ramshackle but inviting hotel has 11 individually decorated rooms. Some are airy, some bright and some have private terraces. An extra mattress can be added for a child. The terrace is very social at breakfast and offers panoramic views, while the owner is a wealth of local info. Minimum two-night stay.

Apollo Tourist House (Map p518; ☎ 22410 32003; www.apollo-touristhouse.com; Omirou 28c; s/d incl breakfast €65/70; 🖥) This small pension has tastefully furnished rooms with wooden four-poster and traditional captain's beds. Splashes of colour and lengths of muslin make it all the more homey. Enjoy the view from your room or head out to the terrace.

Hotel Via Via (Map p518; ☎/fax 22410 77027; www .hotel-via-via.com; Lisipou 2; d €70; 🕑 year-round; 🛇 🖥) Each eclectic room here is unique – some with subtle blues and others with vibrant greens. They're not plush but comfortable and colourful. Embellished with plants, the rooftop terrace offers excellent views.

Domus Rodos Hotel (Map p518; ☎ 22410 25965; info@domusrodoshotel.gr; Platonos; d €80; 🕑 year-round; 🛇 🖥) These well-maintained, comfortable rooms are some of the few available all year-round in the Old Town. The only drawback is noise from nearby bars. Back rooms have balconies and the friendly owner has plenty of local info. Call ahead in winter.

Hotel Spot (Map p518; ☎ 22410 34737; www.spot hotelrhodes.gr; Perikleous 21; s/d/tr incl breakfast €70/90/140; 🛇 🖥 🛜) Heavy wood furniture and orange, red and golden hues give the rooms in this small boutique hotel a Rajasthan feel. It has a comfortable terrace and rooftop terrace, a small book exchange and a friendly host.

Lydia Hotel (Map p517; ☎ 22410 22871; www.lydia hotel.com; Martiou 25; s/d €80/90; 🛇 🖥 🛜) Close to the seaside, shopping and cafes and just a stroll away from the Old Town lies this classy hotel. What the comfortable rooms lack in character is more than made up for by the bar, lobby area and garden.

Hotel Cava d'Oro (Map p518; ☎ 22410 36980; www .cavadoro.com; Kisthiniou 15; d/tr incl breakfast €85/120;

🅿 🛇) Stone walls and wrought-iron furniture give you the feeling that this hotel hails from another era. Then again, the building is 800 years old. A family suite has a cool loft area and all rooms have a stylish touch. Taxis can come to the door.

Marco Polo Mansion (Map p518; ☎ 22410 25562; www .marcopolomansion.gr; Agiou Fanouriou 40-42; d incl breakfast from €90) Set in a 15th-century, carefully restored mansion and bursting with atmosphere, the rooms here have a rustic yet plush feel to them with fabric and furnishings from India and Turkey. Think warm colours, high ceilings and four-poster beds. Right in the heart of the old town, it's a cool, shady retreat.

TOP END

Nikos & Takis Hotel (Map p518; ☎ 22410 70773; www.niko stakishotel.com; Panetiou 29; d from €150; 🅿 🛇 🖥 🛜) This boutique hotel offers atmospheric, individually decorated rooms. Check out the Moroccan-themed Marokino, with its marble tub, ornately tiled floor and authentic slippers. All rooms have music piped into the bathroom and plush amenities. Breakfast is taken on a banana-tree-shaded patio.

Avalon Boutique Hotel (Map p518; ☎ 22410 31438; www.hotelavalon.gr; Charitos 9; d €300; 🛇 🖥 🛜) This peaceful oasis has stunningly luxurious rooms that ooze with character. Opt for one with a fireplace or Jacuzzi. All have flat screen TVs and individual furnishing. The lovely garden and rooftop terrace are ideal for serious relaxation.

Eating

BUDGET

Old Town

Avoid the restaurant touts along Sokratous and around Plateia Ippokratous. Hit the backstreets to find less touristy eateries.

Prince Bakery Cafe (Map p518; Plateia Ippokratous; snacks €1-5; 🕑 10am-11pm) Tucked in the corner of the square, this place has a designer feel to it. Sink into the leather seats and tuck into freshly baked breads and pastries or get something to go. There's a deli for sandwiches, an orange-juicer and a well-stocked bar. If you're more peckish, go for the sausage plate or grills.

gelaterie.gr (Map p518; ☎ 22410 38925; www .gelaterie.gr; Plateia Ippokratous 1; snacks €3-5) Organic crêpes, smoothies and mountains of ice cream will call to you from across the square. Try a rum-and-banana crêpe or spend ages perusing the smoothie options like Love Potion,

Fountain of Youth or Hangover Blaster. There are no tables but the nearby fountain makes a lovely place to slurp and watch the world go by.

O Meraklis (Map p518; Aristotelous 30; soup €4; ⏰ 3am-8am) After a night out on the tiles a plate of tripe and entrails soup is what's needed – according to the Greek hangover cure. That's pretty much all it serves. An experience you *might* want to try.

Walk Inn (Map p518; ☎ 22410 74293; Plateia Dorieos 1; mains €3-7; ⏰ 10am-11pm) With a good mix of tourists hanging out and locals playing chess, this low-key, backpacker-style place serves up homemade pizza, pasta and pita sandwiches.

New Town

our pick Koykos (Map p517; ☎ 22410 73022; Mandilana 20-26; mains €2-8) Popular with Rhodes younger crowds, Koykos is Greek kitsch. From the architecture to the copper-tray-swinging waiters, it would almost be tacky if it weren't so enjoyable. Crowds huddle around chess and card games while others focus on the savoury pies, seafood dishes, salads and mezes. Accompany your meal with barrel wines, ouzo or retsina. The in-house bakery makes divine sweets and breads for you to take home.

Niohori (Map p517; ☎ 22410 35116; I Kazouli 29; mains €3-8) This essentially nontouristy eatery makes little concession to appearance, but if you're a meat-lover you'll forget all about that. The owner is a butcher and serves his own country sausage and veal liver with oil and oregano.

Yachting Club Cafe (Map p517; ☎ 22410 75723; Plateia Alexandrias; snacks €3-10) Slightly pretentious but with lovely sun-filled views across the bay, this is the place to be seen. Everything is rather pricey but very good quality. Come for breakfast and try the brioche, crêpes or flaky croissants, washed down with strong coffee.

Indigo (Map p517; ☎ 6972663100; New Market 105-106; mains €5-12; ⏰ dinner) Unexpectedly located in the New Market, this small restaurant has colourful tablecloths and Greek traditional dishes with creative salads. Try the house salad with croutons, rocket, walnut and garlic or the hazelnut salad with blue cheese. Handy if you're just off the bus.

MIDRANGE & TOP END
Old Town

To Megiston (Map p517; ☎ 22410 29127; Sopokelous; mains €8-15; ⏰ year-round) This family-run taverna whips up amazing food, including a country-style Greek salad, swordfish and specialities from Kastellorizo. The desserts are mouth-watering and the service is exceptionally friendly.

our pick Mandala (Map p518; ☎ 22410 38119; Sofokleos 38; mains €8-15; ⏰ lunch Sun & dinner daily winter; lunch & dinner daily summer) Lively and popular, the hip Mandala dishes up creative cuisine, such as chèvre-and-fig starters, salmon pasta or Moroccan chicken. The eatery offers excellent service, a well-stocked bar and frequent live music make it that much more of a treat.

Nireas (Map p518; ☎ 22410 31741; Sofokleous 45-47; mains €8-16) The fish will taste just as good whether you dine outside under a canopy of greenery or inside in the classy yellow rooms. Seared or sesame-encrusted tuna, steamed mussels with garlic and white wine – the list seems endless. Popular with families for lunch, Nireas opens onto a quiet square. To find it, just follow your nose.

Hatzikelis (Map p518; ☎ 22410 27215; Alhadef 9; mains €9-16) With a high-beamed ceiling and heavy velvet curtains, Hatzikelis is a step back in time. Popular with local families, it's well known for shellfish. Look for mussels, scallops with garlic butter and *kefalotyri* (sheep's-milk cheese), fresh clams or sea-urchin roe. The menu is in Greek only but the helpful waiters speak English.

New Town

To Meltemi (Map p517; ☎ 22410 30480; cnr Plateia Kountourioti & Rodou; mains €7-15) With traditional music and open sea views, Meltemi occupies a prime spot just north of Mandraki harbour. Grills and fish are locally revered and the creative salads are fantastic: try the Meltemi, with rocket, apple, walnut, pine nuts and dried fruit.

Drinking & Entertainment

Rhodes Town is brimming with cool places to hang out in the evening. Bars and watering holes are stylish and atmospheric – great places to mingle with the locals and unwind after a hard day of lounging on the beach.

OLD TOWN

The majority of the nightlife happens around Platonos and Ippokratous squares. Also check out Mandala (above) for live local music on Sundays and some evenings.

DODECANESE

Rogmitou Chronou (Map p518; ☎ 22410 25202; www.rogmitouxronou.gr; Plateia Arionos; ☺ 10pm-5am; ⓐ) With lots of stonework and heavy wood, the Music Cafe spreads over two floors. Downstairs has a cosy, medieval feel to it and live acoustic music on Mondays, while upstairs has a hint of the '50s with red bar stools and live rock bands on Fridays. The rest of the week sees various DJs; check the on-line events listing.

Apenadi (Map p518; ☎ 22410 21055; Evripidou 13-15) Step into the set for Arabian Nights and sink into some colourful cushions, strewn beneath exquisite chandeliers. And let's not forget the funky music, mezes, cocktails and friendly service.

ourpick **Cafe Chantant** (Map p518; ☎ 22410 32277; Dimokratou 3; ☺ midnight-early) Locals sit at long wooden tables, drinking ouzo or beer and listening to live, traditional music. It's dark in here and you won't find snacks and nibbles, but the atmosphere is palpable and the band is lively. It's an experience you won't soon forget.

NEW TOWN

Locals hang out along the bar-lined I Dragoum, while the tourist haunts are found along Akti Miaouli, Orfanidou and Griva.

ourpick **Methexi Cafe** (Map p517; ☎ 22410 33440; 29 Oktovriou, cnr Griva) This colonial-style mansion is filled with black-and-white photos and stacks of magazines. The comfortable, homey feeling draws a relaxed young crowd who come for live Greek music or to drink beer on the terrace.

Christo's Garden (Map p517; Griva; ☺ 10pm-late) Prop yourself up at the grotto-style bar surrounded by lush greenery, seemingly worlds away from the city. Traditional buildings surround the inner courtyard where you can have a relaxed drink amongst the fairy lights.

Sound & Light Show (Map p518; ☎ 22410 21922; www.hellenicfestival.gr; admission €7) Squeezing many centuries of history into a show with lights, voices and music, the Sound & Light Show is something you'll either love or hate. Shows take place from Monday to Saturday next to the walls of the Old Town, off Plateia Rimini and near the D'Amboise Gate. English-language sessions are staggered, but in general begin at either 9.15pm or 11.15pm. Other languages offered are French, German and Swedish.

Shopping

You'll find lots of recognisable high-street shops in Rhodes, particularly along Lambraki (good for shoes and umbrellas) and Karpathou, a pedestrianised street with cafes and shops galore. The eastern half of 28 Oktovriou is where you'll find the posh shops and cafes.

New Market is filled with mostly tacky souvenirs. In the Old Town, look out for gold and silver jewellery, leather goods and ceramics: most shops are along Sokratous.

ourpick **Byzantine Iconography** (Map p518; ☎ 22410 74127; Kisthinioy 42) Visiting the studio of Basilios Per Sirimis is an experience you shouldn't miss. A teacher and accomplished artist, he follows the traditional methods of iconography, producing paintings for churches and families throughout Greece. All of his materials are natural, including gold leaf and pigments mixed with egg and vinegar. You can see paintings in various stages of production and Basilios will fascinate you with his knowledge. Paintings go for €210 to €2000.

Getting Around

Local buses leave from the **urban bus stop** (Map p517; Mandraki) on Mandraki Harbour and charge a flat €1. Bus 11 does a circuit around the coast, up past the Aquarium and on to the Acropolis. Hopping on for a loop is a good way to get your bearings. Bus 2 goes to Analipsi, bus 3 to Rodini, bus 4 to Agios Dimitrios and bus 5 to the Acropolis. Buy tickets on board.

EASTERN RHODES

The majority of Rhodes' long stretches of sandy beaches are along its east coast. Consequently, that's much more developed, with a number of villages made-over into summer resorts that tend to be filled with young package-holidaymakers and endless strips of tourist bars. If you do find yourself based in one of these resorts, you could make the most of the beach and then hire a car or hop on a bus to explore more remote beaches, the interior and the south or west coast.

From Rhodes Town, there are frequent buses to Lindos, but some of the beaches en route are a bit of a hike from the road. The obvious bonus to this is that it's still possible to find uncrowded stretches of sand even at the height of summer.

Restored to its former glory, **Kalithea Thermi** (☎ 22410 65691; Kallithea; www.kallitheasprings.gr; admission €2.50; ☼ 8am-8pm April-Oct, 8am-5pm Nov-Mar) was originally an Italian-built spa, just 9km from Rhodes Town. With grand buildings, colonnades, domed ceilings and countless archways delivering stunning sea views, it's worth a wander. Exhibitions inside show the many films made here (including scenes from *Zorba the Greek*) as well as local artwork. You'll also find a cafe and a small, sandy beach that's good for swimming. The as-yet-uncompleted, vast expanses of *hohlakia* (black-and-white pebble mosaic floors) have taken 14 years to complete so far.

Ladiko Beach, touted locally as 'Anthony Quinn Beach', is in fact two back-to-back coves with a pebbly beach on the north side and volcanic rock platforms on the south. The swimming is good, though the water is noticeably colder here.

Further down the coast, a right turn at Kolymbia takes you along a pine-fringed road to the **Epta Piges** (Seven Springs), 4km away. Head here if you're feeling parched or deprived of greenery. The springs bubble into a river, which flows into a shaded lake. You can reach the lake by following a footpath or by walking through a narrow, dark tunnel that's ankle-deep with fast flowing river water. If you're claustrophobic or tall, opt for the path. The lake itself has a magical colour and is home to turtles. It was built by the Italians who damned the river to irrigate the Kolymbia plains. There's a cafe next to the springs and a kitsch children's playground. There are no buses to Epta Piges; take a Lindos bus and get off at the turn-off.

Back on the coast, the beaches of **Kolymbia** and **Tsambika** are sandy but can get crowded in summer. On the left, a steep signposted road takes you 1.5km up to the 300 steps leading to **Moni Tsambikas**. Inside the small white chapel you'll find an 11th-century icon of Mary, found on the mountaintop by an infertile couple who soon after had a child. Since then, the site has become a place of pilgrimage for women hoping to conceive. On 18 September, the monastery's festival day, women climb up on their knees and make offerings of wax babies and silver plaques, which you'll see crowding the front of the church. The frescoes and ancient altar are worth seeing, as is the magnificent 360-degree view outside.

Further up the road is a turn-off to sandy, idyllic **Stegna Beach**. Another 4km along is a

turning for Haraki from where you'll find a path up to the ruins of the 15th-century **Castle of Faraklos**. Once a prison for recalcitrant knights and the island's last stronghold to fall to the Turks, it offers great views. Nearby is the sandy cove of **Agathi**.

Lindos Λίνδος
pop 1090
Topped with an impressive acropolis and spilling down into stunning twin bays, Lindos is one of Rhodes' most picturesque villages. Following the narrow, winding alleyways will lead you through a maze of dazzling white **17th-century houses**, once the dwellings of wealthy admirals and many boasting courtyards with *hohlakia*.

Of course, the loveliness of Lindos has not gone unnoticed and it's become a bit of a tourist hotspot. Most of the day-trippers congregate between 10am and 4pm; you could visit early in the morning or spend the night to see Lindos *au naturel*. Even in the bustle of the day, head off from the teeming main thoroughfares lined with tourist shops and cafes, and you'll find quiet corners of the village to explore.

HISTORY
Lindos is the most famous of the ancient cities of the Dodecanese and was an important Doric settlement because of its excellent vantage point and good harbour. It was first established around 2000 BC and is overlaid with a conglomeration of Byzantine, Frankish and Turkish remains.

After the founding of the city of Rhodes, Lindos declined in commercial significance, but remained an important place of worship. The ubiquitous St Paul landed here en route to Rome. Later, the Byzantine fortress was strengthened by the knights, and also used by the Turks. The 15th-century Church of Agios Ioannis, within the Acropolis, is festooned with 18th-century frescoes.

ORIENTATION & INFORMATION
The village is totally pedestrianised. All vehicular traffic terminates on the central square of Plateia Eleftherias, from where the main drag, Acropolis, begins. The donkey terminus for rides up to the Acropolis itself is a little way along here. Turn right at the donkey terminus to reach the post office, after 50m.

DODECANESE

THE CAPTAIN'S HOUSE *Korina Miller*

During the 17th century, ship captains from Lindos grew increasingly prosperous. Many of them poured their new-found wealth into building lofty homes that towered over the traditional village houses.

I'm standing inside the oldest of these captain's houses. It was built 400 years ago and is small but very grand. The whitewashed walls stretch upward to a soaring resin ceiling, intricately painted with elaborate, colourful patterns and still scorched in the corner above where the original family cooked. You might be tricked into believing that the captain's family has just stepped out – except for the rather incongruous flat-screen TV and the stylish sofas and coffee tables. Savvas Kornaros is here doing a little repainting and tells me the story of the building.

'This house has been in my wife's family for 150 years. Her great-great grandfather bought it in the 19th century. Her father turned it into a bar 33 years ago, for local people and tourists. He lived here with his family at first, with the bar in the courtyard. But everyone wanted to come inside and see the ceiling and so after a couple of years he moved into the building next door and made the house part of the bar.

The bed is a traditional *penga* (raised wooden sleeping platform) where the whole family slept. The bed and the cupboards on either side, as well as the decor, are pretty much as they were when the captain lived here. Captains' houses didn't need to be large as they spent so much time at sea. The windows in these houses are up very high. This was to let the heat out in summer and also so that the captain's wife could watch the sea for the arrival of her husband's ship. The stone doorway is hand carved and each picture or symbol has meaning. Corn means good harvest, birds mean peace, the cross brings safety and the sunflowers sunlight. The number of ropes carved around the perimeter of the door shows how many ships the captain had. You'll see these symbols on lots of doorways around Lindos.'

We go outside into the courtyard with its intricately laid stone floor. 'This *hohlakia* (black-and-white pebble mosaic) floor is from 1911. It takes a lot of work to make. First the masons have to find enough stones of a similar shape and size. They create the pattern and then use a little bit of cement to put down the black stones and then fit the white ones around them. This kind of floor is expensive; I think the very best price you'd get is €200 for a square metre. That would be a very good deal. But all of the houses and courtyards in Lindos have these floors. They look good and they're long lasting. It's tradition.'

He has just finished cleaning the floor for the summer season. 'In the summer we get very busy here; everyone wants to see inside the house. If you do come in July or August, Sundays and Mondays are probably the quietest days. But the best times to visit Lindos are May and October when the weather is good. In the winter I only open if a cruise ship comes in. Otherwise I fix the place up. I do all of the maintenance myself.'

Savvas heads behind the courtyard bar to pour drinks for some locals who have wandered in. I ask him how tourism has changed Lindos over the years. 'I don't know what you mean. It hasn't. We've had the same people coming here for the past 25 years.'

By the donkey terminus is the Commercial Bank of Greece, with an ATM. The National Bank of Greece, located on the street opposite the Church of Agia Panagia, also has an ATM.

Lindianet (☎ 22440 32142; per hr €3.60; ☺ 9.30am-9pm Mon-Sat, 4-9pm Sun) Internet access plus wi-fi. In lower village.

Lindos Library & Laundrette (☎ 22440 31333; Acropolis; per load €7.50) Laundry service and second-hand English books. Also hires out fans.

Lindos Sun Tours (☎ 22440 31333; www.lindosun tours.gr; Acropolis) Has room-letting services, hires cars

and motorcycles and can assist with airport transfers, babysitting, etc.

Medical Clinic (☎ 22440 31224) Near the church.

Municipal Tourist Office (☎ 22440 31900; Plateia Eleftherias; ☺ 7.30am-9pm) Helpful, although too few staff, too many tourists. You may have to wait a while.

www.lindos-holiday.com A handy private website with a number of alternative villa accommodation options.

SIGHTS & ACTIVITIES
Acropolis of Lindos

Spectacularly perched atop a 116m-high rock is the **Acropolis** (☎ 22440 31258; admission €6;

8.30am-2.40pm Tue-Sun Sep-May, until 6pm Tue-Sun Jun-Aug). Once inside, a flight of steps leads to a large square. On the left (facing the next flight of steps) is a trireme, hewn out of the rock by the sculptor Pythocretes; a statue of Hagesandros, priest of Poseidon, originally stood on the deck of the ship. The steps ahead lead to the Acropolis via a vaulted corridor. A sharp left leads through an enclosed room to a row of storerooms on the right, while the stairway on the right leads to the remains of a 20-columned **Hellenistic stoa** (200 BC). The Byzantine **Church of Agios Ioannis**, with its ancient frescoes, is to the right of this stairway. The wide stairway behind the stoa leads to a 5th-century-BC propylaeum, beyond which is the 4th-century **Temple to Athena**, the site's most important ancient ruin. Athena was worshipped on Lindos as early as the 10th century BC and this temple has replaced earlier ones on the site. From its far side there are splendid views of Lindos village and its beach.

Donkey rides to the Acropolis cost €5 one way – be aware that the poor creatures should not be carrying anyone over 50kg (112lbs), though this stipulation is rarely enforced. To get here on your own steam, head straight into the village from the main square, turn left at the church and follow the signs. The last stretch is a strenuous 10-minute climb up slippery steps. There's no shade at the top; pack a hat and some water.

Beaches

The **Main Beach** is to the east of the Acropolis and is sandy with warm water. You can follow a path north to the western tip of the bay to the smaller **Pallas Beach** where there are some tavernas and a jetty. Avoid swimming near the jetty as it's home to black stinging anemones. On the western side of the Acropolis is the sheltered **St Paul's Bay** with its warm, turquoise water. It's a bit more of a trek to get to but often quieter than the main beach.

SLEEPING

Accommodation can be expensive, hard to find or already reserved. Be sure to call ahead.

Anastasia Studio (☎ 22440 31751; www.lindos -studios.gr; d/tr €45/60; P ☒) On the eastern side of town, these modern apartments are spacious and comfortable, with fantastic flower bedecked verandas affording sea views. Each has a well equipped kitchen and separate bedroom and there's a minimarket across the road.

Electra (☎ 22440 31266; s/d €45/55; ☒) Thankfully, Lindos' true budget option is brilliant. Electra has an expansive and popular roof terrace with superb views and a beautiful shady garden of lemon trees. The 11 rooms are airy and spacious. Each has a fridge and there's a communal kitchen. Follow the donkey route to find it.

Filoxenia Guest House (☎ 22440 31266; www.lindos -filoxenia.com; d/ste incl breakfast €90/140; ☒ ▢) Inside a traditional home, these simple rooms are embellished with wrought-iron bed frames, antique furnishing, tiled floors or raised sleeping platforms. Family rooms are also available. All rooms have fridge and kitchenette.

our pick Melenos (☎ 22440 32222; www.melenoslin dos.com; ste incl breakfast €385; ☒ ▢ ☏) The kind of place most of us dream of staying, Melenos is pure luxury. Built in 17th-century style, almost everything has been handmade, hand-carved or hand-stitched – from the sandstone motifs to the mosaic floors, painted ceiling, woven fabrics and cedar sleeping platforms. Artefacts embellish the already gorgeous rooms while the verandas offer privacy, more comfort and stunning views. Head up to the rooftop bar for your evening aperitif.

EATING

Valanda's Crepes (☎ 22440 31673; crêpes €3-5) You'll smell your way to this crêperie en route to the Acropolis. Watch the crêpes flipped in front of you within the cool blue interior. Choose from sweet and savoury fillings.

Captain's House (☎ 22440 31235; snacks €3-6) This atmospheric, shaded courtyard is an oasis after a trip up to the Acropolis. Sit on sofas in the shaded courtyard or head inside the traditional captain's house. Refresh with iced coffees, beer on tap, cocktails and juice or munch on baguettes or toasted sandwiches. Follow signs left from the Acropolis.

Eklekto (☎ 22440 31286; mains €3-6) Popular with locals and expats, this leafy courtyard and comfortable cafe has sandwiches, tortillas and salads – try Cleopatra's with dried figs, rocket and pine nuts. It's just east off the main drag.

Kalypso (☎ 22440 32135; mains €6-12) Set in one of Lindos' historic buildings, this is a family-run restaurant that's stood the test of time. Ignore the touristy outdoor appearance; inside you'll find traditional decor and a warm atmosphere. Dine on the rooftop on feta flutes, fresh tuna, sausages in mustard, or rabbit stew in red

DODECANESE

wine. The menu is enormous, with vegetarian and children's options. Take the second right off the main drag to find it.

DRINKING

Lindos has plenty of trendy bars and clubs, many of which come and go in fashion with each summer season. Just follow the throngs.

WESTERN RHODES & THE INTERIOR

Greener and more forested than the east coast, Western Rhodes makes for a great road trip with a number of worthwhile sights. It's also windier so the sea tends to be rough and the beaches are mostly pebble. The east–west roads that cross the interior have great scenery and very little traffic. If you have transport, they're well worth exploring. It's also good cycling territory if you have a suitably geared bicycle.

Ancient Ialysos Αρχαία Ιαλυσός

The Doric city of **Ialysos** (adult €3; 8.30am-3pm Tue-Sun) was built on Filerimos Hill, an excellent vantage point, and attracted successive invaders over the years. Over time, it became a hotchpotch of Doric, Byzantine and medieval remains. As you enter, stairs lead to the ancient remains of a 3rd-century-BC temple and the restored 14th-century **Chapel of Agios Georgios** and **Monastery of Our Lady**. All that's left of the temple are the foundations but the chapel is a peaceful retreat.

Take the path left from the entrance to a 12th-century **chapel** (looking like a bunker) filled with frescoes. They're not well preserved but worth a look. To the right of the entrance lies a ruined and no longer accessible **fortress** used by Süleyman the Magnificent during his siege of Rhodes Town.

There is a sign requesting that visitors dress 'properly'. Although there's no elaboration, out of respect, shoulders should be covered and women should wear long skirts or trousers. Outside the entrance you'll find a small kiosk, a whole lot of peacocks and a popular tree-lined path with the **Stations of the Cross**. There are also ruins of a **Byzantine church** below the car park. Ialysos is 10km from Rhodes, with buses running every half hour.

Ialysos to Petaloudes

Heading south from Ialysos, you'll come to the small but interesting **Bee Museum** (22410

48200; www.mel.gr; admission €2; 8.30am-3pm), with lots of English explanations. You'll learn about the process of honey-making and collecting, equipment from past and present, and the history of beekeeping on Rhodes. See bees at work, dress up in beekeepers outfits and watch demonstrations of making honey. The gift shop is a great place to stock up on souvenirs: honey rum, honey soap, honey sweets and just plain honey. To reach the museum, join the super-smooth Tsairi–Airport motorway towards Kalithies; it's on the right, just past Pastida.

From here it's a short trip to **Marista** from where the scenic road takes you up over pine forested hills to **Psinthos**, where you'll find a lively square lined with lunch spots. **To Stolidi Tis Psinthoy** (22410 59998; mains €7-9) has a country feel to it with wooden beams, checked tablecloths and family photos on the walls. Try spicy pork, dolmadhes and freshly baked country bread.

Petaloudes Πεταλούδες

Northwest of Psinthos, **Petaloudes** (adult €3; 8.30am-4.30pm) is better known as the Valley of the Butterflies. Visit in June, July or August when these colourful creatures mature, and you'll quickly see why. They're actually moths (*Callimorpha quadripunctarea*) drawn to this gorge by the scent of the resin exuded by the storax trees. In summer, this is a very popular sight frequented by tour buses. Come out of season and you'll miss the winged critters but you'll have the gorgeous forest path, rustic footbridges, streams and pools to yourself.

While the moths have undoubtedly benefited from having a reserve of their own, their numbers are under threat due to noise disturbance. You're therefore asked not to clap your hands or make any other disruptive noise.

Ancient Kamiros Αρχαία Κάμειρο

The extensive **ruins** of the Doric city of Kamiros stand on a hillside above the west coast, 34km south of Rhodes Town. The ancient city, known for its figs, oil and wine, reached the height of its powers in the 6th century BC. By the 4th century BC it had been superseded by Rhodes. Most of the city was destroyed by earthquakes in 226 and 142 BC, leaving only a discernible layout. Ruins include a **Doric temple**, with one column still standing, **Hellenistic houses**, a **Temple to Athena** and a 3rd-century **great stoa**. It was built on top of a huge 6th-century cistern that supplied the houses with rainwater through an advanced drainage system.

At the time of research, the entire site was closed due to destruction by forest fires. Check with EOT (p516) to see if it has reopened.

Ancient Kamiros to Monolithos
Αρχαία Κάμειρος προς Μονόλιθο

Skala Kamirou, 13.5km south of ancient Kamiros, serves as the access port for travellers heading to and from the island of Halki (p530). The small harbour itself is north of town and very picturesque. Even if you're not waiting for a ferry, it's worth stopping for lunch at **O Loukas** (☎ 22460 31271; mains €7-12). With big, sea views, appropriately nautical decor and a relaxed atmosphere, it serves up very fresh fish, seafood and homemade burgers.

Just south of the harbour, before the town of Skala, is a turning for Kritinia. This will lead you to the ruined 16th-century **Kritinia Castle** with awe-inspiring views along the coast and across to Halki. It's a magical setting where you expect to come across Romeo or Rapunzel.

The road south from here to Monolithos has some stunning scenery. From Skala Kamirou the road winds uphill, with a turning left for the wine-making area of Embonas (below) about 5km further on. The main road continues for another 9km to **Siana**, a picturesque village below Mt Akramytis (825m), famed for its honey and *souma* – a spirit made from seasonal fruit.

The village of Monolithos, 5km beyond Siana, has the spectacularly sited 15th-century **Castle of Monolithos** perched on a sheer 240m-high rock and reached via a dirt track. To enter, climb through the hole in the wall. Continuing along this track, bear right at the fork for **Moni Agiou Georgiou**, or left for the very pleasant shingled **Fourni Beach**.

Wine Country
From Salakos, head inland to **Embonas** on the slopes of Mt Attavyros (1215m), the island's highest mountain. Embonas is the wine capital of Rhodes and produces some of the island's best tipples. The red Cava Emery or Zacosta and white Villare are good choices. Taste and buy them at **Emery Winery** (☎ 22410 41208; www.emery.gr; Embonas; admission free; ⏲ 9.30am-4.30pm April-Oct), which offers tours of its cottage

production. You'll find it on the eastern edge of town.

Embonas is no great shakes itself, despite being touted by the tourism authorities as a 'traditional village'. Detour around Mt Attavyros to **Agios Isidoros**, 14km south of Embonas, a prettier and still unspoilt wine-producing village en route to Siana.

SOUTHERN RHODES
South of Lindos, the island is lush and less developed. As you head further south, it takes on a windswept appearance and the villages seem to have a slower pace. It's well worth exploring – strike out along a quiet country road and you're sure to stumble upon lovely views, quiet villages and family tavernas pleased to whip you up a hearty meal.

Just 2km south of Lindos, sandy **Pefki Beach** is deservedly popular. If it's too crowded, try **Glystra Beach**, just down the road and a great spot for swimming.

The flourishing village of **Laerma** is 12km northwest of Lardos. From here it's another 5km through hilly, green countryside to the beautifully sited 9th-century **Moni Tharri** (entrance by donation), the island's first monastery, which has been re-established as a monastic community. It's a bit of a trek but worth the drive if you're into frescoes. Every inch of the chapel's interior is covered in ornate 13th-century paintings which are very well preserved. The monastery is generally left unlocked during the day.

Further down the coast is the turning for **Asklipieio**, with the ruins of a castle and the 11th-century **Church of Kimisis Theotokou**, with more Byzantine wall paintings.

Gennadi Γεννάδι
pop 655

A patchwork of narrow streets and white-washed houses set several hundred metres back from the beach, Gennadi (ye-*nah*-dhi) is a quiet village with enough facilities to make it a decent southern base. You'll find a fruit market, bakery, cafes, supermarket, internet access, car hire and a couple of cocktail bars to keep you going.

Effie's Dreams Apartments (☎ 22440 43410; www .effiesdreams.com; d/tr €54/58; 🚫 🖵) is next to an enormous 800-year-old mulberry tree and has simple, clean studios with small kitchenettes and lovely rural and sea vistas from the communal balcony. You'll also find a cafe and

DODECANESE

bar serving drinks and filling snacks, such as country-style sausage with onions and peppers. The beach is a 10-minute walk away.

Mama's Kitchen (☎ 22440 43547; pasta €5-6) looks pretty average but makes fresh pizza in front of you. Try one with feta, olives and swordfish. There are also pasta and grills.

Gennadi to Prasonisi Γεννάδι προς Πρασονήσι

From Gennadi an almost uninterrupted beach of pebbles, shingle and sand dunes extends down to **Plimmyri**, 11km south.

Watch for a signposted turning to **Lahania**, 2km off the main highway. The top road of Lahania is less than special, but head downhill into the old town (the first left if you're coming from the coast) to find a village of winding alleyways and traditional buildings that makes it onto very few tourist itineraries. Surrounded by lemon trees and flowers, **Agios Georgios** is a pretty church in the main square with a star-strewn ceiling and a plethora of chandeliers.

If a rural holiday takes your fancy but you want to do it in comfort, stay at the **Four Elements** (☎ 6939450014; studio/apt per week €515/550; ✉ ▯ ▨) with its exceptionally homey and spacious apartments. Some have sea views and one has a traditional open fireplace. All have full kitchens and there's a divine pool, kid's pool, outdoor grill and garden. One of the apartments is wheelchair accessible.

While in Lahania, stop for lunch at **Taverna Platanos** (☎ 22440 46027; mains €3-5), a relaxed taverna tucked behind the church in the main square. With traditional decor and a flower-filled patio, it's a great place to take a break.

The main coastal road continues south past countless chapels to **Kattavia**, Rhodes' most southerly village. It's a friendly place that doesn't see a lot of tourist traffic. Stop in at **Penelope's** (☎ 6944794342; mains €5-12) in the main square for fresh fish, handmade chips and Greek salad made with lots of local greens.

From Kattavia, a 10km road snakes south across windswept terrain to remote and gorgeous **Cape Prasonisi**, the island's southernmost point. Once joined to Rhodes by a narrow sandy isthmus, it's now split by encroaching seas. If you're looking for lunch or a bed, there's a resort here that caters to windsurfers and has surfer-dude-style restaurants and hostels. Outside of the summer season it's totally shut.

Kattavia to Monolithos Κατταβία προς Μονόλιθος

Lonely and exposed, Rhodes' southwest coast doesn't see many visitors. Forest fires in recent years have devastated many of the west-facing hillsides but it's nevertheless a beautiful place to visit with an edge-of-the-earth feeling. The beaches along here are prone to strong winds and currents. About 10km north of Kattavia, a turn-off to the right leads to the serene 18th-century **Moni Skiadi**, with terrific views down to the coast.

HALKI ΧΑΛΚΗ

pop 310

Tiny Halki (*hal*-ki) rests in relative obscurity, just a stone's throw from Rhodes. Rocky and bare, it draws those who come for its relaxation value. Visitors park themselves for weeks at a time in restored stone villas that once belonged to sea captains, and spend their days doing little more than chilling out and socialising with the growing, seasonal expat community.

In the days of antiquity, before water had to be carted over from Rhodes, the island's wells supported a population of 7000 who produced wheat and copper (from which the island's name is derived). In later years, sponge-fishing became the main industry and its demise led to waves of emigration. The largest group departed for Florida in 1911, where they established a strong Greek community that continues to support the island. Halki existed in almost forgotten silence until the vacation boom of the 1970s and 1980s saw its fortunes rise once more.

Despite its barren appearance, Halki is humming with more life than you might think. With 14 types of butterflies, over 40 kinds of birds, fields of oregano and marjoram, countless bee boxes and around 6000 goats, it's a wonder there's room for the sun loungers at all. Visit in spring to see the island blanketed in wild flowers.

Getting There & Away

There is a daily boat from Skala Kamirou on Rhodes with a connecting bus to Rhodes Town every day but Sunday. Walk 150m from the Skala Kamirou ferry quay to the main road to find the bus stop.

Ferries also connect Halki with Sitia on Crete, Karpathos, Santorini and

quarterly *Halki Visitor* is a good source of local information.

There's a DodecNet ATM at the information booth on the harbour although there's no bank on the island.

Chalki Tours (☎ 22460 45281; fax 22460 45219) For assistance on accommodation, travel, excursions and currency exchange.

Clinic (☎ 22460 45206; ⏱ 9am-noon & 6-8pm Mon-Fri) Weekend numbers posted at clinic for emergencies.

Information Hut (quay) Local info posted.

Police and Port Police (☎ 22460 45220) On the harbour.

Post office (⏱ 9am-1.30pm Mon-Fri) On the harbour.

www.chalki.gr A useful (though slightly dated) reference point.

www.halki-travel-guide.com Packed with lots of local info.

Zifos Travel (☎ 22460 45082; zifostravel.gr) Helps with accommodation, travel, excursions and currency exchange.

Piraeus. Tickets are available from Chalki Tours and Zifos Travel in Emborios (see below). For more information, see Island Hopping (p751).

Getting Around

The majority of people get around the island on foot. In summer, a minibus runs hourly between Emborios and Moni Agiou Ioanni (€2). The island also has a lone taxi usually found parked near the post office. Prices and telephone numbers are posted at kiosks. There's also a water taxi that serves the main beaches and you can find excursion boats to the uninhabited island of Alimia (€30), with fields of wild herbs. There are no hire cars or motorcycles on Halki.

EMBORIOS ΕΜΠΟΡΕΙΟΣ
pop 50

The picturesque port village of Emborios is draped around a narrow horseshoe bay of crystal-blue waters. The mansions surrounding it were once the homes of sea captains who took inspiration for the large Venetian-style shuttered windows from their travels across the Mediterranean. Cars are banned from the harbour once the ferries have come and gone, so the waterside enjoys a relaxing, vehicle-free setting.

Orientation & Information

Boats arrive at the centre of Emborios' harbour and most services and accommodation are within easy walking distance. The free

Sights

The old **mansions** that festoon the harbour are a visual feast. Many have been, or are being, restored to their former glory, while others rest in a complete state of disrepair. Together they give Halki a picturesque look and make wandering around the harbour a popular pastime.

The impressive stone **clock tower** at the southern side of the harbour is a gift from the Halki community in Florida. The tower looks resolutely impressive but don't rely on it for the time.

The **Church of Agios Nikolaos** has the tallest belfry in the Dodecanese and boasts an impressive pebbled courtyard on the east side. A small upstairs **museum** (adult €2; ⏱ 6-7pm Mon & Fri, 11am-noon Sun) houses ancient bibles, icons and other ecclesiastical displays.

Sleeping

Most accommodation is prebooked months in advance by foreign tour companies, so booking ahead is best. Both travel agents in town can help you find a room.

Captain's House (☎ 22460 45201; capt50@otenet .gr; d €40) This snug 19th-century house has slightly dated decor and period furniture in comfortable rooms. The tranquil tree-shaded garden is a lovely place to relax. Bookings are always recommended.

Mouthouria (☎ 22460 72755; www.halkimouthau ria.com; house €90) Once the home of a Turkish Governor, this house is decorated in deep reds

DODECANESE

and yellows, with an intricately painted ceiling. With two bedrooms, it can accommodate up to six people and its fully equipped kitchen, garden and view-filled balcony make it ideal for longer stays.

Villa Fiona (☎ 44 01363 83343; www.villafiona.com; house per week €375) This charming restored home will make you want to stay forever. Sleeping up to six, its two bedrooms and lounge are simple and airy. The separate, bright kitchen will inspire you to whip up home-cooked meals. Relaxation is enhanced with books, games, music and sea views from the balcony. It's a minute's walk to a ladder descending into the clear harbour water.

Eating

Mavri Thalassa (☎ 22460 45021; mains €4-6) Found on the south side of the harbour, this place specialises in seafood and is popular with locals and visitors. Try the whole grilled calamari or local, minuscule Halki shrimps – eaten whole.

Maria's Taverna (☎ 22460 45300; mains €4-7) Under the shade of trees, fill up on pasta and local home-cooked specialities like Halki lamb stew. Its central location makes it a popular lunch spot.

Avra (☎ 6945148196; mains €4-7) With a long, tempting menu, Avra's Georgian owners serve excellent chicken and seafood dishes downed with draught white wine.

Remezzo (☎ 22460 45010; mains €5-7) Is your tummy feeling homesick? Give it a break from Greek salad and treat it to pizza, pasta, Mexican salad and apple dessert.

AROUND HALKI

In the next bay south, sandy **Podamos Beach** is the nearest and best beach. Only 1km from Emborios in the direction of Horio, it has shallow water that's ideal for kids. You'll find a basic taverna and loungers and umbrellas for hire. Pebbly **Ftenagia Beach**, past the headland and 500m to the south of Emborios, is excellent for rock swimming and snorkelling. The **Ftenagia Beach Taverna** (☎ 6945998333; mains €5-7; ⊗ lunch & dinner) is a cosy waterside eatery.

Horio, a 30-minute walk (3km) along Tarpon Springs Blvd from Emborios, was once a thriving community of 3000 people, but it's now almost completely derelict. The **church** contains beautiful frescoes but is only unlocked for festivals. On 14 August the entire island climbs up here for a ceremony devoted to the Virgin Mary, the church's icon. A barely per-

ceptible path leads from Horio's churchyard up to the **Knights of St John Castle**. It's a steep 15-minute walk with spectacular views.

Moni Agiou Ioanni is a two-hour, unshaded 8km walk along a broad concrete road from Horio. The church and courtyard, protected by the shade of an enormous cypress tree, is a quiet, tranquil place that comes alive each year on 28 and 29 August during the feast of the church's patron, St John. You can sometimes stay in simple rooms in exchange for a donation to the church.

KARPATHOS
ΚΑΡΠΑΘΟΣ

pop 6080

Despite its soaring mountains, colourful harbours and sandy beaches, Karpathos (*kar*-pa-thos) has long sat in the shadow of its northern neighbours, giving it an off-the-beaten-track quality that's now drawing tourists. The island's windswept coastline has become a magnet for surfers and hits the spotlight each summer when it hosts an international kitesurfing competition. Be prepared for gusts and gales at any time of year.

Over the years, many of the islands' inhabitants have migrated to the USA, from where they slowly trickle back to invest their overseas earnings. The consequence is a vibrant mix of contemporary and traditional culture. In the north of the island lies Olymbos, a small community that was isolated for years from the south by rugged mountains. Today it's still home to a unique culture that has survived the onslaught of modernity and offers a window into the past.

Getting There & Away

Karpathos has an airport with regular links to Athens, Kasis, Sitia and Rhodes. **Olympic Air** (☎ 22450 22057; www.olympicairlines.com, cnr Apodimon Karpathion & 25 Martiou St, Pigadia) is on the central square in Pigadia.

Scheduled ferries service Rhodes, Piraeus, Kasos, Sitia, Agios Nikolaos, Milos and Santorini. Tickets can be bought from Possi Travel (p534) in Pigadia. A small local caïque also runs three times weekly between Finiki (Karpathos) and Fry (Kasos).

For more information, see Island Hopping (p752).

KARPATHOS

0   6 km
0   4 miles

Karpathos Strait

Cape Paraspori

Cape Parthori

Saria

Tristomo

Cape Vroukounda • Vroukounda
Moni Agiou Ioanni

Avlona

Vananda Beach

Moni Agiou Konstantinou • Diafani

Mt Profitis Ilias (716m) ▲ Olymbos

To Halki (50km); Rhodes (60km)

Papa Mina Bay

SEA OF CRETE

Agios Minas

Spoa

Mesohori • Agios Nikolaos

Apella Beach

Karpathos

Excursion Boat

Roman Cistern

Lefkos Pine Tree Studios

Lefkos Beach

Kali Limni (1215m)

Mertonas

Kyra Panagia Beach

Kato Lakos Beach

Aperi

Ahata Beach

Volada

Adia • Pyles • Othos

Cape Proni

Vrondi Bay

Kamarakia Beach

Flaskia Gorge

Pigadia

Agios Georgios Beach

Basilica of Agia Sophia & Acropolis

Finiki

Menetes

Agios Nikolaos Beach

Arkasa

Ammoöpi

Cape Volakas

Cape Agios Theodoros

Afiartis Bay

Cape Akrotiri

Cape Lingi

Cape Kastello

To Kasos (10km); Crete (80km); Piraeus (420km)

Getting Around
TO/FROM THE AIRPORT

There is no airport bus. Hop in a taxi to Pigadia (€15) and beyond.

BOAT

From May to September there are daily excursion boats from Pigadia to Diafani with a bus transfer to Olymbos (€23). Boats depart Pigadia at 8.30am. Tickets are available from Possi Travel (p534). There are also frequent boats to the beaches of Kyra Panagia and Apella (€10). Tickets can be bought at the quay.

From Diafani, excursion boats go to nearby beaches and occasionally to the uninhabited islet of Saria, where there are some Byzantine remains. See p537 for details.

BUS

Pigadia is the transport hub of the island; a schedule is posted at the **bus terminus** (☎ 22450 22338; M Mattheou) and the tourist info kiosk (p534). Buses (€2; July and August only; daily except Sunday) serve most of the settlements in southern Karpathos, including the west-coast beaches. There is no bus between Pigadia and Olymbos or Diafani.

CAR, MOTORCYCLE & BICYCLE

On the eastern side of Pigadia, **Rent A Car Circle** (☎ 22450 22690/911; 28 Oktovriou) hires cars and motorcycles. Possi Travel (p534) also arranges car hire.

The precipitous, and at times hairy, 19.5km stretch of road from Spoa to Olymbos is being slowly graded and will one day be sealed. You can drive it with care; do not tackle this road by motorcycle or scooter. If you hire a vehicle and plan to drive to Olymbos, opt for a small jeep and fill up your tank before you leave.

TAXI

Pigadia's **taxi rank** (☎ 22450 22705; Dimokratias) is close to the centre of town where you'll find current rates posted. A taxi to Ammoöpi costs €8, the airport €15, Arkasa and Pyles €16, and Kyra Panagia €20.

PIGADIA ΠΗΓΑΔΙΑ
pop 1690

While it may feel a little forsaken by the rest of the Dodecanese, Pigadia (pi-*gha*-dhi-ya) is laden with restaurants, hotels and bars. Small and compact, it spills down to the edge

DODECANESE

of Vrondi Bay, where boats bob in a small harbour. The architecture is nothing special (mostly cement blocks erected in the 1960s and '70s) but, with its lively atmosphere and sandy beach, it's a pleasant spot to base yourself.

Orientation & Information

The ferry quay is at the northeastern end of the wide harbour. It's a short walk to the centre of Pigadia, which is punctuated by the main street, Apodimon Karpathion. This in turn leads west to the central square of Plateia 5 Oktovriou. For the sandy beach, head west 300m to Pigadia Bay.

Avra Tourist Shop (☎ 22450 22388; fax 22450 23486; 28 Oktovriou 50) Sells maps for driving and hiking.

Cyber Games (☎ 22450 22110; seafront; per hr €2; ⏰ 9am-1am) Get online amongst gaming teenagers.

National Bank of Greece (Apodimon Karpathion) Has an ATM.

Police (☎ 22450 22224) Near the hospital at the western end of town.

Possi Travel (☎ 22450 22235; possitvl@hotmail.com; Apodimon Karpathion) The main travel agency for ferry and air tickets.

Post office (Ethnikis Andistasis) Near the hospital.

Pot Pourri (☎ 22450 29073; Apodimon Karpathion; per hr €3; ⏰ 7am-1am) Internet access amidst a comfortable cafe.

Tourist information office (☎ 22450 23835; ⏰ Jul-Aug) In a kiosk in the middle of the seafront.

www.inkarpathos.com Locally maintained with articles, news and info.

Sights

Looking down over the town from a small seaside bluff, the **Archaeological Museum of Karpathos** (admission free; ⏰ 9am-1pm & 6-8.30pm Tue, Thu & Sat, 8.30am-3pm Wed, Fri & Sun) houses local artefacts including coins, an early baptismal font, and ceramics.

Follow the coast southwest from town to find a sandy stretch of beach and, after 2km, the ruins of the early Christian **Basilica of Agia Fotini** resting on the seashore. If you head east along the coast and past the ferry quay, you'll come to a peaceful **chapel** high on the hill with stunning views back to town and across the sea.

Sleeping

Pigadia's accommodation is plentiful, with lots of budget options. A few enterprising owners meet the boats.

Hotel Karpathos (☎ 22450 22347; fax 22450 22248; r €25; 🖫) A little worn but spotlessly clean, these

rooms have a fridge and well-scrubbed bathrooms. They're small but you can escape onto the balcony. The top floors have sea views.

Rose's Studios (☎ 22450 22284, 6974725427; www .rosesstudios.com; r €30; 🖫) Slightly characterless but very well maintained rooms have kitchenettes and great balconies with views to the sea. Rooms facing the back are a little cheaper. The lovely owners live downstairs and are a wealth of local info.

Elias Rooms (☎ 22450 22446, 6978587924; www .eliasrooms.com; s/d €30/35, s/d apt €35/40; 🛜) As you climb the rather steep stairs to this hotel, you can console yourself knowing that the view is well worth it. The three rooms are small and plain while the apartments have more character, tiled floors and, in one, a traditional raised sleeping area. The friendly owner has lots of info to dole out.

Amarylis Hotel (☎ /fax 22450 22375; www.amarylis.gr; s/d €30/40; 🖫) These very dated but amazingly spacious rooms are great for families. Many sleep up to four and all have kitchenettes and big balconies.

Hotel Titania (☎ 22450 22144; www.titaniakarpa thos.gr; s/d €40/55; 🖫) With bedspreads so dated they're almost back in style, these rooms are cramped and overpriced. However, in winter they may be all that's open. Ask for a sea view or a room facing the courtyard, or put up with the noisy road outside.

Lemon Tree Apartments (☎ 22450 22081; www .inkarpathos.com/lemontree; s/d €50/60; 🖫) Newly refurbished rooms aren't huge but they've got excellent kitchenettes and big balconies, some with sea views. Doubles have queen-sized beds!

Eating

Amongst the plethora of indistinguishable waterfront establishments are a few gems. Watch for the local speciality, *makarounes* (homemade pasta cooked with cheese and onions). For self-catering, head to the large supermarket across from the taxi rank.

Pastry Shop (☎ 22450 22530; Dimokratias; sweets €1-4) With towering stacks of local sweets, Karpathian baklava, ice cream and waffles, this is the place to indulge with the locals, all washed down with fresh juice or coffee. You can also pick up savoury pies for a seaside picnic.

To Helliniko (☎ 22450 23932; Apodimon Karpathion; mains €4-9; ⏰ year-round) Popular with locals, To Helliniko offers a fantastic dining experience.

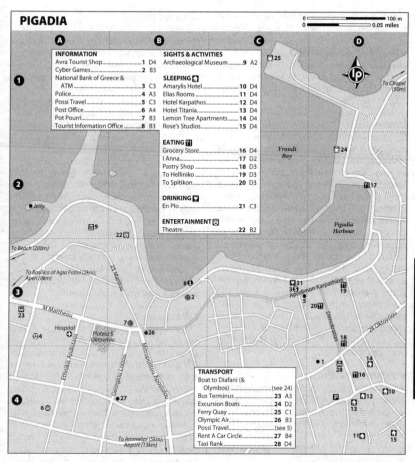

PIGADIA

INFORMATION	
Avra Tourist Shop........................**1** D4	
Cyber Games...............................**2** B3	
National Bank of Greece &	
ATM..**3** C3	
Police...**4** A3	
Possi Travel................................**5** C3	
Post Office..................................**6** A4	
Pot Pourri...................................**7** B3	
Tourist Information Office........**8** B3	

SIGHTS & ACTIVITIES	
Archaeological Museum............**9** A2	
SLEEPING	
Amarylis Hotel.........................**10** D4	
Elias Rooms..............................**11** D4	
Hotel Karpathos.......................**12** D4	
Hotel Titania............................**13** D4	
Lemon Tree Apartments..........**14** D4	
Rose's Studios...........................**15** D4	
EATING	
Grocery Store...........................**16** D4	
I Anna......................................**17** D2	
Pastry Shop..............................**18** D3	
To Helliniko.............................**19** D3	
To Spitikon...............................**20** D3	
DRINKING	
En Plo.......................................**21** C3	
ENTERTAINMENT	
Theatre....................................**22** B2	

TRANSPORT	
Boat to Diafani (&	
Olymbos)..........................(see 24)	
Bus Terminus...........................**23** A3	
Excursion Boats.......................**24** D2	
Ferry Quay...............................**25** C1	
Olympic Air..............................**26** B3	
Possi Travel...............................(see 5)	
Rent A Car Circle.....................**27** B4	
Taxi Rank.................................**28** D4	

To Chapel (50m)

Vrondi Bay

Pigadia Harbour

Jetty

To Beach (200m)

To Basilica of Agia Fotini (2km); Aperi (8km)

Hospital

Plateia 5 Oktovriou

To Ammoópi (5km); Airport (13km)

DODECANESE

With lots of seating but a cosy atmosphere, you'll be served smoked sardines, Karpathian cheese, stuffed artichokes and goat cooked in tomato purée. Be sure to check out the specials board.

I Anna (☎ 22450 22820; Apodimon Karpathion; mains €5-9) You'll quickly forget about the slightly tacky decor as you dig into Pigadia's freshest fish, caught daily off the owner's own boats. Try the fisherman's macaroni with octopus, shrimps and mussels, or the Karpathian sardines in oil.

To Spitikon (☎ 22450 23675; Dimokratias; mains €7-10) A rustic, family atmosphere and attentive service makes this a popular stop. Traditional dishes are served alongside more unusual options like potatoes stuffed with peppermint

and sour cream, spring rolls with crabmeat and bacon, balsamic chicken and *kalamari* (squid) stuffed with dill and feta. The pizza is slightly greasy but satisfying and can be ordered for takeaway.

Drinking & Entertainment

Beneath the museum you'll find a new, open-air **theatre** where music and cultural events are often hosted in summer. For an evening drink, head to the seaside, which is lined with bars and cafes, particularly west of the info kiosk. Try **En Plo** (cocktails €6; 🕐 8am-late), just below the National Bank, for a huge list of cocktails and coffees in a funky, friendly atmosphere. If you're looking for somewhere to boogie, **Heaven Club** (🕐 until 1am nightly, Fri & Sat only in winter) offers a free bus service to patrons who want to reach the isolated dance club out of town.

SOUTHERN KARPATHOS

The south of the island has some sandy beaches and quiet towns to relax in. Scenic walking tracks criss-cross the land; pick up a map in Pigadia.

Ammoöpi Αμμοöπή

If you are seeking sun and sand, plus some of the clearest water for snorkelling in the whole of the Aegean, head for Ammoöpi (amm-oh-oh-*pee*), 5km south of Pigadia. It's a scattered beach resort without any real centre, although you'll find a bus stop and some small shops.

Wind- and kitesurfers head for the broad **Afiartis Bay** in droves to enjoy some world-class conditions. A further 8km south of Ammoöpi, the bay caters for advanced surfers at the crazily windy northern end (nicknamed 'Devil's Bay') and beginners in the sheltered Makrygialos Bay lagoon at the southern end. For lessons, tours and equipment, visit **Pro Center** (☎ 22450 91062; www.chris-schill.com; Afiartis). To learn more about the annual international kitesurfing competition, check out **Speed World Cup** (www.speedworldcup.com).

SLEEPING & EATING

Hotel Sophia (☎ /fax 22450 81078; www.hotelsophia -karpathos.gr/sophia; d €40; ✷ ▨) With a burgeoning garden and cool, well-maintained rooms at the northern end of the settlement, Hotel Sophia is a great deal. All rooms have kitchenettes but ask for one with a balcony to dine over waterfront views.

Vardes (☎ /fax 22450 81111; www.hotelvardes.com; s/d €57/62; ✷ ▨) These simple, spacious studios are set back against the hillside among a lush olive grove and a few banana palms. Chill on the shaded balconies or at the laid-back bar. Some rooms can sleep up to five and it's an easy walk to the beach.

Ammoöpi Taverna (☎ 22450 81138; mains €4-7) At the far northern end of Ammoöpi and right on the beach, the food here is uniformly good. Look for the daily specials – the clove-laced *mousakas* (sliced aubergine and mincemeat arranged in layers and baked) is excellent.

Taverna Helios (☎ 22450 81148; mains €5-7) Just back from the main beach and handy for lunch after a swim, Helios offers Greek and international cuisine with large portions.

Menetes Μενετές
pop 450

Perched precariously atop a sheer cliff, the picturesque village of Menetes (me-ne-*tes*) overlooks rolling landscape. The main street is lined with pastel-coloured neoclassical houses, backed by narrow, stepped alleyways that wind between modest whitewashed dwellings. The village has a small but well-presented **museum** (admission free; ✷ on request) on the right as you come in from Pigadia. Ask the owner of Taverna Manolis to open it.

Menetes is a pleasant place to while away an afternoon. If you decide to stay, try **Mike Rigas Domatia** (☎ 22450 81269; d/tr €20/25), a traditional Karpathian house set in a lush garden. Stop by **Taverna Manolis** (☎ 22450 81103; mains €5-7) for generous helpings of grilled meat, or try **Dionysos Fiesta** (☎ 22450 81269; mains €5-7) for local dishes, including an artichoke omelette and Karpathian sausages. **Pelagia Taverna** (☎ 22450 81135; mains €5-8), just below town, serves free-range goat and lamb along with local cheeses and excellent mashed fava lentils.

Arkasa Αρκάσα

Once a traditional Karpathian village, Arkasa (ar-*ka*-sa) is now a low-key resort and comes to an utter standstill in winter. The village itself sits up from the water, 9km from Menetes, with its beachside resort below. For internet access, visit the Partheon Cafe in town, where you'll also find a supermarket and a string of nondescript cafes with lovely sea views.

Follow a turn-off for 500m from the bottom of the village to the remains of the 5th-century **Basilica of Agia Sophia**, where two chapels stand amid mosaic fragments and columns. Below it you can walk along the coast to an ancient **acropolis**. Just south across the headland from here is **Agios Nikolaos Beach**. About 600m off the main road, it's small and sandy and gets busy in summer with a volleyball net and clear water. Kip out on the water's edge at **Glaros Studios** (☎ 22450 61015; glaros@greekhotel.com; Agios Nikolaos; studios €65), where rooms are decorated in traditional Karpathian style. There's a relaxed adjoining restaurant.

On the road to Finiki, **Eleni Studios** (☎ /fax 22450 61248; www.elenikarpathos.gr; Arkasa; s/d €35/40; ▨) has breezy rooms with touches of colour and kitchenettes. Relax in the on-site bar or the gorgeous pool overlooking the sea. Family rooms are available here too. For something a little plusher, try **Arkasa Bay Hotel** (☎ 22450

61410; www.arkasabay.com; apt €100; ⚡ 🛜 🖵) with its relatively grand rooms, cocktail bar and spectacular views. Located at the southern end of town, it caters well to families with its apartments and children's pool.

Finiki Φοινίκι

The quaint fishing village of Finiki (fi-*ni*-ki) lies 2km north of Arkasa. The best local swimming is at **Agios Georgios Beach**, between Arkasa and Finiki, while the small, sandy cove at Finiki is okay for wading in but mainly used for fishing boats. **Kamarakia Beach**, signposted before Agios Georgios, is a narrow cove with strong sea currents.

Park your bags at **Finiki View Hotel** (☎ 22450 61400; www.finikiview.gr; r €50-60, apt €60; ⚡ 🛜 🖵) where you soak up the view in an outdoor pool. Rooms are simple but spacious and the pricier ones have traditional design including raised sleeping quarters. It's just above the village, overlooking the bay.

Dine on stuffed vine leaves, spicy cheese salad, chicken souvlaki and fresh fish galore at **Marina Taverna** (☎ 22450 61100; mains €4-7; 🕑 year-round) where locals relax to traditional music and tables spill out along the harbour.

Nestled in a verdant garden some 9km north of Finiki are the secluded **Pine Tree Studios** (☎ 6977369948; www.pinetree-karpathos.gr; Adia; d €35, apt €45-70; ⚡). Rooms at this rural retreat are comfortable and spacious with kitchenettes and views over to Kasos. The apartments are fantastic – one with a fireplace and traditional bed and the other with stone walls and oodles of character. The on-site restaurant draws locals from around the island, serving fresh fruit and vegetables from the garden in a relaxed outdoor setting.

Walkers can head up the **Flaskia Gorge**, or as an easier option hike to the nearby **Iliondas Beach**.

Lefkos Λευκός
pop 120

You'll find Lefkos (lef-*kos*) 2km down towards the sea from the main coastal road. In summer it's a burgeoning resort centred on a series of sandy coves but in winter you'd be hard-pressed to find anyone around at all.

Archaeology buffs explore the underground remains of a **Roman cistern**, reached by heading up the approach road and looking for sign on the left to the 'catacombs'. Drive to the very

end of the rough road and then strike out along trail K16.

If you decide to stay in this neck of the woods, try **Le Grand Bleu** (☎ /fax 22450 71400; www.legrandbleu-lefkos.gr; studio/apt €50/90; 🖵) for a homey, well-equipped apartment overlooking the curving Gialou Horafi middle beach in Lefkos. You'll also find an excellent, shady **Taverna** (mains €7-12) on-site with mezedhes like garlic mushrooms and *imam baïldi* (aubergine in oil with herbs), or try the Karpathian mixed platter of sausages, cheese, capers and sardines.

There are daily buses to Lefkos, and a taxi from Pigadia costs €24. **Lefkos Rent A Car** (☎ /fax 22450 71057; www.lefkosrentacar.com) is a reliable outlet that will deliver vehicles, free of charge, to anywhere in southern Karpathos.

NORTHERN KARPATHOS

As you head north, the scenery becomes more dramatic and rugged as the road ascends into the pine-forested mountains. Most people hop on a boat to reach the north; however, the somewhat treacherous road does offer spectacular coastal views as you drive along the mountains' spine. The beaches in the north are pebbly and many are good for swimming and snorkelling and there is plenty of opportunity for walking.

Diafani Διαφάνι
pop 250

Diafani is Karpathos' small northern port and a lazy kind of place in contrast to its busy sister port of Pigadia. Scheduled ferries call at the wharf and a summertime excursion boat arrives daily from Pigadia, to be met by buses that transport visitors to Olymbos. Otherwise, scheduled buses leave for Olymbos daily at 7.30am, 2.30pm and 5pm all year-round.

Most people just pass through Diafani; if you do decide to stay, you'll likely have the beaches and trails to yourself. You can exchange currency at the Travel Agency of Nikos Orfanos but there's no bank or ATM in town, so bring cash with you. There's also no post office or car hire facilities, but you will find wi-fi access in a few restaurants. For local info, check out www.diafani.com.

ACTIVITIES

Join an excursion trip on the *Captain Manolis* to the remote and otherwise inaccessible reaches of Karpathos and to the satellite island of **Saria**.

DODECANESE

Boats leave from the stone jetty from the centre of town at around 10am, returning at 5pm. You need to take all supplies with you.

Walkers should pick up the Road Editions *1:60,000 Karpathos-Kasos* map (available in Pigadia) or visit the Environment Management office near Diafani's seafront. Walks are signposted with red or blue markers or stone cairns. Follow a half-hour coastal track for 4km north through the pines to **Vananda Beach**. You can also head south through the olive groves to the shaded **Papa Mina Bay** (one hour, around 9km). A more strenuous, two-hour walk takes you 11km northwest to the Hellenistic site of **Vroukounda**. En route you'll pass the agricultural village of **Avlona**. Take all your food and water with you as there are no facilities.

SLEEPING & EATING

You'll find quite a few small hotels in Diafani. Head to **Balaskas Hotel** (☎ 22450 51320; www.balaskashotel.com; s/d €30/40; ✷) where spic-and-span rooms overlook a pretty garden. Set back from the waterfront, all rooms have a fridge and some have small kitchenettes. At the northern end of the bay, **Thalassa Apartments** (☎ 22450 22130, 6948629267; www.karpathosbay.com; apt €60; ✷) offers comfortable rooms that are handy for a quick swim off the pebbled harbour beach.

The waterfront is lined with restaurants. **Rahati** (☎ 22450 51200; mains €4-7) uses lots of organic ingredients in local dishes like green beans in tomato sauce, octopus in red wine and fresh fish. Near the fountain is **La Gorgona** (☎ 22450 51509; mains €4-7) where the Italian owner whips up a mean pasta. Sip cappuccino or homemade *limoncello* (lemon liqueur) on the terrace or dive into her freshly baked cakes. You can also buy sandwiches and pizza picnics for the beach.

Olymbos Ολυμπος
pop 330

Clinging to the ridge of Mt Profitis Ilias (716m), Olymbos is a living museum. While it's true that the village's main income is now tourism and the hordes of visitors can give it a theme-park feel, come here out of season or stay behind after the day-trippers clamber back down the mountainside and you'll be spellbound by Olymbos' magic.

Olymbos was built high in the mountains to protect the inhabitants from pirates. Long isolated from the outside world, the locals still speak a dialect that contains traces of an ancient Dorian Greek. It's often called

'Women's Village' as men have traditionally been carted off to war or in search of work. The older women continue to wear traditional dress of bright embroidered skirts, waistcoats, headscarves and goatskin boots. The interiors of the houses are decorated with embroidered cloth and their facades feature brightly painted, ornate plaster reliefs.

Before the tourists came to town, Olymbos was an agricultural centre, at times supporting the entire island. The areas surrounding it continue to be farmed. You'll find the remains of 75 windmills in and around the village; four are still in operation, grinding flour for the local bread baked in outdoor communal ovens.

Once you're inside the village, Olymbos is only negotiable by foot, with narrow alleys and stairs. The valley rolls down its east side to Diafani while the west side drops sharply down to the crashing sea. You won't find banks or post offices here. Basic provisions are available from a couple of shops at the southern end of the village.

SLEEPING & EATING

Small hotels and restaurants are springing up at a quick tempo but if you're visiting out of season, be sure to call ahead. At the far end of Olymbos and close to the central square, **Hotel Aphrodite** (☎ 22450 51307; filippasfilipakkis@yahoo.gr; d €40) has comfortable, airy rooms with verandas looking out over the windmills to the sea. The sunset views are incredible. You'll also find simple rooms at **Mike's** (☎ 22450 51304; r €25) at the southern edge of town and more upscale versions at **Astro Hotel** (☎ 22450 51421; €40) near the centre.

Makarounes is served in most restaurants in Olymbos. You should also aim to try some of the locally made bread. Head for the atmospheric **Taverna O Mylos** (☎ 22450 51333; mains €4-8) at the northwestern end of the village. Built around a restored and working windmill, the excellent food is cooked in a wood oven and features organic meat and vegetables, including goat in red-wine sauce, artichokes and filling *pites* (pies).

Near the centre, just south of the church, is **Blue Garden** (mains €5-10), a rooftop pizzeria with stunning views. At the southern edge of the village is **Mike's Restaurant** (☎ 22450 51304; mains €3-7; ✷ year-round). With its open fire, singing birds and traditional decor, it's worth stopping here for soup, salad or daily specials made fresh by the friendly Sophia.

KASOS ΚΑΣΟΣ

pop 980

The remote outpost of Kasos (*ka*-sos) is the Dodecanese' southernmost island. Curled up close to Karpathos and not far from Crete, it sees few tourists. The slow-paced community greets those who bother to visit with a warm welcome. Don't come here for beaches, sights or nightlife. Instead, come to relax amid olive and fig trees, dry-stone walls, meandering sheep and the craggy peaks shrouded in mist. You may end up staying longer than you anticipated.

History

Despite being diminutive and remote, Kasos has an eventful history. During Turkish rule the island flourished, and by 1820 it had 11,000 inhabitants and a large mercantile fleet. (It's hard to imagine how they didn't sink the island.) Mohammad Ali, the Turkish governor of Egypt, regarded this fleet as an impediment to his plan to establish a base on Crete and on 7 June 1824 his men landed on Kasos and killed around 7000 inhabitants. This massacre is commemorated annually on the anniversary of the slaughter (known locally as Holocaust Day), and Kasiots return from around the world to participate. During the late 19th century many Kasiots emigrated to Egypt where around 5000 of them helped build the Suez Canal, and during the last century many emigrated to the USA.

Getting There & Away

There are regular flights from Kasos to Rhodes, Karpathos and Crete with **Olympic Air** (☎ 22450 41555; Kritis Airport). There are also regular boat departures to Rhodes, Piraeus, Sitia and Finiki on Karpathos.

For more details, see Island Hopping (p753).

Getting Around

The local bus serves all the island villages with a dozen or so scheduled runs; tickets are €0.60. There are two **taxis** (☎ 6977944371, 6973244371) on the island. Scooters or cars can be hired from **Oasis – Renta-a-Car & Bikes** (☎ 22450 41746) in Fry.

FRY ΦΡΥ

pop 270

Fry (*free*) is the island's capital and port. It's a pleasant, ramshackle kind of place with little tourism, though it attracts many returned Kasiot Americans. Its narrow whitewashed streets are usually busy with locals in animated discussion. The village's focal point is the cramped yet picturesque fishing harbour of Bouka. The annexe settlement of Emborio is located less than 1km east of Fry.

Orientation & Information

The large harbour complex abuts the port village right next to its main square, Plateia Iroön Kasou. Fry's main street is Kritis. The airport is 1km west along the coast road. Turn left from the harbour to get to Emborio.

A stand-alone Commercial Bank ATM is next to the port entrance, while there's a Co-operative Bank of the Dodecanese branch, with ATM, on Plateia Iroön Kasou.

ACS Internet (☎ 22450 42751; ⏲ 10am-2pm & 5pm-12am) Offers wi-fi.

Farmacy (☎ 22450 41164) For all medicinal needs.

Health Centre (☎ 22450 41333) Often unattended; you may need to call ahead.

Kasos Maritime & Travel Agency (☎ 22450 41495; www.kassos-island.gr; Plateia Iroön Kasou) For all travel tickets.

Police (☎ 22450 41222) On a narrow paved street running south from Kritis.

Port police (☎ 22450 41288) Behind the Agios Spyridon Church.

Post office (☎ 22450 41255; ⏲ 7.30am-2pm Mon-Fri) Diagonally opposite the Police.

www.kasos.gr An informative website in Greek and English.

Sights & Activities

Fry's minuscule **Archaeological Museum** (☎ 22450 41865; admission free; ⏲ 9am-3pm, summer only) displays the islands treasures but won't turn heads. See objects pulled from ancient shipwrecks, a collection of ancient oil lamps and finds from Polis such as inscribed Hellenistic stone slabs.

The **Athina excursion boat** (☎ 22450 41047, 6977911209; return €15) travels daily in summer to the uninhabited Armathia Islet, departing Fry harbour at 3pm and returning at 7pm. The speck of an island has superb sandy beaches but you'll need to bring all of your own supplies.

Sleeping

With the exception of the days on either side of 7 June (Holocaust Memorial Day), a room can normally be found quite easily in summer. Out of season, be sure to call ahead.

Fantasis (☎ 6977905156; www.fantasishotel.gr; d €40; ❄) These six simple rooms are 300m

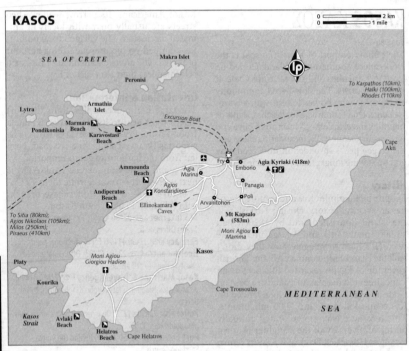

KASOS

SEA OF CRETE

Makra Islet

Peronisi

To Karpathos (10km);
Halki (100km);
Rhodes (110km)

Lytra

Armathia
Islet

Marmara
Beach

Pondikonisia

Karavostasi
Beach

Excursion Boat

Cape
Akti

Ammounda
Beach

Fry

Agia Kyriaki (418m)

Emborio

Agia
Marina

Panagia

Andiperatos
Beach

Agios
Konstandinos

Poli

Ellinokamara
Caves

Arvanitohon

To Sitia (80km);
Agios Nikolaos (105km);
Milos (250km);
Piraeus (410km)

Mt Kapsalo
(583m)

Moni Agiou
Mamma

Kasos

Moni Agiou
Giorgiou Hadion

Platy

Kourika

Cape Trousoulas

MEDITERRANEAN
SEA

Kasos
Strait

Avlaki
Beach

Helatros
Beach

Cape Helatros

0 ————— 2 km
0 ————— 1 mile

outside Fry and make for a good, quiet retreat. All have balconies, a fridge and TV. Savour home-grown figs at breakfast.

Evita Village (☎ 22450 41731, 6972703950; evitavillage@ mail.gr; s/d €45/50; ❄) Meticulously equipped studios are airy, spacious and tasteful. They sport every kitchen appliance imaginable, along with TV and DVD, and sleep up to three people.

Angelica's (☎ 22450 41268, 6992673833; www.an gelicas.gr; apt with/without sea view €65/45; ❄) With simple white walls, wrought-iron beds and beautifully hand-painted floors, these four apartments in a converted traditional home offer tranquillity and comfort. Each airy unit has a full kitchen and a courtyard; some have sea views.

Eating & Drinking

Fry is not overly endowed in the eating stakes, but there are a few decent places to dine.

O Mylos (☎ 22450 41825; Plateia Iroön Kasou; mains €3-5) A reliable eatery in a cosy corner overlooking the west side of the port. Wholesome food includes fish, meat, casserole dishes and local specials. Ask for *roïkio* – an unusual, locally produced green salad.

Apangio (☎ 22450 41880; Bouka; mezedhes €3-5; ❄ 9am until late) Enjoying a very atmospheric Bouka harbour location, the Apangio is a classy *ouzerie*-cum-cafe, serving select mezedhes and late breakfasts.

Cafe Zantana (☎ 22450 41912; Bouka) Kasiots congregate at this trendy cafe, admiring the view of Bouka harbour with a cocktail or cappuccino in hand.

AROUND KASOS

The original trading post of Kasos, tiny **Emborio** is now a satellite port of Fry used for pleasure and fishing boats. With a sandy beach and clear water, it's the nearest place to Fry for a quick dip.

The rather mediocre **Ammounda Beach**, beyond the airport near the blue-domed church of Agios Konstandinos, is the next nearest to Fry. There are slightly better beaches further along this stretch of coast, one of them being the fine-pebble **Andiperatos Beach** at the end of the road system.

The island's best beach is the isolated pebbled cove of **Helatros**, near Moni Agiou Georgiou Hadion, 11km southwest of Fry along a paved road. The beach has no facilities and you'll need your own transport to reach it. **Avlaki** is another decent yet small beach here, reached along a track from the monastery. None of Kasos' beaches offer shade.

Agia Marina, 1km southwest of Fry, is a pretty village with a gleaming white-and-blue church. On 17 July the **Festival of Agia Marina** is celebrated here. Agia Marina is also the starting point for a 3km-long hike to the former rock shelter known as **Ellinokamara**, with its odd, stone-blocked entrance. Follow the Hrysoulas signpost at the southern end of Agia Marina, proceed to the end of the road and follow a path between stone walls for about 10 minutes. Look for a track upwards and to the left to reach the cave.

From Agia Marina, the road continues to verdant **Arvanitohori**, with abundant fig and pomegranate trees. **Poli**, 3km southeast of Fry, is the former capital, built on the ancient acropolis. **Panagia**, between Fry and Poli, now has fewer than 50 inhabitants; its once-grand sea captains' and many ship owners' mansions are either standing derelict or under repair.

Monasteries

The island has two monasteries. The uninhabited **Moni Agiou Mamma**, on the south coast, is a 1½-hour walk from Fry or a 20-minute scooter ride (8km) through a dramatic, eroded landscape. A lively festival takes place here on 2 September. Detour to the chapel of **Agia Kyriaki** (no obvious sign) for eyrie-like views over Fry and the basin villages.

Similarly, there are no monks at **Moni Agiou Georgiou Hadion**, but there is a resident caretaker for most of the year. The festival at Agiou Georgiou Hadion takes place during the week after Easter.

KASTELLORIZO (MEGISTI)
ΚΑΣΤΕΛΛΟΡΙΖΟ (ΜΕΓΙΣΤΗ)

pop 430

Kastellorizo (ka-stel-*o*-rizo) is Greece's most far-flung island. Omitted on many maps, this speck of territory is tucked snugly beneath the underbelly of Turkey, approximately 130km east of Rhodes. Its nearest neighbour is the Turkish port of Kaş, clearly visible across a mere 5km of water. Kastellorizo was named by the Knights of St John after the island's towering red cliffs which give the impression of a medieval castle. The ruins of the Knights' own castle gaze down on the charming, well-preserved harbour with its crystal-clear water. If it all looks familiar, you may have seen the 1991 Italian movie *Mediterraneo*, which was filmed here. In recent decades Australians have arrived in large numbers in search of their parents' or grandparents' homeland. Many have reclaimed and restored homes and set up businesses, giving the island's economy a much-needed boost.

If you're not a film buff or long-lost grandchild, Kastellorizo is not an easy place to get to and doesn't have a lot of draws. But if you're curious and determined enough to get here, you'll likely enjoy uncovering the island's hidden charms. Snorkel in clear inlets, take in a few unique sights and soak up some tangible peace and quiet.

History

Kastellorizo has a tragic history. Once a thriving trade port serving Dorians, Romans, Crusaders, Egyptians, Turks and Venetians, Kastellorizo came under Ottoman control in 1552. The island was permitted to preserve its language, religion and traditions, and its cargo fleet became the largest in the Dodecanese, allowing the islanders to achieve a high degree of culture and advanced levels of education.

Kastellorizo lost all strategic and economic importance after the 1923 Greece–Turkey population exchange. In 1928 it was ceded to the Italians, who severely oppressed the islanders. Many islanders chose to emigrate to Australia, where approximately 30,000 continue to live.

During WWII Kastellorizo suffered bombardment and English commanders ordered the few remaining inhabitants to abandon the island. Most fled to Cyprus, Palestine and Egypt. When they returned they found their houses in ruins and many re-emigrated. While the island has never fully recovered from this population loss, in recent years returnees have brought a period of resurgence and resettlement. Many returning Aussies are locked in land claim battles over their family's property where locals have been squatting since the 1950s.

DODECANESE

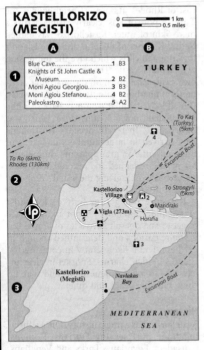

KASTELLORIZO (MEGISTI)

Blue Cave...........................1 B3	
Knights of St John Castle &	
Museum.............................2 B2	
Moni Agiou Georgiou........3 B3	
Moni Agiou Stefanou.........4 B2	
Paleokastro.......................5 A2	

Getting There & Away

You can hop on a flight to Rhodes or wait for a ferry or catamaran, although boat services from the island are often tenuous and always infrequent. See p753 for more details. For flight and ferry tickets, visit **Papoutsis Travel** (☎ 22460 70630, 6937212530; www.kastelorizo.gr) in Kastellorizo Village.

Getting Around

To reach the airport, take the sole island **taxi** (☎ 6938739178) from the port (€5), or the local community bus (€1.50). The bus leaves the square by the port 1½ hours prior to each flight departure.

BOAT

Excursion boats go to the spectacular **Blue Cave** (Parasta), famous for its brilliant, mirror-like blue water, produced by refracted sunlight. Visitors are transferred from a larger caïque to a small motorised dingy in order to enter the very low cave entrance – claustrophobics be warned. Inside, the cave reaches up 35m and is home to pigeons and seals. Visitors are usually allowed a quick dip. The excursion

costs about €15; look for **Georgos Karagiannis** (☎ 6977855756) who runs the *Varvara* and *Agios Georgios* daily from the harbour. Boats leave at 9am and return around 1pm.

You can also take day trips to the islets of **Ro** and **Strongyli** for swims and picnics. The trips cost about €20 and boats depart around 9am from the harbour.

Join islanders on one of their frequent shopping trips to **Kaş** in Turkey. A day trip costs about €20 and is available from boats along the middle waterfront. Passports are required by the police 24 hours beforehand.

KASTELLORIZO VILLAGE

pop 275

Besides Mandraki, its satellite neighbourhood over the hill and to the east, Kastellorizo Village is the main settlement on the island. Built around a U-shaped bay, the village's waterfront is skirted by imposing, spruced-up, three-storey mansions with wooden balconies and red-tiled roofs. The labyrinthine backstreets are slowly being restored and rebuilt. The village has a strong Aussie presence, adding an upbeat energy to an otherwise subdued community.

Orientation & Information

The quay is at the southern side of the bay. The central square, Plateia Ethelondon Kastellorizou, abuts the waterfront almost halfway round the bay, next to the yachting jetty. The settlements of Horafia and Mandraki are reached by ascending the wide steps at the east side of the bay.

First Aid (☎ 22460 45206) For emergencies and basic health needs.

National Bank of Greece (☎ 22460 49054) ATM equipped.

Papoutsis Travel (☎ 22460 70630, 22460 49356; papoutsistravel@galileo.gr) For air and sea tickets.

Police station (☎ 22460 49333) On the bay's western side.

Port police (☎ 22460 49333) At eastern tip of the bay.

Post office (☎ 22460 49298) Next to the police station.

Radio Café (☎ 22460 49029; internet per hr €3) For internet access.

Sights

Follow a rickety metal staircase up to the **Knights of St John Castle** for splendid views of Turkey. Below the castle stands the **museum** (☎ 22460 49283; admission free; 🕑 7am-2pm Tue-Sun) with a collection of archaeological finds, costumes and photos. Beyond the museum, steps lead down to a coastal pathway from where more steps go up the cliff to a rock-hewn **Lycian tomb** with an impressive Doric facade dating back as far as the 4th century BC. There are several along the Anatolian coast in Turkey, but they are very rare in Greece.

Moni Agiou Georgiou is the largest of the monasteries that dot the island. Within its church is the subterranean Chapel of Agios Haralambos, reached by steep stone steps. Greek children were given religious instruction here during Turkish times. The church is kept locked; ask around the waterfront for the whereabouts of the caretaker. To reach the monastery (approximately 1.5km), ascend the conspicuous zigzagging white stone steps behind the village.

Moni Agiou Stefanou, on the north coast, is the setting for one of the island's most important celebrations, the feast of Agios Stefanos on 1 August. The path to the little white monastery begins behind the post office. From the monastery, a path leads to a bay where you can swim.

Paleokastro was the island's ancient capital. Within the old city's Hellenistic walls are an ancient tower, a water cistern and three churches. To reach it (1km), follow the concrete steps, just beyond a soldier's sentry box on the airport road.

Sleeping

Many of Kastellorizo's hotels stay open year-round. Book ahead in high season to be sure of a bed.

Damien & Monika's (☎ 22460 49028; www.kastel lorizo.de; r €40; ✷ ▯) These bright, comfy rooms in the centre of town have that homey touch. Each is slightly unique with traditional furnishings, a fridge and lots of windows. You'll also find a book exchange and heaps of local info.

Poseidon (☎ 22460 49257, 6945710603; www.kaste lorizo-poseidon.gr; s/d €50/60) The Poseidon's two restored houses offer large rooms with a touch of colour and character. Ground-floor rooms have private verandas; 1st-floor rooms have small balconies with big sea views. It's on the west side of the harbour, one block back from the waterfront.

Mediterraneo (☎ 22460 49007; www.mediterraneo -kastelorizo.com; r €70-85) Designed and run by an architect, these stylish waterfront rooms have rustic charm with arches, stone walls

and unique furnishings. All have garden or sea views and include breakfast. The hotel is at the far western tip of the harbour and very convenient for a quick harbour dip.

Eating

With tables perched precariously over the harbour edge, dining in Kastellorizo is both atmospheric and adventuresome – one false move and you are in for a swim.

Radio Café (☎ 22460 49029; breakfast & snacks €2-6; ▯) Other than internet access, this cafe makes a mean coffee and dishes up filling breakfasts, light snacks and pizzas. Sunset views are thrown in for free.

Kaz Bar (☎ 22460 49067; mezedhes €3-6; ▯) For an alternative take on mezedhes, drop by this bar-cum-bistro on the middle waterfront. Dig into pizza, chicken wings and spring rolls, as well as original salads, all washed down with Greek wine.

To Mikro Parisi (☎ 22460 49282; mains €5-7) Going strong since 1974, To Mikro Parisi still serves generous helpings of grilled fish and meat. Fish soup is the house speciality, but the rich *stifadho* (sweet stew cooked with tomato and onions) is equally satisfying.

Entertainment

It ain't no Rio, but Kastellorizo's nightlife has picked up the pace in recent years and the summer influx of Aussies certainly adds fuel. The harbour is lined with small bars and cafes that spill out onto the water's edge as the night wears on. Kaz Bar and Meltemi are staunchly popular but follow the noise and fellow revellers and you can't really go wrong.

SYMI ΣΥΜΗ

pop 2610

Arriving at the main harbour of Symi (*see* me) is like sailing into a postcard. Restored, colourful sea captains' houses nestle the shoreline while bright boats bob in the blue-green sea. Most visitors congregate in the cafes here, alongside the growing expat community, but the island is also home to a surprisingly green interior, a sprinkling of scattered beaches and an enormous monastery that is one of the few religious sites that warrants its own ferry connection.

Symi is one of the most popular day-trip destinations from Rhodes and a popular port

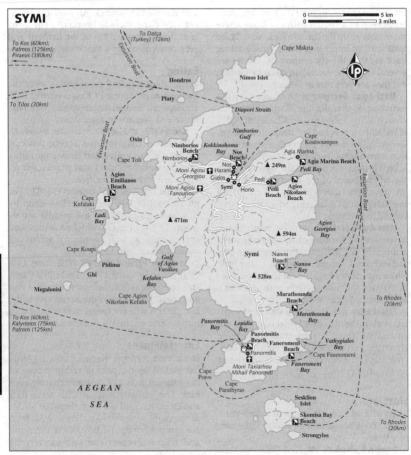

SYMI

0 ———— 5 km
0 ———— 3 miles

To Kos (60km);
Patmos (125km);
Piraeus (380km)

To Datça
(Turkey) (12km)

Cape Makria

To Tilos (30km)

Hondros

Nimos Islet

Platy

Diapori Straits

Oxia

Nimborios
Gulf

Cape
Koutsoumpos

Nimborios
Beach

Kokkinohoma
Bay

Nos
Beach

Agia Marina

Cape Toli

Nimborios

Nos
Harani

▲ 249m

Agia Marina Beach

Pedi Bay

Agios
Emilianos
Beach

Moni Agiou
Georgiou

Gialos

Pedi

Symi

Horio

Agios
Nikolaos
Beach

Moni Agiou
Fanouriou

Pedi
Beach

Cape
Kefalaki

Ladi
Bay

▲ 471m

Agios
Georgios
Bay

Cape Koupi

Pidima

Gulf
of Agios
Vasilios

Symi

Nanou
Beach

Nanou
Bay

Ghi

Kefalos
Bay

▲ 528m

▲ 594m

Megalonisi

Cape Agios
Nikolaos Kefalis

Marathounda
Beach

To Rhodes
(20km)

To Kos (60km);
Kalymnos (75km);
Patmos (125km)

Panormitis
Bay

Lopidia
Bay

Marathounda
Bay

Panormitis
Beach

Panormitis

Faneromeni
Beach

Vathygialos
Bay

Cape Faneromeni

Panormitis

Faneromeni
Bay

AEGEAN

SEA

Cape
Potos

Moni Taxiarhou
Mihail Panormiti

Cape
Parathyras

Sesklion
Islet

Skomisa Bay

Beach

To Rhodes
(20km)

Strongylos

of call for yachties and other sea-struck travellers. It's also an increasingly popular holiday destination in its own right.

History

Symi has a long tradition of both sponge diving and shipbuilding. During Ottoman times it was granted the right to fish for sponges in Turkish waters. In return, Symi supplied the sultan with first-class boat builders and top-quality sponges scooped straight off the ocean floor.

This exchange brought prosperity to the island. Gracious mansions were built and culture and education flourished. By the beginning of the 20th century, the population was 22,500 and the island was launching some 500 ships a year. But the Italian occupation, the introduction of the steamship and Kalymnos' rise as the Aegean's principal sponge producer put an end to Symi's prosperity.

The treaty surrendering the Dodecanese islands to the Allies was signed in Symi's Hotel (now Pension Catherinettes, p546) on 8 May 1945.

Getting There & Away

Catamarans, excursion boats and **ANES** (☎ 22460 71444; www.anek.gr) run regular boats between Symi and Rhodes, as well as to islands further north and to Kastellorizo. One service calls in at Panormitis on the south side of the island. See Island Hopping (p762) for details.

Symi Tours (p546) runs Saturday excursions from Gialos to Datça in Turkey (including Turkish port taxes, €40).

Getting Around

BOAT

Several excursion boats do trips from Gialos Harbour to Moni Taxiarhou Mihail Panormiti and Sesklion Islet, where there's a shady beach. Check the boards for the best-value tickets. There are also boats to Agios Emilianos beach, on the far west side of Symi.

The small **water taxis** (☎ 22460 71423) *Konstantinos* and *Irini* go to many of the island's beaches (€10 to €15), leaving at 10.15am and 11.15am respectively.

BUS & TAXI

The bus stop and taxi rank are on the south side of the harbour in Gialos. The **grey minibus** (☎ 6945316284) makes hourly runs between Gialos and Pedi beach (via Horio; flat fare €1). The **blue minibus** (☎ 22460 71311) departs Gialos at 10am and 3pm daily for Panormitis. Taxis depart from a rank 100m west of the bus stop.

CAR

Near the Gialos clock tower, **Glaros** (☎ 22460 71926, 6948362079; www.glarosrentacar.gr; Gialos) hires cars for around €25 and scooters for €10.

GIALOS ΓΙΑΛΟΣ

pop 2200

Gialos, Symi's port, is a visual treat. Neoclassical mansions in a medley of colours are heaped up the hills flanking its harbour of crystal-clear water. Most facilities and transport are based here, along with lots of seaside cafes where you can sip iced coffee and watch the slow bustle of the harbour.

The old town, Horio, is a steep climb from the harbour but is a great place to lose yourself for a while. Stepped alleys and zigzagging lanes take you past traditional homes, cafes, derelict buildings and churches, with gorgeous views down to the sea.

Orientation & Information

The town is divided into two parts: Gialos, the harbour; and Horio above it, crowned by the *kastro* (castle). Arriving ferries, hydrofoils and catamarans dock just to the left of the quay's clock tower; excursion boats dock a little further along. Ferries can depart from either side of the harbour so check when you buy your ticket. The harbour and the promenade running southwest from its centre are the hub of Gialos activity. Kali Strata, a broad stairway, leads from here to hilltop Horio.

There is no official tourist office in Symi Town. The *Symi Visitor* is a free English-and-Greek-language newspaper distributed by portside newspaper vendors and restaurants.
Kalodoukas Holidays (☎ 22460 71077; www.kalodoukas.gr) At the beginning of Kali Strata; rents houses and organises excursions.
National Bank of Greece (☎ 22460 72294) On the western side of the harbour with an ATM. There's a second ATM at the Co-operative Bank across the harbour.
Police (☎ 22460 71111) By the ferry quay.
Port police (☎ 22460 71205) By the ferry quay.
Post office (☎ 22460 71315) By the ferry quay.
Roloï bar (☎ 22460 71595; internet per hr €2; ☻ 9am-3am) For internet access; a block back from the waterfront.
Symi Tours (☎ 22460 71307; fax 22460 72292; www.symitours.com) Half a block back from east side of harbour. Does excursions, including to Datça in Turkey.
Symi Visitor Office (☎ 22460 72755) Small yellow building on the harbour front.
Victoria Laundry (☎ 22460 70065) At the foot of Kali Strata.
www.symivisitor.com A useful source of island information with an accommodation-booking service.

Sights

Horio is a warren of narrow streets zigzagging between brightly coloured buildings and crumbling remnants. This old town is still very much lived in, with a number of churches, a school and plenty of homes. It's a pleasant place to wander but looking for somewhere in particular is a bit like a scavenger hunt; it's a good idea to ask directions as you go.

Perched at the top of Horio is the **Knights of St John Kastro**. The *kastro* incorporates blocks from the ancient acropolis and the **Church of Megali Panagia** is within its walls. You can reach the castle through the maze of Horio's cobbled pedestrian streets or along a road that runs southeast of Gialos.

En route to the *kastro* and signposted from the stop of Kali Strata, the **Archaeological & Folklore Museum** (admission €2; ☻ 10am-2pm Tue-Sun) has Hellenistic, Byzantine and Roman exhibits, as well as some folkloric material. The nearby **Chatziagapitos House** is a restored 18th-century mansion that you can look around when the museum is open.

Take a left from the top of Kali Strata for the ruins of **Pontiko Kastro**, a stone circle thought to

DODECANESE

date back to the Neolithic period. The site is only partially excavated and was locked at the time of research but offers great views.

Behind the **children's playground** in the port of Gialos, the **Nautical Museum** (admission €2; ⊗ 11am-4pm Tue-Sun) details Symi's shipbuilding history and has wooden models of ships and other naval memorabilia.

Activities

Symi Tours (☎ 22460 71307; fax 22460 72292) has multilingual guides who lead **guided walks** around the island, often ending with a boat ride back to Galios. The publication *Walks in Symi* by Lance Chiltern lists 20 walks on the island for novices and pros alike. Call into the **Symi Visitor Office** (☎ 22460 72755) to purchase a copy.

Sleeping

Hotel Fiona (☎ 22460 72088; www.symivisitor.com/Fiona .htm; Horio; d €50; ❄) With welcome breezes and big sea views from the balcony, Fiona's is a comfortable place to stay. Rooms are very clean with hand-painted furnishings, tiled floors and a small fridge. To reach it, turn left at the top of the stairs and walk for 50m.

Hotel Kokona (☎ 22460 71549, 6937659035; kokonafo@ otenet.gr; Gialos; d €50; ❄) One block inland from the harbour and not far from the children's playground, this hotel has comfortable, tidy rooms that are a stone's throw from the action but in a quieter corner of town. A few have balconies overlooking a small square with a church.

Pension Catherinettes (☎ 22460 71671; marina -epe@rho.forthnet.gr; Gialos; d €55; ❄ 🖳) The historic Catherinettes is on the north side of the harbour. Rooms are basic but large and airy. The halls have traditional hand-painted ceilings, as do a few of the rooms. Small balconies overlook the harbour.

Hotel Pantheon (☎ 6932329202; Kali Strata, Horio; d from €80; ❄) Located halfway up Kali Strata, this restored traditional house has five plush new rooms decked out with antique wooden furniture and well-equipped kitchenettes. Rooms vary in size and layout but all are comfortable and homey. The rooftop veranda offers stellar views.

Eating

In Gialos eateries line the harbour; in Horio they tend to be clustered at the top of Kali Strata.

GIALOS

Stani (☎ 22460 71307; sweets €1-4) Tucked away on a pedestrian street, a block up from the middle harbour, this divine bakery creates local sweets, truffles, cakes and crème brûlée. The perfect stop for some gourmet picnic treats.

Mythos Restaurant (☎ 22460 71488; mezedhes €6-12) This lively harbour-side taverna serves up imaginative food. Try fisherman's risotto, calamari stuffed with pesto, or fish-fillet parcels in a saffron cream sauce. And don't miss the pears stuffed with honey and almond for pudding. Live music and dancing accompanies dinner in the evenings.

O Meraklis (☎ 22460 71003; mains €7-10) A block back from the seafront, this deservedly popular restaurant whips up some amazing dishes. Try macaroni with pistachio and swordfish or stuffed tomatoes. Tables overflow onto the pedestrianised street.

HORIO

our pick **Olive Tree** (☎ 22460 72681; Horio; light meals €2-5; ⊗ 8am-8pm year-round) A cool retreat where you can relax on comfy sofas while savouring excellent home baking (like yummy muffins and cookies), homemade quiche or fresh rolls made to order. There are lots of vegie options (try cheese and red-pepper chutney toasties) and the kids will be kept busy with crayons and books. It's a particularly good spot for breakfast – smoothies, yoghurt with honey and fruit salad or homemade muesli will set you up for the day. Takeaway available. It's across from Hotel Fiona.

Restaurant Syllogos (☎ 22460 72148; Kali Strata; mains €5-7) At the top of the stairs, Syllogos offers imaginative fare such as chicken with prunes, pork with leek, fish with rosemary and tomato, plus vegetarian options like artichokes in egg and lemon sauce, or *spanakopita* (spinach pie).

Giorgos (☎ 22460 71984; mains €6-9) The menu here changes regularly but has enticing oven-cooked dishes like chicken stuffed with rice, herbs and pine nuts, lamb in vine leaves, or stuffed onions.

Drinking

Akrogiali Cafe (☎ 6948191637; ⊗ year-round) Right on the water's edge on the east side of the harbour, this is a great place to sip fresh juice, coffee or something stronger from the well-stocked bar.

Eva (☎ 22460 71372) A Havana-like vibe has seeped into this cool cafe, with antique sofas, funky music and a view across the harbour. In the day, get your caffeine fix here; in the evenings, it's a great place for drinks.

Jean and Tonic Bar (☎ 22460 71819; Kali Strata; ☽ 9pm-late) Feeling homesick for the 80s? Join Barry White, Tina Turner and the expat crowd for a G&T or two.

AROUND SYMI

Pedi is a little fishing village and busy mini-holiday resort in a fertile valley 2km downhill from Horio. It has some sandy stretches on its narrow beach and there are private rooms and studios to rent, as well as hotels and tavernas. The **Pedi Beach Hotel** (☎ 22460 71981; www .blueseahotel.gr; Pedi; d €90; ✻) has simple rooms decorated in white and dark wood that open on to the beach. Walking tracks down both sides of Pedi Bay lead to **Agia Marina** beach on the north side and **Agios Nikolaos** beach on the south side. Both are sandy, gently shelving beaches, suitable for children.

Nos is the closest beach to Gialos. It's a 500m walk north of the clock tower at Panormitis Bay. There you'll find a taverna, bar and sun beds. **Nimborios** is a long, pebbled beach 3km west of Gialos. It has some natural shade, as well as sun beds and umbrellas. You can walk there from Gialos along a scenic path – take the road by the east side of the central square and continue straight ahead; the way is fairly obvious, just bear left after the church and follow the stone trail. Over this way you can stay at **Niriides Apartments** (☎ 22460 71784; www.niriideshotel.com; apt €70-80). The rooms are fairly standard but the views are excellent and you're just steps from the beach.

Moni Taxiarhou Mihail Panormiti

Μονή Ταξιάρχου Μιχαήλ Πανορμίτη

A winding sealed road leads south across the island, through scented pine forests, before dipping in spectacular zigzag fashion to the large, protected Panormitis Bay. This is the site of Symi's biggest attraction – the large **Moni Taxiarhou Mihail Panormiti** (Monastery of Archangel Michael of Panormitis; admission free; ☽ dawn-sunset). The large monastery complex occupies most of the foreshore of the bay.

A monastery was first built here in the 5th or 6th century, however the present building dates from the 18th century. The principal church contains an intricately carved wooden iconostasis, frescoes, and an icon of St Michael that supposedly appeared miraculously where the monastery now stands. St Michael is the patron saint of Symi, and protector of sailors. When pilgrims and worshippers ask the saint for a favour, it's tradition to leave an offering; you'll see piles of these, plus prayers in bottles that have been dropped off boats and found their own way into the harbour.

The large monastery complex comprises a **Byzantine museum** and **folkloric museum**, a bakery with excellent bread and apple pies and a basic restaurant-cafe to the north side. Accommodation is available at the fairly basic **guest house** (☎ 22460 72414; s/d €20/32), where bookings in July and August are mandatory.

The monastery is a magnet for day-trippers, who commonly arrive at around 10.30am on excursion boats; it's a good idea to visit early or after they have left. Some ferries call in to the monastery and there is a minibus from Gialos. A taxi from Gialos costs €45. Dress modestly to enter the monastery.

TILOS ΤΗΛΟΣ

pop 530

Basking in relative obscurity, tiny Tilos (*tee*-loss) sees more migratory birds arriving on its shores than tourists. In fact, with rare species like the Eleonora's falcon, the Mediterranean shag and the Bonelli's eagle nesting here, many tourists who do arrive are avid birdwatchers. Others are drawn by the many walking trails that take you across serene mountains, valleys and meadows to small, isolated beaches surrounded by majestic limestone cliffs. Recognised as a Special Protected Area by the EU, and home to countless rare orchids and mammals such as sea turtles and the Mediterranean monk seal, Tilos is beginning to embrace a greener way of life and open its doors to ecotourism.

Often quietly ignored by the major transport companies, Tilos tends to be overshadowed by its more illustrious neighbours. Known in earlier years for its agricultural prowess rather than for its maritime eminence, it sometimes feels as if it has fallen off the map. If you're looking for a green adventure on a lost island, this is the place for you.

History

Mastodon bones – midget elephants that became extinct around 4600 BC – were found in a cave on the island in 1974. The **Harkadio Cave**

DODECANESE

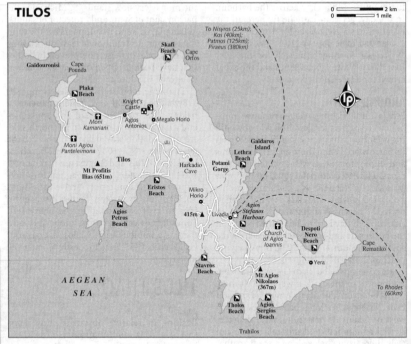

TILOS

To Nisyros (25km);
Kos (40km);
Patmos (125km);
Piraeus (380km)

Skafi Beach
Cape Orfos

Gaïdouronisi
Cape Pounda

Plaka Beach

Knight's Castle

Agios Antonios
Megalo Horio

Moni Kamariani

Moni Agiou Panteleimona

Tilos

Mt Profitis Ilias (651m)

Harkadio Cave

Potami Gorge

Gaïdaros Island

Lethra Beach

Eristos Beach

Mikro Horio

Agios Petros Beach

415m

Livadia

Agios Stefanos Harbour

Church of Agios Ioannis

Despoti Nero Beach

Cape Rematiko

Stavros Beach

Mt Agios Nikolaos (367m)

Yera

To Rhodes (60km)

AEGEAN SEA

Tholos Beach

Agios Sergios Beach

Trahilos

0 ———— 2 km
0 ———— 1 mile

DODECANESE

(closed indefinitely) is signposted from the Livadia–Megalo Horio road and is brilliantly illuminated at night. Erinna, one of the least known of ancient Greece's female poets, lived on Tilos in the 4th century BC. Elephants and poetry aside, Tilos' history shares the same catalogue of invasions and occupations as the rest of the archipelago.

In more recent times, locals have fought for a ban on hunting, which brought over 200 hunters each autumn. This ban was put in place in 1987, renewed in 2001 and is being proposed as a permanent sanction.

Getting There & Away
The Tilos-owned **Sea Star** (☎ 22460 44000; fax 22460 44044) connects the island with Rhodes. Mainland ferries erratically link Tilos to Piraeus, Rhodes and nearby islands in the Dodecanese. See Island Hopping (p763) for more details. Tickets are sold at Stefanakis Travel (opposite) in Livadia.

Getting Around
A bus ploughs up and down the island's main road seven times daily, with the first departure

from Livadia at 8.20am and the last return from Megal Horio at 10.15pm. The timetable is posted at the bus stop in the square in Livadia. Stops include Megalo Horio (€1), Eristos Beach (€1.20) and Agios Andonis (€1.50). On Sunday there is a special excursion bus to Moni Agiou Panteleimona (€4 return), leaving Livadia at 11am with one hour at the monastery. For taxis ring ☎ 6944981727 or ☎ 6945200436.

During summer there are various excursions offered from Livadia to isolated beaches. Look for posters around Livadia for more information.

LIVADIA ΛΙΒΑΔΕΙΑ
pop 470
The main village and port, Livadia is a sleepy, pleasant place. It's got no wow factor with architecture or sights but knows how to relax. The waterfront walkway is great for strolling, with the sea lapping at your feet and a handful of cafes and restaurants lining the shore. In the village you will find most services and shops, as well as most of the island's accommodation.

Orientation & Information

All arrivals are at Livadia. The small port is 300m southeast of the village centre. Tilos has no official tourist bureau. The Bank of the Dodecanese has a branch and an ATM in Livadia. The post office is on the central square.

Clinic (☎ 22460 44171; ☯ noon-5pm) Behind the church.

Kosmos (☎ 22460 44074; www.tilos-kosmos.com; internet per hr €5; ☯ 9.30am-1pm & 7-11.30pm) A gift shop with internet access. Its website is a useful source of information on Tilos. It also has a book exchange and new books for sale.

Police (☎ 22460 44222) In the white Italianate building at the quay.

Port police (☎ 22460 44350) On the harbour.

Remetzo (☎ 22460 44214; internet per hr €2) Next to the ferry dock. Play pool or nibble at the deli while waiting for one of two computers.

Sea Star (☎ 22460 44000; sea-star@otenet.gr) Sells tickets for the Sea Star catamaran.

Stefanakis Travel (☎ 22460 44310) Between the port and Livadia village; has ferry tickets and car hire.

Tilos Park Association (☎ 22460 70880; www .tilos-park.org.gr) An umbrella group promoting ecological conservation on Tilos. Has a summertime kiosk on the waterfront.

Tilos Travel (☎ 22460 44294; www.tilostravel.co.uk) At the port; has helpful staff but open in summer only. Credit card withdrawals and currency exchange are available, as well as book exchange and car and mountain-bike hire.

Sights & Activities
MIKRO HORIO

Not far from Livadia, Tilos' original settlement was built inland as protection from pirates. The last inhabitants left in the 1960s, mainly due to water scarcity. Wandering around is fascinating, with houses in various states of abandonment. A couple have even been restored, with owners hoping to return.

WALKS

Due to its agricultural past, Tilos is riddled with terraced landscapes and trails once used by farmers to reach distant crops. Today many of these trails are used by those wanting to stretch their legs.

A 3km walk heads north of Livadia to **Lethra Beach**, an undeveloped pebble-and-sand cove with limited shade. The trail starts at the far north side of the port; follow the tarmac behind Ilidi Rock Hotel to the start of the footpath. The path is well maintained, fairly easy and very scenic; even if you don't make it as far as the beach, it's a worthwhile jaunt. Returning via the very picturesque **Potami Gorge** brings you to the main island highway.

A second walk is a longer return track to the small abandoned settlement of **Yera** and its accompanying beach at **Despoti Nero**. From Livadia, follow the road south around Agios Stefanos Bay, past the Church of Agios Ioannis on the east side of the bay, and keep walking. Allow half a day for this 6km-long hike.

Tilos Trails (☎ 22460 44128, 6946054593; www.tilos trails.com; per person €25) are licensed guides who conduct a number of walks of various levels around the island.

Sleeping

Kosmos Studios (☎ 22460 44164; www.tilos-kosmos .com; apt €45) Set in a garden close to the beach, these four self-catering units are spacious and private. Each has a sunny front balcony and a shaded veranda at the back. Call into Kosmos gift shop in town to enquire.

Olympus Apartments (☎ 22460 44324; www.tilos island.com; d/tr €50/60; ☷) All rooms have amazingly well-equipped kitchens, good sea views and balconies. Village-style rooms have added character with built-in beds and traditional decor. There's also a family room with loft, but no views.

Anna's Studios (☎ 22460 44334; www.annas-studios .com; d €55) Just above the ferry dock on the north side of the bay, Anna's rooms are very homey and spacious. Gorgeous views and big balconies, kitchenettes and hand-painted wood furnishings make it a perfect home away from home. Family rooms have a second bedroom.

Hotel Irini (☎ 22460 44293; www.tilosholidays.gr; s/d incl breakfast €50/65; ☷) Set back a little from the waterfront, this hotel is ensconced in a citrus garden with a palm-fringed pool. Rooms are comfortable though simple, all with balconies and some with sea views. The lobby and lounging areas are bright and cheerful. The hotel has a cafe, serving fresh juice, homemade cakes and sandwiches.

Livadia Beach Apartments (☎ 22460 44397; www .tilosisland.com; apt €70-85; ☷ ☐) Right on the seafront and set around a colourful garden, these spacious, modern rooms are extremely comfortable with tiled balconies, plush sofas and great kitchens. There's also an alfresco cafe.

Eating

For picnics and self-catering, there are three grocery stores in Livadia with lots of fresh local produce.

Spitico (☎ 22460 44340; snacks €2-3) Overlooking the square, this cafe makes great coffee, cheese pies and local sweets. Sit on the big veranda and watch the world go by.

our pick **To Mikro Kare** (snacks €2-5; mains €3-12; ☽ 6.30pm-late Mon-Fri, 4pm-late Sat & Sun) A recently renovated traditional stone house, this seaside eatery oozes atmosphere. Wooden rafters, portholes and nautical embellishments make it very cosy. Have sandwiches and salads while playing board games in the bar or head up to the dining room for fresh seafood.

Armenon (☎ 22460 44134; mains €3.50-7) On a lively seaside veranda, dine on shrimp baked with feta and tomato or pork with rosemary, thyme and honey. All produce is local, including Armenon's own honey and olive oil.

Taverna Trata (☎ 22460 44364; mains €8-12) The friendly proprietors serve up fresh fish, *kalamari*, goat in tomato sauce and shrimp. Dine on the tree-canopied veranda amidst pretty lanterns and watch them prepare your meal on the outdoor grill. Follow your nose up from the seafront, 100m past the square.

Drinking

Cafe Bar Georges (☎ 22460 44257) This stone building located on the square is very much a working-men's hangout – the kind of place you can lounge in for hours. It might take you that long to take in the random collection of orchids, Chinese New Year ornaments and nautical paraphernalia found here. Drink at handmade wooden tables and join in the local banter.

Paralia Cafe Bar (☎ 22460 44442) With a glass wall providing a huge view of the lapping waves, this stylish bar serves cocktails, coffees and an excellent selection of teas. Relax on big cushions and comfy sofas while listening to Greek pop music or playing monopoly.

Shopping

A number of shops in Livadia have come up aces with local goods to sell. Head to **Nefeli** (☎ 22460 44246) on the square for honey, preserves (like aubergine or cherry) and dried spices all produced locally.

MEGALO HORIO ΜΕΓΑΛΟ ΧΩΡΙΟ

pop 50

Megalo Horio, the island's tiny capital, is a quiet whitewashed village with winding alleyways. If you're looking for a taste of rural life, it can make a good alternative base during the summer season. The little **museum** (admission free; ☽ 8.30am-2.30pm, summer only) on the main street houses mastodon bones from Harkadio Cave. From Megalo Horio, you can also visit the **Knight's Castle**, a taxing 40-minute upwards walk along a track from the north end of the village. Along the way you will pass the **ancient settlement** of Tilos, which once stood precariously on rocky ledges overlooking Megalo Horio.

Miliou Studios (☎ 22460 44204; d €40) has rooms in a tree-shaded garden. Each has a balcony looking towards the sea. Dine at the **Castle** (☎ 22460 44232; mains €5-6.50), on the village's south side, with beautiful views of the bay. The menu features charcoal-grilled meats, including organic goat, locally raised pork and fresh fish. There's also a small grocery store in town.

On the road to Livadia or a short footpath away from Megalo Horio is the splendid **Joanna's Resto-Bar** (☎ 22460 44145; mains €8-12; ☽ 7pm-late, May-Sep). Set in a lush, peaceful garden, Joanna's serve authentic Italian antipasto, stone-baked pizza and homemade cakes and puddings.

Megalo Horio's bus station is at the bottom of town.

AROUND MEGALO HORIO

Just before Megalo Horio, a turn-off to the left leads 2.5km to the tamarisk-shaded **Eristos Beach**, a mixture of gritty sand and shingle. You'll find a payphone, seasonal kiosk and volleyball net that sees action in the summer. In winter, the beach has its share of rubbish but it's cleaned up for the summer. Buses don't stop here on Sundays or out of season unless you ask the driver.

Just off the beach is **Eristos Beach Hotel** (☎ /fax 22460 44025; d €32; ☒ ☒), surrounded by orange, lemon and palm trees. Decent-sized balconies look out to sea; airy studios with kitchenettes sleep up to four. There is also an on-site restaurant, a bar and a lovely pool.

Nafsika Cafe (☎ 22460 44306; mains €4-8) has big windows, lots of light and tables in the flower-filled garden. The menu is standard but all home cooked, the coffee is great and the atmosphere is tranquil. **Tropicana Taverna**

DODECANESE

(☎ 22460 44020; mains €3.60-5.50), on the road up from the beach, serves traditional food with fresh vegies from its farm. Try the scrumptious *revythokeftedhes* (chickpea rissoles).

A signposted turn-off to the right from the junction leads to the quiet settlement of **Agios Antonios**. A further 3km west is the undeveloped, pretty **Plaka Beach**. It's situated in a cove where the water is slightly warmer and has natural shade in the afternoon. Once you wade in a little, the rock shelves are good for snorkelling.

The 18th-century, uninhabited **Moni Agiou Panteleimona** is 5km beyond here, along a scenic, winding road. It's uninhabited but fairly well maintained. Inside, the frescoes have mostly disappeared but the wooden altar is intricately carved and painted and the masonry is quite compelling. There are picnic benches and a stream-fed spout, ready for the lively three-day **festival** that takes place from 25 July. Outside of that, you probably won't find anyone here; in fact they may just leave the key in the door. On summer Sundays the island's minibus driver runs excursions here.

NISYROS ΝΙΣΥΡΟΣ

pop 950

Nisyros (*ni*-see-ross) tumbles down to the sea from its central volcano. Nearly round and built of pumice and rock, the island's volcanic soil makes it phenomenally fertile, drawing botanists and gardeners from around the world to see its unique flora. You don't come to Nisyros for its beaches (which aren't great). You come to stand in the centre of its hissing volcano, to explore its less touristy villages, to hike along its lush slopes and to dine on amazing local produce. Most visitors only make it for a day trip. Spend a couple of days to truly appreciate its beauty.

Getting There & Away

Nisyros is linked by regular ferries to Rhodes, Kos and Piraeus. The *Dodekanisos Pride* catamaran calls in with connections to neighbouring Dodecanese islands. Two small local ferries link Mandraki with Kardamena on Kos and Kos Town. See Island Hopping (p757) for more details.

DODECANESE

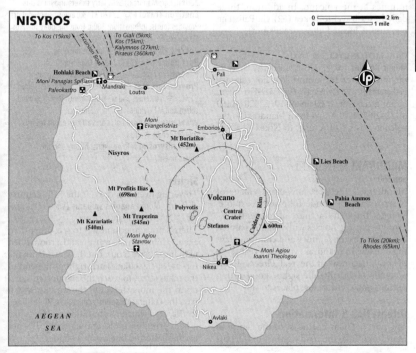

NISYROS

UNSPRUNG

With a steaming volcano set in the middle of the Aegean Sea, it seems only natural that Nisyros would also be home to hot springs. In fact, since the time of Hippocrates, folks have been visiting the springs at Pali for their supposed medicinal properties. The Egyptians loved the springs so much, they built a luxurious palace around them for regular bathing in the early 1800s. When the owner of the palace died, his son emptied the palace of its bling and hit the sea, leaving the building to turn to rubble.

Generations later, the springs called again and a great-grandson returned to rebuild in the 1980s. He planned a luxury hotel and got as far as erecting the outer structure, which continues to dominate Pali's coastline. Unfortunately, for reasons unverified he packed up and left, leaving an empty, half-built hotel and no access to the springs. If you listen carefully, you might still hear the springs' muted call from beneath the concrete, but you'll have to be satisfied with steaming yourself at the volcano's caldera instead.

Getting Around

BOAT

In July and August there are excursion boats (return €10) to the pumice-stone islet of Giali, where there's a relaxing, sandy beach.

BUS

In summer, bus companies run up to 10 excursion buses daily between 9.30am and 3pm (€7.50 return) that give you about 40 minutes at the volcano. In addition, three daily buses travel to Nikea (€2) via Pali. The bus stop is located at Madraki's port.

CAR, MOTORCYCLE & TAXI

Manos Rentals (☎ 22420 31029) on the quay is the most handy for motorbikes. For cars, try **Diakomihalis** (☎ 22420 31459, 6977735229) in town.

For a cab call ☎ 6989969810, 22420 31460 or 22420 22420. A taxi from Mandraki to the volcano costs €20 return, to Nikea €11 and to Pali €5.

MANDRAKI ΜΑΝΔΡΑΚΙ

pop 660

Mandraki is the port and main village of Nisyros and is a wonderful place to explore. Wander through the maze of residential alleyways, passing houses with brightly painted balconies, drying laundry and children playing outside. In Mandraki you get a real sense of sneaking a peak at the 'real' Greece. It has a couple of worthwhile sights, good eating options and comfortable places to stay.

Orientation & Information

The port is 500m northeast of the centre of Mandraki. Take the road right from the port and you will hit the town centre. A couple of blocks up, you'll come to a Y-junction. Head left to reach the tree-shaded Plateia Ilikiomenis, Mandraki's focal point. Head right along the main drag for signs for the monastery and castle.

The Co-operative Bank of the Dodecanese has an ATM at the harbour and a branch in Mandraki.

Diakomihalis (☎ 22420 31015; diakomihalis@kos .forthnet.gr; Mandraki) Sells ferry tickets and hires cars.

Enetikon Travel (☎ 22420 31180; agiosnis@otenet.gr) Provides tourist information; 100m from the quay towards Mandraki.

Police (☎ 22420 31201) Opposite the quay.

Port police (☎ 22420 31222) Opposite the quay.

Post office (☎ 22420 31249) Opposite the quay.

Proveza Internet Cafe (☎ 22420 31618; per 30min €1.40; ⊚) Internet and wi-fi along with freshly ground coffee and MTV videos. On the waterfront.

www.nisyros.com Photos and articles about Nisyros, contributed by readers.

www.nisyros.gr Info on sights, history and the environment.

Sights

Towering over Mandraki is the 14th-century cliff-top **Moni Panagias Spilianis** (Virgin of the Cave; ☎ 22420 31125; admission by donation; ⊙ 10.30am-3pm). There's not a huge amount to see, other than a few exhibits on the way up and a room lined with impressive icons, but the views from the top are spectacular. Turn right at the end of the main street to reach the signposted stairs up to the monastery. On the way up, you'll pass the **Cultural Museum** (admission €0.50; ⊙ 10am-3pm May-Sep), which has traditional objects like a bed, grinding tools, and clothing. It's not earth-shattering but worth a gander.

Nearby, near the seafront and beneath the original cave of the monastery, lies the **Church Museum** (admission €0.50; 🕐 10am-3pm May-Sep). It's small but impressive with glittering ecclesiastic objects from churches and homes around the island. Altars, cups, fonts and objects dating back as far as the 1st century are crammed in here.

In town, the brand new **Archaeological Museum** was due to open at the time of research. If a sneak peek was anything to go by, it's definitely worth a visit.

Above Mandraki, the impressive Mycenaean-era acropolis, **Paleokastro** (Old Kastro) has restored 4th-century Cyclopean walls built from massive blocks of volcanic rock that you can perch atop for breathtaking views. There are good explanatory notes in English throughout the site. Follow the route signposted '*kastro*', heading southwest from the monastery steps. This eventually leads up some stairs and becomes a path through beautiful, lush scenery. At the road, turn right and the *kastro* is on the left. You can drive here too.

Hohlaki is a black-stone beach and can usually be relied upon for swimming unless the wind is up, when the water can get rough. It's on the western side of Moni Panagias Spilianis and is reached by a paved footpath around the headland. Don't attempt this walk in bad weather as you can get washed right off the path. The small sandy **Mandraki beach**, halfway between the port and the village centre, is popular and OK for swimming but sometimes covered in seaweed.

Sleeping

Mandraki has fairly limited accommodation options. Book ahead to be assured of a bed in July and August.

Three Brothers Hotel (☎ 22420 31344; iiibrothers@kos.forthnet.gr; s/d/studio €30/40/60; 🔀) This welcoming, family-run hotel has smallish but well-maintained rooms with balconies and a few spacious, high-ceilinged studios with kitchenettes and verandas. All rooms have a small fridge and most have sea views. Next to the port, it's very handy for ferries.

Hotel Xenon (☎ 22420 31011; d incl breakfast €50; 🔀 🖳) These spotless, standard rooms are nothing special but are positioned right over the water. The hotel has a seaside pool.

Hotel Porfyris (☎ 22420 31376; diethnes@otenet.gr; d incl breakfast €55; 🔀 🖳) Near Plateia Ilikiomenis, this hotel was once grand but has now relaxed

into a comfortable state. Standard rooms with new bathrooms are none too big but have balconies with views of the sea or the mountain. Breakfast on the veranda and swim in the refreshing pool.

Ta Liotridia (☎ 22420 31580; www.nisyros-taliotridia.gr; apt €100; 🔀) Along the waterfront, this stone building used to house oil presses. They're now luxurious rooms decorated in traditional style with raised beds, stone archways and classic furnishings. Expect fantastic sea views from the balcony. Apartments sleep four and have full kitchens.

Eating

Ask for the island speciality, *pitties* (chickpea and onion patties) and wash them down with a refreshing *soumada*, a nonalcoholic local beverage made from almond extract.

Bakery Pali (☎ 22420 31448; snacks €1-3) A block up from the waterfront, this is the place to come for traditional Nisirian breads and cakes, pastries and pies. Pack them along for a picnic or, if you can't wait that long, polish them off sitting by the fountain outside.

Taverna Panorama (☎ 22420 31185; grills €3-5) Just off Plateia Ilikiomenis, heading towards Hotel Porfyris, this little family-run joint dishes up traditional fare. Try the *seftelies* (Cypriot-style herb-laced sausages).

Restaurant Irini (☎ 22420 31365; Plateia Ilikiomenis; mains €3-6) Ignore the big tourist boards outside; dining here may make you wonder if you've entered Irini's own dining room. You'll be treated like family with big dishes of great home cooking. Try the excellent dolmadhes, aubergine salad, grilled meat and fish dishes and leave room for the amazing puddings.

Kleanthes Taverna (☎ 22420 31484; mains €6-12) On the seafront with views of the monastery and Kos, this restaurant is popular with locals for its fresh fish soup, mussels with rice, grilled beefburgers and baked feta.

Drinking

Plateia Ilikiomenis is lined with cafes and bars, as is the waterfront. Ta Liotridia (above) has an atmospheric music bar for an evening drink and Three Brothers Hotel (left) has a relaxed, hip cafe-bar with big windows out to sea. In Plateia Ilikiomenis, try **Beggou** (☎ 22420 03158) where a chill-out lounge is hidden behind a nondescript exterior, complete with white leather sofas and big orange cushions. It has a well-stocked bar and lots of teas, too.

AROUND NISYROS
The Volcano Το Ηφαίστειο

Nisyros is on a volcanic line that passes through the islands of Aegina, Paros, Milos, Santorini, Nisyros, Giali and Kos. The island originally culminated in a mountain of 850m, but the centre collapsed 30,000 to 40,000 years ago after three violent eruptions. Their legacy are the white-and-orange pumice stones that can still be seen on the northern, eastern and southern flanks of the island, and the large lava flow that covers the whole southwest, around Nikea village.

Another violent eruption occurred in 1422 on the western side of the caldera depression (called Lakki); this, like all other eruptions since, emitted steam, gases and mud, but no lava. The islanders call the volcano Polyvotis because, during the Great War between the gods and the Titans, the Titan Polyvotis annoyed Poseidon so much that the god tore off a chunk of Kos and threw it at him. This rock pinned Polyvotis under it and became the island of Nisyros. The hapless Polyvotis from that day forth has been groaning and sighing while trying to escape.

Descending into the **caldera** (admission €2.50; 9am-8pm) is other-worldly. Cows graze near the crater's edge, amidst red, green and orange rocks. A not-so-obvious and unsignposted path descends into the largest of the five craters, **Stefanos**, where you can examine the multicoloured fumaroles, listen to their hissing and smell their sulphurous vapours. The surface is soft and hot, making sturdy footwear essential. Don't stray too far out as the ground is unstable and can collapse. Also be careful not to step into a fumarole as the gases are 100°C and corrosive. Another unsignposted but more obvious track leads to **Polyvotis**, which is smaller and wilder looking, but doesn't allow access to the caldera itself. The fumaroles are around the edge here so be very careful.

You can reach the volcano by bus, car or along a 3km-long trail from Nikia. Get there before 11am and you may have the place entirely to yourself.

Emborios & Nikea Εμπορειός & Νίκαια

Emborios and Nikea perch on the volcano's rim. From each, there are stunning views down into the caldera. Only a handful of inhabitants linger on in Emborios. You may encounter a few elderly women sitting on their doorsteps crocheting, their husbands at the *kafeneio* (coffee house).

our pick Ainria Taverna (☎ 22420 31377; Embrosios; mains €3-12), located behind the church, is the big draw in Embrosiois. It's impossible to go wrong with this menu: the country salad, meatballs, stuffed peppers, baked cheese, tomato and aubergine, and seafood are all truly gourmet. The bright decor of the traditional wooden building makes it a comfortable place to linger over a scrumptious meal.

In contrast to Emborios, picturesque Nikea, with 35 inhabitants, buzzes with life. It has dazzling white houses with vibrant gardens and a lovely mosaic-tiled central square. The bus terminates on Plateia Nikolaou Hartofyli from where Nikea's main street links the two squares. At the edge of town is the **Volcanological Museum** (☎ 22420 31400; 11am-3pm May-Sep) detailing the history of the volcano and its effects on the island. In the village's main square, **Cafe Porta Pangiotis** (☎ 22420 31285) is a cheerful, homey place to get coffee or a cool drink.

The steep path down to the volcano begins from Plateia Nikolaou Hartofyli. It takes about 40 minutes to walk it one way. Near the beginning you can detour to the signposted **Moni Agiou Ioanni Theologou**, where there is an annual **feast** on 25 to 26 September.

Pali Πάλοι

Pali is a small harbour with fishing boats and yacht anchorage. While its own beach is not very good, it's en route to **Lies**, Nisyros' most usable beach, about 5.5km around the coast. The first narrow stretch of Lies is the sandiest, with black, volcanic sand. You can also walk an extra kilometre from the end of the road along an occasionally precarious coastal track to **Pahia Ammos**, a broad expanse of gravelly volcanic sand. Bring your own shade.

If you decide to stick around Pali, head for one of the 12 comfy self-contained studios at **Mammis' Apartments** (☎ 22420 31453; www.mammis.com; d €50; year-round;), on the road to Mandraki. Set back from the sea in lush gardens, they each have a private entrance and balcony with views.

For dining in Pali, head for **Captain's House** (☎ 22420 31016; mains €4-8), where you can watch the fishermen unravel their nets as you breakfast on eggs, local sausage or yoghurt and honey. Later in the day, come here for *mousakas* and fresh fish.

KOS ΚΩΣ

pop 17,890

With some of the Dodecanese' very best beaches, impressive archaeological sites and a lush interior, it's hardly surprising that Kos (*koss*) is such a popular destination. Kos Town has a wonderful vibe and is an excellent base, catering to everyone from upmarket tourists to backpackers after a party. When you tire of the crowds, there are plenty of places to spread out – long, sandy beaches, hilltop villages and remote coves. You won't have the island to yourself, but some things are worth sharing.

History

Kos' fertile land attracted settlers from the earliest days. So many people lived here by Mycenaean times that it sent 30 ships to the Trojan War. During the 7th and 6th centuries BC, Kos prospered as an ally of the powerful Rhodian cities of Ialysos, Kamiros and Lindos. In 477 BC, after suffering an earthquake and subjugation to the Persians, it joined the Delian League and again flourished.

Hippocrates (460–377 BC), the Ancient Greek physician known as the founder of medicine, was born and lived on the island. After Hippocrates' death, the Sanctuary of Asclepius and a medical school were built, which perpetuated his teachings and made Kos famous throughout the Greek world.

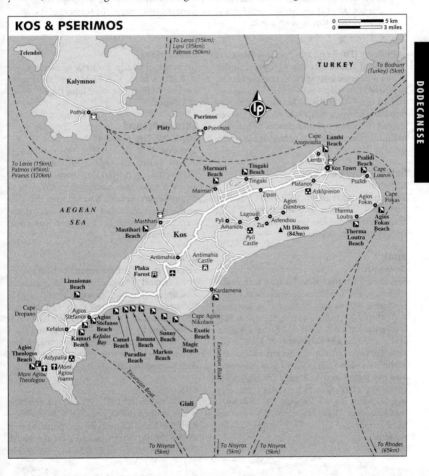

KOS & PSERIMOS

0 — 5 km
0 — 3 miles

Telendos

To Leros (15km);
Lipsi (35km);
Patmos (50km)

Kalymnos

TURKEY   To Bodrum (Turkey) (5km)

Pothia

Pserimos

Platy   Pserimos

Cape   Lambi
Ammoudia   Beach

Lambi   Psalidi Beach

Kos Town   Cape Louros

To Leros (15km);
Patmos (45km);
Piraeus (320km)

Marmari Beach   Tingaki Beach

Tingaki   Psalidi

Marmari   Platanos

Zipari   Asklipieion   Agios Fokas   Cape Fokas

AEGEAN SEA

Agios Dimitrios

Lagoudi

Mastihari   Pyli   Zia   Asfendiou   Therma Loutra   Agios Fokas Beach

Mastihari Beach   **Kos**   Amaniou   ▲ Mt Dikeos (843m)   Therma Loutra Beach

Pyli Castle

Antimahia   Antimahia Castle

Plaka Forest

Limnionas Beach

Kardamena

Cape Drepano

Agios Stefanos

Agios Stefanos Beach

Cape Agios Nikolaos

Kefalos

Kamari Beach   Kefalos Bay   Camel Beach   Banana Beach   Sunny Beach   Exotic Beach

Agios Theologos Beach   Astypalia   Paradise Beach   Markos Beach   Magic Beach

Moni Agiou Theologou   Moni Agiou Ioanni

Excursion Boat

Giali

To Nisyros (5km)   To Nisyros (5km)   To Nisyros (5km)   To Rhodes (65km)

DODECANESE

DROPPING IN ON THE NEIGHBOURS

From most of the Dodecanese Islands, Turkey looms large on the horizon. At times it appears so close, you feel like you can reach out and touch it. And you can. Day and overnight excursions run from a number of ports, making it easy to get a glimpse into the rich culture next door. Here are a few of the options.

■ Rhodes to Marmaris – A tourist hotspot, Marmaris (p515) has a bustling harbour and bazaar, a buzzing nightlife and is the yachty capital of Turkey. Not far away is an unspoilt, azure coastline backed by pine-covered mountains.

■ Kastellorizo to Kaş – Kaş (p542) is a mellow town where you can relax in shady tea gardens, watch fishermen bring in their catch or wander through the shops and boutiques. There are some nearby ruins and an increasing array of adventure activities to keep you busy. Paragliding anyone?

■ Symi to Datça – With small sandy beaches and a pretty harbour, Datça (p545) appeals to European tourists and trendy Istanbulis and is a family-friendly destination. With no sights, it's a good place to just kick back and absorb Turkish culture.

■ Kos to Bodrum – Bodrum (below) may be a big resort town with an influx of tourists, but it's also got lots of charm, stylish restaurants and a gorgeous new marina. The Museum of Underwater Archaeology is worth a visit.

Ptolemy II of Egypt was born on Kos, thus securing it the protection of Egypt, under which it became a prosperous trading centre. In 130 BC Kos fell under Roman domination, and in the 1st century AD it was administered by Rhodes, with whom it has since shared the same ups and downs of fortune, including the influential tourist trade of the present day.

Getting There & Away
AIR

There are regular flights to Athens, Rhodes, Leros and Astypalea with **Olympic Air** (☎ 22420 28330; Vasileos Pavlou 22). See Island Hopping (p754) for more details.

BOAT
Domestic

Kos is well connected to Piraeus and all the islands in the Dodecanese, as well as to the Cyclades, Samos and Thessaloniki. Services are offered by three ferry companies: **Blue Star Ferries** (☎ 22420 28914), **G&A Ferries** (☎ 22420 28545) and the **ANE Kalymnou** (☎ 22420 29900). Catamarans are run by Dodekanisos Seaways at the interisland ferry quay. Local passenger and car ferries run to Pothia on Kalymnos from Mastihari. For tickets, visit the very helpful **Fanos Travel & Shipping** (☎ 22420 20035; www.kostravel.gr; 11 Akti Kountourioti, Kos Town) on the harbour. See Island Hopping (p754) for more details.

International

In summer daily excursion boats leave at 8.30am from Kos Town to Bodrum in Turkey (return €34, one hour), and return at 4.30pm.

Getting Around
TO/FROM THE AIRPORT

The **airport** (☎ 22420 51229) is 24km southwest of Kos Town. An Aegean Airlines bus (€4) ferries passengers from Kos Town, leaving the airline's office two hours before the Athens flights depart. Kefalos-bound buses also stop at the big roundabout near the airport entrance. A taxi from the airport to Kos Town costs around €22.

BOAT

From Kos Town there are many boat excursions around the island and to other islands. Examples of return fares: Kalymnos €10; Pserimos, Kalymnos and Platy €20; Nisyros €20. There is also a daily excursion boat from Kardamena to Nisyros (€14 return) and from Mastihari to Pserimos and Kalymnos. In Kos Town these boats line the southern arm of Akti Koundourioti.

BUS

The **bus station** (☎ 22420 22292; Kleopatras 7, Kos Town) is just west of the Olympic Air office. Buses regularly serve all parts of the island, as well as the all-important beaches on the south

DODECANESE

side of Kos. A bus to the beaches will cost around €3.60.

CAR, MOTORCYCLE & BICYCLE
There are numerous car, motorcycle and moped-hire outlets; always ask at your hotel as many have special deals with hire companies. Cycling is very popular in Kos and you'll be tripping over bicycles for hire; prices range from €5 per day for a boneshaker to €10 for a half-decent mountain bike. In Kos Town try **George's Bikes** (☎ 22420 24157; Spetson 48; per day €3) for decent bikes at reasonable prices.

KOS TOWN
pop 14,750
Palm-fringed and colourful, with the Castle of the Knights picturesquely perched at its centre, Kos Town's harbour hints at the lush, vibrant town that spreads beyond it. Located on the northeast coast, Kos Town is the island's capital and main port. With an abundance of palms, pines, oleander and hibiscus, its lively squares and shopping streets are balanced with impressive Hellenistic and Roman ruins seemingly strewn everywhere. Much of the Old Town was destroyed by an earthquake in 1933 but that which still exists is a wonderful place to wander around, with trendy shops, fantastic restaurants and bars. Even though you probably came to Kos for the beaches rather than the town, you'll be easily charmed by the capital.

Orientation
The ferry quay is north of the castle and Akti Koundourioti is the street edging the harbour. The central square of Plateia Eleftherias is south of here along Vasileos Pavlou. What's left of Kos' Old Town is centred around the pedestrianised Apellou Ifestou.

Southeast of the castle, the waterfront is called Akti Miaouli. It continues as Vasileos Georgiou and then Georgiou Papandreou, which leads to the beaches of Psalidi, Agios Fokas and Therma Loutra.

Information
BOOKSHOPS
News Stand (☎ 22420 30110; Riga Fereou 2) Sells foreign-language newspapers and publications, as well as guides to Kos.

EMERGENCY
Police (☎ 22420 22222) Shares the Municipality Building with the tourist police.

Port police (cnr Akti Koundourioti & Megalou Alexandrou)
Tourist police (☎ 22420 22444)

INTERNET ACCESS
Del Mare (☎ 22420 24200; Megalou Alexandrou 4; per hr €2; ☒ 9am-1am; ☎) A popular bar with a few computers and wi-fi access.

e-global (☎ 22420 27911; cnr Artemisias & Korai; per hr €1.70-2; ☒ 24hr) Countless computers with rates that vary depending on the time of day.

G-gates (☎ 22420 26257; cnr Irodotou & Omirou; per hr €2; ☒ 9am-midnight) A very comfortable cafe where you can play Scrabble or drink at the bar between email sessions.

inSpot (☎ 22420 25262; Ioanou Tehologou, Old Town; per hr €1.20-2.40; ☒ 24hr) Oodles of computers with cheap rates after midnight.

INTERNET RESOURCES
www.travel-to-kos.com Comprehensive guide to most of Kos' attractions.

LAUNDRY
Rose Laundries (Zervanou; wash & dry €6) Clean clothes in a day!

MEDICAL SERVICES
Hospital (☎ 22420 22300; Ippokratous 32) In the centre of town.

MONEY
Alpha Bank (El Venizelou) Has a 24-hour ATM.
National Bank of Greece (Riga Fereou) With ATM.

POST
Post office (Vasileos Pavlou)

TOURIST INFORMATION
Municipal Tourist Office (☎ 22420 24460; www .kosinfo.gr; Akti Kountouriotou; ☒ 8am-2.30pm & 3-10pm Mon-Fri, 9am-2pm Sat May-Oct) General information on Kos in the office and on-line.

Sights & Activities
ARCHAEOLOGICAL MUSEUM
Cool and calm, the **archaeological museum** (☎ 22420 28326; Plateia Eleftherias; admission €3; ☒ 8am-2.30pm Tue-Sun) is a pleasant place to take in local sculptures from the Hellenistic to Late Roman era. The most renowned statue is that of Hippocrates; there's a 3rd-century-AD mosaic in the vestibule that's worth seeing.

CASTLE OF THE KNIGHTS
You can now reach the once impregnable **Castle of the Knights** (☎ 22420 27927; Leoforos Finikon;

KOS TOWN

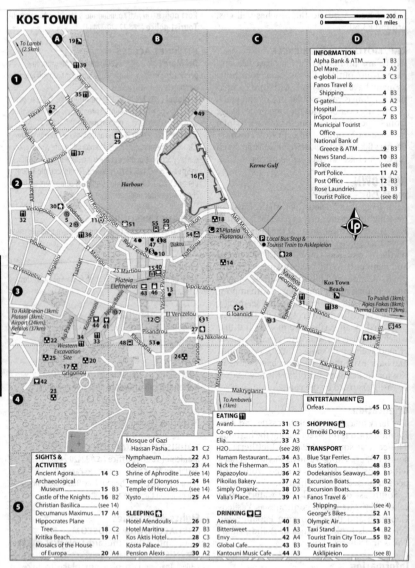

0 — 200 m
0 — 0.1 miles

admission €4; ☻ 8am-2.30pm Tue-Sun) by crossing a bridge over Finikon from Plateia Platanou. The castle, which had massive outer walls and an inner keep, was built in the 14th century and separated from the town by a moat (now Finikon). Damaged by an earthquake in 1495 and restored in the 16th century, it was the knights' most stalwart defence against the encroaching Ottomans. These days you'll find six resident tortoises as well as performances of Hippocrates' works in the summer.

ARCHAEOLOGICAL SITES

The **ancient agora** (admission free; ☻ 8am-2pm) is an open site south of the castle. A massive 3rd-century-BC stoa, with some reconstructed columns, stands on its western side. On the north side are the ruins of a **Shrine of Aphrodite**, **Temple of Hercules** and a 5th-century **Christian basilica**.

North of the agora is the lovely cobblestone Plateia Platanou, where you can sit in a cafe while paying respects to the once magnificent **Hippocrates Plane Tree**, under which Hippocrates is said to have taught his pupils. Plane trees don't usually live for more than 200 years; this ancient one is held up with scaffolding. Beneath it is an old sarcophagus converted by the Turks into a fountain. Opposite the tree is the 18th-century, boarded-up **Mosque of Gazi Hassan Pasha**.

On the other side of town is the **western excavation site**. Two wooden shelters at the back of the site protect the 3rd-century **mosaics of the House of Europa**. The best-preserved mosaic depicts Europa's abduction by Zeus in the guise of a bull. In front of here is an exposed section of the **Decumanus Maximus** (the Roman city's main thoroughfare), which runs parallel to the modern road then turns right towards the **nymphaeum**, which consisted of once-lavish latrines, and the **xysto**, a large Hellenistic gymnasium with restored columns. A short distance to the east, the **Temple of Dionysos** is overgrown but has a few ruins that can be viewed from above.

On the opposite side of Grigoriou is the impressive 2nd-century **odeion**. It was initially a venue for the senate and musical competitions and was restored during the Italian occupation when it was discovered, filled with sculptures (many now in the Archaeological Museum).

BEACHES

On the east side of town, **Kos Town Beach** has a thin strip of sand and deep water for swimming. It tends to be dominated by the restaurants and hotels along this stretch. West of town, **Kritika Beach** is a long sandy stretch that's polka-dotted with umbrellas in the summer. It gets crowded but is within easy walking distance from the town centre.

Sleeping

Pension Alexis (☎ 22420 28798; fax 22420 25797; Irodotou 9; d €40-50; ⊠) Going since the 1970s and with little redecoration since, these big, airy rooms have bold, mismatched wallpaper and a very homey feel. All have lovely balconies; room 4 has the best harbour view. The owner is keen to dole out local info and lets you use her kitchen. The only drawbacks are thin walls and shared bathrooms.

Hotel Afendoulis (☎ 22420 25321; www.afendoulis hotel.com; Evripilou 1; s/d €30/50; ⊠ 💻 🛜) The owners of this very relaxed, family-style hotel will make you feel at home. Rooms are a little dated and on the small side but comfortable and quiet. If you opt for breakfast, expect niceties like homemade fig and apricot marmalade, fresh bread and omelettes.

Kosta Palace (☎ 22420 22855; www.kosta-palace .com; cnr Akti Kountourioti & Averof; d €70; 🕙 year-round; ⊠ 💻 🛋) Easily spotted on the harbour's northern side, these rooms don't have a lot of character but are spacious and impeccably clean. Some have spectacular harbour views and there's a cafe and rooftop pool. Very friendly staff; the beach is just a short walk away.

Hotel Maritina (☎ 22420 23511-3; www.maritina .gr; Vyronos 19; 🕙 year-round; s/d incl breakfast €50/75; ⊠ 💻) The halls may feel a little down-at-heel but the rooms are very comfortable – stylish if anonymous – with lots of amenities and a small balcony. There's a huge breakfast and very friendly service. Substantial discounts are available out of season.

Kos Aktis Hotel (☎ 22420 47200; www.kosaktis .gr; Vasileos Georgiou 7; s/d from €140/178; ⊠ 💻 🛜) You'll fall asleep to the sound of lapping waves at this boutique hotel, set on a small beach yet close to the town centre. Very plush and very stylish, with flat-screen TVs, amazing tubs with sea views and glass balconies; you'll be well pampered. Expect big discounts out of season.

Eating

ourpick **Valia's Place** (☎ 22420 27877; www.valiasplace .gr; Averof 38; mains €3-6) Hidden behind a giant tree, this place has an old jazz club feel to it, complete with lots of wood, worn leather and old photographs. With a patio on the beach, it's a popular haunt with locals and often hosts live local folkstyle music. Fill up on drunk chicken, aubergine *boureki* (pies), salads and sandwiches.

ourpick **Elia** (☎ 22420 22133; Appelou Ifestou 27; mains €4-8) With their images painted beneath the wooden rafters, you will certainly feel like you're dining with the gods here. Start with chunky bread and olive pâté and then try the pumpkin balls, grilled vegies with haloumi, pork with mustard and capers or the Byzantine chicken with leek and spices. With local music, bright preserves lining the walls and a decent house wine, this stone building packs in as much

DODECANESE

atmosphere as flavour and is amazing value for money.

Nick the Fisherman (☎ 22420 23098; Averof 21; mains €5-12) This lively open-air restaurant is frequented by locals and is a relaxed place to try fresh seafood with a gourmet twist. Dishes like squid stuffed with cheese, seafood spaghetti and mussels with red sauce keep customers coming back.

Avanti (☎ 22420 20040; Vasileos Georgiou 4; mains €8-14) Ignore the hotel lobby atmosphere, this vaguely classy restaurant serves top-notch Italian-style pizza and pasta. Watch the chefs flip and cook it in the open stone oven. You can also get takeaway.

Hamam Restaurant (☎ 22420 21444; Diagora; mains €10-20; ☽ dinner) Once a traditional Turkish bath, this 16th-century building has become a distinctive dining experience. It's filled with lots of deep pinks, incense, candles and cushions, a garden lit with twinkly lights and wafting chill-out music. The menu is equally creative with swordfish souvlaki, pork with orange sauce and lots of salads and pastas.

H2O (☎ 22420 47200; Vasileos Georgiou 7; mains €15-20, snacks €5-10) Away from the hubbub of town, this is where stylish locals come to dine before huge sea views. Exceptionally stylish and ultracool, the food lives up to the decor. Try the linguine with shrimp, peppers and ouzo, or garlic lamb with rosemary and local cheese. Or just opt for an aperitif and classy snacks on the patio.

If you're self-catering, head to the well-stocked **Co-op** (Verroiopoulou). For something more organic, including fresh bread and produce, try **Papazoylou** (☎ 22420 24668; cnr Megalou Alexandrou & 31 Martiou). At the other end of town, **Simply Organic** (☎ 22420 20554; Vasileos Georgiou) has bulk snacks and baby food. For bread, sweets and tempting cakes, visit **Pikoilas Bakery** (☎ 22420 26200; cnr Salaminos & Kanari).

Drinking & Entertainment

On weekends locals congregate at Plateia Eleftherias from morning till night to drink coffee and gossip in the many cafes. Kos' nightlife geared for partying tourists is centred a block south of the harbour, along Diakou. There's also a plethora of similar bars along the waterfront on Kritika Beach. Along this stretch is Valia's Place (p559) where you can drink and listen to live music with the locals until the sun comes up. If you're looking for clubs, they pass in and out of favour so just follow the crowds.

Aenaos (☎ 22420 26044; Plateia Eleftherias) Built into the side of a mosque, this tiny place has red velvet sofas inside and a huge sea of tables beneath a tree outside. Sit for hours with coffees and fresh juices or something a little stronger in the evening.

Envy (☎ 22420 00827; Grigoriou) Denlike, with cool blue cube lighting, red chandeliers and velvet sofas, local DJs pump Greek and English music out of this traditional stone building until the wee hours.

Kantouni Music Cafe (☎ 22420 22862; Apellou 12) Popular with locals, this little place has a well-stocked bar and plays Greek pop music. Revellers squeeze inside or sit at the roadside tables.

Bittersweet (☎ 22420 26003; Apellou Ifestou) Disguised as a simple crêperie from the outside, inside you'll find a lounge-like affair with moody lighting, sofas, a fantastic garden and almost anything you can dream of drinking. Not surprisingly, the music is lounge.

Global Cafe (☎ 22420 26044; Ioannidi) Painted like a Tibetan monastery but belting out less than peaceful music, this backpacker-style cafe serves cocktails, coffees and teas. Relax on the small patio beneath palm and banana trees.

Orfeas (☎ 22420 25036; www.cine-orfeas.gr; Plateia Eleftherias; tickets adult/child €7/5) If you're suffering movie withdrawal, this cinema shows English films with Greek subtitles along with some local flicks.

Shopping

For high street-style-shops head to the eastern end of Ioannidi and the pedestrian streets south of Ippokratous. For more boutique options, visit the western end of Ioannidi, just north of the Old Town. **Dimoiki Dorag** (Plateia Eleftherias) is a market with local honey, preserves, spices and herbs that make great souvenirs.

Getting Around
BUS

Urban buses depart from Akti Miaouli and have two ticket prices: Zone A (€0.80) and Zone B (€1). Tickets from vending machines are slightly cheaper than those bought on board. You'll find one in front of the Blue Star Ferries office on the harbour. For schedules, check the Local Bus Office.

TAXI

Taxis congregate at a stand on the south side of the port.

TOURIST TRAIN
In summer, a good way to get your bearings is to hop on the city's vehicular Tourist Train's city tour (€4, 20 minutes), which runs from 10am to 2pm and 6pm to 10pm, starting from the bus station on Akti Kountouriotou. You can also take a train to the Asklipieion and back (€3.50), departing on the hour from 10am to 5pm Tuesday to Sunday, from the bus stop on Akti Miaouli.

AROUND KOS
Kos' main road runs southwest from Kos Town, with turn-offs for the mountain villages and the resorts of Tingaki and Marmari. Between the main road and the coast is a quiet road, ideal for cycling, which winds through flat agricultural land as far as Marmari.

The nearest decent beach to Kos Town is the crowded **Lambi Beach**, 4km to the northwest and an extension of Kritika Beach. Further round the coast is a long, pale-sand stretch of beach, divided into **Tingaki**, 10km from Kos Town, and **Marmari Beach**, 14km west and slightly less crowded. Windsurfing is popular at all three beaches. In summer there are boats from Marmari to the island of Pserimos.

Vasileos Georgiou in Kos Town leads to the three busy beaches of **Psalidi**, 3km from Kos Town, **Agios Fokas** (8km) and **Therma Loutra** (12km). The latter has hot mineral springs that warm the sea.

Asklipieion Ασκληπιείον
The island's most important ancient site is the **Asklipieion** (☎ 22420 28763; Platani; adult/student €4/3; ☼ 8am-7.30pm Tue-Sun), built on a pine-covered hill 3km southwest of Kos Town, with lovely views of the town and Turkey. The Asklipieion consisted of a religious sanctuary devoted to Asclepius (the god of healing), a healing centre and a school of medicine, where training followed the teachings of Hippocrates. Until AD 554, when an earthquake destroyed the Asklipieion, people came from far and wide for treatment.

The ruins occupy three levels. The **propylaea** (approach to the main gate), Roman-era public **baths** and remains of guest rooms are on the 1st level. On the 2nd level is a 4th-century-BC **altar of Kyparissios Apollo**. West of this is the **first Temple of Asclepius**, built in the 4th century BC. To the east is the 1st-century-BC **Temple to Apollo**. On the 3rd level are the remains of the once-magnificent 2nd-century-BC **Temple of Asclepius**.

The hourly bus 3 and the Tourist Train (left) go to the site. It's also a pleasant cycle or walk.

Mastihari Μαστιχάρι
Known for its party scene but also gaining popularity with families, little Mastihari caters to independent travellers after a beach holiday and is a popular alternative to Kos Town. With a wide, sandy beach that gets a summer breeze, the village itself feels somewhat like a seasonal resort and is *very* quite outside summer. If the scene gets too much for you, excursion boats run to the island of Pserimos, where you can escape for a day to its protected sandy beach and convenient tavernas. Just 30km from Kos Town, Mastihari is also an arrival/departure point for ferries to Pothia on Kalymnos.

You'll find plenty of places to stay a block back from the seafront. **Athina Studios** (☎ 22420 59030; www.athinas-studios.gr; d €35) offers bougainvillea-strewn apartments that are airy, immaculate and feel like new, with full kitchen facilities. On the same street, **To Kyma** (☎ 22420 59045; www.kyma.kosweb.com; s/d €30/35) is a family-run hotel with smallish, simple rooms right next to the beach. Half enjoy sea views.

The beachfront is lined with restaurants and cafes, many offering children's menus. Right on the harbour, the busy **Kali Kardia Restaurant** (☎ 22420 59289; fish €6-12) is popular with locals. With fresh seafood, decent pasta and a sea breeze, you can see why.

Chill-Out Cafe (☎ 22420 59192) offers a bit of an escape in the day and is a cool place to hang out in the evening. Look for greeting-card-style swirly decor, a well-stocked bar and comfy chairs.

Mountain Villages
The villages scattered on the northern green slopes of the Dikeos mountain range are a great place for exploring. At **Zipari**, 10km from the capital, a road to the southeast leads to **Asfendiou**. En route, 3km past Zipari, stop in at **Taverna Panorama** (☎ 22420 69367; mains €6-10; ☼ lunch & dinner) for coastal views, traditional cuisine and good mezedhes served to a primarily Greek clientele.

From Asfendiou, a turn-off to the right leads to the village of **Zia**, which pulls in coachloads of

DODECANESE

tourists for its sunset views. The main square of Zia is chock-a-block with restaurants. Head to **Niotis Jazz Cafe** (☎ 6947412440; mains €3-7) for friendly service and great music; the food here is simple (salads, pasta, crêpes and burgers). If you find Zia too packed, the **Village Tavern** (☎ 22420 69918; mains €2-6) offers sausages, *gyros* (meat slivers cooked on a vertical rotisserie; usually eaten with pitta bread), zucchini balls and grilled feta that you can take away to find your own roadside view. At the top of the village, follow the rough staircase to **Kefalovrysi** (☎ 22420 69605; mains €5-8) for well-priced, first-class traditional dishes in leafy surroundings with a great vista.

Returning north from Zia, take a left and follow signs for **Pyli**. Just before the village, a left turn leads to the extensive ruins of the medieval village of **Old Pyli** where a well-marked trail leads past the remains of houses and up to the castle. A number of the chapels on the site are currently being restored and many of the Byzantine gates and archways are still largely intact. Watch out for tortoises, too! Good footwear and a little stamina are a must. It's a great place to picnic; stock up in the grocery stores and bakeries of Pyli.

Kamari & Kefalos Bay Καμάρι & Κέφαλος

South from Mastihari, join the main road at Antimahia and continue southwest to the huge Kefalos Bay, fringed by a 12km stretch of incredible sand. Don't be put off by the tacky strip of tourist shops, restaurants and hotels behind on the main road. These divine beaches are idyllic, backed by green hills and lapped by warm water. The stretch is roughly divided into seven, each signposted from the main road. The most popular is **Paradise Beach**, while the most undeveloped is **Exotic Beach**; **Banana Beach** (also known as Langada Beach) is a good compromise.

Agios Stefanos Beach, at the far western end, is reached along a short turn-off from the main road and worth a visit to see the island of **Agios Stefanos**. Within swimming distance, this tiny island is home to the ruins of two 5th-century basilicas and to another lovely, sandy beach.

Further down the road, you'll reach **Kamari Beach,** an elongated holiday resort strip packed with restaurants, accommodation and shops that have spread to the main road with English brekkies and Yorkshire puddings. The bay itself is filled with bobbing fishing boats and the beach is most accessible east of the resort.

You'll find a small Tourism Office next to the beachside bus stop and an ATM on the top road. Excursion boats leave from here for Nisyros (€16) two or three times weekly. There are also daily boats to Paradise Beach in the summer, departing at 10.30am and returning at 5.30pm

About 150m north of the Kamari seafront bus stop you'll find accommodation at **Anthoula Studios** (☎ 22420 71904; studios €40), a spotless set of airy, roomy studios surrounded by a vegetable garden.

For something a little more authentic, head up to **Kefalos**, a traditional village perched high above the beach that indulges little in tourism. Have a coffee with the locals, dine in time-honoured tavernas and wander about to catch a glimpse of village life. For a surreal experience, visit **Cafe Neo** (snacks €1-3). Entering this blue stone building, you'll feel like you've wandered into someone's home. With a couple of benches, a wood stove, walls filled with photos and an owner who makes a mean coffee, marmalade and lace, this is a popular haunt with neighbours. You'll find it behind the church. The central square, where the bus from Kos Town terminates, has a post office and bank with an ATM.

The southern peninsula has the island's wildest and most rugged scenery. **Agios Theologos Beach** is at the end of a winding road that's dotted with tiny churches. The beach is surf-battered and the waters tempestuous but it's a beautiful setting and worlds away from resort-land. On the beach is the seasonal **Restaurant Agios Theologos** (☎ 6974503556; mains €6-15), which enjoys the best sunsets in Kos. The huge menu is filled with food from the owner's land, including homemade feta, olives, bread and goat. The rest is sourced locally – honey, seafood, burgers and vegies.

ASTYPALEA
ΑΣΤΥΠΑΛΑΙΑ

pop 1240

Flung so far west you'd be forgiven for thinking it was part of the Cycladic Islands, Astypalea (ah-stih-*pah*-lia) appeals to those after an alternative holiday experience. Outside of the bustling port of Skala and cubist hill-top town of Hora, the land is bare and rocky with nary a tree in sight. The beaches are scattered, but most are lovely; the rough terrain offers off-road thrills to adventurers; and the fresh fish and lobster thrill gastronomes. Mass foreign tourism has not yet arrived here, but in July and August Athenians descend in force.

Getting There & Away

There are regular flights from Astypalea to Athens, Leros, Kos and Rhodes. Astypalea Tours (p564) in Skala is the agent for Olympic Air.

Astypalea has ferry services to Piraeus and Rhodes with various stops along the way. They dock at the rather isolated small port of Agios Andreas, 6.5km north of Skala. A bus is scheduled to meet all arriving ferries, but don't bank on it. The Kalymnos-based ferry F/B *Nissos Kalymnos* links the island with Kalymnos and islands further north in the Dodecanese, and docks at Skala. Ferry tickets are available from **Paradisos Ferries Agency** (☎ 22430 61224; fax 22430 61450) or from Astypalea Tours, both in Skala. For more transport info, see Island Hopping (p746).

Getting Around

The airport is 8km northeast of Skala. Flights from Athens and Rhodes are usually met by the local bus, though a pick-up is a more reliable option.

In summer, buses run half-hourly from Skala to Hora and Livadi (€1), and hourly from Hora and Skala to Analipsi (Maltezana; €1.50) via Marmari Beach. Services are scaled back the rest of the year. There are only three taxis on the island and as many car- and scooter-hire agencies. **Vergoulis** (☎ 22430 61351) in Skala is a reputable agency.

From June to August, you can hop on **Thalassopouli** (☎ 6974436338) for boat excursions to the remote western beaches of Agios Ioannis, Kaminakia and Vatses, or to the islets of Koutsomytis or Kounoupa. When the weather is good, longer round-island excursions are offered. Tickets (€10 to €15) can be bought on the boat.

SKALA & HORA ΣΚΑΛΑ & ΧΩΡΑ

The main settlement of Astypalea consists of the port of Skala (known officially as Pera Yialos) and the picturesque hill-top village of

DODECANESE

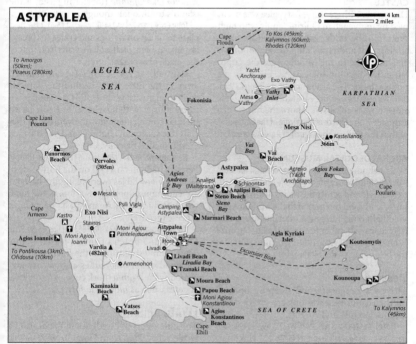

Hora, crowned by an imposing 15th-century castle. Skala has a fairly popular sand-and-pebble beach but most visitors head uphill to the cooler Hora for stunning views of the port and surrounds. The main square in Hora is backed by several restored windmills. Leading upwards from here to the castle is a series of narrow streets with dazzling-white cubic houses sporting brightly painted balconies.

Information

Astypalea Tours (☎ 22430 61571; Skala) For air tickets.

Commercial Bank (☎ 22430 61402; Skala) Has an ATM on the waterfront.

Municipal Tourist Office (☎ 22430 61412; 🕓 10am-noon & 6-9pm; Hora) In a restored windmill.

Police (☎ 22430 61207; Skala) In a Italianate building on the waterfront.

Port police (☎ 22430 61208; Skala) Shares premises with the police.

Post office (☎ 22430 61223; Hora) At the top of the Skala–Hora road.

www.astypalaia.com For history, pictures, facilities and sights.

Sights

CASTLE

During the 14th-century, Astypalea was occupied by the Venetian Quirini family who built the imposing **castle** (admission free; 🕓 dawn-dusk), adding to it and renovating throughout their 300-year rule. In the Middle Ages the population lived within the castle walls to escape pirate attacks. The last inhabitants left in 1953, following a devastating earthquake in which the stone houses collapsed. Above the tunnel-like entrance is the **Church of The Virgin of the Castle** and within the walls is the **Church of Agios Georgios**.

ARCHAEOLOGICAL MUSEUM

Skala is home to a small **archaeological museum** (☎ 22430 61206; admission free; 🕓 11am-1pm Tue-Sun) with treasures found across the island, from the prehistoric Mycenaean period to the Middle Ages. Highlights include grave offerings from two Mycenaean chamber tombs and a little bronze Roman statue of Aphrodite. The museum is at the beginning of the Skala–Hora road.

Sleeping

There's a range of good sleeping options on the island. Reservations are pretty much essential in July and August.

Hotel Australia (☎ 22430 61275, 6973224996; australia_roomsstudios@yahoo.gr; d/tr €45/50; 🆗) This long-popular hotel has simple, well-kept rooms with balcony views to the sea and castle. Each room has a fridge and the beach is only 50m away. You'll find it tucked away on the north side of Skala harbour.

Avra Studios (☎ 22430 61363, 6972134971; d €50; 🆗) Right on the beach, these older, quaint rooms have kitchenettes and balconies. You can literally fall out of bed onto the sand.

Akti Rooms (☎ 22430 61114; www.aktirooms.gr; d/studio incl breakfast €80/85; 🆗) Beautiful wooden furnishings, traditional touches and balconies make these rooms restful. Studios have kitchenettes; mountain-view rooms are somewhat cheaper. Swim from the private platform and enjoy the resortlike facilities. It's on the northeast side of the harbour.

Studio Kilindra (☎ 22430 61131; www.astipalea.com.gr; d/apt €150/170; 🆗 🖥 🏊) This boutique hotel sits just below the castle in Hora, providing amazing sea views. Rooms are luxurious with character added through traditional splashes. And the pool is divine.

Eating

There aren't many eating options in Astypalea. *Astakomakaronadha* (lobster in pasta) is the island's traditional (though pricey) dish.

Jolly Café (☎ 22430 22430; breakfast €5-6) The best place to fill up on waffles and coffee for breakfast is slap-bang on the Skala waterfront under the shade of a tamarisk tree.

Maïstrali (☎ 22430 61691; mains €5-8) Tucked away in the little street behind the harbour and popular with yachties, this is a good place to try lobster with spaghetti. The fish-based menu is complemented with oven-baked specials like succulent lemon goat. Dine alfresco on the shaded balcony.

Restaurant Akti (☎ 22430 61114; mains €5-8.50) Perched high up on a cliff on the north side of Skala, the few tables overlooking the harbour are enormously popular. So, too, is the food, which includes fisherman's pasta or *poungia* (cheese turnovers).

To Akrogiali (☎ 22430 61863; mains €5.50-9.50) Dine on the beach or on a pleasant patio. The yummy smells from the kitchen hint at the good-quality mezedhes at this cosy taverna. Try the *tigania* (pork cubes) or soft local cheeses, such as *hlori* or *ladotyri*.

LIVADI ΛΕΙΒΑΔΙ

The little resort of Livadi lies in the heart of a fertile valley, 2km from Hora. Its wide pebble beach is one of the best on the island and can get fairly crowded in summer. On the seafront, **Hotel Manganas** (☎ 22430 61468, 697657853; astyroom@otenet.gr; studios €50-60; ⊠) offers comfortable, simple rooms with kitchenette, shaded balconies and mini-washing machines to extract all of that sand. For a plusher option, head to **Fildisi Hotel** (☎ 22430 62060; www.fildisi.net; studios from €130; ⊠ ⊜ ⊠) with posh, spacious rooms that combine modern and traditional touches. Feel at home with your own kitchenette and home theatre.

The handful of places to eat at Livadi are strung out along the tree-shaded waterfront. **Trapezakia Exo** (☎ 22430 61083; mains €4-7) is at the western end and serves sandwiches and daily fish specials, while **Astropelos** (☎ 22430 61473; mains €6-9) has a small but imaginative range of seafood dishes.

WEST OF SKALA

Heading west of Skala you hit the big Astypalea outback – gnarled, bare and rolling hills with scarcely a sealed road to speak of. It's just about driveable; you'll need a solid 4WD. The road eventually leads to the **Kastro** ruins and **Moni Agiou Ioanni**, situated next to each other above the coast. From here, the strictly fit may venture downwards on foot to **Agios Ioannis beach**. An equally rough road leads to **Panormos Beach** which you'll likely have to yourself.

On the south coast, an *extremely* rough track winds downwards to **Kaminakia beach**, where there is a good seasonal restaurant, **Sti Linda** (☎ 6932610050; mains €4-7; ⊠ Jul-Sep), serving hearty fish soups, oven-baked goat and home-made bread. If your nerves aren't shattered, detour to the pretty, tree-shaded **Agios Konstantinos beach** on the south side of Livadi Bay.

EAST OF SKALA

Marmari, 2km northeast of Skala, has three bays with pebble and sand beaches and is home to **Camping Astypalea** (☎ 22430 61900; camp sites per adult/tent €6/4; ⊠ Jun-Sep). This tamarisk tree-shaded and bamboo-protected camping ground is right next to the beach and has good facilities like 24-hour hot water, a kitchen, cafe and minimarket. **Steno Beach**, 2km further along, is one of the better least frequented beaches on the island. It's sandy, shady and well protected. The island is just 2km wide here.

Analipsi (also known as Maltezana) is 7km up the road in a fertile valley on the isthmus. A former Maltese pirates' lair, it's a scattered, pleasantly laid-back settlement. On its outskirts are remains of the **Tallaras Roman baths** with mosaics. **Analipsi Beach** is southeast of town and is long, with sand, pebbles, shade and clean, shallow water.

For accommodation in Analipsi, head to **Villa Varvara** (☎ /fax 22430 61448; studios €55; ⊠), which has comfortable blue-and-white studios overlooking a vegetable garden, just 100m from the beach; all have a kitchenette and balcony. The large **Hotel Maltezana Beach** (☎ 22430 61558; www.maltezanabeach.gr; s/d incl breakfast €80/115; P ⊠ ⊠) has lovely rooms in a complex kitted out with countless amenities like a spa, pool bar, playground and family rooms. There aren't many dining options in Maltezana, with the usual seaview tavernas serving traditional fare.

Continuing east, remote **Mesa Vathy** hamlet is an indolent yacht harbour in a sheltered bay. The swimming isn't good, but you can fish for your lunch or dine at the laid-back **Galini Café** (☎ 22430 61201; mains €3-5; ⊠ Jun-Oct), which offers meat and fish grills and oven-baked specials.

KALYMNOS ΚΑΛΥΜΝΟΣ

pop 16,440

Once renowned for its sponge-fishing, Kalymnos (*kah*-lim-nos) still sees a daily catch of sponges sorted through at the harbour's edge. Today the island is working hard to reinvent itself as a tourist destination and with a lively main town, beautiful beaches, and perpendicular cliffs where climbers flock to test their mettle, the island has lots to offer. The island's resorts cater mainly to individuals, and walkers will find a network of ready-to-walk trails and paths that criss-cross the landscape.

Getting There & Away

AIR

Kalymnos is linked to Athens and neighbouring islands by Olympic Air, represented by **Kapellas Travel** (☎ 22430 29265; kapellastravel@gal lileo.gr; Patriarhou Maximou 12, Pothia). The airport is 3.5km northwest of Pothia and the seaplane terminal is 1.5km east. See Island Hopping (p752) for more information.

BOAT

Kalymnos is linked to Rhodes, Piraeus and islands in between via car-ferries, hydrofoils

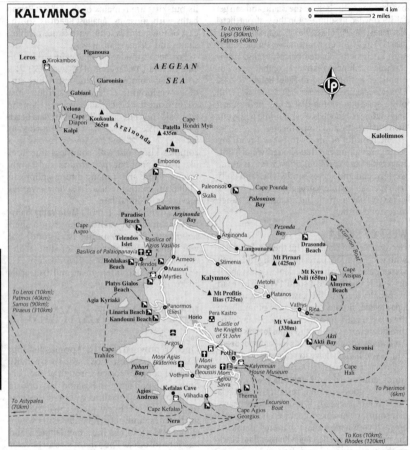

and catamarans. Services are provided by local boats and **Blue Star Ferries** (☎ 22430 26000), **G&A Ferries** (☎ 22430 23700), **Dodecanese Seaways** (☎ 22430 28777; Pothia quay) and **ANE Kalymnou** (☎ 22430 29612), and tickets can be bought from Magos Travel (opposite). For more details, see Island Hopping (p752).

Getting Around
BOAT

In summer there is a daily excursion boat from Myrties to Emborios (€8), leaving at 10am and returning at 4pm. Day trips to **Kefalas Cave** (€20), impressive for its 103m corridor filled with stalactites and stalagmites, run from both Pothia and Myrties. There are also regular boats from Pothia to Pserimos, with its big,

sandy beach and tavernas. The large sailboat **Katerina** (☎ 6938325612) does regular excursions around Kalymnos.

BUS

There are 10 departures daily from Pothia to Elies, Kandouni, Myrties and Masouri, the first leaving at 6.50am and the last returning at 9.40pm. There are also four daily return trips to Vathys at 6.30am, 7.45am, 2.10pm and 5pm. Buy tickets from the Municipality of Kalymnos ticket office by the bus stop in Pothia.

CAR & MOTORCYCLE

There are plenty of vehicle-hire companies on the island, mainly concentrated in Pothia. Try

Rent-a-Bike (☎ 6937980591) or **Automarket Rental** (☎ 22430 51780, 6927834628).

TAXI

Shared taxi services cost a little more than buses and run from the Pothia **taxi stand** (☎ 22430 50300; Plateia Kyprou) to Masouri. The taxis can also be flagged down en route. A regular taxi costs €10 to Myrties and €15 to Vathys.

POTHIA ΠΟΘΙΑ
pop 10,500

Pothia (*poth*-ya), the port and capital of Kalymnos, is a fairly large town by Dodecanese standards. Built amphitheatrically around the slopes of the surrounding valley, it's a visually arresting melange of colourful mansions and houses draped over the hills and spilling down to an equally colourful harbour. Pothia is not, however, a languid island town. It's a bustling, lively commercial centre with plenty of shops and restaurants that are filled with locals going about their busy lives, seemingly oblivious to the tourist trade. With an excellent museum, good hotels, great seafood and lots of energy, it'll keep you on your toes.

Orientation & Information

Pothia's quay is located at the southern side of the port. Most activity, however, is centred on the waterfront square, Plateia Eleftherias. The main commercial centre is on Venizelou. Stay constantly alert while walking around Pothia; traffic hurtles up and down its narrow footpath-less roads.

The Commercial, National and Ionian Banks, all with ATMs, are close to the waterfront.

Heaven @ Cafe (☎ 22430 50444; internet per hr €3; ⏰ 9am-late) Small but handily located on the waterfront.

Kapellas Travel (☎ 22430 29265; fax 22430 51800; Patriarhou Maximou 12) For air tickets.

Magos Travel (☎ 22430 28777; www.magostravel.gr) Hydrofoil and catamaran tickets, including a 24-hour ticket machine outside.

Main post office A 10-minute walk northwest of Plateia Eleftherias. There is a more convenient agency south of Plateia Ethinikis Andistasis.

Neon Internet C@fe (☎ 22430 59120; per hr €3; ⏰ 9.30am-midnight) Popular teen hangout with internet, gaming and bowling!

Police (☎ 22430 29301; Venizelou)

Port police (☎ 22430 29304; 25 Martiou)

Tourist Information (☎ 22430 59056; 25 Martiou)

www.kalymnos-isl.gr Informative site hosted by the Municipality of Kalymnos.

Sights

The brand new **Archaeological Museum** (☎ 22430 23113; adult/student €5/3; ⏰ 8.30am-2.30pm Tue-Sun) is stunningly impressive and packed with a vast array of artefacts dating back as far as 2500 BC and found as recently as 2001. One of the most striking pieces is a large, arresting bronze statue of a woman in a detailed chiton from the 2nd-century BC, found off the coast of Kalymnos. Behind the main building is the **mansion of Nickolas Vouvalis**, a wealthy 19th-century sponge trader who was the island benefactor. Inside, rooms appear as they did when he lived here.

In the centre of the waterfront is the **Nautical & Folklore Museum** (☎ 22430 51361; admission €2; ⏰ 8am-1.30pm Mon-Fri, 10am-12.30pm Sat & Sun, May-Sep), with displays on traditional regional dress and the history of sponge diving. For an even bigger eyeful of sponge, visit the exporting factory of **NS Papachatzis** (☎ 22430 28501), overflowing with sponges of every conceivable shape and size. You can also see sponges hauled in every afternoon in the main square.

Sleeping

Greek House (☎ 22430 23752, 6972747494; s/d/studios/apt €25/35/40/55) Inland from the port, this pleasant budget option has four cosy wood-panelled rooms with kitchen facilities. More expensive and better-equipped studios are also available, as is a self-contained, large apartment in town.

Arhodeko Hotel (☎ 22430 24051; fax 22430 24149; s/d €30/40; ⏰ year-round; ⚡) Conveniently located on the harbour, this hotel has a long history. Built in the 19th-century and a bakery from 1909 until the 1980s, it has a well-preserved exterior and interior stone archways. Room 21 has the original wood-burning oven. Rooms are basic with a fridge and views over the harbour.

Hotel Panorama (☎ 22430 23138; smiksis2003@ yahoo.gr; s/d incl breakfast €30/45; ⏰ year-round; ⚡) Set on a hill on the south side of town, this simply but homey hotel has amazing views from the rooms' small balconies and the communal veranda. The friendly owner has lots of local info.

Evanik Hotel (☎ 22430 22057; d incl breakfast €55; ⚡) Newly renovated and plush for the price, rooms here aren't full of character but are

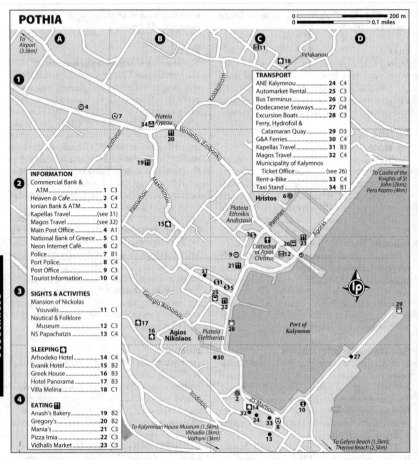

POTHIA

0 — 200 m
0 — 0.1 miles

To Airport (3.5km)

Pelakanou

Plateia Kyprou

Venizelou (Emboriki)

To Castle of the Knights of St John (2km); Pera Kastro (4km)

Hristos

Plateia Ethnikis Andistasis

Cathedral of Agios Christos

Plateia Eleftherias

Agios Nikolaos

Port of Kalymnos

To Kalymnian House Museum (1.5km); Vlihadia (3km); Vothyni (3km)

25 Martiou

To Gefyra Beach (1.5km); Therma Beach (2.5km)

DODECANESE

---

clean and very comfortable with a small balcony. Service is attentive and there's a stylish bar. Ask for a quieter room at the back. It's located a few blocks inland.

Villa Melina (☎ 22430 22682; antoniosantonoglu@yahoo .de; d ind breakfast €55; 🏊 🖭) With a lobby that speaks of faded glamour, this pink mansion on the hill is a unique place to stay. The doubles in the main house are individually decorated, with the quirky layout that older houses afford. The veranda overlooks the harbour and a deep pool is set in a lush garden. Surrounding the garden are plainer studios with kitchenettes.

Eating

Gregory's (☎ 22430 51888; snacks €2-4) It's true, it's part of a chain, but Gregory's deli and its co-

habitant, Coffee Right, are a great stop for a quick bite. Near busy Plateia Kyprou, it's bright, popular and offers good value sandwiches, salads, smoothies, coffees, croissants and *spanakopita*.

Mania's (☎ 22430 29014; mains €5-10) One of the more atmospheric seafood restaurants along the waterfront, this colourful, comfortable place serves fresh fish, ouzo octopus, grilled calamari and *saganaki* (fried cheese). Traditional instruments hang on the walls and are played some evenings.

Pizza Imia (☎ 22430 24809; pizza €7-12) Ignore the tacky pictures of burgers and tourist food outside – come to Pizza Imia for the pizza! Loaded and thin-crusted, the pizzas are cooked in a wood oven and are delicious.

OUTDOOR ADVENTURE

In recent years Kalymnos has become something of a mecca for **rock climbers**. Spectacular limestone walls attract legions of climbers looking for seriously challenging extreme sport. There are over 20 documented climbs awaiting the adventurous, pulling in visitors from March onwards. The best place for the low-down is the **Climber's Nest** (☎ 6938173383; www.climbers-nest.com; Armeos). You'll find equipment, maps, guidebooks, guides and a notice board.

The annual **Diving Festival** held in mid-August offers participants the chance to compete in underwater target shooting, cliff diving, scuba-diving through wrecks and even hunting for lost treasure. See the **Municipality's website** (www.kalymnos-isl.gr) for further details.

Hiking has become enthusiastically organised on Kalymnos. There are 10 established hiking routes scattered all over the island and detailed on the excellent 1:25,000 *Kalymnos Hiking Map* published by **Anavasi** (☎ 21032 18104; www.mountains.gr; Stoa Arsakiou 6a, Athens). A popular hike is the Vathys-Pothia B1 4.25km 'Italian Road', a stone pathway built by the Italians at the beginning of the 20th century. A more arduous hike is the 9km circuit Patella Castle loop (C3 and C4), along the mountain ridge backing Emborios.

The house red is rather port-esque but the service is friendly.

If you're self-catering, head for **Vidhalis Market** (☎ 22430 59230), a well-stocked supermarket on the waterfront, and to **Anash's Bakery** (☎ 22430 29426) at the back of town for baked goods like olive bread and local treats.

Drinking

Pothia's harbour is hopping in the evening. The bars that line the waterfront, particularly around Plateia Eleftherias, are stylish hangouts with tables taking over the square. To the west you'll find more old-boy haunts where you can mingle with the locals over fishing stories.

AROUND POTHIA

South of Pothia, the road to Moni Agiou Savra takes you past **Kalymnian House Museum** (☎ 33420 51635; admission €2; ☆ 9am-2pm & 4-8pm May-Sep), a small traditional home where you'll learn about local customs through guided tours in English.

Running northwards from the port is a busy valley with a series of settlements. The ruined **Castle of the Knights of St John** (Kastro Hrysoherias) looms to the left of the Pothia–Horio road with a small **church** inside its battlements.

On the east side of the valley, **Pera Kastro** was a pirate-proof village inhabited until the 18th century. Within the crumbling walls are the ruins of stone houses and six tiny, 15th-century churches. Check out the few remaining frescoes in the Church of Transfiguration. Steps lead up to Pera Kastro from the end of the main road in **Horio**; it's an unshaded climb with incredible views.

A tree-lined road continues from Horio to **Panormos**, a pretty village 5km from Pothia. Its original name of Elies (olive trees) was replaced following the destruction of the trees during WWII. A postwar mayor planted countless trees and flowers to create beautiful 'panoramas' from which its present-day name is derived. The beaches of **Kandouni** and **Linaria** are a stone's throw from one another and within walking distance of Panormos. Kandouni is a particularly pretty cove surrounded by mountains, with cafes, bars and hotels overlooking the water and a small sandy beach. You can also rock climb from here and there is an annual cliff-diving competition (see above).

For dining and sleeping, Linaria is slightly quieter. **Giorgio's Family Restaurant** (☎ 22430 47809; mains €6-12), at the northern end of Linaria beach, has creative salads, fresh fish and seafood. Try the chilli feta, *saganaki* shrimp or 'god's fish' with garlic sauce alongside a glass of local wine. Rest your head at **Sevasti Studio** (☎ 22430 48779; d/apt €40/50; ☒). A block up the road and away from the party scene, it has cheerful, spacious rooms and a veranda with gorgeous sea views. Apartments have kitchenettes.

Up the road, **Platys Gialos** is a bit more of a trek from Panormos. The beach here is less developed and pebbly.

MYRTIES, MASOURI & ARMEOS
ΜΥΡΤΙΕΣ, ΜΑΣΟΥΡΙ & ΑΡΜΕΟΣ

From Panormos the road continues to the west coast, with stunning views of Telendos Islet perched like a giant castle in the sea. **Myrties** (myr-*tyez*), **Masouri** (mah-*soo*-ri) and **Armeos** (ar-me-*os*) are busy resort centres and essentially one long street, packed head to tail with restaurants, bars, souvenir shops and minimarkets. With lots of trees and a pretty outlook, they're much more relaxed and attractive than the average Greek resort strip. The beach here is divided into two sections by an extinct volcano plug – Myrties beach with Melitsahas harbour, and the marginally better Masouri and Armeos beaches to the north. The beaches have dark sand but aren't so great.

Spread throughout all three centres there are currency-exchange bureaus, a Dodecanet ATM and car- and motorcycle-hire outlets like the reliable **Avis Rental** (☎ 22430 47145; Myrties). To get on-line, visit **Babis Bar** (☎ 22430 47864; per hr €2).

Of the three towns, Myrties is the quietest place to stay. The comfy, spacious studios of **Villa Myrtia** (☎ 22430 47046, 6937942404; www.villamyrtia .gr; d/tr €35/60; 🍴) have waves lapping at their large shaded verandas and are set amidst a gorgeous flowering garden. Next door, **Acroyali** (☎ 22430 47521; www.acroyali-Kalymnos.com; d/tr €50/55; 🍴) has large traditional, village-style studios with colourful touches and wide private balconies.

Take the first turning to the left to find the seafront **To Psirri** (☎ 6932808049; mains €4-12), a long-favoured family restaurant that serves sausages, grilled burgers, fisherman spaghetti and specialities like fresh sea urchins.

From Myrties there are regular small boats to Telendos Islet (€2).

TELENDOS ISLET ΝΗΣΟΣ ΤΕΛΕΝΔΟΣ

The tranquil, traffic-free islet of Telendos is a bit of a creative outpost and an excellent escape from the busy resort strip opposite. Once part of Kalymnos, it was separated by an earthquake in AD 554.

The islet's only settlement surrounds the colourful quay. Head right for the ruins of the early Christian **basilica** of Agios Vasilios. From here you can also follow a footpath to the **basilica** of Palaiopanayia. Further along the coast, there are several small pebble-and-sand beaches including **Paradise Beach** (sometimes popular with nudists). Heading left from the quay and turning right just before Zorba's will bring you to the larger, fine-pebbled **Hohlakas Beach**. It's windswept and wild.

Telendos is a popular climbing destination; pop into Cafe Naytikos for oodles of info. The small **Katerina** (☎ 6944919073) taxis climb-

ers from Myties to sites on Telendos (€20), departing at 7am and returning at 2pm.

Hotels, rooms and restaurants are spread alongside the quay and on the eastern side of the island. Head right from the quay for the homey **On the Rocks Rooms** (☎ 22430 48260; www .otr.telendos.com; d €45; 💻) that sleep up to four and have a balcony, fridge, mossie nets and fan. You can also hire kayaks and dine at the popular cafe which has traditional fare and a gigantic cocktail menu.

A little further along the coast is **Hotel Porto Potha** (☎ 22430 47321; portopotha@klm.forthnet .gr; d incl breakfast €45, apt €45; 🍴 💻), with comfortable rooms, gorgeous views and a very friendly owner.

To fill your belly, head for **Zorba's** (☎ 22430 48660; mains €3-8). Done up like a quirky sea shanty, you'll enjoy the decor as much as the local seafood soup, fresh salads and tasty fetastuffed squid. There are also simple rooms for rent upstairs (double €30).

ourpick Cafe Naytikos (☺ year-round) offers coffee (or something a little stronger). With hanging paper boats and other local artwork, eclectic music and very comfy seats, you could relax here all day.

For self-caterers, there's a small minimarket opposite the quay but you'd be wise to bring any essentials with you.

Caïques for Telendos depart regularly from the Myrties quay between 8am and 1am (one way €2).

EMBORIOS ΕΜΠΟΡΕΙΟΣ

The scenic west-coast road winds a further 11.5km from Masouri to tiny Emborios, where there's a shaded sand-and-pebble beach. The beachside **Artistico Café** (☎ 22430 40115; mains €4-8) offers dinner and regular live music.

ourpick Harry's Paradise (☎ 22430 40062; www .harrys-paradise.gr; mains €5-9; 🍴 💻) is found at the end of what feels like a secret garden. Incredibly lush and secluded, it's a lovely place to dine. The creative menu changes regularly; past delights have included grilled, stuffed mushrooms, filo with smoked cheese, and pork in wine and garlic. The olive oil, eggs, butter, marmalade and edible flowers are all from Emborios. The rooms here (double €45) are extremely cosy and each is individually decorated with artistic flair. All have kitchenettes and balconies overlooking the garden and (from the 1st floor) the sea beyond. Book ahead!

VATHYS & RINA ΒΑΘΥΣ & ΡΙΝΑ

Vathys, set in a long fertile valley on the east coast of Kalymnos, is one of the most beautiful and peaceful parts of the island. Vathys, meaning 'deep', refers to the slender fjord that cuts through high cliffs. Narrow roads wind between citrus orchards, bordered by high stone walls called *koumoula*.

Rina is Vathys' harbour and is a friendly little town, although there's not much to see or do. There's no beach here but if you're careful of fishing boats, you can swim off the jetty at the south side of the harbour. **Water taxis** (☎ 22430 31316, 6947082912) take tourists to quiet coves, such as nearby **Almyres** and **Drasonda** bays. There are a number of churches you can hike to from Pina, including **Hosti** with 11th-century frescoes, found on the western slope of the harbour. An annual cliff-diving competition also takes place at Vathys as part of the International Diving Festival (see p569).

The small, colourful harbour is lined with restaurants. Stop for lunch at **Harbor Taverna** (☎ 22430 31206; mains €4-9) where they've been dishing up scrumptious meals since 1916. Try the calamari with garlic, butter and wine, the fried chicken or the swordfish souvlaki.

Vathys is 13km northeast of Pothia. From here, a new road winds through the mountains from Emborios, making it a speedier way of reaching the north than via the west coast.

LEROS ΛΕΡΟΣ

pop 8210

Laid-back Leros (*leh*-ros) feels both remote and happening. With a beautiful port town, cool cafes, some great dining and lovely vistas, it's a popular spot with domestic travellers but doesn't see many foreign guests. The island is crowned with a stunning medieval castle, one of a number of worthwhile sights, and its small, sandy beaches offer good swimming. If you're after relaxation in comfort, Leros is a very good choice.

Getting There & Away

There are regular flights to Athens, Rhodes, Kos and Astypalea. **Olympic Air** (☎ 22470 22844) is in Platanos, before the turn-off for Pandeli.

Leros is on the main north-south route for ferries between Rhodes and Piraeus, with daily departures from Lakki. Buy tickets at **Blue Star Ferries** (☎ 222470 26000; Lakki) or **Leros Travel** (☎ in Lakki 22470 24000, in Agia Marina 22470 22154). In summer, hydrofoils and catamarans depart daily from Agia Marina on their trip through the Dodecanese, with tickets available on the quay. The **Anna Express** departs from Agia Marina for Kalymnos, Lipsi, Arki, Marathi and Agathonisi. A caïque also services Myrties on Kalymnos.

See Island Hopping (p755) for more transport details.

Getting Around

The **airport** (☎ 22470 22777) is near Partheni in the north. There is no airport bus and the local bus does not accommodate arriving or departing flights. A taxi from the airport to Alinda will cost €8.

The hub for Leros' buses is Platanos. There are three buses daily to Partheni via Alinda and four buses to Xirokambos via Lakki (€1 flat fare).

Car-, motorcycle- and bicycle-hire outlets are mainly on the Alinda tourist strip. **Motoland** (☎ 22470 24584) offers bikes and scooters. For a taxi, ring ☎ 22470 23340, 22470 23070 or 22470 22550.

PLATANOS & AGIA MARINA ΠΛΑΤΑΝΟΣ & ΑΓΙΑ ΜΑΡΙΝΑ

pop 3500

Platanos (*plah*-ta-nos), the capital of Leros, is a bustling village spilling over a narrow hill to the picturesque, colourful port of Agia Marina (ay-*i*-a ma-*ri*-na) to the north. With waterside cafes and good restaurants, the busy port has a strong social vibe and is a great place to unwind, surrounded by relaxed locals and bobbing fishing boats. While there's nowhere to stay right in Agia Marina, Kritonia, Alinda and Paneli offer good accommodation nearby.

Orientation & Information

The focal point of Platanos is the central square, Plateia N Roussou. From this square, Harami leads down to Agia Marina. The Platanos bus station and taxi rank are both about 50m in the other direction, along the Platanos–Lakki road. In Agia Marina, taxis wait at the quay.

The National Bank of Greece is on Platanos' central square. There are two ATMs

DODECANESE

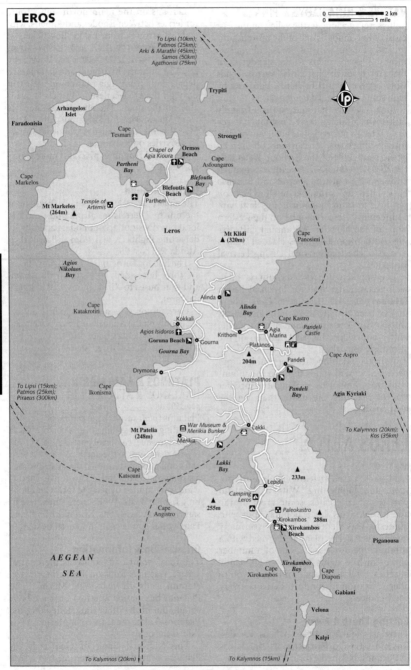

LEROS

0 — 2 km
0 — 1 mile

To Lipsi (10km);
Patmos (25km);
Arki & Marathi (45km);
Samos (50km);
Agathonisi (75km)

Trypiti

Arhangelos
Islet

Faradonisia

Cape
Tesmari

Strongyli

Chapel of
Agia Kioura

Ormos
Beach

Partheni
Bay

Blefoutis
Bay

Cape
Asfoungaros

Cape
Markelos

Blefoutis
Beach

Temple of
Artemis

Partheni

Mt Markelos
(264m)

Leros

Mt Klidi
(320m)

Cape
Panosimi

Agios
Nikolaos
Bay

Cape
Katakrotiri

Alinda

Alinda
Bay

Cape Kastro

Pandeli
Castle

Kokkali

Agios Isidoros

Krithoni

Agia
Marina

Goruna Beach

Gourna

Platanos

Cape Aspro

Gourna Bay

204m

Pandeli

Drymonas

Vromolithos

Pandeli
Bay

Agia Kyriaki

Cape
Ikonisma

To Lipsi (15km);
Patmos (25km);
Piraeus (300km)

To Kalymnos (20km);
Kos (35km)

Mt Patelia
(248m)

War Museum &
Merikia Bunker

Lakki

Merikia

Cape
Katsouni

Lakki
Bay

Lepida

233m

Camping
Leros

255m

Paleokastro

Cape
Angistro

Xirokambos

288m

Xirokambos
Beach

Piganousa

AEGEAN

SEA

Cape
Xirokambos

Xirokambos
Bay

Cape
Diapori

Gabiani

Velona

Kalpi

To Kalymnos (20km)

To Kalymnos (15km)

at Agia Marina, including a handy one at the port itself.

Enallaktiko Café (☎ 22470 25746; internet per hr €2; 🕑 10am-midnight) Opposite the quay, a very cool place to get on-line with a cocktail in hand.

Laskarina Tours (☎ 22470 24550; fax 22470 24551) In Platanos; ferry tickets and island cruises.

Police (☎ 22470 22222) In Agia Marina.

Post Office (☎ 22470 22929) West of the quay in Agia Marina.

Tourist Information Kiosk (☎ 22470 222244) On the quay in Agia Marina.

www.leros.org.uk Info on local history and facilities.

XTreme Net (☎ 22470 24041; internet per hr €3) Lots of computers in an office-like setting.

Sights

Perched high on the hill and overlooking the harbour, **Pandeli Castle** (☎ 22470 23211; admission castle €2, castle & museum €3; 🕑 8am-12.30pm & 4-8pm) is worth visiting for its breathtaking 360-degree views from the ramparts. The castle walls are largely intact and the ornate church inside has impressive, colourful frescoes and icons. Running south from the castle is a picturesque string of recently renovated **windmills**. To reach the castle, you can drive from Platanos or walk east of the main square and follow the arrows to the lengthy, scenic staircase.

The **Archaeological Museum** (☎ 22470 24775; admission free; 🕑 8am-2.30pm Tue-Sun May-Sep) is in a restored 19th-century building and has artefacts collected on and around Leros. You'll pass it on the edge of Agia Marina, en route up the hill to Platanos.

Eating

To Iponradiko (Agia Marina; mains €7-12; 🕑 year-round) Across from the harbour, on the corner of Harami, this popular restaurant has a touch of elegance with a high ceiling, white furnishings and fancy chandeliers. Fill up on smoked mackerel, grilled salmon or shellfish – it's all fresh.

Taverna Mylos (☎ 22470 24894; Agia Marina; mains €6-15; 🕑 year-round) With a home-grown, artsy feel to it, this restaurant is built right over the sea with the watermill just beyond. The creative take on local dishes makes for some tempting dining. Try pasta with smoked salmon, cream and broccoli, calamari with pesto, or chicken with mushroom sauce.

ourpick To Paradosiakon (☎ 22470 25500; sweets €0.50-3) Housed in the big yellow building on the harbour, this family bakery sells

outrageously good desserts, using local ingredients like honey and walnuts. Try the almond bites.

For self-caterers, there is a small supermarket in Agia Marina as well as a fresh fish market near the harbour. Head up to Platanos for fresh fruit and veg sold in the main square.

Drinking

The cafes along the quay are very comfortable places to await the ferry or just to sit and relax next to the water. Enallaktiko Cafe (left) is a hip place for a drink and a game of pool, while **Meltemi Bar** (Agios Marina; 🕑 6pm-late) is a tiny, popular bar with a nautical theme. You may even feel it sway after a few drinks.

PANDELI ΠΑΝΤΕΛΙ

Head south from Platanos and you'll quickly reach Pandeli, a little fishing village with a sand and shingle beach. The main draw is for a pillow under your head and a full belly.

On the east side of the bay, the blue-and-white **Rooms to Rent Kavos** (☎ 22470 25020, 6972154102; d €35) has large unfussy rooms with balconies, fan and fridge. Grab a front room for a harbour view.

Pension Happiness (☎ 22470 23498; www.studios -happiness-leros.com; d/studio/apt €45/55/70; 🕄) has two brand-new apartments that sleep three. More like large studios, they are spacious and very comfortable with full kitchens and verandas overlooking the sea and castle. Rooms and studios here are older but well-maintained.

Taverna Psaropoula (☎ 22470 25200; mains €5-8) is one of many restaurants right on the beach. Its popular menu includes fresh crayfish, big bowls of shellfish and prawn souvlaki.

VROMOLITHOS ΒΡΩΜΟΛΙΘΟΣ

Continue around the headland and you'll stumble upon Vromolithos, with a narrow shingly beach and some shade.

Up on the hill is the always popular **Pension Rodon** (☎ 22470 22075; d €30; 🕑 year-round), a reliable and welcoming choice with comfortable rooms and big sea views. Next door, **Bald Dimitris** (☎ 22470 25626; mezedhes €3-7) offers innovative dishes under a canopy of trees. The hallmark chicken in retsina or pork in wine sauce both satisfy solidly.

ourpick Cafe Del Mar (☎ 22470 24766; www.leros cafedelmar.com; snacks €3-8) sits in a hidden corner of the bay, at the eastern end of the beach. The stylish, glassed-in dining room affords

DODECANESE

phenomenal views. This ranks as Leros' coolest place to chill, with big comfy deck chairs and an amazing bar. In the day, grab a smoked trout sandwich or pancakes and stay till evening when the DJs spin.

LAKKI ΛΑΚΚΙ
pop 2370

Arriving at Lakki (lah-*kee*) by boat is akin to stepping into a long-abandoned Federico Fellini film set. Grandiose buildings and wide tree-lined boulevards attest to its creation during the Italian occupation. Few linger in Lakki, though chances are you'll end up passing through. The port has internet access at the quayside **Kinezos Café** (☎ 22470 2259; per hr €3) and there's a number of ATMs throughout the town. The island's largest grocery store is on the road to Platanos.

Even if you're not a history buff, it's worth detouring to the engrossing **War Museum** (☎ 22470 25520; admission €3; ⏰ 9.30am-1.30pm), a short drive west towards Merikia. Who knew that such a decisive WWII battle took place on this wee island? While the Germans captured Leros from the Italians and British in 1943, locals hid in these bunkers which are now home to countless war-time objects.

If you have an early morning ferry from Lakki, consider staying at **Hotel Miramare** (☎ 22470 22052; georvirv@otenet.gr; d €45; ❄). An old-fashioned family place, the hotel has clean, comfortable rooms with some sea views. You'll find the place one block back from the waterfront.

Plenty of restaurants line the harbour but if you're after something fresh and affordable, grab a bite with the locals at **To Polntimo** (☎ 22470 23323; sandwiches €2-4). Choose your sandwich fillings from the well-stocked deli, have it toasted and wash it down with fruit smoothies and coffee.

XIROKAMBOS ΞΗΡΟΚΑΜΠΟΣ

Southern Xirokambos Bay has a somewhat isolated feel to it. It's a resort in as much as it has a handful of hotels and a restaurant alongside a few village homes. The beach is pebble and sand with some good spots for snorkelling. En route to Xirokambos a signposted path leads up to the ruined fortress of **Paleokastro** for pretty views.

Xirokambos is home to Leros' only camping ground, **Camping Leros** (☎ 22470 23372, 944238490; camp sites adult/tent €6.50/4; ⏰ Jun-Sep). Shaded sites

are in an olive grove, 500m from the beach with a restaurant and basic facilities. Look for it on the right, 3km from Lakki. It's also home to **Panos Diving Club** (☎ 22470 23372; divingleros@hotmail.com; 🖳), offering a series of wreck dives and training courses.

Just up from the beach, **Villa Alexandros** (☎ 22470 22202, 6972914552; d €55; ❄) has comfortable, self-contained studios with kitchenettes, overlooking a flower garden. Right on the beach, **To Aloni** (☎ 22470 26048; mains €4-8) is a pleasant fish taverna that draws clientele from around the island.

KRITHONI & ALINDA
ΚΡΙΘΩΝΙ & ΑΛΙΝΤΑ

Within easy reach of Agia Marina, Krithoni and Alinda sit next to each other on Alinda Bay and attract the lion's share of visitors in summer. That said, they remain small and very relaxed. Most of the action is at Alinda while, just down the road, Krithoni offers a quieter area to stay.

Leros' best beach is at Alinda – although narrow, it's long, shaded and sandy with clean, shallow water and, in summer, the occasional lifeguard on duty. **Alinta Seasport** (☎ 22470 24584) hires out row boats, canoes and motor boats. On the bay, the **Historic & Folklore Museum** (admission €3; ⏰ 9am-12.30pm & 6.30-9pm Tue-Sun) is in what was once a stately home. Displays take you through the social history of Leros.

On Krithoni's waterfront there is a poignant **war cemetery**. After the Italians surrendered in WWII, Leros saw fierce fighting between German and British forces; the cemetery contains the graves of 179 British, two Canadian and two South African soldiers. You'll find various articles kept in the register box beside the gate.

Hotel Alinda (☎ 22470 23266; fax 22470 23383; Alinda; s/d €30/40; ❄) is right on the beachfront with a shaded bar out front and a pleasant taverna. It has a bit of that holiday-camp feel but has great value, comfortable rooms with lovely views.

With the reception in a neoclassical mansion next to the road, **Boulafendis Bungalows** (☎ 22470 23290; www.boulafendis.gr; Alinda; studio/apt €68/100; ❄ 🖳 🛒) offer standard rooms around a gorgeous, palm-fringed pool and garden.

ourpick **Nefeli Hotel** (☎ 22470 24611; www.nefeli hotels.com; studio €80, apt €100-130; 🅿 ❄) has spacious, comfy rooms. Village-style architecture with kitchens and peaceful balconies is made all the more homier with elegant bohemian touches like local art and textiles. Top-floor rooms have sea views.

Set amid a lush garden of flowers, shrubs and shady trees and backed by a small vineyard, the old-style mansion **To Arhontiko tou Angelou** (☎ 22470 22749; www.hotel-angelou-leros.com; Alinda; s/d incl breakfast €90/155; ❄) has beautiful rooms with antique furnishings, wrought-iron bed and wooden floors.

Alinda is lined with lots of stylish cafes and restaurants. Where the bay bends east, **Osteria Del Buon Mangiare** (Alinda; mains €5-10) is a cheerful restaurant serving authentic Italian meals. A few doors south, **Ionos** (☎ 6977781874; mains €6-12) has a homey, old-fashioned feel with an open fire, traditional tiled floors and lots of photos on the walls. Play chess while you wait for your rabbit with fresh tomato sauce, skewered swordfish, or pork with mango sauce.

Alinda has a number of bars lining the waterfront. Head toward Krithoni for **Nemesis** (☎ 22470 22070), a lounge-style bar with sangria, cocktails and coffee and plenty of comfy sofas.

NORTHERN LEROS

The north of the island is quiet and dotted with small fishing communities, beehives and rugged, windswept terrain. Just west of the airport, the **Temple of Artemis** is from the 4th century BC but is yet to be excavated. On the site are the remains of a newer church where the altar is still used to make offerings.

East of here, **Blefoutis Beach** is a narrow stretch of sand and pebble on an enclosed bay. The setting is pretty and it's very quiet, with a seasonal taverna as the only facility.

PATMOS ΠΑΤΜΟΣ

pop 3040

Shrouded in spiritual mystery, Patmos has an atmosphere unlike any of the other Dodecanese. It's as if the island itself knows it's special. Even the light here is unusual, bathing the landscape in warm hues, and the islanders are a mix of proud locals and long-term expats drawn by the lure of harmony. It was here that St John the Divine ensconced himself in a cave and wrote the Apocalypse (see the boxed text, p577). Since then, it has become a place of pilgrimage for both Orthodox and Western Christians and is, without doubt, the best place to experience Orthodox Easter. Beyond the tolling bells of the chapels, it's easy to locate dazzling beaches, great nosh and relaxing places to lay your head. The hard part is leaving.

History

In AD 95 St John the Divine was banished to Patmos from Ephesus by the pagan Roman Emperor Domitian. While residing in a cave on the island, St John wrote the Book of Revelations. In 1088 the Blessed Christodoulos, an abbot who came from Asia Minor to Patmos, obtained permission from the Byzantine Emperor Alexis I Komninos to build a monastery to commemorate St John. Pirate raids necessitated powerful fortifications, so the monastery looks like a mighty castle.

Under the Duke of Naxos, Patmos became a semi-autonomous monastic state, and achieved such wealth and influence that it was able to resist Turkish oppression. In the early 18th century a school of theology and philosophy was founded by Makarios and it flourished until the 19th century.

Gradually the island's wealth became polarised into secular and monastic entities. The secular wealth was acquired through shipbuilding, an industry that diminished with the arrival of the steamship.

Getting There & Away

Patmos is connected with Piraeus, Rhodes and a number of islands in between through mainline services with Blue Star Ferries and G&A Ferries. The F/B *Nissos Kalymnos* and *Anna Express* provide additional links to neighbouring islands. The local **Patmos Star** (☎ 6977601633) serves Lipsi and Leros while the **Delfini** (☎ 22470 31995) and *Lambi II* go to Marathi and Arki. Hydrofoils and catamarans also link Patmos with Samos and the rest of the Dodecanese. Boat tickets are sold by Apollon Travel (p577) in Skala. See Island Hopping (p757) for more details.

Getting Around

BOAT

Excursion boats go to Psili Ammos Beach from Skala, departing around 10am and returning about 4pm.

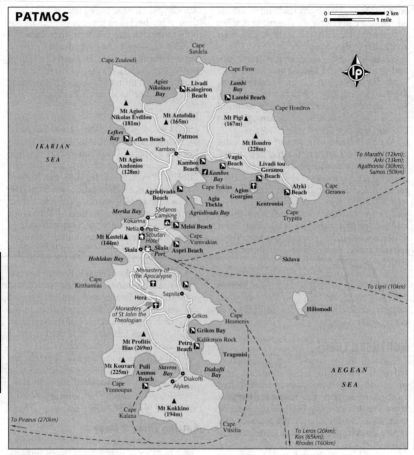

PATMOS

0 — 2 km
0 — 1 mile

Cape Sardela

Cape Zouloufi

Cape Firos

Agios Nikolaos Bay

Livadi Kalogiron Beach

Lambi Bay

Lambi Beach

Cape Hondros

Mt Agios Nikolas Evdilou (181m)

Mt Aetofolia (165m)

Mt Pigi (167m)

Lefkes Bay

Lefkes Beach

Patmos

Mt Hondro (228m)

IKARIAN SEA

Kambos

Mt Agios Andonios (128m)

Kambos Beach

Kambos Bay

Vagia Beach

Livadi tou Geranou Beach

To Marathi (12km); Arki (13km); Agathonisi (30km); Samos (50km)

Agriolivado Beach

Cape Fokias

Agios Georgios

Alyki Beach

Cape Geranos

Agia Thekla

Kentronisi

Merika Bay

Stefanos Camping

Agriolivado Bay

Cape Trypitis

Kokarina

Netia

Porto

Meloï Beach

Mt Kasteli (144m)

Scoutari Hotel

Cape Vamvakias

Sklava

Skala

Skala Port

Aspri Beach

Hohlakas Bay

To Lipsi (10km)

Monastery of the Apocalypse

Cape Krithamias

Sapsila

Hiliomodi

Hora

Monastery of St John the Theologian

Grikos

Cape Hesmenis

Grikos Bay

Mt Profitis Ilias (269m)

Petra Beach

Kalikatsos Rock

Tragonisi

AEGEAN SEA

Mt Kouvari (225m)

Psili Ammos Beach

Stavros Bay

Diakofti Bay

Diakofti

Cape Yennoupas

Alykes

To Piraeus (270km)

Cape Kalana

Mt Kokkino (194m)

Cape Vitsilia

To Leros (20km); Kos (65km); Rhodes (160km)

BUS

From Skala, there are six return buses daily to Hora and four to Grikos and Kambos. Fares are a standard €1.

CAR & MOTORCYCLE

There are several car- and motorcycle-hire outlets in Skala. Competition is fierce, so shop around. Some have headquarters in the pedestrian street behind Skala's main harbour, including **Moto Rent Express** (☎ 22470 32088), **Avis** (☎ 22470 33025) and **Theo & Girogio** (☎ 22470 32066).

TAXI

You can catch a **taxi** (☎ 22470 31225) from Skala's taxi rank opposite the police station.

SKALA ΣΚΑΛΑ

You may find Patmos' port town of Skala (*ska*-la), draped around a curving bay, slightly more glitzy than expected. Large cruise ships are often anchored offshore, while yachts anchor at the new marina. Skala certainly sees its fair share of tourists, resulting in lots of excellent accommodation and restaurants. Despite its bustle, the people here seem to be in perpetual holiday mode and relaxing is easy.

Orientation & Information

All transport arrives at the centre of the long quay, smack bang in the middle of Skala. To the right the road leads to a narrow, sandy beach, the yacht port and on to the north of

ST JOHN THE DIVINE & THE APOCALYPSE

The island of Patmos is home to the Cave of the Apocalypse where St John the Divine was allegedly visited by God and instructed to write the tell-all Book of Revelations, also known as the Book of the Apocalypse. He is often believed to be John the Apostle of Jesus or John the Evangelist, though many would dispute this due to his exile in AD 95 to Patmos by the pagan Roman Emperor Domitian. (John the Apostle would have been very, very old by then.) In the Book of Revelations, John wrote about two apocalyptic visions he had received.

The first (1:11-3:22) describes 'one like unto the Son of man, clothed with a garment down to the foot, and girt about the paps with a golden girdle', speaking with 'a great voice, as of a trumpet'. The second vision comprises the remainder of the book (4-22) and begins with 'a door...opened in the sky'. It goes on to describe the end of the world – involving the final rebellion by Satan at Armageddon, God's final defeat of Satan, and the restoration of peace to the world.

'Revelation' is considered to be open to interpretation at best and is not afforded the serious scholarly study that it would seem to merit – perhaps because of the obscure and essentially hard-to-interpret symbolism of the work. Some critics have even suggested that it was the work of a deranged man. Whatever you choose to believe, it's worth visiting the cave where it all supposedly took place. Who knows – you may even have a bit of a revelation yourself.

the island. To the left the road leads to the south side of the island. From a roundabout near the ferry terminal, a road heads inland and up to Hora. The bus terminal and taxi rank are at the quay and all main services are within 100m.

There are three ATM-equipped banks in Skala: the National Bank of Greece, the Emporiki Bank and the Commercial Bank.

AB Food Market (☎ 22470 34023) A well-stocked grocery store 100m along the Hora road in Skala.

Apollon Travel (☎ 22470 31324; apollontravel@ stratas.gr) Ticketing for flights and ferries.

Apyos News Agent (☎ 22470 32431) Selling international papers, paperbacks, maps and traditional Greek music.

Dodoni Gelateria (☎ 22470 32202; internet per hr €4; ☉ 9am-9pm) Get online while scoffing ice cream.

Hospital (☎ 22470 31211) Two kilometres along the road to Hora.

Just like Home Laundry (☎ 22470 33170; wash & dry per load €10) Behind the new marina. A high cost for cleanliness.

Meltemi (☎ 22470 31839; internet per hr €4) Speedy computers next to the beach.

Municipal Tourist Office (☎ 22470 31666; ☉ summer) Shares the same building as the post office and police station.

Oxerolas Bookshop (☎ 22470 32251) Secondhand books in English, French, Dutch and German.

Police (☎ 22470 31303) On the main waterfront.

Port police (☎ 22470 31231) Behind the quay's passenger-transit building.

www.patmos-island.com Lots of local listings and info.

www.patmosweb.gr A slightly flashier site with history, listings and photos.

Sights & Activities

Skala has a couple of religious sites, including the place where St John first baptised the locals in 96 AD, just north of the beach. To find out more and to see religious objects from across the island, visit the **Orthodox Culture & Information Centre** (☎ 22470 33316; ☉ 9am-1pm Thu-Tue & 6-9pm Mon, Tue, Thu & Fri) in the harbour-side church.

If you feel like a workout, climb up to the remains of an ancient **acropolis** on the hillside to the west of town. The route is not well signposted; head for the prominent chapel then follow the dirt trail across the fields full of wildflowers and lizards. The views from the top are stunning.

Sleeping

At the port you'll find a small **info bureau** (☎ 22470 32899) with details on private rooms, studios and apartments for rent. Hotel and studio owners often meet boats at the port, but it's best to call ahead and arrange a pick-up.

Pension Maria Pascalidis (☎ 22470 32152; s/d €25/35) This longstanding traveller-friendly budget option is on the road leading to Hora. Simple but presentable rooms are part of a family home and set amid a fragrant citrus-tree garden.

Casteli Hotel (☎ 22470 31361; fax 22470 51656; s/d incl breakfast €50/70; P ⊗ ⊠) With '70s retro telephones and funky tiles in the bathroom, this place is dated but well loved. Rooms aren't huge but have great views of the harbour and Hora and there's a rooftop pool.

Hotel Chris (☎ 22470 31001; www.patmoschrishotel.gr; d back/sea view €50/80; ❄) This hotel's age shows in the slightly down-at-heel lobby and halls but the renovated rooms have tiled floors and lovely wooden furniture. Some have four-poster double beds and sea-view rooms have balconies. A little pricy but well situated next to the beach with a popular cafe out front.

Captain's House (☎ 22470 31793; www.captains-house.gr; s/d incl breakfast €55/75; ❄ ☎) This welcoming hotel next to the port has small but comfortable rooms with fridges and a lovely pool to cool off in. The front rooms have sea views, but can get street noise.

Studios Siroco (☎ 22470 33262; fax 22470 34090; d €80; ❄) Next to the beach on Hohlakas Bay, these big, new studios are very comfortable with separate kitchens, brick and tiled floors and spacious verandas. You'll fall asleep to the pounding surf.

Kalderimi Apartments (☎ 22470 33008; www .kalderimi.com; apt incl breakfast from €110; ❄) At the foot of the path up to the monastery and secluded by trees, these gorgeous apartments have traditional design with wooden beams and stone walls, along with lots of swish extras. A full kitchen, shaded balcony and lots of privacy make them a perfect retreat for longer-term stays.

Blue Bay Hotel (☎ 22470 31165; www.bluebay.50g .com; s/d/tr incl breakfast €78/116/144; ❄ ▢ ☎) Just south of town, this hotel has an airy veranda and breakfast room. Rooms don't have much character but are spacious, well maintained and have lovely sea views from the balconies.

Eating

Meltemi (☎ 22470 31839; full breakfast €5; ☾ 9am-late; ▢) Start your morning off right, filling up on a home-cooked breakfasts at tables on the sand. Later in the day, come here for milk-shakes, quiche and coffee while the waves lap at your toes.

Tzivaeri (☎ 22470 31170; mains €4-7; ☾ dinner) All old-fashioned elegance with china, a record player and black-and-white photos, this beachside restaurant serves traditional dishes. The service is fast and courteous and the upstairs looks out over the harbour.

Kiliomothi (☎ 22470 34808; mains €5-9; ☾ dinner) A block up the road to Hora, this quaint res-

taurant has a less touristy feeling than many of its neighbours. Try aubergine or octopus pancakes or fresh fish with garlic sauce.

Ostria (☎ 22470 30501; mains €7-12) Easily recognisable by the boat on its roof, this place doesn't look that special but packs in seafood connoisseurs all day long. Stuffed *kalamari*, shrimp with tomato and feta, and swordfish souvlaki are just a few of the tempting dishes.

Vegghera (☎ 22470 32988; mains €17-28) High-society diners head for this swish restaurant opposite the yacht marina. The cuisine is a melange of French and Greek with dishes like mushroom risotto, spaghetti with smoked turkey or shrimp on halva. And don't miss the chocolate soufflé.

Drinking

George's Juice Place (drinks €4-5; ☾ 8am-8pm) George whips up smoothies and fresh juice from pears, pomegranates, mangoes, carrots – you name it. Have it with milk, coconut milk or yoghurt and add a dash of booze for an extra kick. Follow the road off the main square to the back of town.

Koukoumavia (☎ 22470 32325) Sip your cocktail on the mosaic bar of this very funky drinking hole. A great selection of music, friendly staff and unique artistic creations will keep you lingering. You'll find it a block north of the turn-off for Hora.

Arion (☎ 22470 31595) Right on the harbour, this popular spot has high-beamed ceilings, polished wood tables and looks more Cuban than Greek. Join a good mix of locals and tourists at any time of day, swinging your cocktail, beer or coffee to an eclectic mix of music.

Anemos (☎ 22470 33008; ☾ 9pm-late Thu-Sun) Just outside Skala on the hill heading up to Kambos, this trendy beer house and music bar in an old stone house draws crowds on the weekends.

Shopping

There's a creative streak running through Patmos, which leads to some interesting shopping. **Koukoumavla** (☎ 22470 32325; www .patmos-island.com/koukoumavia) has funky hand-made clothing and accessories; on the harbour, **Selene** (☎ 22470 31742) has work by 40 artists from around Greece. Browse through Byzantine effigies, wooden carvings, games, pottery and jewellery. Behind the main square, **Jewel Kalogero** (☎ 22470 32453) sells locally made silver jewellery with unique designs.

DODECANESE

On a more practical note, **Blue Fin** (☎ 22470 85500; New Marina) can equip you with everything you need for diving and fishing, including oxygen refilling and live bait.

HORA ΧΩΡΑ

High on the hill, huddled around the Monastery of St John, are the immaculate whitewashed houses of Hora, a legacy of the island's great wealth in the 17th and 18th centuries. A stroll through the mazelike streets evokes a timeless atmosphere.

The immense **Monastery of St John the Theologian** (☎ 22470 31398; admission free; 8am-1.30pm daily, plus 4-6pm Tue, Thu & Sun) crowns the island of Patmos. Attending a service here, with plumes of incense, religious chants and devoted worshippers, is like no other experience you'll have in Greece. Outside of services, you'll get a chance to see the intricate decor. To reach it, many people walk up the Byzantine path which starts from a signposted spot along the Skala–Hora road.

Some 200m along this path, a dirt trail to the left leads through pine trees to the **Monastery of the Apocalypse** (☎ 22470 31234; admission free, treasury €6; 8am-1.30pm daily, plus 4-6pm Tue, Thu & Sun), built around the cave where St John received his divine revelation. Inside you can see the rock that the saint used as a pillow, and the triple fissure in the roof from where the voice of God issued. The finest frescoes of this monastery are those in the outer narthex. It's also worth taking a peak at the icons and ecclesiastical ornaments found in the treasury.

A five-minute walk west of St John's Monastery, the **Holy Monastery of Zoodohos Pigi** (admission free; 8am-noon & 5-7pm Sun-Fri) is a women's convent with incredibly impressive frescoes. On Good Friday, a beautiful candle-lit ceremony takes place here.

Just east of St John's Monastery, **Andreas Kalatzis** (☎ 22470 31129) is a Byzantine icon artist who lives and works in a 1740s traditional home. Inside, you'll find an interesting mix of pottery, jewellery and paintings by local artists.

our pick **Archontariki** (☎ 22470 29368; www.arch ontariki-patmos.gr; ste €200-400) will do the trick if you're in need of a little luxury. Inside a 400-year-old building, four gorgeous suites are equipped with every convenience, traditional furnishings and plush touches. Relaxing under the fruit trees in the cool and quiet

garden, you'll wonder why the hotel isn't named Paradise.

Loza (☎ 22470 32405; starters €3-8, mains €10-19) is hard to miss as you enter Hora. With stunning views over Skala, it serves up reasonably priced salads and starters, along with some interesting mains like sweet and sour feta in filo and ouzo prawns with basmati rice. Up the stairs and left from here is the tiny **Pantheon** (☎ 22470 31226; mains €5-12) with views of the harbour. Dolmadhes, aubergine with garlic and fish are all well prepared and great value.

Dine in the square or in the secluded garden at **Vangelis Taverna** (☎ 22470 31967; mains €6-10), with its traditional food and family ambience. For a drink, head to **Stoa Cafe** (☎ 22470 32226;), a hip oasis across the square.

NORTH OF SKALA

The narrow, tree-shaded **Meloï Beach** is just 2km northeast of Skala. If you've brought your tent, head for **Stefanos Camping** (☎ 22470 31821; camp sites per person/tent €7/2; May-Oct). It's clean and well equipped with bamboo-enclosed and tree-shaded sites, a minimarket, cafe-bar and motorcycle-hire facilities. The beach itself has a taverna as well.

Just north of Skala, on the road to Kambos, is the plush **Porto Scoutari Hotel** (☎ 22470 33123; www.portoscoutari.com; d incl breakfast €80-180;). While the reception is overflowing with impressive but stuffy antiques, the rooms are tastefully decorated and the pool is divine. You pay more for a room with gob-smacking views.

Further up the road is the inland village of Kambos, from where the road descends to the relatively wide and sandy **Kambos Beach**, perhaps the most popular and easily accessible beach on the island. Situated on a fairly enclosed bay, it's great for swimming and you can hire kayaks and sun beds.

our pick **George's Place** (☎ 22470 31881; snacks €3-7) is a fantastic beachside spot for lunch with a big selection of gourmet salads and snacks. The mint iced tea is very satisfying. Kick back and play backgammon, listen to the tunes and watch the waves roll in.

The main road soon forks left to **Lambi**, 9km from Skala, where you wind down to an impressive beach of multicoloured pebbles. High above the beach on the approach road, the warm and welcoming **Leonidas** (☎ 22470 33232; mains €4.50-8) rustles up a wide range of home-cooked dishes like Greek sausage, pork

DODECANESE

souvlaki and fresh fish. The view of the green hills rolling into the sea is very peaceful. On the beach itself, the popular **Lambi Fish Tavern** (☎ 22470 31490; mains €5-14) serves stuffed vine leaves and zucchini flowers, chicken souvlaki, octopus cooked in wine and daily platters of seasonal greens. Oh, and fish too.

Under the protected lee of the north arm of the island are several more beaches, including **Vagia Beach**. Overlooking the beach is **Cafe Vagia** (☎ 22470 31658; mains €3-5; ⏰ 9am-7pm) with its amazing vegie pies, hearty omelettes and local desserts, all served in a lush garden. It's especially popular with families.

Further west is the shaded **Livadi tou Geranou Beach**, with a small church-crowned island opposite. The road here is narrow and slightly treacherous but stunning. For lunch, stop at the cute **Livadi Geranou Taverna** (☎ 22470 32046; mains €3-5) overlooking the sea from a shaded garden.

SOUTH OF SKALA

Small, tree-filled valleys and picturesque beaches fill the south of Patmos. Closest to Skala is the tiny settlement of **Sapsila**, ideal for those wanting peace and quiet. **Mathios Studios** (☎ /fax 22470 32583; www.mathiosapartments .gr; d €40-65; 🅿 💻) has studios set in a beautiful garden. Relaxed and very comfortable, they have a homey quality and are just 200m from the beach. Dine at **Benetos** (☎ 22470 33089; Sapsila; mains €7-14; ⏰ dinner Tue-Sun), just up the road. It's a working boutique farmhouse and specialises in Mediterranean fusion dishes with an occasional Japanese kick. Try zucchini blossoms stuffed with mushrooms and cheese, or the herb-crusted, pan-seared tuna. Finish up with a fresh, vodka-laced *sgroppino*, a lemon sorbet drink.

Grikos, 1km further along over the hill, is a relaxed low-key resort with a long, sandy beach and warm shallow water. The bay is lined with tavernas and popular with yachties; be aware that the southern section of the beach doubles as a road. In Grikos is the chapel of **Agios Ioannis Theologos**, built upon ancient public baths where many believe St John baptised islanders. At the southern end of the bay is **Ktima Petra** (☎ 22470 33207; mains €4-7), with organic, homegrown produce. The stuffed and wood-oven-baked goat melts in your mouth and the organic cheese and vegetables are scrumptious.

Just south, **Petra Beach** is very peaceful with sand, pebbles and lots of shade. A spit leads out to the startling **Kalikatsos Rock**. A rough coastal track leads from here to **Diakofti**, the last settlement in the south. (You can also get here by a longer sealed road from Hora.) From here you can follow a half-hour walking track to the long, sandy, tree-shaded **Psili Ammos Beach** where there's a seasonal taverna. You can also get here by excursion boat (p575).

LIPSI ΛEIΨOI

pop 700

Blink on the deck of your ferry and you might miss Lipsi (lip-*see*). Long ago discovered by Italians and latterly by French travellers, who treat it as a well-kept secret, this tiny island's drawcard is its relative anonymity, its fine beaches, its lack of demands on visitors – no clubs, pubs or sights to speak of – and a sense that you have the island to yourself, apart from two or three days in August when pilgrims and revellers descend upon Lipsi for its main religious festival. Everything moves more slowly here.

Getting There & Away

Sea connections with Lipsi are tenuous, although it is linked with Piraeus through long-haul ferries and neighbouring islands via the catamaran, a Kalymnos-based ferry, the local **Anna Express** (☎ 22479 41215) and the larger *Patmos Star*. See Island Hopping (p756) for more details.

Getting Around

Stretching only 8km end to end, Lipsi is small – really small – and you can reach most places on foot. In summer, a minibus departs Lipsi Village hourly to the beaches of Platys Gialos, Katsadia and Hohlakoura (each €1) between 10.30am and 6pm. Two **taxis** (☎ 6942409677, 6942409679) operate on the island; you'll find them roaming around Lipsi Village. You can also hire **motorcycles** (☎ 22479 41358) in Lipsi Village.

LIPSI VILLAGE

pop 600

Hugging the deep harbour, Lipsi Village is a cosy community with a small, atmospheric old town and blue-shuttered homes. This tiny town's scattering of restaurants and hotels is the hub of Lipsi's action.

Orientation & Information

All boats dock at Lipsi Port, where there are two quays. Ferries, hydrofoils and catamarans all dock at the larger, outer jetty, while excursion boats dock at a smaller jetty nearer the centre of Lipsi Village. The *Anna Express* docks close to the large main church in the inner port.

The post office is opposite the church on the upper, central square in the old town. The lower, harbour-side square is home to a **tourist office** (☉ summer only), which opens for most ferry arrivals, along with a shaded children's playground. The Co-operative Bank of the Dodecanese on the port changes money and has an ATM.

Cave (☎ 22470 44328; internet per hr €4) Internet access near the outer jetty.

Leski Internet (Old Town; per hr €4) A few computers in someone's front room, near the church.

Lipsos Travel (☎ 22470 44125) Issues tickets for the *Anna Express* and organises excursions.

Police (☎ 22470 41222) In the port.

Port police (☎ 22470 41133) In the port.

Ticket office (☎ 22470 41250; ☉ 30min prior to departures) A small office on the outer jetty issuing boat tickets.

www.lipsi-island.gr A useful resource about the island.

Activities

Liendou Beach is on the edge of the village so, naturally, is the most popular beach. With a narrow strip of sand and pebbles and shallow, calm water, it's good for swimming. It's just north of the ferry port over a small headland.

Rena and Margarita offer **boat trips** (day trip per person €20) to Lipsi's offshore islands for a sail, picnic and swim. Both excursion boats can be found at Lipsi's smaller jetty and depart at around 10am daily.

Festivals & Events

The annual religious festival of **Panagia tou Harou** takes place near the end of August when the island fills up with visitors. Following a procession, expect all-night revelry in the lower village square.

An annual **wine festival** takes place for three days during August with dancing and free wine. Check locally for the exact dates.

DODECANESE

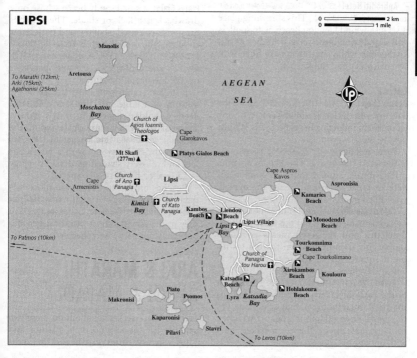

LIPSI

0 — 2 km
0 — 1 mile

Manolis

Aretousa

To Marathi (12km);
Arki (15km);
Agathonisi (25km);

*A E G E A N
S E A*

Moschatou
Bay

Church of
Agios Ioannis
Theologos

Cape
Glarokavos

Mt Skafi
(277m) ▲

Platys Gialos Beach

Cape Aspros
Kavos

Aspronisia

Cape
Armenistis

Church
of Ano
Panagia

Lipsi

Kamaries
Beach

Kimisi
Bay

Church
of Kato
Panagia

Kambos
Beach

Liendou
Beach

Monodendri
Beach

Lipsi
Bay

Lipsi Village

To Patmos (10km)

Tourkomnima
Beach

Cape Tourkolimano

Church of
Panagia
tou Harou

Xirokambos
Beach

Kouloura

Katsadia
Beach

Piato

Lyra

Katsadia
Bay

Hohlakoura
Beach

Makronisi

Psomos

Kaparonisi

Pilavi

Stavri

To Leros (10km)

To Leros (10km)

DODECANESE

Sleeping

Panorama Studios (☎ 22470 41235; studios/apt from €50/80; ✖) The studios here are clean with great sea vistas, while the apartments have balconies on which you could happily spend your whole holiday.

Apartments Galini (☎ 22470 41212, 6932037511; matsouri@yahoo.gr; d €55) Right on the harbour, these simple, immaculate rooms have kitchenettes, proper double beds and small balconies with great views.

Apartments Poseidon (☎ 22470 41130; www.lipsi-poseidon.gr; d incl breakfast €65; ✖) Spacious new apartments sleeping up to four, with lovely trimmings like local pottery. Each has a full kitchen and a big balcony with an uninterrupted sea view. It's between the two quays.

Rizos Studios (☎ 6976244125; fax 22470 44225; www.annaexpress-lipsi.services.officelive.com/rizos.aspx; d €65) Like cosy cottages, these studios have lots of personal touches such as local art, fabric and plenty of cushions. Kitchens are amazingly well stocked, stone-paved floors stay cool and the spacious balconies have a view over Liendou Bay. Phone ahead for a lift from the port.

Aphroditi Hotel (☎ 22470 41000; www.hotel-aphroditi.com; s/d/apt €50/70/125; ✖) This sprawling place is set just behind Liendou Beach, with spotless and slightly grandiose rooms. Studios have a kitchenette while apartments are huge with two balconies and full kitchen.

Eating

Bakery Shop (☎ 22470 41150; sweets €1-3) Sit on the balcony with the locals, sipping coffee, licking ice cream or indulging in baked goods. It's just next to the playground.

Porto Grill House (☎ 22470 41130; mezedhes €2-6) Between the quays. The kebabs in pita, grilled meats, stuffed tomatoes and salads here are great value. Enjoy from the shaded, view-filled patio.

Cafe de Moulin (mains €3-6) It doesn't have the most inspiring menu, but the fresh yoghurt, omelettes and skewered meats go down well at this friendly place in the old town's main square. Exchange books and meet fellow travellers.

Pefko (☎ 22470 41404; mains €4.50-8) The newest of the harbour tavernas, Pefko has perhaps the most imaginative menu selection. Try the *ambelourgou* (lamb in yoghurt wrapped in vine leaves), or the oven-baked beef with aubergine.

Manolis Tastes (☎ 22470 41065; mains €4-10) With mouth-watering dishes like seafood risotto, lamb in lemon sauce and traditional Lipsi pork chops, you'd do well to nab one of the handful of outdoor tables at this tiny restaurant. Find it in a small square in the Old Town and consider the takeaway window for your picnic lunch.

Tholari (☎ 22470 41060; mains €6-12) With stone walls and traditional sofas, this lovely harbourside restaurant does homestyle meals like sharkfish with garlic dip, beef casserole and baked chicken.

AROUND THE ISLAND

Lipsi has quite a few beaches, most of which are small and without any facilities. Getting to them makes for pleasant walks through countryside dotted with olive groves, cypress trees and endless views. The minibus services the main beaches.

Just 1km beyond Lipsi Village, **Kambos Beach** offers some shade and is narrower but sandier than its neighbour Liendou. The water is also deeper and rockier underfoot.

From here, a further 2.5km brings you to **Platys Gialos**, a small sandy beach whose only drawback is a lack of shade. The water is turquoise-coloured, shallow and perfect for children. Above the beach is **Kostas Restaurant** (☎ 6944963303; grills €4.50-6.50; ⏰ 8am-6pm Jul-Aug), for fish and grill dishes. It stays open later on Wednesday and Saturday.

Just 2km south from Lipsi Village at the bottom of a large hill, the sandy **Katsadia Beach** is wilder, especially if it's windy. Tamarisk trees offer some shade and on the beach is the **Dilaila Cafe Restaurant** (☎ 22470 41041; mains €5-8; ⏰ Jun-Sep), with a beach-bar feel and a lovely shaded garden. Try spicy 'mad feta' or the fried-rice specials.

Beaches on the east coast are more difficult to reach. Due to rough roads, neither taxis nor buses come here. Some locals claim they're the island's most beautiful beaches but many are rocky and shadeless.

ARKI & MARATHI
ΑΡΚΟΙ & ΜΑΡΑΘΟΙ

Serious solace seekers chill out on these two satellite islands just north of Patmos and Lipsi where yachties, artists and the occasional backpacker mingle. There are neither cars nor motorbikes – just calmness. Pack your bathers, books and iPod and leave the rest behind.

Getting There & Away

In summer there are frequent excursion boats and caïques from Lipsi and Patmos. A boat also stops regularly en route between Patmos and Samos. For more details see Island Hopping (p746).

ARKI ΑΡΚΟΙ

pop 50

Only 5km north of Lipsi, tiny Arki has rolling hills and secluded, sandy beaches. Its only settlement is the little west-coast port, also called Arki. Away from the village, the island seems almost mystical in its peace and stillness. The island sustains itself with fishing and tourism.

There is no post office or police on the island, but there is one cardphone. The **Church of Metamorfosis** stands on a hill behind the settlement with superb sea views. To visit, ask a local for the key and follow the cement road between Taverna Trypas and Taverna Nikolaos to the footpath. Several **sandy coves** can be reached along a path skirting the north side of the bay.

Tiganakia Bay, on the southeast coast, has a good sandy beach. To walk there from Arki village, follow the road heading south and then the network of goat tracks down to the water. You'll recognise it by the incredibly bright turquoise water and offshore islets.

Arki has a few tavernas with comfortable, well-maintained rooms; bookings are necessary in July and August. To the right of the quay, **O Trypas Taverna & Rooms** (☎ 22470 32230; tripas@12net.gr; d €35, mains €5-7) has simple rooms and serves excellent *fasolia mavromatika* (black-eyed beans) and *pastos tou Trypa* (salted fish). Nearby, **Taverna Nikolaos Rooms** (☎ 22470 32477; d €35, mains €5-8) dishes up potatoes au gratin, stuffed peppers with cheese, or the local goat cheese called *sfina,* which is like a mild form of feta. Rooms have sunset views.

MARATHI ΜΑΡΑΘΙ

Marathi is the largest of Arki's satellite islets, with a superb sandy beach. Before WWII it had a dozen or so inhabitants, but now has only two families. The old settlement, with

an immaculate little church, stands on a hill above the harbour. There are two tavernas on the island, both of which rent rooms. **Taverna Mihalis** (☎ 22470 31580; d €30, mains €4-6) is the more laid-back and cheaper of the two, while **Taverna Pandelis** (☎ 22470 32609; d €40, mains €4-6) at the top end of the beach is a tad plusher.

AGATHONISI
ΑΓΑΘΟΝΗΣΙ

pop 160

Agathonisi (agh-atho-*ni*-see) shows up on few travellers' radar and remains a quiet little getaway isle. Like its neighbours, it's rocky and dry, has few settlements and little organised entertainment. Accommodation is fine yet simple, food is unfussy but good quality, and there's little to do other than reflect, read and get ready for the next swim.

Getting There & Away

Agathonisi has regular ferry links with Samos and Patmos. A hydrofoil also links the island with Samos and destinations further south. Ferry agent **Savvas Kamitsis** (☎ 22470 29003) sells tickets at the harbour prior to departures. For more information see Island Hopping (p745).

Getting Around

There is no local transport, and it's a steep and sweaty 1.5km uphill walk from Agios Georgios to the main settlement of Megalo

DODECANESE

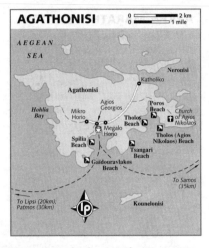

Horio; somewhat less to Mikro Horio. From Megalo Horio, the island's eastern beaches are all within a 3km walk.

AGIOS GEORGIOS ΑΓΙΟΣ ΓΕΩΡΓΙΟΣ

The village of Agios Georgios (*agh-*ios ye-*or-*yi-os) is a languid settlement at the end of a protected fjord-like bay, with a curved, pebble beach. **Spilia Beach**, 900m southwest around the headland, is quieter and better for swimming; a track around the far side of the bay will take you there. A further 1km walk will bring you to **Gaïdouravlakos**, a small bay and beach where water from one of the island's few springs meets the sea.

Orientation & Information

Boats dock at Agios Georgios, from where roads ascend right to Megalo Horio and left to Mikro Horio. There is no tourist information, post office, bank or ATM.

The police are in a prominently marked white building at the beginning of the Megalo Horio road.

Sleeping & Eating

In the middle of the waterfront, **Pension Maria Kamitsi** (☎ 22470 29003; fax 22470 29101; d €35) has comfortable rooms that are easy to find. Above and behind Glaros Restaurant, **Domatia Giannis** (☎ 22470 29062; d/tr €40/50; ✹ ▣) has airy, modern rooms with harbour views.

There's a handful of harbour-side eateries. **Glaros Restaurant** (☎ 22470 29062; mains €4.50-7) serves *markakia* (feta in vine leaves), grills and fish dishes, all made from predominantly organic produce.

AROUND AGATHONISI

Megalo Horio is the only village of any size on the island. Sleepy and unhurried for most of the year, it comes to life with the annual religious festivals of **Agiou Panteleimonos** (26 July), **Sotiros** (6 August) and **Panagias** (22 August), when the village celebrates with abundant food, music and dancing.

To the east of Megalo Horio there's a series of accessible beaches: **Tsangari Beach, Tholos Beach, Poros Beach** and **Tholos (Agios Nikolaos) Beach**, close to the eponymous church. All are within easy walking distance although Poros Beach is the only sandy option.

If you're after a very quiet stay, **Studios Ageliki** (☎ 22470 29085; s/d €30/35) in Megalo Horio has four basic but comfortable studios with kitchenettes and stunning views over a small vineyard and down to the port. Eating in the village is limited to the reliable **Restaurant I Irini** (☎ 22470 29054; mains €5-6) on the central square, or the **Kafeneio Ta 13 Adelfia** (mains €3-4) on the square's south side, serving budget snacks and meals.

Northeastern Aegean Islands Τα Νησιά του Βορειοανατολικού Αιγαίου

These richly varied islands offer some of Greece's most unique and intriguing sights. Less visited than other island groups, their singular identities cultivate a strong and memorable sense of place. And, since they're somewhat off the beaten track, intrepid travellers can escape the crowds here, while experiencing old-fashioned island cuisine, culture and celebrations.

Eccentric Ikaria, marked by dramatic and diverse landscapes, pristine beaches and a laid-back, leftist population, is one of Greece's most remarkable islands, as is Chios, an ecotourism paradise full of flowers and fruit trees and the only place on the planet where gum is produced from mastic trees. The islands range from sprawling Lesvos, Greece's third-largest island and producer of half the world's ouzo, to midsize islands like sultry Samos and breezy Limnos, to specks in the sea like Inousses and Psara – islands which, however tiny, loom large in the illustrious histories of Greek maritime commerce and naval greatness. Other small islands stand out too, like Samothraki, with its ancient Thracian Sanctuary of the Great Gods and lush mountain waterfalls, and the serene archipelago of Fourni, renowned for its fresh seafood.

This group is less compact than other Greek island chains. Thasos and Samothraki are only accessible from Northern Greece ports, while Ikaria is just a skip across the water from Mykonos. The southernmost islands also neighbour on the Dodecanese, while Lesvos, Chios and Samos offer easy connections to Turkey's coastal resorts and historical sites.

HIGHLIGHTS

- **Dive In** Swimming in the clear waters of Ikaria's remote, white-pebble Seychelles Beach (p592)

- **Get Spiritual** Gazing out over Lesvos from the elevated Byzantine monastery of Moni Ypsilou (p624), home of priceless medieval manuscripts and ecclesiastical treasures

- **Lose Yourself** Wandering the winding stone alleyways of Mesta (p610) in southern Chios

- **Total Immersion** Wading through the river to wooded waterfalls in northwest Samos, followed by swimming and a drink on chilled-out Potami Beach (p603)

- **Sunset Solitude** Watching from high above as the gentle folds of the Fourni archipelago fade into dusk (p594)

- **Hot Pursuit** Careening through old-growth forests in lush Thasos' annual international mountain bike race (p640)

- **Seafood Symphony** Watching the fishermen untangle their colourful nets, and then dining on the day's catch in the seafood tavernas of Myrina (p630) in Limnos

★ Thasos

Myrina

Moni Ypsilou ★

Mesta ★

★ Potami Beach

Seychelles Beach ★

Fourni ★ Archipelago

NORTHEASTERN AEGEAN ISLANDS

- POPULATION: 204,160

- AREA: 3842 SQ KM

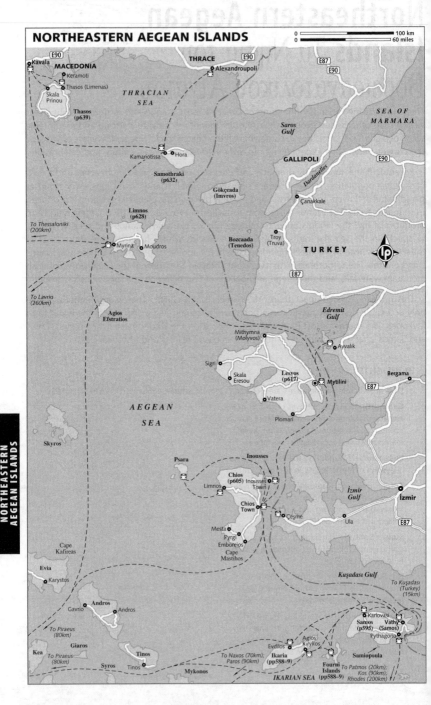

NORTHEASTERN AEGEAN ISLANDS

NORTHEASTERN AEGEAN ISLANDS

IKARIA & THE FOURNI ISLANDS ΙΚΑΡΙΑ & ΟΙ ΦΟΥΡΝΟΙ

area 255 sq km

Ikaria and the Fourni archipelago are arguably the most magical of the northeastern Aegean Islands. Ikaria's dramatic and varied terrain comprises deep, forested gorges, rocky moonscapes and hidden beaches where aquamarine waters gently lap, while the bare, sloping hills of Fourni's little islets overlap across the horizon, running elliptically into a lobster-rich sea.

These islands have eclectic, even mythical histories. As a former hideout for nefarious pirates and other scallywags, Fourni proved a constant vexation for Byzantine and subsequently Ottoman rulers. More recently, Ikaria (ih-kah-*ree*-ah) became a dumping ground for Communist sympathisers during Greece's 1946–49 Civil War – the KKE (Greek Communist Party) remains popular on the island today. Intriguingly, Ikaria is named for Icarus, son of Daedalus, the legendary architect of King Minos' Cretan labyrinth. When the two tried to escape from Minos' prison on wings of wax, Icarus ignored his father's warning, flew too close to the sun and crashed into the sea, creating Ikaria – a rocky reminder of the dangers of overweening ambition.

Greek myth also honours Ikaria as the birthplace of Dionysos, god of wine; indeed, Homer attested that the Ikarians were the world's first wine-makers. Today travellers can enjoy the signature local red here, along with fresh and authentic local dishes in a serene environment far from the crowds; the same is doubly true for Fourni, renowned for its seafood and dotted by isolated sandy coves.

Along with the total tranquillity these islands provide, plenty of activities will keep you busy. Hiking, swimming and cycling are all excellent, while Ikaria's light-hearted summertime *panigyria* (festivals; annual celebrations of saints' days) are truly festive events, involving much food, drink, traditional dance and song – a fun-loving commingling of Orthodox Christianity and Ikaria's deeper Dionysian roots.

Being somewhat small and remote, Ikaria and the Fourni islands are fairly sleepy out of high season, with most, if not all, accommodation options likely to be closed.

Getting There & Away

AIR

For flight schedules from Ikaria, see Island Hopping (p751). **Olympic Air** (☎ 22750 22214; www.olympicairlines.com) in Agios Kirykos, and **Nas Travel** (☎ 22750 31947) in Evdilos sell tickets. There's now an airport bus, serving only Agios Kirykos and Faros. Otherwise, use airport taxis (to/from Agios Kirykos, €10).

BOAT

A caïque leaves Agios Kirykos at 1pm on Monday, Wednesday and Friday for Fourni (€4), stopping at Fourni Korseon, the capital, plus Hrysomilia or Thymena. Day-trip excursion boats to Fourni also go from Agios Kirykos and Evdilos (€20).

For ferry and hydrofoil information from Ikaria, see Island Hopping (p751). Get tickets in Agios Kirykos at **Icariada Holidays** (☎ 22750 23322; depy@ikariada.gr), **G&A Ferries** (☎ 22750 22426), or **Dolihi Tours Travel Agency** (☎ 22750 23230).

Getting Around

BOAT

Water taxis are helpful for nondrivers, or anyone desiring a good boat ride. Summer daily water taxis go from Agios Kirykos to Therma (€2 return). Heading the other way, there's a summertime caïque every Monday, Wednesday and Friday from Agios Kirykos to Karkinagri, a southwest-coast fishing village, stopping first at Maganitis and the idyllic Seychelles Beach. During high season, this boat sometimes goes daily, and represents the only realistic way for nondrivers to reach this remote corner of Ikaria.

BUS & TAXI

Theoretically, buses operate on Ikaria, though the system exists more for transporting schoolchildren than tourists. A twice-daily bus from Agios Kirykos to Hrisos Rahes, via Evdilos and Armenistis, operates (€7). If you don't hire a car, share a taxi; from Agios Kirykos to Evdilos costs around €40, though drivers may use their meter instead.

NORTHEASTERN AEGEAN ISLANDS

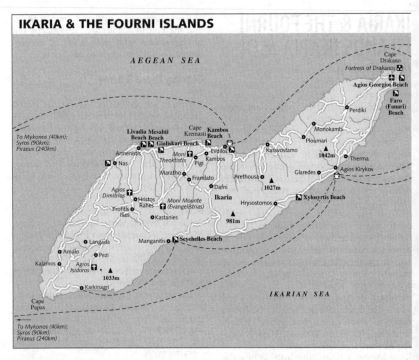

CAR & MOTORCYCLE

It can be a good idea to hire a car or scooter for travel beyond the main towns (though hitchhiking is still accepted by locals). Try **Dolihi Tours Travel Agency** (☎ 22750 23230) in Agios Kirykos, and **Aventura Car & Bike Rental** (aventura@otenet.gr) in Evdilos (p590) and Armenistis (p593).

AGIOS KIRYKOS ΑΓΙΟΣ ΚΗΡΥΚΟΣ
pop 1880

Ikaria's capital is a dated but dependable Greek port, with clustered old streets, tasty restaurants, hotels and domatia with the necessary services. It has elementary nightlife and radioactive hot springs, while Xylosyrtis Beach (4km southwest) is the best of Agios Kirykos' pebble beaches.

Orientation

The ferry quay is 150m south of the town centre; for the *plateia* (square), turn right onto the main road. Leaving the quay, turn left on the square for the bus stop, just west. Excursion boats and hydrofoils dock near Dolihi Tours Travel Agency.

Information

ATM-equipped banks line the *plateia*. The post office is left of it. Useful online resources include www.island-ikaria.com and www .ikaria.gr.

Dolihi Tours Travel Agency (☎ 22750 23230) Helpful agency can arrange accommodation; located below the police station.

Icariada Travel (☎ 22750 23322; depy@ikariada .gr) Waterfront agency sells ferry and plane tickets, and arranges accommodation.

Police (☎ 22750 22222) Above Dolihi Tours.

Port police (☎ 22750 22207)

Tourist police (☎ 22750 22222)

Sights & Activities

Opposite the police station, Ikaria's **radioactive springs** (admission €5; ⏰ 7am-2.30pm & 5-9pm Jun-Oct) are famed for their salutary effects, which include curing arthritis and infertility.

Agios Kirykos' small **archaeological museum** (☎ 22750 31300; admission free; ⏰ 10am-3pm Tue-Wed & Fri-Sun Jul-Aug) boasts local finds, highlighting the large, well-preserved *stele* (500 BC) depicting a seated mother and family. Although the (signposted) museum is near the hospital, at the

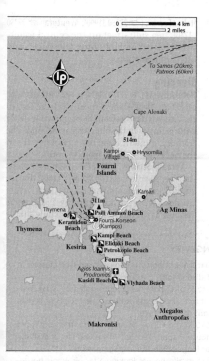

time of writing a new museum was planned for a different location – the old *gymnasio* (high school).

The **Icarus Festival for Dialogue between Cultures** (☎ 22940 76745; www.icarus-festival.ikaria.gr; per event €10; ☷ performances from 9.30pm Jul & Aug) is a summer-long, island-wide series of concerts, dramatic works and other cultural events held since 2005. The festival highlights individuals and groups who espouse multicultural values and cooperation; among them are some quite prominent Greek and international artists. Buses are organised for festival-goers.

A quirky, appropriately Ikarian event held for over 30 years is the Ikaria International Chess Tournament, organised by local chess aficionado **Savas Kyriakou** (☎ 6932478386; www .chess.gr/ikaros), If you're game, this battle of wits is held each July – the winner walks off with €1000, and special cash prices are allotted for 'ladies and veterans' as well.

Sleeping

Pension Maria-Elena (☎ 22750 22835; www.island-ikaria .com/hotels/mariaelena.asp; s/d €35/45; ☒ ☎ ☲) Some 500m from the port near the hospital, this small pension enjoys a garden setting and offers 16 simple but clean rooms with balconies overlooking the sea, plus a few suites. It's open year-round.

Hotel Akti (☎ 22750 23905; s/d €35/50; ☒) A budget choice on the rocks overlooking sea and port, Akti has small but attractive rooms with fridge, TV and mosquito netting, plus friendly, English-speaking owners. Follow the steps just right of Alpha Bank.

Hotel Kastro (☎ 22750 23480; www.island-ikaria.com/ hotels/kastro.asp; d €50; ☒ ☲) This well-appointed hotel has handsome rooms with balconies and all mod cons. There's a bar, and even a rooftop pool. From atop the stairs leading from Dolihi Tours, it's 20m to the left.

Eating & Drinking

Filoti (☎ 22750 23088; mains €4-7) This tasty eatery 30m from the square offers Agios Kirykos' best-value meals (including decent pizzas).

Taverna Klimataria (☎ 22750 22686; mains €6-9) A back-street taverna, strong on grilled meats, with a lovely summer courtyard.

Restaurant Dedalos (☎ 22750 22473; mains €7-12) Beside the square, this busy eatery serves tasty, if pricey, fresh fish.

AROUND AGIOS KIRYKOS

The **hot springs of Lefkada** (☎ 6977017014; admission €5; ☷ 7am-2.30pm & 5-9pm Jun-Oct), 2km north of Agios Kirykos, are therapeutic and relaxing, and reportedly cure many ailments. Ikaria's eastern tip boasts the 2km-long **Faro Beach**, 10km north along the coast road, and the 3rd-century BC **fortress of Drakanos**, which sponsored religious rites dedicated to Eilythia, a fertility deity. Although still not fully excavated, it's worth seeing. A path from a small chapel here leads to the sandy **Agios Georgios Beach**.

While a few tavernas hug this beach, it's more tranquil than the major northwest-coast beaches. Just up from it on the main road, the friendly Greek-Australian Evon Plakidas at **Rooms Evon** (☎ 22750 32580, 6977139208; evon.plakidas@ gmail.com; www.evonsrooms.com; ste €50-110; ☐) rents clean, high-quality suites, some with spiral stairs, all with kitchenettes. The studios hold up to six people. The adjoining cafe, where breakfast is served, has internet access.

EVDILOS ΕΥΔΗΛΟΣ
pop 460

Evdilos, Ikaria's second port, is 41km northwest of Agios Kirykos; they're connected by

NORTHEASTERN
AEGEAN ISLANDS

Ikaria's main road. If you haven't a car, take a taxi (€40). The memorable trip takes in high mountain ridges, striking sea views and slate-roof villages. Evdilos itself is sleepy, though its streets are narrow and poorly planned for the summer influx, as attested by the chronic vehicle congestion. It features stately old houses on winding streets (follow Kalliopis Katsouli, the cobbled street leading uphill from the waterfront square). For the local beach, walk 100m uphill from the *plateia*, then take the path down past the last house on the left.

Information

The waterfront has ATMs, and the ticket agencies for **NEL Lines** (☎ 22750 31572) and **Hellas Ferries** (☎ 22750 31990). **Aventura** (☎ 22750 31140), in a side street off the central waterfront, has car and bike hire, sells tickets and offers information.

Sleeping

Hotel Atheras (☎ 22750 31434; www.atheras-kerame.gr; s/d €50/60; ✕ ⚑) The almost Cycladic feel to the Atheras derives from its bright white decor contrasting with the blue Aegean beyond. The friendly, modern hotel has a pool bar. It's in the backstreets, 200m from the port.

Kerame Studios (☎ 22750 31434; www.atheras-kerame.gr; studio/apt from €70; ✕ ⚑) These diverse studios, apartments and rooms 1km before Evdilos have beach access nearby. Prices are as variable as the quarters, which include simple

---

REVEALED: THE SECRETS OF IKARIAN LONGEVITY

In 2009 Greek and foreign media announced that Ikarians enjoy the longest average lifespan in Europe. To what can be attributed this mark of distinction?

To be sure, the time-honoured, laid-back lifestyle of remote Ikaria, untroubled by mass tourism or the stresses of modern life, is a factor. But to really get the story on the secrets of Ikarian longevity, it's best to go, as reporters say, straight to the source.

Take Ioannis Tzantas: born on 9 February 1910 in the village of Akamanatra, this contented chap sitting outside the local *kafeneio* (coffee house) happily recounts his island life, and all the little things that have gone into extending it far longer than the average person's.

By the age of 14, the bespectacled centenarian recalls, he was looking after his whole household, as his father's health problems left him incapable. 'I sold goats, and worked for my family every day and night,' recounts Ioannis. 'In those days, we would walk everywhere, all day long, following the sheep – walking is very good for you, you know.'

Ioannis was married at 26, and recalls the vibrant life of a village that has since become sleepy due to emigration. 'We had many festivals, with lots of singing and dancing,' he says, 'And I would drink some wine, but I never got drunk, not once!'

Indeed, Ioannis is firm about steering clear of vices. Although he was a pipe smoker for 18 years, he never touched cigarettes. 'Life is very good, even though there are always problems that can't be avoided,' he says, 'But other potential problems can be avoided – like drunkenness and drugs. It makes me very sad when I see people with these problems.'

Instead, Ioannis prescribes two glasses of wine a day, 'but without getting drunk, of course. And no smoking!' With a twinkle in his eye, he adds, 'and be sure to have lots of sex.' (At this, Ioannis' septuagenarian sons erupt with laughter from the corner.)

It takes a hardy and disciplined diet to keep up a man's vitality, of course. Ioannis advises eating lots of eggs, cheese and milk. 'I once even had 32 eggs in one day!' (More laughter.)

For a man of his years, Ioannis has a sharp memory. As his life lessons meander into tangents, he recalls a sometimes harrowing childhood in wild Ikaria, and a facet of life that perhaps helps explain its Communist tendencies. 'In those days, the pirates attacked our island very often,' he says. 'That's why nobody wanted to have lots of things – the pirates would steal them anyway!' He also recalls WWII, when he was stationed in the north, near Albania. Although precisely 225 of his comrades were killed, 'thanks to God, I escaped every time!'

Indeed, having outlived five wars, Ioannis knows something about conflict management. Personal strife, however, endangers one's lifespan most, he believes. The village elder saves this, perhaps his most important lesson, for the end. 'It's very bad for one's health to be jealous of other people's happiness. When others have success, we should also feel joy… *afta* [That's all].'

RELIGIOUS REVELRY ON THE ISLAND OF WINE

Pagan god Dionysos may no longer reign over Ikaria's vineyards, but his legacy lives on in Christianised form in the summertime *panigyria* (festivals; all-night celebrations held on saints' days across the island). There's no better way to dive headfirst into Greek island culture than drinking, dancing and feasting while honouring a village's patron saint. Bring your wallet, however: *panigyria* are important fundraisers for the local community. Use this fact to explain away any overindulgences as well-intended philanthropy.

Western Ikaria *panigyria* occur on the following dates:

Kambos 5 May

Agios Isidoros 14 May

Armenistis 40 days after Orthodox Easter

Pezi 14 May

Agios Kirykos & Ikarian Independence Day 17 July

Hristos Rahes & Dafne 6 August

Langada 15 August

Evdilos 14–17 August

Agios Sofia 17 September

---

but well-maintained studios and apartments for four people, with separate kitchen. Rooms have spacious decks with views; the restaurant is built into a windmill.

Hotel Evdoxia (☎ 22750 31502; www.evdoxia.gr; d €70; ⊠) Although it's a bit of a climb, this B-class hotel has attractive modern rooms and many facilities, like a minimarket, laundry service, currency exchange and traditional restaurant. Advance, multiday reservations get you free pick-up from the ferry.

Eating

Tsakonitis (☎ 22750 31684; Plateia Evdilou; mezedhes €4-7) This *ouzerie* (place that serves ouzo and appetisers) on the waterfront is a local favourite known for its homemade Greek yoghurt.

To Steki (☎ 22750 31723; Plateia Evdilou; mains €5-9) This harbour-side dining 'hang-out' (as its name implies in Greek) is a dependable year-round option for taverna fare, like cheese pies and *soufiko* (an Ikarian speciality, like a Greek ratatouille).

WEST OF EVDILOS

Kambos Κάμπος

pop 94

Little Kambos, 3km west of Evdilos, was once mighty Oinoe (derived from the Greek word for wine), Ikaria's capital. Traces of this ancient glory don't remain, though the village does boast a ruined Byzantine palace, Ikaria's oldest church and a small museum. Kambos' other main attractions are its sand-and-pebble beach and scenic hill walks.

INFORMATION

Kambos is fairly self-explanatory but for insider info, track down long-time local tourism provider Vasilis Kambouris. If he's not at his village shop (on the right when arriving from Evdilos, and also site of Kambos' post box and telephone), Vasilis can be found catering to guests at his Rooms Dionysos (below). Vasilis can also help organise taxis, car hire and ferry tickets.

SIGHTS & ACTIVITIES

On the right-hand side when entering Kambos from Evdilos stand the modest ruins of a **Byzantine palace**. Kambos' small **museum** (☎ 22750 31300; admission free) displays Neolithic tools, geometric vases, classical sculpture fragments, figurines and ivory trinkets. If it's closed, ask Vasilis Kambouris to open it. Adjacent stands Ikaria's oldest surviving Byzantine church, **Agia Irini Church** (12th century). Built on the site of a 4th-century basilica, it contains some columns from this original. Alas, Agia Irini's frescoes remain covered with whitewash because of no funds to pay for its removal.

SLEEPING & EATING

our pick **Rooms Dionysos** (☎ 22750 31300; dionisos@ hol.gr; www.ikaria-dionysosrooms.com; roof-terrace beds/ d/tr €10/40/50; 🛜 🖳) The many happy guests who return every year attest to the magical atmosphere of this pension run by the charismatic Vasilis 'Dionysos' Kambouris, his Australian wife Demetra and brother Yiannis.

MOUNTAIN WALKS & MONKS SKULLS

With its solitude and wild nature, Ikaria's perfect for mountain walks. One that's invigorating, but not too hard on the bones, is the one-day circular walk along dirt roads from **Kambos** south through **Dafni**, the remains of the 10th-century **Byzantine Castle of Koskinas**, and picturesque **Frandato** and **Maratho** villages.

When you reach **Pigi**, look for the Frandato sign; continue past it for the unusual little **Byzantine Chapel of Theoskepasti**, tucked into overhanging granite. You must clamber upwards to get to it, and duck to get inside. Provided the row of old monks' skulls don't creep you out, the chapel makes for a wonderfully peaceful visit and is near **Moni Theoktistis**, with frescoes dating from 1686. The nearby *kafeneio* (coffee house) is good for a relaxed coffee or juice with Maria, the kindly owner.

Rooms are simple but well maintained, with private bathrooms, while the rooftop terrace beds are a steal at €10. The lovely shaded patio overlooking nearby Kambos Beach is where Vasilis serves his trademark big breakfasts, and where guests can enjoy the relaxed conviviality of the place over an evening drink. There's even a book exchange. To find it, ask at Vasilis' village shop or look for the blue-painted trees.

Balcony (☎ 22750 31604; d/tr €40/60) There are fantastic views from the six apartments at family-run Balcony, a bit of a hike to reach. Classic wrought-iron furniture distinguishes the studios, which have a kitchen and loft-sleeping area with twin mattresses. French-style doors lead to a private sitting area with coastal views.

Partheni (☎ 22750 31995; mains €6-8) On Kambos Beach, the Partheni serves simple but tasty Greek food, and great *kalamari* (fried squid). It also does nourishing *mayirefta* (ready-cooked meals), and makes a relaxing place to eat after a swim.

Pashalia (☎ 22750 31346; mains €6-10) A family-run taverna with tradition, the Pashalia offers tasty homemade mezedhes (appetisers), like wild mushrooms, fresh wild asparagus and goat's cheese, and is frequented by the locals.

Kambos to the Southwest Coast

From Kambos, two roads head west: the main road, which hugs the northern coast until the Armenistis resort, and then becomes a secondary road continuing down the north-western coast; and another secondary road, mostly dirt but doable with a good car, which ribbons slightly southwest through the stunning moonscapes of central Ikaria to remote Karkinagri on the southern coast. The latter is ideal for those seeking off-the-beaten-track adventures, while the former is the obvious choice for beach lovers.

The southern coast road through central Ikaria accesses **Moni Theoktistis** and the tiny **Chapel of Theoskepasti** (see boxed text, above), just northwest of Pigi. From Pigi, continue south to Maratho, then west for the impressive **Moni Mounte**, also called Moni Evangelistrias. Some 500m beyond it lies a kid-friendly duck pond with giant goldfish and croaking frogs.

After this, the road forks northwest and southwest: follow the signs and either will arrive at **Hristos Rahes**, an eclectic hillside village and good hiking base, once known for its late-night shopping. Along with various traditional products, there's a useful walking map, *The Round of Rahes on Foot* (€4), sold at most shops; proceeds go to maintaining the trails.

After Hristos Rahes, follow the road south through rustic **Profitis Ilias**. Head south when the road forks; after 1km take the left towards **Pezi**. The landscape now becomes even more rugged and extreme, with wind-whipped thick green trees clinging to bleak boulders, and rows of old agriculturalists' stone walls snaking across the terrain. The bouncy, dusty ride opens onto stunning views of the badlands interior and, after you turn left at Kalamos, of the sea far below. The road finally terminates at tiny **Karkinagri**, which has a few tavernas, rooms and a nearby beach.

In summer this fishing village also has a thrice-weekly boat service to Agios Kirykos (see p587). This highly recommended voyage follows Ikaria's rugged and partially inaccessible southern coast. The boat calls in at **Manganitis** village; nearby is a gorgeous, secluded stretch of white pebbles and crystal-clear waters – the appropriately named **Seychelles Beach** tucked within a protected cove and flanked by a cave.

Alternatively, if coming to Seychelles Beach by car along the coastal road connecting Manganitis with Evdilos and Agios Kirykos, you'll see an unmarked parking area on the right-hand side, after a tunnel; park here and clamber down the boulder-strewn path (a 20-minute walk) to the beach.

SLEEPING & EATING

Hotel Raches (☎ 22750 91222; Hristos Rahes; s/d €25/40) Simple but clean and inexpensive domatia have balconies with views, a communal area and friendly owners – book ahead in high season.

Kaza Papas (☎ 22750 91222; Karkinagri; d/apt €45/55; 🕹) These simple but new Karkinagri domatia and apartments have great sea views. Facing the water, turn right behind the tavernas and walk 100m along the waterfront to reach them, though it's better to reserve ahead.

O Karakas (☎ 22750 91214; Karkinagri; mains €6-9) On a bamboo-roofed seafront patio, this excellent family-run taverna does good fresh fish and salads. Try Ikaria's tasty vegetable stew speciality, *soufiko*.

Armenistis to Nas Αρμενιστής Προς Να

Armenistis, 15km west of Evdilos, is Ikaria's humble version of a resort. It boasts two long, sandy beaches separated by a narrow headland, a fishing harbour and a web of hilly streets to explore, but nothing traditional. Cafes line the beach. Moderate nightlife livens up Armenistis in summer, but it's far more subdued than the typical Greek island resort. **Dolihi Tours** (☎ 22750 71480), by the sea, organises walking tours and jeep safaris. **Aventura** (☎ 22750 71117), by the patisserie before the bridge, offers car hire and ticket sales.

Just 500m east of Armenistis is **Livadi Beach**, where currents are strong enough to warrant a lifeguard service and waves are sometimes big enough for surfing. Beyond Livadi are two other popular beaches, **Mesahti** and **Gialiskari**.

Westward 3.5km from Armenistis lies the pebbled beach of **Nas**, located far below the road and a few tavernas. This nudist-friendly beach has an impressive location at the mouth of a forested river, behind the ruins of an ancient **Temple of Artemis**.

Nas has become slightly upscale and preserving the equilibrium has prompted the Greek police to dismantle the impromptu beach hovels made by the hapless hippies the place attracts. They usually retreat into the river forest to camp, and are generally benign.

SLEEPING

Rooms Fotinos (☎ 22750 71235; www.island-ikaria.com/hotels/PensionFotinos.asp; Armenistis; d from €40; 🕹 May-Oct; 🕹) This family-run Armenistis pension, 150m above the curving beach, has seven rooms, all clean and modern, with a lovely, relaxing garden. The owners are friendly and helpful.

Gallini (☎ 22750 71293; www.galinipension.gr; Armenistis; d €60; 🕹 May-Oct) These 12 domatia also hover above Armenistis. They're small but beautifully furnished, with walls of inset stone and big windows. Studios are larger, with slanting, loft-style ceilings and kitchenettes. All enjoy great sea views.

Atsachas Rooms (☎ /fax 22750 71226; www.atsachas.gr; Livadia Beach; d €60) Right on Livadia Beach, the Atsachas has clean, well-furnished rooms, some with sophisticated kitchens. Most have breezy, sea-view balconies. The cafe spills down to the lovely garden, and the restaurant has also won plaudits.

Villa Dimitri (☎ /fax 22750 71310; www.villa-dimitri.de; Armenistis; 2-person studios & apt with private patio €50-70; 🕹 Mar-Oct; 🕹 🖳) This assortment of separate, secluded apartments set on a cliff amid colourful flowers has a Cycladic feel. It's 800m west of Armenistis and requires advance bookings and a minimum of one week.

Panorama (☎ 22750 71177; www.ikaria-panorama.com; Nas; studios €80; 🅿) This collection of five self-catering studios is located up a steep driveway before the village. Rooms fit up to four people and feature handsome combinations of wood and marble, all with new fixtures and sea views.

EATING

Pashalia Taverna (☎ 22750 71302; Armenistis; mains from €5; 🕹 Jun-Nov) Meat dishes like *katsikaki* (kid goat) or veal in a clay pot are specialities at this, the first taverna along the Armenistis harbour road.

Taverna Nas (☎ 22750 71486; Nas; mains €6-10) This simple taverna on the high bluff over Nas beach has superb views of the western sea at sunset. Although a bit touristy, it serves hearty portions of Greek standbys and fresh fish.

Kelari (☎ 22750 71227; Gialiskari; mains €6-13) Taking the fish straight off the boat, Kelari serves the best seafood available at this laid-back beach east of Armenistis.

THE FOURNI ISLANDS ΟΙ ΦΟΥΡΝΟΙ

pop 1470

The Fourni archipelago is one of Greece's great unknown island gems. Its low-lying vegetation clings to gracefully rounded hills that overlap, forming intricate bays that conceal sandy beaches and little ports where caïques bob on a placid sea. A sort of Outer Hebrides in the Mediterranean, this former pirates' lair is especially beautiful at dusk, when the setting sun suffuses its multifaceted terrain into shades of pink, violet and black – the effect is especially dramatic when viewed from an elevated point.

In centuries past, Fourni's remoteness and quietude attracted pirates seeking refuge, though today those seeking refuge – and some of the Mediterranean's best seafood – are inevitably travellers seeking a peaceful respite from the outside world. Nevertheless, Fourni's swashbuckling past is still evoked in the very appellation of the archipelago's capital, Fourni Korseon; the Corsairs were French privateers with a reputation for audacity, and their name became applied generically to all pirates and scallywags then roaming the Eastern Aegean.

Nowadays, Fourni Korseon offers most of the accommodation and services, plus several beaches. Other settlements include the much smaller Hrysomilia and Kamari to the north, plus another fishing hamlet opposite, on the island of Thymena. In the main island's very south, the monastery of Agios Ioannis Prodromos stands serene over several enticing beaches.

Orientation & Information

Fourni Korseon's waterfront, where ferries dock, is lined with tavernas and some accommodation options. Perpendicular to the central waterfront, the main street runs inland via the *plateia*; this nameless thoroughfare hosts a National Bank of Greece with ATM, travel agencies, a post office and the village **pharmacy** (☎ 22750 51188). Adjacent to it is an **internet cafe** (per hr €3; ⊗ 11am-midnight). There's also a free wi-fi connection at the terrace cafe-restaurant of the Archipelagos Hotel.

Fourni Korseon also has a **doctor** (☎ 22750 51202), **police** (☎ 22750 51222) and **port police** (☎ 22750 51207).

For further information online, see www.fourni.com.

Sights & Activities

Although Fourni is ideal for relaxing, the active-minded can enjoy hiking in the island's rolling hills and swimming at its pristine beaches. The nearest to town, **Psili Ammos Beach**, is a five-minute walk 600m north on the coast road. It has umbrellas and a summer beach bar that also operates at night.

Further from town, a string of popular beaches line the coast road south. **Kampi Beach**, after 3km, is excellent. Further along, **Elidaki Beach** has two sandy stretches and one pebble beach. Beyond is the pebbled **Petrokopeio Beach**.

Near Fourni's southernmost tip, near the **Church of Agios Ioannis Prodromos**, the fine, sandy **Vlyhada Beach** lies before the more secluded **Kasidi Beach**.

Fourni's other main settlements, **Hrysomilia** and **Kamari**, are 17km and 10km from Fourni Korseon respectively (approximately a 30-minute drive on winding but freshly paved uplands roads). Both are placid fishing settlements with limited services, though they offer tranquil settings and beaches. The trip is spectacular, opening onto myriad views of Fourni's sloping hills and hidden coves.

Finally, along with the tiny hamlet of Kampi, Fourni has another inhabited island, **Thymena**, which hosts an eponymous fishing hamlet and enticing **Kermaidou Beach**.

Sleeping

Most Fourni accommodation is in Fourni Korseon, though sleeping in the smaller settlements is possible, as is free beach camping.

Nectaria's Studios (☎ 22750 51365; Fourni Korseon; d/tr €35/45) on the harbour's far side, offers clean, simple rooms.

To Akrogiali (☎ 22750 51168, 6947403019; Kamari village; self-catering apt from €50) In Kamari village, Maria Markaki's two self-catering apartments overlooking the sea are fully-equipped studios with double beds. In high season, book ahead.

ourpick **Archipelagos Hotel** (☎ 22750 51250; www.archipelagoshotel.gr; Fourni Korseon; s/d/tr €45/54/72; P ⊠ ⊛) This elegant new hotel on the harbour's northern edge comprises Fourni's most sophisticated lodgings. From the patio restaurant, set under flowering stone arches, to the well-appointed rooms painted with soft tones complemented by matching marbled baths, the Archipelagos combines traditional yet imaginative Greek architecture with modern luxuries like wireless internet and all-natural Athenian designer soaps. Staff are friendly and helpful.

Eating
Fourni is famous for seafood – and especially, *astakomakaronadha* (lobster with pasta).

Ta Delfinakia (☎ 22750 51064; mains €3-7) When the other waterfront tavernas are taking their afternoon siesta, this is the only place to grab a bite.

Taverna Almyra (☎ 6979141653; Kamari village; fish €5-9) Up in Kamari, this relaxing fish taverna on the waterfront has subtle charm and, locals attest, the island's best fresh fish and *astakomakaronadha*.

Taverna Kali Kardia (☎ 22750 51217; mains €6-9) Hearty Kali Karida on the *plateia* does excellent grilled meats, and is enlivened by animated old locals.

Psarotaverna O Miltos (☎ 22750 51407; Fourni Korseon; mains €7-10) Excellent lobster and fresh fish are expertly prepared at this iconic waterfront taverna.

Archipelagos Hotel Restaurant (☎ 22750 51250; www.archipelagoshotel.gr; Fourni Korseon; mains €7-12) Fourni's foremost hotel offers a refined, romantic dining experience on its patio overlooking the harbour. Come after sunset for an artfully prepared dinner of fresh seafood and a glass of Greek wine.

Getting There & Away
Fourni is connected to Ikaria (Agios Kyrikos) and Samos by ferry and hydrofoil services.

For more information see Island Hopping (p751). **Fourni Island Tours** (☎ 22750 51546; Fourni Korseon; www.fourniisland.ssn.gr) provides information and sells tickets.

Getting Around
Gleaming new asphalt roads connect Fourni Korseon with Hrysomilia and Kamari; however, enjoying these Fourni freeways requires befriending a local, renting a motorbike, hitching or taking the island's lone **taxi** (☎ 22750 51223, 6977370471), commandeered by the ebullient Manolis Papaioannou.

At the time of writing, car hire was being planned; until then, hire a scooter at **Escape Rent a Motorbike** (☎ 22750 51514; gbikes@hotmail.com) on the waterfront.

Alternatively, go by **boat**. Two weekly caïques serve Hrysomilia, while another three go to Thymena year-round, departing at 7.30am.

SAMOS ΣΑΜΟΣ

pop 32,820 / area 477 sq km
Lying seductively just off the Turkish coast, semitropical Samos is one of the northeastern Aegean Islands' best-known destinations. Yet beyond the low-key resorts and the lively capital, Vathy (also called Samos), there are numerous off-the-beaten-track beaches and quiet spots in the cool, forested inland mountains, where traditional life continues more or less unchanged.

NORTHEASTERN AEGEAN ISLANDS

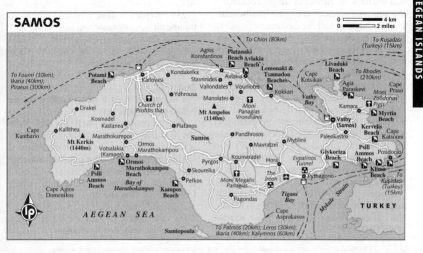

SAMOS

TURKISH CONNECTIONS

Visiting the main resorts and historical sites of Turkey's Aegean coast from Samos, Chios and Lesvos is easy. While boat itineraries, prices and even companies change often, the following explains how things generally work.

From Samos (p595), boats leave twice daily from Vathy (Samos) for **Kuşadası**, a fun resort near **ancient Ephesus**. The *Samos Star* leaves at 8.30am, and a Turkish-flagged vessel departs at 5pm. Additionally, from Pythagorio, a once-weekly boat serves Kuşadası. In low season, two ferries go weekly from Vathy. Tickets cost around €45 open return and €35 one way (plus €10 port taxes). Daily excursions run from May through October; the Sunday trip includes a visit to Ephesus (€25 extra). For tickets and more information, try **ITSA Travel** (☎ 22730 23605; www .itsatravelsamos.gr; Themistokleous Sofouli), opposite Vathy's ferry terminal. The ticket office takes your passport in advance for port formalities, though Turkish visas, where required, are issued in Turkey. Visas aren't necessary for day trips.

From Chios, boats depart year-round from Chios Town (p606) for **Çeşme**, a port near bustling **İzmir**, though they're most frequent in summer. From May to October, daily ferries to Çeşme leave Chios at 8.30am, returning at 6.30pm; on Sunday, however, they return at 5pm. Tickets cost €20 one way and €30 return. Get information and tickets from **Hatzelenis Tours** (☎ 22710 20002; mano2@otenet.gr; Leoforos Aigaiou 2) or **Sunrise Tours** (☎ 22710 41390; Kanari 28), which usually does a combination boat–bus day trip to İzmir via Çeşme (€40 return). Turkish visas, where required, are issued in Çeşme.

From **Lesvos**, boats leave Mytilini Town (p618) for **Dikeli** port, which serves **Ayvalik**. A Turkish company, Costar, leaves Mytilini Town to Dikeli every Tuesday, Thursday and Saturday at 9am (€20 return), returning at 6pm. The Thursday boat also offers onward buses to Ayvalik (€6), while the Tuesday and Saturday trips include a free bus to **ancient Pergamum**. Another Turkish company, Turyol, serves **Fokias** port near **İzmir** each Wednesday, leaving at 8.30am and returning at 6pm (€35).

Most Mytilini Town travel agencies sell Turkish tours; try **Olive Groove Travel** (☎ 22510 37533; www.olive-groove.gr; 11 P Kountourioti; ✆ 7.30am-10pm).

Famous for its sweet local wine, Samos is also historically significant. It was the legendary birthplace of Hera, and the sprawling ruins of her ancient sanctuary, the Ireon – where archaeological excavations continue – are impressive. Both the great mathematician Pythagoras and the hedonistic father of atomic theory, the 4th-century BC philosopher Epicurus, were born here. Samos' scientific genius is also attested by the astonishing Evpalinos Tunnel (524 BC), a spectacular feat of ancient engineering that stretches for 1034m deep underground.

Samos is a convenient ferry hub for the Eastern Aegean, with connections extending to the northern isles, the Dodecanese in the south and the Cyclades to the west; it's also the jumping-off point for Turkey's coastal resort of Kuşadası, and the nearby ruins of ancient Ephesus.

Samos' proximity to Turkey and slightly larger size make it somewhat lively in winter, though even then only a few hotels remain open, in Vathy.

Getting There & Away

For air and boat services from Samos, see Island Hopping (p760).

AIR

Samos' airport is 4km west of Pythagorio. **Olympic Air** (www.olympicairlines.com) Vathy (☎ 22730 27237; cnr Kanari & Smyrnis); Pythagorio (☎ 22730 61213; Lykourgou Logotheti) sells tickets in both major towns, as do travel agencies.

BOAT

For information on trips to Turkey, see the boxed text, above.

The exceptionally helpful **ITSA Travel** (☎ 22730 23605; www.itsatravelsamos.gr; Themistokleous Sofouli), directly opposite the ferry terminal in Vathy (Samos), provides detailed information, offers free luggage storage (without a catch) and sells tickets, including to Turkey. Considering that the boss, Dimitris Sarlas, owns four ferries operating from Samos, it's no surprise that ITSA has the most up-to-date information on schedule changes.

In Pythagorio, double-check ferry and hydrofoil schedules with the **tourist office** (☎ 22730 61389) or the **port police** (☎ 22730 61225).

Getting Around
TO/FROM THE AIRPORT
There's no airport shuttle bus; taxis from the airport cost €12 to Vathy (Samos) or €5 to Pythagorio, from where there are local buses to other parts of the island.

BOAT
Summer excursion boats travel four times weekly from Pythagorio to Patmos (return €45), leaving at 8am. Daily excursion boats go from Pythagorio to Samiopoula islet (including lunch, €30), while a round-island boat tour begins from Pythagorio's harbour twice weekly (€50).

BUS
From Vathy (Samos) **bus station** (☎ 22730 27262; Ioannou Lekati) seven daily buses serve Kokkari (€1.40, 20 minutes). Twelve serve Pythagorio (€1.50, 25 minutes) while six go to Agios Konstantinos (€2, 40 minutes) and Karlovasi (€3.50, one hour). Five serve the Ireon (€2.10, 25 minutes) and Mytilini (€1.40, 20 minutes).

Additionally, from Pythagorio itself, five daily buses reach the Ireon (€1.40, 15 minutes) while four serve Mytilini (€1.70, 20 minutes). Buy tickets inside. Services are reduced on weekends.

CAR & MOTORCYCLE
Pegasus Rent a Car (☎ 22730 24470, 6972017092; pegasus samos@hotmail.com; Themistokli Sofouli 5), opposite the port entrance and next to ITSA Travel in Vathy (Samos), offers the best rates on car, jeep and motorcycle hire. International car-hire outlets include **Hertz** (☎ 22730 61730; Lykourgou Logotheti 77) and **Europcar** (☎ 22730 61522; Lykourgou Logotheti 65).

If in Pythagorio, try **John's Rentals** (☎ 22730 61405; www.johns-rent-a-car.gr; Lykourgou Logotheti).

TAXI
The **taxi rank** (☎ 22730 28404) in Vathy (Samos) is by the National Bank of Greece. In Pythagorio the **taxi rank** (☎ 22730 61450) is on the waterfront at Lykourgou Logotheti.

VATHY (SAMOS) ΒΑΘΥ (ΣΑΜΟΣ)
pop 2025
Vathy (also called Samos) is the island's capital, and enjoys a striking setting within the fold of a deep bay. As in most Greek port towns, the curving waterfront is lined with bars, cafes and restaurants. However, the historic quarter of Ano Vathy, filled with steep, narrow streets and curious old folk features red-tiled 19th-century hillside houses and some atmospheric tavernas. The town centre boasts two engaging museums and a striking century-old church.

Vathy (Samos) also has two pebble beaches, the best being Gagou Beach (about 1km north of the centre); along the way there, you'll pass a string of cool night bars clinging to the town's northeastern cliff side, just before the Pythagoras Hotel, more refined and aesthetically pleasing than the cacophonous waterfront cafes.

Orientation
Facing inland from the ferry terminal, turn right for Plateia Pythagorou on the waterfront, recognisable by its four palm trees and lion statue; this square is partly a wi-fi zone. A little further along, and a block inland, are the leafy municipal gardens. The waterfront road is named after the most illustrious modern Samian, Themistoklis Sofoulis, a pioneering archaeologist and Greek prime minister during the 1946–49 civil war. The bus station is on Ioannou Lekati.

Information
ATM-equipped banks line Plateia Pythagorou and the waterfront. Pythagoras Hotel (p599) has computers and wi-fi internet access (€3 per hour).

Diavlos NetCafe (☎ 22730 22469; Themistokleous Sofouli 160; per hr €4; 🕑 8.30am-11.30pm) Internet access.

Municipal tourist office (☎ 22730 28582) Summer-only office north of Plateia Pythagorou; can find accommodation.

Port police (☎ 22730 27890)

Post office (Smyrnis)

Samos General Hospital (☎ 22730 27407) Well-supplied, efficient hospital, opposite Pythagoras Hotel.

Tourist police (☎ 22730 27980; Themistokleous Sofouli 129)

Sights
Along with the **Ano Vathy** old quarter, the relaxing **municipal gardens** and **Roditzes and Gagou Beaches**, the town's main attraction is its **archaeological museum** (☎ 22730 27469; adult/ student €3/2, Sun free; 🕑 8.30am-3pm Tue-Sun, last entry

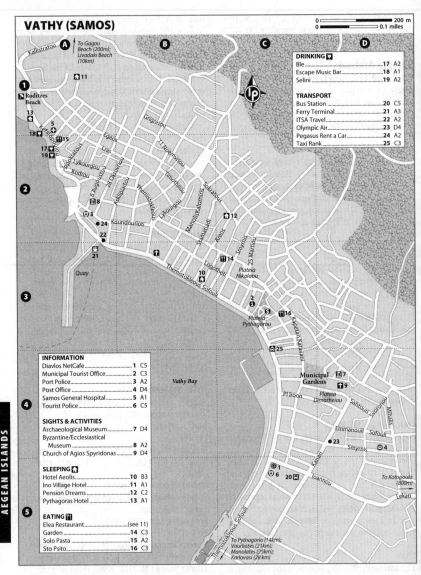

VATHY (SAMOS)

DRINKING	
Ble	**17** A2
Escape Music Bar	**18** A1
Selini	**19** A2
TRANSPORT	
Bus Station	**20** C5
Ferry Terminal	**21** A3
ITSA Travel	**22** A2
Olympic Air	**23** D4
Pegasus Rent a Car	**24** A2
Taxi Rank	**25** C3

INFORMATION	
Diavlos NetCafe	**1** C5
Municipal Tourist Office	**2** C3
Port Police	**3** A2
Post Office	**4** D4
Samos General Hospital	**5** A1
Tourist Police	**6** C5
SIGHTS & ACTIVITIES	
Archaeological Museum	**7** D4
Byzantine/Ecclesiastical Museum	**8** A2
Church of Agios Spyridonas	**9** D4
SLEEPING	
Hotel Aeolis	**10** B3
Ino Village Hotel	**11** A1
Pension Dreams	**12** C2
Pythagoras Hotel	**13** A1
EATING	
Elea Restaurant	(see 11)
Garden	**14** C3
Solo Pasta	**15** A2
Sto Psito	**16** C3

2.45pm). One of the best in the islands, it contains finds starting from the rule of Polycrates (6th century BC), the most famous being the gargantuan (5.5m) *kouros* (male statue of the Archaic period), plucked from the Ireon (Sanctuary of Hera; p602) near Pythagorio – the largest standing *kouros* known. Many other statues, most also from the Ireon, as well as bronze sculptures, *stelae* and pottery, are also exhibited.

Vathy's **Ecclesiastical Museum** (Byzantine Museum; 28 Oktovriou; adult/student €3/2, Sun free; 8.30am-3pm Tue-Sun, last entry 2.45pm) houses rare manuscripts, liturgical objects of silver and gold, as well as exceptional painted icons dating from the 13th to 19th centuries.

Samos owes some of this holy loot to its status as a bishopric (administering also Ikaria and Fourni) and thus also has some splendid churches, like the **Church of Agios Spyridonas** (Plateia Dimarheiou; 7.30-11am & 6.30-7.30pm), near Plateia Dimarheiou. Built in 1909, the ornate church has icons, impressive pillars hewn of marble from Izmir and, unusually, a silver candelabra from India and decorative columns on the iconostasis, inspired by ancient Greek and Byzantine motifs.

Sleeping

Pension Dreams (22730 24350; Areos 9; d with/ without balcony €35/30;) This small but central pension overlooks the harbour from a hill-top, and boasts an expansive rooftop studio; if that's taken, grab a balcony room with garden views. The friendly owner speaks several languages.

Pythagoras Hotel (22730 28422, 69445 18690; www.pythagorashotel.com; Kallistratou 12; s/d/tr incl breakfast €20/35/45; Feb-Nov;) The Pythagoras, just up from the port, is perfect for independent travellers and attracts a younger crowd than most Vathy hotels. The great kindness and hospitality of Stelios Mihalakis and family is only part of what makes this budget hotel special. Many rooms have breezy, sea-facing balconies (at the time of writing, air conditioning was being planned). There's also a well-stocked shop, wi-fi connection plus computers, and a pebble beach below the shaded breakfast patio. For free pick-up from the ferry or bus station, ring Stelios, or enquire at ITSA Travel.

Hotel Aeolis (22730 28377; www.aeolis.gr; Themistokleous Sofouli 33; s/d incl breakfast €50/70;) This grandiose and very central waterfront hotel attracts a slick Greek crowd and some foreigners, drawn by its two pools, Jacuzzi, taverna and bar. Rooms are ample and modern, though with less of a personal touch than at the smaller places in town. Light sleepers should factor in the nocturnal street noise from the cafe strip below.

Ino Village Hotel (22730 23241; www.inovillage.gr; Kalami; s/d/tr incl breakfast from €65/80/100;) With its courtyard pool flanked by ivy-clad, balconied white buildings, Ino Village is a citadel of subdued elegance high above Vathy. While this miniresort is sometimes booked by tour groups, it never endangers the stylish quietude of the hotel, which also boasts a fine restaurant.

Eating

Sto Psito (22730 80800; Plateia Pythagorou; souvlaki €3) Hearty portions of souvlaki and other light grills are served at this very popular place sprawling across the square.

Kotopoula (22730 28415; Vlamaris; mains €6-8) This local favourite known for its spit-roasted chicken is 800m inland along Ioannou Lekati, in the shade of a plane tree.

Garden (22730 24033; Manolis Kalomiris; mains €6-9) Greek specialities stand out at this soothing spot off Lykourgou Logotheti, on a tree-filled outdoor terrace within a garden.

Solo Pasta (22730 23699; Kefalopoulou 13; mains €7-12) With a spic-and-span interior and brisk service, this Italian joint opposite the hillside bars does inventive salads, good bruschettas and various fancy pasta dishes.

Elea Restaurant (22730 23241; Kalami; mains €8-12) Ino Village Hotel's patio restaurant has contemplative views over Vathy and its harbour below, and serves invigorated Greek cuisine and international dishes, while doing fine renditions of classics like swordfish souvlaki (cubes of meat on skewers). Samian wines are well represented. Beware charismatic barman Dimitrios when he tries to whip you up one of his patented shots of tequila with lemon and ground coffee.

Drinking

Vathy's nightlife is more Hellenic than in Pythagorio's blonder, Northern European–frequented bars. While most cafes and bars cling to the waterfront, the coolest ones overlook the water along Kefalopoulou. They include **Escape Music Bar**, **Ble**, and **Selini**. All play modern Greek and Western pop, plus more ambient music matching their outside lighting, which shines on the gently rippling water below to dazzling, hypnotic effect.

AROUND VATHY (SAMOS)

For something different, head 4km northeast to Arkoudolakas and the **Panouris Ranch** (6942704950; www.samostour.dk; Arkoudolakas village; 9am-noon & 6-9pm) for horse-riding expeditions in nearby forests (€10 per hour). Since the horses are well trained and docile, it's suitable for beginners. The ranch offers free pony rides for kids, and free drinks.

Beaches

The beaches east of Vathy are some of Samos' best and least crowded. Follow the north-coast road out of town for 10km and look for a signposted dirt road left leading to **Livadaki Beach**. Here, tropical azure waters lap against soft sand in a long sheltered cove with facing islets. Only Greeks in the know come to Livadaki, which has a beach bar with colourful and comfy soft chairs, and music day and night. The water is warm and very shallow for a long way out, and Livadaki's hedonistic yet mellow summer beach parties easily spill into it. Free kayaking and palm-frond umbrellas are available.

Back at the turn-off for Livadaki Beach, continue east 5km to the fishing hamlet of **Agia Paraskevi**, which has a shady pebble beach and multicoloured boats moored offshore. This beach, popular with Greek families, has a meat-and-seafood taverna, **Restaurant Aquarius** (☎ 22730 28282; Agia Paraskevi; mains €5-8).

Several other small beaches line the coast road south; for these a 4WD is advisable.

PYTHAGORIO ΠΥΘΑΓΟΡΕΙΟ
pop 1330

Down on the southeastern coast opposite Turkey, pretty Pythagorio has a yacht-lined harbour, and Samos' main archaeological sites. The waterfront is lined with touristy restaurants and, when crowded with Scandinavian package tourists, does give one the feeling of a Viking invasion. Since it's not far from Vathy (Samos), you can day-trip it from there for the fine nearby beaches and archaeological sites, though there's accommodation should you prefer to stay.

All boats travelling south of Samos dock at Pythagorio, from where day trips also depart to Samiopoula islet.

Orientation

From the ferry quay, turn right and follow the waterfront to the main street, Lykourgou Logotheti, a turn-off to the left. Most services are here. The central square (Plateia Irinis) is further along the waterfront. The bus stop is on Lykourgou Logotheti's south side.

Information

Commercial Bank (Lykourgou Logotheti) Has ATM.
Digital World (☎ 22730 62722; Pythagora; internet per hr €4; ⏰ 11am-10.30pm) Has internet access.

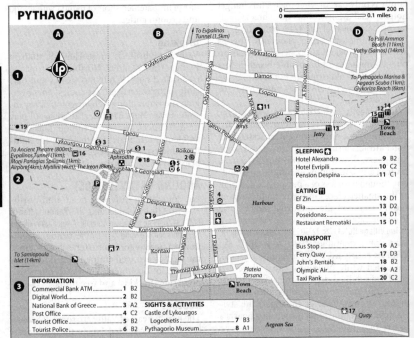

PYTHAGORIO

SLEEPING
Hotel Alexandra 9 B2
Hotel Evripili 10 C2
Pension Despina 11 C1

EATING
Ef Zin 12 D1
Elia 13 D2
Poseidonas 14 D1
Restaurant Remataki 15 D1

TRANSPORT
Bus Stop 16 A2
Ferry Quay 17 D3
John's Rentals 18 B2
Olympic Air 19 A2
Taxi Rank 20 C2

INFORMATION
Commercial Bank ATM 1 B2
Digital World 2 B2
National Bank of Greece 3 A2
Post Office 4 C2
Tourist Office 5 B2
Tourist Police 6 B2

SIGHTS & ACTIVITIES
Castle of Lykourgos
Logothetis 7 B3
Pythagorio Museum 8 A1

National Bank of Greece (Lykourgou Logotheti)
Port police (☎ 22730 61225)
Post office (Lykourgou Logotheti)
Tourist office (☎ 22730 61389; deap5@otenet.gr;
Lykourgou Logotheti; ☺ 8am-9.30pm) The friendly and
informative staff advise about historical sites and sleeping
options, provide maps, bus timetables and ferry info, and
also exchange currency.
Tourist police (☎ 22730 61100; Lykourgou Logotheti)
Left of the tourist office.

Sights & Activities

Samians took the lead locally in the 1821
War of Independence; the major relic of
that turbulent time is the **Castle of Lykourgos
Logothetis** (☺ 9am-7pm Tue-Sun), built in 1824 by
resistance leader Logothetis on a hill at the
southern end of Metamorfosis Sotiros, near
the car park. The **city walls** extend from here
to the Evpalinos Tunnel, a 25-minute walk
along this path.

The **Pythagorio Museum** (☎ 22730 61400; Town
Hall, Plateia Irinis; admission free; ☺ 8.45am-2.30pm Tue-
Sun) contains finds from the Ireon, though
the best are in the Vathy (Samos) museum.

Exiting Pythagorio northeast, traces of an
ancient theatre appear on a path to the left.
The right fork past the theatre reaches a cave
monastery, **Moni Panagias Spilianis** (Monastery of
the Virgin of the Grotto; ☎ 22730 61361; ☺ 9am-8pm) –
a welcome respite from summer heat.

EVPALINOS TUNNEL ΕΥΠΑΛΙΝΕΟ ΟΡΥΓΜΑ
Back in 524 BC, when Pythagorio (then
called Samos) was the island's capital and
a bustling metropolis of 80,000, securing
sources of drinking water became crucial.
To solve the problem, ruler Polycrates put
his dictatorial whims to good use, ordering labourers to dig into a mountainside
according to the exacting plan of his ingenious engineer, Evpalinos; many workers
died during this dangerous dig. The result
was the 1034m-long **Evpalinos Tunnel** (☎ 22730
61400; adult/student €4/2; ☺ 8.45am-2.45pm Tue-Sun),
which can be partially explored today.
In mediaeval times locals used it to hide
from pirates.

The Evpalinos Tunnel is actually two
tunnels: a service tunnel and a lower water
conduit visible from the walkway. While the
tunnel itself is wide enough, not everyone
can enter, as the entrance stairway is both
low and has very narrow walls, with no
grease provided.

The tunnel is quite cold: as sudden exposure to low temperatures on a hot day is not
healthy, wait until the sweat subsides before
entering, and perhaps pack an extra shirt to
wear while inside.

If walking, reach the tunnel from
Lykourgou Logotheti. If driving, a sign points
to the tunnel's southern mouth after entering
Pythagorio from Vathy (Samos).

DIVING

Along with swimming and sunbathing, try
scuba diving with **Aegean Scuba** (☎ /fax 22730
61194; www.aegeanscuba.gr; Pythagorio marina; ☺ year-
round). Professional instructors lead dives in
search of moray eels, sea stars, octopuses,
lobsters and other critters lurking in the
sponge-covered crevices around Pythagorio.
Snorkelling (€25) is also offered.

A dive with full equipment costs €60,
while two dives in one day costs €85.
Multiday, pay-in-advance diving gets you
discounts. Aegean Scuba also offers several
levels of beginner's courses, a scuba review
course for lapsed divers, emergency response
and rescue dive courses. For those seeking
professional PADI certification, there's a
special dive-master course.

Sleeping

Hotel Alexandra (☎ 22730 61429; Metamorfosis Sotiros
22; d €35) It has only eight rooms, but they are
lovely and some have sea views. There's also
an attractive garden.

Pension Despina (☎ 22730 61677; pensiondespina@
yahoo.gr; A Nikolaou; s/d €35/50) A clean, quiet pension on Plateia Irinis, the Despina offers
simple studios and rooms with balconies
(some have kitchenettes), plus a relaxing
back garden.

Hotel Evripili (☎ 22730 61096; Konstantinou Kanari;
s/d €50/70) This friendly and modern hotel has
well-appointed, cosy rooms off the waterfront; some have balconies.

Eating & Drinking

Poseidonas (☎ 22730 62530; mains €6-12) Next to
Restaurant Remataki, the Poseidonas specialises in seafood with an international flair.

Restaurant Remataki (☎ 22730 61104; mezedhes
€4-6, mains €7-10) Near Elia, this place has a nice
waterfront balcony and some splashy light
meals; salad with rocket leaves, Cretan *dakos*
(tomato and cheese on oil-softened rusks) and

dolmadhes (rice wrapped in vine leaves) are all recommended.

Elia (☎ 22730 61436; mains €7-12) Elia gets high marks from locals for sophisticated Greek and international fare, though it's pricey. It's located at the waterfront's far end.

Ef Zin (☎ 22730 62528; ☸ 10am-late) Also beside Remataki, this cafe-bar on a terrace has nice harbour views and an impressive wine list.

AROUND PYTHAGORIO
The Ireon Το Ηραίον
To judge merely from the scattered ruins of the **Ireon** (☎ 22730 95277; adult/student €4/3; ☸ 8.30am-3pm Tue-Sun), one couldn't imagine the former magnificence of this ancient sanctuary of Hera, located 8km west of Pythagorio. The 'Sacred Way', once flanked by thousands of marble statues, led from the city to this World Heritage–listed site, built at this goddess' legendary birthplace. However, enough survives to provide some insight into the workings of a divine sanctuary that was four times larger than the Parthenon.

Built in the 6th century BC on marshy ground, where the River Imbrasos enters the sea, the Ireon was constructed over an earlier Mycenaean temple. Plundering and earthquakes since antiquity have left only one column standing, though extensive foundations remain. There is something deeply disconcerting about the headless statues of a family, the Geneleos Group, from whose number the giant *kouros* statue in the museum at Vathy (Samos) was taken (see p597). Other remains include a stoa, more temples and a 5th-century Christian basilica. The deep trenches within the site indicate where archaeologists continue to unearth still more buried treasures.

Mytilinii Μυτιληνιοί
Skeletons of prehistoric animals, including forerunners of the giraffe and elephant, are displayed at the **palaeontology museum** (☎ 22730 52055; admission €3; ☸ 10am-2pm), in Mytilini village, northwest of Pythagorio. For more (human) skeletal relics, **Agia Triada Monastery** (☎ 22730 51339; ☸ 8am-1pm Mon-Sun) features an ossuary and a lovely rural setting. Hardy walkers can reach it from the museum.

Beaches
Glykoriza Beach, near Pythagorio, is a clean, pebble-and-sand beach with some hotels. However, sandy **Psili Ammos Beach**, 11km east, is much better. This lovely cove facing Turkey is bordered by shady trees and has shallow waters good for kids. There are tavernas and rooms, the best being **Psili Ammos Apartments** (☎ 22730 80481; s/d €38/65), above the beach's western edge. These family-friendly self-catering apartments with balconies overlooking the sea come with baby cribs and separate kids' rooms.

Buses go from Vathy (Samos) to Psili Ammos, as do excursion boats (€15) from Pythagorio. If driving, take the Pythagorio–Vathy road north and turn east where Psili Ammos is signposted. A unique pond on the left, 1km before it, is animated in spring by cheery pink flamingos.

SOUTHWESTERN SAMOS
Pythagorio to Drakei
Πυθαγόριο προς Δρακαίους
The drive west from Pythagorio traverses spectacular mountain scenery with stunning views of the south coast. This route also features many little signposted huts, where beekeepers sell the superlative but inexpensive Samian honey – stop in for a free sample and you'll walk away with a jar.

Samos' southwest coast is less touristed than the north, though the best beaches are starting to attract the inevitable resorts; however, tourism is still low-key, and secluded wild spots remain.

The drive from Pythagorio to the pebble beach at **Ormos Marathokampou** crosses mountains and the unvisited villages of **Koumaradei** and **Pyrgos**. From the beach, it's a 6km drive inland to **Marathokampos**, which has panoramic views of the immense **Ormos Marathokampou** (Bay of Marathokampos). Some 4km west of Ormos Marathokampou is **Votsalakia** (often called Kambos), with its long, sandy beach. There's an even nicer one 2km further at (the other) **Psili Ammos Beach**. Domatia are available, while beach tavernas prepare fresh fish.

Past Psili Ammos, the rugged western route skirts **Mt Kerkis**. From here until the villages of **Kallithea** and **Drakei,** where the road abruptly terminates, the coast is undeveloped and tranquil.

NORTHERN SAMOS
Vathy to Karlovasi Βαθύ προς Καρλόβασι
From Vathy (Samos), the coast road west passes many beaches and resorts. The first, **Kokkari** (10km), was once a fishing village,

---

A MATTER OF MEASUREMENTS

While the obsession with getting the 'proper pint' may seem modern, the ancient Greeks too were fixated on measuring their alcohol. Pythagoras, that great Samian mathematician (and, presumably, drinker) created an ingenious invention that ensured party hosts and publicans could not be deceived by guests aspiring to inebriation. His creation was dubbed the *dikiakoupa tou Pythagora* (Just Cup of Pythagoras). This mysterious, multiholed drinking vessel holds its contents perfectly well, unless one fills it past the engraved line – at which point the glass drains completely from the bottom, punishing the naughty drinker for gluttony.

Today faithful reproductions of the *dikiakoupa tou Pythagora*, made of colourful, glazed ceramic, are sold in Samos gift shops, tangible reminders of the Apollan Mean (the ancient Greek maxim of Apollo): 'Everything in moderation.'

---

but has become a resort. Windsurfing from its long pebble beach is good when the wind's up in summer. Rooms and tavernas are available. The popular nearby beaches of **Avlakia**, **Lemonaki** and **Tsamadou** are the most accessible for Kokkari-based walkers. The latter two are clothing-optional.

Continuing west, the landscape becomes more forested and mountainous. Take the left-hand turn-off after 5km to reach the lovely mountain village of **Vourliotes**. From here it's a 3km hike to **Moni Panagias Vrondianis**, Samos' oldest surviving monastery, built in the 1550s. Vourliotes' multicoloured, shuttered houses cluster on and above a *plateia*. Walkers can alternatively take a footpath from Kokkari.

Back on the coast road, continue west until the signposted left-hand turn-off for another enchanting village, fragrant **Manolates**, located 5km further up the lower slopes of Mt Ampelos (1140m; known as the 'Balcony of Samos'). Set amidst thick pine and deciduous forests, and boasting truly gorgeous traditional houses, Manolates is nearly encircled by mountains and offers a cool alternative to the sweltering coast. The village's upper part offers impressive views.

The mostly elderly residents of Vourliotes and Manolates are keenly aware of the tourist euro, and shops selling handmade ceramic art, icons and natural products are many. In fairness, you can find good stuff, including the Just Cup of Pythagoras (see the boxed text, above), and the taverna fare is fresh and well prepared. Despite these villages' visible popularity with tourists, they're still worth visiting for a taste of old Samos.

Back on the coast heading west, the road continues through **Agios Konstantinos**, a pretty, flower-filled village before **Karlovasi**, Samos' third port. This workaday place is useful only for

ferry connections. However, just 2km beyond it lies the sand-and-pebble **Potami Beach**, blessed with good swimming and a vaguely Rastafarian beach bar. It's complemented by nearby **forest waterfalls**; head west 50m from the beach and they're signposted on the left. Entering, you'll first encounter a small, centuries-old **chapel**, where pious Greeks light candles. Continuing through the wooded trail along the river brings you, after 10 or 15 minutes, to a deep river channel where you must wade or swim, height depending, through a forested canyon – along with the local eels – before enjoying a splash under the 2m-high waterfalls.

Sleeping

In Kokkari, **EOT** (Greek National Tourist Organisation; ☎ 22730 92217) finds accommodation. It's about 100m after the large church by the bus stop, beside the OTE (national telecom company) building.

Studio Angela (☎ 22730 94478, 21050 59708; Manolates; d €25; ✵) These five studios in Manolates, built into a hillside overlooking the sea, have modern rooms and kitchenettes.

Traditional Greek House (☎ 22730 94331; Manolates; studio €35; ✵) Phone ahead as there's only one studio available in this large old Manolates house behind the Despina Taverna. The room is quiet, romantic and tastefully furnished.

Kokkari Beach Hotel (☎ 22730 92238; Kokkari; d incl breakfast €75; ✵ ✺) This classy establishment 1km west of the bus stop, set back from the road in a pretty yellow building, has modern and comfortably furnished rooms. There's a cafe opposite.

Eating & Drinking

VOURLIOTES

Galazio Pigadi (☎ 22730 93480; Vourliotes; mains €5-7; ✵ 9am-11pm) Right after Vourliotes' *plateia*, this atmospheric place has a variety of traditional Greek mezedhes including *revythokeftedhes* (chickpea rissoles) and *bourekakia* (crunchy filo pastries filled with cheese). Try the house speciality, *kokkoras krasatos* (rooster in wine).

Pera Vrisi (☎ 22730 24181; Vourliotes; mains €5-8; ⊗ 10am-12am) This old-style Samian taverna by the spring at Vourliotes' entrance offers exceptional village cuisine and homemade barrel wine.

MANOLATES

Pigi (☎ 6974984364; Manolates; mains €4-7) Opposite the parking, this outdoor place has great sea views and authentic decor; try the *pitakia* (crunchy pies with cheese and pumpkin). All the food is homemade, with ingredients from the owner's own vegetable patch.

Loukas Taverna (☎ 22730 94541; Manolates; mains €4-8) This well-signposted taverna atop Manolates offers magnificent views of mountains and sea from the outdoor balcony; the offerings, ranging from fried zucchini flowers and hearty meat portions to local muscat wine and homemade cakes, make the walk worthwhile.

Kallisti Taverna (☎ 22730 94661; Manolates; mains €5-7) This intriguing taverna on the square has numerous excellent dishes including *kleftiko* (lamb with vegetables), and desserts, like the tasty orange pie.

Despina Taverna (☎ 22730 94043; Manolates; mains €5-9) This little taverna, halfway up the village in Manolates, serves *mayirefta* and grills.

POTAMI BEACH

Hippies Beach Bar (☎ 22730 33796; Potami Beach; ⊗ 9am-9pm) This appropriately exotic open cafe-bar on Potami Beach combines Greek and South Seas decor with subdued style.

CHIOS ΧΙΟΣ

pop 53,820 / area 859 sq km

Likeable Chios (*hee*-os) is one of Greece's bigger islands, and is significant in national history as the ancestral home of shipping barons. Since many seafaring Chians went abroad to seek their fortunes, the diaspora presence is more conspicuous here than on most Greek islands during summer. Yet Chios is a truly fascinating place even for 'unaffiliated' travellers. Its varied terrain ranges from lonesome mountain crags in the north

to the citrus-grove estates of Kampos, near the island's port capital in the centre, to the fertile Mastihohoria in the south – the only place in the world where mastic (a kind of gum) trees are productive. And the island's coasts are ringed by pristine beaches.

Chians tend to be very kind, and you'll find great hospitality here. Since Chios sees fewer visitors than better-known Greek island getaways, there's more genuine friendliness from the locals, who take great pride in their history, traditions and livelihood. For the visitor, all this translates into excellent opportunities for hands-on interaction with Chian culture, ranging from art and history to hiking and eco activities.

Chios enjoys good regular boat connections throughout the northeastern Aegean Islands, plus an airport. Between them, the ports of Chios Town in the east and Mesta in the southwest offer regular ferries to the intriguing, little-visited satellite islands of Psara and Inousses, which share Chios' legacy of maritime greatness, and to the lively Turkish coastal resorts just across the water.

Chios' large size, proximity to Turkey and shipping interests mean that a modicum of life remains in the capital, Chios Town, in winter. However, outside of high season, its dependencies of Psara and Inousses are almost completely empty.

History

As with Samos and Lesvos, geographic closeness to Turkey (the Karaburun peninsula lies just 8km away, across the Chios Strait) brought Chios both great commercial success before the 1821 revolution and great tragedy during it. Many of Greece's grand old shipping dynasties hail from Chios and its dependencies, Inousses and Psara. Under the Ottomans, Chios' monopolistic production of mastic – the sultan's favourite gum – brought Chians wealth and special privileges.

However, during the 1821–29 War of Independence, thousands of Chians were slaughtered by Ottoman troops. A century later, the Megali Idea ('Great Idea') for the liberation of Greek-majority cities in Anatolia unfolded with a naval assault from Chios – and ended, disastrously, with the Greek armies being driven back into the sea, as waves of refugees from Asia Minor flooded Chios and neighbouring islands.

NORTHEASTERN AEGEAN ISLANDS

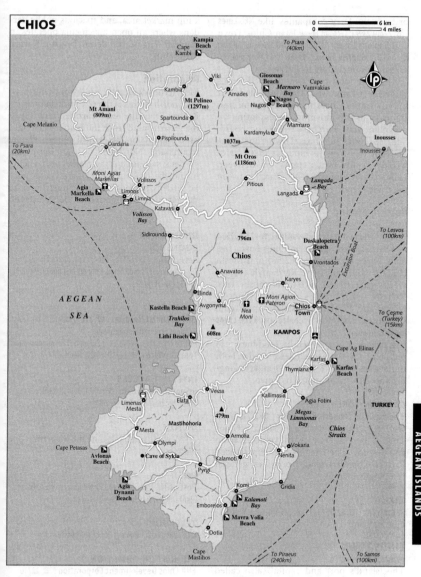

Getting There & Away

For information on flight and ferry access from Chios, see Island Hopping (p748).

AIR

The airport is 4km from Chios Town. There's no shuttle bus; an airport taxi to/from the town costs €6. Travel agen-cies, like Hatzelenis Tours (p607), are in Chios Town.

BOAT

For information on trips to Turkey, see the boxed text, Turkish Connections (p596).

Buy tickets from travel agencies like Hatzelenis Tours (p607), opposite the port, or from the ferry companies, like **NEL Lines** (☎ 22710 23971; Leoforos Egeou 16) in Chios Town and **Miniotis Lines** (☎ 22710 24670; www.miniotis.gr; Neorion 23). **Sunrise Tours** (☎ 22710 41390; Kanari 28) sells tickets, including to Turkey.

The little local boat *Oinoussai III* serves Inousses (€4 one way, 1¼ hours, daily). It mainly leaves Chios in the afternoon and Inousses in the morning, necessitating an overnight stay. Purchase tickets on board. Sunrise Tours in Chios Town runs summertime day trips to Inousses (€20) twice weekly. Daily water taxis go between Langada and Inousses (€40, shared between the passengers).

Getting Around
BUS
From the **long-distance bus station** (☎ 22710 27507; www.ktelchios.gr; Leoforos Egeou) in Chios Town, five daily buses serve Pyrgi (€2.50) and Mesta (€3.50), while four serve Kardamyla (€3.00) via Langada (€1.60). Two weekly buses serve Volissos (€4.10). Buses also go to Kampia, Nagos and Lithi beaches. For up-to-date schedules, visit the website of **KTEL-Chios** (www.ktelchios.gr).

Karfas Beach is served by the blue (city) bus company, with schedules posted at both the **local bus station** (☎ 22710 22079) and the long-distance bus station in Chios Town.

CAR & MOTORCYCLE
The reliable **Chandris Rent a Car** (☎ 22710 27194, 6944972051; info@chandrisrentacar.gr; Porfyra 5) is Chios Town's best agency, with vehicles from €30 per day. The friendly and experienced Kostas Chandris gladly provides general island information.

TAXI
A **taxi rank** (☎ 22710 41111) is on Plateia Vounakiou in Chios Town.

CHIOS TOWN
pop 23,780
The island's port and capital (also called Chios) is on the central east coast, and home to almost half of the inhabitants. Like many island capitals, it features a long waterfront lined with cafes and a noisy boulevard hugging the water. Behind it, however, is a quieter, intriguing old quarter, where some lingering traditional Turkish houses stand around a Genoese castle and city walls. There's also

a fun market area, and spacious public gardens where an open-air cinema operates in summer. The nearest decent beach is Karfas, 6km south.

Orientation
Most ferries dock at the waterfront's northern end; north of this is the old Turkish quarter, Kastro. From the ferry, turn left and follow the waterfront to reach the centre. Turn right onto Kanari for the central square, Plateia Vounakiou. Northwest of it are the public gardens; southeast is the market area. Facing inland, the local bus station is right of the public gardens; the long-distance bus station is to the left. Most hotels are near the waterfront, opposite the port.

Information
BOOKSHOPS
News Stand (☎ 22710 43464; cnr Leoforos Egeou & Rodokanaki) Sells multilingual papers and books, including Lonely Planet guides.

EMERGENCY
Chios General Hospital (☎ 22710 44302; El Venizelou 7) About 2km north of the centre.
Police (☎ 22710 44427; cnr Polemidi 1 & Koundouriotou)
Tourist police (☎ 22710 44427; Neorion)

INTERNET ACCESS
InSpot Internet Café (☎ 22710 83438; Leoforos Egeou 86; per hr €2.50; ☽ 24hr)

MONEY
ATM-equipped banks line the waterfront and *plateia*.

POST
Post office (☎ 22710 44350; Omirou 2; ☽ 7.30am-7pm) One block behind the waterfront.

TELEPHONE
OTE (Dimokratias Roidou) Public telephone.

TOURIST INFORMATION
ENA Chios Development Corporation (☎ 22710 44830; www.chios.gr, www.enachios.gr; Agios Isodoros, Petrokokklinou, Kampos) This official tourism information unit in Kampos, financed by the prefecture of Chios, offers free tours with professional guides to Kampos, Anavatos, Olympi, Nea Moni and Chios Castle.
Municipal Tourist Office (☎ 22710 44389; infochio@ otenet.gr; Kanari 18; ☽ 7am-10pm Apr-Oct, until 4pm Nov-Mar) Information on accommodation, car hire, bus

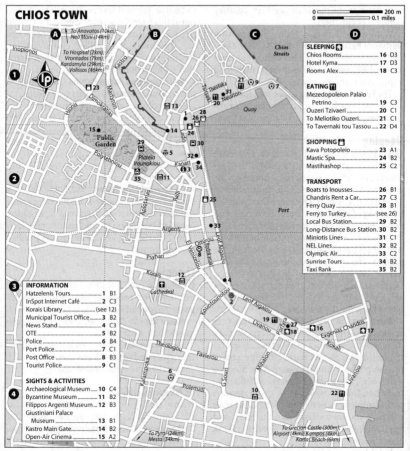

CHIOS TOWN

0 _____ 200 m
0 _____ 0.1 miles

INFORMATION
Hatzelenis Tours	1 B1
InSpot Internet Café	2 C3
Korais Library	(see 12)
Municipal Tourist Office	3 B2
News Stand	4 C3
OTE	5 B2
Police	6 B4
Port Police	7 C1
Post Office	8 B3
Tourist Police	9 C1

SIGHTS & ACTIVITIES
Archaeological Museum	10 C4
Byzantine Museum	11 B2
Filippos Argenti Museum	12 B3
Giustiniani Palace Museum	13 B1
Kastro Main Gate	14 B2
Open-Air Cinema	15 A2

SLEEPING
Chios Rooms	16 D3
Hotel Kyma	17 D3
Rooms Alex	18 C3

EATING
Mezedopoleion Palaio Petrino	19 C3
Ouzeri Tzivaeri	20 C1
To Meliotiko Ouzeri	21 C1
To Tavernaki tou Tassou	22 D4

SHOPPING
Kava Potopoleio	23 A1
Mastic Spa	24 B2
Mastihashop	25 C2

TRANSPORT
Boats to Inousses	26 B1
Chandris Rent a Car	27 C3
Ferry Quay	28 B2
Ferry to Turkey	(see 26)
Local Bus Station	29 B2
Long-Distance Bus Station	30 B2
Miniotis Lines	31 C1
NEL Lines	32 B2
Olympic Air	33 C2
Sunrise Tours	34 B2
Taxi Rank	35 B2

and boat schedules, plus a useful free book, *Hiking Routes of Chios*.

Port Authority (☎ 22710 44432; Neorion)

Thomas Karamouslis (☎ 22710 22838, 6937786213) Affable Thomas has a vast knowledge of the history of Chios, Greece and more, and leads guided tours of important cultural monuments for the ENA Chios Development Corporation (see opposite). A man of impeccable manner and wide learning, he recounts the island's history from a refreshingly objective (and often humorous) perspective.

TRAVEL AGENCIES

Hatzelenis Tours (☎ 22710 20002; mano2@otenet .gr; Leoforos Aigaiou 2) Opposite the port, this dependable full-service travel agency sells ferry and air tickets, plans excursions, finds accommodation and offers car hire.

Sights

The **Filippos Argentis Museum** (☎ 22710 23463; Korais; admission €1.50; ☼ 8am-2pm Mon-Fri, 5-7.30pm Fri, 8am-12.30pm Sat), located beside the impressive **Korais Library**, contains displays of embroideries, traditional costumes and portraits of the wealthy Argentis family. Born in Marseilles in 1891, Argentis devoted his life to researching Chian history, writing many significant works.

The **archaeological museum** (☎ 22710 44239; Mihalon 10; admission €2; ☼ 8.30am-2.45pm Tue-Sun) contains sculptures, pottery and coins dating from the Neolithic period. Closed at the time of writing, the **Byzantine Museum** (☎ 22710 26866; Plateia Vounakiou) occupies a former mosque, the Medjitie Djami, and contains sculptures from the 14th- to 15th-century Genoese occupation.

Within the Kastro's main gate, the tiny **Giustiniani Palace Museum** (☎ 22710 22819; admission Tue-Sat €2, Sun €1; ⏱ 9am-3pm Tue-Sun) contains restored Byzantine wall paintings, including important 13th-century frescoes.

The **Public Gardens** make a nice spot for relaxing; in summer Hollywood hits play at an enclosed **open-air cinema** (tickets €6) nightly at 9pm.

Sleeping

OUR PICK **Chios Rooms** (☎ 22710 20198, 6972833841; www.chiosrooms.gr; Leoforos Egeou 110; s/d/tr €25/35/45) An eclectic, hostel-like neoclassical house on the waterfront, Chios Rooms is the inspiration of its owner, native New Zealander Don. Marked by vintage furnishings, traditional rugs and lofty ceilings, the place has real character. More than half of the rooms have private bathrooms (the others have bathrooms separate from the rooms). The rooftop 'penthouse' has its own terrace. Having spent over 30 years in Greece, Don has much wisdom to impart about Greek life, and life in general, and will readily do so over a beer; the dude abides.

Rooms Alex (☎ 22710 26054; Livanou 29; s/d €30/45) A bright roof garden adorned with various flags increases the visibility of this friendly place. If the interior seems dark, imagine you're in a ship's hull: kindly owner Alex Stoupas was a sea captain for 21 years, and his lovingly handmade model ships decorate each of the simple but clean rooms. The *kapetanios* will pick you up for free from the ferry, and speaks English, French and Spanish. Book ahead in summer.

Hotel Kyma (☎ 22710 44500; kyma@chi.forthnet .gr; Evgenias Handri 1; s/d/tr incl breakfast €71/90/112; ▨ ☎) This century-old converted mansion impresses from the first sight of its central marble stairway (from 1917). The old wing's rooms live up to this promise, with stately decor, billowing curtains and sea-view balconies with red marble walls (ask for room 29). What makes the Kyma more than just another period hotel is its service; owner Theodoros Spordilis wants you to fall in love with Chios, and solves problems in English, Italian and German. Stays in the Kyma's sister hotel (opposite) in Kardamyla can be arranged.

Eating

Ouzeri Tzivaeri (☎ 22710 43559; Neoreion 13; mezedhes €3-8) The sort of food strong enough to soak up ouzo (the Tzivaeri serves 10 kinds) is dished out at this friendly portside eatery. You might need a cast-iron gut to lay into oil-drenched sun-dried tomatoes, grilled cod strips and traditional Chios sausages – but then again, that's what a good *ouzerie* is all about.

Mezedopoleion Palaio Petrino (☎ 22710 29797; Leoforos Egeou; mezedhes €4-7) This well-decorated and friendly place offers great mezedhes, like *tyrokafteri* (spicy cheese dip) and *ktapodi krasato* (octopus in wine sauce).

To Meliotiko Ouzeri (☎ 22710 40407; Neoreion; mains €4-7) The hearty portions served at the Meliotiko, on the port, help you fill your stomach before long ferry trips.

To Tavernaki tou Tassou (☎ 22710 27542; Livanou 8; mains €6-8) This family-friendly eatery near the sea offers standard taverna fare, Chios' own Kambos lemonade and an adjoining kid's land that will help keep restless ones pacified during dinner.

Shopping

Mastihashop (☎ 22710 81600; Leoforos Egeou 36) Get mastic-based products like lotions, toothpaste, soaps and condiments here.

Mastic Spa (☎ 22710 28643; Leoforos Egeou 12) Sells mastic-based cosmetics.

Kava Potopoleio (☎ 22710 23190; Inopionos 4) Find fine wines and myriad European beers in this shop below the Public Gardens.

CENTRAL CHIOS

North of Chios Town, **Vrontados** is site of Homer's legendary stone chair, the **Daskalopetra**. Immediately south of Chios Town is **Kampos**, a lush area with citrus trees, where wealthy Genoese and Greek merchant families summered from the 14th century onwards. You can see the walled mansions, some restored, others crumbling, and elaborate gardens – especially beautiful when flowers blossom in spring. Being fairly extensive, Kampos is best toured by bicycle, moped or car.

Citrus Memories (☎ 22710 31513; www.citrus-chios .gr; Argenti 9-11, Chios Town), a museum and shop founded in 2008, aims to revive the history of citrus fruit production in Kampos over the centuries, including organised visits, and tastings, of local desserts made from citrus fruits, like marzipan, lemon and vanilla sweets. The museum's atmospheric lodgings are on an estate dating from 1742. Other dignified Kampos mansions are being transformed into atmospheric guesthouses.

The nearby resort of **Karfas** (6km south of Chios Town) has accommodation and eating, but gets hectic.

At the island's centre is **Nea Moni** (admission free; ☯ 8am-1pm & 4-8pm), a World Heritage–listed 11th-century Byzantine monastery. Since it's undergoing renovations, some buildings may be closed. Nea Moni was built to commemorate the miraculous appearance of an icon of the Virgin Mary before three shepherds. Once one of Greece's richest monasteries, Nea Moni attracted pre-eminent Byzantine artists to create the mosaics in its *katholikon* (principal church of the monastic complex).

Disastrously, during the Greek War of Independence, the Turks torched the monastery and massacred its monks. Macabre monastic skulls are lined in the ossuary at the little chapel. Another catastrophe occurred with an 1881 earthquake that demolished the *katholikon* dome, damaging mosaics. Despite this, they still rank among Greece's greatest surviving examples of Byzantine art. Nea Moni is now a nunnery.

Another solemn site lies 10km northwest, at the end of a silent road. **Anavatos**, filled with abandoned grey-stone houses, was built on a precipitous cliff over which villagers hurled themselves to avoid capture during Turkish reprisals in 1822. Note that the narrow, stepped pathways leading between the houses to the summit can be dangerous, and the route is often closed.

More happily, nearby **Avgonyma** village, distinguished by mediaeval stone architecture, is currently enjoying a revival, and offers accommodation.

The central-west-coast beaches are quiet and good for solitude seekers, though they're not Chios' most spectacular. **Lithi Beach**, the southernmost of these, is most popular.

Sleeping

Perleas Mansion (☎ 22710 32217; www.perleas.gr; Vitiadou, Kampos; s/d/tr incl breakfast €90/120/150; P ✖) One of Kampos' best restored mansion guesthouses, the Perleas offers seven well-appointed apartments. This relaxing estate, built in 1640, exemplifies high Genoese architecture. The restaurant serves traditional Greek cuisine, using homegrown organic produce.

Spitakia (☎ 22710 81200; www.spitakia.com; Avgonyma village; r from €90; P ✖) This collection of studios and cottages, spread across five locations in a striking village of mediaeval stone houses

surrounded by olive and pine forests, has fantastic ambience. Although traditional, all rooms have kitchenettes and mod cons like air conditioning, TV and central heating (in winter); some have sublime sea views.

NORTHERN CHIOS

Lonesome northern Chios, once home of shipping barons, features craggy peaks (Mt Pelineo, Mt Oros and Mt Amani), deserted villages and barren hillsides. The drive north from Chios Town along the east coast is an astonishing trip through bizarre, boulder-strewn mountains that seem from some other planet.

After the small coastal settlements of **Vrontados** and **Langada** are the main villages, **Kardamyla** and **Marmaro**, ancestral homes of many wealthy ship-owning families – though you wouldn't know it from the humble architecture. Streets are so narrow, in fact, that some buildings have lines painted on the walls so buses won't barge into them. Marmaro has an earthy sand beach, but there are better pebble beaches 5km further at **Nagos** fishing village, and at **Giosonas**, 1km beyond. The beaches have very clear water and a few tavernas, but little shade.

After Nagos, the coast road heads northwest and upwards into remote terrain, skirting craggy Mt Pelineo (1297m). **Amades** and **Viki** are two tiny villages before **Kambia**, high up on a ridge overlooking bare hillsides and the sea. Here choose between turning south on the central road through the mountains, or continuing along the coast.

The latter option passes through wild, empty hills on a jagged road, reaching the pebbly **Agia Markella Beach** and **monastery** above it, also named after Agia Markella, the island's patron saint. Some 3km southeast is **Volissos**, Homer's legendary birthplace, with its impressive Genoese fort. Volissos' port, **Limnia**, isn't striking but has a taverna. From Volissos the coastal road continues south until Elinda, then returns eastwards to Chios Town.

Sleeping

Hotel Kardamyla (☎ 22720 23353; kyma@chi.forthnet .gr; Marmaro; s/d/tr €91/114/140; P ✖) Although the 1970s architecture is somewhat dated, the simple rooms are clean and well maintained at this quiet beachfront hotel in Marmaro. Repeat visitors come for the warm hospitality of the joint Greek-Turkish Spordilis family, who invite guests for a patio lunch. This is the sister hotel of Chios Town's Hotel Kyma (p608), and stays can be arranged from there.

SOUTHERN CHIOS

Unique southern Chios is arguably the island's best destination. Here and nowhere else grows the gum-producing mastic tree, throughout a fertile, reddish territory known as the Mastihohoria (Mastic villages). This region of rolling hills, criss-crossed with elaborate stone walls running throughout olive and mastic groves, is highly atmospheric.

Ottoman rulers' penchant for mastic made the Mastihohoria wealthy for centuries. Some architectural wonders remain in the villages of Pyrgi and Mesta. The former features houses decorated in unusual colourful patterns, while the latter is a car-free, walled fortress settlement built by the Genoese in the 14th century.

Other unique southern Chios attractions include Byzantine churches, the striking Cave of Sykia with its stalactites and stalagmites, and beaches. The port of Limenas Mesta, which offers seafood tavernas, is also a convenient jumping-off point for ferries to Psara (for ferry information, see p748).

Pyrgi Πυργί
pop 1040

Located 24km southwest of Chios Town, Pyrgi (peer-*ghi*), the Mastihohoria's largest village, juxtaposes traditional and modern architecture. Its vaulted, narrow streets pass buildings with facades decorated in intricate grey and white patterns, some geometric and others based on flowers, leaves and animals. The technique used, called *xysta*, requires coating walls with a mixture of cement and black volcanic sand, painting over it with white lime and then scraping off parts of the lime with the bent prong of a fork to reveal the matt grey beneath.

Pyrgi's central square is flanked by tavernas, shops and the little 12th-century **Church of Agios Apostolos** (☎ 10am-1pm Tue-Thu & Sat). The church's 17th-century frescoes are well preserved. On the square's opposite side, the larger church's facade has Pyrgi's most impressive *xysta* designs.

On the main road, east of the square, note the house with a plaque attesting to its former occupant – one Christopher Columbus.

Although definitely worth seeing, Pyrgi is better as a drive-by than a sleepover destination. However, there are signposted domatia, and **Giannaki Rooms** (☎ 22710 25888, 6945959889; d/q €40/70; ❄) offers regular rooms plus a house for up to eight people (€100).

Emboreios Εμπορειός

Six kilometres southeast of Pyrgi, Emboreios was the Mastihohoria's port back when the mastic producers were real high-rollers. Today it's much quieter, though it does boast **Mavra Volia Beach**, named for its black volcanic pebbles. There are domatia and, for food, the shady, atmospheric **Porto Emborios** (☎ 22710 70025; mains €5-9), decorated with fishing nets, hung chillies and garlic.

Mesta Μεστά

Mesta (mest-*aah*) is a truly memorable village, and one of Greece's most unusual. Here, appealing stone alleyways, intertwined with flowers and intricate balconies, are completely enclosed by thick defensive walls – the work of Chios' former Genoese rulers, who built this fortress town in the 14th century to keep pirates and would-be invaders out. Mesta is an ingenious example of mediaeval defensive architecture, featuring a double set of walls, four gates and a pentagonal structure. Since the rooftops are interconnected, with the right guide you can actually walk across the entire town. Dastardly locals have been known to settle scores by dumping water on an adversary's head from above.

In mediaeval times, mastic was a hot commodity, prized for its medicinal powers, meaning Mesta had to be especially well fortified. As a car-free village, it's a relaxing, romantic place where children can run around safely. Mesta also makes a good base for hill walking, exploring hidden southern beaches and caves, and participating in cultural and eco activities.

Village life converges on the central square, near the enormous church of the Taxiarhon, with small cafes and restaurants; on the tranquil, secluded laneways, rooms for rent are indistinguishably attached to the residences of bemused elders, who sit outside while the occasional cat darts past and the laughter of running children fills the air.

ORIENTATION

Buses stop outside of the village walls, on the main road; the *plateia* here is known locally as

Gyros. Facing the town from the bus shelter, turn right and then immediately left; a sign points to Mesta centre. Head down to the central square (Plateia Taxiarhon) for tourist information, rooms and eating options.

SIGHTS

There are two **churches of the Taxiarhon** (Archangels). The older and smaller one dates from Byzantine times and features a magnificent 17th-century iconostasis. The larger, 19th-century church, on the square, was built entirely from the townspeople's donations and labour. It has an ornate outer patio, huge, glittering chandeliers and very fine frescoes.

ACTIVITIES

To participate in traditional Chian farming, cooking and cultural activities, plus various outdoor activities, find Vassilis and Roula at **Masticulture Ecotourism Activities** (☎ 22710 76084, 6976113007; www.masticulture.com; Plateia Taxiarhon) by the restaurant on the square. This very kind and helpful couple provide unique ecotourism opportunities that introduce visitors to the local community, its history and culture. Some activities include mastic cultivation tours (€18), grape stomping with local winemakers (€25), cooking classes and pottery classes (€20).

Masticulture sells boat tickets, finds accommodation in Mesta, Limenas Mesta, Olympi and elsewhere, and provides general information. It's the official port agent for Limenas Mesta, and can arrange boat tickets and advance accommodation for those visiting Psara.

SLEEPING & EATING

Masticulture Ecotourism Activities can arrange rooms, or else ask in the adjacent Mesaonas restaurant for the proprietors listed below.

Anna Floradis Rooms (☎ /fax 22710 76455; floradis@ internet.gr; s/d €40/50; ✷) The friendly Anna Floradis, who speaks French and some English, has rooms, studios and self-catering suites throughout Mesta, all with TV and air-con.

Dhimitris Pipidhis Rooms (☎ 22710 76029; house €60; ✷) The friendly, English-speaking Dhimitris and Koula Pipidhis rent two traditional houses in Mesta. Each has two bedrooms, a *pounti* (the traditional small

Mesta house atrium), kitchen and washing machine. Book ahead in summer.

Mesta Medieval Castle Suites (☎ 22710 76345; www.medievalcastlesuites.com; d/tr incl breakfast €94/117; ✷ 🖳) These luxury suites for the discerning, spread throughout Mesta, seem to blend in seamlessly with the neighbouring houses. Open the door, however, and you have ultrachic rooms with all modern amenities, including flat-screen TVs and laptops; the only thing lacking, perhaps, is a bathtub. Decor is minimalist and obeys the contours of the space. The helpful staff can retrieve guests from the ferry or airport.

our pick Mesaonas (☎ 22710 76050; Plateia Taxiarhon; mains €5-10) With tables spread across Plateia Taxiarhon, this venerable old favourite appeals to locals and tourists alike, and serves hearty portions of *mayirefta* and grills. Everything is local, right down to the *souma* (mastic-flavoured firewater). Order the mixed meat plate to share, but be sure to get the incredibly delicious beef *keftedhes* (rissoles) before they're all gone.

Limani Meston (☎ 22710 76389; Limenas Mesta; fish €6-12) For excellent and unique seafood dishes, try this waterfront fish taverna. The *astakomakaronadha* and special *atherinopita* (small fried fish with onions) are both recommended. Remarkably, it even does fresh breakfast-time *tyropita* (cheese pie) and *bougatsa* (creamy semolina pudding wrapped in a pastry envelope and baked) if you're waiting for the ferry to Psara.

GETTING AROUND

Mesta is a walking-only town; excepting the regular buses to Chios town, it can be hard to see other major sites from here. Fortunately, the friendly, English-speaking **Dimitris Kokkinos** (☎ 6972543543) provides taxi services to major destinations. Sample fares from Mesta: Limenas Mesta €6; Pyrgi €11; Olympi €20; Vessa €23; Kampos €30; Chios Town €35.

Around Mesta

Mesta's west-coast port, **Limenas Mesta** (also called Limenas Meston), is a pretty harbour of colourful fishing boats and tavernas, with nearby pebble beaches, the best being **Avlonia Beach** (7.3km west of Mesta).

Some 3km southeast of Mesta is **Olympi** – like Mesta and Pyrgi, a mastic-producing village characterised by its defensive architecture.

Continue 5km south to the splendid **Cave of Sykia** (admission incl tour €4; ☉ 10am-8pm Tue-Sun), a 150-million-year-old cavern discovered accidentally in 1985. Some 57m deep, the cave's filled with weird, multicoloured stalactites and other rock formations, shaped like giant white organs and phantasms. Selectively lit by floodlights and connected by a series of platforms with handrails, the cave is safe, though somewhat slippery. With its marvellous lighting and colours, the cave could be the set for some adventure movie: think Indiana Jones. Guided tours run every 30 minutes, the last at 7.30pm.

The good dirt road south from here passes a little-used military range, as the signs (unhelpfully, Greek-only) warn. Although there's no danger, this is not a place for random hiking; stick to the road. After 2km the road ends at a small church overlooking **Agia Dynami Beach**, a curving, sandy cove where the water is a stunning combination of blues and greens, flecked with white wavelets. The beach is completely pristine and undeveloped, and you're likely to have it to yourself.

INOUSSES ΟΙΝΟΥΣΣΕΣ

pop 1050 / area 14 sq km

Just northwest of Chios, placid Inousses is ancestral home to about one-third of Greece's shipping barons (the so-called *arhontes*), whose wealthy descendents return here annually for summer vacations from their homes in London, Paris or New York. Inousses was settled in 1750 by ship-owning families from Kardamyla in northeastern Chios, and some amassed huge fortunes during the 19th and early 20th centuries; lingering traces of this history are visible in Inousses' grand mansions and ornate family mausoleums high above the sea.

Although Inousses is little-visited by foreign tourists, it does get a bit lively in high season, with an open-air cinema, cafes and night-time beach parties. Nevertheless, it has retained its serenity and remains an escapist destination, with only one hotel and a few rooms and villas for rent.

The island's port and only town, also called Inousses, attests to its seafaring identity. Arriving by ferry, you'll see a small and green sculpted mermaid watching over the harbour – the Mother of Inoussa (Mitera

Inoussiotissa), protector of mariners. And, along with the port village's white stone houses crowned by two churches, Inousses boasts a well-disciplined merchant marine academy and an eclectic museum of model ships, bequeathed by a former shipping baron. Refreshingly, the placid waterfront is lined by colourful boats where the plaintive cry of seagulls, and not domatia owners hawking rooms, greets arriving visitors.

Orientation & Information

Disembarking from the ferry, walk left along the waterfront and turn right to the *plateia*, site of the tavernas, museum and services. Further along the waterfront are cafes and, above them, a small church. A post office and National Bank of Greece stand adjacent, around the corner from the Nautical Museum. However, there's no ATM; locals explain that having one would make one of the bank's two workers redundant.

Doctor (☎ 22710 55300)

Dimarhio (Town Hall; ☎ 22710 55326) Local officials keep lists of available domatia and can phone them for you.

Police (☎ 22710 55222) Just above Hotel Thalassoporos.

Post office (☎ 22710 55398; ☉ 9.30am-2pm Mon-Fri)

Sights & Activities

Inousses has numerous hill-walking opportunities and untouched beaches. There's no tourist information, so enquire at the *dimarhio* (town hall) or the helpful Hotel Thalassoporos.

Bilali Beach, 2km from town, is the best nearby beach, with summer night parties. Also, a summertime **open-air cinema** (tickets €4) near the central waterfront brings Hollywood hits to Inousses, nightly at 9.30pm.

The fascinating **Nautical Museum** (☎ 22710 44139; Stefanou Tsouri 20; admission €1.50; ☉ 10am-1pm Mon-Fri) celebrates Inousses' seafaring past. To create it, local shipping magnate Antonis Lemos donated his priceless collection of model ships, which include early 20th-century commercial ships, whaling ships made of ivory and whalebone, and ivory models of French prisoner-of-war vessels from the Napoleonic Wars. However, the museum is more eclectic; along with these models (accompanied by vintage maritime paintings by eminent painter Aristeides Glykas), there's a swashbuckling collection of 18th-century muskets and sabres, a WWII-era US Navy diving helmet, a hand-cranked lighthouse made in 1864, antiquarian maps of Greece and (of

NORTHEASTERN AEGEAN ISLANDS

course) a 6th-century-BC stone scarab seal, and various Bronze Age antiquities.

In true Greek style, the museum is timed to close just before the afternoon ferry from Chios arrives and to open after the morning boat back to Chios has left. Therefore you may have to stay for two nights just to see it, unless you can get someone to open it out of hours (Eleni at Hotel Thalassoporos can sometimes help).

To experience the significance of Inousses' heritage, walk 10 minutes up the hill from the museum to the **Church of Agia Paraskevi**; in its leafy courtyard above the sea stands the **Mausoleum of Inousses** (Nekrotafion Inousson), where the island's ship-owning dynasties have endowed the tombs of their greats with huge chambers, marble sculptures and miniature churches. It's a melancholy, moving place, and speaks volumes about the worldly achievements and self-perception of the extraordinary natives of these tiny islands.

Sleeping

Ask at the *dimarhio* about private rooms.

Hotel Thalassoporos (☎ 22720 51475; s/d incl breakfast €40/50; ✖ ⌨) This recently revitalised old hotel has clean, simple rooms with TV, fridge and small balconies, plus views of Inousses town's rooftops and the waterfront. Co-owner Eleni can provide general information, and help arrange house rental elsewhere on Inousses. The hotel is a three-minute walk up a steep street on the ferry-dock side of the waterfront.

Eating & Drinking

Inomageireio To Pateroniso (☎ 22720 55586; mains €5-8) This whimsical taverna near the *plateia* serves Greek standbys and fresh fish, like the heads-and-all fry-up of *atherinia* (minnows) and onions.

Naftikos Omilos Inousson (☎ 22720 55596; ✆ 9am-3am) At the waterfront's east end, the Inousses Yacht Club's long bar and outdoor patio are filled mostly with young Greeks (and their vacationing diaspora relatives), and pop music plays till late.

Getting There & Away

The little *Oinoussai III* (€4 one way, 1¼ hours, one daily) usually leaves from Inousses in the afternoon and returns in the morning (from Chios), warranting overnight stays. Purchase tickets on board,

or from **Sunrise Tours** (☎ 22710 41390; Kanari 28) in Chios Town. There are twice-weekly summertime day excursions (€20), again with Sunrise Tours.

Daily **water taxis** (☎ 6944168104) travel to/from Langada on Chios. The one-way fare is €35, split between passengers. Comparably priced water taxis serve Chios Town, too.

Getting Around

Inousses has neither buses nor car hire; ask around for its one taxi.

PSARA ΨΑΡΑ

pop 420 / area 45 sq km

Celebrated Psara (psah-*rah*), accompanied by its satellite islet of Antipsara, is one of maritime Greece's true oddities. A tiny speck in the sea two hours northwest of Chios, this island of scrub vegetation, wandering goats and weird red rock formations has one settlement (also called Psara), a remote monastery and pristine beaches. However, it's visited mostly by diaspora Greeks and thus remains something of an unknown commodity for foreign travellers. Nevertheless, it's easily accessible from Chios, and decent accommodation and eating options exist. Free camping on remote beaches is tolerated too (if you can get there).

For an island its size, Psara looms inordinately large in modern lore. The Psariot clans (once owners of around 4000 vessels) became wealthy through shipping, and participated in

PSARA

0 ___ 2 km
0 ___ 1 miles

Moni Kimisis Theotokou
▲ (546m)

Aegean Sea

Tourlia Beach

Agios Dimitrios Beach

Psara

Psara

Katsounis Beach

Kavos Beach

Antipsara

Psara

Kato Gialos Beach

Cape Agios Georgios

To Limnos (20km); Chios Town (80km)

the 1821–29 War of Independence. However, as in Chios, their involvement sparked a brutal Ottoman reprisal that depopulated the island in 1824 (it's still commemorated each year). Decades would pass before Psara recovered.

In the late 19th and early 20th centuries, many Psariots put their sailing and fishing skills to use on the high seas, some settling eventually in America and other foreign lands. Their descendents still return every summer, so don't be surprised if the first person you meet speaks English with a Brooklyn accent.

Orientation & Information

Psara town is tucked within a long bay on the island's southwest. When you disembark the ferry, straight on is the jagged hill from which the Psariot women and children are said to have hurled themselves during the 1824 Ottoman assault. Right of this hill, a beach with some accommodation and tavernas lies across the water. The central waterfront, stretched out across the bay, has cafes, shops and restaurants. Beyond the harbour's far side lies Katsounis Beach, with another restaurant.

Behind the waterfront, the small streets conceal houses, two churches and a monument to national hero Konstantine Kanaris (see the boxed text, below), the post office and a National Bank of Greece with ATM. There's an island **doctor** (☎ 22740 61277) and **police** (☎ 22740 61222) for emergencies, and plenty of hearty sailors. The road towards the **Moni Kimisis Theotoukou** (12km), and other beaches, is signposted.

Tourist information is scarce, and neither car nor motorbike hire existed at the time of writing (though this may change). In Chios, for general information, ferry tickets and accommodation, contact Masticulture Ecotourism Activities (p611) in Mesta, which is also the port agent for boats from Limenas Mesta to Psara. If on Psara, track down the helpful Diane Kantakouzenou at Psara Travel on the central waterfront. In any case, the presence of Greek-Americans in summer and the long foreign experience of Psariot sailors means you'll find English speakers to assist you.

Throughout town, you will notice Psara's memorable red-and-white flag waving proudly in the breeze. Emblazoned with the revolutionary slogan *Eleftheria i Thanatos* (Freedom or Death), it features a red cross at its centre, with an upturned spear jutting from one side, while on the other is an anchor apparently impaling a green snake; as if the reference to the Islamic

---

THE ADMIRABLE ADMIRAL OF PSARA

The fact that one of modern Greece's greatest heroes was born on tiny Psara might seem odd to visitors today, but it in fact speaks volumes about the bygone power and prestige of this proud, seafaring island.

One of the dominant figures of 19th-century Greek military and political affairs, **Konstantine Kanaris** (1793–1877) played a leading role in the fight to liberate Greece from the Ottoman Empire during the 1821–29 War of Independence; the heroic stature thus acquired propelled him, six times, to the position of prime minister, before his death at the age of 84.

Orphaned at an early age, Kanaris (like many of his fellow Psariots) turned to the sea. Working on an uncle's brig, he acquired sailing skills that would prove handy when Psara affirmed its readiness for revolution on 10 April 1821. The islanders turned their vast commercial sailing fleet into a veritable navy. Under leaders like Kanaris, the Psariots proved a force to be reckoned with, mounting several successful attacks on Turkish warships.

Kanaris quickly become known for a fearlessness that bordered on the suicidal. While shepherding small boats laden with explosives towards Turkish warships, he would allegedly murmur to himself, 'Konstanti, you are going to die.'

One of Kanaris' most famous operations occurred on the night of 6 June 1822. In revenge for Turkish massacres on Chios, the Psariots destroyed Turkish admiral Nasuhzade Ali Pasha's flagship while the unsuspecting enemy was holding a post-massacre celebration. Kanaris' forces detonated the powder keg of the Ottoman ship, blowing up 2000 sailors and the admiral himself. Through 1824 Kanaris led three more high-profile attacks against the Sultan that significantly affected the Turks' abilities to quell the Greek insurrection elsewhere. However, this success would come at

rule of the Turks wasn't apparent enough, there's an upside-down crescent moon and star under these items for good measure. The yellow dove of freedom flutters to one side.

Sights & Activities

The **Monastery of Kimisis Theotokou** (Monastery of the Dormition of the Virgin), 12km north of town, is Psara's main cultural attraction. Unless you find a lift, it's a two-hour walk past the rolling hills, scrubland and weird red rocks that comprise the island's topography. You may see only goats and beehives (Psara is famous for its invigorating thyme honey) on the way, so check ahead to be sure the monastery will be open.

Psara allegedly has 65 other churches (most, family-maintained chapels). In town, the **Church of Metamorfosi tou Sotiris** (Church of the Metamorphosis of the Saviour) is a five-minute walk inland from the waterfront. This grand, white-and-blue structure built around 1770 is richly decorated with icons. Since renovation work is ongoing, it's not always open. Just before it to the left is a small park containing the **Monument to Konstantine Kanaris**, where Greeks pay their respects to this national hero, who's actually buried in Athens (though his heart is apparently kept in the Naval Museum in Piraeus).

Hill walking is possible – just pick a direction, and you'll find yourself alone in nature. However, since Psara lacks trees, there's no shade.

Several pristine pebble-and-sand beaches stretch along Psara's jagged edges. The closest (except for the two town beaches) from town are the west-coast **Agios Dimitrios Beach** and **Tourlia Beach**. There's good swimming in similarly clear waters at **Kato Gialos Beach** (opposite the cliff, beneath Restaurant Ilionas Ilema) and the more secluded **Kavos Beach**, beyond the harbour's far side.

If in Psara on the last Sunday in June, attend the **religious commemoration** of the 1824 Ottoman massacre. It occurs on the jagged hill opposite the port, and is followed by folk dancing and other cultural activities in town.

Sleeping

Psara Town has domatia and even hotels; just show up, or arrange from Chios with Masticulture Ecotourism Activities (p611) in Mesta. Escapists can enjoy free camping on remote beaches (providing you can get there and can bring your own supplies).

Domatia Fotis Xaxoulis (☎ 22740 61180; studios from €40) Cheery islander Fotis rents 15 well-equipped studio apartments in town, lined by palms.

a heavy price for the Psariots. Determined to crush the islanders' revolt, Sultan Mahmud II was forced to entreat the powerful, semi-independent Ottoman viceroy Mohammad Ali (1769–1849) in Kavala. Together with his son, Ibrahim Pasha, Mohammad Ali commanded a personal army and navy of 100,000 men, many Egyptian. (He also enlisted French mercenary sailors left jobless after Napoleon's defeat.) To win the wily Ali's support against the Greeks, Mahmud II was forced to reward him with the very auspicious headship of Crete. It was the beginning of the end for the Ottomans' central control over their increasingly fractious empire.

The Turkish-Egyptian fleet proved just as ruthless as the Sultan had been promised. When Psara was captured on 21 June 1824 thousands who had failed to escape were butchered or sold into slavery; island lore recounts that women and children flung themselves from a craggy cliff (visible when arriving at Psara port) rather than suffer such an ignominious fate.

Despite the tragic destruction of his island, Kanaris continued to successfully harass the Turks. Still, it took the combined forces of Britain, Russia and France to completely destroy the Ottoman navy, at the Battle of Navarino off the Peloponnese on 20 October 1827.

After Greece was liberated, Konstantine Kanaris became an admiral in the new navy. Upon retiring from duty, he went into politics and was a high-ranking minister in various governments before serving briefly as prime minister in 1844, a post he held another five times. He didn't live to see Psara itself liberated (during the First Balkan War, in 1912).

The admirable admiral of Psara has been honoured frequently by the Greek Navy. Since 1941 several destroyers have been named after him. British and American naval vessels have also been transferred to Greece, and graced with Kanaris' name. The most recent reminder of this maritime legend arrived in 2002, in the form of a pretty kick-ass frigate, the FFG *Kanaris*.

Kato Gialos Apartments (☎ 22740 61178, 6945755321; s/d/apt 40/50/70) Just up from Restaurant Ilionas Ilema, Spiros Giannakis rents out clean, bright rooms and self-catering apartments overlooking Kato Gialos Beach.

Eating & Drinking

Udrohoos (☎ 22740 61182; waterfront; ☻ 8am-midnight) Right on the waterfront, this old cafe also does light breakfasts.

Kafe-Bar Baka Marianna (☎ 22740 61295; waterfront; ☻ 7am-1am) This whimsical *kafeneio* with tables just above the bobbing caïques of Psara is a relaxing place for a Greek coffee or espresso.

Restaurant Ilionas Ilema (☎ 22740 61121; mains €5-8; Kato Gialos Beach; ☻ 6am-2am) Excellent island specialities like stuffed goat and octopus with aubergines are served at this friendly restaurant with tables overlooking Kato Gialos Beach.

Spitalia (Katsounis Beach; mains €5-9; ☻ 9am-1am) Formerly an Ottoman hospital, this restaurant on Katsounis Beach, beyond the far side of the waterfront, is atmospheric and serves nourishing Greek dishes.

Ta Delfinia (☎ 22740 61352; fish €7-12; ☻ 6am-1am) With a proud 20-year tradition behind him, Manolis Thirianos offers some of Psara's best seafood at this *psarotaverna* (fish taverna) on the central waterfront.

ourpick **Petrino** (waterfront; ☻ 7pm-late) This handsomely restored, wood-and-stone bar on the harbour's far side has become Psara's hotspot for young people. Petrino's waterfront terrace is nice for an evening coffee, and on summer nights it gets packed with local and visiting partiers.

Getting There & Away

For ferry information, see Island Hopping (p759). Get tickets from the port agent of Limenas Mesta in Chios, Masticulture Ecotourism Activities (p611). Chios Town travel agencies can also provide tickets for boats departing from there.

Getting Around

Good luck! With neither car nor motorbike hire offered at the time of writing, you'll have to walk, unless you can enlist an islander to give you a lift. While hitchhiking is generally safe, don't count on it, as Psara's remote back roads see little traffic.

LESVOS (MYTILINI)
ΛΕΣΒΟΣ (ΜΥΤΙΛΗΝΗ)

pop 93,430 / area 1637 sq km

Greece's third-largest island, after Crete and Evia, Lesvos (Mytilini) is also one of its most breathtaking, marked by constantly changing landscapes. Long sweeps of rugged, desert-like western plains give way to sandy beaches and salt marshes in the elliptical centre, leading to thickly forested mountains and dense olive groves (some 11 million olive trees are cultivated here) further east. The island's port and capital, Mytilini Town, is a fun-loving place filled with exemplary *ouzeries*, dynamic nightlife and good accommodation, while the north-coast town of Mythimna (also called Molyvos) is an aesthetic treat, with old stone houses clustered on winding lanes overlooking the sea. Lesvos' must-see cultural attractions range from modern art museums to Byzantine monasteries.

Despite its undeniable tourist appeal, hard-working Lesvos makes its livelihood firstly from agriculture. Olive oil is a highly regarded local product, as is ouzo; indeed, the island's farmers produce around half of the aniseed-flavoured national firewater sold worldwide, and its wines are also well known.

Nature lovers will be richly rewarded here, with endless opportunities for hiking and cycling, while birdwatching is another major draw (over 279 species, ranging from raptors to waders, are seen here). Lesvos also boasts therapeutic hot springs that gush with some of the warmest mineral waters in Europe.

Lesvos' great cultural legacy stretches from the 7th-century-BC musical composer Terpander and poet Arion to 20th-century figures like Nobel Prize–winning poet Odysseus Elytis and primitive painter Theofilos. The great ancient philosophers Aristotle and Epicurus also led an exceptional philosophical academy here. Most famous, however, is Sappho, one of ancient Greece's greatest poets. Her sensuous, passionate poetry, apparently created for her female devotees, has fuelled a modern-day cult that draws lesbians from around the world to Skala Eresou, the west Lesvos beach village where she was born (c 630 BC).

The largest of the northeastern Aegean islands, Lesvos is also the one that has the most

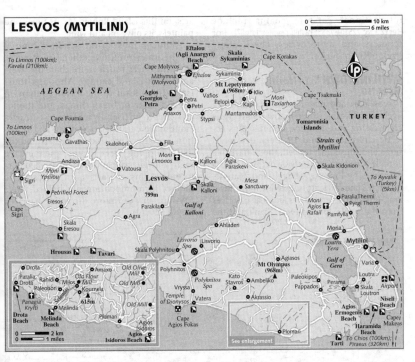

LESVOS (MYTILINI)

life year-round, chiefly thanks to its young university population, size and economic importance. It's the only island in the chain that feels somewhat lively out of high season, though this action is almost entirely to be found in the capital, Mytilini Town.

Getting There & Away

For flights and ferries from Lesvos, see Island Hopping (p755).

AIR

The airport is 8km south of Mytilini Town; a taxi costs €8.

Olympic Air (☎ 22510 28659; www.olympicairlines .com; Kavetsou 44) and **Aegean Airlines** (☎ 22510 61120; www.aegeanair.com) have offices in Mytilini Town and the airport, respectively. Mytilini Town travel agents sell tickets too.

BOAT

For information on trips to Turkey, see the boxed text, Turkish Connections (p596).

In Mytilini Town, ferry ticket offices on Pavlou Kountourioti's eastern side include Zoumboulis Tours (p619), **Samiotis Tours** (☎ 22510 42574; Pavlou Kountourioti 43) and Olive Groove Travel (p619), which also offers Turkey excursions.

Getting Around

BUS

From Mytilini's **long-distance bus station** (☎ 22510 28873; El Venizelou), near Agias Irinis Park, three daily buses serve Skala Eresou (€8.90, 2½ hours) via Eresos; four serve Mithymna (Molyvos; €6.20, 1¾ hours) via Petra (€5.80, 1½ hours); and two reach Sigri (€9.40, 2½ hours). Five daily buses serve Plomari (€4.10, 1¼ hours), five serve Agiasos (€2.60, 45 minutes) and four end at Vatera (€5.60, 1½ hours), the latter via Polyhnitos. Travelling between these smaller places often requires changing in Kalloni, which receives four daily buses from Mytilini (€4.10, one hour). Also, five daily buses go north from Mytilini town to Moni Taxiarhon (€3.80, one hour).

CAR & MOTORCYCLE

Discover Rent-a-Car (☎ 6936057676; Venezi 3; ⏱ 7:30am-1am) is a small local outfit, with good new cars and flexible service. Mytilini's international car-hire chains include **Hertz** (☎ 22510 37355; Pavlou Kountourioti 87). For scooters and motorcycles, check along Pavlou Kountourioti.

MYTILINI TOWN ΜΥΤΙΛΗΝΗ
pop 27,250

Lesvos' port and major town, Mytilini, is a lively and likeable student town with some great eating and drinking options, plus eclectic churches, grand 19th-century mansions and museums; indeed, the remarkable Teriade Museum, just outside of town, boasts paintings by Picasso, Chagall and Matisse. Mytilini's laid-back attitude to life may reflect long-term leftist tendencies, but it also derives from the locals' love of food, drink and the arts, on this island known for its poets and painters, its olive oil and wine.

Although most of the action is centred on the waterfront, like other Greek ports, Mytilini offers much more than the average Greek island capital. Although tourism is significant to the local economy, it doesn't make or break things, and the locals tend to be friendly and down-to-earth. Handmade ceramics, jewellery and traditional products are sold on and around the main shopping street, Ermou, and there are many fine *ouzeries* and student-fuelled bars to enjoy. Plus, the arrival of atmospheric budget accommodation has helped make Mytilini an even more attractive base for island adventures.

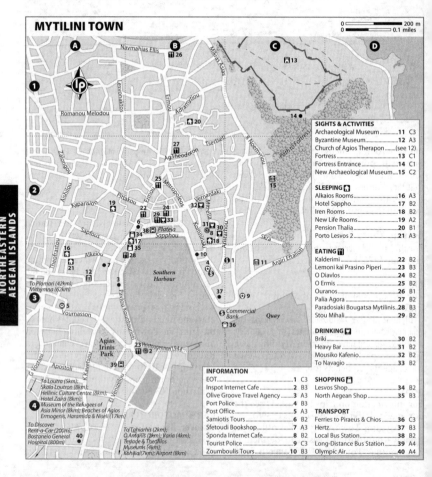

MYTILINI TOWN

0 ──────── 200 m
0 ──────── 0.1 miles

SIGHTS & ACTIVITIES	
Archaeological Museum	**11** C3
Byzantine Museum	**12** A3
Church of Agios Therapon	(see 12)
Fortress	**13** C1
Fortress Entrance	**14** C1
New Archaeological Museum	**15** C2

SLEEPING	
Alkaios Rooms	**16** A3
Hotel Sappho	**17** B2
Iren Rooms	**18** B2
New Life Rooms	**19** A2
Pension Thalia	**20** B1
Porto Lesvos 2	**21** A3

EATING	
Kalderimi	**22** B2
Lemoni kai Prasino Piperi	**23** B3
O Diavlos	**24** B2
O Ermis	**25** B2
Ouranos	**26** B1
Palia Agora	**27** B2
Paradosiaki Bougatsa Mytilinis	**28** B3
Stou Mihali	**29** B2

DRINKING	
Briki	**30** B2
Heavy Bar	**31** B2
Mousiko Kafenio	**32** B2
To Navagio	**33** B2

SHOPPING	
Lesvos Shop	**34** B2
North Aegean Shop	**35** B3

TRANSPORT	
Ferries to Piraeus & Chios	**36** C3
Hertz	**37** B3
Local Bus Station	**38** B2
Long-Distance Bus Station	**39** A4
Olympic Air	**40** A4

INFORMATION	
EOT	**1** C3
Inspot Internet Cafe	**2** B3
Olive Groove Travel Agency	**3** A3
Port Police	**4** B3
Post Office	**5** A3
Samiotis Tours	**6** B2
Sfetoudi Bookshop	**7** A3
Sponda Internet Cafe	**8** B2
Tourist Police	**9** C3
Zoumboulis Tours	**10** B3

Navmahias Ellis
Lesvonaktos
Ermou
Adramytiou
Romanou Melodou
Tsetseti
8 Noemvriou
Ag.Theodoron
Zaloggou
Aishliou
Pittakou
Kyparisiou
Mitropoleos
Vernardaki
Sapfous
Theofrastou
Alkeiou
Mitrelia
Komninaki
Kornarou
Skra
Argin Eftaliou
Southern Harbour
Plateia Sapphou
To Plomari (42km);
Mithymna (62km)
Vournasson
Pavlou Kountourioti
Commercial Bank
Quay
Agias Irinis Park
Apostoli
Glostani
K Xavelsou
Vellestou
Hrinougennon 1944
To Loutra (5km);
Skala Loutron (8km);
Hellinic Culture Centre (8km);
Hotel Zaira (8km);
Museum of the Refugees of Asia Minor (8km); Beaches of Agios Ermogenis, Haramida & Niseli (17km)
To Discover Rent-a-Car (200m);
Bostaneio General Hospital (800m)
To Tahiarhis (2km);
O. Antoniis (3km); Varia (4km);
Teriade & Theofilos Museums (4km);
Kohlia (7km); Airport (8km)
Path to Fortress

Orientation

Ferries dock at the northern end of Mytilini's long and curving waterfront thoroughfare, Pavlou Kountourioti. Further along it is Plateia Sapphou (where a statue of Sappho stands), with nearby restaurants, cafes and hotels. The shopping street, Ermou, links this southern harbour with the disused, ancient northern port. East of the harbours, a large mediaeval fortress stands surrounded by pines.

The long-distance bus station is beside Agias Irinis Park and the local bus station is on Pavlou Kountourioti, near Plateia Sapphou. The airport is 8km south on the coast road.

Information

BOOKSHOPS

Sfetoudi Bookshop (☎ 22510 22287; Ermou 51) Sells good maps from Greece's leading Road Editions series and books on Lesvos.

EMERGENCY

Port police (☎ 22510 28827)
Tourist police (☎ 22510 22776) On the quay.

INTERNET ACCESS

InSpot (☎ 22510 45760; Hristougennon 1944 12; per hr €2.40)
Sponda Internet Café (☎ 22510 41007; 29-33 Komninaki; 10am-1am) Near Iren Rooms.

INTERNET RESOURCES

www.lesvos.com Online information on Lesvos.

MEDICAL SERVICES

Bostaneio General Hospital (☎ 22510 57700; E Vostani 48)

MONEY

Numerous banks equipped with ATMs line Pavlou Kountourioti.

POST

Post office (Vournasson)

TOURIST INFORMATION

EOT (☎ 22510 42512; Aristarhou 6; ☽ 9am-1pm Mon-Fri)
Port authority (☎ 22510 40827)

TRAVEL AGENCIES

Olive Groove Travel (☎ 22510 37533; www.olive -groove.gr; 11 Pavlou Kountourioti; 7.30am-10pm)

Friendly, all-purpose travel agency on the central waterfront; sells tickets for ferries and boat trips to Turkey.
Zoumboulis Tours (☎ 22510 37755; Pavlou Kountourioti 69) Sells ferry and plane tickets, runs boat trips to Turkey and rents rooms.

Sights & Activities

Mytilini's imposing early Byzantine **fortress** (adult/student €2/1; ☽ 8am-2.30pm Tue-Sun) was renovated in the 14th century by Genoese overlord Francisco Gatelouzo. The Turks enlarged it again. It's popular for a stroll and is flanked by pine forests.

The **archaeological museum** (☎ 22510 28032; adult/child €3/2; ☽ 8.30am-3pm Tue-Sun), one block north of the quay, has impressive finds from Neolithic to Roman times, including ceramic somersaulting female figurines and gold jewellery. The ticket grants entry to the **new archaeological museum** (8 Noemvriou; ☽ 8am-7.30pm), 400m away, which portrays island life from the 2nd century BC to the 3rd century AD, including spectacular floor mosaics under glass.

The bulbous dome of the **Church of Agios Therapon** crowns Mytilini's skyline. The church's ornate interior boasts a huge chandelier, an intricately carved iconostasis, a priest's throne and a frescoed dome. The **Byzantine Museum** (☎ 22510 28916; admission €2; ☽ 9am-1pm Mon-Sat) in its courtyard boasts valuable icons.

TERIADE & THEOPHILOS MUSEUMS

From Pavlou Kountourioti's northernmost section, take a local bus 4km south to **Varia**, unlikely host of the **Teriade Museum** (☎ 22510 23372; adult/student €2/1; ☽ 8.30am-2pm, 5pm-8pm Tue-Sun), with its astonishing collection of paintings by world-renowned artists like Picasso, Chagall, Miro, Le Corbusier and Matisse.

The museum honours the Lesvos-born artist and critic Stratis Eleftheriadis, who Gallicised his name to Teriade in Paris. Significantly, Teriade brought the work of primitive painter and fellow Lesvos native Theophilos to international attention.

The **Theophilos Museum** (☎ 22510 41644; admission €2; ☽ 9am-1pm & 4.30-8pm), located next door, houses works commissioned by Teriade; several prestigious Greek museums and galleries display other, more famous paintings by Theophilos, whose story followed the old pattern of many a great artist – living in abject poverty, painting coffee-house walls for his daily bread and eventually dying in the gutter.

NORTHEASTERN
AEGEAN ISLANDS

Sleeping

BUDGET

ourpick **Alkaios Rooms** (☎ 22510 47737, 6945507089; www.alkaiosrooms.gr; Alkaiou 16 & 30; s/d/tr €30/40/50; ⊠) This collection of 30 clean, well-kept rooms nestled discreetly in several renovated traditional buildings is Mytilini's most attractive budget option. It's a two-minute walk up from Paradosiaka Bougatsa Mytilinis (below) on the waterfront.

Iren Rooms (☎ 22510 22787; cnr Komninaki & Imvrou; s/d/tr €40/50/60; ⊠) Friendly Iren has reasonably priced rooms of a good standard, though most don't have the ambience of sister establishment Alkaios Rooms. However, it's a closer walk if coming from the ferry dock, and next to an internet cafe.

New Life Rooms (☎ 22510 23400, 6947365944; Ermou 68; s/d/tr €35/50/70) New Life has bright and well-furnished rooms, a new outdoor bar and a quiet setting on a central side street. There's not always someone there, so call ahead.

MIDRANGE

Hotel Sappho (☎ 22510 22888; sappho@microchip.gr; Pavlou Kountourioti 31; s/d/tr €45/60/70; ⊠) This perfunctory place on the central waterfront frequently fills up because of its position. Despite being dated, it has the necessary amenities and, fortunately for late-night ferry arrivals, 24-hour reception.

Porto Lesvos Hotel (☎ 22510 41771; www.porto lesvos.gr; Komninaki 21; s/d/tr incl breakfast €50/60/70; ⊠ ▣) and **Porto Lesvos Hotel 2** (☎ 22510 21217; www.portlesvos.gr; Alkaiou 15; s/d/tr €50/60/70; ⊠ ▣) are central sister hotels, which aspire to a slightly higher standard (as witnessed by the complimentary toiletries, bathrobe and slippers). The hotels have all mod cons, though rooms are a tad snug for the price.

Eating

Paradosiaka Bougatsa Mytilinis (22510 26918; Kountouriotou 19; bougatsa €2; ⊗ Mon-Sat) Whether you're stumbling off an early-morning ferry or out for a breakfast stroll, this busy waterfront place has Mytilini's very best sweet *bougatsa*, plus various coffees.

O Diavlos (☎ 22510 22020; Ladakia 30; mezedhes €3-6) This central *ouzerie* has excellent ambience, set inside a lofty, wood-beamed building, with (purchasable) artwork lining the walls. Laid-back owner Panayiotis Molyviatis serves up unique and tasty mezedhes, like *giouslemes* (a crunchy cheese pie) and *sfongatoa* (a sort

of oven-baked cake made of zucchini, egg, onion and cheese). Also try the Turkish-flavoured beef kebabs on pitta bread with onions and *yiaourtlou kebab* (Greek yoghurt). Music ranges from relaxed to *rembetika* (Greek blues).

Ouranos (☎ 22510 47844; Navmahias Ellis; mezedhes €3-6) A popular *ouzerie* that looks across at Turkey from a breezy patio on the ancient northern port. Tempting mezedhes include *kolokythoanthi* (fried pumpkin flowers stuffed with rice), *ladotyri mytilinis* (the oil-drenched local cheese) and hefty servings of *kalamari*.

Stou Mihali (☎ 22510 43311; Ikarias 7, Plateia Sapphou; mains €3.50-5; ⊗ 9am-9pm) If you're after good *mayirefta* at a good price, this is the place. Unlike many other such eateries, here you can combine half-portions and thus enjoy more variety. Try the *soutzoukakia* (tomato-soaked beef rissoles), *imam baïldi* (roast eggplant with herbs) and Greek salad.

Palia Agora (☎ 22510 91118; cnr Agion Theodoron & Ermou; mains €4-6; ⊗ 8am-1am) This appealing place, usually playing old *rembetika* music, is a good and inexpensive choice for fish dishes and mezedhes. The decor is authentic, the service friendly.

ourpick **O Ermis** (☎ 22510 26232; cnr Kornarou & Ermou; mezedhes €5-8) This friendly, family-run restaurant with outdoor seating serves very tasty salads and mezedhes in portions that seem small at first, but are in the end just right. It began life in 1800 as a Turkish cafe, and the intriguing traditional decor within reveals bits and pieces of its long history since. Good Macedonian and Limnos wines are offered, and the brown bread is warm and fresh.

Lemoni kai Prasino Piperi (☎ 22510 42678; cnr Pavlou Kountourioti & Hristougennon 1944; mains €10-15; ⊗ 7pm-1am) The poshest place in town, this upstairs restaurant has great waterfront views and even better food, especially the Italian dishes. Try the simple yet exquisite tomato and mozzarella salad or *tagliatelle amatriciana* (spicy tomato and bacon sauce) or *tagliatelle alfredo* (cream cheese and parmesan sauce with garlic) with salmon.

Drinking

Mytilini's loud waterfront cafes are inevitably busy, though the best watering holes are found in the backstreets.

ourpick **Mousiko Kafenio** (cnr Mitropoleos & Vernardaki; ⊗ 7.30am-2am) Even if the stairs are no longer strong enough to allow you to sit upstairs in this old student favourite, the eclectic paintings, mirrors and well-worn wooden fixtures foster a relaxed, arty vibe, making it one of the most fun places in town.

To Navagio (☎ 22510 21310; Arhipelagous 23) A popular cafe-bar on Plateia Sapphou with comfy couches, perfect for a leisurely backgammon game and coffee.

Briki (cnr Hiou & Mitrelia; ☼ 8am-3am) This cool new hole-in-the-wall bar plays jazz, funk and ambient sounds, and has occasional art exhibits.

Heavy Bar (☎ 6945605383; cnr Mitrelia & Ladadika; ☼ 9pm-3am) Rock on! Mytilini's long-haired hard-rock bar is probably the only place on Lesvos where you'll find someone wearing a jean jacket in high summer. The elevated video screen means you can not only hear, but also see Axl Rose, Angus Young and Co.

Shopping

Lesvos Shop (☎ 22510 26088; Pavlou Kountourioti 33) This waterfront shop near the Hotel Sappho sells local natural products, from ouzos, olive oil and soap, to jams, handmade ceramics, wine and cheese. Proceeds benefit the municipality.

North Aegean Shop (☎ 22510 26918; Pavlou Kountourioti 21) Next to Paradosiaka Bougatsa Mytilinis, the shop sells traditional products like Greek sweets, with unusual varieties involving watermelon, olive and nuts.

Getting There & Away

Mytilini's **local bus station** (Pavlou Kountourioti), near Plateia Sapphou, serves in-town destinations and nearby Loutra, Skala Loutron and Tahiarhis. All other buses depart from the **long-distance bus station** (☎ 22510 28873; El Venizelou) near Agias Irinis Park.

SOUTH OF MYTILINI

The small, olive-groved peninsula south of Mytilini has several unique attractions. Following the coast road 7km south, opposite the airport, you'll find a long pebble beach hosting the decadent beach bar, **Kohilia** (☎ 6978773203; ☼ 8am-3am). Pulsating with house and techno music, and frequented by swimsuited students lounging on colourful couches and four-poster beds, Kohilia is a chilled-out hang-out on summer days that doubles as a night bar.

Somewhat more edifying is **Skala Loutron**, a fishing village 8km southwest of Mytilini

on the Gulf of Yera. Here the **Hellenic Culture Centre** (☎ 22510 91660, in Athens 210 523 8149; www .hcc.edu.gr; 2-week courses €650) conducts intensive summer Greek-language courses in a century-old olive-oil factory near the harbour, now restored as the **Hotel Zaira** (☎ 22510 91188; www .hotel-zaira.com; Skala Loutron; s/d €45/60), distinguished by lofty wood beams, nice stonework and home-cooked Greek food. Nonstudents can stay, too.

Also in Skala Loutron, the new **Museum of the Memorial of the Refugees of 1922** (☎ 22510 91086; admission free; ☼ 5-8pm) commemorates Anatolia's lost Greek culture, abruptly ended after 2000 years by the Greek-Turkish population exchanges of 1923. The museum features the photographs, documents, handmade clothes and silverwork of the refugees, plus large wall maps showing over 2000 villages formerly populated by Greeks – and the places in Greece where the refugees were resettled. The museum will be gladly opened outside of normal hours if you ask around.

Some 9km south, the peninsula wraps around to the popular sand-and-pebble **Agios Ermogenis Beach** and **Haramida Beach**. The eastern stretch of the latter, **Niseli Beach**, is secluded under a bluff and separated by a headland from the main beach. There's free camping provided by the municipality, with toilets and showers, under pine trees on the bluff above the beach. The camping ground is located near the lovably eccentric **Karpouzi Kantina** (☎ 6977946809), a drinks-and-snacks wagon named after its mascot – an old skiff, painted like a giant watermelon. Enthusiastic owner Fanis also oversees the camping ground.

NORTHERN LESVOS

With rolling hills garbed in pine and olive trees, peaceful beaches and the aesthetically harmonious town of Mithymna (usually called by its old name, Molyvos), northern Lesvos offers both spots for solitude and some low-key resort action. Seaside hot springs, unvisited traditional villages and intriguing Byzantine monasteries round out the region's offerings.

Moni Taxiarhon Μονή Ταξιάρχον

Some 36km north of Mytilini Town, near Mantamados village, stands one of Lesvos' most important pilgrimage sites: **Moni Taxiarhon** (Monastery of Taxiarhon; Mantamados village; admission free; ☼ 8am-8pm). An axis of Orthodoxy, myth and militarism, this grand 17th-century monastery dedicated to the Archangels is pretty full-on: note the fighter plane parked out front. It all begins to make sense when you recall that the Archangel Michael is the patron saint of the Hellenic Air Force. Indeed, you may meet the odd pious soul here who firmly attests that, even though those mischievous Turks may harass Greek airspace in their F16s on a daily basis, the saint's invisible presence prevents them from flying over the monastery itself.

While numerous reported miracles draw the faithful from around Greece, you don't have to be a believer to marvel at the monastery's magnificent architecture. Mentioned first in 1661 as a working monastery, the current church was built in 1879 as a three-aisled basilica. It's surrounded by leafy grounds (where a snack shop and toilets are conveniently located).

The voluminous interior is marked by grand columns and decorated by icons, the most venerated being an earth-toned depiction of the Archangel. Legend attests that it was created in the 10th century, after a Saracen pirate raid decimated the monastery. While the pirates were massacring the monks, the last survivor climbed to the rooftop; there the Archangel miraculously appeared, sword drawn, driving the Saracens off. To show his gratitude, the monk painted the icon, supposedly, by mixing mud with the blood of his dead comrades. In 1766, the icon was placed in a special case and the shiny faux silver markers you will see dangling before it symbolise worshippers' prayers that have been answered. There are also ornamental shoes left as sacred offerings (the alleged imprint of the Archangel's foot is in the floor near the iconostasis).

While at the monastery, visit the shop of the **Agricultural Co-op of Mandamados** (☎ 22530 61096; asmadama@otenet.gr), which sells numerous natural products from local farmers, like the unique hard cheese, *ladotyri*, made from sheep's milk.

Mithymna (Molyvos) Μήθυμνα (Μόλυβος)
pop 1500

Mithymna, more commonly called Molyvos, is a well-preserved Ottoman-era town of narrow cobbled lanes and stone houses with jutting wooden balconies, complemented by a clean pebble beach below. Drawing a mix of independent travellers and package tourists to its waterfront hotels, Molyvos is a curious place. Yet, factoring in the intimate upper town, crowned by a grand 14th-century Byzantine castle, and good nearby beaches, Molyvos becomes a nice enough spot to spend some time while exploring northern Lesvos.

ORIENTATION
The bus stops on the main north–south road bisecting the town. Below this road is the waterfront, with a beach, several hotels and restaurants, and cafes on the northern end. Above the central road begins the upper town, consisting of narrow, winding streets, where the more atmospheric accommodation and restaurants are located. The so-called *agora* (market), clustered with tourist shops, is further up. Above this is the castle.

INFORMATION
ATM-equipped banks are centrally located.
Central Internet Café (per hr €4) On the port road.
Medical Centre (☎ 22530 71702)
Municipal tourist office (☎ 22530 71347) This small office on the left of Kastrou, between the bus stop and the fork in the central road, can provide info but has had mixed reviews regarding accommodation advice.
Post office (Kastrou)

SIGHTS & ACTIVITIES
Mithymna (Molyvos) is ideal for wandering; the upper town's small streets are lined with bright-shuttered, traditional stone houses wreathed in flowers. A 14th-century **Byzantine-Genoese castle** (☎ 22530 71803; admission €2; ☺ 8.30am-7pm Tue-Sun) stands guard above; the steep climb is repaid by sweeping views of the town, sea and even Turkey shimmering on the horizon. Back in the 15th century, before Lesvos fell to the Turks, feisty Onetta d'Oria, wife of the Genoese governor, repulsed a Turkish onslaught after donning her husband's armour and leading the fight from here. In summer it hosts a **drama festival** (ask at the tourist office).

Beach-lovers can take an **excursion boat** at 10.30am daily for Petra, Skala Sykaminias and Eftalou (from €20). Sunset cruises and boat 'safaris' are also available. Enquire with the portside **Faonas Travel** (☎ 22530 71630; tekes@otenet.gr).

SLEEPING
Budget
Over 50 registered, good-quality domatia are available. Look for signs, or ask the municipal

tourist office. Even more expensive waterfront options sometimes give discounted rates.

Municipal Camping Mithymna (☎ 22530 71169; camp sites per adult/tent €7/3; ☒ Jun-Sep) This publicly run camping ground occupies an excellent shady site 1.5km from town and is signposted from near the municipal tourist office. If arriving before or after high season, call ahead.

Nassos Guest House (☎ 22530 71432, 6942046279; www.nassosguesthouse.com; Arionos; s/d €20/35; ☎) Head up to the old town's only blue house to reach one of Lesvos' most beautiful – and best-priced – sleeping spots. This refurbished Turkish mansion with a small enclosed garden features brightly painted, lovingly decorated traditional rooms with balconies overlooking the harbour. One room has a private bathroom. Friendly Dutch manager Tom provides local information, plus a book on hiking routes (€8). Check directly with him regarding availability to avoid missing out.

Captain's View (☎ 22530 71241; meltheo@otenet .gr; 2-bedroom house €90-150; ☒) This restored old house has a well-equipped kitchen, spacious balcony and lounge. There are two bedrooms and a loft, sleeping up to six people. There are no minimum-stay requirements, but book ahead in summer.

Midrange

Molyvos Hotel (☎ 22530 71496; www.molyvos-hotels .com; waterfront; d incl breakfast €65; ☒) Although it works with package-tour operators, this handsome waterfront hotel is also a good choice for independent travellers, with well-kept, modern rooms overlooking the sea, friendly service and a good breakfast spread. You can usually park in the narrow lane out front.

Amfitriti Hotel (☎ 22530 71741; s/d/tr incl breakfast €65/90/100; ☒ ☒) Just 50m from the beach, this snazzy traditional stone hotel has modern, tiled rooms and a garden pool. It fills up fast and deals with package tourists, but independent travellers are welcome.

EATING & DRINKING

our pick **Alonia** (☎ 22530 72431; mains €4.50-6) Locals swear by this unpretentious place just outside of town, on the road to Eftalou Beach. Although the decor is nothing special, Alonia is the best Mithymna choice for fresh fish at good prices.

Betty's (☎ 22530 71421; 17 Noemvriou; mains €6-9) This restored Turkish pasha's residence, vis-

ible under a red overhanging balcony on the upper streets, offers tasty *tyropitakia* (small cheese pies), savoury lamb souvlaki and baked eggplant with cheese. Best of all are the unusual seafood specialities, like Betty's spaghetti shrimp.

O Gatos (☎ 22530 71661; www.gatos-restaurant.gr; mains €6.50-9) Near the arch by the castle entrance, this restaurant is a bit touristy but enjoys spellbinding views over the water – good for dinner before dusk.

Sunset (☎ 22530 71093; waterfront; ☒ 8am-1am) On the waterfront, close to the Molyvos Hotel, this friendly all-day cafe has a great selection of coffees and attentive service.

Molly's Bar (☎ 22530 71209; ☒ 6pm-late) With its thickly painted walls and blue stars, beaded curtains and bottled Guinness, this whimsical British-run bar on the waterfront's far eastern side is always in shipshape condition. Molly's caters to an older, international crowd. It's flanked by another couple of watering holes that get festive in summer.

Around Mithymna (Molyvos)

Beyond Molyvos, northern Lesvos is largely unvisited; for some scenic routes, consult Tom at Nassos Guest House (left), who sells a useful hiking guide (€8).

The best-known local destination, **Petra**, is a very overrated beach village 5km south, and inexplicably a package tourism favourite. The beach itself comprises coarse sand and pebbles, while spearlike wooden poles stand ominously submerged in the water. Petra's one cultural site, situated above the giant overhanging rock for which the village was named, is the 18th-century **Panagia Glykofilousa** (Church of the Sweet-kissing Virgin), accessible on foot up 114 rock-hewn steps.

While Petra has accommodation, the village itself is barely a strip of souvenir shops and some restaurants. It's far nicer to stay in Molyvos; better yet for solitude-seekers, head a couple of kilometres northeast to **Eftalou Beach** (also called Agii Anargyri Beach). You can either park where the path heads down to the beach, or drive further to reach the Hrysi Akti Hotel and Restaurant, and further beaches beyond that.

Backed by a cliff, the narrow, pebbled Eftalou Beach has pristine waters and offers total serenity. It also boasts the **Mineral Baths of Eftalou** (old bathhouse/new bathhouse €3.50/5; ☒ old bathhouse 6-8am & 6-10pm, new bathhouse 9am-6pm), with their clear, cathartic 46.5°C water. The old bathhouse has a pebbled floor; the new one offers private bathtubs. These springs treat rheumatism, arthritis, neuralgia, hypertension, gall stones, and gynaecological and skin problems. Or you can also just try to find the one spot on the beach in front of the bathhouse where the hot mineral water filters into the cool sea, and enjoy from there.

Beyond the baths, the beachfront **Hrysi Akti** (☎ 22530 71879; Eftalou Beach; s/d €35/45) offers simple rooms with bathrooms in an idyllic setting, right on a practically private pebbled cove. The friendly owners also own a similarly named **restaurant** (☎ 22530 71947; mains €4.50-6) just above the beach; enjoying a contemplative drink overlooking the sea here is a perfect way to wind up a Lesvos summer day.

WESTERN LESVOS

Spectacular, lonesome western Lesvos is the afterthought of massive, primeval volcanic eruptions that fossilised trees and all other living things, making it one of the world's most intriguing sites for prehistoric treasure hunters. The striking, bare landscape, broken only by craggy boulders and the occasional olive tree, is dramatically different from the rest of Lesvos.

Byzantine spiritualists in their high monastic refuges were inspired by the barren, burnt moonscapes of the west and, well before them, a certain Sappho, the 7th-century-BC poet who was dubbed 'the 10th muse' by Plato. Such was the power of her literary seduction that even the usually level-headed ancient ruler Solon despaired that he too must be taught Sappho's song, because he wanted 'to learn it and die'.

However, it is the sensuous, erotic nature of Sappho's surviving poems, and the fact that she taught them to an inner circle of female companions, that made her into a latter-day lesbian icon. Skala Eresou, her birthplace and a lesbian-frequented southwestern coastal resort, has fine beaches, seafood and sunset cocktail bars.

Kalloni to Sigri Καλλονή προς Σίγρι

After driving 34km west from Kalloni, stop for a coffee or lunch break in **Andissa**, a jovial, rustic village of narrow streets kept cool by the two enormous plane trees that stand over its *plateia*. Listen to the crickets and the banter

of old-timers over a Greek coffee or frappe, while farmers hawk watermelons from the back of their trucks.

Escapists will enjoy the little-visited north-coast **Gavathas Beach**, signposted a couple of kilometres before Andissa. This long, sandy stretch lying beside a tiny fishing hamlet has warm and shallow waters ideal for children, and humble sleeping and eating options. Halfway down the main road behind the beach, look left for **O Tsolias Guest Rooms** (☎ 22530 56537; Gavathas Beach; s/d/tr €40/50/60). The kind family who runs these simple but clean rooms with bathrooms also maintains a tasty taverna below.

Some 9km west of Andissa, the Byzantine **Moni Ypsilou** (Monastery of Ypsilou; admission free; ☹ 7.30am-10pm) stands atop a solitary peak surrounded by volcanic plains. Founded in the 8th century, this storied place includes a flowering arched courtyard, a sumptuously decorated church, and a small but spectacular museum with gold and silver reliquaries, antique liturgical vestments, centuries-old icons and Byzantine manuscripts dating back to the 10th century. From the top of the monastery stairs, you can gaze out over the fortress-like walls upon the desolate ochre plains stretched out against the sea.

Some 4km beyond the monastery a signposted left-hand road leads, after another 4.9km, to Lesvos' celebrated **petrified forest** (☎ 22530 54434; www.petrifiedforest.gr; admission €2; ☹ 8am-5pm) – more honestly, a petrified desert. The 20-million-year-old stumps that decorate this baking, shadeless valley are few and far between, though experts insist many more lurk under the ground, waiting to be dug up.

The best specimens are in the **Natural History Museum of the Lesvos Petrified Forest** (☎ 22530 54434; admission €5; ☹ 8am-8pm 15 Jun-18 Oct, 8.30am-4.30pm 5 Oct-5 Jun) in Sigri, a coastal village 7km west. This engaging modern museum manages to make old rocks and dusty fossils interesting, helped by interactive displays and a veritable mother lode of glittering amethyst, quartz and other semiprecious stones.

Sleepy **Sigri** is a fishing port with a sometimes operational ferry port. The village has beautiful sea views, especially at sunset, and there are idyllic, little-visited beaches just southwest. A good-quality dirt coastal road pointing south passes these beaches; it's about a 45-minute drive to Skala Eresou, western Lesvos' most popular destination.

Skala Eresou Σκάλα Ερεσού

pop 1560

All historic places are burdened by their past, but the once-quiet fishing village of Skala Eresou has learned to profit from its. This bohemian beach town, where sensuous songstress Sappho was born in 630 BC, is supposedly ground zero for the lesbian internationale – though this reputation has been overblown. In fact, with its shiatsu, fruit smoothies, healing arts and laptopped cafes, it resembles nothing so much as a New England college town (with a decidedly better climate). All in all Eresou is benign.

Skala Eresou's mainstream appeal derives from its 2km-long beach, good seafood, and low-key nightlife, while the Women Together festival each September marks the apogee of the season for lesbians.

ORIENTATION & INFORMATION

The central square of Plateia Anthis and Evristhenous abuts the waterfront; the beach extends laterally. Restaurants and bars are found here, the latter on the eastern waterfront; most cafes here offer free wi-fi internet. Behind the *plateia* is the Church of Agias Andreas. Further west along Gyrinnis are the major services and ATMs. There's also a **doctor** (☎ 22530 53947; ☽ 24hr).

The full-service **Sappho Travel** (☎ 22530 52140; www.sapphotravel.com) provides information and car hire, sells tickets, arranges accommodation and exchanges currency. It organises women-only sunset cruises and the two-week **Women Together** festival each September. The event brings lesbians from all over for workshops, music, art, therapies and socialising.

SIGHTS

Eresos' **archaeological museum** contains Greek and Roman antiquities, but was still closed at the time of writing. The nearby remains of the early Christian **Basilica of Agios Andreas** include partially intact 5th-century mosaics.

SLEEPING

Skala Eresou has reasonable domatia options, as well as (fairly pricey) hotels. Some former women-only places have gone metrosexual, though two currently remain just for women.

Domatia Maria Pantermou (☎ 22530 53267; pantermou@in.gr; s/d/tr €20/30/40; ☒) Across from the Mascot Hotel, kindly old Marianthi and Giorgios Pantermou rent these small but clean rooms with balconies.

Hotel Eressos (☎ 22530 53560; s/d €35/45; ☽ Mar-Dec; ☒) Decorated with African furnishings the owner brought from her travels, this eccentric place has well-kept, clean rooms in a quiet location, a couple of streets in from the water.

Villa La Passione (☎ 6944602080; s/d/tr €40/50/60) Self-caterers will appreciate these modern, well-outfitted studios, located near Eresou's central parking area.

Hotel Antiopi (☎ 22530 53311; s/d €35/50) A women-only hotel that benefited when the Hotel Sappho went co-ed, the Antiopi has well-maintained but slightly cramped rooms that might strike one as either kitsch and cool or too cute.

Mascot Hotel (☎ 22530 52140; www.sapphotravel.com; s/d €40/60; ☒) There's no sign reading 'males forbidden', but rest assured that the Mascot is female-only. A few blocks back from the beach, it's a bohemian place with 10 snug modern rooms with balconies. Book through Sappho Travel.

Hotel Sappho (☎ 22530 53233; www.sapphohotel.com; s/d €40/60; ☽ 1 Apr-15 Oct; ☒ ☏) The Sappho was the village's first women-only hotel, but has since gone co-ed. While it has thus lost some street cred among the lesbian set, the Sappho still has a prime waterfront setting, smartly appointed rooms and free wi-fi.

EATING

Skala Eresou's restaurants and bars line the beach, the latter to the eastern side. On clear days Chios emerges on the horizon.

Eressos Palace (☎ 22530 5385; mains €6-10) A good *psarotaverna* on the western edge, it also does grills and purveys local Eressos cheese.

Soulatso (☎ 22530 52078; fish €6-13) This busy beachfront place with outdoor patio specialises in fresh fish and other seafood.

DRINKING

Skala Eresou's limited nightlife consists of a contiguous series of cafe-bars strung along the eastern waterfront, several quite pretty.

Tenth Muse (☎ 22530 53287) The first place along the main *plateia* is an old favourite of females, strong on fruit drinks, Haagen-Dazs ice cream and conviviality.

Parasol (☎ 22530 52050) With its orange lanterns further down on the waterfront, it does cocktails that match its South Seas decor.

NORTHEASTERN AEGEAN ISLANDS

Margaritari (☎ 22530 53042) Recognisable by its orange furnishings, it's another nice outdoor cafe with great sweets.

Breez (☎ 22530 537108) An ever-so-slick nightspot more popular with young Greeks.

Zorba the Buddha (☎ 22530 53777) The place furthest down on the eastern waterfront is a popular old standby that's full til late.

SOUTHERN LESVOS

Interspersed groves of olive and pine trees mark southern Lesvos, from the flanks of Mt Olympus (968m), the area's highest peak, right down to the sea, where the best beaches lie. This is a hot, intensely agricultural place where the vital olive-oil, wine and ouzo industries overshadow tourism. Southern Lesvos has thus retained authenticity in its villages and solitude on its beaches.

Just south of the Mytilini–Polyhtinos road, **Agiasos** is the first point of interest. On the northern side of Mt Olympus, it's a quirky, well-kept traditional hamlet where village elders sip Greek coffees in the local *kafeneia*, unmindful of time, and local artisans hawk their wares to day-trippers from Mytilini Town. Nevertheless, it's a relaxing, leafy place and boasts the exceptional **Church of the Panagia Vrefokratousa**, which hosts an icon-rich **Byzantine Museum** and **Popular Museum**. Atmospheric accommodation is also available.

Alternatively, the road south that hugs the western side of the Gulf of Gera reaches **Plomari**, the centre of Lesvos' ouzo industry and an attractive seaside village with its large, palm-lined *plateia* and waterfront tavernas. Here see the **Varvagianni Ouzo Museum** (☎ 22520 32741; ☷ 9am-7pm Mon-Fri, by appointment Sat & Sun). The popular beach settlement of **Agios Isidoros**, 3km east, absorbs most of Plomari's summertime guests. This beach isn't bad but **Tarti**, a bit further east, is nicer and less crowded. West of Plomari, **Melinda** is a tranquil fishing village with beach, tavernas and domatia.

Melinda to Vatera Μελίντα προς Βατερά
DRIVING TOUR

From Melinda, the road less taken to the beach resort of Vatera passes through tranquil mountain villages and richly forested hills, and winds between steep gorges offering breathtaking views down to the sea.

Driving north, tiny **Paleohori** is the first village, with very narrow streets and gentle elderly villagers who will peer over their thick glasses curiously at you from *kafeneia* in the hamlet's miniature *plateia*. The old church in the upper town is much grander and more ornate than Paleohori would seem to need. It's usually open and the priest can provide information (in Greek) about its history.

Continuing north from Paleohori, there are sweeping views of the sea and glimpses of even tinier villages nestled in the forested mountains opposite. Take the road west to Akrassio, and then north to **Ambeliko**; even though there's a more direct western route, it's safer to go to Ambeliko first and then, just before reaching it, turn left on the signposted, good-quality dirt road pointing downwards to **Kato Stavros**. This road lasts 9km before reverting to asphalt, and passes through serene olive and pine forests. The total driving time from Melinda to Vatera is little over an hour.

HIKING TRAILS

Hikers here can enjoy southern Lesvos' 'olive trails', which comprise paths and old local roads from Plomari and Melinda. The **Melinda–Paleohori trail** (1.2km, 30 minutes) follows the Selandas River for 200m before ascending to Paleohori, passing a spring with potable water along the way. The trail ends at one of the village's two olive presses. You can continue southwest to **Panagia Kryfti**, a cave church near a hot spring and the nearby **Drota Beach**, or take the **Paleohori–Rahidi trail** (1km, 30 minutes), paved with white stone and passing springs and vineyards. Rahidi, which got electricity only in 2001, has several charming old houses and a *kafeneio*.

Another trail heading northeast from Melinda leads to shady **Kournela** (1.8km, 40 minutes) and from there to **Milos** (800m, 20 minutes), where there's an old flour mill. Alternately, hike to Milos directly from Melinda (2km, one hour) on a trail that hugs the river and passes ruined olive mills, one spring and two bridges, as well as orange and mandarin trees. From Milos, follow the river northeast to **Amaxo** (1.75km, one hour) and be treated to refreshing mountain-spring water in plane, poplar and pine forests.

Other, more complicated hiking trails can get you directly from Melinda to Vatera; consult the **EOT** (☎ 22510 42511; Aristarhou 6; ☷ 9am-1pm Mon-Fri) in Mytilini Town or a travel agency for precise details.

Vatera & Polyhnitos Βατερά & Πολυγνίτος

Despite its 9km-long sandy beach, Vatera (vah-ter-*ah*), remains a low-key destination, with only a few small hotels and domatia operating, and even fewer bars. Serene Vatera thus remains a perfect destination for families, couples, or anyone looking to get away from it all.

On its western edge, at Cape Agios Fokas, the sparse ruins of an ancient **Temple of Dionysos** occupy a headland overlooking the sea. In the cove between the beach and the cape, evidence has been found indicating an ancient military encampment; indeed, some historians believe this is the place Homer was referring to in the 'Iliad' as the resting point for Greek armies besieging Troy. Legend also says that nearby Vryssa village was named after a Trojan woman, Vrysseida, who died after being contested by two of the victorious Greek fighters. To this day old women and even the occasional baby girl with the name Vrysseida can be found here; the name is not given anywhere else.

Vatera's most remote history has attracted international attention. Fossils have been found here dating back 5.5 million years, including remains of a tortoise as big as a Volkswagen Bug and fossils of a gigantic horse and gazelle. A small **Museum of Natural History** (☎ 22520 61890; admission €1; ⏰ 9.30am-7.30pm), located in Vryssa'a old schoolhouse, displays these and other significant remains. Ongoing excavations mean that more exciting finds may still be made.

Agricultural **Polyhnitos**, 10km north of Vatera on the road back to Mytilini town, is known for its two nearby **hot springs**, one just to the southeast and the other 5km north, outside Lisvorio village. The former, known as the **Polyhnitos Spa** (☎ 22520 41449; admission €3; ⏰ 7am-noon & 3-8pm) is in a pretty, renovated Byzantine building, and has some of Europe's hottest baths temperatures, at 31°C (87.6°F). Rheumatism, arthritis, skin diseases and gynaecological problems are treated here.

The **Lisvorio Spa** (☎ 22530 71245; admission €3; ⏰ 8am-1pm & 3-8pm) consists of two small baths situated around a wooded stream. They're unmarked, so ask around for directions; though the buildings are run-down, bathing is unaffected. The temperature and water properties are similar to those at Polyhnitos.

Some 5km northwest of Polyhnitos, the fishing port of **Skala Polyhnitou** lies on the Gulf of Kallonis. It's a relaxing, though unremarkable place, where caïques bob at the docks and fishermen untangle their nets, and is great for low-key fresh seafood dinners with the locals.

Sleeping & Eating

Agiasos Hotel (☎ 22520 22242; Agiasos; s/d/tr €20/25/30) Next to the Church of Panagia in Agiasos, this friendly place has simple, clean rooms near the centre of the action.

Stratis Kazatzis Rooms (☎ 22520 22539; Agiasos; s/d/tr €20/25/30) Right at the entrance of Agiasos, these handsome rooms are also good value for money. Like the Agiasos Hotel, it's a small place to book ahead.

our pick **Hotel Vatera Beach** (☎ 22520 61212; www .vaterabeach.com; Vatera; s/d €65/90; P X 🖳 ☎) This peaceful beachfront hotel regards its guests, many of whom return annually, as dear old friends. The congenial George and Barbara Ballis and family provide for the common needs of travellers with free multilingual newspapers and internet-equipped computers. Service is kind and courteous, while the hotel's excellent restaurant gets most of its ingredients from the owners' organic farm.

our pick **Psarotaverna O Stratos** (☎ 22520 42910; Skala Polyhnitou; fish €6-9; ⏰ 10am-1am) The best of several fish tavernas on Skala Polyhnitou's waterfront, O Stratos offers excellent and inexpensive fresh seafood, plus salads like *vlita* (wild greens) and tasty mezedhes. The small fishing boats moored right before your table add to the ambience. Service is gracious and attentive.

LIMNOS ΛΗΜΝΟΣ

pop 15,225 / area 482 sq km

Isolated Limnos, all alone in the northeastern Aegean save for neighbouring Agios Efstatios, nevertheless has much to offer to those looking for Greek island life relatively unaffected by modern tourism. Its capital, Myrina, has retained its classic Greek fishing harbour feel, while a grand Genoese castle flanked by beaches provides a dramatic backdrop. In high season, the city's chic cafes and shops are frequented by (mostly Greek) tourists but otherwise the island is quiet, especially in its tranquil inland villages.

Although it's not enormous, Limnos does offer variety. The eastern lakes are visited by spectacular flocks of flamingos and the austere

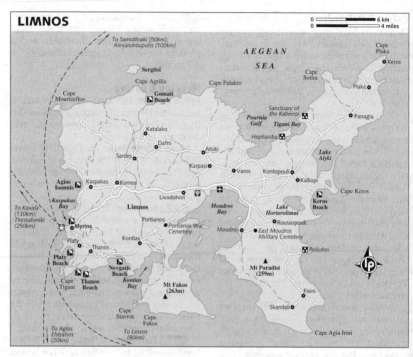

LIMNOS

central plain is filled with wildflowers in spring and autumn. Superb sandy beaches lie near the capital, as well as in more distant and intimate corners of the island. For even more isolation, you can visit Limnos' tiny island dependency of Agios Efstratios (see p631) to the south, which also boasts serene beaches and fresh fish.

Limnos is notorious for its strong summer winds, which make the island great for windsurfing; in late summer, it also suffers the curse of the northernmost Aegean islands: jellyfish. However, to Greeks it's perhaps best known as being the central command post of the Hellenic Air Force – a strategic decision, as Limnos is in an ideal position for monitoring the Straits of the Dardanelles leading into İstanbul. For this very reason the island was used as the operational base for the failed Gallipoli campaign in WW1; a moving military cemetery for fallen Commonwealth soldiers remains near Moudros, where the Allied ships were based.

Limnos, and especially its sparsely populated dependency of Agios Efstratios, are almost unvisited by tourists out of high season, though the steady population of the military

keeps Myrina more active than other small island capitals.

Getting There & Away

For flights and ferries from Limnos, see Island Hopping (p755).

AIR

The airport is 22km east of Myrina; taxis cost about €16.

Olympic Air (☎ 22540 22214; www.olympicairlines .com; Nikolaou Garoufallidou) is opposite Hotel Paris in Myrina.

BOAT

Buy ferry and hydrofoil tickets at Pravlis Travel (opposite) or Myrina Tourist & Travel Agency (opposite). The latter also sells tickets (one way/return €8/15) for day trips to Agios Efstratios on the *Aeolis* ferry, which depart every Sunday at 8am and return at 5pm.

Getting Around

BUS

Limnos' bus service has one diabolical purpose: to bring villagers to town for their morning shopping and to get them home by lunch. Going and returning by bus in the same day is only possible to four destinations, by no means the most interesting ones, either. For example, two morning buses serve Plaka, but only return the next day at 7am and 8.45am (€4.60, 1¼ hours). Similarly, two morning buses go to Skandali, only returning the next day at 7am (€4.60, 1¼ hours) and two morning buses serve Kontias, returning the next day at 7am and 9am (€2.40, 45 minutes). Two daily buses to Katalakos – a measly 25-minute trip – only return at 8.30am and 1.30pm (€1.80).

Also from Myrina, five daily buses serve Moudros, via the airport (€2.80, 30 minutes), with the last return bus leaving at 12.15pm.

Myrnia's **bus station** (☎ 22540 22464; Plateia Eleftheriou Venizelou) displays schedules and has printed copies.

CAR & MOTORCYCLE

Myrina Rent-a-Car (right), near the waterfront, charges from €30 per day. Motorcycle-hire outlets are on Kyda-Karatza.

TAXI

A **taxi rank** (☎ 22540 23033) is on Myrina's central square, by the bus station.

MYRINA MYPINA
pop 5110

Backed by volcanic rock and a craggy Genoese castle, Limnos' capital is a striking place. Despite some tourism, it keeps a certain serenity, harking back to its roots as a fishing port. Here you'll see old fishermen sip Greek coffee while unfolding their nets, and colourful caïques in the harbour. Beyond the castle lies a sandy beach, and another, less windy one beyond that.

In summer Myrina comes to life, with shops selling traditional foods, handicrafts and more in its bustling *agora*. Its white-washed stone houses, old-fashioned barber shops and *kafeneia,* crumbling neoclassical mansions and wood-balconied homes all create a relaxed feel.

The town (and Limnos in general) is mostly frequented by Greek tourists, and this has given a strongly Hellenic flavour to its nightlife, with the most popular places being stylish beachfront bars. Despite the hubbub, however, the castle's overgrown hill is inhabited by shy, fleet-footed deer who dart around at night; in winter, locals say, they even wander through the *agora* – presumably, to do their shopping.

Orientation

From the quay turn right onto Plateia Ilia Iliou. Continue past Hotel Lemnos and the town hall, turning left after the derelict Hotel Action, then immediately veer half-left onto the main thoroughfare Kyda-Karatza to reach Myrina's central square. Continue and you'll find Plateia Eleftheriou Venizelou and the bus station.

Information

ATM-equipped banks line the central square. The summertime tourist info kiosk on the quay sometimes works.

Excite-Net (☎ 22540 25525; internet per hr €1.50; ◷ 24hr) Waterfront internet cafe.

Myrina Rent-a-Car (☎ 22540 24476; Kyda-Karatza) Near the waterfront.

Myrina Tourist & Travel Agency (☎ 22540 22460; mirina@lim.forthnet.gr) Full-service agency on the waterfront.

Police station (☎ 22540 22201; Nikolaou Garoufallidou)

Port police (☎ 22540 22225)

Post office (Nikolaou Garoufallidou)

Pravlis Travel (☎ 22540 22471; pravlis@lim.forthnet .gr; Parasidi 15) For ferry tickets.

SAOS Ferries (☎ 22540 29571) Sells ferry tickets from a small compartment on the castle side of the waterfront.

Theodoros Petrides Travel Agency (☎ 22540 22039; www.petridestravel.gr; Kyda-Karatza 116) Offers sightseeing tours on the island, car hire and accommodation bookings.

Sights & Activities

Myrina's **castle** occupies a headland that divides the town from its popular beach. The sea views from here extend to Mt Athos. From the harbour, take the first side street to the left by an old Turkish fountain, where the castle is signposted. At night, sitting in front of the church on the northeastern side of the castle gives great views of the cafe lights down below and, if you're lucky, quick glimpses of bounding deer in the darkness to the left.

Myrina's beaches include the wide and sandy **Rea Maditos**, and a superior **Romeïkos Gialos**, beyond the harbour; it's accessible by taking any left from Kyda-Karatza as you're walking inland. Further on, it becomes **Riha Nera** (shallow water), named for its gently shelving, child-friendly seafloor. There's nightlife here too.

Five minutes south on the road towards Thanos Beach, **Platy Beach** is a shallow, sandy beach popular with locals, and has beach bars and restaurants.

Myrina's **archaeological museum** (admission €2; ◷ 9am-3pm Tue-Sun) occupies a neoclassical mansion overlooking Romeïkos Gialos beach, and contains finds from Limnos' three sites of Poliohni, the Sanctuary of the Kabeiroi and Hephaistia.

From June to September, Theodoros Petrides Travel Agency (p629) organises round-the-island **boat trips** (€20), with stops for swimming and lunch.

Sleeping

Hotel Filoktitis (☎ /fax 22540 23344; Ethnikis Andistasis 14; s/d €40/50; ✹) This welcoming hotel has airy, well-equipped rooms just inland of Riha Nera Beach. Follow Maroulas (the continuation of Kyda-Karatza) and then Ethnikis Andistasis; the hotel is located above the quite fine restaurant of the same name.

Hotel Lemnos (☎ 22540 22153; s/d €45/60; ✹) The harbour-side Lemnos has friendly staff and modern rooms with balconies overlooking the waterfront or castle.

Apollo Pavillion (☎ /fax 22540 23712; www.apollopavilion.com; studios incl breakfast from €60; ✹) Tucked behind the port in a neoclassical house, the popular Apollo Pavillion offers large rooms with kitchenette and balcony. Walk along Nikolaou Garoufallidou from Kyda-Karatza and the sign is 150m along on the right.

Lemnos Village Hotel (☎ 22540 23500; www.lemnosvillagehotel.com; Platy Beach; s/d/tr €50/60/70; ℗ ✹ ✦) Just out of town on Platy Beach, this chic resort-type hotel offers many more amenities for the price than Myrina's simpler places (partly why it's popular with foreign groups).

To Arhontiko (☎ 22540 29800; cnr Sahtouri & Filellinon; s/d/tr €50/65/80; ✹) This restored mansion dating from 1814 has lovely boutique rooms with simple charm, and helpful, friendly staff. It's located on a quiet alley near the main shopping street, one street back from the beach.

Nefeli Guest Rooms (☎ 22540 22825; d/tr/q €100/120/150; ℗ ✹ ▣) This intimate place features handsome stone rooms with great sea views high above the town. It's up the hill from the castle, next to the cafe of the same name.

Eating

our pick **Ouzeri To 11** (☎ 22540 22635; Plateia KTEL; seafood mezedhes €4.50-7) This unassuming little *ouzerie* by the bus depot is the local favourite for seafood. From *kydonia* (mussels with garlic and Venus clams) to limpets, sea urchins, crayfish and more, 'To *En*-dheka' (as it's pronounced) serves all the strange stuff, along with plenty of ouzo to make you forget what you're eating.

O Platanos Taverna (☎ 22540 22070; mains €5-8) *Mayirefta* with an emphasis on meats are served at this iconic place under a giant plane tree, halfway along Kyda-Karatza.

O Sozos (☎ 22540 25085; Platy village; mains €5-8) In the mountain village of Platy, just east of Myrina, O Sozos is popular for its traditional fare. Specialities include *Kokkaras Flomaria* (rooster served with pasta).

Tzitzifies (☎ 22540 23756; fish from €7) Fresh fish and meat dishes are available at this worthwhile taverna with excellent sea views through beachfront trees.

Drinking

Myrina's summer nightlife is centred around the bars above Romeïkos Gialos beach.

Karagiozis (Romeïkos Gialos beach; ◷ 9am-5am) This popular place, on a leafy terrace near the sea, is busy until late.

Kinky Bar (☎ 6973667489; ◷ midnight-5am Wed, Fri & Sat) The island's only real club is a stylish place surrounded by trees and very popular with Greeks. It operates three days a week, from June through August only. Find it in Avlonas (3km from town) on the road towards Agios Ioannis Beach and Kaspakas.

WESTERN LIMNOS

North of Myrina, the road left after **Kaspakas** village accesses the fairly quiet **Agios Ioannis Beach**, with a few tavernas and beach houses. The beach ends with the aptly named **Rock Café**, set nicely beneath a large overhanging volcanic slab.

After Kaspakas, drive east and turn left at **Kornos**, and follow the road northwards to remote **Gomati Beach** on the north coast; a good dirt road gets there from **Katalako**.

Alternatively, drive east from Kaspakas and continue past Kornos, turning south at **Livadohori**. This road passes barren, tawny hills and modest farmlands. Further south along the coast, **Kontias** is a fairly prosaic, plastered old village now inexplicably popular among Northern European property hunters. Below Kontias the road swings southwest back to Myrina, on the way passing the sandy **Nevgatis**

NORTHEASTERN AEGEAN ISLANDS

Beach and **Thanos Beach.** Although they're very popular and get crowded, these beaches are truly idyllic and only a 10-minute drive from Myrina.

CENTRAL LIMNOS

Central Limnos' flat plateaus are dotted with wheat fields, small vineyards and sheep – plus the Greek Air Force's central command (large parts are thus off-limits to tourists). Limnos' second-largest town, **Moudros**, occupies the eastern side of muddy Moudros Bay, famous for its role as the principal base for the ill-fated Gallipoli campaign in February 1915.

The **East Moudros Military Cemetery**, with the graves of Commonwealth soldiers from the Gallipoli campaign, is 1km east of Moudros on the Roussopouli road. Here you can read a short history of the Gallipoli campaign. A second Commonwealth cemetery, **Portianos War Cemetery** (6km south of Livadohori on the road to Thanos Beach and Myrina) is the area's other sombre attraction.

EASTERN LIMNOS

Historical remnants and remote beaches draw visitors to eastern Limnos. Its three **archaeological sites** (admission free; 8am-7pm) include four ancient settlements at **Poliohni** on the southeast coast, the most significant being a pre-Mycenaean city that pre-dated Troy VI (1800–1275 BC). The site is well presented, but remains are few.

The second site, the **Sanctuary of the Kabeiroi** (Ta Kaviria), lies on remote Tigani Bay. The worship of the Kabeiroi gods here actually pre-dates that which took place on Samothraki (p634). The major site, a **Hellenistic sanctuary**, has 11 columns. Nearby, the legendary **Cave of Philoctetes** is supposedly where that Trojan War hero was abandoned while his gangrenous, snake-bitten leg healed. A path from the site leads to the sea cave; there's also a narrow, unmarked entrance to the left past the main entrance.

To reach the sanctuary, take the left-hand turn-off after **Kontopouli** for 5km; from Kontopouli itself, a dirt road accesses the third site, **Hephaistia** (Ta Ifestia), once Limnos' main city. It's where Hephaestus, god of fire and metallurgy, was hurled down from Mt Olympus by Zeus. Little remains, however, other than low walls and a partially excavated theatre.

Limnos' northeastern tip has some rustic, little-visited villages, plus remote **Keros Beach**, popular with windsurfers. Flocks of flamingos sometimes strut on shallow **Lake Alyki**. From Cape Plaka, at Limnos' northeastern tip, Samothraki and Imvros (Gökçeada in Turkish) are visible. These three islands were historically considered as forming a strategic triangle for the defence of the Dardanelles, and thus İstanbul (Constantinople); this was Turkey's case for clinging to Imvros in 1923, even after Greece had won back most of its other islands a decade earlier.

AGIOS EFSTRATIOS
ΑΓΙΟΣ ΕΥΣΤΡΑΤΙΟΣ

pop 370

Little-visited Agios Efstratios lies isolated in the Aegean, south of Limnos (p627). Abbreviated by locals as 'Aï-Stratis', it attracts a few curious visitors drawn by the island's fine, remote beaches and generally escapist feel. They certainly don't come for the architecture: a 1968 earthquake destroyed Agios Efstratios' classic buildings. Nevertheless, this sparsely populated place has domatia, good seafood tavernas, relaxing hill walks and beaches (some accessible only by boat).

Agios Efstratios has had a chequered past. Even before the quake, many dissidents and suspected communists were exiled here, including the composer Mikis Theodorakis and poets Kostas Varnalis and Giannis Ritsos.

Sights & Activities

The **village beach** has dark volcanic sand and warm waters. A 90-minute walk northeast leads to **Alonitsi Beach**, a long, idyllic strand with intriguing facing islets. Take the track from the village's northeast side, starting by a small bridge; when it splits, keep right. **Lidario Beach**, on the west side, is a much tougher walk, so go by local boat to this and other hard-to-reach beaches.

Sleeping & Eating

Book rooms from Limnos with Myrina Tourist & Travel Agency (p629) or Theodoros Petrides Travel Agency (p629), or else find domatia upon arrival; only in high summer might things be crowded. The island's few tavernas offer inexpensive fare and fresh seafood.

Getting There & Away

For ferry and hydrofoil information from Agios Efstratios, see Island Hopping (p745). Buy tickets at Myrina Tourist & Travel Agency (p629) in Myrina. Bad weather can cause unpredictable cancellations and delays.

SAMOTHRAKI
ΣΑΜΟΘΡΑΚΗ

pop 2720 / area 176 sq km

Lush Samothraki sits contentedly alone in the northeastearn Aegean, halfway between the mainland port of Alexandroupoli and Limnos to the south. This thickly forested island is relatively small, with few settlements, and is rarely visited out of high season, though it does boast one of the most important archaeological sites in Greece in the ancient Thracian Sanctuary of the Great Gods. Also here stands the Aegean's loftiest peak, Mt Fengari (1611m), from where Homer recounts that Poseidon, god of the sea, watched the Trojan War unfold.

Samothraki's mountainous interior is totally unpopulated, and full of valleys bursting with massive gnarled oak and plane trees, making it ideal for hiking and mountain biking. Outdoors lovers will especially want to seek out Samothraki's woodlands waterfalls, which plunge into deep, icy pools, providing cool relief on a hot summer's day. The island's remote beaches in the southeast are idyllic and pristine, while the west offers therapeutic hot baths at Loutra (Therma). The main port, sleepy Kamariotissa, is a whimsical fishing village, while the hilly former inland capital, Hora, is bursting with flowers and pretty traditional homes, all overlooking the distant sea.

While the famous electronic music festival seems to have been killed off due to local irritation with its spaced-out guests, the proliferation of safari hats, dreadlocks and Hindu symbols lingers, perpetuating Samothraki's exotic, jungle vibe. Although the island's remoteness and poor transport links mean that it's often forgotten by foreign island-hoppers, devotees of ancient archaeology and outdoors sorts will find this unique and laid-back island very much worth the effort it takes to get here.

Getting There & Away

For ferry and hydrofoil information from Samothraki, see Island Hopping (p760). Niki Tours (opposite) in Kamariotissa sells tickets.

Getting Around

BOAT

In summer the tour boat **Samothraki** (☎ 25510 42266) circles the island (€20), departing Loutra (Therma) at 11am and returning by 6.30pm. The boat passes sights like the Byzantine castle

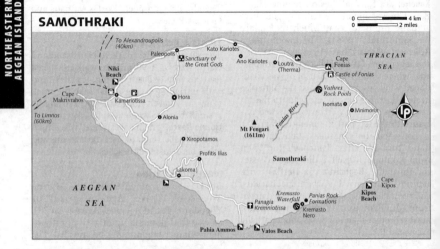

SAMOTHRAKI

0 — 4 km
0 — 2 miles

To Alexandroupolis (40km)

Kato Kariotes
Paleopolis
Sanctuary of the Great Gods
Ano Kariotes
Loutra (Therma)

THRACIAN SEA

Cape Fonias
Castle of Fonias

Niki Beach

Vathres Rock Pools
Isomata
Mnimoria

Cape Makrivrahos
Kamariotissa
Hora

To Limnos (60km)

Alonia

Xiropotamos

Mt Fengari (1611m)

Fonias River

Samothraki

Profitis Ilias

Lakoma

AEGEAN SEA

Kremasto Waterfall
Panagia Kremniotissa
Panias Rock Formations
Kremasto Nero

Cape Kipos
Kipos Beach

Pahia Ammos
Vatos Beach

of Fonias, the Panias rock formations and Kremasto Waterfall, before stopping at 1pm for four hours of swimming and sunbathing at Vatos Beach. A snack bar operates on board. For more information, ask at Petrinos Kipos Taverna in Kamariotissa or call the boat operator.

BUS

In summer 10 buses daily go from Kamariotissa **bus station** (☎ 25513 41533) to Hora (€1) and eight to Loutra (Therma; €2) via Paleopolis (€1). Some Loutra buses continue to the two camping grounds. Five daily buses serve Profitis Ilias (€2) via Alonia and Lakoma.

CAR & MOTORCYCLE

For vehicle hire, on Kamariotissa's waterfront opposite the buses, **X Rentals** (☎ 25510 42272) has cars and small jeeps, as does **Kyrkos Rent a Car** (☎ 25510 41620, 6972839231). **Rent A Motor Bike** (☎ 25510 41057), opposite the quay, offers motorcycles and scooters.

TAXI

Taxis from Kamariotissa access most destinations, including Hora (€5), Pahia Ammos (€15), Profitis Ilias (€7.50), Sanctuary of the Great Gods (€5), Loutra (Therma; €7.50), first camping ground (€8.50), second camping ground (€9.50), Fonias River (€12), and Kipos Beach (€17).

For a taxi, call the English- and German-speaking company **Petros Glinias** (☎ 6972883501) or other **taxi companies** (☎ 25510 41733, 25510 41341, 25510 41077).

KAMARIOTISSA ΚΑΜΑΡΙΩΤΙΣΣΑ
pop 960
Samothraki's port, largest town and transport hub, Kamariotissa has the island's main services and a nearby pebble beach with bars and decent swimming. While most visitors don't linger, it's a likeable enough port town filled with flowers and good fish tavernas, and roughly equidistant from Samothraki's more famous attractions.

Orientation & Information
Turn left from the ferry and you'll find a tourist information kiosk 50m along the road running along the water, on the port side. Buses wait behind this kiosk further east on the waterfront. Across the road are

tavernas, travel and car- and motorcycle-hire agencies, and ATMs. Follow the waterfront further east for 100m to reach Kamariotissa's beach.

Café Action (☎ 25510 41056; internet per hr €4) At the harbour's west end.

Niki Tours (☎ 25510 41465; niki _tours@hotmail.com) A helpful, full-service travel agency, across from the buses.

Port police (☎ 25510 41305) East along the waterfront.

Tourist Information Kiosk (☎ 25510 89242) On the port.

www.samothraki.com General information about Samothraki, including boat schedules.

www.samothrace.gr Another online resource (Greek-only), with important phone numbers.

Activities
Haris Hatzigiannakoudis at Niki Tours runs a **Capoeira Camp** (a Brazilian martial art/dance) with Brazilian master Lua Rasta annually in late June, and can organise **hiking safaris** to Mt Fengari. As many of Samothraki's lush inland hiking trails are poorly marked or unmarked completely, and since the island has no official mountaineering guide, see Haris if interested in serious hiking here.

Festivals & Events
Although disapproving local authorities seem to have pulled the plug on Samothraki's natty-haired world music festival, there's always talk of a resurrection. Meanwhile, the island has somehow become a gathering point for Greek motorcyclists – a sort of Hell's Angels-meets-the-hippies juxtaposition with many intriguing possible outcomes. Check for festival news online or with Niki Tours.

Sleeping
Domatia are arranged at the port-side tourist information kiosk or Niki Tours, and are also signposted.

Niki Beach Hotel (☎ 25510 41545; s/d €45/60) This spacious hotel with large, modern rooms has a lovely garden and is fronted by poplar trees, opposite the town beach.

Hotel Aeolos (☎ 25510 41595; s/d incl breakfast €60/80; 🛏 🌊) Up behind Niki Beach Hotel, the Aeolos stands on a hill overlooking the sea and has comfortable rooms. Front rooms face the large swimming pool and garden, while the back ones have views of Mt Fengari.

Eating

Klimitaria Restaurant (☎ 25510 41535; mains from €6) This waterfront eatery serves an unusual speciality called *gianiotiko*, an oven-baked dish of diced pork, potatoes, egg and more, as well as the usual taverna fare.

I Synantisi (☎ 25510 41308; fish €6-10) For fresh fish at good prices, head to this hard-working outdoor *ouzerie* on the central waterfront. View the daily catch, on ice inside.

HORA ΧΩΡΑ

Set within a natural fortress of two sheer cliffs, and with a commanding view of the sea, Hora (also called Samothraki) was the obvious choice for the island's capital. In the 10th century the Byzantines built a castle on its northwestern peak, though today's substantial remains mostly date from the 15th-century rule of Genoese lord Palamidi Gattilusi, who married into the last Byzantine imperial dynasty, the Palaeologi.

Marked by curving cobbled streets wreathed in flowers and colourful, crumbling traditional houses topped by terracotta roofs, Hora is perfect for ambling and enjoying a leisurely lunch or coffee. The great views and constant interplay of angles, shadows and colour make it fun for photographers, and in summer there's subdued nightlife in Hora's small streets and roof bars.

Orientation & Information

Buses and taxis stop in the square, below the village. Walk upwards along the main street, following the signs for the *kastro* (castle). Here are the OTE, Agricultural Bank and post office. The **police station** (☎ 25510 41203) is in Gattilusi's castle. Cafes and tavernas are found higher on the street and, on the right, there's a small fountain with fresh mountain spring water.

Sleeping

Hora has a few domatia. Midway up the main street, **Kyra Despina** (☎ 6974980263; s/d €45/60), who speaks some English, has fan-only, self-catering studios with sweeping views, sleeping up to four people.

Eating & Drinking

our pick **O Lefkos Pyrgos** (☎ 25510 41601; desserts €4-6; 9am-3am Jul-Aug) The summer-only Lefkos Pyrgos is an excellent and inventive sweets shop run by master desserts inven-

tor Georgios Stergiou and wife Dafni. Only all-natural ingredients are used, without preservatives or artificial flavourings. The lemonade sweetened with honey and cinnamon is very refreshing on a hot summer's day, and some unique variations on traditional fare (like Greek yoghurt flavoured with bitter almond) are also on offer. Exotic teas, coffees and mixed drinks are also served, along with a variety of indulgent cakes and other desserts.

Café-Ouzeri 1900 (☎ 25510 41224; mains €5-9) This relaxing taverna set under a shady trellis left of the fountain offers friendly service and great views of the village's red rooftops, castle and sea. Try the *spetsofaï* (stewed green peppers, tomatoes and sausage in an earthen pot), rice with seafood, or *tzigerosarmades* (goat flavoured with onion, dill and spearmint). The large, colourful menu, printed to look like a newspaper, is a take-home memento.

Meltemi (☎ 25510 41071; 8am-late) Higher up in Hora, the side street to the left, opposite the fountain, leads to this cool bar with great views and roof garden popular by night.

SANCTUARY OF THE GREAT GODS
ΤΟ ΙΕΡΟ ΤΩΝ ΜΕΓΑΛΩΝ ΘΕΩΝ

Some 6km northeast of Kamariotissa, the **Sanctuary of the Great Gods** (admission €3, free Sun 1 Nov-31 Mar & public holidays; 8.30am-4pm Tue-Sun), is one of Greece's most important – and mysterious – archaeological sites. The Thracians built this temple to their Great Gods around 1000 BC. By the 5th century BC, the secret rites associated with the cult had attracted many famous ancient figures. Among the initiates were Egyptian Queen Arsinou and Philip II of Macedon. Remarkably, the Sanctuary operated until paganism was forbidden in the 4th century AD.

The principal deity, the Great Mother (Alceros Cybele), was a fertility goddess; when the original Thracian religion became integrated with the state religion, she was merged with the Olympian female deities Demeter, Aphrodite and Hecate. The last of these was a mysterious goddess associated with darkness, the underworld and witchcraft. Other deities worshipped here were the Great Mother's consort, the virile young Kadmilos (god of the phallus), later integrated with the Olympian god Hermes, and the demonic Kabeiroi twins, Dardanos and Aeton, later integrated with Castor and Pollux (the Dioscuri), the twin sons of Zeus and Leda. These twins were invoked by mariners to protect them while at sea. Samothraki's Great Gods were venerated for their immense power; in comparison, the bickering Olympian gods were considered frivolous, fickle and almost comic characters.

Little is known about what actually transpired here – no surprise, since initiates who revealed the rites were punished by death. The archaeological evidence, however, points to two initiations, a lower and a higher. In the first, the Great Gods were invoked to grant the initiate a spiritual rebirth; in the second, the candidate was absolved of transgressions. Anybody who wanted could be initiated.

The site's most celebrated relic, the *Winged Victory of Samothrace* (now in the Louvre), was found by Champoiseau, the French consul, at Adrianople (present-day Edirne, Turkey) in 1863. Subsequent excavations were sporadic until just before WWII, when Karl Lehmann and Phyllis Williams Lehmann of the Institute of Fine Arts, New York University, directed an organised dig.

Exploring the Site

The site is extensive but well labelled. After entering, take the left-hand path to the rectangular **anaktoron**. At its southern end was a **sacristy**, the antechamber where white-gowned candidates assembled before going to the *anaktoron's* main room for their first (lower) initiation. One by one, each initiate would then enter the small inner temple at the structure's northern end, where a priest would explain the ceremony's symbols. Afterwards the initiates received a sort of initiation certificate in the sacristy.

Sacrifices occurred in the **arsinoein**, southwest of the *anaktoron*. Once a grand cylindrical structure, it was built in 289 BC as a gift to the Great Gods from Egyptian Queen Arsinou. Southeast stands the **sacred rock**, the site's original altar.

Following the initiations, a celebratory feast was held, probably south of the *arsinoein* in the **temenos** – a gift from Philip II. Adjacent is the prominent Doric **hieron**, the sanctuary's most photographed ruin, with five reassembled columns. Initiates received their second (higher) initiation here.

Opposite the *hieron* stand remnants of a **theatre**. Nearby, a path ascends to the **Nike monument** where once stood the magnificent *Winged Victory of Samothrace,* a gift from Demetrius Poliorketes (the 'besieger of cities') to the Kabeiroi for helping him defeat Ptolemy II in battle. The ruins of a massive **stoa**, a two-aisled portico where pilgrims to the sanctuary sheltered, lie to the northwest. Initiates' names were recorded on its walls. Ruins of an unrelated **medieval fortress** lie just north.

A good **site map** is located on the path east from the Nike monument; the path continues to the southern **necropolis**, Samothraki's most important ancient cemetery, used from the Bronze Age to early Roman times. North of the cemetery once stood the sanctuary's elaborate Ionic entrance, the **propylon**, a gift from Ptolemy II.

The site ticket includes the **museum** (☎ 25510 41474; ☉ 8.30am-3pm Tue-Sun), whose exhibits include terracotta figurines, vases, jewellery and a plaster cast of the *Winged Victory of Samothrace.*

AROUND SAMOTHRAKI

Loutra (Therma) Λουτρά (Θερμά)

Loutra (also called Therma) is 14km east of Kamariotissa and near the coast, and represents Samothraki's most popular place to stay. This relaxing village of plane and horse-chestnut trees, dense greenery and gurgling creeks comes to life at night when the young people staying in local domatia or the nearby camping grounds congregate in its laid-back outdoor cafe.

The village's synonymous names refer to its therapeutic, mineral-rich springs; the **thermal bath** (☎ 25510 98229; admission €3; ☉ 7-10.45am & 4-7.45pm Jun-Sep) reportedly cures everything from skin problems and liver ailments to infertility. The prominent white building by the bus stop houses the official bath; however, bathing for free is possible at another indoor bath, 50m up the road to the right, and at two small outdoor baths another 20m up the hill.

SLEEPING & EATING

Samothraki's two popular camping grounds occupy the beach east of Loutra. They are both called 'Multilary Camping' (no, they don't mean 'Military') and are similar. If you come out of season, you can usually stay for free.

Multilary Camping I (Camping Plateia; ☎ 25510 41784; camp sites per adult/tent €4/3; ☉ Jun-Aug) A shady, laid-back place on the left 2km beyond Loutra.

Multilary Camping II (☎ 25510 41491; camp sites per adult/tent €5/3; ☉ Jun-Aug) Just past Multilary

Camping I, with a minimarket, restaurant and showers.

Studios Ktima Holovan (☎ 25510 98335, 6976695591; d/tr €70/80) Located 16km east of Kamariotissa, this relaxing place has very modern, two-room self-catering studios set on a grassy lawn 50m from the beach, and a mini-playground for kids. The price also includes a free hire car.

Mariva Bungalows (☎ 25510 98230; d incl breakfast €80; ☒) These secluded bungalows, with breezy modern rooms, sit on a lush hillside near a waterfall. To reach them, turn from the coast road inland towards Loutra, and then take the first left. Follow the signs to the bungalows (600m further).

Kafeneio Ta Therma (☎ 25510 98325) This big open cafe near the baths is always full, whether for coffee in the morning, beer at night or homemade fruit sweets at any time.

Loutra has fast food like souvlaki, though **Paradisos Restaurant** (☎ 25510 95267; mains €5-8) and **Fengari Restaurant** (☎ 25510 98321; mains €5.50-9) have good sit-down fare; try the latter's stuffed goat or *imam tourlou* (roast eggplant stuffed with potatoes and pumpkin).

Fonias River

After Loutra on the northeast coast is the Fonias River, and the famous **Vathres rock pools** (admission €1). The walk starts at the bridge 4.7km east of Loutra, by the (summer-only) ticket booths. The first 40 minutes are easy and on a well-marked track leading to a large rock pool fed by a dramatic 12m-high waterfall. The cold water is very refreshing on a hot summer's day. The river is known as the 'Murderer', and in winter rains can transform the waters into a raging torrent. The real danger, however, is getting lost: though there are six waterfalls, marked paths only run to the first two; after that, the walk becomes dangerously confusing. For serious hiking here and in the Mt Fengari area, consult Niki Tours (p633) in Kamariotissa.

Beaches

The 800m-long **Pahia Ammos Beach** is a superb sandy beach along an 8km winding road from Lakoma on the south coast. In summer, caïques from Kamariotissa visit. The boat tour from Loutra stops around the headland at the equally superb, nudist-friendly **Vatos Beach**.

The formerly Greek-inhabited island of Imvros (Gökçeada), ceded to Turkey under the Treaty of Lausanne in 1923, is sometimes visible from Pahia Ammos.

Pebbled **Kipos Beach** on the southeast coast, accessed via the road skirting the north coast, is pretty but shadeless; like the others, it's reached in summer by caïque or excursion boat.

Other Villages

The small villages of **Profitis Ilias**, **Lakoma** and **Xiropotamos** in the southwest, and **Alonia** near Hora, are all serene and seldom visited, though they're easily accessible. The hill-side Profitis Ilias, with many trees and springs, has several tavernas; **Vrahos** (☎ 25510 95264) is particularly famous for its roast goat.

THASOS ΘΑΣΟΣ

pop 13,530

One of Greece's greenest and most gentle islands, Thasos lies 10km from mainland Kavala. While similar climate and vegetation gives the feeling that the island is but an extension of northern Greece, it boasts enviable sandy beaches and a gorgeous, forested mountain interior. It's also quite inexpensive by Greek island standards and is one of the most popular with families, as well as young people from the greater Balkan 'neighbourhood' of Bulgaria and the ex-Yugoslav republics. Frequent ferries from the mainland allow independent travellers crossing northern Greece to get here quickly, and the excellent bus network makes getting around easy.

Over its long history, Thasos has often benefited from its natural wealth. The Parians who founded the ancient city of Thasos (Limenas) in 700 BC struck gold at Mt Pangaion, creating an export trade lucrative enough to subsidise a naval fleet. While the gold is long gone, Thasos' white marble – said to be the second whitest in the world – is still being exploited, unfortunately blighting the mountainside with quarries in the process. Environmentalists have criticised this, and the (subdued) exploration for offshore oil between Thasos and Kavala.

For visitors today, however, the island's main source of wealth stems from its natural beauty and some notable historic attractions. The excellent archaeological museum in the capital, Thasos (Limenas) is complemented by the Byzantine Monastery of Arhangelou, with its stunning cliff-top setting, and the ancient Greek temple on the serene southern beach of Alyki.

While some of Thasos' best beaches have been afflicted by shabby package tourism, untouched spots remain. And, considering that the relatively short 'high season' runs essentially from mid-July to mid-August, it's possible at other times to enjoy peaceful moments on this so-called 'emerald isle'.

Living as it does largely from tourism, Thasos' shuttered domatia and hotels were lonely out of season. Only the capital, Limenas, has a few functioning hotels in winter.

Getting There & Away

Thasos is only accessible from Kavala and Keramoti on the mainland (for details, see Island Hopping, p753). In Kavala, ferries dock on the long eastern harbour while hydrofoils wait on the dock opposite the harbour, just behind the main intercity (IC) bus station, beside the small port police kiosk.

On Thasos itself, get ferry schedules at the **ferry ticket booths** (☎ 25930 22318) in Thasos (Limenas) and the **port police** (☎ 25930 22106) at Skala Prinou. The ferry dock for Keramoti is 150m west of Thasos town centre.

Getting Around

BICYCLE

Basic bikes can be hired in Thasos (Limenas), but top-of-the-line models and detailed route information are available in Potos from local mountain biking expert, **Yiannis Raizis** (☎ 25930 52459, 6946955704; www.mtb-thassos.com).

BOAT

The **Eros 2 excursion boat** (☎ 6944945282; day trip €25) makes full-day trips around Thasos four times weekly, with stops for swimming and a barbecue. The boat departs the Old Harbour at 10am. Water taxis run regularly to Hrysi Ammoudia (Golden Beach) and Makryammos Beach from the Old Harbour. Excursion boats of varying sizes, nationalities and alcohol content also set sail regularly from the coastal resorts.

BUS

Frequent buses circle the coast in both directions and service inland villages too. Buses meet arriving ferries at Skala Prinou and Thasos (Limenas), the island's transport hub. The two port towns are connected by eight daily buses (€1.80).

Daily buses go 10 to 12 times a day from Thasos (Limenas) through west-coast villages like Skala Marion (€3.30) to Limenaria (€4), with seven continuing to Potos (€4.20). Five daily buses connect Thasos (Limenas) with Theologos (€5.30). From Thasos (Limenas) four buses daily go further south to Alyki (€3.30) and nearby Moni Arhangelou. From Potos you can follow the same route to these places on to the east coast and Paradise Beach (€3.10), Skala Potamia (€3.90) and nearby Hrysi Ammoudia (Golden Beach) for €4.20.

In summer 10 daily buses go the other way from Thasos (Limenas) to these east-coast villages, servicing Skala Potamia (€1.50) via Panagia (€1.40) and Potamia (€1.40). A full circular tour (about 100km) runs nine times daily (€9.50, 3½ hours), clockwise or anti-clockwise. Helpfully, this round-the-island ticket is valid all day, meaning you can jump on and off without paying extra. The **bus station** (☎ 25930 22162) on the Thasos (Limenas) waterfront, provides timetables.

CAR & MOTORCYCLE

Avis Rent a Car Thasos (Limenas) (☎ 25930 22535); Potamia (☎ 25930 61735); Skala Prinou (☎ 25930 72075) is widespread, though smaller, local companies may be cheaper. In Thasos (Limenas), **Billy's Bikes** (☎ 25930 22490), opposite the newsagent, and **2 Wheels** (☎ 25930 23267), on the Prinos road, offer bike and motorcycle hire.

TAXI

The Thasos (Limenas) **taxi rank** (☎ 25930 22391) is on the waterfront, next to the main bus stop. In Potos, a taxi rank with listed prices is besides the main road's bus stop.

THASOS (LIMENAS) ΘΑΣΟΣ (ΛΙΜΕΝΑΣ)
pop 2610 / area 375 sq km

Thasos (also called Limenas), has the island's most services and year-round life, along with a picturesque fishing harbour, sandy beach, shopping, a few ancient ruins and an archaeological museum. Still, considering the relatively expensive accommodation rates and lacklustre restaurant offerings here, and the superior beaches, mountain forests and nightlife further on, lingering isn't necessary.

Orientation & Information

ATM-equipped banks are near the central square. The town beach, backed by waterfront tavernas and beach bars, is about 100m beyond the old harbour, a 10-minute walk from the town centre.

Billias Travel Service (☎ 25930 24003; www
.billias-travel-service.gr; Gallikis Arheologikis Scholis 2)
All-services travel agency.
Mood Café (☎ 25930 23417; cnr 18 Oktovriou & K
Dimitriadi; per hr €3; ☻ 9.30am-2am) Internet cafe with
fast connection.
Port police (☎ 25930 22106)
Tourist police (☎ 25930 23111)
www.gothassos.com Useful online resource.

Sights

Thasos' **archaeological museum** (☎ 25930 22180;
☻ 9am-3pm Tue-Sun) displays Neolithic utensils
from a mysterious central Thasos tomb, plus
Ancient Greek art, including a 5m-tall 6th-
century BC *kouros* carrying a ram.

Next door stand ruins of the **ancient agora**,
the commercial centre in ancient Greek and
Roman times. The foundations of stoas, shops
and dwellings remain. About 100m east of the
agora, the **ancient theatre** stages performances
of ancient dramas and comedies during the
Kavala Festival of Drama. The theatre is signposted from the small harbour.

From here a path leads to the **acropolis**,
where substantial remains of a medieval
fortress stand. Carved rock steps descend to
the foundations of the ancient town walls on
which the fortress was built. There are magnificent views of the coast from here as well.

Festivals & Events

In July and August plays are held in the ancient theatre during the **Kavala Festival of Drama**.
A free **Full moon concert** occurs each August,
featuring singers from all over Greece. The **EOT**
(☎ 25102 22425) in Kavala has information and
tickets, or ask Thasos' **tourist police** (☎ 25930
23111). The summertime **Thasos Festival** includes
classical drama, painting exhibitions and contemporary Greek music. Programs are available at hotels, cafes and tourist agencies.

Sleeping

BUDGET & MIDRANGE

Hotel Possidon (☎ 25930 22739; www.thassos-possidon
.com; Old Harbour; s/d €40/50; ☒ ☞) This friendly
waterfront hotel's recently renovated lobby
bar straddles both the harbour and main
shopping street of 18 Oktovriou. It's one of
the few local hotels that doesn't work with
package-tour companies. Rooms are modern
and well maintained, many with comfortable
water-view balconies.

Hotel Galini (☎ 25930 22195; Theageneou; s/d €44/50;
☒) This small, slightly worn place opposite
the Amfipolis Hotel has 16 simple but clean
rooms. Service is gruff, though a flowery back
garden restores good cheer.

Hotel Akropolis (☎ /fax 25930 22488; M Alexandrou;
incl breakfast €45/55; ☒) This century-old mansion
offers a classic touch, with eclectic antiques
and a relaxing garden, though rooms are
slightly cramped.

Hotel Angelica (☎ 25930 22387; www.hotel-angelica
.gr; Old Harbour; s/d €50/60; ☒) Another waterfront
hotel, the Angelica is a dependable choice,
though not overwhelming. Bathrooms are a
bit dated but clean.

TOP END

Hotel Timoleon (☎ 25930 22177; Old Harbour; s/d €70/100;
☒) Located next to the Hotel Possidon, the
three-star Timoleon has 30 rooms (15 with
sea view) characterised by smooth fixtures
and spacious interiors; considering the price,
though, perhaps not unique enough.

Amfipolis Hotel (☎ 25930 23101; www.hotelamfipolis
.gr; cnr 18 Oktovriou & Theogenous; s/d/tr/ste incl breakfast
€95/140/165/235; ☻ Jun-Oct; ☒ ☞ ☒) Thasos'
most elegant hotel occupies this national
heritage–listed building with an imposing
blue facade. A hotel since 1938 and previous
to that a tobacco warehouse, the Amfipolis
has elegant rooms with high, wood-panelled
ceilings, and even a garden Jacuzzi.

Eating & Drinking

Simi (☎ 25930 22517; Old Harbour; mains €7-10) At
first glance, Simi looks like all the other Old

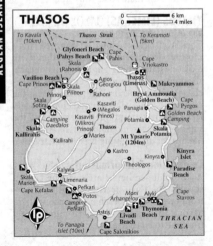

THASOS

0 —————— 6 km
0 —————— 4 miles

To Kavala (10km)
Thasos Strait
To Keramoti (5km)
Glyfoneri Beach
Cape Pahis
Pahys Beach
Skala Rahoniu
Cape Vriokastro
Vasiliou Beach
Cape Prinos
Agios Georgiou
Thasos (Limenas)
Makryammos
Skala Prinou
Rahoni
Prinos
Kasaviti
Hrysi Ammoudia (Golden Beach)
Skala Sotira
(Megalos Prinos)
Panagia
Cape Pyrgos
Golden Beach Camping
Camping Daedalos
Kasaviti (Mikros Prinos)
Thasos
Potamia
Skala Kallirahis
Maries
Mt Ypsario (1204m)
Skala Potamia
Kallirahi
Kastro
Kinyra
Kinyra Islet
Kalyvia
Theologos
Paradise Beach
Skala Marion
Limenaria
Pefkari
Moni Arhangelou
Alyki
Cape Stavros
Cape Kefalas
Potos
Camping Pefkari
Astris
Thymonia Beach
Livadi Beach
THRACIAN SEA
To Panagia Islet (10km)
Cape Salonikios

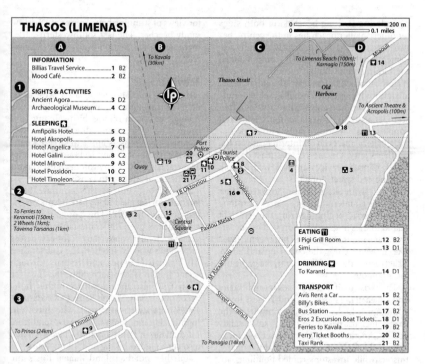

THASOS (LIMENAS)

INFORMATION	
Billias Travel Service	**1** B2
Mood Café	**2** B2

SIGHTS & ACTIVITIES	
Ancient Agora	**3** D2
Archaeological Museum	**4** C2

SLEEPING	
Amfipolis Hotel	**5** C2
Hotel Akropolis	**6** B3
Hotel Angelica	**7** C1
Hotel Galini	**8** C2
Hotel Mironi	**9** A3
Hotel Possidon	**10** C2
Hotel Timoleon	**11** B2

EATING	
I Pigi Grill Room	**12** B2
Simi	**13** D1

DRINKING	
To Karanti	**14** D1

TRANSPORT	
Avis Rent a Car	**15** B2
Billy's Bikes	**16** C2
Bus Station	**17** B2
Eros 2 Excursion Boat Tickets	**18** D1
Ferries to Kavala	**19** B2
Ferry Ticket Booths	**20** B2
Taxi Rank	**21** B2

Harbour tavernas with touting waiters; however, locals agree that it serves Limenas' best fish. There's taverna fare, too.

I Pigi Grill Room (☎ 25930 22941; Central Square; mains €5-7.50; ☺ dinner) This friendly, central restaurant next to a spring does excellent grills; seafood mezedhes and fresh salads are good, too.

Taverna Tarsanas (☎ 25930 23933; mezedhes €4, mains €10-15) Located 1km west of Thasos, Tarsanas offers great fish and unique seafood mezedhes.

To Karanti (☎ 25930 24014; Miaouli) An outdoor *ouzerie* on the Old Harbour frequented by locals and tourists alike, To Karanti has a picturesque setting overlooking fishing boats, complemented by its traditional music and tasty mezedhes.

Karnagio (☎ 25930 23170) Stroll past the Old Harbour to the end for Karnagio, a nice open spot for a quiet sunset drink. The outdoor seating opens onto both sides of a rocky promontory lapped by waves. You can also clamber up the rocks to the small, candle-lit chapel above.

WEST COAST

Thasos' west coast has been assailed by package tourism for years, though there are still a few idyllic spots and quiet sandy beaches. Better still, the inland mountain villages preserve a traditional pace of life and some fine architecture, without much appreciable damage from the masses. There are ATMs in Skala Prinou, Limenaria and Potos, all large villages with numerous services.

Following the coast west from Thasos (Limenas), two average sandy beaches emerge, **Glyfoneri** and then **Pahys Beach**.

Continuing west, the port of **Skala Prinou** has ferries to Kavala, though little else. However, 1km south, the lovely **Vasiliou Beach** stands backed by trees, and the inland, hillside villages of **Mikros Prinos** and **Megalos Prinos** (collectively known as Kasaviti) offer a refreshingly lush break from the touristed coast, with undeniable character and a few places to stay and eat. Further southwest, two small beaches appear at **Skala Sotira** and **Skala Kallirahis**. Some 2km inland from the latter, traditional **Kallirahi** features steep narrow streets and stone houses.

However, the first real point of interest lies further south; the whimsical fishing port of **Skala Marion**. The village has been relatively unaffected by tourism – somewhat surprising, considering its long beaches on both sides (another smaller beach lies in the centre, between two jetties). Still primarily a fishing settlement, Skala Marion could be commissioned for filming some Italian romantic comedy. Its few canopied tavernas overlooking the sea are faithfully populated by village elders shuffling backgammon chips, while little children scamper about. A good choice for families and couples, Skala Marion features a few domatia, a bakery and even an internet cafe on the northern jetty. On the village's feast day (24 June), church services are followed by folk dancing and sweets for all.

Inland from Skala Marion, forested **Maries** makes for an interesting day trip. A 4km-long solid dirt road beginning from the centre of inland Maries hugs a deep, forested ravine, arriving at a manmade but still photogenic **forest lake**. Drive or enjoy the cooler upland air by **hiking** there – the road is straight, the going not too strenuous.

The coast road south passes more beaches and **Limenaria**, Thasos' second-largest town. Although it looks rather ungainly from the road, Limenaria has a nice, though small, sandy beach. Limenaria was created over a century ago for the German Speidel Metal Company; this erstwhile investor's ruined buildings, including a circular tower, still loom over the waterfront.

A few kilometres further south, the fishing-villages-turned-resorts of **Potos** and **Pefkari** have long sandy beaches, the former being especially crammed with cafes and tavernas. Although Potos has a good position for southwestern Thasos activities, including boat excursions, the kitsch and frenetic package-tour presence has scarred it irrevocably.

Although technically nowhere near the west coast, Thasos' medieval and Ottoman capital, **Theologos**, is only accessible from the main road at Potos. The turnoff is signposted, and the road leads inland for 10km before reaching Theologos, set against a rocky white peak and surrounded by forests. This tranquil hamlet of 400 souls is notable for its whitewashed, closely set traditional houses, many with slate roofs. Here see the **Church of Agios Dimitrios** (1803), distinguished by its tall, white-plastered clock tower and grand slate roof. Although buses serve Theologos, accommodation is scarce, making it a better day-trip destination.

From the Theologos-Potos corner of the main road, head southeast round the coast for views of stunning bays, some with pristine sandy beaches. The last southwestern settlement, **Astris**, has a good beach with tavernas and domatia.

Activities

Despite its touristy feel, Thasos' west coast offers worthwhile outdoors activities like scuba diving, mountain biking, birdwatching and more. The rocky, uninhabited **Panagia Islet**, southwest of Potos, is home to Greece's largest sea cormorant colony; **birdwatching boat trips** are arranged by local environmentalist Yiannis Markianos at Aldebaran Pension (below).

Also from Potos, the annual **Thasos International Mountain Biking Race** occurs on the last Sunday in April. This popular amateur event draws over 200 contestants, who race across a circular route from Potos east across the island's wooded interior. The course scales Mt Ypsario (1204m) and returns through scenic Kastro village. Incredibly, the entry fee (only €20) also includes three nights' hotel accommodation. **Yiannis Raizis** (☎ 25930 52459, 6946955704; www.mtb-thassos.com), who hires out high-quality mountain bikes year-round from his domatio in Potos, organises this event and also runs guided biking and hiking tours.

Further north, inland **Rahoni** hosts the **Pine Tree Paddock** (☎ 6945118961; ☑ 10am-2pm & 5pm-sunset), which has mountain ponies and horses (per hour €20), and does guided trail rides (per hour €25). Advance reservations are required.

Scuba-diving lessons for beginners and excursions for the experienced are offered in Potos by Vasilis Vasiliadis of **Diving Club Vasiliadis** (☎ 6944542974; www.scuba-vas.gr), including dives at Alyki's submerged ancient marble quarry.

Sleeping

Camping Pefkari (☎ 25930 51190; camp sites per adult/tent €5/4; ☑ Jun-Sep) This appealing camping ground on a wooded spot above Pefkari Beach is popular with families and has clean bathrooms; a minimum three-night stay is required.

Camping Daedalos (☎ /fax 25930 58251; camp sites per adult/tent €6/4) This beach-front camping ground north of Skala Sotira includes a mini-market and restaurant. Sailing, windsurfing and water-skiing lessons are offered too.

Aldebaran Pension (☎ 25930 52494, 6973209576; www.gothassos.com; Potos; d from €30; ☒) One street back from Potos beach, and set in a relaxing, leafy courtyard, this friendly, family-run pension has rooms with all mod cons and spacious balconies. Owner Yiannis Markianos, who also runs the informative Gothassos.com website, also hires out boats and does birdwatching boat trips to Panagia Islet.

Domatia Filaktaki (☎ 25930 52634, 6977413789; Skala Marion; r from €35; ✖) These simple but air-conditioned rooms are situated above the home of the kind and helpful Maria Filaktaki and family in Skala Marion. It's the first place you'll reach when descending to the waterfront from the bus stop, above the family's restaurant, Armeno.

MTB Yiannis Raizis Domatia (☎ 25930 52459, 6946955704; www.mtb-thassos.com; Potos; d/tr/q €45/60/70; ✖) A good option for large groups, these spacious self-catering studios run by mountainbiking enthusiast Yiannis Raizis fit up to eight people. It's 20m past the church on the Potos main road, and a five-minute walk from the beach. There are sea views from the roof garden, an adjacent pool and shaded lawn bar.

Eating

O Georgios (☎ 25930 52774; Potos; mains €4.50-7) This traditional Greek grill house set in a pebbled rose garden is a local favourite away from the tourist strip on Potos' main road, offering friendly service and big portions.

Taverna Giatrou (☎ 25930 31000; Theologos; mains €5-8) Set 800m on the right side when entering Theologos, this big taverna has great balcony views of village roofs and verdure below. Run by Kostas Giatrou ('the Doctor') and family, the place offers specialities including local roast lamb.

our pick Armeno (☎ 25930 51277; Skala Marion; mains €5-9) This relaxing waterfront taverna in off-beat Skala Marion has tasty fish, plus the full taverna menu. The vegetables and olive oil are organic and from the gardens of the friendly Filaktaki family, who also rent rooms and can help with local information and car hire.

Piatsa Michalis (☎ 25930 51574; Potos; mains €6-10) Potos' 50-year-old beachfront taverna started working well before mass tourism came to town, and sticks to the recipe with specialities like stewed rabbit and octopus in red-wine sauce, plus a full menu of taverna fare.

Restaurant Alphas (☎ 25930 53510; Skala Marion; mains €6-11) There's fine waterside ambience, and some good mezedhes, at this fish taverna on Skala Marion's northern pier.

Psarotaverna To Limani (☎ 25930 52790; Limenaria; mains €8-13) Limenaria's best seafood is served at this waterfront restaurant opposite the National Bank of Greece, though prices can be steep.

Kafeneio Tsiknas (☎ 25930 31202; Theologos) At the beginning of Theologos, right before the church, this charming cafe has balcony seating, coffees and snacks.

EAST COAST

Thasos' sandy east-coast beaches are packed in summer, though the tourist presence is more concentrated than on the west side – partly because the landscape features thick forests that run down from mountains to the sea. Although there are fewer organised activities here, there's a more relaxed feel, and the warm, shallow waters are excellent for families with small children.

The east coast also has photogenic (though touristy) inland villages like **Panagia** and **Potamia**, just south of Thasos (Limenas). Their characteristic architecture includes Panagia's stone-and-slate rooftops and the sumptuously decorated, blue-and-white domed **Church of the Kimisis tou Theotokou** (Church of the Dormition of the Virgin), which has a valuable icon collection. To reach this peaceful quarter, follow the sound of rushing spring water upwards along a stone path heading inland. Less-picturesque Potamia boasts the **Polygnotos Vagis Museum** (☎ 25930 61400; admission €3; ☉ 8.30am-noon & 6-8pm Tue-Sat, to noon Sun & holidays), devoted to Greek-American artist Polygnotos Vagis (born here in 1894). It's beside the main church. The Municipal Museum of Kavala (p307) also exhibits some of Vagis' work.

Potamia also makes a good jumping-off point for climbing Thasos' highest peak, **Mt Ypsario** (1204m), and for general hiking. A tractor trail west from Potamia continues to the valley's end, after which arrows and cairns point the way along a steep path upwards. The Ypsario hike is classified as being of 'moderate difficulty' and takes about three hours. You can sleep at the **Ypsario Mountain Shelter** (per bed €5), but first phone Leftheris of the Thasos Mountaineering Club in Thasos (Limenas) on ☎ 6972198032 to book and get the key. The shelter has fireplaces and spring water, but no electricity.

Both Panagia and Potamia are 4km west of the east coast's most popular beaches: sandy **Hrysi Ammoudia (Golden Beach)**, tucked inside a long, curving bay, and **Skala Potamia**, on its southern end. The latter has very warm, gentle and shallow waters, making it ideal for small children. A bus between the two (€1.30) runs

NORTHEASTERN AEGEAN ISLANDS

every couple of hours. Both have accommodation, restaurants and some nightlife. There's one Commercial Bank ATM in Skala Potamia, rather oddly set alone on the main road, 150m west of the village turn-off.

Further south of Skala Potamia is the deservedly popular **Paradise Beach**, located down a narrow, winding dirt road 2km after tiny **Kinyra** village. Continuing around the main road's southwestern bend, peaceful **Alyki** is Thasos' best place to unwind by the beach – and get some culture, too. This escapist destination features two fine sandy coves, with small snack shops and a taverna on the western one. The beaches are separated by a little olive grove dotted with ancient ruins comprising the **archaeological site of Alyki**. This inscrutable site, deemed Thasos' second-most significant after Limenas, lies alluringly above the southeastern (and more placid) beach. A helpful English-language placard with map explaining the site stands along the stone path connecting the two beaches.

The main attraction, a former **ancient temple** where the gods were once invoked to protect sailors, is situated right above the sea and is studded by column bases. A now submerged nearby **marble quarry** operated from the 6th century BC to the 6th century AD. Clamber along the rocky path from the temple site southward around the peninsula, and you'll also see an **early Christian cave** where hermits once lived.

Continuing west from Alyki, you'll pass **Thymonia Beach** before rising upwards to the cliff-top **Moni Arhangelou** (admission free; ☾ 9am-5pm), an Athonite dependency and working nunnery, notable for its 400-year-old church and stunning views over the sea. Those improperly attired will get shawled up for entry. As at many Orthodox monasteries, pilgrims can stay overnight for free if they attend services.

Heading west from here, the road descends sharply; watch out for the small dirt road to the left, at the road's northernmost curve. It leads to a tranquil swimming spot, **Livadi Beach**. One of Thasos' most beautiful beaches, its aquamarine waters are ringed by cliffs and forests, with just a few umbrellas set in the sand.

Sleeping & Eating

Domatia and small hotels run down the coast, though most are nondescript and dated. There's less accommodation at Kinyra and Alyki than at Hrysi Ammoudia (Golden Beach) and Skala Potamia, and there's no accommodation on

Paradise Beach. Regardless of place, you can just show up and grab a room; outside of July and August, prices are often 20% cheaper.

Golden Beach Camping (☎ 25930 61472; Hrysi Ammoudia; camp sites per adult/tent €5/4; **P**) A party feel pervades Golden Beach Camping, with its minimarket, bar, beach volleyball, and many young people from Greece, Serbia, Bulgaria and beyond. It's a fun place on the beach's best spot.

our pick **Domatia Vasso** (☎ 25930 31534, 6946524706; Alyki; r €50; **P** 🔀) Just east of Alyki's bus stop on the main road, look for the big burst of flowers and sign pointing up the drive to this relaxing set of eight self-catering domatia run by friendly Vasso Gemetzi and daughter Aleka. There's a relaxing outdoor patio with tables and cooking space. Kids stay free. A minimum two-night stay is required.

Semeli Studios (☎ 25930 61612; www.semeli-studios .gr; Skala Potamia; d/tr €50/60; **P** 🔀) The Kamelia's friendly owner Eleni Stoubou also runs these larger, self-catering options just behind. From the bus stop, head towards Hryssi Ammoudia on the main road for 100m; both Hotel Kamelia and Semeli Studios are signposted on the right.

Hotel Kamelia (☎ 25930 61463; www.hotel-kamelia .gr; Skala Potamia; s/d incl breakfast €40/60; **P** 🔀) This beach-front hotel has an understated, arty appeal, with flowery canvases, minimalist wall sculptures and cool jazz playing in the garden bar. The spacious, fresh-smelling rooms have large balconies and all mod cons.

Thassos Inn (☎ 25930 61612; www.thassosinn.gr; Panagia; s/d €50/70) Panagia's best accommodation is ideally set near the church, with sweeping views of the village's clustered slate rooftops. It has all mod cons and good-sized rooms, though the simple floors are uninspiring. The inn is run by the welcoming Tasos Manolopoulos, who proudly shows off his vegetable patch and pool of gigantic goldfish.

Taverna Elena (☎ 25930 61709; Panagia; mains €6-9) Just next to the traditional products shop off Panagia's central square, this classic taverna has mezedhes like *bougloundi* (baked feta with tomatoes and chilli), and excellent roast lamb and goat.

Restaurant Koralli (☎ 25930 62244; Skala Potamia; mains €7-11) This big Skala Potamia taverna serves above-average mushrooms stuffed with shrimp, eggplant baked with mozzarella and parmesan, zucchinis stuffed with crab, carpaccio and 330g sirloin steaks.

NORTHEASTERN AEGEAN ISLANDS

Evia & the Sporades
Εύβοια & Οι Σποράδες

Evia and the four islands known as the Sporades remain largely off the beaten path, but attract more Greeks than most and consequently retain a good deal of local colour. Evia is joined to the mainland by a short drawbridge at Halkida, which spans a narrow gulf.

Only two hours from Athens, both Halkida and nearby Eretria are destinations for car loads of weekend visitors. Across the island, though, the pace slows as the landscape stretches out, dotted by hilltop monasteries, small farms and vineyards. Goats stand in the middle of the road and stare at passing cars. Small beaches await on the north, west and southeast coasts, many of them with crystal-clear bays that elsewhere would be lined with matching umbrellas. The Sporades (in Greek, 'scattered ones') seem like an extension of the forested Pelion Peninsula. In fact, in prehistoric times they were joined. Skiathos, a haven for northern Europeans, claims the sandiest beaches in the Aegean, along with several prime scuba-diving spots. Low-key Skopelos kicks back with a relaxed and postcard-worthy harbour and a good number of pristine bays, and forest meadows threaded with walking trails. Alonnisos, the most remote of the group, anchors the National Marine Park of Alonnisos – established to protect the Mediterranean monk seal – and is a model for ecological awareness throughout Greece. Skyros, the southernmost of the chain, retains a good deal of local character, and is well known for its unique cuisine, woodworking and ceramics, folk traditions that date from Byzantine times when these islands were home to rogues and pirates – something that the good-natured residents are proud to mention.

HIGHLIGHTS

- **Spa Bathing** Soaking in the therapeutic thermal waters at Loutra Edipsou (p647), on Evia
- **Dinner on the Dock** Picking out your favourite from the fresh catch at Kalamakia (p663), on Alonnisos
- **Aegean Adventure** Watching for dolphins while cruising around Greece's only national marine park at Alonnisos (p661)
- **Island Walks** Hiking through olive groves and across pristine meadows on Skopelos (p659)
- **Romantic Meditation** Catching the sunset over wine from Atsitsa Bay (p669), on Skyros
- **Midnight Music** Listening to one of Greece's best bouzouki players above the *kastro* overlooking Skopelos Town (p658)
- **Scuba Diving** Exploring an underwater reef 30m down off Tsougriaki islet, Skiathos (p654), on Skopelos

National Marine Park of Alonnisos ★
★ Kalamakia
★ ★ Kastro
Tsougriaki
Atsitsa ★
★ Loutra Edipsou

- POPULATION: 228,750
- AREA: 4167 SQ KM

EVIA & THE SPORADES

EVIA & THE SPORADES

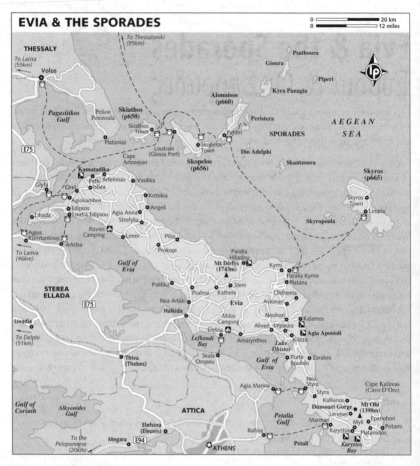

EVIA ΕΥΒΟΙΑ

Evia (*eh*-vih-ah), Greece's second-largest island after Crete and a prime holiday destination for Greeks, remains less charted by foreign tourists. Its attractions include glorious mountain roads, challenging treks, major archaeological finds and mostly uncrowded beaches. A mountainous spine runs north–south, dividing the island's precipitous eastern cliffs from the gentler and resort-friendly west coast. Ferries link the island to the mainland, along with a short sliding drawbridge over the narrow Evripos Channel to the capital of Halkida. The current in the narrow channel reverses direction about seven times daily,

an event whose full explanation has eluded observers since Aristotle.

Getting There & Away

There are regular bus services between Halkida and Athens (€6.20, 1¼ hours, half-hourly), Ioannina (€35.50, one daily) and Thessaloniki (€36, 6 hours, twice daily). There is also a regular train service between Halkida and Athens (normal, €5, 1½/one hour, hourly/four daily), and between Halkida and Thessaloniki (normal/IC express €26/33, 5½/4½ hours, six/four daily). There are regular ferry services from Evia to Skyros, Alonnisos and Skopelos; for details see Island Hopping (p750).

Tickets may be purchased at the dock kiosk at Paralia Kymis (the port of Kymi on Evia).

CENTRAL EVIA

After crossing the bridge to Halkida, the road veers south, following the coastline to Eretria, a bustling resort and major archaeological site. Further on, a string of hamlets and fishing villages dot the route until the junction at Lepoura, where the road forks north towards Kymi. Several branch roads to the sea are worth exploring, and the sandy beach at Kalamos is exceptional. A decent dirt road leads west from Kymi above the north coastline to Paralia Hiliadou.

Young fir, pine, and olive trees are making a comeback along the coastal road south of Eretria, thanks to a joint governmental and private reforestation project, following the tragic forest fires of August 2007.

Halkida Χαλκίδα
pop 54,560
Mentioned in the 'Iliad', Halkida (aka Halkis) was a powerful city-state in the 8th and 7th centuries BC, with several colonies dotted around the Mediterranean. The name derives from the bronze manufactured here in antiquity (*halkos* means 'bronze' in Greek). Today it's a gateway to Evia, and a lively shipping and agricultural centre. As evening approaches, the waterfront promenade by the Old Bridge comes to life.

To glimpse Halkida's interesting religious history, head up Kotsou towards the *kastro* (castle) to find a striking 15th-century **mosque**, and 19th-century **synagogue**, adjacent to Plateia Tzami (Tzami Sq). Then walk south about 150m to find the Byzantine **church** of Agia Paraskevi. An **Archaeological Museum** (☎ 22210 60944; Leoforos Venizelou 13; admission €2; 🕑 8.30am-3pm Tue-Sun) displays a fine torso of Apollo discovered at Eretria.

INFORMATION
Several ATMs cluster near the corner of Venizelou and Voudouri.
Hospital (☎ 22210 21902; cnr Gazepi & Hatzopoulou)
Kiosk (☎ 22210 76718; cnr Boudouri & Douna) International press.
Pharmacy (☎ 22210 25424; Isaiou 6)
Post office (cnr Karamourtzouni & Kriezotou; 🕑 8am-6pm Mon-Fri)
Surf-on-Net Cafe (☎ 22210 24867; Angeli Goviou 7A; internet per hr €1.50; 🕑 24hr)
Tourist police (☎ 22210 77777)

ACTIVITIES
Sport Apollon Scuba Diving Centre (☎ 22210 86369, 6945219619; www.sportapollon.gr; 🕑 9am-1.30pm & 5-9pm) in Halkida organises dives off the nearby Alykes coast, led by dive team Nikos and Stavroula. A one-day dive costs about €40.

SLEEPING & EATING
Best Western Lucy Hotel (☎ 22210 23831; www.lucy-hotel.gr; Voudouri 10; s/d/tr/ste incl breakfast €70/90/137/157; P 🅿 🖭 🖳 🛜) Rooms at the 2009-renovated Lucy are on the modern side, with swank blond furnishings, long desks and large bathrooms. The friendly multilingual staff can also clue you in to the adjacent boardwalk cafe scene.

Ouzerie O Loukas (☎ 22210 60371; Makariou 1; mezedhes €3-6, mains €5-9) On the mainland side of the Old Bridge, this handsome *ouzerie* (place that serves ouzo and light snacks) has first-rate mains and appetisers, from grilled octopus and *horta* (wild greens) to tzatziki and mussels with rice.

Mostar Café-Bar (☎ 22210 81213; Old Bridge; drinks, snacks €3-7; 🖭 🛜) You can't get any closer to the channel or the drawbridge than at this swank ultramodern bar.

GETTING THERE & AWAY
There are regular bus services between Halkida and Athens, Ioannina and Thessaloniki. Regular trains also connect Halkida with Athens and Thessaloniki.

To reach other parts of Evia, there are connections from **Halkida KTEL Bus Station** (☎ 22210 20400, cnr Styron & Arethousis), 3km east of the Old Bridge, to Eretria (€2, 25 minutes, hourly) and Kymi Town (€7.60, two hours, hourly), one of which continues to Paralia Kymis to meet the Skyros ferry. There are also buses to Steni (€2.70, one hour, twice daily), Limni (€7.10, two hours, three daily), Loutra Edipsou (€10.80, 2½ hours, once daily) and Karystos (€10.50, three hours, three daily).

For more information see also Island Hopping (p750).

Eretria Ερέτρια
pop 3160
Heading southeast from Halkida, Eretria is the first place of interest, with a small harbour and a lively boardwalk filled with mainland families who pack its fish tavernas on holiday weekends. There are late Neolithic finds around Eretria, which became a major maritime power and home to an eminent

school of philosophy by the 8th century BC. The modern town was founded in the 1820s, during the War of Independence, by islanders from Psara fleeing the Turkish.

INFORMATION

For emergencies, call the Halkida **tourist police** (☎ 22210 77777). For internet access, head to **Christos Internet Cafe-Bar** (☎ 22290 61604; per hr €2; ☺ 9am-1am) on the waterfront.

SIGHTS

From the top of the **ancient acropolis** there are splendid views over to the mainland. West of the acropolis are the remains of a palace, temple and theatre with a subterranean passage once used by actors to reach the stage. Close by, the excellent **Archaeological Museum of Eretria** (☎ 22290 62206; admission €2; ☺ 8.30am-3pm Tue-Sun) contains well-displayed finds from ancient Eretria. A 200m walk will bring you to the fascinating **House of Mosaics**, and ends 50m further on at the **Sanctuary of Apollo**.

SLEEPING & EATING

Milos Camping (☎ 22290 60420; www.camping-in-evia .gr/index_en.html; camp sites per adult/tent €6.50/4) This clean, shaded camping ground on the coast 1km northwest of Eretria has a small restaurant, bar and narrow pebble beach.

Eviana Beach Hotel (☎ 22290 62113; www.eviana beach.gr; s/d/tr incl breakfast €80/105/145; P ✿ 🖳 🛜) Tucked away 500m east of the waterfront, this 2009-renovated lodging occupies a prime beachfront spot, with spacious tile-floored rooms, plus an inviting tree-shaded beach bar.

Taverna Astra (☎ 22290 64111; Arheou Theatrou 48; mains €4-9) Just past the supermarket, this friendly waterfront taverna is known for well-priced fresh fish, along with appetisers like *taramasalata* (fish roe) and roasted sardines.

GETTING THERE & AWAY

Ferries travel daily between Eretria and Skala Oropou. For details see Island Hopping (p750).

Tickets should be purchased from the dock kiosk at the port of Eretria.

Steni Στενή

pop 1080

From Halkida, it's 31km to the lovely mountain village of Steni, with its gurgling springs and shady plane trees.

Steni is the starting point for a serious climb up **Mt Dirfys** (1743m), Evia's highest mountain. The **Dirfys Refuge** (☎ 22280 24298), at 1120m, can be reached along a 9km dirt road. From there, it's a steep 7km to the summit. Experienced hikers should allow about six hours from Steni to the summit. For refuge reservations, contact **Stamatiou** (☎ Mon-Fri 6972026862, Sat-Sun 22280 25655; per person €12). For more hiking information, contact the EOS-affiliated **Halkida Alpine Club** (☎ 22210 25230; Angeli Gouviou 22, Halkida). For tips on day hikes around Mt Dirfys, contact **Graham Beaumont** (☎ 6936523804; www.eviavillas .co.uk) in Halkida. An excellent topo map (No 5.11), *Mt Dirfys*, is published by Anavasi.

A twisting road continues from Steni to **Paralia Hiliadou** on the north coast, where a grove of maple and chestnut trees borders a fine pebble-and-sand beach, along with a few domatia and tavernas. Campers can find shelter near the big rocks at either end of the beach.

SLEEPING & EATING

Hotel Dirfys (☎ 22280 51217; s/d incl breakfast €30/40) The best of Steni's two hotels is big on knotty pine which dominates the decor, from the lobby walls to most of the furniture. The comfortable and carpeted rooms have perfect views of the forest and stream.

Taverna Kissos (Ivy Taverna; ☎ 22280 51226; mains €4-9) One of a cluster of good brookside eateries, this traditional taverna offers hearty meat grills (steaks sold by the kilo), traditional *mayirefta* (ready-cooked meals) and salads prepared from locally grown greens.

Kymi & Paralia Kymis
Κύμη & Παραλία Κύμης
pop 3040

The workaday town of Kymi is built on a cliff 250m above the sea. Things perk up at dusk when the town square comes to life. The port, Paralia Kymis, 4km downhill, is the only natural harbour on the precipitous east coast, and the departure point for ferries to Skyros.

The excellent **Folklore Museum** (☎ 22220 22011; ☺ 10am-1pm Wed & Sun, 10am-1pm & 4-6.30pm Sat), 30m downhill from the main square, has an impressive collection of local costumes and historical photos, including a display honouring Kymi-born Dr George Papanikolaou, inventor of the Pap smear test.

Kymi is home to **Figs of Kymi** (☎ 22220 31722; www.figkimi.gr; ☺ 9am-3pm Mon-Fri), an agricultural co-op dedicated to supporting local fig farmers and sustainable production in general. It's a fascinating operation to see, and you can buy dried preservative-free figs in the shop.

SLEEPING & EATING

In Paralia Kymis, the reliable **Hotel Beis** (☎ 22220 22604; www.hotel-beis.gr; s/d/tr incl breakfast €40/60; **P** 🟦), a cavernous white block with large and spotless rooms, is opposite the ferry dock for Skyros. A string of tavernas and *ouzeries* lines the waterfront.

Just 3km south in tiny Platana, next to the seawall, try the excellent fish taverna **Koutelos** (☎ 22220 71272; mains €5-9), where Alexandra and Konstantinos will interpret the menu with dramatic pleasure. Up the hill in Kymi, little **Taverna Mouria** (☎ 22220 22629; mains €4-9), 150m north of the square, is great for shrimp grills, *mayirefta* dishes and family-sized Greek salads (€4.50).

NORTHERN EVIA

From Halkida a road heads north to **Psahna**, the gateway to the highly scenic mountainous interior of northern Evia. A good road climbs and twists through pine forests to the woodsy village of **Prokopi**, home of the pilgrimage church of **St John the Russian**. At Strofylia, 14km beyond Prokopi, a road heads southwest to picturesque Limni, then north to quaint Loutra Edipsou, the ferry port at **Agiokambos,** and **Pefki**, a small seaside resort.

Loutra Edipsou Λουτρά Αιδηψού

pop 3600

The classic spa resort of Loutra Edipsou has therapeutic sulphur waters, which have been celebrated since antiquity. Famous skinny dippers have included Aristotle, Plutarch and Sylla. The town's gradual expansion over the years has been tied to the improving technology required to carry the water further and further away from its thermal source. Today the town has Greece's most up-to-date hydrotherapy and physiotherapy centres. The town beach (Paralia Loutron) heats up year-round thanks to the thermal waters which spill into the sea.

INFORMATION

You'll find internet service at **Lan Arena** (☎ 22260 22597; per hr €2.50; ⏰ 10am-1am), opposite the ferry port. For medical needs, contact

English-speaking **Dr Symeonides** (☎ 22260 23220; Omirou 17).

ACTIVITIES

Most of the hotels offer various **spa treatments**, from simple hot baths (€6) to four-hand massages (€160).

The more relaxing (and affordable) of the resort's two big spas is the **EOT Hydrotherapy-Physiotherapy Centre** (☎ 22260 23501; 25 March St 37; ⏰ 7am-1pm & 5-7pm 1 Jun-31 Oct), speckled with palm trees and with a large outdoor pool that mixes mineral and sea water, and terrace overlooking the sea. Hydro-massage bath treatments start at a modest €8.

The ultraposh **Thermae Sylla Hotel & Spa** (☎ 22260 60100; www.thermaesylla.gr; Posidonos 2), with a somewhat late-Roman ambience befitting its name, offers an assortment of health and beauty treatments, from thermal mud baths to seaweed body wraps, from around €60.

Modern spa treatments (including Thai massage) are also available from the **Knossos CitySpa Hotel** (☎ 22260 22460; www.knossos-spa.com; Vyzantinon 19).

SLEEPING & EATING

Hotel Istiaia (☎ 22260 22309; 28th October 2; www.istiaia hotel.com; s/d/tr incl breakfast from €34/50/70; 🟦 💻 🛜) The Istiaia is a handsome vintage hotel with high-ceiling rooms and an old world feel, aside from the smallish bathrooms. A cafewine bar faces out to the seawall.

Hotel Kentrikon (☎ /fax 22260 22502; www .kentrikonhotel.com; 25th Martiou 14; s/d/tr €42/60/70; 🟦 💻 🛜 🖹) This friendly hotel-spa, managed by a Greek-Irish couple, is equal parts kitsch and charm. An inviting thermal pool awaits, along with a massage therapist, Vicky Kavartziki (☎ 6945146374).

Thermae Sylla Hotel & Spa (☎ 22260 60100; www .thermaesylla.gr; Posidonos 2; s/d/ste from €210/250/500; **P** 🟦 💻 🛜 🖹) This posh in-your-mud-masked-face spa offers luxury accommodation along with countless beauty treatments. Day visitors can sample the outdoor pool for €27.

Dina's Amfilirion Restaurant (☎ 22260 60420; 28th October 26; mains €5-10) Beautifully prepared offerings change daily here. A generous plate of grilled cod with oven potatoes, a juicy tomato-cucumber salad and a worthy house wine costs about €12. Look for the small wooden sign with green letters in Greek, 20m north of the ferry dock.

Also recommended:

Captain Cook Self-Service Restaurant (☎ 22260
23852; mains €3-7) A bit of everything, tasty and cheap.

Taverna Sbanios (☎ 22260 23111; mains €4-8) Quality
grills, breakfast omelettes.

GETTING THERE & AWAY

Boat

Regular ferries run between Loutra Edipsou
and mainland Arkitsa, and also between
nearby Agiokambos and mainland Glyfa.
For details see Island Hopping (p750).

Tickets should be purchased from the dock
kiosk at the port of Loutra Edipsou.

Bus

From the **KTEL bus station** (☎ 22260 22250;
Thermopotamou), 200m from the port, buses
run to Halkida (€13, four hours, once daily
at 5.30am), Athens (€12.30, 3½ hours, three
daily via Arkitsa) and Thessaloniki (€22, five
hours, daily at 10am via Glyfa). For more
information on services to/from Athens and
Thessaloniki, see Island Hopping (p743).

Limni Λίμνη
pop 2070

One of Evia's most picturesque ports, little Limni faces seaward, its maze of whitewashed houses and narrow lanes spilling
onto a busy waterfront of cafes and tavernas.
The town's cultural **museum** (☎ 22270 31900;
admission €2; ☼ 9am-1pm Mon-Sat, 10.30am-1pm Sun),
just 50m up from the waterfront, features
local archaeological finds along with antique
looms, costumes and old coins. Seldom visited, Limni is well worth a stopover.

With your own transport, you can visit
the splendid 16th-century **Convent of Galataki**,
(☼ 9am-noon & 5-8pm) 9km southeast of Limni
on a hillside above a coastal road, and home
to a coterie of six nuns. The fine mosaics
and frescoes in its *katholikon* (main church)
merit a look, especially the *Entry of the
Righteous into Paradise*.

SLEEPING & EATING

Rovies Camping (☎ 22270 71120; www.campingevia
.com/evia-holidays.html; camp sites per adult/tent €6.50/free)
Attractive and shaded Rovies sits just above
a pebble beach, 12km northwest of Limni.

Ostria Apartments (☎ /fax 22270 32248; www.os
tria-apartments.gr; apt incl breakfast from €90; P ✗ ℝ)
Olive trees and bougainvillea surround 10

handsome self-catering apartments across
the road from a long beach, 1km northwest
of Limni.

Taverna Arga (☎ 22270 31479; mains €4-12) Pick
an outside table at this waterfront taverna
and enjoy the passing parade of villagers and
visitors, along with well-prepared grilled octopus, *gavros* (anchovies) and *yemista* (stuffed
peppers and tomatoes).

Other village options:

Zaniakos Domatia (☎ 6977936698; r €25; ✗)

Agrabeli Apts (☎ 22270 32312; www.agrabeli.eu;
r €70; P ✗ 💻 ❤ ℝ)

Ouzerie Fiki (☎ 22270 32411; mezedhes €2-5)

SOUTHERN EVIA

Continuing east from Eretria, the road
branches at Lepoura: the left fork leads north
to Kymi, the right south to Karystos. A turn-
off at Krieza, 3km from the junction, leads to
Lake Dhistos, a shallow lake bed favoured by
egrets and other wetland birds. Continuing
south, you'll pass high-tech windmills and
catch views of both coasts as the island narrows until it reaches the sea at Karystos Bay,
near the base of Mt Ohi (1398m).

Karystos Κάρυστος
pop 4960

Set on the wide Karystos Bay below Mt Ohi,
and flanked by two sandy beaches, this remote
but charming coastal resort is the starting point
for treks to Mt Ohi and the Dimosari Gorge.
The town's lively Plateia Amalias (Amalias Sq),
faces the bay and boat harbour.

INFORMATION

You'll find an Alpha Bank **ATM** on the main
square, and **Polihoros Internet & Sports Cafe**
(☎ 22240 24421; Kriezotou 132; per hr €3; ☼ 9am-1am)
next to the Galaxy Hotel.

SIGHTS

Karystos, mentioned in Homer's 'Iliad', was a
powerful city-state during the Peloponnesian
Wars. The **Karystos Museum** (☎ 22240 25661; admission €2; ☼ 8.30am-3pm Tue-Sun) documents the
town's archaeological heritage, including tiny
Neolithic clay lamps, a stone plaque written in
the Halkidian alphabet, 5th-century-BC grave
stelae depicting Zeus and Athena, and an exhibit of the 6th-century *drakospita* (dragon
houses) of Mt Ohi and Styra. The museum
sits opposite a 14th-century Venetian castle,
the **Bourtzi** (admission free; ☼ year-round).

TOURS

South Evia Tours (☎ 22240 25700; fax 22240 29091; www.eviatravel.gr; Plateia Amalias) offers a range of booking services including mainland ferry tickets, excursions in the foothills of Mt Ohi, trips to the 6th-century-BC Roman-built *drakospita* near Styra, and a cruise around the Petali Islands (€35 with lunch). The resourceful owner, Nikos, can also arrange necessary taxi pick-up or drop-off for serious hikes to the summit of Mt Ohi and back, or four-hour guided walks through Dimosari Gorge (€25).

FESTIVALS & EVENTS

Karystos hosts a summer **Wine & Cultural Festival** from early July until the last weekend in August. Weekend happenings include theatre performances and traditional dancing to the tune of local musicians, along with exhibits by local artists. The summer merrymaking concludes with the Wine Festival, featuring every local wine imaginable, free for the tasting. Festival schedules are available at the Karystos Museum (opposite)

SLEEPING & EATING

Hotel Karystion (☎ 22240 22391; www.karystion.gr; Kriezotou 3; s/d incl breakfast €45/55; P ✻ wi-fi) The Karystion is the pick of town lodgings, with modern, well-appointed rooms, along with sea-view balconies and helpful multilingual staff. A small stairway off the courtyard leads to a sandy beach below, great for swimming.

our pick **Cavo d'Oro** (☎ 22240 22326; mains €4-7.50) Join the locals in this cheery alleyway restaurant, one block west of the main square, where tasty mains include goat with pasta (€7.50) and mackerel with rice (€6.50), along with homemade *mousakas* (layers of eggplant or zucchini, minced meat and potatoes, topped with cheese sauce and baked; €6) and salads featuring only local produce and olive oil. The genial owner, Kyriakos, is a regular at the summer wine festival, bouzouki in hand.

Other options:

Hotel Galaxy (☎ 22270 71120; cnr Kriezotou & Odysseos; s/d incl breakfast €45/65; ✻ internet wi-fi) On the waterfront.

Taverna Mesa-Exo (In-Out Taverna; ☎ 22240 23997; mains €5-12) At the western end of the waterfront.

DRINKING

Check out the late-night scene around the *plateia* (square).

Bar Alea (☎ 22240 23085; internet wi-fi) On the *plateia*; delivers decent drinks and sounds.

Club Kohili (☎ 22240 24350) This swank-casual place is on the beach by the Apollon Suite Hotel.

GETTING THERE & AWAY

Boat

There is a regular ferry service between Marmari (10km west of Karystos) and Rafina, and from Nea Styra (35km north of Karystos) to Agia Marina. For details see Island Hopping (p750).

Tickets may be purchased from either the dock ticket kiosk at the port of Mamari, or in advance at **South Evia Tours** (☎ 22240 25700; fax 22240 29091; www.eviatravel.gr) in Karystos.

Bus

From the **Karystos KTEL bus station** (☎ 22240 26303), opposite Agios Nikolaos church, buses run to Halkida (€10.50, three hours, Sunday to Friday) and to Athens (€8.30, three hours, four daily), and Marmari (€1.70, 20 minutes, Monday to Saturday). A taxi to Marmari is about €12.

Around Karystos

The ruins of **Castello Rosso** (Red Castle), a 13th-century Frankish fortress, are a short walk from **Myli**, a delightful, well-watered village 4km inland from Karystos. A little beyond Myli there is an **ancient quarry** scattered with green and black fragments of the once-prized Karystian *cippolino* marble.

With your own transport, or taxi, you can get to the base of **Mt Ohi** where a 1½-hour hike to the summit will bring you to the ancient *drakospita* (dragon house), the finest example of a group of Stonehengelike dwellings or temples, dating from the 7th century BC, and hewn from rocks weighing up to several tons and joined without mortar. Smaller examples near **Styra** (30km north of Karystos) are nearly as fascinating.

Hikers can also head north to the **Dimosari Gorge** where a beautiful and well-maintained 10km trail can be covered in four to five hours (including time for a swim).

With a local map from South Evia Tours (left), you can easily explore the villages and chestnut forests nestling in the foothills between Mt Ohi and the coast.

SKIATHOS ΣΚΙΑΘΟΣ

pop 6160

Blessed with some of the Aegean's most beautiful beaches, it's little wonder that in July and August the island can fill up with sun-starved Europeans, as prices soar and rooms dwindle. At the island's small airport, the arrival board lists mostly incoming charter flights from northern Europe. Despite its popularity, Skiathos remains one of Greece's premier resorts.

Skiathos Town, the island's major settlement and port, lies on the southeast coast. The rest of the south coast is interspersed with walled-in holiday villas and pine-fringed sandy beaches. The north coast is precipitous and less accessible; in the 14th century the Kastro Peninsula served as a natural fortress against invaders. Aside from the ample sun and nightlife, the curious will find striking monasteries, hilltop tavernas and even secluded beaches.

Getting There & Away

See Island Hopping (p761) for details of air and sea connections to other islands and the mainland.

AIR

Along with numerous charter flights from northern Europe, during summer there is one flight daily to/from Athens (€49). **Olympic Air** (☎ 24270 22200) has an office at the airport, not in town.

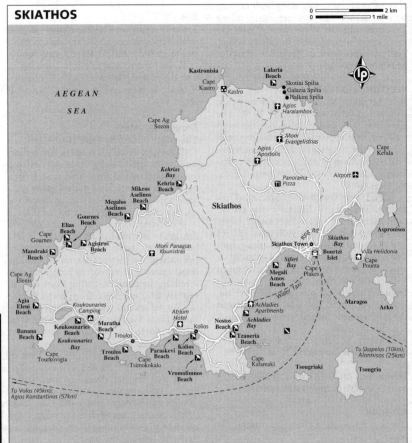

SKIATHOS

0 _____ 2 km
0 _____ 1 mile

AEGEAN

SEA

Kastronisia

Cape Kastro

Kastro

Lalaria Beach

Skotini Spilia
Galazia Spilia
Halkini Spilia

Agios Haralambos

Cape Ag Sozon

Moni Evangelistrias

Agios Apostolis

Cape Kefala

Kehrias Bay

Kehria Beach

Panorama Pizza

Airport

Mikros Aselinos Beach

Megalos Aselinos Beach

Gournes Beach

Elias Beach

Cape Gournes

Agistros Beach

Mandraki Beach

Skiathos

Moni Panagias Kounistras

Skiathos Town

Skiathos Bay

Aspronisos

Villa Helidonia

Cape Pounta

Cape Ag Elenis

Agia Eleni Beach

Banana Beach

Cape Tourkovigia

Koukounaries Camping

Koukounaries Beach

Koukounaries Bay

Maratha Beach

Troulos

Troulos Beach

Atrium Hotel

Kolios

Paraskevi Beach

Cape Tsimokokalo

Kolios Beach

Nostos Beach

Achladies Bay

Tzaneria Beach

Vromolimnos Beach

Siferi Bay

Megali Amos Beach

Bourtzi Islet

Cape Plakes

Water Taxi

Achladies Apartments

Cape Kalamaki

Maragos

Arko

To Skopelos (10km), Alonnisos (25km)

Tsougriaki

Tsougria

Ring Rd

To Volos (45km), Agios Konstantinos (57km)

EVIA & THE SPORADES

BOAT

Skiathos' main port is Skiathos Town, with links to mainland Volos and Agios Konstantinos, and to Skopelos and Alonnisos.

Tickets can be purchased from either **Hellenic Seaways** (☎ 24270 22209; fax 24270 22750) at the bottom of Papadiamantis, or from **GA Ferries** (☎ 24270 22204; fax 24270 22979), next to Alpha Bank.

Getting Around

BOAT

Water taxis depart from the old port for Tzaneria and Kanapitsa beaches (€3, 20 minutes, hourly) and Achladies Bay (€2, 15 minutes, hourly).

BUS

Crowded buses leave Skiathos Town for Koukounaries Beach (€1.20 to €1.50, 30 minutes, every half-hour between 7.30am and 11pm). The buses stop at 26 numbered access points to the beaches along the south coast.

CAR & MOTORCYCLE

Reliable motorbike and car-hire outlets in Skiathos Town include **Europcar/Creator Tours** (☎ 24270 22385) and **Heliotropio Tourism & Travel** (☎ 24270 22430) on the new port.

TAXI

The **taxi stand** (☎ 24270 21460) is opposite the ferry dock. A taxi to/from the airport costs €5.

SKIATHOS TOWN

Skiathos Town, with its red-roofed, white-washed houses, is built on two low hills. Opposite the waterfront lies tiny and inviting **Bourtzi Islet** between the two small harbours and reached by a short causeway. The town is a major tourist centre, with hotels, souvenir shops, galleries, travel agents, tavernas and bars dominating the waterfront and the narrow main thoroughfare, Papadiamanti.

Orientation

The quay (wharf) is in the middle of the waterfront, just north of Bourtzi Islet. To the right (as you face inland) is the newer small boat harbour; to the left is the curving old harbour used by local fishing and excursion boats. Papadiamanti strikes inland from opposite the quay. Plateia Tris Ierarches (Tris Ierarches Sq) is above the old harbour. The bus terminus is at the northern end of the new harbour.

Information

EMERGENCY

Port police (☎ 24270 22017; quay)
Tourist police (☎ 24270 23172; ⏲ 8am-9pm; Ring Rd)

INTERNET ACCESS

Creator Tours (☎ 24270 21384; waterfront; per 30min €1; ⏲ 9am-9pm) Inside Europcar office.
Internet Zone Café (☎ 24270 22767; Evangelistrias 28; per hr €2; ⏲ 10am-3am)

MEDICAL SERVICES

Health Centre Hospital (☎ 24270 22222) Above the old port.
Pharmacy Papantoniou (☎ 24270 24515; Papadiamanti 18)

MONEY

Numerous ATMs are on Papadiamanti and the waterfront.

POST

Post office (upper Papadiamanti; ⏲ 7.30am-2pm)

TRAVEL AGENCIES

For reliable information about Skiathos, or onward travel, try the following:
Creator Tours (☎ 24270 21384; www.creatortours.com; waterfront)
Heliotropio Tourism & Travel (☎ 24270 22430; www.heliotropio.gr; waterfront)
Mathinos Travel (☎ 24270 23351; Papadiamanti 18)

Sights

Skiathos was the birthplace of famous 19th-century Greek novelist and short story writer Alexandros Papadiamanti, whose writings draw upon the hard lives of the islanders he grew up with. Papadiamanti's humble 1860-vintage house is now a charming **museum** (☎ 24270 23843; Plateia Papadiamanti; admission €1; ⏲ 9.30am-1.30pm & 5-8.30pm Tue-Sun) with books, paintings and old photos documenting his life on Skiathos.

Tours

Excursion boats make half- and full-day trips around the island (€10 to €25, approximately four to six hours), and usually visit Cape Kastro, Lalaria Beach and the three *spilies* (caves) of Halkini, Skotini and Galazia, which are only accessible by boat. A few boats also visit the nearby islets of Tsougria and Tsougriaki for swimming and snorkelling; you can take one boat over and return on another. At the old harbour, check out the signboards in front of each boat for a tour and schedule to your liking.

Sleeping

Book early for July and August, when prices quoted here are nearly double those of the low season. There's also a quayside kiosk with prices and room pictures. For last-minute accommodation in high season, try the resourceful agents, **Sotos & Maria** (☎ 24270 23219, 6974716408; sotos-2@otenet.gr).

Lena's Rooms (24270 22009; Bouboulinas St; r €55; ⊠) These six double rooms over the owner's flower shop are airy and spotless, each with fridge and balcony, plus a well-equipped common kitchen and shady, flower-filled veranda.

Villa Orsa (☎ 24270 22430; fax 24270 21952; s/d/f incl breakfast from €70/80/110; ⊠ 💻 🛜) Perched well above the old harbour, this classic cliff-side mansion features very comfortable, traditionally styled rooms with balcony views overlooking a secluded bay. A generous breakfast is served on the garden terrace.

our pick Villa Helidonia (Swallows Villa; ☎ 24270 21370; 6945686542; apt €75-95; Ⓟ ⊠ 💻) This unusually comfortable and secluded lodging sits above the Punta (point), only minutes from town, but a world away otherwise. There are just two apartments (minimum four-night stay), each with full kitchen, satellite TV and overhead fans, along with a fig tree within picking distance. Close by, a hidden snorkelling bay awaits.

Hotel Bourtzi (☎ 24270 21304; Moraitou 8; www .hotelbourtzi.gr; s/d/tr incl breakfast from €90/130/150; Ⓟ ⊠ 💻 🛜 🖭) On upper Papadiamanti, the swank Bourtzi escapes much of the town noise, and features austere-modern rooms, an inviting garden and two small pools, one just for kids.

Also recommended:

Hotel Meltemi (☎ 24270 22493; meltemi@skiathos.gr; s/d/f €55/65/95; ⊠ 💻 🛜) Old-fashioned charmer.

Alkyon Hotel (☎ 24270 22981; www.alkyon.gr; s/d/tr incl breakfast from €63/84/105; Ⓟ ⊠ 💻 🛜 🖭) Large waterfront lodging.

Eating

Skiathos has more than its share of overpriced and touristy eateries with so-so (*etsi-ketsi* in Greek) food. Explore the narrow lanes west of Papadiamanti to find exceptions like these:

Taverna-Ouzeri Kabouria (☎ 24270 21112; mains €4-9) Poke your nose in the kitchen to glimpse the day's catch at the only year-round eatery at the old port. The cheerful owner-cooks prepare great fish grills and seafood mezedhes at moderate prices.

Taverna Alexandros (☎ 24270 22341; Mavrogiali; mains €4-9) Excellent lamb grills, traditional oven-roasted chicken and potatoes, and live acoustic Greek music await at this friendly alleyway eatery under a canopy of mulberry trees.

Taverna Bakaliko (☎ 24270 24024; Club St; mains €4.50-9) You can't get much closer to the bay than at this popular eatery, known for well-prepared and well-priced standards like stuffed cabbage leaves, tomato and parsley salad and fish soup.

Taverna Mesogia (☎ 24270 21440; mains €5-10) Another back street gem, with open kitchen, and summer seating in the narrow lane. Owner Pandelis boasts of his 'simple and traditional' cuisine; his grandfather first opened in 1923.

Medousa Pizza (☎ 24270 23923; Club St; mains €6-8) Just barfing distance from the drink-till-you-drop waterfront clubs, Medousa's wood-oven pizza is worth a trip at any hour, and they deliver.

Taverna Anemos (Wind; ☎ 24270 21003; mains €6-14) Locals know this fine fish taverna up the old harbour steps for its generous portions of fresh cod, lobster and mussels. Best of all, Vassili the cook has probably spent the morning at his other job – fishing and diving for your dinner.

our pick Maria's Pizza (☎ 24270 22292; mains €8-15) The pizza is just the beginning at this flower-filled gem above the old port. If you don't walk inside to see Maria and crew in action, you've missed the point. Highlights include stuffed garlic bread, tagliatelle pasta with prosciutto and asparagus (€12) and salads galore, each a meal in itself.

Other fine options:

Igloo (☎ 24270 24076; Papadiamanti; drinks-snacks €1.50-4; ⏱ 6am-10pm) Cold drinks, breakfast.

No Name Fast Food (☎ 6974426707; Simionos; mains €2) Not that fast, and his name is Aris. Best *gyros* (meat slivers cooked on a vertical rotisserie; usually eaten with pitta bread).

Main Street (☎ 24270 21743; Papadiamanti; breakfasts €2-4) Breakfast, wraps, burgers.

Taverna O Batis (☎ 24270 22288; mains €6-12) Fresh fish, charming service.

Drinking

our pick **Kentavros Bar** (☎ 24270 22980) The long-established and handsome Kentavros, off Plateia Papadiamanti, promises rock, soul, jazz and blues, and gets the thumbs-up from locals and expats alike for its mellow ambience, artwork and good drinks.

Rooftop Bar (☎ 6949096465) A popular place to chill above the old port, with the best happy hour on the waterfront, plus live music Saturday nights.

Rock & Roll Bar (☎ 24270 22944) Huge beanbags have replaced many of the pillows outside this trendy bar by the old port, resulting in fewer customers rolling off. Heaven for frozen strawberry-daiquiri lovers.

Bar Destiny (☎ 24270 24172; Polytechniou) Look for the soft blue light coming from this hip side-street bar with music videos, draught beer and a bit of dancing when the mood hits.

The dancing and drinking scene heats up after midnight along the club strip past the new harbour. Best DJs are at **BBC** (☎ 24270 21190), followed by **Kahlua Bar** (☎ 24270 23205) and **Club Pure** (☎ 6979773854), open till dawn.

Entertainment

Cinema Attikon (☎ 24270 22352; Papadiamanti; admission €7) Catch current English-language movies at this open-air cinema, sip a beer (beer and snacks €2 to €4) and practise speed-reading your Greek subtitles at the same time. (Greece is one of the few countries in Europe to show films in the original language, not dubbed.)

Shopping

Glittery open-air shops fill Papadiamanti. But branch off one of the ever-disappearing side streets to explore another side of Skiathos.

Loupos & his Dolphins (☎ 24270 23777; Plateia Papadiamanti; ⏲ 10am-1.30pm & 6-11.30pm) Look for delicate hand-painted icons, fine Greek ceramics, along with gold and silver jewellery at this high-end gallery shop, next to Papadiamanti Museum.

Galerie Varsakis (☎ 24270 22255; Plateia Trion Ierarhon; ⏲ 10am-2pm & 6-11pm) Browse for unusual antiques like 19th-century spinning sticks made by grooms for their intended brides, plus unusual Greek and African textiles. The collection rivals the best folklore museums in Greece.

Archipelagos Gallery (☎ 24270 22585; Plateia Papadiamanti; ⏲ 11am-1pm & 8-10pm) Work by contemporary Greek and visiting artists stands out at this intimate shop.

AROUND SKIATHOS
Sights & Activities
BEACHES

With some 65 beaches to choose from, beach-hopping on Skiathos can become a full-time occupation. Buses ply the south coast, stopping at 26 numbered beach access points. **Megali Amos** is only 2km from town, but fills up quickly. The first long stretch of sand worth getting off the bus for is the pine-fringed **Vromolimnos Beach**. Further along, **Kolios Beach** and **Troulos Beach** are also good but both, alas, very popular. The bus continues to **Koukounaries Beach**, backed by pine trees and touted as the best beach in Greece. But nowadays its crowded summer scene is best viewed at a distance, from where the 1200m long sweep of pale gold sand does indeed sparkle.

Big Banana Beach, known for its curving shape and soft white sand, lies at the other side of a narrow headland. Skinny-dippers tend to abscond to laid-back **Little Banana Beach** (also popular with gay and lesbian sunbathers) around the rocky corner.

West of Koukounaries, **Agia Eleni Beach** is a favourite with windsurfers. Sandy **Mandraki Beach**, a 1.5km walk along a pine-shaded path, is just far enough to keep it clear of the masses. The northwest coast's beaches are less crowded but are subject to the strong summer *meltemi* (northeasterly winds). From here a right fork continues 2km to **Mikros Aselinos Beach** and 5km further on to secluded **Kehria Beach**.

Lalaria Beach is a tranquil strand of pale-grey, egg-shaped pebbles on the northern coast. It is much featured in tourist brochures, but only reached by excursion boat from Skiathos Town (see Tours, p651).

KASTRO ΚΑΣΤΡΟ

Kastro, perched dramatically on a rocky headland above the north coast, was the fortified pirate-proof capital of the island from 1540 to 1829; an old cannon remains at the northern end. Four of the crumbling town's old churches have been restored, and the views are magnificent. Excursion boats come to the beach below Kastro, from where it's an easy clamber up to the ruins.

EVIA & THE SPORADES

MONI EVANGELISTRIAS ΜΟΝΗ ΕΥΑΓΓΕΛΙΣΤΡΙΑΣ

The most famous of the island's monasteries is the 18th-century **Moni Evangelistrias** (Monastery of the Annunciation; ☎ 24270 22012; ⏱ 9.30am-1.30pm & 5-7pm), poised 450m above sea level and surrounded by pine and cypress trees. It was a refuge for freedom fighters during the War of Independence and the Greek flag was first raised here, in 1807. Today, two monks do the chores, which include wine-making. You can sample, and buy, the tasty results of their efforts in the **museum** (admission €1) shop. An adjacent shed of old olive and wine presses and vintage barrels recalls an earlier era, long before the satellite dish was installed above the courtyard.

MONI PANAGIAS KOUNISTRAS ΜΟΝΗ ΠΑΝΑΓΙΑΣ ΚΟΥΝΙΣΤΡΑΣ

From Troulos (bus stop 20), a road heads north to the 17th-century **Moni Panagias Kounistras** (Monastery of the Holy Virgin; ⏱ morning-dusk), which is worth a visit for the fine frescoes adorning its *katholikon*. It's 4km inland from Troulos.

DIVING

The small islets off the south shore of Skiathos make for great diving. Rates average €40-50 for half-day dives, equipment included.

Dive instructor team Theofanis and Eva of **Octopus Diving Centre** (☎ 24270 24549, 6944168958; www.odc-skiathos.com; new harbour) lead dives around Tsougria and Tsougriaki islets for beginners and experts alike. Call or enquire at their boat.

Skiathos Diving Centre (☎ 24270 24424; www.skiathosdivingcenter.gr; Papadiamanti), and **Dolphin Diving** (☎ 24270 21599, 6944999181; www.ddiving.gr; Nostos Beach) are also popular for first-time divers, with dives off Tsougriaki Islet exploring locations 30m deep.

HIKING

A 6km-long hiking route begins at Moni Evangelistrias, eventually reaching **Cape Kastro**, before circling back through Agios Apostolis. Kastro is a spring mecca for birdwatchers, who may spot long-necked Mediterranean shags and singing blue-rock thrushes on the nearby rocky islets.

THE GREEN BEEKEEPER OF SKIATHOS *Michael Clark*

Bouncing along a dirt road in his old car, Skiathos beekeeper Yiannis talked non-stop about his life before bees and since. 'I had once work with stock markets, and I can't sleep the night. But Hippocrates say, "Give milk and honey"', referring to the 5th-century-BC father of medicine. 'It's clean now, inside me.' Then, laughing, he corrected himself, 'It's a dirty job, but is something good to the land.'

At the bee field, Yiannis, who's in his early 30s, has scattered about 100 blue boxes, each with 7000 to 10,000 bees. 'I'm first one in Skiathos. Hard to find the young person to do this.' With that, he takes out a small 'smoke can', stuffs a handful of green weeds into it, then lights it with a match. Smoke pours out as he waves it around a bee box. 'Smoke to scare the bees. Communicate to queen 'fire danger!' Then queen, she makes more eggs!'

He talks about the honey (in Greek, *meli*) and about different blossoms and trees – *elatos* (fir) and *pefko* (pine) are favourites. 'Bees, the inside, make love the flower'. I wave off some bees who are getting a little too friendly. We are both wearing protective head nets, but our arms and hands are exposed. Yiannis shows little concern: 'The bees, they know me.' As for me, I just mutter, 'I'm with him'.

Opening another box, Yiannis' face lights up: 'Look, is the queen! You must have good queen. She live four years. One good queen, young, make lot of honey'. He reads my mind: 'Fifteen euros to buy new queen. We have Greek queen, Italian queen'.

But a new queen must be accepted by the bee colony. 'Different smell, so bees must accept her.' This entails putting the new and hungry queen in a tiny box with a door made of food. By the time she nibbles her way out 24 hours later, she is usually accepted. 'But if not understand, the bees, they kill her.'

Without partners or assistants, Yiannis works alone, but confides, 'The bees, they help!' His modest goal is to double his production from 100 to 200 boxes. 'We have best honey in all the world.' His pride is contagious, but I'm impressed that he never loses sight of the larger picture: 'The land and the sky have energy. The bee feel this. We need the honey, for the planet. To be careful, the green planet!'

Sleeping & Eating

Koukounaries Camping (☎ /fax 24270 49250; camp sites per adult/tent €10/4; **P**) Shaded by fig and mulberry trees, this family-managed site near the eastern end of Koukounaries Beach features spotless bathroom and cooking facilities, a minimarket and taverna.

Achladies Apartments (☎ 24270 22486; http:// achladies.apartments.googlepages.com; Achladies Bay; d/tr/f incl breakfast €45/60/75; **P**) Look for the hand-painted yellow sign to find this welcoming gem, 5km from Skiathos Town. Along with self-catering rooms (two-night minimum stay) and ceiling fans, it features an eco-friendly tortoise sanctuary and a succulent garden winding down to a taverna and sandy beach.

our pick **Atrium Hotel** (☎ 24270 49345; www. atriumhotel.gr; Paraskevi Beach; s/d/ste incl breakfast from €100/130/200; **P** **X** **X** **Q** **Q** **Q** **Q**) Traditional architecture and modern touches make this hillside perch the best in its class. Rooms are low-key elegant, with basin sinks and large balconies. A lavish breakfast buffet starts the day, and amenities include sauna, children's pool, billiards and ping-pong.

Panorama Pizza (☎ 6944192066; pizzas €7-10; ☼ noon-4pm, 7pm-late) Escape to this hilltop retreat, off the ring road, for pizza and panoramic views.

SKOPELOS ΣΚΟΠΕΛΟΣ

pop 4700

Skopelos is a beautiful island of pine forests, vineyards, olive groves and orchards of plums and almonds, which find their way into many local dishes.

Like Skiathos, the high cliffs of the northwest coast are exposed, while the sheltered southeast coast harbours several sand-and-pebble beaches. There are two large settlements: the capital and main port of Skopelos Town on the east coast; and the unspoilt west coast village of Glossa, 3km north of Loutraki, the island's second port.

In ancient times the island was an important Minoan outpost ruled by Stafylos (meaning 'grape'), the son of Ariadne and Dionysos in Greek mythology, and who is said to have introduced wine-making here. The island endured more recent fame as a filming location for the 2008 movie *Mama Mia!*

Getting There & Away

BOAT

Skopelos has two ports, Skopelos Town and Glossa, both with links to mainland Volos and Agios Konstantinos, and to the other Sporades islands of Skiathos, Skopelos, Alonnisos and Skyros. For details see Island Hopping (p761).

Tickets are available from **Hellenic Seaways** (☎ 24240 22767; fax 24240 23608) opposite the new quay; and **Lemonis Agency** (☎ 24240 22363) in Pension Lemonis towards the end of the new quay. In Glossa, **Hellenic Seaways** (☎ 24240 33435, 6932913748) is opposite the port.

Getting Around

BOAT

A regular water taxi departs late morning for Glysteri Beach (€5 one way), and returns around 5pm.

BUS

There are seven or eight buses per day in summer from Skopelos Town to Glossa/Loutraki (€4.30, one hour) and Elios (€3, 45 minutes), three that go only as far as Panormos (€2.20, 25 minutes) and Milia (€2.60, 35 minutes), and another two that go only to Agnontas (€1.40, 15 minutes) and Stafylos (€1.40, 15 minutes).

CAR & MOTORCYCLE

Several car- and motorcycle-hire outlets line the harbour in Skopelos Town, mostly located at the eastern end of the waterfront, including the friendly and efficient **Motor Tours** (☎ 24240 22986; fax 24240 22602) next to Hotel Eleni, and **Avis** (☎ 24240 23170).

TAXI

Taxis wait by the bus stop. A taxi to Stafylos is €7, to Limnonari €12, to Glossa €25.

SKOPELOS TOWN

Skopelos Town is one of the most captivating ports in the Sporades. It skirts a semicircular bay and clambers in tiers up a hillside, culminating in an old fortress and a cluster of four churches. Dozens of other churches are interspersed among dazzling white houses with brightly shuttered windows and flower-adorned balconies.

Orientation

The town's waterfront is flanked by two quays. The old quay is at the western end of

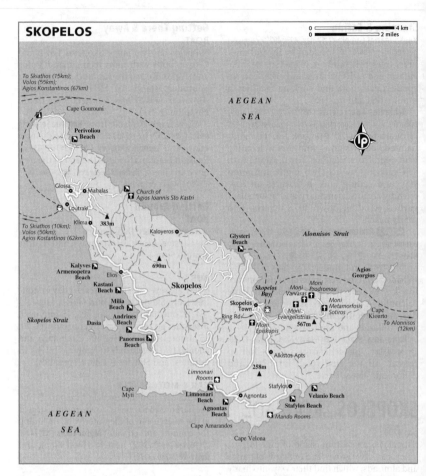

the harbour and the new quay is at the eastern end, used by all ferries and hydrofoils. From the dock, turn right to reach the bustling waterfront lined with cafes, souvenir shops and travel agencies; turn left (20m) for the bus stop. Less than 50m away is Plateia Platanos, better known as Souvlaki Sq.

Information

BOOKSHOPS
International newsstand (☎ 24240 22236; ☻ 8am-10pm) Opposite the bus stop.

EMERGENCY
Health Centre (☎ 24240 22222) On the ring road, next to the fire station.

Police (☎ 24240 22235) Above the National Bank.
Port police (☎ 24240 22180)

INTERNET ACCESS
Blue Sea Internet Café (☎ 24240 23010; per hr €3; ☻ 8am-2am) Beneath the *kastro* steps.
Orange Net Café (☎ 24240 23093; per hr €3; ☻ 9am-midnight) Next to the post office.

LAUNDRY
Blue Star Washing (☎ 24240 22844) Next to the OTE office.

MONEY
There are three ATMs along the waterfront.

POST
Post office (Platanos Sq; ☻ 7.30am-2pm)

TRAVEL AGENCIES

Madro Travel (☎ 24240 22300; www.madrotravel
.com) At the end of the new port, Madro can provide help
with booking accommodation and ticketing, and arrange
walking trips, island excursions, cooking lessons, even
marriages (partners extra).

Thalpos Holidays (☎ 24240 29036; www.holiday
islands.com) The helpful staff at this waterfront agency
offer a range of standard services including apartment and
villa accommodation and tours around the island.

Sights

Strolling around town and sitting at the
waterside cafes might be your chief occupations in Skopelos, but there are also two
small folk museums. The handsome **Folk Art
Museum** (☎ 24240 23494; Hatzistamati; admission €2;
☼ 10am-10pm) features a Skopelean wedding
room, complete with traditional costumes
and bridal bed. At the 2009-opened **Bakratsa
Museum** (☎ 24240 22940; admission €3; ☼ 11am-1pm
& 6-10pm), find out how young women and
men, married and unmarried, dressed in
days gone by new.

Tours

Day-long cruise boats (€25 to €50) depart
from the new quay by 10am, and usually take
in the Marine Park of Alonnisos (p661), pausing en route for lunch and a swim. There's a
good chance of spotting dolphins along the
way. For bookings, contact Thalpos Holidays
or Madro Travel on the waterfront.

Sleeping

Hotel prices quoted are for the July-to-August
high season, but are often reduced by 30%
to 50% at other times. An energetic kiosk
('Rooms') next to the ferry dock can help
with accommodation. Also enquire at Madro
Travel or Thalpos Holidays.

BUDGET

ourpick **Sotos Pension** (☎ 24240 22549; www.skopelos
.net/sotos; s/d €35/50; ⊠ ▯ ⬤) The pine-floored
rooms at this charming waterfront pension
are each a bit different; an old brick oven
serves as a handy shelf in one. There's an
interior courtyard, whitewashed terrace and
communal kitchen, all neatly managed by the
welcoming Alexandra (Alex, for short).

MIDRANGE

Hotel Agnanti (☎ /fax 24240 22722; www.skopelos.net/
agnanti; s/d/tr incl breakfast from €45/65/90; P ⊠ ▯)

Theo and Eleni run the show at this inviting
12-room oasis on the far bay, with ceiling
fans, period furniture, ceramic decorations,
plus a paperback lending library in the
rustic lobby.

Alkistis Studio Apartments (☎ 24240 23006;
www.skopelosweb.gr/alkistis; d/apt from €90/120;
P ⊠ ▯ ⬤ ⬤) Located between Skopelos
Town and Stafylos Beach, this beautifully landscaped and family-friendly complex features
huge studio and apartment units with modern
bathrooms, comfy beds and satellite TV.

Hotel Dionyssos (☎ 24240 23210; www.dionyssos
hotel.com; s/d/tr incl breakfast €100/120/130; P ⊠ ⬤ ⬤)
The low-key Dionyssos occupies a quiet street
between the ring road and the waterfront,
and has a spacious and woodsy lobby. The
upper rooms offer balcony views of the harbour. The hotel pool bar is popular with
town residents.

Also recommended:

Hotel Regina (☎ 24240 22138; www.skopelosweb.gr/
regina; s/d incl breakfast €40/55; ⊠) Vaguely Victorian.

Ionia Hotel (☎ 24240 22568; www.ioniahotel.gr; s/d/
tr/f incl breakfast €76/95/114/137; P ⊠ ▯ ⬤ ⬤)
Stylish and quiet.

Eating

Just 100m up from the dock, Souvlaki Sq is
perfect for a quick bite of *gyros* or, not surprisingly, souvlaki. Skopelos is known for a variety of plum-based recipes, and most tavernas
will have one or two on the menu.

Taverna Ta Kimata (☎ 24240 22381; mains €5-9) The
oldest taverna on the island (and better known
by the owner's name, Angelos) sits at the end
of the old quay. Step inside to look over the
day's *mayirefta* dishes, such as *briam* (mixed
vegies) and octopus with pasta or lamb *stifadho* (meat cooked with onions in a tomato
purée) – both €8.50.

Taverna Englezos (☎ 24240 22230; mains €7-11)
When we asked for a menu at this waterfront prize, the owner-waiter laughed, saying
'I am the menu!' Great grills at good prices –
half a chicken on the spit for €7. Summer
meals often end with fresh fruit, on the
house.

ourpick **To Perivoli Restaurant** (☎ 24240 23758;
mains €7-12) Just beyond Souvlaki Sq, Perivoli
promises excellent Greek cuisine in an elegant
courtyard setting. Specialities include grilled
lamb with yoghurt and coriander, and rolled
pork with *koromila* (local plums) in wine
sauce, plus excellent Greek wines.

EVIA & THE SPORADES

Anna's Restaurant (☎ 24240 24734; Gifthorema; mains €7-19) Look for the palm tree to find this handsome alleyway bistro, serving authentic Skopelos dishes like sautéed veal with plums, or black risotto with cuttlefish.

Other popular spots:

DIA Discount Supermarket (☎ 24240 24340; ⏰ 8.30am-9.30pm)

Michalis (☎ 24240 23591; snacks & cakes €2-5; ⏰ 9am-11pm) Great *tyropita* (cheese pie).

Nastas Ouzerie (☎ 24240 23441; mezedhes €2.50-5, mains €6-10) Opposite Hotel Eleni.

Finikas Restaurant (☎ 24240 23247; mains €5-10) Behind Sunrise Villa.

Drinking

Platanos Jazz Bar (☎ 24240 23661) Near the end of the old quay, this leafy courtyard cafe-bar is open for morning coffee and late-night drinks.

Oionos Blue Bar (☎ 6942406136) Cosy and cool, little Oionos serves up blues and soul along with over 20 brands of beer and single malt whiskies at last count.

Mercurios Music Café-Bar (☎ 24240 24593; 🛜) This snappy veranda bar above the waterfront mixes music, mojitos and margaritas.

For excellent coffees, juices and free wi-fi access, grab a soft chair at either **Anemos Espresso Bar** (☎ 24240 23564; 🛜) or its waterfront neighbour, **En Plo Café-Bar** (☎ 24240 23405; 🛜).

Shopping

Gray Gallery (☎ 24240 24266, 6974641597) Works by island and visiting artists are featured in this hole-in-the-wall fine-arts gallery.

Ploumisti Shop (☎ 24240 22059) Browse this attractive shop for excellent ceramics, handmade jewellery, icons, silk scarves, small paintings and Greek music.

Entertainment

Ouzerie Anatoli (☎ 24240 22851; ⏰ 8pm-2am, summer only) For mezedhes and traditional music, head to this breezy outdoor *ouzerie*, high above the *kastro*. From 11pm onwards you will hear traditional *rembetika* music sung by Skopelos' own exponent of the Greek blues and master of the bouzouki, Georgos Xindaris.

GLOSSA & LOUTRAKI
ΓΛΩΣΣΑ & ΛΟΥΤΡΑΚΙ

Glossa, Skopelos' other settlement, is a white-washed delight, and the upper square is a good place to get a feel for the entire village.

From the bus stop by the large church, a road winds down 3km to the low-key ferry port of Loutraki, with several tavernas and domatia; a smaller lane leads nearby to the business district, with a bank ATM, pharmacy, excellent bakery and a few eateries. A considerably shorter *kalderimi* (cobblestone path) connects both villages as well. Fans of the movie *Mama Mia!* (with Meryl Streep) can start their pilgrimage in Glossa to reach the film's little church, **O Yiannis sto Kastri** (St John of the Castle).

Loutraki means 'small bath' and you can find the remains of ancient **Roman baths**, with details in English, at the 'archaeological kiosk' on the port.

Sleeping & Eating

Hotel Selenunda (☎ 24240 34073; www.skopelosweb.gr/selenunda; Loutraki; d/tr from €40/55; 🅿 ❄ 🛜) Perched well above the port, these self-catering rooms are large and airy. A family apartment sleeps four, and the genial hosts, Karen and Babbis, can suggest ways to explore the area.

Flisvos Taverna (☎ 24240 33856; Loutraki; mains €3-7) Perched above the seawall 50m north of the car park, this friendly family taverna offers fresh fish at decent prices, fresh chips, homemade *mousakas*, and perfect appetisers like *taramasalata* (a thick purée of fish roe, potato, oil and lemon juice) and tzatziki.

Taverna To Steki Mastora (☎ 24240 33563; Glossa; mains €4-7) Look for a small animal roasting on a big spit outside this popular *psistaria* (restaurant serving grilled food), between the church and bakery.

Agnanti Taverna & Bar (☎ 24240 33076; Glossa; mains €8-12) Enjoy the views of Evia from swank Agnanti's rooftop terrace, along with superb Greek fusion dishes like grilled sardines on pita with sea fennel and sun-dried tomatoes.

AROUND SKOPELOS
Sights & Activities
MONASTERIES

Skopelos has several monasteries that can be visited on a beautiful scenic drive or day-long trek from Skopelos Town. Begin by following the road (Monastery Rd), which skirts the bay and then climbs inland. Continue beyond the signposted Hotel Aegeon until the road forks. Take the left fork, which ends at the 18th-century **Moni Evangelistrias**, now a convent. The monastery's prize, aside from the superb views, is a gilded iconostasis containing an 11th-century icon of the Virgin Mary.

The right fork leads to the uninhabited 16th-century **Moni Metamorfosis Sotiros**, the island's oldest monastery. From here a decent dirt road continues to the 17th-century **Moni Varvaras** with a view to the sea, and to the 18th-century **Moni Prodromou** (now a convent), 8km from Skopelos Town.

Moni Episkopis rests within the Venetian compound of a private Skopelian family, about 250m beyond the ring road. Ring **Apostolis** (☎ 6974120450) for details and an invitation. The small chapel within is a wonder of light and Byzantine icons.

BEACHES

Skopelos' best beaches are on the sheltered southwest and west coasts. The first beach you come to is the sand-and-pebble **Stafylos Beach**, 4km southeast of Skopelos Town. From the eastern end of the beach a path leads over a small headland to the quieter **Velanio Beach**, the island's official nudist beach and coincidentally a great snorkelling spot. **Agnontas**, 3km west of Stafylos, has a small pebble-and-sand beach and from here caïques sail to the superior and sandy **Limnonari Beach**, in a sheltered bay flanked by rocky outcrops. Limnonari is also a 1.5km walk or drive from Agnontas.

From Agnontas the road cuts inland through pine forests before re-emerging at pretty **Panormos Beach**, with a few tavernas and domatia. Enquire at **Panormos Travel** (☎ 24240 23380) for accommodation bookings. One kilometre further, little **Andrines Beach** is sandy and less crowded. The next two beach bays, **Milia** and **Kastani**, are excellent for swimming.

Tours

If you can't tell a twin-tailed pascha butterfly from a double leopard orchid, join one of island resident Heather Parson's **guided walks** (☎ 6945249328; www.skopelos-walks.com; tours €15-25). She fights to maintain Skopelos' natural beauty, and her four-hour Panormos walk follows an old path across the island, ending at a beach taverna, with wonderful views to Alonnisos and Evia along the way. Her book, *Skopelos Trails* (€10.25), contains graded trail descriptions and a pull-out illustrated map, and is available in waterfront stores.

Sleeping & Eating

There are small hotels, domatia, tavernas and beach canteens at Stafylos, Agnontas, Limnonari, Panormos, Andrines and Milia.

Limnonari Rooms & Taverna (☎ 24240 23046; www.skopelos.net/limnonarirooms; Limnonari Beach; d/tr/ste €65/80/120; P ⊠) Set back on a beautiful and sandy bay, this well-managed domatio features a well-equipped communal kitchen and terrace, just 30m from the water. The garden taverna serves a perfect vegetarian *mousakas* (€7), along with owner Kostas' homemade olives and feta.

ourpick Mando Rooms (☎ 24240 23917; www.skopelos.net/mando; s/d/tr/f €80/90/110/150; P ⊠) Having its own cove on the bay at Stafylos is a good start at this family-oriented and welcoming pension. Other extras include free coffee, a communal kitchen, satellite TV, and a platform over the rocks to enter the water.

ALONNISOS
ΑΛΟΝΝΗΣΟΣ

pop 2700

Alonnisos rises from the sea like a mountain of greenery with thick stands of pine and oak, along with mastic and arbutus bushes, and fruit trees. The west coast is mostly precipitous cliffs but the east coast is speckled with small bays and pebbly beaches and remains of a 5th-century-BC shipwreck. The water around Alonnisos has been declared a national marine park, and is the cleanest in the Aegean.

But lovely Alonnisos has had its share of bad luck. In 1952 a thriving cottage wine industry came to a halt, when vines imported from California were struck with the disease phylloxera. Robbed of their livelihood, many islanders moved away. Then, in 1965, an earthquake destroyed the hilltop capital of Alonnisos Town (now known as Old Alonnisos or Hora). The inhabitants were subsequently rehoused in hastily assembled dwellings at Patitiri.

Getting There & Away

Alonnisos' main port is Patitiri, which has links to mainland Volos and Agios Konstantinos, and to the other Sporades isles of Skiathos, Skopelos and Skyros. For details see Island Hopping (p745).

Tickets can be purchased from **Alkyon Travel** (☎ 24240 65220), or **Alonnisos Travel** (☎ 24240 65188; book@alonnisostravel.gr), both in Patitiri.

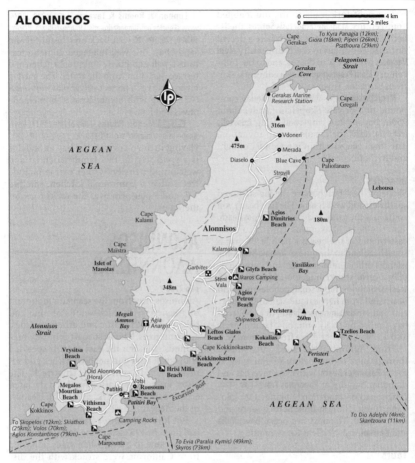

ALONNISOS

AEGEAN SEA

Alonnisos Strait

AEGEAN SEA

Getting Around

BOAT
Alonnisos Travel (☎ 24240 65188) hires out four-person 15hp to 25hp motorboats. The cost ranges from €48 to €60 per day in summer.

BUS
In summer, one bus plies the route between Patitiri (from opposite the quay) and Old Alonnisos (€1.20, hourly, 9am to about 3pm). There is also a service to Steni Vala from Old Alonnisos (€1.30).

CAR & MOTORCYCLE
Several motorcycle-hire outlets can be found on Pelasgon, in Patitiri, including reliable **I'm Bike** (☎ 24240 65010). Be wary when riding down

to the beaches, as some of the sand-and-shale tracks are steep and slippery. For cars, try **Albedo Travel** (☎ 24240 65804), or **Nefeli Bakery & Rent-A-Car** (☎ 24240 66497), both in Patitiri.

TAXI
The four taxis on the island (Georgos, Periklis, Theodoros and Spyros) tend to congregate opposite the quay. It's about €5 to Old Alonnisos, €8 to Megalos Mourtias and €12 to Steni Vala.

PATITIRI ΠΑΤΗΤΗΡΙ
Patitiri ('wine press' in Greek) sits between two sandstone cliffs at the southern end of the east coast. Despite its hasty origins following the devastating 1965 earthquake that levelled the

old hilltop capital (Palia Alonnisos), Patitiri is gradually improving its homely looks. The town is small and relaxed, and makes a convenient base for exploring Alonnisos.

Orientation

Finding your way around Patitiri is easy. The quay is in the centre of the waterfront and two roads lead inland. With your back to the sea, turn left for Pelasgon, or right for Ikion Dolopon. In truth, there are no road signs and most people refer to them as the left-hand road and right-hand road (or main road).

Information

National Bank of Greece ATM (main road)
Play Café (☎ 24240 66119; internet per hr €3; ✆ 9am-2pm & 6-9pm) Opposite the bank.
Police (☎ 24240 65205) Top of main road.
Port police (☎ 24240 65595; quay)
Post office (main road; ✆ 7.30am-2pm)
Techno Plus (☎ 24240 29100; internet per hr €3; ✆ 9am-2pm & 5-9pm) Top of main road.

Sights

FOLKLORE MUSEUM OF THE NORTHERN SPORADES

Largely a labour of love by Kostas and Angela Mavrikis, the **Folklore Museum of the Northern Sporades** (☎ 24240 66250, 6974027465; www.alonnissosmuseum.com; admission adult/child €4/free; ✆ 10am-9pm) includes an extensive and well-signed display of pirates' weapons and tools, a blacksmith's and antique nautical maps. A small cafe with displays by local artists sits atop the museum with views of the harbour, and a gift shop is open to the public. Take the stone stairway at the far west end of the harbour.

NATIONAL MARINE PARK OF ALONNISOS

In a country not noted for ecological long-sightedness, the National Marine Park of Alonnisos is a welcome innovation. Started in 1992, its prime aim has been the protection of the endangered Mediterranean monk seal (*Monachus monachus*). See the boxed text (below).

The park is divided into two zones. The carefully restricted Zone A comprises a cluster of islets to the northeast, including Kyra Panagia. Zone B is home to Alonnisos itself and Peristera.

In summer, licensed boats from Alonnisos and Skopelos conduct excursions through the marine park. Though it's unlikely you'll find the shy monk seal, your chances of spotting dolphins (striped, bottlenose and common) are fairly good.

MOM Information Centre (☎ 24240 66350; www.mom.gr; Patitiri; ✆ 10am-8pm) Don't miss this excellent info centre, all about the protected Mediterranean monk seal, with attractive displays, videos in English and helpful multilingual staff on hand.

Activities

WALKING

Walking opportunities abound on Alonnisos, and the best ones are waymarked. At the bus stop in Old Alonnisos a blue noticeboard details several walks. From Patitiri, a 2km donkey track winds up through shrubbery and orchards before bringing you to Old Alonnisos.

Consider a **guided walk** (☎ 6974080039; www.alonnisoswalks.co.uk; walks €15-30) with island resident Chris Browne. A half-day walk above Patitiri winds through pine forest trails, past

---

THE MONK SEAL

Once populating hundreds of colonies in the Black Sea and the Mediterranean, as well as along the Atlantic coast of Africa, the Mediterranean monk seal has been reduced to about 400 individuals today. Half of these live in waters between Greece and Turkey.

One of the earth's rarest mammals, this seal is on the list of the 20 most endangered species worldwide. Major threats include deliberate killings by fishermen – who see the seal as a pest that tears holes in their nets and robs their catch – incidental capture in fishing gear, decreasing food supply as fisheries decline, habitat destruction and pollution.

Recognising that this seal may become extinct if not protected, Greece established the National Marine Park of Alonnisos (above) in 1992, both to protect the seal and to promote recovery of fish stocks.

For more information, visit the website of **MOM** (Hellenic Society for the Study and Protection of the Monk Seal; www.mom.gr).

churches and olive groves overlooking the sea. His book, *Alonnisos through the souls of your feet* (€15), contains detailed forest and coastal trail descriptions, plus prime snorkelling sites. Also available at waterfront shops is the informative *Alonnisos on Foot: A Walking & Swimming Guide* (€14), by Bente Keller and Elias Tsoukanas.

CYCLING

The best mountain-bike riding is over on the southwest coast around the bay of Megali Ammos. There are several bicycle- and motorcycle-hire outlets on Ikion Dolopon.

Courses

Kali Thea (☎ 24240 65513; www.kalithea.org) offers yoga classes and massage on the outskirts of Old Alonnisos.

Tours

Three professional travel agencies on the waterfront provide maps and arrange popular marine park excursions. Enquire at **Ikos Travel** (☎ 24240 65320; www.ikostravel.com) for popular round-the-island guided excursions aboard the *Gorgona* (a classic Greek boat captained by island native, Pakis Athanasiou), which visit the **Blue Cave** on the northeast coast, and the islets of **Kyra Panagia** and **Peristera** in the marine park, with swimming breaks along the way. **Albedo Travel** (☎ 24240 65804; www.albedotravel .com) runs regular snorkelling and swimming excursions aboard the *Odyssey* to Skantzoura and nearby islands, and even arranges island weddings. **Alonnisos Travel** (☎ 24240 65188; www .alonnisostravel.gr) also runs marine park excursions, aboard the *Planitis*.

Sleeping

Prices here are for the higher July and August season; expect discounts of 25% at other times. A helpful quayside kiosk opens in July and August.

Camping Rocks (☎ 24240 65410; camp sites per adult/tent €6/3) Follow the signposts in town to this basic, clean and shaded coastal spot 1km south of Patitiri.

Pension Pleiades (☎ 24240 65235; www.pleiadeshotel .gr; s/d/tr from €25/35/50; 🅿 🖳 🛜) Take the stairway behind the newsstand to find this bright and welcoming budget option with views over Patitiri Bay.

Ilias Rent Rooms (☎ 24240 65451; fax 24240 65972; Pelasgon 27; d €45, 2-/3-bed studios €50/55; 🅿) Owners

Ilias and Magdalini give their spotless and bright blue-and-white domatia a warm and welcoming touch. Rooms and studios share a communal kitchen.

our pick **Liadromia Hotel** (☎ 24240 65521; www.liadromia.gr; d/tr/ste incl breakfast from €50/70/95; 🅿 ⬛ 🖳 🛜) This welcoming and impeccably maintained hotel overlooking the harbour was Patitiri's first. All the rooms have character to spare, from hand-embroidered curtains and antique lamps to stone floors and period wood furnishings. The gracious owner, Maria, takes obvious delight in making it all work.

Paradise Hotel (☎ 24240 65213; www.paradise-hotel .gr; s/d/incl breakfast €65/80/100; 🅿 ⬛ 🖳) Wood ceilings and stone-tiled floors give a rustic feel to the balconied rooms, which overlook both bay and harbour. Beyond the pool bar, a small stairway leads down to the bay for swimming.

Eating

Ouzerie Archipelagos (☎ 24240 65031; mains €4-8) If you want to get the feel of this very Greek establishment, pick a table toward the back, where locals gather to order round after round of excellent mezedhes, grilled fish and ouzo (or local favourite *tsipouro*, another distilled spirit) as the night rolls on.

Anais Restaurant & Pizzeria (☎ 24240 65243; mains €5-12; ☽ breakfast, lunch & dinner) Patitiri's first restaurant, opposite the hydrofoil dock, is still going strong, with snappy service and a big menu including souvlakia, pasta, hefty Greek salads and house favourite *kleftiko* (slow-oven-baked lamb, €10).

Also recommended:

Café Flisvos (☎ 24240 65307; mains €5-8) Best *mousakas*.

To Kamaki Ouzerie (☎ 24240 65245; mains €5-15) Father-and-son eatery.

OLD ALONNISOS ΠΑΛΙΑ ΑΛΟΝΝΙΣΟΣ

Old Alonnisos (also known as Palia Alonnisos, Hora, Palio Horio or Old Town), with its winding stepped alleys, is a tranquil, picturesque place with panoramic views. From the main road just outside the village an old donkey path leads down to pebbled Megalos Mourtias Beach and other paths lead south to Vithisma and Marpounta Beaches.

Sleeping

Pension Hiliadromia (☎ /fax 24240 65814; Plateia Hristou; d/2-bed studio €35/55; ⬛) Several of the pine-and-stone-floor rooms at the Hiliadromia come with balcony views, and the studios have well-equipped kitchens.

our pick Konstantina Studios (☎ 24240 66165, 6932271540; www.konstantinastudios.gr; s/d incl breakfast €60/80; P ✕ 🖥) Among the nicest accommodation on Alonnisos, these handsome and quiet self-catering studios with traditional styling come with balcony views of the southwest coast. The owner, Konstantina, happily fetches her guests from the dock and offers loads of tips for navigating the island.

Eating & Drinking

our pick Hayati (☎ 24240 66244; Old Alonnisos; snacks €2-4; 🕙 9am-2am) Hayati is a sweets shop (*glykopoleiou*) by day and a piano bar by night, with knock-out views of the island any time of day. Morning fare includes made-to-order Alonnisos *tyropita*. Later, you'll find homemade pastas and juicy souvlaki, handmade desserts, custards and cakes, along with the gracious hospitality of owner-cooks Meni and Angela. It's a five-minute walk from the village square.

Hayati Mezedhopoleio (☎ 24240 65885; Old Alonnisos; mezedhes €2.50-7) The same Hayati whose sweets shop is so good recently opened an excellent little mezedhes-style taverna, 50m from the square. Menu highlights include fried prawns, *skordalia* (garlic and potato dip), *kritamos* (rock samphire salad) and grilled octopus.

Taverna Megalos Mourtias (☎ 24240 65737; mains €4-8; 🕙 breakfast, lunch & dinner) A stone's throw from the surf, this laid-back taverna and beach bar 2km down the hill from the Hora prepares fine salads, *gavros*, fish soup, and several vegie dishes.

Astrofengia (☎ 24240 65182; mains €5-12) Patitiri residents think nothing of driving up to the Hora, just to sample the evening whims of chef Demi. Shrimp with saffron and garlic in filo dough stands out, along with an excellent vegie *mousakas*. For dessert, squeeze in a slice of *galaktoboureko* (homemade custard pie), whether you have room or not.

Aerides Café-Bar (☎ 6936522583; Old Alonnisos; 🕙 9am-5pm & 7pm-2am) Maria makes the drinks, picks the music and scoops the ice cream in summer at this snappy little bar on the square.

AROUND ALONNISOS

Alonnisos' main road reaches the northern tip of the island at Gerakas (19km), home to an EU-funded marine research station. Six kilometres north of Patitiri, another sealed road branches off to the small fishing port and yacht harbour of Steni Vala, and follows the shore past Kalamakia for 5km. A third road takes you from Patitiri to Megalos Mourtias.

Maria's Votsi Pension (☎ 24240 65510; www.pension-votsi.gr; Votsi; d/tr from €30/55; ✕ 🖥 🖥) occupies a perfect little corner of Votsi, just 100m from the bay. Rooms are immaculate and comfortable, and owner Maria's hospitality is everywhere. Nearby, **Milia Bay Hotel Apartments** (☎ 24240 66036; www.milia-bay.gr; d/apt from €85/160; P ✕ 🖥 🖥) spread out over the hillside, with large, well-appointed and self-catering studio apartments.

The island's east coast is home to several small bays and beaches. The first one of note, tiny **Rousoum**, is tucked between Patitiri and Votsi and very popular with local families. Next is the sandy and gently sloping **Hrysi Milia Beach**, another kid-friendly beach. Two kilometres on, **Cape Kokkinokastro** is the site of the ancient city of Ikos, with remains of city walls under the sea. Continuing north, the road branches off 4km to **Leftos Gialos**, with a lovely pebble beach and the superb **Taverna Eleonas** (☎ 24240 66066; mains €5-10), with outstanding versions of traditional *pites* (pies), vegie dolmas (dolmadhes) and excellent wine made by owner Nikos.

Steni Vala, a small fishing village and deep-water yacht port with a permanent population of no more than 30, has two small but decent beaches; pebbly **Glyfa** just above the village and sandy **Agios Petros** just below. There are 50-odd rooms in domatia, a few villas, as well as modest **Ikaros Camping** (☎ 24240 65772; camp sites per adult/tent €5/5), decently shaded by olive trees. Try **Ikaros Café & Market** (☎ 24240 65390) for reliable lodging information and more. The owner, Kostas, also runs the splendid museum in Patitiri. Four tavernas overlook the small marina, with **Taverna Kalimnia** (☎ 24240 65748; mains €4-8) claiming the best views of the harbour.

Kalamakia, 2km further north, is the last village of note, and has a few domatia and tavernas. The fishing boats usually tie up directly in front of **Margarita's Taverna** (☎ 24240 65738; mains €6-15), where the morning catch of fish and lobster seems to jump from boat to plate. Simple and spotless rooms are available at **Pension Niki** (☎ 24240 65989; s/d €30/50; ✕).

Beyond Kalamakia, the sealed road continues 3km to a wetland marsh and **Agios**

THE ORIGINAL CHEESE PIE

Tyropita (cheese pie) is almost deified in its birthplace, the northern Sporades. The popular pie is made with goat cheese which is rolled in delicate filo dough, coiled up, then fried quickly and served hot – a method that evolved in the wood-oven kitchens of Alonnisos.

However, the pie's origins are open to debate. Alonnisos residents claim their delicacy was appropriated by Skopelos in the 1950s, following the collapse of the cottage wine industry. Struggling Alonnisos farmers went to work on neighbouring Skopelos, picking plums. Their salty cheese pie lasted all day in the fields. Not surprisingly, it also made its way into the country kitchens of Skopelos, where residents claim that the treat was a motherly invention. This version has it that, when *spanakopita* (spinach pies) were slowly baking, resourceful mums quieted fussy children by tearing off a piece of filo, throwing in a handful of cheese, and frying it quickly with a reprimand, 'Here, stop your screaming'.

In the 1990s a popular daytime TV host touted the pie, but credited Skopelos with its origin. Predictably, frozen 'Skopelos Cheese Pie' soon showed up on mainland supermarket shelves. Today you can even buy it in the Athens' airport departure lounge, 'the deterioration of an imitation', according to a long-time Alonnisos resident, Pakis. Don't count on the frozen pie resembling the original and superior version.

On both Alonnisos and Skopelos there are now breakfast versions with sugar and cinnamon, and others using wild greens or lamb, especially popular in winter with red wine. But stunned Alonnisos folk still can't get over what's happened to their simple and delicious recipe. As one Skopelos businesswoman, Mahi, confided, 'Basically, we stole it!'

Dimitrios Beach, with a canteen and domatia opposite a graceful stretch of white pebbles. Beyond this, the road narrows to a footpath heading inland.

ISLETS AROUND ALONNISOS

Alonnisos is surrounded by eight uninhabited islets, all of which are rich in flora and fauna. **Piperi**, the furthest island northeast of Alonnisos, is a refuge for the monk seal and is strictly off-limits. **Gioura**, also off-limits, is home to an unusual species of wild goat known for the crucifix-shaped marking on its spine. Excursion boats can visit an old monastery and olive press on **Kyra Panagia**. The most remote of the group, **Psathoura**, boasts the submerged remains of an ancient city and the brightest lighthouse in the Aegean.

Peristera, just off Alonnisos' east coast, has several sandy beaches and the remains of a castle. Nearby **Lehousa** is known for its stalactite-filled sea caves. **Skantzoura**, to the southeast of Alonnisos, is the habitat of the Eleanora's falcon and the rare Audouin's seagull. The eighth island in the group, situated between Peristera and Skantzoura, is known as **Dio Adelphi** (Two Brothers); each 'brother' is actually a small island, both home to vipers, according to local fishermen who refuse to step foot on either.

SKYROS ΣΚΥΡΟΣ

pop 2600

Skyros is the largest of the Sporades group, though it can seem like two islands – the small bays, rolling farmland and pine forests of the north, and the arid hills and rocky shoreline of the south.

In Byzantine times, rogues and criminals exiled here from the mainland entered into a mutually lucrative collaboration with invading pirates. The exiles became the elite of Skyrian society, decorating their houses with pirate booty looted from merchant ships: hand-carved furniture, ceramic plates and copper ornaments from Europe, the Middle East and East Asia. Today, similar items adorn almost every Skyrian house.

In Greek mythology, Skyros was the hiding place of young Achilles. See the boxed text, p667, for more information about the Skyros Lenten Carnival and its traditions, which allude to Achilles' heroic feats.

Skyros was also the last port of call for the English poet Rupert Brooke (1887–1915), who died of septicaemia on a French hospital ship off the coast of Skyros en route to the Battle of Gallipoli. Today a number of expats, particularly English and Dutch, have made Skyros their home.

Getting There & Away

AIR

Skyros airport has flights to/from Athens and Thessaloniki and occasional charter flights from Oslo and Amsterdam. Winter flights operate between Skyros and Thessaloniki three times per week (Tuesday, Wednesday and Saturday). Also in winter, there are flights to Athens twice weekly (Tuesday and Saturday).

For tickets, contact **Olympic Air** (☎ 210 966 6666; www.olympicairlines.com) or visit **Skyros Travel Agency** (☎ 22220 91600; www.skyrostravel.com; Agoras St). For flight details, see Island Hopping (p762).

BOAT

Skyros' main port is Linaria, with ferry links to Evia (Paralia Kymis) and to Alonnisos and Skopelos in summer. For details see Island Hopping (p762).

You can buy tickets from **Achileas ticket office** (☎ 22220 91790; fax 22220 91792; Agoras; 🕑 9am-1pm & 7-10pm) on Agoras in Skyros Town. There is also a ferry ticket kiosk at the dock in Linaria, and another at the dock in Paralia Kymis (Evia).

Getting Around

BUS & TAXI

In high season there are daily buses departing from Skyros Town to Linaria (€1.30) and to Molos (via Magazia). Buses for both Skyros Town and Molos meet the ferry at Linaria. However, outside of high season there are only one or two buses to Linaria (to coincide with the ferry arrivals) and none to Molos. A

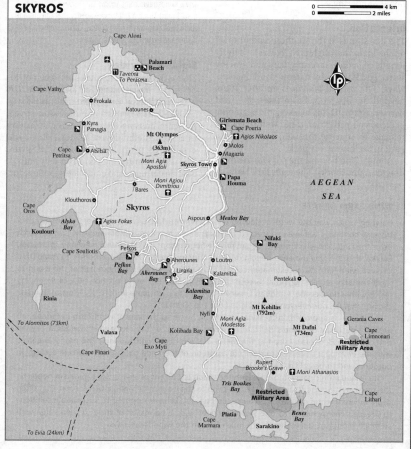

SKYROS

0 ————— 4 km
0 ————— 2 miles

taxi from Skyros Town to Linaria is €13; to the airport it's €20.

CAR & MOTORCYCLE

Cars, motorbikes and mountain bikes can all be hired from **Martina's Rentals** (☎ 22220 92022; 6974752380) near the police station in town. The reasonable **Vayos Motorbikes** (☎ 22220 92957) is near the bus stop, and **Angelis Cars** (☎ 22220 91888) is 200m before the bus stop.

SKYROS TOWN

Skyros' capital is a striking, dazzlingly white town of flat-roofed Cycladic-style houses draped over a high rocky bluff. It's topped by a 13th-century fortress and the monastery of Agios Georgios, and is laced with labyrinthine, smooth cobblestone streets that invite wandering.

Orientation

The bus stop is at the southern end of town on the main thoroughfare (Agoras) – a lively jumble of people, tavernas, bars and grocery stores and flanked by narrow winding alleyways. The central *plateia* is another 100m beyond the bus stop, From there, the road narrows dramatically, marking the beginning of the town's pedestrian zone. Motorbikes still manage to squeeze through, but cars must park in the nearby car park.

About 100m beyond the *plateia*, the main drag of Agoras forks. The right fork leads up to the fortress and Moni Agiou Georgiou, with its fine frescoes and sweeping views. The left fork zigzags to two small museums adjacent to Plateia Rupert Brooke, where a simple bronze statue of a nude Rupert Brooke faces the sea. The frankness of the statue caused an outcry among the local islanders when it was first installed in the 1930s.

From Plateia Rupert Brooke the cobbled steps descend 1km to Magazia Beach.

Information

Mano.com (☎ 22220 92473; Agoras; internet per hr €3; 🕑 9am-2pm & 6.30-11.30pm)
National Bank of Greece ATM (Agoras)
Police (☎ 22220 91274) Behind Skyros Travel Agency.
Post office (Agoras; 🕑 7.30am-2pm)
Skyros Travel Agency (☎ 22220 91600, 6944884588; www.skyrostravel.com; Agoras St; 🕑 9am-2.30pm & 6.30-11pm) This is a full-service agency that can arrange room bookings, travel reservations, car and motorbike hire, diving and excursions around Skyros.

Sights & Activities

Skyros Town has two museums. The not-to-be-missed **Manos Faltaïts Folk Museum** (☎ 22220 91232; www.faltaits.gr; Plateia Rupert Brooke; admission €2; 🕑 10am-2pm & 6-9pm) is a one-of-a-kind private museum housing the outstanding collection of a Skyrian ethnologist, Manos Faltaïts, and detailing the mythology and folklore of Skyros. The 19th-century mansion is a labyrinth of Skyrian costumes and embroidery, antique fur-

---

WIND FARM DEBATE

Gauging which way the wind is blowing is becoming trickier on Skyros, where a running controversy continues between concerned residents and a monastery, Moni Megistis Lavras, which owns the land, and which quietly began private negotiations in 2005 with a mainland contractor, Enteka, and the government's Regulatory Authority for Energy. At stake: whether to establish a massive wind farm (at an estimated cost of €500 million) on the southern half of the island to meet the EU's requirement that Greece utilise renewable energy to provide 20% of its energy needs within the decade. Although Greece is anxious to participate in the EU's effort to mitigate climate change, not everyone is thrilled about the location.

If the plan is approved, little Skyros would be home to the largest wind farm in Europe, effectively putting the island's delicate breeding grounds for the rare and endangered Skyrian pony and the Eleonora's falcon at the mercy of 150m-high wind turbines. The proposal comes with the developer's promise to dedicate a portion of the 'wind park' to the delicate ecology in question, and to be called 'Natura 2000'.

The island municipality, together with the Union of Citizens of Skyros, have joined in opposing the proposal, and the issue has already moved to the Council of State, a Greek court that often hears environmental disputes. Of course, no one on Skyros is opposed to sustainable solutions to Greece's energy needs. As one Skyros resident said, 'It's a matter of scale'. It seems that with so much money at stake, there's not much faith in the wind these days.

SKYROS CARNIVAL

In this wild pre-Lenten festival, which takes place on the last four weekends before Clean Monday (Kathara Deftera, or Shrove Monday – the first Monday in Lent, 40 days before Easter), young men portray their elders' vigour as they don goat masks, hairy jackets and dozens of copper goat bells, often weighing up to 30kg. They then proceed to clank and dance with intricate steps through the town, each with a male partner ('korela'), dressed up as a Skyrian bride but also wearing a goat mask. During these revelries there is singing and dancing, performances of plays, recitations of satirical poems and much drinking and feasting. Women and children join in, wearing fancy dress as well. These strange goings-on are overtly pagan, with elements of Dionysian festivals, including goat worship. In ancient times, as today, Skyros was renowned for its goat's meat and milk.

The transvestism evident in the carnival seems to derive from the cult of Achilles associated with Skyros in Greek mythology. According to legend, the island was the childhood hiding place for the boy Achilles, whose mother, Thetis, feared a prophecy requiring her son's skills in the Trojan War. The boy was given to the care of King Lykomides of Skyros, who raised him disguised as one of his own daughters. Young Achilles was outwitted, however, by Odysseus, who arrived with jewels and finery for the girls, along with a sword and shield. When Achilles alone showed interest in the weapons, Odysseus discovered his secret, then persuaded him to go to Troy where he distinguished himself in battle. This annual festival is the subject of Joy Koulentianou's book *The Goat Dance of Skyros*.

---

niture and ceramics, daggers and cooking pots, vintage photographs and a small gift shop.

The adjacent **Archaeological Museum** (☎ 22220 91327; Plateia Rupert Brooke; admission €2; ⏰ 8.30am-3pm Tue-Sun) features excellent examples of Mycenaean pottery found near Magazia and, best of all, a traditional Skyrian house interior, transported in its entirety from the benefactor's home.

Every year around mid-September, Skyros is host to a **half-marathon** (☎ 22220 92789), which starts in Atsitsa and ends at the town square in Skyros Town, with drummers welcoming the first runners across the finish line. A minimarathon for the children sets the tone, followed by music and dancing.

Courses

Reiki courses are offered by long-time island resident and reiki master **Janet Smith** (☎ 22220 93510; Skyros Town; www.simplelifeskyros.com). It's on the south edge of Skyros Town.

Skyros is home to the British-based holistic holiday centre retreat, the **Skyros Centre** (☎ 22220 92842; www.skyros.com), with facilities both in town and Atsitsa. One- and two-week residential courses feature ever-changing themes ranging from yoga and Greek cooking to sailing and the art of flirting.

Tours

feel ingreece (☎ 22220 93100; www.feelingreece.com; Agora St) is a new endeavour by hard-working local owner Chrysanthi Zygogianni, dedicated to helping sustain the best of Skyrian culture. The focus is on the local arts and the island environment. The office arranges hiking excursions to glimpse wild Skyrian ponies. Boat trips and diving courses, pottery, woodcarving and cooking lessons, scuba diving and Greek dancing are among the offerings. Says Chrysanthi, 'I think tourism should be healthy and supporting something authentic for the community.' Prices start from around €30.

A day-long boat excursion (€35) to the Gerania sea caves on the southeast coast or nearby Sarakino Islet includes lunch and a swim. Contact Skyros Travel for details.

Contact the resourceful **Niko Sekkes** (☎ 22220 92707), manager of the Argo museum shop on upper Agoras, for details on his impromptu tours of the island and the Faltaïts Museum.

Sleeping

BUDGET & MIDRANGE

Hotel Elena (☎ /fax 22220 91738; s/d/tr €30/45/55; P 🐶 🖳) A rooftop bar doubles as a breakfast spot on summer mornings here. Rooms are big and comfy, and it's just 100m past the square, easy to find after a night on the town.

our pick **Atherinis Rooms** (☎ 22220 93510; 6979292976; www.simplelifeskyros.com; d/apt from €45/60; P 🐶) Welcoming owners Dimitris Atherinis

---

TOP FIVE SKYRIAN POTTERY STUDIOS

Skyros is unique for its centuries-old collections of fine and unusual ceramics, dating from the days when passing pirates collaborated with rogue residents, whose houses became virtual galleries for pirate booty, ceramics included. To see the evolution of this island art, make a tour of these favourites:

- Yiannis Komboyiannis (p670)
- Stamatis Ftoulis (opposite)
- Stathis Katsarelias (opposite)
- Ioanna Asnmenou Ceramics (right)
- Efrossini Varsamou-Nikolaou (opposite)

---

and English transplant Janet Smith are constantly attending to detail at these self-catering apartments (300m below the bus stop). Spacious double rooms feature hand-tiled baths and overlook a well-tended garden. Breakfast (€5) includes fresh juice and homemade bread.

Pension Nikolas (☎ 22220 91778; fax 22220 93400; s/d/tr €50/60/70; P ✖) Set back on a small, quiet road, this comfortable and friendly pension is only a five-minute walk to busy Agoras. The upper rooms have air conditioning and balconies; the lower rooms have fans and open onto a shady garden.

TOP END

Hotel Nefeli & Dimitrios Studios (☎ 22220 91964; www .skyros-nefeli.gr; d/studios/ste incl breakfast €125/190/300; P ✖ ☀ ⊕ ☎) This smart hotel on the edge of town has an easy minimalist-meets-Skyrian feel to it, with vintage photographs, handsome furnishings and swank bathrooms. The adjacent family-size studios are part of a remodelled Skyrian house. Both properties share a saltwater swimming pool and bar.

Eating

Skyros welcomes a steady number of visiting Athenians, with the pleasant result that island cooks do not cater to touristy tongues.

Taverna Lambros (☎ 22220 92498; mains €5-8.50) Family-run and roadside Lambros is just 3km south of Skyros Town in Aspous. Generous-sized dishes include lamb and pork grills, fresh fish gumbo and Skyrian cheese bread.

our pick Maryetis Restaurant (☎ 22220 91311; Agoras; mains €6-9) The local favourite, by far, for grilled fish and octopus *stifadho*, Skyrian goat in lemon sauce, along with hearty soups and mezedhes such as black-eyed beans and bean dip.

O Pappous kai Ego (☎ 22220 93200; Agoras; mains €6-9) The name of this small taverna means 'my grandfather and me', and it's easy to see how one generation of family recipes followed another. Mezedhes are excellent, especially broad-bean dip and Skyrian dolmadhes made with a touch of goat's milk.

Drinking

Nightlife in Skyros Town centres mostly around the bars on Agoras; the further north you go away from the *plateia*, the more mellow the sounds.

Kalypso (☎ 22220 92160; Agoras; ⌨) Classy Kalypso plays lots of jazz and blues, and owner-bartender Hristos makes a killer margarita, along with homemade sangria. A side room sports an internet connection.

Rodon (☎ 22220 92168; Agoras) This smart and comfortable late-night hang-out is a mellow spot to end the evening. Bonus points for big drinks and fresh juices.

Agora Café-Bar (☎ 22220 92535; Agoras; ☎) Next to the post office at the back of the main square, this cosy bar offers free wi-fi and a welcoming atmosphere.

Shopping

Argo (☎ 22220 92158; Agoras) Argo specialises in high-quality copies of ceramics from the Faltaïts Museum.

Andreou Woodcarving (☎ 22220 92926; Agoras) Get a close look at the intricate designs that distinguish traditional Skyrian furniture at this handsome shop on upper Agoras.

Leyteris Avgoklouris (☎ 22220 91106) Equally interesting is this open workshop in the nearby village of Aspous.

Ioanna Asnmenou Ceramics (☎ 22220 92723; Agoras) An oasis of fine work near the busy main square.

MAGAZIA & MOLOS
ΜΑΓΑΖΙΑ & ΜΩΛΟΣ

The resort of Magazia, a compact and attractive place of winding alleys, is at the southern end of a splendid, long sandy beach, situated a short distance north of Skyros Town. Skinny-dippers can leave it all behind at **Papa Houma** near the southern end of Magazia.

At the northern end of the beach, once-sleepy Molos now has its own share of decent tavernas and rooms. Its landmark windmill and adjacent rock-hewn Church of Agios Nikolaos are easy to spot.

Activities

Several potters spin their wheels in Magazia without bothering to put up a sign out, but they are happy to see visitors, and some of their exceptional work is for sale. **Stathis Katsarelias** (☎ 22220 92918) runs a studio on the small lane between the main road and Taverna Stefanos; he also offers drop-in pottery workshops for adults, kids and whoever wants to get their hands muddy. The studios of **Efrossini Varsamou-Nikolaou** (☎ 22220 91142) are in the Deidamia Hotel. Just down from Taverna Stefanos, you'll find the workshop of **Stamatis Ftoulis** (☎ 22220 91559).

Sleeping

Georgia Tsakamis Rooms (☎ 22220 91357; gtsakamis @yahoo.gr; Magazia; d/tr €45/50; ✳) You can't get much closer to the sand and sea than at these geranium-adorned domatia 20m from the beach, opposite a handy car park.

Deidamia Hotel (☎ 22220 92008; www.deidamia .com; d/tr/f from €45/50/70; P ✳ 🖳 �) The spacious and tidy Deidamia is on the road entering Magazia, opposite a small market. Look for the bougainvillea garden and rooftop solar panels.

Ariadne Apartments (☎ 22220 91113; www. ariadnestudios.gr; d/apt from €65/95; ✳ 🖳) Just 50m from the beach at Magazia, these inviting studios and two-room apartments enclose a small courtyard and breakfast cafe (with great pastries). Handsome rooms have fully equipped kitchens and are decorated with original artwork.

ourpick **Perigiali Studios** (☎ 22220 92075; www. perigiali.com; d/tr/apt incl breakfast from €75/90/180; ✳ 🖳 ✳) Perigiali feels secluded despite being only 50m from the beach. One part of the compound features Skyrian-style rooms overlooking a garden with pear, apple and apricot trees, while a new upscale wing sports a pool with swank view apartments. English-speaking owner Amalia is full of ideas for travellers.

Eating & Drinking

Juicy Beach Bar (☎ 22220 93337; snacks €2-5; Magazia) Escape the midday sun or chill under the

stars at busy Juicy's, with breakfast throughout the day.

Stefanos Taverna (☎ 22220 91272; mains €4.50-8) Sit on the terrace of this traditional eatery overlooking Magazia Beach, and choose from a range of point-and-eat dishes, wild greens, souvlakia and fresh fish by the kilo. Breakfast omelettes start at €3.50.

Oi Istories Tou Barba (My Uncle's Stories; ☎ 22220 91453; Molos; mains €4-10) Look for the light blue railing above the beach in Molos to find this excellent cafe and *tsipouradhiko* with well-prepared prawn and octopus mezedhes.

Thalassa Beach Bar (Sea; ☎ 22220 92044; Molos) This thoroughly modern beach bar somehow blends in with easy-going Molos. Maybe it's the mojitos and full-moon parties.

AROUND SKYROS

Linaria Λιναριά

Linaria, the port of Skyros, is tucked into a small bay filled with bobbing fishing boats and a few low-key tavernas and *ouzeries*. Things perk up briefly whenever the *Achileas* ferry comes in, its surreal arrival announced with the booming sound of Richard Strauss' *Also Sprach Zarathustra* blasting from the speakers at a hillside bar above the port; the acoustics would make any audio engineer proud.

You can practically stumble off the ferry and into **King Lykomides Rooms to Let** (☎ 22220 93249, 6972694434; soula@skyrosnet.gr; r incl breakfast €45-60; P ✳ 🖳), an efficient domatio managed by the hospitable Soula Pappas. It has well-maintained rooms, each with balcony.

Join the port regulars under the big plane tree at the friendly **Taverna O Platanos** (☎ 22220 91995; mains €5-7), which has well-prepared grilled octopus and fried *gavros*, plus oven-ready chicken and potatoes, and generous Greek salads.

For drinks at sunset there's **Kavos Bar** (☎ 22220 93213; drinks & snacks €2-5). This swank open-air bar, perched on the hill overlooking the port, pulls in Skyrians from across the island.

Atsitsa Ατσίτσα

The picturesque port village of Atsitsa on the island's west coast occupies a woodsy setting, shaded by pines that approach the shore, where **Taverna Antonis** (☎ 22220 92990; mains €4-8) sits opposite a small pier where the family's fishing boat ties up.

our pick **Sunset Café** (☎ 22220 91331; Atsitsa; drinks & snacks €1.50-4) overlooks the bay. This snappy all-organic cafe is a treat. Choose from Greek coffee, wines from Corinth, fresh juices, ice creams, *karidhopita* (walnut cake) and delicate salads, all compliments of Mariana and family. Look for the family's adopted pelican, Poseidon, while you're there.

Nearby, just a few metres from the beach, is the ceramics workshop of **Yiannis Komboyiannis** (☎ 22220 91064; www.artinskyros.gr; Kira Panagia). This ceramics master goes about his work methodically, visitors or no visitors. The yard facing the beach is filled with rope, random sculptures, fishing nets, an old boat pulled ashore and his most recent handiwork drying in the sun. Look for workshops and gallery openings in the summer.

Beaches

Beaches on the northwest coast are subject to strong winter currents and summer *meltemi* winds.

Atsitsa has a small pebble beach shaded by pines, good for freelance camping, but too rocky for swimming. Just to the north (1.5km) is the superior swimming beach of **Kyra Panagia**, named for the monastery on the hill above. Just 1.5km to the south, the tiny and protected north-facing bay at **Cape Petritsa** is also good for swimming.

A beautiful horseshoe-shaped beach graces **Pefkos Bay**, 10km southeast of Atsitsa. Nearby, the beach at **Aherounes** has a gentle sandy bottom, very nice for children, along with two tavernas and domatia.

To the north and near the airport, **Palamari** is a graceful stretch of sandy beach that does not get crowded. Palamari is also the site of a well-marked **archaeological excavation** (www.skyros .gr/ancient-palamari-skyros.html) of a walled Bronze Age town dating from 2500 BC. At the airport junction, the popular roadside **Taverna To Perasma** (☎ 22220 92911; mains €4.50-7) serves excellent *mayirefta* dishes (goat in lemon sauce €6).

Rupert Brooke's Grave

Rupert Brooke's well-tended marble grave is in a quiet olive grove just inland from Tris Boukes Bay in the south of the island, and marked with a wooden sign in Greek on the roadside. The gravestone is inscribed with some of Brooke's verses, beginning with the following apt epitaph:

> If I should die think only this of me:
> That there's some corner of a foreign field
> That is forever England.

From coastal Kalamitsa, just east of Linaria, a road south passes the village of Nyfi, and brings you to Brooke's simple tomb. No buses come here, and travel is restricted beyond this southernmost corner of the island, which is dominated by the Greek Naval station on Tris Boukes Bay.

Ionian Islands
Τα Ιόνια Νησιά

The Ionian Sea is where 'the blue begins', in Lawrence Durrell's haunting phrase, and the Ionian Islands are certainly where Greece begins to seduce with its heat, its intensity of colour and its dazzling light. This is where the grey north relents entirely. The main islands of Corfu, Paxi, Lefkada, Ithaki, Kefallonia and Zakynthos lie scattered down the west coast of mainland Greece like fragments of a mosaic. With their olive groves, cypress trees, starkly beautiful mountains, and countless beaches fringing iridescent waters, they offer something for adventure seekers, culture vultures and beach bums alike. Devastating earthquakes and the formative hands of such occupiers as the Venetians, French and British, have shaped the architecture of the islands while Italy, especially, has inspired a unique Ionian cuisine. In Corfu Town you can admire British neoclassical palaces, drink beneath Parisian-style arcades and wander through Venetian alleyways. Yet, on all the islands, the seductive spirit of Old Greece survives, in Byzantine churches and in village *plateies* (squares) shaded by bougainvilleas and plane trees, or beneath a taverna's vine-covered canopy amid the scent of jasmine.

The islands are, of course, overwhelmed by conspicuous tourism in countless beach resorts, but it is still possible to get off the beaten track to isolated swimming coves, to wander across rugged mountains, or to seek out the dreamy silence of lonely hamlets. Cultural adventurers can explore fortresses, ancient churches and Homeric sites and can visit numerous museums and art galleries of great quality. Outdoor addicts can hike, cycle, windsurf and scuba dive and everyone can enjoy some of the finest food and drink in Greece amid the reassuring spirit of Ionian *filoxenia* (hospitality) and friendliness.

HIGHLIGHTS

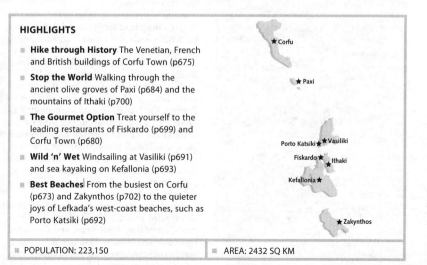

- **Hike through History** The Venetian, French and British buildings of Corfu Town (p675)

- **Stop the World** Walking through the ancient olive groves of Paxi (p684) and the mountains of Ithaki (p700)

- **The Gourmet Option** Treat yourself to the leading restaurants of Fiskardo (p699) and Corfu Town (p680)

- **Wild 'n' Wet** Windsailing at Vasiliki (p691) and sea kayaking on Kefallonia (p693)

- **Best Beaches** From the busiest on Corfu (p673) and Zakynthos (p702) to the quieter joys of Lefkada's west-coast beaches, such as Porto Katsiki (p692)

- POPULATION: 223,150

- AREA: 2432 SQ KM

IONIAN ISLANDS

0 ————— 40 km
0 ————— 20 miles

To Italy
(80km)

Othoni   Erikousa
   Diapondia
      Islands
Mathraki
         Sidhari   Saranda

Agios Stefanos   **Corfu**   **ALBANIA**
                    (p674)
Paleokastritsa

Pelekas   Corfu   Sagiada
             Town
                    To Ioannina
                    (75km)

                         Igoumenitsa

Leflommi

                         GREECE
       South
       Kerkyra
       Straits
       Lakka
Paxi   Parga
(p686)
       Gaios   **EPIROS**

Antipaxi
(p686)   To Athens
                     (350km)

IONIAN
SEA
                    Preveza

             Lefkada   **STEREA**
Lefkada Town   **ELLADA**
(p690)
             Nydri
       Vasiliki   Meganisi

                   Mytikas
                   Kalamos
    Fiskardo
              Frikes   Kastos
Kefallonia Myrtos **Ithaki**
(p694)   Piso   (p694)
          Aetos   To Astakos
   Agia   (5km)
Lixouri Evfymia   Vathy
      Argostoli Sami

         Pesada
                    Poros
                    To Patra
                    (70km)

       Agios Nikolaos
       Zakynthos
       Strait   To Patra
                    (70km)
                Kyllini
Zakynthos   Zakynthos **PELOPONNESE**
(p703)   Town
   Bay of
   Laganas

History

The origin of the name 'Ionian' is obscure, but it's thought to derive from the goddess Io. As yet another of Zeus' paramours, Io fled the wrath of a jealous Hera (in the shape of a heifer), and happened to pass through the waters now known as the Ionian Sea.

If we are to believe Homer, the islands were important during Mycenaean times; however, no traces of palaces or even modest villages from that period have been revealed, though Mycenaean tombs have been unearthed. Ancient history lies buried beneath tonnes of earthquake rubble – seismic activity has been constant on all Ionian islands.

By the 8th century BC, the Ionian Islands were in the clutches of the mighty city-state of Corinth, which regarded them as stepping stones on the route to Sicily and Italy. A century later, Corfu staged a successful revolt against Corinth, which was allied to Sparta, and became an ally of Sparta's arch enemy, Athens. This alliance provoked Sparta into challenging Athens, thus precipitating the Peloponnesian Wars (431–404 BC). The wars left Corfu depleted and it became little more than a staging post for whoever happened to be holding sway in Greece. By the end of the 3rd century BC, the Romans ruled the Ionian Islands. Following the decline of the Roman Empire, the islands saw the usual waves of invaders fastening on Greece. After the fall of Constantinople, the Ionian Islands fell under the control of Venice.

Corfu was never fully a part of the Ottoman Empire, in spite of sporadic and violent visitations. Lefkada was under Turkish control, however, except for occasional Venetian retrenchment, from 1479 until 1684 when Venice finally won back control of the island.

Venice fell to Napoleon in 1797 and two years later, under the Treaty of Campo Formio, the Ionian Islands were allotted to France. In 1799 Russian forces wrested the islands from Napoleon, but by 1807 they were his again. The all-powerful British could not resist meddling, and in 1815, after Napoleon's downfall, the Ionian Islands became a British protectorate under the jurisdiction of a series of lord high commissioners.

British rule was oppressive but the British constructed roads, bridges, schools and hospitals, established trade links, and developed agriculture and industry. However, the nationalistic fervour throughout the rest of Greece soon reached the Ionian Islands and by 1864 Britain had finally relinquished the islands to Greece.

During WWII the Italians invaded Corfu in pursuit of Mussolini's imperialistic ambitions. Italy surrendered to the Allies in September 1943 and, in revenge, the Germans massacred thousands of Italians who had occupied the Ionian Islands. They also bombed Corfu Town and sent 1795 of Corfu's 2000 Jews to be murdered at Auschwitz-Birkenau. On the way to the death camps many died in dreadful conditions that included being transported by sea to Athens in open barges. There is a striking memorial statue to Corfu's Jews in Plateia Solomou, near the Old Port in the area still known as Evraiki, the Jewish Quarter.

The islands saw a great deal of emigration after WWII, and again following the devastating earthquakes of 1948 and 1953. By the 1960s foreign holidaymakers were visiting in increasing numbers and package tourism especially became a feature. Today, tourism is a major influence in the Ionian Islands and future challenges include managing the more negative aspects of the industry in the face of often rapidly changing global trends.

CORFU KEPKYPA

pop 122,670

Corfu – or Kerkyra (ker-kih-rah) in Greek – is the second largest and the greenest Ionian island. It is also the best known. This was Homer's 'beautiful and rich land', Shakespeare reputedly used it as a background for The Tempest and in the 20th century, the writers Lawrence and Gerald Durrell – among others – extolled its virtues. The island's capital, Corfu Town is one of the loveliest towns in Greece.

WWW.PLANNING YOUR TRIP.COM

There are countless websites devoted to the Ionians – here are some of the better ones:

Corfu www.allcorfu.com, www.kerkyra.net
Kefallonia www.kefalonia.gr, www.kefalonia .net.gr
Lefkada www.lefkada.gr, www.lefkas.net
Ionian Islands www.greeka.com/ionian
Ithaki www.ithacagreece.com
Paxi www.paxos-greece.com, www.paxos.tk
Zakynthos www.zakynthos-net.gr, www .zanteweb.gr

Corfu is mountainous in its northern half where the east and west coastlines can be steep and dramatic and where the island's interior is a rolling expanse of peaceful countryside where stately cypresses rise from a pelt of shimmering olive trees. South of Corfu Town, the island narrows appreciably and becomes very flat. Beaches and resorts punctuate the entire coastline, intensively so north of Corfu Town and along the north coast, but less so in the west and south.

Getting There & Away
AIR
Domestic

Corfu has several flights to/from Athens each day. There are at least three flights a week to/from Thessaloniki, Preveza and Kefallonia. **Olympic Air** (☎ 26610 22962; www.olympicairlines.com) is based at the airport. For details see Island Hopping (p748).

International

The budget airline easyJet has daily direct flights between London and Corfu (May to October).

From May to September, many charter flights come from northern Europe and the UK to Corfu.

BOAT
Domestic

Hourly ferries travel daily between Corfu and Igoumenitsa and hydrofoils and car ferries go between Corfu and Paxi and Paxi and Igoumenitsa daily in high season

There are six ferries daily between Lefkimmi, at the southern tip of Corfu, and Igoumenitsa.

Petrakis Lines (Map p676; ☎ 26610 31649; Ethnikis Antistasis 4) operates passenger-only hydrofoils between Corfu and Paxi from May until mid-October. Be sure to book one day prior; places fill quickly.

For details of all domestic boat connections from Corfu see Island Hopping (p748).

Shipping agencies selling tickets are found in Corfu Town near the new port, along Xenofondos Stratigou and Ethnikis Antistasis. **Mancan Travel & Shipping** (p678; ☎ 26610 32664; Eleftheriou Venizelou 38) and **Agoudimos Lines/GLD Travel** (Map p676; ☎ 26610 80030; tickets@gld.gr; Ethnikis Antistasis 1) have helpful staff.

International

Corfu has regular connections with three ports in Italy (Brindisi, Bari and Venice), operated by

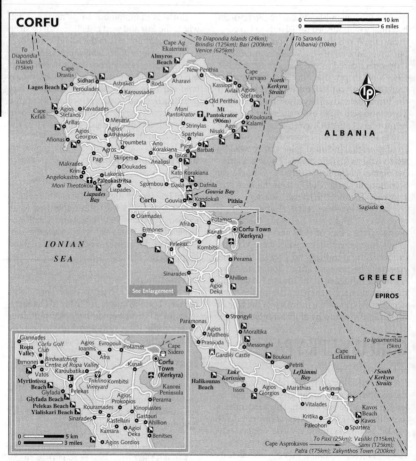

a handful of ferry companies sailing between Italy and Igoumenitsa and/or Patra. (Travellers can also sail between Ancona and Igoumenitsa, then transfer to a local ferry.) Crossings are most frequent in July and August, but there are year-round services at least weekly between Corfu and Brindisi, Bari and Venice.

From Corfu it's possible to cross to Albania, or to visit on a day trip. **Petrakis Lines** (Map p676; ☎ 26610 31649; Ethnikis Antistasis 4) operates hydro-foil services connecting Corfu and Albania. Daily sailings go to/from the Albanian town of Saranda. As well as the ticket price, travellers also pay €10 to obtain a temporary visa for Albania.

Note: the only ferry companies that accept Eurail and Inter-rail passes are Bluestar, Superfast and Agoudimos. All international

ferry companies also have special offers and concessions for seniors, families and last-minute tickets.

BUS
KTEL (☎ 26610 28898) runs buses three times daily (and on Monday, Wednesday and Friday via Lefkimmi in the island's south) between Corfu Town and Athens (€39.50, 8½ hours). There's also a daily service to/from Thessaloniki (€37.70, eight hours); for both destinations budget another €7.50 for the ferry between Corfu and the mainland. Long-distance tickets should be purchased in advance from Corfu Town's **long-distance bus station** (Map p676; ☎ 26610 28927/30627; I Theotoki), between Plateia San Rocco and the new port.

INTERNATIONAL FERRIES FROM CORFU TOWN

Destination	Duration	Fare	Frequency
Ancona (Italy)	15¼hr	€73	1 weekly
Bari (Italy)	8hr	€30	17 weekly
Brindisi (Italy)	5½-6¼hr	€38	12 weekly
Saranda (Albania)	25min	€19	1 daily
Venice (Italy)	25hr	€73	4 weekly

Getting Around

TO/FROM THE AIRPORT

There is no bus service between Corfu Town and the airport. Buses 6 and 10 from Plateia San Rocco in Corfu Town stop on the main road 800m from the airport (en route to Benitses and Ahillion). A taxi between the airport and Corfu Town costs around €12.

BUS

Long-Distance (Green) Buses from Corfu Town

Long-distance KTEL buses (known as green buses) travel from Corfu Town's **long-distance bus station** (Map p676; ☎ 26610 28927/30627; I Theotoki).

Fares cost €1.40 to €3.40. Printed timetables are available at the ticket kiosk. Sunday and holiday services are reduced considerably, or don't run at all.

Destination	Duration	Frequency
Agios Gordios	45min	7 daily
Agios Stefanos	1½hr	5 daily
Aharavi (via Roda)	1¼hr	6 daily
Arillas (via Afionas)	1¼hr	2 daily
Barbati	45min	4 daily
Ermones	30min	4 daily
Glyfada	30min	7 daily
Kassiopi	45min	6 daily
Kavos	1½hr	10 daily
Messonghi	45min	5 daily
Paleokastritsa	45min	6 daily
Pyrgi	30min	7 daily
Sidhari	1¼hr	8 daily
Spartera	45min	2 daily

Local (Blue) Buses in Corfu Town

Local buses (blue buses) depart from the **local bus station** (Map p678; ☎ 26610 28927; Plateia San Rocco) in Corfu Old Town.

Tickets are either €0.90 or €1.30 depending on the length of journey, and can be purchased from the booth on Plateia San Rocco (although tickets for Ahillion, Benitses and Kouramades are bought on the bus). All trips are under 30 minutes.

Destination	Via	Bus No	Frequency
Agios Ioannis	Afra	8	14 daily
Ahillion		10	7 daily
Benitses		22	12 daily
Evropouli	Potamas	4	11 daily
Kanoni		2	half-hourly
Kombitsi	Kanali	14	4 daily
Kondokali & Dasia	Gouvia	7	half-hourly
Kouramades	Kinopiastes	5	14 daily
Pelekas		11	8 daily

CAR & MOTORCYCLE

Car- and motorbike-hire outlets are plentiful in Corfu Town and most of the resort towns on the island. Prices start at around €45 per day (less for longer-term hire). Most international car-hire companies are represented in Corfu Town and at the airport. Most local companies have offices along the northern waterfront.

Recommended agencies:

Budget (Map p676; ☎ 26610 22062; Ioannou Theotoki 132)

Easy Rider (Map p676; ☎ 26610 43026) Opposite the new port; rents out scooters and motorbikes.

International Rent-a-Car (Map p678; ☎ 26610 33411/37710; 20a Kapodistriou) Reliable, long-established company with an office on the Spianada (doubles as the Irish Consulate).

Sunrise (Map p676; ☎ 26610 26511/44325; www .corfusunrise.com; Ethnikis Antistasis 6) A reliable choice along the waterfront near the new port.

CORFU TOWN

pop 28,200

Corfu Town takes hold of you and never lets go. Pastel-hued Venetian-era mansions grace the old town, the Campiello. The seafront is a majestic esplanade, known as the Spianada. It is lined with handsome buildings and an arcaded promenade, the Liston, built by the French as a nostalgic nod to Paris's Rue de Rivoli. Today, the Liston, with its swath of packed cafes, is the town's social focus. At the Spianada's northern end stands the Palace of St Michael and St George, a grand neoclassical gesture that was built as the residence for a succession of British high commissioners. To seaward, across a narrow 'moat', the Contrafossa, lies the famous Palaio Frourio (Old Fortress) originating in the 6th century and massively extended by the Venetians. Inland, from all of this historic glory,

IONIAN ISLANDS

CORFU TOWN (KERKYRA)

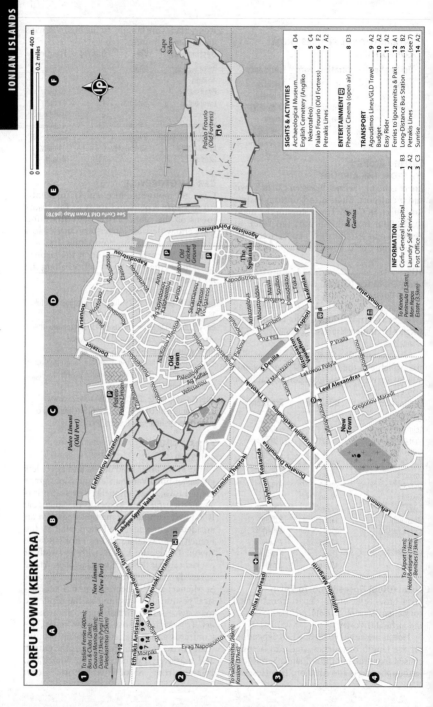

See Corfu Old Town Map (p678)

SIGHTS & ACTIVITIES
Archaeological Museum	4 D4
English Cemetery (Angliko	
Nekrotafeio)	5 C4
Palaio Frourio (Old Fortress)	6 F2
Petrakis Lines	7 A2

ENTERTAINMENT 🎭
Pheonix Cinema (open air)	8 D3

TRANSPORT
Agoudimos Lines/GLD Travel	9 A2
Budget	10 A2
Easy Rider	11 A2
Ferries to Igoumenitsa & Paxi	12 A1
Long-Distance Bus Station	13 B2
Petrakis Lines	(see 7)
Sunrise	14 A2

INFORMATION
Corfu General Hospital	1 B3
Laundry Self Service	2 A2
Post Office	3 C3

marble-paved streets lined with shops lead to the bustling modern town. Corfu Town is known also as Kerkyra.

Orientation

The older districts of Corfu Town lie in the northern section between the Spianada and the Neo Frourio, the monolithic 'New Fortress' begun in the 16th century. The southern section is more modern and is crammed with most services and shops. Its main focus is the brash and busy Plateia San Rocco, also known as Plateia G Theotoki Ioannou.

The Paleo Limani (Old Port) of Kerkyra lies on the northern waterfront. At the time of writing a new yacht marina was being built. The Neo Limani (New Port) with all ferry departures, lies west of the Paleo Limani with the hulking Neo Frourio between them. The local (blue) bus station is on Plateia San Rocco and the long-distance (green) bus station is on I Theotoki (formerly known as Avramiou) between Plateia San Rocco and the new port. The airport is just under 2km southeast of the Spianada.

Information

BOOKSHOPS

Tourmoussoglou (Map p678; ☎ 26610 38451; Nikiforou Theotoki 47) For international newspapers, and a range of guidebooks and paperbacks in Greek, English and German.

EMERGENCY

Tourist police (Map p678; ☎ 26610 30265; 3rd fl, Samartzi 4) Off Plateia San Rocco. There is a manned kiosk outside the entrance.

INTERNET ACCESS

The going rate for internet access is around €3 per hour.

Bits & Bytes (Map p678 ; ☎ 26610 36812; cnr Mantzarou & Rizospaston Voulefton) Convenient, but popular with games players.

Netoikos (Map p678; ☎ 26610 47479; Kaloheretou14) Near the Church of Agios Spyridon; with bar.

LAUNDRY

Laundry Service (Map p676; ☎ 26610 34857; Morpiki; per load €12; 🕑 8.30am-2pm Mon-Sat, plus 6-8pm Wed-Fri) Around the corner from Petrakis Lines.

MEDICAL SERVICES

Corfu General Hospital (Map p676; ☎ 26610 88200; Ioulias Andreadi)

MONEY

There are banks and ATMs around Plateia San Rocco, on Georgiou Theotoki and by Paleo and Neo Limanis.

Alpha Bank (Map p678; Kapodistriou) Behind the Liston.

National Bank of Greece (Map p678; Voulgareos)

POST

Post office (Map p676; ☎ 26610 25544; 26 Leoforos Alexandras)

TELEPHONE

Public telephones can be found on most major streets and squares. Prepaid telephone cards (from €4) are available from kiosks. The scratch card type is hugely better value than the slot-in type.

TOURIST INFORMATION

There is no national tourist office in Corfu Town. During high season, a municipal **tourist kiosk** (Map p678 ; Plateia San Rocco; 🕑 9am-4pm) may operate in Plateia San Rocco, though not on Sundays from April to October. This is the least effective location and the future of even this service may not be certain. A similar kiosk may operate at the ferry arrival port in high season. English-speaking staff at **All Ways Travel** (Map p678; ☎ 26610 33955; www.corfuallwaystravel.com; Plateia San Rocco) are very helpful. Many hotels stock free Corfu maps. The *Corfiot* (€2), an English-language monthly newspaper with listings, is available from kiosks and from shops that sell newspapers.

Sights & Activities

The **Archaeological Museum** (Map p676; ☎ 26610 30680; P Vraïla 5; adult/concession €4/2, Sun free; 🕑 8.30am-3pm Tue-Sun) gives top billing to the massive Gorgon Medusa pediment, one of the best-preserved pieces of Archaic sculpture found in Greece. It was part of the west pediment of the 6th-century-BC Temple of Artemis, a Doric temple that stood on the nearby Kanoni Peninsula. The splendid Lion of Menekrates from the 7th century BC is another plus, as is a fragment of pediment featuring Dionysus and a naked youth.

The **Palace of St Michael & St George** (Map p678), at the north end of the Spianada, houses the fascinating **Museum of Asian Art** (Map p678; ☎ 26610 30443; adult/concession €4/2; 🕑 8.30am-7pm Tue-Sun May-Oct, 8.30am-3pm Tue-Sun Nov-Apr) containing 10,000 objects, including prehistoric bronzes, porcelain plates, jade figurines, coins

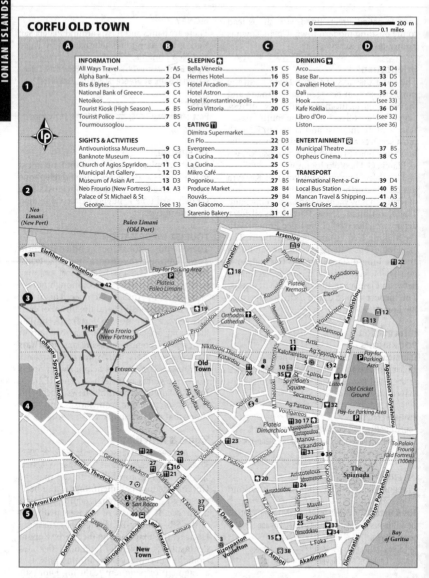

CORFU OLD TOWN

0 — 200 m
0 — 0.1 miles

and artefacts in onyx, ivory and enamel, collected from China, Japan, India, Tibet, Nepal, Korea and Thailand. Apart from the museum, the palace's throne room and rotunda have impressive period furnishings and art work.

Behind the eastern side of the palace is the **Municipal Art Gallery** (Map p678; admission €2; 9am-5pm Tue-Sun). This fine collection features the

work of leading Corfiot painters, a highlight being *The Assassination of Capodistrias* by Charalambos Pachis. There's also a collection of splendid icons. An annexe, showing changing exhibitions, is located in the front east wing of the palace.

Inside the 15th-century Church of Our Lady of Antivouniotissa is the **Antivouniotissa**

Museum (Byzantine Museum; Map p678; ☎ 26610 38313; admission €2; ⏲ 8am-7pm Tue-Sun Apr-Oct, 8.30am-2.30pm Tue-Sun Nov-Mar). This exquisite aisle-less and timber-roofed basilica, located off Arseniou, has an outstanding collection of Byzantine and post-Byzantine icons and artefacts dating from the 13th to the 17th centuries.

It's worth visiting the two fortresses, Corfu Town's most dominant landmarks. The **Palaio Frourio** (Old Fortress; Map p676; ☎ 26610 48310; adult/concession €4/2; ⏲ 8.30am-3pm Nov-Mar, 8.30am-7pm May-Oct) was constructed by the Venetians on the remains of a 12th-century Byzantine castle. The British made further alterations. The gatehouse area houses a Byzantine museum and exhibition space. The summit of the inner outcrop is crowned by a lighthouse and can be reached by a steep climb for superb views. The **Neo Frourio** (New Fortress; Map p678; admission €3; ⏲ 9am-9pm May-Oct) is a gaunt piece of military architecture reached by a steep climb. Again, there are fine views and the interior is an eerie mass of tunnels, rooms and staircases.

The sacred relic of Corfu's beloved patron saint, St Spyridon, lies in an elaborate silver casket in the 16th-century **Church of Agios Spyridon** (Map p678; Agiou Spyridonos). Nearby is the intriguing **Banknote Museum** (Map p678; ☎ 26610 41552; St Spyridon's Sq; admission €2; ⏲ 9am-2pm & 5.30-8.30pm Wed & Fri, 8.30am-3pm Thu, Sat, Sun Apr-Sep, 8am-3pm Wed-Sun Oct-Mar), part of the Ionian Bank. It has a collection of banknotes, including a sixpenny note from the British period.

A haunting survival of British rule is the peaceful garden-like **English Cemetery** (Angliko Nekrotafeio; Map p676; Kolokotroni) off Mitropoliti Methodiou and also known as the British Cemetery, on the southwestern outskirts of town. It has been lovingly tended by its caretaker over many years and contains the graves of soldiers and civilians of the 19th and 20th centuries.

On the southern outskirts of Corfu on the Kanoni Peninsula is the **Mon Repos Estate** (off Map p676; ⏲ 8am-7pm May-Oct, 8am-5pm Nov-Apr), an extensive wooded park surrounding an elegant neoclassical villa. The estate and villa were created in the 1830s by the second British commissioner of the Ionians, Sir Frederick Adam, as a tribute to his Corfiot wife. The British handed over Mon Repos to King George I of Greece in 1864. It was the birthplace, in 1921, of King George's grandson, the UK's current Duke of Edinburgh (Queen Elizabeth II's husband).

Eighteen months later the Duke's parents – and the baby Duke – fled the island on board a British warship when the new Greek Republic banished its then monarch, and Philip's uncle, King Constantine. For many years ownership of Mon Repos was in dispute between the Greek government and Constantine until the Municipality of Corfu took over the estate and turned it into a rather splendid public amenity. Today, the villa houses the excellent **Museum of Palaeopolis** (☎ 26610 41369; adult/concession €3/2; ⏲ 8am-7.30pm Tue-Sun May-Oct), with entertaining displays of archaeological finds and the history of Corfu Town. Rooms on the first floor are furnished in the early-19th-century Regency style of the British era. Tracks and paths lead through the wooded grounds to the ruins of two Doric temples; the first is vestigial, but the southerly one is still quite impressive.

Parking outside the gates of Mon Repos is limited.

Tours

Petrakis Lines (Map p676; ☎ 26610 31649; Ethnikis Antistasis 4) and **Sarris Cruises** (☎ 26610 25317; Eleftheriou Venizelou 13) both organise day trips from Corfu Town, including an excursion to ancient ruins (Butrinti) in Albania for €59; and a boat trip taking in Paxi (and the Blue Caves) and Antipaxi for €40. Transfers are included and Petrakis Lines offers a 15% discount if you book direct. Passports are required for trips to Albania.

Sleeping

Hotels in Corfu Town are not cheap, with 'budget' being relative to the general high prices. The nearest camping ground is Dionysus Camping Village (p682), 8km away. Book ahead for all options in high season. The hotels mentioned are open all year.

BUDGET

Hermes Hotel (Map p678; ☎ 26610 39268; www.hermes-hotel.gr; Markora 12; s/d/tr €50/60/75; ⏲) Located in a busy part of the new town, just up from Plateia San Rocco and near the market, the Hermes has had a complete makeover in recent years and has pleasant, well-appointed rooms with double glazing. Breakfast is €7.

Hotel Bretagne (off Map p676; ☎ 26610 30724; www.corfuhotelbretagne.com; K Georgaki 27; s/d/tr €50/60/80; ⏲) Close to the airport and about 1.5km from the town centre, but a good budget option with trim, well-maintained rooms; those at the back face onto a small grassy garden.

MIDRANGE

Hotel Astron (Map p678; ☎ 26610 39505; hotel_astron@ hol.gr; Donzelot 15; s €75-105, d €80-110, tr €95-125; 🖳 🛜) Overlooking Plateia Palaio Limani (Old Port Sq), and patiently waiting for the Old Port marina to be completed, the Astron is steadily updating its airy, good-sized rooms and installing a gym and a spa. It may rename itself the City Marina. Breakfast is €10.

Hotel Konstantinoupolis (Map p678; ☎ 26610 48716; www.konstantinoupolis.com.gr; K Zavitsianou 11; s/d/tr incl breakfast €88/98/118; 🖳 🛜) Bright decor enhances the refurbished rooms at this atmospheric old Corfiot hotel overlooking Plateia Palaio Limani.

TOP END

Prices quoted here represent high season rates (reduced at other times) and include breakfast.

Hotel Arcadion (Map p678; ☎ 26610 37670; www .arcadionhotel.com; Vlasopoulou 2; s/d/tr €110/150/170; 🖳 🛜) Right on the Liston's busiest corner, the Arcadion has been updated in recent years and its prices likewise.

Bella Venezia (Map p678; ☎ 26610 46500; www .bellaveneziahotel.com; N Zambeli 4; d €170; 🖳 🖳 🛜) Housed in what was once a girls' school, the Venezia has comfy rooms and a stylish ambience. The gazebo breakfast room in the garden is delightful.

Siorra Vittoria (Map p678; ☎ 26610 36300; www .siorravittoria.com; Stefanou Padova 36; s €170-235 d €235-315; 🖳 🛜) Expect luxury and style at this 19th-century mansion where traditional architecture and modern facilities meet. It's in a quiet location and rooms are well appointed. There's a peaceful garden for breakfasting, beneath an ancient magnolia tree.

Eating

An enduring Corfu experience is people watching and gossiping at the Liston's many cafes, although you'll pay around €3.50 to €5 for a coffee or fresh juice here. Corfiot cuisine has been influenced by many cultures, particularly Italian.

Starenio Bakery (Map p678; ☎ 26610 47370; Guilford 59; snacks under €3) This bakery has a huge selection of homemade gourmet pies, breads and the *best* of best cakes.

Evergreen (Map p678; ☎ 26610 28000; Voulgareos 86; snacks €3-7; 🕑 24hr) A useful pit stop, this streetside place does decent fast food.

Mikro Café (Map p678; ☎ 26610 31009; cnr N Theotoki 42 & Kotardhou; snacks €3.50-6) A little cafe-bar at the heart of the old town, Mikro has a leafy raised terrace and seating that clambers up a narrow lane. There's live entertainment at times and you may catch anything from acoustic riffs to very accomplished slackliners walking the wobbly walk on a shaky line slung between buildings.

En Plo (Map p678; ☎ 26610 81813; Faliraki; mains €5.50-12) A stylish place in a blissful waterside location looking across to Palaio Frourio, En Plo is reached down a slip road at the northern end of Kapodistriou, beyond the Palace of St Michael and St George. They do a fine seafood risotto, and mezedhes plates of meat or fish as well as pizzas and daytime snacks.

ourpick La Cucina Guilford (Map p678; ☎ 26610 45029; Guilford 17; mains €5.50-22;) Moustoxidou (Map p678; ☎ 26610 45799; cnr Guilford & Moustoxidou) A long-established restaurant, La Cucina shines for its well-run ethos and its creative cuisine, with hand-rolled pasta dishes to the fore – cajun shrimp with cherry tomatoes, spring onions and mascarpone sauce is delicious. There's a range of creative mezedhes, fresh salads and pizzas, with excellent wines to go with it all. The good news is that a second branch, run by the same owner, has opened a few metres down Guilford at the attractive crossing with Moustoxidou.

Rouvás (Map p678; ☎ 26610 31182; S Desilla 13; mains €8-14; 🕑 lunch) Resilient traditional cooking makes this a favourite lunch stop for many locals. It's just down from the market and has even caught the eye of UK celebrity chef Rick Stein for a TV cooking program.

San Giacomo (Map p678; ☎ 26610 30146; Plateia Dimarchiou; mains €8-22) Located in Town Hall Sq, this fine restaurant has such creative starters as octopus in a vinegar and herb sauce and mains of baked lamb with potatoes, paprika, onions, garlic and feta. The wine list is unassumingly good, as is the house wine.

SELF-CATERING

North of Plateia San Rocco is the bustling **produce market** (Map p678; 🕑 Mon-Sat), open morning to early afternoon and selling fresh fruit, vegetables and fish. A brand new market on the site was still under construction at the time of writing. For groceries try **Dimitra supermarket**

(Map p678; G Markora). Right opposite the supermarket is the traditional food shop **Pogoniou** (☎ 26610 31320; G Markora 17) which is crammed with cheeses, cold meats, spices, olive oil and much more.

Drinking

The bars along the Liston are top places for preening. They include (all on Map p678): Libro d' Oro, Arco, Liston and Kafe Koklia. Clustered near the Cavalieri are small, intimate music bars such as Hook (p678) and Base Bar (p678).

Dali (p678; N Theotoki) There are other great bars of character deeper into town such as this one with comfy indoor seating and mainstream music.

Cavalieri Hotel (p678; Kapadistriou) The rooftop garden bar of this hotel at the southern end of Kapadistriou is a long-time favourite, if you want to rise in the world.

Entertainment

For bigger dance venues, after 11pm, head to Corfu's disco strip, 2km northwest of the new port, along Ethnikis Antistasis (off Map p676; take a taxi – it's a very busy unlit road without walkways). Recommended are the fashionable and mainstream Privilege, the enduring Au Bar (Ω in Greek) for sharper house, R'n'B and Greek music and the biggest of all, Cristal, the ex-Hippodrome, with several bars. There's usually a €10 admission fee that includes one drink.

For visual entertainment, Corfu Town's **Orpheus Cinema** (Map p678; ☎ 26610 39768; G Aspioti) screens English-language films with Greek subtitles. Just across the road is the summertime open air **Pheonix Cinema** (Map p676; ☎ 69366 91419; G Aspioti) run on the same lines, but you can order pizzas from your seat. Tickets for both are about €7.50.

The **Municipal Theatre** (Map p678; ☎ 26610 33598; Mantzarou) is Corfu's cultural power house and stages various classical music, opera, dance and drama performances, some of which are also staged at the theatre next to the Mon Repos Estate (p679).

Shopping

Numerous sweet shops and tourist haunts cram the streets of the tourist-oriented old town. Some reasonable fashion shops – for shoes, swimwear and dress items – are located in the new town, especially along G Theotoki.

NORTH & NORTHWEST OF CORFU TOWN

Much of the coast just north of Corfu Town is overwhelmed with beach resorts such as **Gouvia**, **Dasia** and the linked resorts of **Ipsos** and **Pyrgi**, all with close-quarters humanity and narrow beaches, but with everything for a fun-time holiday for all the family. To explore fully all regions of the island outside Corfu Town your own transport is advised. Beyond Pyrgi the tawny slopes of **Mt Pantokrator** (906m), the island's highest peak, crowd down to the sea and reclaim the coast at some lovely scenic stretches along a winding road.

Just beyond Pyrgi, you can detour to Mt Pantokrator. Initially, the road corkscrews upward through about 25 hairpin bends and later passes through the picturesque villages of **Spartylas** and **Strinylas**. The road then climbs through stark terrain that is transformed by wildflowers in spring to the mountain's summit and to where the monastery, **Moni Pantokrator**, is now dominated by a massive telecommunications tower sprouting from its courtyard. There's a seasonal cafe and there are superb all-round views as far as the mountains of Albania and the Greek mainland, though it's sometimes hazy. There is very little parking at the top and turning can be awkward. At busy times, park before the steeply twisting final stretch and get some exercise.

Hugging the coast north from Pyrgi, the first decent place is **Barbati** where there's a shingle beach and a water-sports centre. Further on is **Agni** renowned for its three competing tavernas – **Taverna Toula** (☎ 26630 91350), **Taverna Nikolas** (☎ 26630 91243) and **Taverna Agni** (☎ 26630 91142), all of which serve excellent food. The bay-side village of **Kalami** is famous for the picturesque White House, perched above the water. For a time it was home to Lawrence and Nancy Durrell. The Durrell family are famously associated with Corfu and lived on the island for many years prior to WWII. Lawrence became an outstanding writer and one of his nonfiction books was *Prospero's Cell*, a lyrical evocation of Corfu. His brother Gerald's equally splendid book, *My Family and Other Animals*, was based on the Durrell family's eccentric and idyllic life on the island during the 1930s. There are tavernas and rooms at Kalami. North again is **Agios Stefanos** another attractive fishing village and resort nestled in a sheltered bay and with a shingle beach.

Avlaki lies beyond a wooded headland north of Agios Stefanos and has a substantial beach with very little development and only a couple of tavernas, including the friendly **Cavo Barbaro** (☎ 26630 81905; mains €5.50-15). It can catch the wind and is popular for windsurfing.

Kassiopi is a likeable, though very busy place, its streets crammed with shops, tavernas and bars. It's noted for fine embroidery and several shops sell pieces. The town's infrastructure was refurbished in 2009 with the harbour area getting an attractive facelift. Kassiopi's strategic headland was an outpost of Corinth and saw Roman and Venetian settlement. Nero is said to have holidayed outrageously here, while today, British politicians have been guests at the Rothschild estate that lies south of Kassiopi behind the best constructed walls in Corfu, while the mega 'yacht' of Russian oligarch Oleg Deripaska has been known to drop anchor offshore. Nero would have been beside himself with excitement.

In Kassiopi's main street, opposite the church of the Blessed Virgin, steps climb to the ruins of the **Venetian castle**, which was being renovated at the time of writing. You can also walk over the headland to the nearby Battaria and Kanoni Beaches. Beyond Kassiopi, the main road heads west along Corfu's north coast past the hugely popular and custom-made resorts of **Aharavi**, **Roda** and **Sidhari**, all served by a succession of beaches. At **New Perithia** halfway between Kassiopi and Aharavi is the **Art of Olive Wood** (☎ 26630 51596; www.olive-wood.gr) a showroom full of authentic artefacts by craftsman Costas Avlonitis. His main workshop is in a lovely setting at Kavadades near Arillas and Agios Georgios (see opposite).

Corfu's other **Agios Stefanos** is on the island's northwest coast and has a large sandy beach. From the nearby fishing harbour regular excursion boats head for the **Diapondia Islands**, a cluster of little-known satellite islands. For excursion details contact **San Stefano Travel** (☎ 26630 51910; www.san-stefano.gr).

Sleeping & Eating
Dionysus Camping Village (☎ 26610 91417; www.dionysuscamping.gr; camp sites per adult/child/car/tent €5.80/3.50/3.50/4, huts per person €11.50; 🛜 🐾) The closest camping ground to Corfu Town, signposted between Tzavros and Dasia and well served by bus 7, has good facilities. Tents can also be hired for €9 per person, or you can opt for simple pine-clad huts with straw roofs

our pick Casa Lucia (☎ 26610 91419; www.casa-lucia-corfu.com; Sgombou; studios & cottages €70-120; 🕑 year-round; 🅿 🐾) A garden complex of lovely studios and cottages, Casa Lucia has a strong artistic and alternative ethos and a warm ambience. There are yoga, t'ai chi and Pilates sessions, art, music and other cultural events. Winter lets are very reasonable. It's on the road to Paleokastritsa and is an ideal base for the entire north of Corfu.

Manessis Apartments (☎ 26610 34990; diana@otenet.gr; Kassiopi; 4-person apt €100; 🐾 🛜) It's hard to pick what's more pleasant – the friendly Greek-Irish owner, or her homely bougainvillea and vine-covered two-bedroom apartments. The location, at the end of Kassiopi's picturesque harbour, makes a lovely base. Top-floor apartments have air-conditioning; others have fans.

Little Italy (☎ 26630 81749; Kassiopi; mains €4.50-18) A longstanding Kassiopi favourite, this restaurant sources its ingredients well. The fresh pasta is the real thing and other pleasures include breast of duck with caramelised oranges and green peppers.

Also recommended:

Taverna Galini (☎ 26630 81492 Agios Stefanos; mains €5-12) Fresh local fish are displayed front of house at this efficient restaurant that does a fine seafood pasta and some creative salads and hefty steaks.

Piedra del Mar (☎ 26630 91566; Barbati; mains €7-22) Beachfront chic goes with terrific Mediterranean and international cuisine at this expensive restaurant.

SOUTH OF CORFU TOWN
The coast road continues south from Corfu Town with a turn-off to well-signposted **Ahillion Palace** (☎ 26610 56245; adult/concession €7/5; 🕑 8.30am-3pm Nov-Mar, 8am-7pm Apr-Oct) near the village of Gastouri. The Ahillion was built in the 1890s by the Empress Elizabeth of Austria, known as Sisi, as a retreat from the world and in tribute to her hero, Achilles. (Poor Sisi was later assassinated on the shores of Lake Geneva by a deranged anarchist.) Kaiser Wilhelm II bought the palace in 1908, extending the themes of both imperialism and self-aggrandisement by adding to the gardens a ferocious statue of Achilles Triumphant, before leaving Corfu for something less than triumph in 1914. The palace is a major coach tour destination. Get there early for a fascinating journey through heavily accented neoclassicism, fabulous furnishings and bold statuary, along a very thin line between style and kitsch.

South of the Ahillion is the resort of **Benitses**, enhanced by its pleasant old village, from where tracks and paths lead into the steep, wooded slopes above. The taverna **O Paxinos** (☎ 26610 72339; Benitses) is noted for its mezedhes and fish dishes (by the kilo). Further south again are the popular beach resorts of **Moraitika** and **Messonghi**, from where the winding coastal road leads south to the tranquil **Boukari** with its little harbour and waterside tavernas, including the good *psarotaverna* (fish restaurant) **Spiros Karidis** (☎ 26620 51205; Boukari). You can stay at the pleasant **Golden Sunset Hotel** (☎ 26620 51853; Boukari; d incl breakfast €60-65, tr incl breakfast €70). A restaurant is attached.

Lefkimmi, just over 10km from Boukari in the southern part of the island, is one of Corfu's most authentic towns, and still gets on with everyday life. Fascinating churches are dotted throughout the older section, and it's divided by a rather quaint, but sometimes odorous, canal. Eat at the **River Restaurant (To Potami)** (☎ 69725 42153; mains €5-15), which has been blessed by UK celebrity chef Rick Stein for his Mediterranean Escapes TV show. They have decent, if slightly old-fashioned, rooms and apartments from €40 to €60.

WEST COAST

Some of Corfu's prettiest countryside, villages and beaches are situated on the west coast. The scenic and very popular resort of **Paleokastritsa**, 26km from Corfu Town, rambles for nearly 3km down a valley to a series of small, picturesque coves hidden between tall cliffs. Craggy mountains swathed in cypresses and olive trees tower above. You can venture to nearby grottoes or one of the dozen or so local beaches by small excursion boat (per person €8.20, 30 minutes), or water taxis can drop you off at a beach of your choice. There's a range of water-boat activities available. Cool sun-seekers can hang out at cafe-bar **La Grotta** (☎ 26630 41006; Paleokastritsa), which is set in a stunning rocky cove with cafe, sunbeds and diving board. It's reached down steps opposite the driveway up to Hotel Paleokastritsa.

Perched on the rocky promontory at the end of Paleokastritsa is the icon-filled **Moni Theotokou** (admission free; 7am-1pm & 3-8pm), a monastery founded in the 13th century (although the present building dates from the 18th century). Just off the monastery's garden – with ivy, vines, roses and pot plants – is a small **museum** (admission free; 9am-1pm & 3-6pm

Apr-Oct). Most interesting is the olive mill exhibition under the museum, with a small shop selling oils and herbs.

From Paleokastritsa a path ascends to the unspoilt village of **Lakones**, 5km inland by road. Be sure to check out the town's only *kafeneio* (coffee house) – Kafeneio Olympia – and the village's growing **photographic archive** (☎ 26630 41771-3) where local man Vassilis Michalas has assembled a remarkable archive of photographs that form a vivid record of island life. Lakones' not-for-profit photographic archive is housed in the Lakones' choral group's practice room in the village's municipal building. Interested visitors can phone ahead.

Quaint **Doukades** has a historic square and pleasant tavernas. The 6km road north from Paleokastritsa to **Krini** and **Makrades** climbs steeply to spectacular views; many restaurant owners have capitalised on the vistas. A left turn towards the coast leads through Krini's miniature town square and on down to **Angelokastro**, the ruins of a Byzantine castle and the most western bastion on Corfu.

Further north, via the village of **Pagi**, are the pleasant beach resorts of **Agios Georgios** and **Arillas** with between them the knuckly headland of **Cape Arillas** with the little village of **Afionas** straggling up its spine.

South of Paleokastritsa, the pebbly beach at **Ermones** is dominated by heavy development, but clings to its claim of being the beach on which Odysseus was washed ashore and where Nausicaa, daughter of King Alcinous, just happening to be sunning herself. Hilltop **Pelekas**, 4km south, is perched above wooded cliffs and one-time hippy beaches. This likeable village still attracts independent travellers.

The **Triklino Vineyard** (☎ 26610 58184, 69458 90285; www.triklinovineyard.gr; adult/under 6yr €7/free; noon-5pm Tue-Sun) 6km from Corfu Town on the Pelekas road near Karoubatika blends culture with viniculture at its delightful complex where some enticing wines are produced from local vines such as Kakotrygis. There's a tour of an olive-oil mill and winery, and wine tasting and Corfiot mezedhes. They also run a series of cultural activities and performances.

Near Pelekas village are two sandy beaches, **Glyfada** and **Pelekas** (marked on some maps as Kontogialos, and also a resort in its own right), with water sports and sunbeds galore. These beaches are quite developed and are backed by large hotels and accommodation options.

IONIAN ISLANDS

A free bus service runs from Pelekas village to these beaches. Further north is the popular, but dwindling (due to erosion) **Myrtiotissa** beach; the former unofficial nudist 'colony' has more or less merged with the happy families section, save for some giant boulders in between. It's a long slog down a steep, partly surfaced road before you see a bottom of any kind (drivers should park in the parking area on the hilltop). The taverna and bar, Elia, part way down, makes a welcome break.

Agios Gordios is a popular resort south of Glyfada where a long sandy beach can cope with the crowds.

Just along the turn off from the main road to Halikounas Beach is the Byzantine **Gardiki Castle**, which has a picturesque entranceway, but is entirely empty inside. Just south of the castle is the vast **Lake Korission**, separated from the sea by a narrow spit that is fronted by a long sandy beach where you can usually escape from the crowds.

Sleeping

Paleokastritsa has many hotels, studios and a few domatia (rooms, usually in private homes) spread along the road. Further south, in the Pelekas area, there are also plenty of sleeping options.

Paleokastritsa Camping (☎ 26630 41204; www .paleokastritsaholidays.com; Paleokastritsa; camp sites per adult/child/car/tent €5/3.10/3.10/3.50) On the right of the main approach road to town is this shady and well-organised camping ground on historic olive terraces.

Hotel Zefiros (☎ 26630 41244/41088; www.hotel -zefiros.gr; Paleokastritsa; d incl breakfast €60-80, tr incl breakfast €75-105, q incl breakfast €90-130; ❄ ✆) On the roadside near the seafront, but a delight and with immaculate, stylish rooms, some with a massive terrace. The downstairs cafe is a bright oasis.

Rolling Stone (☎ 26610 94942; www.pelekasbeach .com; Pelekas Beach; r €30-40, apt €98) The clean and colourful apartments and double rooms surround a big sun terrace with funky trappings at this laid-back place. There's even a resident 'wellness' practitioner (relaxation treatments €10 to €30).

Jimmy's Restaurant & Rooms (☎ 26610 94284; info@jimmyspelekas.com; Pelekas; d/tr €40/50; ❄) These decent rooms with rooftop views are above a popular restaurant (mains €6 to €12), a short distance uphill from the centre and on the road to the Kaiser's Throne.

Yialiskari Beach Studios (☎ 26610 54901; d studio €65; Yialiskari Beach; ❄) Studios with great vistas are perfect for those who want seclusion away from neighbouring Pelekas Beach. The studios are run by the owner of Yialiskari Beach's taverna.

There are two budget options in the Pelekas area, both on the backpackers' circuit and both piled high with facilities and activities; the **Pink Palace** (☎ 26610 53103; www.thepinkpalace .com; Agios Gordios Beach; dm per person incl breakfast & dinner €18-25, r incl breakfast & dinner €22-30; 💻) south of Sinarades and **Sunrock** (☎ 26610 94637; www .sunrockcorfu.com; Pelekas Beach; r per person incl breakfast & dinner €18-24; 💻 ❄). The experience at both is relative to how young you feel.

Eating

There are also a few eating places at Afionas to the north of Paleokastritsa.

Das Blaue (The Blue House; ☎ 26630 52046; Afionas; dishes €4.50-8) Superb balcony views enhance the food at this bright place where the salads are especially good and the desserts heavenly.

Limani (☎ 26630 42080; Paleokastritsa Harbour; mains €4.50-11) Located down by Paleo's harbour, the well-run Limani, with its rose-bedecked terrace, does local dishes with a sure hand. Fish is by the kilo but a generous fish plate for two costs about €38.

Nereids (☎ 26630 41013; Paleokastritsa; mains €6.50-11) Halfway down the winding road to Paleokastritsa beach is this smart place, below road level and with a huge leafy courtyard. Specialities such as pork in a mustard sauce with oregano, lemon, peppers, garlic and cheese are hard to beat.

PAXI ΠΑΞΟΙ

pop 2440

Paxi packs a great deal into a bite-size island. At only 10km by 4km it's the smallest of the Ionian's main holiday islands and has hung on to a reputation for serenity and overall loveliness – a fine escape clause to Corfu's more metropolitan, quicker-paced pleasures. There are three colourful harbour towns – Gaïos, Loggos and Lakka. All have pretty waterfronts with Venetian-style pink-and-cream buildings set against lush green hills. Idyllic coves can be reached by motorboat, if not by car or on foot. The dispersed inland villages sit within centuries-old olive groves, accented

---

CORFU ACTIVITIES

Corfu brims with great outdoor action. Dinghy sailing and windsurfing buffs will find **Greek Sailing Holidays** (☎ 26630 81877; www.corfu-sailing-events.com) at Avlaki, while for chartering try **Corfu Sea School** (www.corfuseaschool.com) or **Sailing Holidays Ltd** (www.sailingholidays.com), both at Gouvia marina.

For **diving** in crystal-clear waters you'll find operators at Kassiopi, Agios Gordios, Agios Georgios, Ipsos, Gouvia and Paleokastritsa.

Corfu has some excellent walking. The **Corfu Trail** (www.corfutrail.org), developed by the devoted islander Hilary Whitton Paipeti, traverses the island north to south and takes between eight and 12 days to complete. For help with accommodation along the trail, contact **Aperghi Travel** (☎ 26610 48713; www.travelling.gr/aperghi). The book *In the Footsteps of Lawrence Durrell and Gerald Durrell in Corfu* (Hilary Whitton Paipeti, 1999) is an excellent buy.

For mountain-biking, especially off-road**,** the **Corfu Mountainbike Shop** (☎ 26610 93344; www .mountainbikecorfu.gr) is based in Dasia and rents out bikes for independent exploration, as well as organising day trips and cycling holidays. Horse riding through olive groves and on quiet trails is another excellent option with **Trailriders** (☎ 26630 23090), based in the village of Ano Korakiana. Not far from Ermones on the island's west coast is the **Corfu Golf Club** (☎ 26610 94220; www.corfu golfclub.com), one of the few such courses in Greece. Birdwatchers should check the **Birdwatching Centre of Ropa Valley** (☎ 26610 94221), who meet regularly at the Corfu Golf Club.

---

by winding stone walls, ancient windmills and olive presses. On the less accessible west coast, sheer limestone cliffs plunge hundreds of metres into the azure sea and are punctuated by caves and grottoes. The old mule trails are a walker's delight. An obligatory purchase is the *Bleasdale Walking Map of Paxos* (€10 or €15), available from the island's travel agencies.

For details on day trips from Parga on the mainland to Paxi and Antipaxi, see p350.

Getting There & Away

BOAT

Ferries dock at Gaïos' new port, 1km east of the central square. Excursion boats dock along the waterfront.

Domestic

Busy passenger-only hydrofoils link Corfu and Paxi (and occasionally Igoumenitsa) from May until mid-October. For information contact **Arvanitakis Travel** (☎ 26620 32007; Gaïos), or Petrakis Lines (p679) in Corfu.

Two car ferries operate daily services between Paxi and Igoumenitsa on the mainland, and Corfu. There's also a **ferry information office** (☎ 26650 26280) in Igoumenitsa.

For details on all domestic connections see Island Hopping (p758).

Sea taxis can be a fast and effective way to travel, especially if there are other people on board. The going rate between Corfu and Paxi is around €180 per boat, shared among

the passengers. Try **Nikos** (☎ 26620 32444, 69322 32072; Gaïos), or www.paxosseataxi.com.

International

You can reach Corfu and Igoumenitsa from the major ports in Italy, then transfer to a local ferry for Paxi. For details on international connections to Corfu see p673, to Igoumenitsa see p353.

BUS

There's a twice-weekly direct bus service between Athens and Paxi (€47, plus €7.50 for ferry ticket between Paxi and Igoumenitsa, seven hours). On Paxi, tickets are available from **Bouas Tours** (☎ 26620 32401; Gaïos). The bus leaves from Plateia Karaiskaki in Athens (note: the terminal changes so always check with Bouas beforehand).

Getting Around

The island's bus links Gaïos and Lakka via Loggos up to four times daily in either direction (€2). Taxis between Gaïos and Lakka or Loggos cost around €12. The taxi rank in Gaïos is located by the car park and bus stop inland from the waterfront.

Daily car hire ranges between €42 and €115 in high season. Reliable agencies are **Arvanitakis Travel** (☎ 26620 32007) and **Alfa Hire** (☎ 26620 32505) in Gaïos. **Rent a Scooter Vassilis** (☎ 26620 32598), opposite the bus stop in Gaïos, has a good range of scooters and mopeds. Hire

IONIAN ISLANDS

PAXI & ANTIPAXI

0 ————— 2 km
0 ————— 1 mile

is about €20 to €25 in high season. Many travel agencies rent out small boats – this is a great way to access beach coves. Rental for a day ranges from €40 to €90 depending on engine capacity. Don't overestimate your needs.

GAÏOS ΓΑΪΟΣ

pop 560

Gaïos hardly needs to try for the 'picturesque' label. It's the island's main town and its pink, cream and whitewashed buildings line the water's edge of a sizeable bay to either side of the main Venetian square. The town is protected from too much open water by the wooded islet of Agios Nikolaos, named after its eponymous monastery. It lies so close to the shore that it creates the illusion of Gaïos being a pretty riverside town. The waterfront is lined with cafes and tavernas and can get crowded mid afternoon when excursion boats arrive.

The main street (Panagioti Kanga) runs inland from the main square towards the back of town, where you'll find the bus stop, taxi rank and car park. Banks and ATMs are near the square and there's an internet room at the waterfront **Bar Pío Pío** (☎ 26620 32662; per hr €5). There isn't a tourist office, but the helpful and efficient staff at **Paxos Magic Holidays** (☎ 26620 32269; www.paxosmagic.com) will happily direct you. They organise island excursions, including boating trips and walks. They can also arrange villa accommodation in advance.

The charming **Cultural Museum** (admission €2; ✆ 10am-2pm & 7-11pm), in a former school on the southern waterfront, has an eclectic collection of fossils, farming and domestic artefacts, pottery, guns, coins and clothing. Brace yourself for the 17th-century wedding night 'facilitator' that might just be described as quaint. A room is devoted to the paintings of the Paxiot priest Christodoulos Aronis.

At the far southern end of the harbour is a striking statue of Georgios Anemogiannis, a local sea captain who died heroically in 1821, aged 23, during the Greek War of Independence. The sea has 'greened' Georgios rather vividly.

Sleeping

San Giorgio Apartments (☎ 26620 32223; s/d/tr €40/70/90) Pink, blue and white are the colours of these airy and clean studios with basic cooking facilities. Head towards town from the port by the lower (pedestrian) harbour road, and follow the signposted steps.

Thekli Studios (Clara Studios; ☎ 26620 32313; d €75; P ⊠ ⬛) Thekli, a local fisher-diver and energetic personality about town, runs these immaculate and well-equipped studios. She will meet you at the port if you call ahead. Otherwise, go up the alleyway to the left of the museum, turn left and then, in 50m, turn right and up some steps for another 50m.

Paxos Beach Hotel (☎ 26620 32211; www.paxos beachhotel.gr; s/d/tr/q incl breakfast from €88/117/146/165, ste €168-380; ⊠) In a prime location 1.5km south of Gaïos these bungalow-style rooms step down to the sea and have a range of rooms from standard to superior. There's a private jetty, tennis court, beach, bar and restaurant.

Eating

Capriccio Café Creperie (☎ 26620 32687; crêpes €3-6) For a cheap and filling sweet or savoury experience, head past the museum to this waterfront crêperie. They do breakfast for €3 to €7.80 and sandwiches for €3 to €4.

Taverna Vasilis (☎ 26620 32596; mains €6.50-14) The owner of this eatery is a former butcher, and knows the best meat for tasty spit-roasts and other meaty servings. It's just back from the mid waterfront.

Karkaletzos (☎ 26620 32729; mains €7-10) Walk up an appetite to this grill house, the locals' choice, 1km behind town. Meat dishes are balanced by some creative fish cuisine.

Taka Taka (☎ 26620 32329; mains €6-22) For up-market seafood (€40 to €75 per kilogram) in attractive surroundings, this popular place is behind the main square. Go left from the left-hand inner corner of the square, then, after 30m, turn right.

The supermarket is west of the central square. Two excellent bakeries, one on the waterfront, the other near the main square, serve Paxiot delights. Gloria's, at the north end of the waterfront, tempts with some deeply sinful ice cream flavours.

LOGGOS ΛΟΓΓΟΣ

Loggos is 5km northwest of Gaïos and is a mini-gem of a place with a pretty waterfront curled round a small bay. Bars and restaurants overlook the water and wooded slopes climb steeply above. There are coves and pebble beaches nearby. **Café Bar Four Seasons** (☎ 26620 31829; per hr €6) has internet facilities.

You can hire boats and scooters from **Julia's Boat & Bike** (☎ 26620 31330) at Arthur House (see below); boats are €60 to €70 per day and scooters about €25.

Sleeping & Eating

Studio (☎ 26620 31397, 26620 31030; d €55) A pleasantly bohemian – and bougainvillea – choice, this studio sits above the gift shop Marbou, just in from the waterfront. It's best to book in advance.

Arthur House (☎ 26620 31330; studio €75, apt €110) These modest and spotless studios are above the owner's house, a two-minute walk from the waterfront. Julia's Boat & Bike (above) hire is part of the family deal.

O Gios (☎ 26620 31735/30062; mains €6-16) A step back from the waterfront is this unvarnished place with good value seafood and grill dishes.

Vasilis (☎ 26620 31587; mains €8-14) An unexpected treat, this well run, stylish place features a clever menu card in the shape of a facsimile newspaper of the 1970s. Specialities include octopus in red wine sauce and lamb casserole as well as pasta and risotto.

Drinking

There are several cafes and bars in Loggos with favourites for cocktails and music being the waterside To Taxidi and Roxy Bar.

Kafeneio Burnaos (Magazia) Don't blink or you'll miss this wonderful 60-year-old *kafeneio*, located in Magazia, several kilometres southwest of Loggos. There are no set hours, but locals gather here to play cards and backgammon (there's even a set from 1957).

Erimitis Bar (☎ 689777 53499; Magazia) A growing reputation has made this out-of-the-way place increasingly popular, especially for sunset viewing. It's down lanes and tracks towards the west coast from Magazia and you need transport.

LAKKA ΛΑΚΚΑ

The picturesque, tranquil and unspoiled harbour of Lakka lies at the end of a protective bay on the north coast. It's a popular yacht anchorage, and there are plenty of facilities as well as bars and restaurants. Small, but reasonable beaches lie round the bay's headland, including Harami Beach, and there are pleasant walks nearby.

Routsis Holidays (☎ 26620 31807/31129; www.routsis-holidays.com) is tucked away inland and **Planos Holidays** (☎ 26620 31744; www.planos-holidays.gr) is on the waterfront. Both are helpful agencies responsible for well-appointed apartments and villas for all budgets.

Paxos Blue Waves (☎ 26620 31162) on the waterfront rents boats for €35 to €65 and scooters for €18 to €20.

For a Bali experience in Corfu, visit the colourful **Il Pareo** (☎ 6972164089) for a great collection of Indonesian Batik and other items.

For accommodation try the immaculate and comfy **Yorgos Studios** (☎ 26620 31807/31129; www.routsis-holidays.com; s/d €50/65; ⊠) next door to the Routsis Holidays office and run by the company. The owners of Il Pareo also have an away-from-it-all **garden studio** (☎ 69721 64089; ste €70).

Unfussy food and drink and internet (€3 per half hour) can be had at the waterside **Arriva Taverna** (☎ 26620 30153; mains €8-13.80). A popular local place is **Diogenis** (☎ 26620 31442; mains €4.20-9.80) in the square at the back of the village. Cuttlefish with spinach and lamb in lemon sauce are well done classics. For something special head along the shore on the right-hand side of the bay to a little beach and to the Italian-influenced **La Bocca** (☎ 26620 31991;

mains €8-18) for proper *caprese* or spaghetti with fresh tuna, amid colourful decor.

ANTIPAXI ΑΝΤΙΠΑΞΟΙ
pop 25

The stunning and diminutive island of Antipaxi, 2km south of Paxi, is covered with grape vines, olives and with the occasional small hamlet here and there. Caïques and tourist boats run daily from Gaïos and Lakka, and pull in at two beach coves, the small, sandy **Vrika Beach** and the pretty, pebbly **Voutoumi Beach**. Floating in the water here – with its dazzling clarity – is a sensational experience.

An inland path links the two beaches (a 30-minute walk), or if you are more of an energetic person you can walk up to the village of **Vigla**, or as far as the lighthouse at the southernmost tip. Take plenty of water and allow 1½ hours minimum each way. Voutoumi Beach has two eateries – Bella Vista and a taverna on the beach. Vrika Beach also has two good competing tavernas – Spiros and Vrika. Main meals at both cost between €7 and €15 and fish dishes can be very pricey.

Accommodation is available through one or two of the beach tavernas. Boats to Antipaxi (from €6 return) leave Gaïos at 10am and return around 5.30pm – there are more services in high season.

LEFKADA ΛΕΥΚΑΔΑ

pop 22,500

Lefkada (or Lefkas), the fourth-largest island of the Ionians, is an absorbing destination, mountainous and in places remote. Yet it has its fair share of holiday resorts and tourism facilities and seems less insular than most, not least because it was once attached to nearby mainland Greece by a narrow isthmus until occupying Corinthians breached the land bridge with a canal in the 8th century BC. A causeway now spans the 25m strait, yet Lefkada remains steadfastly traditional and island-like in the best of ways. In remoter villages you often see older women in traditional dress and the main town of Lefkas has a splendid mid-20th-century period appeal.

Lefkada's mountains rise to over 1000m, and olive groves, vineyards, and pine forests cover huge areas of the landscape. There are 10 satellite islets off the heavily developed east coast, and the less populated west coast boasts spectacular beaches.

Getting There & Away
AIR

Lefkada has no airport, but the airport near Preveza (Aktion) on the mainland, with flights to Athens and Corfu, is about 20km away. For details see Island Hopping (p758).

Also, from May to September there are charter flights from northern Europe and the UK to Preveza.

BOAT

Four Islands Ferries (☎ 210 412 2530) runs a daily ferry service that sails to an ever-changing schedule (and with ever-changing prices) between Nydri and Frikes on Ithaki (€6.40, one hour 30 minutes), Vasiliki on Lefkada and Frikes (€8, two hours) and Vasiliki and Fiskardo on Kefallonia (€6.90, one hour). You can bring a car across to either port on Lefkada – it costs €30 from Fiskardo and €28 from Frikes. For more information on departing from Lefkada, see Island Hopping (p755).

Information and tickets can be obtained from **Borsalino Travel** (☎ 26450 92528; borsalin@ otenet.gr) in Nydri and from **Samba Tours** (☎ 26450 31520; www.sambatours.gr) in Vasiliki.

BUS

Lefkada Town's new **KTEL bus station** (☎ 26450 22364; Ant Tzeveleki) is located about 1km from the centre opposite the new marina complex. Head down Golemi to the busy road junction and go left for 750m. Buses head to Athens (€30.50, 5½ hours, four or five daily), Patra (€14.50, three hours, two to three weekly), Thessaloniki (€39.10, eight hours, one to two weekly and more in high season), Preveza (€2.70, 30 minutes, six to seven daily) and Igoumenitsa (€11, two hours, daily).

Getting Around

There's no reliable bus connection between Lefkada and Preveza's Aktion airport. Taxis are relatively expensive (around €35); a cheaper option is to take a taxi to Preveza and then a bus to Lefkada

From Lefkada Town, frequent buses ply the east coast, with up to 20 services daily to Nydri (€1.40, 30 minutes) and Vlyho (€1.60, 40 minutes) in high season, and four daily to Vasiliki (€3, one hour). There are regular buses to Agios Nikitas (€1.40, 30 minutes). Around six daily services head to the inland village of Karya (€1.40, 30 minutes). One or two buses serve other villages daily. Sunday services are reduced.

Car hire starts at €40 per day, depending on season and model. Cars can be hired from reliable **Europcar** (☎ 26450 23581; Panagou 16, Lefkada Town) or next door at **Budget** (☎ 26450 25274; Lefkada Town). Rent a bike or moped, starting at €15 per day, from **Santas** (☎ 26450 25250; Lefkada Town), next to the Ionian Star Hotel. There are countless car-and bike-hire companies in Nydri and several in Vasiliki.

LEFKADA TOWN

pop 6900

The island's engaging main town is built on a promontory at the southeastern corner of a salty lagoon. Earthquakes are a constant threat here and the town was devastated by one in 1948 (but unaffected in 1953), only to be rebuilt in a distinctively quake-proof and attractive style with the upper storey facades of some buildings in brightly painted corrugated iron.

The town has a relaxed feel, with a vibrant main thoroughfare, a pleasant plaza and handsome churches with separate ironwork bell towers, like small oil rigs, to withstand seismic activity.

Orientation & Information

The town's vibrant main pedestrian strip, Dorpfeld, starts south of the causeway. The street is named after 19th-century archaeologist Wilhelm Dorpfeld, who postulated that Lefkada, not Ithaki, was the home of Odysseus. Dorpfeld leads to Plateia Agiou Spyridonos, the main square, and continues as Ioannou Mela, which is lined with modern shops and cafes. ATMs and the post office are on Ioannou Mela. There's no tourist office. The bus station is on the southern waterfront.

There's an **Internet Café** (Koutroubi; per hr €1.50), just off 8th Merarchias.

Sights

Housed in the modern cultural centre at the western end of Agelou Sikelianou is the **Archaeological Museum** (☎ 26450 21635; adult/concession €2/1; ⌚ 8.30am-3pm Tue-Sun). It contains island artefacts spanning the Palaeolithic Age to the late Roman periods. The prize exhibit is a 6th-century-BC terracotta figurine of a flute player with nymphs.

Works by icon painters from the Ionian school and Russia dating back to 1500 are displayed in an impressive **collection of post-Byzantine icons** (☎ 26450 22502; Rontogianni; admission free; ⌚ 8.30am-1.30pm Tue-Sat, 6-8.15pm Tue & Thu). It's in a classical building and also houses the **public library** off Ioannou Mela.

The 14th-century Venetian **Fortress of Agia Mavra** (⌚ 9am-1.30pm Mon, 8.30am-1pm Tue-Sun) is immediately across the causeway. It was first established by the crusaders but the remains mainly date from the Venetian and Turkish occupations of the island. **Moni Faneromenis**, 3km west of town, was founded in 1634, destroyed by fire in 1886 and later rebuilt. It houses a **museum** (⌚ 9am-1pm, 6-8pm Mon-Sat) with ecclesiastical art from around the island. The views of the lagoon and town are also worth the ascent.

Sleeping

Hotel Santa Maura (☎ 26450 21308, fax 26450 26253; Dorpfeld; s/d/tr incl breakfast €55/70/86; ❄) A decent hotel with a mix of rooms, all in pleasantly pale decor. The rooms onto Dorpfeld overlook a busy evening scene.

Pension Pirofani (☎ 26450 25844; fax 26450 24084; Dorpfeld; d/tr €85/100; ❄) There's a colourful character to this small hotel and its stylish rooms, all in lush colours and with sparkling facilities. There's even tea- and coffee-making kit.

Ionian Star Hotel (☎ 26450 24762; www.ionion-star.gr; s/d/tr incl breakfast €100/115/130; ⊠ ❄ 💻 🏊) Comfortable, light and spacious rooms mark out this business-class hotel that overlooks an attractive open area just in from the waterfront. The breakfasts are filling and there's a bar and big lounge.

Eating & Drinking

Faei Kairos (☎ 26450 24045; Golemi; mains €4.50-11) Unashamed nostalgia for the good old days of cinema defines this excellent eatery on Lefkada Town's waterfront. The eye-catching motifs go well with such treats as *spetsofai*, local sausage in a tomato sauce, or *rigamato*, pork in cream and oregano sauce or fish plates for one or two.

Ey Zhn (☎ 69746 41169; Filarmonikis 8; mains €9-13) 'Live Well' is the name here. Backstreet rather than scenic, but with an attractive interior, the food is excellent, from the filling starters such as mushroom risotto to a seafood paella

LEFKADA & MEGANISI

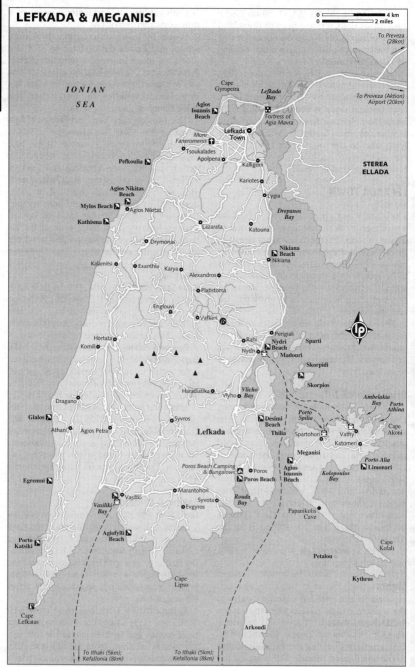

0 ────── 4 km
0 ────── 2 miles

To Preveza
(28km)

IONIAN
SEA

Cape
Gyropetra

Lefkada
Bay

To Preveza (Aktion)
Airport (20km)

Agios
Ioannis
Beach

Fortress of
Agia Mavra

Lefkada
Town

Moni
Faneromenis

Tsoukalades

Apolpena

Kalligoni

STEREA
ELLADA

Pefkoulia

Kariotes

Lygia

Agios Nikitas
Beach

Drepanos
Bay

Mylos Beach

Agios Nikitas

Lazarata

Katouna

Kathisma

Drymonas

Nikiana
Beach
Nikiana

Kalamitsi

Exanthia

Karya

Alexandros

Platistoma

Englouvi

Vafkeri

Hortata

Komili

Rahi

Perigiali

Nydri
Beach
Nydri

Sparti

Madouri

Skorpidi

Skorpios

Ambelakia
Bay

Porto
Athina

Haradiatika

Vlyho

Vlicho
Bay

Porto
Spilia

Spartohori

Vathy

Cape
Akoni

Dragano

Desimi
Beach
Thilia

Katomeri

Gialos

Meganisi

Porto Alia

Athani

Agios Petra

Lefkada

Syvros

Agios
Ioannis
Beach

Kolopoulos
Bay

Limonari

Egremni

Poros Beach Camping
& Bungalows

Poros

Poros Beach

Papanikolis
Cave

Vasiliki

Marantohon

Syvota

Rouda
Bay

Vasiliki
Bay

Evgyros

Cape
Kefali

Porto
Katsiki

Agiofylli
Beach

Petalou

Kythros

Cape
Lefkatas

Cape
Lipso

Arkoudi

To Ithaki (5km);
Kefallonia (8km)

To Ithaki (5km);
Kefallonia (8km)

for two at €18, or shrimps in garlic sauce. Evenings only.

Also recommended on the Golemi strip and with similar prices are the *ouzeries* **Frini Sto Molo** (☎ 26450 24879) and **Burano** (☎ 26450 26025), both offering well-prepared Greek classics.

Stylish bars and cafes line the western side of the waterfront; **Karma** (Dorpfeld), at the start of Dorpfeld, is the place to be seen. Plateia Agiou Spyridonos is crammed with cafes and crowds.

Self-caterers can pick up supplies from the **supermarket** (Golemi) next to the bus station or from the well-stocked **bakery** (Ioannou Mela 182).

EAST COAST & SURROUNDS

Lefkada's east coast has seen heavy tourist development over the years with the main focus at Nydri, once a fishing village but now a crowded strip of tourist shops and with not much of a beach. You can escape inland, however, to another world of scattered villages, local tavernas and pleasant walks. From Nydri itself there is another escape seaward on cruises to the islets of **Madouri**, **Sparti**, **Skorpidi** and **Skorpios**, plus **Meganisi**. Numerous excursions go to Meganisi and stop for a swim near Skorpios (€15 to €25), and some visit Ithaki and Kefallonia as well (€20). Helpful **Borsalino Travel** (☎ 26450 92528; borsalin@otenet .gr; Nydri) on the main street can organise just about everything.

Amblers might enjoy the lovely walk to **waterfalls** 3km out of Nydri (and another 400m past the taverna). The walk follows a path through a ravine; be careful on the slippery rocks.

The small harbour of **Syvota**, 15km south of Nydri, has a relaxed airy appeal. It's popular with yachts and the local fishing fleet is still active. There's no beach to speak of and you need your own transport to get the best of it.

Sleeping & Eating

Poros Beach Camping & Bungalows (☎ 26450 95452; www.porosbeach.com.gr; Poros Beach; camp sites per adult/car/ tent €9/5/5, studio €60-90; **P** 🟰 🖳 🖳) Twelve kilometres south of Nydri is this unpretentious complex overlooking pretty Poros Beach. It has studio apartments and a shaded camping area, plus restaurant, minimarket, bar and swimming pool.

Ionian Paradise (☎ 26450 92268; www.ionianparadise .gr; Nydri; r €75; 🟰) Nicely located off the main drag, the recently refurbished Ionian still has

an old-fashioned welcome and its rooms are pleasantly functional. Breakfast is €5. It's down a side street diagonally opposite the Avis car-hire office.

Apartments Sivota (☎ 26450 31347, fax 26450 31151; Syvota; r €45, 2-person studio €100, 3-person apt €110; 🟰) In Syvota, these very pleasant apartments are set slightly back from the waterfront, but have balconies and good views. Steps lead up from the waterfront road.

Spiridoula (☎ 26450 31989; Syvota; mains €5.50-15) The first of the harbourside tavernas in Syvota has ice storage drawers from which you can choose fish from local landings. Meat dishes feature also, but the fish soup is a rewarding choice.

Pinewood (☎ 26450 92075; Nydri; mains €6-16.50) Popular with locals and offering some subtle classics such as lamb in a red wine and herb sauce, this well-run place is at the quiet northern end of Nydri's main street.

VASILIKI ΒΑΣΙΛΙΚΗ

Vasiliki has a stony beach, but is a hot spot for the tanned and toned, mainly because it's one of the best water-sports venues in the Mediterranean. This is due to the configuration of the resort's square-cut bay where soft breezes in the morning make it ideal for instructing beginners. In the afternoon, winds whip down the flanking mountains for some serious action by aficionados. It's not all fast sailing though; the winding waterfront, with eucalyptus and canopy-covered eateries is a pleasant place in which to relax. Caïques take visitors to the island's better beaches and coves including **Agiofylli Beach**, south of Vasiliki.

Along the beach, water-sports outfits have staked their claims with flags, equipment and with their own hotels for their guests. **Wildwind** (www.wildwind.co.uk) is a main operator of all-inclusive one- and two-week action holidays ranging from €563 to €921 depending on season. **Healthy Options** (www.healthy-option.co.uk) is a linked program offering a swath of activities including yoga and Pilates, dance and fitness as well as water sports and eco-walking trips. Contact both of the above for possible short-term options.

Club Vassiliki Windsurfing (☎ 26450 31588; www .clubvass.com) organises windsurfing sessions for €25. For diving try **Nautilus Diving Club** (☎ 69361 81775; www.underwater.gr), which has a range of options, including a snorkelling safari for €30, a discover scuba diving course for €50 and an open-water course for €360. It also has sea kayaking half days for €30.

All the activities have beach stations.

Helpful **Samba Tours** (☎ 26450 31520; www .sambatours.gr) in the main street can organise car and bike hire, and answer most queries regarding the region. Other car-hire places are **Christo's Alex's** (☎ 26450 31580) near the bus stop.

Sleeping, Eating & Drinking

Vassiliki Beach Camping (26450 31308; campkingk@ otenet.gr; camp sites per person/tent/car €8/5/6) A well-run and compact camping option with easy access to the beach.

Pension Holidays (☎ 26450 31426; nicol60@ windowslive.com; s/d €60/65; ☺ year-round; ⚇) Friendly Spiros and family offer Greek hospitality, breakfast (€5) on the balcony with views of the bay and harbour, and simply furnished but well-equipped rooms. Above the ferry dock; prices vary according to length of stays.

Vasiliki Bay Hotel (☎ 26450 31077; www.hotelvassiliki bay.gr; s/d incl breakfast €60/70; ⚇ ☎) A few blocks inland from the waterfront is this well-appointed hotel behind Alexander Restaurant. Prices drop substantially outside August. The same family has lovely villas outside the village. Phone for details.

Delfini (Dolphin; ☎ 26450 31430; mains €6.50-13) The best of the harbour haul, the food at this traditional place is freshly cooked to order and is popular locally.

Zeus (☎ 26450 31560) Current hot club on Vasiliki's main drag, Zeus is revved up by the young water-sports crowd. You can always spill over into the next door **Yacht Café** (☎ 26450 31890).

WEST COAST & AROUND

Serious beach fanciers should head straight for Lefkada's west coast where the sea lives up to the brochure clichés; it's an incredible turquoise blue and most beaches are sandy. The best beaches include remote **Egremni** and breathtaking **Porto Katsiki** in the south. You'll pass by local stalls selling olive oil, honey and wine. The long stretches of **Pefkoulia** and **Kathisma** in the north are also lovely (the latter beach is becoming more developed and there are a few studios for rent here).

Word is out about the picturesque town of **Agios Nikitas**, and people flock here to enjoy the holiday village's pleasant atmosphere, plus the lovely **Mylos Beach** just around the headland (to walk, take the path by Taverna Poseidon. It's about 15 minutes up and over the peninsula, or for €3 you can take a water taxi from tiny Agios Nikitas beach). The town's accommodation options are plentiful, and include **Camping Kathisma** (☎ 26450 97015; www.camping-kathisma.gr; camp sites per person/tent/car €7/5/6), 1.5km south of town. Or try the modest, Greek-Canadian-run **Olive Tree Hotel** (☎ 26450 97453; www.olivetree -lefkada.com; Agios Nikitas; s/d incl breakfast €70/90) – ask a local for directions. Right on the beach is the excellent **Sapfo** (☎ 26450 97497; Agios Nikitas; fish per kilogram €40-60), Agios Nikitas' established fish taverna.

CENTRAL LEFKADA

The spectacular central spine of Lefkada, with its traditional farming villages, lush green peaks, fragrant pine trees, olive groves and vines – plus occasional views of the islets – is well worth seeing if you have time and transport. The small village of **Karya** is a bit of a tourist haunt but it boasts a pretty square with plane trees, around which are tavernas and snack bars. There's a car park just as you approach the village. Karya is famous for its special embroidery, introduced in the 19th century by a remarkable one-handed local woman, Maria Koutsochero. Visit the **Museum Maria Koutsochero** (admission €2.50; ☺ 9am-9pm) for an interesting display of embroidery paraphernalia and local artefacts all laid out in a quite haunting way throughout a traditional house. There's a cafe at the museum, though note that hours may vary. You can walk up steeply from the village or turn up a sign-posted road just before the village entrance coming from Lefkada Town.

For food, **Taverna Karaboulias** (☎ 26450 41301; Karya plateia; mains €5-13.50) is recommended for its traditional dishes, including *yemista*, tomatoes and peppers stuffed with rice and herbs and a marvellous bread-based salad. For accommodation options ask British Brenda Sherry at **Café Pierros** (☎ 26450 41760; Karya) who can arrange all (as well as a cup of tea and signature toasted sandwich).

The island's highest village, **Englouvi**, is renowned for its honey and lentil production and is only a few kilometres south of Karya.

MEGANISI ΜΕΓΑΝΗΣΙ
pop 1090

Meganisi, with its verdant landscape and deep bays of turquoise water, fringed by pebbled beaches, is the escape clause for too much of Nydri. It can fit into a day visit or a longer, more relaxed stay. There are three settlements; **Spartohori**, with narrow lanes and pretty, bougainvillea-bedecked houses, all perched on a plateau above Porto Spilia (where the ferry docks; follow the steep road or steps behind). Pretty **Vathy** is the island's second harbour, and 800m behind it is the village of **Katomeri**. With time to spare you can visit remote beaches such as **Limonari**.

Helpful **Asteria Holidays** (☎ 26450 51107), at Porto Spilia, is in the know for all things relating to the island.

Sleeping & Eating

Hotel Meganisi (☎ 26450 51240; Katomeri; d incl breakfast €100; ✿ ☕) Bright rooms with sea and country views from their balconies are enhanced by this pleasant hotel's generous-sized pool and terrace. It also has a good restaurant. Follow signs once you get to Katomeri.

Decent dining options include **Taverna Porto Vathy** (☎ 26450 51125; Vathy; mains €7-14), the undisputed favourite fish taverna (fish by the kilo) cast out on a small quay in Vathy; **Tropicana** (☎ 26450 51486; Spartohori), which serves excellent pizzas in Spartohori; or **Laki's** (☎ 26450 51228; Spartohori; mains €5.50-9.50), a classic taverna, also in Spartohori.

Getting There & Away

The Meganisi ferry boat runs about six times daily between Nydri and Meganisi (per person/car €2/13, 25 to 40 minutes). It calls at Porto Spilia before Vathy (the first ferry of the day stops at Vathy, then Porto Spilia).

A local bus runs five to seven times per day between Spartohori and Vathy (via Katomeri) but it's worth bringing your own transport on the car ferry.

KEFALLONIA
ΚΕΦΑΛΛΟΝΙΑ

pop 39,500

Kefallonia is the largest of the Ionian Islands and is big hearted with it. It boasts rugged mountain ranges, rich vineyards, soaring coastal cliffs, golden beaches, caves and grottoes, monasteries and antiquities. The 1953 earthquake devastated many of the island's settlements and much of the island's archi-

tecture is relatively modern in style. Enough untouched traditional villages and individual buildings survive, however, to make exploration worthwhile. Kefallonia also has a reputation for fine cuisine and great wines.

The capital is Argostoli and the main port is Sami. Other high points include the picturesque village of Fiskardo in the north of the island.

Getting There & Away

AIR

There are daily flights between Kefallonia and Athens and connections to Zakynthos and Corfu. For details see Island Hopping (p753). **Olympic Air** (☎ 26710 41511) is based at the airport.

From May to September, many charter flights come from northern Europe and the UK to Kefallonia.

BOAT

Domestic

There are frequent ferry services to Kyllini in the Peloponnese from Poros and Argostoli. One ferry links Sami with Astakos via Piso Aetos on Ithaki. In August there are direct ferries from Sami to Astakos on alternate days.

Strintzis Lines (www.ferries.gr/strintzis) has two ferries daily connecting Sami with Patra and Vathy or Piso Aetos.

There are ferries between Fiskardo and Frikes on Ithaki and between Fiskardo and Vasiliki on Lefkada. Information and tickets for these routes can be obtained from **Nautilus Travel** (☎ 26740 41440; Fiskardo), on the Fiskardo waterfront.

From the remote port of Pesada in the south there are two daily high-season services to Agios Nikolaos on the northern tip of Zakynthos (an alternative is to sail from Argostoli to Kyllini in the Peloponnese, and from there to Zakynthos Town). Getting to and from Pesada and Agios Nikolaos without your own transport can be difficult (and costly if you rely on taxis). To get to the ferry point in Pesada from Argostoli, you can catch one of two daily buses (in high season only and except Sundays). On Zakynthos, there are two buses per week to and from Agios Nikolaos to Zakynthos Town (via villages).

One ferry a day runs between Argostoli and Kyllini (three hours, €14) and up to five run between Poros and Kyllini (1½ hours, €9.90). One

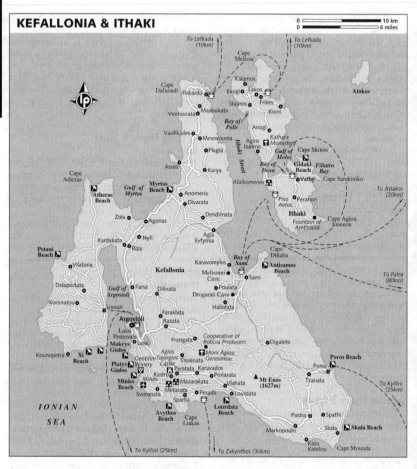

KEFALLONIA & ITHAKI

ferry a day runs between Fiskardo and Frikes (55 minutes, €3.80) and between Fiskardo and Vasiliki (one hour, €6.90). Sami has two daily connections with Vathy (45 minutes, €5.60), Patra (2¾ hours, €16.90) and Piso Aetos (30 minutes, €2.80) and one daily with Astakos (three hours, €10). In summer there are two ferries a day between Pesada and Agios Nikolaos (1½ hours, €7).

For more information, see Island Hopping (p753).

International

In high season there are regular ferries between Sami and Bari (€45, 12 hours) in Italy. To get to other ports in Italy, take the ferry first from Sami to Patra.

Tickets and information can be obtained from **Vassilatos Shipping** (☎ 26710 22618; Antoni Tristi 54, Argostoli), opposite the port authority, and from **Blue Sea Travel** (☎ 26740 23007; Sami), on Sami's waterfront.

BUS

Four daily buses connect Kefallonia with Athens (€37.10, seven hours), via Patra (€21, four hours) using the various ferry services (to/from Argostoli, Sami and Poros) to the mainland.

For information contact the **KTEL bus station** (☎ 26710 22276/81; kefaloniakteltours@yahoo.gr; A Tristi 5, Argostoli) on the southern waterfront in Argostoli. The office produces an excellent printed schedule.

IONIAN ON THE VINE

The Ionian Islands would not be the same without wine and Kefallonia especially has a reputation for outstanding vintages, most notably from the unique Robola grape. High in the mountains southeast of Argostoli, at the heart of verdant Omala Valley, is the winery of the **Cooperative of Robola Producers of Kefallonia** (☎ 26710 86301; www.robola.gr; Omala; ☒ 9am-8.30pm Mon-Fri Apr-Oct, 7am-3pm Mon-Fri Nov-Mar) Here, grapes from about 300 individual growers are transformed into the yellow-green Robola, a dry white wine of subtle yet lively flavours. The Robola is said to have been introduced by the Venetians and its wine was a favourite of The Doge. It grows exuberantly on high ground and the light soils, wet winters and arid summers of Kefallonia are ideal for its cultivation. Other varieties of grape enhance the viniculture on Kefallonia. A visit to the cooperative includes wine tasting.

A smaller and very distinguished winery is **Gentilini** (☎ 6932718730; ☒ tastings 10.30am-2.30pm & 5.30-8.30pm Mon-Sat Jul-Aug, tours & tastings 5.30-8.30pm Tue, Thu, Sat Jun–mid-Sep). Here, in a charming setting, a range of superb wines, including the scintillating Classico, is produced. The winery is 2km south of Argostoli on the airport road and you can also arrange visits by appointment.

Getting Around

TO/FROM THE AIRPORT

The airport is 9km south of Argostoli. There's no airport bus service; a taxi costs around €15.

BOAT

Car ferries run hourly (more frequently in high season) from 7.30am to 10.30pm between Argostoli and Lixouri, on the island's western peninsula. The journey takes 30 minutes, and tickets cost €1.80/4.50/1.20 per person/car/motorbike.

BUS

From Argostoli's **KTEL bus station** (☎ 26710 22281, 26710 25222) on the southern waterfront there are 11 buses daily heading to the Lassi Peninsula (€1.40), with four buses to Sami (€4), two to Poros (€4.50), two to Skala (€4.50) and two to Fiskardo (€5). There's a daily east-coast service linking Katelios with Skala, Poros, Sami, Agia Evfymia and Fiskardo. No buses operate on Sunday.

CAR & MOTORCYCLE

The major resorts have plenty of car- and bike-hire companies. A very reliable local company is **Greekstones Rent a Car** (☎ 26710 42201; www.greek stones-rentacar.com) They deliver to the airport and within a 15km radius of their base at Svoronata (7km from Argostoli, near the airport). **Europcar** (☎ 26710 42020) has an office at the airport.

ARGOSTOLI ΑΡΓΟΣΤΟΛΙ

pop 8900

Argostoli is a hugely likeable and lively town. It suffered enormous damage during the 1953 earthquake and was not rebuilt in its former Venetian splendour. Today, its style is one of broad boulevards and pedestrianised shopping streets lined with the chunky, light-coloured buildings typical of Mediterranean urban architecture of the later 20th century. The central focus is an attractive, if overlarge, square, Plateia Valianou, that has drawn some life away from the long waterfront.

Orientation & Information

The main ferry quay is at the northern end of the waterfront and the bus station is at its southern end. Plateia Valianou, the large palm-treed central square, is a few blocks in from the waterfront off 21 Maïou, and its nearby surrounds. Other hubs are pedestrianised Lithostrotou, lined with smart shops, and the waterfront Antoni Tristi. There are banks with ATMs along the northern waterfront and on Lithostrotou.

Bookmark (☎ 26710 27616; 4 Lithostrotou) A bibliophile's corner, just off busy Lithostrotou, Bookmark has a menu of new and used English-language books, for sale or, indeed, for rent.

EOT (Greek National Tourist Organisation; ☎ 26710 22248; ☒ 8am-8pm Mon-Fri, 9am-3pm Sat Jul-Aug, 8am-2.30pm Mon-Fri Sep-Jun) The tourist office is on the northern waterfront beside the port police.

Excelixis (☎ 26710 25530; cnr Minoos & Asklipiou; per hr €3) Well-run internet, including wi-fi, is available upstairs at this computer shop.

Post office (Lithostrotou)

Sights & Activities

The **Korgialenio History & Folklore Museum** (☎ 26710 28835; Ilia Zervou 12; admission €4; ☒ 9am-2pm Mon-Sat)

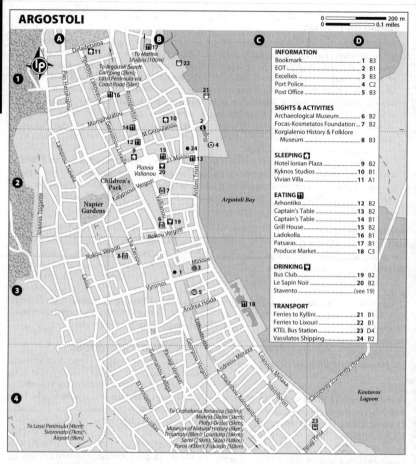

ARGOSTOLI

INFORMATION	
Bookmark..................................	**1** B3
EOT.......................................	**2** B1
Excelixis................................	**3** B3
Port Police..............................	**4** C2
Post Office..............................	**5** B3

SIGHTS & ACTIVITIES	
Archaeological Museum..............	**6** B2
Focas-Kosmetatos Foundation ...	**7** B2
Korgialenio History & Folklore	
Museum................................	**8** B3

SLEEPING	
Hotel Ionian Plaza.....................	**9** B2
Kyknos Studios........................	**10** B1
Vivian Villa............................	**11** A1

EATING	
Arhontiko...............................	**12** B2
Captain's Table.......................	**13** B2
Captain's Table.......................	**14** B1
Grill House............................	**15** B2
Ladokolla...............................	**16** B1
Patsaras...............................	**17** B1
Produce Market........................	**18** C3

DRINKING	
Bus Club................................	**19** B2
Le Sapin Noir..........................	**20** B2
Stavento...............................	(see 19)

TRANSPORT	
Ferries to Kyllini......................	**21** B1
Ferries to Lixouri.....................	**22** B1
KTEL Bus Station......................	**23** D4
Vassilatos Shipping...................	**24** B2

and **Focas-Kosmetatos Foundation** (☎ 26710 26595; Vallianou; admission €3; ⏱ 9.30am-1pm & 7-10pm Mon-Sat) provide interesting insights into Argostoli's cultural and political history. The Focas-Kosmetatos Foundation museum also manages the **Cephalonia Botanica** (☎ 26710 26595; ⏱ 8.30am-2.30pm Tue-Sat), a lovely garden, about 2km from the centre of town, full of native flora and shrubs. The Cephalonia Botanica carries out much research into resources and climate change. Entrance to the gardens is included in the Focas-Kosmetatos Foundation ticket and you can get a leaflet with directions at the foundation's museum. Argostoli's **Archaeological Museum** (☎ 26710 28300; Rokou Vergoti; admission €3; ⏱ 8.30am-3pm Tue-Sun) has a collection of island relics, including Mycenaean finds.

Six kilometres from Argostoli in Davgata is the **Museum of Natural History** (☎ 26710 84400; admission €2.50; ⏱ 9am-3pm), with fascinating exhibits on the geological and natural phenomena of the island, and an excellent topographical model of the island in relief.

The town's closest and largest sandy beaches are **Makrys Gialos** and **Platys Gialos**, 5km south. Regular buses serve the area.

Lourdata, 16km from Argostoli on the Argostoli–Poros road, has an attractive long beach set against a mountainous green backdrop.

To get closer to Kefallonia's coast and sea contact **Monte Nero Activities** (☎ 69340 10400, 69329 04360; www.monte-nero-activities.com) for well-organised sea kayaking. Day tours are €55 with lunch and snorkelling gear and there are multi-day options and instructional courses. They also organise cycling and hiking tours in the island's coastal regions. At the time of writing the company was planning a name change to Sea Kayaking Kefalonia.

Tours

KTEL Tours (☎ 26710 23364) runs excellent-value tours of Kefallonia (€18) on Wednesdays and Sundays, visiting several towns and villages around the island. It also takes tours to Ithaki every Friday (€35). Bookings can be made at the KTEL bus station building.

Sleeping

Argostoli has a fair number of standard hotels, although there are several places with character. **KTEL Tours** (☎ 26710 23364) has a selection of apartments and hotel options available and will organise these via email.

Argostoli Beach Camping (☎ 26710 23487; www.argostolibeach.gr; camp sites per adult/car/tent €7.50/3.50/4.50) This pleasant and quiet camping spot is near the lighthouse on the northernmost point of the peninsula.

Kyknos Studios (☎ 26710 23398; p-krousos@otenet.gr; M Geroulanou 4; d/tr €55/60) An old well in a quirky little garden sits in front of these seven attractive, if a little faded, studios, each with a small verandah and in a quiet part of town

Marina Studios (☎ 26710 26455; maristel@hol.gr; Agnis Metaxa 1; r €55, studio €65-75; 🖭) Located in a quiet street right at the northern end of the waterfront and just across from the Naval College, the rooms here are spacious and comfy and the studios have lovely beamed angle ceilings. Subtle prints and paintings enhance the mood.

Vivian Villa (☎ 26710 23396; www.kefalonia-vivianvilla.gr; Deladetsima 9; s/d/tr €55/70/85, apt €120; 🖭) Highly recommended for its big, bright rooms and friendly owners. There are tea-making facilities in each room, and some have kitchens. The top-floor apartment is excellent. Prices are discounted for longer stays. There's a lift to upper floors.

Hotel Ionian Plaza (☎ 26710 25581; www.ionianplaza.gr; Plateia Valianou; s/d/tr €96/125/169; 🖭 🖭) Argostoli's smartest hotel has a marble-decorated lobby, stylish public areas and well-appointed rooms with balconies.

Eating

There are numerous cafes around the edges of Plateia Valianou and along Lithostrotou.

Ladokolla (☎ 26710 25522; Xarokopou 13; dishes €1.90-7; 🕒 1pm-1am) Forget table-top conventions, this is the 'Table Top' in every sense, where piping hot chicken, pork, lamb, kebabs, pittas and souvlaki are delivered without plates and onto very clean disposable covers. They'll bring a plate for anything saucy, but this is cracking down-to-earth noshing, hugely popular locally and with lively service.

Grill House (gyros €2.20) Cheap and cheerful fast food among the pricier cafes on Plateia Valianou, next to Hotel Aeon.

Patsuras (☎ 26710 22779; Antoni Tristi 32; mains €5.50-12) A local favourite on the waterfront road, with a great range of authentic Greek dishes and plentiful helpings.

Captain's Table waterfront (☎ 26710 27170; 1 Metaxa; mains €5.50-24.90) plateia (3 Risospaston) The seafront arm of this popular eatery offers reasonable traditional dishes. The more upmarket arm is just along from the central square.

our pick **Arhontiko** (☎ 26710 27213; 5 Risospaston; mains €6.50-8.80; lunch & dinner) Top Kefallonian cuisine is on offer here, with starters such as a soufflé of spinach, cheese and cream, or shrimps and *saganaki* (fried cheese). For mains try *exohiko*, pork stuffed with tomatoes, onions, peppers and feta cheese. Even the house wine matches a good bottled vintage.

You can pick up a range of self-catering supplies from the waterfront produce market and from bakeries and supermarkets nearby.

Drinking

The Plateia Valianou area has several breezy music bars and cafes that fairly bounce by late evening. Popular venues are Le Sapin Noir, Bus Club and Stavento.

SAMI & SURROUNDS ΣΑΜΗ
pop 2200

Sami, 25km northeast of Argostoli and the main port of Kefallonia, was also flattened by the 1953 earthquake. Its exposed long strip is made up of tourist-oriented cafes, but beyond this it's an attractive place, nestled in a bay and flanked by steep hills. There are several monasteries, ancient castle ruins, caves, walks and nearby beaches that reflect the region's rich history. All facilities, including a post office and banks, are in town. Buses for Argostoli usually meet ferries, and car hire is available through **Karavomilos** (☎ 26740 23769). Sami's **tourist office** (🕒 9am-7pm May-Sep) is at the northern end of town. An informative website is www.sami.gr.

Sights & Activities

The Municipality of Sami has published a simple brochure called *Walking Trail,* which outlines enjoyable walks through the local area. The brochures are available from the tourist office.

Antisamos Beach, 4km northeast of Sami, is a long, stony beach in a lovely green setting backed by hills. The drive here is also a highlight, offering dramatic views from cliff edges.

The rather overrated **Melissani Cave** (admission incl boat trip adult/child €7/4; ☺ 8am-8pm May-Oct), a subterranean sea-water lake that turns a distinctive blue in sunlight, is only worth visiting when the sun is overhead between noon and 2pm. It's 2.5km west of Sami. The **Drogarati Cave** (☎ 26740 22950; adult/child €5/3; ☺ 8am-8pm Jul-Aug) is a massive (natural) chamber with stalactites. Its fragile infrastructure seems to be suffering erosion from too much human pressure.

About 7km from Argostoli, on the road to Sami, a side road leads south into the heart of Robola grape country where a visit to the Cooperative of Robola Producers (see p695) is worthwhile. Near the winery is the **Moni Agiou Gerasimou** dedicated to Kefallonia's patron saint. The monastery is cared for by nuns. There's a pile of wraps outside the chapel and, out of respect, bare arms and shoulders, at least, should be covered before entering. Inside the chapel is a famous cave where Gerasimos escaped from the rigours of monastic life to even greater self-abnegation. Descent, *with great care,* is via a steep metal ladder into a small chamber 6m below. From this chamber a narrow squeeze leads to another tiny chamber. There are lights, but it's not for the claustrophobic – or the unsaintly.

Sleeping

Karavomilos Beach Camping (☎ 26740 22480; www .camping-karavomilos.gr; Sami; camp sites per adult/car/tent €7.50/3.50/6; ▣ ☜) This is a large, award-winning camping ground in a great beachfront location, with plenty of facilities.

Hotel Melissani (☎ 26740 22464; Sami; d/tr €65/78) Unashamed retro style welcomes you at this very tall, very slim building some way in from the waterfront. Even the bar goes all out with swivelling vinyl bar stools, marble floors and groovy tiles. The smallish rooms have balconies with views of either mountains or sea.

Hotel Kastro (☎ 26740 22656; www.kastrohotel .com; Sami; s/d/tr €70/95/120) At the heart of town, the Kastro is essentially resort modern, but a reasonable option.

Eating

Sami's waterfront is lined with fairly standard eateries.

Dolphins (☎ 26740 22008; mains €5-20) The best of the waterfront line-up, Dolphins adds value very cleverly by staging lively Greek music nights. The food is excellent Kefallonian traditional with favourites such as baked rabbit, while fish lovers can dig into a sizable seafood platter.

Paradise Beach (☎ 26740 61392; mains €6.50-13, fish per kilogram €48-52; Agia Evfymia) Bear right past the harbourfront tavernas at Agia Evfymia and keep going until the road ends at the famous Paradise, where the cast of an equally famous movie used to eat every night. Penny and Nick may be long gone, but the dolmadhes and Kefallonia meat pie are still fantastic, as is the salted cod in garlic sauce, while the welcome is unfailingly upbeat and the views outstanding.

ASSOS ΑΣΟΣ

Tiny Assos is an upmarket gem of whitewashed and pastel houses, straddling the isthmus of a peninsula on which stands a Venetian fortress. The fortress is a pleasant place to hike to and around, with superlative views and a great historical ambience.

For accommodation, try the **Pension Gerania** (☎ 26740 51526; www.pensiongerania.gr; d incl breakfast €85; ✖). It does what it says on the label at this pension with its lush garden full of geraniums, while the light and appealing rooms have pleasant views. Follow the *pension* (and parking) sign at the top of the hill as you enter town.

Cosi's Inn (☎ 26740 51420, 69367 54330; www .cosisinn.gr; 2-/3-person studio €113/129; ✖) is not typically 'Greek' but has the marks of the young and hip interior designer owner: iron beds and sofas, frosted lights and white decor feature strongly.

For eating, **Platanos** (☎ 69446 71804; mains €5.50-13) is in an attractive shady setting near the waterfront. Strong on meat dishes, there are also fish and vegetarian options such as a tasty eggplant, feta and parmesan pie.

AROUND ASSOS

One of Greece's most breathtaking and picture-perfect beaches is **Myrtos**, 8km south of

MEMORIES WITHOUT MANDOLINS

Down at the Paradise Beach taverna, the irrepressible Stavros Dendrinos still does exuberance when it comes to memories. As a youngster during WWII, Stavros longed to escape from the strictures of island life. 'Every time I saw a distant sail, my heart leapt with excitement,' he says with a smile.

Then, aged 12, during WWII, Stavros joined his uncle in running a tiny sailing motor boat to and from Kefallonia and Piraeus. They carried passengers and small amounts of local produce within strict limits imposed by the German occupiers. Under curfew rules, they had to pull ashore wherever they could, as soon as darkness fell. Years of worldwide seagoing followed and then Stavros settled in Athens until memories of Kefallonia and the bright sea of his childhood drew him back to become one of the island's best known taverna owners.

Oh… did someone mention *Captain Corelli's Mandolin* and Penelope Cruz (who is said to have dined at the Paradise taverna every night while on location)? 'Lovely lady,' says Stavros, graciously, but with his eyes on the sea and distant sails.

Assos along an exciting stretch of the west coast road. From a roadside viewing area, you can admire and photograph the white sand and shimmering blue water set between tall limestone cliffs far below and you can reach the beach from sea level at Anomeria. Be aware that the beach drops off quickly and sharply, but once you are in the water it's a heavenly experience. Think clichéd turquoise and aqua water.

FISKARDO ΦΙΣΚΑΡΔΟ
pop 230

Fiskardo, 50km north of Argostoli, was the only Kefallonian village not devastated by the 1953 earthquake. Framed by cypress-mantled hills and with fine Venetian buildings, it has an authentic picturesque appeal and is popular with well-keeled yachting fans. It has some outstanding restaurants. There's a car park above the harbour at the south end of the village.

Nautilus Travel (☎ 26740 41440) towards the ferry quay end of the waterfront is an efficient agency that can help with all your needs. **Pama Travel** (☎ 26740 41033; www.pamatravel.com) on the harbour front has foreign exchange facilities and can help with travel services including car and boat hire. It also has internet access (15 minutes €2).

Sleeping

Fiscardo has quite a fair mix of sleeping options and some seriously top-level restaurants.

Regina's Rooms (☎ 26740 41125; d/tr €50/60) Friendly Regina runs a popular place that has colourful rooms dotted with plastic flow-ers. Some rooms have kitchenettes and/or balconies enjoying views over the water. It's alongside the main car park at the south end of the village.

Villa Romantza (☎ 26740 41322; www.villa-romantza .gr; r/studio €50/70, apt €80-110; 🐾) An excellent budget choice with simple and clean rooms. It's found next door to Regina's rooms on the car park. Cheaper out of season.

Stella Apartments (☎ 26740 41211; www.stella -apartments.gr; d €105, apt €210; 🐾) Located on the quiet southern outskirts of the village about 800m from the main car park. these apartments have immaculate, spacious studios with kitchens and balconies. There's a communal dining area.

Emelisse Hotel (☎ 26740 41200; www.arthotel.gr; d €480-630, ste €510-1800, apt €770-800; 🕑 year-round; 🐾 🐾) In a superb position overlooking the unspoiled Emplisis Bay, this stylish and luxurious hotel has every facility for the pampered holiday. The rooms are beautifully appointed, leafy terraces surround the lavish swimming pool and there's even a gym and tennis court. Breakfast is included.

Eating & Drinking

Café Tselenti (☎ 26740 41344; mains €7.50-23) Housed in a lovely 19th-century building, owned by the Tselenti family since 1893, with a romantic outdoor terrace at the heart of the village, the cuisine at this noted restaurant is outstanding. Starters of cheese and mushroom patties and aubergine rolls are superb, as are such mains as linguine with prawns, mussels and crawfish in a tomato sauce or the pork fillet with sundried apricots, dates and fresh pineapple.

Tassia (☎ 26740 41205; mains €10-25) A complete refurbishment in 2009 has added even more lustre to this Fiskardo institution run by Tassia Dendrinou, celebrated chef and writer on Greek cuisine. Everything is a delight, but specialities include *kolokythokeftedhes,* baby marrow croquettes and a fisherman's pasta incorporating finely chopped squid, octopus, mussels and prawns in a magic mix that even includes a dash of cognac. Meat dishes are equally splendid and Tassia's desserts are famous.

Gaeta Art Bar (☎ 69322 57027) At the heart of waterfront Fiskardo, the Gaeta is the place for watching the world go by over coffee by day and for cocktails, drinks and good company at night.

Getting There & Away
You can get to/from Fiskardo by ferry to/from Lefkada and Ithaki (for details see Island Hopping, p753) or by bus to/from Argostoli. The ferry is at one end of the waterfront; ask the bus to drop you at the turn-off; or it's a 10-minute walk from the car park to the ferry.

ITHAKI ΙΘΑΚΗ

pop 3700
Sheltered Ithaki dreams happily in its lake-like setting between Kefallonia and mainland Greece. The island is celebrated as being the mythical home of Homer's Odysseus, where loyal wife Penelope waited patiently, while besieged by unsavoury suitors, for Odysseus's much delayed homecoming. This tranquil island is made up of two large peninsulas that are joined by a narrow isthmus. Sheer cliffs, precipitous mountains and vast swaths of olive groves and cypresses gild this Ionian gem. Attractive villages (much rebuilt after the 1953 earthquake) and hidden coves with pebbly beaches add to the charm, while monasteries and churches offer Byzantine delights and splendid views.

Getting There & Away
Strintzis Lines (www.ferries.gr/strintzis-ferries) has two ferries daily connecting Vathy or Piso Aetos with Patra via Sami on Kefallonia. The ferry *Ionian Pelagos* runs daily (sometimes twice a day) in high season between Piso Aetos, Sami and Astakos on the mainland.

Other ferries run to ever-changing schedules from Vasiliki and Nydri (Lefkada) to Frikes (Ithaki) and Fiskardo (Kefallonia). For details see Island Hopping (p752).

Information and tickets for the routes can be obtained from Delas Tours (below) on the main square in Vathy.

One ferry a day runs from Frikes to Fiskardo (€3.80, 55 minutes) and from Frikes to Nydri (€7, 1½ hours). Two ferries a day run from Vathy to Patra (€17.60, 3¾ hours) and two ferries a day run from Piso Aetos to Patra (€17.60, three hours).

Getting Around
Piso Aetos, on Ithaki's west coast, has no settlement; taxis often meet boats, as does the municipal bus in high season only. The island's one bus runs twice daily (weekdays only, more often in high season) between Kioni and Vathy via Stavros and Frikes (€3.90), and its limited schedule is not well suited to day-trippers. Taxis are relatively expensive (about €30 for the Vathy–Frikes trip), so your best bet is to hire a moped or car (or a motorboat) to get around. In Vathy, **Rent a Scooter** (☎ 26740 32840) is down the lane opposite the port authority. For cars, try Happy Cars – contact Polyctor Tours (below) or **Alpha Bike & Car Hire** (☎ 26740 33243) behind Alpha Bank.

VATHY ΒΑΘΥ
pop 1820
Ithaki's pretty main town sprawls along its elongated and square-cut waterfront and has a central square, lined with cafes and restaurants, as the social hub. Narrow lanes wriggle inland from the waterfront.

The ferry quay is on the western side of the bay. To reach the central square (Plateia Efstathiou Drakouli), turn left and follow the waterfront.

Ithaki has no tourist office. **Delas Tours** (☎ 26740 32104; www.ithaca.com.gr) and **Polyctor Tours** (☎ 26740 33120; www.ithakiholidays.com), both on the main square, can help with tourist information. The main square also has banks with ATMs; the post office; and internet access – try **Net** (per hr €4).

Sights & Activities
Behind Hotel Mentor is an interesting **archaeological museum** (☎ 26740 32200; admission free;

HOT HIKES AFTER HOMER

Ithaki's compact size ensures dramatic scenery changes over short distances on walks that can reveal 360-degree views of the ocean and surrounding islands. Thanks to the efforts of islander Denis Sikiotis and his band of helpers, several cleared and marked trails exist around the island. Mr Sikiotis has prepared brief notes and maps that should be available from the town hall in Vathy. Enjoyable guided walks, including the popular Homer's Walk on Wednesdays, explore little seen parts of the island and are organised through **Island Walks** (☎ 69449 90458; www.xs4all.nl/~rienz/iwalks). Routes are from 5km to 13km and cost €15 to €25.

🕙 8.30am-3pm Tue-Sun) with some notable ancient coins depicting Odysseus. The equally entertaining and informative **nautical & folklore museum** (admission €1.50; 🕙 10am-2pm & 5-9pm Tue-Sat) is housed in an old generating station one block behind the square.

Boat excursions on the **Albatross** (☎ 69769 01643) leave from Vathy harbour in the summer months and include day trips around Ithaki and to Fiskardo (€30); Lefkada (€35); and 'unknown islands' that include Atokos and Kalamos (€35). There's also a water taxi to **Gidaki Beach**. Note: the only way to access this beach on foot is to follow the walking track from Skinari Beach.

Sleeping

Grivas Gerasimos Rooms (☎ 26740 33328; d/tr €75/88) Spacious studios with pot plants, small balconies and a seaside vista are a good bet at this pleasant place. Turn right at the Century Club on the waterfront and then go first left at the road parallel to the sea. The studios are 50m on your right. There may be a discount, depending on the length of stay.

Odyssey Apartments (☎ 26740 33400; www.ithaki -odyssey.com; apt €110-170; 🞉 🞉) You need to head right along the waterfront then turn up right, signed Skinos and Odyssey Apartments, for another 500m to this excellent option. There are light, breezy studios and apartments with balconies, and a magical view of the yacht harbour and beyond.

Hotel Perantzada (☎ 26740 33496; www.arthotel.gr/ perantzada; Odissea Androutsou; s €200, d €316-388, ste €459-707; 🞉 🖳 🛜 🞉) Part of the Emelisse group,

this stylish boutique hotel is in a transformed neoclassical building of 19th-century vintage. It all glows with modernist chic and the vibrant designs of such names as Philip Stark and Ingo Mauer. A new extension is even more dazzling and includes an infinity pool. Breakfasts are every bit as svelte.

Eating & Drinking

Vathy's waterfront eateries are fairly standard and with identical menus, although there are exceptions.

For a sweet experience, try *rovani*, the local speciality made with rice, honey and cloves, at one of the patisseries on or near the main square.

Café Karamela (☎ 26740 33580; snacks €2.50-6) The western quay is home to this welcoming place, where you have a genuine picturesque view of the bay through a massive window. Board games, books and TV, plus home-made snacks cakes and pastries make it all even more pleasant.

Dracoulis (☎ 26740 33453; snacks €5-9) Housed in a dignified old seafront villa, this bar-cafe has drinks, sandwiches, mixed plates and music. Note the little mooring pool in front of the mansion and ponder on sea level rise. The below-road channel was once navigable by small boats. You'd need a mini-sub now.

Gregory's Taverna/Paliocaravo (☎ 26740 32573; mains €5.50-19) This long-standing family concern serves fish and tasty specialities such as *savoro*, fish marinated in vinegar and raisins. It's 1km north along Vathy's waterfront and overlooks the yacht marina.

Drosia (☎ 26740 32959; mains €6-15) This well-known taverna serves authentic Greek dishes and throws in a touch of Venezuelan influence as well. Popular for its charcoal grill dishes you may also catch some impromptu dancing to the playing of bouzoukis. It's 1km up the narrow road to Filiatro from the inner corner of the harbour.

AROUND ITHAKI

Ithaki proudly claims several sites associated with Homer's tale, the 'Odyssey'. Finding the hyped-up locations can be an epic journey – signage is a bit scant. Many seem to be myths themselves, so vague are their locations, but there's no questioning the classical spirit of this island. The **Fountain of Arethousa**, in the island's south, is where Odysseus' swineherd, Eumaeus, is believed to have brought his pigs to drink. The exposed and isolated hike – through unspoilt landscape with great sea views – takes 1½ to two hours (return) from the turn-off; this excludes the hilly 5km trudge up the road to the sign itself. Take a hat and water.

The location of Odysseus' palace has been much disputed and archaeologists have been unable to find conclusive evidence; some present-day archaeologists speculate it was on **Pelikata Hill** near Stavros, while German archaeologist Heinrich Schliemann believed it to be at **Alalkomenes**, near Piso Aetos. Also in Stavros visit the small **archaeological museum** (☎ 26740 31305; admission free; ◷ 9am-2.30pm Tue-Sun).

Take a break from Homeric myth and head north from Vathy along a fabulously scenic mountain road to sleepy **Anogi**, the old capital. Its restored church of **Agia Panagia** (claimed to be from the 12th century) has incredible Byzantine frescoes and a Venetian bell tower. You can obtain the keys from the neighbouring *kafeneio*. About 200m uphill are the small but evocative ruins of Old Anogi within a rock-studded landscape.

Further north again is the little village of **Stavros** above the Bay of Polis, also reached along the west coast road. Heading northeast from Stavros takes you to the tiny, understated seafront village of **Frikes** clasped between windswept cliffs and with a swath of waterfront restaurants, busy bars and a relaxed ambience. It's the ferry departure point for Lefkada. From Frikes a twisting road hugs the beautiful coastline to end at **Kioni**, another small seafront village that spills down a verdant hillside to a miniature harbour where yachts overnight and tavernas and bars eagerly await them.

Sleeping & Eating

Mrs Vasilopoulos' Rooms (☎ 26740 31027; Stavros; s/d/apt €40/50/65) These homely studios, with overhead fans, are reached by going up the leftmost lane to the left of Café To Kentro from the main square in Stavros. The pretty garden overlooks olive and cypress groves.

Captain's Apartments (☎ 26740 31481; www .captains-apartments.gr; Kioni; d €65, 4-person apt €90; ◷ year-round; P ☼) Well-run and definitely ship-shape are these well-maintained studios and apartments that are signposted halfway down the twisting road to the harbour at Kioni.

Fatouros Taverna (☎ 26740 31385; Stavros; mains €5-12) A pleasant unvarnished place behind its red-brick facade, this popular eatery exults in spit-roast meat dishes and Greek standards.

Yiannis (☎ 26740 31363; Stavros; mains €5-12) Friendly Yiannis does a good line in pizzas and sturdy mezedhes as well as Greek main dishes. Breakfasts are about €5.

Rementzo (☎ 26740 31719; Frikes; mains €6.80-11.60) Among the usual swathe of waterside tavernas in Frikes, Rementzo does good value Greek standards.

ZAKYNTHOS
ΖΑΚΥΝΘΟΣ

pop 38,600

Zakynthos (*zahk*-in-thos), also known by its Italian name Zante, is a fascinating island, unfairly known perhaps for conspicuous and heavy package tourism along its eastern and southeast coasts, but essentially a beautiful island whose western and central regions are mountainous, green and inspiring. The Venetians called it the Flower of the Orient. Its people are welcoming and its cuisine a delight. Too much tourism is, however, endangering more than the aesthetics of island life. The loggerhead turtle (see At Loggerheads, p707) struggles in the face of commercial development.

Getting There & Away
AIR

There are at least one or two daily flights between Zakynthos and Athens and connections to other Ionian Islands including Kefallonia and Corfu. **Olympic Air** (☎ 26950 28322; Zakynthos Airport; ☎ 8am-10pm Mon-Fri) can help with information and bookings. For details see Island Hopping (p763).

From May to September, many charter flights come from northern Europe and the UK to Zakynthos.

BOAT
Domestic

Depending on the season, between five and seven ferries operate daily between Zakynthos Town and Kyllini in the Peloponnese. Tickets can be obtained from the **Zakynthos Shipping Cooperative** (☎ 26950 22083/49500; Lombardou 40) in Zakynthos Town.

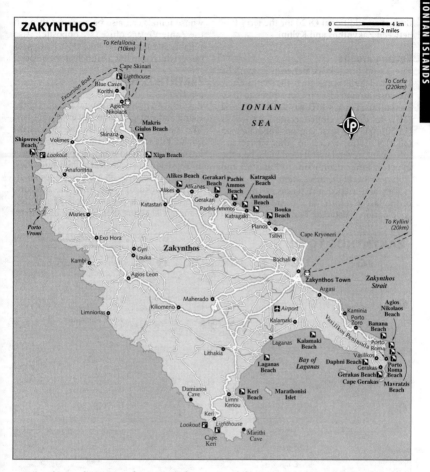

ZAKYNTHOS

From the northern port of Agios Nikolaos a ferry service shuttles across to Pesada in southern Kefallonia twice daily from May to October. In high season, there are only two buses a week from Zakynthos Town to Agios Nikolaos and two buses daily from Pesada (Kefallonia) to Argostoli (Kefallonia) making crossing without your own transport difficult. An alternative is to cross to Kyllini and catch another ferry to Kefallonia.

For ferry details see Island Hopping (p763).

International

Hellenic Mediterranean Lines (www.hmlferry.com) has July and August services once or twice a week between Brindisi and Zakynthos (€69, 15½ hours).

BUS

The smart new **KTEL bus station** (☎ 26950 22255) has recently opened on the bypass to the west of Zakynthos Town. On Monday to Friday, from early morning until 3pm, a mini-bus runs every hour or so to the new bus station from the site of the **old bus station** (42 Filita St).

KTEL operates four buses daily between Zakynthos Town and Patra (€6.80, 3½ hours), and four daily connections to/from Athens (€23.20, six hours) via the Corinth Canal road (€16.60, five hours). There's also a twice-weekly service to Thessaloniki (€44.30).

Budget an additional €8.20 for the ferry fare between Zakynthos and Kyllini.

Getting Around

There's no bus service between Zakynthos Town and the airport, 6km to the southwest. A taxi costs around €10. Frequent buses go from Zakynthos Town's **KTEL bus station** (☎ 26950 22255) to the developed resorts of Alikes (€1.50), Tsilivi, Argasi, Laganas and Kalamaki (all €1.40). Bus services to other villages are infrequent. Several useful local buses take the upper or lower main roads to Katastari and Volimes. Ask at the bus station.

Car- and moped-hire places are plentiful in the larger resorts. In Zakynthos Town a good option is **Motor Club Rentals** (☎ 26950 53095)

whose rentals can also be arranged through the Zante Voyage office (see opposite). Also reliable is **Europcar** (☎ 26950 41541; Plateia Agiou Louka), which also has a branch at the airport.

ZAKYNTHOS TOWN
pop 11,200

Zakynthos Town is the capital and port of the island and straggles round an enormous bay. The town was devastated by the 1953 earthquake, but was reconstructed to its former layout with arcaded streets, imposing squares and gracious neoclassical public buildings. A Venetian fortress on a hill provides an attractive backdrop. The town has a strong Greek feel and is patently more of a vibrant commercial centre than a tourist one. It still

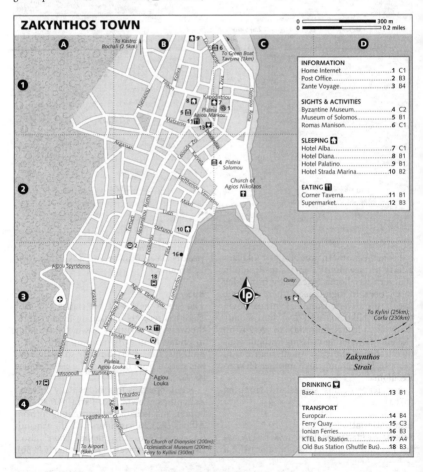

ZAKYNTHOS TOWN

INFORMATION	
Home Internet	**1** C1
Post Office	**2** B3
Zante Voyage	**3** B4

SIGHTS & ACTIVITIES	
Byzantine Museum	**4** C2
Museum of Solomos	**5** B1
Romas Manison	**6** C1

SLEEPING	
Hotel Alba	**7** C1
Hotel Diana	**8** B1
Hotel Palatino	**9** B1
Hotel Strada Marina	**10** B2

EATING	
Corner Taverna	**11** B1
Supermarket	**12** B3

DRINKING	
Base	**13** B1

TRANSPORT	
Europcar	**14** B4
Ferry Quay	**15** C3
Ionian Ferries	**16** B3
KTEL Bus Station	**17** A4
Old Bus Station (Shuttle Bus)	**18** B3

has some outstanding cultural attractions, however, while the northern area (around Plateia Agiou Markou) has plenty of cafes, bars, and restaurants.

Orientation & Information

Plateia Solomou is at the northern end of the waterfront road of Lombardou, opposite the ferry quay. Plateia Agiou Markou is behind it. The bus station is out on the western by-pass. The main thoroughfare is Alexandrou Roma, running several blocks inland, parallel to the waterfront.

Zakynthos Town has no tourist office. The helpful **Zante Voyage** (☎ 26950 25360; 12 Agiou Dionysou) promises 'travel solutions' and does a good job of delivering on queries, accommodation, car hire and tours.

There are banks with ATMs along Lombardou and just west of Plateia Solomou. The **post office** (☎ 26950 44875; Tertseti 27; ⏰ 7am-2pm) is one block west of Alexandrou Roma. **Home Internet** (12 L Ziva; per hr €3; ⏰ 10am-1am) has reasonable connection.

Sights & Activities

The **Byzantine museum** (☎ 26950 42714; Plateia Solomou; admission €3; ⏰ 8.30am-3pm Tue-Sun) houses two levels of fabulous ecclesiastical art, rescued from churches razed by the earthquake. It's all displayed in a beautiful setting overlooking the main plaza. Inside, the 16th-century St Andreas Monastery has been artfully 'replicated' to house its restored frescoes. The nearby **Museum of Solomos** (☎ 26950 28982; Plateia Agiou Markou; admission €4; ⏰ 9am-2pm) is dedicated to Dionysios Solomos (1798–1857), who was born on Zakynthos and is regarded as the father of modern Greek poetry. His work *Hymn to Liberty* became the Greek national anthem. The museum houses his memorabilia and archives. Just north of Plateia Agiou Markou is the fascinating **Romas Mansion** (☎ 26950 28343; 19 Louka Karrer; admission €5; ⏰ 10am-2pm Mon-Sat Apr-Oct). Built in the 17th century by an English merchant, the house was British-owned (Gladstone addressed the locals from its balcony) until bought by the Romas family during the 1880s. The house suffered badly in the 1953 earthquake but was partly rebuilt a few years later. Its period furnishings and decor are splendidly intact and the library has an astonishing 10,000 volumes.

The **Church of Dionysios**, the patron saint of the island, in Zakynthos Town's south has

some amazing gilt work and notable frescoes. Behind the church is an **ecclesiastical museum** (admission €2; ⏰ 9am-1pm & 5-9pm). It contains intriguing icons from the Monastery of Strofades, home to Dionysios, plus speech scrolls from the 13th and 14th centuries and a 12th-century book in Ancient Greek.

The peaceful, shady and pine tree-filled **Kastro** (☎ 26950 48099; admission €3; ⏰ 8.30am-2.30pm Tue-Sun), a ruined Venetian fortress high above Zakynthos Town, makes for a pleasant outing. It's 2.5km from town in the viewpoint village of Bochali (take Dionysiou Roma north and turn left at Kapodistriou; it's signed from here). There's a big car park as you enter Bochali and a one-way system thereafter. You are strongly advised not to try driving up to the castle, which is 300m above Bochali's main square. There's a walkway. Bochali has several cafes and tavernas with glorious views over Zakynthos Town.

Sleeping

Tour groups tend to monopolise many out-of-town hotels, but the following are safe bets for independent travellers and all are open throughout the year.

Hotel Alba (☎ 26950 26641; www.albahotel.gr; L Ziva 38; s/d/tr incl breakfast €48/68/96; ✂) A reasonable, if slightly dull, hotel but convenient for the centre of town. Rooms are slowly being refurbished and you pay a general €6 to €14 more for renovated ones.

Hotel Strada Marina (☎ 26950 42761; hotel@strada marina.gr; Lombardou 14; s/d incl breakfast €60/90; ✂ ▣) A good location on the main harbourfront road makes this business standard hotel a good option. Rooms are well equipped and the upper balconies have a great view of the bay. The rooftop area has a small pool.

Hotel Diana (☎ 26950 28547; Plateia Agiou Markou; s/d/tr incl breakfast €70/90/100; ✂ ▣ ⏣) Slightly ponderous decor does not mar this comfortable and well-appointed hotel in a good, central location.

Hotel Palatino (☎ 26950 27780; www.palatino hotel.gr; Kolokotroni 10; s/d/tr €75/110/125; ✂ ▣ ⏣) Business style is the measure of this well-appointed hotel with its comfortable rooms and smooth decor.

Eating & Drinking

There are plenty of tavernas and restaurants around Plateia Agiou Markou, but they tend to be overpriced and not entirely inspiring. There are decent options here, all the same, and elsewhere in town.

Green Boat Taverna (☎ 26950 22957; Krionerou 50; mains €4-15) It's a bit of a hike of about 1km north along the waterfront but the Green Boat is worth it for its fish and excellent Greek dishes such as *melitzanes*, eggplant in tomato sauce with feta cheese. Grilled king prawns are €12 and a plate of small fish is €10.

Corner Taverna (☎ 26950 42654; Plateia Agiou Markou; mains €6-19.80) Bang at the heart of the action and very proactive in catching custom, this busy place does offer reasonable grills and pastas.

Base (☎ 26950 42409; Plateia Agiou Markou; cappuccino €3.50) In a perfect location, Base commands the flow through Plateia Agiou Markou dispensing coffees, drinks and music to a very relaxed, sometimes posey, people-watching, gossipy local crowd.

There's also a well-stocked **supermarket** (cnr Filioti & Lombardou).

AROUND ZAKYNTHOS

Transport of your own is really the way to unlock the charms of Zakynthos.

A major feature of the island are the loggerhead turtles (see At Loggerheads, opposite) that come ashore to lay their eggs on the golden-sand beaches of the huge Bay of Laganas, a national marine park on Zakynthos' south coast. Unfortunately, the turtles share the bay with holidaymakers, who are often unaware of the situation concerning turtle breeding while protective legislation covering the loggerheads is often flouted by local tourism interests.

The **Vasilikos Peninsula** is the pretty green region southeast of Zakynthos Town, and fringing Laganas Bay. It's being heavily developed and has several settlements off the main road, all with tavernas and accommodation. **Banana Beach**, a long and narrow strip of golden sand on the peninsula's northern side, has plenty of action: crowds, water sports and umbrellas. Zakynthos' best beach is the long, sandy and much-coveted **Gerakas**. It's on the other side of the peninsula, facing into Laganas Bay. This is one of the main turtle-nesting beaches, and access to the beach is forbidden between dusk and dawn during May and October. On the northeastern side of Vasilikos Peninsula is the reasonable beach of **Kaminia**.

With transport, you can reach the far southwest of the island where, beyond the

very traditional village of **Keri,** a road leads past a taverna boasting the allegedly biggest Greek flag and flagpole in the country to **Cape Keri** and its lighthouse above sheer cliffs, where some care should be taken on paths that descend to the very abrupt cliff edge.

Fascinating and sometimes happily confusing roads lead north from here through beautiful wooded hill country where the welcoming locals sell honey and other seasonal products. The way leads to appealing west coast coves, such as **Limnionas** or **Kambi** and to such inland gems as **Kiliomeno** whose church of **St Nikolaos** features an unusual roofless campanile. The bell tower of the church of **Agios Leon** was formerly a windmill. **Louka** is a lovely village that seems more northern European, with its surrounding woodland and lush greenery. The hamlet of **Exo Hora** has a collection of dry wells and what is reputed to be the oldest olive tree on the island. **Volimes** is the unashamed sales centre for all traditional products.

North of Zakynthos Town the east coast is lined with resorts but the further north you go, the more remote and lovely the island becomes until the road begins to run out at the ferry point and small resort of **Agios Nikolaos**, where development is slight. Carry on beyond and you reach the breezy Cape Skinari from where boats leave for the coastal **Blue Caves**, sea-level caverns that pierce the limestone coastal cliffs. The boats enter the caves, where the water is a translucent blue. The boats also go to the famous **Shipwreck Beach**, whose photos grace virtually every tourist brochure about Zakynthos, in Navagio Bay, about 3km west of Volimes at the northwest tip of the island. It's overhyped, inevitably, and definitely over patronised by excursion boats. There's a precariously perched lookout platform (signposted between Anafonitria and Volimes). **Potamitis Trips** (☎ 26950 31132; www.potamitisbros.gr) offers worthwhile trips in glass-bottomed boats from Cape Skinari (Blue Caves only €7.50, Shipwreck Beach and Blue Caves €15).

Sleeping

Earth Sea & Sky can arrange short- or long-term stays in villas and cottages around the Vasilikos Peninsula – book through **Ionian Eco Villagers** (☎ UK 0871 711 5065; www.relaxing-holidays .com). Alternatively, you could try your luck for a spontaneous booking with the same company at its wildlife information kiosk in Gerakas.

AT LOGGERHEADS

The Ionian Islands are home to the Mediterranean's loggerhead turtle *(Caretta caretta)*, one of Europe's most endangered marine species. The turtles bury their eggs on large tracts of clean, flat sand, unfortunately the favoured habitat of basking tourists. The implications are obvious.

Zakynthos hosts the largest density of turtle nests in the Ionian – an estimated 1100 along the 5km Bay of Laganas. During hatching time (July to October), surviving hatchlings emerge after a 60-day incubation period in the sand. Bizarrely, wooden frames with warning notes attached are placed by conservation agencies over the buried hatching sites, often alongside the sunbeds and windbreaks of tourists. Many of the nests are destroyed by sun brollies and bikes. Young turtles often don't make it to the water – they are often disoriented by sunbeds, noise and lights.

Conservation lobbyists have clashed with local authorities, tourist operators and the government. In 1999, following pressure from the EU, the Greek government declared the Bay of Laganas area a national marine park. Strict regulations were put in force regarding building, boating, mooring, fishing and water sports in designated zones.

All designated nesting beaches are completely off-limits between dusk and dawn during the breeding season (May to October). Despite this, dozens of illegal bars and tavernas operate in the area, illegal umbrellas and sunbeds are rented out to tourists, and sightseeing boats 'guarantee' turtle sightings and inevitably get too close to the creatures, an intrusion that causes stress at a crucial point in the turtles' breeding cycle.

In July 2009 savage wildfires around Laganas Bay, several allegedly started by human action, were feared to have damaged some sections of breeding areas, especially in the Daphni Beach area where dozens of holidaymakers had to be rescued. Daphni is one of the turtle beaches where protective legislation continues to be flouted.

The Greek government has been condemned by the European Court of Justice for failing to implement EU nature protection legislation. Meanwhile, WWF (Worldwide Fund for Nature), Archelon (the Sea Turtle Protection Society of Greece) and Medasset (Mediterranean Association to Save the Sea Turtles) continue their lobbying efforts. Volunteers from **Archelon** (www.archelon .gr) and the national marine park provide informal beach wardens and run excellent education and volunteer programs. For further information, visit the wildlife information centre at Gerakas Beach.

Visitors can also be aware of the following and make their judgements accordingly:

- Avoid using umbrellas on dry sand (use the wet part of the beach).
- Do not enter nesting beaches between dusk and dawn, and avoid visiting Daphni Beach.
- Be aware of boating trips – where they go and what's on offer.
- Seek information on the area's sea turtle conservation efforts and protective regulations.

Tartaruga Camping (☎ 26950 51967; www.tartaruga -camping.com; camp sites per adult/car/tent €5/3/3.60, r per person €20-50; P 🍴 💻) A great place for happy campers – amid terraced olive groves, pines and plane trees that sprawl as far as the sea. It has a small store and a taverna (mains €4-8), and rooms for rent. It's well-signed on the road from Laganas to Keri.

Panorama Studios (☎ 26950 31013; panorama -apts@ath.forthnet.gr; Agios Nikolaos; s/d/tr €40/45/55) The English-speaking hosts at this place in Agios Nikolaos offer excellent studio accommodation on the main road 600m uphill from the port, but set back in a lovely garden area.

Revera Villas (☎ 26950 27524, 69748 75171; www .revera-zante.com; d €70, studio €80, 4-/6-person villa €150/200; P 🍴 💻 🏖) This complex of Italian-feel villas is located 4km southwest of Limni Keriou village (and 500m southwest of Keri village), just off the road to the lighthouse. The buildings and individually decorated, luxury rooms incorporate exposed stonework. Mountain bikes are available free of charge.

Anna's Villas (☎ 69772 36243, 69772 36243; apt €90; Limni Keriou; P 🍴) Two good-value studio apartments, in a garden setting and with kitchen facilities. They're set a block or so back from Limni Keriou's waterfront.

Windmill (☎ 26950 31132; Cape Skinari; www.potami tisbros.gr; 2-/4-person windmills €90/120; 🛌) There are two converted windmills at Cape Skinari in a fantastic cliff-top location. The bigger one has cooking facilities, and an adjoining cafe-bar, with excellent rooms (€70) and an apartment (€120) above, all with stunning views. Steps lead down to a lovely swimming area and one of the departure points for boat trips to the Blue Caves and Shipwreck Beach (p706).

Louha's Coffee Shop (☎ 26950 48426; mains €4-7; Louka; 🕑 lunch & dinner) Head along the lane to the Church of St John the Theologian, who would have enjoyed eating under Louha's vine-shaded terrace opposite the church. Very traditional and good local wine goes with soothing views of cypress and pine-tree dotted hills.

To Litrouvio (☎ 26950 55081; mains €6.50-16; Lithakia; 🕑 lunch & dinner) An olive-oil stone presser and various traditional artefacts add to the experience at this popular place, where good local dishes come in plentiful helpings.

Directory

CONTENTS

ACCOMMODATION

There is a range of accommodation available in Greece to suit every taste and pocket. All places to stay are subject to strict price controls set by the tourist police. By law, a notice must be displayed in every room, stating the category of the room and the price charged in each season. The price includes a 4.5% community tax and 8% VAT.

Accommodation owners may add a 10% surcharge for a stay of less than three nights, but this is not mandatory. A mandatory charge of 20% is levied if an extra bed is put into a room (although this often doesn't happen if the extra bed is for a child). During July and August accommodation owners will charge the maximum price, but in spring and autumn prices can drop by 20%, and then drop even further in winter.

Rip-offs rarely occur, but if you do suspect that you have been exploited by an accommodation owner, make sure you report it to either the tourist police or the regular police, and they will act swiftly.

Throughout this book we have divided accommodation into budget (up to €80 in Athens; up to €60 elsewhere), midrange (€80 to €150 in Athens; €60 to €150 elsewhere) and top end (€150+) categories. This is based on the rate for a double room in high season (July and August). Unless otherwise stated, all rooms have private bathroom facilities. It's difficult to generalise accommodation prices in Greece as rates depend entirely on the season and location. Don't expect to pay the same price for a double on one of the islands as you would in central Greece or Athens.

Camping

Camping is a good option, especially in summer. There are almost 350 camping grounds in Greece, found in the majority of regions and islands (with the notable exception of the Saronic Gulf Islands), with many situated in picturesque locations. Standard facilities include hot showers, kitchens, restaurants and minimarkets – and often a swimming pool.

Most camping grounds are open only between April and October. The **Panhellenic Camping Association** (Map pp112–13; ☎ /fax 210 362 1560; www.panhellenic-camping-union.gr; Solonos 102, Exarhia, Athens) publishes an annual booklet list-

---

BOOK YOUR STAY ONLINE

For more accommodation reviews and recommendations by Lonely Planet authors, check out the online booking service at www.lonelyplanet.com/hotels. You'll find the true, insider low-down on the best places to stay. Reviews are thorough and independent. Best of all, you can book online.

ing all its camping grounds, their facilities and months of operation.

Camping fees are highest from 15 June through to the end of August. Most camping grounds charge from €5 to €7 per adult and €3 to €4 for children aged four to 12. There's no charge for children under four. Tent sites cost from €4 per night for small tents, and from €5 per night for large tents. Caravan sites start at around €6; car costs are typically €4 to €5.

If camping in the height of summer, bring a silver fly sheet to reflect the heat off your tent. Otherwise, dark tents that are all the rage in colder countries become sweat lodges. Between May and mid-September the weather is warm enough to sleep out under the stars. Many camping grounds have covered areas where tourists who don't have tents can sleep in summer; you can get by with a lightweight sleeping bag. It's a good idea to have a foam pad to lie on and a waterproof cover for your sleeping bag.

Domatia

Domatia (literally 'rooms') are the Greek equivalent of the British bed and breakfast, minus the breakfast. Once upon a time, domatia comprised little more than spare rooms in the family home that could be rented out to travellers in summer; nowadays,

---

PRACTICALITIES

- Use the metric system for weights and measures.

- Plug your electrical appliances into a two-pin adaptor before plugging into the electricity supply (220V AC, 50Hz).

- Keep up with Greek current affairs by reading the daily English-language edition of *Kathimerini* that comes with the *International Herald Tribune*.

- Channel-hop through a choice of nine free-to-air TV channels and an assortment of pay TV channels.

- Be aware that Greece is region code 2 when you buy DVDs to watch back home.

---

many are purpose-built appendages to the family house. Some come complete with fully equipped kitchens. Standards of cleanliness are generally high.

Domatia remain a popular option for budget travellers. Expect to pay from €25 to €50 for a single, and €35 to €65 for a double, depending on whether bathrooms are shared or private, the season and how long you plan to stay. Domatia are found throughout the mainland (except in large cities) and on almost every island that has a permanent population. Many are open only between April and October.

From June to September domatia owners are out in force, touting for customers. They meet buses and boats, shouting 'Room, room!' and often carrying photographs of their rooms. In peak season it can prove a mistake not to take up an offer – but be wary of owners who are vague about the location of their accommodation.

Hostels

Most youth hostels in Greece are run by the **Greek Youth Hostel Organisation** (Map p108; ☎ 210 751 9530; www.athens-yhostel.com; Damareos 75, Pangrati, Athens). There are affiliated hostels in Athens, Olympia, Patra and Thessaloniki on the mainland, and on the islands of Crete and Santorini.

Hostel rates vary from around €10 to €20 for a bed in a dorm and you don't have to be a member to stay in them. Few have curfews.

GREEN STAYS

Park your bags in the countryside and bunk down in luxurious digs that also happen to be sustainable. Top green stays:

- **Achladies Apartments** (Achladies Bay, Skiathos; p655)

- **Harry's Paradise** (Kalymnos, Dodecanese; p570)

- **Milia** (Kissamos, Crete; p498)

- **Pine Tree Studios** (Karpathos, Dodecanese; p537)

- **Red Tractor Farm** (Korissia, Cyclades; p455)

For more ideas, visit www.guestinn.com and www.agrotravel.gr. Both sites have oodles of traditional rural accommodation options, listed by interests like farm stays, walking holidays or vineyard routes.

Hotels

Hotels in Greece are divided into six categories: deluxe, A, B, C, D and E. Hotels are categorised according to the size of the rooms, whether or not they have a bar, and the ratio of bathrooms to beds, rather than standards of cleanliness, comfort of beds and friendliness of staff – all elements that may be of greater relevance to guests.

As one would expect, deluxe, A- and B-class hotels have many amenities, private bathrooms and constant hot water. C-class hotels have a snack bar and rooms with private bathrooms, but hot water may only be available at certain times of the day. D-class hotels may or may not have snack bars; most rooms will share bathrooms, but there may be some with private bathrooms; and they may have solar-heated water, which means hot water is not guaranteed. E-class hotels do not have a snack bar; bathrooms are shared and you may have to pay extra for hot water.

Prices are controlled by the tourist police and the maximum rate that can be charged for a room must be displayed on a board behind the door of each room. The classification is not often much of a guide to price. Rates in D- and E-class hotels are generally comparable with domatia. In C class you can pay from €35 to €60 for a single in high season and €45 to €80 for a double. Prices in B class range from €50 to €85 for singles and from €90 to €150 for doubles. A-class prices are not much higher.

Mountain Refuges

There are 55 mountain refuges dotted around the Greek mainland, Crete and Evia. They range from small huts with outdoor toilets and no cooking facilities to very comfortable modern lodges. They are run by the country's various mountaineering and skiing clubs. Prices start at around €7 per person, depending on the facilities. The EOT (Greek National Tourist Organisation) publication *Greece: Mountain Refuges & Ski Centres* has details about each refuge; copies are available at all EOT branches (see p722).

Pensions

Pensions are indistinguishable from hotels. They are categorised as A, B or C class. An A-class pension is equivalent in amenities and price to a B-class hotel, a B-class pension is equivalent to a C-class hotel, and a C-class pension is equivalent to a D- or E-class hotel.

Rental Accommodation

A really practical way to save on money and maximise comfort is to rent a furnished apartment or villa. Many are purpose-built for tourists while others – villas in particular – may be owners' homes that they are not using. The main advantage is that you can accommodate a larger number of people under one roof, and you can also save money by self-catering. This option is best for a stay of more than three days. In fact, some owners may insist on a minimum week's stay. A good site to spot prospective villas is www.greekislands.com.

If you're looking for long-term accommodation, it's worth checking the classified section of the *Athens News* – although most of the places are in Athens. For rural areas and islands, local websites are a good place to start your search.

ACTIVITIES
Cycling

With over 4000km of coastal road on the mainland alone and 80% mountainous terrain, Greece is gaining popularity as a cycling destination. While it's possible to rent a bike for a day, many people choose cycling as their main form of transport. Bicycles can be taken on trains and ferries for free and there are an increasing number of tour companies specialising in cycling holidays.

Cycle Greece (www.cyclegreece.gr) runs road- and mountain-bike tours across most of Greece for various skill levels. **Hooked on Cycling** (www .hookedoncycling.co.uk/Greece/greece.html) offers boat and bike trips through the islands and tours of the mainland. **Bike Greece** (www.bikegreece .com) specialises in mountain biking, with various week-long tours for beginners and the experienced.

Much of Greece is very remote. Be sure to carry a repair and first-aid kit with you. Motorists are notoriously fast and not always travelling in the expected lane, and extra caution on corners and narrow roads is well warranted. In July and August most cyclists break between noon and 4pm to avoid sunstroke and dehydration. For lots of information and routes, check out Anthony Campbell's website at www.acampbell.ukfsn.org/cycling/greece .index.html. Also see Road Rules (p735).

Diving & Snorkelling

Snorkelling can be enjoyed just about anywhere along the coast of Greece. Especially good places are Ammoöpi (p536) in southern Karpathos, Velanio (p659) on Skopelos and Paleokastritsa (p683) on Corfu.

Greek law insists that diving be done under the supervision of a diving school in order to protect the many antiquities in the depths of the Aegean. Until recently dive sites were severely restricted, but many more have been opened up and diving schools have flourished. You'll find diving schools on the islands of Corfu, Evia, Hydra, Leros, Milos, Mykonos, Paros, Rhodes, Santorini and Skiathos; in Agios Nikolaos and Rethymno on Crete; in Glyfada near Athens; and in Parga on the mainland.

Hiking

The majority of Greece is mountainous and, in many ways, is a hikers' paradise. The most popular routes are well walked and maintained; however, the **EOS** (Greek Alpine Club; ☎ 210 321 2429; Plateia Kapnikareas 2, Athens) is grossly underfunded and consequently many of the lesser-known paths are overgrown and inadequately marked. You'll find EOS branches in Epiros (p338), Crete (Mountaineering & Skiing Club of Iraklio; p466) and Evia (Halkida Alpine Club; p646). See p719 for information on hiking maps.

The Louisos Gorge (p197) and the Mani (p209), both in the Peloponnese, are two of the best places in Greece to explore on foot.

On small islands you will encounter a variety of paths, including *kalderimia,* which are cobbled or flagstone paths that have linked settlements since Byzantine times. Other paths include shepherds' trails *(monopatia)* that link settlements with sheepfolds or link remote settlements via rough unmarked trails. Be aware that shepherd or animal trails can be very steep and difficult to navigate.

A number of companies run organised hikes. The biggest is **Trekking Hellas** (www.trekking.gr), which offers a variety of hikes ranging from a four-hour stroll through the Lousios Valley to a week-long hike around Mt Olympus and Meteora. The company also runs hikes on Crete and in the Cyclades.

Kitesurfing

Also known as kiteboarding, this action sport has taken off in a big way in Greece and you'll find beaches festooned with athletic surfers. The **Greek Wakeboard and Kite Surf Association** (☎ 69445 17963; www.gwa.gr) has details of popular kitesurfing locales. Each summer, Ammoöpi (p536) on Karpathos hosts an international kitesurfing competition.

Skiing

Greece provides some of the cheapest skiing in Europe. There are 16 resorts dotted around the mountains of mainland Greece, mainly in the north. The main skiing areas are Mt Parnassos (p246), 195km northwest of Athens, and Mt Vermio (p313), 110km west of Thessaloniki. There are no foreign package holidays to these resorts; they are used mainly by Greeks. They have all the basic facilities and can be a pleasant alternative to the glitzy resorts of northern Europe.

The season depends on snow conditions but runs approximately from January to the end of April. For further information pick up a copy of *Greece: Mountain Refuges & Ski Centres* from an EOT office (p722). Information may also be obtained from the **Hellenic Skiing Federation** (Map pp110-11; ☎ 210 323 0182; press@ski.org.gr; Karageorgi Servias 7, Syntagma, Athens). You'll find information about the latest snow conditions on the internet at www.snowreport.gr.

Waterskiing

There are three islands with waterskiing centres: Kythira, Paros and Skiathos.

Given the relatively calm and flat waters of most islands and the generally warm waters of the Aegean, waterskiing can be a very pleasant activity. August can be a tricky month, when the *meltemi* (northeasterly wind) can make conditions difficult in the central Aegean. The island of Poros near Athens is a particularly well-organised locale with one organisation, **Passage** (☎ 22980 42540; www.passage.gr; Neorion Bay), hosting a popular school and slalom centre.

White-Water Rafting

The popularity of white-water rafting and other river adventure sports has grown rapidly in recent years as more and more urban Greeks, particularly Athenians, head off in search of a wilderness experience.

Trekking Hellas (www.trekking.gr) offers half a dozen possibilities, including the Ladonas and Alfios Rivers in the Peloponnese, the Arahthos River in Epiros and the Aheloos River in Thessaly. **Alpin Club** (☎ 210 675 3514/5; www.alpinclub.gr) specialises in the Alfios River and the Evinos River, near Nafpaktos in Sterea Ellada. **Eco Action** (☎ 210 331 7866; www.ecoaction.gr;

Agion Anargyron, Psyrri) offers rafting and kayaking on the Ladonas River, which hosted the kayaking at the 2004 Olympics, as well as on another three rivers throughout Greece.

Windsurfing

Windsurfing is a very popular water sport in Greece. Hrysi Akti (p404) on Paros and Vasiliki (p691) on Lefkada vie for the position of best windsurfing beach. According to some, Vasiliki is one of the best places in the world to learn the sport, while Afiartis (p536) on Karpathos is for more experienced windsurfers.

You'll find sailboards for hire almost everywhere. Hire charges range from €10 to €15 an hour, depending on the gear. If you are a novice, most places that rent equipment also give lessons.

Sailboards can be imported freely from other EU countries, but the import of boards from other destinations, such as Australia and the USA, is subject to regulations. Theoretically, importers need a Greek national residing in Greece to guarantee that the board will be taken out of the country again. Contact the **Hellenic Windsurfing Association** (Map pp110-11; ☎ 210 323 3696; Filellinon 4, Syntagma, Athens) for more information.

Yachting

Yachting is an amazing way to see the Greek islands. Nothing beats the experience of sailing the open sea, and the freedom of being able to visit remote and uninhabited islands.

The free EOT booklet *Sailing the Greek Seas,* although long overdue for an update, contains lots of information about weather conditions, weather bulletins, entry and exit regulations, entry and exit ports, and guidebooks for yachties. You can pick up the booklet at any GNTO/EOT office either abroad or in Greece (see p722 for locations).

If your budget won't cover buying a yacht, there are several other options open to you. You can hire a bare boat (a yacht without a crew) if two crew members have a sailing certificate. Prices start at €1000 per week for a 28-footer that will sleep six. It will cost an extra €850 per week to hire a skipper.

Individuals can check out week-long island cruises offered by **Ghiolman Yachts & Travel** (Map p116; ☎ 210 325 5000; www.ghiolman.com; 8 Propileon, Acropoli, Athens), operating weekly from early

May to the end of September. **Hellenic Yachting Server** (www.yachting.gr) has information about yachting and chartering yachts. For more information see Cruising (p732).

BUSINESS HOURS

Banks are open from 8am to 2.30pm Monday to Thursday, and from 8am to 2pm Friday. Some banks in large towns and cities also open from 3.30pm to 6.30pm on weekdays and from 8am to 1.30pm on Saturday.

Post offices are open from 7.30am to 2pm Monday to Friday. In the major cities they stay open until 8pm, and open from 7.30am to 2pm on Saturday.

In summer the usual opening hours for shops are from 8am to 3pm on Monday, Wednesday and Saturday, and from 8am to 2.30pm and from 5pm to 8.30pm on Tuesday, Thursday and Friday. Shops open 30 minutes later during winter. These times are not always strictly adhered to. Many shops in tourist resorts are open seven days a week and keep later hours.

Department stores and supermarkets are open from 8am to 8pm Monday to Friday, and from 8am to at least 3pm on Saturday. They are closed on Sunday.

Periptera (street kiosks) are open from early morning until late at night. They sell everything from bus tickets and cigarettes to razor blades and shaving cream.

Restaurant hours vary enormously. Most places are normally open for lunch from 11am to 3pm and for dinner from 7pm to 1am, while restaurants in tourist areas remain open all day. Cafes normally open at about 10am and stay open until midnight.

Bars open from about 8pm until late. Discos and nightclubs don't usually open until at least 10pm; it's rare to find much of a crowd before midnight. They close at about 4am, later on Friday and Saturday.

CHILDREN

Greece is a safe and easy place to travel with children. Greeks will generally make a fuss over your children, who will find themselves on the receiving end of many small gifts and treats. Teaching your children a few words in Greek will ingratiate them further.

Matt Barrett's website (www.greektravel .com) has lots of useful tips for parents, while daughter Amarandi has put together some tips for kids (www.greece4kids.com).

Practicalities

Travelling is especially easy if you're staying at a resort hotel by the beach, where everything is set up for families with children. As well as facilities like paddling pools and playgrounds, they also have cots and highchairs.

Elsewhere, it's rare to find cots and highchairs, although most hotels and restaurants will do their best to help. The fast service in most restaurants is good news when it comes to feeding hungry kids. Ordering lots of small dishes to share gives your kids the chance to try the local cuisine, and you can almost always find omelettes, chips or spaghetti on the menu. Many hotels let small children stay for free and will squeeze an extra bed in the room.

Unless you head straight for the beach, a holiday in Greece can necessitate a lot of walking. If your kids aren't old enough to walk on their own for long, consider a sturdy carrying backpack; pushchairs are a struggle in towns and villages with slippery cobbles and high pavements. Nevertheless, if the pushchair is a sturdy, off-road style, you should be OK.

Fresh milk is available in large towns and tourist areas, but harder to find on smaller islands. Supermarkets are the best place to look. Formula is available almost everywhere, as is condensed and heat-treated milk. Disposable nappies are also available everywhere.

Travel on ferries, buses and trains is free for children under four. They pay half-fare up to the age of 10 (ferries) or 12 (buses and trains). Full fares apply otherwise. On domestic flights, you'll pay 10% of the adult fare to have a child under two sitting on your knee. Kids aged two to 12 pay half-fare. If you plan to rent a car, it's wise to bring your own car or booster seat as many of the smaller local agencies won't have these.

Sights & Activities

Most towns will have at least a small playground, while larger cities often have fantastic, modern play parks. These offer a great opportunity for your children to play with local kids. Children seem to have an innate ability to overcome language barriers through play. Children also enjoy climbing and exploring at the many ancient sights; young imaginations go into overdrive when let loose somewhere like the 'labyrinth' at Knossos.

The Hellenic Children's Museum (p136) is an excellent diversion, where your kids can join Greek cooking and craft classes.

CLIMATE

Greece can be divided into a number of main climatic regions.

Northern Macedonia and northern Epiros have a climate similar to the Balkans, with freezing winters and very hot, humid summers. The Attica Peninsula, the Cyclades, the Dodecanese, Crete, and the central and eastern Peloponnese have a more typically Mediterranean climate, with hot, dry summers and milder winters.

Snow is rare in the Cyclades, but the high mountains of the Peloponnese and Crete are covered in snow during the winter and it occasionally snows in Athens. In July and August the mercury can soar to 40°C (over 100°F) in the shade just about anywhere in the

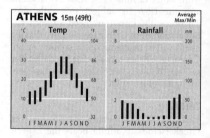

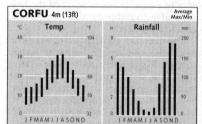

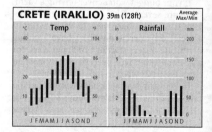

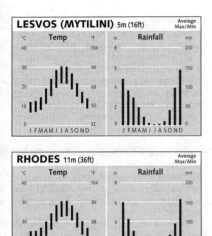

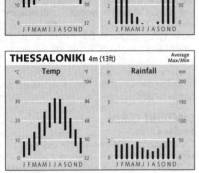

country. July and August are also the months of the *meltemi*, a strong northerly wind that sweeps the eastern coast of mainland Greece (including Athens) and the Aegean islands, especially the Cyclades. The wind is caused by air pressure differences between North Africa and the Balkans. The *meltemi* is a mixed blessing: it reduces humidity, but plays havoc with ferry schedules and sends everything flying – from beach umbrellas to washing hanging out to dry.

The western Peloponnese, western Sterea Ellada, southwestern Epiros and the Ionian Islands escape the *meltemi* and have less severe winters than northern Greece, but are the areas with the highest rainfall. The Northeastern Aegean Islands, Halkidiki and the Pelion Peninsula fall somewhere between the Balkan-type climate of northern Greece and the Mediterranean climate. Crete stays warm the longest – you can swim off the island's southern coast from mid-April to November.

Mid-October is when the rains start in most areas, and the weather stays cold and wet until February – although there are also occasional winter days with clear blue skies and sunshine.

For tips on the best times to visit Greece, see p19.

COURSES

Cooking

It is possible to do cooking courses on Santorini, Kea, Ikaria and Crete. See p82 for more information.

Dance

The Dora Stratou Dance Theatre (p148) in Plaka and the Nelly Dimoglou Dance Company (p521) in Rhodes Town run courses in traditional Greek dance for foreigners.

Language

If you are serious about learning the Greek language, an intensive course at the start of your stay is a good way to go about it. Most of the courses are based in Athens (see p136), but there are also special courses on the islands in summer.

The **Athens Centre** (Map p108; ☎ 210 701 2268; www.athenscentre.gr; Arhimidou 48, Mets, Athens) is located in the suburb of Mets, and also runs courses on the island of Spetses in June and July. Three-week courses cost €1190, and involve 66 hours of classwork.

The **Hellenic Culture Centre** (☎ 22750 61139/40; www.hcc.gr; ☼ May-Oct), in the village of Arethousa, 7km from Evdilos, offers courses in Greek language, culture and literature. All levels of language proficiency are catered for.

CUSTOMS

There are no longer duty-free restrictions within the EU. Upon entering the country from outside the EU, customs inspection is usually cursory for foreign tourists and a verbal declaration is usually all that is required. Random searches are still occasionally made for drugs.

You may bring the following into Greece duty-free: 200 cigarettes or 50 cigars; 1L of spirits or 2L of wine; 50mL of perfume; 250mL of eau de cologne; one camera (still or video) and film; a pair of binoculars; a portable musical instrument; a portable radio or tape recorder; a laptop computer; sports equipment; and dogs and cats (with a veterinary certificate). Restrictions apply to the importation of sailboards into Greece (see p713).

Importation of works of art and antiquities into Greece is free, but they must be declared on entry so that they can be re-exported. Import regulations for medicines are strict; if you are taking medication, make sure you get a statement from your doctor before you leave home. It is illegal, for instance, to take codeine into Greece without an accompanying doctor's certificate.

An unlimited amount of foreign currency and travellers cheques may be brought into Greece. If you intend to leave the country with foreign banknotes in excess of US$1000, you must declare the sum upon entry.

It is strictly forbidden to export antiquities (anything over 100 years old) without an export permit. This crime is second only to drug smuggling in the penalties imposed. It is an offence to remove even the smallest article from an archaeological site. The place to apply for an export permit is the Antique Dealers and Private Collections section of the **Athens Archaeological Service** (Map pp110-11; Polygnotou 13, Plaka, Athens).

Vehicles

Cars can be brought into Greece for six months without a carnet; only a green card (international third-party insurance) is required. If arriving from Italy your only proof of entry into the country will be your ferry ticket stub, so don't lose it. From other countries, a passport stamp will be ample evidence.

DANGERS & ANNOYANCES
Adulterated & Spiked Drinks

Adulterated drinks (known as *bombes*) are served in some bars and clubs in Athens and resorts known for partying. These drinks are diluted with cheap illegal imports that leave you feeling worse for wear the next day.

Many of the party resorts catering to large budget-tour groups are also unfortunately the scene of drunk and disorderly behaviour – some of it just purely annoying and some of it frighteningly violent. Spiked drinks are not uncommon; keep your hand over the top of your glass. More often than not, the perpetrators are foreign tourists rather than locals.

Bar Scams

Bar scams continue to be an unfortunate fact of life in Athens, particularly in the Syntagma area. The basic scam is some variation on a solo male traveller being lured into a bar, where charming girls appear and ask for what turn out to be ludicrously overpriced drinks, leaving the traveller footing an enormous bill. See p107 for the full rundown on this scam.

Theft

Crime, especially theft, is traditionally low in Greece, but unfortunately it is on the rise. The worst area is around Omonia in central Athens – keep track of your valuables here, especially on the metro and at the Sunday flea market.

The vast majority of thefts from tourists are still committed by other tourists; the biggest danger of theft is probably in dormitory rooms in hostels and at camping grounds. Make sure you do not leave valuables unattended in such places. If you are staying in a hotel room, and the windows and door do not lock securely, ask for your valuables to be locked in the hotel safe – hotel proprietors are happy to do this.

DISCOUNT CARDS
Senior Cards

Card-carrying EU pensioners can claim a range of benefits such as reduced admission to ancient sites and museums, and discounts on bus and train fares.

Student & Youth Cards

The most widely recognised form of student ID is the International Student Identity Card (ISIC). These cards can entitle the holder to half-price admission to museums and ancient sites, and discounts at some budget hotels and hostels. In some cases only Greek student cards will be accepted but it's always worth flashing your international student card just in case. The Euro26 card is available for anyone up to the age of 30 and which can provide discounts of up to 20% at sights, shops and for some transport.

Some travel agencies in Athens are licensed to issue ISIC and Euro26 cards. For ISIC cards you must show documents proving you are a student, provide a passport photo and cough up €10. For Euro26 you just need proof of age, a photo and €14. Visit www.isic.org and www.euro26.org for more details.

Aegean Airlines offers student discounts on some domestic flights, but there are none to be had on buses, ferries or trains. Students can often find good deals on international airfares.

EMBASSIES & CONSULATES

All foreign embassies in Greece are in Athens and its suburbs, with a few consulates in Thessaloniki.

Albania (Map pp114-15; ☎ 210 687 6200; Vekiareli 7, Athens GR-152 37)

Australia (Map pp114-15; ☎ 210 870 4000; cnr Leoforos Alexandras & Leoforos Kifisias, Ambelokipi, Athens GR-115 23)

Bulgaria (☎ 210 674 8105; Stratigou Kalari 33a, Psyhiko, Athens GR-154 52)

Canada (Map pp114-15; ☎ 210 727 3400; Genadiou 4, Athens GR-115 21)

Cyprus (Map pp114-15; ☎ 210 723 7883; Irodotou 16, Athens GR-106 75)

France (Map pp114-15; ☎ 210 361 1663; Leoforos Vasilissis Sofias 7, Athens GR-106 71)

Germany (Map pp114-15; ☎ 210 728 5111; Dimitriou 3, cnr Karaoli, Kolonaki, Athens GR-106 75)

Ireland (Map p108; ☎ 210 723 2771; Leoforos Vasileos Konstantinou 5-7, Athens GR-153 34)

Italy (Map pp114-15; ☎ 210 361 7260; Sekeri 2, Athens GR-106 74)

Japan (Map p108; ☎ 210 775 8101; Athens Tower, Mesogion 2-4, Athens GR-115 27)

Netherlands (Map p108; ☎ 210 723 9701; Leoforos Vasileos Konstantinou 5-7, Athens GR-106 74)

New Zealand (☎ 210 687 4701; Kifisias 268, Halandri, Athens 152 26)

Turkey Athens (Map pp114-15; ☎ 210 724 5915; Leoforos Vasileos Georgiou 8, Athens GR-106 74); Thessaloniki (Map pp284-5; ☎ 23102 48452; Agiou Dimitriou 151, Thessaloniki)

UK Athens (Map pp114-15; ☎ 210 723 6211; Ploutarhou 1, Athens GR-106 75); Thessaloniki (Map pp284-5; ☎ 23102 78006; Tsimiski 43, Thessaloniki)

USA Athens (Map pp114-15; ☎ 210 721 2951; Leoforos Vasilissis Sofias 91, Athens GR-115 21); Thessaloniki (Map pp284-5; ☎ 23102 42905; Tsimiski 43, Thessaloniki)

It's important to know what your embassy – the embassy of the country of which you are a citizen – can and can't do to help if you get into trouble. Generally, it won't be much help in emergencies if the trouble you're in is remotely your own fault. Remember that you are bound by the laws of the country you are in. Your embassy will not be sympathetic if you commit a crime locally, even if such actions are legal in your own country.

In genuine emergencies you might get some assistance, but only if other channels have been exhausted. For example, if you need to get home urgently, a free ticket is exceedingly unlikely. If you have all your money and documents stolen, your embassy will usually assist with getting a new passport, but a loan for onward travel is very unlikely.

Some embassies used to keep letters for travellers, but these days the mail holding service has usually been stopped.

FESTIVALS & EVENTS

See the Events Calendar (p23) for the top festivals and events throughout Greece.

FOOD

For large cities and towns, restaurant listings in this book are given in the following order: budget (under €15), midrange (€15 to €40) and top end (over €40). Prices refer to a main dish for one person unless otherwise noted in the review. Within each section the restaurants are listed in budget order. For information on Greek cuisine, see p76.

GAY & LESBIAN TRAVELLERS

In a country where the Church still plays a prominent role in shaping society's views on issues such as sexuality, it should come as no surprise that homosexuality is generally frowned upon by many locals – especially outside the major cities. While there is no legislation against homosexual activity, it pays to be discreet.

Some areas of Greece are, however, extremely popular destinations for gay and lesbian travellers. Athens has a busy gay scene, but most gay and lesbian travellers head for the islands. Mykonos has long been famous for its bars, beaches and general hedonism, while Skiathos also has its share of gay hang-outs. The island of Lesvos (Mytilini), birthplace of the lesbian poet Sappho, has become something of a place of pilgrimage for lesbians.

Information

The *Spartacus International Gay Guide,* published by Bruno Gmünder (Berlin), is widely regarded as the leading authority on the gay travel scene. The Greek section contains a wealth of information on gay venues everywhere from Alexandroupoli to Xanthi.

DIRECTORY

There is also stacks of information on the internet. **Roz Mov** (www.geocities.com/WestHollywood/2225) has info on gay health, press, organisations, events and legal issues – and links to lots more sites. Also check out **Gayscape** (www.gayscape.com/gays cape/menugreece.html).

HOLIDAYS

Many sites (including the ancient sites in Athens) offer free entry on the first Sunday of the month, with the exception of July and August. You may also gain free entry on other locally celebrated holidays, although this varies across the country.

Public Holidays

All banks and shops and most museums and ancient sites close on public holidays. National public holidays in Greece:

New Year's Day 1 January
Epiphany 6 January
First Sunday in Lent February
Greek Independence Day 25 March
Good Friday March/April
Orthodox Easter Sunday April/May. Orthodox Easter Sunday falls on 4 April in 2010, 24 April in 2011 and 15 April 2012.
Easter; most sights stay open
May Day (Protomagia) 1 May
Whit Monday (Agiou Pnevmatos) May/June/July; 50 days after Easter Sunday. Schools and offices close but museums, major sites and shops usually stay open.
Feast of the Assumption 15 August
Ohi Day 28 October
Christmas Day 25 December
St Stephen's Day 26 December

School Holidays

The school year is divided into three terms. The main school holidays are in July and August.

INSURANCE

A travel insurance policy to cover theft, loss and medical problems is a good idea. Some policies offer lower and higher medical-expense options; the higher ones are chiefly for countries such as the USA, which have extremely high medical costs. There is a wide variety of policies available, so check the small print.

Some policies specifically exclude 'dangerous activities', which can include scuba diving, motorcycling and even hiking. A locally acquired motorcycle licence is not valid under some policies.

You may prefer a policy that pays doctors or hospitals directly rather than requiring you to pay on the spot and claim later. If you have to claim later make sure you keep all documentation. Some policies ask you to call back (reverse charges) to a centre in your home country where an immediate assessment of your problem is made. For more information on health insurance, see p764.

Paying for your ticket with a credit card sometimes provides limited travel insurance, and you may be able to reclaim the payment if the operator doesn't deliver. In the UK, for instance, credit card providers are required by law to reimburse consumers if a company goes into liquidation and the amount in contention is more than UK£100.

Buy travel insurance as early as possible. If you buy it just before you fly, you may find you're not covered for such problems as delays caused by industrial action. Worldwide travel insurance is available at www.lonelyplanet .com/travel_services. You can buy, extend and claim online anytime – even if you're already on the road.

INTERNET ACCESS

Greece has long since embraced the convenience of the internet. There has been a huge increase in the number hotels and businesses using the internet, and where available, websites are listed throughout this book. For a selection of useful websites about Greece, see p22.

Internet cafes are everywhere, and are listed under the Information section for cities and islands where available. Many hotels also offer internet and wi-fi access, although hot spots are often located in the lobby rather than in your room. You'll also find many cafes offering wi-fi.

LEGAL MATTERS
Arrests

It is a good idea to have your passport with you at all times in case you are stopped by the police and questioned. Greek citizens are presumed to always have identification on them; foreign visitors are similarly presumed to by the police. If you are arrested by police insist on an interpreter (*the*-lo dhi-ermi-*nea*) and/or a lawyer (*the*-lo dhi-ki-*go*-ro). Travellers should also note that they can be prosecuted under the law of their home country regarding age of consent, even when abroad.

Drugs

Greek drug laws are the strictest in Europe. Greek courts make no distinction between possession and pushing. Possession of even a small amount of marijuana is likely to land you in jail.

MAPS

Unless you are going to hike or drive, the free maps given out by the EOT will probably suffice, although they are not 100% accurate. On islands where there is no EOT office, there are usually tourist maps for sale for around €1.50 but, again, these are not very accurate, particularly maps of towns and villages.

The best overall maps for coverage are published by the Greek company **Road Editions** (☎ 210 345 5575; www.road.gr; Kozanis 21, cnr Amfipoleos, Votanikos, Athens), whose maps are produced with the assistance of the Hellenic Army Geographical Service. There is a wide range of maps to suit various needs, starting with a 1:500,000 map of Greece. Motorists should check out the company's 1:250,000 series covering Thrace, Macedonia, Thessaly and Epiros, Central Greece, the Peloponnese and Crete. Even the smallest roads and villages are clearly marked, and the distance indicators are spot-on – important when negotiating your way around the backblocks. The company also produces a Greek island series and a Greek mountain series, which is essential for any serious hiking.

Hikers should also consider the *Topo* series published by **Anavasi** (☎ 210 321 8104; www.mountains.gr; Stoa Arsakiou 6a, Athens), with durable plasticised paper and detailed walking trails for many of the Aegean islands. **Emvelia** (☎ 210 771 7616; www.emvelia.gr; Navarinou 12, Athens) publishes detailed maps, including some excellent plans of the region's main towns, each with a handy index booklet. All maps can be bought online or at major bookstores in Greece.

MONEY

Greece has been using the euro currency since the beginning of 2002. There are eight euro coins, in denominations of two and one euros, then 50, 20, 10, five, two and one cents, and six notes: €5, €10, €20, €50, €100 and €200.

See inside the front cover for currency exchange rates and p19 for information on costs in Greece.

ATMs

ATMs are found in every town large enough to support a bank and in almost all the tourist areas. If you've got MasterCard or Visa, there are plenty of places to withdraw money. Cirrus and Maestro users can make withdrawals in all major towns and tourist areas. Be warned that many card companies can put an automatic block on your card after your first withdrawal abroad as an antifraud mechanism. To avoid this happening, inform your bank of your travel plans. Also be aware that many ATMs on the islands can lose their connection for a day or two at a time, making it impossible for anyone (locals included) to withdraw money. It's useful to have a backup source of money.

Automated foreign-exchange machines are common in major tourist areas. They take all the major European currencies, Australian and US dollars and Japanese yen, and are useful in an emergency, although they charge a hefty commission.

Cash

Nothing beats cash for convenience – or for risk. If you lose cash, it's gone for good and very few travel insurers will come to your rescue. Those that will, normally limit the amount to approximately US$300. It's best to carry no more cash than you need for the next few days. It's also a good idea to set aside a small amount of cash, say US$100, as an emergency stash.

Note that Greek shopkeepers and small-business owners have a perennial problem with having any small change. If buying small items it is better to tender coins or small-denomination notes.

Credit Cards

The great advantage of credit cards is that they allow you to pay for major items without carrying around great wads of cash. Credit cards are now an accepted part of the commercial scene in Greece, although they're often not accepted on many of the smaller islands or in small villages. In larger places, credit cards can be used at top-end hotels, restaurants and shops. Some C-class hotels will accept credit cards, but D- and E-class hotels rarely do.

The main credit cards are MasterCard and Visa, both of which are widely accepted in Greece. They can also be used as cash cards to draw cash from the ATMs of affiliated Greek banks in the same way as at home. Daily withdrawal limits are set by the issuing bank and are given in local currency only. American Express and Diners Club are widely accepted in tourist areas but unheard of elsewhere.

Tipping

In restaurants a service charge is normally included in the bill, and while a tip is not expected (as it is in North America), it is always appreciated and should be left if the service has been good. Taxi drivers normally expect you to round up the fare, while bellhops who help you with your luggage to your hotel room or stewards on ferries who take you to your cabin normally expect a small gratuity of between €1 and €3.

Travellers Cheques

The main reason to carry travellers cheques rather than cash is the protection they offer against theft. They are, however, losing popularity as more and more travellers opt to put their money in a bank at home and withdraw it at ATMs as they go.

American Express, Visa and Thomas Cook cheques are available in euros and are all widely accepted and have efficient replacement policies. Maintaining a record of the cheque numbers and recording when you use them is vital when it comes to replacing lost cheques – keep this separate from the cheques themselves.

PHOTOGRAPHY & VIDEO

Digital photography has taken over in a big way in Greece and a range of memory cards can now be bought from camera stores. Film is still widely available, although it can be expensive in smaller towns. You'll find all the gear you need in the photography shops of Athens and major cities.

It is possible to obtain video cassettes in larger towns and cities, but be sure to buy the correct format. It is usually worth buying at least a few cassettes duty-free to start off your trip.

Restrictions & Etiquette

Never photograph a military installation or anything else that has a sign forbidding photography. Flash photography is not allowed inside churches, and it's considered taboo to photograph the main altar.

Greeks usually love having their photos taken but always ask permission first. The same goes for video cameras, probably even more annoying and offensive for locals than a still camera.

At archaeological sites you will be stopped from using a tripod as it marks you as a 'professional'.

POST

Tahydromia (post offices) are easily identifiable by the yellow signs outside. Regular post boxes are also yellow and may be labelled *esoteriko* for domestic and *exoteriko* for overseas. The red boxes are for express mail only.

Postal Rates

The postal rate for postcards and airmail letters up to 20g is €0.60 to Europe and €0.80 to North America and Australasia. Post within Europe takes between three and seven days; to the USA, Australia and New Zealand it takes five to 12 days. Express service *(katepiogonda)* costs about €3 and shaves a couple of days off. Some tourist shops and kiosks also sell stamps, but with a 10% surcharge.

Parcels can often only be sent from main towns and cities. In Athens, parcels weighing over 2kg should be taken to the parcel post office (p107); elsewhere, take it to the parcel counter of a regular post office. You must leave the box open for inspection; bring your own tape to shut it as it's not usually sold at post offices.

Receiving Mail

You can receive mail by poste restante (general delivery) at any main post office. The service is free, but you are required to show your passport. Ask senders to write your family name in capital letters and underline it, and also to mark the envelope 'poste restante'. It is a good idea to ask the post office clerk to check under your first name as well if letters you are expecting cannot be located. After one month, uncollected mail is returned to the sender. If you are about to leave a town and expected mail hasn't arrived, ask at the post office to have it forwarded to your next destination, c/o poste restante. In Athens, both Athens Central post office (p107) and Syntagma post office (p107) hold poste restante mail.

Parcels are not delivered in Greece; they must be collected from the parcel counter of a post office.

SHOPPING

Shopping is big business in Greece. At times a tourist town can look like one big shop with all kinds of goods and trinkets on display. Shops and kiosks in major tourist centres are often overpriced and it's often better to find out where the locals shop. That said, Athens' flea market (p151) has a bewildering array of items on sale and you can find some good bargains. Throughout Greece, shoes and clothes are often excellent buys, especially in post-seasonal sales. If you have room in your suitcase or backpack there are some really excellent quality artisanal works to be picked up from small boutiques and galleries, including pottery, jewellery and metalworked *objets*.

Bargaining

Getting a bit extra off the deal through bargaining is sadly a thing of the past in Greece. You might be offered a 'special deal' but the art and sport of bargaining per se has gone the way of the drachma. Instead, know your goods and decide for yourself if the price you are being offered is worth it before accepting the deal.

SMOKING

In July 2009 Greece brought in antismoking laws similar to those found throughout most of Europe. Smoking is now banned inside public places, with the penalty being fines placed on the business owners. Greece is home to some of the heaviest smokers in Europe, so it will be a challenge for these laws to be enforced and many believe they will be imposed in only a nominal way in remote locations.

SOLO TRAVELLERS

Greece is a great destination for solo travellers, especially in summer when the Greek islands become an international meeting point. Hostels and other backpacker-friendly accommodation are good places to meet up with other solo travellers. Dining solo in restaurants is not an issue with restaurant owners and there are no real disadvantages to travelling solo – other than that you are unlikely to stay solo for long.

TELEPHONE

The Greek telephone service is maintained by the public corporation known as OTE (pronounced o-*teh*; Organismos Tilepikoinonion Ellados).

The system is modern and reasonably well maintained. There are public telephones just about everywhere, including in some unbelievably isolated spots. The phones are easy to operate and can be used for local, long-distance and international calls. The 'i' at the top left of the push-button dialling panel brings up the operating instructions in English.

Note that in Greece the area code must always be dialled when making a call (ie all Greek phone numbers are 10-digit).

Mobile Phones

The number of mobile phones in Greece now exceeds the number of landline phones. If you have a compatible GSM mobile phone from a country with an overseas global roaming arrangement with Greece, you will be able to use your phone in Greece. You may need to inform your mobile phone service provider before you depart in order to have global roaming activated. US and Canadian mobile phone users won't be able to use their mobile phones, unless their handset is equipped with a dual- or tri-band system.

There are several mobile service providers in Greece, among which Panafon, CosmOTE and Wind are the best known. All offer 2G connectivity. Of these three, CosmOTE tends to have the best coverage in remote areas, so try retuning your phone to CosmOTE if you find mobile coverage is patchy. All three companies offer pay-as-you-talk services by which you can buy a rechargeable SIM card and have your own Greek mobile number. The Panafon system is called 'à la Carte', the Wind system 'F2G' and the CosmOTE system 'Cosmokarta'.

Note: the use of a mobile phone while driving in Greece is prohibited, but the use of a Bluetooth headset is allowed.

Phonecards

All public phones use OTE phonecards, known as *telekarta*, not coins. These cards are widely available at *periptera*, corner shops and tourist shops. A local call costs around €0.30 for three minutes.

It's also possible to use payphones with the growing range of discount-card schemes. This involves dialling an access code and then punching in your card number. The OTE version of this card is known as 'Hronokarta'. The cards come with instructions in Greek and English and the talk time is enormous compared to the standard phonecard rates.

TIME

Greece maintains one time zone throughout the country. It is two hours ahead of GMT/UTC and three hours ahead on daylight-saving time – which begins on the last Sunday in March, when clocks are put forward one hour. Daylight saving ends on the last Sunday in October.

TOILETS

Most places in Greece have Western-style toilets, especially hotels and restaurants that cater for tourists. You'll occasionally come across Asian-style squat toilets in older houses, *kafeneia* (coffee houses) and public toilets.

Public toilets are a rarity, except at airports and bus and train stations. Cafes are the best option if you get caught short, but you'll be expected to buy something for the privilege.

One peculiarity of the Greek plumbing system is that it can't handle toilet paper; apparently the pipes are too narrow. Whatever the reason, anything larger than a postage stamp seems to cause a problem; flushing away tampons and sanitary napkins is guaranteed to block the system. Toilet paper etc should be placed in the small bin provided next to every toilet.

TOURIST INFORMATION

Tourist information is handled by the Greek National Tourist Organisation, known by the initials GNTO abroad and EOT within Greece. The quality of service from office to office varies dramatically.

Local Tourist Offices

The EOT in Athens dispenses information, including a very useful timetable of the week's ferry departures from Piraeus, and details about public transport prices and schedules from Athens. Its free map of Athens is urgently in need of an update, although most places of interest are clearly marked. The office is about 500m from Ambelokipi metro station.

EOT offices can be found in major tourist locations, though they are increasingly being supplemented or even replaced by local municipality tourist offices (such as in the Peloponnese).

Athens (Map pp110–11; ☎ 210 331 0392; www.gnto .gr; Leoforos Vasilissis Amalias 26a, Syntagma; ⏰ 9am–7pm Mon-Fri, 10am-4pm Sat & Sun) See also p107.

Crete (Map p462; ☎ 2810 246 299; Xanthoudidou, Iraklio; ⏰ 8.30am-8.30pm Apr-Oct, 8.30am-3pm Nov-Mar) See also p463.

Dodecanese (Map p517; ☎ 22410 35226; www.ando .gr; cnr Makariou & Papagou, Rhodes Town, Rhodes; ⏰ 8am-2.45pm Mon-Fri) See also p516.

Ionian Islands (Map p696; ☎ 26710 22248; Argostoli, Kefallonia; ⏰ 8am-8pm Mon-Fri & 9am-3pm Sat Jul-Aug, 8am-2.30pm Mon-Fri) See also p695.

Macedonia (Office of Tourism Directorate; Map pp284–5; ☎ 2310 221 100; tour-the@otenet.gr; Tsimiski 136, Thessaloniki; ⏰ 8am-8pm Mon-Fri, 8am-2pm Sat) See also p286.

Northeastern Aegean Islands (Map p618; ☎ 22510 42512; Aristarhou 6, Mytilini Town, Lesvos; ⏰ 9am-1pm Mon-Fri) See also p619.

Peloponnese (Info Center; Map p171; ☎ 2610 461 740/1; www.infocenterpatras.gr; Othonos Amalias 6, Patra; ⏰ 8am-10pm) See also p170.

Tourist Police

The tourist police work in cooperation with the regular Greek police and the EOT. Each tourist police office has at least one member of staff who speaks English. Hotels, restaurants, travel agencies, tourist shops, tourist guides, waiters, taxi drivers and bus drivers all come under the jurisdiction of the tourist police. If you think that you have been ripped off by any of these, report it to the tourist police and they will investigate. If you need to report a theft or loss of passport, then go to the tourist police first, and they will act as interpreters between you and the regular police. The tourist police also fulfil the same functions as the EOT and municipal tourist offices, dispensing maps and brochures, and giving information on transport. They can often help to find accommodation.

TRAVELLERS WITH DISABILITIES

Access for travellers with disabilities has improved somewhat in recent years, largely thanks to the Olympics. Improvements are mostly restricted to Athens, where there are more accessible sights, hotels and restaurants. Much of the rest of Greece remains inaccessible to wheelchairs, and the abundance of stones, marble, slippery cobbles and stepped alleys creates a further challenge. Visually or hearing impaired people are also rarely catered to.

Careful planning before you go can make a world of difference. The British-based **Royal Association for Disability & Rehabilitation** (Radar;

☎ 020 7250 3222; www.radar.org.uk; 12 City Forum, 250 City Rd, London EC1V 8AF) publishes a useful guide called *Holidays & Travel Abroad: A Guide for Disabled People,* which gives a good overview of facilities available to travellers with disabilities in Europe. Also check out www.greecetravel.com/handicapped for links to local articles, resorts and tour groups catering to physically disabled tourists. Some options:

Christianakis Travel (www.greecetravel.com/handi capped/christianakis/index.htm) Creates tailor-made itineraries and can organise transportation, hotels and guides.

Sailing Holidays (www.charterayachtingreece.com /DRYachting/index.html) Two-day to two-week sailing trips around the Greek islands in fully accessible yachts.

Sirens Resort (www.hotelsofgreece.com/central/ loutraki/sirens-wheelchair-accessable-resort/index. html; Loutraki, Skaloma, Central Greece) Family-friendly resort with accessible apartments, tours and ramps into the sea.

VISAS

The list of countries whose nationals can stay in Greece for up to three months without a visa includes Australia, Canada, all EU countries, Iceland, Israel, Japan, New Zealand, Norway, Switzerland and the USA. Other countries included are the European principalities of Monaco and San Marino and most South American countries. The list changes – contact Greek embassies for the full list. Those not included can expect to pay about US$20 for a three-month visa.

Visa Extensions

If you wish to stay in Greece for longer than three months, apply at a consulate abroad or at least 20 days in advance at the **Aliens Bureau** (Map pp114–15; ☎ 210 770 5711; Leoforos Alexandras 173, Ambelokipi, Athens; ☾ 8am–1pm Mon–Fri) in the Athens Central Police Station. Take your passport and four passport photographs along. You may be asked for proof that you can support yourself financially, so keep all your bank exchange slips (or the equivalent from a post office). These slips are not always automatically given – you may have to ask for them. Elsewhere in Greece apply to the local police authority. You will be given a permit that will authorise you to stay in the country for a period of up to six months.

Many travellers get around the need for an extension by visiting Bulgaria or Turkey briefly and then re-entering Greece. If you overstay your visa, you will be slapped with a huge fine upon leaving the country.

WOMEN TRAVELLERS

Many women travel alone in Greece. The crime rate remains relatively low and solo travel is probably safer than in most European countries. This does not mean that you should be lulled into complacency; bag snatching and rapes do occur, particularly at party resorts on the islands.

The biggest nuisance to foreign women travelling alone is the guys the Greeks have nicknamed *kamaki.* The word means 'fishing trident' and refers to the *kamaki's* favourite pastime: 'fishing' for foreign women. You'll find them everywhere there are lots of tourists: young (for the most part), smooth-talking guys who aren't in the least bashful about sidling up to women in the street. They can be very persistent, but they are usually a hassle rather than a threat. The majority of Greek men treat foreign women with respect, and are genuinely helpful.

WORKING

EU nationals don't need a work permit, but they need a residency permit and a Greek tax file number if they intend to stay longer than three months. Nationals of other countries are supposed to have a work permit.

Bar & Hostel Work

The bars of the Greek islands could not survive without foreign workers and there are thousands of summer jobs up for grabs every year. The pay is not fantastic, but you get to spend a summer in the islands. April and May are the times to go looking. Hostels and travellers hotels are other places that regularly employ foreign workers.

English Tutoring

If you're looking for a permanent job, the most widely available option is to teach English. A TEFL (Teaching English as a Foreign Language) certificate or a university degree is an advantage but not essential. In the UK, look through the *Times* educational supplement or Tuesday's edition of the *Guardian* newspaper for opportunities; in other countries, contact the Greek embassy.

Another possibility is to find a job teaching English once you are in Greece. You will see language schools everywhere. Strictly speaking, you need a licence to teach in these schools, but many will employ teachers without one. The best time to look around for such a job is late summer.

The noticeboard at the Compendium in Athens (p106) sometimes has advertisements looking for private English lessons.

Street Performance

The richest pickings are found on the islands, particularly Mykonos, Paros and Santorini. Plaka is the place to go in Athens; the area outside the church on Kydathineon is the most popular spot.

Volunteer Work

There are lots of opportunities to volunteer in Greece. Here are a few of the options:

Earth Sea & Sky (www.earthseasky.org) Conservation and research based in the Ionian Islands.

Hellenic Society for the Study & Protection of the Monk Seal (Map pp112-13; ☎ 210 522 2888; fax 210 522 2450; Solomou 53, Exarhia, Athens) Volunteers are used for monitoring programs on the Ionian Islands.

Hellenic Wildlife Hospital (Elliniko Kentro Perithalpsis Agrion Zoön; ☎ 22970 28367; www.ekpaz.gr, in Greek; ⏰ 10am-7pm) Welcomes volunteers in Aegina, particularly during the winter months. For more information see p360.

Sea Turtle Protection Society of Greece (Map pp112-13; ☎ /fax 210 523 1342; www.archelon.gr; Solomou 57, Exarhia, Athens) Monitor turtles on the Peloponnese.

WWOOF (World Wide Opportunities on Organic Farms; www.wwoof.org/independents.asp) Volunteer at one of around 35 farms in Greece.

Other Work

There are often jobs advertised in the classifieds of English-language newspapers, or you can place an advertisement yourself if you wish. EU nationals can also make use of the Organismos Apasholiseos Ergatikou Dynamikou (OAED), which is the Greek National Employment Service, in their search for employment. The OAED has offices throughout the country.

Seasonal harvest work is handled by migrant workers from Albania and other Balkan nations, and is no longer a viable option for travellers.

Transport

GETTING THERE & AWAY

Flights, tours and rail tickets can be booked online at www.lonelyplanet.com/travel_services.

ENTERING THE COUNTRY

Visitors to Greece with EU passports are rarely afforded more than a cursory glance. If entering from another EU nation passports are not checked, but customs and police may be interested in what you are carrying. EU citizens may also enter Greece on a national identity card.

Passports

Visitors from outside the EU usually require a visa. This must be checked with consular authorities before you arrive. For visa requirements, see p723.

AIR

Most visitors to Greece arrive by air, which tends to be the fastest and cheapest option, if not the most environmentally friendly.

Airports & Airlines

Greece has three main international airports that take chartered and scheduled flights.
Athens (Eleftherios Venizelos International Airport; code ATH; ☎ 210 353 0000; www.aia.gr)

Iraklio (Nikos Kazantzakis International Airport, Crete; code HER; ☎ 2810 228401)
Rhodes (Diagoras Airport, Dodecanese; code RHO; ☎ 22410 83222)
Thessaloniki (Macedonia International Airport, Northern Greece; code SKG; ☎ 2310 473 700)

Many of Greece's other international airports, including Rhodes, Corfu, Crete and Mykonos, have begun taking scheduled international flights with easyJet. Kos and Araxos also take direct flights from Germany. Other international airports across the country include Santorini, Karpathos, Samos, Skiathos, Hrysoupoli, Aktion, Kefallonia and Zakynthos. These airports are most often used for charter flights from the UK, Germany and Scandinavia.

AIRLINES FLYING TO/FROM GREECE

Olympic Air (OA; ☎ 801 114 4444; www.olympicairlines.com) is the country's national airline with the majority of flights to and from Athens. Olympic flies direct between Athens and destinations throughout Europe, as well as to Cairo, İstanbul, Tel Aviv, New York and Toronto.
Aegean Airlines (A3; ☎ 801 112 0000; www.aegeanair.com) has flights to and from destinations in Spain, Germany and Italy as well as to Paris, London, Cairo and İstanbul. The safety record of both airlines is exemplary. The contact details for local Olympic and Aegean offices are listed throughout the book.

Other airlines with offices in Athens:
Aeroflot (code SU; ☎ 210 322 0986; www.aeroflot.org)
Air Berlin (AB; ☎ 210 353 5264; www.airberlin.com)

THINGS CHANGE...

The information in this chapter is particularly vulnerable to change. Check directly with the airline or a travel agent to make sure you understand how a fare (and ticket you may buy) works and be aware of the security requirements for international travel. Shop carefully. The details given in this chapter should be regarded as pointers and are not a substitute for your own careful, up-to-date research.

CLIMATE CHANGE & TRAVEL

Climate change is a serious threat to the ecosystems that humans rely upon, and air travel is the fastest-growing contributor to the problem. Lonely Planet regards travel, overall, as a global benefit, but believes we all have a responsibility to limit our personal impact on global warming.

Flying & Climate Change

Pretty much every form of motor travel generates CO_2 (the main cause of human-induced climate change) but planes are far and away the worst offenders, not just because of the sheer distances they allow us to travel, but because they release greenhouse gases high into the atmosphere. The statistics are frightening: two people taking a return flight between Europe and the US will contribute as much to climate change as an average household's gas and electricity consumption over a whole year.

Carbon Offset Schemes

Climatecare.org and other websites use 'carbon calculators' that allow jetsetters to offset the greenhouse gases they are responsible for with contributions to energy-saving projects and other climate-friendly initiatives in the developing world – including projects in India, Honduras, Kazakhstan and Uganda.

Lonely Planet, together with Rough Guides and other concerned partners in the travel industry, supports the carbon offset scheme run by climatecare.org. Lonely Planet offsets all of its staff and author travel.

For more information check out our website: lonelyplanet.com.

Air Canada (AC; ☎ 210 617 5321; www.aircanada.ca)
Air France (AF; ☎ 210 353 0380; www.airfrance.com)
Alitalia (AZ; ☎ 210 353 4284; www.alitalia.it)
American Airlines (AA; ☎ 210 331 1045; www.aa.com)
British Airways (BA; ☎ 210 890 6666; www.british airways.com)
Cyprus Airways (CY; ☎ 210 372 2722; www.cyprusair .com.cy)
Delta Airlines (DL; ☎ 210 331 1660; www.delta.com)
easyJet (U2; ☎ 210 967 0000; www.easyjet.com)
EgyptAir (MS; ☎ 210 353 1272; www.egyptair.com.eg)
El Al (LY; ☎ 210 353 1003; www.elal.co.il)
Emirates Airlines (EK; ☎ 210 933 3400; www .emirates.com)
Gulf Air (GF; ☎ 210 322 0851; www.gulfairco.com)
Iberia (IB; ☎ 210 323 4523; www.iberia.com)
Japan Airlines (JL; ☎ 210 324 8211; www.jal.co.jp)
KLM (KL; ☎ 210 353 1295; www.klm.com)
Lufthansa (LH; ☎ 210 617 5200; www.lufthansa.com)
Qatar Airways (QR; ☎ 210 950 8700; www.qatarair ways.com)
SAS (SK; ☎ 210 361 3910; www.sas.se)
Singapore Airlines (SQ; ☎ 210 372 8000, 210 353 1259; www.singaporeair.com)
Thai Airways (TG; ☎ 210 353 1237; www.thaiairways .com)
Turkish Airlines (TK; ☎ 210 322 1035; www.turkish airlines.com)
Virgin Express (TV; ☎ 210 949 0777; www.virgin xpress.com)

Tickets

Purchasing airline tickets has never been easier. Most airlines sell tickets online, offering good deals and eliminating the fear of losing your precious ticket while on holiday. Airlines will also text or email you with any changes to the flight. EasyJet offers some of the cheapest tickets between Greece and the rest of Europe and covers a huge range of destinations. If you're coming from outside Europe, consider a cheap flight to a European hub like London and then an onward ticket with easyJet. Some airlines also offer cheap deals to students. If you're planning to travel between June and September, it's wise to book ahead.

Asia

Most Asian countries offer fairly competitive deals, with Bangkok, Singapore and Hong Kong the best places to shop around for discount tickets.

Khao San Rd in Bangkok is the budget travellers' headquarters. Bangkok has a number of excellent travel agencies, but there are also some suspect ones; ask the advice of other travellers. **STA Travel** (☎ 02-236 0262; www.statravel .co.th) is a good place to start.

In Singapore, **STA Travel** (☎ 6737 7188; www .statravel.com.sg) offers competitive discount fares for most destinations. Singapore, like

Bangkok, has hundreds of travel agencies to choose from, so it is possible to compare prices. Chinatown Point shopping centre on New Bridge Rd has a good selection of travel agencies.

In Hong Kong, **Four Seas Tours** (☎ 2200 7760; www.fourseastravel.com) is recommended, as is **Shoestring Travel** (☎ 2723 2306; www.shoestring travel.com.hk).

Australia

STA Travel (☎ 1300 733 035; www.statravel.com.au) has its main office in Melbourne but also has offices in all major cities and on many university campuses. Call for the location of your nearest branch. **Flight Centre** (☎ 13 16 00; www.flightcentre .com.au) has its central office in Sydney and dozens of offices throughout Australia.

Qantas no longer flies direct to Athens, but you could fly via London with a British Airways connection to Athens. Thai Airways and Singapore Airlines both have convenient connections to Athens as do three of the Persian Gulf airlines – Emirates, Gulf and Qatar Airways. If you're planning on doing a bit of flying around Europe, it's worth looking around for special deals from the major European airlines, including KLM and Lufthansa.

Canada

Canada's national student travel agency is **Travel CUTS** (☎ 800 667 2887; www.travelcuts.com), which has offices in all major cities. **Flight Centre** (☎ 1 877 967 5302; www.flightcentre.ca) has offices in most major cities and offers discounted tickets. For online bookings go to www.expedia.ca or www.travelocity.ca.

Olympic Air has flights from Toronto to Athens via Montreal. There are no direct flights from Vancouver, but there are connecting flights via Toronto, Amsterdam, Frankfurt and London on Air Canada, KLM, Lufthansa and British Airways.

Continental Europe

Athens is linked to every major city in Europe by either Olympic Air or the flag carrier of each country. Amsterdam, Frankfurt, Berlin and Paris are all major centres for cheap airfares.

France has a network of travel agencies that can supply discount tickets to travellers of all ages. They include **OTU Voyages** (☎ 01 40 29 12 22), which has branches across the country. Other recommendations include

Voyageurs du Monde (☎ 01 40 15 11 15; www.vdm .com) and **Nouvelles Frontières** (☎ 0825 000 747; www.nouvelles-frontieres.fr).

In Germany, **STA Travel** (☎ 01805 456 422; www .statravel.de) has several offices around the country. For online fares, try **Expedia** (☎ 0180 500 6025; www.expedia.de).

In Denmark, **My Travel** (☎ 7010 2111; www .mytravel.dk) and in the Netherlands, **Airfair** (☎ 020-620 5121; www.airfair.nl) are recommended.

Cyprus

Olympic Air and Cyprus Airways share the Cyprus–Greece routes. Both airlines have flights between Larnaca and Athens, as well as to Thessaloniki. Cyprus Airways also flies between Pafos and Athens once daily while Olympic has two flights weekly between Larnaca and Iraklio.

Turkey

Olympic Air, Aegean Airlines and Turkish Airlines all fly between İstanbul and Athens. There are no direct flights from Ankara to Athens; all flights go via İstanbul.

UK

Discount air travel is big business in London. Advertisements for many travel agencies appear in the travel pages of the weekend broadsheet newspapers, in *Time Out*, the *Evening Standard* and the free magazine *TNT*.

STA Travel (☎ 0871 230 0040; www.statravel.co.uk) has discounted tickets for students and travellers under 26, while **Flight Centre** (☎ 0870 499 0040; www.flightcentre.co.uk) offers competitive rates and also has deals for students. Both agencies have offices in most cities. Other recommended travel agencies in London include **Trailfinders** (☎ 020 7938 3939; www.trailfinders.co.uk), **Travel Bag** (☎ 0870 814 6614; www.travelbag.co.uk) and **ebookers** (☎ 0800 082 3000; www.ebookers.com). Online, check out www.charterflights.co.uk and www.cheapflights.co.uk.

The cheapest scheduled flights are with **easyJet** (☎ 0871 750 0100; www.easyjet.com), the no-frills specialist, which has flights from Luton and Gatwick to Athens. Pricing varies wildly depending on departure days and times. See the website for current rates.

Greece's two main airlines have regular flights between the UK and Athens and offer good deals for online booking. **Olympic Air** (www.olympicairlines.com) has services from Manchester, Heathrow and Gatwick while

Aegean Airlines (www.aegeanair.com) operates flights from Heathrow, Stansted and Manchester. From Athens, you can connect with domestic flights to reach the islands.

USA

STA Travel (☎ 800 781 4040; www.statravel.com) has offices in most major cities that have a university. For online bookings try www .cheaptickets.com, www.expedia.com and www.orbitz.com.

New York has the widest range of options to Athens. The route to Europe is very competitive and there are new deals almost every day. Olympic Air and Delta Airlines both have direct flights but there are numerous other connecting flights.

While there are no direct flights to Athens from the west coast, there are connecting flights to Athens from many US cities, either linking with Olympic Air in New York or flying with one of the European national airlines to their home country, and then on to Athens.

LAND

Travelling by land offers you the chance to really appreciate the landscape, as well as the many experiences that go along with train or bus travel. International train travel, in particular, has become much more feasible in recent years with speedier trains and better connections. You can now travel from London to Athens by train and ferry in less than two days. By choosing to travel on the ground instead of the air, you'll also be reducing your carbon footprint. It's a win-win situation.

Border Crossings
ALBANIA
There are four crossing points between Greece and Albania. The main one is at Kakavia, 60km northwest of Ioannina (see p340), and it can have intensely slow queues. The other crossings are at Sagiada, 28km north of Igoumenitsa; Mertziani, 17km west of Konitsa; and Krystallopigi, 14km west of Kotas on the Florina–Kastoria road.

BULGARIA
There are three Bulgarian border crossings: one located at Promahonas, 109km northeast of Thessaloniki and 41km from Serres; one at Ormenio in northeastern Thrace; and a new 448m tunnel border crossing at Exohi, 50km

north of Drama. As Bulgaria is part of the EU, crossings are usually quick and hassle free.

FORMER YUGOSLAV REPUBLIC OF MACEDONIA (FYROM)
There are three border crossings between Greece and FYROM. These are at Evzoni, 68km north of Thessaloniki; Niki (p317), 16km north of Florina; and Doïrani, 31km north of Kilkis. A new crossing at Markova Noga, near Agios Germanos, was being discussed at the time of research.

TURKEY
The crossing points are at Kipi, 43km east of Alexandroupoli, and at Kastanies (p333), 139km northeast of Alexandroupoli. Kipi is probably more convenient if you're heading for İstanbul, but the route through Kastanies goes via the fascinating towns of Soufli and Didymotiho in Greece, and Edirne (ancient Adrianoupolis) in Turkey.

Albania
BUS
The **Greek Railways Organisation** (OSE; www.ose .gr) operates a daily bus between Athens and Tirana via Ioannina and Gjirokastra. The bus departs Athens daily from Sidiridromou 1 near the Larisis train station, arriving in Tirana the following day.

See Florina (p317) and Ioannina (p340) for alternative public transport options to Albania.

Bulgaria
BUS
The OSE operates a bus from Athens to Sofia (15 hours, six weekly). It also operates Thessaloniki–Sofia buses (7½ hours, four daily). There is a private bus service to Plovdiv (six hours, twice weekly) and Sofia (seven hours, twice weekly) from Alexandroupoli.

TRAIN
There is a daily train to Sofia from Athens (18 hours) via Thessaloniki (nine hours). From Sofia, there are connections to Budapest and Bucharest.

Former Yugoslav Republic of Macedonia (FYROM)
TRAIN
There are two trains daily from Thessaloniki to Skopje (five hours), crossing the border

between Idomeni and Gevgelija. They continue from Skopje to the Serbian capital of Belgrade (13 hours).

There are no trains between Florina and FYROM, although there are one or two trains a day to Skopje from Bitola (4½ hours) on the FYROM side of the border.

Russia

TRAIN

There is a summer-only direct weekly train service from Thessaloniki to Moscow (70 hours).

Turkey

BUS

The OSE operates a bus from Athens to İstanbul (22 hours, six weekly), leaving the former Peloponnese train station in Athens in the evening and travelling via Thessaloniki (seven hours) and Alexandroupoli (13 hours). Students qualify for a 20% discount and children under 12 travel for half price. See each city's Getting There & Away sections for information on where to buy tickets.

Buses from İstanbul to Athens leave the Anadolu Terminal (Anatolia Terminal) at the Topkapı *otogar* (bus station).

TRAIN

There are no direct trains between Athens and İstanbul. Travellers must take a train to Thessaloniki and connect with one of two daily services running to the Turkish city. The best option is the Filia–Tostluk Express service, leaving Thessaloniki in the evening (11½ hours) and arriving in İstanbul the next morning. The other service is the indirect Intercity IC90 service to Orestiada from Thessaloniki; passengers for İstanbul change at Pythio on the Greece–Turkey border.

Western Europe

Overland enthusiasts can reach Greece on a fascinating route through the Balkan peninsula, passing through Croatia, Serbia and the Former Yugoslav Republic of Macedonia. If you're keen to reach Greece without taking to the air but fancy a bit more convenience and speed than offered by buses and cars, it's easily done. All you need to do is train it to the western coast of Italy (there are connections throughout most of Europe) and then hop on a ferry to Greece. Not only will you be doing your bit for the earth, but you'll see some gorgeous scenery from your window as well.

A sample itinerary from London would see you catching the Eurostar to Paris and then an overnight sleeper train to Bologna in Italy. From there, a coastal train takes you to Bari where there's an overnight boat to Patra on the Peloponnese. From Patra, it's a 4½-hour train journey to Athens. The journey will land you in Athens within two days of leaving London.

CAR & MOTORCYCLE

Most intending drivers these days drive to an Italian port and take a ferry to Greece. The most convenient port is Venice, with Ancona a close second. The route through Croatia, Serbia and the Former Yugoslav Republic of Macedonia takes, on average, 2½ days from Venice to Athens, whereas a high-speed ferry from Venice to Patra can be completed in around 26 hours. From Patra to Athens is a further 3½ hours' driving.

TRAIN

Reaching Greece by train does take some effort. You cannot buy a single ticket from Western Europe to Greece; instead you'll need multiple tickets to cover the journey. Travel agents can do this for you, or look online at www.raileurope.com.

Greece is part of the Eurail network. Eurail passes can only be bought by residents of non-European countries and are supposed to be purchased before arriving in Europe. They can, however, be bought in Europe as long as your passport proves that you've been here for less than six months. In London, head for the **Rail Europe Travel Centre** (☎ 08705 848 848; 179 Piccadilly). Check the Eurail website (www.eurail .com) for full details of passes and prices.

If you are starting your European travels in Greece, you can buy your Eurail pass from the OSE office at Karolou 1-3 in Athens, and at the stations in Patra and Thessaloniki.

Greece is also part of the Inter-Rail Pass system, available to those who have resided in Europe for six months or more. See the Inter-Rail website (www.interrailnet.com) for details.

SEA

Albania

Corfu-based **Petrakis Lines** (☎ 26610 38690; www .ionian-cruises.com) has daily hydrofoils to the Albanian port of Saranda (25 minutes).

Cyprus & Israel

Passenger services from Greece to Cyprus and Israel have been suspended indefinitely. **Salamis Lines** (www.viamare.com/Salamis) still operates the route, but carries only vehicles and freight.

Italy

There are ferries to Greece from the Italian ports of Ancona, Bari, Brindisi and Venice.

The ferries can get very crowded in summer. If you want to take a vehicle across it's wise to make a reservation beforehand. In the UK, reservations can be made on almost all of these ferries through **Viamare Travel Ltd** (☎ 020-7431 4560; www.viam are.com).

You'll find all the latest information about ferry routes, schedules and services online at www.greekferries.gr. Main ferry companies serving Italy include Agoudimos Lines, ANEK Lines, Blue Star Ferries, Hellenic Seaways, Minoan Lines, Superfast Ferries and Ventouris Ferries. For contact details in Greece and websites, see Island Hopping (p739).

The following ferry services are for high season (July and August), and prices are for one-way deck class. On these services, deck class means exactly that. If you want a reclining, aircraft-type seat, you'll be up for another 10% to 15% on top of the listed fares. All companies offer discounts for return travel. Prices are about 30% less in the low season.

ANCONA

In summer there are at least three daily sailings between Ancona and Patra with Superfast Ferries, Minoan Lines and ANEK (€53 to €78, 20 hours). There's also a weekly ferry between Ancona and Corfu (€73, 15 hours).

All ferry operators in Ancona have booths at the *stazione marittima* (ferry terminal) off Piazza Candy, where you can pick up timetables and price lists and make bookings. You can also buy tickets through **Morandi & Co** (☎ 071-20 20 33; Via XXIX Settembre 2/0) or at **ANEK Lines** (☎ 071-207 23 46; Via XXIX Settembre 2/0). Superfast Ferries accepts Eurail passes.

BARI

Superfast Ferries (☎ 080-52 11 416; Corso de Tullio 6) has daily sailings to Patra (€53, 14½ hours) via Corfu (€30, eight hours) and Kefallonia (€45, 14 hours). Eurail passes are accepted.

Ventouris Ferries (☎ 080-52 17 609; www.ventouris .gr; Stazione Marittima) has daily boats to Corfu

(€53, 10 hours) and Igoumenitsa (€53, 11½ hours).

BRINDISI

The trip from Brindisi was once the most popular crossing, but it now operates only between April and early October. **Hellenic Mediterranean Lines** (☎ 0831-54 80 01; Costa Morena) offers services to Patra (€53, 15 hours), calling at Igoumenitsa on the way. It also has services that call at Corfu (€38, six hours), Kefallonia (€51, 12 hours) and Zakynthos (€69 to €99, 15 hours). Eurail passes are accepted.

VENICE

In summer there are up to 12 weekly sailings between Venice and Patra (€70 to €80, approximately 30 hours) with Minoan Lines and ANEK Lines. The boat also calls in at Corfu (€73, 25 hours).

Turkey

There are regular ferry services between Turkey's Aegean coast and the Greek islands. See the boxed text, p596, for more information about these services. Tickets for all ferries to Turkey must be bought a day in advance. You will almost certainly be asked to turn in your passport the night before the trip, but don't worry, you'll get it back the next day before you board the boat. Port tax for departures to Turkey is around €15.

See also the relevant sections under individual island entries in the destination chapter for information on the following services. It's also possible to take a day trip over to Turkey from the Dodecanese; see p556.

CHIOS

There are daily Çeşme–Chios boats from May to October (one-way/return €20/30, 1½ hours).

KOS

There are daily summertime ferries and excursion boats between Kos and Bodrum (€34, one hour). Port tax is extra.

LESVOS

In summer there are daily boats between Lesvos and Dikeli (€10, one hour). There are also daily excursion boats from Greece in the summer (€20 return).

TRANSPORT

RHODES

There is a daily catamaran from Rhodes' Commercial harbour to Marmaris, Turkey (€36, 50 minutes), departing twice daily in summer. There is also a passenger and car ferry service on this same route (car/passenger €95/49 including taxes, 1¼ hours), running four or five times a week in summer. Open return tickets cost €46 plus €29 tax.

SAMOS

There are two boats daily between Kuşadası (for Ephesus) and Samos in summer (€35, 1½ hours). Port tax is extra.

GETTING AROUND

Greece is an easy place to travel around thanks to a comprehensive public transport system. Buses are the mainstay of land transport, with a network that reaches out to the smallest villages. Trains are a good alternative, where available. If you're in a hurry, Greece also has an extensive domestic air network. To most visitors, though, travelling in Greece means island hopping on the multitude of ferries that crisscross the Adriatic and the Aegean. See Island Hopping (p738) for details on ferries and flights between the islands.

AIR

See Island Hopping (p738) for details on flights between the mainland and the islands and between the islands themselves.

The vast majority of domestic mainland flights are handled by the country's national carrier, **Olympic Air** (☎ 801 114 4444; www.olympic airlines.com), and its main competitor **Aegean Airlines** (☎ 801 112 0000; www.aegeanair.com). Both offer competitive rates. Olympic has offices wherever there are flights, as well as in other major towns.

The prices listed in this book are for full-fare economy, and include domestic taxes and charges. There are discounts for return tickets for travel between Monday and Thursday, and bigger discounts for trips that include a Saturday night away. You'll find full details on the airline's website, as well as information on timetables.

The baggage allowance on domestic flights is 15kg, or 20kg if the domestic flight is part of an international journey. Olympic offers a 25% student discount on domestic flights, but only if the flight is part of an international journey.

BICYCLE

Cycling is not popular among Greeks; however, it's gaining kudos with tourists. You'll need strong leg muscles to tackle the mountains or you can stick to some of the flatter coastal routes. Bike lanes are rare to nonexistent and helmets are not compulsory. The island of Kos is about the most bicycle-friendly place in Greece, as is anywhere flat, such as the plains of Thessaly or Thrace. See p711 for more details on cycling in Greece.

Hire

You can hire bicycles in most tourist places, but they are not as widely available as cars and motorcycles. Prices range from €5 to €12 per day, depending on the type and age of the bike.

Purchase

Bicycles are carried free on ferries. You can buy decent mountain or touring bikes in Greece's major towns, though you may have a problem finding a ready buyer if you wish to sell it on. Bike prices are much the same as across the rest of Europe, anywhere from €300 to €2000.

BOAT

See Island Hopping (p738) for details on getting around by boat.

BUS

All long-distance buses, on the mainland and the islands, are operated by regional collectives known as **KTEL** (Koino Tamio Eispraxeon Leoforion; www.ktel.org). Every prefecture on the mainland has a KTEL, which operates local services within the prefecture and to the main towns of other prefectures. Details of inter-urban buses throughout Greece are available by dialling ☎ 14505; at the time of research it was only available in Greek but an English translation was planned.

The bus network is comprehensive. With the exception of towns in Thrace, which are serviced by Thessaloniki, all the major towns on the mainland have frequent connections to Athens. The islands of Corfu, Kefallonia and Zakynthos can also be reached directly from

TRANSPORT

CRUISING

Cruise ships aren't everyone's cup of tea but, not surprisingly, in a country with countless islands and gorgeous azure waters, they're a popular way of seeing Greece. There is something very special about sailing into the colourful harbours of the islands. The upside is you won't have to deal with the fluctuations and general havoc of ferry schedules; you don't have to pre-book or hunt accommodation; and you know everything will be open as the islands take out all the stops when a cruise ship arrives in town.

There are, of course, the downsides. International cruise ships tend to be enormous floating hotels and can easily dwarf a small island. Two thousand passengers disembarking can lead to large queues and crowds. These big boats are also rarely able to dock in the small island harbours and you'll need to wait for your turn on the little boats running guests to shore.

More fitting for the Greek islands are smaller, local cruise ships. We're not talking dinghies – these boats still accommodate 500 to 800 people and have the expected amenities like spas, gyms, shops, bars and pools. They're able to dock in the island harbours and the smaller number of passengers disembarking means you're likely to have a more meaningful experience on the islands.

The most popular Greek cruise line is **Louis Cruises** (☎ 21032 14980; www.louiscruises.com), with a wide range of reasonably priced trips and various types of accommodation. A week-long cruise through the islands and to Turkey starts from €470, while a three-day cruise begins at €175. Booking through a travel agency means you may get a few days in Athens and even a discount flight from Europe tacked on. Try **Fantasy Travel** (www.fantasytravelofgreece.com), **Seafarer Cruises** (www.seafarercruises.com) or **Brendan Tours** (www.brendanvacations.com).

If you opt for the big boys, **Thomas Cook** (www.thomascook.com) has lots of cruises that include the Greek islands, including some family-friendly options. Their smallest boat, the *Calypso*, takes only 486 passengers and is an adult-only liner that visits the Aegean. Seven nights starts from €540 if you book online. **easyCruise** (www.easycruise.com) has three-day cruises from €330. Like the airline, they're cheap and cheerful.

Prices on cruises include meals, port fees and portage but there are often fuel and gratuity charges that are extra. Children often only pay port fees if they bunk in with parents. Excursions are generally additional as well and can range from €40 to €60, depending on what's included. You should be able to go to shore independent of the excursion but double check before you book; some larger cruises dock at distant ports and the only way to reach the destination is by purchasing a place on the tour.

For information on cruising the islands by yacht, see p713.

Athens by bus – the fares include the price of the ferry ticket.

The KTEL buses are safe and modern, and these days most are air conditioned – at least on the major routes. In more-remote rural areas they tend to be older and less comfortable.

Most villages have a daily bus service of some sort, although remote areas may have only one or two buses a week. They operate for the benefit of people going to town to shop, rather than for tourists, and consequently leave the villages very early in the morning and return early in the afternoon.

On islands where the capital is inland rather than a port, buses normally meet boats. Some of the more remote islands have not yet acquired a bus, but most have some sort of motorised transport – even if it is only a bone-shaking, three-wheeled truck.

Larger towns usually have a central, covered bus station with seating, waiting rooms, toilets and a snack bar selling pies, cakes and coffee. It is important to note that big cities like Athens, Iraklio, Patra and Thessaloniki may have more than one bus station, each serving different regions. Make sure you find the correct station for your destination.

In small towns and villages the 'bus station' may be no more than a bus stop outside a *kafeneio* (coffee house) or taverna that doubles as a booking office. In remote areas, the timetable may be in Greek only, but most booking offices have timetables in both Greek and Roman script. The timetables give both the departure and return times – useful if you are making a day trip. Times are listed using the 24-hour clock system.

When you buy a ticket you may be allotted a seat number, which is noted on the ticket. The seat number is indicated on the *back* of each seat of the bus, not on the back of the seat in front; this causes confusion among Greeks and tourists alike. You can board a bus without a ticket and pay on board but, on a popular route or during high season, this may mean that you have to stand. Keep your ticket handy for checking.

It's best to turn up at least 20 minutes before departure to make sure you get a seat, and buses have been known to leave a few minutes before their scheduled departure. Buses on less-frequented routes do not usually have toilets on board and they don't have refreshments available, so make sure you are prepared on both counts. Buses stop about every three hours on long journeys. Smoking is prohibited on all buses in Greece.

Costs

Fares are fixed by the government and bus travel is very reasonably priced. A journey costs approximately €5 per 100km. Some major routes include Athens–Patra (€17, three hours), Athens–Volos (€25, five hours) and Athens–Corfu (€48 including ferry, 9½ hours).

CAR & MOTORCYCLE

No one who has travelled on Greece's roads will be surprised to hear that the country's road fatality rate is the highest in Europe. More than 2000 people die on the roads every year, with overtaking listed as the greatest cause of accidents. Ever-stricter traffic laws have had little impact on the toll; Greek roads remain a good place to practise your defensive-driving techniques.

Heart-stopping moments aside, your own car is a great way to explore off the beaten track. The road network has improved enormously in recent years; many roads marked as dirt tracks on older maps have now been asphalted, particularly in more remote parts of Epiros and the Peloponnese. It's important to get a good road map (for more information, see p719).

There are regular (if costly) car-ferry services to almost all islands. For more information and sample prices for vehicles, see p741.

Automobile Associations

Greece's domestic automobile association is **ELPA** (Elliniki Leschi Aftokinitou kai Periigiseon; ☎ 210 606 8800; www.elpa.gr in Greek; Leoforos Mesogion 395, Agia Paraskevi).

Bring Your Own Vehicle

EU-registered vehicles are allowed free entry into Greece but may only stay six months without road taxes being due. A green card (international third-party insurance) is all that's required. Your only proof of the date of entry – if requested by the police – is your ferry ticket if you arrive from Italy, or your passport entry stamp if entering from elsewhere. Non-EU-registered vehicles may be logged in your passport.

Driving Licence

Drivers with an EU driving licence can drive with it in Greece. If your driving licence comes from outside the EU, Greece requires that you possess an International Driving Permit, which should be obtained before you leave home.

Fuel & Spare Parts

Fuel is available widely throughout the country, though service stations may be closed on weekends and public holidays. On the islands, there may be only one petrol station; check where it is before you head out. Self-service pumps are not the norm in Greece, nor are credit-card pumps, so it is always advisable to keep the reservoir level up just in case. Petrol in Greece is cheaper than in most other European countries, but by American or Australian standards it is expensive. Prices are generally set by the government, but can vary from region to region. Super (leaded) and *amolyvdi* (unleaded) is always available, as is *petreleo kinisis* (diesel).

Spare parts for most Japanese and European cars are available everywhere, although you may need to wait for them to be ferried to the islands.

Hire

CAR

Hire cars are available just about everywhere, but it's best to hire from major cities where competition offers better opportunities to bargain. All the big multinational companies are represented in Athens, and most have branches in major towns and popular tourist

TRANSPORT

ROAD DISTANCES (KM)

	Alexandroupoli	Athens	Corinth	Edessa	Florina	Igoumenitsa	Ioannina	Kalamata	Kastoria	Kavala	Lamia	Larisa	Monemvasia	Nafplio	Patra	Pyrgos	Sparta	Thessaloniki	Trikala	Tripoli
Athens	854																			
Corinth	884	84																		
Edessa	427	569	596																	
Florina	497	592	251	353																
Igoumenitsa	816	473	393	380	353															
Ioannina	702	447	364	298	320	96														
Kalamata	1055	284	175	767	763	501	467													
Kastoria	535	489	519	108	67	286	204	690												
Kavala	177	682	655	250	320	615	525	878	358											
Lamia	643	214	244	355	360	353	263	415	274	466										
Larisa	493	361	389	218	231	309	209	561	239	323	151									
Monemvasia	1156	350	266	869	855	613	579	156	756	976	505	655								
Nafplio	947	165	63	659	664	482	427	163	582	770	307	455	215							
Patra	828	220	138	567	513	281	247	220	483	664	193	341	332	201						
Pyrgos	924	320	234	636	643	367	347	119	542	747	284	432	275	208	96					
Sparta	1025	225	145	737	759	517	483	60	660	848	385	533	96	119	236	180				
Thessaloniki	349	513	544	89	159	452	362	715	220	169	303	154	807	610	488	584	711			
Trikala	554	330	356	227	233	247	148	520	159	377	115	62	597	419	310	400	501	216		
Tripoli	964	194	110	713	681	457	430	90	639	820	324	472	157	81	176	155	61	624	466	
Volos	556	326	355	278	293	371	271	518	301	383	115	62	620	417	308	408	524	214	124	435

destinations. The majority of islands have at least one outlet. By Greek law, rental cars have to be replaced every six years and so most vehicles you rent will be relatively new.

High-season weekly rates with unlimited mileage start at about €280 for the smallest models, such as a Fiat Seicento, dropping to about €200 per week in winter. These prices don't include local tax (known as VAT). There are also optional extras such as a collision damage waiver of €12 per day (more for larger models), without which you will be liable for the first €295 of the repair bill (much more for larger models). Other costs include a theft waiver of at least €6 per day and personal accident insurance. The major companies offer much cheaper prebooked and prepaid rates.

You can find better deals at local companies. Their advertised rates can be up to 50% cheaper, and they are normally open to negotiation, especially if business is slow. On the islands, you can rent a car for the day for around €30 to €50, including all insurance and taxes.

Always check what the insurance includes; there are often rough roads or dangerous routes that you can only tackle by renting a 4WD. If you want to take a hire car to another country or onto a ferry, you will need advance written authorisation from the hire company, as the insurance may not cover you. Unless you pay with a credit card, most hire companies will require a minimum deposit of €120 per day. See the Getting Around sections of cities and islands for details of places to rent cars.

The minimum driving age in Greece is 18 years, but most car-hire firms require you to be at least 21, or 23 for larger vehicles.

For current rates of some of the major car-hire players in Greece, see the following websites:

Avis (☎ 210 322 4951; www.avis.gr)
Budget (☎ 210 349 8800; www.budget.gr)
Europcar (☎ 210 960 2382; www.europcar.gr)
Hertz (☎ 210 626 4000; www.hertz.gr)

MOTORCYCLE

Mopeds, motorcycles and scooters are available for hire wherever there are tourists to rent them. Most machines are newish and in good condition. Nonetheless, check the brakes at the earliest opportunity.

To hire a moped, motorcycle or scooter you must produce a licence that shows proficiency to ride the category of bike you wish to rent; this applies to everything from 50cc up. British citizens must obtain a Category A licence from the Driver and Vehicle Licensing Agency in the UK (in most other EU countries separate licences are automatically issued).

Motorcycles or scooters are a cheap way to travel around. Rates start from about €15 per day for a moped or 50cc motorcycle, to €30 per day for a 250cc motorcycle. Out of season these prices drop considerably, so use your bargaining skills. Most motorcycle hirers include third-party insurance in the price, but it's wise to check this. This insurance will not include medical expenses. Helmets are compulsory and rental agencies are obliged to offer one as part of the hire deal. Police will book you if you're caught without a helmet.

Warning

Greece is not the best place to initiate yourself into motorcycling. There are still a lot of gravel roads – particularly on the islands. Novices should be very careful; dozens of tourists have accidents every year. Scooters are particularly prone to sliding on gravelly bends. Try to hire a motorcycle with thinner profile tyres. If you are planning to use a motorcycle or moped, check that your travel insurance covers you for injury resulting from a motorcycle accident. Many insurance companies don't offer this cover, so check the fine print!

Insurance

Insurance is always included in any vehicle hire agreements, but you are advised to check whether it is fully comprehensive or third party only. Otherwise you may be up for hefty costs in the event of any damage caused to your vehicle if you are at fault.

Road Conditions

Main highways in Greece have been improving steadily over the years but many still don't offer smooth sailing. Some main roads retain the two-lane/hard shoulder format of the 1960s which can be confusing, if not downright dangerous. Roadwork can take years and years in Greece, especially on the islands where funding often only trickles in. In other cases, excellent new tarmac roads may have appeared that are not on any local maps.

Road Hazards

Slow drivers – many of them unsure and hesitant tourists – can cause serious traffic events on Greece's roads. Road surfaces can change rapidly when a section of road has succumbed to subsidence or weathering. Snow and ice can be a serious challenge in winter, and drivers are advised to carry snow chains. Animals in rural areas may wander onto roads, so extra vigilance is required. Roads passing through mountainous areas are often littered with fallen rocks that can cause extensive damage to a vehicle's underside or throw a bike rider.

Road Rules

In Greece, as throughout Continental Europe, you drive on the right and overtake on the left. Outside built-up areas, traffic on a main road has right of way at intersections. In towns, vehicles coming from the right have right of way. This includes roundabouts – even if you're in the roundabout, you must give way to drivers coming onto the roundabout to your right.

Seat belts must be worn in front seats, and in back seats if the car is fitted with them. Children under 12 years of age are not allowed in the front seat. It is compulsory to carry a first-aid kit, fire extinguisher and warning triangle, and it is forbidden to carry cans of petrol. Helmets are compulsory for motorcyclists if the motorcycle is 50cc or more.

Outside residential areas the speed limit is 120km/h on highways, 90km/h on other roads and 50km/h in built-up areas. The speed limit for motorcycles up to 100cc is 70km/h and for larger motorcycles, 90km/h. Drivers exceeding the speed limit by 20% are liable to receive a fine of €60; exceeding it by 40% costs €150.

The police have also cracked down on drink-driving – at last. A blood-alcohol content of 0.05% can incur a fine of €150, and over 0.08% is a criminal offence.

If you are involved in an accident and no one is hurt, the police will not be required to write a report, but it is advisable to go to a nearby police station and explain what happened. A police report may be required for insurance purposes. If an accident involves injury, a driver who does not stop and does not inform the police may face a prison sentence.

HITCHING

Hitching is never entirely safe in any country in the world, and we don't recommend it.

TRANSPORT

TRANSPORT

Travellers who decide to hitch should understand that they are taking a small but potentially serious risk. People who do choose to hitch will be safer if they travel in pairs and should let someone know where they are planning to go. In particular, it is unwise for females to hitch alone; women are better off hitching with a male companion.

Some parts of Greece are much better for hitching than others. Getting out of major cities tends to be hard work and Athens is notoriously difficult. Hitching is much easier in remote areas and on islands with poor public transport. On country roads it is not unknown for someone to stop and ask if you want a lift, even if you haven't stuck a thumb out.

LOCAL TRANSPORT
Bus
Most Greek towns are small enough to get around on foot. All the major towns have local buses, but the only places you're likely to need them are Athens, Patra, Kalamata and Thessaloniki. The procedure for buying tickets for local buses is covered in the Getting Around section for each city.

Metro
Athens is the only city in Greece large enough to warrant the building of an underground system. For more details, see p157. Note that only Greek student cards are valid for a student ticket on the metro.

Taxi
Taxis are widely available in Greece except on very small or remote islands. They are reasonably priced by European standards, especially if three or four people share costs.

Yellow city cabs are metered, with rates doubling between midnight and 5am. Additional costs are charged for trips from an airport or a bus, port or train station, as well as for each piece of luggage over 10kg. Grey rural taxis do not have meters, so you should always settle on a price before you get in.

Many younger taxi drivers now have satnav systems in their cars, so finding a destination is a breeze as long as you have the exact address.

Some taxi drivers in Athens have been known to take unwary travellers for a financial ride. If you have a complaint about a taxi driver, take the cab number and report your complaint to the tourist police. For more

information see p107. Taxi drivers in other towns in Greece are, on the whole, friendly, helpful and honest.

TOURS
Tours are worth considering if your time is very limited or if you fancy somebody else doing all of the organising. In Athens, you'll find countless day tours (p137), with some agencies offering two- or three-day trips to nearby sights. For something on a larger scale, try **Intrepid Travel** (www.intrepidtravel.com). With offices in Australia, the UK and the USA, Intrepid offers a 15-day tour of the Greek Islands (£1105/US$2120 plus €200) and an eight-day tour from Athens to Santorini (£645/US$1230 plus €200), including everything except meals and flights. **Encounter Greece** (www.encountergreece.com) offers a plethora of tours; a 10-day tour across the country costs €1595 while three days on the mainland is €375. Flights to Greece are not included.

More adventurous tours include guided activities involving hiking, climbing, whitewater rafting, kayaking, canoeing or canyoning. **Alpin Club** (www.alpinclub.gr) in Athens operates out of Karitena in the Peloponnese, while outfits like **Trekking Hellas** (www.trekking.gr) or **Robinson Expeditions** (www.robinson.gr) run tours from the centre and north of Greece. For more information on activity-based tours, see p711.

TRAIN
Trains are operated by **Greek Railways Organisation** (Organismos Sidirodromon Ellados; www.ose .gr), always referred to as the OSE. You'll find information on fares and schedules on the website. Information on domestic departures from Athens or Thessaloniki can be sought by calling ☎ 1440.

The biggest problem with the Greek railway network is that it is so limited. There are essentially only two main lines: the standard-gauge service from Athens to Alexandroupoli via Thessaloniki (p154), and the Peloponnese network (p173). Despite these limitations the train is an excellent way to get around most of the major towns in Northern Greece (Macedonia and Thrace) – mountainous Epiros being the only mainland prefecture lacking train tracks. The train is also a useful way to get from Patra to Athens if arriving by ferry from Italy, and the round-Peloponnese rail ride is an attraction in itself. Trains also run to Kalambaka (Meteora) and the Pelion port of Volos for onward links to the Sporades islands. The services that do exist are of a good standard, and are improving all the time.

Classes

There are two types of service: regular (slow) trains that stop at all stations and faster, modern intercity (IC) trains that link most major cities.

The slow trains represent the country's cheapest form of public transport: 2nd-class fares are absurdly cheap, and even 1st class is cheaper than bus travel.

The IC trains that link the major Greek cities are an excellent way to travel. The services are not necessarily express – the Greek terrain is far too mountainous for that – but the trains are modern and comfortable. There are 1st- and 2nd-class tickets and a cafe-bar on board. On some services, meals can be ordered and delivered to your seat.

Costs

For a 2nd-class slow-train trip from Athens to Thessaloniki expect to pay €28 (six hours).

A trip from Thessaloniki to Alexandroupoli costs €9 (eight hours).

Ticket prices for IC services are subject to a distance loading charged on top of the normal fares. Seat reservations should be made as far in advance as possible, especially during summer. Sample 2nd-class fares: Athens to Thessaloniki €36 (five hours); and Athens to Alexandroupoli €49 (10 hours). There is an additional nonstop Athens–Thessaloniki express service for €48 (four hours).

A comfortable night service runs between Athens and Thessaloniki, with a choice of couchettes (from €20), two-bed compartments (€31) and single compartments (€54).

Train Passes

Eurail and Inter-Rail cards are valid in Greece, but it's generally not worth buying one if Greece is the only place where you plan to use them. Prices for Inter-Rail passes are tiered, depending on which countries you plan to travel in. For Greece and a host of other countries (including ferries between Greece and Italy), three/eight days' train travel within a month costs €71/149 for travellers 26 years-old and under, and €109/229 for those over 26. For fewer countries (and no ferries), a three-/eight-day pass valid for a month costs €45/90 for those 26 and under, and €69/139 for those over 26-years. In addition to this, you'll have to pay supplements for IC and sleeper car tickets and these can be costly. Whatever pass you have, you must have a reservation to board the train. On presentation of ID or passports, passengers over 60 years-old are entitled to a 25% discount on all lines except in July, August and over the Easter week.

Island Hopping

CONTENTS

In Greece, getting there really is half the adventure and island hopping remains an essential part of the Greek experience. Whether you're sailing into a colourful harbour, sitting on the sun-drenched deck with the surf pounding below, or flying low over the azure waters in a propeller-driven twin-engine plane, you will undoubtedly be filled with a sense of adventure and see the islands at their most tantalising. It is still possible to board one of the slow boats chugging between the islands and to curl up on deck in your sleeping bag to save a night's accommodation, but Greece's domestic ferry scene has undergone a radical transformation in the past decade and these days you can also travel in serious comfort and at a decent speed.

The trade off is, of course, that sea travel can be quite expensive these days. A bed for the night in a cabin from Piraeus to Rhodes can be more expensive than a discounted airline ticket. Nevertheless, deck class is still very reasonable, cabins are like hotel rooms and the experience of staying overnight on a boat is one you shouldn't pass up too quickly. The key is to choose carefully – you can still find the chug-a-lug voyages with all-night noise and insalubrious bathrooms, or you can opt for vessels more akin to the Love Boat. Try mixing your experiences – zipping over the water in a catamaran, slowly ploughing the sea aboard a slow ferry, and soaring from one island airport to the next in a tiny plane.

In the summer, lots of boats and planes connect the islands to one another and the mainland. However, travelling at peak times and between smaller islands and island groups can take some careful planning. Many local travel agents have a good handle on the transport available and can help you build an itinerary and book all necessary tickets. Out of season, planning ahead is even more essential as the number of boats and planes diminishes considerably.

Ferry and airline timetables change from year to year and season to season, and planes and boats can be subject to delays and cancellations at short notice due to bad weather and strikes. No timetable is infallible, but the comprehensive weekly list of departures from Piraeus put out by the EOT (known abroad as the GNTO, the Greek National Tourist Organisation) in Athens is as accurate as possible. The people to go to for the most up-to-date ferry information are the local *limenarhio* (port police), whose offices are usually on or near the quayside.

You'll find lots of information about ferry services on the internet and many of the larger ferry companies also have their own sites (see opposite).

A couple of very useful websites:

Danae Travel (www.danae.gr) This is a good site for booking boat tickets.

Greek Travel Pages (www.gtp.gr) Has a useful search program and links for flights and ferries.

This chapter deals with domestic flight and boat connections. For international services, see p725 or the individual sections of each destination chapter.

PRACTICALITIES

THE GREEK FLEETS

With a network covering every inhabited island, the Greek ferry network is vast and varied. The slow, rust-buckets that used to ply the seas are nearly a thing of the past. You'll still find slow ferries, but high-speed ferries are more popular and cover most of the long-haul routes. Local ferries, excursion boats and tiny, private fishing boats called caïques often connect neighbouring islands and islets. You'll also find water taxis that will take you to isolated beaches and coves. At the other end of the spectrum, hydrofoils and catamarans can cut down travel time drastically. Hydrofoils have seen their heyday but continue to link some of the more remote islands and island groups. Catamarans have taken to the sea in a big way, offer more comfort and cope better with poor weather conditions.

While the largest and most popular islands tend to have airports, many of the smaller ones don't. Flights tend to be short and aeroplanes are small, often making for a bumpy ride. In addition to the national airlines, there are a number of smaller outfits running seaplanes or complementing the most popular routes.

For information on cruise ships, see Cruising (p732).

OPERATORS
Who's Who in the Air?
The biggest player in the sky is Olympic Air, followed closely by Aegean Airlines which often offers great discounts. Airlines often have local offices on the islands (see the relevant destination chapter for details).

Aegean Airlines (☎ 801 112 0000, 210 626 1000; www.aegeanair.com)

Athens Airways (☎ 210 669 6600; www.athensairways.com)

Olympic Air (☎ 801 114 4444; www.olympicairlines.com)

Sky Express (☎ 28102 23500; www.sky express.gr)

Who's Who in the Water?
Ferry companies often have local offices on many of the islands; see the relevant destination chapter for details of these as well as small, local ferries and caïques.

Aegean Flying Dolphins (☎ 210 422 1766) Hydrofoils linking Samos with Kos and islands in between.

Aegean Speed Lines (☎ 210 969 0950; www.aegeanspeedlines.gr) Super-speedy boats between Athens and the Cyclades.

Agoudimos Lines (☎ 210 414 1300; www.agoudimos-lines.com) Ferries connecting the Cyclades and mainland. Also travels to Italy via Corfu.

Alpha Ferries (☎ 210 428 4001/02; www.alphaferries.gr) Traditional ferries from Athens to the Cyclades.

ANE Kalymnou (☎ 22430 29384) Kalymnos-based hydrofoils and old-style ferry linking some of the Dodecanese and the Cyclades.

ANEK Lines (☎ 210 419 7420; www.anek.gr) Cretan-based long-haul ferries.

ANES (☎ 210 422 5625; www.anes.gr) Symi-based old-style ferries servicing the Dodecanese.

Anna Express (☎ 22470 41215; www.annaexpress-lipsi.services.officelive.com) Small, fast ferry connecting northern Dodecanese.

Blue Star Ferries (☎ 210 891 9800; www.bluestarferries.com) Long-haul high-speed ferries and Seajet catamarans between the mainland and the Cyclades.

Cyclades Fast Ferries (☎ 210 418 2005; www.fastferries.com.gr) Comfortable ferries to the most popular Cyclades.

Dodekanisos Seaways (☎ 22410 70590; www.12ne.gr) Runs luxurious catamarans in the Dodecanese.

Euroseas (☎ 210 413 2188; www.ferries.gr/euroseas) Linking the Saronics with services to the mainland.

Evoikos Lines (☎ 210 413 4483; www.glyfaferries.gr in Greek) Comfortable short-haul ferry services between Glyfa on the mainland and Agiokambos in northern Evia.

GA Ferries (☎ 210 419 9100; www.gaferries.gr) Old-style, long-haul ferries serving a huge number of islands.

Hellenic Seaways (☎ 210 419 9000; www.hellenicseaways.gr) Conventional long-haul ferries and catamarans from the mainland to Cyclades and between the Sporades and Saronic islands.

Ionian Ferries (☎ 210 324 9997; www.ionianferries.gr) Large ferries serving the Ionian Islands.

LANE Lines (☎ 210 427 4011;www.ferries.gr/lane) Long-haul ferries.

Minoan Lines (☎ 210 414 5700; www.minoan.gr) High-speed luxury ferries between Piraeus and Iraklio, and Patra, Igoumenitsa and Corfu.

NEL Lines (☎ 22510 26299; www.nel.gr) High-speed, long-haul ferries.

SAOS Lines (☎ 210 625 0000; www.saos.gr) Big, slow boats calling in at many of the islands.

Sea Jets (☎ 210 412 1001) Catamarans calling at Athens, Crete, Santorini (Thira), Paros and many islands in between.

Sea Star (☎ 22460 44000; www.net-club.gr/tilosseastar.htm) High-speed catamaran connecting Tilos with Rhodes, Halki and Nisyros.

Skyros Shipping Company (☎ 22220 921164; www.sne.gr) Slow-boat between Skyros and Kymi on Evia.

Strintzis Ferries (☎ 26102 40000; www.strintzisferries.gr) Larger, older ferries in the Sporades.

Superfast Ferries (www.superfast.com) As the name implies, speedy ferries from the mainland to Crete, Corfu and Patra.

ISLAND HOPPING

FERRY ROUTES

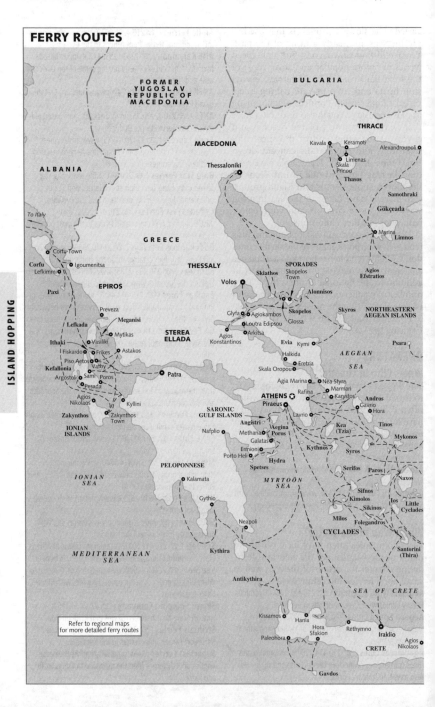

Ventouris Sea Lines (☎ 210 411 4911; www.ventouris sealines.gr) Big boats from the mainland to the Cyclades.

Zante Ferries (☎ 26950 49500; www.zanteferries .gr) Older ferries connecting the mainland with the western Cyclades.

TICKETS
Ticket Purchase

As ferries are prone to delays and cancellations, for short trips it's often best not to purchase a ticket until it has been confirmed that the ferry is leaving. During high season, or if you need to reserve a car space, you will need to book in advance. High-speed boats like catamarans tend to sell out long before the slow chuggers. For overnight ferries it's always best to book in advance, particularly if you want a cabin or particular type of accommodation. If a service is cancelled you can usually transfer your ticket to the next available service with that company.

Many ferry companies have online booking services or you can purchase tickets from their local offices or most travel agents in Greece. Agencies selling tickets line the waterfront of most ports, but rarely is there one that sells tickets for every boat, and often an agency is reluctant to give you information about a boat they do not sell tickets for. Most have timetables displayed outside; check these for the next departing boat or ask the *limenarhio*.

To find specific details on where to buy tickets and other important local information for the islands, see the specific island's Getting There & Away section in the destination chapters throughout this book.

Costs

Ferry prices are fixed by the government, and are determined by the distance of the destination from the port of origin. The small differences in price you may find at ticket agencies are the results of some agencies sacrificing part of their designated commission to qualify as a 'discount service'. (The discount is seldom more than €0.50.) Ticket prices include embarkation tax, a contribution to NAT (the seamen's union) and 10% VAT.

High-speed ferries and hydrofoils cost about 20% more than the traditional ferries, while catamarans are often a third to double the price of their slower counterparts. Caïques and water taxis are usually very reasonable while excursion boats can be pricey but very useful to

ISLAND HOPPING

FEELING WOOZY?

Even those with the sturdiest stomachs can feel seasick when a boat hits rough weather. Here are a few tips to calm your tummy:

■ Gaze at the horizon, not the sea. Don't read or stare at objects that your mind will assume are stable.

■ Drink plenty and eat lightly. Many people claim ginger biscuits and ginger tea settle the stomach.

■ Don't use binoculars.

■ If possible stay in the fresh air – don't go below deck and avoid hydrofoils where you are trapped indoors.

■ Try to keep your mind occupied.

■ If you know you're prone to seasickness, consider investing in acupressure wrist bands before you leave.

---

reach out-of-the-way islands. Children under five travel for free while those between five and ten are usually given half-price tickets.

Almost all islands are served by car ferries, but they are expensive. Sample prices for vehicles up to 4.25m include Piraeus-Mykonos, €80; Piraeus-Crete (Hania and Iraklio), €90; and Piraeus-Samos, €86. The charge for a large motorcycle is about the same as the price for a deck-class passenger ticket. If you're planning to island hop, you're better off renting vehicles at each destination.

Classes

On smaller boats, hydrofoils and catamarans, there is only one type of ticket available and these days, even on larger vessels, classes are largely a thing of the past. The public spaces on the more modern ferries are generally open to all. What does differ is the level of accommodation that you can purchase for overnight boats.

Your 'deck class' ticket typically gives you access to the deck and interior with no accommodation option. It's still a very economical option and if you're one of the first to board, you can usually find somewhere to curl up in your sleeping bag, either inside or on the deck. Next up, aeroplane-type seats give you a reserved, reclining seat in which to hopefully sleep. Then come various shades of cabin accommodation: four-berth, three-berth or two-berth interior cabins are cheaper than their equivalent outside cabins with a porthole. On most boats, cabins are very comfortable, resembling a small hotel room with a private bathroom. While these cost the equivalent of a discount airline ticket,

you also need to factor in that your ticket also buys you a night's accommodation. At the other end of the spectrum are luxury cabins with a view to the front of the ship. These resemble standard cruise-ship cabins and are generally very pricey.

Unless you state otherwise, you will automatically be given deck class when purchasing a ticket. Unless otherwise indicated, prices quoted in this book are for deck-class tickets and economy flight tickets.

CONNECTIONS

Transport information is always vulnerable to change – nowhere is this truer than in Greece. It's important to remember that ferry companies and airlines can change routes and timetables faster than a catamaran can zip between the islands. Every year or two, the ferry companies may 'win' the contracts for operating different routes; thus, they can change annually. Outside of the summer season, most services are less frequent. Always check online schedules, operators or travel agencies for up-to-the-minute info.

This section includes transport information for specific island chains, such as options for travelling from the mainland and individual islands. Refer to the departure timetables for individual islands and mainland ports (from p744) to find out how to hop from where you are to your next destination, and then from there to the next destination and so on.

Details on services from individual islands and mainland ports are listed alphabetically in this chapter. References to 'port' in the table headings throughout this chapter refer to the port of departure, not the destination port.

ATHENS

Most people begin their island hopping in Athens, from where it's an easy trip to the nearby mainland ports of Piraeus, Rafina and Lavrio. Countless ferries, catamarans and hydrofoils set sail from these ports to many of the island groups. If you're beginning your journey from Athens, see p746 for the detailed tables on departures to the various islands. For more general information on Athens, see also p101.

CRETE

As one of Greece's major destinations, Crete is very well connected by boat and air with the rest of the country and even with some international airports/destinations. Given the size and wealth of the island, it's no surprise that some of the biggest transport companies (such as the maritime Minoan Lines and Aegean Airlines) were founded by Cretan businessmen. For more general information on this region see also p457.

CYCLADES

Olympic Air provides regular flights between Athens and the Cyclades. Large high-speed boats and catamarans are a regular feature on Cyclades' routes from about mid-June to mid-September. Their travel times are usually half those of regular ferries. Ferry routes separate the Cyclades into western, northern, central and eastern subgroups. Most ferry services operating within the Cyclades connect one of these subgroups with the ports of Piraeus, Lavrio or Rafina on the mainland. The eastern Cyclades (Mykonos, Paros, Naxos, Ios and Santorini) are the most visited and have the best ferry links with the mainland, usually to Piraeus.

The small islands south of Naxos – Iraklia, Schinousa and Koufonisia – make up the main grouping known as the Little Cyclades.

For more general information on this region see also p372.

DODECANESE

There are regular direct flights between many of the Dodecanese and Athens, along with flights between some of the larger islands in this group. Overnight ferries between Piraeus and Rhodes stop at many of the Dodecanese

en route, albeit at some fairly antisocial hours. Within the Dodecanese are a vast array of high-speed catamarans and older clunkers, calling in at the majority of the island group.

For more general information on this region see also p511.

EVIA & THE SPORADES

Skiathos and Skyros airports handle domestic flights from Athens (as well as occasional charter flights from Oslo and Amsterdam).

From Athens' Terminal B station (p153) there are buses departing to Halkida and Paralia Kymis, for Skyros; and to Agios Konstantinos, for the Sporades. From Athens' Mavromateon terminal (p153), there are frequent buses to Rafina, for Evia.

There are daily ferries to the Sporades from both Agios Konstantinos and Volos, and weekly ferries from Thessaloniki to the Sporades, as well as regular ferry routes connecting Evia to the mainland. There are frequent daily hydrofoil links from both Agios Konstantinos and Volos to the Northern Sporades (Skiathos, Skopelos and Alonnisos only). In 2009, a new service started between Skopelos, Alonnisos and Skyros (via Paralia Kymis, Evia).

For more general information on this region see also p643.

IONIAN ISLANDS

Corfu, Kefallonia and Zakynthos have airports; Lefkada has no airport, but Aktion airport, near Preveza on the mainland, is about 20km away. The four airports have frequent flights to/from Athens. There are interisland connections between Corfu and Preveza, Preveza and Kefallonia and between Kefallonia and Zakynthos.

KTEL long-distance buses connect each major island with Athens and Thessaloniki, and usually also with Patra or Kyllini in the Peloponnese. Buses to Corfu, Lefkada, Kefallonia, Ithaki and Zakynthos depart from Athens' Terminal A bus station.

The Peloponnese has two departure ports for the Ionian Islands: Patra for ferries to Corfu, Kefallonia and Ithaki; and Kyllini for ferries to Kefallonia and Zakynthos. Epiros has one port, Igoumenitsa, for Corfu (island) and Paxi; and Sterea Ellada has one, Astakos, for Ithaki and Kefallonia (although this service is limited to high season).

For more general information on this region see also p671.

ISLAND HOPPING

NORTHEASTERN AEGEAN ISLANDS

The northeastern Aegean Islands are fairly well connected to various ports in mainland Greece and other island chains (notably the Cyclades and the Dodecanese) though not all of them have airports. However, they are not all well interconnected among themselves and here especially travellers will need to take a patient and flexible approach when planning trips. Budget in a few extra days to be on the safe side, especially when setting sail for the smaller and more remote islands. Services out of summer can be much reduced and, when the weather is stormy, result in delays.

Just five of the northeastern Aegean Islands have airports – though none is very large. From these airports (Samos, Chios, Lesvos, Limnos and Ikaria) you can fly directly to Athens and Thessaloniki. While interisland flights are possible, most go via Athens. However, the new carrier Sky Express has several direct flights to the islands.

Although they enjoy a plethora of ferry connections, the northeastern Aegean Islands can be very vexing to circumnavigate. The northernmost of them, Thasos and Samothraki, are currently only accessible via the northern Greece mainland, while other islands too sometimes fall victim to the grand wars of one-upmanship between Greece's shipping barons that continue to wreak havoc with ferry schedules. New lines and companies spring up, others shut down, and unscheduled 'ghost ships' set sail in the early morning hours. No surprise, therefore, that the crafty pirates of the Aegean found these islands so attractive for centuries.

The northeastern Aegean Islands are also significant for their frequent boats to various resorts and historical sites on the Turkish coast; for details see the boxed text Turkish Connections (p596). For information on other excursion boats and special short-haul lines, see the specific island sections in the northeastern Aegean Islands chapter, p585.

NORTHERN GREECE

Getting to the islands from northern Greece is possible by flying (usually via Athens) and by boat. However, the great distances between northern ports and most of the Greek islands mean that it's a long, tiring and relatively expensive haul (with the notable exceptions of Thasos and Samothraki). However, if you need to take a vehicle from the mainland to an island, travelling by boat becomes the only option.

While ferries to Thasos and Samothraki are frequent and reliable in summer, boats to more far-flung destinations are less frequent and prone to unexpected changes, so always check well in advance.

For more general information on this region see also p279.

PELOPONNESE

The major ferry services in the Peloponnese run from the ports of Patra and Kyllini (to the Ionian Islands), Gythio (to Kythira) and Neapoli (to Kythira). In eastern Peloponnese, high-speed services run from Porto Heli, Ermioni and Galatas to a combination of Spetses, Hydra and Poros. Services to Italy are served by companies in Patra.

For more general information on this region see also p166.

SARONIC GULF ISLANDS

The Saronic Gulf Islands have regular links to and from each other and Piraeus. At the time of writing only fast ferries ran from Piraeus to Hydra and Spetses and Ermioni and Porto Heli on the mainland. Tickets for these ferries are often substantially more expensive than those for conventional ferries. An alternative, cheaper way of reaching Poros, Hydra and Spetses is to travel overland through the Peloponnese and then to take local ferries to your island of choice.

For more general information on this region see also p355.

INDIVIDUAL ISLANDS & MAINLAND PORTS
Aegina
Saronic Gulf Islands; see also p356

BOAT SERVICES FROM AEGINA

Destination	Port	Duration	Fare	Frequency
Angistri (Skala)	Aegina Town	15min	€5	1 daily
Angistri (Skala)*	Aegina Town	10min	€6	8 daily
Methana	Aegina Town	40min	€5.70	2-3 daily
Piraeus	Aegina Town	1hr 10min	€9.50	8-10 daily
Piraeus	Agia Marina	1hr	€9.50	3-4 daily
Piraeus	Souvala	1hr 35min	€8.50	3-4 daily
Piraeus*	Aegina Town	40min	€14	hourly
Poros	Aegina Town	1hr 50min	€8.60	4 daily

*high-speed services

Agathonisi
Dodecanese; see also p583

BOAT SERVICES FROM AGATHONISI

Destination	Port	Duration	Fare	Frequency
Arki	Agios Georgios	45min	€8	2 weekly
Lipsi	Agios Georgios	1hr	€8	2 weekly
Patmos	Agios Georgios	2hr	€7	4 weekly
Rhodes*	Agios Georgios	5hr	€46	1 weekly
Samos	Agios Georgios	1hr	€5	4 weekly

*high-speed services

Agios Efstratios
Northeastern Aegean Islands; see also p631–2

BOAT SERVICES FROM AGIOS EFSTRATIOS

Destination	Port	Duration	Fare	Frequency
Chios (Mesta)	Agios Efstratios	3½hr	€35	1 weekly
Kavala	Agios Efstratios	8hr	€19	3 weekly
Lavrio	Agios Efstratios	8½hr	€24-50	3 weekly
Lesvos (Sigri)	Agios Efstratios	3hr	€9	1 weekly
Limnos	Agios Efstratios	8½hr	€6-13	4 weekly
Psara	Agios Efstratios	3hr	€35	1 weekly

Agios Konstantinos
Central Greece (mainland port); see also p255–6

BOAT SERVICES FROM AGIOS KONSTANTINOS

Destination	Port	Duration	Fare	Frequency
Alonnisos*	Agios Konstantinos	3½-3¾hr	€44	1 daily
Alonnisos**	Agios Konstantinos	3hr	€44	1-2 daily
Skiathos*	Agios Konstantinos	2hr	€33	1 daily
Skiathos**	Agios Konstantinos	2hr	€33	2-3 daily
Skopelos*	Agios Konstantinos	3hr	€44	1 daily
Skopelos**	Agios Konstantinos	2½hr	€44	1-2 Mon-Fri, 2-3 Sat & Sun

*fast-ferry services **hydrofoil services

Alexandroupoli
Northern Greece (mainland port); see also p329

AIR
Alexandroupoli's airport serves only Sitia Airport in Crete directly. Check with local travel agents or on the websites of Greek air carriers for the cumulative fares of flights from Alexandroupoli to other islands via Athens.

DOMESTIC FLIGHTS FROM ALEXANDROUPOLI

Destination	Airport	Duration	Fare	Frequency
Crete (Sitia)	Alexandroupoli	1½hr	€100	3 weekly

BOAT
Alexandroupoli is the major ferry port for Samothraki; at time of research, the time-honoured onward service to Rhodes via the Northeast Aegean Islands and other islands in the Dodecanese had been inexplicably terminated, though it may again resume (double-check in advance). Summer hydrofoils usually serve Samothraki, but are unpredictable; check locally.

BOAT SERVICES FROM ALEXANDROUPOLI

Destination	Port	Duration	Fare	Frequency
Samothraki	Alexandroupoli	2hr	€13	2 daily

Alonnisos
Evia & the Sporades; see also p659

BOAT SERVICES FROM ALONNISOS

Destination	Port	Duration	Fare	Frequency
Agios Konstantinos*	Alonnisos	3½hr	€44	1 daily
Agios Konstantinos**	Alonnisos	4hr	€44	1 daily
Skopelos (Glossa)*	Alonnisos	1hr	€13	3 daily
Skiathos	Alonnisos	2hr	€10	4 weekly
Skiathos*	Alonnisos	1½hr	€16	3 daily
Skopelos	Alonnisos	30min	€5	4 weekly
Skopelos*	Alonnisos	20min	€9	3 daily
Volos	Alonnisos	4½hr	€23	2 weekly
Volos*	Alonnisos	3hr	€38.50	2 daily

*hydrofoil services **fast-ferry services

Amorgos
Cyclades; see also p420

BOAT SERVICES FROM AMORGOS

Destination	Port	Duration	Fare	Frequency
Aegiali	Katapola	50min	€4.50	1-2 daily
Donousa	Katapola	2hr 20min	€6.50	1-2 daily
Folegandros*	Katapola	3hr 5min	€35	1 daily
Ios	Katapola	5hr 20min	€11.50	1 weekly
Iraklia	Katapola	1¾hr-5hr	€8.50-10.50	2-3 daily
Kos	Katapola	5hr	€22.50	2 weekly
Leros	Katapola	3hr 10min	€18	2 weekly
Milos*	Katapola	4¼hr	€39	1 daily
Naxos	Katapola	1-4hr	€7.50	1-3 daily
Paros	Katapola	3-7hr	€12.20-15	1-2 daily
Patmos	Katapola	2hr	€18	2 weekly
Piraeus	Katapola	9hr	€30	4 weekly
Piraeus*	Katapola	7hr 25min	€58	1 daily
Rhodes	Katapola	10hr	€25.50	2 weekly
Schinousa	Katapola	1hr 40min	€8-10.50	2-3 daily
Santorini (Thira)*	Katapola	1½hr	€32	1 daily
Syros	Katapola	5¼hr	€29.80	4 weekly

*high-speed services

ISLAND HOPPING

Anafi

Cyclades; see also p439

BOAT SERVICES FROM ANAFI

Destination	Port	Duration	Fare	Frequency
Folegandros	Anafi	5hr	€21	5 weekly
Ios	Anafi	3hr	€8.80	5 weekly
Karpathos	Anafi	6hr	€16.30	5 weekly
Kea	Anafi	16hr 40min	€46.80	2 weekly
Kythnos	Anafi	15hr	€43.90	2 weekly
Naxos	Anafi	7hr 25min	€14.30	5 weekly
Paros	Anafi	7hr 25min	€17.90	3-4 weekly
Piraeus	Anafi	11hr 20min -13½hr	€29.60	3 weekly
Rhodes	Anafi	11hr 40min	€22.20	5 weekly
Santorini (Thira)	Anafi	1hr	€8	5 weekly
Sikinos	Anafi	4hr	€19.60	4 weekly
Syros	Anafi	9hr 10min	€36.30	4 weekly

Andros

Cyclades; see also p374

BOAT SERVICES FROM ANDROS

Destination	Port	Duration	Fare	Frequency
Kea	Gavrio	5hr 50min	€17.20	1 weekly
Kythnos	Gavrio	4hr 20min	€25.20	1 weekly
Mykonos	Gavrio	1¼hr	€10-13	4 daily
Naxos	Gavrio	4hr 10min	€15.70	2 weekly
Rafina	Gavrio	2½hr	€12-14	4-8 daily
Syros	Gavrio	2hr 20min	€16	7 daily
Tinos	Gavrio	1hr 35min	€8-11	4 daily

Angistri

Saronic Gulf Islands; see also p361

BOAT SERVICES FROM ANGISTRI

Destination	Port	Duration	Fare	Frequency
Aegina*	Skala	10min	€6	6 daily
Piraeus*	Skala	55min	€15	6 daily
Piraeus	Skala	1½hr	€10	1-2 daily

*high-speed services

Arki & Marathi

Dodecanese; see also p583

The F/B *Nissos Kalymnos* calls in up to four times weekly as it shuttles between Patmos and Samos on its vital milk run. The Lipsi-based, speedy *Anna Express* links Arki with Lipsi (15 minutes) twice weekly. In summer, Lipsi-based excursion boats and Patmos-based caïques do frequent day trips (return €20) to Arki and Marathi. A local caïque runs between Marathi and Arki (1¼ hours).

BOAT SERVICES FROM ARKI & MARATHI

Destination	Port	Duration	Frequency
Patmos	Arki/Marathi		4 weekly
Samos	Arki/Marathi		4 weekly
Lipsi	Arki	15min	2 weekly
Arki	Marathi	1¼hr	

Astakos

Central Greece (mainland port); see also p251

BOAT SERVICES FROM ASTAKOS

Destination	Port	Duration	Fare	Frequency
Kefallonia (Sami)	Astakos	3hr	€8	1 daily
Ithaki (Piso Aetos)	Astakos	2¼hr	€10	2 daily

Astypalea

Dodecanese; see also p563

AIR

Olympic has three flights per week to Leros (€41, 20 minutes), Kos (€47, one hour) and Rhodes (€47, 1½ hours).

BOAT SERVICES FROM ASTYPALEA

Destination	Port	Duration	Fare	Frequency
Kalymnos	Agios Andreas	2½hr	€11	4 weekly
Kalymnos	Skala	2¾hr	€12	3 weekly
Kos	Agios Andreas	3½hr	€15	1 weekly
Naxos	Agios Andreas	3½hr	€23	4 weekly
Paros	Agios Andreas	5hr	€29	4 weekly
Piraeus	Agios Andreas	10hr	€34	4 weekly
Rhodes	Agios Andreas	9hr	€29	1 weekly

Athens

Mainland port; see also p152

AIR

Olympic Air has flights to all islands with airports, and the more popular islands are also serviced by Aegean Airlines and Athens Airways.

Aegean Airlines has eight flights daily to Rhodes, seven flights daily to Iraklio, six to Santorini (Thira), five daily to Hania, three to Lesvos (Mytilini) and Mykonos, at least two daily to Corfu and Kos and at least one daily to Chios, Kefallonia, Samos and Limnos.

Athens Airways has flights to Hania, Chios, Iraklio, Kefallonia, Lesvos, Mykonos, Rhodes and Santorini.

The following table indicates starting prices (including tax).

ISLAND HOPPING

DOMESTIC FLIGHTS FROM ATHENS

Destination	Duration	Fare	Frequency
Alexandroupoli	65min	€77	14 weekly
Astypalea	1hr	€54	5 weekly
Chios	50min	€77	20 weekly
Corfu	1hr	€77	14 weekly
Crete (Hania)	50min	€77	30 weekly
Crete (Iraklio)	50min	€77	40 weekly
Crete (Sitia)	1hr 10min	€89	4 weekly
Ikaria	55min	€60	6 weekly
Kavala	1hr	€77	13 weekly
Kefallonia	65min	€111	13 weekly
Kos	55min	€89	14 weekly
Kythira	45min	€65	7 weekly
Leros	1hr	€68	7 weekly
Lesvos (Mytilini)	50min	€89	27 weekly
Limnos	55min	€77	14 weekly
Milos	45min	€50	10 weekly
Mykonos	40min	€77	27 weekly
Naxos	45min	€80	8 weekly
Paros	40min	€79	16 weekly
Preveza	1hr	€95	3 weekly
Rhodes	1hr	€77	35 weekly
Samos	1hr	€77	27 weekly
Santorini (Thira)	50min	€77	35 weekly
Skiathos	50min	€71	7 weekly
Skyros	35min	€43	3 weekly
Syros	35min	€95	2 weekly
Thessaloniki	55min	€77	58 weekly
Zakynthos	1hr	€95	11 weekly

BOAT

Athens' main port, Piraeus, is the departure point for an overwhelming number of island destinations. The smaller east coast ports of Rafina and Lavrio service the Cyclades and Evia. See also p153.

BOAT SERVICES FROM ATHENS

to Crete

Destination	Port	Duration	Fare	Frequency
Agios Nikolaos	Piraeus	12hr	€30	2 weekly
Souda (Hania)	Piraeus	8½hr	€30	2 daily
Souda (Hania)*	Piraeus	4½hr	€55	daily
Iraklio	Piraeus	8hr	€36-37	2 daily
Iraklio*	Piraeus	6½hr	€33.50	3 weekly
Rethymno	Piraeus	10hr	€30	2 daily
Rethymno*	Piraeus	6hr	€57	1 daily
Sitia	Piraeus	14½hr	€32.10	2 weekly

*high speed services

to the Cyclades

Destination	Port	Duration	Fare	Frequency
Amorgos*	Piraeus	7hr 25min	€58	1 daily
Amorgos	Piraeus	9hr	€30	4 weekly
Anafi	Piraeus	11hr 20min	€29.60	3 weekly
Andros	Rafina	2hr	€12-14	4 daily
Donousa	Piraeus	7hr 10min	€30	4 weekly
Folegandros*	Piraeus	4hr	€55	1-3 daily
Folegandros	Piraeus	13hr	€30.50	4 weekly
Ios	Piraeus	7hr	€31.50	4-5 daily
Ios*	Piraeus	5½hr	€46	3 daily
Iraklia	Piraeus	7hr 20min	€30	1-2 daily
Kea (Tzia)	Lavrio	50min	€12.70	3-5 daily
Kimolos	Piraeus	9hr 20min	€24.50	5 weekly
Kimolos*	Piraeus	5¼hr	€48	3 weekly
Koufonisia	Piraeus	8hr	€30	1-2 daily
Koufonisia*	Piraeus	7hr	€58	1 daily
Kythnos	Piraeus	3hr 10min	€18	1-2 daily
Milos	Piraeus	8hr	€30.50	1-2 daily
Milos*	Piraeus	3-4hr	€49	2-3 daily
Mykonos	Piraeus	4¾hr	€30.50-39.50	2 daily
Mykonos*	Piraeus	3hr	€43	3 daily
Mykonos	Rafina	4½hr	€23	2-3 daily
Mykonos*	Rafina	2hr 10min	€41	4-5 daily
Naxos	Piraeus	4¾hr	€30	4-5 daily
Naxos*	Piraeus	3½hr	€45	3 daily
Naxos*	Rafina	3hr	€43	1 daily
Paros	Piraeus	5hr	€29-31	4 daily
Paros*	Piraeus	2½hr	€439.50	6 daily
Paros*	Rafina	2½hr	€49.50	1 daily
Santorini (Thira)	Piraeus	9hr	€33.50	4-5 daily
Santorini (Thira)*	Piraeus	5¼hr	€47-65	3 daily
Santorini (Thira)*	Rafina	4¾hr	€49	1 daily
Schinousa	Piraeus	7½hr	€30	1-2 daily
Serifos	Piraeus	5hr	€22.50	2 daily
Serifos*	Piraeus	2¼hr	€40	2 daily
Sifnos	Piraeus	5¼hr	€28	5 daily
Sifnos*	Piraeus	2hr 25min	€44	3 daily
Sikinos	Piraeus	12hr	€29.69	4 weekly
Syros	Piraeus	4hr	€26-29	4 daily
Syros*	Piraeus	2½hr	€44.50	3 daily
Syros*	Rafina	2hr 50min	€45	2 weekly
Tinos	Piraeus	4¾hr	€28	1 daily
Tinos*	Piraeus	3¾hr	€44	3 daily
Tinos*	Rafina	2hr	€40	4-5 daily
Tinos	Rafina	4hr	€19	4 daily

*high speed services

ISLAND HOPPING

ISLAND HOPPING

to the Dodecanese

Destination	Port	Duration	Fare	Frequency
Astypalea	Piraeus	10hr	€34	4 weekly
Kalymnos	Piraeus	13hr	€44	3 weekly
Karpathos	Piraeus	17hr	€58	2 weekly
Kasos	Piraeus	19hr	€35	3 weekly
Kos	Piraeus	10hr	€46	4 weekly
Leros	Piraeus	8hr	€35	1 daily
Lipsi	Piraeus	12hr	€42	2 weekly
Nisyros	Piraeus	18hr	€46	3 weekly
Patmos	Piraeus	7hr	€34	4 weekly
Rhodes	Piraeus	13hr	€53	1 daily
Symi*	Piraeus	15hr	€64	2 weekly
Tilos	Piraeus	19hr	€46	2 weekly

*via Rhodes

to Evia

Destination	Port	Duration	Fare	Frequency
Evia (Marmari)	Rafina	1hr	€7	4-6 daily

to the Northeastern Aegean Islands

Destination	Port	Duration	Fare	Frequency
Chios	Piraeus*	6-9hr	€25-33	2 daily
Fourni	Piraeus	10hr	€30	2 weekly
Ikaria (Agios Kirykos)	Piraeus	10½hr	€35	3 weekly
Ikaria (Agios Kirykos)	Piraeus*	4¼hr	€52	2 weekly
Lesvos (Mytilini Town)	Piraeus	8½-13hr	€27-37	2 daily
Limnos	Lavrio	9½-14hr	€28.60	3 weekly
Limnos	Piraeus	21hr	€30.50	1 weekly
Samos (Vathy)	Piraeus	7-13hr	€41	1-2 daily

*high-speed services

to the Saronic Gulf Islands

Destination	Port	Duration	Fare	Frequency
Aegina	Piraeus	1hr	€8	hourly
Aegina*	Piraeus	40min	€14	hourly
Angistri*	Piraeus	55min	€15	6 daily
Angistri	Piraeus	1½hr	€10	1-2 daily
Hydra*	Piraeus	50min-1½hr	€28.40	10 daily
Poros	Piraeus	2¼hr	€13.30	4 daily
Poros*	Piraeus	1hr	€25.20	4-6 daily
Spetses*	Piraeus	2hr 10min	€39	7 daily

*high-speed services

to the Peloponnese

Destination	Port	Duration	Fare	Frequency
Ermioni*	Piraeus	2hr	€30	4 daily
Kythira	Piraeus	6½hr	€23	2 weekly
Methana	Piraeus	2hr	€12	1-3 daily
Porto Heli*	Piraeus	2hr	€29.50	4 daily

*high-speed services

Chios

Northeastern Aegean Islands; see also p605

DOMESTIC FLIGHTS FROM CHIOS

Destination	Airport	Duration	Fare	Frequency
Athens	Chios	45min	€90	7 weekly
Thessaloniki	Chios	50min	€80	5 weekly

BOAT SERVICES FROM CHIOS

Destination	Port	Duration	Fare	Frequency
Agios Efstratios	Mesta	4¼hr	€35	1 weekly
Inousses	Chios	1-1¼hr	€4-10	1 daily
Kalymnos	Chios	6¾hr	€21	1 weekly
Kos	Chios	8hr	€22	1 weekly
Lavrio	Mesta	4hr	€50	1 weekly
Lesvos (Mytilini Town)	Chios	3hr	€13-19	2 daily
Lesvos (Sigri)	Chios	3hr	€15	1 weekly
Limnos	Chios	10-12hr	€22	4 weekly
Limnos	Mesta	5hr	€40	1 weekly
Mykonos	Chios	3hr	€28.50	2 weekly
Piraeus	Chios	6-9hr	€25-33	2 daily
Psara	Chios	3½hr	€10.70	1 daily
Psara	Mesta	45min	€6-13	2 weekly
Rhodes	Chios	12hr	€34	1 weekly
Samos (Karlovasi)	Chios	2½hr	€11	2 weekly
Samos (Vathy)	Chios	3½hr	€12	2 weekly
Syros	Chios	3½hr	€30.50	5 weekly
Thessaloniki	Chios	13-20hr	€37	3 weekly

Corfu

Ionian Islands; see also p673

DOMESTIC FLIGHTS FROM CORFU

Destination	Airport	Duration	Fare	Frequency
Athens	Corfu	1hr	€60	2 daily
Kefallonia	Corfu	1hr 20min	€39	3 weekly
Preveza	Corfu	30min	€39	3 weekly
Thessaloniki	Corfu	55min	€69	3 weekly

BOAT SERVICES FROM CORFU

Destination	Port	Duration	Fare	Frequency
Igoumenitsa	Corfu	1¼hr	€7	hourly
Igoumenitsa	Lefkimmi	1hr 10min	€5.60	6 daily
Patra	Corfu	6½hr	€30	2 weekly
Paxi*	Corfu	40min	€16.40	1-3 daily
Paxi	Corfu	3½hr	€8.50-57	3 weekly
Zakynthos	Corfu	8¾hr	€32	1 weekly

*high-speed services

Crete
See also p457

AIR
Crete's major Nikos Kazantzakis Airport in Iraklio receives the bulk of the island's national and international flights, though Hania in the west is also busy. Sitia in the far northeast has been pegged for expansion, but remains much less used. For this reason, air tickets are sometimes cheaper from mainland Greece to Sitia, though you will want to factor in the cost of ongoing ground transport, logistics and time that will accrue if you are not planning on staying in this remote area.

To reach Crete by air from other Greek islands usually requires changing in Athens, except for some flights operated by newcomer Sky Express; the direct flight offers between Crete and other islands in the tables here are all offered by Sky Express. However, all travel agents and the online booking websites of the other individual airlines can provide actual cumulative prices that involve flying via Athens. Note, cheaper Sky Express flights restrict baggage to 12.5kg.

In the high season, it's best to book in advance, as Crete is a very popular destination and tickets may sell out quickly for the dates you wish to travel. Remarkably, international direct flights to Crete are sometimes cheaper than flying to the island from elsewhere in Greece, even from Greek carriers themselves. Aegean Airlines has direct scheduled flights from Iraklio to Milan, Rome and other European cities, while Olympic serves even more airports abroad.

If coming from a Western European country, it may be possible to score a cheap seat on a charter flight operating for package tourists – without actually having to buy the rest of the package (accommodation, food etc.). However, you'll have to check with a travel agency in such a country to see if it's feasible.

European budget airlines are also starting to serve Crete in summer months.

BOAT
While ferry schedules to and from Crete tend to stay more stable than with other islands, you should always check ahead as routes and prices may change without much notice. Since Crete is such a large island, many visitors choose to drive while here; prices for bringing a car from Athens start at around €90.

Crete's major ferry ports are all on the north coast. Iraklio is the major one, followed by Souda (for Hania), Rethymno and Sitia in the east. The small western port of Kissamos (Kastelli) exists exclusively to service Gythio in the Peloponnese and the nearby island of Kythira.

Crete also has several southern ports. From Paleohora and Hora Sfakion, it's possible to visit the most southerly point in Europe, Gavdos, two hours south in the Libyan Sea. There's also an important ferry route that hugs the coast between Paleohora and Hora Sfakion – otherwise separated by impassable mountains – making stops along the way at Sougia, Agia Roumeli and Loutro.

Finally, numerous minor excursion boats and boat taxis run by local travel agencies and even fishermen serve small coastal towns and satellite islands such as Paximadia

DOMESTIC FLIGHTS FROM CRETE

Destination	Port	Duration	Fare	Frequency
Alexandroupoli	Sitia	1½hr	€100	3 weekly
Araxos (Patra)	Iraklio	1hr	€127	2 weekly
Athens	Hania	1hr	€100	1 daily
Athens	Iraklio	1hr	€110	2 daily
Ikaria	Iraklio	55min	€127	2 weekly
Kalamata	Iraklio	1hr	€100	3 weekly
Kos	Iraklio	35min	€110	4 weekly
Lesvos (Mytilini)	Iraklio	50min	€110	2 weekly
Mykonos	Iraklio	30min	€80	12 weekly
Rhodes	Iraklio	45min	€110	11 weekly
Samos	Iraklio	50min	€110	2 weekly
Thessaloniki	Hania	1½hr	€120	1 daily
Thessaloniki	Iraklio	1½hr	€130	2 daily

ISLAND HOPPING

and Gaidouronisi (Hrysi) in the south and Spinalonga in the north.

Information given in the below table pertains only to north-coast ports. For schedules, prices and other information involving the south-coast ports and local excursion boats, see the relevant sections of the Crete chapter (see p457).

BOAT SERVICES FROM CRETE

Destination	Port	Duration	Fare	Frequency
Gythio	Kissamos	7hr	€23	5 weekly
Ios	Iraklio	5¼hr	€42	2 weekly
Karpathos	Iraklio	7½hr	€19.60	2 weekly
Kassos	Iraklio	6¼hr	€17.90	2 weekly
Kythira	Kissamos	4hr	€17	5 weekly
Kythira	Rethymno	6hr	€20	1 weekly
Mykonos	Iraklio	6¾hr	€66.50	2 weekly
Paros	Iraklio	6hr	€65	2 weekly
Piraeus	Agios Nikolaos	12hr	€30	2 weekly
Piraeus	Iraklio	8hr	€36-37	2 daily
Piraeus	Iraklio	6½hr	€33.50	3 weekly
Piraeus	Rethymno	10hr	€30	2 daily
Piraeus*	Rethymno	6hr	€57	1 daily
Piraeus	Sitia	14½hr	€32.10	2 weekly
Piraeus	Souda (Hania)	8½hr	€30	2 daily
Piraeus*	Souda (Hania)	4½hr	€55	daily
Rhodes	Agios Nikolaos	12hr	€26.40	2 weekly
Rhodes	Iraklio	12hr	€27.50	2 weekly
Rhodes	Sitia	10hr	€26.40	2 weekly
Santorini (Thira)	Iraklio	4½hr	€16.30	4 weekly
Santorini (Thira)*	Iraklio	1¾hr	€41	1 daily
Santorini (Thira)	Rethymno	2hr 20min	€46	3 weekly

*high speed services

Donousa

Cyclades; see also p418

BOAT SERVICES FROM DONOUSA

Destination	Port	Duration	Fare	Frequency
Amorgos	Donousa	2hr 20min	€6.50	1-2 daily
Iraklia	Donousa	2hr 20min-4hr	€7.50-14.40	1-2 daily
Naxos	Donousa	3hr-3hr 50min	€11.50-€14	2-3 daily
Paros	Donousa	2hr 30min	€10.30-12.50	1-3 daily
Piraeus	Donousa	7hr 10min	€30	4 weekly
Schinousa	Donousa	2hr	€7.50-	1-2 daily
Syros	Donousa	4hr20min	€15	4 weekly

Evia

Evia & the Sporades; see also p644

BOAT SERVICES FROM EVIA

Destination	Port	Duration	Fare	Frequency
Agia Marina	Evia (Nea Styra)	45min	€3.50	6-8 daily
Arkitsa	Evia (Loutra Edipsou)	40min	€3.30	10-12 daily
Glyfa	Evia (Agiokambos)	20min	€2	8-12 daily
Rafina	Evia (Marmari)	1hr	€7	4-6 daily
Skala Oropou	Evia (Eretria)	25min	€1.40	hourly
Skyros	Evia (Paralia Kymis)	1¾hr	€9	1-2 daily

Folegandros

Cyclades; see also p441

BOAT SERVICES FROM FOLEGANDROS

Destination	Port	Duration	Fare	Frequency
Amorgos*	Folegandros	3hr 20min	€35.50	1daily
Anafi	Folegandros	4¾hr	€21.20	5 weekly
Ios	Folegandros	1hr 20min	€11.50	1-2 daily
Kea	Folegandros	11hr 25min	€38.20	2 weekly
Kimolos	Folegandros	1½hr	€7	5 weekly
Koufonisia*	Folegandros	3hr	€35	1 daily
Kythnos	Folegandros	7¼hr	€16	2 weekly
Milos	Folegandros	2½hr	€8	5 weekly
Milos*	Folegandros	1¼hr	€16	4 weekly
Naxos	Folegandros	5hr 35min	€33.20	4 weekly
Piraeus	Folegandros	13hr	€30.50	4 weekly
Piraeus*	Folegandros	4hr	€55	1-3 daily
Paros	Folegandros	4-6hr	€15-16.70	5 weekly
Santorini (Thira)	Folegandros	2½hr	€7.50	1-3 daily
Santorini (Thira)*	Folegandros	30min	€19	1 daily
Serifos	Folegandros	7hr 40min	€16	5 weekly
Serifos*	Folegandros	1¾hr	€23	4 weekly
Sifnos	Folegandros	4½hr	€13.50	1-3 daily
Sifnos*	Folegandros	1hr	€18	4 weekly
Sikinos	Folegandros	40min	€5.50	1-3 daily
Syros	Folegandros	5hr	€23.90	4 weekly

*high-speed services

Fourni Islands

Northeastern Aegean Islands; see also p587

BOAT SERVICES FROM FOURNI

Destination	Port	Duration	Fare	Frequency
Ikaria (Agios Kirykos)	Fourni	1½hr	€5	1-3 daily
Piraeus	Fourni	10hr	€30	2 weekly
Samos (Karlovasi)	Fourni	1-3hr	€5	1-3 daily
Samos (Vathy)	Fourni	3-5hr	€8	1-2 daily*

*except Fridays

Halki

Dodecanese; see also p530

Two local ferries, the *Nissos Halki* and *Nikos Express*, run daily between Halki and Skala Kamirou on Rhodes (€10, 30 minutes).

BOAT SERVICES FROM HALKI

Destination	Port	Duration	Fare	Frequency
Karpathos	Emborios	3hr	€12	4 weekly
Piraeus	Emborios	19hr	€63	2 weekly
Rhodes	Emborios	2hr	€10	4 weekly
Rhodes*	Emborios	1¼hr	€21	2 weekly
Santorini (Thira)	Emborios	15hr	€30	2 weekly

*high-speed services

Hydra

Saronic Gulf Islands; see also p364

BOAT SERVICES FROM HYDRA

Destination	Port	Duration	Fare	Frequency
Ermioni*	Hydra	50min	€9.50	7 daily
Piraeus*	Hydra	1½hr	€28.40	7 daily
Poros*	Hydra	1hr 50min	€12.50	7 daily
Porto Heli*	Hydra	50min	€11.50	7 daily
Spetses*	Hydra	1hr	€14.50	7 daily

*high-speed services

Igoumenitsa

Northern Greece (mainland port); see also p353

BOAT

Igoumenitsa is a major port for ferries to Italy, and also has frequent boats to the Ionian islands of Corfu and Paxi, as well as Athens' port of Piraeus. Boats generally leave mornings and evenings. Hydrofoils to/from Corfu and Paxi usually run in summer; check locally.

BOAT SERVICES FROM IGOUMENITSA

Destination	Port	Duration	Fare	Frequency
Corfu	Igoumenitsa	1- 2¼hr	€7-9	15-20 daily
Paxi	Igoumenitsa	3¾hr	€8	1-2 daily
Patra	Igoumenitsa	5-7¾hr	from €33	2-6 daily
Sami	Igoumenitsa	4¾hr	€50	5 weekly

Ikaria

Northeastern Aegean Islands; see also p587

DOMESTIC FLIGHTS FROM IKARIA

Destination	Airport	Duration	Fare	Frequency
Athens	Ikaria	45min	€80	1 daily
Crete (Iraklio)	Ikaria	55min	€127	2 weekly

BOAT SERVICES FROM IKARIA

Destination	Port	Duration	Fare	Frequency
Chios	Agios Kirykos	4½hr	€13	1 weekly
Fourni	Agios Kirykos	1½hr	€5	1-3 daily
Kavala**	Agios Kirykos	21½hr	€37	1 weekly
Lesvos (Mytilini Town)	Agios Kirykos	8hr	€21	1 weekly
Limnos	Agios Kirykos	13¾hr	€30	1 weekly
Mykonos	Agios Kirykos	3½hr	€15	3 weekly
Piraeus	Agios Kirykos	10½hr	€35	3 weekly
Piraeus**	Agios Kirykos	4¼hr	€52	2 weekly
Samos (Karlovasi)	Agios Kirykos	2-3½hr	€13	1-2 daily*
Samos (Vathy)	Agios Kirykos	3½hr	€12	1-2 daily*

*except Friday
**high-speed services

Inousses

Northeastern Aegean Islands; see also p613

BOAT SERVICES FROM INOUSSES

Destination	Port	Duration	Fare	Frequency
Chios	Inousses	1¼hr	€4-10	1 daily

Ios

Cyclades; see also p423

BOAT SERVICES FROM IOS

Destination	Port	Duration	Fare	Frequency
Amorgos	Ios	50min	€4.50	1-2 daily
Anafi	Ios	3hr	€8.80	5 weekly
Folegandros	Ios	1hr 20min	€11.50	1-2 daily
Iraklio*	Ios	2½hr	€58	1 daily
Kera	Ios	10hr 40min	€40.40	2 weekly
Kimolos	Ios	2½hr	€20.80	5-6 weekly
Kythnos	Ios	8½hr	€16	2 weekly
Lavrio	Ios	11hr 35min	€43.30	2 weekly
Milos	Ios	3½hr	€29.50	5-6 weekly
Naxos	Ios	1hr 35min	€9.90-€18	1-3 daily
Naxos*	Ios	50min	€20.50	1-2 daily
Paros	Ios	2½-3hr 10min	€11	2 daily
Paros*	Ios	1hr	€27	1-2 daily
Piraeus	Ios	7hr	€31.50	4-5 daily
Piraeus*	Ios	5½hr	€46	3 daily
Santorini (Thira)	Ios	1¼hr	€8	5 daily
Santorini (Thira)*	Ios	40-50min	€18	3 daily
Sifnos	Ios	6hr	€13.50	4 weekly
Serifos	Ios	7hr 10min	€16	4 weekly
Sikinos*	Ios	10min	€12	1 weekly
Sikinos	Ios	20min	€8	1-4 daily
Syros	Ios	5hr 35min	€30.80	4 weekly

*high-speed services

Iraklia

Cyclades; see also p415

BOAT SERVICES FROM IRAKLIA

Destination	Port	Duration	Fare	Frequency
Amorgos	Iraklia	1¾-4hr 40	€8.50-10.50	2-3 daily
Donousa	Iraklia	2hr 20min-4hr	€7.50-14.40	1-2 daily
Koufonisia	Iraklia	1hr	€5	2-3 daily
Naxos	Iraklia	1hr	€6.50	2-3 daily
Paros	Iraklia	2¼hr	€12.50	1-2 daily
Piraeus	Iraklia	7hr 20min	€30	1-2 daily
Schinousa	Iraklia	15min	€4.50	2-3 daily
Syros	Iraklia	3hr 35min	€22.70	4 weekly

Ithaki

Ionian Islands; see also p700

BOAT SERVICES FROM ITHAKI

Destination	Port	Duration	Fare	Frequency
Fiskardo	Frikes	55min	€3.80	1 daily
Nydri	Frikes	1½hr	€7	1 daily
Patra	Vathy	3¾hr	€17.60	2 daily
Patra	Piso Aetos	3hr 10min	€17.60	2 daily
Sami	Piso Aetos	30min	€2.60/15.90	2 daily
Sami	Vathy	45min	€5.60/26.70	2 daily

Kalymnos

Dodecanese; see also p565

AIR

Olympic has daily flights to Athens (€65, 20 minutes).

BOAT

Small, local car and passenger ferries leave three times daily from Pothia to Mastihari on Kos. The fast Lipsi-based *Anna Express* links Pothia with Leros and Lipsi three times weekly. There's also a daily caïque from Myrties to Xirokambos (€8) on Leros and Emborios (€8) in the north of Kalymnos. A caïque runs between Myrties and Telendos Islet (€2) throughout the day.

BOAT SERVICES FROM KALYMNOS

Destination	Port	Duration	Fare	Frequency
Astypalea	Pothia	3½hr	€11	3 weekly
Kos*	Pothia	35min	€15	1 daily
Kos	Pothia	50min	€4	3 daily
Leros*	Pothia	50min	€20	1 daily
Leros	Pothia	1½hrs	€7	1 daily
Lipsi*	Pothia	1hr 20min	€20	6 weekly
Patmos*	Pothia	1hr 40min	€26	6 weekly
Piraeus	Pothia	13hr	€44	3 weekly
Rhodes	Pothia	4½hr	€20	3 weekly

*high-speed services

Karpathos

Dodecanese; see also p532

AIR

Flights with Olympic Air head daily to Kasos (€21) and Sitia (€43), twice daily to Rhodes (€28) and three times per week to Athens (€69).

BOAT SERVICES FROM KARPATHOS

Destination	Port	Duration	Fare	Frequency
Halki	Diafani	2hr	€17	4 weekly
Kasos	Pigadia	1½hr	€15	2 weekly
Milos	Pigadia	16hr	€36	2 weekly
Piraeus	Pigadia	17hr	€58	2 weekly
Rhodes	Pigadia	5hr	€22	3 weekly
Santorini (Thira)	Pigadia	11hr	€25	2 weekly
Sitia	Pigadia	4hr	€18	2 weekly

Kasos
Dodecanese; see also p539

AIR
Olympic offers daily flights to Karpathos (€21, 10 minutes) and Sitia (€38, 40 minutes) and five flights per week to Rhodes (€34, one hour).

BOAT SERVICES FROM KASOS

Destination	Port	Duration	Fare	Frequency
Karpathos	Fry	1½hr	€15	2 weekly
Piraeus	Fry	19hr	€35	3 weekly
Rhodes	Fry	7hr	€24	3 weekly
Sitia	Fry	2½hr	€12	3 weekly

Kastellorizo (Megisti)
Dodecanese; see also p542

AIR
Olympic has three flights per week to Rhodes (€22, 20 minutes) from where you can get connections to Athens.

BOAT SERVICES FROM KASTELLORIZO (MEGISTI)

Destination	Port	Duration	Fare	Frequency
Piraeus	Kastellorizo	23hr	€53	1 weekly
Rhodes	Kastellorizo	4hr 40min	€17	2 weekly
Rhodes*	Kastellorizo	2½hr	€25	1 weekly

*high-speed services

Kavala/Keramoti
Northern Greece (mainland port); see also p309

AIR
From Kavala's Alexander the Great Airport, all island flights go via Thessaloniki or Athens. For cumulative fares involving these routes, check locally or with the websites of Greek air carriers.

BOAT
Kavala is one of two ports serving Thasos, and in summer has frequent ferries and hydrofoils to the island's ports of Skala Prinou and Limenas. It's also a ferry hub for the Northeast Aegean Islands. Thasos (Limenas) also has frequent connections during summer from Keramoti, 46km east of Kavala and closer to the mainland airport.

BOAT SERVICES FROM KAVALA/KERAMOTI

Destination	Port	Duration	Fare	Frequency
Agios Efstratios	Kavala	7½hr	€19	3 weekly
Chios (Chios Town)	Kavala	15hr	€31	2 weekly
Ikaria (Agios Kirykos)	Kavala	20¾hr	€37	1 weekly
Lavrio	Kavala	15½-19hr	€39	3 weekly
Lesvos (Mytilini Town)	Kavala	11hr	€26	2 weekly
Lesvos (Sigri)	Kavala	11hr	€26	1 weekly
Limnos	Kavala	5½hr	€15	5 weekly
Samos (Karlovasi)	Kavala	19hr	€37	1 weekly
Samos (Vathy)	Kavala	19hr	€37	1 weekly
Thasos (Limenas)	Keramoti	40min	€3.30	hourly
Thasos (Limenas)*	Kavala	40min	€10	4 daily
Thasos (Skala Prinou)	Kavala	1¼hr	€3.50	hourly
Thasos (Skala Prinou)*	Kavala	40min	€10	4 daily

*high-speed services

Kea (Tzia)
Cyclades; see also p455

BOAT SERVICES FROM KEA (TZIA)

Destination	Port	Duration	Fare	Frequency
Andros	Kea	5hr 50min	€17.20	1 weekly
Folegandros	Kea	7hr 40min	€16	5 weekly
Ios	Kea		€10.40-40.40	2 weekly
Kimolos	Kea	13½hr	€32	2 weekly
Kythnos	Kea	1hr	€12.80	7 weekly
Lavrio	Kea	50min	€12.70	3-5 daily
Milos	Kea	14½hr	€25.20	2 weekly
Paros	Kea	7hr.50min	€31.20	2 weekly
Naxos	Kea	8¾hr	€31.20	2 weekly
Sikinos	Kea	11hr 10min	€41.40	2 weekly
Syros	Kea	2hr 50min	€20.40	4 weekly
Tinos	Kea	4hr	€22.20	4 weekly

Kefallonia
Ionian Islands; see also p693

DOMESTIC FLIGHTS FROM KEFALLONIA

Destination	Airport	Duration	Fare	Frequency
Athens	Kefallonia	55min	€71	2 daily
Zakynthos	Kefallonia	20min	€32	3 weekly
Preveza	Kefallonia	30min	€34	3 weekly

ISLAND HOPPING

BOAT SERVICES FROM KEFALLONIA

Destination	Port	Duration	Fare	Frequency
Astakos	Sami	3hr	€10	1 daily
Igoumenitsa	Sami	4¼hr	€13	1 weekly
Ithaki (Frikes)	Fiskardo	55min	€3.80	1 daily
Ithaki (Piso Aetos)	Sami	30min	€2.80	2 daily
Ithaki (Vathy)	Sami	45min	€5.60	2 daily
Kyllini	Argostoli	3hr	€14	1 daily
Lefkada (Vasiliki)	Fiskardo	1hr	€6.90	1 daily
Patra	Sami	2¾hr	€16.90	2 daily
Poros	Kyllini	1½hr	€9.90	3-5 daily
Zakynthos (Agios Nikolaos)	Pesada	1½hr	€7	2 daily

Kimolos

Cyclades; see also p447

BOAT SERVICES FROM KIMOLOS

Destination	Port	Duration	Fare	Frequency
Folegandros*	Kimilos	1½hr	€7	5 weekly
Ios	Kimilos	2½hr	€20.80	5-6 weekly
Kea	Kimilos	13½hr	€32	2 weekly
Kythnos	Kimilos	5hr 50min	€11	2 weekly
Milos	Kimilos	35min	€5.70-9.50	8 weekly
Naxos	Kimilos	4hr 35min	€25.60	2 weekly
Paros	Kimilos	3hr 20min	€20.80	2 weekly
Piraeus	Kimilos	9hr 20min	€24.50	5 weekly
Piraeus*	Kimilos	5¼hr	€48	3 weekly
Santorini (Thira)	Kimilos	3½hr	€7.20	2 weekly
Sifnos	Kimilos	3hr	€6	5 weekly
Serifos	Kimilos	4hr 10min	€8.50	5 weekly
Syros	Kimilos	5¼hr	€25.20	5 weekly

*high-speed services

Kos

Dodecanese; see also p556

AIR

Olympic Air has two daily flights to Athens (€44; 55 minutes) and three weekly to Rhodes (€41; 20 minutes), Leros (€41; 15 minutes) and Astypalea (€47; one hour).

BOAT SERVICES FROM KOS

Destination	Port	Duration	Fare	Frequency
Leros	Kos Town	1hr 40min	€22	1 daily
Kalymnos	Mastihari	1hr	€4	3 daily
Kalymnos*	Kos Town	30min	€15	1 daily
Nisyros	Kos Town	1hr 20min	€8	4 weekly
Nisyros*	Kos Town	45min	€16	2 weekly
Patmos	Kos Town	4hr	€13	2 weekly
Patmos*	Kos Town	2½hr	€29	6 weekly
Piraeus	Kos Town	10hr	€46	4 weekly
Rhodes	Kos Town	3hr	€26	1 daily
Rhodes*	Kos Town	2½hr	€30	1 daily
Samos	Kos Town	5½hr	€19	1 daily
Symi*	Kos Town	1½hr	€22	1 daily
Thessaloniki	Kos Town	21hr	€47	1 weekly

*high-speed services

Koufonisia

Cyclades; see also p417

BOAT SERVICES FROM KOUFONISIA

Destination	Port	Duration	Fare	Frequency
Amorgos	Koufonisia	1hr 5min-1hr 40min	€7.50	3 daily
Donousa	Koufonisia	1¼hr	€5.50	1-2 daily
Folegandros*	Koufonisia	3hr	€35	1 daily
Iraklia	Koufonisia	1hr	€5	2-3 daily
Milos*	Koufonisia	3hr 40min	€39	1 daily
Naxos	Koufonisia	2hr 20min	€7.50	1-2 daily
Paros	Koufonisia	4½hr	€15.50	1-2 daily
Piraeus	Koufonisia	8hr	€30	2-3 daily
Piraeus*	Koufonisia	7hr	€58	1 daily
Schinousa	Koufonisia	40min	€4.50	2-3 daily
Syros	Koufonisia	4½hr	€12.70	4 weekly

*high-speed services

Kythira

Ionian Islands; see also p231

BOAT SERVICES FROM KYTHIRA

Destination	Port	Duration	Fare	Frequency
Gythio	Kythira	2½	€11	2 weekly
Kalamata	Kythira	4½	€17	1 weekly
Kissamos (2 via Antikythira)	Kythira	4hr	€17	3 weekly
Neapoli (Diakofti)	Kythira	1hr	€11	1 daily
Rethymno	Kythira	6hr	€20	1 weekly

Kythnos

Cyclades; see also p453

BOAT SERVICES FROM KYTHNOS

Destination	Port	Duration	Fare	Frequency
Folegandros	Kea	11hr 25min	€38.20	2 weekly
Ios	Kea	2½hr	€20.80	5-6 weekly
Kea	Kea	1hr	€12.80	7 weekly
Kimolos	Kea	8½hr	€16	2 weekly
Milos	Kea	3¼hr-4hr	€18-16	1-2 daily
Paros	Kea	6hr 40min	€27.40	2 weekly
Piraeus	Kea	3hr 10min	€18	1-2 daily
Santorini (Thira)	Kea	8hr	€16	2 weekly

ISLAND HOPPING

Serifos	Kea	1hr 20min	€15	1-2 daily
Sifnos	Kea	2½hr	€13.50	1-2 daily
Syros	Kea	2hr	€9.90	4 weekly

Lefkada

Ionian Islands; see also p688

DOMESTIC FLIGHTS FROM LEFKADA

Destination	Airport	Duration	Fare	Frequency
Athens	Preveza /Lefkada	1hr	€97	2 daily
Corfu	Preveza /Lefkada	25min	€39	3 weekly

BOAT SERVICES FROM LEFKADA

Destination	Port	Duration	Fare	Frequency
Fiskardo via Frikes	Nydri	2½hr	€6.90	1 daily
Frikes	Nydri	1½hr	€6.40	1 daily
Fiskardo	Vasiliki	1hr	€6.90	1 daily
Frikes	Vasiliki	2hr	€8	1 daily

Leros

Dodecanese; see also p571

AIR

Olympic flies from Leros to Athens (€55, one hour) six times each week, and to Rhodes (€47, two hours), Kos (€41, 20 minutes) and Astypalea (€41, 15 minutes) three times per week.

BOAT

The Lipsi-based **Anna Express** (☎ 22479 41215) departs from Agia Marina and links Leros with Kalymnos three times per week, calling at Arki once each week. The caïque *Katerina* leaves Xirokambos each morning for Myrties on Kalymnos (€7).

BOAT SERVICES FROM LEROS

Destination	Port	Duration	Fare	Frequency
Kalymnos*	Agia Marina	50min	€20	6 weekly
Kos	Lakki	3¼hr	€11	daily
Kos*	Agia Marina	1hr	€22	6 weekly
Lipsi*	Agia Marina	20min	€14	6 weekly
Patmos*	Agia Marina	45min	€16	6 weekly
Piraeus	Lakki	8hr	€35	1 daily
Rhodes	Lakki	3½hr	€25	3 weekly
Rhodes*	Agia Marina	4hr	€41	6 weekly

*high-speed services

Lesvos (Mytilini)

Northeastern Aegean Islands; see also p616

DOMESTIC FLIGHTS FROM LESVOS (MYTILINI)

Destination	Airport	Duration	Fare	Frequency
Athens	Mytilini Town	55min	€110	7 weekly
Thessaloniki	Mytilini Town	45min	€105	7 weekly
Crete (Iraklio)	Mytilini Town	50min	€110	2 weekly

BOAT SERVICES FROM LESVOS (MYTILINI)

Destination	Port	Duration	Fare	Frequency
Chios	Mytilini Town	2-3¼hr	€13-20	2 daily
Kavala	Mytilini Town	11hr	€26	3 weekly
Karlovasi (Samos)	Mytilini Town	6½hr	€22	2 weekly
Limnos	Mytilini Town	6hr	€19	4 weekly
Mykonos	Mytilini Town	5½hr	€36	2 weekly
Piraeus	Mytilini Town	8½-13hr	€27-37	2 daily
Syros	Mytilini Town	6½hr	€34	5 weekly
Thessaloniki	Mytilini Town	14hr	€36	3 weekly
Vathy (Samos)	Mytilini Town	7¼hr	€17	2 weekly

Limnos

Northeastern Aegean Islands; see also p627

DOMESTIC FLIGHTS FROM LIMNOS

Destination	Airport	Duration	Fare	Frequency
Athens	Limnos	55min	€100	7 weekly
Thessaloniki	Limnos	35min	€105	6 weekly

BOAT SERVICES FROM LIMNOS

Destination	Port	Duration	Fare	Frequency
Agios Efstratios	Limnos	1½hr	€6-13	3 weekly
Alonnisos	Limnos	3hr	€37	1 weekly
Chios	Limnos	11hr	€22	3 weekly
Chios (Mesta)	Limnos	5½hr	€40	1 weekly
Ikaria (Agios Kirykos)	Limnos	15½hr	€30	1 weekly
Kavala	Limnos	5hr	€15	5 weekly
Lavrio	Limnos	9½-14hr	€28.60	3 weekly
Lesvos (Mytilini)	Limnos	6hr	€19	3 weekly
Lesvos (Sigri)	Limnos	5hr	€13	1 weekly
Piraeus	Limnos	21hr	€30.50	1 weekly
Psara	Limnos	4¼hr	€48.50	1 weekly
Samos (Karlovasi)	Limnos	14½hr	€30	1 weekly
Samos (Vathy)	Limnos	14hr	€28	2 weekly
Skiathos	Limnos	5hr	€39	1 weekly
Skopelos	Limnos	4hr	€38	1 weekly
Thessaloniki	Limnos	8½hr	€23	2 weekly
Volos	Limnos	7¼hr	€40	1 weekly

Lipsi
Dodecanese; see also p580

BOAT
The small local, but speedy **Anna Express** (☎ 22479 41215) links Lipsi with Kalymnos and Leros three times per week, and runs to Arki twice weekly.

BOAT SERVICES FROM LIPSI

Destination	Port	Duration	Fare	Frequency
Agathonisi	Lipsi	3hr	€8	4 weekly
Agathonisi*	Lipsi	40min	€13	1 weekly
Kalymnos	Lipsi	1½hr	€8	2 weekly
Kalymnos*	Lipsi	20min	€20	1 daily
Kos*	Lipsi	5hr 50min	€29	6 weekly
Leros	Lipsi	1hr	€8	2 weekly
Leros*	Lipsi	20min	€14	6 weekly
Patmos	Lipsi	25min	€5	1 daily
Patmos*	Lipsi	10min	€13	5 weekly
Piraeus	Lipsi	12hr	€42	2 weekly
Rhodes*	Lipsi	5½hr	€45	6 weekly

*high-speed services

Milos
Cyclades; see also p445

DOMESTIC FLIGHTS FROM MILOS

Destination	Airport	Duration	Fare	Frequency
Athens	Milos	40min	€41	2 weekly

BOAT SERVICES FROM MILOS

Destination	Port	Duration	Fare	Frequency
Folegandros	Milos	2½hr	€8	5 weekly
Folegandros*	Milos	1¼hr	€16	4 weekly
Ios	Milos	3½hr	€29.50	5-6 weekly
Iraklio	Milos	7hr 25min	€21.70	3 weekly
Kea	Milos	14½hr	€25.20	2 weekly
Kimolos	Milos	35min	€9.50	8 weekly
Kythnos	Milos	3¾hr-4¼hr	€18-16	1-2 daily
Naxos	Milos	2¼hr	€13.60	4 weekly
Paros	Milos	4¼hr	€24.70	4 weekly
Piraeus	Milos	8hr	€30.50	1-2 daily
Piraeus*	Milos	2hr 50min-3hr 55min	€49-51	2-3 daily
Santorini (Thira)	Milos	4hr	€17	2 weekly
Santorini (Thira)*	Milos	2hr	€34	1 daily
Sifnos	Milos	3hr 40min	€13.50	1-2 daily
Serifos	Milos	4hr 40min	€16	1-2 daily
Serifos*	Milos	1½hr	€16	1-3 daily
Sifnos*	Milos	1hr	€14	1-3 daily
Syros	Milos	4hr 20 min	€25.20	5 weekly

*high-speed services

Mykonos
Cyclades; see also p386

DOMESTIC FLIGHTS FROM MYKONOS

Destination	Airport	Duration	Fare	Frequency
Athens	Mykonos	50min	€52-103	3-5 daily
Thessaloniki	Mykonos	1hr	€100	3 weekly
Santorini (Thira)		30min	€85	1-2 daily

BOAT SERVICES FROM MYKONOS

Destination	Port	Duration	Fare	Frequency
Andros	Mykonos	2¾hr	€13	3-4 daily
Chios	Mykonos	3hr	€28.50	2 weekly
Ios*	Mykonos	1½hr	€28	2-3 daily
Iraklio*	Mykonos	1½hr	€66.50	1-2 daily
Lesvos (Mytilini)	Mykonos	5hr 35min	€35.50	2 weekly
Naxos	Mykonos	1¾hr	€12	1 weekly
Naxos*	Mykonos	40min	€18.50	2 daily
Paros*	Mykonos	1hr	€19	3 daily
Piraeus	Mykonos	4¾hr	€30.50-€39.502	1 daily
Piraeus*	Mykonos	3hr	€43	3 daily
Rafina	Mykonos	4½hrn	€23	2-3 daily
Rafina*	Mykonos	2hr 10min	€41	4-5 daily
Santorini (Thira)*	Mykonos	2hr 10min	€38	2-3daily
Syros	Mykonos	1½hr	€8-11	2-3 daily
Syros*	Mykonos	30min	€13	3 daily
Tinos	Mykonos	30min	€4.50-€6	5 daily
Tinos*	Mykonos	15min	€10.50	5-6 daily

*high-speed services

Naxos
Cyclades; see also p406

DOMESTIC FLIGHTS FROM NAXOS

Destination	Airport	Duration	Fare	Frequency
Athens	Naxos	45min	€62	1 daily

BOAT SERVICES FROM NAXOS

Destination	Port	Duration	Fare	Frequency
Amorgos	Naxos	3hr-3hr 50min	€11.50-14	2-3 daily
Anafi	Naxos	7¼hr	€14.30	5 weekly
Astypalea	Naxos	5½hr	€23	5 weekly
Donousa	Naxos	1-4hr	€7.50	1-3 daily
Folegandros	Naxos	3¼hr	€14.30-€20.20	5 weekly
Ios	Naxos	1hr 35min	€9.90-€18.10	1-3daily
Ios*	Naxos	50min	€20.50	1-2 daily
Iraklia	Naxos	1hr	€6.50	2-3 daily
Kalymnos	Naxos	4¾hr	€19.50	2 weekly
Kastellorizo	Naxos	16hr 20min	€38.50	2 weekly
Kea	Naxos	8¼hr	€18.70	1 weekly

Kimolos	Naxos	4hr 35min	€25.60	2weekly
Kos	Naxos	8¼hr	€23	2 weekly
Koufinisia	Naxos	2hr-2hr-40min	€7.50-9	2 daily
Kythnos	Naxos	8hr 20min	€19.20	1 weekly
Lavrio	Naxos	10hr	€24	1 weekly
Milos	Naxos	5hr 35min	€33.20	4 weekly
Mykonos	Naxos	1¾hr	€12	1 weekly
Mykonos*	Naxos	40min	€18.50	2 daily
Paros	Naxos	1hr	€7	6 daily
Paros*	Naxos	45min	€13	3 daily
Piraeus	Naxos	4¾hr	€30	4-5 daily
Piraeus*	Naxos	3½hr	€45	4 daily
Rafina*	Naxos	3hr	€43	1 daily
Rhodes	Naxos	14hr	€32	2 weekly
Santorini (Thira)	Naxos	3hr	€15.50	5 daily
Santorini (Thira)*	Naxos	1½hr	€27.50	2-3daily
Schinousa	Naxos	2hr 20min	€7.50	1-2 daily
Sikinos	Naxos	2¼hr	€13.60	3-4 weekly
Syros	Naxos	3hr	€10.80	1daily
Syros*	Naxos	1¾hr	€20	4 weekly
Tilos	Naxos	9hr 35min	€23	2 weekly
Tinos	Naxos	4¼hr	€13	1 daily

*high-speed services

Nisyros
Dodecanese; see also p551

BOAT
The small local ferry *Agios Konstantinos* links Mandraki with Kardamena on Kos (€8, two hours, daily), while the larger *Panagia Spyliani* links Nisyros with Kos Town (€10, daily).

BOAT SERVICES FROM NISYROS

Destination	Port	Duration	Fare	Frequency
Kalymnos	Mandraki	2½hr	€7	4 weekly
Kos	Mandraki	1¼hr	€8	1 weekly
Kos*	Mandraki	45min	€16	1 weekly
Piraeus	Mandraki	18hr	€46	3 weekly
Rhodes	Mandraki	4½hr	€15	3 weekly
Rhodes*	Mandraki	2¾hr	€28	2 weekly
Symi	Mandraki	3¾hr	€11	2 weekly

*high-speed services

Paros
Cyclades; see also p397

DOMESTIC FLIGHTS FROM PAROS

Destination	Airport	Duration	Fare	Frequency
Athens	Paros	35min	€60	1 daily

BOAT SERVICES FROM PAROS

Destination	Port	Duration	Fare	Frequency
Amorgos	Paros	3-7hr	€12.20-15	1-2 daily
Anafi	Paros	7hr 25min	€17.90	3-4 weekly
Astypalea	Paros	4hr 50min	€28.50	5 weekly
Donousa	Paros	2½hr	€10.30-12.50	1-3 daily
Folegandros	Paros	4-6hr	€15-16.70	5 weekly
Ios	Paros	2½hr-3hr 10min	€11	2 daily
Ios*	Paros	1hr	€27	1-2 daily
Iraklia	Paros	2¼hr	€12.50	1-2 daily
Iraklio*	Paros	3hr 40min	€65	1 daily
Kalymnos	Paros	7½hr	€19.50	2 weekly
Kastellorizo	Paros	17hr 35min	€40	2 weekly
Kea	Paros	7hr 50min	31.20	2 weekly
Kimolos	Paros	3hr 20min	€20.80	2 weekly
Kos	Paros	7-7½hr	€23	2 weekly
Koufinisia	Paros	4½hr	€15.50	1-2 daily
Kythnos	Paros	6hr 40min	€27.40	2 weekly
Milos	Paros	4¼hr	€24.70	4 weekly
Mykonos*	Paros	1hr	€19	3 daily
Naxos	Paros	30min	€15	2 daily
Naxos	Paros	1hr	€7	5 daily
Piraeus	Paros	4¾hr	€29-€31	6 daily
Piraeus*	Paros	2½hr	€39.50	4 daily
Rafina*	Paros	2½hr	€49.50	1 daily
Rhodes	Paros	13hr 20min	€32	2 weekly
Santorini (Thira)	Paros	3-4hr	€16.50	5 daily
Santorini (Thira)*	Paros	2¼hr	€36	2-3 daily
Schinousa	Paros	2hr 20min	€10	1-2 daily
Serifos	Paros	2½hr	€10.10	2 weekly
Sifnos	Paros	2hr	€5.40	3 weekly
Sikinos	Paros	3hr 10min	€15.10	3-4 weekly
Syros*	Paros	45min	€8.20	3 daily
Tilos	Paros	10hr 50min	€23	2 weekly
Tinos	Paros	1¼hr	€21.50-€24.503	1 daily

*high-speed services

Patmos
Dodecanese; see also p575

BOAT
The local *Patmos Star* leaves Patmos daily for Lipsi and Leros (return €8) while the *Delfini* goes to Marathi daily each morning in high season and twice weekly out of season (return €15), calling twice each week at Arki. The local *Lambi II* goes to Arki, Marathi and Lipsi three times each week. The Lipsi-based *Anna Express* connects Patmos with Lipsi and Leros three times each week.

ISLAND HOPPING

BOAT SERVICES FROM PATMOS

Destination	Port	Duration	Fare	Frequency
Agathonisi	Skala	55min	€8	4 weekly
Kalymnos*	Skala	1hr 40min	€26	6 weekly
Kos*	Skala	3hr	€29	6 weekly
Leros	Skala	2hr	€8	1 weekly
Leros*	Skala	40min	€16	6 weekly
Lipsi*	Skala	25min	€13	1 weekly
Piraeus	Skala	7hr	€34	4 weekly
Rhodes	Skala	6hr	€40	3 weekly
Rhodes*	Skala	5hr	€46	6 weekly
Samos	Skala	5hr	€9	4 weekly
Symi*	Skala	4hr	€44	5 weekly

*high-speed services

Paxi

Ionian Islands; see also p685

BOAT SERVICES FROM PAXI

Destination	Port	Duration	Fare	Frequency
Corfu*	Paxi	40min	€16.40	1-3 daily
Corfu	Paxi	3½hr	€8.50	3 weekly
Igoumenitsa	Paxi	2hr	€7.50	2 daily

*high-speed services

Peloponnese

See also p166

BOAT

Boats between Galatas (Peloponnese) and the island of Poros run approximately every 15 to 30 minutes.

BOAT SERVICES FROM THE PELOPONNESE

Destination	Port	Duration	Fare	Frequency
Corfu	Patra	6-7½hr	€30	4 weekly
Corfu	Patra	6-7½hr	€33	1 daily
Crete (Kissamos)	Gythio	7hr	€24	1 weekly (via Kythira & Antikythira)
Crete	Kalamata	7hr	€40	1 weekly (via Kythira)
Gythio	Kythira	2½hr	€11	2 weekly
Hydra*	Ermioni	25min	€15	4 daily
Hydra	Ermioni	1hr	€9.50	4 daily
Hydra*	Porto Heli	25min	€15	4 daily
Ithaki (Piso Aetos)	Patra	3¾hr	€18	1 daily
Ithaki (Vathy)	Patra	5hr	€18	1 daily
Kefallonia (Argostoli)	Kyllini	2hr	€13	1 daily
Kefallonia (Lixouri)	Kyllini	2¼hr	€14	1 daily
Kefallonia (Poros)	Kyllini	1½hr	€8	5 daily
Kefallonia (Poros)	Kyllini	1hr	€10	1 daily
Kefallonia (Poros; by bus)	Patra	3hr	€18	
Kefallonia (Sami)	Patra	2¾hr	€17	3 weekly
Kefallonia (Sami)	Patra	2¾hr	€18	2 daily
Kythira	Kalamata	4½hr	€17	1 weekly
Kythira (Diakofti)	Neapoli	1hr	€11	1 daily
Lefkada (by bus)	Patra	3hr	€14.50	2 weekly
Piraeus*	Ermioni	2hr	€29.50	4 daily
Piraeus*	Porto Heli	3hr 20min	€35.50	4 daily
Poros*	Ermioni	1hr	€15	3 daily
Poros	Methana	30min	€4.20	2-3 daily
Poros*	Porto Heli	1hr 40min	€19	2 daily
Spetses*	Ermioni	25min	€7.50	2 daily
Spetses*	Porto Heli	15min	€5.50	4 daily
Zakynthos (by bus)	Kyllini	3½hr	€15	3 on Sun
Zakynthos	Kyllini	1¼hr	€6.80	4-6 daily

*high-speed services

Preveza

Northern Greece (mainland port); see also p349

DOMESTIC FLIGHTS FROM PREVEZA

Destination	Airport	Duration	Fare	Frequency
Athens	Preveza	1hr	€95	5 weekly
Corfu	Preveza	30min	€39	3 weekly
Kefallonia	Preveza	30min	€34	3 weekly
Zakynthos	Preveza	1hr 20min	€43	3 weekly

Poros

Saronic Gulf Islands; see also p361

BOAT SERVICES FROM POROS

Destination	Port	Duration	Fare	Frequency
Aegina	Poros	1¼hr	€8.60	4 daily
Hydra*	Poros	30min	€12.50	6 daily
Methana	Poros	30min	€4.20	4 daily
Piraeus	Poros	2½hr	€13.30	8-10 daily
Piraeus*	Poros	1hr	€25.20	4 daily
Spetses*	Poros	1hr	€14.50	7 daily

*high-speed services

Psara

Northeastern Aegean Islands; see also p616

BOAT SERVICES FROM PSARA

Destination	Port	Duration	Fare	Frequency
Chios	Psara	3½hr	€11	6 weekly
Mesta (Chios)	Psara	45min-2hr	€6-13	2 weekly
Lavrio	Psara	5hr	€45	1 weekly
Agios Efstratios	Psara	3¼hr	€35	1 weekly
Limnos	Psara	4hr	€48.50	1 weekly

Rhodes

Dodecanese; see also p514

AIR

Olympic Air has at least five flights daily to Athens (€58), around six per week to Karpathos (€28), three weekly to Kasos (€34), five weekly to Kastellorizo (€22), three weekly to Thessaloniki (€110), three weekly to Astypalea (€47) and two weekly to Samos (€37). Aegean Airlines also offers daily flights to Athens (€64) and Thessaloniki (€90).

BOAT

In addition to the departures listed below, there are local ferries running daily between Skala Kamirou, on Rhodes' west coast, and Halki (€10, one hour). From Skala Kamirou services depart at 2.30pm, and from Halki at 6am. There are also excursion boats to Symi (€22 return) daily in summer, leaving Mandraki Harbour at 9am and returning at 6pm. You can buy tickets at most travel agencies, but it's better to buy them at the harbour, where you can check out the boats personally.

BOAT SERVICES FROM RHODES

Destination	Port	Duration	Fare	Frequency
Agathonisi*	Commercial Harbour (Rhodes Town)	5hr	€46	1 weekly
Alexandroupoli	Commercial Harbour (Rhodes Town)	29hr	€46	1 weekly
Astypalea	Commercial Harbour (Rhodes Town)	10hr	€30	1 weekly
Halki*	Commercial Harbour (Rhodes Town)	1¼hr	€21	2 weekly
Halki	Commercial Harbour (Rhodes Town)	2hr	€10	4 weekly
Kalymnos*	Commercial Harbour (Rhodes Town)	3hr	€38	1 daily
Kalymnos	Commercial Harbour (Rhodes Town)	4½hr	€20	3 weekly
Karpathos	Commercial Harbour (Rhodes Town)	5hr	€22	3 weekly
Kasos	Commercial Harbour (Rhodes Town)	8hr	€25	4 weekly
Kastellorizo*	Commercial Harbour (Rhodes Town)	2½hr	€25	1 weekly
Kastellorizo	Commercial Harbour (Rhodes Town)	4hr 40min	€17	2 weekly
Kos*	Commercial Harbour (Rhodes Town)	2½hr	€30	1 daily
Kos	Commercial Harbour (Rhodes Town)	3hr	€26	1 daily
Leros*	Commercial Harbour (Rhodes Town)	3½hr	€41	6 weekly
Leros	Commercial Harbour (Rhodes Town)	5hr	€25	3 weekly
Lipsi*	Commercial Harbour (Rhodes Town)	5½hr	€45	6 weekly
Lipsi	Commercial Harbour (Rhodes Town)	8hr	€40	2 weekly
Nisyros*	Commercial Harbour (Rhodes Town)	2¾hr	€28	2 weekly
Nisyros	Commercial Harbour (Rhodes Town)	4½hr	€15	3 weekly
Patmos*	Commercial Harbour (Rhodes Town)	5hr	€46	6 weekly
Patmos	Commercial Harbour (Rhodes Town)	6hr	€40	3 weekly
Piraeus	Commercial Harbour (Rhodes Town)	13hr	€53	1 daily
Sitia	Commercial Harbour (Rhodes Town)	10hr	€28	3 weekly
Symi*	Commercial Harbour (Rhodes Town)	50min	€15	1 daily
Symi	Mandraki	2hr	€12	1 daily
Thessaloniki	Commercial Harbour (Rhodes Town)	21hr	€55	1 weekly
Tilos*	Commercial Harbour (Rhodes Town)	2hr	€25	2 weekly
Tilos*	Mandraki Harbour (Rhodes Town)	1½hr	€24	6 weekly
Tilos	Commercial Harbour (Rhodes Town)	2½hr	€15	4 weekly

*high-speed services

Samos

Northeastern Aegean Islands; see also p596

DOMESTIC FLIGHTS FROM SAMOS

Destination	Airport	Duration	Fare	Frequency
Athens	Samos	45min	€80	7 weekly
Iraklio (Crete)	Samos	50min	€110	2 weekly
Thessaloniki	Samos	50min	€90	5 weekly

BOAT SERVICES FROM SAMOS

Destination	Port	Duration	Fare	Frequency
Chios	Karlovasi	2½hr	€11	2 weekly
Fourni	Vathy	1½-2hr	€8	1-3 daily
Ikaria (Agios Kirykos)	Vathy	2hr	€6	1-2 daily
Ikaria (Evdilos)**	Vathy	1hr	€11.50	1 daily*
Kalymnos	Vathy	4hr	€18	1 weekly
Kavala	Vathy	18hr	€37	1 weekly
Kos	Vathy	5¼hr	€19	1 weekly
Lesvos (Mytilini)	Karlovasi	6¼hr	€22	1 weekly
Lesvos (Sigri)	Karlovasi	6hr	€23.50	1 weekly
Limnos	Vathy	13hr	€30	1 weekly
Mykonos	Vathy	6½hr	€23	3 weekly
Naxos**	Vathy	3½hr	€29	1 daily*
Paros**	Vathy	4½hr	€30	1 daily*
Piraeus	Vathy	7-13hr	€41	1-2 daily
Rhodes	Vathy	9¼hr	€30	1 weekly
Thessaloniki	Karlovasi	15½hr	€42	1 weekly

*except Mondays
**high-speed services

Samothraki

Northern Greece; see also p632

BOAT SERVICES FROM SAMOTHRAKI

Destination	Port	Duration	Fare	Frequency
Samothraki	Alexandroupoli	2hr	€13	2 daily

Santorini (Thira)

Cyclades; see also p428

DOMESTIC FLIGHTS FROM SANTORINI (THIRA)

Destination	Port	Duration	Fare	Frequency
Athens	Santorini (Thira)	45min	€68	10 daily
Iraklio	Santorini (Thira)	30min	€85	5 weekly
Rhodes	Santorini (Thira)	1hr	€112	2 daily

BOAT SERVICES FROM SANTORINI (THIRA)

Destination	Port	Duration	Fare	Frequency
Amorgos*	Santorini (Thira)	1hr	€32	1 daily
Anafi	Santorini (Thira)	1hr	€8	5 weekly
Folegandros	Santorini (Thira)	2½hr	€7.50	1-2 daily
Folegandros*	Santorini (Thira)	30min	€19	1 daily
Iraklio	Santorini (Thira)	4½hr	€24	1 daily
Iraklio*	Santorini (Thira)	1¾hr	€42	1 daily
Karpathos	Santorini (Thira)	8hr	€25	5 weekly
Kimolos	Santorini (Thira)	3½hr	€7.20	2 weekly
Kos	Santorini (Thira)	4¼hr	€28.50	2 weekly
Kythnos	Santorini (Thira)	8hr	€16	2 weekly
Lavrio	Santorini (Thira)	16hr 20min	€50	2 weekly
Milos	Santorini (Thira)	4hr	€17	2 weekly
Milos*	Santorini (Thira)	2hr	€34	1 daily
Mykonos*	Santorini (Thira)	2hr 10min	€38	2-3daily
Naxos	Santorini (Thira)	3hr	€15.50	5daily
Naxos*	Santorini (Thira)	1½hr	€30	2-3daily
Paros	Santorini (Thira)	3-4hr	€16.50	5 daily
Paros*	Santorini (Thira)	2¼hr	€36	2-3 daily
Piraeus	Santorini (Thira)	9hr	€33.50	4-5 daily
Piraeus*	Santorini (Thira)	5¼hr	€47-65	3 daily
Rafina*	Santorini (Thira)	4¾hr	€49	1 daily
Rethymno	Santorini (Thira)	2hr 20min	€46	3 weekly
Rhodes	Santorini (Thira)	13hr 10min	€27	1-2 daily
Serifos	Santorini (Thira)	9hr	€16	2 weekly
Sifnos	Santorini (Thira)	7hr 20min	13.50	2 weekly
Sikinos	Santorini (Thira)	2¾hr	€14.10	1-4 daily
Sikinos*	Santorini (Thira)	55min	€18	1 weekly
Syros	Santorini (Thira)	5¼hr	€22	2 weekly

*high-speed services

Schinousa

Cyclades; see also Little Cyclades p415

BOAT SERVICES FROM SCHINOUSA

Destination	Port	Duration	Fare	Frequency
Amorgos	Schinousa	1hr 40min	€8-10.50	2-3 daily
Donousa	Schinousa	2hr	€7.50	1-2 daily
Iraklia	Schinousa	15min	€4.50	2-3 daily
Koufonisia	Schinousa	40min	€4.50	2-3 daily
Naxos	Schinousa	2hr-2hr 40min	€7.50-9	1-2 daily
Paros	Schinousa	2hr 20min	€10	1-2 daily
Piraeus	Schinousa	7½hr	€30	1-2 daily
Syros	Schinousa	4hr	€22.20	4 weekly

Serifos

Cyclades; see also p450

BOAT SERVICES FROM SERIFOS

Destination	Port	Duration	Fare	Frequency
Folegandros	Serifos	7hr 40min	€16	5 weekly
Folegandros*	Serifos	1¾hr	€23	4 weekly
Ios	Serifos	7hr 10min	€16	4 weekly
Kimolos	Serifos	4hr 10min	€8.50	5 weekly
Kythnos	Serifos	1hr 20	€15	1-2 daily
Milos	Serifos	4hr 40min	€16	1-2 daily
Milos*	Serifos	1½hr	€16	1-3 daily

ISLAND HOPPING

Paros	Serifos	2½hr	€10.10	3 weekly
Piraeus	Serifos	5hr	€22.50	2 daily
Piraeus*	Serifos	2¼hr	€40	3 daily
Santorini (Thira)	Serifos	9hr	€16	2 weekly
Sifnos	Serifos	50min	€11-13.50	1-2 daily
Sifnos*	Serifos	25min	€13	1-2 daily
Syros	Serifos	2hr 50min	€9.90	4 weekly

*high-speed services

Sifnos

Cyclades; see also p448

BOAT SERVICES FROM SIFNOS

Destination	Port	Duration	Fare	Frequency
Folegandros	Sifnos	4½hr	€13.50	1-3 daily
Folegandros*	Sifnos	1hr	€18	4 weekly
Ios	Sifnos	6hr	€13.50	4 weekly
Kythnos	Sifnos	2½hr	€13.50	1-2 daily
Kimolos	Sifnos	3hr	€6	5 weekly
Milos	Sifnos	3hr 40min	€13.50	1-2 daily
Milos*	Sifnos	1hr	€14	1-3 daily
Paros	Sifnos	2hr	€5.40	3 weekly
Piraeus	Sifnos	5¼hr	€28	2 daily
Piraeus*	Sifnos	2hr 40min	€44	3 daily
Santorini (Thira)	Sifnos	7hr 20min	€13.50	2 weekly
Serifos	Sifnos	50min	€11-13.50	1-2 daily
Serifos*	Sifnos	25min	€13	1-2 daily
Syros	Sifnos	4hr 10min	€17.70	5 weekly

*high-speed services

Sikinos

Cyclades; see also p439–40

BOAT SERVICES FROM SIKINOS

Destination	Port	Duration	Fare	Frequency
Anafi	Sikinos	4hr	€19.60	4 weekly
Folegandros	Sikinos	40min	€5.50	1-3 daily

Ios	Sikinos	20min	€8	1-4 daily
Ios*	Sikinos	10min	€12	1 weekly
Kea	Sikinos	12¼hr	€41 40	2 weekly
Kythnos	Sikinos	11hr	€32	2 weekly
Naxos	Sikinos	2¼hr	€13.60	4 weekly
Paros*	Sikinos	4hr 10min	€50-55	1-2 daily
Piraeus	Sikinos	12hr	€29.60	4 weekly
Santorini (Thira)	Sikinos	2¾hr	€8	4 weekly
Santorini (Thira)*	Sikinos	55min	€19	1 weekly
Syros	Sikinos	5hr	€15	1-3 daily

*high-speed services

Skiathos

Evia & the Sporades; see also p650

AIR

During summer there's one flight daily to/from Athens (€49).

BOAT SERVICES FROM SKIATHOS

Destination	Port	Duration	Fare	Frequency
Agios Konstantinos	Skiathos	2hr	€32	1 daily
Agios Konstantinos*	Skiathos	2hr	€33	2 daily
Alonnisos	Skiathos	2½hr	€9.50	1 daily
Alonnisos*	Skiathos	1½hr	€16	4-5 daily
Skopelos (Glossa)	Skiathos	40 min	€5.50	1 daily
Skopelos (Glossa)*	Skiathos	20min	€9.50	3-4 daily
Skopelos (Skopelos Town)*	Skiathos	45min	€16	4-5 daily
Skopelos	Skiathos	1¼hr	€9	1 daily
Thessaloniki*	Skiathos	4¼hr	€55	1 daily
Volos	Skiathos	2½hr	€18	2 daily
Volos*	Skiathos	1½hr	€30	3 daily

*hydrofoil services

Skopelos

Evia & the Sporades; see also p655

BOAT SERVICES FROM SKOPELOS

Destination	Port	Duration	Fare	Frequency
Agios Konstantinos*	Skopelos*	3½hr	€44	1 daily
Agios Konstantinos**	Skopelos**	2½hr	€44	1-3 daily
Alonnisos	Skopelos (Skopelos Town)	30min	€5	4-5 weekly
Alonnisos**	Skopelos (Glossa)	50min	€13	4-5 daily
Alonnisos**	Skopelos (Skopelos Town)	20min	€8.50	4-5 daily
Skiathos	Skopelos (Skopelos Town)	1hr	€9	1 daily
Skiathos*	Skopelos (Skopelos Town)	50min	€15.50	4-5 daily
Skiathos**	Skopelos (Glossa)	20min	€9.50	4-5 daily
Volos	Skopelos (Glossa)	3½hr	€19.50	1 daily
Volos	Skopelos (Skopelos Town)	4hr	€23	1-2 daily

*fast-ferry services
**hydrofoil services

ISLAND HOPPING

Skyros

Evia & the Sporades; see also p665

DOMESTIC FLIGHTS FROM SKYROS

Destination	Port	Duration	Fare	Frequency
Athens	Skyros	25min	€40	3 weekly
Thessaloniki	Skyros	35min	€68	3 weekly

BOAT

A regular ferry service is provided by *Achileas* between the port of Kymi (Evia) and Skyros. On Friday and Sunday the ferry (usually) makes two crossings; on the remaining days, just one crossing.

BOAT SERVICES FROM SKYROS

Destination	Port	Duration	Fare	Frequency
Evia (Paralia Kymis)	Skyros	1¾hr	€9	1-2 daily
Alonnisos	Skyros	5hr	€21	2 weekly
Skopelos	Skyros	6hr	€22	2 weekly

Spetses

Saronic Gulf Islands; see also p368

BOAT SERVICES FROM SPETSES

Destination	Port	Duration	Fare	Frequency
Hydra	Spetses	30min	€13	7 daily
Ermioni*	Spetses	1hr	€10	2 daily
Piraeus*	Spetses	2hr 10min	€39	7 daily
Poros	Spetses	70min	€14.50	7 daily
Porto Heli*	Spetses	10min	€7	5 daily

*high-speed services

Symi

Dodecanese; see also p544

BOAT

In summer, daily excursion boats run between Symi and Rhodes (€15). The Symi-based *Symi I* and *Symi II* usually go via Panormitis.

BOAT SERVICES FROM SYMI

Destination	Port	Duration	Fare	Frequency
Kalymnos*	Gialos	2hr	€31	1 daily
Kos*	Gialos	1½hr	€22	1 daily
Leros*	Gialos	3hr	€40	1 daily
Patmos*	Gialos	4hr	€44	1 daily
Piraeus	Gialos	15hr	€64	2 weekly
Rhodes	Gialos	2hr	€132	1 daily
Rhodes*	Gialos	1hr	€15	1 daily
Rhodes*	Gialos	50min	€21	1 daily
Tilos	Gialos	2hr	€8	2 weekly

*high-speed services

Syros

Cyclades; see also p381

DOMESTIC FLIGHTS FROM SYROS

Destination	Airport	Duration	Fare	Frequency
Athens	Syros	35min	70	2 weekly

BOAT SERVICES FROM SYROS

Destination	Port	Duration	Fare	Frequency
Anafi	Syros	9hr	€36.30	2-3 weekly
Amorgos	Syros	4½hr	€19	4 weekly
Andros	Syros	2hr 20min	€16	4 weekly
Astypalea	Syros	6¼hr	€20.50	3 weekly
Chios	Syros	3hr 20min	€30.50	5 weekly
Donousa	Syros	4hr 20min	€15	4 weekly
Folegandros	Syros	6hr	€15.10	3 weekly
Ios	Syros	2¼hr	€42	1 daily
Iraklia	Syros	3hr 35min	€22.70	3-4 weekly
Kea	Syros	3hr	€12.30	2 weekly
Kimilos	Syros	3¾hr	€15.10	4 weekly
Kos	Syros	7hr 40min	€32	3 weekly
Koufonisia	Syros	4½hr	12.70	4 weekly
Kythnos	Syros	2hr	€9.90	4 weekly
Lavrio	Syros	3½hr	€18.50	3 weekly
Leros	Syros	4hr 35min	€28	3 weekly
Milos	Syros	4hr 20min	€25.20	4 weekly
Mykonos	Syros	1hr 20min	€8	1 daily
Mykonos*	Syros	40min	€14.50	4 daily
Naxos	Syros	1hr 25min-2hr 50min	€9.20-€11.50	2 daily
Paros	Syros	1¾hr	€8.50	1-3 daily
Patmos	Syros	3hr 25min	€26	3 weekly
Piraeus	Syros	4hr	€26-€29	4 daily
Piraeus*	Syros	2½hr	€44.50	3 daily
Rafina*	Syros	2hr 50min	€45	2 weekly
Rhodes	Syros	9hr 25min	€38.50	3 weekly

*high-speed services

Thasos

Northeastern Aegean Islands; see also p637

BOAT SERVICES FROM THASOS

Destination	Port	Duration	Fare	Frequency
Keramoti (Limenas)	Thasos	40min	€3.30	hourly
Kavala* (Limenas)	Thasos	40min	€10	4 daily
Kavala (Skala Prinou)	Thasos	1¼hr	€3.50	hourly
Kavala* (Skala Prinou)	Thasos	40min	€10	4 daily

*high-speed services

ISLAND HOPPING

Thessaloniki

As Greece's second city, the mainland port of Thessaloniki has plenty of air and boat connections and is an important ferry hub for the Northeast Aegean Islands. It usually has hydrofoils to the Sporades as well, but these are unpredictable, so check locally. See also p295.

AIR

Some of Thessaloniki's island flights go via Athens; the following table lists direct island flights. Note that a few island flights are multistop, but don't involve change of aircraft.

DOMESTIC FLIGHTS FROM THESSALONIKI

Destination	Airport	Duration	Fare	Frequency
Chios	Thessaloniki	55min	€90	4 weekly
Corfu	Thessaloniki	50min	€75	4 weekly
Crete (Hania)	Thessaloniki	1¼hr	€100	7 weekly
Crete (Iraklio)	Thessaloniki	1¼hr	€100	2 daily
Kefallonia	Thessaloniki	1¾hr	€100	3 weekly
Kos	Thessaloniki	1¼hr	€100	3 weekly
Lesvos (Mytilini)	Thessaloniki	50min	€90	11 weekly
Limnos	Thessaloniki	30min	€75	6 weekly
Mykonos	Thessaloniki	1hr	€100	3 weekly
Rhodes	Thessaloniki	1¼hr	€100	2 daily
Samos	Thessaloniki	1hr	€90	3 weekly
Santorini (Thira)	Thessaloniki	1¼hr	€100	3 weekly

BOAT SERVICES FROM THESSALONIKI

Destination	Port	Duration	Fare	Frequency
Chios	Thessaloniki	13-20hr	€35	3 weekly
Kalymnos	Thessaloniki	20hr	€46	1 weekly
Kos	Thessaloniki	19¼hr	€47	1 weekly
Lesvos (Mytilini)	Thessaloniki	15hr	€35	2 weekly
Lesvos (Sigri)	Thessaloniki	9½hr	€33	1 weekly
Limnos	Thessaloniki	8½hr	€22	2 weekly
Rhodes	Thessaloniki	25hr	€57	1 weekly
Samos (Karlovasi)	Thessaloniki	15½hr	€42	1 weekly
Samos (Vathy)	Thessaloniki	23hr	€39	1 weekly

Tilos

Dodecanese; see also p548

BOAT SERVICES FROM TILOS

Destination	Port	Duration	Fare	Frequency
Kos	Livadia	3hr	€9	2 weekly
Kos*	Livadia	1½hr	€22	2 weekly
Nisyros	Livadia	1hr	€7	6 weekly
Nisyros*	Livadia	40min	€13	2 weekly
Piraeus	Livadia	19½hr	€46	2 weekly
Rhodes	Livadia	2½hr	€15	4 weekly
Rhodes*	Livadia	1½hr	€24	6 weekly
Symi	Livadia	2hr	€8	2 weekly

*high-speed services

Tinos

Cyclades; see also p378

BOAT SERVICES FROM TINOS

Destination	Port	Duration	Fare	Frequency
Andros	Tinos	1hr 35min	€9.60	4 daily
Lavrio	Tinos	8¾hr	€16	1 weekly
Mykonos	Tinos	30-40min	€5.50-6	4 daily
Mykonos*	Tinos	15-25 min	€7-10.50	5 daily
Naxos	Tinos	1hr 25min	€13	2 weekly
Paros	Tinos	1hr 25min	€21.50-24.50	3 daily
Piraeus*	Tinos	3¾hr	€44	3 daily
Piraeus	Tinos	4¾hr	€28	1 daily
Rafina	Tinos	3hr 50min	€19	5 daily
Rafina*	Tinos	2hr 10min	€40	5 daily
Syros	Tinos	2hr	€5	7 daily

*high-speed services

Volos

Central Greece (mainland port); see also p261

BOAT SERVICES FROM VOLOS

Destination	Port	Duration	Fare	Frequency
Alonnisos	Volos	5hr	€24	3 weekly
Alonnisos*	Volos	3hr	€40	2 daily
Skiathos	Volos	2½hr	€18.50	1-2 daily
Skiathos*	Volos	1½hr	€31	2 daily
Skopelos (Skopelos Town)	Volos	4hr	€24	1 daily
Skopelos (Skopelos Town)*	Volos	2½hr	€40	2 daily
Skopelos (Glossa)	Volos	3hr	€20.50	3 weekly
Skopelos (Glossa)*	Volos	2hr	€34	2 daily

*hydrofoil services

Zakynthos

Ionian Islands; see also p702

DOMESTIC FLIGHTS FROM ZAKYNTHOS

Destination	Airport	Duration	Fare	Frequency
Athens	Zakynthos	55min	€77	2 daily
Kefallonia	Zakynthos	20min	€32	3 weekly
Preveza	Zakynthos	1hr 20min	€43	3 weekly

BOAT SERVICES FROM ZAKYNTHOS

Destination	Port	Duration	Fare	Frequency
Corfu	Zakynthos Town	8¾hr	€32	2 weekly
Kyllini	Zakynthos Town	1hr	€8.20	7 daily
Kefallonia (Pesada)	Agios Nikolaos	1½hr	€7	2 daily

ISLAND HOPPING

Health

CONTENTS

BEFORE YOU GO

Prevention is the key to staying healthy while abroad. A little planning before departure, particularly for pre-existing illnesses, will save trouble later. Bring medications in their original, clearly labelled containers. A signed and dated letter from your physician describing your medical conditions and medications, including generic names, is also a good idea. For example, taking codeine into Greece is strictly prohibited unless accompanied by a doctor's certificate. See also p716.

If carrying syringes or needles, be sure to have a physician's letter documenting their medical necessity. If you are embarking on a long trip, make sure your teeth are OK and take your optical prescription with you.

INSURANCE

If you're an EU citizen, a European Health Insurance Card (EHIC; formerly the E111) covers you for most medical care but not emergency repatriation home or nonemergencies. It is available from health centres, and post offices in the UK. Citizens from other countries should find out if there is a reciprocal arrangement for free medical care between their country and Greece. If you do need health insurance, make sure you get a policy that covers you for the worst possible scenario, such as an accident requiring an emergency flight home. Find out in advance if your insurance plan will make payments directly to providers or reimburse you later for overseas health expenditures.

RECOMMENDED VACCINATIONS

No jabs are required to travel to Greece, but a yellow-fever vaccination certificate is required if you are coming from an infected area. The World Health Organization (WHO) recommends that all travellers should be covered for diphtheria, tetanus, measles, mumps, rubella and polio.

INTERNET RESOURCES

The WHO's publication *International Travel and Health* is revised annually and is available online at www.who.int/ith. Other useful websites include www.mdtravelhealth.com (travel health recommendations for every country; updated daily), www.fitfortravel.scot.nhs.uk (general travel advice for the layperson), www.ageconcern.org.uk (advice on travel for the elderly) and www.mariestopes.org.uk (information on women's health and contraception).

IN TRANSIT

DEEP VEIN THROMBOSIS (DVT)

Blood clots may form in the legs during plane flights, chiefly because of prolonged immobility (the longer the flight, the greater the risk). The chief symptom of DVT is swelling or pain of the foot, ankle, or calf, usually but not always on just one side. When a blood clot travels to the lungs, it may cause chest pain and breathing difficulties. Travellers with any of these symptoms should immediately seek medical attention. To prevent the development of DVT on long flights you should walk about the cabin, contract the leg muscles while sitting, drink plenty of fluids and avoid alcohol and tobacco.

JET LAG

To avoid jet lag drink plenty of nonalcoholic fluids and eat light meals. Upon arrival, get exposure to natural sunlight and re-adjust your schedule (for meals, sleep etc) as soon as possible.

IN GREECE

AVAILABILITY & COST OF HEALTH CARE

If you need an ambulance in Greece call ☎ 166. There is at least one doctor on every island and larger islands have hospitals. Pharmacies can dispense medicines that are available only on prescription in most European countries, so you can consult a pharmacist for minor ailments.

All this sounds fine but, although medical training is of a high standard in Greece, the public health service is badly underfunded. Hospitals can be overcrowded, hygiene is not always what it should be and relatives are expected to bring in food for the patient – which could be a problem for a tourist. Conditions and treatment are much better in private hospitals, which are expensive. All this means that a good health-insurance policy is essential.

TRAVELLER'S DIARRHOEA

If you develop diarrhoea, be sure to drink plenty of fluids, preferably in the form of an oral rehydration solution such as dioralyte. If diarrhoea is bloody, persists for more than 72 hours or is accompanied by fever, shaking, chills or severe abdominal pain you should seek medical attention.

ENVIRONMENTAL HAZARDS
Bites, Stings & Insect-Borne Diseases

Keep an eye out for sea urchins lurking around rocky beaches; if you get some of their needles embedded in your skin, olive oil should help to loosen them. If they are not removed they will become infected. You should also be wary of jellyfish, particularly during the months of September and October. Although jellyfish are not lethal in Greece, their stings can hurt. Dousing the affected area with vinegar will deactivate any stingers that have not 'fired'. Calamine lotion, antihistamines and analgesics may help reduce any reaction you experience and relieve the pain of any stings. Much more painful than either of these, but thankfully much rarer, is an encounter with the weever fish. The fish buries itself in the sand of the tidal zone with only its spines protruding, and injects a painful and powerful toxin if trodden on. Soaking your foot in very hot water (which breaks down the poison) should solve the problem but if a child is stung, medical at-

tention should be sought. Weever-fish stings can cause permanent local paralysis in the worst case.

Greece's dangerous snakes include the adder and the less common viper and coral snakes. To minimise the possibilities of being bitten, always wear boots, socks and long trousers when walking through undergrowth where snakes may be present. Don't put your hands into holes and crevices, and be careful when collecting firewood. Snake bites do not cause instantaneous death and an antivenin is widely available. Keep the victim calm and still, wrap the bitten limb tightly, as you would for a sprained ankle, and attach a splint to immobilise it. Seek medical help, if possible with the dead snake for identification. Don't attempt to catch the snake if there is a possibility of being bitten again. Tourniquets and sucking out the poison are now comprehensively discredited.

Always check all over your body if you have been walking through a potentially tick-infested area as ticks can cause skin infections and other more serious diseases. If a tick is found attached, press down around the tick's head with tweezers, grab the head and gently pull upwards. Avoid pulling the rear of the tick's body as this may squeeze the tick's gut contents through the attached mouth parts into the skin, increasing the risk of infection and disease.

Greece is now officially rabies-free, however even if the animal is not rabid, all animal bites should be treated seriously as they can become infected or can result in tetanus.

Mosquitoes can be an annoying problem in Greece so some precautions may be needed, though there is no danger of contracting malaria. The electric plug-in mosquito repellents are usually sufficient – and more bearable than coils – to keep the insects at bay at night. Nonetheless choose accommodation that has flyscreen window-protection wherever possible. Mosquito species can vary as can your reaction to their bites. Mosquitoes in northern Greece can provoke a severe reaction. The Asian tiger mosquito (*Aedes albopictus*) may be encountered in mountainous areas and can be a voracious daytime biter. It is known to carry several viruses, including Eastern equine encephalitis, which can affect the central nervous system and cause severe complications and death. Use protective sprays or lotion if you suspect you are being bitten during the day.

HEALTH

Invisible bedbugs can be a major irritation if encountered. Symptoms are lots of pinprick bites that you may initially assign to mosquitoes – even if you are covered up. There is no protection other than to change to a noninfected bed. Airing the mattress thoroughly in the sun may alleviate the problem.

Heatstroke

Heatstroke occurs following excessive fluid loss with inadequate replacement of fluids and salt. Symptoms of heatstroke include headache, dizziness and tiredness. Dehydration is already happening by the time you feel thirsty – aim to drink sufficient water to produce pale, diluted urine. To treat heatstroke drink water and/or fruit juice, and cool the body with cold water and fans.

Hypothermia

Hypothermia occurs when the body loses heat faster than it can produce it. As ever, proper preparation will reduce the risks of getting it. Even on a hot day in the mountains, the weather can change rapidly so carry waterproof garments, warm layers and a hat, and inform others of your route. Hypothermia starts with shivering, loss of judgment and clumsiness. Unless rewarming occurs, the sufferer deteriorates into apathy, confusion and coma. Prevent further heat loss by seeking shelter, warm dry clothing, hot sweet drinks and shared bodily warmth.

Water

In much of Greece, tap water is drinkable and safe. However, in small villages and on some of the islands, this is not always the case. Always ask locally if the water is safe and, if in doubt, drink boiled or bought water. Even when water is safe, the substances and microbacteria in it may be different than you are used to and can cause vomiting or diarrhoea. If you suffer from either of these and think water might be the cause, stick to the bottled variety.

TRAVELLING WITH CHILDREN

Make sure children are up to date with routine vaccinations and discuss possible travel vaccines well before departure as some vaccines are not suitable for children under a year old. Lonely Planet's *Travel with Children* (Brigitte Barta et al) includes travel health advice for younger children. Children are often more susceptible to diarrhoea and dehydration, and bites and stings can have a greater impact on their smaller body mass. Keep a first-aid kit handy.

SEXUAL HEALTH

Condoms are readily available but emergency contraception may not be, so take the necessary precautions.

Language

CONTENTS

The Greek language is believed to be one of the oldest European languages, with an oral tradition of 4000 years and a written tradition of approximately 3000 years. Its evolution over the four millennia was characterised by its strength during the golden age of Athens and the Democracy (mid-5th century BC); its use as a lingua franca throughout the Middle Eastern world, spread by Alexander the Great and his successors as far as India during the Hellenistic period (330 BC to AD 100); its adaptation as the language of the new religion, Christianity; its use as the official language of the Eastern Roman Empire; and its proclamation as the language of the Byzantine Empire (380–1453).

Greek maintained its status and prestige during the rise of the European Renaissance and was employed as the linguistic perspective for all contemporary sciences and terminologies during the period of Enlightenment. Today, Greek constitutes a large part of the vocabulary of many Indo-European languages, and much of the lexicon of scientific repertoire.

The modern Greek language is a southern Greek dialect which is now used by most Greek speakers both in Greece and abroad. It is the result of the mixing of ancient vocabulary with words from Greek regional dialects, namely Cretan, Cypriot and Macedonian.

Greek is spoken throughout Greece by a population of just over 10 million, and by some 5 million Greeks living abroad.

PRONUNCIATION

All Greek words of two or more syllables have an acute accent (′), which indicates where the stress falls. For instance, άγαλμα (statue) is pronounced *aghalma*, and αγάπη (love) is pronounced *aghapi*. In our pronunciation guides, italic lettering indicates where stress falls, eg *a*·ghal·ma. Note also that **dh** is pronounced 'th' as in 'there' and **gh** is a softer, slightly guttural version of 'g'. See the box on p769 for more details.

ACCOMMODATION

I'm looking for ...
Ψάχνω για ...   *psa*·hno ya ...
  a hotel
  ένα ξενοδοχείο   *e*·na kse·no·dho·*khi*·o
  a room
  ένα δωμάτιο   *e*·na dho·*ma*·ti·o
  a youth hostel
  έναν ξενώνα   *e*·nan kse·*no*·na
  νεότητας   ne·*o*·ti·tas

I'd like to book ...
Θα ήθελα να κλείσω ... tha *i*·the·la na *kli*·so ...
  a bed
  ένα κρεββάτι   *e*·na kre·*va*·ti
  a single room
  ένα μονόκλινο   *e*·na mo·*no*·kli·no
  δωμάτιο   dho·*ma*·ti·o
  a double room
  ένα δίκλινο   *e*·na *dhi*·kli·no
  δωμάτιο   dho·*ma*·ti·o
  a room with a double bed
  ένα δωμάτιο με   *e*·na dho·*ma*·ti·o me
  δυό κρεββάτια   dhy·o kre·*va*·ti·a
  a room with a bathroom
  ένα δωμάτιο με   *e*·na dho·*ma*·ti·o me
  μπάνιο   *ba*·ni·o

Where's a cheap hotel?
Πού είναι ένα φτηνό ξενοδοχείο;
pou *i*·ne *e*·na fti·*no* xe·no·do·*hi*·o

What's the address?
Ποια είναι η διεύθυνση;
pya *i*·ne i dhi·*ef*·thin·si

Could you write the address, please?
Παρακαλώ, μπορείτε να γράψετε τη διεύθυνση;
pa·ra·ka·*lo* bo·*ri*·te na *ghra*·pse·te ti dhi·*ef*·thin·si

Are there any rooms available?
Υπάρχουν ελεύθερα δωμάτια;
i·*par*·chun e·*lef*·the·ra dho·*ma*·ti·a

I'd like to share a dorm.
Θα ήθελα να μοιράσω ένα κοινό δωμάτιο
με άλλα άτομα
tha *i*·the·la na mi·*ra*·so e·na ki·*no* dho·*ma*·ti·o me al·la a·to·ma

How much is it ...?	Πόσο κάνει ...;	*po*·so ka·ni ...
per night	τη βραδυά	ti ·vra·*dhya*
per person	το άτομο	to *a*·to·mo

May I see it?
Μπορώ να το δω;
bo·*ro* na to dho

Where's the bathroom?
Πού είναι το μπάνιο;
pou *i*·ne to ba·ni·o

I'm/We're leaving today.
Φεύγω/φεύγουμε
fev·gho/fev·ghou·me
σήμερα
si·me·ra

CONVERSATION & ESSENTIALS

Hello.
Γειά σας.
ya·sas (pol)
Γειά σου.
ya·su (inf)

Good morning.
Καλημέρα.
ka·li·*me*·ra

Good afternoon/evening.
Καλησπέρα.
ka·li·*spe*·ra

Good night.
Καληνύχτα.
ka·li·*nikh*·ta

Goodbye.
Αντίο.
an·*di*·o

Yes.
Ναι.
ne

No.
Όχι.
o·hi

Please.
Παρακαλώ.
pa·ra·ka·*lo*

Thank you.
Ευχαριστώ.
ef·ha·ri·*sto*

That's fine./You're welcome.
Παρακαλώ.
pa·ra·ka·*lo*

Sorry. (excuse me, forgive me)
Συγγνώμη.
sigh·*no*·mi

What's your name?
Πώς σας λένε;
pos sas *le*·ne

My name is ...
Με λένε ...
me *le*·ne ...

Where are you from?
Από πού είστε;
a·*po* pou *i*·ste

I'm from ...
Είμαι από ...
i·me a·*po* ...

I (don't) like ...
(Δεν) μ' αρέσει ...
(dhen) ma·*re*·si ...

Just a minute.
Μισό λεπτό.
mi·*so* lep·to

DIRECTIONS

Where is ...?
Πού είναι ...;
pou *i*·ne ...

Straight ahead.
Όλο ευθεία.
o·lo ef·*thi*·a

Turn left.
Στρίψτε αριστερά.
strips·te a·ri·ste·*ra*

Turn right.
Στρίψτε δεξιά.
strips·te dhe·*ksia*

at the next corner
στην επόμενη γωνία
stin e·*po*·me·ni gho·*ni*·a

at the traffic lights
στα φώτα
sta *fo*·ta

behind	πίσω	*pi*·so
in front of	μπροστά	bro·*sta*
far/near (to)	μακριά/κοντά	ma·kri·*a*/kon·*da*
opposite	απέναντι	a·*pe*·nan·di

acropolis	ακρόπολη	a·*kro*·po·li
beach	παραλία	pa·ra·*li*·a
bridge	γέφυρα	ye·fi·ra
castle	κάστρο	*ka*·stro
island	νησί	ni·*si*
market	αγορά	a·gho·*ra*
museum	μουσείο	mu·*si*·o
old quarter	παλιά πόλη	pa·li·*a* po·li
ruins	αρχαία	ar·*he*·a
sea	θάλασσα	*tha*·las·sa
square	πλατεία	pla·*ti*·a
temple	ναός	na·*os*

SIGNS	
ΕΙΣΟΔΟΣ	Entry
ΕΞΟΔΟΣ	Exit
ΠΛΗΡΟΦΟΡΙΕΣ	Information
ΑΝΟΙΧΤΟ	Open
ΚΛΕΙΣΤΟ	Closed
ΑΠΑΓΟΡΕΥΕΤΑΙ	Prohibited
ΑΣΤΥΝΟΜΙΑ	Police
ΑΣΤΥΝΟΜΙΚΟΣ ΣΤΑΘΜΟΣ	Police Station
ΓΥΝΑΙΚΩΝ	Toilets (women)
ΑΝΔΡΩΝ	Toilets (men)

LANGUAGE

THE GREEK ALPHABET & PRONUNCIATION

Greek	Pronunciation Guide		Example		
A α	**a**	as in 'father'	αγάπη	a·*gha*·pi	love
B β	**v**	as in 'vine'	βήμα	*vi*·ma	step
Γ γ	**gh**	a softer, guttural 'g'	γάτα	*gha*·ta	cat
	y	as in 'yes'	για	ya	for
Δ δ	**dh**	as in 'there'	δέμα	*dhe*·ma	parcel
E ε	**e**	as in 'egg'	ένας	*e*·nas	one
Z ζ	**z**	as in 'zoo'	ζώο	*zo*·o	animal
H η	**i**	as in 'feet'	ήταν	*i*·tan	was
Θ θ	**th**	as in 'throw'	θέμα	*the*·ma	theme
I ι	**i**	as in 'feet'	ίδιος	*i*·dhyos	same
K κ	**k**	as in 'kite'	καλά	ka·*la*	well
Λ λ	**l**	as in 'leg'	λάθος	*la*·thos	mistake
M μ	**m**	as in 'man'	μαμά	ma·*ma*	mother
N ν	**n**	as in 'net'	νερό	ne·*ro*	water
Ξ ξ	**x**	as in 'ox'	ξύδι	*xi*·dhi	vinegar
O o	**o**	as in 'hot'	όλα	*o*·la	all
Π π	**p**	as in 'pup'	πάω	*pa*·o	I go
P ρ	**r**	as in 'road', slightly trilled	ρέμα ρόδα	*re*·ma *ro*·dha	stream tyre
Σ σ, ς	**s**	as in 'sand'	σημάδι	si·*ma*·dhi	mark
T τ	**t**	as in 'tap'	τόπος	*to*·pos	site
Y υ	**i**	as in 'feet'	ύστερα	*is*·te·ra	later
Φ φ	**f**	as in 'find'	φύλλο	*fi*·lo	leaf
X χ	**kh**	as the 'ch' in Scottish 'loch', or	χάνω	*kha*·no	I lose
	h	like a rough 'h'	χέρι	*hye*·ri	hand
Ψ ψ	**ps**	as in 'lapse'	ψωμί	pso·*mi*	bread
Ω ω	**o**	as in 'hot'	ώρα	*o*·ra	time

Combinations of Letters
The combinations of letters shown here are pronounced as follows:

Greek	Pronunciation Guide		Example		
ει	**i**	as in 'feet'	είδα	*i*·dha	I saw
οι	**i**	as in 'feet'	οικόπεδο	i·*ko*·pe·dho	land
αι	**e**	as in 'bet'	αίμα	*e*·ma	blood
ου	**u**	as in 'mood'	πού	pou	who/what/where
μπ	**b**	as in 'beer'	μπάλα	*ba*·la	ball
	mb	as in 'amber'	κάμπος	*kam*·bos	forest
ντ	**d**	as in 'dot'	ντουλάπα	dou·*la*·pa	wardrobe
	nd	as in 'bend'	πέντε	*pen*·de	five
γκ	**g**	as in 'green'	γκάζι	*ga*·zi	gas
γγ	**ng**	as in 'angle'	αγγελία	an·ge·*li*·a	announcement
γξ	**ks**	as in 'minks'	σφιγξ	sfinks	sphynx
τζ	**dz**	as in 'hands'	τζάκι	*dza*·ki	fireplace

The pairs of vowels shown above are pronounced separately if the first has an acute accent, or the second a dieresis (¨), as in the examples below:

Κάιρο	*kai*·ro	Cairo
γαϊδουράκι	gai·dhou·*ra*·ki	little donkey

Some Greek consonant sounds have no English equivalent. The υ of the groups αυ, ευ and ηυ is generally pronounced 'v'. The Greek question mark is represented with the English equivalent of a semicolon (;).

TRANSLITERATION & VARIANT SPELLINGS: AN EXPLANATION

The issue of correctly transliterating Greek into the Roman alphabet is a vexed one, fraught with inconsistencies and pitfalls. The Greeks themselves are not very consistent in this respect, though things are gradually improving. The word 'Piraeus', for example, has been variously represented by the following transliterations: *Pireas*, *Piraievs* and *Pireefs*; and when appearing as a street name (eg Piraeus St) you will also find *Pireos*!

This has been compounded by the linguistic minefield of the two forms of the Greek language. The purist form is called *Katharevousa* and the popular form is *Dimotiki* (Demotic). The *Katharevousa* form was never more than an artificially and *Dimotiki* has always been spoken as the mainstream language, but this means there are often two Greek words for each English word. Thus, the word for 'bakery' in everyday language is *fournos*, but the shop sign will more often than not say *arto-poieion*. The baker's product will be known in the street as *psomi*, but in church as *artos*.

A further complication is the issue of Anglicised vs Hellenised forms of place names: Athens vs Athina, Patra vs Patras, Thebes vs Thiva, Evia vs Euboia – the list goes on and on. The existence of both an official and everyday name for a place can explain why you see variations such as Corfu/Kerkyra, Zakynthos/Zante, and Santorini/Thira. In this guide we usually provide modern Greek equivalents for town names, with one well-known exception, Athens. For ancient sites, settlements or people from antiquity, we have tried to stick to the more familiar classical names; so we have Thucydides instead of Thoukididis, Mycenae instead of Mykines.

Problems in transliteration have particular implications for vowels, especially given that Greek has six ways of rendering the vowel sound 'ee', two ways of rendering the 'o' sound and two ways of rendering the 'e' sound. In most instances in this book, **y** has been used for the 'ee' sound when a Greek *upsilon* (υ, Υ) has been used, and **i** for Greek *ita* (η, Η) and *iota* (ι, Ι). In the case of the Greek vowel combinations that make the 'ee' sound, that is οι, ει and υι, an **i** has been used. For the two Greek 'e' sounds αι and ε, an **e** has been employed.

As far as consonants are concerned, the Greek letter *gamma* (γ, Γ) usually appears as **g** rather than **y** throughout this book. For example, *agios* (Greek for male saint) is used rather than *ayios*, and *agia* (female saint) rather than *ayia*. The letter *fi* (φ, Φ) can be transliterated as either **f** or **ph**. Here, a general rule of thumb is that classical names are spelt with a **ph** and modern names with an **f**. So Phaistos is used rather than Festos, and Folegandros is used rather than Pholegandros. The Greek *chi* (χ, Χ) has usually been represented as **h** in order to approximate the Greek pronunciation as closely as possible. Thus, we have Hania instead of Chania and Polytehniou instead of Polytechniou. Bear in mind that the **h** is to be pronounced as an aspirated 'h', much like the 'ch' in 'loch'. The letter *kapa* (κ, Κ) has been used to represent that sound, except where well-known names from antiquity have adopted by convention the letter **c**, eg Polycrates, Acropolis.

Wherever reference to a street name is made, we have omitted the Greek word *odos*, but words for avenue (*leoforos*, abbreviated *leof* on maps) and square (*plateia*) have been included.

EATING OUT

For more on food and drink, see p85.

I want to make a reservation for this evening.
Θέλω να κλείσω ένα τραπέζι για απόψε.
the·lo na kli·so e·na tra·pe·zi ya a·po·pse

A table for... please.
Ένα τραπέζι για... παρακαλώ.
e·na tra·pe·zi ya ... pa·ra·ka·lo

I'd like the menu, please.
Το μενού, παρακαλώ.
to me·nu, pa·ra·ka·lo

Do you have a menu in English?
Έχετε το μενού στα αγγλικά;
e·hye·te to me·nu sta ang·li·ka

I'd like ...
Θα ήθελα ...   *tha i·the·la ...*

Please bring the bill.
Το λογαριασμό, παρακαλώ.
to lo·ghar·ya·zmo pa·ra·ka·lo

I'm a vegetarian.
Είμαι χορτοφάγος.
i·me hor·to·fa·ghos

I don't eat meat or dairy products.
Δε τρώω κρέας ή γαλακτοκομικά προϊόντα.
dhen tro·o kre·as i gha·la·kto·ko·mi·ka pro·i·on·da

HEALTH

I'm ill.   Είμαι άρρωστος.   *i·me a·ro·stos*
It hurts here.   Πονάει εδώ.   *po·na·i e·dho*

EMERGENCIES

Help!
Βοήθεια!   vo·*i*·thya
There's been an accident.
Έγινε ατύχημα.   ey·i·ne a·*ti*·hi·ma
Go away!
Φύγε!   fi·ye

Call ...!	Φωνάξτε ...!	fo·*nak*·ste ...
a doctor	ένα γιατρό	e·na yi·a·*tro*
the police	την αστυνομία	tin a·sti·no·*mi*·a

I have ...
Έχω ...   e·ho ...
  asthma
  άσθμα   asth·ma
  diabetes
  ζαχαροδιαβήτη   za·ha·ro·dhi·a·*vi*·ti
  diarrhoea
  διάρροια   dhi·a·ri·a
  epilepsy
  επιληψία   e·pi·lip·*si*·a

I'm allergic to ...
Είμαι αλλεργικός/   i·me a·ler·yi·*kos*/
αλλεργική ...   a·ler·yi·*ki* ... (m/f)
  antibiotics
  στα αντιβιωτικά   sta an·di·vi·o·ti·*ka*
  aspirin
  στην ασπιρίνη   stin a·spi·*ri*·ni
  penicillin
  στην πενικιλλίνη   stin pe·ni·ki·*li*·ni
  bees
  στις μέλισσες   stis *me*·li·ses
  nuts
  στα φυστίκια   sta fi·*sti*·ki·a

contraceptive	προφυλακτικό	pro·fi·lak·ti·*ko*
medicine	φάρμακο	farm·a·ko
sunblock cream	κρέμα ηλίου	kre·ma i·*li*·u
tampons	ταμπόν	tam·*bon*

LANGUAGE DIFFICULTIES

Do you speak English?
Μιλάτε αγγλικά;   mi·*la*·te an·gli·*ka*
Does anyone speak English?
Μιλάει κανείς αγγλικά;   mi·*lai* ka·*nis* an·gli·*ka*
How do you say ... in Greek?
Πώς λέγεται ... στα   pos *le*·ghe·te ... sta
ελληνικά;   el·li·ni·*ka*
I understand.
Καταλαβαίνω.   ka·ta·la·*ve*·no

I don't understand.
Δεν καταλαβαίνω.   dhen ka·ta·la·*ve*·no
Please write it down.
Γράψτε το, παρακαλώ.   *ghrap*·ste to pa·ra·ka·*lo*
Can you show me on the map?
Μπορείτε να μου το   bo·*ri*·te na mou to
δείξετε στο χάρτη;   *dhi*·xe·te sto *har*·ti

NUMBERS

0	μηδέν	mi·*dhen*
1	ένας (m)	e·nas
	μία (f)	*mi*·a
	ένα (n)	e·na
2	δύο	dhi·o
3	τρεις (m&f)	tris
	τρία (n)	tri·a
4	τέσσερεις (m&f)	te·se·ris
	τέσσερα (n)	te·se·ra
5	πέντε	*pen*·de
6	έξη	e·xi
7	επτά	ep·*ta*
8	οχτώ	oh·*to*
9	εννέα	e·ne·a
10	δέκα	*dhe*·ka
20	είκοσι	ik·o·si
30	τριάντα	tri·*an*·da
40	σαράντα	sa·*ran*·da
50	πενήντα	pe·*nin*·da
60	εξήντα	e·*xin*·da
70	εβδομήντα	ev·dho·*min*·da
80	ογδόντα	ogh·*dhon*·da
90	ενενήντα	e·ne·*nin*·da
100	εκατό	e·ka·*to*
1000	χίλιοι (m)	*hi*·li·i
	χίλιες (f)	*hi*·li·ez
	χίλια (n)	*hi*·li·a
2000	δυό χιλιάδες	dhi·o hi·*li*·a·dhez

PAPERWORK

name
  ονοματεπώνυμο   o·no·ma·te·*po*·ni·mo
nationality
  υπηκοότητα   i·pi·ko·o·ti·ta
date of birth
  ημερομηνία   i·me·ro·mi·*ni*·a
  γεννήσεως   yen·*ni*·se·os
place of birth
  τόπος γεννήσεως   *to*·pos yen·*ni*·se·os
sex (gender)
  φύλον   fi·lon
passport
  διαβατήριο   dhia·va·*ti*·ri·o
visa
  βίζα   *vi*·za

QUESTION WORDS

Who/Which?

Ποιος/Ποια/Ποιο;	pi·os/pi·a/pi·o (sg m/f/n)
Ποιοι/Ποιες/Ποια;	pi·i/pi·es/pi·a (pl m/f/n)

Who's there?

Ποιος είναι εκεί;	pi·os i·ne e·ki

Which street is this?

Ποια οδός είναι αυτή;	pi·a o·dhos i·ne af·ti

What?

Τι;	ti

What's this?

Τι είναι αυτό;	ti i·ne af·to

Where?

Πού;	pu

When?

Πότε;	po·te

Why?

Γιατί;	yi·a·ti

How?

Πώς;	pos

How much?

Πόσο;	po·so

How much does it cost?

Πόσο κάνει;	po·so ka·ni

SHOPPING & SERVICES

I'd like to buy ...

Θέλω ν' αγοράσω ...	the·lo na·gho·ra·so ...

How much is it?

Πόσο κάνει;	po·so ka·ni

I don't like it.

Δεν μου αρέσει.	dhen mu a·re·si

May I see it?

Μπορώ να το δω;	bo·ro na to dho

I'm just looking.

Απλώς κοιτάζω.	ap·los ki·ta·zo

It's cheap.

Είναι φτηνό.	i·ne fti·no

It's too expensive.

Είναι πολύ ακριβό.	i·ne po·li a·kri·vo

I'll take it.

Θα το πάρω.	tha to pa·ro

Do you accept ...?	Δέχεστε ...;	dhe·he·ste ...
credit cards	πιστωτική κάρτα	pi·sto·ti·ki kar·ta
travellers cheques	ταξιδιωτικές επιταγές	tak·si·dhi·o·ti·kes e·pi·ta·ghes
more	περισσότερο	pe·ri·so·te·ro
less	λιγότερο	li·gho·te·ro
smaller	μικρότερο	mi·kro·te·ro
bigger	μεγαλύτερο	me·gha·li·te·ro

I'm looking for ...	Ψάχνω για ...	psach·no ya ...
an ATM	μια αυτόματη μηχανή	mya af·to·ma·ti mi·kha·ni
a bank	μια τράπεζα	mya tra·pe·za
the church	την εκκλησία	tin ek·kli·si·a
the city centre	το κέντρο της πόλης	to ken·dro tis po·lis
the ...	την ...	tin ...
embassy	πρεσβεία	pres·vi·a
a local internet cafe	το τοπικό καφενείο με διαδίκτυο;	to to·pi·ko ka·fe·ni·o me thi·a·thik·ti·o
the market	τη λαϊκή αγορά	ti lai·ki a·gho·ra
the museum	το μουσείο	to mu·si·o
the post office	το ταχυδρομείο	to ta·hi·dhro·mi·o
a public toilet	μια δημόσια τουαλέττα	mya dhi·mo·sia tu·a·let·ta
the tourist office	το τουριστικό γραφείο	to tu·ri·sti·ko ghra·fi·o

TIME & DATES

What time is it?	Τι ώρα είναι;	ti o·ra i·ne
It's (2 o'clock).	είναι (δύο η ώρα).	i·ne (dhi·o i o·ra)
When?	Πότε;	po·te
in the morning	το πρωί	to pro·i
in the afternoon	το απόγευμα	to a·po·yev·ma
in the evening	το βράδυ	to vra·dhi
today	σήμερα	si·me·ra
tomorrow	αύριο	av·ri·o
yesterday	χθες	hthes
Monday	Δευτέρα	dhef·te·ra
Tuesday	Τρίτη	tri·ti
Wednesday	Τετάρτη	te·tar·ti
Thursday	Πέμπτη	pemp·ti
Friday	Παρασκευή	pa·ras·ke·vi
Saturday	Σάββατο	sa·va·to
Sunday	Κυριακή	ky·ri·a·ki
January	Ιανουάριος	ia·nou·ar·i·os
February	Φεβρουάριος	fev·rou·ar·i·os
March	Μάρτιος	mar·ti·os
April	Απρίλιοςq	a·pri·li·os
May	Μάιος	mai·os
June	Ιούνιος	i·ou·ni·os
July	Ιούλιος	i·ou·li·os
August	Αύγουστος	av·ghous·tos
September	Σεπτέμβριος	sep·tem·vri·os
October	Οκτώβριος	ok·to·vri·os
November	Νοέμβριος	no·em·vri·os
December	Δεκέμβριος	dhe·kem·vri·os

TRANSPORT
Public Transport

What time does the ... leave/ arrive?	Τι ώρα φεύγει/ φτάνει το ...;	ti *o*·ra fev·yi/ *fta*·ni to ...
boat	πλοίο	*pli*·o
(city) bus	αστικό	a·sti·*ko*
(intercity) bus	λεωφορείο	le·o·fo·*ri*·o
plane	αεροπλάνο	ae·ro·*pla*·no
train	τραίνο	*tre*·no

I'd like (a) ...	Θα ήθελα (ένα) ...	tha *i*·the·la (e·na) ...
one-way ticket	απλό εισιτήριο	a·*plo* i·si·ti·ri·o
return ticket	εισιτήριο με επιστροφή	i·si·*ti*·ri·o me e·pi·stro·*fi*
1st class	πρώτη θέση	*pro*·ti the·si
2nd class	δεύτερη θέση	*def*·te·ri the·si

I want to go to ...
Θέλω να πάω στο/στη ...
the·lo na *pao* sto/sti ...

The train has been cancelled/delayed.
Το τραίνο ακυρώθηκε/καθυστέρησε
to *tre*·no a·ki·ro·thi·ke/ka·thi·*ste*·ri·se

the first
το πρώτο   to *pro*·to
the last
το τελευταίο   to te·lef·*te*·o
platform number
αριθμός αποβάθρας   a·rith·*mos* a·po·*va*·thras
ticket office
εκδοτήριο εισιτηρίων   ek·dho·*ti*·ri·o i·si·ti·*ri*·on
timetable
δρομολόγιο   dhro·mo·*lo*·gio
train station
σιδηροδρομικός   si·dhi·ro·dhro·mi·*kos*
σταθμός   stath·*mos*

Private Transport

I'd like to hire a ...	Θα ήθελα να νοικιάσω ...	tha *i*·the·la na ni·ki·*a*·so ...
car	ένα αυτοκίνητο	e·na af·to·*ki*·ni·to
4WD	ένα τέσσερα επί τέσσερα	e·na tes·se·ra e·pi tes·se·ra
(a jeep)	(ένα τζιπ)	(e·na tzip)
motorbike	μια μοτοσυκλέττα	mya mo·to·si·*klet*·ta
bicycle	ένα ποδήλατο	e·na po·*dhi*·la·to

Is this the road to ...?
Αυτός είναι ο δρόμος για ...
af·*tos* i·ne o *dhro*·mos ya ...

Where's the next service station?
Πού είναι το επόμενο βενζινάδικο;
pu *i*·ne to e·*po*·me·no ven·zi·*na*·dhi·ko
Please fill it up.
Γεμίστε το, παρακαλώ.
ye·*mi*·ste to pa·ra·ka·*lo*
I'd like (30) euros worth.
Θα ήθελα (30) ευρώ.
tha *i*·the·la (tri·*an*·da) ev·*ro*

diesel	πετρέλαιο κίνησης	pet·*re*·le·o *ki*·ni·sis
leaded petrol	σούπερ	*su*·per
unleaded petrol	αμόλυβδη	a·*mo*·liv·dhi

Can I park here?
Μπορώ να παρκάρω εδώ;
bo·*ro* na par·*ka*·ro e·*dho*
Where do I pay?
Πού πληρώνω;
pu pli·*ro*·no

The car/motorbike has broken down (at ...)
Το αυτοκίνητο/η μοτοσυκλέττα χάλασε στο ...
to af·to·*ki*·ni·to/i mo·to·si·*klet*·ta *kha*·la·se sto ...
The car/motorbike won't start.
Το αυτοκίνητο/η μοτοσυκλέττα δεν παίρνει μπρος.
to af·to·*ki*·ni·to/i mo·to·si·*klet*·ta dhen *per*·ni· bros
I have a flat tyre.
Επαθα λάστιχο.
e·pa·tha *la*·sti·cho
I've run out of petrol.
Εμεινα από βενζίνη.
e·*mi*·na a·*po* ven·zi·ni
I've had an accident.
Επαθα ατύχημα.
e·pa·tha a·*ti*·chi·ma

TRAVEL WITH CHILDREN
Are children allowed?
Επιτρέπονται τα παιδιά;
e·pi·*tre*·pon·de ta pe·*dhya*

Do you mind if I breastfeed here?
  Μπορώ να θηλάσω εδώ;
  bo·ro na thi·la·so e·dho

Is there a/an ...? Υπάρχει ...;   i·par·chi ...
I need a/an ... Χρειάζομαι ...   chri·a·zo·me ...
  baby change μέρος ν' αλλάξω   me·ros na·lak·so
  room το μωρό   to mo·ro
  car baby seat κάθισμα για   ka·this·ma ya
  μωρό   mo·ro

children's menu μενού για παιδία   me·nu ya pe·dhya
(disposable) πάννες Pampers   pan·nez pam·pers
  nappies/diapers
(English- μπέιμπι σίττερ   ba·bi sit·ter
  speaking) (που μιλά   (pu mi·la
  babysitter αγγλικά)   an·ghli·ka)
highchair παιδική καρέκλα   pe·dhi·ki ka·rek·la
potty γιογιό   yo·yo
stroller καροτσάκι   ka·ro·tsa·ki

Also available from Lonely Planet:
Greek Phrasebook

Glossary

For culinary terms see the Food Glossary (p85), and also see Where to Eat & Drink (p78).

Achaean civilisation – see *Mycenaean civilisation*
acropolis – citadel; highest point of an ancient city
agia (f), agios (m) – saint
agora – commercial area of an ancient city; shopping precinct in modern Greece
Archaic period – also known as the *Middle Age* (800-480 BC); period in which the city-states emerged from the *'dark age'* and traded their way to wealth and power; the city-states were unified by a Greek alphabet and common cultural pursuits, engendering a sense of national identity
arhon – leading citizen of a town, often a wealthy bourgeois merchant; chief magistrate
arhontika – 17th- and 18th-century AD mansions, which belonged to *arhons*
askitiria – mini-chapels or hermitages; places of solitary worship

baglamas – small stringed instrument like a mini bouzouki
basilica – early Christian church
bouleuterion – council house
bouzouki – long-necked, stringed lutelike instrument associated with *rembetika* music
bouzoukia – any nightclub where the *bouzouki* is played and low-grade blues songs are sung
Byzantine Empire – characterised by the merging of Hellenistic culture and Christianity and named after Byzantium, the city on the Bosphorus that became the capital of the Roman Empire; when the Roman Empire was formally divided in AD 395, Rome went into decline and the eastern capital, renamed Constantinople, flourished; the Byzantine Empire (324 BC-AD 1453) dissolved after the fall of Constantinople to the Turks in 1453

caïque – small, sturdy fishing boat often used to carry passengers
Classical period – era in which the city-states reached the height of their wealth and power after the defeat of the Persians in the 5th century BC; the Classical period (480-323 BC) ended with the decline of the city-states as a result of the Peloponnesian Wars, and the expansionist aspirations of Philip II, King of Macedon (r 359-336 BC), and his son, Alexander the Great (r 336-323 BC)
Corinthian – order of Greek architecture recognisable by columns with bell-shaped capitals that have sculpted, elaborate ornaments based on acanthus leaves; see also *Doric* and *Ionic*

Cycladic civilisation – the civilisation (3000-1100 BC) that emerged following the settlement of Phoenician colonists on the Cycladic islands
cyclops (s), cyclopes (pl) – mythical one-eyed giants

dark age – period (1200-800 BC) in which Greece was under *Dorian* rule
domatio (s), domatia (pl) – room, usually in a private home; cheap accommodation option
Dorians – Hellenic warriors who invaded Greece around 1200 BC, demolishing the city-states and destroying the *Mycenaean civilisation;* heralded Greece's *'dark age'*, when the artistic and cultural advancements of the *Mycenaean* and the *Minoan civilisations* were abandoned; the Dorians later developed into land-holding aristocrats which encouraged the resurgence of independent city-states led by wealthy aristocrats
Doric – order of Greek architecture characterised by a column that has no base, a fluted shaft and a relatively plain capital, when compared with the flourishes evident on *Ionic* and *Corinthian* capitals

Ellada or Ellas – see *Hellas*
ELTA – Ellinika Tahydromia; the Greek post office organisation
EOT – Ellinikos Organismos Tourismou; main tourist office (has offices in most major towns), known abroad as *GNTO*

Filiki Eteria – Friendly Society; a group of Greeks in exile; formed during Ottoman rule to organise an uprising against the Turks
filoxenia – hospitality
frourio – fortress; sometimes also referred to as a *kastro*

Geometric period – period (1200-800 BC) characterised by pottery decorated with geometric designs; sometimes referred to as Greece's *'dark age'*
GNTO – Greek National Tourist Organisation; see also *EOT*

Hellas – the Greek name for Greece; also known as *Ellada* or *Ellas*
Hellenistic period – prosperous, influential period (323-146 BC) of Greek civilisation ushered in by Alexander the Great's empire building and lasting until the Roman sacking of Corinth in 146 BC
hora – main town (usually on an island)
horio – village

IC – intercity (sometimes express) train service

Ionic – order of Greek architecture characterised by a column with truncated flutes and capitals with ornaments resembling scrolls; see also *Doric* and *Corinthian*

kastro – walled-in town; also describes a fort or castle

katholikon – principal church of a monastic complex

kore – female statue of the *Archaic period*; see also *kouros*

kouros – male statue of the *Archaic period*, characterised by a stiff body posture and enigmatic smile; see also *kore*

KTEL – Koino Tamio Eispraxeon Leoforion; national bus cooperative; runs all long-distance bus services

laïka – literally 'popular (songs)'; mainstream songs that have either been around for years or are of recent origin; also referred to as urban folk music

leoforos – avenue; commonly shortened to 'leof'

limenarhio – port police

meltemi – northeasterly wind that blows throughout much of Greece during the summer

Middle Age – see *Archaic period*

Minoan civilisation – Bronze Age (3000-1100 BC) culture of Crete named after the mythical King Minos, and characterised by pottery and metalwork of great beauty and artisanship

moni – monastery or convent

Mycenaean civilisation – the first great civilisation (1600-1100 BC) of the Greek mainland, characterised by powerful independent city-states ruled by kings; also known as the *Achaean civilisation*

nisi – island

odos – street

OSE – Organismos Sidirodromon Ellados; Greek railways organisation

OTE – Organismos Tilepikoinonion Ellados; Greece's major telecommunications carrier

Panagia – Mother of God or Virgin Mary; name frequently used for churches

panigyri (s), panigyria (p) – festival; the most common festivals celebrate annual saints' days

Pantokrator – painting or mosaic of Christ in the centre of the dome of a Byzantine church

periptero (s), periptera (pl) – street kiosk

plateia – square

rembetika – blues songs commonly associated with the underworld of the 1920s

Sarakatsani – Greek-speaking nomadic shepherd community from northern Greece

stele (s), stelae (pl) – upright stone (or pillar) decorated with inscriptions or figures

stoa – long colonnaded building, usually in an *agora;* used as a meeting place and shelter in ancient Greece

tholos – Mycenaean tomb shaped like a beehive

Vlach – traditional, seminomadic shepherds from Northern Greece who speak a Latin-based dialect

The Authors

KORINA MILLER Coordinating Author, Dodecanese, Island Hopping

Korina first ventured to Greece as a backpacking teenager, sleeping on ferry decks and hiking in the mountains. She has since found herself drawn back to soak up the dazzling Greek sunshine, lounge on the beaches and consume vast quantities of Greek salad and strong coffee. Korina grew up on Vancouver Island and has been exploring the globe since she was 16, working, studying and travelling in 36 countries en route. She now resides in England's Sussex countryside while she plots her next adventure. Korina has been writing travel guides for Lonely Planet for the past decade with 15 titles under her belt. Korina also wrote the Destination Greece, Getting Started, Events Calendar, Itineraries, Environment, Directory, Transport, Health and Glossary chapters.

KATE ARMSTRONG Peloponnese

Having studied history and fine arts, Kate headed to Greece aeons ago to view her first (noncelluloid) *kouros* (male statue of the Archaic period), and fell in love with the country. On several subsequent visits she's rubbed shoulders with many ghosts of mythical beings in the Peloponnese, her all-time favourite region. She devoured kilos of feta and olives (to the delight of locals), several pigs (to the dismay of her vegetarian partner) and was treated to more hospitality than Aphrodite herself. When not wandering in mountainous terrains, Kate sets her itchy feet in Australia. A freelance travel writer, she contributes to Lonely Planet's African, South American and Portuguese titles as well as Australian newspapers, and is the author of educational children's books.

MICHAEL STAMATIOS CLARK Central Greece, Evia & the Sporades

Michael's Greek roots go back to the village of Karavostamo on the Aegean island of Ikaria, home of his maternal grandparents. He was born into a Greek-American community in Cambridge, Ohio, and recently became a Greek citizen. His first trip to Greece was as a deckhand aboard a Greek freighter, trading English lessons for Greek over wine and backgammon. When not travelling to Greece, Michael teaches English to international students in Berkeley, California, listens to Greek *rembetika* (blues) after midnight and searches for new ways to convert friends to the subtle pleasures of retsina.

THE AUTHORS

LONELY PLANET AUTHORS

Why is our travel information the best in the world? It's simple: our authors are independent, dedicated travellers. They don't research using just the internet or phone, and they don't take freebies in exchange for positive coverage. They travel widely, to all the popular spots and off the beaten track. They personally visit thousands of hotels, restaurants, cafes, bars, galleries, palaces, museums and more – and they take pride in getting all the details right, and telling it how it is. Think you can do it? Find out how at **lonelyplanet.com**.

CHRIS DELISO   Northern Greece, Northeastern Aegean Islands, Crete

Chris Deliso was drawing maps of the Aegean by the age of five, and 20 years later he ended up in Greece while labouring away on an MPhil in Byzantine Studies at Oxford. Ever since studying Modern Greek in Thessaloniki in 1998, he has travelled frequently in Greece, including a year in Crete and a long sojourn on Mt Athos. Chris especially enjoyed stumbling upon the unexpected on remote isles like Psara, imbibing heartily in the wineries of Macedonia, gawking at the vultures ripping apart carrion in Thrace, and feasting himself on those incomparable Cretan sweet cheese pies – the *myzithropitakia*.

DES HANNIGAN   Saronic Gulf Islands, Cyclades, Ionian Islands

Des first surfaced (literally) in Greece many years ago in an Aegina harbour, having jumped off a boat into several feet of unexpected water. Ever since, he's been drifting around the country whenever he can, although home is on the edge of the cold Atlantic in beautiful Cornwall, England. In a previous life Des worked at sea, valuable experience for coping with the Greek ferry system. One day he'd really like to hop round the islands in a very fast yacht with all sails set, although he would happily settle for an old caïque with just one sail. Des worked on the previous editions of Lonely Planet's *Greece* and *Greek Islands* and has written guidebooks to Corfu and Rhodes for other publishers.

VICTORIA KYRIAKOPOULOS   The Culture, Food & Drink, Athens

Victoria Kyriakopoulos is a Melbourne-based journalist who morphs effortlessly into an Athenian whenever she hits the motherland. She just clocked up her 269,010th kilometre getting to Greece, has travelled widely around the country and moved there for a while (2000–04), hoping to get it out of her system. Victoria wrote Lonely Planet's first pocket *Athens* guide in 2001, did a stint as editor of *Odyssey* magazine, covered the 2004 Olympics for international media and worked on several television shows about Greece. She returns regularly for research (and pleasure), including for Lonely Planet's latest *Athens Encounter* and *Crete*. An occasional food critic back home, when not writing or making documentaries, she is working through her extensive Greek cookbook collection.

CONTRIBUTING AUTHORS

Gina Tsarouhas Born in Melbourne with Greek blood flowing through her veins, Gina packed her little suitcase at the tender age of four and took off for Greece. Gina flitted across various continents over the years until she discovered she could travel vicariously as an editor of travel guides, as well. When not editing she's co-authoring and contributing to all things Greek at Lonely Planet, including *Greece* and the *Greek Islands*; or tending to her beloved fig and olive trees in the backyard. Gina worked on the previous edition of *Greece*, and wrote the Architecture and History chapters for this guidebook.

Richard Waters Richard's first of taste of travel was as a 21-year-old driving around Central America in an old jalopy; it took him through Guatemala's civil war and gave him his first taste of wanderlust. He's been travelling ever since: across Southeast Asia, Europe, the US and Africa. His first visit to Laos in '99 brought the Hmong guerrillas to his attention and in 2002 he was among the first to creep into the Special Zone in search of their story. He's since contributed to three books on Laos for Lonely Planet. He lives with his partner, son and daughter in Brighton and works as a freelance writer and photographer for British newspapers and magazines. You can see his work at: www.richardwaters.co.uk. Richard wrote A Who's Who of the Ancient Greek Pantheon for this book.

Behind the Scenes

THIS BOOK

This 9th edition of *Greece* was updated by Korina Miller, Kate Armstrong, Michael Stamatios Clark, Chris Deliso, Des Hannigan, Victoria Kyriakopoulos and Gina Tsarouhas, with contributions from Richard Waters. Janet White contributed to the boxed text, The Meteora: Geology of a Rock Forest. Paul Hellander authored on *Greece* 8 with contributions from Will Gourlay and Gina, along with Richard, Kate, Michael, Chris, Des and Victoria. Paul, Kate, Michael, Chris, Des and Victoria all worked on the previous editions, as did Miriam Raphael and Andrew Stone. This guidebook was commissioned in Lonely Planet's London office, and produced by the following:

Commissioning Editors Fiona Buchan, Joanna Potts, Sally Schafer
Coordinating Editor Gina Tsarouhas
Coordinating Cartographer Diana Duggan
Coordinating Layout Designer Wendy Wright
Managing Editor Annelies Mertens
Managing Cartographers Adrian Persoglia, Herman So
Managing Layout Designer Indra Kilfoyle
Assisting Editors Janice Bird, Monique Choy, Kate Evans, Paul Harding, Stephanie Pearson, Martine Power, Erin Richards, Fionn Twomey

Assisting Cartographers Anita Banh, Ildiko Bogdanovits, Dennis Capparelli, Birgit Jordan, Khanh Luu, Marc Milinkovic, Peter Shields
Assisting Layout Designers Carol Jackson, Cara Smith
Cover Image research provided by lonelyplanetimages.com
Project Manager Eoin Dunlevy
Language Content Laura Crawford

Thanks to Lucy Birchley, Chris Girdler, Mark Griffiths, Sally Darmody, Laura Jane, Rebecca Lalor, Trent Paton

THANKS
KORINA MILLER

A huge thank you to the countless people we met on the road for answering my unending questions and making us – and particularly my daughter – feel so very welcome. Thank you to the following people for their generosity of time and knowledge: Anastasios Pissas at GNTO, London; Mary Thymianou at EOT, Rhodes; Adriana Miska in Rhodes Town; Kalliope Karayianni at Nisyros Town Hall; Fokas Michellis in Skala, Patmos; Stavros, his parents and grandmother in Mandraki, Nisyros; and Thanasis Argyroudis in Krithoni, Leros. At Lonely Planet, a big thanks to Jo Potts and Sally Schafer for their patience and assistance, to Fiona Buchan for giving me

THE LONELY PLANET STORY

Fresh from an epic journey across Europe, Asia and Australia in 1972, Tony and Maureen Wheeler sat at their kitchen table stapling together notes. The first Lonely Planet guidebook, *Across Asia on the Cheap,* was born.

Travellers snapped up the guides. Inspired by their success, the Wheelers began publishing books to Southeast Asia, India and beyond. Demand was prodigious, and the Wheelers expanded the business rapidly to keep up. Over the years, Lonely Planet extended its coverage to every country and into the virtual world via lonelyplanet.com and the Thorn Tree message board.

As Lonely Planet became a globally loved brand, Tony and Maureen received several offers for the company. But it wasn't until 2007 that they found a partner whom they trusted to remain true to the company's principles of travelling widely, treading lightly and giving sustainably. In October of that year, BBC Worldwide acquired a 75% share in the company, pledging to uphold Lonely Planet's commitment to independent travel, trustworthy advice and editorial independence.

Today, Lonely Planet has offices in Melbourne, London and Oakland, with over 500 staff members and 300 authors. Tony and Maureen are still actively involved with Lonely Planet. They're travelling more often than ever, and they're devoting their spare time to charitable projects. And the company is still driven by the philosophy of *Across Asia on the Cheap*: 'All you've got to do is decide to go and the hardest part is over. So go!'

the opportunity, and to Michala Green for an insightful brief. Thank you also to Eoin Dunlevy and his production crew and to Herman So in cartography. A big cheer to my co-authors, particularly Victoria Kyriakopoulos and Des Hannigan for their wisdom and support. And finally, love and appreciation to my husband Paul and daughter Simone for keeping up with my schedule on the road and making it a fabulous adventure.

KATE ARMSTRONG
Ευχαριστώ πολύ (thank you very much) to the enthusiastic patriotic Greeks who know when to share and share so much, and to fellow travellers for their insights of every kind. In Stemnitsa: Nena and Koula – thanks dear, generous friends; in Patra: Maria Dometiou and Andreas at the best tourist office in Greece; in Corinth: Elena in Hotel Ephira; in Gerolimenas: Alexandros Kyrimis; in Kalavryta: Marios at Helmos Hotel; in Monemvasia: Isabelle and Christos for their generosity of spirits; and, to friend-in-crime Anne Sinclair, alias Annie Esmerelda – for her guidance in all things to do with shoes, Greek salads and beaches. Finally in Nafplio, yet again to the friendly Zotos Brothers for just about everything. To my Lonely Planet team, editors, cartographers and Jo Potts, and especially to fellow authors and Korina Miller for the e-insights.

MICHAEL STAMATIOS CLARK
Ευχαριστώ (thank you) to those who made my travels through Greece so enjoyable, among them: Jay Melch, Tolis Choutzioumis (Athens); Yiannis and Christos Christopoulos, Dr Elena Partida (Delphi); Yiannis Karakantas (Kalambaka); George Tsiotsis, Anastasia, Sissy (Volos); Keyrillos Sinioris (Evia); Eirini-Georgia Kampouromyti (Alonnisos); Chrysanthi Zygogianni (Skyros). MJ Keown (Long Beach) was instrumental. Kostas and Nana Vatsis provided invaluable help, not to mention drip-free wine. Special thanks to my fellow authors, to Korina Miller and Jo Potts, for putting it all together with grace. And to my splendiferous family – Janet, Melina and Alexander – Greek kisses on both cheeks for all.

CHRIS DELISO
Without the help of many my work would have been much less useful and interesting for the reader. Those whose assistance proved truly indispensable include George, Apostolis, Grigoris, Anastasia, Vassilis and Roula. Others deserving credit include Eri, 'Johnny Dendro' and the Zigouris clan (Epiros); Ilias, Katerina, 'Billas ', Stellios

Boutaris and Vangelis Gerovassiliou (Macedonia); Anna, Nikos and family (Thasos); Jenny Ballis, the Polytihniou Clinic staff, and the musclemen of Loutra (Lesvos); Vassilis and Dimitra (Ikaria); Don (Chios); Stellios and family, and the Geniko Nosokomeio Samou (Samos); Toula and Manolis (Fourni); and in Crete, Nikos Karellis, Dr Giorgos Nikitas, Kyria Rena and Anna, Yiannis, Costas, Eleftheris, Hristos, Manolis, Nikolas, Giorgos and Chris in Plakias – ya mas! I also should thank my fellow scribes, especially our ever-patient coordinating author, Korina Miller, commissioning editor Jo Potts, Sally Schafer, Mark Griffiths and his merry mapmakers, and the hard-working production crew. Finally, I must thank Buba for holding down the fort, and Marco, for giving me the energy and inspiration to keep on truckin' on.

DES HANNIGAN
Warmest thanks and affection to my many friends and acquaintances in Greece who helped and advised me, as always, with characteristic good humour, wit and patience. Greatest thanks to those who know the business best of all; to John van Lerberghe and his staff on Mykonos, Lisos Zilelides on Santorini, Flavio Facciolo on Folegandros and Theresa Pirpinias-Ninou on Milos. Special thanks, as always, to Kostas Karabetsos on Mykonos for the nightlife run. Thanks, also to my fellow authors for entertaining and helpful e-conferences and to Jo Potts, at Lonely Planet's London office, and coordinating author Korina Miller, for their help and for their stoic patience in holding it all together.

VICTORIA KYRIAKOPOULOS
Sincere thanks to Vicky Valanos for her invaluable assistance and to my dear Athens host and friend, Eleni Bertes. Athens wouldn't be as much fun without Antonis Bekiaris, Maria Zygourakis, Eleni Gialama, Mary Retiniotis and Xenia Orfanos. Thanks also to Georgios Xylouris, Vicki Theodoropoulou, Tobias Judmaier, Athena Lambrinidou, George Hatzimanolis, Colin Dodd, Maria Rota and Ray Jones. At Lonely Planet, thanks to Sally Schafer and Jo Potts in London; and to patient coordinator Korina Miller and fellow authors for their efforts. Finally to my loving partner Chris Anastassiades for his support and encouragement and to Rosanna De Marco for always being there.

GINA TSAROUHAS
Thanks to all who provided valuable advice. And a big nod to the Lonely Planet crew, of course, and to my co-authors, for their support. My eternal gratitude to my folks (and grandfolks, too)

BEHIND THE SCENES

for inspiring my pride and deep passion for our heritage. Ευχαριστώ to George and Vicki for their love and μάκια (kisses) to Peter, Katerina and Chris for being too cute. Hugs also to those darling friends and family, who are happy to argue, philosophise and even soliloquise Greek history at the dinner table – always engaging. Finally, my heart sings with thanks to Lisa Baas, for everything *(όχι εσύ!)*.

OUR READERS

Many thanks to the travellers who used the last edition and wrote to us with helpful hints, useful advice and interesting anecdotes:

A Martin Andersen, Betsy Arthur, Yannis Assimakopoulos **B** Kevin Baglow, Dimos Birakos, Tormod Bjørnerud **C** Hilde Calberson, Elliot Capp, Gilly Carr, Jen Carter, Heather Chaplow, Andriana Chronopoulos, John Connelly, Bill Cook, Anastasia Corellis, Lawrence Court, Elisabeth Cox, John Cox **D** Line Dalene, Robert Derash, Eydokia Despotidou, Monica Devold, Karen Deyerle, Alain Diette, Lucia Donetti **E** Helen Ellis, Ruth Emerson **F** Norman Field, Rita Frumin **G** Ron Gabb, Heather Gabb, Saki Galaxidis, Stephanie Giannakeas, Sara Gordon **H** Michael Haluschak, Brendan Haynes, Stephen Hill, Christian Hoffmann, Theresa Hollers **I** Mustafa Ispir, Gerbert **J** José Jansen Groothuis, Jos Janssen **K** Iris Kaeslin Grogg, Jennifer Klein, Gordon Knight, Ira Koenig, Giorgos Koutsogiannopoulos **L** Michael Leese, Jens Jakob Legarth, Karine Ligneau, Paula Lyons **M** Olli Makila, Kristin Markay, Anne Matheson, Kate McLoughlin, Fin McNicol, Clare McNicol, Raene Mewburn, Brock Millet, Dennis Mogerman **N** Dylan Nichols, Simos Nikitas, Pelle T Nilsson, Lisa Nolan **O** Meaghan O'Brien **P** Sharon Pask, Emma Peacocke, Helena Pereira, Sandy Peters, Sundiep Phanse, Megan Philpot **R** Julie Rand, Kasper Rassmussen **S** Akis Sartzetakis, Roxane Schury, Colin Scott, Rob Seal, Lloyd Sethill, Penny Smith, Nick Smith, Tom Stockman **T** Klaas Tjoelker, Antonis Trohalakis

SEND US YOUR FEEDBACK

We love to hear from travellers – your comments keep us on our toes and help make our books better. Our well-travelled team reads every word on what you loved or loathed about this book. Although we cannot reply individually to postal submissions, we always guarantee that your feedback goes straight to the appropriate authors, in time for the next edition. Each person who sends us information is thanked in the next edition and the most useful submissions are rewarded with a free book.

To send us your updates – and find out about Lonely Planet events, newsletters and travel news – visit our award-winning website: **lonelyplanet.com/contact**.

Note: we may edit, reproduce and incorporate your comments in Lonely Planet products such as guidebooks, websites and digital products, so let us know if you don't want your comments reproduced or your name acknowledged. For a copy of our privacy policy visit lonelyplanet.com/privacy.

V Katrine Voldby **W** Stuart Watson, Carol Weinrich, Ken West, James Wilkinson, Rita Williams, Sean Windsor **Z** Manuele Zunelli

ACKNOWLEDGMENTS

Many thanks to the following for the use of their content:

Globe on title page ©Mountain High Maps 1993 Digital Wisdom, Inc.

Index

INDEX

GREENDEX

The following attractions, accommodation, shops and restaurants have been selected by Lonely Planet authors because they demonstrate a commitment to sustainability. We've selected restaurants and hotels that aim to safeguard the environment by using organic ingredients or practising water conservation. We've listed shops that help to sustain the local economy by selling locally produced organic goods. And we've hunted down attractions that are involved in conservation or environmental education.

Greece is getting greener by the day – if you find someone we've not included in our GreenDex who should be listed here, email us at http://www.lonelyplanet.com/contact. For more tips about travelling sustainably in Greece, turn to Getting Started (p20) and for further information about sustainable tourism and Lonely Planet, see www.lonelyplanet.com/responsibletravel.

Accommodation
  Achladies Apartments 655
  Casa Lucia 682
  Harry's Paradise 570
  Milia 498
  Pine Tree Studios 537
  Red Tractor Farm 455

Activities
  2407 Mountain Activities 215
  feel ingreece 667
  Gialova Lagoon 223
  Healthy Options 691
  Masticulture Ecotourism
    Activities 611
  Octopus Sea Trips 404
  Serpentine Organic Garden 267, 4

Conservation
  desalination plant 415
  Hellenic Wildlife Hospital 359
  Library of Zagora 264

Drinking
  George's Juice Place 578
  Mercouri Estate 225

Food
  Armenon 550
  Benetos 580
  Castle 550
  Cavo d'Oro 649
  Costas Prekis 385
  gelaterie.gr 522
  Glaros Restaurant 584
  Harry's Paradise 570
  Kaleris 234
  Kritsa Restaurant & Hotel 263
  Ktima Petra 580
  Lena's Bio 143
  Nico's Taverna 423
  Olive Tree 546
  Pantopoleion 393
  Papazoylou 560
  Pure Bliss 144
  Rahati 538
  Restaurant Agios Theologos 562
  Simply Organic 560
  Sunset Café 670
  Taverna A-B 264
  Taverna O Mylos 538
  Taverna Palia Istoria 271
  Taverna Panellinion 277

Taverna Paradisos 278
Taverna Vakhos 245
To Paradosiakon 573
Tropicana Taverna 550-1
Yiantes 146

Shopping
  Era 412
  Figs of Kymi 646

Sights
  Cephalonia Botanica 696
  Figs of Kymi 646
  Gialova Lagoon 223
  Manos Faltaïts Folk Museum 666-7
  Museum of the Olive & Greek Olive
    Oil 201-2
  Serpentine Organic Garden 267, 4

Transport
  bus (Parikia) 398

INDEX

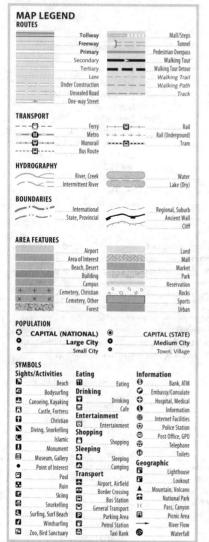

MAP LEGEND

ROUTES

Tollway	Mall/Steps
Freeway	Tunnel
Primary	Pedestrian Overpass
Secondary	Walking Tour
Tertiary	Walking Tour Detour
Lane	Walking Trail
Under Construction	Walking Path
Unsealed Road	Track
One-way Street	

TRANSPORT

Ferry	Rail
Metro	Rail (Underground)
Monorail	Tram
Bus Route	

HYDROGRAPHY

River, Creek	Water
Intermittent River	Lake (Dry)

BOUNDARIES

International	Regional, Suburb
State, Provincial	Ancient Wall
	Cliff

AREA FEATURES

Airport	Land
Area of Interest	Mall
Beach, Desert	Market
Building	Park
Campus	Reservation
Cemetery, Christian	Rocks
Cemetery, Other	Sports
Forest	Urban

POPULATION

CAPITAL (NATIONAL)	CAPITAL (STATE)
Large City	Medium City
Small City	Town, Village

SYMBOLS

Sights/Activities
- Beach
- Bodysurfing
- Canoeing, Kayaking
- Castle, Fortress
- Christian
- Diving, Snorkelling
- Islamic
- Monument
- Museum, Gallery
- Point of Interest
- Pool
- Ruin
- Skiing
- Snorkelling
- Surfing, Surf Beach
- Windsurfing
- Zoo, Bird Sanctuary

Eating
- Eating

Drinking
- Drinking
- Cafe

Entertainment
- Entertainment

Shopping
- Shopping

Sleeping
- Sleeping
- Camping

Transport
- Airport, Airfield
- Border Crossing
- Bus Station
- General Transport
- Parking Area
- Petrol Station
- Taxi Rank

Information
- Bank, ATM
- Embassy/Consulate
- Hospital, Medical
- Information
- Internet Facilities
- Police Station
- Post Office, GPO
- Telephone
- Toilets

Geographic
- Lighthouse
- Lookout
- Mountain, Volcano
- National Park
- Pass, Canyon
- Picnic Area
- River Flow
- Waterfall

LONELY PLANET OFFICES

Australia (Head Office)
Locked Bag 1, Footscray, Victoria 3011
☎ 03 8379 8000, fax 03 8379 8111
talk2us@lonelyplanet.com.au

USA
150 Linden St, Oakland, CA 94607
☎ 510 250 6400, toll free 800 275 8555
fax 510 893 8572
info@lonelyplanet.com

UK
2nd fl, 186 City Rd,
London EC1V 2NT
☎ 020 7106 2100, fax 020 7106 2101
go@lonelyplanet.co.uk

Published by Lonely Planet Publications Pty Ltd
ABN 36 005 607 983

© Lonely Planet 2009

© photographers as indicated 2009

Cover photograph: Caryatids of the Erechtheion (p121), Athens, George Tsafos/Lonely Planet Images. Many of the images in this guide are available for licensing from Lonely Planet Images: lonelyplanetimages.com.

Printed by China Translation and Printing Services Ltd
Printed in China

Mixed Sources
Product group from well-managed forests and other controlled sources
www.fsc.org Cert no. SGS-COC-005002
© 1996 Forest Stewardship Council
FSC